THE LETTERS OF Sean O'Casey 1910-41

THE LETTERS OF Sean O'Casey

1910-41

VOLUME I

Edited by
DAVID KRAUSE

CASSELL • LONDON

CASSELL & COMPANY LTD
an imprint of
Cassell & Collier Macmillan Publishers Ltd
35 Red Lion Square, London WC1R 4SG
and at Sydney, Auckland, Toronto, Johannesburg

and an affiliate of Macmillan Publishing Co., Inc., New York

First published in Great Britain 1975

ISBN 0 304 29608 2

Printed and bound in the United States of America

CONTENTS

INTRODUCTION

A Self-Portrait of the Artist as a Man

THE informal and unguarded self-portrait Sean O'Casey drew of himself in his letters may turn out to be one of the greatest characters he created. It was not a conscious creation, and yet it is no accident that the total man who emerges here, larger than life size in his aspirations and achievements, all too human in his frailties and defeats, assumes the dimensions of an heroic figure in a modern legend of the artist as a man. As a man and as a dramatist, he made himself out of a unique yet most unpromising quality of clay. While he never conquered the adversity and near-blindness of his eighty-four years—fifty-four of them recorded in these letters—he learned to live with his afflictions; and though he endured many personal tragedies, in the final reckoning his life is not a tragedy. It is a transfiguration and a triumph.

Since he was so very much a man and artist of his time, in many ways ahead of his time, the legend that grows out of the letters encompasses a public as well as a private account of the central issues of life and art in the twentieth century. In his unending struggle to shape and assert his authentic voice of integrity and innovation, he may well be the radical conscience of us all as he goes forth to fight against all forms of exploitation that would deny the dignity of man, and all forms of regimentation that would diminish the freedom of the artist. No less than a Dante or a Swift, he is determined to measure out rewards and punishments for his friends and enemies, and we should not be surprised that the latter, often his fellow Irishmen, outnumber the former. His private hell is hot and crowded, for he never forgot and seldom forgave a calculated transgression or a personal affront, no matter how slight the offense.

And his chief instruments of retribution are language and laughter, for like the ancient Irish bards he realized that sticks and stones can only break bones, but accurately aimed words loaded with comic ironies can inflict deep wounds and break hearts. Nevertheless, he can also win hearts and heal them; he can use warm words with a tender grace, especially when dealing with women or the young; and he can use a wide range of humorous and satiric responses that function as a comic catharsis. On special occasions he can charm the deserving birds out of the bushes. His letters show him to be an intensely sympathetic and demanding companion who never spares himself, never covers up, for his complex and sometimes paradoxical nature reveals a generous and vindictive, proud and compassionate being, with all the warts and wounds exposed, all the passions and principles accessible.

His letters reveal a succession of tenacious loyalties and broken friendships, long years of artistic neglect and financial hardship, when he had only his stoical courage and rough humor to sustain himself. They reveal all the significant and controversial aspects of his life and work, in which there are extravagances of outrage and genius but not an ounce of shabbiness or shame. In later years some reviewers of his autobiography accused him of cowardice for attacking men like A.E. and George Orwell only after they were dead and could not fight back; but his letters to both men, some of them suppressed, indicate that when the two were very much alive he told them directly and forcefully what he thought of them. He often made carbon copies of his letters, and many that were refused publication by nervous editors of newspapers and journals, among them the pointed reply to Orwell, are now printed here for the first time. Many letters that were edited and cut are now restored to their original versions.

What O'Casey once wrote about his father might be applied to him: he was "famed by all as one who spat out his thoughts into the middle of a body's face." If he was imprudent in his candor, he was motivated by a passion for truth. If he was a tough and relentless fighter, he had to be because he was invariably outnumbered and isolated, and he might have justified his behavior the way his Fluther Good replied to the British soldiers in Dublin during the 1916 Easter Rising: "Fight fair! A few hundhred scrawls o' chaps with a couple o' guns an' Rosary beads, again' a hundhred thousand thrained men with horse, fut, an' artillery—an' he wants us to fight fair! D'ye want us to come out in our skins an' throw stones?" So the constantly ambushed O'Casey threw his barrage of words; he fought back with new plays, with new volumes of autobiography, with new books of essays, and with his artillery of openhearted letters to the world. He was an eloquent and prodigious word-fighter.

In his beginning and in his ending, words were the weapons of his idealism and discontent. Words for him were a delight and a defense, a way of playing with dramatic images and developing his working-class values, a way of compensating for his lack of formal education; but ultimately and of necessity words were a way of defending himself in an Ireland torn by economic and political revolt, religious conflict and literary backbiting. If he was poor in material things, he could be rich, even profligate with words. In some of his earliest extant letters he is in his most characteristic moods when as a St. Laurence O'Toole piper in 1910 he defends the glory of the ancient Irish war pipes, in English and later in Gaelic; and when as an unemployed railway laborer in 1913 he defends Irish freedom and socialism in a letter to the *Irish Worker* that is subtitled, "A Challenge to Verbal Combat." He was to spend the rest of his life piping the tragicomic music of Irish life and seeking verbal combat whenever honor was at stake. He was incapable of turning away from a fight; he courted conflict, even when it was apparent that he would probably win the argument but lose the battle. As he once wrote about himself in later years in the persona of "The Green Crow": "Some Latin writer once said, 'If a crow could feed in quiet, it would have more meat.' A thing this Green Crow could never do: it had always, and has still, to speak and speak while it seeks and finds its food, and so has had less meat than it might have had if only it had kept its big beak shut." Suffering in silence would have been an unbearable sign of humiliation and defeat—to him the ultimate despair, and a sin against the Holy Ghost which he never committed.

Exile and cunning, yes, and after he left Ireland in 1926 the letters grew in volume and self-vindication as he grew more confident in his isolation and artistry. The regular habit of writing and receiving letters became a compulsive ritual of faith that continued until the very last weeks of his life in 1964. After Yeats and the Abbey Theatre rejected *The Silver Tassie* in 1928, O'Casey was deprived of a regular theatre audience for his new plays, and in the years ahead he was often forced to write for publishers rather than for theatres. Thus, as the result of an urgent and compensatory need, the hundreds of people all over the world with whom he exchanged letters became his own private audience, his intimate and immediate contact with everyday reality.

But from the start he had also maintained that contact through his public letters, the hundreds of letters he wrote to newspapers and journals in Ireland, England, America, and Russia. In these letters he takes a stand on the major issues of our time, on labor and nationalism, religion and politics, war and peace, God and man, freedom and censorship, sex and society, capitalism and communism, literature and culture. And for half a century his private and public letters become more than a defense of his own plays, for they tell a tale of the theatre in three cities, Dublin and London and New York, as he comments on plays and playwrights and productions. From the 1920s onward he becomes the radical conscience of the modern theatre and its need to experiment with new forms and visions of drama.

* * *

Volume I covers the years 1910 to 1941, his life from age thirty to sixty-one—the crucial years of his coming to maturity and notoriety. After the success of his first play, *The Shadow of a Gunman,* at the Abbey Theatre in 1923, he met and developed a beautiful though eventually heartbreaking friendship with the aristocratic Lady Gregory. He also found two warm companions in Barry Fitzgerald and Gabriel Fallon, part-time actors at the Abbey. He was to open his mind and heart to Lady Gregory and Fallon in many important letters over the years.

In 1926 the letters show him fighting a series of battles in defense of *The Plough and the Stars*: when some Abbey actors objected to the play, and again when some nationalist and religious groups rioted in the theatre and Yeats stood up for O'Casey by shouting down the mob with his famous "You have disgraced yourselves again" speech. O'Casey was drawn into public debate and a letter-writing controversy with the widow of an Irish martyr, Mrs. Hanna Sheehy-Skeffington, with whom he was later to become reconciled. He went to London in 1926 to receive the Hawthornden Prize for *Juno and the Paycock,* there establishing friendships with men like Bernard Shaw and Augustus John, and falling in love with the Irish-born actress, Eileen Reynolds Carey. His self-exile from the bitterness of his native land had begun. His love-hate quarrel with Ireland came to a head in 1928 when Yeats, Lady Gregory, and Lennox Robinson rejected his new play, *The Silver Tassie*. O'Casey fought back in a series of blistering letters to the Irish press. In 1929 some irate nationalists in Limerick prevented a production of *The Plough* and burned the film of *Juno* in an anti-O'Casey street demonstration. In 1930 an Irish priest launched a vituperative attack against *The Silver Tassie* which led to the cancellation of a Dublin production of the play.

Through the 1930s, as O'Casey continued to experiment with symbolic forms of drama, he was a dramatist without a theatre. The English producer C. B. Cochran urged him to cease writing "fine things" and instead write for "material reward," something he could never do. "It might be good for me," he replied, "but bad for my conception of drama." He exchanged a number of lively letters with Shaw, but on one occasion Shaw's wife Charlotte begged O'Casey to avoid controversy. He wrote to her protesting that he hated fighting: "If I be damned for anything, I shall be damned for keeping the two-edged sword of thought tight in its scabbard when it should be searching the bowels of knaves and fools." He was never to be damned on this point, for he went on swinging his sword at his Irish and British critics. He became involved in a savage exchange of letters with A.E. over modern art. In an angry letter to the *Irish Times* in 1932 he rejected the offer of membership in Yeat's newly formed Irish Academy of Letters. In 1933 a London printer refused to set the type for one of his short stories on the grounds that it was immoral; and a year later the Irish censorship board banned his book *Windfalls* for similar reasons (five years later the board was to ban the first volume of his autobiography, *I Knock at the Door,* again for alleged immorality). When the London critics, led by the waspish James Agate, wrote unfavorable reviews of *Within the Gates* in 1934, O'Casey swung his two-edged sword often and accurately at the formidable Agate. But as usual, O'Casey was winning verbal battles and losing financial wars.

His letters reveal that he needed help from his aristocratic friends, Lady Astor and Lady Londonderry, when he went to America in 1934 for the opening of *Within the Gates.* Again the play was an artistic success which lost money at the box office. One important asset of his American trip, however, was his new friendships with Eugene O'Neill, George Jean Nathan, and Brooks Atkinson—especially the two drama critics, who became champions of his work and to whom he was to write many significant letters during more than twenty years. Predictably, *Within the Gates* was banned in Boston in 1935, and again O'Casey swung into action against the Catholic and Methodist clergy who had condemned it as "blasphemous and obscene." Meanwhile Yeats had a change of heart over *The Silver Tassie* and produced it at the Abbey in 1935, an occasion that led to a reconciliation between the two men. The production raised a storm of controversy in Dublin when some religious groups conducted a campaign against the "blasphemous tassie filled in a sewer."

In 1936 his London publisher and friend, Harold Macmillan, tried to urge O'Casey to remove some of the critical sting from *The Flying Wasp,* his collection of essays attacking the mediocrity of the modern theatre. He replied in a letter of characteristic candor and accuracy: "Everything I have written, up to the present, has been 'combative,' and the sword I have swung so long is now stuck to my hand, and I can't let go." In a series of public letters, he went on swinging his sword at Ethel Mannin in a controversy over propaganda in art, at Kingsley Martin over censorship, at Malcolm Muggeridge over the validity of the Moscow Trials, at Lady Rhondda over the ideals of Marxism; he did, however, put aside his sword when he joined Shaw in a communist embrace, or when he cheerfully assured his friends in Ireland, England, and America that they were all unconscious communists. "You want the best that can be given to the art of the theatre," he wrote to George

Jean Nathan, "and that is the creed of the Communist." Sometimes what he called his communism was inspired by the Holy Ghost as well as Karl Marx, for as he wrote to Harold Macmillan, he was a communist who followed in the footsteps of Christ.

When one considers the bulk of his published writing, and the conditions of hardship and near-blindness under which he wrote, it is surprising that he found the time and sheer energy to write all his letters. He wrote eighteen full-length plays, seven one-act plays, four unproduced early plays, a six-volume autobiography, the equivalent of four volumes of songs, poems, stories, essays, history, and close to a hundred articles and reviews. These works total about six thousand pages or roughly one and three-quarter million words. His surviving letters thus far also total about six thousand pages and another one and three-quarter million words. He began writing in his mid-twenties and he apparently turned out an estimated total of three and a half million words over a sixty-year span, though most of it was written during his last forty years.

This is to say nothing of the hundreds of letters which were lost or destroyed or still remain to be located; or the many thousands of words he wrote in his younger days in Dublin during the first two decades of the century when he was the ubiquitous secretary: secretary of the St. Laurence O'Toole Pipers' Band, secretary of the St. Laurence O'Toole Athletic and Dramatic Club, secretary of the Red Hand Hurling Club, secretary of the Drumcondra Branch of the Gaelic League, secretary of the Women and Children's Relief Fund during the 1913 general strike and lock-out, secretary of the Wolfe Tone Memorial Committee, secretary of the Irish Citizen Army, secretary of the Release Jim Larkin Committee. Unfortunately none of his minute-books and only a few of those early letters have survived, for during the years of "The Trouble," 1916–23, the War of Independence and the Civil War, one had to travel light and often; possibly incriminating papers were wisely destroyed, or burned by the Black and Tans, especially anything written and signed by the obviously Republican name of "Sean O'Cathasaigh," for at that time O'Casey had gaelicized his name, John Casey, as a protest against British tyranny.

Up to the time he achieved his initial success as a playwright at the Abbey Theatre when he was forty-three, when he changed his name to Sean O'Casey, he had worked as a common laborer in Dublin so that he had to do his writing in the night hours after a long hard day with a pick and shovel. After his marriage four years later in 1927 to Eileen Reynolds Carey, an Irish-born actress working in England, when he lived briefly in London and then settled in Devon, he became such a devoted family man that he spent most of his daytime hours with his wife and three children, or reading, again turning to his writing in the quiet of the evening, usually working into the early morning. He wrote the first drafts of his manuscripts with pen and ink, then typed them by a two-finger method, making constant revisions until he had a final version, which contained more revisions.

For his letters he resorted to the impulse of the moment, writing straight off with a pen or directly on the typewriter. As a result the style of his letters often has the fresh quality of Dublin speech, is more relaxed and less "literary" than the style of his formal writing. Sometimes he drew satiric sketches in his letters, many of which have survived. During the last ten years of his life when his left eye was gone and only a flicker of sight remained in his fading right eye, he stabbed at the keys of his typewriter in such a hit-and-miss fashion that he often picked up his pen and added an apology for the errors. For reading and writing he had to hold the paper so close to his thick lensed glasses that his nose almost touched the page. His wife often helped him with his correspondence by picking out the main points in letters he received and writing out the key phrases in inch-high words so that he could read them and write his replies.

In the summer of 1965 in Dublin I had an opportunity to meet Dr. L. B. Somerville-Large, a noted Irish eye surgeon and one-time colleague of the late Dr. Joseph D. Cummins, O'Casey's very good friend and eye doctor who had treated him when he was a young man in Dublin. Dr. Somerville-Large told me that he and Dr. Cummins had often talked about and considered the cause of O'Casey's infected eyes, and they decided that he had contracted chronic trachoma as a child. Trachoma, he explained, is a contagious form of conjunctivitis, characterized by the formation of inflammatory granulations on the inner eyelid and eyeball, and is usually caused by unsanitary conditions.

When I last saw O'Casey in early September of 1964 at his home in St. Marychurch—as it turned out, only two weeks before he died of a heart attack—he was practically blind, but there was an unfinished letter in his typewriter, and a pile of letters to be answered on his writing table.

* * *

During the first thirty years of his life, up to the time of his first extant letter in 1910, he was often exposed to the pains and conflicts of life on the depressed north side of Dublin. When he was born as John Casey on 30 March 1880 in a tenement at 85 Upper Dorset Street, the last of thirteen children, eight of whom had already died of infant diseases, his lower-middle-class Protestant parents were in a state of economic decline. His father, Michael Casey, the last-born child of a mixed marriage, Catholic father and Protestant mother, had been raised in his mother's faith after his father, a Limerick farmer, died at an early age. Michael's brothers and sisters had been brought up as Catholics, and as a result of religious tensions in the family he cut away and went to Dublin as a young man, eventually marrying a Protestant girl, Susan Archer, the daughter of a Wicklow auctioneer. Michael earned his living as a commercial clerk and for many years worked for the Irish Church Mission, a proselytizing organization which would have employed only militant Protestants, at a much lower salary than he would have received in the business world. During his last years when he was often ill he became caretaker of the tenement house on Upper Dorset Street, which meant free rent for his family; but he died of a spinal injury in 1886 at the age of forty-nine, when his youngest son was six years old, and thereafter the family situation declined steadily.

The young O'Casey was a sickly child who in infancy had contracted a chronic eye disease which impaired his sight and prevented him from living a normal childhood. His weak and suppurating eyes had to be treated every day with soakings and ointments and bandages, which meant many years of regular trips with his mother to the public dispensary of St. Mark's Ophthalmic Hospital, a demeaning experience that he shared with the destitute Catholics who filled the crowded waiting room, though his mother was able to pay the sixpence-a-month fee. For the bewildered boy it meant a psychological as well as a physical wound, to be isolated in semidarkness, surrounded by human misery, and treated as something of a cripple. For his mother, a proud Protestant now surviving on contributions from the salaries of her older children and forced to measure out every penny, it was an ironic humiliation that they had more in common with their poor Catholic neighbors than with the remote and largely indifferent Protestants in the city. Thus, the religion into which O'Casey had been born was itself an alienating factor, when one considers what it meant to exist at the lower levels of society as a Protestant in the Dublin of the 1880s, where eighty percent of the population of two hundred and fifty thousand were Catholic and predominantly poor, while most of the Protestant minority were prosperous or titled Anglo-Irish.

Formal education was an irregular and impossible experience for the half-blind boy. Although he was sent to a Protestant church school for several years, he was often absent and his poor eyesight prevented him from learning to read and write. Due to the diligence of his mother, however, a devout churchgoer who daily read the Bible to him, he had memorized so many passages of scripture that when he was seven years old he won a Sunday-school prize "For Proficiency in Holy Scripture and Church Formularies." When he was ten, with the help of his older brother Archie who was active in a local amateur theatre group, he was memorizing speeches from the plays of Shakespeare and Boucicault, and the two Casey brothers often performed scenes together.

Five years later he had an unexpected opportunity to act in public for the first time at the old Mechanics Theatre in Abbey Street. This was the same theatre which, nine years later in 1904, was to be taken over by W. B. Yeats and Lady Gregory and, with the adjoining city morgue, rebuilt as the Abbey Theatre. It happened that the touring company of Charles D'Alton, the Irish comedian and actor-manager, was performing Boucicault's *The Shaughraun* at the Mechanic's Theatre, and when one of the actors became sick a distress call went out for a last-minute replacement. D'Alton's son Louis (later to become a popular playwright at the Abbey), who was in the company and who several years earlier had acted in scenes from Boucicault's plays with the Casey brothers at the local amateur group, called in the fifteen-year-old Johnny, who was unusually tall and ascetic-looking for his age, to take over the role of Father Dolan, the patriotic priest who defends a Fenian rebel. He played that part on the stage where twenty-eight years later his own first play was to be performed by the Abbey Theatre company.

Although he remained interested in drama and became involved in amateur theatre groups as he grew older, the labor movement ultimately became the dominant experience and conviction of his young manhood. But first he had to prepare himself for life, and a number of enthusiasms held his interest. With the aid of his sister Isabella, who was a teacher at one of the Protestant church schools, he had begun in his early teens to teach himself to read and write. When he was fourteen he earned his first money, three shillings and sixpence for a sixty-hour week, working as a stock boy for a wholesale chandlers firm. In his twenties he took odd jobs as a common laborer, and he began to haunt the Dublin bookstalls, gradually building up his own library by buying and sometimes stealing secondhand copies of his favorite authors, the works of Shakespeare, Dickens, Scott, Balzac, Milton, Byron, Keats, Shelley, Goldsmith, Sheridan, Ruskin. He taught Sunday school at St. Barnabas Church and became a close friend of the rector, the Rev. Dr. Edward Morgan Griffin, the father figure of his youth. In his thirties he joined the Gaelic League and learned the Irish language; he learned to play the Irish war pipes and became a founder-member and secretary of the St. Laurence O'Toole Pipers' Band; he wrote songs and sketches which he sang and read at meetings of the St. Laurence O'Toole Club; he joined the secret Irish Republican Brotherhood; and he finally found a steady job as a handyman and then bricklayer's assistant on the Sutton branch of the Great Western Railway. He worked on the railroad from 1903 to 1911, when he was sacked for his strong labor sympathies and his membership in Jim Larkin's new Irish Transport and General Workers' Union.

It was the dynamic Larkin who now became the most important force in the shaping of the young O'Casey; Larkin the socialist champion of the unskilled laborers of Ireland; Larkin the liberator and fiery street orator who came to Dublin to save the people from the money-changers with his "divine mission of discontent." For Irish nationalists the Easter rising of 1916 was the crucial event in Irish history; but for the Irish labor movement, and for O'Casey, it was Larkin's general strike of

1913 which struck the first blow for the liberation of the Irish people. As he did throughout his life, O'Casey put his socialism before his nationalism and turned out for the strike but not the rising. Both events were tragic failures which were eventually transformed into psychological and moral victories; but whereas the British army inadvertently provided the martyrs for the rising, the Irish capitalists during the prolonged strike fought a battle of attrition in which there was little room for heroism, and as a result the birth of militant labor in Ireland was a decisive but unspectacular occasion.

O'Casey was active in the general strike and served with Larkin as secretary of the union's Irish Citizen Army; and he began to write his first public letters and articles for Larkin's labor journal, the *Irish Worker*. Some years later Augustus John, the Welsh artist who had painted a portrait of O'Casey, was distressed by O'Casey's working-class loyalties and wrote to him in a letter of 21 October 1929: "I don't see why you need to attach yourself to any *class*. A poet, an artist is really no class at all." Such a detached view of the artist might have been all right for some aesthetes and literateurs of independent means, but O'Casey could not have been an artist at all if he had not as a man of conscience attached himself, by experience and by choice, to the working class. For him there was no such thing as a classless artist, or a classless man. For him the artist even more than the ordinary man had a responsibility to his fellow-men which was inseparable from his responsibility to his art. Perhaps the basis of O'Casey's humanity, his faith in democracy or socialism—or communism as he often insisted on calling it precisely because the term had been debased by those he considered to be the enemies of the people—can be found in Jim Larkin's labor motto: "An injury to one is the concern of all."

The decade of Ireland's revolutionary labor and nationalist movements, 1912–22, was probably the most desperate period of O'Casey's life. An unskilled, unemployed, and unhealthy laborer whose union convictions made it impossible for him to get a steady job, he was often destitute during this time and barely survived. He contracted beriberi, he had to have an operation to remove tubercular glands from his neck, his mother died and he was completely on his own, and his weak eyes continued to deteriorate. Only his pride grew stronger. On one occasion when his Pipers' Band had arranged to play at some function outside Dublin, the members were expected to pay for their own train fare, which meant that the penniless O'Casey could not make the journey. When several of his friends volunteered to buy him a ticket, "Sean the Proud," as he was known in those days, replied in a phrase that characterized his whole life: "I wouldn't go to heaven on a free ticket." If he made it to heaven in the end, he paid his own way. The quality of his life and art was his ticket.

TEXT AND ACKNOWLEDGMENTS

ALL the letters in this edition are printed in their entirety, exactly as O'Casey wrote them. In a number of instances, mainly in his typed letters to newspapers and magazines, I have been able to restore cuts made by editors, which I have indicated by square brackets, since he often made carbon copies. Thanks to these carbon copies, which I found among his private papers, I have also been able to preserve letters which editors have refused to publish, letters which private owners have refused to let me see or copy, letters which their owners have destroyed or lost, and letters to people whom I have been unable to locate.

Although O'Casey's handwriting and typing became very erratic in his final years when he was practically blind and wrote largely by instinct and determination, I have, with only a few exceptions, been able to transcribe his writing with what I trust is complete accuracy. His spelling was remarkably accurate, though in some instances I have corrected a misspelled word or name which he had previously spelled correctly. When in his near-blindness or haste he hit the wrong keys on the typewriter, I have made the logical corrections. Where some letters are undated I have been able to supply close or approximate dates. Return addresses are given in full only once or twice after a change, and are abbreviated thereafter. Irregularities in the use of the apostrophe in the name O'Cathasaigh in some of the early letters are explained by the Irish practice of placing the apostrophe over the Ó, rather than after it, O'. Since few printers then had fonts of Irish type, the O often appears without the apostrophe or in the anglicized form with the apostrophe after the O. All letters to newspapers and magazines would normally be addressed "To the Editor of *Irish Times,*" but here this introduction has been shortened: "To *Irish Times.*"

For the transcription and translation of his letters in the Irish language, I have relied upon the valuable aid and counsel of Mr. Alfrid MacLochlainn and Mr. Pádraig O'Neill, who have assured me that O'Casey's uneven and sometimes ungrammatical Irish makes up in feeling and style what it may lose through awkward and archaic constructions. (In the notes, the Gaelic is repeated only to correct an ungrammatical usage.) Considering that he had no opportunity to speak the language after he left Ireland in 1926, it is remarkable that he was able to retain a reading and writing knowledge of it throughout his life.

A collection of letters which gives only one side of the natural dialogue in a correspondence can be very frustrating to the reader. In the hope of alleviating some if not all of this frustration, I have tried to supply the other side of the dialogue in some instances by including letters written to him (when they were available and pertinent), letters to newspapers and magazines written about him, controversial articles and reviews to which he responded directly, and also news stories which supply important information about his life or his views. I have had to follow some measure of restraint in the introduction of this material, however, for otherwise this already substantial edition would have overflowed into several more volumes.

I have also tried to tell some of the story behind the letters by providing the necessary background and context in the footnotes. Because O'Casey was always vitally curious about playwrights and plays, I have tried to identify and date the plays he mentions; and because he was always deeply concerned about which actors appeared in his plays, I have included the casts of his premieres, as well as the leading players in some notable productions. For books and other references cited in the notes, full bibliographical information is given for the first citation, but only the date for repeated citations.

My personal friendship with O'Casey during the last decade of his life proved to be an invaluable aid in clearing up many vague and puzzling references that came up in the letters. Particularly during the final two and a half years of his life I was able to ask him direct questions about specific situations and controversies. His replies were always straight and unequivocal. If he didn't know exactly when certain events took place—he was vague about dates—he had a phenomenal memory of what had happened and why it had happened. This edition of his letters could not have been completed in its present form without his great good help, and also the very kind and generous assistance of his wife.

Over a period of twelve years I collected more than two thousand letters, one thousand eight hundred of which appear in the three volumes of this edition. I know of the existence of at least two hundred more letters, of which I have been unable to obtain copies. For example, the New York University Library has refused to give me permission to see or make copies of one hundred twenty-six letters from O'Casey to Jack Carney—see the carbon copy of O'Casey's letter to Carney, 18 September, note 1—letters which they claim were purchased only for graduate student research, not for publication. Fortunately, however, the other libraries which own O'Casey letters believe that their publication is essential for research. I suspect that many hundreds of letters have been lost or destroyed, and that many hundreds more will continue to turn up in the years ahead. In Volume III I will indicate the final count of the letters I have collected, with a catalogue of the printed and unprinted letters. All the unprinted letters will be deposited in the National Library in Dublin.

The letters are divided into three separate volumes, covering the following years: Volume I, 1910–41; Volume II, 1942–54; Volume III, 1955–64.

Volume I contains 653 letters by O'Casey; 124 letters to or about O'Casey; 21 news reports and reviews by or about O'Casey; a total of 798 entries.

* * *

I have used the following code to identify the nature of the original letter:

MS. Manuscript copy
TS. Typescript copy
TC. Typed carbon copy
PC. Printed copy

The location of each letter can be found in the following table of sources.

A. Institutions

Henry W. and Albert A. Berg Collection, New York Public Library
British Museum, London
Bucknell University Library, Lewisburg, Pennsylvania
State University of New York Library at Buffalo
Colby College Library, Waterville, Maine
Cornell University Library, Ithaca, New York
National Library of Ireland, Dublin
London University Library
Macmillan and Co. Ltd., London

Macmillan Publishing Co., Inc., New York
Society of Authors, London
Southern Illinois University Library, Carbondale
Texas University Library, Austin
Yale University Library, New Haven, Connecticut

B. Periodicals
An Poblacht (The Republic), Dublin
Country Life, London
Daily Express, London
Daily Telegraph, London
Daily Worker, London
Dublin Evening Telegraph
Dublin Saturday Post
Forward, Glasgow
International Literature, Moscow
Irish Freedom, London
Irish Independent, Dublin
Irish Press, Dublin
Irish Statesman, Dublin
Irish Times, Dublin
Irish Worker, Dublin
John O'London's Weekly, London
The Leader, Dublin
Manchester Guardian
Modern Drama, Lawrence, Kansas
Nation and Athenaeum, London
New Statesman and Nation, London
Newsweek, New York
New York Times
Nineteenth Century, London
The Observer, London
Picture Post, London
Sinn Fein, Dublin
The Star, Dublin
Sunday Times, London
Time and Tide, London
Totnes Times, Devon
Tribune, London
Voice of Labour, Dublin

C. Books
Lady Gregory's Journals, 1916–30 (1947), ed. Lennox Robinson
Letters of T. E. Lawrence (1938), ed. David Garnett
Winifred Loraine, *Robert Loraine: Soldier, Actor, Airman* (1938)
Eileen O'Casey, *Sean* (1971)

Sean O'Casey, *Rose and Crown* (1952)
Sean O'Cathasaigh, *Story of the Irish Citizen Army* (1919)
Letters of W. B. Yeats (1954), ed. Alan Wade

D. Private Owners
Nancy Viscountess Astor, London
Brooks Atkinson, New York
Guy Boas, London
Richard C. Boys, Ann Arbor, Michigan
John Bradley, South Hadley, Massachusetts
Ivor Brown, London
Maira Lady Bury, Newtown Ards, County Down
Cyril Clemens, Kirkwood, Missouri
Jack Daly, Oxford
Dorothy Elmhirst, Totnes, Devon
Lehman Engel, New York
Bertha Gaster, London
Lillian Gish, New York
Oliver D. Gogarty, Dublin
Major Richard Gregory, Guildford, Surrey
Mrs. Augustus John, London
James Kavanagh, Dublin
Christine Lady Longford, Dublin
Mrs. Maude O'Connor, Dublin
Timmie McElroy, London
Pegeen Mair, London
Herbert Marshall, London
Erna Meinel, London
Mrs. Isabella Murphy, Dublin
Peter Newmark, Guildford, Surrey
B. Douglas Newton, London
Mrs. Eileen O'Casey, London
Sean O'Casey, Torquay, Devon
Micheál O h-Aodha, Dublin
Betty Purdon, Ontario, Canada
Horace Reynolds, Belmont, Massachusetts
Mrs. Lennox Robinson, Dublin
Leo Rush, Dublin
James Shiels, Dublin
Mrs. Iris Wise, London

For kind permission to publish copyrighted material, in letters written to or about O'Casey, and in articles and reviews on O'Casey, I am grateful to the following: the James Agate reviews by permission of the Estate of James Agate; the Lady Astor letter by permission of the Honorable

David Astor; the Gordon Beckles letter and review by permission of the *London Express* News and Feature Services; the Ernest Blythe letter by permission of Ernest Blythe; the St. John Ervine letter by permission of the Society of Authors in behalf of the Estate of St. John Ervine; the Oliver St. John Gogarty poem "O Boys, O Boys" from the *Collected Poems,* copyright © 1954 by Oliver St. John Gogarty, by permission of The Devin-Adair Co. and Constable & Co.; the Ronald Gow letters by permission of Ronald Gow; the Lady Gregory letters by permission of the Estate of Lady Gregory; the Augustus John letter by permission of Romilly John; the James Joyce letter by permission of the Trustees of the Estate of James Joyce; the T. E. Lawrence letter by permission of Jonathan Cape Ltd.; the Wyndham Lewis letter by permission of Mrs. G. A. Wyndham Lewis; the Ramsay MacDonald letter by permission of Malcolm MacDonald; the Ethel Mannin letter by permission of Ethel Mannin; the Kingsley Martin letter by permission of A. D. Peters and Co.; the Malcolm Muggeridge letters by permission of Malcolm Muggeridge; the George Jean Nathan article by permission of *Newsweek;* the Eugene O'Neill letters by permission of Yale University as legatee under the will of Carlotta Monterey O'Neill; the Raymond Postgate column by permission of Professor J. R. Postgate and the Executors of the Estate of Raymond W. Postgate; the Lennox Robinson letters by permission of Mrs. D. L. Robinson; the George Russell (AE) letter by permission of A. M. Heath and Co. Ltd.; the George Bernard Shaw letters, © 1975, by permission of the British Museum, the Governors and Guardians of the National Gallery of Ireland and Royal Academy of Dramatic Art; the Charlotte F. Shaw letters by permission of the Trustees of the Will of Mrs. Bernard Shaw; the James Stephens letter by permission of the Society of Authors in behalf of the Estate of James Stephens; the William Butler Yeats letters by permission of Mr. Michael Yeats and Miss Anne Yeats.

While it would be impossible to list everyone who has helped me in my work, I must express a very deep debt of thanks to those who have given me valuable aid, counsel, and information—first singling out these heroic helpers: Mr. Timothy O'Keeffe; Mr. Alfrid MacLochlainn; Mr. Liam Miller; Mr. Alick Bartholomew; Mr. R. L. DeWilton; Mr. Richard Garnett—and also the following: Mr. Ronald Ayling; Miss M. Cairns; Mrs. Mina Carney; Mr. and Mrs. Cyril Cusack; Mr. Reginald Davis-Pointer; Mr. Michael Durkan; Mrs. Rhiannon Gooding; Mr. Eric Gorman; Mr. Martin Green; Dr. Richard Hayes; Mr. Patrick Henchy; Mr. Michael Hewson; Dr. Robert Hogan; Mrs. R. Kloegman; Dr. Emmet Larkin; Dr. Dan H. Laurence; Mr. Francis MacManus; Mr. Michael Martin; Mr. Francis Mins; Dr. Daniel Murphy; Mrs. Fergus O'Connor; Mr. Micheál O h-Aodha; Mr. Pádraig O'Neill; Mr. John O'Riordan; Mrs. Dorren O'Siochru; Mr. Jack Paris; Mr. and Mrs. James

Plunkett; Mr. James Scully; Mr. Seamus Scully. I must also acknowledge a special debt of gratitude and appreciation to Mr. Ray A. Roberts, whose sense of dedication and editorial wisdom brought the whole edition to life; to Miss Susan Morrow for her editorial endeavors in preparing the manuscript for the printer, for her excellent advice and great good judgment; and to Mrs. Lorraine V. Steurer, who coped with the massive set of galleys and brought her X-ray vision to the final pages and the indexes.

Finally, this edition could not have been completed without the generous help of two grants from the American Council of Learned Societies and the Bronson Fellowship of Brown University, and three Summer Stipends from Brown University.

And through the final years of the work I have been fortified and blessed by the love of my wife Anne.

O'CASEY CHRONOLOGY

1880	March 30	Born at 85 Upper Dorset Street, Dublin, to Michael and Susan Casey
	July 28	Baptized John Casey at St. Mary's Church, Church of Ireland
1883		Family moves to 7 Innisfallen Parade, off Dorset Street
1885		Briefly attends St. Mary's Infant's School, Lower Dominick Street
1886	September 6	Father Michael Casey dies at age forty-nine
1887		Wins a second class prize for oral proficiency in Holy Scripture and Church Formularies at St. Mary's Sunday School
1888		Family moves to a two-room attic flat in St. Mary's School, Lower Dominick Street, where his sister Isabella works as a teacher
	April	Attends St. Mary's National School, until February 1889. His early schooling is irregular, often interrupted due to bad eyesight, as a result of chronic trachoma contracted as an infant

1889		Family moves to 22 Hawthorne Terrace, North Wall, in the parish of St. Barnabas
1890		Briefly attends St. Barnabas' National School
1894		Gets his first job as stock boy at Hampton and Leedom, wholesale chandlers in Henry Street, and works there for over a year
1895		Acts the role of Father Dolan, the patriotic priest, in Dion Boucicault's *The Shaughraun* at the old Mechanics Theatre in Abbey Street, which nine years later is rebuilt as the Abbey Theatre
1896		Works as a van boy for Eason and Son, wholesale newsagents in Lower Abbey Street, but is dismissed after one week for disobedience
1897		Family moves to 18 Abercorn Road, North Wall, near St. Barnabas Church
1898	March 29	Confirmation in the Church of Ireland at Clontarf Parish Church
1900		Teaches Sunday school at St. Barnabas Church until 1903
1903		Begins to work as a common laborer on the Great Northern Railway of Ireland, and remains at this job for the next nine years
1906		Learns Irish language, joins the Drumcondra Branch of the Gaelic League, and gaelicizes his name to Seán Ó Cathasaigh
1907		Joins the St. Laurence O'Toole Club, and writes his first stories and articles for the Club's Manuscript Journal, which was read at meetings
	May 25	First publication, an article, "Sound the Loud Trumpet," *The Peasant and Irish Ireland*
1908		Joins the Irish Republican Brotherhood Secretary of the Drumcondra Branch of the Gaelic League
1910		Founder-member and Secretary of the St. Laurence O'Toole Pipers' Band

1911		Joins Jim Larkin's Irish Transport and General Workers' Union
	December	Dismissed from his job at the Great Northern Railway of Ireland after nine years, mainly due to his union membership
1912	June	Begins to write articles for Jim Larkin's *Irish Worker*
1913	July	Secretary of the Wolfe Tone Memorial Committee
	October	Secretary of the Women and Children's Relief Fund during the general strike and lockout
1914	February 6	Brother Tom Casey dies at age 44
	March	Secretary of the Irish Citizen Army; resigns in October
	May	Begins to write a regular column, "By the Camp Fire," for the Citizen Army in the *Irish Worker*
1915	August 15	Enters St. Vincent's Hospital, Dublin, for an operation on his neck for tubercular glands which had troubled him since his youth
1917		Meets Maurya Keating, his first steady girl-friend, at the St. Laurence O'Toole Dramatic Club
	November 25	Acts in the St. Laurence O'Toole Dramatic Club's production of Thomas K. Moylan's *Naboclish* at the Empire Theatre, now the Olympia
1918	January 1	Sister Isabella Casey Beaver dies at age fifty-two
		Publications under the name of Sean Ó Cathasaigh: *The Story of Thomas Ashe; The Sacrifice of Thomas Ashe; Songs of the Wren No. 1; Songs of the Wren No. 2; More Songs of the Wren*
	November 9	Mother Susan Casey dies at age eighty-one
1919		Publication of *The Story of the Irish Citizen Army*
1920	January 26	Abbey Theatre rejects his first two plays, *The Harvest Festival* and *The Frost in the Flower*
		Moves to a tenement at 35 Mountjoy Square to share a room with Micheál Ó Maolain

		Works as a janitor at the Old Forester's Hall, 10 Langrishe Place, Summerhill
1921		Moves into a room at 422 North Circular Road
	November	Secretary of the Release Jim Larkin Committee and the Jim Larkin Correspondence Committee
1922	April 15	Abbey Theatre rejects *The Seamless Coat of Kathleen*
	September 28	Abbey Theatre rejects *The Crimson in the Tricolour*
	November 17	Abbey Theatre accepts *The Shadow of a Gunman*
1923	April 12	*The Shadow of a Gunman* opens at the Abbey Theatre
	October 1	*Cathleen Listens In* opens at the Abbey Theatre
1924	March 3	*Juno and the Paycock* opens at the Abbey Theatre
	June 7	His first visit to Lady Gregory's home at Coole Park, Galway
	September 29	*Nannie's Night Out* opens at the Abbey Theatre
1925	February	Publication of *Two Plays* (*Gunman* and *Juno*)
1926	February 8	*The Plough and the Stars* opens at the Abbey Theatre
	February 10	Nationalist riots in the Abbey Theatre against *The Plough and the Stars*
	March 23	Receives the Hawthornden Literary Prize of £100 in London for *Juno and the Paycock*
	April	Publication of *The Plough and the Stars*
		Lives at 7 Lansdowne Place, Guilford Street, London, W.C.1
		Moves to 2 Trafalgar Square, Chelsea, S.W.3
	May	Has his portrait painted by Augustus John
	July	Moves to 32 Clareville Street, South Kensington, S.W.7

1927	September 23	Marries Eileen Reynolds Carey in the Roman Catholic Church of All Souls and the Redeemer, Chelsea
1928	January	Moves to 19 Woronzow Road, St. Johns Wood, N.W.8
	April 20	Abbey Theatre rejects *The Silver Tassie*
	April 30	Birth of his son Breon
	June	Publication of *The Silver Tassie*
1929	October 11	*The Silver Tassie* opens in London at the Apollo Theatre
1930	September 22	Film of *Juno and the Paycock* is released
	October 24	*The Silver Tassie* opens in New York at the Greenwich Village Theatre
	November 10	Film of *Juno and the Paycock* is burned in the street in Limerick by Nationalists
1931	September	Moves to 2 Misbourne Cottages, Chalfont St. Giles, Buckinghamshire
	October	Moves to Hillcrest, Chalfont St. Giles, Buckinghamshire
	November	Writes his first autobiographical sketch, "A Child is Born," which later becomes the opening chapter of *I Knock at the Door* (1939)
1932	July	Writes *A Pound on Demand,* a one-act play
1933	May	His short story, "I Wanna Woman," is censored by the printer of *Time and Tide*
	December	Publication of *Within the Gates*
1934	February 7	*Within the Gates* opens in London at the Royalty Theatre
	September 13	Leaves Southampton on the *Majestic* and arrives in New York on September 19 for American premiere of *Within the Gates*
	October	Publication of *Windfalls,* a collection of early poems, four short stories, and two one-act plays

	October 22	*Within the Gates* opens in New York at the National Theatre
	November 16	Gives the Morris Gray Poetry Talk at Harvard University on "The Old Drama and the New"
	December 4	*Windfalls* is banned by the Irish Censorship of Publications Board
	December 12	Leaves New York on the *Britannic* and arrives in Liverpool on December 23
1935	January 15	Birth of his son Niall
	January 15	*Within the Gates* is banned by the Mayor of Boston, forcing the cancellation of a scheduled tour of thirteen cities
	August 12	*The Silver Tassie* opens at the Abbey Theatre
	September	Returns to Dublin for the last time on a two-week visit, and meets Yeats on friendly terms
	October	Publication of *Five Irish Plays* (*Gunman, Juno, Plough, End of the Beginning, Pound on Demand*)
1936	February	Gives a talk, "The Holy Ghost Leaves England," to the Shirley Society of St. Catharine's College, Cambridge
1937	February 8	*The End of the Beginning* opens at the Abbey Theatre
	March	Publication of *The Flying Wasp,* a collection of essays, articles, and reviews
	March 15	Film of *The Plough and the Stars* is released
1938	September	Moves to Tingrith, Totnes, Devon
1939	March	Publication of *I Knock at the Door,* first volume of autobiography
	May 16	*I Knock at the Door* is banned by the Irish Censorship of Publications Board
	September 28	Birth of his daughter Shivaun
1940	February	Publication of *The Star Turns Red*

	March 12	*The Star Turns Red* opens in London at the Unity Theatre
	June 10	Becomes a member of the new Advisory Board of the London *Daily Worker*
	November	Publication of *Purple Dust*
1941	July	Finishes writing *Pictures in the Hallway,* second volume of autobiography

THE LETTERS OF Sean O'Casey 1910-41

I

SOME KNOCKS AT IRELAND'S DOORS, 1910-19

I AM one of those who has entered into the labour of our fathers; one of those who declare—by the fame of our forefathers; by the murder of Red Hugh; by the anguished sighs of the Geraldine; by the blood-dripping wounds of Wolfe Tone; by the noble blood of Emmet; by the death-wasted bodies of the famine—that we will enter into our inheritance or we will fall one by one. Amen."

"The right to toil till the blood is dried in our veins; the right to bless the land that gives us what it thinks we are worth; the right to suffer starvation, and misery, and disease, and then thank God that such light affliction work an exceeding weight of glory! Workers, ye are fools to train and drill for anything less than complete enfranchisement, for the utter alteration of the present social system, for liberty to ensure the natural and absolute development of every Irishborn man and woman."

The young O'Casey was a man of deep Irish loyalties which he defended with considerable idealism and anger, and many of his early letters are colored by contrasting moods of lyrical enthusiasm and fierce contention, as well as by his characteristic sense of irony and comedy. Although few of his letters in the Irish language have survived, one to Lord Castletown reflects his fervent yet improbable vision of working-class Irishmen devoting their lives to Celtic music and culture. During these early years, 1911–13, he was also trying to reconcile the principles of Irish nationalism with those of the Irish labor movement. It was the failure of this reconciliation—then and throughout his lifetime—which led O'Casey to reject the heroics of fanatical nationalism and fight for the democratic socialism of Jim Larkin. He chose to be a rebel worker rather than a rebel patriot. This decision cost him the only steady job he ever had as a common laborer for the Great Northern Railway when he was sacked for joining Larkin's new union of unskilled workers and openly professing his socialist as well as Irish loyalties.

Thereafter he was irrevocably committed to verbal combat in defense of an Irish socialist republic. He challenged the G.N.R.I. to justify his dismissal; and in his continuing attempt to unite the aims of Irish labor and nationalism, apparently an impossible task, he challenged "Euchan," the Irish Volunteers, James MacGowan, and anyone who questioned his concept of the new Ireland, free from capitalism as well as England. Two major events in modern Irish history were beginning to take shape, the 1913 general strike of labor, and the 1916 Easter rising of nationalism; and true to his working-class principles, O'Casey was active only in the former. His reaction to the events of 1916 is limited to several satiric letters and cartoons. It is significant to note that while he was at first enthusiastic about Padraig Pearse's festival in honor of a Gaelic Ireland, he was soon disenchanted when he learned that a national leader like Pearse had acted as a scab by riding the Dublin trams during the strike. O'Casey maintained his republican ideals but he was disinclined to become involved in a middle-class rising. Unemployed, hungry, and proud, he remained secretary of the Wolfe Tone Committee, and most of his energy went into the labor movement at Liberty Hall where, as an unpaid assistant to Larkin, he was secretary of the Women and Children's Relief Fund and secretary of the Irish Citizen Army.

Meanwhile he was playing in the pipers' band and acting in plays at the St. Laurence O'Toole Club; he was writing comic skits which he read at club meetings; his letters and articles on labor and nationalism were appearing in the press; he was writing comic and republican ballads and pamphlets for his first publisher, Fergus O'Connor; and Maunsel published his first book in 1919, *The Story of the Irish Citizen Army*. In 1919 he also wrote his first two plays, *The Harvest Festival* and *The Frost in the Flower,* both of which he had submitted to the Abbey Theatre. Now seeking an artistic voice for his radical views, he was knocking at many Irish doors.

To . . . . . .[1]

PC. NAT LIB, DUBLIN

ATH CLIATH,
DATE [1910]

A Chara,[2]

This Club has been formed to organize a Pipers' Band for the Parish, and to cultivate a love for the priceless Music of our Country, particularly that of the Irish War Pipes. It is also proposed that the Club, which will be strictly non-sectarian and non-party, will encourage the study of Irish History and Irish Language.

The expenses necessary to equip a Pipers' Band are heavy—about £50;—and we earnestly appeal and confidently expect financial help from the Parishioners.

Subscriptions, which will be duly acknowledged, may be sent to the Trustees, Treasurer, or Secretary, or given to the Collectors who will be appointed for the purpose.

We earnestly ask you to do a little to revive again the majestic music which led the Irishmen to victory on many a hard fought field, the last of which was the charge of the Brigade at Fontenoy.

The following Subscriptions have already been received:—

	£	s.	d.
Rev. James Brady, P.P., Seville Place,	1	0	0
A. Byrne, T.C., Talbot Street,	1	0	0
Hon. Wm. Gibson,	1	0	0
Edward Martyn, Esq.,	1	0	0
T. Byrne, Esq., Donnycarney,	0	10	0
P. O'Toole, Esq., Sheriff Street,	0	10	0

[1] This form letter was printed as a fund-raising circular which accompanied the 14 May 1911 letter to Lord Castletown. The St. Laurence O'Toole Pipers' Band was founded in the summer of 1910 and the letter was written later that year.

[2] A Chara: Friend.

Rev. James Breen, C.C.,	0	5	0
Misses Tierney's, Seville Place,	0	5	0
Mr. Buckley, Maynooth,	0	5	0
John O'Byrne, Esq.,	0	5	0
Mr. Downey, Sheriff Street,	0	5	0
J.P. Farrelly, T.C., Sheriff Street,	0	5	0
Miss Dawson, Sheriff Street,	0	5	0
Mr. Lennox, Newfoundland Street,	0	5	0
Shane Leslie,	0	5	0
H. O'Hehir, Esq.,	0	5	0
Mrs. Noone, Commons Street,	0	2	6
Dr. Douglas Hyde,[3]		5	0
Stephen Gwynn, M.P.,		5	0
W. Curtis, Esq.,		10	0
Cathal Brugha, Esq.,		5	0

"Bíodh ceól na píbe fé mhear ag Gaedhealaibh." [4]

Mise,

S. Ó Cathasaigh,[5]

Hon. Sec.

[3] The last four names—Hyde, Gwynn, Curtis, Brugha—were added in O'Casey's handwriting.

[4] "Let the music of the pipes be in the hands of the Gaels."

[5] O'Casey was christened John Casey and went by that name until his mid-twenties when he became a nationalist and Irish language enthusiast and gaelicized his name to Sean Ó Cathasaigh. Thereafter he was known as Jack Casey, John O'Casey, or Sean Ó Cathasaigh, until the Abbey Theatre accepted *The Shadow of a Gunman* in 1923 and he became Sean O'Casey.

To Lord Castletown of Upper Ossory [1]

CUMANN PÍOBAIRÍ
NAOIṀ LORĊAIN UÍ ṪUAṪAIL

ST. LAURENCE O'TOOLE'S PIPERS' CLUB.)

[1] Lord Castletown of Upper Ossory, Bernard Edward Barnaby Fitzpatrick (1848–1937), Irish peer and supporter of the movement to revive the Irish language. The drawing of the piper which accompanied this letter is colored in red, green, and black ink. A translation of the sentence under the drawing reads: Long live the St. Laurence O'Toole Pipers' Club. The initials J.K.C. stand for John Casey.

MS. Nat Lib, Dublin

Bealtaine XIV, 1911
18 Abercorn Road, Dublin

A chara fíor-uaisle:—

Bhuaileadh fé áthás mé, uair fágadh fúm an dilleóg atá taobh istigh annseo—ar a deineadh trácht ar Chumainn Píobaireachta—'seoladh fé do dhéin, chun éilimh ort beagán cabhra cuir i dtreo lucht a stiurigte, leis a n-iarracht a neartugadh is a buanughadh 'nar measg. Lucht oibre 'seadh daoine ár ndúthaighe, as is fíorbheag an tsuim cuirtear i leithead de Chonnradh na Gaedhilge, nó, fós, aon nidh baineanns léi. Gidh gur ceangailte atathar do nóseanna na nGall, 'támuid a' fághail togha cabhra uatha i gcóir neartighthe ár noibre. Cheapadh go deinfidh ar gCumann-sa obair tairbheach le na n-iompodh cun slighe na nGaedheal, agus cuirfidh fuireann Píobairí ós a gcomhair go deas as go brioghmar cad is cuid de tréithibh agus noseannaibh a sinnsir ann. Beidh an Cumann, le congnamh Dé, mar coinneal atá suidhthe i gcoinnleor i lár seomra a gnidheas solas dá gach a bhfuil istigh. 'Támuid féin taréis moráin do deineamh. Íoceann sinn as costus Áruis, soluis, leabhair ceoil, feadáin, agus culaiththe eadaigh i gcóir fuirinn píobairí; tá cuid maith againn ag eirige ana-chlisde ar na píbibh, bhailigh sinn go dtí anois suas le fiche púnt; atá buidhin mhaith Gaedhilge agus 'támuid á' fhoghluim go dían. Sé mar a dhéineam agus is leor do Mhiceál boict a dhicheall. 'Támuid ag braith ar cáirdibh anois go bhfuil suim acú i ndúil na nGaedheal beagan cabhra chuir chughainn agus ní in aisge 'glaochadh orra.

Tá súil agam go dtiochfaidh sé t-aigne cuidín 'chuir le cad tá againn cheana, is a thainig ó cáirdibh atá suidhte ar lic ár dteineadh féin, is ó cáirdibh comhnuidheanns taobh amuigh dhínn.

Go neirghidh go geal le gach Gaedheal, go mbeidh

"An saoghal suaimhneach, sitheach, shóghach
"Gan pléidh gan bhuaidhirt gan bhruighin gan bhrón,
"Beidh an spéir gan duartan suim ar neoin
"Gan fraoch gan fuacht gan teimheal gan cheo."

Mise, agus meas agam ort,
S. Ó Cathasaigh,
Runaidhe.

Lord Castletown of Upper Ossory
Doneraile
Co. Cork

14 MAY 1911

My very dear Sir:—

I was delighted when it was left to me to send you on the enclosed leaflet, in which there is an account of a Pipers' Club, to appeal to you to send a little help to those who are directing it, to strengthen and make permanent their work amongst us. The people of our district are working class and they take little interest in such things as the Gaelic League, or indeed anything connected with it. Even though they are attached to the customs of the Foreigner [the English], we are getting the best of help from them for the strengthening of our work. It was thought that our Club might do good work to turn them to the way of the Gael, and a pipers' band will put before them nicely and in a lively fashion something which is part of the manners and customs of their ancestors. The Club will, with the help of God, be as a candle which is placed in a candlestick in the middle of a room and gives light to all who are within.

We ourselves have done much. We pay the cost of rent, light, music books, whistles, and uniforms for the Pipers' Band; some of us are getting very clever on the pipes. Up to now we have collected about £20. There is a good Irish class and we are studying the language hard. That's how we're doing, and his best is enough for poor Michael [ie., no man can do more than his best]. We are depending on friends now who have interest in the aims of the Gaels to send us a little help and it is not in vain they have been called upon.

I hope you will see your way to add something to what we have already, and which has come from friends who are on our own hearthstone, and from friends who live away from us.

May it go well with all the Gaels, and

"May life be restful, peaceful, pleasant,
Without acrimony or trouble, without fighting or sorrow,
And the sky will be cloudless at evening,
Without fury or cold, without mist or any blemish."

I am, respectfully yours,
S. O'Casey,
Secretary

To Irish Worker

9 MARCH 1912

18 ABERCORN ROAD [DUBLIN]

4 FEBRUARY 1912

A Chara—I would be glad if you would kindly publish the following correspondence which recently passed between myself and the Secretary of the Great Northern Railway.

Perhaps it will demonstrate the "sweet simplicity" of those who cherish the reflection that the people who sit in high places are always ready to hearken unto their protests and complaints. Subsequent to receiving notice of dismissal [1] from Foreman Reid—a circumspect and most edifying man, of the Engineering Department—I addressed the following letter to the Secretary of the Great Northern Railway:—

7 DECEMBER 1911

The Secretary G.N.R.

Dear Sir,—On the eve of Tuesday, the 28th November, I was apprised by Foreman Reid that Engineer Whilden had ordered him to signify to me that the Company had decided to dispense with my services after the 8th inst. On asking for a reason some intangible charges [2] were made by Foreman Reid at the instance of Engineer Whilden. The charges, which I deny emphatically, were made in a very indifferent way, and I may add, with the greatest assurance, that Foreman Reid knows them to untrue. As the imputation of these assertions against me may possibly allow them to become an obstacle in the way of filling a position which I may essay to obtain subsequently, I now respectfully demand that the charges alleged against me be made again, definitely, in the presence of your Board, and that an opportunity be furnished me to defend myself.

I have been in the company's service now for nearly ten years, and can hardly be expected to tamely submit to ignominious dismissal for reasons that exist in neither substance [n]or fact, but which, I believe, have been generated by a strong desire on the part of Foreman Reid

[1] After working for the Great Northern Railway of Ireland as a common laborer from 1902 to 1911, O'Casey was dismissed in December 1911.

[2] The unspecified charges presented to O'Casey merely indicated that his work was "unsatisfactory." Actually, he had been overheard attacking the working conditions at the Great Northern Railway of Ireland and praising Jim Larkin and the Irish Transport and General Workers' Union, of which he was now a member. The G.N.R.I. was owned by antilabor Northern Irishmen from Belfast.

to separate me from the company's service. I will now thank you to place this letter before your Board at your earliest convenience, and to let me have an answer to same.—I am, sincerely yours,

J. O'Casey
(Late of Engineering Department, G.N.R.I.)

(Acknowledgment)

SECRETARY'S OFFICE, G.N.R.
9 DECEMBER 1911

Dear Sir,—I beg to acknowledge receipt of yours of the 7th inst. re dismissal, and to say that it will receive attention.

T. Morrison, Secretary

(Reply)

SECRETARY'S OFFICE, G.N.R.
12 DECEMBER 1911

Dear Sir,—Your letter of the 7th inst., has been laid before my Directors, and in reply thereto, I am desired to say that the Company do not require your services.—Yours faithfully,

T. Morrison, Secretary

In answer to above the following reply was sent by me.

18 DECEMBER 1911

The Secretary G.N.R.
Dear Sir,—I beg to acknowledge yours of the 12th inst., and to thank you for placing mine of the 7th inst., before your Board. May I point out the unsatisfactory nature of the Board's reply. The subject matter of same does not even pretend to deal with the letter I had the honour of sending for the generous consideration of your Board. They say that the "Board do not require my services." My services had previously been dispensed with by their Foreman, which fact I was aware of. Not reinstatement in my old position, nor employment in any other, but an opportunity to defend myself from charges made against me by Engineer Whilden through Foreman Reid was the privilege I asked the Board to concede to me. I demand this again, and am bold to ask the following questions:—

Was I dismissed on the 28th November, when I received notice from Foreman Reid; or on the 12th December, when I had the honour of receiving notice from the Directors?

What charges have been made against me, that have caused your Directors to approve of my dismissal, and may I hope that an opportunity will be afforded me of answering these without delay.—Sincerely yours,

J. O'Casey

[20 DECEMBER 1911]

J. O'Casey

Dear Sir,—I beg to acknowledge your of the 18th inst., re dismissal, and to say that it shall receive attention.—Faithfully yours,

T. Morrison,
Secretary, G.N.R.I.

The following letter was subsequently received by me:—

G.N.R.I., SECRETARY'S OFFICE
AMIENS STREET
5 JANUARY 1912

Dear Sir,—With further reference to your letter of the 18th ultimo, I beg to say that my Board are not cognizant of any charges against you, and that notice was given to you terminating your engagement with the company as your service was no longer required.—Yours faithfully,

T. Morrison, Sec.

There's the courageous and justice-loving G.N.R. for ye. Sure there's no necessity for union; the Board, God bless them, are always ready to hear any grievance of the least of their poor employees. This statement is a frost-covered lie, cold and bitter to the hand that is foolish enough to touch it. The men on the G.N.R. are at the mercy of their foremen and managers, and the mercy of those time-servers is always strained finely. In the department in which I worked (the engineering) the unfortunate men were at the feet of a sleeven English engineer named Whilden. Well, God made him, so we'll call him a man; and a cold, wolfish-hearted foreman named Reid, in whom is neither truth, honour, nor candidness. Of these more anon.[3]

Men, there is no hope outside iron-hearted Union. Here is a man, ten years' service, missing about six quarters during that time; a total

[3] He wrote six articles on the G.N.R.I. for the *Irish Worker,* the Union newspaper edited by Larkin, exposing some of the grim working conditions: "Great Northern Railway, Ireland, Some of Its Works and Pomps: The Charity of Its Officials," 8 June 1912; "Chiefs of the G.N.R.I., I," 25 January 1913; "Chiefs of the G.N.R.I., II," 8 February 1913; "Chiefs of the G.N.R.I., III," 15 February 1913; "Some Slaves of the G.N.R.I. and Others," 1 March 1913; "The Recent Tragedy on the G.N.R.I.," 12 July 1913. The first five articles are reprinted in *Feathers From the Green Crow, Sean O'Casey, 1905–1925,* ed. Robert Hogan (Columbia, University of Missouri Press, 1962).

abstainer; ill during his service about a fortnight—nine days due to accident—yet dismissed because he refused to be a slave to an Irish cur or an English importation.—Sincerely yours,

J. O'Casey

To Irish Worker

8 February 1913

Dear Mr. Editor,

I would like to know what Euchan [1] means when he writes that "Ireland's sub-conscious mind is away in the glories of the past." "The past, however, is past, Ireland can never be again the glorious nation she was." [2] What does the writer mean by Ireland's sub-conscious mind, and what does he know about Ireland's past? Can he see farther than the soldiers, the saints and the sages of Eireann? Has he received this message from Balor of the Evil Eye, or does he write the words whispered in his ear by Manconan Mac Lir? Does Euchan think Labour will lay a detaining hand on Ireland's shoulder? Is the hand of Euchan about to write *ne plus ultra* on Ireland's soul? 'Twill want to be steady and true, and very, very strong. How like is Euchan's words to those written long ago which the Gael has not forgotten: "The Gael is gone with a vengeance, Laus Deo!" The Gael is here still, Euchan, stronger to suffer than Hell can harm, and it is highly improbable that our hearts shall shake before the words of Euchan. So the Labour Party is "not making pikes," but is "making intelligent voters." So, Euchan, you sneer at the pike. It's not the first sneer that winked at the Gael from the face of *The Worker*. The weapon only bruises the hand that flings it. And we learn that new gods have come to Eireann with gifts of intelligence in their hands, and Euchan is one of them. Ah! I fear we Irish will prove unpleasantly unreceptive. Attacks, ignorant and presumptive, upon our cherished ideals will do no good to the Labour Movement. The Labour Movement can afford to lose some of its friends; 'tis wise to convert

[1] Andrew Patrick Wilson, journalist, actor, playwright, wrote a regular column in the *Irish Worker* under the pseudonym of "Euchan." He was also an actor at the Abbey Theatre, served briefly as manager of the theatre (1914–15) and had two of his own plays produced there; he became director of the Scottish National Players in 1921. In Ireland he called himself A. Patrick Wilson, in Scotland, Andrew P. Wilson.

[2] "Euchan," "The Rebel Movement: Labour and Its Relation to Home Rule," *Irish Worker*, 1 February 1913. O'Casey's letter is a reply to this article.

an enemy to friendship, who will dare to say that it is wise to ignorantly offend a friend?

But we laugh at Euchan; "Ireland will never again be the glorious nation she was", is comically equal to the statement by the same writer, "that Bobbie Burns was, perhaps, the greatest of all Scots."—Perhaps he was, Euchan!

S. O'Cathasaigh

"EUCHAN'S" REPLY

Through the courtesy of the Editor of the WORKER I have been handed the foregoing letter, so that I may make any reply I may deem fitting.

Though I have read the letter with the gravest and greatest attention I can find nothing in it that is worth replying to. If my good critic would try to write less prettily and more logically I might endeavour to make something of his charges. As it is, I must say a suitable reply seems hopeless. If I say that Ireland's "past is past," I can't for the life of me see how I can be said to be laying a "detaining hand on Ireland's shoulder." Will my critic read the article again, without prejudice, in full and not in part, and then he may realise that I was discussing the commercial present and not the romantic past. If he reads the article as I suggest, he may also see that when I talk about "pikes" I am not sneering at them. Pikes have served their day, but their day is past, that's all. When it comes to be a case of removing corrupt politicians from a nation's progress, I submit once more that intelligent voters are of more use than pikes. What does my critic think?

As to his closing remarks about Robert Burns, I am afraid I'm once more at a loss regarding my critic's meaning. It may be my density, or, again, it may be that the writer's logic has been lost amidst his powers of rhetoric.

Briefly re-stated, the arguments of the article were:—

(a) That the present is purely a commercial age.

(b) That the coming of Home Rule will bring Ireland into commercial line with its neighbours.

(c) That the battle of the future in Ireland will be between Capital and Labour.

(d) That the workers of Ireland must prepare now for that battle.

An intelligent critic will either attempt to refute or to further these arguments in whole or in part. Would he mind writing again after he has *read* the article.

"Euchan"

To Irish Worker

22 February 1913

"EUCHAN" AND IRELAND: A CHALLENGE TO A VERBAL COMBAT

'Tis man aspires
To link his present with his country's past
And live anew in knowledge of his sires.
Samuel Ferguson

Are you ready, "Euchan"? On guard, then!

I asked "Euchan" some questions. He did not answer them. He says they were not worth answering. He stated "Ireland's past is past," and that "Ireland can never again be the glorious nation she was." I asked him what reasons he held for making such an assertion. But though probably reasons are, with "Euchan," as plentiful as blackberries, he will not give us one; the question is "not worth answering." The question will be answered for him. Surely "Euchan" did not think my brief letter was a criticism of his article. I therein asked for a fuller meaning of some astonishing announcements concerning the National faith of all Irishmen. "Euchan" should have READ my letter. Here are now my opinions on the various points raised by "Euchan": (a) "That the present age is purely commercial."

God forbid! This age has seen the rekindling of many nations; this age has witnessed in many lands the stirring of the dry bones of the toilers. Bohemia, which regarded more fondly her language and her literature than her linen and her glass, Finland and the Balkan States are all heaving in the throes of a National Revival. Nationalists are being hurried into gaol in Egypt for preaching Egypt for Egyptians; and Hindu and Mussulman, in India, are chanting Bande Bataram; in our own dear country Fleming, O'Growney and Rooney, among many have proclaimed that "the life is more than meat and the body more than raiment." Life is stirring everywhere; democratic States are appearing everywhere—even in China—but still the fountain remains unpure; the people still cling to the mire. In my opinion this is far from being a "purely commercial age," but is the age rather of an excitedly awakening democracy. Ireland never was, never will be the slave of Commercialism. Her glens and valleys will never be furnace-burned like the Vale of Dura. In the past, "Euchan," Commercialism was far from her shores; in the present, she, in her language, national and dramatic revival, has turned her back upon Mammon.

"Euchan" tells us that (b) "Home Rule will bring Eire into commercial line with our neighbours." Evidently, he thinks, too, Home Rule is the final settlement. Don't you think, "Euchan," the people have something to say to that? Ireland's soul is not symbolised by the buzz of Jacob's machinery, nor are her energies confined between the four walls of Irwin's paper mills (although Irwin once issued a Municipal election leaflet in Irish). Ireland's nearest neighbour is England. In language, industrialism or ultimate ideal Ireland will never be linked with her. Ireland will look for better things than an Old Age Pension, State Insurance Act, or Meals for Necessitous Children. Gaelic Ireland will have no room but a grave space for the persecutor and the oppressor. Our work will be, not to link our country with commercial England, but to make her feed as large a number of people as possible: making every sod productive, every tree a defence, and every son and daughter of our mother happy. "Euchan" further says (c) that "the battle of the future will be with Labour and Capital." Here again "Euchan" suggests that Home Rule is our final political settlement with England. Not so, "Euchan"—not so. And to supplement this "Euchan" adds that the Labour movement is the only rebel movement in Ireland, and "Euchan" is going to arm his rebels with votes. Good man, "Euchan"! but don't you think the revolution will be a tame one? But they'll have intelligence, too, says "Euchan." Aye, so had "O'F" and so had Richardson. Intelligence sometimes has its price and can be used against the very power it was expected to aid. Give me the men who simply did what's good, who'd hesitate to give the reason why; devotion to sacred principle is greater than acquired wisdoms. "Euchan" asks me if votes intelligently given are not more effective than pikes? I believe they are useless without power to resist their nullification. The votes of our Volunteers were useless when they handed up their arms; the votes of the French National assembly would have been choked in their blood were not behind them the people with arms in their hands. Ireland's future battle will be, "Euchan," the continuance of the fight that has gone on since the thievish Normans came to Ireland with their English civilisation. We are out to overthrow England's language, her political government of our country, good and bad; her degrading social system; her lauded legal code which are blossoms on the tree which springs, not from the centre of the Dublin Corporation, nor from the Halls of Westminster, but which has its roots in the heart of the English race.

Now, "Euchan," place between the alphabetical points which constitute the analysis of your first article these phrases, which I suppose, as you say, are not worth answering: "Ireland's past is past"; "Ireland can never be again the glorious Nation she was." What are we to infer? Come, "Euchan," be honest as well as logical; add to this, "The Labour Movement is now the only Rebel Movement in Ireland." And what are we to think? Why, what else but that all our love for, and inspiration in Ireland's past is vanity, and that the glory of Ireland's future is framed in the Labour Party's pamphlet. You prate of logic, and you say that in your article you dealt with the Commercial Present and not with the Romantic Past. But you tell us, "Euchan," that Ireland's past, our past, is past, and thereby deal with our country's history in a way which we resent and which we challenge. You say that you dealt with the Commercial Present, and you add that "Ireland will never again be the glorious nation she was." Does this phrase not deal with Ireland's future? Aye, in a way that we resent and that we challenge. Past indeed! I tell you that where one ten years ago thought of Ireland's past, hundreds now are studying it. "Beidh tracht agus iomradh ar mo gniomhaibh fos," [1] said Ireland's incomparable hero, and it is so. Sunday last the athletes of ten counties met in hurling and football to provide funds to erect a visible sign that a great Gael, whose life is now part of Ireland's past, is not forgotten. Now "Euchan" of the logic and the intelligence, I challenge you to debate with me that "this is purely in Ireland a commercial age"; "that Home Rule will link Ireland with her commercial neighbours"; "that Ireland's past is past" and "that she can never be the glorious Nation she was." You have already the advantages of intelligence and a logical mind; I will add to these: You can choose your own place —where you are most at home for preference—select your audience from the Transport Union Workers to whom, I presume, you are well known —I will not ask one of my friends to attend the debate—choose your own chairman—Jim [2] if you wish—and behold, it shall be made manifest to-morrow (Sunday) week, the 2nd ulto, or that day week, or afterwards when you will, that the Faith of the Gael is even more potent than the prophecies of "Euchan."

With regard to the failure of "Euchan" to understand my reference to Bobbie, "the greatest of Scots, and the herald of democracy," which he attributes to his density or my rhetoric, I fear "Euchan's" failure is due to density and ignorance. If "Euchan" be a Scotsman his statement that Bobbie "was, perhaps, the greatest of Scots" proclaims him ignorant of the history of his sires. It was not Burns of whom it was written, "Fortissimus heros Scotorum." The statement that he was the "herald of democracy," I leave to "Euchan" himself. His statements about Ireland manifest—if he be an Irishman—how ignorant an Irishman he is; but if "Euchan" be of the English breed, he is naturally trying to speak profoundly of things about which he knows next to nothing.

[1] "There will yet be comment and discourse on my heroic deeds."

[2] Jim Larkin (1876–1947), the leading figure in the Irish labor movement; founded the Irish Transport and General Workers' Union in 1909; founder-editor of the *Irish Worker,* 1911–14; 1924–25; 1930–32; leader of the Dublin general strike in August 1913. See O'Casey's characterization of Larkin as "Red Jim" in *The Star Turns Red* (London, Macmillan, 1940); and the chapter about Larkin, "Prometheus Hibernica," *Drums Under the Windows* (London, Macmillan, 1946).

Ceangal [3]

The delivery of Ireland is not in the Labour Manifesto, good and salutary as it may be, but in the strength, beauty, nobility and imagination of the Gaelic ideal. I am one of those who has entered into the labour of our fathers; one of those who declare—by the fame of our forefathers; by the murder of Red Hugh; by the anguished sighs of the Geraldine; by the blood-dripping wounds of Wolfe Tone; by the noble blood of Emmet; by the death-wasted bodies of the famine—that we will enter into our inheritance or we will fall one by one. Amen.

S. O'Cathasaigh

[3] Ceangal, 'Envoi.

From "Euchan" (A. Patrick Wilson) to Irish Worker

1 MARCH 1913

THE GOOD OLD PAST!
"Rip Van Winkle" Wakens Up
By "Euchan"

The other week an article of mine called "The Rebel Movement" was published in this paper.

By the "Rebel Movement" I meant the Labour Movement, and I still hold today, as I did then, that "the Labour Movement is the only Rebel Movement now existing in Ireland."

I based my contention principally on my belief that this is a commercial age; further, that all government today is essentially commercial government; and that, when Home Rule comes, the workers of Ireland will recognise that fact more fully than they now do, and that they will rally into the ranks of the Rebel Labour Movement in order that they may fight the commercial capitalist-controlled Government, and thus enable the workers to obtain justice or, at least, some measure of it.

That was the scope of the article. It was essentially a Labour article written for THE WORKER, because this particular paper is the only paper devoted to the interests of Labour.

Out of the many thousand readers of THE WORKER there is one who has taken exception to my article, and last week, by the courtesy of the Editor, he was allowed to meander over a considerable portion of the front page with a vague but lengthy article, which, I presume, he considered criticism.

Now my colleagues on THE WORKER know full well that I welcome criticism—nay, more, the policy of THE WORKER is to welcome criticism, for in many cases it helps to elucidate some debatable point, and bring the meaning more clearly before the minds of the readers.

With this policy before me, therefore, I have given careful attention to this particular article I refer to, and as I do not know the writer or anything at all about him, I could read his article quite dispassionately.

Having done so I am bound to say that his article is not criticism at all. It was two columns of aimless futility, tinged here and there with obvious spite. I can understand the futility, but with regard to the spite I neither understand it nor am I concerned about it.

My critic (if I may so call him for convenience sake) heads his article—"Euchan and Ireland." He honours me too much in bracketing me thus, for he must know that I am just as unworthy of such a position as—well, let us say my critic himself.

I suppose the unconscious reason he had for doing so was the old one of kinship between great love and strong hate. My critic evidently loves Ireland well, and he hates "Euchan" much, so, unconsciously, his rather wild and untutored mind brackets his two prevailing passions when he sits down to write.

I do not blame him for loving Ireland—I could honour him for that if I had any proof of his sincerity—neither do I blame him for hating "Euchan," but if I may use his article as evidence against him I would suggest that Ireland, or the Irish workers, will reap just as much benefit from his love as "Euchan" will reap discomfort from his hate, and the quantity of each can safely be reckoned "Nil."

Judging by the article I would say that my critic is a dreamer—a man going about with his head deeply immersed in the mists of the good old past. We meet them from time to time, but not very often nowadays. The last one I met was in Sligo, and in his drunken enthusiasm he said just the sort of things my critic wrote.

I do not suggest that my critic was drunk when he wrote his article—far from it; but he had just awakened from a dream, and it was my article that awakened him.

He either bought or got the loan of THE WORKER and started to read it under the impression that it was a journal for historic research. When he read my article he got a shock. He discovered that THE WORKER was a real live workers' paper, written by workers in the interests of the workers, and with his mind away back amid the serfdom and slavery of feudal times; he was considerably jarred.

He read my article again on the look out for insults to his dream world, and, not finding any, he manufactured some, and now has gulled himself into the belief that he actually found them.

Good old Rip Van Winkle! Good old Dreamland!

Rip Van Winkle is enraged. He imagines I have trod upon his

prehistoric corns, and he challenges me to mortal combat, or rather to a verbal onslaught.

"Are you ready, 'Euchan'?" says he. "On guard, then!"

I don't know whether he takes me for an ancient man-at-arms or a boy scout, I presume the former.

He might have said more appropriately under the circumstances—

"Lay on, Macduff;
And damned be him that first cries 'Hold, enough!' "

But I suppose even Shakespeare himself is too modern for this dreamland crusader.

THE CHALLENGE

As for the challenge to the verbal combat, it strikes me as the funniest thing I have read for a long time.

Poor old Rip Van Winkle shakes the fungus from his limbs and wants to fight. He is rather sorry that he has been awakened out of his dreams, but now that he is awake he will break a lance with "Euchan" who disturbed his slumbers, or if he cannot break a lance with him he will at least try to drown him in a flood of sentimentality.

Poor old Rip takes himself seriously, so seriously indeed that he cautions me to be "on guard." Good heavens, does Rip think that I am as foolish or as dream-ridden as he himself apparently is. On guard! forsooth. On guard against what? Surely I don't require to be told to be on guard against the motley collection of prehistoric red-herrings which Rip chooses to draw across my path? They are old and stale enough, Rip, to speak for themselves never you fear.

Rip challenges me to debate. I may select my own hall, my own audience. In other words, I may pack the place with my friends, and all that Rip wants is that those friends of mine will see Rip eat "Euchan" up. Rip also suggests that I get Jim [Larkin] to take the chair. He also wants Jim to see "Euchan" being swallowed. Why, I don't know, unless it be that Jim might take the hint and instal the victorious Rip in the dead "Euchan's" place.

This challenge of Rip's protests too much to be genuine, but his suggested date appeals to me as the crowning piece of futility of a futile mind. He will debate with me on the "2ND ULT"! Good old Rip! But if he can debate upon a date long since past I can't. That, of course, is a quibble; but, perhaps my readers will see more readily from that than anything else how much behind this critic of mine is.

I do not propose accepting Rip's challenge. If he thinks I have nothing better to do with my time than waste it on a platform trying to nail him to an argument when he would be scouting around two thousand years or more of history and sentiment, then he is welcome to his opinion; but I am not prepared to search hayricks for needles, and waiting for a sensible argument from this critic would just be as futile in my opinion.

Besides all that there is a much better reason than that why this matter cannot be thrashed, or rather "chased," out on a public platform.

Rip Van Winkle has chosen to question my right to write the article I did. The article was published in this paper, and any criticism arising about it or from it must also be published in the paper, as, we must presume, the readers, are to a certain extent interested in the matter.

Does Rip realise that there is not a public hall in Dublin capable of holding even a fourth of the readers of THE WORKER? Rip has tried to criticise my article; he has chosen to condemn me for things I haven't said, and now he wants to dodge behind an avalanche of sentiment in order to finish the matter. You'll say all you have to say about me or what I write, Rip, in these columns and not anywhere else. I'm "on guard," Rip, and don't you forget it. I detest red-herrings, especially when they are stale, and it will take a much earlier riser than you, Rip, to catch "Euchan" napping.

I have purposely refrained from making a reply to the article of Rip in detail. I hold that the article is a piece of futility, and as such is not worth replying to. Possibly this will make him come to the point. I trust it will. Let my critic drop all his silly little spiteful allusions to "Euchan," and let him hit out as hard as he likes. "Euchan" really doesn't mind what Rip Van Winkle thinks of him, and if he thinks that by saying nasty things about the writer will make his own case more plain, then Rip is welcome to say them, for his case meantime is painfully obscure.

When a man says, as this critic of mine does, "that the present age is not a commercial one," then the natural inclination of anyone listening would be to look around for the man's keeper and not argue with him.

If it is not a commercial age then there is no justification for the existence of THE IRISH WORKER—there is no reason for Trade Unions—and the Labour Party may just as well never have been born.

I never suggest for a minute that the granting of Home Rule is the last word in the Irish Political scheme of things. It is but the first step in a total national upheaval, but in that upheaval it is the workers who will come off worst as they always have done unless they waken up now and join forces with the Rebel Labour Movement. It is not to the Rip Van Winkles like my critic that the workers must look to for help. These good people live in a dream world of their own. "The delivery of Ireland is not in the Labour Manifesto," says my critic.

It may be so, but one thing at least is certain THAT THE DELIVERY OF THE IRISH WORKERS IS CONTAINED IN THE LABOUR MANIFESTO, and my critic can drop all his fine talk and poetical allusions and assail that principle IF HE DARE.

The fight of the future in Ireland is between Capital and Labour, and if my critic doesn't realise that then it is time for him to again fall into that long sleep from which he has just arisen. It concerns the workers very little whether their employers talk English, Dutch, or even Irish. Without combination the workers will be sweated and robbed.

Ireland as a part of the British Empire or the completely separated land my critic desires will still be governed by the capitalist class unless the workers combine now. Will my critic tell me or the readers of this paper how the Irish workers can better their condition outside of the Labour Movement? If he is out to assail the Labour Movement he had better do sc in his next attempt. If he is merely out for the purpose of trying to belittle "Euchan," then he is only wasting his time, for all that "Euchan" cares.

This is a Labour paper—not a journal for historic research—and my critic should get that into his head first and foremost.

I said nothing in my article derogatory to the history of Ireland in spite of Rip's inflamed imagination. I am writing for the workers of the present with an eye open for future developments, national and political.

The only history I am concerned with as a Labour writer is Industrial history, and from it I learn that the toilers of any and every age have been degraded, robbed, and sweated. It is to change that sorry scheme of things that Labour has been organised, and my critic is either with that attitude or against it—he can't be both.

To Irish Worker

8 March 1913

"EUCHAN" AND A CRITIC
THE CRITIC

I am seriously inclined by the promptings of Charity to say no more for Euchan's sake. I never anticipated that my few questions—which he has not answered, and my few remarks—could create such a hysterical commotion in poor Euchan's soul. But Truth is greater than Charity. I really wish Euchan would TRY to be logical. He says he said nothing derogatory of Ireland's History, and he heads his reply "The Good Old Past," and in the text he uses the phrase "motley collection of prehistoric red-herrings." What do these phrases mean? I wonder what does the writer of the "Coming of Cuchullain," Standish O'Grady,[1] think of

[1] Standish O'Grady (1846–1928), scholar, historian and novelist of Celtic mythology, often called "the father of the Irish literary revival." O'Casey refers to his popular novel, *The Coming of Cuchulain* (London, Methuen, 1894).

Euchan's opinion of Ireland's Past? Euchan says he bases his contentions principally on his BELIEF.

Upon what conditions, arguments and premises, does he base his belief? He may believe anything; he may say what he believes, but if he knew even the first elements of logic, he would realise that in no dispute or debate can belief be expected to carry conviction.

Does he expect all of us to fall down and worship when he chants his logical stanza, Credo Euchan! He still holds the "Labour Movement is the only Rebel Movement in Ireland." This is only an opinion; let him prove it. I suppose he is still content to arm his "Rebels" with votes! If he armed each of them even with a halberd of an ancient man-at-arms, or the stick of a boy scout, they'd have a better chance of success. It was the rifle on Bunker Hill, not the VOTES of the American Representatives, that won American Independence. It was the same power that overthrew the French Monarchy.

To-day, even in the very ward where the Transport Union is strongest, the VOTES of the electors have declared that Jim Larkin is their councillor. What prevents him from sitting in the Corporation, Euchan? British Law. The votes were no use to him. Surely, these points are clear enough for you. You tell us that as a Labour Writer you are only concerned in Industrial History. But do you not know, Euchan, that you cannot separate the Industrial History of Ireland from their National and Political records?

James Connolly [2] could give you some valuable information on this question. You say again that *The Irish Worker* is a labour paper, not a journal of historic research.

Your amusing mistakes have revealed that to me. I suppose it is because you have such a contempt for history in general that you make statements that historically are laughable, such as "He was the herald of Democracy," and "the greatest of the Scots," and that you try to hold up your beliefs by the arm with historical references, such as "Ireland's Past is Past," and "We are not Forging Pikes," etc.

I think your contention that *The Worker* is simply a Labour Paper is nonsense. The other week there was a long review of a recently issued volume of poetry, called "The Agate Lamp," [3] which, according to Euchan, had nothing to do with Labour whatever. And the Editor recently, in a sub-leader, advised all his readers to go and see pictures exhibited in the Central Branch of the Gaelic League, which, according

[2] James Connolly (1868–1916), a leader of revolutionary socialism, labor, and nationalism in Ireland; author of many books and articles on these subjects; one of the architects and martyrs of the 1916 Easter rising.

[3] Eva Gore-Booth, *The Agate Lamp* (London, Longmans, 1912), a book of poems, reviewed by A. Patrick Wilson ("Euchan"), *Irish Worker*, 18 January 1913.

to Euchan, had nothing to do with Labour. Are not the men of science and art and literature labourers, too? Ruskin says they are. What does Euchan think?

Euchan calls me a dreamer. I thank him for the word. He seems to think the dreamer who lives in the inspiration of the past is a fool. This is another of Euchan's "beliefs." The dreamers were and are the salt of all nations. Ruskin was a dreamer; so was Burns, the "greatest of Scots—perhaps"; so was Robert Emmet; and only the other week, in one of his articles, The O'Grady said that without imagination nothing can be done. But the most amusing part of Euchan's "reply" is his anxiety about his miserable job. What a bold bad man I must be to try a Jacobean trick on "Euchan" and supplant him in the good opinion of Jim. Why, years ago I argued some labour and historical questions with Jim himself in Drumcondra, and though Jim in his reply said I "spoke straight and hit hard", he never expressed any fear of losing his job.

"Euchan" refuses to give any reasons for the various statements he has made, and is definite—very definite—in one point only—he won't debate with me. He is afraid. Along with the fear of losing his job, his other reasons are: "The hall could not contain the readers of *The Worker*"; "I would spend my time scouting in the history of two thousand years ago." Now, I challenge him again to debate these questions with me—one or all of them.

1. "That the Labour Movement is the only Rebel Movement in Ireland";
2. "That this is purely a Commercial Age";
3. "That the Coming of Home Rule will link Ireland with her Commercial Neighbours";
4. "That the Delivery of the Irish Workers is in the Labour Manifesto."

Now "Euchan", I will sign an agreement in the presence of any witnesses you like that, in the eventuality of victory or defeat in a debate upon any one or all of the above subjects, I will not take your job from you; and if you do not wish Jim to behold your discomfiture—you know you never can tell—choose as your chairman the Labour Councillor for Kilmainham, W. P. Partridge. I am satisfied he will show no favour to either side.

If Liberty Hall[4] cannot contain the readers of *The Worker,* the "old spot by the river" will do me equally well, or the Fifteen Acres if you like, for the matter of that; and I will further give "Euchan" a guarantee that my remarks shall not go back a thousand years, but will be confined to the incidents, facts, and history of the Present Generation.

[4] Liberty Hall, Dublin, headquarters of the I.T.G.W.U.

Now, "Euchan", surely you need be afraid no longer, but give us an answer for the hope that is in you. "Euchan's" premises, which lead him to assert my criticisms were largely due to spite, are beneath contempt. His logical deductions consequent upon meeting in Sligo are equally contemptible. His passing remark that I either bought a copy of *The Worker* or got a LOAN of it, is another brilliant example of "Euchan's" arguments. His insinuation that a contributor who sent in a criticism over his true name was after his job is an example of his sense of fair play and of his courtesy.

"Euchan" has already many obvious advantages. I have added all I could to these. It is his business now to accept my challenge and prove the things he says are or will be. It is an article of logic that no one can be called upon to prove a negative. This is my last word. If "Euchan" refuses then I declare that he is a poor, shadowy Labour writer, ignorant of history, unacquainted with the first elements of logic, unworthy to play a part in the Movement which he does not understand.

S. O'Cathasaigh

"EUCHAN'S" ANSWER

To hear from my critic in his opening sentence this week that he is "seriously inclined from the promptings of charity, to say no more," strikes me as funny; but his further remark that it is "for Euchan's sake" he is so inclined strikes me as being even more funny still.

I, on the other hand, am seriously inclined to think that the inflated sense of importance with which this relic of the past regards himself will be sufficient to carry him altogether off his feet some day, and then there will be more German airship scares when his swelled head is seen floating round in the heavens.

Talk of charity comes well from this writer, considering the fact that a "charitable" (?) phrase of his had to be deleted from his first article to save THE WORKER from being suppressed.

What a complicated piece of decayed mechanism this writer's brain must be. He has wasted columns of our space in writing to make out that when I said "Ireland's past is past" I was trying to insult Ireland's great dead. I have waited for any substantiation of any such absurd argument, but it looks as if I must wait in vain.

This week he again tries to conjure my heading of last week's article, "The Good Old Past," into an insult, and he further grumbles about my use of the word "prehistoric." These grumbles and tricks of his, however, reveal to me now that he doesn't know the meaning of the English Language. When I write "good" he evidently thinks I mean "bad," and when I write "prehistoric" he evidently thinks I should have written "historic"; but the fact that I have not done as he would wish doesn't make the slightest difference to the terrific onslaught he makes upon THE THINGS I HAVE NOT WRITTEN.

I put it to my readers that no person outside a lunatic asylum could debate with this critic of mine. He tries, moreover, to drag Standish O'Grady to his side by the same misrepresentation. Well, if Standish O'Grady said that this wasn't a commercial age, as "Rip" has done, I'd make a solemn vow never to put pen to paper again in this life.

Last week I made a chance shot, which has evidently told. He says that my "insinuation that a contributor who sent in a criticism over his true name was after his job is an example of his sense of fairplay and of his courtesy." He says other things on the same score throughout his article, and this repetition shows, if anything, that the shot rankles. But about his remarks re "fair play and courtesy": In good sooth, but these come well from him—I don't think. Fairplay! the miserable hound! When only two weeks ago in the course of his article he sought to bracket my name with "O.F." and Richardson.

If I had cared to be bought I could have been bought long ago by just those imitation patriots like my critic who love to write their names in Irish, but they did not seem to realise that "Euchan" wrote for THE WORKER because he liked to do so; and that in consequence he wasn't for sale. I do not intend to deal further with this purely personal side of the case, but that this critic should write of fair-play in the face of the insinuations he made, either out of spite or malice, are enough to make an honest man turn sick.

Knowing something of the unseen influences and their power in this city, I am inclined to wonder if my critic attacked me on his own initiative, or does he only hold a brief!

As to his renewed challenge to debate. It is but a further proof of the man's inflated notions of himself. He says, "I am afraid." Well, I'm quite content to leave it at that, if he gets any satisfaction from his idea, but for my part I would not waste either my own time or that of an audience in letting this relic pose around on a platform trying to obtain a large advertisement for himself.

One point I have succeeded in bringing him to, and that is that he doesn't believe in the Labour Party. I believe that his posing as an expert historian is all a sham, and that the only real thing about him is this feeling of his against the Labour Party. Well, I'm not a Labour speaker, and it would raise a distinctly novel precedent had every writer to be challenged to debate by his irate critics, but if my dear old Rip is very badly wanting to knock spots off the Labour Party why shouldn't he tackle one of their recognised speakers. I'm sure they will be most happy to oblige.

That I should say that his remarks about Euchan were obviously tinged with spite is, according to Rip, beneath contempt. Very good. I suppose then, Rip, you won't mind my putting your reiterated spiteful remarks about Burns into the same category, and say that they also are beneath contempt. You've a big, swelled head, Rip (the result of consorting with a crowd of boys, possibly) but you have a very small mind. Take care that the mind doesn't sweep you off your feet some day.

"Euchan"

To Irish Worker

7 JUNE 1913

THE IRISH FETE IN JONES'S ROAD [1]

"Neart i n-ar lamhaibh, Firinne i n-ar mbealaibh, agus glaine i n-ar geroidhthibh." [2]—The Fenian character

"There shall yet old men and old women dwell in the streets of Jerusalem, every man with his staff in his hand for very age. And the streets of the city shall be full of boys and girls playing in the streets thereof."
—Zechariah 8:4–5

St. Enda's College—Is it a great thing to be asked to help in the strengthening of the one natural Gaelic School in Ireland? Workers for Ireland, let us help now to fertilize the seed sown by Padraig Mac Piarais by instant help and vigorous sympathy, that it may grow and bring forth fruit a hundred-fold to the glory of God and the honour of Ireland. Slaves, and worse than slaves, are we if it should be that this man's hope and this man's effort are as water spilled upon the ground. St. Enda's is the beginning, a glorious beginning—the acorn that may contain a forest of oak trees—ours now to do and say, "Live and flourish!" "We refuse," says P. Mac Piarais, "to worship the gods of Hume Street." Isn't it time for Irish Irelanders, not only to refuse to worship these

[1] Here O'Casey makes one of his many attempts to unite labor and nationalism by urging the workers to attend the Irish pageant produced by Padraig Mac Piarais (Padraig Pearse, 1879–1916, who was to become one of the martyrs of the 1916 rising) to raise funds for his St. Enda's College, a school for boys to be educated in the Irish language and culture. O'Casey helped Pearse organize the publicity for the pageant, which was based on "The Cattle Raid of Cooley" (*Táin Bó Cuailnge*), the great epic tale of the Red Branch or Ulster Cycle. For O'Casey's glowing attitude toward Pearse and an extended account of the pageant, see "In This Tent, the Rebubblicans," *Drums Under the Windows* (1946). For a contrasting view, see his reply to James MacGowan, "Volunteers and Workers," *Irish Worker,* 21 February 1914, where he says "Pearse is worse than all" because he was a strike-breaker and often rode the trams during the Dublin tram strike that began in August 1913, which helps to explain his sometimes ambivalent attitude toward Pearse.

[2] "Strength in our arms, Truth in our mouths, and purity in our hearts."

gods, but to take them out, smash them to pieces, and grind the pieces to powder in the Temple of Irish Ireland? How better to weaken what is strong than to strengthen what is weak? Every penny given to Scoil Enna [3] is a link in the defensive armour of Ireland. Any Gael who refuses to help, or neglects to help, the efforts being made to strengthen and extend the influence of St. Enda's College, let him be anathema!

The Fete will commence on Monday, June the 9th, and go on every evening till Saturday, June the 14th. All kinds of amusements will make the Fete attractive to everybody, such as Shooting Galleries, Hobbie Horses, Aunt Sally Shows, Swing boats, etc. As well, there will be exhibitions of drill, tent-pitching, and skirmishing by the Dublin National Boy Scouts. Pipers' Bands, and Brass and Reed Bands will enliven the hours with gay and stirring tunes. Open-air concerts will be held every night, at which every time will be as the handbills declare —"New, fresh, and good."

Irish Dancing on the sward may be indulged in by all who love the merry gig and reel for a very nominal fee. The principal attraction will be the elaborate pageant, "The Defense of the Ford," depicting one of the grandest episodes in Ireland's Heroic Past.

Two hundred performers will take part in this pageant. Here will be shown the Boy Corps of Ulster hurling on the field. The news of Cuchulain's wounding; the march of the boys to defend the frontiers till the Hero recovers; the scene of the men of Ireland around their Camp Fires; the attack by the Boy Corps of Ulster; and, finally, in the last act, the "Battle of the Ford" between the two Heroes, Cuchulain and Feardiadh. Admission to Grounds is only 3d., so that it certainly is possible for almost everyone to come upon one of the nights to witness a unique and instructive Festival. Three-day tickets may be had for one shilling; season tickets, admitting to all functions throughout the week, two and sixpence.

In one of his latter paragraphs in "An Macaomh," St. Enda's Manual, enumerating the teachers, Padraig Mac Piarais says, "Bow to us, and pass on." We bow to you, A Phadraig, but we will not pass on. Our hopes are your hopes; your work shall be our work; we stand or fall together. Scoil Enna for Ireland, Ireland for Scoil Enna, amen, a Thigbearna! [4]

Craobh na nDealg [5]

[3] Scoil Enna, St. Enda's School.

[4] a Thighearna!, Oh Lord!

[5] Craobh na nDealg, The Thorny Branch, one of O'Casey's pseudonyms, and an ironic comment on the well-known pseudonym of the founder of the Gaelic League, Dr. Douglas Hyde, An Craoibhínn Aoibhinn, The Pleasant Little Branch.

Irish Worker

19 JULY 1913

WOLFE TONE COMMITTEE [1]

The following amounts have been received in aid of the Wolfe Tone Memorial—

Collected on Cards, 2/6 per card—T. Shine, J. McGrath, E. Cicham, Madame Marie, T. Kelly, G. Irvine, F. Fahy, Sean Murphy. W. Murray (subscription per T. Clarke), 2/6.

Collections—Jones's Road, July 6th, 8/6; Dolphin's Barn Aeridheacht, 10/9; Swords, 3/4½; Kilkenny, 14/8; Ballymore Feis, 7/–; Mullingar Feis, 9/8.

Both (per Leo Casey Hurling Club), July 13th.—Carlow Feis £1 8s. 9½d.; Dolphin's Barn, 6/2½. Interest on Corporation Stock, £3 16s. 6d.; Robert Emmet Literary Club, Butte, Montana, U.S.A. (per J. J. MacCarthy), £10.

All delegates to attend Quarterly Meeting to be held on Friday, July 25th. Any delegate who may have received no notification is asked to forward his address to S. O'Cathasaigh, 18 Abercorn Road.

All monies for Bodenstown Pilgrimage is to be handed in at once to allow the account to be closed.

[1] This report in the *Irish Worker* indicates that "S. O'Cathasaigh" was secretary of the Wolfe Tone Memorial Committee.

To Sean T. O'Kelly [1]

MS. KRAUSE [2]

18 ABERCORN ROAD
DIA SATHAIRN
[20 JULY 1913]

[1] Sean T. O'Kelly (1882–1966), member of the Irish Volunteers during the 1916 rising, one of the founders of the Irish Republic, second president of Ireland, 1945–59. In 1913 O'Kelly was a town councillor of Dublin, and he and O'Casey met often in the Parnell Street tobacco and newspaper shop of Tom Clarke. For some time he had been trying to get a job for O'Casey, who had been out of work for a year and a half, since he was dismissed from the Great Northern Railway (see 9 March 1912 letter to *Irish Worker*), and O'Casey sent him this message as a reminder. O'Casey had placed the stamp of George V upside down as a protest against England. O'Kelly finally found a temporary job for O'Casey as a laborer through Patrick Tobin, secretary of the Improvements Committee of the Dublin Corporation. Mr. O'Kelly gave me this information in an interview in the summer of 1963.

[2] Postcard. Christine Lady Longford of the Dublin Gate Theatre very kindly presented me with the original postcard, which hung on the wall of her office in the theatre for many years.

S. T. O'KELLY, T.C.
8 BELVEDERE AVENUE
NORTH CIRCULAR ROAD

A Sheán, is dócha go bhfuair tú an cárta posta do chuir mé cughat tamaillín ó soin ann? Bí eagla orm gur imtigheadh amuigha é.

Sean Ó C.

[SATURDAY]

[Dear Sean, I suppose you got the postcard which I sent to you a short time ago? I was afraid it had gone astray.]

To Irish Worker

18 OCTOBER 1913

Correspondence

STRIKING FOR LIBERTY [1]

"Say, are ye Friends to Freedom?"

Evidences are everywhere manifesting themselves of the Gael's determination to stand by the workers in their magnificent fight to vindicate the liberties of man. The G.A.A.[2] has nobly taken its stand with the workers. Go neartighidh Dia e.[3]

There are many Irish Irelanders, I feel sure, who are anxious to help us in this historic battle, and I would like to suggest that they may help to strengthen the funds of the workers by contributing to the Strike Fund or by collecting among their friends. All information about collecting will be gladly given at Liberty Hall, and I shall be glad to receive or call for any subscriptions that Irish Irelanders may be willing to give towards preserving the elemental Rights of Man.

It is our right to decide for ourselves the best means of protecting ourselves. Freedom of speech and freedom of action—who will deprive us of them? Shall we be slaves for ever?

Sean O'Cathasaigh

[1] The Dublin tram strike began on 26 August 1913, after Jim Larkin had tried to organize the tram workers. The employers countered with a lock-out, the unions declared a general strike, and by the end of August 25,000 men in Dublin were out of work. The strike and lock-out lasted until February 1914. O'Casey was writing as secretary of the Strike Relief Fund Committee.

[2] The Gaelic Athletic Association.

[3] God give it strength.

To Irish Worker

26 NOVEMBER 1913

RELIEF FUND COMMITTEE

LIBERTY HALL, BERESFORD PLACE,
DUBLIN, 26 NOVEMBER 1913

Dear Sir,—My Committee take the liberty of claiming the hospitality of your paper to announce the receipt of a subscription of £5 from the Mary Street Cinema Company. Especially do we wish to acknowledge through your columns the encouraging and generous help we have received from the Dorset Street Picture House in the shape of a subscription of £10, and a promise of £5 weekly till further notice. We wish to convey to the management our earnest appreciation of their sympathy with our work, expressed in such a substantial and practical manner. The Dorset Street Picture House has invariably stood by the workers and the poor when in especial difficulties, and we are not surprised at their generous action on this occasion. Our Committee sincerely hope that the kindness of the Dorset Street Picture House will act as an incentive to other firms of a like nature to help the good work we have in hand by subscriptions or by benefit performances or, preferably, by both. Many other contributions we have received will shortly be published.

Sincerely yours,
P. Lennon,[1]
Sean O'Cathasaigh,
Hon. Secretaries

[1] Patrick Lennon, a horse-lorry driver. With the help of Lennon and his lorry, O'Casey traveled throughout Dublin raising funds for strike relief.

To Irish Worker

10 JANUARY 1914

WOMEN AND CHILDREN
(Of Locked-out Workers)
RELIEF FUND

No. 4 COMMITTEE ROOM,
LIBERTY HALL,
DUBLIN, 5 JANUARY 1914

Dear Sir,—We are requested by our Committee to make public the fact that owing to the kindness and generosity of the subscribers of the "Herald" League Fund, 1,335 children of the locked-out workers have been fully dressed with serviceable warm clothing, including a second supply of underclothing, during the period between 12th November and 31st December, 1913.

In eighty maternity cases within same period the mothers and babies have also been fully dressed.

A large quantity of the clothing has been sent direct from the "Herald" League branches in England, Scotland, and Wales, the largest supplies being sent from London, Glasgow, and Plymouth.

A local Committee has also worked energetically in collecting funds for the same meritorious object, and have succeeded in materially helping the Ladies' Committee in providing the necessities of life for Dublin's destitute poor.

In addition to the clothing referred to, a sum of £509 has been expended for same purpose, and there remain thousands of children yet to be clad.

On an average between 2,500 and 3,000 children get breakfast of cocoa, bread, and about 75 women with their babies get dinner daily, this dinner being varied every day.

Much credit is due to the courteous Paddy Murtagh (of hornpipe fame), who not only looks after the cooking, but ably assists in attending on the children at breakfast.

John O'Brien, tramway man, in the same manner takes charge of and looks after the women's dinner, both men being assisted by the locked-out women and girls.

These dinners and breakfasts are also supplied by the "Herald" League.

In recognition of the untiring efforts of Miss [Delia] Larkin and Miss Grace Neale, we commend the work that has been done, and confidently ask for additional support, that comfort may not be to Dublin's poor only a day's joy, but till such time as Christianity and reason may bring about such a condition of things that no human being shall starve in a land of plenty.

Sincerely yours,
Patrick Lennon, Hon. Sec.
Sean O'Cathasaigh, Assistant Sec.

To Irish Worker

24 JANUARY 1914

AN OPEN LETTER TO WORKERS IN THE VOLUNTEERS [1]

In a word, we demand Ireland for the Irish, not for the gentry alone.
John Mitchel

Many of you have been tempted to join this much talked of movement by the wild impulse of genuine enthusiasm. You have again allowed yourselves to be led away by words—words—words! You have momentarily forgotten that there can be no interests outside of those identified with your own class. That every worker must separate himself from every party—every movement that does not tend towards the development of the faith that all power springs from and is invested in the people.

The volunteer movement now shouts for the support of all classes, but hopes to build its battalions from flank to flank and from front to rear with massed bodies of workers.

Workers, do you not think it is high time to awake from your sleep and yield allegiance to no movement that does not avow the ultimate destiny of the workers. Ye stood by the farmers in the Land War, by the Revivalists in the fight for the Gaelic Language, largely by the Separatists in the Sinn Fein Movement, and what have ye gained? Now you are cuddled with dear words about Nationality and Country to devote the power of reason and the force of energy to a movement which silently disregards your claim to be anything but a slave to a class that has always opposed, and will always oppose National aspira-

[1] The Irish Citizen Army, a labor militia with the aim of protecting the workers against police brutality, was organized during the 1913 general strike and lock-out by the Irish Transport and General Workers' Union, under the leadership of Larkin and Connolly, with O'Casey serving as secretary. In November 1913, a month after the founding of the Citizen Army, a rival group organized the nationalistic Irish Volunteers. Patriotic, middle-class, and antilabor, the Volunteers began to draw recruits from the ranks of the Citizen Army, which prompted O'Casey's open letter. See also his *The Story of the Irish Citizen Army* (Dublin and London, Maunsel, 1919) for a full account of this struggle between labor and nationalism in Ireland.

tions that may be opposite to their monetary and commercial interests. "To secure and maintain the liberties and rights common to all Irishmen"—they say they stand for this. We know the liberties and rights we enjoy.

The right to toil till the blood is dried in our veins; the right to bless the land that gives us what it thinks we are worth; the right to suffer starvation, and misery, and disease, and then thank God that such light affliction work an exceeding weight of glory! Workers, ye are fools to train and drill for anything less than complete enfranchisement, for the utter alteration of the present social system, for liberty to ensure the natural and absolute development of every Irishborn man and woman.

We, workers, know too, the rights that are common to many Irishmen; rights that are organised robbery and oppression; rights that give them the robber's privilege to enjoy exclusively by the wealth that was created for all.

Workers, the leaders of this movement will try to cajole you with terms of Wolfe Tone and Mitchel whom they never knew, or did not understand. They will impress upon you the will to pay from your hard-earned wages a weekly premium to support an organisation that may be used, subsequently, to preserve the so-called interests of the employing class—your enemies and your country's enemies. They will tempt money from you to deck you in uniforms of scarlet or grey, or green and gold, while they will ignore and cause you to forget the hundreds of your fellow-countrymen and country-women gliding through Dublin's streets naked and unashamed in sin, misery and want.

Workers, this movement is built on a re-actionary basis, that of Grattan's Tinsel Volunteers. Are you going to be satisfied with a crowd of chattering well-fed aristocrats and commercial bugs coming in and going out of College Green? Are you going to rope Ireland's poor outside the boundaries of the Nation? Do you know what Mitchel said of Grattan's precious Parliament? This:—"This Parliament is a very fine thing to talk or sing about; it has association of a theatrical sort, but no Irish workman or Irish peasant will ever draw a trigger to restore it."

They tell us, too, the Volunteers are for all classes. How often have we heard that thrice-blessed statement before! Whenever we hear that we may know that the workers are welcome so long as they are content to lie at the feet of others. It is stated their manifesto is signed by a member of the Sinn Fein Executive, the U.I.L.[2] Executive, and the A.O.H.[3] Executive—a blessed and impeachable political Trinity!

[2] The United Irish League, a home-rule organization under the leadership of John Redmond.

[3] The Ancient Order of Hibernians, an exclusively Roman Catholic organization under the leadership of Joseph Devlin of Belfast, a conservative opposed to both the labor and national movements.

To you I would say, don't make d——— fools of yourselves! Stand by no movement that does not avow the principles of Tone and Mitchel and Lalor. Remember "equal citizenship" is no use to us as long as we have to work day and night, year in and year out, to avoid starvation for a pitiful wage in the workshop of another.

Use, or reserve for ultimate use, all your mental and physical energies towards the advancement of your own class.

S. O'Cathasaigh

From James MacGowan
To Irish Worker

7 February 1914

THE VOLUNTEERS AND THE WORKERS
A Reply to Seaghan O'Cathasaigh

In a recent issue of the "Irish Worker" I regret to see that Seaghan O'Cathasaigh sounds the discordant note on the question of the newly-formed Irish National Volunteers. He is very much perturbed lest the workers of Ireland should give any countenance or assist the new movement, and in order to add weight to his arguments he invokes the name of John Mitchel. Surely to goodness there is something wrong somewhere when a man calling himself an Irish Republican and a believer in the principles of Mitchel and Tone should raise his voice at this hour in an attempt to wean the workers away from their allegiance to those principles to create disunion (not the disunion anathematised by the Parliamentarian humbugs) but the real disunion that most assuredly will militate against the progress of Ireland towards the goal of national freedom and consequently of social and intellectual emancipation. He says that the workers are again being led away by words; that they have momentarily forgotten there can be no interests outside of those identified with their own class. Now, I hold no brief for the privileged classes. In fact, I detest as heartily as Seaghan O'Cathasaigh does the selfishness, corruption, and lack of patriotism which all through the history of their country they as a body have displayed; but I do say this: if Seaghan's dictum had been the guiding principle of all classes in Ireland her history would, indeed, have been an inglorious one. We would have no Lord Edward or Tone or Napper Tandy to look back to for inspiration in '98, no Emmet or Russell in 1803, no Mitchel or O'Brien or Fintan Lalor in '48, no Kickham or O'Leary or Luby in '67, no George Henry Moore, no Parnell. All these men, it seems, lived and laboured under a delusion: they thought they had other interests to serve besides their own, and acted accordingly. And in our own day we have the Casements, the George Russells, and the Captain Whites making fools of themselves in the same way.

The Volunteer movement provides a common meeting ground for the best and most progressive elements in Irish life. It is a movement that will enable different sections to come to a better understanding with each other. The intermingling of Protestant and Catholic, Home Ruler and Republican, Larkinite and Hibernian, cannot but have a healthy influence on the nation as a whole. It will generate a spirit of comradeship, a spirit of brotherhood, among all Irishmen, the lack of which has been the curse of our race in the past, and which has enabled the forces of sectarianism, Imperialism, and industrial tyranny to maintain their diabolical sway over our people, to the detriment of our common country.

Seaghan O'Cathasaigh seems to forget that Irishmen in general differ not as to the end to be attained, but only in regard to the means to be used. That end is the National independence of Ireland and the happiness and prosperity of her children; next the prosperity indicated by an increased banking account or a growth in the value of imports and exports, which more often than not are the causes of more real misery among the workers than anything else I know of.

Irishmen to-day are being misled by the cries of party. The old shibboleths which divided our fathers before us still in large measure serve the purpose of the self-seeking politicians whose only aim is their own aggrandisement and who care as little for the interests of their deluded followers as the Keoghs and Sadliers of old.

A real union of the Irish people can only be effected on the basis of a military movement, and the organisers of the Volunteers provide us with such a movement. It is not modelled on the lines of the Volunteers of 1782; its basic principle is freedom for the nation and for the individual; it is not a reactionary body. The same spirit that animated the '98 men, the spirit that caused the revolution of '48 to rise from the pauper graves of the Famine years, the spirit that nerved the Fenians to make another brave and not altogether futile attempt to smash their country's chains, once more manifests itself, and calls on the men of Ireland to rally to the standard of Irish liberty.

This movement in spite of the croaking of self-constituted prophets like Seaghan O'Cathasaigh will yet make history, and if the workers of Ireland prove true to their traditions an Irish Republic may be an event of the near future. The fact that men like Pearse, Macken and honest Tom Kelly are identified with the organisation is sufficient guarantee that the interests of the workers shall not be trampled upon. Only in an Irish Republic can the worker come into his full inheritance. Seaghan O'Cathasaigh is only doing the work of the English Government in trying to injure the Volunteers, and it is that Government that is responsible for all the blood that was shed in Dublin for the last six months.

James MacGowan

To Irish Worker

21 FEBRUARY 1914

VOLUNTEERS AND WORKERS

> I wish to say I am more than ever convinced that the way I have been taking is the only true way to deal with the "Government," to right the wrongs of working men, and to achieve liberty for my country.
>
> John Mitchel in Newgate Gaol

James MacGowan, standing proudly 'neath the fluttering banners —I suppose they will have fluttering banners—of the new Irish Volunteers, complains because the workers are beginning to dribble into public places, beginning to examine the different banners of political parties; beginning to study the symbols thereon and ask their meaning; beginning to ponder these things in their hearts, if these things mean to them bread and life.

The cries and bitter interjections of hunger and disease and pain must always fall discordantly on ears closed to all sounds but honey'd words from Leaders dressed well and fed well by those who follow them in efforts that are bound to leave the workers' last state equally as bad as their first.

Does James MacGowan mean to plead for a development of silent cowardice when the time has come to speak? Does he think that the stick which beats the workers now, will, in the hand of a Nationalist prophet, blossom and bear almonds like the rod of Aaron?

I am chided for using the name of Mitchel. I quote Mitchel because I am a Republican in principle and practice; because he denounced tyranny everywhere he found it, in the English Parliament, in the Irish convention; because he stood for the Irish worker against the English Lord and the Irish aristocrat, because tho' present day ranting extreme Nationalists conjure with his sacred name they ignore, I believe they deliberately ignore, the fact that he stood for, and fought for, the class they elect to despise and pass by.

James MacGowan condemns the writer's criticisms because they may be calculated to upset the fraternal feelings of Volunteers recruited from various political societies, but he makes it clear he does not mean the "unity" so jealously guarded by the "Parliamentary humbugs."

Well, Mr. MacGowan knows, I'm sure, there are humbugs that are not gilded with Parliamentarian glamour, and well he ought to know that the pretence of one is equal to the pretence of the other. He suggests there must be something wrong because I venture to criticise the Volunteers. There certainly is something wrong in the implied suggestion that we should receive all activities with acclamation, dumbfoundedly, that are heralded with the shrill bugle note of Nationality.

Is not this Unity, which seems like a king, to be hedged with an impenetrable divinity, another name for placid hypocrisy? How can there be any affinity of thought, any unity of action between a Republican and a member of the Board of Erin? [1]

How can there be any semi-mutual understanding between a man starving, because he exercises a right that should "be common to all men," and an individual who denies him this right? Have not greater men than those who prance the National Stage of Ireland now, tried and failed to unite all Irishmen in a common bond? Davis tried and failed; so did Mitchel, and even O'Connell displayed at his meetings, on his breast ribbons of orange and green. The Gaelic League was to bring about this blessed consummation, and so was the Sinn Fein movement, and where all these failed we are asked to believe the Volunteer movement will succeed! There can be no unity amongst men save the unity engendered by a common heritage of pain, oppression and wage-slavery.

Picture the embrace of him who in the oath of allegiance bows lowly obeisance to an English king with the Separatist whose vision stretches to the grave of Wolfe Tone!

It has come to a nice pass when Nationalists declare that sweet is bitter and bitter is sweet. Well for you, Wolfe Tone, that you are in your shroud and safe!

James MacGowan makes the point of declaring that national freedom surrounds social and intellectual emancipation. This statement would certainly be sublime if it were not ridiculous. He further alleges that had the workers always fought for their own interests they would never have recourse to the baptism of fire from the souls of such men as Tone, Mitchel, and Kickham. For whom were they fighting in '98, '48, and '67? Will he answer us that? And were such men as Mitchel and Tone decorated with ribbons and stars and a' that? We toilers will welcome the help of all men who realise, as Mitchel realised, that "the life of one labourer is worth the life of one nobleman; no more nor no less."

This correspondent tells us that the Volunteers are "not modelled on the lines of the Volunteers of '82." Has he read the official organ

[1] Board of Erin, synonymous with the Ancient Order of Hibernians, a conservative Catholic organization. In 1906 the Ulster Catholics, led by Joseph Devlin, national president of the A.O.H. in Belfast and Nationalist M.P. for West Belfast, formed the Board of Erin as a wing of the A.O.H., to protect the interests of Catholics.

of the society, which teems with detail regarding the formation, official government, apparel, and principles of the glorious soldiers of '82? Has he read the article contributed to the *Evening Herald* of blessed memory, by Arthur Griffith, holding up for the worship of Dublin's workers the kinemacoloured defenders of the privileged classes? Has he noticed the appeals in *Irish Freedom* to all Irishmen to follow in the steps of the men whom the aristocracy subsidised to repel the spread of Republicanism from France to Ireland? Maybe when he has read all these he will allow that there may be some justification for assuming that the inspiration of '82 is being used to make unfortunate men struggle to perpetuate the things they ought to destroy.

He says they are animated with a spirit identical with the spirit of '48 and '67. Does he think his readers are devoid of the rudiments of common sense? Fancy John McNeill or Laurence Kettle claiming kinship with the Fenians!

Picture the most Christian members of the Board of Erin tearing up the Pastorals that denounce Fenianism!

My critic reminds me "that Irishmen in general differ, not as to the end to be attained, but only in regard to the means to be used." Surely he ought to consider before he makes such a statement as this. Is it not clear that Irishmen differ very widely as to the end to be attained and the means to be used, and that on these points there can be no apparent or actual union?

There is a wide difference between Home Rule, a Republic, or a Co-operative Commonwealth. There was a wide difference even between the opinions of a Mitchel and those of Thomas Davis. There is an essential or unbridgable difference between Physical Force, Constitutionalism, Arrangement by Agreement and Devolution.

Personally, I hold the workers are beside themselves with foolishness to support any movement that does not stand to make the workers supreme, for these are the people, and without them there can be no life nor power.

The time is passing, and soon all workers shall realise that it is good to die for one's friend, but foolish to die for one's enemy.

This correspondent also ventures the statement that the presence of Tom Kelly, P. Macken, and P. H. Pearse in the Volunteers movement makes assurance doubly sure for the worker.

There seems to be a little of Browning's theory that "God's in his heaven and all's well with the world" in that statement. It provokes a smile to think of every wearer of the Red Hand being received into the Volunteer movement in the name of Pearse, Macken, and Kelly!

How is it that while Honest Tom Kelly held a high position on the Sinn Fein Executive the official organ slashed unmercifully at the workers in the throes of an industrial struggle?

Pearse is worse than all. When the workers of Dublin were waging a life and death struggle to preserve some of the "liberties" which ought to be common to all Irishmen, this leader of democratic opinion consistently used the trams on every possible occasion, though the controller of the Dublin tramway system was the man who declared the workers could submit or starve.

No sir: we have certainly made progress sufficient to be mentally independent on questions such as these, and beg leave to be allowed the common liberty we have been advised to practise, namely, to think for ourselves.

It is true that the British Government spilled the blood of the Dublin workers; it is equally true that the Irish mercantile Shylocks of Dublin created the conditions that gave the Government their sweet opportunity.

I have nothing to say regarding the observations made of myself. I challenge the officials of the Volunteers to tell us what they stand for. Is it for Home Rule? Is it for "the King, Lords, and Commons of Ireland"? Is it for a politically-free oligarchy? Is it for an Independent Irish Republic?

I challenge them to explain the meaning of "the liberties and rights common to all Irishmen." I challenge them to tell us if it be prudent to excitedly discuss the colours and distinctions of Volunteer uniforms, to beg for money to gratify their craving for pomp and show, while in Dublin alone twenty thousand families are wriggling together like worms in a putrid mass in horror-filled one-room tenements.

The preservation of one life is rather to be chosen than the decking of a thousand men in uniforms of green or scarlet and gold.

Not in the shouts of the deluded wage-slave Volunteers, but in the hunger-cry of the nation's poor is heard the voice of Ireland.

Sean O'Cathasaigh

From Seamus [James] MacGowan
To Irish Worker

28 February 1914

SHOULD THE WORKERS JOIN THE VOLUNTEERS?

Sean O'Cathasaigh in a series of vague generalities, which are to say the least of it unconvincing, endeavours to justify his attitude on the Volunteer question, and at the same time to confound my arguments. In this case he makes the initial mistake of misrepresenting—I don't say wilfully—what I have written on the subject. Those who have so far followed this little controversy can see plainly that he misinterprets my epistle in its entirety. He evades the unanswerable points I made, but makes an onslaught on what he considers the vulnerable parts of my armour. Curiously enough that onslaught leaves my position unaffected. His wordy arrows seem to have gone off at a tangent, as I still occupy the same vantage point I held in the beginning. Sean is very fond of a text on which to base his case. In this instance he goes to Mitchel for his inspiration. This to my mind is a very unfortunate circumstance —for Sean. His position, as I understand it, may be summed up in one sentence—Don't join the Volunteers because they have not placed in the forefront of their programme Sean O'Cathasaigh's views on the Labour question! And because of this omission the workers of Ireland are counselled to boycott the only movement which in our day has caused a flutter in the dovecotes of Downing street and Dublin Castle. Don't arm, says Sean O'Cathasaigh, with the manacled figure of Mitchel in his mind's eye; manacled workers of Ireland because a gullible people disregards his glorious message in '48—a message embodied in the one word: "Arm." That message comes thundering down the years to us to-day, and now when his countrymen have at last hearkened to the appeal of the great apostle of Irish Nationalism, a man who claims political kinship with the mighty dead dons the garb of faction and seeks to close the ears of those to whom that appeal has been directed.

As far as my position as a Volunteer is concerned I am proud of it, but when Sean O'Cathasaigh says I complain because the workers are beginning to dribble into high places, he states what he above all others knows to be absolutely untrue. He seems to forget who was his chiefest support in other quarters on this very question of the rights of the workers. But, let that pass. I do not complain because the workers are beginning to elevate themselves from the slough of despair to which hunger, disease and pain, combined with oft-repeated treachery on the part of alleged leaders, had so often consigned them in the past. I rejoice as heartily as he does in the re-awakening of the wage-slaves of Ireland to a sense of their own power, to a consciousness of the noble destiny that awaits them if they only prove true to themselves in this the critical moment of the struggle.

But to proceed. I do not mean to plead for a development of silent cowardice when the time has come to speak. I plead with the class to which I belong, that they may render allegiance to the teachings of Mitchel and Emmet and Tone. I plead for the loyalty of my class to the grand ideal of Irish nationhood. I plead for the unwavering adherence of my fellow-workers to the cardinal principle of our Nationalist faith. That principle is that every Irishman should arm, and thus be in a position to win back and defend the political independence of his country. I appeal to them to cherish the spirit of '98, '48 and '67. Take away that spirit and there is nothing left but ashes.

In his reference to the rod of Aaron, Sean O'Cathasaigh pretends to believe what he knows will never come to pass. That is that the

Volunteer will be used sometime in the dim and misty future to keep the workers down in the abyss of industrial serfdom. He says he quotes Mitchel because he is a Republican in principle and practice. Is it I ask, the principle and practice of a Republican to tell a people, oppressed and disarmed for centuries by a hostile foreign power to remain in that helpless plight, when they have the opportunity to enrol in a National Guard formed to gain and defend our stolen liberties? Is it the principle and practice of a Republican to try and find flaws in a movement which, like all things human, cannot be perfect no matter how noble and inspiring its immediate objects may be? Is it the principle and practice of a Republican to stand aside when the Irish people have at last realised the meaning of Mitchel's mission in life, when with a spontaneous outburst of genuine patriotism they have responded to the call of the Motherland, and joined hands in a holy and unbreakable band of brotherhood beneath the fluttering banners of the Irish National Volunteers? Is it, I repeat, the principle and practice of a Republican to stand aside at such a time contributing nothing to the movement but the counsels of despair and the poisoned arrows of spiteful criticism?

The Volunteer movement, it is hardly necessary to say, is one of the most democratic movements of our time. In its constitution it is more democratic than the old Fenian movement. Yet where is the man calling himself a Nationalist who is not ready to doff his hat to the memory of the gallant men of '67? When James Stephens and John O'Mahony started the Irish Republican Brotherhood was the Co-operative Commonwealth inscribed on their banner? No! Farseeing men that they were they knew that there could be no permanent improvements effected in the conditions of the Irish working class while the Union Jack floated within a stone's throw of College Green and while the hired assassins of England in their uniforms of red and blue paraded the streets of our great cities and towns. These men (God rest their immortal souls) realised the eternal truth that all Ireland's misfortunes are traceable directly or indirectly to that foul abomination known as English Government in Ireland, and so they devoted all their intellect and all their energies to securing its overthrow. The one question for Irish Nationalists to consider to-day is how to achieve that glorious consummation.

Sean O'Cathasaigh talks of the "ranting extreme Nationalists" who ignore the fact that Mitchel fought for the class they elect to despise. One would imagine from this that these individuals were high and mighty ones who regarded the world as their own and the workers as their bondslaves. Yet some of these men—leaders at that—have scarcely a second coat to put on their backs.

When I speak of the unity of Irishmen of all creeds and parties, which I believe the Volunteers will accomplish, I mean the unity which will spring from knowledge of the fact that one and all are soldiers prepared, if need be, to fight and die for the independence of their country. All sections of Irishmen coming together will learn to know each other better. The differences that kept them apart in the past and that loomed so large in their eyes will vanish to a considerable extent. Because, remember the disunion we have always had in Ireland, against which Davis, Mitchel and Tone directed their fiercest attacks was not the result of any inherent love for internecine strife on the part of the Irish people, rather was it because their gullibility encouraged every self-seeking politician with a tongue of silver and a cheek of brass to delude them with meaningless platitudes about Irish freedom while the poor people contributed to keep those political corner-boys in luxury. The unity which I speak of is not another name for placid hypocrisy, but it is the unity that shall yet mean the downfall of English rule in Ireland. There may not be any affinity of thought between a Republican and a member of the Board of Erin, but it is possible, aye probable, that the latter may have Republican principles drilled into him in the ranks of the volunteers.

With regard to the criticisms of my friend, I do not condemn any criticism so long as it is honest, but I do condemn criticism which is intended to damn in the eyes of the workers of Ireland a movement fraught with great possibilities for their future and the future of their country.

Sean is of opinion that because, as he alleges, Davis, Mitchel and O'Connell, the Gaelic League and Sinn Fein failed to unite the people of Ireland, the Volunteer movement will also fail to bring about such a glorious result. The statement if it were true is not in consonance with logic. But I deny that either Davis or Mitchel failed to unite our countrymen. Davis died before his teachings had time to take root, and whatever chance they had of doing so, was blasted by the famine, a disaster which could have been prevented were it not that wiseacres like my friend were out preaching to the people the folly of arming. Mitchel was carried off in chains before his policy had developed.

As space is limited I have not time to go into all the points raised in Sean's article. But one or two I cannot refrain from noticing. I did not say that National Freedom surrounds social and intellectual emancipation. What I did say was that National Freedom is essential to the social and intellectual emancipation of our people, quite a different thing. Again, I said if Tone, Lalor and Kickham had done as Sean would have the workers do, that is act on all questions as the interests of their class dictated, we would not now look back on the stainless records of their lives with pride. He says, "We, toilers, will welcome the help of all men who realise, as Mitchel realised, that the life of one labourer is worth the life of one nobleman." Quite right, Sean. But if the classes have other interests besides their own, does it not follow that the workers have other interests besides their own? In other words, the interests of the country overshadow the interests of any section or party.

Sean reiterates the statement that the Volunteers are modelled on the lines of the Volunteers of '82. Had he read the constitution he would see that in essentials they are as widely divergent as the Poles. The Volunteers of to-day are open to all Irishmen, irrespective of creed or party. Was that one of the principles of the men of '82? He asks me have I read certain papers. I have read all and have found nothing in them to give the lie to anything I have written. To the statement that Irishmen differ, not as to the end to be attained, but only in regard to the means to be used towards the attainment of that end, I still adhere. That end is the happiness and prosperity of the people as I said before. Republics, Co-operative commonwealths and all the other panaceas are only means to that end.

With regard to Pearse, if he has done what this correspondent alleges, I do not intend to try and excuse him. But the record of Kelly as a champion of the rights of the workers is too well known to be dilated on here. "It is true," says Sean O'Cathasaigh, "that the British Government spilled the blood of the Dublin workers; it is equally true that the Irish Mercantile Shylocks of Dublin created the conditions that gave the Government their sweet opportunity."

Granted that these Shylocks created the conditions that gave the Government their opportunity, who created those same Shylocks? Are they not the products of England's so-called civilization? The evils of capitalism were unknown in free Gaelic Ireland, but they shall remain to blight our country and her people until the day when a revivified Ireland shall rise from the ashes of the past glorious, immortal and free, strong in the devotion of her daughters, invincible in the courage of her sons. That day shall only come when the Irish race, armed to the teeth, gives the signal that shall hurl the British Empire to eternal damnation unwept, unhonoured, and unsung.

Seamus MacGowan,
Pound Street, Sligo

To Irish Worker

7 MARCH 1914

IRISH WORKERS AND IRISH VOLUNTEERS

Appearances to save his only care,
So things seem right no matter what they are.

At the risk of irritating *The Worker* readers, I venture to send a last reply to James MacGowan. My opponent justifies his appeal upon the workers to fall into the Volunteer Movement by

Appealing to them to render allegiance to the principles of Tone, Emmet and Mitchel;

By the statement that it is "one of the most democratic movements of our time";

By the belief that he holds that in the Volunteer movement is the power to evolve a Bond of Union for all Irishmen;

By asserting the hope or belief that this movement will hasten the day when "Ireland armed to the teeth, will hurl the British Empire to eternal damnation!"

Because it is the only movement in our day that has caused a "flutter in Dublin Castle!"

Yet neither from these beautiful flowers culled from Sligo, and held like a nosegay to be smelled by the workers, nor from any indication in official headquarters do we pluck a promise, stated or implied, that this movement guarantees us any fuller life, nor the bestowal upon us of that for which we are fighting—the Moral and National Ownership of Ireland.

I venture to point out to James MacGowan that the workers are, and cannot help being true to the pessimism of Tone and Mitchel.

As one of the leaders of the Volunteer Movement says in February's *Freedom*—"However the leaders may have failed, *the instinct of the people has always been unerring*." At a meeting held in Navan recently, in answer to a question John MacNeill, one of the secretaries to the Volunteers, told us that the Volunteers would be under the supreme control of the Irish Parliament, which, according to Mr. J. Redmond, will be under the control of the English Imperial Parliament.

What do the Separatist and Republican members of the Volunteers think of that statement? Why, even the Chocolate Soldiers of '82 would not submit to such a bandaging, for they were independent of Grattan's property loving Parliament. James MacGowan's time would be well spent in trying to insure that Tone and Mitchel were something more than useful games to the advanced Nationalists who are said to deny themselves so rigidly that they "have scarcely a second coat to put upon their backs!"

"The most democratic movement!" The same was said of the Gaelic League and Sinn Fein.

Will the officials of the Volunteers explain why, that while every National body, society and club, U.I.L., B.O.E., G.A.A., Sinn Fein received invitations to attend the initial meeting, held to start the movement, the Transport Union, that largest union of unskilled workers in Ireland, was ignored? That in a celebrated article entitled "The Coming Revolution," contributed to *An Claidheamh,* before the founding of the Volunteers, P. H. Pearse expressed the wish to see every member of Sinn Fein, B.O.E., U.I.L., and the Transport Union armed; that subsequently, dealing with the Volunteers in *Irish Freedom,* he mentions all these organisations but omits the Transport Union.

That while A. Griffith, dealing with the same movement in *The Irish American,* mentions the names of these organisations, but does not articulate the name of the Transport Union. Speaking some time ago to a prominent Volunteer, while criticising the principles of the new movement, he told me arrangements were being made to hold special drills for the leaders, who doubtlessly felt it would be injudicious to rub shoulders with the ordinary workers of Dublin.

Can the officials explain that, acting on a suggestion I made to Captain White, I myself wrote to a leading Volunteer with a view of possibly arranging for the use of the Dublin Halls at present engaged by the Volunteers, mutually by them and The Citizen Army, I received no reply to the communication sent?

Why is it that in the official organ reference was made in the speeches reported or articles contributed to every organisation in Irish National life, save and except the Labour movement?

This canting cry of all creeds and all classes is worn to a ghastly shadow: it is the cry of all societies deaf to the appeals of the subject workers of the Nation: it is the long arm that chucks the aristocracy under the chin, who have always been in Ireland a selfish materialistic crew, exemplifying in their life that it is indeed a dangerous disease to eat too much cake. These people, whom the Gaelic League and Sinn Fein were, and whom the Volunteers now are afraid to shock, were the weakness and bane of every National movement. It was they who succeeded in preventing the Volunteers of '82 from opening their ranks to the then subject class, the Catholics of Ireland—and when new men with democratic ideals began to organise the enslaved Catholics, the patriotic Henry Grattan drew attention to "the alarming drilling of the lowest classes of the populace. The old, the original Volunteers had become respectable, because they represented the property of the Nation; but attempts had been made to arm the poverty of the kingdom. They had originally been the armed property—were they now to become the armed beggary?" The modern Board of Erin and milk-hearted Republicans are apparently as anxious as Grattan was to maintain entire the respectability of the Volunteers and to prevent the inclusion of an armed beggary clamourous for the fuller exercise of human development and freedom.

I do not understand how Mr. MacGowan's logical mind construed an appeal to the workers to have nothing to do with the Volunteers into a declaration that no physical effort should be made by them to fulfill the first law of nature—to act and fight for their self-preservation. If ever an Irish leader called upon the people to arm for themselves, that was Mitchel. Speaking of the movement which in his day "stirred thro' Ireland from sea to sea," he says: "It is essentially not only a National movement, but *also*—why not admit it?—*a class movement*. Why should the gentry not join us? Why not lead us? Why? Surely because their interest is the other way—they know the end of British dominion here would be the end of them."

Arm indeed! Arm for what? Is it to preserve J. Redmond in the Cabinet Ministry of Ireland? Is it to "secure and maintain liberties and rights common to all Irishmen" which was denied and trampled upon by the very men who pose as leaders in the movement called together to secure and maintain them? Is it to preserve a system which compels thousands of our unfortunate fellow-slaves to rot in places declared by an unsympathetic Board to be unfit for human habitation? Let the Provisional Committee of the Volunteers give in their "Glorious Constitution," "The Rights of Man," an equal place with the "Rights of Ireland," and then the workers may have reason to disbelieve the statement that "National Liberty is not worth the shedding of a drop of blood."

Dealing with the question of the Union of all Irishmen, Mr. MacGowan says, "that coming together we shall grow to know each other better." We already know some of the leaders too well, and beg to say that there can be no Union of Light and Darkness. My opponent says that my contention of the failure of Mitchel and Davis to unite all Ireland foreshadows a similar failure on the part of the Volunteers is not logical. Well, let him prove the affirmative.

Certainly, where men like Mitchel and Davis, progressive, turbulent, majestically minded nerves failed, it is hardly conceivable that reactionary, unprogressive baby-trained leaders will succeed. Mitchel declares the failure of Davis. When Davis joyfully hailed an article in the *Evening Mail* as an indictment of "the appearance in the sanctuary of the Orange Heart of the Angel of Nationality," Mitchel says—"He was too sanguine. In the sanctuary of the Orange Heart no angel dwells—of the better species." Mr. MacGowan makes the point that the reasons of Mitchel's opponents' failure was that he was transported before his policy had time to wash the people. But in *Irish Freedom* for March, 1913, "Lucan," a well-known contributor, remarks that "Mitchel's gospel went thro' Ireland like lightning; the people loved it and forced their leaders to adopt it."

But my opponent perhaps is right. Mitchel failed not, but the other timid-soul'd leaders failed to grasp at the greatness of the class war Mitchel preached, and to-day the Volunteer leaders aim at a union with a class that has nothing in common with Ireland and ignore the masses that contain the will and the power to make Ireland, not a Nation in name, but a Nation in spirit and in truth.

I fear the Ezekielian vision of our friend of "the British Empire being hurled by the 'Irish Race' armed to the teeth to eternal damnation," conjures up, in my mind, that he is a frequent visitor to the picture theatres.

Mr. MacGowan sings the praises of the Volunteers because "it is the only movement in our day that has caused a flutter in the dove-cotes of Dublin Castle."

Still trusting on the fame of the workers' sentimental imaginations, of which we begin to tire: we ask for bread and they give us a stone.

But dealing with the point: Who were they who caused the Castle Authorities to imagine they saw recently in the streets of Dublin the Birth of a Revolution? Who were they who were charged with sedition and conspiracy to disturb the Peace of His Majesty's subjects? Were they the leaders of the Volunteers? Dublin Castle again sleeps in peace; the Revolution was stillborn. But then, it is still in the hearts of the people; as Newman says—"a whole wherever it is, unapproachable and incapable of being grasped, as being the result of causes far deeper than political or other visible agencies, the spiritual awakening of spiritual wants."

I challenge again the leaders of the Volunteers to explain their constitution; to tell us if Eoin MacNeill's statement be true; to declare if they stand for Home Rule, Grattan's Parliament, or an Irish Republic; to give in their constitution the Rights of Man an equal place with the Rights of Ireland, as the United Irishmen did; to tell us why they allow a paternal welcome to those who have attempted to prevent workers from preserving the elemental right to join the union of their choice.

Let them cease to rave about the principles of '98 and '67. Let them demonstrate unmistakably that they are not afraid to realise that Tone and Mitchel stood for something more than a politically free Ireland. That these men saw that the People were greater than the pride of power and the influence of Property. Let the leaders of the Volunteers have the courage to tell us which they prefer—The Aristocracy and the propertied Class, or the long-suffering but all-powerful People. Leaders of the Irish Volunteers! Why halt ye between two opinions; choose ye to-day whom ye shall serve!

Sean O'Cathasaigh

From Seamus [*James*] *MacGowan*
To Irish Worker

14 MARCH 1914

A Last Word to Sean O'Cathasaigh

I have no desire to any further prolong the discussion which has filled the columns of the "Worker" for weeks past in connection with the attempt of the gentleman above—an ineffectual attempt I may say—to smash the Volunteers. His last contribution dealing with this question shows the agility with which he is able to jump over the troublesome points of my last letter. He makes great capital out of the fact that the Volunteer leaders have not declared for a Republic. What an unpardonable omission that is, to be sure. However, that could be remedied if Sean would only intimate to the Provisional Committee his wishes on that point.

Sean seems to forget that when Wolfe Tone, the first of Irish Republicans, started the United Irishmen he did not declare for an Irish Republic. However, that did not prevent the movement declaring itself when the time was opportune. His reference to my attendance at picture houses I pass over as beneath notice. The whole tone of his letters is evidence of the spite which frustrated ambition engenders. In them is reflected the narrow-mindedness, the shallowness and the pessimism which are the chief characteristics of the cynic and the sceptic.

Seamus MacGowan

PS. *Story Irish Citizen Army* [1]

To Irish Trades Bodies

IRISH CITIZEN ARMY HEADQUARTERS
LIBERTY HALL, DUBLIN
[? APRIL 1914]

Manifesto Sent to Irish Trades Bodies

The Secretary.......................Trades Union.

A Chara,—In view of the present situation it has been decided to reorganise and develop the scope of the Irish Citizen Army. No one knows what a day may bring forth. We have the Ulster Volunteers preparing for eventualities in the North, and the National Volunteers actively organising themselves in various parts of Ireland, while all the time the Labour Hercules leans foolishly and lazily on his club.

Would it not be a shame if the forces of Labour alone were content to believe all things, suffer all things, endure all things; to starve rather than take, to be stricken and not to strike back?

[1] As secretary of the Irish Citizen Army, O'Casey wrote the manifesto, the handbill, the membership card, the original draft of the constitution, and the poster. This material appears as the appendix of his *The Story of the Irish Citizen Army* (1919), pp. 68–72.

Believing that Labour will shake itself to action, we have formed a Provisional Council to develop the power and influence of the Citizen Army in Labour circles, and we hope their efforts will receive the co-operation of your Trades Union. We propose to hold a meeting in your .... shortly, and, in the meantime, we appeal to you to use your efforts to prevent the members of your Union from joining any organisation, however attractive its name or principles may seem, till we have the opportunity of fully explaining to them the principles, objects and aims of the Irish Citizen Army.

We enclose copies of Constitution, posters and handbills, and hope that these will show that the Irish Citizen Army is the only suitable organisation for the workers of Ireland.

Fraternally yours,
President, Captain White, D.S.O.,
Hon. Secretary, Sean O'Cathasaigh,
Irish Citizen Army.

FIRST HANDBILL ISSUED BY IRISH CITIZEN ARMY

WHY IRISH WORKERS SHOULD NOT JOIN THE NATIONAL VOLUNTEERS!

1. Because many members of the Executive are hostile to the workers.
2. Because it is controlled by the forces that have always opposed Labour.
3. Because many of its officials have locked out their workers for asserting their right to join the Trades Union of their choice.
4. Because they refuse to definitely declare that they stand for the Democratic principles of Wolfe Tone and John Mitchel.
5. Because they welcome into their organisation creatures that are proved renegades to their own class.

REASONS WHY THE WORKERS SHOULD JOIN THE IRISH CITIZEN ARMY

1. Because it is controlled by Leaders of your own class.
2. Because it stands for Labour and the principles of Wolfe Tone, John Mitchel and Fintan Lalor.
3. Because it has the sympathy and support of the Dublin Trades Council.
4. Because it refuses to allow in its ranks those who have proved untrue to Labour.

WORKERS, don't be misled; trust only those ye know and have suffered for your class.

JOIN THE CITIZEN ARMY NOW!

COPY OF MEMBERSHIP CARD

Front Page

THE IRISH CITIZEN ARMY

MEMBERSHIP CARD

1913

President:

Captain White, D.S.O.

Hon. Secretary:

Sean O'Cathasaigh

Hon. Treasurers:

Countess Markievicz

Richard Brannigan

Army Headquarters:

Liberty Hall, Dublin

Go gCuiridh Dia an Rath Orainn.[2]

Back Page

"The Land and Sea and Air of Ireland for the People of Ireland. That is the gospel the heavens and earth are proclaiming; and that is the gospel every Irish heart is secretly burning to embrace."—*John Mitchel.*

THE CONSTITUTION OF THE IRISH CITIZEN ARMY

1.—That the first and last principle of the Irish Citizen Army is the avowal that the ownership of Ireland, moral and material, is vested of right in the people of Ireland.

2. That its principal objects shall be:—

a. To arm and train all Irishmen capable of bearing arms to enforce and defend its first principle.

b. To sink all differences of birth, privilege and creed under the common name of the Irish People.

3.—That the Citizen Army shall stand for the absolute unity of Irish Nationhood and recognition of the rights and liberties of the World's Democracies.

4.—That the Citizen Army shall be open to all who are prepared to accept the principles of equal rights and opportunities for the People of Ireland and to work in harmony with organised Labour towards that end.

5.—Every enrolled member must be, if possible, a member of a Trades Union recognised by the Irish Trades Union Congress.

GOD SAVE THE PEOPLE.

[2] Go gCuiridh Dia an Rath Orainn, May God bring us good luck.

COPY OF FIRST POSTER ISSUED BY CITIZEN ARMY COUNCIL, 1914

"Train your hands and your sons' hands, gentlemen of the earth, for you and they will have to use them."—Fintan Lalor.

TO THE PEOPLE OF IRELAND

This is the Time for Action. All political organisations are preparing for the future. Shall labour remain apathetic? Remember, workers, that

THE PRICE OF LIBERTY IS ETERNAL VIGILANCE.

Put the advice of Labour in practice by joining now

THE IRISH CITIZEN ARMY,

which stands for the Cause of Labour and erects its Constitution on the principles of

WOLFE TONE and JOHN MITCHEL.

Enlist at once and help us create

THE IRISH CO-OPERATIVE COMMONWEALTH.
GOD SAVE THE PEOPLE.

All particulars from

THE HONORARY SECRETARY,
Irish Citizen Army,
Liberty Hall,
Dublin.

To Irish Worker

9 May 1914

BY THE CAMP FIRE [1]

Labour Challenge to the Irish Volunteers.[2]

The following challenge has been sent to the Provisional Executive of the Irish Volunteers, and copies of the challenge have been forwarded to the "Evening Mail", "Evening Telegraph", and the "Irish Times". It will be interesting, we feel sure, to the rank and file of the Volunteers to watch the action taken by the Volunteers' Executive with the workers simple and straight, appeal to the Volunteer Executive to explain definitely their insidious and silent attempt to crib, cabin and confine the efforts of Labour to secure a fuller and more abundant recognition.

To the Provisional Executive of the
Irish National Volunteers.

Whereas the Provisional Executive of the Irish National Volunteers have claimed from public platforms and in the Press the support of the Irish workers; and

Whereas, the rank and file of the movement are almost wholly composed of members of the working class; and

Whereas, the conviction is growing stronger in labour circles considering the ambiguous principles of the Volunteers' Constitution and the class basis of the Provisional Executive and the Ladies' Auxiliary Committee, and the strong elements co-operating with the movement which have been consistently antagonistic to the lawful claims of labour,

We, the members of the Council of the Irish Citizen Army, representative of organised labour, now challenge the Executive of the Irish National Volunteers in public debate to justify this appeal for the sympathy and support of the Irish working class.

Details of debate to be arranged by three members of the Volunteers' Executive and three members of the Council of the Irish Citizen Army.

(Signed) *S. O'Cathasaigh,*
Hon. Sec.

[1] Beginning with the 4 April 1914 issue of the *Irish Worker,* O'Casey wrote a regular column under this title devoted to news about the Citizen Army.

[2] On 14 May 1914 Tom Clarke, one of the martyrs of the 1916 rising, wrote in a letter to John Devoy: "Larkin's people for some time past have been making war on the Irish Volunteers. I think this is largely inspired by a disgruntled fellow named O'Casey." *Devoy's Post Bag,* eds. William O'Brien and Desmond Ryan (Dublin, C. J. Fallon, 1948, 1953), 2 vols., p. 445.

To Irish Worker

13 JUNE 1914

The Citizen Army and National Volunteers

Some time ago the Citizen Army Council suggested to the National Volunteers by a public challenge that they should give reasons to justify their persistent appeals to the workers to support the movement. The challenge sent to the Secretaries of the Volunteers elicited the appended reply from Professor John MacNeill, and subsequently from the Assistant Secretary, Mr. Gogan. The replies are eloquent testimonies to the workers that the National Volunteers' attachment to Democracy are built upon foundations of hay and straw and stubble:—

19 HERBERT PARK, DUBLIN

Dear Sir—I received your letter last night at the Volunteers Headquarters and I gather from its contents that you think that there is a distinction being made by the Volunteer Executive between the noble and obscure, the rich and the poor, and that you wish to discuss the matter in public debate.

I am ignorant of the existence of such a distinction. I never heard much or little of such till I read your letter. It is impossible for me to enter into a discussion upon a matter about which I know nothing.

Sincerely yours,
(Signed) *Eoin MacNeill*

To Sean O'Cathasaigh.

THE IRISH VOLUNTEERS,
206 GT. BRUNSWICK ST.,
MAY 1914

Dear Sir—With reference to your challenge to public debate, the Provisional Committee regret to say that they cannot see their way to participate.

Yours fraternally,
The Honorary Secretaries,
Per L. G. Gogan,
Assistant Secretary.

The Secretary,
Irish Citizen Army.

We venture to draw your readers' attention to the fact that the challenge was first answered by Professor MacNeill himself without consulting his Executive—a singular action; and also that the subsequent letter from the Assistant Sec. includes the rejection of the suggestion of a conference between three members from each Council to discuss the whole question. Is it any wonder that Labour looks dubiously upon a movement which is afraid or unwilling to give an answer for the hope that is in it.

Sincerely yours,
Hon. Sec.,
Irish Citizen Army
[*Sean O'Cathasaigh*]

To Leo Rush [1]

MS. RUSH [2]

[DUBLIN]
[? OCTOBER 1915]

[1]Leo Rush, a carpenter in the St. Laurence O'Toole parish, who at this time was working in Kilkenny. O'Casey had been in St. Vincent's Hospital, Dublin, from 15 August to 1 September 1915, for an operation on his neck to remove some tubercular glands that had troubled him since his youth; and after the operation he grew a beard. See "St. Vincent Provides a Bed," *Drums Under the Windows* (1946).

[2] The letter that went with the drawing is lost.

To James Shiels [1]

MS. Shiels

Dublin
14 June 1916

Jimmy Mo mhile stoir: [2]

Ever so glad to hear you are well, safe and happy so-so. It is very gratifying to hear ye are now allowed to talk together and to enjoy yourselves as far as circumscribed circumstances will permit. We had a horrible time in our district; death was facing us back and front for days, but there must have been more righteous men amongst us than were found in Sodom and Gomorrah, for most of us came out safely, and could now listen to the "ping" of bullets as serenely as to the chirrup of "the little dickie birds sitting in the tree."

We were all glad when we heard from your sister, Bridie, that a letter had been received from you, which informed us you "like Hope, had for a Season bade the world farewell."

We have made great friends with "Kitty"; she is a great youngster, full of buoyancy and promise. Enclosed is a sketch of "Dear Francis," [3] collecting on the Quays for the National Aid Association (Cumann Cosanta na nGaedhael) with a sweet little colleen, and he took the opportunity, as the sketch will show, to declare

[1] James Shiels of the St. Laurence O'Toole Club. A member of the Irish Citizen Army, he was captured by the British during the 1916 Easter rising and was a prisoner in England when this letter was written.

[2] My dearest Jimmy, literally, Jimmy my thousand treasures.

[3] Frank Cahill, a lay teacher at the Christian Brothers' school in the St. Laurence O'Toole parish, and a founder-member of the St. Laurence O'Toole Club in 1907. The writing on the drawing reads: "Frank kicks two birds with the wan stone." "Paddy Mac felt ashamed" refers to Patrick MacDonnell of the St. Laurence O'Toole Club.

Springtime is ringtime, come on & don't be slow,
Change your name, go on be game
My Irish Molly Oh! Oh! Oh!

The ohs are those last notes which are so often found in Irish music.

I hope you will soon be amongst us again, and all the boys, to whom I want to be kindly remembered.

Give them my best wishes.

My dearest regards to yourself.

Your sincere friend,
Sean Ó Cathasaigh

To James Shiels

MS. SHIELS

DUBLIN
17 JULY 1916

My Dear Jimmy:

Greeting and health to you, and to all your fellow prisoners. I am sorry I could not, or, perhaps, did not, is more true—answer your letter to me before this.

All goes well in Dublin still: clergy preach; the Salvation Army still trolls out under the Customs House Bridge: "Glory for me, glory for me; that'll be glory, glory for me!" The pubs are doing their best to satisfy their patrons; the children in the slums still run about naked & hungry; the hospitals and the theatres are always full; and the sneering moon looks down and laughs quietly at us all. Oh! Life, Life! Oh, Man, Oh, Man! Today a worm; tomorrow a god; today a god; tomorrow a worm again!

Just as you say, Seumas, I try to laugh at the world—nay, I do not laugh *at* the world, but with the world, for a cheerful spirit will serve a man in Heaven or in Hell. List to Omar:—

> Ah! fill the Cup—what boots it to repeat
> How Time is slipping underneath our Feet:
> Unborn Tomorrow and Dead Yesterday,
> Why fret about them if Today be sweet!

Sorry to read that my "sketch" of "Frank and Somebody Else" was a source of enjoyment. Viewed in the "Perspective"—to use a war expert term—it is a cause for heart searching and general deprecation. However, I have spoken to Father Breen about the matter, and he promised to speak to Frank seriously about his unedifying & reprehensible conduct. I hope you will all enjoy your new quarters in Frongoch.[1]

We have made great friends with Bridie, and Frank was terribly put out because she gave me a rose; she's a charming little Irish Cailin,[2] but for Hearing's sake don't say—"let on" is better—I was talking—writing is better—about her.

Frank was fit to be tied because the Emeralds won from Geraldines, & are almost certain to win the Championship. He said xxx--?!!x-x--?? !!!!!--I'm sure the Censor wouldn't let it pass, so use your own imagination. He—Frank, of course—will never die happy till the "Emeralds" are dead and buried; so the enclosed "Sketch"[3] shows the Parish "Lohengrin," or "Jack the Giant Killer" out on the warpath to slay the horrible monstrosity.

Farewell, old, young friend for the present. Give my love to all the Boys. Tell them they are still fondly remember'd by

poor old Sean O'Cathasaigh

[1] Shiels had been transferred to the internment prison at Frongoch in Wales.

[2] cailín, girl or colleen.

[3] The sketch has been lost. I have included two other sketches of the rising which O'Casey sent to Shiels around this time. One reads: "Dodging Bullets in Dublin during the Revolt, JKC." The other: "Be the Holy!/Before/After. Scene in the Slums after the Looting. J.K.C."

Dodging Bullets in Dublin during
the Revolt. J.K.C.

Be the Holy.
After.
Before.
Scene in the Slums
after the Looting. J.K.C.

To Dublin Saturday Post

22 SEPTEMBER 1917

Labour and Sinn Fein.[1]

Dear Sir,—Last week's meeting of the Dublin Trades Council indicates a yawning awakefulness on the part of the Labour movement. It is indeed hopeful to see Labour making an effort even to mend the thatch to keep the rain out. Too long have we submitted to the control and dictation of lesser powers; too long has the infant governed the nurse.

It is surprising that Labour is only now beginning to realize that it must work out its own salvation apart, not only apart from, but through the different movements now stirring the dry bones of Irish political life.

I venture to offer a few opinions in the face of those expressed by several of the Labour delegates.

Two of those maintained that Labour should not interfere with any political movement; "that we should stick together for Labour, and not for any other political party." But this is impossible.

The Trades Council could, no doubt, live in the desert, and elect to spend its time in sweet and ravishing meditation. But I think all will agree that the Trades Council is not the whole Labour movement. Labour overflows from the Trades Hall, and we find it everywhere, in the Gaelic League, in Sinn Fein, in the Orange camp, and it will always be so, for humanity has many interests and many pleasures beside a loaf of bread and a few fish.

What I think the Labour movement ought to do is to make the workers, by education and propaganda, a power in all these organisations, particularly in those that appeal to the national sentiments of the people. By all means let us all forget Sinn Fein when we discuss Labour problems, but when we discuss Sinn Fein, we should never forget that we are of the working class. If the workers must or will attach themselves to organisations other than Labour, then let their activities in these movements be such as to make them recognise and submit to the claims and aspirations of the working class. Then will the danger Mr. Winston fears be removed. The Labour movement will never clash with Sinn Fein for then Sinn Fein would not dare clash with the Labour movement. So far from neglecting to interfere with any organisation we must interfere with them all.

[1] This is a continuation of the struggle between the labor movement and nationalism. Sinn Fein, literally "Ourselves Alone," the slogan of the Irish nationalists, was originally used by Arthur Griffith, but later was taken over by more militant groups. O'Casey's letter is based on a news story in the 15 September issue of the *Saturday Post* giving a report of the Dublin Trades Council meeting.

We must be more than "careful," as Mr. MacPartlin [2] advises; we must be aggressive. By lectures and pamphlet propaganda we must teach the workers that they are the prop of all things; then they will, in the power of evolution, teach the several organisations to which they are connected, that without them they can do nothing. "Courtesy" is worth little; deference is what we want; all political movement must be made to obey the Labour movement.

Mr. O'Brien's [3] contention that even if Labour put forward the worst possible candidate for popular selection acceptance should follow is a dangerous policy. Labour must select its best. Labour will always be unhappy, will always be beaten, till the workers are educated to demand and to select the wisest amongst them to govern their activities. Labour is no more immune from natural law than any other movement: it must grow wiser or die!

Then we hear Mr. Winston proclaiming that no attack should be made on Sinn Fein! Jove is being robbed of his thunder. Formerly it was don't embarrass the Party—now it is, don't embarrass Sinn Fein! Finally, it is unfair and it is useless to blame any single member of the Labour Party for the contemptuous way in which we have been deceived. All are culpable. I have been told two delegates were sent by the Trades Council to the recent Sinn Fein convention to explain the hopes and ideals of Labour and then retire. They elected to remain and they voted upon several questions, and fully participated in the Convention proceedings, and still no rebuke was administered subsequently by the Trades Council. We strain at gnats and swallow camels. We have all contributed to Labour's weaknesses. It is time to become strong. It was prophesied at the Trades Congress in Derry that the class war would begin when Ireland's political aims had been achieved. If that prophecy is to become true we must begin to fulfil it now. "Here or nowhere, now equally as at any time." Then, though we become a very strife to our neighbours, we shall at least be no longer a scorn to our enemies.

Sean O'Cathasaigh

Dublin
17 September 1917

[2] Thomas MacPartlin, president of the Dublin Trades Council.

[3] William O'Brien, an official of the Irish Transport and General Workers' Union, as well as a member of the Dublin Trades Council, and later to become a bitter anti-Larkinite. See O'Casey's letters to O'Brien in November 1921.

To Dublin Saturday Post

6 OCTOBER 1917

THOMAS ASHE [1]

Republican and Internationalist.

Many tributes have been paid to this dead leader. All activities of Irish life have sensibly and earnestly manifested the homage of approval over his sacred remains. To-day the fairest wreath above his grave, invisible to material sight, is the garland of love, bound together by the one thought, woven by the hands of Nationality, Labour, Nationalism and Education.

We all knew Thomas Aghas as the Gaelic Leaguer, the Commandant of Fianna Fail, but few realised that he was a true Republican and a firm and convinced advocate of the rights of Labour. It will be a surprise to many to hear that he loved the working classes as ardently and as fearlessly as he loved Ireland. Some of us remember well the human and inexhaustible sympathy he displayed with the fighting workers during the stirring and bloody days of the Great Strike of 1913. I remember the scathing and almost bitter terms he used towards many prominent Nationalists who thought it a respectable thing to condemn or ignore the fight the workers were then making for the elemental principles of Liberty.

Tom Ashe was always a warm supporter of the Ideals of Labour, voiced then by Labour's great leader, Jim Larkin, and between them there existed a close and unbreakable intimacy. Many times did Jim pronounce the eulogy that Tom Ashe has proved he so well deserved: "Tom Ashe is a man."

Someone writing in a morning paper recently, said that the late leader "divided mankind into two classes—Irish, and the others." This is not true; were it so it would go to show that Tom Ashe's thoughts were not so high and broad as we know them to have been. He was by no means insular in thought, save with respect to the language and traditions of his country—would to Heaven all rampant Sinn Feiners followed his example in this matter—but he never believed in the nonsensical "Wall of Brass" theory, and he took a keen interest in all peoples who were endeavouring to secure for themselves, by culture and progress, an honourable place in the sun.

[1] Thomas Ashe (1882–1917), teacher, Gaelic Leaguer, and Republican martyr, commanded the Volunteer forces at Ashbourne during the 1916 rising; was sentenced to death by court martial, but the sentence was commuted to life imprisonment in England. He was released in general amnesty of 17 June 1917, but was shortly re-arrested for making speeches against the British authorities in Ireland. As a prisoner at Mountjoy Prison he went on a hunger strike for a week, was forcibly fed, and died shortly after on 26 September 1917. See O'Casey's letter to Fergus O'Connor, 17 February 1918, note 4.

But he went farther than this: he understood and sympathised with the working-classes of all countries in their efforts to evolve a better life for themselves against their capital-controlled National Governments. He acknowledged that social regeneration must follow, or, conceivably, go before political emancipation. While he always remembered he was a Nationalist, he never forgot that he was a Republican. He avowed the Brotherhood of Man. He was a Republican as Wolfe Tone and John Mitchel were Republicans: he prophesied that the Labour Strike was the beginning of the Irish Revolution. The symbol of the Brotherhood of Man, the Red Flag—should have draped his body as well as the Irish Republican tri-colour.

Labour has reason to mourn the loss of Tom Ashe: he was ever the workers' friend and would always have been their champion. It never made him less Irish to love and to fix his hope on the ultimate Emancipation of the Masses. It never made him less Irish to accept the gospel of Mitchel: "The land, the sea, and the air of Ireland for the People of Ireland." Were the working-classes of Ireland to-day as Irish as the Irish of Ballyvourney or Macroom, that would still be the "gospel the heavens and earth would preach," and that would be the "gospel every Irish heart would be burning to embrace." That was the social faith of Tom Ashe: it was no less. He was a leader amongst the leaders of Irish Republicanism. It would be well if every Sinn Feiner followed in his steps. The least, however, they ought to do, if they cannot follow in the broad path in which he walked, is to follow in narrow insular way in which he first walked, and learn to read and to speak the language, without which the land Thomas Aghas loved will surely die.

Sean O'Cathasaigh

Dublin Saturday Post

1 DECEMBER 1917

The O'Toole Concert [1]

Under the auspices of the O'Toole Club a concert was held at the Empire Theatre on last Sunday night. We understand that several of the artistes offered their services and the theatre was placed at the disposal of the promoters free of charge. The total proceeds of the concert will

[1]The St. Laurence O'Toole Club's "Concert and Play" was performed on Sunday, 25 November 1917, at the Empire Theatre, Dublin (now the Olympia Theatre), "to provide Meals for Necessitous Children and the Poor."

be devoted to provide meals for necessitous children and the poor of Dublin. It was a big undertaking for the O'Tooles, and it is a pleasure to be able to record that their praiseworthy efforts were rewarded with unqualified success. Five minutes before the performance started there was not a square inch of unoccupied space in any part of the theatre, and hundreds of people were unable to gain admission.

The outstanding item on the programme was, of course, the singing of Miss Joan Burke. She sang "My Dark Rosaleen," and had to respond to an imperative *arís.*[2] "The Brave Volunteers," sung by Miss Connie O'Hanlon, was a popular item. Sean Mag Fhloinn and John Neilan sang, "Wrap the Green Flag" and "The West's Awake," respectively, and dances were contributed by Tom Bolger, Joseph Brewer and Miss Bridie McKenna. Liam Paul was accorded a great reception in recitations, but the applause of the night was reserved for Messrs. [Michael] Smyth and [Sean] O'Cathasaigh in the topical song, "The Constitutional Movement Must Go On," [3] and, in response to an *arís,* "I Don't Believe It, Do You?"

"Nabocklish," a comedy in two acts, by Thomas K. Moylan,[4] was performed by the O'Toole players. The idea of the play is good, but the author hardly made the most of his opportunities in the comedy line. The parts were capably filled. Pride of place must be given to Miss Bridie Shiels, as "Molly." She was the most natural of the players and was always distinct in her conversations. Paddy McDonnell, as "Jeremiah Cullinan," was good, though he displayed a certain amount of excitement and nervousness. Michael Smyth caused much amusement as the Car-driver, and Sean O'Cathasaigh strove valiantly in a part that was altogether unsuited to him.[5] M. Colgan was easily the best of the others, and in "make up" he was the best of all. The great reception which the play received should encourage the O'Toole players to still greater effort.

[2]*arís,* encore.

[3]"The Constitutional Movement Must Go On," a song written by O'Casey and Fergus O'Connor. See O'Casey's letter to Fergus O'Connor, 4 March 1918, note 1.

[4] Thomas King Moylan, *Naboclish* (Dublin, Duffy, 1913). The title is taken from the Irish, ná bac leis, never mind.

[5] This is one of the rare comments on the young O'Casey as an actor, particularly in the role of a stage-Englishman. He played one of the leading parts, that of George Herbert Chantilly Smith, a dim-witted English tourist who wants to meet some genuine Irish rebels; and apparently O'Casey had some difficulty in affecting a British manner and accent. Small wonder, since he had a thick Dublin brogue, which he retained throughout his life. See his letter to the *Irish Times,* 5 February 1949, Vol. II, where he makes a brief remark about his bad acting on this occasion.

To Fergus O'Connor [1]

MS. O'CONNOR

DUBLIN
[? JANUARY 1918]

Sinn Fein Election Ballad
"Hurrah For Ireland and Sinn Fein"
Air: "God Save Ireland"

1.

Ireland's hour is striking now,
Sinn Fein's hand is at the plough
And the people all are pressing to the goal,
Like a river's urgent flow,
Foreign rule to overthrow,
And emancipate our Country's Irish Soul!

Chorus
Hurrah for Ireland and for Sinn Fein!
Now or never is the call!
March we with the true and brave,
For the freedom of the slave
And for Ireland, blessed Ireland over all!

2.

Long we thought that Liberty,
Like a proudly cultured tree
Would produce a golden fruit in ſoreign clay;
But at last we know the truth
And we'll plant its spreading root
In the Native Soil of Ireland here today!
Chorus.

3.

Long we spurned the call of Tone
That our Land could stand alone,
And we hid his body, darkly, in the grave;
But the flag he loved to see—
Symbol of a people free—
O'er a joyous Irish People soon shall wave!
Chorus.

4.

The wondrous Stone of Lia Fail,
Proclaims as Queen our Granuaile,

[1] Fergus O'Connor (1875–1952), publisher of song books, music, Republican and labor pamphlets, and greeting cards for all occasions; arrested after the 1916 rising and interned at Frongoch, Wales.

And the Irish people gather 'round her throne:
Ne'er again the Gaelic Tribe
Shall accept a Saxon bribe,
But shall stand together, free, erect, alone!
Chorus.

Dear Fergus: Sending you on this additional effort to show that I have really made an effort to do as you ask. Find it hard to concentrate thought on any work other than that at which I am busy. Excuse writing—first attempt with a Fountain Pen.

Yours as Ever,
Sean O'Cathasaigh

To Dublin Evening Telegraph

11 FEBRUARY 1918

CASE OF PATRICK HIGGINS

Sir—Efforts have frequently been made to induce the Government to regard the majesty of the law as being thoroughly vindicated in the case of the unfortunate Patrick Higgins, who in 1913 was sentenced 10 years penal servitude for an offence committed in the heat and turmoil of the Dublin strike that then surged through the city of Dublin. Five years have since passed, and many things have happened, and surely the time has come for the people of Dublin to bring pressure to bear upon a flinty-hearted authority to strain out of its nature a little mercy towards this poor man who has languished for such a long time in a convict prison. It was mentioned at the trial that it was shocking that such an offence should have been committed on Christmas Day; but four Christmas Days have since come and gone, and these judicial teachers of the poor workers have lost as many opportunities to practically display the truth and earnestness of their Christian charity. Surely they, who say they know better, display a bitterness by keeping this unfortunate man in confinement, which is somewhat inconsistent with the expressions of Peace and Goodwill. How can they expect us workers to banish bitterness from our natures, when they refuse to have pity upon us? There is a threefold punishment in this case—upon the man himself, upon his wife, and upon his unfortunate children. His comrades of the coal trade have not forgotten him, and are determined that the measure of pity meted out to others, because, presumably, they occupied a more influential position in the social scale, shall be extended to their comrade, Higgins. Why the law must always take its course with a coal heaver, when it can be set aside for the sake of others, is a question now being discussed by this man's fellow-workers, and they are convinced that an answer should be given to this question, and given without undue delay. We hope the Dublin workers in general will help us in our efforts to restore Higgins to his suffering wife and children, so that charity may not remain a monopoly of the rich and influential.—Yours faithfully,

Sean O Cathasaigh

Dublin
10 February 1918

To Fergus O'Connor

MS. O'CONNOR

DUBLIN
13 FEBRUARY 1918

A Chara.

Re. what we were speaking of today: Those who want to publish stuff from my pen are—I have got their consent to reveal their identity—are a Mr. King, a traveller, and W. Kelly,[1] the latter interested in two shops, one [in] Seville Place & the other shop in Amiens St. The proposed conditions are: the two named above to be financially responsible for printing, & to undertake sales & distribution; I to contribute the reading matter.[2] Terms: equal division of profit, and guarantee to me of a minimum of Two Pounds for each effort. Certainly, appearing to be a fair offer, I must say that I feel inclined to consider it, for two reasons: I believe my opinions concerning Labour and Sinn Fein are pregnant with truth & foreknowledge; secondly, I am anxious to avoid refusing the chance of a few pounds if I can secure them—this is a frank & an honest confession. I think all my future publications ought to bear on cover the

[1] William Kelly, a close friend of the young O'Casey, owned a newspaper and tobacco shop in Seville Place, near the Five Lamps, the intersection of Amiens Street, Portland Row, North Strand Road, and Seville Place. Tom Clarke had owned two such shops, one at 75 Parnell Street and the other at 77 Amiens Street—both frequented by O'Casey—and after Clarke was executed in 1916, Kelly took over the Amiens Street shop. O'Casey made his first visit to the Abbey Theatre with Kelly and his wife Anne during the week of 11 December 1917 to see *Blight: The Tragedy of Dublin,* by "Alpha and Omega" (Oliver St. John Gogarty and Joseph O'Connor).

[2] The publishing firm of Kelly and King, which was to print the writings of O'Casey, never materialized.

name Shaun O'Casey, because many of my friends fail to discover me under the usual title that appears thereon. What about a 6[d] Edition of the Democratic Poems & Recitations of Boyle O'Reilly? [3]

Re. 6[d] Edition of my own songs, would not enclosed be a good 6[d] Line—
Should you want me drop me a card as I cannot go up so frequently now on account of the continued feebleness of my mother who has nobody to look after her but myself.

Sincerely yours,
Sean O'Cathasaigh

P.S.

I think you ought to advertise Songs of the Wren [4] in "Irish Opinion".[5] I know the agent, Johnny Lynch & could give the add to him if you wish.

S O'C.

[3] John Boyle O'Reilly (1844–90), Fenian journalist and poet, born in County Meath, joined the British army for the purpose of recruiting Irish soldiers for the Fenian movement; was court martialed and deported to Australia, but escaped to America where he continued to work for Irish freedom through his editorship of the Boston *Pilot* and his poems. Some of O'Casey's early songs and writing were influenced by the patriotic rhetoric of O'Reilly. O'Casey and O'Connor never came to an agreement about the proposed edition of O'Reilly's poems and speeches.

[4] Sean Ó Cathasaigh, *Songs of the Wren,* New Series No. 1 (Dublin, Fergus O'Connor, n.d. [1918]), a seven-page booklet of five songs, price one penny. On the cover the title is printed in Irish and English, with the following description: *Amhráin an Dreoilín, Songs of the Wren,* Humourous and Sentimental, by the author of "The Grand Oul' Dame Britannia." The title was inspired by an old Irish song, "An Dreoilín" (The Wren), which was sung by the insurgent Wren Boys on St. Stephen's Day. O'Casey's song, "The Grand Oul' Dame Britannia," first appeared in the *Worker's Republic,* 16 June 1916, by An Gall Fada (The Tall Foreigner or Protestant), his first pseudonym. O'Connor brought out two more editions of O'Casey's songs later in 1918, *Songs of the Wren,* New Series No. 2, n.d., an eight-page booklet of five songs, price one penny; and *More Wren Songs,* n.d., an eight-page booklet of four songs, price twopence. Ten of the above songs, plus "The Grand Oul' Dame," are reprinted in *Feathers From the Green Crow* (1962). Lady Gregory printed "The Grand Oul' Dame Britannia" in her *Kiltartan History Book* (London, T. Fisher Unwin, 1926; expanded 2nd edition), as part of a group of anonymous "Broadsheet Ballads of the Wars," for she did not know O'Casey had written it.

[5] Between 1916–18, O'Casey wrote six articles and a song that appeared in *Irish Opinion,* a weekly labor magazine: "Irish Protestants and Real Home Rule," 1 July 1916; "Cork University and Socialism," 8 July 1916; "Experiments in Communism," 13 January 1917; "Room For the Teachers," 12 January 1918; "As I Wait in the Boreen for Maggie," 12 January 1918, a song reprinted in *Songs of the Wren,* New Series No. 1; "Down With the Gaedhilge!," 9 March 1918; "The Gaelic Movement Today," 23 March 1918. The last three articles and the song are reprinted in *Feathers* (1962).

To Fergus O'Connor

MS. O'CONNOR

DUBLIN
17 FEBRUARY 1918

A Chara:

I thank you for your kind letter. Do not think for a moment that I shall not call to see you occasionally. I fear you think it was because I suggested better terms that I was afraid to speak to you face to face. That is not so. My mother is ailing for a long time, & will hardly ever be strong again. However, I could call up now and again, but should you not be in I cannot wait as I formerly used to do, for since my sister died,[1] I have to do all the washing, cooking & scrubbing in the house, unless I am prepared to reign in dirt, which I am not prepared to do. So for the preface.

Now, about future lines: I have got back an article from "Irish Opinion" on "Griffith & English Labour" which, I think, King & Kelly want to publish. Perhaps, you would like to dispose of some of these in the provinces. It might be possible to imprint on them, as being issued from the "Labour Press", so that it might not appear that they emanated from you. I have an invitation to call to see the Editor of "Irish Opinion" & I could talk about the matter with him. I am glad to say that the above mentioned article was in the file for publication, & that it was reluctantly returned, so that you are not to think it was *Rejected*. I will show you the letter from the sub-Editor that accompanied it back. I am working home on the Poems of J. B. O'Reilly—They are a revelation to me and are a wonderful production. They will make a splendid 6[d] or 1/line. You will want to get them in hands at once.

Do you remember months ago I suggested the publishing of Fintan Lalor's works, & you laughed at the idea. Have you noticed that these are advertised as about to be issued in all the National Weeklies. A splendid opportunity lost, a chara.

I will leave my Songs with you shortly, for the promised 6[d] Edition.

Will you settle up that account of the £3.10.0 you gave me. This has been annoying me; looks very like charity, & I'd rather not do anything than that this should present itself even in *appearance*.

As against this you have from me,

[1] Isabella Casey Beaver, his married sister, died on 1 January 1918, at the age of 51. His mother, Susan Casey, died ten months later on 9 November 1918, at the age of 81. They were buried in Mount Jerome Cemetery, Dublin, in Lot A35+247, beside his father, Michael Casey (1838–1886), and his brother Tom Casey (1869–1914). All these deaths are described in the autobiography. His brother Michael Casey (1866–1947) also lies in the family lot.

Songs of the Wren, No. 1.
Voices from the Dead O'Reilly [2]
" " " " Connolly [3]
Sacrifice of Thomas Ashe (Reprint) [4]

I ask £2.10.0 for Songs of the Wren No. 1. 2.10. 0
Sacrifice of Thomas Ashe, 2d line. 3.10. 0
V. from the Dead (O'Reilly) 6d line.
" 1½d per copy published with an 5. 0. 0
on account

Relative to the same line (Connolly) if this is to be published at a 6d line, it must be increased and improved which I will undertake, in a 2d line.

Songs of the Wren Book 6d Line,
same as other 6d lines. 3. 0. 0.

I could write up a pamphlet on lines suggested by you on England's atrocities in Ireland. Will talk about it to you.

Yours as Ever,
Sean O'Cathasaigh

Relating to 6d lines there will be no necessity for you to keep an account of number published. I shall be happy, indeed to take your word for all. I have never doubted it, & I am grateful for past favours.

Sean O'Cathasaigh

P.S. Do not hesitate to ask me for any ideas relating to schemes of your own. My brains—such as they are—will always be at your service.

[2] "Voices From the Dead, O'Reilly," not published.
[3] "Voices From the Dead, Connolly," not published.
[4] Sean O'Cathasaigh, *The Sacrifice of Thomas Ashe* (Dublin, Fergus O'Connor, 1918), a slightly expanded second edition of *The Story of Thomas Ashe* (Dublin, Fergus O'Connor, 1918); the former is reprinted in *Feathers From the Green Crow* (1962).

To Fergus O'Connor

MS. O'Connor

Dublin
4 March 1918

A Chara:

I called up to see you about Boyle O'Reilly's Poems but you were out each time. I am eager to get these out at once, but, perhaps, you have had enough stuff from me for awhile. Should you not be ready to deal with these, I would like to make other arrangements for their publication. Should you have too much on hands, then, I will call up to get the poems I have already left with you.

I hope "The Songs of the Wren" are going well. Would you be prepared to take any of the Pamphlet "Griffith & English Labour" when it comes out? Let me know if you will; it will be a Twopenny line.

Your Patrick's Day Cards are very pretty—you see the brighter colours enhance them greatly.

I shall be glad if you would lay aside some Xmas Cards on which are verses similar to those you want me to write for you.

The music of the Constitutional Movement [1] was sent to Clonmel recently. (Manuscript music).

Yours,
Sean O'Cathasaigh

[1] "The Constitutional Movement Must Go On," a song written by O'Casey and Fergus O'Connor. After the 1916 rising, John Redmond, the leader of the Irish Parliamentary Party, declared that in spite of the rebellion "the constitutional movement must go on," which inspired the writing of this satiric song. Among Fergus O'Connor's private papers I located four stanzas written in O'Casey's hand and seven others typed, with no indication of which were written by O'Casey or O'Connor. In his 17 April 1936 letter to Horace Reynolds, O'Casey says that O'Connor wrote the first two stanzas and O'Casey the rest.

To Dublin Evening Telegraph

7 March 1918

MR. P. T. DALY & RUMOURS [1]
Relations with Tom Clarke and Sean MacDermott [2]

Dear Sir—Regarding the "gossip mongering and rumours" circulating respecting Mr. P. T. Daly, I venture to place before your readers the following facts:—

In 1912 an earnest effort was made to link up the National Movement, as then represented by the "Freedom" clubs and the Labour movement, the guiding power of which at that time was Jim Larkin. A committee to discuss the question and take action was formed from the clubs, members of which included Tom Clarke, Shaun MacDermott, Peadar Maicin, Sean O'Cathasaigh, and others. It was decided that in

[1] The "rumours" were that Patrick Thomas Daly, an official of the Irish Transport and General Workers' Union and secretary of the Irish Trades Union Congress (1910–14), had been accused of dishonesty. Since he remained a trusted aide of Jim Larkin, however, as well as a friend of O'Casey, O'Casey came to his defense.

[2] With Clarke, Sean McDermott was one of the martyrs of the 1916 rising.

election Labour should be asked to help National candidates and to admit articles dealing with National aspirations into its press, and Progressive Nationalism was to act in the same friendly way towards Labour. Sean MacDermott and Sean O'Cathasaigh were sent as a deputation to Jim Larkin, and in Liberty Hall I was witness to the warm and friendly intimacy that evidently existed between Sean MacDermott and "Paddy" Daly. I can say with perfect knowledge that the same cordial friendliness was manifested by Tom Clarke towards P. T. Daly against whom Tom Clarke often assured me he had nothing to say, but the most friendly feeling existed between them. Now, if what has been said of P. T. Daly is true, these two men were either afraid of Daly, or were acting hypocritically. To those who knew them it is easy to realise they were afraid of nothing. Many people knew the painful candour of Thomas Clarke while all knew the honest, earnest sincerity of Sean MacDermott. There is not the least shadow of doubt that Daly held the confidence of these two leaders, and I speak not on an acquaintance of a few months, but an intimate friendship of many years, which I am glad to say, notwithstanding differences of opinion, endured cordially to the end—Sincerely yours.

Sean O'Cathasaigh

To Fergus O'Connor

MS. O'Connor

Dublin
8 March 1918

Dear Fergus:

I have seen today the proof—the cover of the reprint of No 1 Songs of the Wren, & it is most attractive & splendidly turned out. I really believe you ought to charge 2^{d} for it. It is really too good value for one Penny. When I compare it with the rubbish that sells at a penny the reflection is a painful one. I have been considering your remark about the risk of publishing 6^{d} lines for the last hour or so: Now, I know that my style is a peculiarly personal one, & I feel it is bound to interest. I have read pamphlets issued at 3^{d} & 4^{d} and they are rotten. Doubtless you imagine this assurance is born of vanity, but it has really been evolved by the assurance given by hard work and mental sweat and blood. Take [Darrell] Figgis or [Sean] Milroy, ay, or even [Arthur] Griffith, & give me one half hour with them on the same platform, & let those who are present judge as to the force, fire and originality of each. Why their vision is poor and rudimentary. I have weighed Life not in one balance alone, but in many. However, I do not want you to take any risks, for that would not be fair. So I shall be only too pleased to take back the poems of Boyle O'Reilly from you, or to seek another channel for the outflow of the continuing series of Voices From the Dead; or for any other line that will run to the important extent of a sixpenny issue. In fact I believe my effort to focus the thoughts of John Mitchell into abbreviated form would extend to a shilling line.

Just you examine Hegarty's book on Mitchell: [1] Here we have a "scholar" peering into Mitchell's Soul, & finding that Mitchell's Soul rejects every luminating ray but the green variety!

So I will call up when opportunity permits to get the selection of O'Reilly's Poems I left with you. The girls can set them aside for me.

Yours as Ever
Sean O'Cathasaigh

[1] Patrick S. O'Hegarty, *John Mitchel* (Dublin and London, Maunsel, 1917).

To Fergus O'Connor

MS. O'Connor

Dublin
9 March 1918

Dear Fergus:

Enclosed is a poem on John Redmond as you suggested.[1] I think it is good satire, but contains nothing vulgarly offensive. I submit it for publication to you first. You can have it for 25/–. Should you consider it unsuitable I shall be pleased if you return it as soon as possible. It is written in Boyle O'Reilly's style. I must confess I am tired of writing Christmas Greetings—it is most difficult to write to order. However, I have ten good ones done, and I want you to send me on the price you are prepared to give for thirty of them before I do any more, for I don't care a lot for the job.[2]

[1] The occasion was the recent death of John Redmond (1856–1918).

[2] On the back of O'Casey's 4 March 1918 letter to O'Connor, O'Connor had composed a draft of a reply to O'Casey, saying at one point, "I want about 24 Heart to Heart, personal, Irish, Sincere, Homely Greetings." Mrs. Fergus O'Connor kindly allowed me to examine her husband's private papers, and among them I found six Christmas card verses written in O'Casey's hand. They appear at the end of this letter. In 1963 O'Casey told me that O'Connor paid him the princely sum of one shilling for each verse, and that his total earnings for songs, poems, and Christmas card verses written for Fergus O'Connor came to about £5, "a small fortune for me then."

I called on Saturday but you were out. I thought you might have had the Poems of B. O'Reilly laid aside for me, which I must ask you to do, for I'm most anxious to have them published immediately. I can see that at present you are fairly choked with stuff, & I would not have written enclosed poem had you not suggested it yourself.

Please don't forget to let me have the poems of Boyle O'Reilly back, so that I may hasten their publication. Don't forget to let me have a look over the proofs of "Voices from the Dead" (O'Reilly) No. 2 of Songs of the Wren, & the Reprint of No 1 of same.

I shall be glad to receive as soon as is convenient to you the money for the 10,000 reprint of No 1 of the Wren Songs.

Sincerely yours,
Sean O'Cathasaigh

John Redmond. Dead, 1918

"Less than justice was done in the House of Commons to his efforts to rally Ireland to the Cause of the Empire and Civilization"—*Daily Mail*

1.

Busy the Empire's front extending,
While the life of his own dear land was ending;
Mimic fights he fought for the rights of man,
Far in the rear of the Nation's van;
The Hand of Oblivion his tomb is sealing—
From the People's ban there is no appealing!

2.

On the lid of coffin wreaths are piling—
And the People marching on are smiling—
For Wealth and Power honors weak behaviour,
And strew brave flowers on their slavish Saviour:
But, the Seed of Liberty's Tree is sowed
Wherever the People's blood has flowed!

3.

A Son of Ireland? Yes, but finding
Joy in his country's hapless binding;
Fearful of Energy's wrathful pleading,
He stumbled down in his task of leading;
Then he shrank aside from Freedom's violence,
And is shrouded now in a Nation's silence!

4.

No tremulous sob weakens Ireland's Voice,——
And Charity checks her desire to rejoice;
With the helpless, now, he is safely numbered,
And he frees the land that he long encumbered:
Knowledge and Thought in Strength returning,
Shall save the land like a brand from the burning!

5.

In the bloody throes of the world's collision,
His age-blind eyes saw a miraged vision,
And his life passed into a firm oration
For the sake of the world's poor civilization:
And he laboured to fix on the toiling masses
A Yoke, that a lifetime's toil surpasses!

6.

He struck at the torch that Freedom was raising,
And burned himself in its fiercer blazing,
The foeman's altar he served untiring
Tho' the flame licked the blood of his land expiring—
But dumb let us be—for his works deride him:
Let the generous Breast of his Country hide him!

Sean O'Cathasaigh

[Christmas Card Verses by O'Casey]

Throughout your Life may Fortune smile,
Each day with buoyant Hope surrounding;
And Christmas thoughts of Peace and Love
Link firm your heart with Joy abounding.

As the Rose far excels all the flowers of the field
In fragrance and loveliness too—
May this Christmas all Festival Seasons surpass
In its Joy and Sweet Pleasure to you!

May Christmas Joys in powerful measure
Drive from your Heart all thoughts that grieve you,
And finding there a welcome fair,
Remain in peace and never leave you.

May you, dear Friend, this Christmas find
The Fruit you seek on the Tree of Desire;
The trusty friend, the joy that lasts,
And Ireland warmed by Freedom's Fire.

May Nature give us day by day,
Joy after Joy—just as we need them—
The strength to show our love for man—
The will to strive for Ireland's Freedom!

Around your life may Christmas shed,
  Her Joys that banish thoughts depressing,
And furnish you, dear friend, instead,
  With Peace and Love and every Blessing.

To Dublin Evening Telegraph

14 MARCH 1918

MRS. T. CLARKE, P. T. DALY, AND SEAN O'CATHASAIGH.[1]

Dear Sir—Allow me to claim the indulgence of a last word from me respecting above subject. I am sure that many who have known me in the Gaelic League, in the national organisations, and in the labour movements will readily admit that Sean O'Cathasaigh never hesitated, even to save himself unpleasantness, to speak what he believed to be truth. They will do me more justice in this respect than Mrs. T. Clarke is evidently inclined to do. The statements I made relative to Sean MacDermott's cordiality towards P. T. Daly in Liberty Hall are true, whether Mrs. Clarke elects to believe them or not. But, perhaps, should Mrs. Clarke persist in assuring herself that I am an unreliable witness for the defence, the following incidents, which were public, will help us to come to a just and an honest conclusion:—

In 1915 when Daly stood for the Councillorship of the North Dock Ward, Mr. T. Clarke came down and voted for him. In October, 1914, a meeting was arranged to be held under the auspices of the Irish Volunteers, to which, I believe, Jim Larkin was invited. Eoin MacNeill refused to allow the labour leader on the platform, and a separate meeting held, at which Messrs. Clarke, MacDermott, Partridge, and Larkin spoke; P. T. Daly was the chairman of that meeting. If P. T. Daly did not possess the confidence of the militant leaders of the Volunteers, why was he allowed to preside at this meeting?

Personally, may I venture to assure Mrs. Clarke that my definite juncture with Labour did not break off my friendly relations with either

[1] On 11 March 1918 the *Dublin Evening Telegraph* printed a letter from Mrs. Kathleen Clarke, the widow of Tom Clarke, in which she replied to O'Casey's letter of 7 March, insisting that her husband and Sean MacDermott had broken with P. T. Daly and O'Casey "some years previous to Easter, 1916."

Tom Clarke or Sean MacDermott. Subsequently, at Bodenstown, with Larkin, in connection with the working activities of the Wolfe Tone Memorial Association, and with aeridheachta [2] celebrations in aid of St. Enda's, I have had many cordial talks with both of these leaders. I crave Mrs. Clarke's pardon if anything I have said assumed the grotesque shape of a boast. Such an effort was, indeed, far from my intention. During a hard and toilsome life I have never sought the favour or patronage of any individual or party, and I will continue to occupy that independent, if perilous position, I hope, till the grave closes on me.

In conclusion, I just wish to say that it is pitiful that national life seems to be reverting to the pre-historic law of the club and claw, and is beginning again, apparently, to pant to make, in a most unjust way, martyrs of its own flesh and blood.—I am, sincerely yours,

Sean O'Cathasaigh

Dublin
13 March 1918

[2] Aeridheachta: open-air entertainments or festivals. See above, "The Irish Fete in Jones's Road," *Irish Worker,* 7 June 1913.

To Fergus O'Connor

MS. O'Connor

Dublin
16 March 1918

A Chara:—

At last night's meeting of "The Irish Socialist Party," it was decided to give the issue of Jim Connolly's songs to wholesalers—Easons, J. J. Walsh & O'Hanrahan's being particularly mentioned—on the following terms:—

1/6 Per Doz of 13 copies, in not less than 1 Gross Quantities.

Retail Price—2/3 per doz of, I think, 12 copies.

The Booklet sells at 3d net. I did not mention your name for fear you should not have wished it. However, as Hanrahan's & J. J. Walsh are getting supplies, I thought it might interest you to know details. You can get particulars by applying to:

The Secretary
Irish Socialist Party
Room 3
Liberty Hall, Dublin

Yours,
Sean O'Cathasaigh

I hope you have got the Poems of O'Reilly. I have had a good deal of patience you must admit, & I shall be grateful if you would send them on to me without delay.

S O'C

To Fergus O'Connor

MS. O'Connor [1]

Dublin

6 April 1918

Dear Fergus:—

Yours of the 5th received, for which I thank you. Glad to think you are convinced that I have a little business intelligence. I'm afraid I must differ from you respecting my business transactions with Stanley,[2] or any other Publisher. I cannot see how the sale of anything I may write is to be decided by any business differences that may exist between you & him or them. Selling anything that my mind may produce to anybody willing to buy is neither dishonorable nor illegitimate.

With regard to Christmas Verses I may say I have written Christmas, Easter, & St. Patrick's Day Greetings to friends on Cards painted by myself more than a year before I ever met you; indeed some of those I gave you first were copies of ones I sent long before to personal friends including—

Father Brady P.P. St. Lawrence's Parish [3]

Rev. E. M. Griffin, Rector Barnabas Parish [4]

Sister Gonzaga, St. Vincent's Hospital [5]

[1] This letter was written on the stationery of the St. Laurence O'Toole Pipers' and Athletic Club, 17 Lower Oriel Street, Dublin.

[2] Joseph Stanley, publisher of the Gaelic Press, later Juverna Press, located in Parnell Street and Liffey Street.

[3] Rev. James Canon Brady, P.P., St. Laurence O'Toole's Church, a close friend of the young O'Casey.

[4] Rev. Edward Morgan Griffin, rector of St. Barnabas Church. The Protestant parish of St. Barnabas and the Roman Catholic parish of St. Laurence O'Toole overlapped in the North Wall section of Dublin. Many years later O'Casey dedicated the second volume of his autobiography, *Pictures in the Hallway* (London, Macmillan, 1942), "To the memory of the Rev. E. M. Griffin, B.D., M.A., one-time Rector of St. Barnabas, Dublin, a fine scholar; a man of many-branched kindness, whose sensitive hand was the first to give the clasp of friendship to the author." Rev. Griffin was rector from 1899–1918, when he retired. He died in 1923.

[5] O'Casey met and became friendly with Sister Gonzaga, a nurse in St. Vincent's Hospital, Dublin, when he went into the hospital to have some tubercular glands in his neck removed by surgery, 15 August–1 September 1915. See "St. Vincent Provides a Bed," *Drums Under the Windows* (1946).

& many members of the O'Toole Club. The only idea you gave me was to turn the talent—if such it be—to commercial purposes—which you now, apparently, strongly object to. Surely, you cannot expect me to look upon other Publishers as enemies because they happen to be business rivals, & as Stanley has seen my verses in your cards & has asked me to submit some to him, would it be fair to myself to refuse the recognition of merit, which his request undeniably demonstrates?

I'm grateful for your kind offer of recommendation to an English Firm, but any author who would bind himself to one publisher would be a fool, & I am egotistical enough to feel that I am not one of the world's fools. I think I have acted generously in not seeking the sale of the verses I wrote in the highest market, but instead sent them on to you first to make your selection, & to give you a chance of being first in the field. I, too, have given *you* some ideas a few of which you acted upon, others which you rejected—foolishly I think—and I never complained of your using them for your own profit, & I never would complain.

Best Wishes
Sean O'Cathasaigh

P.S. Let me have the verses you reject as soon as possible.

To Fergus O'Connor

MS. O'Connor

Dublin
9 April 1918

Dear Fergus:

The letter enclosed [1] has been held back by me to see if mature thought would alter the complexion of any ideas it contains. But, after long consideration, I still am convinced that your objection to my having business with Stanley—even for the supply of Christmas Card Verses—is pre-eminently absurd. "The first Social Right of man is the right to live," says Connolly, and alas! I have to try to live as well as any other mortal.

You have told me that you have no idea when the reprint of No 1 "Songs of the Wren" will be accomplished, so I gather you are full up, & can't accept any more of my effusions at present. I shall be pleased, therefore, if you will allow me to submit the continuing numbers of "Voices from the Dead" series to another publisher.

[1] The letter of 6 April 1918.

Please don't forget to let me have the number of the Christmas Card Verses that you think unsuitable.

I suppose you have read De Valera's repudiation of [Joseph] Devlin's charges respecting De Valera's antagonism to Labour. It indicates strongly the growing power of Labour opinions.

Truth is mighty & shall prevail.

Yours as Ever,
Sean O'Cathasaigh

To Fergus O'Connor

MS. O'CONNOR

DUBLIN
10 APRIL 1918

A Chara dhilis: [1]

Enclosed is a picture taken from the Socialist paper "Satire", which may prove useful as a subject for a picture-postcard. Should you use it, please mention source from which it is taken, or, if you think proper, write for permission to the

Editor
"Satire"
127, Ossulston Street
London N.W.1.

Hope you won't forget to send me on as soon as possible the No. of each verse you will not take, & let me know if I can hand over subsequent numbers of "Voices From the Dead" to Stanley.

Yours Fraternally
Sean O'Cathasaigh

PS. Am enclosing a song "The Girl From the County Kildare." If you do not think it worth an offer will you return it in any letter you may be sending me.[2]

S. O'C.

[1] A Chara dhilis, My very dear Friend.

[2] In the draft of a reply, O'Connor writes that he cannot use the cartoon, the song, or any future numbers of "Voices From the Dead," and he is returning the cartoon and song. However, he must have made a copy of the song before he returned it, for I found it among his private papers and include it with this letter.

The Girl From the County Kildare

Air: "Twenty-Four Strings to My Bow"

Whenever the plough I am driving
Into Mother Earth's passionate breast,
My own heart I'm thinking I'm riving
With sharp thoughts that give me no rest;
For, faith, I am sorely entangled
In Love's wide, unbreakable snare—
And I'd rather be dead if I am not to wed
The sweet girl from the County Kildare!

Chorus

The girl from the County Kildare—
In my heart Love has lighted a flare,
Oh, I am the lad would be joyful and glad
With the girl from the County Kildare.

Dear maid, when the valleys are blazing
With wild flowers of many a hue,
They seem to be pensively praising
The much sweeter beauty of you.
For the fairest of all the fair flowerets
That are splendidly blossoming there,
Would not dare say to me, I'm fairer than she—
The sweet girl from the County Kildare.

Chorus

The girl from the County Kildare,
Sure, the wild flowers in chorus declare
That the gems of the field in their beauty must yield
To the girl from the County Kildare.

When the sun in his rapture's arraying
The morn in a ravishing dress,
To my mind every beam is displaying
The glow of each radiant tress;
The rich flame of the sun cannot equal
The gleam of her shimmering hair—
When she stands near the stile the sun seems to smile
On the girl from the County Kildare.

Chorus

The girl from the County Kildare—
The sun whispers now everywhere,
There's no stars in the skies like the bright flashing eyes
Of the girl from the County Kildare.

Bright joy in my bosom is dancing,
And Hope builds a nest in my soul,
For my heart in its task is advancing
To rob hers, now, for mine that she stole!
And soon I'll have courage to ask her,
If the rest of her life she can spare,
To give a poor boy a long life-time of joy
With the girl from the County Kildare.

Chorus
The girl from the County Kildare—
Sure Life will not muster a care,
When at home by the fire sits my heart's one desire,
The sweet girl from the County Kildare.

To Fergus O'Connor

MS. O'CONNOR

DUBLIN
15 APRIL 1918

A Chara:

I have received the verses you have returned which is a singular action, I think, on your part considering the importunity used to induce me to write them for you. However, your temperament is a curious one, and I have enough of patience to bear with you

> "When the rash humour which your mother (or father) gave you makes you forgetful" [1]

I cannot humiliate myself so as to allow you to become the arbiter as to whom I shall, or shall not, sell the poor effusions of my mind. From the bitter tone of your letter I have assumed that you wish to break off, immediately, all business intimacy, and, though I regret the differences, yet, owing to the circumstances which have occasioned the rupture, I feel that my personal freedom of action is immeasurably preferable to the pleasure of possible transactions with you in the future.

Wishing you every success,

Sean O'Cathasaigh

[1] A modification of Cassius's remarks to Brutus, in Shakespeare's *Julius Caesar,* IV, iii.

To Fergus O'Connor

MS. O'CONNOR
DUBLIN
25 MAY 1918

A Chara:—

I am herewith returning the little book you lent me from which to take materials for a phamplet, but, which for reasons that will be obvious to you, has now lost that utility, unless I employed it for issue through another channel which I am not prepared to do.

I shall be glad if you will leave aside for me the "Feilire na nGaedhilge",[1] the Booklet on the '98 Centenary Celebration, the Daily Mail Yearbook, the History of the G.A.A. and the Book on History Lessons, containing portraits of historic Irishmen, with any other materials you may have had from me, which I shall call up to take away in the near future.

I shall also be gratified if you would give me a full list of all the humorous songs you took from me, so that I may be certain that any of these I hand over for publication may not contain any you have purchased from me. Kindly let me know when I may call for above books.

I hope the present crisis has not materially interfered with your business, & I trust your mother and Mrs O'Connor are in the best of health.

Best of wishes,
Sincerely yours,
Sean O'Cathasaigh

[1] Féilire ná nGaedhilge, the calendar of the Irish.

To Fergus O'Connor

MS. O'CONNOR
DUBLIN
22 NOVEMBER 1918

Dear Fergus:—

I had abandoned forever the thought of writing the usual stuff called "songs", indeed I wrote a few which I have placed in a dust-filled pidgeon hole.

However, I am venturing to send you on a song dealing with the coming elections, which may suit your requirements. You did not say whether you wanted a serious or a humorous effort, so I have sent on a humorous item. I don't think much of it myself, but it may go well, which is the main point.

Could you make any suggestions yourself for a serious ballad? If you could suggest a good air I might be able to put words to it.

I might call up to see you soon & discuss the matter.

Yours As Ever,
Sean O'Cathasaigh

Sinn Fein Election Song
Hurrah! for Ireland and Sinn Fein
Air: "The Peeler and the Goat"

1.

Ses Johnny Dillon with a sigh,
    Things badly need arranging O,
Sinn Fein is now the battle-cry
    And things are sadly changing O;
I've play'd the Irish pantaloon
    On England's stage so clever O,
I thought I'd never hear the tune
    Of Ireland now or never, O!

Chorus
    Hurra for Ireland and Sinn Fein—
    Our star is in the ascendant O;
    The fight for Progress we'll maintain
    Till Ireland's Independent O!

2.

Ses Johnny Dillon now I feel
    The ground beneath me slippin' O,
Sinn Fein with undiminished zeal
    My Party wings are clippin' O;
Ses De Valera, Johnny dear,
    Your days of power are numbered O
Sinn Fein united soon will clear
    The land you long encumbered O!
Chorus:

3.

Ses Dillon, as he shed a tear,
    We'll ne'er survive this tacklin' O;

"We'll lose four hundred pounds a year,"
The Party Geese kept cacklin' O.
Ses De Valera, Ireland's Soul's
Above your paltry sellin' O,
No mean or gen'rous English doles
Can buy an Irish Felon O!
Chorus:

4.
Ses Dillon in Westminster Hall
We'll never more be talkin' O
In answer swift to Ireland's call,
The Saxon to be baulkin' O;
Ses De Valera, here's the place
To fight for Ireland's Freedom O
At home the suffering Irish Race
Will find the men to lead them O!
Chorus:

5.
Ses Dillon when we lose our posts
We'll all be well-nigh starvin' O,
Sinn Feiners will be drinkin' toasts,
And nice things they'll be carvin' O.
Ses De Valera, when you're weak,
Your light we'll not be quenchin' O.
Sinn Fein will Dillon kindly keep
Upon an Old Age Pension O!
Chorus:

From Bernard Shaw

MS. O'CASEY

10 ADELPHI TERRACE WC2
[LONDON]
3 DECEMBER 1919

Dear Sir,

I like the forword and afterword much better than the shouts, which are prodigiously overwritten.[1]

[1] O'Casey had sent Shaw the manuscript of a little book, "Three Shouts on a Hill," composed of three essays based on his articles on Irish labor, nationalism, and the Gaelic language in the *Irish Worker* and *Irish Opinion*. He asked Shaw to write a preface. The book was never published.

Why do you not come out definitely on the side of Labor & the English language?

I am afraid the National question will insist on getting settled before the Labor question. That is why the National question is a nuisance and a bore; but it can't be helped.

Of course the publishers will publish it with a preface by me; but how will that advance *you* as an author? Besides, my prefaces mean months of work. I'm asked for prefaces three times a week. It is quite out of the question. You must go through the mill like the rest and get published for your own sake, not for mine.

You ought to work out your position positively & definitely. This objecting to everyone else is Irish, but useless.

In great haste—I am busy rehearsing.

G. Bernard Shaw

Shaun O'Casey, Esq.
18 Abercorn Road
Dublin

II

THE TEMPLE OF THE ABBEY, 1920-25

I HAVE been thinking of Synge, Hugh Lane, Robert Gregory—standing on the galley deck of The Shadowy Waters, 'blue & dim, with sails & dresses of green and ornaments of copper'—and Ledwidge, the young, pale poet; all now of the dead; and you, Yeats, Stephens & Shaw, still, happily, of the living. Aristocrats, middle-class and worker: 'Three in One & one in three.' When one remembers those that have died; & these that still live, one, when thinking of Ireland, can still murmur: blessed is the womb that bore them, & the paps that they have sucked."

"I have written this primarily to show that no savage attack upon me by you or by Mr. F. J. McCormack will prevent me from venturing to give an answer for the hope that is in me, and to point out that while the Abbey Players have often turned water into wine, they may occasionally, (as in this instance, in my opinion) turn wine back again into water."

Yeats and Lady Gregory said no. They rejected O'Casey's first two plays, *The Harvest Festival* and *The Frost in the Flower,* but they saw signs of promise in these crude hand-written scripts, especially Lady Gregory, who offered encouragement because she felt instinctively that this unknown "writer has something in him." O'Casey submitted two more plays, *The Crimson in the Tri-colour* and *The Seamless Coat of Kathleen,* but they were also rejected, the former after much deliberation and dispute in 1921.

In her critique of *The Crimson in the Tri-colour,* Lady Gregory remarked that this "puzzling play—extremely interesting—" had several excellent characters, and contained some good ideas about Labour and Sinn Fein which were however too provocative to be staged during the Irish rebellion. She might have been anticipating the riots over *The Plough and the Stars.* In his critique of *The Crimson in the Tri-colour,* Yeats, by objecting to the new writer's direct exposure of the Irish audience's prejudices, and lamenting the fact that this type of popular drama was replacing his own style of verse drama, was anticipating some significant differences between his heroic theatre and the tragicomic theatre of O'Casey: "On the other hand it is so constructed that in every scene there is something for pit & stalls to cheer or boo. In fact it is the old Irish idea of a good play—Queens Melodrama brought up to date would no doubt make a sensation—especially as everybody is ill mannered as possible, & all truth considered as inseperable from spite and hatred. If Robinson wants to produce it let him do so by all means & be damned to him. My fashion has gone out."

In spite of these complaints, Yeats was wise enough, along with Lady Gregory and Lennox Robinson, to accept O'Casey's fifth script in 1923, *On the Run,* which was performed as *The Shadow of a Gunman.* The doors of the Abbey had finally opened to Sean O'Cathasaigh, the self-educated Dublin laborer who now became the dramatist Sean O'Casey. But while he was writing his plays he still maintained an active public life, serving as secretary of the Jim Larkin Correspondence Committee when the labor leader was in prison in America in 1921; and he continued his controversial letter writing on Irish problems, particularly the debate over the Irish language. Although he was a fluent Irish speaker, he was against the compulsory teaching of Irish to the poor children of the Dublin slums, whose need for proper food and clothing was a more urgent concern: "My sympathies were always with the rags and tatters that sheltered the tenement-dwelling Temples of the Holy Ghost."

He remained loyal to those sympathies after his successes with *Gun-*

man and *Juno,* and in his new friendship with the aristocratic Lady Gregory, who invited him to Coole Park and nurtured his genius. Lennox Robinson also offered a helping hand, but O'Casey was still "terrified" by the magisterial Yeats. Two of his best friends now were part-time Abbey actors, Gabriel Fallon and Barry Fitzgerald. O'Casey was among the first to recognize the comic genius of Fitzgerald and wrote the role of Captain Boyle for him. Fallon became his closest and most trusting companion. But in 1925 there were early signs of trouble for O'Casey at the Abbey. He had incurred the wrath of two leading actors, M. J. Dolan and F. J. McCormick, for his honest but imprudent criticism of their work in Shaw's *Man and Superman*; and the script of his new play, *The Plough and the Stars,* had provoked the government representative among the directors, Dr. George O'Brien, to demand the censorship of the language and characters of the Dublin slums. O'Casey was now learning by bitter experience that, contrary to Yeats's opinion, truth was indeed becoming inseparable from spite and hatred for him at the Abbey and in Ireland.

From Abbey Theatre

TS. O'CASEY

ABBEY THEATRE
26 JANUARY 1920

DIRECTORS—W. B. YEATS, LADY GREGORY
MANAGER—LENNOX ROBINSON

Reader's Opinion

"The Harvest Festival" and
"The Frost in the Flower" [1]

This play is interestingly conceived but not well executed. It is seldom dramatic and many of the characters suffer from being too typical of their class or profession (Williamson, Sir J. Vane, for instance). They are conventional conceptions, as unreal as the "Stage Irishman" of 20 years ago. If the author has got these typical figures firmly planted in his imagination we should advise him to try to replace them by figures drawn as accurately as possible from his own experience.

In "The Frost in the Flower" the characters are much more life like,

[1] These were the first two plays O'Casey submitted to the Abbey Theatre, in 1919.

and the faults we have to find with it are that it is set too much in the one key throughout, and the endless bickerings of the family end by becoming wearisome. The decision of the hero to throw up his job is too well prepared for and does not come as a surprise (we think it did in the first version).

We are afraid that we liked the first version better except for the character of Shawn who was stilted and who is in this version quite natural, though the author seems to have gone to the other extreme and made him almost common-place, we should like him to stand out from the others without becoming unnatural.

We are sorry to have to return these plays for the author's work interests us, but we don't think either would succeed on the stage.

From James O'Connor (Seamus O'Concubhair)

TS. O'CASEY

57 DAME STREET
DUBLIN
27 JUNE 1921

A Sheain a chara,[1]

Your letter of the 19th inst. was received and read with greatest pleasure. Needless to say Mr. Moore[2] is receiving and will receive the very best attention and services that it is possible for me to give, bearing as he does credentials from an old and valued friend.[3]

I got busy at once and obtained copy of the will and copy of the Schedule of Assets showing the property Mr. Weston died possessed of. I fear, however, that Mr. Moore will have great difficulty in sustaining his contention unless he throws all energy possible into seconding my efforts. I need, and need very badly an interview with a couple of the witnesses who were present when the will was made and some ingenious

[1] Dear Sean.

[2] John Moore, who lived with his family in the flat above O'Casey's room at 422 North Circular Road, was the victim of the faulty will explained in the letter. This situation provided the plot for the Boyle family in *Juno and the Paycock* (1924). Faulty wills apparently remained a problem in Ireland as late as 1965 when the question was raised in a Dáil Éireann debate and the situation in *Juno* was cited as a warning that the government must move to protect heirs from ambiguous wills. (25 May 1965, *Parliamentary Debates,* Dublin, Vol. 215, No. 14, p. 2015.)

[3] O'Casey had known James O'Connor when he was Seamus O'Concubhair and both were members of the Irish Republican Brotherhood and the Red Hand Hurling Club of Drumcondra some ten years earlier.

person to draw the schoolmaster—against whom, by the way, I have a distinct grievance, as a good trade unionist!

Please ask Mr. Moore, therefore, to get hold of those witnesses and you should give him the benefit of your advice as regards getting some information from the schoolmaster. All this is of the utmost importance, otherwise I fear that the first and second cousins would come in and with the investigations etc. necessary, would stretch out the final distribution of the estate to a very far distant date.

I should be very glad to see you some evening whether you are well or badly clad for although I belong to a class which an Act of Parliament made gentlemen, I have not kept up the fiction and would feel it as a distinct personal loss should any of my old friends keep away from me because they imagined that owing to my so-called rise in life I had no time for the friends whom I made during those splendid years when the hitting of a hurley ball and the best make of a hurley stick were the things best worth thinking of.

Ever your friend,
S. O'Concubhair

Sean O Cathasaigh Uasal,[4]
422 N.C.R.
Dublin.

[4] Mr. Sean Ó Cathasaigh.

To Lennox Robinson [1]

MS. ROBINSON

422 N. CIRCULAR ROAD
DUBLIN
5 AUGUST 1921

Dear Sir:

I suppose I should have heard from you had you found the Play [2] I sent to you. The task of re-writing the work from memory terrifies me, but I suppose there is no other alternative.

[1] Lennox Robinson (1886–1958), playwright, actor, director, chosen by Yeats to be manager of the Abbey Theatre in 1910, served as a director of the Abbey from 1923 to 1956.

[2] *The Crimson in the Tri-colour,* the third play O'Casey had submitted to the Abbey Theatre.

I shall wait another while, and then if Fortune fails me, I shall bend my back to the galley oar.

I'm sure you will be good enough to let me know if you come across the work.

Yours
Sean O'Casey

To Lennox Robinson

MS. Robinson
Dublin
9 October 1921

Dear Sir:

I have just received your announcement of the discovery of the "Crimson in the Tricolour". I was delighted to hear such good tidings of great joy.

I sincerely hope, now that I shall have the happiness of seeing it performed in the Abbey.

It is essentially a Futurist work, evolved from the passions, ideas & activities of the present.

Many, many thanks for your kindness.

Sincerely Yours
Sean O'Casey

From A. de Staic (Austin Stack) [1]

TS. O'Casey
Dáil Éireann.
Department of Home Affairs
21 October 1921

To:
Sean O Cathasaigh,
422, N.C. Road.

A Chara,

Fireproof Dwellings Co. 10, Commons St., Dublin

I am in receipt of your statement in this matter.

If proceedings are instituted against any tenant in the British Court

[1] Austin Stack (1879–1929), minister for home affairs in the insurgent Irish Republic, and in charge of the Republican Courts in defiance of the official British Courts.

the tenant may apply to the Republican Courts for an Order restraining the landlords from further proceedings in the enemy Courts. If the Court makes such an Order it will be handed to the Republican Police whose duty it will be to see that the Order is obeyed. The application should be made immediately the summons or Civil Bill in the enemy Courts is served.

If the Agent of the landlord uses abusive language towards the tenants or assaults any of their children, the necessary proceedings may be instituted against him in the Republican Courts by the parties affected.[2]

Mise,

A. de Staic

[2] This incident formed one of the tragicomic subplots in *The Shadow of a Gunman* (1923). See the scene between Mrs. Henderson, Mr. Gallogher, and Davoren, and Mr. Gallogher's letter.

Play critique by Lady Gregory

MS. Southern Illinois

[? October 1921]

The Crimson in the Tricolour—(a very good name)

This is a puzzling play—extremely interesting—Mrs. Budrose is a jewel, & her husband a good setting for her—I don't see any plot in it, unless the Labour unrest culminating in the turning off of the lights at the meeting may be considered one. It is the expression of ideas that makes it interesting (besides feeling that the writer has something in him) & no doubt the point of interest for Dublin audiences—But we could not put it on while the Revolution is still unaccomplished—it might hasten the Labour attack on Sinn Fein, which ought to be kept back till the fight with England is over, & the new Government has had time to show what it can do—

I think Eileen's rather disagreeable flirtation with O'Regan shd. be cut—their first entrance—or rather exit (or both) seems to be leading to something that doesn't come—In Act II a good deal of O'Regan & Nora shd be cut—

In Act III almost all the O'Malley & Eileen part shd. be cut—The end is I think good, the entry of the Workmen, & Fagan & Tim Tracy—

I feel that there is no personal interest worth developing—but that with as much as possible of those barren parts cut, we might find a possible play of ideas in it.

I suggest that (with the author's leave) it shd. be worth typing the play at theatre's expense—with or without those parts—For it is impossible to go through it again—or show it—or have a reading of it—while in hand-writing—

A.G.[1]

[1] A.G., Augusta Gregory.

From Lennox Robinson

TS. O'Casey

Abbey Theatre
5 November 1921

Dear Mr. O'Casey,

I read your play again and I liked a great deal of it but thought some of it not necessary and not very good. I sent it then to Lady Gregory and I tell you exactly what she says about it, but I would like you to treat her opinion as confidential.

> "The Crimson in the Tricolour" (a very good name) "This is a puzzling play—extremely interesting. Mrs. Budrose is a jewel and her husband a good setting for her. I don't see any plot in it, unless the Labour unrest culminating in the turning off of the lights at the meeting may be called one. It is the expression of ideas that makes it interesting (besides feeling that the writer has something in him). But we could not put it on while the Revolution is still unaccomplished—it might hasten the Labour attack on Sinn Fein, which ought to be kept back till the fight with England is over and the new Government has had time to show what it can do. I think Eileen's rather disagreeable flirtation with O'Regan should be cut—their first entrance—or rather exit—or both, it seems to be leading to something that doesn't come. In Act II a good deal of O'Regan and Nora should be cut. In Act III almost all of the O'Malley and Eileen part should be cut. The end is, I think, good, the entry of the workmen, and Fagan and Tim Tracy. I feel that there is no personal interest worth developing—but that with as much as possible of those barren parts cut, we might find a possible play of ideas in it. I suggest that (with the author's leave) it would be worth typing the play at the Theatre's expense with or without those parts. For it is impossible to go through it again—or show it, or have a reading of it while in handwriting."

I should like to know what you think and wonder whether you could come down and see me towards the end of next week say, Friday evening about 8-30. Let me know.

Yours Truly,
Lennox Robinson

To William O'Brien [1]

TS. NAT LIB, DUBLIN [2]

Litir Chumainn Sheumais Ui Lorcain
(The Jim Larkin Correspondence Committee) [3]

BANBA HALL
BAILE ATHA CLIATH
[?] NOVEMBER, 1921

To:———

Dear Comrade,

The above Committee in the course of its activities have decided to ask the Irish Workers, and the Irish People in general, to forward a special Christmas Greeting to Jim, that his solitude may be peopled with the happy and encouraging reflections that his comrades and co-workers have not forgotten him.

You will find enclosed a sample card,[4] which we request you to display in a prominent place in the hall or house in which you hold your meetings. The card[s], one penny each, will be on sale in the various shops in your district. Should you find any difficulty in procuring them, kindly communicate with us.

The Committee is representative of Republican and Labour Activities united in the bonds of admiration and affection for the great Irish Labour Leader who fearlessly did so much for Irish Labour and the cause of Irish Freedom.

There can hardly be any necessity for us to appeal to you to strenuously assist us in this effort to show Jim we have not forgotten one who

[1] William O'Brien (1881–1968), a leading figure in the Irish labor movement, and a bitter rival of Jim Larkin; president of the Irish Trade Union Congress, 1913, 1918, 1925, 1941; general treasurer of the Irish Transport and General Workers' Union in 1919, and several years later general secretary, until 1946.

[2] A mimeographed letter.

[3] Jim Larkin was in prison in America. In October 1914 he had gone to America to raise funds for the Irish labor movement, but due to World War I, and the disinclination of the American and British authorities to allow him to go back, he was unable to return to Ireland. He became active in the I.W.W. and the radical wing of the Socialist Party, which became the Communist Party, and in 1919 he was arrested for "criminal anarchy" and sentenced to Sing Sing Prison for ten years. In 1921 O'Casey helped organize and became secretary of The Release Jim Larkin Committee and the Jim Larkin Correspondence Committee. Larkin was pardoned in 1923 by New York's Governor Al Smith. When he returned to Ireland, he discovered that William O'Brien was in control of the Irish Transport and General Workers' Union, and in 1924 Larkin founded the rival Workers' Union of Ireland.

[4] The Christmas greeting card to Jim Larkin which appears at the end of the next letter was given to me by the late Mrs. Maude O'Connor, widow of Fergus O'Connor. O'Casey told me he designed the card and made the drawing of the plough, gun, and hammer, colored in the green, white, and orange of the Irish tricolor flag.

did so much for Liberty and Truth. His present condition testifies to his unbreakable fealty to the Cause of the People. His is the prison cell, the convict garb, and the felon's cap. He never sold the workers for a handful of silver, nor ever left them for a riband to stick in his coat. There can be said of Jim Larkin that which Boyle O'Reilly, the Irish Rebel, said of a true man:—

"His reward?—nor Cross, nor ribbon,
But all others high above;
They have won their glittering symbols—
He has earned the People's Love."

Fraternally yours
Sean O'Cathasaigh,
Hon. Sec.

In remembrance of Jim, our Leader,
and in the Cause of Labour and Ireland.

To William O'Brien

MS. NAT LIB, DUBLIN

Litir Chumainn Sheumais Ui Lorcain
(The Jim Larkin Correspondence Committee)

BANBA HALL
PARNELL SQUARE, DUBLIN
10 NOVEMBER 1921

Comrade William O'Brien
a chara:

Would you be good enough to grant the undersigned an interview of about ten minutes?

I have called twice to your offices in Parnell Square, but on each occasion failed to see you.

You will surely remember Sean O'Cathasaigh &, he is confident that, on account of past efforts in the Irish Labour Movement, you will readily grant the favour he requests of you. He is willing to suit your own convenience, any hour between the "rising of the sun & the going down of the same"—or after.

Sean O'Cathasaigh

Post Card

JIM LARKIN
77,161 Sing Sing,
354 Hunter Street,
OSSINING,
State of New York, U.S.A.

Published by Fergus O'Connor, Dublin, for the Committee

Ireland which is I
And I who am Ireland
Have not Forgotten You.
Christmas 1921.
From:
Address.

Send a Christmas Greeting to
JIM LARKIN
Greeting Cards on Sale Everywhere
Price One Penny
Show You Have Not Forgotten
One Who Is In
JAIL FOR YOU

What you have to do:

1. Write your name and address on the back of the card in the space provided.
2. Fix a Three Halfpenny Stamp on the face of the card, and then drop it in the nearest Pillar Box.

That's All
Will you neglect to write a few words
or refuse to spend 2½d. for the sake of
Jim Larkin
Who loved you, worked for you, and is now in
Jail For You
Cards Published by Fergus O'Connor, Dublin
The Gael Co-Operative Printing Society Ltd.,
73 Lr. Mount Street, Dublin

To Lennox Robinson

TS. ROBINSON

DUBLIN
10 APRIL 1922

I am sending you, herewith, an allegorical play [1] in one act dealing with the present situation in Ireland—from my point of view. A hope is buoyant in my breast that you may be willing and able to produce it—if suitable—before the Season closes. It is critical of many things, and touches humour here and there. There is no doubt that it would be very interesting, and would probably be the recipient of an equal amount of applause and deprecation. I am sending on a copy to Jim Larkin, on whose committee there are people prominent in the Dramatic world of America.

By the way, I suppose nothing further has been done with my

[1] Sean O'Cathasaigh, "The Seamless Coat of Kathleen," originally written as an allegorical tale of the same title which appeared in *Poblacht Na h-Eireann* (Republic of Ireland), 29 March 1922; reprinted in *Feathers From the Green Crow* (1962). It is based on the biblical theme of the tossing of dice for the seamless garment of Christ, in this instance the seamless garment of Kathleen Ni Houlihan. The play was never performed.

other play—"The Crimson in the Tri-colour?" Jim asked me some time ago to send him a copy of it, but, as you know, that was impossible.

Would it be possible when you are getting it typed to do one for me? I am gathering together the material for "On The Run," [2] and have actually started it. I am sure you will thank a kindly Providence when you perceive that my present play—"The Seamless Coat of Kathleen"—is in typescript.[3] However I may again afflict you with bad plays, I will never again afflict you with damned bad writing.

Very Sincerely yours,
Sean O Cathasaigh

[2] "On the Run," the original title of *The Shadow of a Gunman.*
[3] He had bought a secondhand typewriter.

From Lennox Robinson

TS. O'CASEY
[ABBEY THEATRE]
15 APRIL 1922

Dear Mr. O Cathansaigh,[1]

The Directors and I have read your play [2] and like a great deal of it—its humour and the element of phantasy in it. At the same time it is too definite a piece of propaganda for us to do it—even if our season was not just at an end, and it may be completely out of date in a few weeks time. Would there be no chance of getting it put on at Liberty Hall? I hope you will try us again with a play that is not so topical of the moment. Meanwhile I shall go over "The Crimson in the Tricolour" again.

Yours sincerely,
[Lennox Robinson]

[1] The name was misspelled by Robinson.
[2] *The Seamless Coat of Kathleen.*

To Lennox Robinson

TS. ROBINSON
[DUBLIN]
23 APRIL 1922

Dear Mr. Robinson:

Received the returned play [1] all right; expected you would not produce a play containing so much propaganda.

[1] *The Seamless Coat of Kathleen.*

I shall be only too happy to submit any play I may write to the Abbey, for that Theatre, the country, the National Gallery and the Botanic Gardens —with certain Authors—are the only things I worship.

A Commandant [2] of the Leix I R A has written to me saying that the local School Teacher has a Dramatic Class there, and requests me to send him on the words of "Duty".[3] I have asked several about it but nobody can tell me where I can get it; could you? If you can let me know where I can get the words I shall be very grateful.

Sincerely yours,
Sean O Cathasaigh

[2] Sean Shelley, an I.R.A. commandant who was an officer in the Irish Citizen Army when O'Casey first met him some years earlier, probably 1914.

[3] Seumas O'Brien's *Duty,* a one-act comedy first performed at the Abbey Theatre on 16 December 1913, directed by Lennox Robinson.

Play critique by W. B. Yeats [1]

MS. SOUTHERN ILLINOIS
[19 JUNE 1922]

The Crimson in the Tricolour

I find this discursive play very hard to judge for it is a type of play I do not understand. The drama of it is loose & vague. At the end of Act I Kevin O'Regan is making very demonstrative love to Eileen Budrose, & the curtain falls on what (in all usual stage manners) should have been her early seduction. In Act II without a word of explanation one finds him making equally successful love to Nora. In Act III one learns for the first time that Eileen has married Shemus O'Malley. We have not even been told that they were courting. We have only seen her refuse his escort to supper. Regan talks constantly of his contempt for organised opinion & suddenly at the end we discover him as some kind of labour leader—one organized opinion exchanged for another. It is a story without meaning—a story where nothing happens except that a wife runs away from a husband, to whom we had not the least idea that she was married, & the Mansion House lights are turned out because of some wrong to a man who never appears in the play.

On the other hand it is so constructed that in every scene there is something for pit & stalls to cheer or boo. In fact it is the old Irish idea of a good play—Queens Melodrama brought up to date would no doubt

[1] W. B. Yeats (1865–1939), Irish poet and playwright; a founder-director of the Abbey Theatre in 1904; senator of the Irish Free State, 1922–28; winner of the Nobel Prize in 1923; one of the most important poets and literary figures of the twentieth century.

make a sensation—especially as everybody is as ill mannered as possible, & all truth considered as inseperable from spite and hatred.

If Robinson wants to produce it let him do so by all means & be damned to him. My fashion has gone out.

W B Yeats

From Lennox Robinson

TS. O'CASEY
ABBEY THEATRE
28 SEPTEMBER [1922]

Dear Mr. O'Cathasaigh,

I've kept your play a very long time, but it got held up in the country and you know what that means. Here is one of our Reader's opinion of it: [1]

> "The drama of it is loose and vague. At the end of Act I Kevin O'Regan is making very demonstrative love to Eileen Budrose and the curtain falls on what (in all usual stage manners) should have been her early seduction. In Act 2, without a word of explanation, one finds him making equally successful love to Nora. In Act 3 one learns for the first time that Eileen has married Shamus O'Malley. We have not even been told that they were courting, we have only seen her refuse his escort to supper. Regan talks constantly of his contempt for organised opinion and suddenly at the end we discover him as some kind of labour leader—one organised opinion exchanged for another. It is a story without meaning, a story where nothing happens except that a wife runs away from a husband to whom we had not the least idea she was married and the Mansion House lights are turned out because of some wrong to a man who never appears in the play."

On the other hand, though I must agree with certain of these criticisms, I persist in finding the play very interesting. I have felt an attraction to all your work. If you still are interested in the subject of this play we might be able to make it over again and make a play of it. I think you have got the scenario—the shape of the play wrong, or if you have another play in your mind will you come and talk over the idea and we will work out a scenario together?

I apologise again for the delay.

Yours sincerely,
Lennox Robinson

[1] For the full comment see play critique by W. B. Yeats, 19 June 1922. O'Casey told me that Robinson shortly afterward identified the "Reader" as Yeats.

To Lennox Robinson

TS. ROBINSON

[DUBLIN]
9 OCTOBER 1922

Dear Mr. Robinson—

I have received the returned play [1] safely. I was terribly disappointed at its final rejection, and felt at first as if, like Lucifer, I had fallen never to hope again.

I have re-read the work and find it as interesting as ever, in no way deserving the contemptuous dismissal it has received from the reader you have quoted.

Let me say that I do not agree with his criticism: I cannot see that because a man makes "demonstrative love to a girl" it necessarily follows that he must seduce her. If this be the usual stage manners then they are bad manners—I am writing now of what I know very little about. And what could be more loose and vague than life itself? Are we to write plays on the framework of the first of Genesis; And God said let there be light and there was light; and he separated the light from the darkness and he called the light day, and the darkness he called night; and the morning and evening were the first Act.

It is the subtle vagueness in such writers as Shaw and Ibsen that—in my opinion—constitute their most potent charm.

"Regan talks constantly of his contempt for organised opinion, and suddenly we discover him as some kind of labour leader—one organised opinion exchanged for another." Well, what then? Every thinker has a contempt—more or less—for organised opinion; but he may have a decided regard for organised action. I know Republican philosophers who have a supreme contempt for the organised opinion of the Free State, but who have, when bullets are flying about, a wholesome regard for that opinion in action. Besides it has often happened that a thinker suddenly leaves his solitude to oppose a general or particular act of injustice: Voltaire did so, and Zola, W B Yeates [sic] and "AE" did so in 1913 during the strike.[2]

I was thinking of changing the play into a comedy, making Mrs

[1] *The Crimson in the Tri-colour.*

[2] During the 1913 general strike and lock-out in Dublin, A.E. and Yeats wrote open letters to the press in defense of the strikes: A.E., "To the Masters of Dublin," *Irish Times,* 7 October 1913; W. B. Yeats, "Dublin Fanaticism," *Irish Worker,* 1 November 1913.

Budrose the supreme character. Should I do [so] would it be re-considered?

One other point: the reader adversely criticises the fact that an action is performed for a man that never appears on the stage. I am glad this is mentioned, for I was thinking of writing a play around Jim Larkin —The Red Star [3]—in which he would never appear though [be] responsible for all the action.

Many, many thanks for your own kind expression of appreciation. I shall certainly take advantage of your generous invitation to go to see you and talk of my work.

I am engaged on a play at present—On The Run—the draft of the first act is finished and most of the second. Would it be well to wait till this is completed and then make the bringing of the work to you an opportunity of having a talk with you? It deals with the difficulties of a poet who is in continual conflict with the disturbances of a tenement house, and is built on the frame of Shelley's phrase: "Ah me, alas, pain, pain ever, forever."

Sincerely yours,
Sean Ó Cathasaigh

[3] He wrote this play eighteen years later as *The Star Turns Red* (1940).

To Lennox Robinson

TS. Robinson

Dublin

17 November 1922

Dear Mr. Robinson:—

I have just completed 'On The Run.' [1] It is a tragedy in two acts—at least I have called it so. The play is typed—not faultlessly, I'm afraid—but the result is obviously immeasurably above my fiendish handwriting. I have to thank you and Lady Gregory for the self-sacrifice displayed by the reading of such a manuscript as 'The Crimson In The Tri-colour.'

[1] This two-act tragedy was accepted, but O'Casey had to change the title to *The Shadow of a Gunman* (Robinson told him there already was a play called *On the Run*), and it opened at the Abbey Theatre on 12 April 1923, directed by Lennox Robinson, with the following cast: Arthur Shields as Donal Davoren, F. J. McCormick as Seumas Shields, Michael J. Dolan as Tommy Owens, P. J. Carolan as Adolphus Grigson, May Craig as Mrs. Grigson, Gertrude Murphy as Minnie Powell, Eric Gorman as Mr. Mulligan, G. V. Lavelle as Mr. Maguire, Christine Hayden as Mrs. Henderson, Gabriel J. Fallon as Mr. Gallogher, Tony Quinn as An Auxiliary.

I will bring over 'On The Run' on Tuesday night; should you not be in the Theatre on that night, I shall come again on Wednesday.

Ever Sincerely Yours.
S. O' Cathasaigh

To Michael J. Dolan [1]

TC. O'CASEY
DUBLIN
[? MAY 1923]

Dear Mr Dolan—

Enclosed is script of the Play, "The Crimson in the Tri-colour."

Included is the criticism of Mr Yeates [sic], as I wish to be absolutely frank with you.

I shall be happy to show to you, to Mr [Arthur] Shields and to Mr [F. J.] McCormick the much more favourable criticism of Lady Gregory—on one condition: that it shall be considered confidential. It was made so to me, and you must give me your word that it will be confidential to you.

Should it happen that you should decide to use the play, the latter criticism will, I think, be valuable to you in any alteration thought necessary in the work.

I should be glad if you could arrange with the parties aforesaid to take tea with me some evening in the Broadway,[2] so as to discuss the matter. Any evening except Wednesday will do. say about seven.

Sincerely Yours,
S Ó Cathasaigh

[1] Michael J. Dolan (1884–1954), actor and play director at the Abbey Theatre. Although the Abbey had officially rejected *The Crimson in the Tri-colour,* O'Casey wanted Dolan to direct the play on a Sunday in the off-season when the Abbey actors gave special performances on their own to supplement their earnings.

[2] The Broadway Soda Fountain Parlour in O'Connell Street, where many of the Abbey Theatre people, who preferred not to spend the night drinking in the pubs, often gathered for coffee and talk. O'Casey was a teetotaler, a habit he picked up from Jim Larkin. Until Larkin came to Dublin to organize the unskilled laborers in the Irish Transport and General Workers' Union in 1909, many of the men were paid in pubs and often drank up their wages before they could bring them home to their wives.

From Michael J. Dolan

TS. O'CASEY
ABBEY THEATRE
DUBLIN
7 MAY 1923

Dear Mr. O'Casey,

In the words of Father Harte "—I'm sorry to be the bearer of what must be rather disappointing news to you".[1] Having read the "Crimson on the Tricolour" I was reluctantly compelled to the conclusion that it is not a good proposition for the Stage. However I did not take my own opinion as final; I asked both Mr [Arthur] Shields and Mr [F. J.] McCormick to come down one morning last week to listen to it and give me their verdict. They were in absolute agreement with my opinion. I detest to say this to you; but I feel to put it on would mean undoing your good work of the "Gunman". I am not very good at expressing myself on paper, and would prefer to have a talk with you. I am engaged from 7 o.c. every evening this week; but could see you any time before that if you care to make an appointment. If you can come to the theatre any evening before say 6 o.c. I shall be glad to see you and say all I have left unsaid in this.

Yours sincerely,
Michael J. Dolan

[1] T. C. Murray's *Maurice Harte*, first performed by the Abbey Players on 20 June 1912 at the Royal Court Theatre, London.

To Lennox Robinson

TS. ROBINSON
[DUBLIN]
29 DECEMBER 1923

Dear Mr Robinson—

I was delighted with the volume of Tchehov's Plays for two reasons: because I wanted to read them—I have read some by the same Author, lent to me by Arthur Shields, The Cherry Orchard, etc—and was anxious to read more; and because your name is in the book, a fact of which I shall be a little proud. It was a thoughtful gift and a kindly tribute, and

I thank you very much. I spent a most enjoyable evening on Friday looking at, and listening to your White-headed Boy.[1]

It is a glorious work—I mean *glorious,* mind you—and as you envy every word of Lady Gregory's Jackdaw,[2] I envy you every word of the White-headed Boy.

This is no hasty opinion, for I read the Play before I went to see it, and though honestly, I thought at first, I was going to be disappointed, I soon found myself laughing, and it takes a good man to make me laugh, now.

Very Sincerely Yours,
Sean O'Casey

[1] A revival of Lennox Robinson's *The Whiteheaded Boy,* first performed at the Abbey Theatre on 13 December 1916.

[2] Lady Gregory's *The Jackdaw* was first performed at the Abbey Theatre on 23 February 1907.

From W. B. Yeats

TS. O'CASEY [1]

82, MERRION SQUARE,
DUBLIN
26 MARCH 1924

Dear Mr O'Casey.

Will you come in on Monday March 31 at 8-15? My play the "Hawk's Well" [2] is being done that evening with masks, costumes and music by Edmund Dulac.

W. B. Yeats.

P.S. The gathering will be quite informal. We are only asking people connected with the arts. No day passes without my hearing praise of your play.[3]

[1] The letter was typed and the P.S. was added in Yeats's handwriting.

[2] *At the Hawk's Well.* See O'Casey's account of this performance in *Inishfallen, Fare Thee Well* (1949), *Autobiographies* II (London, Macmillan, 1963), pp. 232–35.

[3] *Juno and the Paycock* opened at the Abbey Theatre on 3 March 1924, directed by Michael J. Dolan, with the following cast: Barry Fitzgerald as "Captain" Jack Boyle, Sara Allgood as Juno Boyle, Arthur Shields as Johnny Boyle, Eileen Crowe as Mary Boyle, F. J. McCormick as Joxer Daly, Maureen Delany as Mrs. Maisie Madigan, Michael J. Dolan as Needle Nugent, Christine Hayden as Mrs. Tancred, P. J. Carolan as Jerry Devine, Gabriel J. Fallon as Charlie Bentham, Maurice Esmonde as First Irregular, Michael J. Dolan as Second Irregular, Peter Nolan as First Furniture Remover and Sewing-machine Man, Tony Quinn as Second Furniture Remover and Coal-block Vendor, Eileen O'Kelly and Irene Murphy as Two Neighbours.

From Lady Gregory [1]

MS. O'Casey

Coole Park, Gort
Co Galway
26 May 1924

A Chara,

June is coming & the sun is gaining strength—and I am hoping you will find your way here & spend a couple of weeks with me. There are the woods to wander in, & there is quiet for writing. I am alone, & have no amusements to offer, but I think you would find the library an interest, it is a good one. It will be a great pleasure to me to see you here.

Yours always sincerely
A Gregory

[1] Isabella Augusta Persse, Lady Gregory (1852–1932), playwright, popularizer of Irish mythology, co-director of the Abbey Theatre. When her husband (Sir William Gregory, a former governor of Ceylon) died in 1892, she began a career in literature and drama. She helped Yeats found the Irish Literary Theatre in 1898, and in 1905 she became co-director with Yeats and Synge of the Abbey Theatre. Until her death on 23 May 1932, she remained with Yeats a guiding force of the theatre and wrote a number of one-act plays that have become classics in Irish drama.

To Lady Gregory

MS. Gregory

Dublin
2 June 1924

Dear Lady Gregory.

You are very kind, & I thank you for your generous invitation to Coole Park.

I have a few reasons for being half afraid to accept, & many for being wholly afraid to refuse. Isnt it a pity that there are no amusements there? How splended it would be if the Woods of Coole were vibrating with throngs of Joywheels and Charoplanes.

I am arranging to go down on Saturday or Monday next, if that should please you.[2]

Very Sincerely Yours.
Sean O'Casey

[2] This was the occasion of O'Casey's first visit to Coole Park. He arrived on Saturday, 7 June, and stayed a week.

To Society of Authors

TS. SOCIETY OF AUTHORS

DUBLIN
19 JUNE 1924

THE SECRETARY,
SOCIETY OF AUTHORS AND PLAYWRIGHTS.

Dear Sir—

I am desirous of becoming a member of the Dramatic section of your Society. Three of my plays [1] have been produced by the Abbey Theatre, Dublin, and James Stephens, the poet, has kindly allowed me to mention his name as an introduction. P O for £1-1-0 enclosed.

Sincerely Yours,
Sean O Casey

[1] The third play was *Cathleen Listens In,* which opened at the Abbey Theatre on 1 October 1923.

To Irish Statesman

5 JULY 1924

THE GAELICISATION OF IRISH EDUCATION.

Dear Sir,—I frankly but vainly believe that I represent the ordinary type of the Irish peasant mind. I have been a reader of the STATESMAN since its first issue. In the articles dealing with education, particularly the "Gaelicising of Irish Education," [1] I take a special interest. In his article, Dr. Garrett says:—"Is not Ireland more likely to express her individuality through her own mode than through the one now in use?" In that very question, in the words "in her own mode" lies the fundamental difficulty confronting all present-day theories, on which a true modern system of

[1] Dr. L. Garrett, "The Gaelicising of Irish Education," *Irish Statesman,* 24 May and 14 June 1924, a two-part article.

Irish education must eventually be built. What is Ireland's own mode? The mentality and habits of thought of, say, the average Midland peasant are fundamentally distinct from those of a resident of the Gaeltacht. There is no gainsaying that statement. History and economics, based on rich pastures versus mountain, account for it. In the process of education should not language be in harmony with thought? Is it educationally sound, or a threatened metempsychosis of the mind of the poor Irish Midlander of to-day, the attempt to Gaelicise his education, *on a similar basis,* as the effort made to Gaelicise the education of the youth of Ballinskelligs, Tourmakeady and the Glenties? In doing so are we attempting on the youth of the Pale what Whately was charged with in the "thirties", and what the Irish hedge schools under popular control long before Whately's time, attempted to do, viz., the enforcement of a foreign education on the minds of thousands of Irish children? Briefly, the mentality and tradition of most of the children of the Gaeltacht to-day is, let us say, "Irish." Outside the Gaeltacht it is "English" if you will. Is it "educational" to have the same basic programme of instructors for primary and secondary schools for these two sections? These are questions that parents, who are neither "scholars" nor "enthusiasts," are now discussing. It shows a healthy sign to have these matters discussed by plain ordinary folk. Again, is a distinct language essential, as Dr. Garrett thinks, that a nation may be recognised as a distinct entity? The present-day views of many men of moderate thinking run counter to Dr. Garrett's views in this respect. The more light thrown on these subjects the better. The pity of it was that in the past discussions on such questions were chiefly left to "enthusiasts" and wielders of "epithets" and "shibboleths." Extra biassed minds reason wrongly except by chance. Yours faithfully,

Sean O Cathasaigh

To Lady Gregory

MS. GREGORY

DUBLIN
12 JULY 1924

Dear Lady Gregory—

For the past few weeks my eyes have been a little troublesome, & I cannot write the letter I find my heart prompting me to write.

However, I cannot put off any longer the sending of my full and earnest appreciation of your great kindness to me during my stay in Beautiful Coole.

You will be glad to hear that I have given an absolute absolution to Gort, freeing it from all its sordid sins because of the loveliness of Coole. Besides, is it not written that, "through much tribulation we shall enter the Kingdom of Heaven"?

I have long pondered over whether the beautiful pictures & statuary, the glorious books, or the wonderful woods, river & Lake of Coole deserve the apple of praise—for they are like the three competitors that stood before & showed their charms to Paris—but I think I must choose the woods, the Lake and the river. I am sending you a few thoughts builded on the delightful memories of Coole.

I received safely your Cuchulain of Muirthemne [1] and thank you for the gift.

With this note I am enclosing the Bureau key & trust it will prove satisfactory.[2]

I am wondering how you fared in the land of the Philistines,[3] and hope you have succeeded in arranging for the restoration of the treasures they have taken from our Temple.[4]

Thanks, & again thanks to you.

Sincerely Yours.
Sean O'Casey

[1] Lady Gregory, *Cuchulain of Muirthemne* (London, Murray, 1902), her rendering of the Cuchulain legends in the Kiltartan dialect of her native Galway.

[2] The key to her writing bureau was bent and O'Casey had it fixed for her.

[3] England.

[4] The Lane pictures. Sir Hugh Lane (1875–1915), art collector and critic, nephew of Lady Gregory, lost his life on the *Lusitania,* which was torpedoed off the coast of Ireland by a German submarine on 7 May 1915. In February 1915 he wrote the controversial codicil to his will, giving his collection of modern paintings to Ireland on the condition that a gallery would be provided for them within five years of his death. But the codicil was unwitnessed and contested by the English National Gallery, which had possession of the paintings. After forty-four years of controversy the British and Irish authorities finally reached a compromise plan in 1959: the Lane pictures were divided into two groups, one in London and the other in Dublin, and they were to be exchanged every five years for the following twenty years.

To Lady Gregory

MS. GREGORY

DUBLIN
22 JULY 1924

Dear Lady Gregory—

Many thanks for your kind letter, and the little Book [1] containing possible treasures of thought for use on divers occasions. I have not yet

[1] Lady Gregory, *The Kiltartan History Book* (Dublin and London, Maunsel, 1909; 1st edition), illustrated by Robert Gregory, her son.

continued the reading of Joan,[2] for I am busy riding in galloping chariots; listening to the clanging of buckler, spear & sword, and joining in the Battle Shouts of the Knights of the Red Branch—in other words, I am reading Cuchulain.

So glad to hear that you think the desire for the return of the Lane Pictures will probably be gratified. We cannot afford to quietly abandon even one ray from even one gem of Beauty we may possess, for these are the manifestations that God is with us. I have read of a Rainbow around God's Throne: these are a Rainbow around His Footstool.

I am glad that De Valera is out again,[3] & read that he says we must go back to 1917. I wish he would read Back to Methuselah, and long a little less earnestly for the salvation of his countrymen. A great many of us are really too anxious about the souls of other men.

The other day I spent wandering around Howth Hill with two Bobbin Testers [4]—young lassies of eighteen; one of them my niece [5]—over on a holiday from Lancashire. And I thought it strange that we may have passed over ground once trodden by Cuchulain, & Fionn with his seven battle battalions of Fianna. They had never heard of either, but they had an intangible idea that Brian Boru had some connection with them.

I am working at "Penelope's Lovers",[6] but have not yet started the more ambitious Play "The Plough & the Stars".

I shall send on Joan as soon as I read it; I hope I'm not keeping it too long.

Very Sincerely Yours.
Sean O'Casey

[2] Samuel Langhorne Clemens, *Personal Recollections of Joan of Arc*, by the Sieur Louis de Conte [pseud.] (New York and London, Harper, 1899).

[3] On 16 July 1924 Eamon de Valera was released from Arbour Hill Prison where he had been held by the Irish Free State government for eleven months for Republican activities.

[4] He wrote about this experience in the form of a short story which appeared as "Gulls and Bobbin Testers," *Irish Statesman*, 6 September 1924; reprinted in *Feathers From the Green Crow* (1962).

[5] The daughter of his brother Isaac Archer Casey (1873–1931), who had emigrated to Liverpool late in 1916, and there changed his name to Joseph Casey.

[6] The first version of *Nannie's Night Out*, which opened at the Abbey Theatre on 29 September 1924.

To James Stephens[1]

MS. WISE

[DUBLIN]
12 AUGUST 1924

Dear Mr. Stephens—

Delighted to learn of the honour given to you by the Taillteann Literary Adjudicators.[2] I am glad for two reasons: because you deserve it; and because you are such a lovable man.

Very Sincerely Yours
Sean O'Casey

[1] James Stephens (1882–1950), Irish novelist, short-story writer, poet, essayist, probably best known for his mythic novel, *The Crock of Gold* (London, Macmillan, 1912).

[2] Stephens had just received first prize for fiction for his *Deirdre* (London, Macmillan, 1923) at the revival of the Tailteann Games in 1924. This competitive festival of arts and sports, comparable to the Greek Olympic Games, had been celebrated in ancient Ireland every four years on 1 August, Lammastide or Lugnasad. The festival was held in 1928 and 1932, and then abandoned.

From Daniel Macmillan
To James Stephens

TS. O'CASEY

JAMES STEPHENS, ESQ.
NATIONAL GALLERY OF IRELAND,[1]
MERRION SQUARE, DUBLIN.

ST. MARTIN'S STREET
LONDON, W.C.2.
27 AUGUST 1924

Dear Sir,

You may be interested to hear that we have arranged to publish Mr. Sean O'Casey's two plays.[2] We are very much obliged to you for

[1] Stephens was registrar of the National Gallery of Ireland from 1918–25. When he gave up the position in 1925, Lady Gregory urged O'Casey to take it, but he refused, and it was filled by Brinsley Macnamara, the playwright and novelist.

[2] Sean O'Casey, *Two Plays* (London, Macmillan, 1925), *The Shadow of a Gunman* and *Juno and the Paycock*.

introducing Mr. O'Casey to us, and we agree with you that his plays are very remarkable.

As Mr. O'Casey is comparatively unknown in this country, we think it would be a great advantage if you would write a few words by way of preface to his book.[3] We have not made this suggestion to Mr. O'Casey, but no doubt you are in touch with him.

We wonder if you would mind us quoting in our Autumn Announcement List your opinion that Mr. O'Casey is the greatest dramatic find of modern times?

we are,
Yours faithfully,
Daniel Macmillan

[3] This idea was abandoned.

To Lady Gregory

MS. GREGORY

DUBLIN
29 AUGUST 1924

Dear Lady Gregory—

I am sending back Mark Twain's Joan of Arc, having enjoyed the reading of it in an exceeding great measure. The whole story is very moving in its deep earnestness and sweet simplicity.

The burning stake in Rouen has become one of God's Pillars of fire. The story of Mark Twain is a worthy supplement to the Play by Shaw.

I am glad to say that I expect The Gunman and Juno (in one volume) to be published shortly. I have just signed an agreement with Macmillan & Co; so I am looking forward to the pleasure of being allowed to send a copy to Lady Gregory.

Very Sincerely Yours
Sean O'Casey

To Gabriel Fallon[1]

MS. Texas

[Dublin]
2 September 1924

Dear Gaby.

Come up tomorrow, Wednesday, say about 7-30 up to 8 o'c.

It's a straight walk up Portland Row & N.C. Road; cross over Dorset st. & continue up the N.C.R. passing Cahill's Chemist shop on the left-hand side as you cross. The house (422) on the corner of a lane has a small sycamore growing in the front garden, and is about fifty steps from Cahill's, the Chemists.

Yours,
Sean O'Casey

[1] Gabriel J. Fallon (1898–), Abbey Theatre actor and dramatic critic; met O'Casey at the Abbey in 1923, and played in the original cast of *The Gunman, Juno,* and *The Plough;* a director of the Abbey since 1959, and resigned in 1974; author of *Sean O'Casey, The Man I Knew* (London, Routledge & Kegan Paul, 1965).

From Lady Gregory

PS. Modern Drama[1]

Coole Park, Gort, Co. Galway
3 September [1924]

A Chara

Thank you for returning Joan. I think it a beautiful telling of the story—

That is good news that your plays are to be published and Macmillan is a good firm.

I have just had the real pleasure of Reading "Irish Nannie"[2]—a fine and witty piece of ironical comedy—I look forward to seeing it on the stage. L. Robinson says he saved Nannies life—and I applaud him—I should not easily have forgiven her death—Perhaps she may come into another play one day—

[1] From a copy made by A. C. Edwards and printed in *Modern Drama,* May 1965.

[2] Sean O'Casey, *Nannie's Night Out,* a one-act comedy first performed at the Abbey Theatre on 29 September 1924, as an after-piece to a revival of Shaw's *Arms and the Man* (1894). The play is printed in *Feathers From the Green Crow* (1962).

I write this quickly—for I am setting out bye and bye for London—to give evidence before the Lane pictures Committee—an ordeal—but I have gone through many in these last 9 years on this matter—with my high hopes moving sometimes down to the bottomless pit so far:—

always your truly,
A Gregory

To Lady Gregory

MS. GREGORY

DUBLIN
28 SEPTEMBER 1924

Dear Lady Gregory—

Yesterday Miss Bushel[1] told me you had the night previously phoned for me to join you and Dr. Yeats at the Father Mathew Hall to see "The Merchant of Venice".[2]

I am very sorry, indeed, that I wasn't there to receive it.

On Wednesday I was in the Green Room, & heard you were in the Theatre, with the rather terrifying epilogue that you were accompanied by Mr. Yeats, so that I feared if I came to speak to you, I should be disturbing you & him. So when you did not come up to the Green Room, I presumed you had forgotten, or had changed your mind.

I am enclosing a copy of the "Irish Worker," which may interest you. It contains an article about Hugh Lane, a reference to the late John Quinn, & some photographs of violent attacks made upon the I.W.W. in California. The particulars attached to the pictures are undoubtedly true, & little Lena, the "Wobbly Nightingale", is suffering terribly from scalds.

I'm afraid the stars on the American Flag are having a baleful influence upon the American people.

Yours Sincerely
Sean O'Casey

[1] Miss Bushell worked in the Abbey Theatre box-office.

[2] Shakespeare's *The Merchant of Venice* was performed by the Father Mathew Players, an amateur company, directed by Frank Fay, on 27 September 1924 at the Father Mathew Hall, Dublin.

To James Stephens

MS. Wise

[Dublin]

28 September 1924

Dear Mr. Stephens—

I got your letter last night.

As a Playwright I will be honoured if you should do as Messrs Macmillan suggest; [1] as a Buttie I shall be delighted, delighted, delighted.

Yours Sincerely,

Sean O'Casey

[1] See Daniel Macmillan's letter to James Stephens, 27 August 1924, printed above.

To Lady Gregory

MS. Gregory

Dublin

October 1924

Dear Lady Gregory—

I am returning the little book, "The Singing Jail Birds" [1] to you, & thank you for the loan.

Honestly, I dont think much of it as Drama, & very little of it as an expression of life. The Play is, I think, hysterical. It reminds me of Crashaw's Magdalen's weeping eyes:

> "Two walking baths; two weeping motions
> Portable and compendious Oceans!"

The miseries of the workers are not housed in the jails. Imprisonment during a fight is very often an exhilaration: it is in our homes; in the hospitals; in the fields, factories and workshops, during the piping times of peace, carrying out "the daily round & common task" that hunger, hardship & disease assail us. It is far easier to sing in jail with comrades, than to sing when one is "by one's lone" looking for a job.

The Play is not comparable to either O'Neill's "Hairy Ape", or

[1] Upton Sinclair, *The Singing Jailbirds* (Pasadena, California, 1924; published by author).

Toller's "Masses & Men". The sentiments expressed seem to me to be the old lust for martyrdom, as dangerous in the Labour Movement as it is in Politics. The incidents are, I believe, true, but the suffering borne by the workers isn't that against which I vehemently protest—but the conditions that arrest human development. Stifling the desire, & destroying the power of creation, and deadening the faculty to understand and enjoy the higher things of life. To me the play is to Labour what street preaching is to religion.

"Nannie's Night Out" [2] went well; Mr. Perrin tells me the "houses" were remarkably good: I don't like the play very much myself.

Many, many thanks for your kind intimation that if I wish to go down to Coole, I shall be welcome. I will certainly avail myself of your goodness in the Spring, if not before. At present I am very busy laying down linoleum in my room; having the floor sides stained & waxed & the window frames painted, and all the bother makes me feel far from friendly towards civilization. The proofs of Juno & The Gunman are beginning to pour in from Macmillan's so that I fear I shall have to make "the night joint labourer with the day". As well, I am anxious to start work on "The Plough & the Stars" which, dealing with Easter Week, will bring to our Remembrance "old unhappy, far off days, & battles long ago!" I have just re-read your "Irish Theatre",[3] & have harboured a feeling of regret that I wasn't with the Abbey in the great fight that did so much for Ireland's Soul, and Ireland's body.

I have been thinking of Synge, Hugh Lane, Robert Gregory—standing on the galley deck in The Shadowy Waters, "blue & dim, with sails & dresses of green and ornaments of copper"—and Ledwidge,[4] the young, pale poet; all now of the dead; and you, Yeats, Stephens & Shaw, still, happily, of the living. Aristocrats, middle-class and worker: "Three in One & one in three". When one remembers those that have died; & these that still live, one, when thinking of Ireland, can still murmur: blessed is the womb that bore them, & the paps that they have sucked.

Yours.

Sean O'Casey

[2] O'Casey's *Nannie's Night Out,* a one-act comedy, was first produced at the Abbey Theatre on 29 September 1924, directed by Michael J. Dolan, with the following cast: Maureen Delany as Mrs. Polly Pender, Barry Fitzgerald as Oul Johnny, Michael J. Dolan as Oul Jimmy, Gabriel J. Fallon as Oul Joe, Sara Allgood as Irish Nannie, Gerald Breen as Robert, F. J. McCormick as A Ballad Singer, Arthur Shields as A Young Man, Eileen Crowe as A Young Girl.

[3] Lady Gregory, *Our Irish Theatre* (London, Putnam, 1914).

[4] Francis Ledwidge (1891–1917), Irish poet killed in action during World War I.

To R. M. Fox[1]

MS. University of London

[Dublin]

27 October 1924

Dear Mr. Fox:

Many thanks for your two kind letters.

I'm afraid you'll have to write your article without any help from me. Desire for quietude is stronger in me than desire for publicity—the spirit is stronger than the flesh. It's not due to modesty; I'd love to blow my own trumpet, but the work's too hard. And even if others supply the trumpet, they expect you to provide the wind. This refusal isn't singular; I have just declined to allow an artist to sketch my face, simply because I was too lazy.

Yours

Sean O'Casey

[1] R. M. Fox (1899–1969), author, journalist, dramatic critic of the Dublin *Evening Mail* from 1939 to 1962; wrote *The History of the Irish Citizen Army* (Dublin, Duffy, 1943), *James Connolly* (Dublin, Duffy, 1947), *Jim Larkin: Rise of the Underman* (London, Lawrence & Wishart, 1957).

To Lady Gregory

MS. Gregory

Dublin

17 December 1924

Dear Lady Gregory—

Many thanks for your kindness in sending me the cutting. It was very interesting & it has been incorporated with the symphony of praise I already possess.

I am looking forward to seeing "The would be Gentleman";[1] I'm sure Barry Fitzgerald will be delightful in the part. The "Playboy" is going well; it seems as if, at last, we had decided to call him comrade.

"The Passing"[2] was played splendidly, though I dont think very much of the play.

Sincerely Yours

Sean O'Casey

[1] See O'Casey's letter to Lady Gregory, 18 March 1925, note 1.

[2] Kenneth Sarr's *The Passing* opened at the Abbey Theatre on 9 December 1924. Kenneth Sarr was the pseudonym of District Justice Kenneth Reddin, and his one-act tragedy with a cast of two was played by Sara Allgood and Michael J. Dolan.

To The Leader

20 DECEMBER 1924

In our issue of December 6th we described Mr. O'Casey's sketch or article in the *Hairy Fairy's Weekly* [1] as "an affected and shallow attack on Irish in the schools." And we added: "All these people hate Irish. After all, Irish is our flag." We have re-read the sketch, and we can make nothing out of it beyond an attack on the teaching of Irish. [D. P. Moran] [2]

We have received the following:—

Dear Sir,—In last week's issue of the LEADER you had the kindness to refer to an article of mine on Irish in the Schools, which appeared in *The Statesman*. By implication you say that I hate the Irish language. That statement isn't true. No paragraph or phrase in the article stated or implied such an attitude. But I know that the Dublin children hate what is being taught to them as the Irish language; and I have good reason to believe that the majority of the teachers hate it just as heartily, though they haven't the guts to say so; and that the parents of our Dublin children don't care a damn about it.

I happen to know the Dublin workers a little better than you, sir, and I unhesitatingly say that, if a quiet referendum, without speech-making or leaflet-writing were taken, 95 per cent of them would vote against Irish, compulsory or voluntary, and, in my opinion, they would be right.

It is very charming to read that Irish is your flag. I'm afraid the flag is a small one: something like those sold on Language Day; an inch square, with 'An Gaedhilge Abu' [3] written timidly across them. I venture to propose an interesting suggestion to test the dimensions of that flag; it is this: that a debate be held between you and me as to whether the teaching of compulsory Irish to the Dublin children of the workers be commendable or not. The debate to be exclusively in Irish; the debaters to speak and not to read their arguments; no one but those qualified to wear the gold ring to be admitted. I am sure that such a debate, as well as being interesting, would show where the love was, and where the hate lay.—Very sincerely yours,

Sean O'Casey

[1] Sean O'Casey, "Irish in the Schools," *Irish Statesman,* 29 November 1924. By referring to A.E.'s *Irish Statesman* as "the *Hairy Fairy's Weekly,*" Moran is making the then current joke about the bearded mystic.

[2] David Patrick Moran (1871–1936) founded *The Leader* in 1900 and remained its editor until his death.

[3] "Up the Irish Language."

To Lady Gregory

MS. GREGORY

DUBLIN
20 DECEMBER 1924

Dear Lady Gregory.

I am sending you a copy of "The Leader" that may be interesting to you. The Editor, criticising an Article of mine that appeared in the Statesman, said that the [Horace] Plunkett coterie all hated Irish. I sent him the letter which he published; he wrote asking for verification—he was doubtful that I had sent it—I replied the second time vigorously in Irish, repeating the challenge. As you will see by what he writes, he's evidently wiser than to meet me in an Irish debate, for I'm sure he knows very little of it.[1] It is these kind of hypocrites that make me mad! Bawling Irish, Irish, Irish!, and not more than a chara, & Is mise le meas mor,[2] at them!

The paper contains articles on Irish Drama,[3] and on the Poetry of AE.[4]

Yours Sincerely—Sean O'Casey

[1] Below O'Casey's letter in *The Leader,* 20 December 1924, D. P. Moran wrote a long explanation of why it would be useless to debate O'Casey in Irish, since O'Casey hated the language and Moran loved it. O'Casey's explanation was that he was fluent in the language and Moran was not.

[2] Friend, & I am, with great respect yours.

[3] "The Growth of Irish Drama" by "Theo."

[4] "Neo Pantheism" by "Watchman."

To Lady Gregory

MS. GREGORY

DUBLIN
[?] JANUARY 1925

Dear Lady Gregory—

Forgive me for not replying earlier to your very kind letter. I shall be delighted to receive a loan of Orpen's book.[1] You may be certain I

[1] Sir William Orpen, R.A., *Stories of Old Ireland and Myself* (London, Williams & Norgate, 1924). Chapter 10 is an account of Orpen's friendship with Jim Larkin and includes some drawings Orpen made during the 1913 general strike of "Larkin at Work in Liberty Hall" and "The Soup Kitchen at Liberty Hall."

will take every care of it, and return it safely to you. I very much wish, with your permission, to type the article about Jim, & give him a copy.

I recently had dinner with him and a Communist organiser, & we spoke, among other things, of Hugh Lane. Jim told us of a dinner he had with Sir Hugh in America, & talked of the various Artists represented in the Hugh Lane Gift to our City. He mentioned that he remained quiet about the matter for fear his championship would have the effect of hardening the hearts of those anxious to retain them.

He has asked me to write to ask you to permit him to play "The Risin O the Moon" in the Queen's Theatre on Sunday next. The Union is holding a Concert there, and Jim would like to show the work of an Abbey Playwright to many who had never been inside of the Abbey Theatre.

There is a very bitter article in this month's "Catholic Bulletin" about the recent happenings around the publication of "Tomorrow".[2] It is so vulgar in its tone that I am reluctant to send it on to you.

Sincerely Yours,
Sean O'Casey

[2] *To-Morrow,* a magazine edited by Francis Stuart and Cecil Salkeld, appeared only twice, August and September 1924, and was forced to discontinue after its second issue when a controversy arose over a short story in the first issue by Lennox Robinson, "The Madonna of Slieve Dun," which the Dublin printer refused to print and had to be printed in Manchester. The tale is about a young peasant girl named Mary who is seduced by a tramp, dreams that she will bear the Christ Child in His Second Coming, then bears a girl and dies in childbirth. Although Robinson tells the story with sympathetic restraint, many people agreed with the Dublin printer that the story was blasphemous, and a heated controversy followed. Leading the attack against the magazine and its contributors, among whom were Yeats, Robinson, Liam O'Flaherty, Francis Stuart, F. R. Higgins, Cecil Salkeld, and Arthur Symons, was the *Catholic Bulletin,* and in its January issue, which O'Casey felt was too bitter and vulgar for Lady Gregory's sensibilities, the editor, after a long tirade, condemned "the filthy Swan Song of Senator W. B. Yeats ["Leda and the Swan"] and the ribald obscenities and brutal blasphemies of the prose story signed 'Lennox Robinson.'" The controversy led to the dismissal of Robinson from his position as secretary of the Carnegie Library Committee as a result of the protests of two clerical members of the committee, one Roman Catholic and the other Church of Ireland.

To Lady Gregory

MS. GREGORY

[? JANUARY 1925]
WEDNESDAY.

Dear Lady Gregory—

Received book this morning, many, many thanks, Am telling Jim Larkin of your kind permission to play "The Risin o the Moon".

I shall be delighted to see you if you come to Dublin.

Sincerely Yours,
Sean O'Casey

To Irish Statesman

10 JANUARY 1925

THE INNOCENTS AT HOME

Dear Sir,—I have been often advised to read Mark Twain's *Innocents Abroad,* but good patriot as I am, I am satisfied with the intense amusement derived from the antics of our own dear innocents at home. They are sprinkled everywhere, in the political parties, in the Dail and the Senate, and some have recently been chirruping at the Conference of the Catholic Truth Society about the saintly lives of the poor in the tenements.

They have turned Ireland into a huge crystal ball in which they see visions, and over which they dream dreams.

And not the least of the innocents of Ireland is Miss [Mary] MacSwiney, of Cork, and 'Iliam O Rinn,[1] of Dublin of the Golden Goblets

[1] In letters to the *Irish Statesman,* 6 December 1924, Mary MacSwiney and Liam Ó Rinn attacked O'Casey and the *Irish Statesman* as enemies of the Irish language movement, mainly because of O'Casey's short story, "Irish in the Schools," *Irish Statesman,* 29 November 1924. Ó Rinn called the story a "crude and long-drawn sneer." The following bit of dialogue from the story, between two unemployed Dublin laborers, illustrates the type of O'Casey irony which angered Ó Rinn and Miss MacSwiney:

"Jim was silent for a moment, then he murmured softly, 'Still, Jack, we ought to have an Ireland not only free, but Gaelic as well; the first thought towards our children is to make them Irish.'

" 'The first thought towards our children,' responded Jack, 'is their life, rather than their language; to see that the tissues of life get every necessary nourishment, and every possible protection, to provide them with clothes that will leave them cool in the Summer and clothes that will keep them warm in the Winter. And you know, as well as I do, Jim, that the sparrows on the housetops are better fed, and the dolls that are born for Christmas are better clothed than the children of the workers.' "

and the slums. 'Iliam asks me if it be my contention that because the body is starved that the mind should be starved as well. For the sake of the child—yes. How can a half-starved child be educated? The torture of semi-starvation is bad enough, but 'Iliam wants the mind in the half-starved body to be tortured as well. I have no hesitation in saying that I am against the torture of animals, even though it be done "for the glory of God and the honour of Ireland." Our half-starved children are a shame and a reproach to the State, and *is* and *'ta* are not even the shadow of equivalents for bread and butter. Man doth not live by bread alone, but, all the same, he lives by bread. If he thinks this view demonstrates a contempt for the education of the workers' children, he is very simple indeed; it is because of the importance of education (after life) that I stress the necessity of food.

But there are other reasons that induce me to oppose the teaching of Irish, compulsory or voluntary, to the children of the working-class. One is that the attachment to Irish on the part of the elders of the nation is a fancy fraud and a gigantic sham. They know it to be a sham, and, consequently, wish to give it the semblance of reality by forcing it down the throats of the defenceless children. This view is supported by an Irish-Ireland Moses and many of the prophets. In the issue of this week's *Fainne An Lae* we are told by "Cu Uladh" [2] that in the recent election in Tirchonaill the election literature of both parties was written exclusively in English; and that all the official work was wholly performed in English. He tells us that in the districts where English was known those that listened to the speakers became impatient when Irish was spoken for more than a few moments. He tells us that English is used in all the activities of the law, politics, commerce and trade; he says that the young everywhere are turning to the English. "Cu Uladh" complains that he heard that Irish isn't spoken by the clergy in two of the most Irish of the Tirchonaill parishes, and ejaculates that "this is an insufferable and a damned scandal!"

He plaintively tells of having met a man, twenty years younger than himself, who couldn't ask in English for even a half-glass of whiskey, and how he felt that he could have fallen on his neck and kissed him. Perhaps it's just as well he didn't, for the man might have decided that English was the safer if it wasn't the better tongue of the two.

Recently in a Dublin weekly there was a discussion on the force and quality of the dramas by Synge by two contributors, one of whom, I presume, wears the Fainne [3] (undoubtedly he is qualified), the other a native speaker. The discussion, up to the present, and I think it has almost concluded, has been written wholly in English, save for a quotation

[2] "Gairm Sgoile" ("A Call to Arms"), *Fáinne An Lae*, 3 January 1925, a leading article by "Cu Uladh" (Hound of Ulster), pseudonym of P. T. McGinley (1857–1942), president of the Gaelic League and the Fáinne.

[3] The Fáinne, an emblem of proficiency in the Irish language.

by one of the contributors from Geoffrey Keating. Now, why, if the desire for Irish be what it is said to be, should this discussion between two Irish speakers be carried on in English? The reason is obvious: one wished the readers of the paper to understand her attacks on Synge, and the other wished them to appreciate his defence of the dramatist, and the English language served admirably for both purposes.

Out of thirty-four advertisements in *Fainne An Lae,* three are in Irish, and the rest are in the much-abused but ever serviceable English.

Why, the very teaching of the Irish in the schools, in spite of the fierce blasts on the Barr Buadh,[4] is, perhaps, the biggest sham of all. The compulsory learning of Irish is as detestable to the teachers as it is to the children; I'll venture to say that the unhappiest days of a teacher's life (the most of them, anyhow) are those on which they crowd together to read, mark, learn and inwardly digest some of the textbooks that have added copiously to the thorns that are so lavishly scattered in the way of poor Kathleen Ni Houlihan. Of course, they all pretend to be supremely happy, and at the end of the session present a peace-offering to their Irish teacher in the shape of a bangle or a fountain pen. But their efforts, I fear, are like the efforts of Sisyphus, the stone they roll up during the session slips away from them during the rest of the year, and they have to grapple with the stone again, till, I feel sure, some of them wish the Stone of Destiny had never come to Ireland.

And if the teachers find it difficult to learn the language, how can the children find it easy? They don't learn it, and the time spent trying is, in my opinion, a criminal waste. Only a few months ago I had in my room a hardy specimen of a worker's son, red-headed and bare-footed. He had been attending Phibsboro School for some years, and had been learning Irish half an hour a day for twelve months. He is a particularly bright and vivid boy, yet all he knew were a few sentences and the numerals up to ten.

And there is one thing certain even if the rest be lies, and that is that the parents of these children don't care a damn about the Irish language, for they have something else to think of. Let 'Iliam O Rinn on his way from Sackville Gardens to the town call to the tenements in Summerhill, in Hutton's Lane, in Gardiner Lane or Middle Gardiner Street, knocking at every door and entering every room; let him speak to the people there of the glories of Brian the Brave, and I can tell him he finds, as far as these people are concerned, that the days of that hero are o'er. And let him remember that these places form but a tiny portion of the multitude of the Dublin tenements.

Let us take the question of culture pure and simple: what is the teaching of the Irish in the schools going to do for culture; what can it do?

[4] The ancient Celtic victory horn.

In this manner culture can come to the children only through the teachers; and they, forlorn enough as they are in English, a language which they know, how can they excel in Irish, a language which they don't know?

Supposing, however, that the circumstances of our Dublin children were as comfortable and as reassuring as they ought to be, and that the teachers were able effectively to teach the things that belong unto their peace; are we blindly to believe that

> A Thomaisin an cheoil, ciacu is fearr leat an bhean Chriona no an bhean og?
>
> Is fearr liom an bhean chriona mar 'si thugan an bainne beirithe dhom,[5]

and the like, are any better than "Casabianca" or "Under a spreading chestnut tree the village smithy stands"?

Even if teachers and pupils were, after many years of study, able to read the ancient Irish classics, would they be able to understand and enjoy them, or would they know them in the fashion of those that have won honours in the Intermediate?

We have had twenty-five years of "The Gaedhilge, the Gaedhilge", and we have no modern writer of Irish—with the happy exception of Padruig O Conaire[6]—worth reading. The best book of the day—*The Black Soul,* by 'Iliam O Flaherty[7]—written by a Gaelic speaker, has been written in English.

Miss MacSwiney, with a vigorous push of her gentle hand, hurls all who are opposed to the compulsory teaching of Irish into the shadowy Limbo of howling hypocrites. Oh, Miss MacSwiney, Miss MacSwiney, what about your own collection of noisy camp followers? Have we not often had to run like hell from the valiant green-plumed knights, galloping hither and thither, trying to prod our backs with their lances, and forced, when caught, to read the mystical pennant scroll of "A chara, agus is mise le meas mor."[8]

While we are waiting for that Irish Government that "will rigidly insist on the restoration of the Irish language to its proper place," will Miss MacSwiney insist on the restoration of the Irish language to its proper place among her own young Republican soldiers? She durst not; for her life she durst not.

And we have the G.A.A.[9] vehemently resolving (a few years

[5] Thomas of the music, which would you prefer—the old woman or the young woman?

I prefer the old woman because she gives me hot milk.

[6] Pádraig O Connaire (1883–1928), the well-known Gaelic story-teller.

[7] Liam O'Flaherty, *The Black Soul* (London, Jonathan Cape, 1924).

[8] "Friend, and with very great respect," the conventional opening and closing of a formal letter in Irish.

[9] The Gaelic Athletic Association.

previously) that the Irish language would be the language of the 1917 Convention; when, as a matter of fact, the Convention of 1924 is as (or more) English than ever.

We learn that, out of seven thousand members of An Fainne, only five hundred forwarded their yearly subscription of one shilling, and that this is not an occasional but an invariable omission. Perhaps it would be well for Miss MacSwiney to know that "the fairy tale" of opposition to compulsory Irish by the Ard Fheis [10] of Sinn Fein has been exploited by some other than those whom she is pleased to call hypocrites.

In *Fainne An Lae* for December 27th, the editor, complaining of the weakening of the Gaelic League for the current year, stresses the sharp necessity for the continuance of the movement on account of what is happening every day under the Free State Government, *and of what recently happened at the Ard Fheis of Sinn Fein.*

Unable to force the big people, Miss MacSwiney and the rest of them are determined to make national Atlases of the little ones, bearing up what she is pleased to call the nation on their frail little backs.

In conclusion, I wish to say that, while I believe my knowledge of the circumstances of the children of the Dublin workers to be greater than that of 'Iliam O Rinn, I am convinced that his sympathy with them and for them is no less than mine—I remember the collection he made for us in the Gaelic League during the lock-out of 1913—but he must try to forgive me when I laugh, for the rash humour my mother gave me makes me occasionally forgetful.—Yours faithfully,

Sean O Casey

[10] High Council.

To Irish Statesman

7 FEBRUARY 1925

BARR BUADH AND PICCOLO

Dear Sir,—'Liam O Rinn by writing in Irish [1] gives an additional proof of the fragile hold of the language in the actual life of the people, for his views probably remain unread by 95 per cent of the readers of the *Statesman,* just as the readers of a contemporary probably pass by the articles of Father Dinneen without even waiting to ask themselves what they may be all about.

I did not say, nor did I mean to say that the writers arguing around the works of Synge should have written in Irish. That is an ancient

[1] Liam Ó Rinn replied in a long letter in Irish, *Irish Statesman,* 24 January 1925. Mary MacSwiney also replied to O'Casey in this issue.

method of attack of which I have grown weary. I said it was strange that two Irish speakers wrote in English; asked why, and gave myself the reason, namely, that they wished their views to be understood by as many as possible so writing in English, they demonstrated the enormous strength of the English with the weakness of the Irish language.

'Liam, abhorring the fact that great numbers of school-going children are improperly and insufficiently fed, argues that since they must attend school, the education received there should be good and strongly Irish. "Throw the Irish language", says he, "out of the schools, and the hungry children will be hungry still."

Agreed. But at least they will escape a torture and a strain their circumstances will not allow them to bear. You cannot give a good education, either English or Irish, to a barely-nourished child—let that be a law unto itself; it is unassailable. But, since they are forced, ill-fed as they are, to go to school, I hold that the efforts required of them, and the calls upon their impoverished energy should be as few and as bearable as possible, so as to leave them some of the resisting force necessary to withstand the physical dangers surrounding them. We see when any epidemic is rife how weak this resistance is, for the schools are usually the places most likely to be flooded with its havoc. We can again see its weakness in the Dublin Eye and Ear Hospital, in the various Union Dispensaries, and in the country Sanatoria. And this addition, if it weakens the resistance of the children to the diseases that are always flourishing around them, is an added burden to their parents, and what this burden is only a poverty-stricken woman with an ailing child can know. Then, with all respect to 'Liam O Rinn and his comrades, neither he nor they have any right whatsoever, to do anything calculated to add to the already almost intolerable hardships of their more unfortunate brothers and sisters.

That it is easier for the children to learn English than it is for them to learn Irish seems to be painfully obvious to me. They have a good knowledge of it before they begin to go to school. The fundamentals of geography are learned by the locality of the places connected with the street in which they live; of arithmetic by the counting used in their games, and the division of money when sent on messages for their parents, and, by the use of pencil and chalk, they learn the elements of writing. I would venture to say that a teacher who had gone through two or three sessions of intensified study of Irish, would have an infantile grip of the language, compared with the grip of English a child of ten would have on the day of its entering school for the first time in its life.

While the learning of the language may be difficult to older people, admits 'Liam, the learning of it by the children, he contends, is a comparatively easy task: "To my own children", he goes on, "I have spoken nothing but Irish since the day on which they first saw the light; and, though English is spoken to them by their mother and all those who speak to them during my absence, they readily understand everything I may say to them."

That is, I presume, the children of 'Liam speak Irish to the one and English to the many. If they speak English to their mother and to every, or almost every, other individual whom they know, then, I think, their ultimate current of thought will, in the nature of things, be a flow towards an English, an ebb away from an Irish influence.

Again, what comparison can there be between a family group of children to whom Irish only is spoken by the father and the tens of thousands of family groups to whom only English is spoken by father, mother, sister, brother, and all others with whom they live and have their being? Does 'Liam think that these children will, does he think they can, make use of whatever of the "teachers' Irish" they can remember in the homes in which not a word of it is understood? One would think that the appalling impossibility of the thing would shake the confidence, if it didn't undermine, the faith of the most fanatical Gaelic Leaguer.

I can hear 'Liam crowing when he says that never did he meet Gael, Gall or Jew who, having learned a little Irish did not like it. Of course; we all like it; but this interesting fact is what astronomers would call a "light year's distance" from the difficulty of making the Irish language the living tongue of the plain people.

'Liam cannot agree that the teachers are against the language, and says that the few who have written to the papers against the compulsory teaching of Irish are not representative of the rest. I think they are, and, what is more, I think that the clamour of the few is not half so eloquent as the silence of the many. Their jobs grip them by the throat, and, to use a phrase of the common workers, "when the gaffer laughs we all have to laugh." The first prostrate consent to its imposition may have been due to the hidden thought that their love for the glory of Ireland would deliver them from a reduction in their salaries. The teachers have yet to learn that the Labour Movement is something more than affiliation with the Trades Union Congress. It would be interesting to examine the mind of the teachers through a secret ballot.

'Liam introduces a comrade who teaches a teacher's class through the post; we are told that the class has a high knowledge (Ard-eolas) of the language and of its literature, and love for both. The high knowledge of and the love for the Gaelic is really becoming as comic as

> Eileen alanna, Eileen asthore,[2]
> Faithful I'll be to the colleen I adore—

but what else would the comrade say: did anyone ever hear of a correspondence school that wasn't at least an inch or two above perfection?

[2] Terms of endearment: My darling Eileen.

I am advised that if I speak to the residents of the tenements of the poetry of Yeats, of Milton, or of Shakespeare, I will find that there isn't, never has been, and never will be, a surrender to their beauty, power, and inspiration. Exactly; one can hardly look for the blossoming of roses in these sun-forgotten places. It isn't a question of English or Irish culture with the inanimate phantasies of the tenements, but a question of life for the few and of death for the many. Irish-speaking or English-speaking, they are what they are, convalescent homes of plague, pestilence, and famine.

I should be delighted to know that little lad that is such a devil for Irish that he "nearly ates his Irish book, and then rams it under the pilla goin' to bed, so as to be at it the first thing in the mornin'", and who, probably, in the meantime, dreams of Deirdre and the Children of Ua Uisnuigh.

'Liam is kind enough to think that I am not using the hungry children of the tenements as a buckler to hide an attack on the teaching of Irish, but this expression seems to suggest that others do. My sympathies were always with the rags and tatters that sheltered the tenement-living Temples of the Holy Ghost. Years ago I was at a gathering of these in a huge hall—probably once a stable—lying at the back of the Grenville Street tenements, organised by some friends from Trinity College. A number of Gaelic Leaguers were present to entertain the little ones. I see still the slim little shadows violently prancing through the Waves of Tory and the Walls of Limerick; I can hear a young lady telling the heap of atrophied life before her of the strength and glory of the Hound of Ulster; I laughingly listen still to a little, ragged elf trolling out a terribly smutty song, that shocked the Leaguers, causing one of them to shake over us all the incense of "Sing O hurrah, let England quake, we'll watch till death for Erin's sake." I see Miss Nelli O Brien dancing a jig on a kitchen table amid the dignified applause of the visitors and the wild cries of the little savages of the slums. And Grenville Street is here to-day, a little older, but as ugly and as horrible as ever.

I am worried that if I continue the criticism of the language that I will separate the sympathies of the Leaguers from the children of the tenements: Well, God's will be done! If they harden their hearts to the misery of the places where the language is dead, let them soften their hearts to the misery of the places where the language is living.

I am urged to cease blathering, and to put forward a plan that will make the tenements fall like the walls of Jericho; 'Liam says he is willing to blow a blast on one of the ram's horns. I am sure he would, but the days of the ram's horns are over. Each of us, from President Cosgrave to Mr. de Valera, is woven into the fabric of responsibility for the continuance of the slums. Conscious or unconscious of it, they have corrupted each of our souls with a spot of their own leprosy. It is a National problem that cannot be solved by a conjuring trick.

The question of the general revival of Irish must be left to a future letter. It would be well if we tried to determine whether the panel we seek is of such value that it is worth the sale of all the others we possess.

I have gently but determinedly set aside 'Liam's invitation to continue the discussion in Irish. It is strange that Irish should be defended by the English language; but it is only natural, for Irish as a defence to itself is only a toy sword. But it would be ridiculous to defend the English in the Irish tongue, for we would be looking at a huge giant, armed, not with a weapon like a weaver's beam, but with a wisp of straw that would only tickle when it strikes.

If 'Liam decides, like Roderick Dhu, to throw away his target, then he must take the consequences of additional wounds from a rapier held in a hand that thrusts indifferently at friend or foe.

Yours faithfully,
Sean O Casey

To Lady Gregory

MS. GREGORY

[DUBLIN]

22 FEBRUARY 1925

Dear Lady Gregory—

Thanks for accepting the Two Plays: [1] I have a proud vision of the little volume expanding itself in the company of superior associations in the great Library of Coole. This to me is a tremendous pleasure and a positive pride.

You are, I think perfectly right about "The [Catholic] Bulletin"; it is coarse, without strength or picturesque fanaticism. It is ignorant, without sincerity: it has a knowledge of evil and no knowledge of good.

I sent in to the Theatre the beginning of the week the Revised

[1] Sean O'Casey, *Two Plays* (London, Macmillan, 1925), *The Shadow of a Gunman* and *Juno and the Paycock*. The book is dedicated "To Maura and to the Abbey Theatre." Maura refers to Maura Keating, his sweetheart in Dublin from 1918–26. For his comments on her see "Nora Creena" in "The Girl He Left Behind Him," *Inishfallen, Fare Thee Well* (London, Macmillan, 1949), and "Sheila Moorneen" in *Red Roses for Me* (1942). See also Sean McCann, "The Girl He Left Behind," *The World of Sean O'Casey,* ed. Sean McCann (London, Four Square, 1966). McCann, a cousin of Miss Keating, prints some excerpts from O'Casey's letters to her, and a number of poems he wrote to her. Miss Keating, married and living in Dublin, deposited the letters and poems in the National Library of Ireland, not to be opened to the public until 1980.

Version of "Kathleen Listens In", & am again working slowly at "The Plough and the Stars".

It is indeed very sad for young Dudley Persse to look upon the charred remains [2] of what to him must be very tender memories. But this is a sad thing to the whole of us; the ruins of all these lovely houses constitute a desolate monument of shame to Irish humanity.

I am enclosing a clipping from the Leader that may interest you.

Very Sincerely Yours,
Sean O'Casey

[2] Roxborough, the Persse mansion, Lady Gregory's family home, near Loughrea, County Galway, was burned to the ground during the Irish Civil War in 1922. Dudley Persse (1901–) is a great-nephew of Lady Gregory.

To Lady Gregory

MS. GREGORY
DUBLIN
18 MARCH 1925

Dear Lady Gregory—

I am sending you your book that you so kindly sent to me, & thank you sincerely for the loan. The book is, I think, naked of any merit—except the pictures.

I hear your "Would Be Gentleman",[1] is to go on at Easter, & I am looking forward to having a very pleasant few hours with Moliere—and Lady Gregory.

My own play is going forward slowly; about half way to its journey's end—or rather, to the day, when, through the enchanted gate of the Abbey, it may take its first step into the life of the world.

I saw Anti-Christ [2] last night, and, I didn't care a lot for the play.

The papers tell us that Canon O Hanlon, P.P. of Roscommon and Sceilg na Sceol [3] (The Editor of the Catholic Bulletin) had a desperate (almost) encounter on the declaration day of the local elections. Accord-

[1] *The Would-Be Gentleman,* Lady Gregory's translation of Molière's play into Kiltartan dialect, produced at the Abbey Theatre on 4 January 1926. She had earlier done similar translations of *The Doctor in Spite of Himself* (1906), *The Rogueries of Scapin* (1908), *The Miser* (1909). See *The Kiltartan Molière* (London and Dublin, Maunsel, 1910).

[2] Frank Hugh O'Donnell's *Anti-Christ* was produced at the Abbey Theatre on 17 March 1925. This is an indication that O'Casey was now going to first nights at the Abbey.

[3] Sceilg na Sceol, pen-name of Sean O Cellaig (J. J. O'Kelly, 1872–1957), Editor of *The Catholic Bulletin.*

ing to each the other was anything but a gentleman. The poor people of our Slums will have to look to their laurels if the Canons and the Sceilg no Sceols start! And these are they that only can teach us the gentleness, patience and refinement of the Prince of Peace. Instead of the poor Devil there are quite a number of Saints going about like roaring lions seeking whom they may devour.

The Republicans have got a bad set back; they are threatened with an irremediable division. The waving of Father O Flannigan's[4] stole is I think, beating the party into two elements that will possibly dissolve the unified power of the party.

Personally, I'm glad, for I have always thought that diversity & not Unity, is our fairest friend.

Best of Wishes
Very Sincerely Yours,
Sean O'Casey

[4] Father Michael O'Flanagan (1876–1942), Republican priest and Gaelic League enthusiast who, due to his radical views, often clashed with secular and religious authorities. In 1915 when he was a curate at Cliffoney, Country Sligo, the Congested Districts Board announced that the turf banks which had been available to Cliffoney people for generations were to be restricted to tenants of the area, whereupon Father O'Flanagan urged his destitute people to go out and cut the turf, and accompanied them in breaking the law.

To Gabriel Fallon

MS. TEXAS

THE KIP PALACE OF VARIETIES
DUBLIN
THURSDAY
[? MAY 1925]

Dear Gaby—

Many thanks for card. Glad to hear that all's well. Interesting article on The Abbey in this month's Dublin M. by A E Malone.[1] Says "Portrait" is poor; "The Old Man" worse, & Anti-Christ terrible. Advocates enlargement of the Abbey Directorate: probably means the inclusion of AE malone. I never read before such an aggressively egotistical critic—a

[1] Andrew E. Malone, "From the Stalls: Propaganda and Melodrama," *Dublin Magazine,* May 1925. He reviews Dorothy MacArdle's *The Old Man,* which opened at the Abbey Theatre on 24 February 1925; Frank Hugh O'Donnell's *Anti-Christ,* which opened at the Abbey Theatre on 17 March 1925; Lennox Robinson's *Portrait,* which opened at the Abbey Theatre on 31 March 1925.

Malvolio among the Dramatic Critics. Will keep the magazine for you to read.

Had Joyce Chancellor,[2] Brugère [3] & Will [4] with me on Thursday evening. The Brugère Butterfly was comically fluttherin' around the chancellorian Rose all the evening. Poor little Joyce! a wistful little body, full of quaint charm.

I have received a letter from Harry Clarke [5] asking us down to the Studio on Tuesday at 11. or 11.30. So will you meet me at Findlater's Theological Music Hall [6] at 11 oc. or will you come to my place first —say at 10.30? Am writing to Brugère to meet us at The Studio or thereabouts.

Haven't received my fees yet for performances of "The Gunman" in Father Mathew Hall. Well, if I don't get them soon, the Franciscans'll feel a furious tug at their girdles.

Jasus, I forgot. There's an article on the Queen's Royal Theatre in the Dublin M. this month by Holloway [7]—it's gloriously funny: a bewildering storm of wildly blown statistics. It would make Aristotle turn in his grave. But then what can one expect from anything with letters after its name?

Best wishes to all the company, especially to you, & to Johnny.[8] Don't forget to secure Johnny's address for me.

Got a letter from AE asking me & Brugère to go up on Sunday; think I'll have to go.

Yours,
Sean O'Casey

[2] Joyce Chancellor, an Abbey Theatre actress.

[3] Raymond Brugère, a young French professor from L'École Normale who was spending a year at Trinity College. See his article, "Sean O'Casey et le Théâtre irlandais," *Revue Anglo-Américaine,* III, 1926.

[4] Will Shields (Barry Fitzgerald).

[5] Harry Clarke (1889–1931), the Irish stained-glass artist.

[6] Findlater's Theological Music Hall, the Abbey Presbyterian Church at the top of Parnell Square, commonly known as Findlater's Church.

[7] Joseph Holloway, "Some Pages out of the Strange Eventful History of the Old Queen's Royal Theatre, Dublin," *Dublin Magazine,* May 1925.

[8] John Perrin, secretary of the Abbey Theatre.

To Bernard McCabe[1]

TC. O'CASEY

DUBLIN

15 MAY 1925

My Dear Sir—

Replying to yours of the 14th. inst, I feel I ought to say that the fact of your Committee giving the matter consideration does not provoke one to the chanting of a Te Deum.

Before the performances[2] were given I received from you and from Father Laurence letters framing (one of them in gold) an assurance that the fees would be paid. I was innocent enough to believe that they would be paid in the usual way.

Some days ago, a representative of the Kincora Players visited me and offered the fee, but, from what was said, I concluded that the payment presented great difficulty to the company. You will probably think it strange, but I cannot allow myself to suffer the indignity of being paid in this way. I refused the fee, and, made aware that the takings had gone to the Committee, told the representative that under the circumstances, I would apply to you for payment.

I have received no reply to a letter sent to the Dublin Repertory Company.

Your statement that "the troupes received prize money far in excess of the takings," is interesting, but unconvincing to me, and you really must permit me to ignore it.

This damned trouble of writing for what is due to one is irritating when other work has to be done, and should an additional effort be required, I shall place the matter in the hands of the English Society of Authors and Playwrights.

I am,
Very Sincerely Yours,
[*Sean O'Casey*]

[1] Bernard McCabe, Committee, Father Mathew Feis (Festival).

[2] The Kincora Players, an amateur company, performed *The Shadow of a Gunman* on 22 April 1925 in the dramatic competition of the Father Mathew Feis at the Father Mathew Hall, Dublin.

To Lady Gregory

MS. GREGORY

DUBLIN

29 JUNE 1925

Dear Lady Gregory.

I am enclosing article that appeared in "Honesty"; you will find it very funny. I also send a picture—taken from a Russian Paper—of a young village girl who recently won a prize offered by the Russian Soviet Government for the organization of the best equipped village library—a contrast to the lordly Irish Bishop who is afraid the Irish people may drown themselves in the Pierian Spring! [1]

Gaby Fallon (of the Abbey) and myself were at St Joan [2] the other evening. The Play was delightful, beautiful and worthy of our fellow-countryman Shaw.

The Scene in which occurs the Kiltartan sneeze [3] was particularly lovely.

The acting was splendid. Jacques of the Independent gave the Play a very bad criticism; [4] but swine can only trample on the pearls that may be cast before them.

A young carpenter,[5] living in the house with me, after some persuasion, went to see "Joan", and was so delighted, that he is now reading the Play.

However, he had spent a Novitiate in the Abbey, and was ready to enjoy "things of beauty that are joys for ever".

Gaby Fallon and myself are beginning to talk of Poetry, & to read it together—Keats and Masefield—presently, and, later on, "The Dynasts". I think he has the desire to become a writer, and he is intensely interested in the Drama. I am looking forward to "Man & Superman" & to "The Would Be Gentleman" in The Abbey.

Sincere Wishes.
Sean O'Casey

[1] See Pope's *Essay on Criticism,* II, 14–17:
A little learning is a dangerous thing;
Drink deep, or taste not the Pierian spring:
There shallow draughts intoxicate the brain,
And drinking largely sobers us again.

[2] Bernard Shaw's *Saint Joan* opened on 22 June 1925 at the Gaiety Theatre, Dublin, produced by Charles MacDona, with Dorothy Holmes-Gore in the title role.

[3] Shaw met Lady Gregory when he was writing his play, and he told her about the scene at the siege of Orleans when the wind changes to aid the attack. She told him: 'In Gort we often sneeze when the wind changes. Why don't you use a Kiltartan sneeze in your play?" Which he did. Lady Gregory had mentioned this to O'Casey, and he told me about it in the summer of 1963.

[4] "Jacques" (J. J. Rice) in his review in the *Irish Independent,* 23 June 1925, was not impressed by *Saint Joan:* "There is nothing wrong with this play except that it is dull. Most of the characters are Shavian puppets."

[5] Jim Kavanagh.

To Lady Gregory

MS. GREGORY

DUBLIN
12 AUGUST 1925

Dear Lady Gregory—

Thanks for your two very kind letters. I was waiting to reply to the first as soon as I had a definite idea as to the moment I could record for the finishing of the Play.[1] Today, I have to type the Caste, and then, after a final look at the Script, bring it with hope to the Abbey Theatre Directorate.

I have really worked very hard at it for the last few months, & am glad the "Labourer's task is o'er"—for the present.

I shall be delighted to take advantage of your brimming kindness, and plunge enthusiastically into the wonderful woods of Coole. I have told some of my friends of these woods that seem to be crowded with the quiet revelries of the fairy people, and they all envy me.

Let me know when it may be convenient to you for me to go down.

Very Sincerely Yours,
Sean O'Casey

[1] *The Plough and the Stars.*

To Michael J. Dolan

TC. O'CASEY

13 AUGUST 1925

Dear Mr. Dolan,

Now that the tumult and the shouting, consequent upon the expression of an opinion critical of the recent performance of "Man and Superman" [1] has died down, let me say on further thought that my first

[1] Bernard Shaw's *Man and Superman* was revived at the Abbey Theatre on 10 August 1925, directed by Michael J. Dolan, with the following cast: Barry Fitzgerald as Roebuck Ramsden, Shelah Richards as The Maid, Arthur Shields as Octavius Robinson, F. J. McCormick as John Tanner, Eileen Crowe as Ann Whitefield, Maureen Delany as Mrs. Whitefield, May Craig as Miss Ramsden, Ria Mooney as Violet

impressions have been confirmed and intensified. The performance was, in my opinion, bad from every point of view. The acting (the first essential in Drama) the settings and the general balance and interpretation of the play were painfully imperfect.

Let us take the acting first. Tanner and Ann were bad in the sense that the first was too strong and the second too weak. Indeed, if you will pardon this expression, they presented to me the appearance of a roaring lion and a cooing dove. The vehemence of Tanner was overwhelming; he overthrew everything and everybody, and grievously upset the balance of the play. And if the balance of a play be upset, then the whole work becomes a collection of warring and discordant elements. It is generally accepted, I believe, that the plays of Shaw are not star-ridden plays, that one part is as important as another, and that all together weave a sympathetic and unified pattern. But Tanner in his vehemence was a star of the first magnitude and repelled or rejected the wandering forces around as the whim moved him. He dominated the play, and, apparently, frightened everybody else, not only out of their full, but even out of a plausible interpretation of their parts. Why, even in the second scene, he downed Straker! Now, speaking in the spirit, rather than in the letter of Shaw, Tanner was liked by all (except, possibly, Miss Ramsden) even by Violet, though she says she hated him, and, really by Ramsden, even though he feared him. Now could anyone like the unspeakable bounder, Tanner, as he was played on Monday? Nobody but yourself, Mr. Dolan.

In fact, I have no hesitation in saying that, in my opinion, it was this extravagant vehemence that marred the whole pattern of the play, and the thing that astonishes me is that you seem to fail to see it. Starting from this as the central point of imperfection, they were all bad (except Ria Mooney) and some of them realise it. Ann was the weakest manifestation of the surging life force one could imagine. In her smile there was little of that conquering mystery that is said to be in the smile of the Mona Lisa. In the last act she looked (to me) like a nice little girl out for a holiday, instead of a soul-absorbed huntress about to spring on her prey. Even in the episode in the latter part of the same act, she failed to show any of the terrible fascination of a siren, and hooked Tanner as easily as a fisher would hook a gudgeon.

Roebuck Ramsden admits he was bad, so there is no necessity to

---

Robinson, Michael J. Dolan as Henry Straker, Tony Quinn as Hector Malone, Gabriel J. Fallon as Old Malone.

After the performance O'Casey went backstage to tell the actors what the reviewers confirmed the next day, that the production was poor; and the bitter argument that followed, mainly with Dolan and McCormick, led to the beginning of O'Casey's farewell to Inishfallen. For his account of the argument see the last two pages of "The Temple Entered," *Inishfallen, Fare Thee Well* (1949). For another description of the incident see Gabriel Fallon's *Sean O'Casey, The Man I Knew* (1965), pp. 74–77.

say anything about him—I have already told him what I thought of him. Though there is this to be said: Barry Fitzgerald is a fine actor, and the part of Ramsden is vividly drawn. Now why did Ramsden fail to impress? Because the potentialities of the part were whirled away by the storm of Tanner's fierceness: that's why. Now, you yourself, indirectly admitted playing badly by remarking that Straker could not be played without the motorcar. Let me candidly say that I venture to think this expression less sublime than ridiculous. Is it not putting the machine before the art of the actor with a vengeance. One might as well say that Broadbent could not be played without the pig; or Joan play her part without carrying the stake around in her arms like a doll. There is no part which I can appreciate more than that of Straker: I not only can feel, but I know the man, and I must honestly say that I never saw such an apologetic "engineer" as the one I saw on Monday night.

There is [no] use in trying to fool me with the thought that I thought the play bad because of lack of action. I have seen "Misalliance", a play in which there is less action than in "Man and Superman", performed in the Abbey, and the production was infinitely greater than the production of "Man and Superman".

The settings werent, in my opinion, perfect either, especially the second scene: this to me appeared to be shocking. The last, evidently meant to be gorgeous, was grotesque. And when the characters were moving confusedly about, it was a comical picture indeed. I shouldnt have been a bit surprised if one or more of them had given us a song and a dance.

I have written this primarily to show that no savage attack upon me by you or by Mr. F. J. McCormack will prevent me from venturing to give an answer for the hope that is in me, and to point out that while the Abbey Players have often turned water into wine, they may occasionally, (as in this instance, in my opinion) turn wine back again into water.

I am,
Sincerely Yours,
[*Sean O'Casey*]

To Lady Gregory

MS. Gregory

Dublin

19 August 1925

My dear Lady Gregory—

Saturday I cross the Shannon into Conacht, and on to Coole of the Woods.[1]

I shall be delighted to meet Mr. & Mrs. Jack Yeats. I remember well feeling first his wonderful vitality in the pictures illustrating "Ceachta Beag Gaedhilge".[2] I have never forgotton "Do dhun se a dha dhorn" [3] or "Ta an ngas in ngob bhur nge".[4]

And I am looking forward to many a gentle talk with you about the things that we believe to belong unto our Country's place.

Yours Sincerely
Sean O'Casey

[1] He went to Coole Park for his second visit on Saturday, 22 August, and stayed for two weeks.

[2] *Ceachta Beag Gaedhilge,* Irish reading lessons, compiled by Norma Borthwick, with illustrations by Jack Yeats (Dublin, Irish Book Co., 1902).

[3] "He closed his two fists," as in a fighting pose.

[4] "Your green stalk is in the gob of the goose."

To Gabriel Fallon

MS. Texas

Coole Park

Gort, Co. Galway

Wednesday [26 August 1925]

Dear Gaby—

Am taking advantage of a damp morning to write a line or two. The weather here, up to now, has been ideal. I have spent most of my time by the lake, in the woods & on the river. Jack Yeats & I have become great butties. I sincerely hope "Juno" is going well this week, which is, perhaps, a little too much to expect.

Lady Gregory received my play [1] on Saturday night from Switzerland, sent by Lennox Robinson who had read it to W. B. Yeats. Their opinion is that "it is probably the best thing O'Casey has done". Lady Gregory read it publicly to us—the first Act on Sunday, & the following

[1] *The Plough and the Stars.*

acts on Monday evening—and she thinks it a fine play, terribly tragic. It was rather embarrassing to me to hear her reading the saucy song sung by Rosie & Fluther in the second act, but she is an extraordinarily broad-minded woman, & objects only to the line "put your leg over mine, Nora"; not because it is objectionable, but because she's afraid it may provoke a laugh from the wrong people. The play has now been sent to Mr. George O'Brien for final decision, so that production is almost certain.

I am still very anxious about the Caste, & it's a pity I didn't read it to you & to Barry Fitzgerald, before The Abbey opened, so as to get suggestions. I wonder ought I to chance young [Shelah] Richards for the part of Nora? Or Ria Mooney? Which of the two would you suggest? I was thinking of Eileen Crowe for the part of the "young daughter of the Digs". And [John P.] Stephenson for either the "figure in the window;" or for the part of Jack Clitheroe.

However, I may have time to read it to you (if you don't mind) before the Caste is chosen.

Remember me affectionately to Will [Barry Fitzgerald], and to Doctor Larkey [2] and his Orchesthra. And affectionately, as well, to Peter Judge [F. J. McCormick].

Your Sincere Buttie
Sean

[2] Dr. John F. Larchet (1884–1967), Irish composer, conductor, teacher of music; musical director and conductor of the orchestra at the Abbey Theatre.

To Gabriel Fallon

MS. TEXAS

I've forgotten the number of your flat 139 or 130? Will you get & keep for me last Saturday's Independent?

COOLE PARK,
GORT, CO. GALWAY
SUNDAY [30 AUGUST 1925]

My dear Gaby—

Writing letters is a talent the gods have denied me. I must have been a Secretary in a previous existence.

Delighted to hear your "Candles End" has been accepted. I didn't mention it in my first letter for fear you hadn't heard & any reference to it might have depressed you. You see I was right when I thought the effort infinitely greater than any of your previous attempts, & I'm certain you will do much better still. You will renew your youth like the eagle when you see it in print.

I'm not sure yet about Sheila Richards. What do you mean by a "good Producer"? I'm anxious that Lennox Robinson should produce the play. As soon as he returns to Dublin I'll ask him.

And "The figure at the window" is an important personage. The force of the 2nd Act depends upon this character, & if [John P.] Stephenson plays Clitheroe, whom shall I get to play the figure? I can think of no-one with a resonant voice. I have asked "JP" to give you the MM.S to read. I hope you got it. If you have read it, you will understand why I am troubled, too, about the part of Mrs. Gogan. [Maureen] Delaney is too merry for the part, & [May] Craig is, I think, impossible. I should choose, myself, Helena Moloney; but I'm afraid that's almost out of the question.

Isn't it terrible that Peter Judge should be content to constitute himself an echo? I'm thinking of writing to him telling him the play has passed, suggesting he should play "The Young Covey" & asking his opinion of the play.

What about yourself for the part of Peter [Flynn]? If you can't or won't do this then the Covey or Peter must be played by Stephenson and McCormack; each in either part, I think.

Thanks for getting me "Plays for Dancers".[1] Sorry I can't see "Autumn Fire" [2] again.

Just been in the orchard collecting apples with Lady Gregory. By the way, Gaby, me son, address letter "care of Lady Gregory" and tell Barry Fitzgerald to eat his . . . . . bun! Remember me to Muriel—if she's back—and to Miss McQuaid.

Yours as Ever
Sean

[1] W. B. Yeats, *Four Plays for Dancers* (London, Macmillan, 1921).
[2] A revival of T. C. Murray's *Autumn Fire* (1924).

From George O'Brien[1]
To W. B. Yeats

TS. NAT LIB, DUBLIN

40 NORTHUMBERLAND ROAD
DUBLIN
5 SEPTEMBER 1925

Dear Mr. Yeats,

I have read O'Casey's new play and am convinced that it would be quite as successful as any of his others if produced. There are, however, certain particulars in which I think the play in its present form would seriously offend the audience and I think that it must be amended in certain respects before it can be staged.

The love scene between Clitheroe and his wife in Act I does not read true, and I am inclined to think that it could be easily improved. But even if it is let stand as it is there are a couple of phrases which I think would annoy the audience. These are:—

"You can; come on, put your leg
against mine—there."
"Little rogue of th' white breast."
(Act I, p. 19).

My most serious objection is to Act II where, in my opinion, the introduction of the prostitute is quite unnecessary to the action. Of course the mere introduction of a prostitute as a character in the play is not in itself objectionable but I think that the character as presented by Mr. O'Casey is objectionable. The lady's professional side is unduly emphasised in her actions and conversation and I think that the greater part of this scene should be re-written. In view of this general objection I shall not trouble you with the particular phrases in this act to which I take exception as they are very numerous and I think could not possibly be allowed to stand. The song at the end is an example of what I mean.

My only other objections to the play are to particular phrases and modes of expression which could easily be omitted or altered without in any way interfering with the main structure of the play. I will go through these seriatim.

(1). The words "Jesus" "Jasus" and "Christ" occur frequently (e.g., Act I p.12, Act III p.8, Act IV pp.15 and 18.) These words used as expletives would certainly give offence.

[1] Dr. George O'Brien (1892–1974), professor of economics, University College, Dublin, appointed by the Irish government to serve as a director of the Abbey Theatre, along with Yeats, Lady Gregory, and Robinson, on 20 July 1925 when the theatre received its first annual subsidy of £850. See *Lady Gregory's Journals, 1916–1930,* ed. Lennox Robinson (London, Putnam, 1946), pp. 87–99, for her account of the objections of O'Brien and Michael J. Dolan to O'Casey's new play.

(2). On Act I p.11 there is a speech "I'll leave you to th' day when th' all-pitiful, all-merciful, all-lovin' God'll be rievin' an' roastin' you; tearin' an' tormentin' you; burnin' an' blastin' you!"

There are similar phrases to be found in Act III, p.10 (near the top) and Act IV, p.3 (at the bottom). These speeches would offend the audience and must be altered.

(3). On Act II, p.10 the speeches of Bessie Burgess and Mrs. Gogan contain objectionable expressions which could be considerably toned down with advantage.

(4). The vituperative vocabulary of some characters occasionally runs away with itself. As examples of what I mean I would refer to the last words of The Covey before his exit on Act I, p.17, the last two speeches on Act II, p.16, and the last speech on Act III, p.13. I think that the numerous references to "lowsers" and "lice" should be changed.

(5). The word "bitch" occurs on Act I, p.15, Act III, p.4, and Act IV p.17. I think this should be altered.

I think you will agree with me that the play would be improved if the foregoing suggestions were accepted, and hope that Mr. O'Casey can be prevailed on to take the same view. I do not think that any of these alterations will materially alter the main action of the play, which, while excellent in its conception and execution, could not possibly be produced in precisely its present form.

Yours sincerely
George O'Brien

To Lady Gregory

MS. Gregory

Dublin
9 September 1925

Dear Lady Gregory—

By this you will have learned that your picture was inadvertently left behind. We had a wild rush to catch the train, and in a furious gripping of my case the handle broke, & I had to carry it like a sick child. It was by a brief moment that we caught the train. You must keep the picture for me, or, possibly when you next come to Dublin, you may be good enough to bring it with you if it does not inconvenience you too greatly. I am feeling not a little strange in my old room, listening to all the (now) unfamiliar noises.

I have written to Lennox Robinson asking him to produce "The Plough and the Stars", and expect to see him in the Theatre tonight. Mr. [John] Perrin was telling me the receipts for last night (Monday) were almost £40: not too bad for the "Gunman".[1]

Many, many, many thanks to you for your indefatigable kindness to me during my stay in Coole. I posted your letters in the station of Athenry.

Sincerely Yours.
Sean O'Casey

[1] *The Shadow of a Gunman* was revived at the Abbey Theatre on 7 September 1925, for the usual one-week run, with the original cast, except that Ria Mooney played the role of Minnie Powell. Chekhov's *The Proposal,* a one-act farce, was the curtain-raiser.

From W. B. Yeats and Lennox Robinson To George O'Brien

TC. NAT LIB, DUBLIN

82 MERRION SQUARE
DUBLIN
10 SEPTEMBER 1925

Dear O'Brien,

We agree with you about Clitheroe and his wife, that love scene in the first act is most objectionable and, as you say, does not read true. What is wrong is that O'Casey is there writing about people whom he does not know, people he has only read about. We had both decided when we first read the play that he should be asked to try and modify these characters, bringing them within the range of his knowledge. When that is done the objectionable elements will lose their sentimentality and thereby their artistic offence. We decided that if he cannot do this that the dialogue would have to be greatly modified in rehearsal.

Now we come to the prostitute in Act 2; she is certainly necessary to the general action and idea as are the drunkards and wastrels. O'Casey is contrasting the ideal dream with the normal grossness of life and of that she is an essential part. It is no use putting her in if she does not express herself vividly and in character, if her "professional" side is not emphasised. Almost certainly a phrase here and there must be altered in rehearsal but the scene as a whole is admirable, one of the finest O'Casey has written. To eliminate any part of it on grounds that have nothing to do with dramatic literature would be to deny all our traditions.

The other passages you mention are the kind of thing which are dealt with in rehearsal by the producer (in almost every one of O'Casey's plays the dialogue here and there has been a little modified and he has never objected to our modifications) but we are inclined to think that the use of the word "bitch" in Act 4 is necessary. It occurs when Bessie on receiving her mortal wound turns furiously on the women whose delirium has brought it on her. The scene is magnificent and we are loath to alter a word of it.

If you do not feel that this letter entirely satisfies you we can have a Directors' meeting on the subject.[1]

Yours sincerely,
[W. B. Yeats
Lennox Robinson]

[1] On 13 September 1925 O'Brien replied to Yeats and Robinson in part, ". . . I quite see your point that 'to eliminate any part of it on grounds that have nothing to do with dramatic literature would be to destroy all our traditions.' I feel however that there are certain other considerations affecting the production to which it is, in a peculiar way, my duty to have regard. One of these is the possibility that the play might offend any section of public opinion so seriously as to provoke an attack on the theatre of a kind that would endanger the continuance of the subsidy. Rightly or wrongly, I look upon myself as the watchdog of the subsidy. Now, I think that the play, just as it stands, might easily provoke such an attack. . . ." (TS. Nat. Lib., Dublin)

To Lady Gregory

MS. Gregory

[Dublin]
11 September 1925

Dear Lady Gregory—

Thanks for your very kind letter. I am just beginning to realize that I am in Dublin. They are mending the road just outside my window, & a lumbering road-engine, with its monstrous, monotonous rumble has taken the place of the cock. He had a rare three-course meal the last day I was with him—bread & butter, barm-brack and ginger-cake.[1]

I am going up on Sunday to Mr. Yeats to speak about some cuts in my play—he has asked me to come—and, of course, I've no objection to cuts made by him, or you or Mr. Robinson.

My little song, I think, has to go.[2] Speaking to me across the

[1] During his stay at Coole Park, a cock flew up to his window sill every morning at breakfast time.

[2] Rosie Redmond's bawdy song about the tailor and sailor at the end of Act Two, which was omitted in the first production, and has never been sung in revivals of the play at the Abbey down to the present day.

telephone, Mr. Yeats said he thought The Plough & the Stars a wonderful play, and I am very pleased to rank with you, and Yeats, Robinson & Synge in the great glory of the Abbey Theatre.

I find I made a mistake when I said Sally Allgood was playing in "The Proposal". I thought she would be, but I have discovered she isn't, so I am correcting the error.

I am enclosing a cutting from "The Catholic Pictorial" about the Abbey—a poor thing indeed; and another from The Statesman (which you may not have noticed) giving an explanation for the name of "Solomon's Seal".[3]

I am glad to think that the Coole workers like me. They were all very kind, & I am very fond of them.

Jim Larkin had a great meeting here on Wednesday night. His men were jubilant, for five boats laden with coal, purchased by the Union, had berthed in the Liffey, and some food ships are expected too.

He spoke again of "the little Theatre, over the river", at the meeting, and I know that many coal-heavers, dockers, Carters & labourers have been in the Abbey, & good is sure to come from their visits. Many grumbling to me because they couldn't get in wanted to know "why the hell we didn't take the Tivoli!"[4]

I got a pass yesterday night for the woman neighbour that lives in the kitchen of our house & her "buttie" that lives in the top of the house, & off the pair of them went in all their Sunday splendour.

I'm afraid I should have preferred the picture to the luncheon, for I ate nothing till I got home, & then supped royally on eggs & tea, cake & grapes. With very many happy remembrances.

Sincerely Yours,
Sean O'Casey

[3] The leaves of this plant are believed to have special healing powers.
[4] A well-known music-hall theatre on the south bank of the Liffey.

To James Stephens

MS. WISE
DUBLIN
11 SEPTEMBER 1925

My dear Seumas—

I'm sure you will be interested to hear that my new play, "The Plough and the Stars", has been accepted by the Abbey, & will soon be going into rehearsal.

Lady Gregory, W. B. Yeats & Lennox Robinson think it a fine play, & speaking to me on the phone, W. B. Yeats said he thought it "wonderful".

They all think it the finest thing I have yet written, so your opinion of me may be justified at least a little.

Best wishes to Mrs. Stephens, to your boy, to Iris & to yourself.

Yours,
Sean

To Lady Gregory

MS. Gregory

Dublin
15 September 1925

Dear Lady Gregory—

"Professor Tim" [1] was played to a crowded house, and apparently, thoroughly enjoyed by all. Parts of the play are very amusing indeed, & the acting was excellent—particularly the work of Barry Fitzgerald, Sally Allgood & F. J. McCormack. The play itself is, I think, a poor one, but it would be absurd to try to criticise the obvious innocency of the work.

George Shiels is very fond of fashioning hearts of gold & hearts of silver, & here & there, a heart of oak, & one or two ever labouring to be deceitful above all things, & desperately wicked, but then eventually become the broken & contrite hearts that no-one dare despise, and those who do not get a crown, at least will get a palm branch.

I always feel panic-stricken & frantic to run for shelter when he starts at the end of his plays to bomb us with conversions, and seals all his characters with his own funny seal of righteousness.

It's really terrible when you look into it.

It was delightful to look back at the fine audience, & in the front row of stalls were two old comrades of mine in the far away & long ago activities of the Irish Movement, now Colonels in the Free State Army. One of them spent many a night in the little town of Kinvarra, & knew Coole & Clare-Galway well. I'm sure the Abbey has an active future in front of it, & that many who had never even known where it was, will become part of its being.

[1] George Shiels's *Professor Tim* opened at the Abbey Theatre on 14 September 1925.

I hope you are continuing to think of another volume to your "Irish Theatre"; I should be delighted to figure in the volume, for I am, honestly, a little jealous of the first book because I then hadn't then even reached the horizon that gave me a distant glimpse of Ireland's Dramatic Pillar of Fire.

Best of Wishes
Sincerely Yours
Sean O'Casey

From James Stephens

MS. EILEEN O'CASEY [1]

LONDON
21 SEPTEMBER 1925

My dear Sean:

As is to be expected, I have mislaid your letter & (so) your address, & have been waiting for it to turn up, which it hasnt. I am delighted to know that you are pleased with your new play. Tis all rubbish what people say—that an author isn't a good judge of his own work. Given that he *is* a writer he knows better than anyone else will ever know, and if the rest of the world is against him then the rest of the world is an ass. After all, my dear lad, you are the White Man's hope, in drama anyway; & tis the very deuce and the very devil, & the very diamond-point and pinnicle of responsibility (not to have that said of one but) to have that to say to oneself when the times seem meagre & the winds at the east.

A friend of mine in America (Major W. Van R. Whitall,[2] Pelham, New York) wants you to go out there on a (modified) lecture trip. He thought (in conversation with me) that he (with Dudley Digges & Kerrigan [3] & a few others helping) could see to it that you got enough "speeches" to pay your way there & back & leave something over, & that it would be a bit of a change, & a bit of an experience for you. If you can do it you ought to go. Twould be interesting. And, I assure you,

[1] This letter is among O'Casey's private papers, and Richard J. Finneran, who is editing a collection of James Stephens's letters, has kindly given me permission to use the letter here.

[2] Whitall, a bibliophile whom Stephens met on his first American tour, died several months later. But O'Casey showed no interest in the proposed lecture tour.

[3] J. M. Kerrigan (1885–1964) had acted at the Abbey Theatre in its early days and was now working in theatre and films in America. See O'Casey's exchange of letters with Dudley Digges, 24 November 1931, 22 July 1932, and Digges's letter to O'Casey, 27 December 1931.

you can depend on Van Whitall—He is All White. He wants you to stay with him, & he is the decentest soul, & the generousest that you can stay with. As for Digges—There are few men I like better, or would trust further, and I dont think there is any man whose word is so authorative, or wise either, in theatrical America than Dudley Digges' is. It would be a stimulating holiday for you; and, if Whitall has written you—He arranged with me that he would do so—dont balk or jib at the well-meant offer—Just go to it, and do it, America is really wonderful, when you get a bit into it. And New York is the wonderfullest kind of thing that is on the globe, except the simple kindness of Americans, & that, in every part of America & in New York, is the principal thing that beats New York. You should send Whitall, or Digges a copy of your new play with a view to American production. Digges can advise you as to this, & I am certain that his advice would be as honest as your own. If you see AE (lucky man to be actually able to see AE whenever you want) give him my love, & say that I do never forget him.

Mise
[*"I am"*]
James Stephens

To Lady Gregory

MS. Gregory

Dublin
25 September 1925

Dear Lady Gregory—

I am very sorry that I could not see & speak with you again before you returned to Coole. My cold became worse, & threatened an attack of bronchitis; I went to The Abbey on Wednesday night, but I felt so ill, that I returned home almost immediately.

Since then I have been forced to look at life from my room window.

Well, as Marcus Aurelius has said, "Nothing happens to [me] that cannot in the course of things happen to man", & so we must rest content. If one wasn't so hoarse, one could sing, & that would be something.

Books on Renoir, Monet, Cezanne & Chavanne arrived to-day, surrounded by six new Balzac novels (Heaven bless "Juno & the Paycock") so, with Dostoevsky, there'll be rare company in the tenement for the next few weeks.

Best of Wishes.
Sean O'Casey

To Lady Gregory

MS. GREGORY

DUBLIN
2 OCTOBER 1925

Dear Lady Gregory—

It was very good & very kind of you to send me the big & beautiful box of grapes. Bacchus was my favourite god while they lasted.

I am very much better now, & the fear of having to spend some weeks in hospital has passed away. Your picture looks splendid in the centre of the main wall of my room. You have been very kind, very indulgent & very human in your goodness to me. I felt most deeply of all, your placing at my disposal the books of your dear son, and I wish, not to thank you for this, for it was too deep a thing for thanks, but to say how I felt this kind & sincere & generous favour to me.

The Abbey is still doing very well, indeed: the last few nights have seen fine audiences for "A Doll's House".[1] I am convinced that our Theatre (permit me the honour of including myself in its possession) will be better known & more appreciated than ever. Gaby Fallon & I were speaking of the length we have travelled on the road towards a knowledge of Art & Literature, & we both realised how much we owed to the Abbey Theatre.

Kind regards to all at Coole. Congratulations to the young fishers upon catching Pike and Perch: were I the fisher the Pike and Perch would catch me.

Yours.
Sean O'Casey

[1] Ibsen's *A Doll's House* was revived at the Abbey Theatre on 28 September 1925; it was first performed at the theatre on 22 March 1923.

To Sara Allgood[1]

MS. O h-Aodha
Dublin
21 October 1925

Dear Sally,

Thanks for your kind letter. I have wired and written to Mr. [J. B.] Fagan about *Juno*.[2] The Abbey hold the right, but I'm almost certain they will agree to the play's production by Mr. Fagan.

Robinson is to let me know if permission be granted and then, I will wire.

Glad that *The Playboy* went so well.[3] Ay, but when are *you* coming back to the Abbey??? Here I've had everything packed and ready, parked and ready for months in *The Plough and the Stars* and off you pop leaving me stranded for someone to play "Bessie Burgess".

"The cur—God forgive me for goin' to curse!"

Best of wishes, anyhow.
Yours sincerely—Sean

[1] Sara Allgood (1883–1950), one of the outstanding actresses of the Abbey Theatre, having been with the company since its beginning in 1904, distinguishing herself in the plays of Yeats, Lady Gregory, J. M. Synge, and O'Casey. She gave notable performances as Maurya in Synge's *Riders to the Sea,* and as Juno Boyle in *Juno* and Bessie Burgess in *The Plough;* the latter was written especially for her by O'Casey. Her last performance on the stage was in a revival of *Juno* in New York in 1940; thereafter she appeared only in films. She was the sister of Abbey actress Maire O'Neill (Molly Allgood).

[2] James Bernard Fagan (1873–1933), actor-manager, producer and playwright, born in Belfast. For his production of *Juno* see O'Casey's letter to Lady Gregory, 17 November 1925, note 1.

[3] J. M. Synge's *The Playboy of the Western World* was revived at the Royalty Theatre, London, on 25 October 1925. Miss Allgood played the role of the Widow Quinn.

To Gabriel Fallon

MS. Texas
[Dublin]
26 October 1925

Dear Gaby—

As you know already I expected you would be available to play the part of "Peter Flynn" in "The Plough & the Stars", shortly to be produced by the Abbey.

Now your resignation from the Company has made the selection of a substitute a complex problem to me.

Consequently, I must ask you, if at all possible, to soften your determination to the extent of playing the part of "Peter" in "The Plough & the Stars".[1]

Very Sincerely Yours,
Sean O'Casey

[1] Fallon played the role of Captain Brennan in *The Plough*. For the full cast see O'Casey's letter to Sara Allgood, 10 February 1926, note 1.

To Lady Gregory

MS. GREGORY
DUBLIN
1 NOVEMBER 1925

Dear Lady Gregory—

Thanks for your very kind letter. I have mixed feelings about the London production of "Juno": there is loss as well as gain in the exaltation. My heart was set on Sally Allgood to play "Bessie Burgess", in "The Plough & the Stars", and now she is gone, and "the glory has departed from Israel!"

To me "Juno & the Paycock" has gone to live among the Shades, while the new Play is waiting to have breathed into it the breath of life, and however great its biogenesis may be, it will feel the loss of Sally's soul.

She wrote to me telling me of her "little secret" of asking the Theatre for a loan, & of the refusal. I cannot help feeling that this refusal was a mistake. However, one thing is certain: the Theatre is greater than even Sally.

I have altered the love scene in the first act of The Plough & the Stars, & the alteration has eliminated any possible objectionable passage.

One Tuesday last Earnest Blythe[1] came over to my place, & we spent a vivacious evening talking of "old, and happy far off things, and battles long ago".[2]

[1] Ernest Blythe, an Ulster Protestant, whom O'Casey had originally met when they were young members of the Gaelic League and the Irish Republican Brotherhood, 1906–08. Blythe became minister for finance in the Irish Free State government, 1922–32, and he was instrumental in obtaining the first annual government subsidy for the Abbey Theatre in July 1925. For Blythe's account of his early friendship with O'Casey, see his *Trasna Na Bóinne* (Dublin, Sairséal Agus Dill, 1957), "Crossing the Boyne," by Earnan de Blaghd. See Blythe's letter to O'Casey, 29 October 1928, note 1.

[2] From Wordsworth's "The Reaper."

I happened to mention to a German Labour comrade, whom I met in the Abbey, that I was thinking of writing in the future a Labour play to be called "The Red Star". Since then I have received appeals from Leningrad & Moscow to let them know when the play is to be commenced & when finished, & to send on the work to them Scene by scene & act by act so as to avoid all possible delay in production! Well, comrades and all as they are, they will have to wait till the proper time may come for the new birth.

I haven't yet finished [Dostoievsky's] "The Idiot", but am reading it with reverent avidity: it is a great story, and I am very glad you placed it in my way. The central figure is a Christ that was born in Russia. Not Revolutions, but men must bring about the Brotherhood of Man.

Best of Wishes & Kindest Regards to you, Lady Gregory, & to all in Coole.

Sean O'Casey

To Sara Allgood

MS. NAT LIB, DUBLIN

DUBLIN
7 NOVEMBER 1925

Dear Sally—

Never mind what I said; I was simply joking. It can't be helped that you aren't here to play Bessie; you'll surely add laurels to my fame where you are. I haven't the slightest doubt that "Juno" is going to be a big success, & that the Company will "quit themselves like men" (as St. Paul would say).

If the O'Casey banner is lowered in Dublin, it's only that it may be raised in London, and, since we cannot divide you into two equal parts, "we must be satisfied" (as Synge would say).

I have just received a splendid review of the "Two Plays" from the "Langues Modernes" in which the French writer hails the Plays as the works from the hands of a master, & hopes for an O'Casey to appear among the French Dramatists.

From what you tell me, you all must be working hard at the Rehearsals, & Mr. [J. B.] Fagan's motto evidently is, "Whatsoever thy hand findeth to do, do it with all thy might."

The Abbey is playing "Professor Tim" to good houses. The "Plough" will not be going on till after Christmas. Best wishes to you, & to all The Irish Players.

Yours as ever,
Sean

To Lady Gregory

MS. GREGORY

DUBLIN
17 NOVEMBER 1925

My dear Lady Gregory—

Many thanks for your kind hopes about the London production of "Juno."[1]

I have remained quietly in Dublin, and spent the evening yesterday with my friend Doctor Cummins.[2] I shall be glad of the play's success as much for the sake of the Abbey as for my own. I am indeed glad that anything I may have done has given another ray to the fairest jewel in Irelands Breastplate. The Abbey Theatre. There is a paragraph in the current number of "The Observer"[3] that would seem to imply I was ready to forget the kindly & essential encouragement I first received from the Abbey. I enclose a copy of a brief letter sent to Mr. Fagan (at his request) which demonstrates that this is not so.

I don't think you should have been depressed about the Abbey;

[1] *Juno and the Paycock* opened at the Royalty Theatre, London, on 16 November 1925, presented by Dennis Eadie, directed by J. B. Fagan, with the following cast: Arthur Sinclair as "Captain" Jack Boyle, Sara Allgood as Juno Boyle, Harry Hutchinson as Johnny Boyle, Kathleen O'Regan as Mary Boyle, Sidney Morgan as Joxer Daly, Maire O'Neill as Mrs. Maisie Madigan, J. A. O'Rourke as Needle Nugent, Kitty Kirwan as Mrs. Tancred, David Morris as Jerry Devine, Eric Page as Charlie Bentham, Barney Mulligan as An Irregular Mobiliser, Edmund O'Grady as A Coal-Block Vendor, Christopher Steele as A Sewing Machine Man, Edmund O'Grady as A Furniture Removal Man, Joyce Chancellor and Mollie Mackay as Two Neighbours.

[2] Dr. Joseph Dominick Cummins, chief eye surgeon at the Royal Eye and Ear Hospital, Dublin, who had treated O'Casey's ulcerated corneas for many years. See O'Casey's letter to Dr. Cummins, 26 November 1942, Vol. II.

[3] The statement in the "Dramatis Personae" column of *The Observer*, 15 November 1925, reads: "If in the full course of time Mr. O'Casey fulfils the promise of these two plays [*Gunman* and *Juno*] and becomes an original genius, he will be able to assume the dignity of a genius and say that he did without god-parents; as a young playwright with great promise ahead of him, his god-parents are still the founding and directing geniuses of a small theatre in a back street in Dublin, Mr. Yeats, Lady Gregory, Mr. Lennox Robinson."

Caesar cannot be always conquering new countries. Besides, one never knows what may be born in the day of small things. Hail, and Hail again to the Abbey Theatre!

Sincerely yours
Sean

To Sara Allgood

MS. Nat Lib, Dublin

Dublin
7 December 1925

My dear Sally—

A dramatic success is as big a nuisance as a dramatic failure. I have been flooded with letters, till I feel, like Job, I could curse God & die!

All the same, Sally, I'm delighted "Juno" is going so well, & sincerely hope she may have a long and useful life.

I hope you are pleased with the grand notices you are getting; while they make your heart flutter, I hope they won't fill your head with contempt for your poorer brothers and sisters.

The best way is to take them quietly & murmur—Well, what the hell else could they say. I cannot offer you congratulations, for you have done nothing that I did not know was in you to do.

I'm sorry I can't send you MS of "The P & the Stars"; had only 3 copies; one at Abbey, one to the agents, & one to Macmillan & Co who are going to publish it. As soon as it is published, you will have one of the first copies. J. B. Fagan has asked me for the E. & American rights, & I hope I may be able to come to terms with him.

Hope you will accept enclosed photo; if any other member of the Company would like one, let me know.

Yours,
Sean

To Gabriel Fallon

MS. TEXAS

DUBLIN
9 DECEMBER 1925

Dear Gaby—

Hope all goes merry as a (Jasus, I didn't know how to spell marraige) marriage bell, in Cork.[1] Christmas is busy here making the poor people as dull & as gloomy as possible. Every—or almost every—dial appears to wear a look of desperation. Thousands are treading the mournful climb of the Calvary of Christmas. Sweating multitudes in Woolworths. Gold, but neither frankincense nor myrrh.

Hope the Company is pleasing the Cork people. I read an account of the first night of "Professor Tim", & great praise was given to play & performance.

Have been very busy since answering letters, & busier still leaving them unanswered. "Juno", I understand, is going well still. I have to see Robbie tomorrow in the Theatre at 11 oc *A M*. which early hour is a weight on my conscience. Am going with a carpenter tomorrow night to see "Major Barbara".[2]

Best of Wishes to Johnnie, & to the Company, and to you.

Yours as Ever
Sean

[1] The Abbey Theatre Company traveled to Cork to put on a group of plays at the Cork Opera House for the week of 7–12 December: George Shiels's *Professor Tim,* Lady Gregory's *Hyacinth Halvey,* T. C. Murray's *Spring,* Shaw's *Arms and the Man,* O'Casey's *The Shadow of a Gunman.*

[2] Bernard Shaw's *Major Barbara* opened at the Abbey Theatre on 7 December 1925, with Shelah Richards in the title role.

To Lady Gregory

MS. GREGORY

DUBLIN
10 DECEMBER 1925

Dear Lady Gregory—

The letters I have received lately seem to outnumber the stars of the sky and the sands of the seashore in multitude, and I would fain flee away into the solitude of the desert. However, I take the burden philosophically, for I leave the most of them unanswered.

I hope you and all in Coole are well, & rejoice that your household are glad with me about the success of "Juno".

From the first fruits, I have bought a bookcase, books and a filing-cabinet to help in the organization of any work I may yet have to do.

I shall be glad if you would kindly send me the address of Mr Jack Yeats, for I wish to open negotiations for the possible purchase of a picture,[1] and let the gods so speed me that I may find him willing!

I am venturing to send you a "Royalty" programme of "Juno", & hope you will be good enough to accept this simple souvenir of a success in which you had such a vital part.

I'm sure you will be in Dublin for the production of "The Would Be Gentleman",[2] & hope to see you then.

Ever Sincerely Yours,
Sean

[1] He bought a Jack Yeats painting, "The Tops of the Mountains."
[2] See O'Casey's letter to Lady Gregory, 18 March 1925, note 1.

To Sara Allgood

MS. NAT LIB, DUBLIN

DUBLIN
21 DECEMBER 1925

Dear Sally—

Thanks for letter, and glad to hear that "Juno" is still winning you laurels which you needn't hesitate to wear.

Hope W[inston] Churchill liked the play—don't care a damn whether he did or not.

The American Rights of "The Plough" are in the hands of Curtis Brown. J. B. Fagan has written offering terms for the English & American rights; I have replied to him—I should like if possible to contract with him—and I haven't heard from him yet. I don't know that I could stipulate that you should play Bessie B. in England and in N. Y. If we could lop you in two there would be no difficulty, but, alas, we can't, & even Sally can be in one place only at a time!

What do you mean by someone buying "Juno" from [James] Brady of New York? What the hell has he got to do with it? I agreed with Duncan & Cheney about the American rights, & I presume they are to produce it & not Brady.

As a matter of fact, I refused it long ago to Mr. Brady.

I'll send on the rest of the photos shortly. Remember me to Syd.

Best Wishes,
Sean

To New York Times

27 December 1925

Sir—A cutting from your paper of the date of Nov. 15, sent in by your Dublin correspondent (presumably), has been sent to me, and I wish to counter two statements that he must have known, or ought to have known, were far away from the facts.

The statements are (a) "Sean O'Casey, repeated too often, began to pall." The fact is that *Juno and the Paycock,* and the *Shadow of a Gunman,* when last performed (August and September), were played to record houses.

Statement (b) "*Nannie's Night Out* went west because the principal character spent most of her time off-stage, and the minor character failed to be interesting", isn't even on the horizon of fact.

The play was held back because Sara Allgood, who played Nannie magnificently, at the time was suffering from her throat, and the author would permit no other artist to take her place.

The Abbey Directors finally allowed the author to withdraw the work because he felt the character of Nannie deserved the richer picture of a three-act play.[1]

These are the facts, and they can be proved in spite of statements of "J.J.H."[2]

Please be good enough to publish above at your earliest convenience.

Sean O'Casey

DUBLIN,
8 DECEMBER 1925

[1] The expanded version of *Nannie's Night Out* was to be called *The Red Lily,* but O'Casey didn't write it.

[2] J. J. Hayes, secretary of the Irish Dramatists League, and "the Dublin Correspondent."

To Sara Allgood

MS. NAT LIB, DUBLIN

DUBLIN
28 DECEMBER 1925

Now, now, now, Sally!

"Provided I think you're good enough to play 'Bessie Burgess' ". There's a little bit of a joke in that, Sally, but I'll forgive you since Christmas is behind us. My difficulty is this: it's almost certain that I should come to terms with J. B. Fagan for the English rights of "The Plough," & possibly, the American Rights as well; plus a possible tour of "Juno" in the Provinces. Now, how is Sally going to play Juno in the Provinces; Bessie in New York & both in Dublin?? And the same difficulty arises with A. Sinclair, M. O'Neill [1] & others of the London Co. You see, Sally, a great artist is both a blessing and a nuisance: he or she can only be in one place at a time. That you will play Bessie somewhere, is certain; or Drama will lose a genius, for if you refused, there'd be a death, and it wouldn't be mine!

I think you're wrong about [Augustin] Duncan. The negociations with him were carried on through Curtis Brown, and, I understand. he is a reputable producer, one time Director of The Theatre Guild. Mr. [James] Brady certainly made me an offer two years or so ago, through Curtis; but the offer was such that I wrote Curtis telling them Brady could go to the devil.

I'll send on photos for the rest of the Co in a day or two.

Thanks, Sally, for kind wishes & pretty card. I'm busy now looking over typescript of "The Plough" for the Publishers.

I see where Robbie [Lennox Robinson] read the last act of the play at a lecture he gave in the Liverpool University. He thinks the last act splendid, & Bessie has a fine part in it. I'm looking forward to seeing you enthrall audiences in the interpretation.

The photos have just arrived & I'm sending on more copies with this; should any member of the Co still be without one, & a copy is wished for, let me know.

What do all the Excursions & Alarums about "Biddy" mean?

Lady Gregory was in great form last night.

Best Wishes,
Sean

[1] The one-time Abbey actors Arthur Sinclair and Maire O'Neill (Molly Allgood, Sara's sister).

III

FAREWELL TO INISHFALLEN, 1926-27

Nora voices not only the feeling of Ireland's women, but the women of the human race. The safety of her brood is the true mark of every woman. A mother does not like her son to be killed—she doesn't like him even to get married."

"The people that go to football matches are just as much a part of Ireland as those who go to Bodenstown, and it would be wise for the Republican Party to recognize this fact, unless they are determined to make of Ireland the terrible place of a land fit only for heroes to live in."

Early in 1926 O'Casey was fighting numerous battles on many fronts in defense of *The Plough and the Stars*. The public riot broke out in the Abbey Theatre on 10 February, three nights after the opening, but a month earlier on 10 January he had been confronted by a backstage rebellion of the actors who refused to say some of his earthy dialogue and objected to playing his rough characters from the slums. The directors had already insisted on some changes (the love scene between the Clitheroes in Act One was modified, Rosie Redmond's randy song at the end of Act Two was entirely omitted), but when the actors demanded more changes O'Casey threatened to withdraw his play. Thanks to the courage of Yeats and Lady Gregory, however, the play went on, and then the prudery of the actors was outdone by the super-patriotism of the nationalists who tried to wreck the theatre. The police were called in and Yeats tried to shout down the mob with his famous speech from the stage: "You have disgraced yourselves again. Is this to be an ever-recurring celebration of the arrival of Irish genius? Synge first and then O'Casey. The news of the happenings of the past few minutes will go from country to country. Dublin has once more rocked the cradle of genius. From such a scene in this theatre went forth the fame of Synge. Equally the fame of O'Casey is born here tonight. This is his apotheosis."

But this "apotheosis" was also the beginning of his alienation. From this time onward and throughout his life he was to be attacked by the nationalists and anti-Larkinites as an enemy of Ireland. He was drawn into a letter-writing controversy and a public debate by Mrs. Hanna Sheehy-Skeffington, one of the leaders of the riot. He had to defend himself and his play against the charge that he had mocked the sacred heroes of the Easter rising, and he felt that the fanatical nationalists were transforming Ireland into a "terrible place of a land fit only for heroes to live in." Such a place was obviously unfit for O'Casey, who had become something of an exile in his own land even before he left it.

Although he had been reviled and humiliated—he was "overcome by a temporary weakness" of embarrassment during the debate and had to sit down—he had no immediate intention of forsaking Ireland when he went to London in March 1926. He went to oversee the West End production of *Juno* and to receive the Hawthornden Prize, but he had paid his rent for his room in Dublin up to May. Gradually, however, a world of new friends, experiences and ideas was opening up to him. While he still wrote faithfully to Gabriel Fallon and Lady Gregory, both of whom urged him to return to Ireland, he was now developing what were to become lifelong friendships with men like Bernard Shaw and Augustus John, who painted his portrait, and he had fallen in love with Eileen Carey, the beautiful young Irish-born actress who was temporarily playing the role of Nora Clitheroe in the London production of *Plough*. He was no longer exposed to the savage accusations of Dublin and he was enjoying his new freedom. Like Joyce, a copy of whose banned *Ulysses* he had finally "ferreted out" and was now reading, he was discovering in exile a personal and artistic freedom which he had been unable to find in Ireland. By 20 June he was writing to Fallon that he was finished with Dublin: "I must say I feel at home in London now."

Through 1927 he continued to write warmly to his Dublin friends, even about a return visit, but his life and work were now being fulfilled in London. He married Eileen Carey, and he was finishing a new play, *The Silver Tassie.*

To Lennox Robinson

TS. ROBINSON

[DUBLIN]
10 JANUARY 1926

Dear Mr Robinson—

I have carefully and (I hope) impartially re-read The Plough and the Stars, lingering thoughtfully over those passages that have irritated or shocked some of the members of the Caste, and I cannot admit into my mind any reason for either rejection or alteration.

Miss Crowe's hesitation over part of the dialogue of Mrs Gogan [1] seems to me to be inconsistent when I remember she was eager to play the central figure in "Nannie's Night Out", which was as low (God help us) and, possibly lower, than the part of Mrs. Gogan.

Neither can I see any reason standing beside the objection to such words as Snotty,[2] Bum, Bastard or Lowsey. To me it isnt timidity but cowardice that shades itself from them. Lowsey is in "Paul Twyning": [3] is it to be allowed in that play and rejected in mine? Bastard in "The Devil's Discipline" [4] is said with all the savagery of a callous bigot to a young child: is the word to flourish in that play and wither in mine? Snotty is simply an expression for sarcastic or jeering.

The play itself is (in my opinion) a deadly compromise with the

[1] Eileen Crowe objected to many of her speeches and, after consulting her priest, refused to say the line, "Ne'er a one o' Jinnie Gogan's kids was born outside of th' bordhers of the Ten Commandments." She was replaced in the role by May Craig

[2] F. J. McCormick, Miss Crowe's husband, cast in the role of Jack Clitheroe, refused to say the word "snotty," and during performances he always slurred the word making it indistinguishable; but Shelah Richards, who played Nora Clitheroe and had to repeat the word after he said it, always pronounced it with special clarity to make certain the audience did not miss it.

[3] George Shiels's *Paul Twyning* was first produced at the Abbey Theatre on 3 October 1922.

[4] Bernard Shaw's *The Devil's Disciple* was first produced at the Abbey Theatre on 10 February 1920.

actual; it has been further modified by the Directors but I draw the line at a Vigilance Committee of the Actors.

I am sorry, but I'm not Synge; not even, I'm afraid, a reincarnation. Besides, things have happened since Synge: the war has shaken some of the respectability out of the heart of man; we have had our own changes, and the U.S.S.R. has fixed a new star in the sky. Were corrections of this kind to be suffered the work would be one of fear, for everyone would start a canonical pruning, (As a matter of fact Miss Mooney has complained to me about the horror of her part)[5] and impudent fear would dominate the place of quiet courage.

As I have said, these things have been deeply pondered, and under the circumstances, and to avoid further trouble, I prefer to withdraw the play altogether.

Sincerely Yours,
Sean O'Casey

[5] Ria Mooney played the role of the prostitute, Rosie Redmond.

To Sara Allgood

MS. Nat Lib, Dublin

Dublin
10 February 1926

My dear Sally—

Ah, thanks indeed to you for your very kind telegram wishing me success,[1] & thanks again & more than thanks for your message to Delany.[2]

You'll never be able, Sally, to close up your warm & generous heart!

The play went splendidly, & the bookings have broken all records. Maureen was really very good, & worked like a Trojan woman.

We had a little trouble when the play was being cast, Miss Crowe

[1] *The Plough and the Stars* opened at the Abbey Theatre on 8 February 1926, directed by Lennox Robinson, with the following cast: F. J. McCormick as Jack Clitheroe, Shelah Richards as Nora Clitheroe, Eric Gorman as Peter Flynn, Michael J. Dolan as The Young Covey, Barry Fitzgerald as Fluther Good, Maureen Delany as Bessie Burgess, May Craig as Mrs. Gogan, Kitty Curling as Mollser, Gabriel J. Fallon as Captain Brennan, Arthur Shields as Lieutenant Langon, Ria Mooney as Rosie Redmond, P. J. Carolan as A Barman, Eileen Crowe as A Woman, J. Stephenson as The Voice, P. J. Carolan as Corporal Stoddard, J. Stephenson as Sergeant Tinley.

[2] Maureen Delany played the role of Bessie Burgess, originally promised to Sara Allgood, because Miss Allgood was at the time playing Juno Boyle in the London production of *Juno and the Paycock*.

objecting to a good deal of the dialogue in her part (grand dialogue too) & May Craig had to take her place.

Sheila Richards was, I think, magnificent in the part of young Nora: she has, I believe, in her something of the genius of Sally Allgood—and that's saying a hell of a lot!

I have heard you have had a bad cold, & I hope you are all right by now.

My own eyes are troubling me, and the surgeon has ordered no writing or reading for a little time, so I have to be as brief as possible, but I couldn't stay easy from sending you my best thanks.

Yours,
Sean

From Mrs. Hanna Sheehy-Skeffington [1]
To Irish Independent

15 February 1926

[Dear Sir] Your editorial misses what was apparent in your report regarding the Abbey Theatre protest.[2] The demonstration was not directed against the individual actor, nor was it directed to the moral aspect of the play. It was on national grounds solely, voicing a passionate indignation against the outrage of a drama staged in a supposedly national the-

[1] Mrs. Hanna Sheehy-Skeffington (1877–1946), ardent Republican and widow of Francis Sheehy-Skeffington (1878–1916), pacifist and champion of women's rights who was brutally executed during the Easter rising for no official reason by a British officer who was later declared to be insane. (For her reconciliation with O'Casey, see the news story, "The Plough and the Stars," *Irish Independent,* 2 March 1926, note 2.)

[2] *The Plough and the Stars* opened on Monday, 8 February; there were minor disturbances in the audience on Tuesday, and on Wednesday night a full-scale riot broke out in the theatre. Before the violence erupted, the initial speech-making protest had been organized by Mrs. Sheehy-Skeffington and Frank Ryan, I.R.A. leader and Marxist, and up to this time time a close friend of O'Casey's. (For his reconciliation with Ryan, see O'Casey's letters to Horace Reynolds, 19 March 1937, note 2, and to F. R. Higgins, 5 June 1939, note 1.) During the riot some people tried to leap on the stage, the air was filled with flying objects and stink bombs, and the second act was often played in complete dumb-show amid the uproar. Finally the police were called in, the curtain was lowered, and Yeats stepped forward to make his famous speech: "You have disgraced yourselves again. Is this to be an ever-recurring celebration of the arrival of Irish genius? Synge first and then O'Casey. The news of the happenings of the past few minutes will go from country to country. Dublin has once more rocked the cradle of genius. From such a scene in this theatre went forth the fame of Synge. Equally the fame of O'Casey is born here tonight. This is his apotheosis." (*Irish Times* and *Irish Independent,* 12 February 1926).

atre, which held up to derision and obloquy the men and women of Easter Week.

The protest was made, not by Republicans alone, and had the sympathy of large numbers in the house. There is a point beyond which toleration becomes merely servility, and realism not art, but morbid perversity. The play, as a play, may be left to the judgment of posterity, which will rank it as artistically far below some of Mr. O'Casey's work. It is the realism that would paint not only the wart on Cromwell's nose, but that would add carbuncles and running sores in a reaction against idealisation. In no country save in Ireland could a State-subsidised theatre presume on popular patience to the extent of making a mockery and a byword of a revolutionary movement on which the present structure claims to stand.

I am one of those who have gone for over 20 years to performances at the Abbey, and I admire the earlier ideals of the place that produced "Kathleen Ni Houlihan," that sent Sean Connolly out on Easter Week; that was later the subject of a British "Royal" Commission; the Abbey, in short, that helped to make Easter Week, and that now in its subsidised, sleek old age jeers at its former enthusiasms.

The incident will, no doubt, help to fill houses in London with audiences that come to mock at those "foolish dead," "whose names will be remembered for ever."

The only censorship that is justified is the free censorship of popular opinion. The Ireland that remembers with tear-dimmed eyes all that Easter Week stands for, will not, and cannot, be silent in face of such a challenge.

[*Mrs. H. Sheehy-Skeffington*]

To Irish Independent [1]

20 February 1926

Sir—A space, please, to breathe a few remarks opposing the screams and the patter antagonistic to the performance of "The Plough and the Stars" in the Abbey Theatre.

In her letter to the "Irish Independent" Mrs. Sheehy-Skeffington does not drag before us the parts of the play that spread irritating thoughts over the minds of herself and her allies, but a talk with some of the young Republican women which I had after the disturbance enabled me

[1] A shorter version of this letter appeared in the *Irish Times* on 19 February.

to discover that the National tocsin of alarm was sounded because some of the tinsel of sham was shaken from the body of truth.

They objected to Volunteers and men of the I.C.A. visiting a public-house. Do they want us to believe that all these men were sworn teetotallers? Are we to know the fighters of Easter Week as "The Army of the Unco' Guid"? Were all Ireland's battles fought by Confraternity men? The Staff of Stonewall Jackson complained bitterly to him of the impiety of one of their number. "A blasphemous scoundrel," said the General, "but a damned fine artillery officer." Some of the men of Easter Week liked a bottle of stout, and I can see nothing derogatory in that.

They objected to the display of the Tricolour, saying that that flag was never in a public-house. I myself have seen it there. I have seen the Green, White and Gold in strange places. I have seen it painted on a lavatory in "The Gloucester Diamond"; it has been flown from some of the worst slums in Dublin; I've seen it thrust from the window of a shebeen in "The Digs"; but perhaps the funniest use it was put to was when it was made to function as a State robe for a Southern Mayor.

They murmured against the viewpoint of Nora Clitheroe, saying it did not represent the feeling of Ireland's womanhood. Nora voices not only the feeling of Ireland's women, but the women of the human race. The safety of her brood is the true mark [2] of every woman. A mother does not like her son to be killed—she doesn't like him even to get married.

The Republican women shouted with a loud voice against the representation of fear in the eyes of the fighters. If this be so, what is the use of sounding forth their praises? If they knew no fear, then the fight of Easter Week was an easy thing, and those who participated deserve to be forgotten in a day, rather than to be remembered for ever. And why is the sentiment expressed in "The Plough and the Stars" condemned, while it goes unnoticed (apparently) in other plays?

In "The Old Man" (written by a Republican),[3] during a crisis, the many fall back, only the few press forward. In "Sable and Gold" [4] (played by the Republican Players), a volunteer who is a definite coward, is one of the principal characters, and yet no howl has proclaimed the representation to be false or defaming. And are the men of Easter Week greater than those whose example they are said to have followed? Were they all unhuman in that they were destitute of the first element in the nature of man?

"Upon the earth there is not his like," says Job, "who is made with-

[2] In the *Irish Times* letter this word appears as "morality."

[3] Dorothy Macardle's *The Old Man* was produced at the Abbey Theatre on 24 February 1924.

[4] Maurice Dalton's *Sable and Gold* was produced at the Abbey Theatre on 16 September 1918.

out fear." Even the valiant Hector, mad with fear, was chased around the walls of Troy. And do the Republicans forget the whisper of Emmet to the question of the executioner. "Are you ready, sir?" "Not yet . . . not yet."

I wonder do the Republicans remember how Laoghaire and Conall, two of the champions of the Red Branch, ran, as rabbits would run, from what they believed to be the certainty of death; and how Cuchullain alone remained to face death, with "pale countenance, drooping head, in the heaviness of dark sorrow."

One of the young Republicans whispered to me in admiration the name of Shaw, inferentially to my own shame and confusion. Curious champion to choose, and I can only attribute their choice to ignorance, for if ever a man hated sham, it is Shaw.

Let me give one example that concerns the subject I am writing about. Describing in "Arms and the Man", a charge of cavalry. Bluntschli says: "It's like slinging a handful of peas against a window-pane: first one comes, then two or three close behind him, then all the rest in a lump." Then Raina answers with dilating eyes (how like a young Republican woman!): "Yes, first One! the bravest of the brave!" followed by the terrible reply: "Hm; you should see the poor devil pulling at his horse!"

As for vanity, I think I remember a long discussion in "The Volunteer" over the adoption of the green and gold, scarlet and blue, black, white and crimson plumed costumes of the Volunteers of "82" for the Volunteers of "13"; and though these were rejected—they had to be—there was still left a good deal of boyish vanity in the distribution of braids, tabs, slung swords and Sam Brown belts. And how rich (to me) was the parade of the stiff and stately uniformed men. "The solemn looking dials of them," as Rosie Redmond says in the play, and they marching to the meeting very serious, very human, but damnably funny.

I am glad that Mrs. Sheehy-Skeffington says that the demonstration was not directed against any individual actor. As Mr. F. J. McCormack told the audience, the author alone is responsible for the play, and he is willing to take it all.

The politicians—Free State and Republican—have the platform to express themselves, and heaven knows they seem to take full advantage of it; the Drama is my place for self-expression, and I claim the liberty in Drama that they enjoy on the platform (and how they do enjoy it!), and am prepared to fight for it.

The heavy-hearted expression by Mrs. Sheehy-Skeffington about "The Ireland that remembers with tear-dimmed eyes all that Easter Week stands for" makes me sick. Some of the men can't get even a job. Mrs. Skeffington is certainly not dumb, but she appears to be both blind and deaf to all the things that are happening around her. Is the Ireland that is pouring to the picture houses, to the dance halls, to the football matches, remembering with tear-dimmed eyes all that Easter Week stands for? Tears may be in the eyes of the navvies working on the Shannon scheme, but they are not for Ireland.

When Mrs. Skeffington roars herself into the position of a dramatic critic, we cannot take her seriously: she is singing here on a high note wildly beyond the range of her political voice, and can be given only the charity of our silence.

In refutation of a story going round, let me say that there never was a question of a refusal to play the part of Rosie Redmond (splendidly acted by Miss Mooney): the part declined by one of the players was the character of "Mrs Gogan."

I have no intention of noticing the poor stupid things written by the Kellys, Burkes, Sheas, and the Finigans.

Sean O Casey

From Mrs. Hanna Sheehy-Skeffington
To Irish Independent

23 February 1926

"THE PLOUGH AND THE STARS"
Reply to Mr. O'Casey

[Dear Sir,] In his letter Mr. O'Casey sets himself the task of replying to certain criticisms of his play. Since receiving Mr. Yeats' police-protected "apotheosis" Mr. O'Casey appears to take himself over-seriously, not sparing those of us who decline to bow the knee before his godhead. His play becomes "the shaking of the tinsel of sham from the body of truth": an over-statement surely, for of the body of truth as portrayed in "The Plough and the Stars" one may only discern a leprous corpse.

As Arthur Griffith wrote nearly twenty years ago, when last police assisted at an Abbey production: "If squalidness, coarseness, and crime are to be found in Ireland, so are cancer, smallpox, and policemen."[1] But because these are to be found it would not be true to claim that nothing but these are present in Ireland. Because Mr. O'Casey has seen the tricolour painted on a lavatory wall he claims the right to parade it in a public-house as typical of the custom of the Citizen Army and the Volunteers. Because indecent and obscene inscriptions are similarly so found one may not exalt them as great literature.

[1] Griffith wrote these remarks against Synge's *Playboy of the Western World* in 1907 when the play provoked a riot in the Abbey Theatre.

Mr. O'Casey's original version, as is now generally known, was pruned before production. One wonders on what basis certain parts were excluded and others retained. This may, indeed, be the reason for the lopsidedness of some scenes, suffering, as sometimes the picture plays do, from a drastic, ill-concealed cut. Will the original version now appear in London and elsewhere, benefiting by the réclame of a "succès de scandale," a réclame that is usually ephemeral?

As to Mr. O'Casey's ransacking of literature to find soldiers that show fear or vanity, all that is beside the point. Whether the sight of men parading before an action that will lead many of them to their death is "damnably funny," or whether it might be pitiful and heartrending, is also a matter of presentment and point of view. The Greeks, who knew not Mr. O'Casey, used to require of a tragedy that it evoke feelings in the spectator of "pity and terror," and Shakespeare speaks of holding the "mirror up to nature." Submitted to either criteria, "The Plough and the Stars" is assuredly defective. But no doubt Mr. O'Casey would regard such standards as sadly out of date.

A play that deals with Easter Week and what led up to it, that finds in Pearse's words (spoken in almost his very accents) a theme merely for the drunken jibe of "dope," in which every character connected with the Citizen Army is a coward, a slacker, or worse, that omits no detail of squalid slumdom, the looting, the squabbling, the disease and degeneracy, yet that omits any revelation of the glory and the inspiration of Easter Week, is a "Hamlet" shown without the Prince of Denmark.

Is it merely a coincidence that the only soldiers whose knees do not knock together with fear and who are indifferent to the glories of their uniform are the Wiltshires? Shakespeare pandered to the prejudices of his time and country by representing Joan of Arc as a ribald, degraded camp-follower. Could one imagine his play being received with enthusiasm in the French theatre of the time, subsidised by the State?

I learn that Mr. O'Casey's personal knowledge of the Citizen Army does not extend beyond 1914–15. To those, however, who remember the men and women of 1916 such presentation in a professedly "National" theatre seems a gross libel.

Mourning for the men of Easter Week is not incompatible with sympathy for the suffering survivors. The Ireland that is "pouring to the picture houses, the dance halls and the football matches" is the Ireland that forgets—that never knew. It is the Ireland that sits comfortably in the Abbey stalls and applauds Mr. O'Casey's play. It is the Ireland of the garrison, which sung twenty years ago "God Save the King" (while Mr. Yeats then, too, enforced the performance of the "Playboy" with the aid of the police). These do not shed tears for the navvy on the Shannon nor for the men of Easter Week nor for the sorrows of the slums.

Mr. O'Casey accords me as a critic in a shrieking paragraph or two the "charity of his silence." Unfortunately for his play, the professional critics are for the most part on my side, justifying my opinion that his latest play is also his poorest. For (pace Mr. Yeats) the police do not necessarily confer immortality, nor is it invariably a sign of a work of genius to be hissed by an Irish audience.

Arthur Griffith wrote thus in "Sinn Fein" of a similar episode:—"Mr. Yeats has struck a blow" (by calling in police and arresting certain members of the audience who protested against the "Playboy") "at the freedom of the theatre in Ireland. It was perhaps the last freedom left to us. Hitherto, as in Paris or in Berlin or in Athens 2,000 years ago, the audience in Ireland was free to express its opposition to a play. Mr. Yeats has denied this right. He has wounded both art and his country."

May I suggest that when Mr. O'Casey proceeds to lecture us on "the true morality of every woman" he is somewhat beyond his depth. Nora Clitheroe is no more "typical of Irish womanhood" than her futile, snivelling husband is of Irish manhood. The women of Easter Week, as we know them, are typified rather in the mother of Padraic Pearse, that valiant woman who gave both her sons for freedom. Such breathe the spirit of Volumnia, of the Mother of the Gracchi.

That Mr. O'Casey is blind to it does not necessarily prove that it is non-existent, but merely that his vision is defective. That the ideals for which these men died have not been achieved does not lessen their glory nor make their sacrifices vain. "For they shall be remembered for ever" [2] by the people if not by the Abbey directorate.

[*Mrs. H. Sheehy-Skeffington*]

[2] An often-quoted line about the patriotic Irish martyrs from Yeats's early nationalistic play, *Cathleen Ni Houlihan* (1902).

To Sara Allgood

MS. Nat Lib, Dublin

Dublin

23 February 1926

Dear Sally—

Sorry the run of "Juno" is ending, but the play had a fairly gay time of it.[1]

[1] Instead of closing, *Juno and the Paycock* ended its run at the Royalty Theatre on 6 March and was then transferred to the Fortune Theatre where it continued on 8 March.

I am still negociating with Mr. Fagan about "The Plough and the Stars."

The play has raised something of a whirlwind in Dublin.

Am unable to write more: both of my eyes are very bad & painful. Doctor's orders to do as little as possible.

Best Wishes,
Sean

To Irish Independent

26 February 1926

Sir—In a letter on 15th inst. Mrs. Sheehy-Skeffington said that "the demonstration was not directed to the moral aspect of the play. It was on National grounds solely." Yet in her letter of 23rd she viciously affirms what she had before denied, and prancing out, flings her gauntlet in the face of what she calls the "obscenities and indecencies" of the play. She does more: in the righteousness of her indignation, she condemns, by presumption, what she has neither seen nor heard.

This is her interpretation of the Rights of Man. Evidently the children of National light in their generation are as cute as the children of National darkness by placing a puritanical prop under the expression of National dissatisfaction, even though the cuteness requires an action that can be called neither fair nor just.

We know as well as Mrs. Sheehy-Skeffington that obscene and indecent expressions do not make great literature, but we know, too, that great literature may make use of obscene and indecent expressions, without altogether destroying its beauty and its richness. She would hardly question the greatness in literature of Shakespeare (somebody a year or so ago wrote asking if Shakespeare wrote thirty plays without a naughty word, why couldn't O'Casey write them), but in the condemnation of an O'Casey play the green cloak is concealed by the puritanical mantle. Indeed, her little crow over the possible horror of the censored part of the play seems to whisper that the wish is father to the thought, and that, when the play is published, nothing less (or more) will satisfy her than that the united church bells of Dublin, of their own accord, in a piercing peal will clang together—"This is a bad, bad, bad, bad play!"

There is no use of talking now of what Mr. Arthur Griffith thought of or wrote about "The Playboy." Now the world thinks, and I think so, too, that "The Playboy" is a masterpiece of Irish drama. If these Greeks knew not Mr. O'Casey (how the devil could they), O'Casey knows the Greeks, and hopes that the Republican Players will one of these days produce one of their works dealing with ancient gods and heroes. At present he himself is interested in men and women.

Mrs. Skeffington's statement that "every character connected with the Citizen Army is a coward and a slacker" is, to put it plainly, untrue. There isn't a coward in the play. Clitheroe falls in the fight. Does Mrs. Skeffington want him to do any more? Brennan leaves the burning building when he can do nothing else; is she going to persist in her declaration that no man will try to leap away from a falling building? Will she still try to deny that in a man (even in the bravest) self-preservation is the first law? She may object to this, but, in fairness, she shouldn't blame me.

Langon, wounded in the belly, moans for surgical aid. Does she want me to make him gather a handful of his blood and murmur, "Thank God that this has been shed for Ireland?" I'm sorry, but I can't do this sort of thing.

She complains of the Covey calling sentences of The Voice, dope. Does she not understand that the Covey is a character part, and that he couldn't possibly say anything else without making the character ridiculous? Even the Greeks wouldn't do this. And it doesn't follow that an author agrees with everything his characters say. I happen to agree with this, however; but of these very words Jim Connolly himself said almost the same thing as the Covey.

The Tommies weren't represented without fear; but isn't it natural that they should have been a little steadier than the Irish fighters? Even Mrs. Skeffington will not deny that the odds were terribly in their favour, and that they were comparatively safe. Sixty or more to one would make even a British Tommy feel safe.

The people that go to football matches are just as much a part of Ireland as those who go to Bodenstown, and it would be wise for the Republican Party to recognise this fact, unless they are determined to make of Ireland the terrible place of a land fit only for heroes to live in.

Sean O'Casey

To Voice of Labour

Saturday, 27 February 1926

O'CASEY AND "THE VOICE."

I.

THE ABBEY THEATRE,
DUBLIN
20 FEBRUARY 1926

Sir,—Permit me to correct a statement appearing in your paper connecting me with "internal events in the I.C.A.[1] when the late James Connolly was preparing that body for armed revolution." [2]

I had no connection whatever, direct or indirect, with the I.C.A. at that time: I had left, abandoned, deserted, fled from (take your choice of terms) the I.C.A. long before James Connolly had begun to "prepare that body for armed revolution." [3]

Tommy Irwin asks "the author to show us the tenements in Dublin with the three-room flats." He knows of none. The original script has: "The home of the Clitheroes. It consists of the front and back drawing-rooms of a fine old Georgian house." The alteration was made to suit the limitations of the Abbey stage.

May I beg of you for God's sake, and for the reputation of the Irish Labour movement (such as it is) to prevent poor Tommy Irwin from framing his stupidities by trying to write about the Drama?—Sincerely yours,

Sean O'Casey

II

Mr. O'Casey denies one of several statements made in last week's VOICE OF LABOUR. But he was not able to deny his connection with a discreditable cabal against a prominent member [4] of the I.C.A. while he was still a member of that organisation. Really, the particular moment at which his connection with the I.C.A. was ignobly severed doesn't matter, but at the time the late James Connolly *was* preparing for revolution. We can no more accept the statement of Mr. Sean O'Casey now than

[1] Irish Citizen Army.

[2] This statement appeared in a review of *The Plough and the Stars* by Tom Irwin, a member of the Plasterers' Union and secretary of the Dublin Workers' Council, "Tom Irwin at the Abbey: A Dublin Workingman on O'Casey's Play," *Voice of Labour,* 20 February 1926.

[3] O'Casey resigned from the Irish Citizen Army in October 1914 as the result of a controversy over the Countess Markiewicz (Constance Gore-Booth). At a time when the Irish Citizen Army and the Irish Volunteers were rival organizations, he maintained that by holding office in both groups she compromised her position and confused the diminishing ranks of the Citizen Army.

[4] Countess Markiewicz.

we did when the widow of the late Thomas J. Clarke was constrained by decency to write to the "Evening Telegraph" in March, 1918: [5] "Mr. Sean O Cathasaigh makes the statement that Mr. P. T. Daly was an intimate friend of my husband (the late Tom Clarke) and Sean McDermott up to their end. In making that statement Mr. O Cathasaigh must know that he states what is not the truth. . . . As to Mr. O Cathasaigh's boasted friendship and intimacy, well, so far as I know, it came to an abrupt end long before Easter, 1916." There is no difference between the O Cathasaigh of 1914 or 1918 and the O'Casey of 1926.

That a Dublin man who works and is a son of the tenements should write what he feels about a performance at the Abbey seems to have cut pretty close to the bone of a genius at his apotheosis. It's too bad. Playwrights ought to be protected from workingmen in the Press, as they are (sometimes) from hostile demonstrations in the theatre. At all events, Tom Irwin has compelled the admission that at least one "alteration was made to suit the limitations of the Abbey stage." That isn't a bad achievement for a working-class critic. How many other changes—to suit the spirit of the Abbey directorate—were made the Abbey deities alone know.
—Ed., VOICE OF LABOUR.[6]

[5] See O'Casey's letters to the Dublin *Evening Telegraph*, 7 and 14 March 1918.

[6] Editor Cathal O'Shannon and the *Voice of Labour* were bitterly anti-Larkinite as well as anti-O'Casey. The paper regularly denounced Larkin, and several months later the same Tom Irwin wrote a strong attack on him.

Irish Independent

2 March 1926

"THE PLOUGH AND THE STARS"
AUTHOR REPLIES TO REPUBLICAN'S CHARGES
A PIQUANT DEBATE [1]

There was a piquant development last night in the controversy over Mr. Sean O'Casey's play, "The Plough and The Stars," when the author and the leader of the Abbey opposition, Mrs. Sheehy-Skeffington, debated its merits.

Mrs. Sheehy-Skeffington contended that the play was a travesty of Easter Week, and that it concentrated on pettiness and squalor, unrelieved by a gleam of heroism.

[1] As a result of *The Plough* riots and the exchange of letters between Mrs. Sheehy-Skeffington and O'Casey, she challenged him to debate the issue and he accepted. The following is a news story of the debate.

Mr. O'Casey declared that Mrs. Sheehy-Skeffington saw everything through the eyes of a politician, and he through the eyes of a dramatist.

He also said he was not trying, and never would try, to write about heroes. He wrote only about the life he knew and the people he knew.

The dramatist and the leader of the opposition to the play met under the auspices of the Universities' Republican Club in the Mills' Hall, Merrion Row, last night, Prof. A. E. Clery presiding.

Lecturing on the controversy, Mrs. Sheehy-Skeffington said the main point of controversy turned on whether an audience had a right to express disapproval. Most authors and actors agreed that audiences had a right to express approval, and, therefore, the question was, whether an audience had a right to express disapproval by the usual method of hissing and boohing.

She thought that it was necessary that a protest should be made to hit the Abbey directorate in the eye.

There was no other way by which that could be done at present. "The Plough and the Stars" did not strike her as an anti-war play, but as an Anti-Easter week play.

Dealing with National Theatres, she personally regretted, not as a Republican, but as a lover of freedom and of the theatre, that the Abbey Theatre had been subsidised by the Government. It was now a "kept" house, "and any theatre lost more than the subsidy it received by giving up its freedom," and should in the natural course of events "kow tow" to the powers that be. Would it be possible in a subsidised theatre in Belfast for the Ulster Players to produce such a travesty as the "Plough and the Stars" of Carson's Volunteers before Sir James Craig and Lord Carson? Would not the theatre be wrecked by the indignant supporters of these two gentlemen?

"With regard to Mr. O'Casey," she continued, "my own impression of him is that he has 'a grouch.' He likes to see rather the meanness, the littleness, the squalor, the slum squabbles, the women barging each other, and the little vanities and jealousies of the Irish Citizen Army. He has rather the art of the photographer rather than the art of the dramatist.

"These scenes are all put together," and the natural conclusion is that this is a typical picture of the men of 1916.

"There is not a single gleam of heroism throughout 'The Plough and the Stars.'

"The theme of the play right through is the folly of it. That is why it cut to the bone, because we looked to see some of the heroism that did produce Easter Week."

The present Abbey motto was to see the squalor.

"I am sorry for Mr. O'Casey," she proceeded, "because I do realise that his plays have the mark of genius. He has taken Easter Week for what is, after all, rather a comedy than a tragedy. We do wish that a dramatist will arise who will deal with what is great and fine in 1916." (hear, hear).

Mr. Sean O'Casey, who rose to propose a vote of thanks to the lecturer, only uttered a few sentences when he was overcome by a temporary weakness and had to sit down for a short period.[2]

In the meantime Mr. [Lyle] Donaghy, a T.C.D. student, carried on the debate.

Mr. O'Casey resumed and said that Mrs. Sheehy-Skeffington saw everything through the eyes of a politician, while he saw most things through the eyes of a dramatist. She seemed to pay a great deal of attention to what England or America thought of them. He cared nothing for what these countries thought of Irishmen—even if they thought half of them were pookhas and the other half leprecauns.

Referring to the flag in the play, he said that it was not symbolical or representative of any one county or province, or of the Republicans, but was symbolical of the whole of Ireland, and if it represented the whole of Ireland it would have to take its place amongst the Bessie Burgesses, Jinnie Gogans, and Fluther Goods—even the Rosie Redmonds, as it did amongst the President of the Dail, the President of the Seanad, and President of a Republican convention. One of the golden stars on the

[2] There have been various uncomplimentary explanations of O'Casey's "temporary weakness," and many years later Mrs. Sheehy-Skeffington's son, Senator Owen Sheehy-Skeffington, provided the most likely account of what had happened. Shortly before the premiere in Dublin of O'Casey's *The Bishop's Bonfire* on 28 February 1955, the rabidly Roman Catholic weekly newspaper, *The Standard,* on 18 and 25 February ran a series of unsigned front-page attacks against O'Casey and his as yet unseen play. In the 25 February issue a Tomás O'Maolain stated in a letter that O'Casey was a coward as well as a dangerous writer, supporting his claim by saying he had seen O'Casey "collapse" from "a pitiable lack of guts" in his 1926 debate with Mrs. Sheehy-Skeffington. In the 4 March issue, in which the whole front page and many inside columns were devoted to reviewing and attacking O'Casey and his play, Senator Owen Sheehy-Skeffington in a letter replied to Mr. O'Maolain:

"Starting off the debate, my mother put her point of view as effectively as she could, in the full expectation of getting a rattling good reply. She was a good speaker, and the audience was almost 100 per cent with her. Then Sean O'Casey stood up to answer her. As she told it to friends afterwards, he was clearly unwell, his sight was apparently not good, he had difficulty in reading his notes, and he was under great emotional stress before an unfriendly audience. When he was unable to go on and had to stop dead, my mother's reaction was one of genuine sympathy. She was big enough to understand that a writer's greatness and sincerity are not necessarily coupled with the gift for public speaking—and she was well aware that *she* had started with the initial sympathy of the audience.

"Mr. O'Maolain will believe me, I know—and may therefore somewhat modify his view of Mr. O'Casey [he didn't]—when I say that I have direct and indirect evidence that in all the years since that debate Sean O'Casey has never spoken or written of my mother save in the highest terms of appreciation and admiration.

"Moreover, I would affirm that were my mother alive to-day she would feel nothing but disgust for the current STANDARD hate-campaigns conducted by anonymous character-assassins. She was, indeed, old-fashioned enough to regard felon-setting as an un-Irish activity."

See also O'Casey's letter to Dr. Owen Sheehy-Skeffington, 22 July 1961, Vol. III.

tricolour was Easter Week, and in his opinion another was Irish drama. That flag had also to take the spots of disease, of hunger, hardship.

He was not trying, and never would try, to write about heroes. He could write only about the life he knew, and the people he knew.

"These people formed the bone and sinew, and ultimately," he believed, "they were going to be the brain of the country as well."

Mr. O'Casey then went on to reply in detail to the criticisms, and referring to the publichouse scene said that Mrs. Sheehy-Skeffington evidently wanted to bring everyone out of the publichouse.

Mrs. Sheehy-Skeffington—Hear, hear.

Mr. O'Casey—"I am anxious to bring everyone into the publichouses to make them proper places of amusement and refreshment. The play, in my opinion, is the best of the three produced. It has been said I have been writing for England. I am not writing for England. I am writing for England as well as for Ireland, and I don't see why I should not.

"The Plough and the Stars" was handed in and passed for production long before there was a word of the London production of "Juno and the Paycock."

"All my plays were written for Dublin" (applause).

Referring to the critics, he said: "Do not mind the critics. No dependence can be placed on the critics. To my mind, the critics of England and Ireland, and particularly in Ireland, are the Bunsbys of the dramatic movement" (hear, hear).

Mrs. McCarville seconded the vote of thanks, and said that the play was an anti-Pearse play.

Mr. Gabriel Fallon spoke of the protest against the play as mob censorship.

Mr. E. O'Rahilly, Mr. F. J. O'Donnell, and Madame Gonne MacBride also spoke.

To Gabriel Fallon

MS. Texas

The Fortune Theatre
Drury Lane
London
Friday
5 March 1926

Dear Gaby—

Arrived safely & in good fettle—except for me bloody eye—. Had a rough passage across the "Seas of Moyle" [1] but tramped the quarter-deck like a man head on to the wind, & felt at home on the billows!

Having a busy time with photo-men & reporters.

Going to Oxford tomorrow with [J. B.] Fagan—fine fellow.

Going to Broadcast for a few moments on Sunday. Wonder shall I never know peace no more?

Best Wishes
Yrs
Sean

[1] The North Channel between Ireland and Scotland.

To Gabriel Fallon

MS. Texas

The Fortune Theatre
London
9 March 1926

Dear Gaby—

Have seen nothing so far but lifts, taxi cars, Restaurants & Policemen. Lunched today with Lady Gregory. Going tomorrow with Lady Londonderry to see "The Immortal Hour".[1]

Saw "Uncle Vanya": [2] bad acting; splendid production. Fine first night in The Fortune.[3] Cheers and prolonged applause. Flowers flung at

[1] *The Immortal Hour,* a musical drama by Rutland Boughton and Fiona MacLeod, opened at the Kingsway Theatre on 30 January 1926.

[2] Chekhov's *Uncle Vanya* opened at the Barnes Theatre on 16 January 1926, directed by Theodore Komisarjevsky.

[3] O'Casey was still in Dublin and missed the opening of the London production of *Juno and the Paycock* at the Royalty Theatre on 16 November 1925, but he was present when the play was transferred to the Fortune Theatre on 8 March 1926, and the occasion was treated as a gala opening night, with a curtain speech by the playwright.

the members of company. Spoke: more cheers & prolonged applause. Interviewers like the Breastplate of St Patrick.

Interesting to hear that "Dormidus" was played under the protection of the police. Tell us more about this. The full facts urgently requested.

Eyes very bad: had to telegraph to Dr Cummins for prescription of remedy.

Can't write any more.

Yours Affectionately.
Sean

To Huntly Carter

MS. COLBY LIBRARY

FORTUNE THEATRE
LONDON
20 MARCH 1926

Dear Huntly Carter,

I have been very busy, & only now am able to whip a moment from the flying hours to reply to your kind letter. All my plays written before the first accepted work have been ruthlessly destroyed: they were bad.

I fear the Drama in Ireland is not in a very flourishing condition. No Dramatist has sprung from the Revolutionary Movement—at least not yet. [Brinsley] Macnamara, of course, preceded it. The modern trend of the European Drama has hardly reached us yet.

I have just ordered your Theatre in Soviet Russia,[1] & am sure it will prove to be a fascinating work. I was delighted with your Modern Drama in Europe.[2] When Rehearsals of my new play "The Plough & the Stars" have ended—they have just begun—I hope to have the honour and the pleasure of being able to have a talk with you.

Best of Wishes.
Yours Sincerely,
Sean O'Casey

[1] Huntly Carter, *The New Theatre and Cinema of Soviet Russia* (London, Chapman & Dodd, 1924).

[2] Huntly Carter, *The New Spirit in the European Theatre, 1914–1924* (London, Ernest Benn, 1925).

Irish Times

24 March 1926

LONDON HONOURS MR. O'CASEY
AWARD OF HAWTHORNDEN PRIZE
From Our Own Correspondent

London, Tuesday.

Mr. Sean O'Casey, author of "Juno and the Paycock" and "The Plough and the Stars," this afternoon, at the AEolian Hall, was presented with the Hawthornden Literary Prize of £100 by Lord Oxford and Asquith. A large gathering of men and women of letters and of play-goers assembled to see Mr. O'Casey receive his reward.

The prize was instituted in 1919 by Miss Alice Warrender, sister of the late Admiral Sir George Warrender, for the best work of imaginative literature, in prose or verse, published during the previous twelve months. Both the achievement and promise of the author were to be taken into account in the adjudication, the only condition being that the writer should not be over forty years of age.[1]

The Committee of Selection included Miss Warrender, the donor of the prize; Mr. Laurence Binyon, and Mr. Robert Lynd, Mr. Edward Marsh, and Mr. J. C. Squire.

In making the presentation, Lord Oxford said that in all the domain, varied as it was of what could be called imaginative literature, there was no particular department in which, it seemed to him, were we, and indeed the rest of the world, so far behind, for the time being, as in the production of new works of enduring quality and character for the drama. There was no department in which we and other countries were more in need of a fresh outlook and a new departure.

Play-goers were one of the most intelligent classes in the community, and they became sick of the reproductions of what was called the sex problem, with its triangles and its complexes and its more or less thinly disguised indecencies, both of language and of situation. We should hail the prospect of emancipation from this too prolonged, and now outworn, interlude in the history of the drama.

During the last twelve months we had had a relief and a revelation in the discovery of a still young man, who satisfied the conditions of the Hawthornden Prize, in that he was under forty years of age, and he had produced on the stage in London a work which, said Lord Oxford, I do not hesitate to describe as the most moving and impressive drama that

[1] At this time O'Casey thought he had been born on 30 March 1884, so that he would have been just under 40 when *Juno and the Paycock* was first performed at the Abbey Theatre on 3 March 1924. Many years later when he had to obtain a birth certificate, he discovered that the year was 1880.

we have seen for ten, fifteen or twenty years—the drama of "Juno and the Paycock."

It was perfectly true, he continued, that the play had the advantage of the incomparable acting, individually and collectively, of what he believed to be the finest company of actors upon any stage in Europe at this moment, those who were artistically brought up, nurtured and trained in the Abbey Theatre, of Dublin.

But, great as Mr. O'Casey's debt was to the actors, those who had seen the play—and he (Lord Oxford) himself had seen it more than once—would agree with him that, in the delineation of character, in the rich variety and appropriateness of the dialogue, in the invention of situations, in pathos, and in humour, the play was, in the truest and most adequate sense of the word, a great work of art.

The author, on his title page, described it as a tragedy, and tragedy, in a very real and very true sense, it was; but the tragic atmosphere, which from first to last hovered round it, and sometimes enveloped it—that tragic atmosphere was shot through now and again by the intervention of what George Meredith used to call "the comic spirit," and all who had seen the play, or who had read it, would agree with him that, in the characters of Captain Jack Boyle and his satellite, Joxer, they had a pair who were entitled to take their part in the long procession of inseparable pairs which great geniuses of comedy, from Shakespeare and Cervantes downwards, had used to provoke, and to provoke incessantly, and with ever-growing appreciation, the intelligent laughter of mankind.

From both points of view, and from the larger point of view—that of a real creative artist—those who were disposed to be despondent, as he was at the moment, about the present position and immediate prospects of the British drama, might feel that they had a new source of hope and promise in Mr. O'Casey's work.

Mr. Sean O'Casey, on rising to return thanks, had a great reception. He was dressed in a grey lounge suit, with a varicoloured cardigan. His first sentences were fervently spoken in Gaelic. Lapsing into English, he thanked his friends and comrades very much for the praise they had bestowed on his work. He would always be very proud of the prize. It would be a happy memento of his visit to England, and, to use his own words, "a very darling example" of his visit. Furthermore, he would like to accept the prize as a tribute to the drama of the Abbey Theatre and the wonderful acting of the Abbey players.

Lady Gregory, who was present, and was one who did much to encourage the young dramatist in the early days of his writings, gave an interesting outline of Mr. Sean O'Casey's career.

She was very proud of Mr. Sean O'Casey, she said, because he was the latest-born child of the Abbey Theatre. The O'Casey family were very poor, but the father was a lover of books, having a big collection.

The mother of the young dramatist was a woman with a high heart and a sense of humour. After the father's death the family had to live in poverty, and they were glad if they could have bread and tea twice a day. At the earliest age possible young O'Casey went to work at four shillings a week, and then got nine shillings a week at a news-agent's. After that, for some years, he was on the railroad, but after his first play had been put on—"The Shadow of a Gunman"—he had become master of his own fate. In the first years of his life, owing to bad eyesight, he was not able to learn to read, but when he was sixteen years of age he taught himself. His studies gradually progressed, and, after studying other volumes, he read Shakespeare, from which time his dramatic education began.

He went on spending his little money in books, and amassed quite a good collection. With the revival of the Gaelic League, he became a great enthusiast for the language, which was the oldest in Europe except that of the Greeks. He not only learned to speak Gaelic fluently, but he wrote it. Learning a second language was, in some ways, a classical education. Then he began to write stories, and essays, and patriotic ballads, before going to the Abbey Theatre. They looked forward in London to his third play, which was a great and moving piece of writing.

Mr. J. C. Squire proposed a vote of thanks to Lord Oxford and others.

In reply, Lord Oxford referred to Lady Gregory as "the Fairy Godmother of the Abbey Theatre."

To Gabriel Fallon

MS. TEXAS

THE FORTUNE THEATRE
27 MARCH 1926

Dear Gaby—

Very glad indeed to hear that you and Miss Donnellan have "made it up". Give her my best wishes. Another of Cyril Fagan's prophecies gone WEST! What Fagan ought to do is to Stop in bed. Still having a busy time of it: It looks as if "Juno" was going to run for some time longer: business going up. Fagan (not Cyril) expects it to last the Season. What with taxis (or should it be taxii) Buses (or Busi) Tubes, and trains, the life of London seems to be "a getting in and a getting out". However, I like it well, and may stay here forever. Saw last night in

The Barnes "The Three Sisters": [1] wonderful (using this word with its full meaning) production. Great buttie now of Sybil Thorndike: very natural kind, & lovable woman. Haven't been to a Revue yet! Have to lunch with Maurice Macmillan—made him wait a fortnight. That's the stuff to give them! Longing for a cup o' tea be th' oul' fireside with you & the boul' Will [Shields], to whom be the honour & good parts, world without end, AMEN! Hear "Juno" is going well in Dublin. An you still play Bentham? The young man that does it here to "Mary" is I imagine a man, who if he couched with a woman, she'd have to lift him on top of her.

Haven't said a prayer in St Paul's yet, nor have I heard a word spoken in The House of Commons.

Remember me to Arthur [Shields] & P. Carolan & Johnny Perrin. Have just been elected a MEMBER of the Garrick Club.

Expect to be playing golf in Hyde Park tomorrow. Will go down some day next week to make myself an honorary member of the Thames Lightermen.

Hope the Republic is still functioning in the hearts of the Irish People. Had a letter from a Charwoman today asking me to help her to write a play. Told her to write it herself & to send it on to Fagan.

Best of Wishes
Your Buttie. Sean

[1] Chekhov's *The Three Sisters* opened at the Barnes Theatre on 16 February 1926, directed by Theodore Komisarjevsky.

To Gabriel Fallon

MS. TEXAS

J. B. FAGAN'S SEASON
FORTUNE THEATRE
29 MARCH 1926

Dear Gaby.

Haven't the bastard's address. Wrote to him (can't think of his name Van something) c/o of a hotel in Enniskerry. Got no answer. [Liam] O'Flaherty couldn't tell me his number in Fitzwilliam Sqr. or Street. Since believed O'F was having a joke with me built up on the impossibly cheap rent & O F's possible idea of my parsimoniousness. O'F has a funny sense of humour. I sensed the joke even before I wrote to Van der Something.

Sean

To An Poblacht *(The Republic)*

[DUBLIN]
2 APRIL 1926

"Mr. Seán O'Casey and St. Patrick's Night"

Mr. Seán O'Casey, writing from the Fortune Theatre, London, objects strongly to the paragraph published in these columns a fortnight ago which described him as attending the Irish Club banquet at which the Prince of Wales was also a guest. Mr. O'Casey says:

"Is it a surprise to you to learn that I think more of the drama than I do of a dinner, even though the Prince of Wales be present with a bunch of shamrocks in his coat? St. Patrick's night was spent by me—on the invitation of Sybil Thorndike—in the company of an old buttie whom I first met about twenty golden years ago named Billy Shakespeare. I enjoyed his company during a fine performance of 'Henry the VIII' . . . I didn't even wear a shamrock in the course of the day. The statement made in your paper is a vulgar lie."

We apologize to Mr. O'Casey and regret that we commented on what now proves not to have been a fact.

To Gabriel Fallon

MS. TEXAS
FORTUNE THEATRE [LONDON]
2 APRIL 1926

Dear Gaby—

A favour from you, a favour, a favour: I want you to get for me the preliminary speeches (specially written) bringing Stephenson to the Window in "The Plough" before he began on the actual lines in the Script.[1] Stephenson will probably remember them, & be able to write them down—if he doesn't remember—then let him be anathema, marán-anathema! [2]

[1] John Stephenson played The Voice, the figure who orates the words of Padraic Pearse outside the pub in the second act of *The Plough*.

[2] morán, an intensive prefix meaning "very."

And look in "An Poblacht" for me to see if they published a note from me contradicting a statement that at the Dinner given by The IRISH club I sat on the Prince's lap. Curious to think of condemning a man for trying to honour The Blood Royal, when the same man would kiss De Valera's Arse.

As I write The Foundlings are playing their band, and walking solemnly around the grounds opposite my window, offering up prayers (I'm sure) in the little hearts in gratitude for the generosity & loving kindness of their brother-men who have stretched out helping hands & clothed them in white pinafores (the girls) & decent blue suits (the boys) & thanking God for giving them ears to hear the voices of their Masters shouting, "Form Fours!"

Yr Buttie, Sean

To Jim Kavanagh [1]

MS. KAVANAGH

THE FORTUNE THEATRE [LONDON]
[? APRIL 1926]

Dear Jim—

Thanks again for sending me on letters.

Enclosed is One Pound for Rent which, I think, will bring payment up to the 8th of May. Out of the second Pound enclosed, will you give Mrs. Leonard 5/– to wash out room; 2/6 to the man to clean windows, & take a few drinks yourself with the rest of the £1. Enclosed, too, is ten bob, to be given, if you will kindly do it, to Young Curley, in parts of 2/6 each week. Hope Mrs. Kavanagh & Vera are well. How is Mary Moore? [2] Busy still with Rehearsals of "The Plough."

Hear the play is to go on next week at the Abbey.[3] If so Bring

[1] Jim Kavanagh, O'Casey's carpenter friend and neighbor at 422 North Circular Road. The fact that O'Casey had sent money to pay for a month's rent for his room indicates that the letter was probably written in the first week of April, and that O'Casey still intended to return to Dublin at this time.

[2] Mary Moore, one of the neighbors at 422, had provided some of the background material for *Juno and the Paycock*. She had been in love with an I.R.A. man who shot a Free-stater and was in turn ambushed and killed in Finglas. And the Moore family had trouble with a faulty will, for some of the background of which see the letter from James O'Connor, 27 June 1921.

[3] A revival of *Juno and the Paycock*.

enclosed note to the Secretary, & he will give you tickets for two seats.

Best of Wishes, Jim, & thanks.

Your Buttie
Sean

Enclosures:
two One Pound notes.
One ten shilling note
One letter.

To Gabriel Fallon

MS. Texas

c/o A. K. Leishman
7, Lansdowne Place
Guilford Street
[London] W.C.1.
12 April 1926

Dear Gaby—

Thanks for cutting from Ireland's Premier Paper. "Juno" still going well.

Stephenson is right about the additional words—he gave them back to me, and they are, God only knows where, in Dublin. I thought he might possibly have remembered them. It can't be helped: Mea Culpa, mea culpa.

Purchased last week a nice copy of "The Sleeping Venus"; the woman in Dublin'll have a fit when she sees it—oh, it's a shockin' picture! And I got one of Jack Yeats'—"The Tops of the Mountains"—yesterday. He is holding an exhibit in New Bond Street. I am sending you herewith a copy of "The Plough".

This is a lonely City after all: I wish sometimes I was singing "Goodbye Piccadilly Farewell Leicester Square", for they're so damned busy here, they haven't time to make friends.

Saw last night in The Kingsway a lovely little Miracle Play called "The Marvellous Adventures of St Bernard".[1]

The B. Virgin, St Nicholas & Gabriel in heaven speaking to the

[1] Henri Ghéon's *The Marvellous Adventures of St. Bernard,* translated and directed by Sir Barry Jackson, opened at the Kingsway Theatre on 7 April 1926.

saints on earth: the divil & the Deadly sins, & all that sort of thing. But it was really very beautiful, & I wish you had been with me.

Autumn Fire [2] is running this week in the Little Theatre. How did "Look at the Heffernans" go? [3] If you saw some of the things here that they call plays—Holy God, it's awful! Poor Dolan! I suppose The Abbey will soon be in the close season, breeding new activeness & newer plays for the future. But as an Orator said in Hyde Park last Sunday—"I thank Gawd for wot I am, and were I am!" God Almighty has locked up in steel the English sense of humour.

Best of Wishes to Will, & to Rose. Glad you are enjoying yourself at last. Oh, be God, I ferreted out a copy of "Ullyses" [4] at last!

Best Wishes to Johnny, to Sheila Richards, "Tay Pay" [5] oh, Jasus!

Yours
Sean

[2] T. C. Murray's *Autumn Fire* (1924).
[3] Brinsley Macnamara's *Look at the Heffernans!* opened at the Abbey Theatre on 12 April 1926.
[4] James Joyce's *Ulysses* (Paris, Shakespeare & Co., 1922).
[5] T. P. O'Connor, the journalist.

To Lady Gregory

MS. GREGORY

THE FORTUNE THEATRE
[23 APRIL 1926]

Dear Lady Gregory—

I received your lovely little History Book,[1] and I thank you very much for it indeed.

I will be leaving Lansdowne Place at the end of the week for a flat in Chelsea. I spent Tuesday evening with Alec Martin [2] and his family in Richmond. How fond he is of his children! What an unhappy thing it is to be able to love so strongly.

I have sent to T.P. [O'Connor] an autographed copy of "The Plough & the Stars", as a tribute to his work for the restoring of the Lane Pictures to Dublin.

Best of Wishes.
Sean O'Casey

[1] Lady Gregory, *The Kiltartan History Book* (London, T. Fisher Unwin, 1926), expanded new edition.
[2] See O'Casey's letter to Sir Alec Martin, 1 September 1948, Vol. II.

To Gabriel Fallon

MS. Texas

c/o Mrs. Spanner
2, Trafalgar Square
Chelsea. S.W.3.
26 April 1926

Dear Gaby—

Here I am just flitted from Bloomsbury to Chelsea, and thinking of stopping in London till God calls me away.

What's happening to the Abbey at all? Is Macnamara's play as bad as Yeats thinks it is? Perhaps, it may not be so bad even as you imagine. I'm very sorry I didn't see it before I came here, for some of the stuff here is so terrible that a bad play might possibly be a great one. Going on Thursday night to Hammersmith to see "She Stoops to Conquer" play by [Frank] Benson & his company.

So poor Morrier thinks I'll die a Catholic! Bar the women, I'm half living a Catholic already. Remember me to him; I'll send him a card if you send me his address: to send it to the Theatre might hurt him.

By the way, can you think of anyone who'd fit the character of Clitheroe here? The chap that's rehearsing's no good. There's a possibility of getting Donovan [Fred O'Donovan], but it's not certain.

And when is the Abbey Season coming to an end (Between ourselves) Fagan's thinking of asking Will [Barry Fitzgerald] to play Shotover & "The W.B. Gentleman" in Oxford in May. I hear it's genuine about O'Flaherty writing a bio of Tim.[1] Is it to be poor Tim, or poor O'Flaherty? What a strange thing for him to try to do!

So Arthur [Shields]'s beginning to practice looping the loop is he? I'm not surprised. He that humbleth himself, &c.

I've just sent an article "London's Passer By" to Curtis Brown, with a minimum price of £25.—He that exactheth (forgotten how to spell it; will have to buy a Bible) himself, &c.

What a great article the Independent had about Murray.[2] And the way they left out portions that followed. One of them, from "The Morning Post" praised Murray, & then spoke of him as a better Craftsman than I. The Independent quoting says: "Better Craftsman etc: moving

[1] Liam O'Flaherty, *The Life of Tim Healy* (London, Jonathan Cape, 1927).

[2] T. C. Murray's *Autumn Fire* opened in London at the Little Theatre on 13 April 1926, and on 16 April the *Irish Independent* printed an article quoting from the favorable reviews the play received from the London critics.

play. His people are veracious. . . . They are not only veracious—they are memorable".

What was written is this: "Murray's characters are veracious" . . . "O Casey's characters are not only veracious, they are memorable".

There's a bit of Catholic Irish Journalism for you.

Regards to Sheila, Will, Johnny, to Rose & to You.

Your Buttie
Sean

To Gabriel Fallon

MS. Texas

Chelsea
[?] May 1926

Dear Gaby,

Got your letter & telegram alright . . thanks. The General Strike has reduced everything to a terrible state of chassis.[1] Expect all theatres to close down, &, of course, The Fortune as well. So I cannot reply to your query about [P. J.] Carolan.

Don't be too hard on W. B. [Yeats]. After all he's a greater man than O Rahilly the 2nd [2] & as good a Theologian I'll warrant. Just listen to this schoolboy cant: "These devoted men have abandoned lawful human pleasure & honour, they have sacrificed their (what does this mean?) educating poor Irish boys to be useful and even lives to the humble patient obscure drudgery of eminent citizens".[3] Either O'Rahilly or the Editor

[1] The general strike began on 5 May and continued for practically the rest of the year.

[2] Alfred O'Rahilly (1884–1969), teacher, Catholic apologist, and priest; professor of mathematical physics at University College, Cork, 1916–43; president of University College, Cork, 1943–54; became a priest in 1955 at the age of 71. By calling him "O'Rahilly the 2nd," O'Casey meant to distinguish him from his brother, Thomas F. O'Rahilly (1882–1953), "the 1st," Celtic scholar and professor of Irish at Trinity College, Dublin. See also O'Casey's letter to the *Irish Times,* 12 April 1961, note 3, Vol. III, which was refused publication because O'Casey called Alfred O'Rahilly "that curious little ecclesiastical cuckoo-clock."

[3] Prof. Alfred O'Rahilly, "Mr. Yeats as Theologian." *Irish Tribune,* Cork, 23 April 1926. A line was probably dropped out of the printed article, which explains the confusion O'Casey mentions. The Yeats-O'Rahilly controversy grew out of Yeats's defense of the well-known "Cherry Tree Carol." A Christian Brother, editor of a Catholic boys' newspaper, confiscated all copies of a London magazine containing the "Cherry Tree Carol" and burned them as "devilish literature." Yeats wrote an article on the incident and sent it to the *Irish Statesman,* but A.E., the editor, rejected it explaining that "this essay would endanger the magazine's exist-

(probably both) of "The Irish Tribune" deserve to be hanged. O'Rahilly, I'm sure, would denounce "The Marvellous Adventures of St Bernard" as a blasphemy: so would the Christian Brothers.

Hope "The P & the Strs" will go uproariously.

I haven't seen the article by Yeats, but I've asked The Press-Cutting Agency to try to get it for me, & if they do, I'll send it on to you.

Had tea yesterday with Augustus John: a fine, simple, great man.

Remember me to all the staff of the Abbey.

You'll have to take care of yourself & not be catching colds: why the hell don't you see that the grass is dry? or bring out a waterproof sheet?

An Ancient Irish Night—Good God! I've looked at the book & I find that the copy of the Plough I have is a second edition: your note made me look: it was the first time I learned of it.

Eyes not too well: saw Bishop Harman: wearing spectacles—cure o' God on them!

Have you heard or seen anything of Tess Power lately? Tell Carolan nothing can be done at present.

Yours
Sean

---

ence." He then sent it to the *New Criterion* where it appeared in the April 1926 issue, under the title "Our Need For Religious Sincerity." Yeats pointed out that Douglas Hyde gives an Irish version of the Carol in his *Religious Songs of Connacht* (London, T. Fisher Unwin, 1906), and then he drew an analogy between the burning of the Carol and the controversy that raged over Lennox Robinson's supposedly blasphemous story, "The Madonna of Slieve Dun," which led to the suppression of *To-Morrow* magazine (see O'Casey's letter to Lady Gregory, ? January 1925, note 2). In reply to O'Rahilly, Yeats stated: 'I have a right to condemn a system which has left the education of Irish children in the hands of men so ignorant that they do not recognize the most famous Carol in the English language." O'Rahilly defended the Christian Brother who burned the Carol on the grounds that it was blasphemous: "Mr. Yeats regards himself as a much better judge of blasphemy than a mere Christian Brother. In his eyes 'the poem is a masterpiece, the most famous Carol in the English language.' This literary appraisement is quite irrelevant; a masterpiece may be famous—and blasphemous."

To Gabriel Fallon

MS. TEXAS

CHELSEA

13 MAY 1926

Dear Gaby,

"The Plough & the Stars" was last night produced for the first time in the land of the Omnipotent.[1] Went well. Am tired and a little weary of many things. No, no: no woman has anything to do with it.

Nine weeks here now, & haven't yet clicked with a woman.

Sitting tomorrow to have my picture done by Augustus John; & the end thereof shall be honour and great glory. He is holding an exhibit in a week's time & wants my face there. Augustus John says Tuohy's picture of me is a splendid drawing of somebody else! [2]

Father Kearney, P.P. of Covent Garden Party sat through the entire rehearsal of "The Plough" (Dress Rehearsal) heard even the song, & never jibbed at it. Said the play "was wonderful, wonderful, & intensely Catholic!" Am enclosing cuttings from the Morning Post & from the Observer to compare with the notice about Murray that appeared in the Independent.

They don't appear to be playing the game. Keep them—the cuttings for me, oul' son.

Have made a great buttie of Augustus John. He's a splendid fellow, & utterly unspoiled. Says I'm a great Dramatist & slaps me on the back for breaking every damned rule of the Stage.

Got a great ovation last night. Met Peggy Sheridan the Prima Donna from Italy who is to sing in Covent Garden shortly. She's a darlin' girl, & from Dublin too!

[1] *The Plough and the Stars* opened in London at the Fortune Theatre on 12 May 1926, directed by J. B. Fagan, with the following cast: David Morris as Jack Clitheroe, Eileen Carey as Nora Clitheroe, J. A. O'Rourke as Peter Flynn, Sidney Morgan as The Young Covey, Sara Allgood as Bessie Burgess, Maire O'Neill as Mrs. Gogan, Joyce Chancellor as Mollser, Arthur Sinclair as Fluther Good, Henry Hutchinson as Lieutenant Langon, Felix Irwin as Captain Brennan, Edwin Ellis as Corporal Stoddart, Christopher Steele as Sergeant Tinley, Kathleen Drago as Rosie Redmond, E. J. Kennedy as A Bar Tender, Barney Mulligan as The Figure in the Window.

[2] Patrick J. Tuohy, R.H.A., drew a portrait of O'Casey in Dublin in 1925. O'Casey disliked and disowned the portrait, which is now in the Dublin Municipal Gallery, and Lady Gregory told him: "Tuohy has made you look like a butcher." See his comments on the portrait in "Dublin's Gods and Half-Gods," *Inishfallen, Fare Thee Well* (1949), *Autobiographies II*, p. 158.

She says I'm better—or as well—known in Italy as England.

Sally [Allgood] was great as Bessie. And Maire O Neill was really splendid as Mrs. Gogan—

The bloody telephone is ringing like hell—so I must go & close—

Your old Buttie
Sean

To Eileen Carey[1]

MS. Eileen O'Casey

Chelsea
[14? May 1926]

My dear Eileen Carey—

Be brave and be confident in the power and possibilities that are in you. Fight firmly against the disadvantages that are wrestling with you, & the effort will give you a strength that will bring you to a strength that is greater still.

You have done well, and you will do better.

If you should want any help in any way, any advice about a particular phrase or incident, ask me & all the fullness of sympathetic help that is in me will be freely given to you.

With Best Wishes,
Sean O'Casey

[1] Eileen Carey, an unknown young actress who up to this time had acted only minor roles in musical comedy, had been engaged to play Nora Clitheroe in *The Plough and the Stars* for the first week of the run when Kathleen O'Regan became ill. Several actresses auditioned, and O'Casey himself chose the inexperienced but attractive Miss Carey. She was unsure of herself in the role, and he wrote this letter several days after the opening. He was to marry her the following year on 23 September 1927.

To Gabriel Fallon

MS. Texas

Chelsea
16 May 1926

Dear Gaby—

Very busy altering the Caste of The Plough. It is going splendidly, & promises a long run. The Withdrawal of "Juno" was due to circumstances that I will tell you of when I see you. I may possibly go over to Dublin next week for a few days.

At present I'm trying to decide whether it shall be Dublin or London.

Augustus John has painted a picture of me—in one sitting from 11. a m till 4.30: he is delighted & thinks it the best work he's done yet. It is a marvellous portrait: uncanny, powerful, embarrassingly vivid: an alert concentration wearing a look of (to me) shuddering agony.

He is already half-way through a second picture of me, & is evidently intensely interested in what he sees behind what is understood as my face. He is a delightful man.

Starting some hours later to continue the writing of this, I find that it may not be possible for me to go over to Dublin next week. Kathleen O'Regan, who was ill, is to take up her part, & a change is to be made in the part of Clitheroe (you have probably heard that Fagan has sent for P. Carolan)[1] so all this will mean more Rehearsals. Besides, I have to speak at a Dinner the London Critics are to give soon—I have forgotten exactly when: I'll have to look it up—so I'll have to leave it for the following week, I think.

Had a letter from T. C. Murray full of fulsome congratulations, and asking me why K[athleen] Drago, who is playing in "Autumn Fire" is in the Cast of "The Plough". The fact is, I understand, she was engaged long ago for "The Plough", & though not bound in any way, & getting more money in Murray's play, she prefers to play Rosie in "The Plough". I'm not going to answer this letter.

I've got a few more copies of "Two Plays" [2] for presentation, & I see that the book is in its fourth Edition.

Did you see the criticism of A. E. Malone in The Tribune of May the 7th? [3] He says:—"The Dramatist strives after a literary quality of speech which is entirely Alien to the dwellers of the Dublin slums . . . The life of a tenement house is pictured with an actuality that may well be envied by realistic Dramatists".

Andrew E. Malone—and let this saying of Sean O'Casey go down to posterity—is either a whore of an idiot, or an idiot of a whore!

And now, my dear Gaby, what about yourself? Are you doing Any writing these times? Is the wreath of myrtle greater to you than the wreath of bays?

Well, we'll talk of this when I see you in Dublin, or you see me in London, & I hope Rose may be with us to give the deciding vote.

[1] Patrick J. Carolan (1899–1938) of the Abbey Theatre was called over from Dublin to replace David Morris as Jack Clitheroe.

[2] Sean O'Casey, *Two Plays* (1925), *Juno and the Paycock* and *The Shadow of a Gunman.*

[3] In this issue of the *Irish Tribune,* Cork, Andrew E. Malone reviewed the recently published *The Plough and the Stars.*

Had a letter from Tom McGreevey yesterday asking me to come to see him. He is working in "The Connoisseur". Wishes to Johnny, Will, Sheila: to you & to your Sweetheart.

Your Buttie
Sean

P.T.O.

Sending this to The Abbey Address of last letter of Yours.—Oh damn it—the Abbey may be closed. Sending it to
139 Stephen's Green
Are you there still?

To Macmillan & Co. Ltd.

MS. MACMILLAN, LONDON

CHELSEA
19 MAY 1926

Dear Sirs,

Augustus John had just painted a picture of me which I should very much like to have as a frontispiece to any new Edition of "Two Plays" & "The Plough & the Stars."

The picture is a wonderful work, & it must, if at all possible, be added to the "Two Plays," & supersede the one done by Tuohy in "The Plough & the Stars." [1]

Can this be done? I shall be glad to share in or pay the whole of the cost of having the picture added.

Yours,
Sean O'Casey

[1] See O'Casey's letters to Gabriel Fallon, 13 May 1926, note 2, and to Maurice Macmillan, 13 November 1926.

To Gabriel Fallon

MS. TEXAS

FORTUNE THEATRE [LONDON]
2 JUNE 1926

Wednesday

Dear Gaby—

Can't come over this week. Complications (a few) with the F. Theatre.

Having lunch tomorrow with Augustus John & B. Shaw. Wonder what the hell it all means. More puzzled than ever.

Sincerely Yours
Sean

To Jim Kavanagh

MS. KAVANAGH

CHELSEA
[? JUNE 1926]

Dear Jim—

Enclosed explains itself. Your letter from Liverpool took 3 days to reach me, & I forwarded enclosed immediately on receipt: it has just returned, & I am sending it on to Dublin.

I'm terribly sorry, but the fault wasn't mine.

When you got no reply, why didn't you send a telegram?

Please accept enclosed, & if you are ever in want of a bob or two, if it is to be got, you know your Buttie's at your service.

Yours.
Sean

To Gabriel Fallon

MS. TEXAS

CHELSEA
5 JUNE 1926

Dear Gaby—

Read enclosed cutting. I am tortured with an attack of eye inflammation, & am unable to write much.

We expect to be leaving The Fortune Theatre at the end of next week, possibly for The New Theatre in St Martin's Street.

Say nothing about this, Gaby, till the thing's done.

Curious wage sheet, that of The Abbey! Are they being paid during the holidays? And what did they play in Cork? How is F. J. [McCormick] & [Fred] O'D[onovan]? I see O'Flaherty's new book, "The Tent" [1] is to be published this month.

Best of Wishes to Yourself & to Rose. Hope Will is well.

Your Buttie
Sean

[1] Liam O'Flaherty, *The Tent* (London, Jonathan Cape, 1926), a collection of short stories.

To Gabriel Fallon

MS. TEXAS

CHELSEA
17 JUNE 1926

Dear Gaby—

No rest yet, no rest yet. Just getting into my stride. I have decided to come to Dublin as soon as I can—to arrange to bring over my things for residence in London! I'd have been over last week only that circumstances surrounding the Play prevented me. J. B. Fagan and I have drawn our swords! God such a poor, weak creature! For a long time we've been sick of The Fortune—a kip, Gaby a kip; & I've been forcing the pace to get them to clear out of it. Fagan and his "Can't get a Theatre, impossible; no Theatre to be had anywhere" etc. "Royalty wouldn't consider the question" "New" turned it down Cold! So there was nothing for it but to seek myself & I sought. In a week Gaby I had Dennis Eadie of the Royalty doing a faint, because we wouldn't take his Theatre; and an Agreement signed with "The New Theatre" one of the finest houses in the

West End. So we open in The New on Monday week the 28th Inst. It's a big venture, but hopes are high.

I've just had a note from Sheila Richards saying she's coming here on Saturday. What about you?

F. J. [McCormick] & Miss [Eileen] Crowe are here, but they haven't come to see or even asked after me. Well, well, well!

Have you written anything since? I've just sent word to Curtis Brown that no article can be written under £100, and even then, only by the grace o' God! I am arranging for the production of "The Gunman" here, after the run of "The Plough". Thinking of O'Flaherty V.C.[1] with the "Gunman".[2] What do you think?

Fred O'Donovan joins the Caste tomorrow. By the way, why did you leave Will? Had a note from Lennox R. this morning asking me to write to him. Colum has sent "Grasshopper" [3] to Fagan for London production. I wonder how would it go. Plays are failing here every week.

Best of Wishes to you & Rose.

Sean

[1] Bernard Shaw's *O'Flaherty, V.C.* (1915), a one-act play.

[2] *The Shadow of a Gunman* opened in London at the Court Theatre on 27 May 1927, with the following cast: Harry Hutchinson as Donal Davoren, Arthur Sinclair as Seumas Shields, Brian O'Dare as Tommy Owens, Sydney Morgan as Adolphus Grigson, Maire O'Neill as Mrs. Grigson, Eileen Carey as Minnie Powell, Felix Irwin as Mr. Mulligan, Tony Quinn as Maguire, Sara Allgood as Mrs. Henderson, J. A. O'Rourke as Mr. Gallogher, Edwin Ellis as An Auxiliary. The play was preceded by J. M. Synge's *Riders to the Sea,* with Sara Allgood as Maurya.

[3] *The Grasshopper,* by Padraic Colum and E. Washburn Freund, adapted from a German play by Keyserling, was first performed at the Abbey Theatre on 24 October 1922.

To Gabriel Fallon

MS. TEXAS

CHELSEA
20 JUNE 1926
SUNDAY NIGHT

My dear Gaby—

Thanks ever so much for your inquisitive and clever card.

You have probably got my letter by this explaining the position of things. Besides being furiously occupied with the change from one Theatre to another, & an attack of eye trouble, I am looking for a flat in which to lie down comfortably to the task of more work.

I have just spent the evening with Sheila Richards—as irresponsible as ever. A good little soul all the same. I expect to be in Dublin when "The Plough" settles down in the New [Theatre], or if it fails to draw & comes off, to gather together my Dublin property & bring it over here to London. I must say I feel at home in London now. It feels funny to read the Irish correspondents writing about Ireland in the London papers. The Free State—what the hell, & where the hell is it anyhow! I am going to a Dance on Thursday given by The English-Speaking Union: imagine a Gael going to an event like that—however the night is a "Theatrical" one, & possibly that may partly explain it. Do you ever see [Liam] O'Flaherty now? Is he in Dublin still? Tell Lyle Donaghy,[1] should you see him, that I was asking for him. Is he still thinking of producing Prometheus Bound? Isn't it strange that all my Irish friends have so quickly faded from my memory—all except yourself. Seems a little sad too, when I come to think of it. I find it difficult to visualise any of them. There is a likelihood of The Gunman being produced here after "The Plough" has run its course.

Hope you are well.
Good Wishes
Sean

[1] John Lyle Donaghy (1902–49), Irish poet and teacher.

To Mrs. L. L'Estrange Malone

MS. O'CASEY [1]
CHELSEA
[? JUNE 1926]

Dear Mrs Malone—

Yes; I've seen by the papers that you have cancelled the Matinee, and, in my opinion a nice blunder you've made of the whole damned thing.

You got the Artists, you got the Theatre and you got the play—what more did you want? The Manager of the Theatre thought—rightly or wrongly—that he risked too much, I suppose, by the permission given to Mr [A. J.] Cook to speak; the producer, Mr [J. B.] Fagan disagreed

[1] Rough draft of a letter to Mrs. L. L'Estrange Malone, who, with the cooperation of O'Casey, J. B. Fagan, the actors, and the management of the Fortune Theatre, had arranged a special matinee performance of *The Plough and the Stars* for the benefit of the striking miners, idle since the beginning of the general strike on 5 May 1926. As the letter indicates, however, the plan collapsed when permission was refused to A. J. Cook, secretary of the Miner's Federation, to make a speech during one of the intervals.

with this arrangement too; some of the Artists—possibly all of them—held the same opinion: do you think it was possible for me—or you—or the Committee to ram a different opinion down their throats?

Was the primary need that of hearing Mr Cook speak, or of getting funds for the women & the children of the Miners? Whatever the primary reason may have been, you've now lost the two advantages.

It was, in my opinion, a stupid thing to do—as stupid for your Committee to cancel the Matinee because Mr. Cook wouldn't be permitted to speak, as it was stupid for the T.U.C. to refuse help because it came from Russia.

If the alternatives had been—get the Theatre with the loss of Mr. Cook's speech, or lose the Theatre with the gain of Mr. Cook's speech, there would have been something attempted if nothing were done, but you have lost the one without gaining the other, and it would be sometimes useful if we learned that there is a time to keep silent as well as a time to speak. (You'll find this in the Bible)

Besides,—& this is most important of all—I'm not going to permit Mr. Cook or Mr. [Stanley] Baldwin, God or devil, prince or proletariat to interfere with the action by a speech, or in any other way, whatsoever, in any interval between the acts of any play of mine.

If you will let me know the expenses you have incurred in advertising the Matinee, I shall be glad to pay them for you.

Sincerely Yours
[Sean O'Casey]

To Gabriel Fallon

MS. TEXAS

[CHELSEA]

13 JULY 1926

Dear Gaby—

Coming to Dublin on Thursday. Expect to be there in the evening.

Have taken a flat for 3 years in Chelsea, & am going back to London as soon as I can.

Hope to see you soon.

Best Wishes to you & to Mrs. Fallon.

Yours
Sean

To Eileen Carey

MS. EILEEN O'CASEY

32 CLAREVILLE STREET
S. KENSINGTON. S.W. 7
KEN 6038
[? JULY 1926]

Dear Eileen—

I am very glad indeed to hear that your health is so good, and that you are working. I must go to see you in "The Street Singer".[1] Where is it to be shown?

Yes, I shall be delighted to go some evening & have a plain meal with you & a chat.

I wonder would you take a simple dinner with me in a little Chelsea Restaurant on Thursday or Friday night.

If you can, & will, let me know. A word or two on the 'Phone will be answered any morning before 11 oc.

Very Sincerely Yours
Sean O'Casey

[1] *The Street Singer,* libretto by Frederick Lonsdale, music by H. Fraser-Simon, lyrics by Percy Greenbank, opened in London on 27 June 1924, and ran for three hundred and sixty performances. Eileen Carey was rehearsing in the part of Violette, the soubrette, with a touring company of the musical which was to play the London music-hall circuit from 9 August to 27 November 1926. The show began a week's run at the Chelsea Palace on 6 September, where O'Casey saw it.

To Bertha Gaster[1]

MS. GASTER

KENSINGTON
[12 AUGUST 1926]

Miss Bertha Gaster.

Yes, of course, my dear Miss Gaster, I could "find it in my heart to come down to you", but the difficulty would be to find it in my head to get up to you.

[1] Miss Gaster, a student at University College, London, had asked O'Casey to give a lecture on drama to the university literary society.

Imagine me in the University College of London! Like Peter in the Court of Pilate, I might begin to curse and to swear, saying—oh, a whole lot of things.

Should you ever be in South Kensington, in the afternoon, give me a phone and come up and have a cup o' tea.

No, no, I won't lecture.

Sincerely yours,
Sean O'Casey

To Gabriel Fallon

MS. Texas

Kensington
4 September 1926

Dear Gaby—

I should have written before this, but I have been occupied, pre-occupied and post occupied with a thousand things and many more. I hope both you and Rose are well. I daresay you've heard The Plough ended its London run on Saturday.

Juno goes to Preston on Monday, & then to Harrogate, Liverpool & Birmingham.

I hope you liked "Mr. Murphy's Other Island".[1] Is it true Elizabeth Harte & Lennox Robinson are twins?

I have settled down fairly well in the new flat, but some furnishing remains to be done yet. I expect in a week or two to commence work again.

Have you done anything since? How strange it is to see the Autumn leaves falling in London! And still the Buses rush, push, tear through & roll lumberingly along, & the people push, tear rush & force their way everywhere, and, lo all is vanity and vexation of Spirit.

Only today in Hyde Park I met a young man who used to come into Kirwan's tobacco shop, opposite Findlater's Church, and he told me—after he had hoped I was well, as it left him at present—that De Valera had approved of the Shannon Scheme. Be good enough to ascertain if this statement be true, & wire accordingly.

The Theatres here are terrible. London's one play now is "Escape" by Galsworthy.

[1] *Mr. Murphy's Island,* a Black and Tan comedy produced at the Abbey Theatre on 16 August 1926, directed by Lennox Robinson, was written by "Elizabeth Harte," who was never identified publicly. Ernest Blythe, director of the Abbey, told me that the author was Elizabeth Healy, the daughter of Tim Healy.

Barry Jackson's Kingsway,[2] however, are shortly to start a season of Shaw & Ibsen; & December will see Sybil Thorndike playing Macbeth in the Prince's. I am getting into touch with a little Theatre in Floral St. Covent Garden who are giving a season of Gorki, Capek O'Neill & others, but the place is very humble & poor, but still, better than the damned gilt of the Commercial Theatre. I have just invested in a complete set of Maupassant. Remember me to Will, Boss, Sheila & Ria Mooney & Johnny. Best Wishes to you & Rose.

Hope you'll get this all right.

Sean

[2] Sir Barry Jackson's company took over the Kingsway Theatre in 1925.

To Gabriel Fallon

MS. TEXAS

KENSINGTON
1 OCTOBER 1926

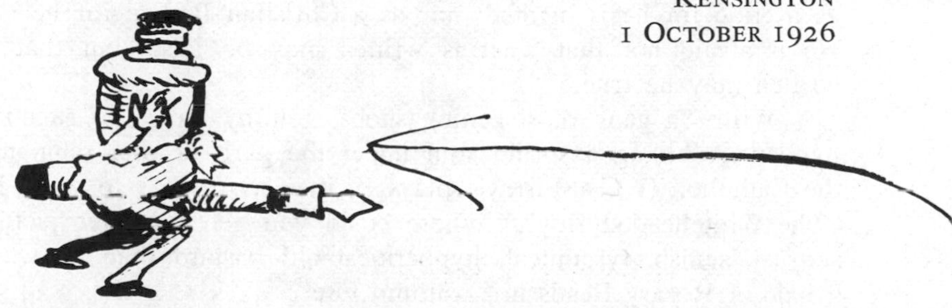

Dear Gaby—Thanks for your two letters to which I am replying at last.

Impossible to get Last Night of Don Juan or M.H. of St Bernard [1] in English—I hope the French Editions may be of some use.

Don't bother sending me on O'Flaherty's address, & don't give him mine: he and I never can be butties. I never lose an opportunity of speaking about his work to others, & this is the only way I can appreciate (God Almighty is *this* spelt correctly?) him and his great work.

Thanks, too, for Donaghy's book of poems.[2] Let me know the price of a copy of each of the forthcoming volumes & I'll forward a CHEQUE.

Thanks too three for news—my God what a Country! Isn't it strange that the biggest bastard I've met over here is an Irishman, and

[1] Two plays by Henri Ghéon, *The Last Night of Don Juan* and *The Marvellous History of St. Bernard*. Ghéon (1875–1943) was a leader of the modern revival of religious drama in France.

[2] Lyle Donaghy, *At Dawn Above Aherlow* (Dublin, Cuala Press, 1926).

a Catholic (or was) as well. However the most adorable woman I ever met was Irish and a good Catholic too, so the whole thing remains a mystery. What a pity I missed "The Importance of Being Earnest" [3]—by the way, there's a bit of a joke in the title. "When a decision has to be come to" why wasn't "when a decision has to be arrived at" said? "threw these plays back into costume"—threw them back, flung them back, pushed them back it doesn't much matter whether these plays are played in plus fours—poor Will; what we want is Revolution—Revolution, be Jasus. Revolution!—or costumes—why not play them in their skins? Comedies of Manners are dead to Art & to Humanity—they are in the Hearse of Time on the way to the Grave.

And a good job for Lyle Donaghy that his poems are a hell of a lot better than his criticism.[4] "Though far from presenting us with Lady Bracknell Maureen Delany, (the comma in the wrong place) satisfies us with her acting because it is definite". Very definite I'd swear. "The experiment in Costume & the decorations add greatly to the interest of the play". Lyle Donaghy, Lyle Donaghy what sort of vile and bloody stuff is this? Good enough (too good) for "T.C.D." but there is nothing in it of The Mark of War. Best of Wishes to Lyle.

Who is Archbishop Sheehan? [5] He (it seems to me) cannot speak as a critic for he is bigoted; nor as a Christian Prelate for he is unjust. He is afraid not that what is written may be false, but that what is written may be true.

Write "a gang of sickening snobs, a filthy crowd of sanctimonious hypocrites, hiding a sordid soul under the garb of oral religion" about the Catholic, T. C. Murray's plays, & it is as true as to write it about "The Whiteheaded Boy".[6] Where could you get a greater picture of a sensual, selfish, tyrannical, hypocritical old bastard than he who wears a halo of Rosary Beads in "Autumn Fire"?

The Archbishop points to the good that was in E. Burke because of his Catholic extraction. Can he prove that what he would call bestial & filthy in Joyce or O'Flaherty was due to their Protestant extraction? Why does he say of a Novelist whom he deplores "Whose name I will not give", & of another "whose name I will also suppress" while he banners aloft the names of Yeats, Robinson & Russell! Because these are Catholics & those are Protestants, and (I think) particularly those are Anglo-Irish & these are Gaelic. And what's the use of talking about the Bronze of the Irish Classics. They're dead too. Does he think that Finn McCoul & Cuchullin will one day be members of An Dail? Can he

[3] Oscar Wilde's comedy was first performed at the Abbey Theatre on 6 November 1926.

[4] Donaghy reviewed the Abbey production of *Earnest* for the student magazine of Trinity College, Dublin, *T.C.D.*: A College Miscellany.

[5] Archbishop Michael Sheehan of Sydney, Australia.

[6] Lennox Robinson's *The Whiteheaded Boy* opened at the Abbey Theatre on 13 December 1916.

not remember that the Free Staters yelled of the Republicans & that the Republicans bawled of the Free Staters, & that the Northern boyos screamed of the other two parcel of Saints things that no Realistic Author would care to publish. And poor Robbie's poor story [7] is easily passed by [George] Moore and [Anatole] France both (I think) reared in the Catholic tradition. It's a wonder his grace hadn't a slam at me.

I assure you, Gaby, I know nothing of the putting on or the taking off of either "The Plough" or "The Gunman". I've written to Johnny Perrin, but I didn't discuss affairs of the Theatre. Robbie sent me a copy of "White Blackbird & Portrait",[8] which I (shamefully) didn't even acknowledge yet.

I've just commenced work on a new play. The ideas of each act have been arranged in my head, & I've found a good opening for the first Act, & the rest will, I hope, be filled in while the Earth is spinning once around the Sun.

Not married, nor any intention of marrying yet.

Of course Will [Barry Fitzgerald] ought to see about his eyes. [Dr. Joseph] Cummins will be all that a Surgeon can be to him. Tell him not to mind writing till he has time & is well. If Will wants to die a martyr to the cause, nothing I could say would move him. If he does he's a ——— ———.

And best
wishes to you,
Rose, Will &
Lyle.
Sean

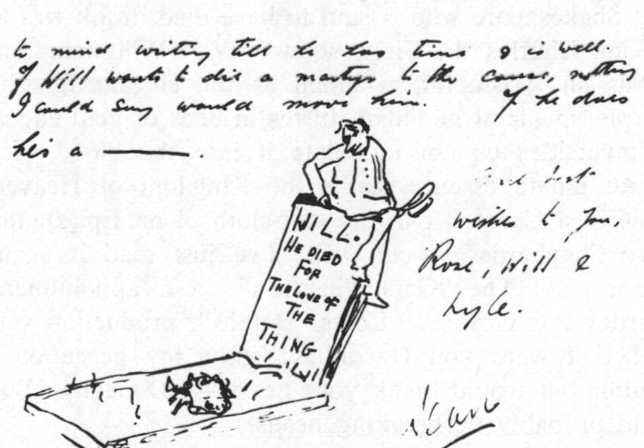

[7] Lennox Robinson, "The Madonna of Slieve Dun," *To-Morrow*, August 1924. See O'Casey's letter to Lady Gregory, ? January 1925, note 2.

[8] Lennox Robinson's *The White Blackbird* opened at the Abbey Theatre on 12 October 1925, and *Portrait* on 31 March 1925.

To Gabriel Fallon

MS. Texas

Kensington
3 October 1926

My dear Gaby—

Will was here on Thursday—looking well and bright, fairly happy and a little nervous. He has crossed over to Paris, and has promised to call again before returning to Dublin. Sorry you didn't think much about "The Big House" [1] Sheila seems to think it a good play, & so does Lady Gregory. And Starkie in "The Statesman" [2] dons the Aristotelean Robe & murmurs "This is a play".—

A cushion here, a cushion there—
A cup of tea to stay us
With Aristotle standing by
Bring order out o' chaos.
And Starkie murmuring, yes, yes, yes;
That passage subtle meant a
Fierce flaming truth held up the sleeve
Like a la Benavente.

God Almighty does poor Lennox think that dining in the evening; wearing dress clothes; conventional education and an accidental birth creates an Aristocrat! Shakespeare who is said to have died drunk was an Aristocrat. So was King Charles the First; so was Walt Whitman. And Francis of Assissi was an Aristocrat as much as the elegant Ignatius Loyola. Robes of purple, meals at midnight, births in beds of gold education in hot-house Universities cannot inoculate it into the blood of a Boor swamee; it is an innate essence, as is the Kingdom of Heaven, sheltered in the purple of a Caesar or in the serf-cloth of an Epi[c]tetus.

Hope "The Two Shepherds" [3] went well: I've just read it again, & after all, it's a poor play. The "Gate Theatre's" [4] a disappointment, Gaby. I saw on Saturday last Gorkie's "Lower Depths"; production very poor; acting terrible! If I were you I wouldn't stake my peace on a similar venture in Dublin—it would break your heart—& Donaghy (Best Wishes to him) would probably be breaking heads.

[1] Lennox Robinson's *The Big House* opened at the Abbey Theatre on 6 September 1926.

[2] Dr. Walter Starkie's review of Robinson's play, in the *Irish Statesman*, 11 September 1926.

[3] A revival of G. Martínez Sierra's *The Two Shepherds*, translated by Helen and Harley Granville-Barker, which originally opened at the Abbey Theatre on 12 February 1924.

[4] The Gate Theatre in London, a club theatre on Floral Street under the management of Peter Godfrey.

You surely should have written something since I left "me native land". Seven months, Gaby, and nothing garnered. Shame.

I get The Statesman every week & hope to see "The man who saw Death" shortly.

All the Best
Sean

Enclosed is a cutting from Evening News

To Macmillan & Co. Ltd.

MS. MACMILLAN, LONDON

KENSINGTON
19 OCTOBER 1926

Dear Sirs,

A paragraph in one of the London papers (Sunday) has been pointed out to me in which was said that I "saw the genius of Eimar O'Duffy, introduced the author to the publishers, & in various ways commended his work."

May I say that I never had the honour of meeting Mr. O'Duffy, & have never read any work by him so far, &, should the statement concerning recommendation as published be by any possible circumstance believed by you, allow me to say that I am in no way responsible. Of course I wish the book [1] every success, & I intend to read the work very soon.

Yours,
Sean O'Casey

[1] Eimar O'Duffy, *King Goshawk and the Birds* (1926), a mock-epic novel on ancient and modern Ireland, published by Macmillan.

To Maurice Macmillan [1]

MS. MACMILLAN, LONDON

KENSINGTON

13 NOVEMBER 1926

Dear Mr. Macmillan,

I'm almost certain that I wrote to you (oh a long time ago) asking if it would be possible to substitute a reproduction of John's portrait for the present picture appearing in "The Plough & the Stars." [2]

Since seeing the work of John, Tuohy's picture has become a daymare (I sleep well o' nights) to me, & I am very anxious that John's picture should cancel the mistake of Tuohy.

Indeed I would prefer a photograph to the present effort.

Very sincerely yours,
Sean O'Casey

[1] Maurice Macmillan (1853–1936), publisher.

[2] See O'Casey's letters to Macmillan & Co. Ltd., 19 May 1926, and to Gabriel Fallon, 13 May 1926, note 2.

To Lady Gregory

MS. GREGORY

KENSINGTON

CHRISTMAS EVE 1926

My dear Lady Gregory.

I suppose you think (forgive me for not writing to you) I have allowed former memories to be submerged by Glamour of London. I haven't, & feelings for & remembrance of you are as deeply affectionate as ever.

I am living here as quietly as I have lived in Dublin; abiding alone even throughout the Christmas Festival. I am now—very tranquilly—working on a new play.

Keeping away from dinners, luncheons, parties & dances prevents me from doing very much for the Lane Pictures. Augustus John & I have come to be very fond of each other.

I have just got from him a lovely "Head of a Girl", which I shall keep during my life, & then—if they will take it from me—I will give it to the Dublin M. Art Gallery, or, if you like, to be added to the Lane Collection.

Up to the present, this is all I can do for Dublin.
I sincerely hope the Abbey is doing well.
"The Whiteheaded Boy" is doing splendidly here.
Please give my love to all my worker friends in Coole.

Affectionately Yours.
Sean

To Gabriel Fallon

MS. TEXAS

KENSINGTON
5 JANUARY 1927

Dear Gaby—

Salutations and Greetings & the soul-clasping of hands to you. The Play [1] writes well—a double event of a joking pun. Haven't much of it done yet—two characters are shadowing the main theme of the play. And, by the way it is building itself on a song I heard a friend sing here—a Scotchman in whose blood is the salt of a thousand seas. He bellows it out at the top of his voice. He went with his son—a young salt just home from Panama—to "The Plough".

The little manager—born within view of Oxford University—when he met me the next evening complained: "Your two friends disturbed the audience, shouting 'it's a bloody great play, it tis thawt!' He says he's coming again—shall we admit him?" So I gently tapped the little evening-clad pumpkin on his dainty shoulder & said—"The next time George comes to the play prevent him from going to the stalls: show him into a box!"

7.2. 27

I have had a busy time: Russia, Germany & Sweden writing, talking, arguing, pleading, about translations & productions, & I whispering, murmuring, yelling—Go to hell, the whole o' Yous!

Sincerely hope Rose is well, & that the worst of the trouble is over. Johnnie [Perrin] has written saying that Poor Brinsley's play has been rejected.[2] Sorry for him, for he's a decent fellow. But I'm afraid he's not much of a Dramatist.

I suppose you've heard of Will's [Barry Fitzgerald] flight over here, & his winged return to Dublin. Has he told you of his thoughts about

[1] *The Silver Tassie.*

[2] Brinsley Macnamara's *The Three Thimbles.* It was finally produced at the Abbey Theatre on 24 November 1941.

coming to London? I don't think there's a comedian here could do anything with him, save to help him to put on his coat. What do you think? And I wish you'd come over here for a few days. It wouldn't cost you much. You could put up at a friend's flat, & provided Rose would let you come, (I wouldn't lead you into any danger) we'd have a quiet time & a gentle talk.

I may go over to Dublin for a few days later on. I wonder where would be the most comfortable place to stay in? I'd like to have a room to receive friends as well as a place in which to sleep—What a disjointed letter this is—but I can't really write to you—a talk or nothing.

Love to you & to Rose.

Yours
Sean

To Jim Kavanagh

MS. KAVANAUGH

KENSINGTON
21 JANUARY 1927

Dear Jim—

I want you to go to Price's Medical Hall, 26. Clare Street—opposite Nassau St end of Lincoln Place—& get a supply of ear drops from the copy of prescription enclosed. I can't find the original, but I'm sure the copy will do. Whenever I get a cold my ear gets bad, & if you could do this for me, it would save me some trouble.

Return by registered post, see that the cork is tight, & pack closely again in the wool, & it will arrive alright.

I enclose £1.0.0. The cost will be about 5/– & you can get some fags with the rest.

Hope all are well.

Sean

To Jim Kavanagh

MS. Kavanagh

Kensington
Thursday.
[? February 1927]

My dear Jim—

Thanks, but I must trouble you again, old son, for it's the wrong stuff—my own stupidity, my own bloody stupidity. The number should be—as on label of bottle enclosed—32. If you could get some for me —thanks. But don't bother if it's too much trouble.

And I enclose a 10/– note. Now for Christ's sake don't be trying to get me to get you to do things for nothing. And *get* fags with whatever may remain.

Working (lazily) on a new play, & hope to have it finished by the time "the robins nest again."

By the way, Jim, how's the work going? Are you toiling now?

And I'm damn glad to hear the war veteran Dan [Breen] has gone into the Free State Dail. His action, in my opinion, is a combination of courage & common-sense. Best wishes to Mrs. K, Vera—she must be a big lassie now—& yourself.

Yours.
Sean

To Bill Blackwood[1]

MS. O'CASEY

30 MARCH 1927

[*Dear Bill,*]

A literateur, a literateur, a Literateur! What the hell's a literateur? How does it look; what does it eat; where does it live? Does it glide along in Evening Dress, or swing about in Plus Fours?

I know these Literateurs: they're graceful creatures, Nancy Boys in Art whose minds are pouncet boxes filled with perfumes; whose dainty, gloved hands will never stretch—

> "To pluck bright honour from the pale-faced moon,
> Or dive into the bottom of the deep
> Where fathom-line would never touch the ground,
> And pluck up drownded honour by the locks." [2]

And they can go to hell, and tell them that from me.

I know very little about politics, but enough to save me from the stupidities of the House of Commons. As there are "tied Houses" so are there tied men, & your "Literateur" is probably one of them: a man whose humanity is as broad as the cheques he gets for the work he does.

And he can go to hell, & tell him that from me.

And I will probably go on jolting my literary & dramatic admirers; let them wash their own feet & comb their own hair for they wont get me to do it. Let them go on Kissing the hand of God & pray for us poor Bolshies who are shaking the devil's paw.

[1] This is a draft of a letter to Blackwood, the editor of *Answers,* a London weekly magazine, who on 29 March had written to O'Casey:

"My dear Sean, What is this I hear about you? Namely, that you have been putting your name to election literature of the most *seditious* nature?

"I happened to mention the other day to a well-known literateur that I had the honour and pleasure of your friendship. He thereupon went off the deep end, cursing you loudly and bitterly for taking part in the recent Leith by-election, and allowing your name to go on some pamphlets which are distributed by the tens of thousands all over that section of my beloved land affected by the election. This morning he sends me a copy of this election document, along with a note urging me in impassioned language to ask you to refrain in future from lending so distinguished a name as yours to the Anti-Christs and the Bolsheviks of Britain!!

"Joking apart, my own idea is that probably you never saw the document in question, and, in any event, I am not sufficient of a politician to be concerned by it either way. But I think seeing your name on such a virulent Red pamphlet has been rather a jolt to some of your literary and dramatic admirers. . . ."

The miners were still on strike since the general strike of the previous year, and O'Casey had sent a five-guinea subscription to support the pro-miner Labour Party candidate in the Leith by-election in Scotland.

[2] Hotspur in *Henry IV,* Part I, Act I, sc. iii.

Maybe I'll go up to your office some day next week—if you're not afraid God's thunder should follow me into the building!

[*Sean*]

To Gabriel Fallon

MS. Texas

Kensington

25 April 1927

My dear Gaby—

Saluta, Salutus, Salutissimus. How are you? Eleven of the clock A.M. & here I am sitting before an open window in the bowels of London looking down a pretty avenue sprinkled with the fresh green of trees that feel the arms of Spring around them.

My dear Gaby there is no use of asking me to go home—I have no home—the foxes have holes & the birds of the air have nests, & I have just a place in which to rest my head—a nice little place all the same, glittering with the sign of Kensington: 6038!

Gaby be honest—oh you are a cute one—e's a cute one, e is! The roads, the bogs & the hillsides; the magenta heather, the sadness of the evenings—what you really desire is, not to restore these things to me, but to bring me back to yourself, which is kind and grand and selfish.

And you know damn well if I came to Ireland again I wouldn't be plungin' into the bogs, or huggin' bushes of heather to my breast, or spreadin' my arms to embrace the sadness of the evenins, but would certainly be on my way from the city to Ballybrack,[1] or you would be comin' from Ballybrack to the City to talk and talk of books & plays and poems, and plays and poems & books. Am I right or am I wrong, Mr. Gallicker?

It's my business to write plays but it's hardly my business to suffer, Gaby—that must remain a privilege, a pleasure and a joy. What are you thinking of? Fleshpots! Do you think I'm like one of the Forty Thieves —up to my neck in a jar? My dear Gaby Sean here's the same as Sean there. The truth is Gaby I'm slapping Pharoah's arse instead of kissing it. And I'll tell you all—or nearly all—when I see you again —which may be—and I hope so—soon.

I have done well with the new play; [2] worked like a nigger during

[1] A suburb of Dublin.
[2] *The Silver Tassie.*

Easter, & have now finished the first act & am starting the second. So much has been done that it has a pull on me now, & my mind will never (like Ireland) be at peace till the work is done.

"Professor Tim" was a bad failure here I'm sorry for Shiels.[3] I think a mistake, a bad mistake, was made in not putting on "Paul Twyning" instead. It is easily his best play, & the title part would have suited [Arthur] Sinclair admirably,—a much better part than Professor Tim. I strongly advised Fagan for Shiel's sake to select "Paul Twyning" but he was all for the "money-getter" & I fear Shiels agreed with him, and now he's lost, I hear, £500 pounds on the play.

Let me know, will you, when—a week in advance if possible—"Juno" or "The Plough" will be going on again. A friend of mine is eager to see Will [Barry Fitzgerald] play in either, & we may go over for a few days.[4]

Best of Wishes to Rose & Love to you.

Sean

[3] George Shiels's *Professor Tim* opened in London at the Vaudeville Theatre on 22 March 1927, directed by J. B. Fagan.
[4] The "friend" he wanted to take to Dublin was Eileen Carey.

To Eileen Carey

MS. Eileen O'Casey

Kensington
Friday
[? June 1927]

Beautiful little Eileen—

I am thinking, thinking, thinking of you, darling. When you are with me I can never, never get close enough to you; when you are away you are never far from me. Bright, fascinating things that often made me linger have lost their colour, & are pale gaunt shadows in the soft light of my love for you. When I lie down you are with me, & when I wake in the morning, behold you are there; your white hand is under my head, & I hear your voice like the distant singing of many birds.

My little Eileen, & she is fair, she is very fair; she is fair to look upon and very graceful, and the kisses of her mouth are desirable and lovely. She comes and the dull things of life creep away; she is here, and lo they are gone, for my love is like unto a spray of apple blossoms in a market-place.

She is my delight on the hills of vision and the touch of her white hand is strength in the shadows of thought.

And I am longing for you, darling, to hold you in my arms again, to fondle you, to kiss, & kiss & kiss again your sweet mouth, & to tell you of my love.

Sean

To Lady Gregory

MS. GREGORY

KENSINGTON
16 AUGUST 1927

My dear Lady Gregory—

I do hope the Dail will be tall enough to look for a moment over the top fringe of their Party Banners so as to see—even in a glass darkly—the brilliant importance of the Lane Pictures.

On Sunday, when I had sent the wire to you, & realizing the swiftness of time's passage, I ventured to send wires to Pres Cosgrave, De Valera, T. Johnston & Capt Redmond, & to Ernie Blythe. There is nothing to prevent them passing the declaration—it would only add dignity to each & to all.

I'm very glad you like the idea, & hope you and all my friends in Coole are in good health.

Very Sincerely Yours
Sean

To Robert Loraine [1]

PS. LORAINE [2]
[? AUGUST 1927]

ROBERT LORAINE,—A friend and I saw you last night, and saw you not; you were a great artist in a great play.

Strindberg, Strindberg, Strindberg, the greatest of them all. Barrie [3]

[1] Robert Loraine (1876–1935) played the Captain in August Strindberg's *The Father,* which opened in London at the Savoy Theatre on 23 August 1927.

[2] Printed in Winifred Loraine's *Robert Loraine: Soldier, Actor, Airman* (London, Collins, 1938).

[3] As a curtain-raiser, J. M. Barrie's *Barbara's Wedding* preceded *The Father.*

mumbling as he silvers his little model stars and gilds his little model suns, while Strindberg shakes flame from the living planets and the fixed stars.

Ibsen can sit serenely in his Doll's House, while Strindberg is battling with his heaven and his hell.

We thank you and your comrades for your and their revelation of *The Father*. Would that I could see you and them playing in *The Dance of Death*.

Kyrie Eleison, Robert Loraine, Christie Eleison.

Eileen Carey, Sean O'Casey

To Gabriel Fallon

MS. TEXAS
KENSINGTON
14 SEPTEMBER 1927

My dear Gaby—

I'm really sorry that no power came, that no spirit spoke unto me to open my mouth to you and to speak of those things that concern me & so concern you, or of things touching you that touch me as well. I have been busy with my play (off & on) & I have just altered a good deal of the second act—an idea came to me after I had passed the middle of the act, & I liked it so well that I felt that idea was meant to leaven the whole lump. I start the 3rd act tomorrow & afterwards the fourth act, & then revision, & then an exultant weariness.

Besides, I've been "keeping company" with a pretty girl, & she has at times pushed my thought away from the play—the two of us may possibly go over soon for a week in Dublin.

And here there's a lot of talk about sending "The Plough" to America with Sinclair's company; could you suggest anyone who might be able to take over the Part of Capt Clitheroe?

If you could I should be glad.

If I go to Dublin I'll see you. If I don't go I'll write again. Hope Rose & the babe are doing well.

Remember me to each to whom you think it may be due, & accept my love.

Sean

To Gabriel Fallon

MS. TEXAS
KENSINGTON
[23 SEPTEMBER 1927][1]

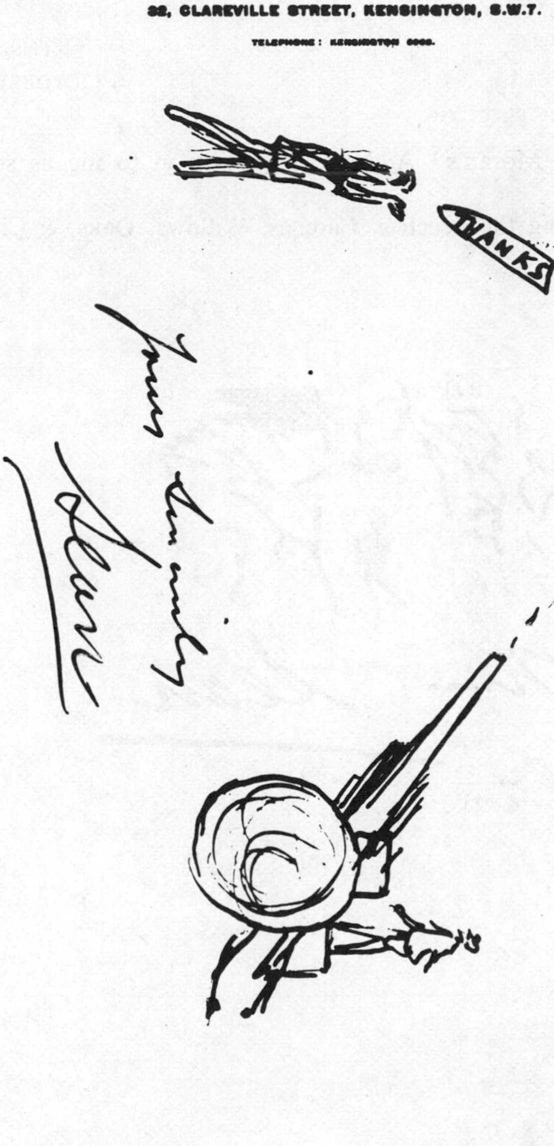

32, CLAREVILLE STREET, KENSINGTON, S.W.7.
TELEPHONE: KENSINGTON [illegible].

Yours Sincerely
Sean

[1] This drawing was postmarked 23 September, the day he married Eileen Reynolds Carey in the Roman Catholic Church of All Souls and the Redeemer, Chelsea.

To Gabriel Fallon

MS. TEXAS

KENSINGTON
9 OCTOBER 1927

My dear Gaby—

Would you get Moran's [1] Address & send it on to me as soon as ever you can.

Bask here among the beeches, Larches, Willows, Oaks, & Chestnut trees of London.

Yours.
Sean

[1] Tom Moran, a young actor at the Abbey Theatre.

To Gabriel Fallon

MS. TEXAS

KENSINGTON
13 OCTOBER 1927

Dear Gaby—

Ever so many thanks for your letter & the trouble you took about Moran. Value has changed since I learn that he is not unemployed. It would be a pity to drag Tom out of his Cornucopica, and, anyhow, we wouldn't take him till he had passed through the fire test of several rehearsals, so that, even though his expenses would be paid, possible rejection would make this hardly fair to him. I think I shall write to [Michael] Scott, & simply ask him would he be willing to take the part, & he will probably explain to me the circumstances he stands in, & then I can judge whether it would be just to call him from the receipt of customs to put on the motley. You might let me know his initials—Tom or Dick or Percival—& I'll write care of The Abbey.

Perhaps Will is right to blanket all risks with The Public Safety Act, & to remain one of those thinly coated sheep that has never gone astray. It would be terrible if Will became one of the Lost Sheep of the House of Robbie.

I've written to Sheila [Richards]: the contracts with [Arthur] Sinclair, Mollie & S. Allgood are, I believe to be written out today, & the company is to sail about the 10th of next month. I'm almost sure Sheila will be taken on the condition of a 3 months' stay.

I suppose you've heard that the American Abbey Tour is off: the agent of the Parties negotiating to bring him out was over here, & told a friend of mine that the attempt had fallen through. I think they came to the conclusion that there wasn't enough of a chance in the money-making side of the scheme.

At present I'm busily engaged trying to solve an Einstein problem of how to buy a £4000 house for 25/– and, incidentally, I'm Working at the Play.

and Best Wishes & Love to
The Baby, Rose & you.
Sean

PS. *Modern Drama*[1]

From Lady Gregory

STANDARD HOTEL, DUBLIN
SUNDAY
[?] NOVEMBER 1927

Dear Sean—

I have seen the seven performances of Juno this last week, and must tell you how well it went and what delight it gave. Of course Sara Allgood's part went, if possible, better than ever—and the Abbey was well filled—last night such a "queue"—all round the corner—and it was grievous that so many had to be turned away. Will Shield and McCormack[2] are better than ever—I wish London could see them—The week has done me good—the Abbey is a "People's Theatre"—I hope, yet fear, for poor George Shiels play[3] this week—his health seems worse—and he is so anxious—

I am here on the old business—Lane pictures—It had to sleep through the elections, and I came up to awaken it. There is to be a deputation to Cosgrave on Tuesday "Men Only," I'm keeping in the background —and then I hope we can begin in the newspapers again—I go home this week—I hope all goes well with you—and your bride—and that you won't forsake us—

Yours sincerely and affectionately
A Gregory

[1] From a copy made by A. C. Edwards and printed in *Modern Drama,* May 1965.

[2] Barry Fitzgerald and F. J. McCormick in their original roles as "Captain" Jack Boyle and Joxer Daly.

[3] George Shiels's *Cartney and Kevney* opened at the Abbey Theatre on 29 November 1927.

To Gabriel Fallon

MS. Texas

Kensington
14 December 1927

Dear Gaby,

Glad to get your letter & to feel the drop curtains—black & gold or blue and gold, or purple & gold—fluttering aside to reveal the old Lady and Will & Cartney & Kevney and yourself

Will coming down to go on!

Lady G. wrote to me many times—I really must write her a letter. Glad to hear too, that Juno still goes well. Understand the Company went to Cork. Who is Seep P. See [1] in "The Statesman?" Curious criticism of Cartney & Kevney there the other week. "Laughter dripping from every pore"—"The corrugg?ated lips of the critics" [2] there's hyperboloxical language for you! I really know nothing about the Plough position in New York.[3] Some say went well, others, went badly; some "won't last 2 weeks", others "it'll have a long run". Heard Shelah [Richards] & [Michael] Scott passed the Majestic American Critics hm, hm alright. How is [T.C.] Murray's soul; hope it's flourishing like the bulls of

[1] Constantine P. Curran, an official in the Dublin Law Courts, friend of A.E. and James Joyce, regular contributor to the *Irish Statesman* under his initials, C.P.C.

[2] From Curran's review of George Shiels's *Cartney and Kevney,* in the *Irish Statesman,* 10 December 1927.

[3] *The Plough and the Stars* opened in New York on 28 November 1927, presented by the Irish Players and staged by Arthur Sinclair, with the following cast: Michael Scott as Jack Clitheroe, Shelah Richards as Nora Clitheroe, J. A. O'Rourke as Peter Flynn, Sydney Morgan as The Covey, Arthur Sinclair as Fluther Good, Sara Allgood as Bessie Burgess, Maire O'Neill as Mrs. Gogan, Margaret O'Farrell as Mollser, Harry Hutchinson as Captain Brennan, Tony Quinn as Lieutenant Langon, Cathleen Drago as Rosie Redmond, E. J. Kennedy as A Barman, Joseph French as The Voice, Edwin Ellis as Corporal Stoddard, Joseph French as Sergeant Tinley. The production received mixed reviews and closed after thirty-two performances.

Basham & the fleshpots of Eshcool. Does he see still visions of bees & butterflies buzzing & fluttering in the smoke of Dublin

Mother:	Hugh!
Wife:	Hugh, Hugh!
Son:	Hugh, Hugh, Hugh!
Hugh:	I'll go; I must go; I shant stop, I'll go; I daren't stay!
Mother:	God, Hugh.
Wife:	God, Hugh, Hugh!
Son:	God, Hugh, Hugh, Hugh! [4]

Mick to Barny (—Curtain, quick, man curtain! Nicely). Poor FXWZ had Anti Christ on at the Kew.[5] Searched all the papers but saw only one notice in "The Post". The play passed unnoticed. Frank must have lost about £150 pounds. One has to pay for production there. Ervine St. John recently had an article in "The Author" [6] denouncing the modus vivus operandi. I warned Frank about it, appealed to him not to have anything to do with it, but his faith in his play was greater than his faith in God. It was the last time before the last that I warned him. While at Kew he never sought to come near me.

Am sending you a few photos. We go to 19. Woronzow Road, London, N.W.8 the first week after Christmas. Will give you a few days notice. It's not the house we sought, much cheaper, & for a lease only of 7½ years. I now own about 150 pounds to keep me & her from the Workhouse. However God may send me some American dollars.

Am just finishing the rough typing of the last page or so of the new play's last act; then for the selection, & remodelling and then a rest. Best Love to Rose, Babe & You.

Sean

[4] A parody of the dialogue in T. C. Murray's *Birthright*, first performed at the Abbey Theatre on 27 October 1910.

[5] Frank Hugh O'Donnell's *Anti-Christ*, which was originally produced at the Abbey Theatre on 17 March 1925, was revived at the "Q" Theatre in London in 1927.

[6] St. John Ervine, "A Curious Contract," *The Author*, July 1927.

IV

THE TASSIE SCORNED, 1928

And one thing is certain—that so long as God or Nature leaves us one atom of strength, we must continue to use that atom of strength to fight on for that which is above & before all governments & parties—Art & Literature which are the mantle & mirror of the Holy Ghost, and the Sword of the Spirit."

"If W. B. Yeats had known me as faintly as he thinks he knows me well, he wouldn't have wasted his time—and mine—making such a suggestion; I am too big for this sort of mean and petty shuffling, this lousy perversion of the truth. There is going to be no damned secrecy with me surrounding the Abbey's rejection of the play. Does he think that I would practice in my life the prevarication and wretchedness that I laugh at in my plays?"

Although he had been outraged by the prudery of the Abbey actors, O'Casey's quarrel over the *Plough* riot in 1926 was with Irish nationalism, not with the Abbey Theatre and its directors, who had defended him and his play. He was living in London now but he was still an Irish playwright, and his plays were a vital part of the Abbey's repertoire. Financially as well as artistically he had saved the Theatre, which needed him as much as he needed it, and he depended upon the royalties from the regular revivals of his first three successes, *Gunman, Juno,* and *Plough*. There was therefore great excitement among the directors, especially Lady Gregory and Lennox Robinson, as they waited for the script of his new play, *The Silver Tassie*. O'Casey himself was so confident the play would be accepted and produced that he sent Robinson a recommended cast list. In his enthusiastic letters to Lady Gregory he was full of anticipation over his return to Ireland as a playwright, and he even added on one occasion—remembering the trouble over *Plough*—"There's no mention of politics throughout the play."

Unfortunately, however, the play was rejected, and this crucial decision and the bitter controversy that followed were to have an irrevocably damaging effect upon the career of O'Casey and the future of the Abbey: for the rest of his life he was to be deprived of a regular working theatre and too often had to write new plays for publication prior to uncertain production, and meanwhile the Abbey languished for want of good plays. Two years earlier Yeats had assailed the rioting Irish mob for its disgraceful behavior and failure to appreciate the genius of O'Casey; but now it was an ailing Yeats just back from Rapallo who disgraced himself and his theatre. It is still an open question whether Yeats was right or wrong in his critical judgment—only time can ultimately assess the value of a challenging work like *The Silver Tassie*—but by his shabby treatment of O'Casey he had committed a serious blunder in closing the door of the theatre to its major playwright. Because of his important contribution to Irish drama, Yeats and the Abbey owed O'Casey a production of his new experimental play. For as O'Casey was quick to point out, the Abbey had been founded to encourage experimental drama, yet was now producing innocuous works far below the quality and conception of *The Silver Tassie*.

The background of the exchange of letters between O'Casey and Lady Gregory around the period of the rejection in late March and April is especially poignant, for apparently she was distressed because she knew and concurred in the decision to say no, while the unsuspecting O'Casey was trying to shake her out of her depression with eloquent praise of her great contribution to Irish culture. Since she had doubts about the rejection, and later regretted it, it was probably a sense of guilt which prompted her to send all the Abbey correspondence to O'Casey. He, prompted by his wounded pride and a need for vindication, sent all the letters, including his own blistering reply to Yeats, to the English and Irish press.

In the midst of the controversy, ten days after the rejection, O'Casey's first child was born. Bernard Shaw came to his defense with several brilliant letters which ridiculed the Abbey directors and hailed O'Casey as a

"Titan"; Macmillan published the play; C. B. Cochran agreed to produce it in London the following year; and the angry titan without a theatre continued his love-hate quarrel with Ireland.

To Lady Gregory

MS. GREGORY

19, WORONZOW ROAD,
ST. JOHN'S WOOD, N.W. 8.
[20? JANUARY 1928]

Dear Lady Gregory—

I am very sorry to trouble you, but I am a little puzzled about royalties which haven't been received, some of which are now a long time due. I have written five times to Mr. Perrin & once to Mr. Robinson, but have received no reply to any of my letters.

One Royalty for the "Gunman" is due since the second week in October last; a week of "Juno" played a little later & the royalties on the "Gunman" played in Cork.

Once before a cheque was sent that never came, & Mr Perrin had to cancel it; later I had to write several times about fees, & when in Dublin I had to personally call for royalties that had been due for a long time.

Maybe Mr. Perrin has been very busy, but it is irritating to have to write about them, & the annoyance is made worse when one can get no answer to inquiries.

I am sorry indeed to trouble you, but I thought it better to see if an explanation can be given for the long delay, & the failure to secure a reply to my letters.

Just left off for a few moments working at the play to write this.

Sincerely hope you are well & all at Coole.

Affectionately Yours
Sean

From Lady Gregory

MS. O'CASEY

COOLE PARK, GORT, CO. GALWAY
25 JANUARY 1928

Dear Sean—

I have just had yours & have written (but post had gone for today) to L. Robinson & Perrin asking about your royalties—I cant understand their having been kept back so long. I wrote enquiring about a small sum owed me—since November as they were generally sent within a week of performance—& Perrin explained they had been in late—& then preparing to audit—very [unfortunate]—but that doesn't explain your earlier ones. But I hope all will be sent promptly now.

I have just found Perrins letter in answer to mine, & [have] the part that refers to business that occupied him—tho' that doesn't account for October *Gunman*. But I hope he will be more punctual in future. His marriage & wedding trip to Wales in the Autumn (September) may have upset his usual tranquil business habits for a time.

Holiday work still keeps me busy here—a household of eleven—besides extra guests, to housekeep for—in the country—takes some thought & foresight: My granddaughter Anne has just come up from the lake with her gun & 3 wild Duck she had shot flying overhead.

I am correcting proofs of my "3 Last Plays"—Sancho, Dave—& W. be Gentleman[1]—haven't quite got through them yet. I was to get to Dublin to stir up that business of building a Gallery but am held here for a while.

It is a comforting thought that you are working to fill your silver tassie!

Affectionately
A. Gregory

[1] Lady Gregory, *Three Last Plays* (London, Putnam, 1928), *Sancho's Master, Dave,* and *The Would-Be Gentleman.*

To Gabriel Fallon

MS. Texas

St. John's Wood
27 February 1928

My dear Gaby—

So sorry you have been so ill, but just as well you were or you wouldn't have looked into yourself, or have let anyone else do it either. It would be all right if illness wasn't so damned expensive. Astonishing all the comfort & big house that come from pain & disease, & you're (we're) (they're) to offer your pain to God, & give your money to the Surgeons!

Glad you saw Oliver St. John [Gogarty]—he's a great skin & he is a Surgeon—he's a buttie of mine now. He was here last night, & I spoke to him about you—and between ourselves ⟵ between ourselves ⟶ he'll let you down lightly. Had a bad few weeks myself with my eyes, & had to go to Harley st to Harley street, to Harley street, but am much better now.

Glad Will did so well as B. B.

Just finishing off the last few corrections in the new play to send it to be properly typed for publication. I believe it to be the best play I've written. "The Silver Tassie." Expect to let the Abbey have it in a fortnight or so. Going to have Gregorian Chant in the second act. Two parts for Will. Second Act is in France.

Write more fully later on. Learning a lot about Gregorian Chant & Plainsong from the Sarum Psalter. "This is the intonation of the first tone, and this is the mediation, & this is the ending."

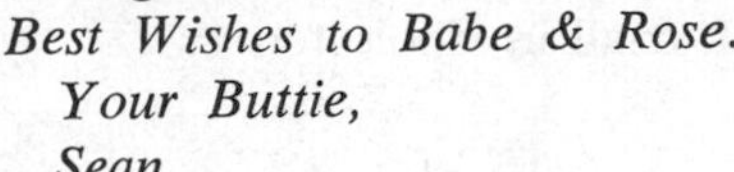

Best Wishes to Babe & Rose.
Your Buttie,
Sean

To Lady Gregory

MS. GREGORY

ST. JOHN'S WOOD
28 FEBRUARY 1928

Dear Lady Gregory—

I have got the Royalties alright from Mr. Perrin, & thank you for your attention to the complaint I made.

I've just finished writing & typing (in my own way) The Silver Tassie, & when I have got a couple of copies typed—which will be in about a fortnight's time—I'll send on a copy to The Abbey, & will send a copy to no-one else till I get word that the play has been received, so that I may be able to say that The Abbey Theatre was the first to get my new effort.

I hope it may be suitable, & that you will like it. Personally, I think the play is the best work I have yet done.

I have certainly put my best into it, & have written the work solely because of love & a deep feeling that what I have written should have been written.

The other week I was offered £500 for a short story for a Film Journal—something with a snap in it—& I told those who offered that they could safely raise the offer to £5000, so as to appear generous with what they had to give away.

Most of the Second Act is to be sung. A good deal to Gregorian chant, & some to the airs of songs & a hymn.

I sincerely hope W. B. Yeats is getting his health again & that you are well, & all in Coole too.

Affectionately Yours.
Sean O'Casey

There's no mention of politics throughout the play.

From Lady Gregory

MS. O'Casey

Coole Park, Gort, Co. Galway
2 March 1928

Dear Sean—

This is such very good news about your Silver Tassie! I long to see it —I'm sure the wine you have filled it with is of the best vintage. There will be great excitement when it comes. I'm afraid I shant be in Dublin when it comes—but of course L[ennox] R[obinson] will send it on to me to read. I am kept tied here by my granddaughters—Anne and Catherine—their mother has left them here—they are very happy riding & running about—& I'd a little work with our clergyman's wife. I have been correcting proofs of my "Last Plays"—the last I mean to write—Sancho's Master—Dave—W[ould] be Gentleman.[1] It is time for me to retire voluntarily & not be like—as I quote—that

"long remembered guest
"Who may not rudely be dismissed
"Yet who has outstayed his welcome while
"And brings the jest without the smile" [2]

It will happily be long before your "jests" will fail—I believe your more settled & easy life will leave the imagination free to make new discoveries and use them. I am so sorry for Lord Oxford's death [3]—he was such a warm admirer of yours. And he was all for us about the Lane pictures. I feel sad just now because here we are on the threshold of this years Patrick's Day—& not able to make a demonstration, because we cant yet announce that a Gallery is to be built. I was in Dublin lately for a few days & I think got a move on—as this reorganization of the local govt of Dublin makes a new check. However [William T.] Cosgrave is in earnest about it & there may be a move on soon.

[1] Lady Gregory, *Three Last Plays* (1928), *Sancho's Master, Dave, The Would-Be Gentleman.*

[2] The last four lines of Coleridge's "Youth and Age" (1834), which read:

Like some poor nigh-related guest,
That may not rudely be dismist;
Yet hath outstay'd his welcome while,
And tells the jest without the smile.

[3] Lord Oxford, Herbert Henry Asquith, died on 15 February 1928 at the age of seventy-five. He presented the Hawthornden Prize to O'Casey in 1926. For his comments on O'Casey's work at the presentation, see the news story in the *Irish Times,* 24 March 1926, printed above.

We are going to do J. G. Borkman [4] for the Ibsen centenary—I saw Doctors Dilemma which went wonderfully well.

Yours sincerely & affectionately
A. Gregory

[4] Ibsen's *John Gabriel Borkman* opened at the Abbey Theatre on 3 April 1928, directed by Lennox Robinson, with F. J. McCormick in the title role.

From Lennox Robinson

MS. O'CASEY

ABBEY THEATRE
WEDNESDAY
[18? MARCH 1928]

Dear Sean,

Your play [1] arrived this morning. Three cheers! I shall read it as soon as possible and send it then to Lady Gregory. Very busy now over *Borkman* and a new Murray.[2]

Yours ever
Lennox Robinson

[1] *The Silver Tassie.*
[2] T. C. Murray's *The Blind Wolf* opened at the Abbey Theatre on 30 April 1928.

To Lady Gregory

MS. GREGORY

ST. JOHN'S WOOD
28 MARCH 1928

My dear Lady Gregory:—

Now, now, now; you shouldn't be sad. It is hardly just to the mind & the vitality that have done so much for Coole & Galway; for Ireland and for womanhood. Shaw once said that you were the most distinguished of living Irishwomen. And now I have thought of our present-day country women, seeking some, seeking even one, that had in her something of Grania, or Emer, or of Maeve, but God, perhaps, has hidden them from mine eyes. And you are with us still, still in front of our women, though no chair has been placed for you in the Senate or the Dail. And, apart from your own personal work altogether, you have done for Art & Literature, not only as much as Ireland would permit, but a great deal more than Ireland would permit you to do. And from what I know of you,—and I know you fairly well now—I don't believe you'll ever really grow old, for there always was, & always will be, a lot of the child in your soul. Like my mother, who aged & aged, but kept her keen, bright eyes, her intelligent mind & her humourful laugh for ever. And one thing is certain—that so long as God or Nature leaves us one atom of strength, we must continue to use that atom of strength to fight on for that which is above & before all governments & parties—Art & Literature which are the mantle & mirror of the Holy Ghost, and the Sword of the Spirit.

My dear Lady Gregory you can always walk on with your head up. And remember you had to fight against your birth into position & comfort as others had to fight against their birth into hardship & poverty, & it is as difficult to come out of one as it is to come out of the other so that power may be gained to bring fountains and waters out of the hard rocks.

My Best Wishes to all at Coole.
Yours Affectionately
Sean

To Macmillan & Co. Ltd.

MS. MACMILLAN LONDON

ST. JOHN'S WOOD
31 MARCH 1928

Dear Sirs,

Enclosed you should find the letter from Messrs Francis, Day & Hunter giving permission to use the air of the Tango "Spain" in "The Silver Tassie."

I haven't included the score in the music sent to you for publication as the air can be easily obtained when wanted for the production.

A young Artist friend of mine [1]—who, if he lives, will make his name—would, I think, do a charcoal sketch portrait as a frontispiece for the book, & I should like to know what you think of the suggestion. There is no doubt about the young fellow's genius, & a sketch by him in my

[1] Evan Walters. See O'Casey's letter to Walters, 8 February 1939, note 1. The sketch appears as the frontispiece of *The Silver Tassie* (London, Macmillan, 1928).

book might help to bring notice to his work, & the drawing would add to the publication.

May I venture to suggest that a higher price might be charged for the play than that linked on to "The Plough & the Stars."

Sincerely yours
Sean O'Casey

From Lady Gregory

PS. *Modern Drama* [1]

COOLE PARK, GORT, CO. GALWAY
2 APRIL 1928

Dear Sean—

Your kind letter has moved and touched me very much—and helped the courage I am keeping alive in spite of some discouraging events—or anxieties—this long fight with the Tate for instance. But one of the comforting things I sometimes take to rest on is this of your great success, so good for us all—and for Ireland. And there comes in with this a little grain of pride in the little finger-touch of help I was once able to give you in your early play-writing days. And I like to think of your present happiness, with wife and house and garden—

Yes, it is true I had to fight to get free of my surroundings—My husband had felt something of the same reproach many, many years ago, when, having been brought up as a strong Tory he supported several measures, in and out of Parliament—such as the disestablishment of the Church—I was called "mad" when I gave my personal help to the Gaelic League—and all that followed—But now I have the happiness, whatever our troubles may be, not only of seeing the flourishing Abbey—but in knowing how the name of one of our dramatists has gone so high—towards the Stars!

The Lane pictures have been a heavy burden this last year; I would not go to London—because we had not yet built a Gallery—and I felt awkward—but I have—ten days ago—spent *one* day in Dublin—went on a deputation with P[hilip] Hanson and [Thomas] Bodkin and Miss [Sarah] Purser to the hard-hearted City Commissioners—and to [William T.] Cosgrave and Senator [Samuel L.] Brown—and now we are to have an

[1] From a copy made by A. C. Edwards and printed in *Modern Drama,* May 1965.

"enquiry publicly as to the need of a Gallery—and my hopes rise again: —My little granddaughter's coming over for the letters—so I must say good by.

With affection and gratitude
A Gregory

To Lennox Robinson

MS. Robinson
St. John's Wood
5 April 1928

Sylvester Heegan	Barry Fitzgerald.
Simon Norton	Gaby Fallon.
Susie Monican	Eileen Crowe.
Mrs Heegan	
Teddy Foran	J Stephenson.
Harry Heegan	F J McCormack.
Barney Bagnal	P Carolan.
Jessie Taite	Sheila Richards.
The Corporal	J Stephenson.
The Visitor	Barry Fitzgerald.
The Surgeon and Croucher	A Shields.
Staff Wallah	M J Dolan.
Mrs Foran	May Craig?
Ward Sister	M Delaney?

Dear Mr. Robinson—

Assuming acceptance of "The Silver Tassie", I send above list of those whom I imagine would fill the principal parts of the play. I have written to Gaby & he is very willing to play, and I am very glad, for I think he would play the part of Simon splendidly.

I was talking yesterday to Sir Barry Jackson, & we spoke about a possible London Season for The Abbey Players. He seemed to be very interested in the idea, & possibly, later on, you might think of it & write to him about a possible arrangement. I'm sure that a six, seven or eight week's run here would be a success—possibly a great success. And the Abbey Players should be seen in London. I spoke to Mr. Yeats about this when he was here last, & he liked the idea.

Best Wishes
Yours
Sean O'Casey

To Lady Gregory

MS. GREGORY

ST. JOHN'S WOOD
20 APRIL 1928

My dear Lady Gregory—

The long fight with the Tate Gallery is a very irritating annoyance indeed, & so is the apathy of the cultured Irish people towards the return of incalculable treasures that are seperated from them really by only one closed door. But fighting is nothing new to you, & I imagine that the fight would be most effective if carried on for a building in which to place the pictures. Surely Ireland has enough of money to do this; or till this be done we could make a space in the National Gallery for them, putting where each picture is to hang an inscription indicative of the present circumstances.

I mean that where "Don Quixote & Sancho Panza" would hang to put the name of the picture & the Artist above an inscription saying: Picture held away from Dublin by The Tate Gallery. "The Toilet" Puvis Chavanne still held from us by the Tate Gallery & so on in each instance. This would be a constant reminder to Dublin & to visitors of the damned and unjustifiable selfishness of the clique over here that hang on to the pictures that Lane undoubtedly gave to Dublin. And near this display of angry remonstrance could be hung a brief account of the happenings (in Large lettering) taken from "The Case for the Return of Sir Hugh Lane's Pictures to Dublin." [1]

If the Press took up the contest again, I would suggest the taking of every possible means of interesting the people in the return of the Pictures —even by flashing on every Cinema Screen in Ireland a demand that they should be given back. And one thing is certain: no harm can ever be done by exciting the ignorant to take a hand in such a fight: it is a passion from which no harm, but good may come. I remember myself siding long ago with the demand for the building of a gallery (in 1913 I think) ignorantly indeed, for I knew nothing then of Corot or Manet or Daumier, or Chavannes; but now I know, & who can say how many, ignorant now, may, later on, vividly enjoy the wonder of Colour, Line & Form?

I wonder could anything be done during the progress or the inception of the coming Tailltеann Games? I imagine a good opportunity was lost

[1] Lady Gregory, *The Case for the Return of Sir Hugh Lane's Pictures to Dublin* (Dublin, Talbot Press, 1926).

for an effective protest at the first Assembly of a United Dail, but that cant be helped now.

And could not the remonstrance be carried to The League of Nations? Wasn't France made to give back things taken during the Napoleonic Wars? And Germany recently? Should not England be pressed back from the pictures by a protest made to the League of Nations? Is it not a meaner thing to steal in peace than to steal in war?

I hope you are keeping well & hopeful. When I go over to Dublin again you must let me go down to Coole for a few days. I have often spoken about you to Eileen, & she is looking forward to seeing Lady Gregory that helped me so much towards Art and the Drama.

I sent my play to Mr. Robinson some weeks ago, & suppose you have read it by now. I think it by far the best work I have done.

The play is, I think, very different to my previous work. I am correcting proofs now, & it will be published in a few months time. You must take from me the first copy sent to anyone.

Warm Regards to all in Coole.
And Sincere Affection to You.
Sean

From Lennox Robinson to Lady Gregory

PS. GREGORY [1]

[? APRIL 1928]

[*Dear Lady Gregory,*]

I was very relieved to get your letter to-day and to find that you agreed with me about O'Casey's play. If you had disagreed with me I should have suspected myself of all sorts of horrid subconscious feelings. I shall send the play at once to W. B. Yeats and avoid writing to Sean until he has read it. We can't do it before the end of this season and if W. B. agrees with you and me Sean will have time to think over his last acts before July and August. It looks to me as if he had put very careful work into Acts I and II, and finished the other two acts haphazard because everyone was beginning to say he would never write a play again and he wanted to show that he could—but the play as it stands won't increase his reputation. I see the end of his play as a single tenement act with the maimed heroes back and everyone sorry they've come and the girl gone

[1] From a copy made by Lady Gregory, in *Lady Gregory's Journals, 1916–1930.* ed. Lennox Robinson (New York, Macmillan, 1947), pp. 104–105.

off with the other fellow. This is obvious, but the idea in Sean O'Casey's plays is always obvious; it is the treatment that makes the difference, makes the genius.

[*Lennox Robinson*]

From W. B. Yeats to Lady Gregory

TC. O'CASEY [1]

25 APRIL 1928

Dear Lady Gregory—

It has just occurred to me that if you agree that we have no choice but to reject Casey's play, if Casey leaves the play in our hands, the most considerate thing for us to do is to suggest that he withdraws it. My letter gives an opinion, but not absolutely reject. He could withdraw the play "for revision" and let that be known to the Press. He could say that he himself had become dissatisfied and had written to ask it back. If he disagrees with our opinions as to its merits he can wait a little and offer it to some London Manager. If the London Manager accepts then our opinions wont matter at all to him. On the other hand if no London Manager accepts it, or if he doesnt offer it there, he can keep it by him revising or not as he pleases. I want to get out of the difficulty of the paragraphs saying the play has been offered to us. I have not told anybody what I think of the play and I will get Lennox not to give his opinion. You have perhaps already written to Casey but even if you have I would like you to write making this suggestion.

W B Yeats.

Could anything equal the assumption of Zeusian infallibility[2]

[1] Lady Gregory sent a copy of this letter to O'Casey.
[2] O'Casey wrote this comment.

From Lady Gregory

PS. *Modern Drama* [1]

COOLE PARK, GORT, CO. GALWAY
27 APRIL 1928

Dear Sean—

I did not answer and thank you for your very kind letter—about Hugh Lane's pictures—and saying you wd. come to Coole again some time (as I still hope you and your wife will do) because I didn't like to say anything about the play [2] until WBY had seen it—His letter has only come today, and I think I ought to mail it to you at once though I am afraid it might hurt you—or at least disappoint you—(as his criticism did me, on my first draft of "Sancho.") But it is right you should at once know what he—what we all—feel and think—I won't make any more comment—I know you will prefer this to any attempt to "soften" things and will believe that I, that we all—feel you would rather have the exact truth than evasions—

Yours very affectionately
A Gregory

April 27—'28
I don't remember exactly what I wrote to L.R. but I wrote in my diary March 28: "I absolutely agree with LR's criticism, the beginning is fine, the two first acts—then such a falling off, especially in the last—the "persons lost in rowdiness"

A.G.

(April 28, 1928)
Saturday morning—Dear Sean, I awoke early—having got to sleep late—and really suffering at what I have had to write and send on—

My comfort is that you have such courage (far beyond mine!) and tenacity that I know you will, as of old, when the "Banner" [3] went back —set your teeth and "turn a defeat to a victory" as you did then—

Always affectionately
A Gregory

[1] From a copy made by A. C. Edwards and printed in *Modern Drama*, May 1965.

[2] *The Silver Tassie*.

[3] O'Casey's *The Crimson in the Tri-colour*. See Yeats's critique of the play, 19 June 1922, printed above.

To Gabriel Fallon

MS. TEXAS

ST. JOHN'S WOOD
1 MAY 1928

My dear Gaby—

Eileen has asked me to get you to stand as Godfather (by proxy) for the son and heir [1]—of all I haven't got—and would you say Yes, please and would you let me know if you will as soon as possible as this leaves me at present—

Sean

[1] Breon O'Casey, born 30 April 1928.

To Lennox Robinson

TS. ROBINSON

ST. JOHN'S WOOD
2 MAY 1928

Dear Mr Robinson—

Lady Gregory has written in her kind way and has given me a full, perfect and sufficient account of the Abbey Theatre Directorate's dislike of "The Silver Tassie."

The rejection of the play was not unexpected—I have said many times to some friends—had a bet about it in fact—to my wife (curious word that for me to be using) and even to Barry Fitzgerald when he was here, that I thought that the play wouldnt be fondled by the Abbey.

Lady Gregory in her kind way again, enclosed portion of a letter from W B Yeats which unfolds the suggestion that the Directorate would be willing to allow me to "withdraw for revision and let that be known to the Press saying that he himself has become dissatisfied and had written to ask it back." This to save my dignity and to deliver me from the curse of the Abbey's rejection when dealing with an English Manager.

If W B Yeats had known me as faintly as he thinks he knows me well, he wouldn't have wasted his time—and mine—making such a suggestion. I am too big for this sort of mean and petty shuffling, this lousy perversion of the truth. There is going to be no damned secrecy with me surrounding the Abbey's rejection of the play. Does he think that I would practice in my life the prevarication and wretchedness that I laugh at in my plays?

Since the play hasnt been accepted, it has been rejected, and let the middle course be cut for those to whom the world is a crawling Limbo.

Any Journalist, Irish or English, who asks me about the Abbey production will be told that the play has been refused by the Abbey because they thought the play a bad one, supplemented by me saying that I believe the play was refused because it was a good one.

A well known English Manager [C. B. Cochran], who thinks the play a great one, has been considering a London production, and, hearing of a business meeting to arrange preliminary matters, I went along and not only told him of the Abbey's rejection, but showed him the entire correspondence received from the Abbey, for if the work be what I believe it to be his rejection or the Abbey's rejection couldnt take a gasp out of a single line of a fine play. (he still thinks it a great play)

I shall be glad if you would return the Typescript of the play to me as soon as possible.

Sincerely Yours,
Sean O'Casey

From Lennox Robinson

MS. O'Casey

Abbey Theatre
9 May [1928]

Dear Sean,

I return the M.S. of "The Silver Tassie". As I write this I hear the audience cheering "The Plough" [1] which makes it very grievous to have to return this play—we had all looked forward to it for so long.

Yours sincerely,
Lennox Robinson

[1] *The Plough and the Stars* was revived at the Abbey Theatre on 9 May 1928 with the original cast.

From W. B. Yeats

MS. O'Casey

Abbey Theatre
9 May [1928]

Dear Casey

I have just had your letter. I write from the Abbey, Lady Gregory, Lennox Robinson my wife & I are here for "The Plough & the Stars"—a packed enthusiastic house. Had my admiration for your genius been less my criticism had been less severe. I think that is true of Lady Gregory and Robinson also.

Yours
W. B. Yeats

From Lady Gregory

PS. *Modern Drama* [1]

82, Merrion Square, Dublin
Thursday, 10 May 1928

Dear Sean—

I am glad of your letter of the 5th, glad of its kind tone,—for I should be very sorry were there any break in a friendship I value. Perhaps I was wrong in sending on those letters to you—no I think you will say I was right—they were the genuine opinion of us writers at the moment, whether mistaken or not—and I believe you would rather have them than a more formal and polite "arranged" document—However, that is over—and I like better to think of the enthusiasm and applause last night as the Plough made its progress—There was an idea this morning of running it on for next week—I should have liked this for my own sake, as I shall be here—But later we were told there is a good deal of booking for the Heffernans [2] and the printing all out—L. R. came round to say this—and that it would be better to begin next season (in June) with it—The programs are to be "slipped" today and tomorrow with an announcement of this—But you are tired of the Plough details

I have been all this morning with Sir Philip H[anson], re pictures. He

[1] From a copy made by A. C. Edwards and printed in *Modern Drama,* May 1965.

[2] Brinsley Macnamara's *Look at the Heffernans!* was revived at the Abbey Theatre on 14 May 1928.

will arrange for a big public meeting, to show the desire of the public for the Gallery, before the "enquiry" that is to be held by the City Commissioners next month. It is the money £120-000 that is the fence to get over—a big sum—but most of this wd. go to labour.

I am having a couple of weeks here, having been tied to Coole all the winter—Yeats is very much better, but has to take care of himself—

I hope mother and child are doing well—I wonder what you have called him—

Always affectionately
A Gregory

From Daniel Macmillan

TS. O'Casey

London
10 May 1928

Dear Mr. O'Casey,

We have read through your correspondence with the Abbey Theatre people with great interest, but we think that on the whole it would be a mistake to publish it in the book as a preface, so I am returning it to you. By the way, I suppose you would still like us to issue the play now instead of waiting till the autumn? [1] We can issue it quite soon, as it is already being printed.

I am,
Yours sincerely,
Daniel Macmillan

[1] The printed text of *The Silver Tassie* was issued in June 1928.

To Gabriel Fallon

MS. Texas

St. John's Wood
11 May 1928

My dear Gaby—

Nonsense, Gaby, you mustn't be sorry for me. It wasn't such a terrible blow at all. It was more than partly expected—in fact I found myself all along, during the writing of the play, & after it had been sent in, forcing into my mind that they would like & take the play. In my own, peculiar, canny way I sensed all that was going to happen. The only sad thing about the affair is that the Abbey seems to be determined to go on making dead trees from the dead leaves of many seasons ago. "You mustn't jump" says Yeats, "till I give the word". But either I wasn't listening, or I didn't hear, so I jumped & knocked him head over tip! The whole business is curious: When Yeats was over here last he came to see me at the Court Theatre, & asked me earnestly if I was going to give my new play to the Abbey. And I said "yes, of course; I'm going to give my new play to the Abbey". And sipping his ginger beer, ginger ale or ginger cordial—yes, be God, it was ginger cordial—he asked was it in my former style. I told him no, & gave him the places of the four scenes, telling him that the second act took place "Behind the trenches, in the Rest Camps out in France", & not a word or a suggestion from him then that "I wasn't interested in the Great War".

I enclose here copies of the letters that have been sent to me, & copies of the letters I have sent to them.

If the play be not an O'Casey play, the letters are O'Casey letters.

Comical & curious to note in his last letter Mr. Yeats writes of a "packed house". Mr. Yeats pines for packed houses. Odd that he seems to have forgotten that a great play may empty a house as well as fill one.

Imagine him saying the play was like a leading article. Well if some or any or one leading article be like the play, there's something to be said for leading articles.

I will think well over your suggestion of a Dublin production, & let you know. The book of the play will be published shortly. Love to Rose Baby & yourself from Eileen & myself.

Sean

To Daniel Macmillan [1]

MS. MACMILLAN LONDON

ST. JOHN'S WOOD
12 MAY 1928

Dear Sir,

I'm sorry you have decided that it would be better not to publish the Abbey's letters to me & my letters to the Abbey.

I have no intention of pressing for their publication in this way, for it

[1] Daniel Macmillan (1886–1965), publisher.

would not be fair to bring Macmillans into the controversy against their wishes.

I am satisfied that I have acted in a square way with your Firm, & nothing more remains to be said about that particular matter.

Now that Mrs. O'Casey is better,[2] I will be able to see about correction in music proofs, & return them as soon as possible so that the play may be ready for publication shortly.

Yrs.

Sean O'Casey

[2] His wife was recovering from the birth of their first child, Breon, on 30 April 1928.

To Lady Gregory

MS. GREGORY

ST. JOHN'S WOOD
14 MAY 1928

Dear Lady Gregory—

I sincerely hope you & Sir Philip Hanson will succeed in bringing a meeting that will abundantly prove that the people desire a gallery. The pictures held in the Tate Gallery would add more than a cubit to Dublin's Stature. Even from a commercial point of view it would be, I think, an asset, for I'm sure many would come to see this wonderful collection of French Impressionism, Daumier, Chavannes, Courbet, Manet, Renoir, Monet, Ingres, Degas housed in Dublin! And not for one week—even civic week—but forever! They would be a coat of arms no Corporation or Commissioners could ever give.

I have made friends here with a young artist [1] from Wales, who will (so says John) [2] be a great man in colour & form. He has painted me a splendid group of blue Hydrangea, full of strength and emotion, and he is to paint a special little vista in our garden presently. The garden & the surroundings here are looking lovely just now—jewelled with masses of Lilac, Laburnum, red & white hawthorn, chestnut-blooms & acacia. And as I write there is a great big fellow of a blackbird hard at his song right in front of my window.

My wife & the young boy are going ahead splendidly. Eileen has decided to call him Brian.[3] She has begun to take a glorious interest in paint-

[1] Evan Walters.
[2] Augustus John.
[3] Several years later they decided to use the Gaelic form of his name, Breon.

ing—not to paint herself of course—which might be terrible—but to love and understand the wonder of colour, Line and form.

She can admire & enjoy, & point out a Cezanne, a Van Gogh, a Matisse, a Segonzac, a Derain, a Daumier, a Manet, a Utrillo, a Degas with the best.

I have three originals here now, & hope, in time, to have at least one room enriched with the work of present day artists.

Best of Wishes
Sean

To Lady Gregory

MS. GREGORY

ST. JOHN'S WOOD
15 MAY 1928

Dear Lady Gregory—

I have just received your "Three Last Plays", & I thank you very much for your kind thought in sending them on to me.

Eileen (Mrs. O'C) is up again, & next week I am bringing her to the Tate to see H. Lane's collection, the Chair by Van Gogh, & John's great Cartoon of Galway.

Warm Regards.
Sean

To Gabriel Fallon

MS. TEXAS

ST. JOHN'S WOOD
16 MAY 1928

Dear Gaby—

That was a very interesting chat that Lyle [Donaghy] had with the Lady. He has had his own trouble, I think, with the apostolical advice & admonition of the Yeatsean City Set on a Hill, with the Robinsonian Banner flying from one Turret & the Georgian Banner flying from the other turret, and poor Lady Gregory, I'm afraid captive inside. Instead

of Lyle running towards Yeats his best thing to do is to run as far away from him as possible. Lyle's world is in front of him; Yeats' world is all behind him: his people aren't our people & his god isn't our God.

I am looking forward to that public statement. I imagine it will be a little difficult for them to say the right thing or the wrong thing; for the right thing might be wrong & the wrong thing might be right. I shouldn't be surprised if they kept a "dead silence".

I'm sure Yeats & Robinson counted on me withdrawing the play "for revision"; or that I would gallop over to Dublin & pant along to Merrion Square to fall for rest and peace at the feet of the torso till it bent down & softly said—my peace be with you—go and sin no more!

I can come to no other conclusion than that the whole thing had been planned by Robinson & Yeats. They were obviously eager to reject the play—too eager in fact, for even from their own point of view, the play was worthy of production. But neither Yeats nor Robinson knew his man: the little irridescent bubble of air & water, as they thought when they pushed their little pin at it, was found to be steel, & that little pin is badly bent.

And did Yeats really say that "if I could only write dialogue like Robinson?" Holy God, he's adding insult to injury!

"How is he? Oh, just Williamish! How did he take it? Just Williamishly." "That's a lie; if you had been in bed your hair would have been ruffled, but it is sleek as sleek". No, more, in God's name, I pray you!

The book's in the Press, & will be published shortly. The play can't be produced here till September—the summer is a bad season for production—besides the work of Casting, getting a theatre, etc is a heavy one. Love to Rose & Baby, & to you.

Sean

To Daniel Macmillan

MS. Macmillan London

St. John's Wood
16 May 1928

Dear Sir,

Yes, of course; publish "The Silver Tassie" as soon as possible.

I forgot to say before that I think the reproduction of the charcoal sketch a very good one indeed.

I am pleased to say that three prominent men in the theatrical world here,—Sir Barry Jackson, Golding Bright, & C. B. Cochran, who have read the play, think it a very great work indeed.

Please reserve to me (60) sixty copies of the first Edition.

Very sincerely yours,
Sean O'Casey

To Gabriel Fallon

MS. Texas

St. John's Wood
17 May 1928

Dear Gaby—

Read Y O's criticism of Donaghy's Ad Perennis Vitae Fontem? [1] It's inside here; have a look at it.

Out of every hush of the air,
Out of every pause of the ocean, life.[2]

Yo Yo finds it vague. So he would since it speaks of Life! Here's one by Eee Ay, Ay Ay, in the paper that has the Criticism. E calls it "Blight." Ay. Ay. The boy stood on the burning deck, etc.

They stilled the sweetest breath of song
Who loosed from love its chains,
Who made it easy to be borne,
A thing that had no pains.

[1] Using his alter-ego initials of Y.O., A.E. reviewed Lyle Donaghy's book of poems, *Ad perennis vitae fontem* (Dublin, Minorea Press, 1928), in the *Irish Statesman,* 19 May 1928.

[2] Y.O./A.E. quoted these two lines from Donaghy's poem "Unborn" as an example of a style he rejected as too "declamatory in a vague philosophical fashion."

A dusk has blighted Pysche's wings
And the wild beauty dies:
The fragrance & the glow were born
From its own agoneyes! [3]

A E, Sir? Ay, Ay, sir. Why so, sir? Y.O., Sir.
Oh, why, sir, Yo, sir? No, no, sir; Ay Ay, sir.

Death of Psyche

Oh, Kathleen Ni Houlihan, your way's a thorny way!
I will send you on a copy of 'The Silver Tassie' as soon as it is published which will be very shortly now.

I wish The Abbey would make that 'Public Statement' soon. It should be very interesting reading. It's rather strange that no word yet has appeared in the Irish Press about the play's rejection.

I suppose it must have been something of a shock to W. B. Yeats when he read my sentences hammering at the very door of his heart. But, I'm afraid this outburst has been secretly jarred up in my soul for quite a long time now, and Yeats's cool impudence has itself to blame in opening the thunderflow of resentment. My God to think of Ireland going to sleep on these air-filled cushions of humbug! Smothering life with their storm of feathers.

Did you see [T.C.] Murray's "Blind Wolf"?

"I did it with me little hatchit!"

What play is going to get the Tailltean First Prize this year?[4] "Young Man from Rathmines",[5] or "Mr. Murphy's Island"? [6] I understand Billy [McElroy] has written to you about coming over here for the production of "The Tassie". I don't know what he has said, but you can tell me what you think of it.

Sean

[3] This poem by A.E., "Blight," appeared in the same issue of the *Irish Statesman* as Y.O.'s review, 19 May, and O'Casey implies that it is "declamatory in a vague philosophical fashion." See also O'Casey's letter to Oliver St. John Gogarty, 20 May 1928, note 6.

[4] In August 1928 the Tailteann Games first prize for drama went to Bernard Shaw's *Saint Joan,* and the first prize for poetry to Yeats's *The Tower*.

[5] M. M. Brennan's *Young Man From Rathmines* opened at the Abbey Theatre on 6 April 1922.

[6] See O'Casey's letter to Fallon, 4 September 1926, note 1.

To Oliver St. John Gogarty [1]

MS. BUCKNELL [2]

ST. JOHN'S WOOD
20 MAY 1928

Dear Oliver,

It was a welcome touch of friendship to get your volume of Wild Apples [3]—not so wild either, for there's a scent of culture in the most of them.

I like the poems in which you put your arms around a woman the best of all, & your 'Aphorism,' thought of before & written after you had read Tolstoy.

Who was Spengler? I imagine the boyo knew a little when he said that 'Culture was a fading tree' [4]—is it a tree at all?—or a bonny Bunch of Roses, O!?

And I'm afraid a rude puff of wind would blow out that blazing halo you've lighted around the head of A.E.,[5] indeed a breath from his own nostrils has shaken it a little. Read this in "The Statesman" last week—

Blight [6]

They stilled the sweetest breath of song
Who loosed from love its chains,
Who made it easy to be borne,
A thing that had no pains.

[1] Dr. Oliver St. John Gogarty (1878–1957), Irish poet, man of letters, and surgeon; senator of the Irish Free State, 1922–36; the original of James Joyce's "Buck Mulligan" in *Ulysses* (1922).

[2] An imperfect copy of this letter appears in James F. Carens, "Four Letters: Sean O'Casey to Oliver St. John Gogarty," *James Joyce Quarterly,* Fall 1970, O'Casey Issue.

[3] Oliver St. John Gogarty, *Wild Apples* (Dublin, Cuala Press, 1928).

[4] A reference to Gogarty's poem, "The Crowing of a Cock":

The knowledgeable Spengler says,
'Twere better far for you and me
To turn to take mechanics up
Than forge a lyric nowadays,
For Culture is a fading tree
That, broadening, withers at the top.
Where Spengler lives that well may be;
But Culture is of small account
Where men are governed by a clock,
Nor hold the Muses paramount
Nor hear the crowing of a cock.

[5] A reference to Gogarty's poem, "To A.E. Going to America."

[6] A.E., "Blight," *Irish Statesman,* 19 May 1928.

A dusk has blighted Psyche's wings
And the wild beauty dies;
The fragrance & the glow were born
From its own agonies.

All beautiful & bright he stood
As born to rule the storm;
A creature of Heroic mould—
A proud tho' childlike form.

No, Oliver, if this be AE the poet then take him away & hang him for his bad verses. Or, to punish him still more, bring him to Trinity College & make him a Doctor of Literature. A god with a body o brass & a head of clay.

Pardon for not acknowledging earlier your kindness, & taking your acceptable gift from a man who is greater than he will permit himself to be.

I stay,

Yours in Friendship,
Sean

To Gabriel Fallon

MS. TEXAS

[ST. JOHN'S WOOD]
23 MAY 1928

Dear Gaby—

It doesn't much matter that Will [Barry Fitzgerald] told the old Lady [Lady Gregory] about C.B.C[ochran]'s interest in the "Tassie", though Will might have kept his mouth shut. The keeping of things quiet for the present has no connection with the action of 'The Abbey' but it is the procedure here till everything is signed sealed & signatured. At present negotiations are still going on, & no publicity will be given till these are ended, & a big splash is made in the Press, or agreement fails to come & other channels must be searched for.

As a matter of fact these are held up by myself at present because I'm not satisfied with the contract C.B.C. has offered to me, & if he can't see his way to see as I see then I must look for someone else who has a keener & a brighter vision. However, I imagine it'll be settled alright shortly.

It is just like Billie's impetuosity to write to you about the production here, but I'll not talk of this to you till things take definite shape, & definite considerations can be put before you. (I should of course love you to have a hand in it all, & perhaps, through this find a crevice through which to creep away from the devastating Civil Service to that which I believe you have been shaped for by God or Nature or something indefinable). I sympathise with Will's dear, sweet, fair, lovely, chaste, strong, determined, persevering sympathy for Lady Gregory. It is indeed a sweet savouring thing to find this blossom blooming in the middle—right in the middle mind you—of the spinning activities, preoccupations & selfish garnerings of this present world. And he couldn't sleep o' nights, too; dear God, this is terrible! But *What* is Lady Gregory fretting about? She thinks & the Duke thinks, and the Duke's Esquire thinks that "The Silver Tassie" is a bad, poor play—nay, they know—and having refused to produce a bad play in the Abbey the Theatre's honour is preserved inviolate. That is nothing to be sad about, but calls for merry-making in the heart, because of the spiritual exhilaration of casting out the things that would defile the soul of Drama—

> "Up with the neck and clap the wing,
> Red cock, and crow!" [1]

For the present we'll leave William saunterin along at his ease hand in hand with Lady Gregory.

The baby's name is Brian. Eileen will soon be writing to Rose, & I suppose you'll hear all & more about it.

Love to Rose, the Baby & yourself.

Yours
Sean

[1] From the first musician's song in Yeats's *The Dreaming of the Bones.* This play was written in 1919, published in *Four Plays For Dancers* (London, Macmillan, 1921), and first performed at the Abbey Theatre on 6 December 1931.

To Timmie McElroy [1]

MS. McElroy [2]

St. John's Wood
26 May 1928

My dear Timmie—

I am so glad to be told by your Daddy that you are getting better, & that you will soon be as well as ever and that the ceiling that fell on you didn't do you so much harm as we were afraid of. It must have been horrible to feel all the plaster and things falling on your head, & the pain of the bruises must have been very bad indeed.

However it will soon be forgotten when you get completely well.

Love from
Sean

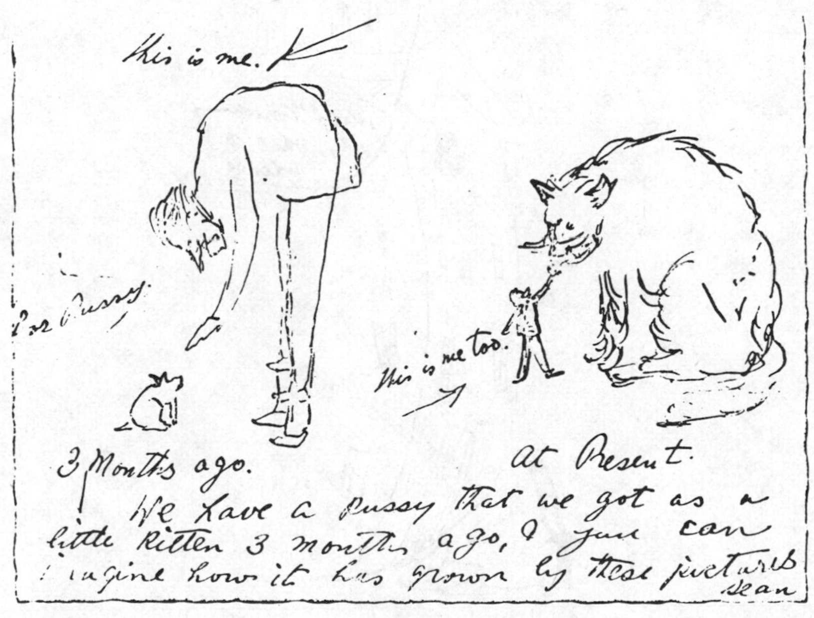

[1] Timmie McElroy, young daughter of William McElroy, who was the best man at O'Casey's marriage on 23 September 1927. McElroy, a coal merchant in London, was the backer of the first London production of *Juno*; and he often sang his favorite song to O'Casey, "The Silver Tassie," which O'Casey used in his play.

[2] A Xerox copy of this letter was sent to me by Michael Coming.

To Gabriel Fallon

MS. TEXAS

[ST. JOHN'S WOOD]
31 MAY 1928

Dear Gaby—

I have sent the correspondence on to "The Observer" &, though they can't publish the whole of it, an important portion of the letters will probably appear in Sunday's issue, or that of the Sunday following.[1]

Best Wishes
Sean O'Casey, Esquire

Ex Past Chief Ranger of the Abbey Theatre Directorate de Triumvirate.

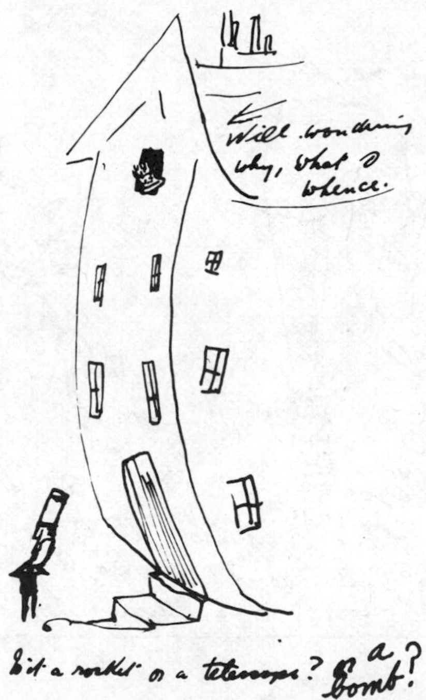

[1] Part of the correspondence between O'Casey and the Abbey Theatre directors appeared in *The Observer*, 3 June 1928. Yeats and Robinson were angry about this unauthorized publication of their letters, but as Yeats indicates in his 4 June letter to Lady Gregory, printed below, he and Robinson now decided that their case would be stronger if the whole correspondence were published, and it appeared in the *Irish Statesman*, 9 June 1928. The full correspondence is printed below.

From Lady Gregory

PS. *Modern Drama* [1]

COOLE PARK, GORT, CO. GALWAY
31 MAY 1928

Dear Sean—

This is to ask your help in this matter of the meeting that is to press for the building of a Gallery—I will put in the formal letter to show you what has been done—I was occupied with this writing while in Dublin—I went to De Valera who was kind, and will speak—I will go up again for the meeting—Sir Philip H[anson] is to read a very energetic opinion—

He writes that someone (I wont give the name—a woman) "says our meeting will be broken up by Larkinites"—

But I don't think this can be a true prophecy—for J. Larkin was always sympathetic to Hugh Lane—If I knew him personally I would write to him—but I think perhaps you would do so—You know what Hugh intended the Gallery to be and what it will be—a place full of beauty that is open to all—and that he hoped would be a place of rest and pleasure to the workers above all—Were you in Dublin I know you would help us in person—

I am alone here, among the trees and flowers—and working indoors to put papers and m.s.s. and old diaries in order, to save my executors trouble. For the death, in the last nine months, of two brothers—leaves me the only survivor of our large family, and I want to leave all in order—I hope all will go well and happily with you and yours—

Sincerely and affectionately
A Gregory

[1] From a copy made by A. C. Edwards and printed in *Modern Drama,* May 1965.

To Lady Gregory

MS. GREGORY

ST. JOHN'S WOOD
1 JUNE 1928

Dear Lady Gregory—

Oh, nonsense, there'll be no interference with the meeting by "The Larkinites".[1]

Why not ask 'Jim' to be a member of the Citizens' Committee?

He knows as much about Literature as most of those on the Council, & more about Art than some of them, &, surely to God he's a greater man than Farren!

Affectionately Yrs.
Sean

[1] When he heard about the meeting of the Citizens' Committee to plan the building of an art gallery for the Lane Pictures, Jim Larkin was reported to have said that the Irish people needed food more than a picture gallery. O'Casey gave me this information in 1963, but he added: "That was Jim Larkin talking to the capitalists of Dublin, but when he talked to the workers of Dublin he always urged them to aim for a bunch of red roses and a book on the table beside the loaf of bread."

From George Russell

THE IRISH STATESMAN
WITH WHICH IS INCORPORATED
THE IRISH HOMESTEAD

MS. O'CASEY

84 MERRION SQUARE,
DUBLIN
1 JUNE 1928

My dear O'Casey

As I wired you today I would be delighted to print letters if you have Yeats & Lennox Robinson's permission to print. The copyright in letters belongs to the writer & I think I am right in saying G. B. Shaw won some case where letters of his were printed without his consent. Naturally as Editor I wish to print these letters. Naturally also I do not wish a legal action if the directors are angry at their letters being printed. If they refuse permission the best thing you could do is to tabulate their objections and send the letters written to W. B. Yeats as your comment on the tabulated objections.

Yours sincerely
George Russell

To George Russell[1]

TC. O'CASEY

ST. JOHN'S WOOD
2 JUNE 1928

THE EDITOR, *Irish Statesman.*
Dear Mr Russell.—

Oh, that doesnt matter in the least. You can take it from me that neither Mr Robinson nor Mr Yeats will mind the publication of the letters. If you will read them again youll see that what really concerned them was the fear that the rejection of the play would be a very great blow to me. The realization that the blow wasnt so great as they thought will be rather a relief to them, and they will welcome instead of objecting to the publication of the letters.

So on you go and print them in the Irish Statesman as soon as you like. Up with the neck and clap the wing, red cock, and crow.

Yours Sincerely,
[*Sean O'Casey*]

[1] George Russell, A.E. (1867–1935), Irish poet, painter, mystic, editor; an organizer of the Irish Agricultural Co-operative Society, and editor of the Society's journal, *Irish Homestead,* 1895–1923; founder and editor of the *Irish Statesman,* 1923–30. His pseudonym, A.E., was a shortening of an earlier one, "Aeon."

To Gabriel Fallon

TS. TEXAS

[ST. JOHN'S WOOD]
2 JUNE 1928

Dear Gaby—

I must be wearying you with all these letters. But I'll chance this one anyway. Got the following telegram from G Russell:

O'Casey: Have you got permission to print letters copyright in which belongs to writers; if so will gladly insert Statesman—Russell.

To which I send this reply today:

EDITOR, *Irish Statesman.*

Dear Mr Russell—

Oh, that doesn't matter in the least. You can take it from me that neither Mr Robinson nor Mr Yeats will mind the publication of the letters. If you will read them again you'll see that what really concerned them was the fear that the rejection of the play would be a very great blow to me. The realization that the blow wasn't so great as they thought will be rather a relief to them, and they will welcome instead of objecting to the publication of the letters.

So on you go and print them in the Statesman soon as you like. Up with the neck and clap the wing, red cock, and crow.

Yours Sincerely etc.

Say nothing about the Observer yet. Sheila Richards rang me up late last night from Dublin and asked me if it was true that the Abbey had refused the play. Said she had heard only a rumour. Surely she must have known positively that the play had been rejected? Asked me would I let her and D[enis] Johnston produce it in Dublin. Answered no. Asked me would I let it be done by [Arthur] Boss Shields; answered no. Told her I didn't care a damn if it was never produced there; she said that that might be how I felt about it, but it wasn't how THEY felt. By the way, Gaby, I want you to keep as clear as possible from this little quarrel; you couldn't tell how it might hurt you in your job.

The book of "The Silver Tassie" is to be published on the 12th of this month, and (of course) I'll send you on a copy as soon as they come to me.

Best of Wishes to Rose, to you and the BABY.

Sean

To Gabriel Fallon

MS. TEXAS

ST. JOHN'S WOOD
4 JUNE 1928

Dear Gaby—

One O'Dea [1]—is it Jimmy—sends telegram asking to perform Tassie under auspices of Jervis St Hospital commencing Nov 12th. Of course I had to refuse. Enclosed is a copy of a letter from AE, & a cutting from Monday's Daily Mail. Have written AE assuring him that it's alright, —there now, there now was it frightened—naughty, naughty Yeats, frighten little AE. Dtch, dtch, the poor little frame is shaking & quivering —bad, bold, naughty Yeats!

I am still reading your letter—why don't you type & keep a copy— & I am still trying to agree with it. I'm afraid I thought the play decidedly anti-Christian.

Am I like Baalam—or was it Baalam—who tried to curse the Lord's people & could only bless them?

No developments yet with Cochrane. Billy [McElroy] will probably be going over to Ireland shortly & if he does, you'll see him, & find him a very remarkable & lovable man.

Sean

[1] Jimmy O'Dea (1900–65), the popular Irish music-hall comedian.

From W. B. Yeats to Lady Gregory

TC. NAT LIB, DUBLIN

82 MERRION SQUARE
DUBLIN
4 JUNE 1928

My dear Lady Gregory,

Please regard this letter as private. Last Sunday's Observer published the bulk of our correspondence with Casey including the part of my letter to you which you forwarded to him, and the Irish Times has reprinted all this morning. Lennox has wired a formal protest to the Observer. Meanwhile Dr. Starkie is very much offended. He is a Director of the Abbey, and the correspondence was sent to O'Casey before he was consulted. Lennox and I have decided that there is only one thing to be done—publication of the whole correspondence with Starkie's opinion added in this week's Irish Statesman. Starkie is in my study at this moment writing that opinion. It is of course of the utmost importance that O'Casey should not know that the writing out of Starkie's opinion has been so long delayed. When you were in Dublin, Starkie gave us his opinion verbally, but O'Casey would not believe this. On Saturday O'Casey sent the correspondence to the Irish Statesman, but A.E. wired that he could not publish without the authors' permission, and on Saturday Lennox wrote Macmillan objecting to its publication with O'Casey's play. Lennox is I think now inclined to think that in the changed circumstances it might be better to permit publication if the correspondence is complete. In view of this possibility I would be very much obliged if you sent me my letter to you about Casey marking that part which you sent him.

So far as Dublin is concerned I think we will gain out of the controversy, and elsewhere when the play is published. The tragedy is that O'Casey is now out of our saga.

[*W. B. Yeats*]

To Irish Times

5 JUNE 1928

[*Statement for the Irish Times*
To be published in full or not at all.] [1]

The correspondence that has passed between the Abbey Theatre directorate and me has been forwarded to *The Irish Statesman* for publication.

I received a telegram and subsequently a letter from the Editor, Mr. G. Russell, saying that 'he would be delighted to publish letters if you have Yeats's and Robinson's permission'. He went on to say that he was afraid of a possible legal action against the *Statesman* should the directors be angry because of their publication. Mr. Russell thinks he remembers a case—I remember it—in which G. B. Shaw figured against the publication of letters written by him without his consent.

I know Mr. Shaw a little personally, and a great deal by his works —'by their works ye shall know them'—(this is a quotation from Christina Rossetti) [2] and I do not hesitate to say that if Mr. Shaw wrote a criticism of a play of mine—or anybody else's—and that criticism was published

[1] Written on a typed carbon of the original letter.

[2] At the time Lennox Robinson had been quoted as saying that Christina Rossetti was a great poet.

with a reply from me—or anybody else—he would be the last man—the very last man to take legal action.

I have written to Mr. Russell venturing to assure him that Mr. Robinson and Mr. Yeats won't mind the publication of the correspondence, unless it be that they are reluctant to stand shoulder to shoulder by their written opinions, which is a feeling one would hardly like to welcome. So in all probability, the correspondence will be published in *The Irish Statesman* shortly, which will save them and me from the trouble of answering a multitude of questions.

Since Mr. Yeats has run up and shouted a lot of things in at O'Casey's window, he shouldn't be surprised, and he mustn't be sulky, when he finds O'Casey hammering at the Yeatsian door. *The Silver Tassie* will be published by Macmillans on the 12th of this month, and anyone who may be interested in the affair can judge for themselves whether the play was, or was not, worthy of production by the Abbey Theatre.

(signed) Sean O'Casey

From W. B. Yeats to the Society of Authors.

TC. NAT LIB, DUBLIN

82 MERRION SQUARE
DUBLIN
5 JUNE 1928

Dear Mr. Thring

I send you a copy of The Observer for Sunday June 3rd, which contains a mass of correspondence which was certainly not written for publication. The Abbey Theatre Directors are accustomed to enter into detailed criticism of the work of their dramatists, to put them into the most complete possession of their minds. This we have done for years and the movement here owes a great deal to that practice. That will be impossible if our correspondence is not looked upon as private, if we have to re-argue every question in public. You will see by the enclosed paper that the Observer has published a letter by me to Lady Gregory, as well as my own letter to Mr. Sean O'Casey himself. The correspondence was sent to Mr. Sean O'Casey by Lady Gregory that he might be fully informed. I need hardly say our permission was not asked. I do not complain of Mr. O'Casey's own action, for he was probably unaware of the general practice, but the Observer has set a precedent which it seems to me should be considered by your Society. The abstract question of Copyright is raised, and a very concrete question. Every author writes many letters to correspondents whom he does not know, or knows only slightly, and he can as a rule count upon the fact that before the publication of those letters his permission will be asked.

If I am right in supposing that letters are under the common law protected from publication where the author's consent has not been obtained, is your Society prepared to take this matter up against The Observer?

Yours very truly
[W. B. Yeats]

From Robert Bell to Lennox Robinson

TS. ROBINSON
The Observer
22 TUDOR STREET,
LONDON, E.C. 4
5 JUNE 1928

LENNOX ROBINSON, ESQ.,
SORRENTO COTTAGE,
DALKEY. CO. DUBLIN.

Dear Mr. Robinson,

The O'Casey correspondence came to us via [St. John] Ervine: O'Casey had written to him asking for publication. He suggests that in view of the early publication of the play, he desires to show that no effort has been made by him to conceal the opinion of the Abbey Directorate that the play is not worthy of production.

Yours sincerely,
Robert Bell

From St. John Ervine

TS. O'CASEY
131 WHITEHALL COURT
LONDON SW1
6 JUNE 1928

My dear O'Casey,

Thank you for your letter, enclosing copies of the correspondence you have had with A.E., whose argument, if seriously-meant, is woolly-witted. But of course, he is excusing himself from publishing the letters because he does not wish to offend Yeats.

You were perfectly justified in publishing the correspondence. The production of a play by you at the Abbey is a matter of public interest. The Abbey is the nearest thing we have to a national theatre in these islands: it is subsidised by the Government of The Free State; and therefore the rejection of a play by an author who, as Yeats himself asserts, saved the theatre from extinction is a matter of considerable public interest. It certainly is of more importance than the stuff spouted by De Valera in the Dail or the immersion of ducks in the Dodder by Dr Oliver Gogarty. I do not object to Yeats regarding himself as the Holy Ghost, but I complain that he is sometimes inclined to regard himself as the entire Trinity. And he isn't.

Even if your play were, as Yeats asserts, a poor one, the Abbey should nevertheless have produced it. You are a distinguished dramatist, and the theatre is admittedly under a heavy debt of gratitude to you. The least of your work has some interest. If the Directors of the Abbey were in the financial situation of a West End manager and likely to be ruined by a failure, I would sympathise with them; but that is not their situation. The production of "The Silver Tassie" would almost certainly have paid its way. On that ground, therefore, there is no case. Yeats, indeed, has not suggested that there is. It seems to me, then, that the proper thing to have done would have been for the Directors to tell you their opinion of your play and, while suggesting that you might wish to re-write it, offer to produce it as it is written. There is no better way of enabling an author to realise the faults in his work than by letting him see it publicly performed. The Abbey can afford to do that for authors of distinction. Lennox Robinson, I notice, says that you are experimenting with form. What better method of testing that form is there than a public performance?

I should be impressed by Yeats's argument if I had ever heard of the rejection of a play by him or by Lady Gregory. Several of them might well have been rejected. When "A.E." experimented with the dramatic form and wrote a play on Deirdre—how Irish authors love to write about that dreary, drivelling woman!—the Directors did not tell him that his play was hopeless. They produced it. I remember "A.E." telling me that it ought to have been done behind a gauze net. This was not, as you may suppose, for the protection of the company, but for the purpose of making the play appear remote. It was remote all right, gauze net or no gauze net!

The whole of this affair seems to have been handled in a very tactless and ill-considered fashion, and the net result of the Directors' brilliant bungling is that a breach has been made between you and the Abbey which may not easily be repaired. I hope, however, that when your justifiable anger has subsided, you will remember that you are an

Irish dramatist, and that the life of the Abbey is more important to Ireland than the life of you or me or Yeats or any other individual. It has kept what mind there is in Dublin—Heaven knows there is not much to boast about—and it must, therefore, not be hurt. Your withdrawal from it may gravely injure it, and I am sure you are too good an Irishman to wish to do that.

Yours sincerely,
St John Ervine

To Irish Statesman

9 June 1928

THE ABBEY DIRECTORS AND MR. SEAN O'CASEY [1]

[1] I found these three drawings of O'Casey and the Abbey Directors among O'Casey's private papers, and I do not believe he sent them to anyone. In the first drawing, the directors gesture No with their hands as O'Casey sprints away with his script; Yeats stands in front of the Abbey, Lady Gregory is on her knees between his legs, and Lennox Robinson is behind them. The dialogue reads:

> Yeats: We decree that thou art a heretic.
> Robbie: Cast out from the unity of the Abbey.
> Yeats: Sundered from her body.
> Robbie: Segregated & abandoned for evermore.
> Lady Gregory: Amen.

In the second drawing, Yeats approaches the edge of the cliff, gazing at the stars, while Lady Gregory carries the banner in front of the procession, with Robinson as the tall figure in the middle. In the third drawing, on page 266, O'Casey goes forth in a fighting pose.

DEAR SIR,—Questions are beginning to fall on top of me about the Abbey's production of "The Silver Tassie" which I find impossible to answer *in toto absolutium questionarii,* and to place before all who may be interested, the full circumstances surrounding the rejection of the play by the Abbey directorate. I shall be glad if you would kindly publish the enclosed correspondence.

If the material should take up too much space in one, then the letters could be spread over two issues of your journal.

The publication would, I'm sure, save me a lot of toil and trouble, fire-burn and cauldron bubble.

If they can't be published in full, then do not publish them at all, for no bread is as good as half a loaf. It will deliver the Abbey Theatre directorate, too, from pity pain which might make them reluctant to declare publicly their assurance of the poverty of my latest play, when they are affronted with my assurance that it is a fine one.—Yours sincerely,

Sean O'Casey

St. John's Wood
30 May 1928

DEAR LADY GREGORY,—I enclose the O'Casey play, which I have read again—in fact, three times in all. The first act is typical O'Casey and very good, I think. The second act in the modern Russo-German manner is very fine, I think, difficult to do and get right, but not impossible, and should be very effective. I like the third and fourth acts much less;

I don't think the mixture of the two manners—the realism of the first act and the unrealism of the second—succeeds, and the characters who were Dublin slum in the beginning of the play end by being of nowhere. The last acts remind me very much of those first O'Casey's, "The Frost in the Flower," etc. I wonder will you agree at all with me. I'm glad that he is groping towards a new manner—he couldn't go on writing slum plays for ever and ever—but I wish the second half of his play was better.—Yours.

L.R.

Abbey Theatre, Dublin

DEAR LADY GREGORY,—I have read Casey's play, and I did so without reading your opinion or Lennox's, and without knowing whether your verdict was favourable or otherwise. I dictated to George my opinion on it in the form of a letter to O'Casey which I enclose. I had meant to keep it until Lennox returned, and let Lennox send it on to O'Casey with a covering letter from myself. I hear now that Lennox may not return for another fortnight, and that seems to be too long to put the matter off, especially as O'Casey has told various journalists that he has sent the play to us and may go on doing so; it seems wrong to allow him to deceive himself. I wonder would you think it well to write a covering letter, enclosing mine, if you agree with it. I am afraid our refusal will be a very great blow to him, but if anybody can soften the blow you can. I did not think it tactful to say in my letter that he has left his material here in Dublin and will in all likelihood never find it anywhere else, because he cannot become a child again and grow up there. I did not say that to him, because I thought he might suspect me of exaggerating some of his faults in order to lure him back.

W. B. Yeats

82 Merrion Square, Dublin, 20 April 1928

MY DEAR CASEY,—Your play was sent to me at Rapallo by some mistake of the Theatre's. It arrived just after I had left, and was returned from there to Dublin. I found it when I myself reached Dublin four days ago. Enclosed with it were the opinions of my fellow-directors, but those opinions I shall not read until I have finished this letter; the letter, however, will not be posted unless their opinion concurs with mine. I had looked forward with great hope and excitement to reading your play, and not merely because of my admiration for your work, for I bore in mind that the Abbey owed its recent prosperity to you. If you had not brought us your plays just at that moment I doubt if it would now exist. I read the first act with admiration; I thought it was the best first act you had written, and told a friend that you had surpassed yourself. The next night I read the second and third acts, and to-night I have read the fourth. I am sad and discouraged. You have no subject.

You were interested in the Irish civil war, and at every moment of those plays wrote out of your own amusement with life or your sense of its tragedy; you were excited, and we all caught your excitement; you were exasperated almost beyond endurance by what you had seen or heard as a man is by what happens under his window, and you moved us as Swift moved his contemporaries. But you are not interested in the Great War; you never stood on its battlefields or walked its hospitals, and so write out of your opinions. You illustrate those opinions by a series of almost unrelated scenes as you might in a leading article; there is no dominating character, no dominating action, neither psychological unity nor unity of action, and your great power of the past has been the creation of some unique character who dominated all about him and was himself a main impulse in some action that filled the play from beginning to end. The mere greatness of the world war has thwarted you; it has refused to become mere background, and obtrudes itself upon the stage as so much dead wood that will not burn with the dramatic fire. Dramatic action is a fire that must burn up everything but itself; there should be no room in a play for anything that does not belong to it; the whole history of the world must be reduced to wallpaper in front of which the characters must pose and speak. Among the things that dramatic action must burn up are the author's opinions; while he is writing he has no business to know anything that is not a portion of that action. Do you suppose for one moment that Shakespeare educated Hamlet and King Lear by telling them what he thought and believed? As I see it, Hamlet and Lear educated Shakespeare, and I have no doubt that in the process of that education he found out that he was an altogether different man to what he thought himself, and had altogether different beliefs. A dramatist can help his characters to educate him by thinking and studying everything that gives them the language they are groping for through his hands and eyes, but the control must be theirs, and that is why the ancient philosophers thought a poet or dramatist Daimon-possessed.

This is a hateful letter to write, or rather to dictate—I am dictating to my wife—and all the more so because I cannot advise you to amend the play. It is all too abstract, after the first act; the second act is an interesting technical experiment, but it is too long for the material; and after that there is nothing. I can imagine how you have toiled over this play. A good scenario writes itself; it puts words into the mouths of all the characters while we sleep, but a bad scenario exacts the most miserable toil. I see nothing for it but a new theme, something you have found and no newspaper writer has ever found. What business have we with anything but the unique?

Put the dogmatism of this letter down to splenetic age and forgive it.

W. B. Yeats

82 Merrion Square, Dublin, 20 April 1928

Saturday, 28 April. This just arrived this morning. I thought it best to put it in for you to see.—A.G.

DEAR LADY GREGORY,—It has just occurred to me that if you agree that we have no choice but to reject Casey's play, if Casey leaves the play in our hands, the most considerate thing for us to do is to suggest that he withdraws it. My letter gives an opinion, but does not absolutely reject. He could withdraw the play "for revision," and let that be known to the Press. He could say that he himself had become dissatisfied and had written to ask it back. If he disagrees with our opinion as to its merits he can wait a little and offer it to some London manager. If the London manager accepts, then our opinion of the play won't matter to him at all. On the other hand, if no London manager accepts it, or if he doesn't offer it there, he can keep it by him, revising or not revising as he pleases. I want to get out of the difficulty of the paragraphs saying that the play has been offered to us. I have not told anybody what I think of the play, and I will get Lennox not to give his opinion. You have perhaps already written to Casey, but even if you have I would like you to write making this suggestion.

W. B. Y.

82 Merrion Square, Dublin, 25 April 1928

LENNOX ROBINSON, ESQ.

DEAR MR. ROBINSON,—Lady Gregory has written in her kind way and has given me full, perfect and sufficient account of the Abbey Theatre Directorate's dislike of "The Silver Tassie".

The rejection of the play was not unexpected—I have said many times to some friends—had a bet about it, in fact—to my wife (curious word that for me to be using), and even to Barry Fitzgerald when he was here, that I thought that the play wouldn't be fondled by the Abbey.

Lady Gregory, in her kind way again, enclosed portion of a letter from W. B. Yeats which unfolds the suggestion that the directorate would be willing to allow me to "withdraw for revision, and let that be known to the Press, saying that he himself has become dissatisfied and had written to ask it back". This to save my dignity and to deliver me from the curse of the Abbey's rejection when dealing with an English manager.

If W. B. Yeats had known me as faintly as he thinks he knows me well, he wouldn't have wasted his time—and mine—making such a suggestion; I am too big for this sort of mean and petty shuffling, this lousy perversion of the truth. There is going to be no damned secrecy with me surrounding the Abbey's rejection of the play. Does he think that I would practice in my life the prevarication and wretchedness that I laugh at in my plays?

Since the play hasn't been accepted, it has been rejected, and let the middle course be cut for those to whom the world is a crawling Limbo.

Any journalist, Irish or English, who asks me about the Abbey production will be told the play has been refused by the Abbey because they thought the play a bad one, supplemented by me saying that I believe the play was refused because it was a good one.

A well-known English manager, who thinks the play a great one, has been considering a London production, and, hearing of a business meeting to arrange preliminary matters, I went along and not only told him of the Abbey's rejection, but showed him the entire correspondence received from the Abbey, for if the work be what I believe it to be, his rejection or the Abbey's rejection couldn't take a gasp out of a single line of a fine play (he still thinks it a great play).

I shall be glad if you would return the typescript of the play to me as soon as possible.—Sincerely yours,

Sean O'Casey

St. John's Wood

DEAR LADY GREGORY,—Recent circumstances prevented me from writing before this. Thank you for your thoughtful telegram and very kind wishes.

I have, of course, received your own, the one from Mr. Yeats, and the copy of letter sent by Mr. Robinson to you. Of your criticism I can only say that I cannot agree with it, and that I think you are mistaken.

I have written to Mr. Yeats telling him what I think of his, and of the criticism given by Mr. Robinson I can only say that the opinion of a critic that would give the Tailteann Festival first prize for drama to "The Passing" evokes no more than a passing hurried thought and—pass along, pass along.

I have read, too, Mr. Yeats's suggestion that I should ask to withdraw the play, telling the Press that I am dissatisfied with it (I am proud of it), and that I want to revise, etc., and I do not thank him for it. Does he take me to be such a dish of skimmed milk that I would do such a shuffling, lying thing as that?

I have already shown the letters to the London manager who is considering the production of the play here. When time permits—a few days—I am bringing them to Macmillan's, who can stop the publishing of the book if they think the criticism more important than the play. If they decide to go on, I shall ask them to publish the letters, with my reply, as a preface to the book.

There's no more to be said at present, except to send you my warm regards.—Yours as ever,

S. O'Casey

St. John's Wood

DEAR MR. YEATS,—There seems to me to be no reason to comment upon whether you read my play in Rapallo or Dublin, or whether you read my play before or after reading your fellow-directors' opinions, or whether the Abbey owed or did not owe its prosperity to me—these things do not matter, and so we'll hang them up on the stars.

And we'll send into exile for the present the "dogmatism and splenetic age," and have a look at the brood of opinions these have left behind them.

You say—and this is the motif throughout the intonation of your whole song—that "I am not interested in the Great War." Now, how do you know that I am not interested in the Great War? Perhaps because I never mentioned it to you. Your statement is to me an impudently ignorant one to make, for it happens that I was and am passionately and intensely interested in the Great War. Throughout its duration I felt and talked of nothing else; brooded, wondered, and was amazed. In Dublin I talked of the Great War with friends that came to see me, and with friends when I went to see them. I talked of the Great War and of its terrible consequences with Lady Gregory when I stayed in Coole. I have talked of the Great War with Doctor Pilger, now the cancer expert in Dublin, who served as surgeon at the front. Only a week before I got your letter I talked of the Great War to a surgeon here. And yet you say I am not interested in the Great War. And now will you tell me the name and give me the age and send me the address of the human being who, having eyes to see, ears to hear and hands to handle, was not interested in the Great War?

I'm afraid your statement (as far as I am concerned) is not only an ignorant one, but it is a silly statement too.

You say "you never stood on its battlefields." Do you really mean that no one should or could write about or speak about a war because one has not stood on the battlefields? Were you serious when you dictated that—really serious, now? Was Shakespeare at Actium or Phillipi? Was G. B. Shaw in the boats with the French, or in the forts with the British when St. Joan and Dunois made the attack that relieved Orleans? And someone, I think, wrote a poem about Tir na nOg who never took a header into the Land of Youth. And does war consist only of battlefields?

But I have walked some of the hospital wards. I have talked and walked and smoked and sung with the blue-suited wounded men fresh from the front. I've been with the armless, the legless, the blind, the gassed and the shell-shocked; one with a head bored by shrapnel who had to tack east and tack west when before he could reach the point he wished to get to; with one whose head rocked like a frantic moving pendulum. Did you know "Pantosser," and did you ever speak to him? Or watch his funny, terrible antics, or listen to the gurgle of his foolish thoughts? No? Ah, it's a pity you never saw or never spoke to

"Pantosser." Or did you know Barney Fay, who got field punishment No. 1 for stealin' poulthry (an Estaminay cock, maybe) behind the trenches, in the rest camps, out in France? And does war consist only of hospital wards and battlefields?

You say: "You illustrate these opinions by a series of almost unrelated scenes as you might in a leading article." I don't know very much about leading articles, though I may possibly have read them when I had the mind of a kid, so I don't quite get your meaning here. And do you know what you are thinking about when you talk of leading articles, or do you know what you are talking about when you think of leading articles? Surely to God, Mr. Yeats, you don't read leading articles!

I have pondered in my heart your expression that "the history of the world must be reduced to wallpaper," and I can find in it only the pretentious bigness of a pretentious phrase. I thank you, out of mere politeness, but I must refuse even to try to do it. That is exactly, in my opinion (there goes a cursed opinion again) what most of the Abbey dramatists are trying to do—building up, building up little worlds of wallpaper, and hiding striding life behind it all.

I'm afraid I can't make my mind mix with the sense of importance you give to "a dominating character." God forgive me, but it does sound as if you peeked and pined for a hero in the play. Now, is a dominating character more important than a play, or is a play more important than a dominating character? You say that "my power in the past has been the creation of a unique character that dominated all round him, and was a main impulse in some action that filled the play from beginning to end." In "The Silver Tassie" you have a unique work that dominates all the characters in the play. I remember talking to Lady Gregory about "The Plough and the Stars" before it was produced, and I remember her saying that "The Plough" mightn't be so popular as "Juno", because there wasn't in the play a character so dominating and all-pervading as "Juno", yet "The Plough" is a better work than "Juno," and, in my opinion—an important one—"The Silver Tassie," because of, or in spite of, the lack of a dominating character, is a greater work than "The Plough and the Stars." And so when I have created the very, very thing you are looking for—something unique—you shout out: "Take, oh, take this wine away, and, for God's sake, bring me a pot of small beer."

It is all very well and very easy to say that "dramatic action must burn up the author's opinions." The best way, and the only way, to do that is to burn up the author himself. What's the use of writing a play that's just as like a camel as a whale? And was there ever a play, worthy of the name of play, that did not contain one or two or three opinions of the author that wrote it? And the Abbey Theatre has produced plays that were packed skin-tight with the author's opinions—the plays of Shaw, for instance.

Whether Hamlet and Lear educated Shakespeare, or Shakespeare educated Hamlet and Lear, I don't know the hell, and I don't think you know either.

Your statement about ". . . psychological unity and unity of action . . . Dramatic action is a fire that must burn up everything but itself . . . the history of the world must be reduced to wallpaper in front of which the characters must pose and speak . . . while an author is writing he has no business to know anything that isn't a part of the action . . ." are, to me, glib, glib ghosts. It seems to me they have been made, and will continue to be spoken forever and ever by professors in schools for the culture and propagation of the drama. (I was nearly saying the Gospel). I have held these infants in my arms a thousand times and they are all the same—fat, lifeless, wrinkled things that give one a pain in his belly looking at them.

You say that after the first and second acts of *The Silver Tassie* there is . . . nothing. Really nothing? Nothing, nothing at all? Well, where there is nothing, where there is nothing—there is God.

Turning to your advice that I should ask for the play back; that I should tell the Press that I want to revise it, and so slip aside from the admonition of the Abbey Directorate, I refer you to what I have written already to Mr. Robinson.

I shall be glad for the return of the script of the play, and a formal note of its rejection.—Best personal wishes,

S. O'Casey

St. John's Wood

To the Editor of the IRISH STATESMAN.

DEAR SIR,—The letters of Abbey Directors to Mr. Sean O'Casey and about Mr. Sean O'Casey were obviously private and should never have been published. However, *The Observer* has decided otherwise, and I prefer a complete to an incomplete publication. I send you some additional passages and letters, including Dr. Starkie's opinion, which Mr. Sean O'Casey has not yet seen.—Yours faithfully,

W. B. Yeats

82 Merrion Square, Dublin.
4 June 1928

Copy of letter from W. B. Yeats to Sean O'Casey.

DEAR O'CASEY,—I have just had your letter. I write from the Abbey. Lady Gregory, Lennox Robinson, my wife and I are here for *The Plough and the Stars*—a packed enthusiastic house. Had my admiration for your genius been less my criticism had been less severe. I think that is true of Lady Gregory and Lennox Robinson also.—Yours,

W. B. Yeats

4 May 1928

Copy of letter No. 2 from Sean O'Casey to W. B. Yeats.
Dated 11 May 1928

You seem, Mr. Yeats, to be getting beautifully worse; you astonish me more and more. There seem to be shallows in you of which no one ever dreamed.

What have packed houses, enthusiastic (cheering, says Mr. Robinson) audiences for *The Plough* got to do with your contention that *The Silver Tassie* is a bad play?

Perhaps this thought is due, as a journalist might say, to your delightful sense of Irish humour.—Farewell,

Sean O'Casey

DEAR W.B.—I have been in Spain for the past two months and when I returned I found Sean O'Casey's play waiting for me. I have read it several times very carefully, and I want to give you my opinion. In order to prepare my mind for *The Silver Tassie* I read over again the three published plays of Sean O'Casey. The present play is a new departure: it is written around a great and noble idea. In *The Plough and the Stars,* when we penetrate beneath the tragedy of Nora Clitheroe, Bessie and Fluther Good we discover that the play is a pacifist one written against war. It is the poor who really suffer and are sacrificed in war. But this moral is dramatically compelling only because we have been excited and moved by the suffering of those characters who came upon the stage and impressed their reality upon us. In *The Silver Tassie* the characters seem to come from a shadow world: they are not beings of flesh and blood. I know Bessie Burgess and Mollser and I shall always remember their faces and their actions. I do not remember the characters of *The Silver Tassie*. I feel that the author had a great idea at the back of his mind and fugitive symbols presented themselves to him, but he was not able to create, as he did before, living men and women. The play seems to me to decline act by act from the beginning. The first act is masterly because the author seemed still to be attached to the roots of his native city. I visualize the scene of that first act in Dublin. The second act struck me as resembling the dream play in Toller's *Masses and Men*. By means of original effects of production I can imagine such a scene with its weird verse-chanting making an appeal. The last acts seemed to me lacking in depth. The characters are fainter, and I feel as if the author was already tired of his creations. I feel that he has seen those hospitals of the war and has suffered, but it is all so huge that it blurs his vision. Many visions, many ideas crowd into his mind, but he is unable to make the synthesis and enclose them within the framework of drama. In spite of all this, I feel that the author is experimenting in a new world of drama; for this reason I feel strongly that the Abbey Theatre should produce the play. Sean O'Casey has given us so many fine works that we ought to leave the final decision with the audience that has laughed and wept with him. He is groping after a new drama outside the conventional stage; at any moment he may make a great discovery.—Yours sincerely,

Walter Starkie

Botanic House, Lansdowne Road, 30 April 1928

To Irish Times

9 JUNE 1928

MR. O'CASEY REPLIES TO HIS CRITICS

The controversy centring round Mr. Sean O'Casey's play, "The Silver Tassie," which was rejected by the Abbey Theatre, Dublin, was advanced a further stage yesterday when we received the following letter from Mr. O'Casey with the headline, "O'Casey and the Big Four":—

"In the *Irish Times* of the other day, Mr. Yeats, speaking of the correspondence that passed between me and the Abbey, is reported to have said—'there were a number of letters, some of which had been addressed to Mr. Robinson.' This is a mistake. I have no letter which had been addressed to Mr. Robinson. Mr. Yeats, in all fairness, must try to keep to facts. I have three letters which, in the first instance, had been addressed to Lady Gregory—one from Mr. Robinson, which contained his criticism of the play; another from Mr. Yeats, asking Lady Gregory to enclose a covering letter to me with his criticism, if she agreed with it, so as 'to soften the blow'; and the third from Yeats again, asking her to put in the form of a personal letter to me his suggestion that 'he should withdraw the play, saying to the Press that he had become dissatisfied with it.'

"Instead of doing what Yeats suggested, Lady Gregory sent the letters on to me, saying she 'felt it right you should know at once what we all feel and think, and that you would prefer this to any attempt to soften things, and that you will believe that I—and we all—feel you would rather have the exact truth than evasions.' (Bravo, Lady Gregory.) And in a subsequent letter: 'Perhaps I was wrong in sending these letters to you—I think you will say I was right—(yes; before God and man, you were right, Lady Gregory) they were the genuine opinions of us writers at the moment, whether mistaken or not, and I believe you would rather have them than a mere formal and polite "arrangement."'

"To use a parable, or an allegory, or simile, Mr. Yeats handed the stone to Lady Gregory, and said—'Go on, you fire it at him.' Instead of throwing it at me, Lady Gregory handed it to me to let me see what sort it was, and immediately, I let fly and socked Mr. Yeats right in the eye with it, and off, yelling he goes now to the Authors' Society, but I would strongly advise him to take the question to The League of Nations.

"And Mr. Yeats should not quibble about the form the rejection of the play took. He knows I was not bothering about his little printed note of refusal—he knows what I wanted was an honest, open and unequivocal rejection of the play.

"But it is very hard to fix Mr. Yeats to simple statements. Ask him about his opinions and he will say (according to the reports) 'My opinions are in the letters'; ask him about the letters and he will say: 'They should never have been published.' What he really means is that they should never have been written.

"I should like to say a word or two about Dr. Starkie's opinion of the play, but it seems impossible to fix him either. I cannot reconcile happily the statements made in the *Irish Times* with the statements made in the *Irish Independent*. Is it altogether impossible for Doctors of Literature to express their opinions in open, plain and comprehensible language? (I'm afraid he'll have to wait in the queue till I am done with Mr. Yeats.) He can go on criticising as much as he likes for the present, but one thing he must not do, and that is to furnish me with motives. He said—or is reported to have said—'Mr. O'Casey's new play was written for the purpose of showing the useless brutality of war.' Now here's a question for Dr. Starkie: Was the cartoon for the Canadian War Memorial by Augustus John drawn to show the useless brutality of war?

"In point of fact my play was written for no such definite purpose at all. If it shows the useless brutality of war that is another matter, which Dr. Starkie, as a critic, ought to know.

"Well, it's inevitable that we should have to differ from the critics, but Holy God, it's hard lines when we have to teach them.

"You know there has been quite a lot of fun in the fight, but the funniest thing of all to me is the declaration by Doctors Starkie and Yeats that O'Casey has written something abstract and elusive."

To Manchester Guardian

12 JUNE 1928

PLOUGHING THE STAR

Dear Sir,

In a sub-Leader in the "Manchester Guardian" for the 4th of June, you write about the rejection of "The Silver Tassie" by the Abbey Theatre Directorate. Now the Star has withstood the test but the Plough hasnt. Quoting Mr Yeats as saying "what business have we with anything but the unique," you go on to add—"for any director of a theatre to deliver such counsel and stand by it is itself so unique that Mr O'Casey can hardly fail to admire the rule."

Mr Yeats delivers the counsel right enough, he delivers it with all the majesty of a dramatic Zeus, but instead of standing up to it, when he isnt running away from it, he's dodging it as cleverly as possible, which is odd, which is funny, but which isnt a proper or a very unique thing to do.

Plays have been produced at the Abbey Theatre, if not under Mr Yeats's blessing, at least under the canopy of his permission, which were unique only in so far as they were commonplace, dull and ineffective. If you will send this to Mr Yeats and he needs to know I shall be happy to tell him the names of the plays I mean. And no mortal has yet ever heard of the rejection of one of the plays written by the Directors themselves, though some of them have been abstract, elusive, and almost destitute of dramatic force—his own for instance.

Now when the Star felt the Plough instead of jumping back, it swung forward and the damned thing I'm afraid has cut Mr Yeats rather badly. When his criticisms were challenged, published and answered he began running about roaring out that the whole thing should have been kept a secret, that the publication of the letters was a breach of copyright, and that he would hale me up before the Authors' Society. (by the way this is certainly a unique thing to do) Now Mr Yeats may be the personification of the Abbey Theatre but he is not that of the Drama as a whole, and the sooner he realises that the better for himself and for the Drama in Ireland.

Mr Yeats is no master of mine; he never was and never will be. As a genius—this is Mr Yeats's thought, and no new one for he mentions the name as late as the 9th of May last—he may criticise me, but he mustnt give me orders. I wouldnt dare to order him as to the shape his poetical genius should take, and whatever dramatic genius I may have will be kneaded and moulded by myself and not by him.

Sean O'Casey

To Gabriel Fallon

MS. TEXAS

ST. JOHN'S WOOD

[13? JUNE 1928]

My dear Gaby—

For the past fortnight I've been very busy attending to a few little things that need arranging each in his own little particular place, & am still engaged in the work, so your letter in which so many interesting things were said about the Silver Tassie,—that you seem to think has in it a little gold and frankincense & myrrh—must wait till we are face to face once more. I suppose you've seen the letters in The Statesman?

Red Cock has crowed at last (a fine title for a play—The Red Cock)

Last week I got a letter from Oh Y in which he asked me had I seen the Irish Times which would show that he was justified in the fear of a legal action if he printed the letters. I replied as follows:—

Now Mr. Russell, now, now don't be trying to act the bloody Gaum. Yours Sincerely S O'Casey.

In a letter to the Times & The Independent I suggested Yeats should take the question to the League of Nations.

Had a letter from PÓL UA FEARGHAIL [Paul Farrell] asking for the play—thought he'd produce it in the Queen's or The Gaiety next November. Was he born at the start in the middle or the end of November? Told him I was terribly sorry that I really couldn't give it to him.

Suppose you got my telegram. If you could send me any cutting of news—only what you really think should be answered—I shall be very much obliged. I have written a few lines about Starkie's criticism as it appears in the Statesman, but am almost convinced it is a waste of time to reply. However I suppose it will go over in the end to show that even the wooden heads of Trinity aren't impregnable. In his first mouthful he says —"To fully prepare my mind for The Silver Tassie, I sat down & read over again the three published plays of Sean O'Casey"—and I have written almost a one-act play around the statement.

I suppose the circulation of the old Statesman's gone up this week.

If you get it read AE's review of Shaw's book: and all about his (AE's) fourth dimensional conceptual conscientious sense of justice.[1]

I saw a cloud of Psyche's limbs,
Wave pearly pink where Karma swims.
I heard a roar of silent hymns
His bloody beard the poet trims.

Yrs.
Sean

[1] In the *Irish Statesman,* 9 June 1928, Y.O. [A.E.] reviewed Bernard Shaw's *The Intelligent Woman's Guide to Socialism and Capitalism* (London, Constable, 1928). He objected to Shaw's concept of social justice, which A.E. claimed is not related to "the three dimensional world of Socialism" but rather to "the fourth dimensional world" of the Karma: "I feel that the sense of this other justice is lacking in the book, that is, that [Shaw] has not allowed his spirituality, his fourth dimensional moral consciousness to dictate a sentence." It was this type of "spirituality" which inspired much of the mirth and anger that O'Casey aimed at A.E. in subsequent letters and in "Dublin's Glittering Guy," *Inishfallen, Fare Thee Well* (1949).

To Lady Londonderry [1]

MS. Lady Bury

St. John's Wood
13 June 1928

Dear Lady Londonderry,

Thanks for your kind letter. I am sorry you have hurt your hand, & hope, if it isn't well, that it is much better now. I send you the letters that have appeared in the Irish Statesman about the Abbey's refusal of "The Silver Tassie." Supplementary letters have appeared in "The Irish Times" since & more & more & more are to follow! It is my opinion that Mr. Yeats & Mr. Robinson had long ago decided, that if at all possible, O'Casey's new play should be rejected. Of course I shall be glad to see you when you come to London.

Perhaps, you would come to us here one of the days & talk and drink some tea, & talk again?

I am sending you a copy of "The Silver Tassie," which I hope you will take from me.

I have often spoken of you to Eileen, & she and I send you our Warm Regards.

Sean O'Casey

[1] Lady Londonderry (1879–1959), 7th Marquess Edith Helen Vaine-Tempest-Stewart; president of Women's Legion between two world wars; first woman J. P. of County Down, 1919; author.

To Irish Statesman [1]

TC. O'CASEY

LONDON

15 JUNE 1928

Dear Sir:

I am very sorry indeed that I have hurt the refined sentimentalities of C.W. Allen [2] by neglecting to use the lavender (not all lavender either) language of the 18th and 19th centuries, and that I did not for his sake or her sake, frill out my thoughts into gentler statements.

But someone (I cant remember his name at the moment) reputed to be one of the most refined and gentlest of men, said to a companion (I cant remember his name at the moment) who could on occasions, curse and swear like a bearded pard, I will give unto thee the keys of the kingdom of heaven, an important gift to one who was evidently a bit of a cave-man.

What I should have done, I suppose, to avoid hurting the feelings of the Nancy Boys of Literature, was to throw away even the rapier, and brain the other Protagonists (if I have made a naughty-meaning improper-use of the learned word, Allen is to blame, for he has shown me how to use it this way) in the dispute with a lady's fan.

Yours sincerely,
[*Sean O'Casey*]

[1] This letter was refused publication by the editor, A.E.

[2] A letter by C. W. Allen appeared in the *Irish Statesman,* 16 June 1928, in which he objected to the "ill-temper and discourtesy" of literary men in the recent controversy over *The Silver Tassie.* He was disturbed that "these men of letters should not only fight with rapiers but resort to even more primitive weapons. The spectacle is not edifying." O'Casey's letter was apparently written a day before the publication date, but this seeming contradiction is explained by the usual practice of distributing magazines several days before the publication date.

From Charlotte F. Shaw

MS. O'CASEY

PASSFIELD CORNER,
LIPHOOK,
HANTS.
17 JUNE 1928

Dear Mr. O'Casey

G.B.S. & I have read The Silver Tassie with *deep interest*. We are both greatly impressed by it—I am most enthusiastic!—& we want to have a chat with you about it, & the whole business.

Could you, & Mrs. O'Casey, come & have luncheon with us at Whitehall Court on Thursday next, the 21st, at 1.30? Do if you possibly can. We would be alone so that we might talk freely (about our friends?!—*no*—about the play!)

Our flat is 130, & you come to Block 4 of the building & the Porter will send you up to us in the Lift.

Hoping to see you both on Thursday.

Yours Sincerely
C. F. Shaw
(Mrs. Bernard Shaw)

We are staying down here with the Sidney Webbs until Wednesday—so please write here.

To Irish Statesman [1]

TC. O'CASEY

[? JUNE 1928]

In the "Irish Statesman" of June the ninth, there is a criticism by Dr. Starkie of "The Silver Tassie", which I had not, as Mr. Yeats says, seen before. Dr. Starkie found the play waiting for him when he returned from Spain. (Curious that Dr. Yeats found the play waiting for him when he returned from Italy, and Dr. Starkie found the play waiting for him when he returned from Spain.) Now I have also read the opinions of Dr. Starkie printed in "The Independent" and in the "Irish Times". The criticism in the "Statesman" and the opinions in the other two Journals pre-

[1] This letter was refused publication by the *Irish Statesman*, and a shorter version of it was rejected by the *Irish Times*.

sent themselves to me as badly dove-tailed contradictions. He seems to think little of the play in the "Statesman", a little more of it in the "Independent", and a great deal more of it in the "Times." However we'll strip these to their funny nakedness a little later on.

Dr. Starkie found "The Silver Tassie" waiting for him when he came back from Spain, and he decided that the play would have to wait a little longer, for he wasnt quite ready for it. He says himself that in order to prepare his mind for "The Silver Tassie", he "read over again the three published plays of Sean O'Casey." He sat down, Dr. Starkie sat down and read over again the three published plays in order to prepare his mind for "The Silver Tassie." And Starkie calls himself a critic, and is a Director on the Board of Ireland's National Theatre. The Critic and the Director sat down and read over again three old plays in order to prepare his mind for a new one. There it was, "The Silver Tassie", in its envelope, sent by Mr. Yeats or by Mr. Robinson, waiting for him when he came home from Spain, but he wouldnt touch it because he had to prepare his mind for the new play. So he read "The Gunman" and he read "Juno" and he read "The Plough", because he had to prepare his mind for "The Silver Tassie." When he came home from Spain and saw the play waiting for him he said:

I must read this play very carefully,
I must assimilate this play very fully,
I must understand this play very thoroughly,

and to do this I must read, not this new play but three old ones. So he took down "The Gunman" and he read that; but he wasnt fully prepared, so he took down "Juno" and he read that; but still he found that his mind wasnt fully prepared, and so he took down and read all over again "The Plough and the Stars," so that his mind might be fully prepared for "The Silver Tassie." And Dr. Starkie calls himself a Critic, and the Free State Government has appointed him as a Director on the Board of Ireland's National Theatre.

What is one to think of a Critic and a Director who thinks that the best way to prepare his mind for a new play is to read over again three other old ones!

But having prepared his mind for "The Silver Tassie" by reading over again the three other plays, he at last sat down and he read the New Play. And what does he find? (His own words) A new departure; a new art; a new technique.

And having discovered this new departure, this new art, this new technique in the new play he proceeds to criticise all these by the old manner, the old art and the old technique of the old plays. And this is a Critic and a Director of Ireland's National Theatre. Dont forget now, when Dr. Starkie wanted to understand a new idea, he saturated his mind with a lot of old ones.

And the old plays gave Dr. Starkie food for thought about the new one. He began to think, and when Dr. Starkie begins to think, things happen; so he thought and thought till his mind was drunk with vivid comprehension. I heard the roar and whirl of his mind over here, so I decided to fly across and have a head to head talk with Dr. Starkie, and here it is:

Dr. Starkie: I've read your play.

O'Casey: Yes?

Starkie: It was waiting for me when I came home from Spain; there's not a hell of a lot in it, you know. I agree generally with Mr. Yeats and Mr. Robinson.

O'Casey: Yes?

Starkie: The characters in the play seem to be fugitive symbols.

O'Casey: Yes?

Starkie: God damn it man, will you try to say something besides yes, yes, yes!

O'Casey: How did I need any helping hand from the Abbey in my attempt to achieve a new technique that I was groping after, as you have said, if the new technique in the play was touched with genius and stood out above all, as you have said as well?

Starkie: I read your three old plays before I read your new one.

O'Casey: You said "The Silver Tassie" has not the motion, the reality and the excitement of the other plays. Will you tell us how a work that is a new departure, a new idea and a new technique touched with genius and standing out above all, could have the same emotion, reality and excitement as the old plays?

Starkie: At any moment you may make a great discovery.

O'Casey: Dont you think that if I have created a new art and a new technique touched with genius and standing out above all, that the discovery is already made?

Starkie: You know it is the poor who really suffer and are sacrificed in war.

O'Casey: Dr. Starkie, Dr. Starkie, you have made a great discovery.

Starkie: Yes, isnt it—I get those flashes sometimes.

O'Casey: In your criticism of "The Silver Tassie" you have really stated two different things: when you talk about the technique and the new idea as being touched with genius and standing out above all, you seem to say that the Drama must not stand still; when you say that the play hasnt the reality and emotion of the other plays, and so ask for "more of the same again", you seem to say the Drama must stand still. Now tell me do you know your right hand from your left hand?

Starkie:I feel uncomfortable. I shall always remember the faces of Mollser and of Bessie Burgess.

O'Casey: Must the reality and emotion of Drama be co-equal—as they

arent in music or painting—at every time and in every place? Is even the reality of the musing of Falstaff exactly similar to the reality of the musing of Lord and Lady Macbeth?
Starkie: Ah, I have you there! There isnt any doubt that Lear and Hamlet educated Shakespeare.
O'Casey: Dr. Starkie, I have made a great discovery.
Starkie: That's interesting; what is it?
O'Casey: That, taking things all round, Dr. Starkie is a bit of a cod.

"The Irish Statesman"

To the Editor:

Dear Sir—Above is a reply to the criticism of Dr. Starkie about "The Silver Tassie" that appeared in the "Irish Statesman." If you will not publish it, be kind enough to return to

Sean O'Casey

From Bernard Shaw

MS. O'Casey[1]

(4 Whitehall Court SW.1)
Passfield Corner
19 June 1928

My dear Sean

What a hell of a play! I wonder how it will hit the public.

Of course the Abbey should have produced it—as Starkie rightly says—whether it liked it or not. But the people who knew your uncle when you were a child (so to speak) always want to correct your exercises; and this was what disabled the usually competent W.B.Y. and Lady Gregory.

Still, it is surprising that they fired so very wide considering their marksmanship. A good realistic first act, like Juno, an incongruously phantasmic second act, trailing off into a vague and unreal sequel: could anything be wronger? What *I* see is a deliberately unrealistic phantasmopoetic first act, intensifying in exactly the same mode into a climax of war imagery in the second act, and then two acts of almost unbearable realism bringing down all the Voodoo war poetry with an ironic crash to

[1] O'Casey printed a shortened version of this letter in "The Silver Tassie," *Rose and Crown* (London, Macmillan, 1952).

earth in ruins. There is certainly no falling-off or loss of grip: the hitting gets harder and harder right through to the end.

Now if Yeats had said "It's too savage: I can't stand it" he would have been in order. You really are a ruthless ironfisted blaster and blighter of your species; and in this play there is none righteous—no, not one. Your moral is always that the Irish ought not to exist; and you are suspected of opining, like Shakespear, that the human race ought not to exist—unless, indeed, you like them like that, which you can hardly expect Lady Gregory, with her kindness for Kiltartan, to do. Yeats himself, with all his extraordinary cleverness and subtlety, which comes out just when you give him up as a hopeless fool and (in this case) deserts him when you expect him to be equal to the occasion, is not a man of this world; and when you hurl an enormous smashing chunk of it at him he dodges it, small blame to him.

However, we can talk about it when we meet, which I understand is to be on Thursday next week. This is only to prepare you for my attitude. Until then.

Cheerio, Titan,
G. Bernard Shaw

From Bernard Shaw to Lady Gregory

PS. Lady Gregory [1]

[?] June 1928

Why do you and W.B.Y. treat O'Casey as a baby? Starkie was right, you should have done the play anyhow. Sean is now *hors concours*. It is literally a hell of a play; but it will clearly force its way on to the stage and Yeats should have submitted to it as a calamity imposed on him by the Act of God, if he could not welcome it as another *Juno*. Besides, he was extraordinarily wrong about it on the facts. The first act is not a bit realistic; it is deliberately fantastic chanted poetry. This is intensified to a climax into the second act. Then comes a ruthless return for the last two acts to give the fiercest ironic realism. But that is so like Yeats. Give him a job with which you feel sure he will play Bunthorne and he will astonish you with his unique cleverness and subtlety. Give him one that any second-rater could manage with credit and as likely as not he will make an appalling mess of it. He has certainly fallen in up to the

[1] From a copy made by Lady Gregory and printed in *Lady Gregory's Journals, 1916–1930* (1946), ed. Lennox Robinson, pp. 110–111.

neck over O'C. But this is not a very nice letter, is it? Consequently the very last letter I want to send you. So I will stop before I become intolerable.

G.B.S.

To Gabriel Fallon

MS. TEXAS

21 JUNE 1928

Dear Gaby—

How are you, how are you–very well, how is yourself?

> 45, Fitzwilliam Sqr. 12.6.28
>
> Chara—I have read your reference to my play 'The Passing' in a letter to Lennox Robinson (it was to Lady G. but that doesn't matter) in the Irish Statesman. What has happened young Sean? (oh, the joy of life!) Has England done this to you? (I am going to join the Conservative Party—God Save the King!) Have you really gone & got a swelled head?
>
> Kenneth Sarr
>
> (Mechanical whistle) [1]

Got a letter from Mrs. Carey [2] saying she was in London (she is) & asking me could I see Her—just for a moment, & if I couldn't (I couldn't) she would come to 'pay her respects to my little, little lovely little wife'. Oh, be God! But the little wife didn't want to be troubled either. Mrs. Carey said she was sure that Yeats & I and Robinson really misunderstood each other. Told her I was equally sure we understood each other now, so what's the use o' worrying! You rogue, you want to lead me now into a dispute with yourself! The sword of the Lord & of Gideon! Well, we are laying up for ourselves a lot of treasures for future discussion in some happy day to come.

And why don't you write something yourself for publication? Who

[1] O'Casey added all the comments in parentheses in this copy of a letter he had received from the Abbey playwright, Kenneth Sarr (District Justice Kenneth Reddin). For the reference to *The Passing* which provoked Sarr's letter, see "The Abbey Directors and Mr. Sean O'Casey," *Irish Statesman*, 9 June 1928, printed above, the letter from O'Casey to Lady Gregory (n.d.), where he points out ironically that Lennox Robinson was one of the judges who awarded the Tailteann Games first prize for drama in 1924 to Sarr's undistinguished one-act tragedy, *The Passing*.

[2] Mrs. May Carey, a Dublin actress who played small parts at the Abbey and Gate Theatres, and directed her own amateur productions.

is he that can write letters as you write them? (I'm not saying now as I agree with everything you say) Why not a book about O'Casey as you know him, & his plays as no one else knows them? I'd rather you'd create something for the talent's there, right enough, but even the work suggested would be something.

I've all your letters about "The Silver Tassie", & you could have them back on loan. Macmillan's might be got to publish it, & it might be the first step away from 26 x 2 = 52.

Yes, I've read the criticism of the geni of The Irish Times who says the second act is realism, that recovery from "religious mania" is a "moral collapse" & that poor Jessie's a "flashy kind of a girl". Oh, what can Dramatists do against the stupidity of CRITICS!

I enclose a letter from Shaw. I sent him the book which I promised long ago, didn't ask his opinion & told him nothing about the row. Got a letter too from Lady Londonderry who says she remembers me telling her long ago that the Abbey wouldn't like the play, which I had forgotten. So the feeling must have been deeply felt when I told it to her, though I like her immensely &, of course, that is why I involuntarily told her the thoughts that were "simmering at the back of my mind".

Yes, I can guess the thoughts at the back of the minds of those that want to produce "The Silver Tassie". "Have *you* got me, Mr. Davoren?"

A comment on the row appeared in THE NATION, & I have sent a brief reply part of which asks the writer to ask Mr. Yeats why the mystery surrounding identity of the author of "Mr. Murphy's Island"; is the author ashamed or proud of the play; & does it hold aloft the "banner of the unique".[3]

Righto, I'll send on the reviews of the play—I imagine they'll hardly know what to say.

Warm Regards to Lyle. Love to you, Rose & the child—all well here. Billy's back here again—his little girl's got the measles so he hurried home to get into everybody's way.

Is Robbie gone to America?

Sean

[3] O'Casey had heard rumors that Mrs. George Yeats was the mysterious author of *Mr. Murphy's Island,* a Black and Tan comedy by "Elizabeth Harte." See O'Casey's letter to Fallon, 4 September 1926, note 1.

To Irish Times [1]

21 June 1928

MR. SEAN O'CASEY'S "LAST WORD." "CROSSING THE BRIDGE."

Mr. Sean O'Casey apparently has said his last word in "The Silver Tassie" controversy, which arose as the result of the rejection of that play by the directors of the Abbey Theatre, Dublin. In a statement received last night by the *Irish Times,* Mr. O'Casey, under the heading of "Tying Things Together," writes:—

"Since Mr. Yeats seems determined to say no more, and has elected to challenge my criticism of his rejection of "The Silver Tassie," by making it a question of law and order, there is little more to be said by me. His contention that to write about war one must be cradled in a cannon, is ridiculous; his statement that a playwright must have no opinions when writing a play is ridiculous, for that would overthrow even Euripides; his zeal for the absolute necessity for what he called a predominant character in a play is, in modern drama, ridiculous; his cute contention that I was out of touch with my environment, and had lost my material, is ridiculous too.

I am now two years in London; the new play was thought out and started more than eighteen months ago, and to toss away in six months the material of a lifetime is more than even Mr. Yeats himself could do. His resolve that nothing but the unique can strut on the Abbey stage is ridiculous, when we remember some of the plays performed there, a few of them written by those with plumes wild on the wind in their hats.

When I lived in Chelsea Mr. Robinson came to me there, kind and eager and anxious to make certain of my promise to give my next play to the Abbey. Dr. Yeats came to me in the Court Theatre in London, kind and eager and anxious to make certain of my promise to give the next play to the Abbey; and it is strange that it should be these two that seem to have been most eager and most anxious to reject the play they were so anxious to secure.

Mr. Yeats asked me then (in the Court Theatre) if the new play was following the lines of the old ones, and he was told that it would be entirely different; he was told the second act was an impression of the great war, and that the play would be written in a new manner. But he sat dumb and opened not his mouth.

During his stay in London he spoke at a reception given in his honour before—if I remember rightly—the Irish Literary Society. He mentioned enthusiastically the receipt of a play (I write from memory)

[1] A copy of this letter appeared on the same day in the *Irish Independent.*

from a young dramatist which contained the promise of a new idea in Irish drama. The first act showed a group of young men making bombs in an underground room or cellar. They had been confined to this room and to this work for a long time, and the act was an expressionistic effort to show the psychological reaction of these young men to their peculiar circumstances.

Here Mr. Yeats praised in one play what he condemned in another. And Mr. Yeats went on to say—I quote from memory—that this act foreshowed a new direction in Irish drama; that O'Casey had built the bridge across which the coming Irish dramatists would pass to a new technique and a new art.

And Mr. Yeats has seemingly waxed faint and furious to find that the first Irish dramatist to cross was the dramatist that built the bridge himself.

Mr. Yeats has evidently decided to stay in his room with the blinds down. Like Aeschylus who is said to have liked to open a play with an awful silence, so Mr. Yeats likes to close a discussion with an awful silence. He is apparently determined to be interested in, to speak to and to dispute with only those who are content to be so many coloured buttons on his dinner jacket.

Mr. Yeats himself has fixed my kinship with Swift, and taking things all round, I imagine that I have done him proud. I feel that the rejection of the play has done more harm to the Abbey than it has done to me, and it would be unhuman of me to say that I was sorry for that. So for the present, good-bye all, and cheerio."

To Lady Gregory

TS. GREGORY

ST. JOHN'S WOOD
21 JUNE 1928

Dear Lady Gregory—

I have received a letter from Mr [John] Perrin enclosing agreement for 'The Plough and the Stars', accompanied by a cheque for four guineas as advance royalties on the play as per paragraph 4.

No agreement has ever been signed by me for this play, and never yet have I received for any play the advance royalties as sent to me now by Mr Perrin.

The only inference I can draw is that Mr Robinson (the cheque is signed by him) thinks that at the last moment I may stop the production of the Plough and so cause inconvenience to the Abbey Theatre.

I wonder would you be good enough to tell Mr Robinson that I dont do this sort of thing.

Warm Regards,
Sean O'Casey

From Lady Gregory

PS. *Modern Drama* [1]

KILMACURRAGH, KILBRIDE, CO. WICKLOW
23 JUNE 1928

Dear Sean—

Your letter has come to me here, where I am staying (with Mrs. Phillimore [2] who has been asking for you—You may remember we had tea with her after you had received that prize [3]) till Monday when I return to Coole—I had not heard anything about the letter of Perrins—it had not come into my thoughts that you would stop the Plough—it would have punished many who don't deserve such disappointment—and wd. have been a grief to me whether or not I deserve it—I will give L. R. your message—

I had meant to write anyhow, to tell you how much your letters—the parts of them that I read—were appreciated at last Sundays meeting—yours and De Valeras—the only ones I read—The pictures looked very well indeed—those that were thrown on the screen—The best point—at least the most applauded, was made by Farren—who said "We don't want to meddle with the 39 articles in England—but we do with the 39 pictures"—

The enquiry at the Town Hall seemed to go well also—and I may go home with my mind easier on that matter than it has been for a long time—

affectionately
A Gregory

[1] From a copy made by A. C. Edwards and printed in *Modern Drama*, May 1965.

[2] Mrs. Robert Phillimore, author of a book on the Gospels.

[3] The Hawthornden Prize for 1926, for *Juno and the Paycock*.

To Nation and Athenaeum

23 JUNE 1928

O'CASEY AND THE ABBEY THEATRE

SIR,—In a comment upon the dispute between Sean O'Casey and the Abbey Theatre which appeared in THE NATION of June 16th, the writer [1] exultingly slaps up the Abbey Theatre's majestic indifference to box office receipts, and the splendid way in which the Abbey Directorate "stoutly uphold the banner of the ideal and the unique."

He can take it from me that the Abbey Theatre is as fond of a "full house" as any theatre in London.

And has the writer of the comment seen every play that has been produced for the last few years at the Abbey Theatre? And, if he has not, why does he make a statement impregnable simply because it has been made by Mr. Yeats? The pole has been held aloft, right enough, but the banner has been very often flying at half-mast. Will the writer of the comment ask Mr. Yeats why there is a mystery surrounding the name of the writer of "Mr. Murphy's Island"; will he ask Mr. Yeats whether the author is ashamed or proud of the play, or whether it holds up to the heavens the banner of the unique and the ideal?

And if the writer of the comment knew what he was talking about, he would know that the play was not "resolutely turned down," and that the shiftiness of the whole proceeding was one of the factors that gave the author cause for complaint.

Your commentator's talk about the "paternal tone" and the "fostering care" of Mr. Yeats is drivel. The Abbey Theatre is not an orphanage for dramatists. And it may conceivably happen that, in some things, the son may know a little more than the father. A stupid thing said by Mr. Yeats (his contention that to write of war one must be cradled in a cannon is obviously stupid) does not become by a miracle a wise thing, and Mr. Yeats must be told this, and, if he be a sensible man, it will do him a lot of good.

So please publish this in your valuable journal, for "fiat justitia, ruat coelum," which is Gaelic, I think, for "if you share out justice, share it out all round."—Yours, &c.,

Sean O'Casey

[1] "Kappa" in his regular column, "Life and Politics."

To The Observer

24 JUNE 1928

SIR BARRY JACKSON [1]

Dear Sir,

Surely Mr. H. M. Harwood ought to know that Mr. St. John Ervine's criticism of the trade in the theatre can have no association whatever with Sir Barry Jackson, and that anyone with even an elementary love of drama takes Barry Jackson simply for what he is. Barry Jackson's cultured love of the drama does not save the merchants—it damns them.

Yours,

Sean O'Casey

[1] A reply to H. M. Harwood's letter, "Business in the Theatre," *Observer*, 17 June 1928, in which Harwood refers to St. John Ervine's article, "At the Play—Sloppy Speech," *Observer*, 10 June 1928.

To Daniel Macmillan

MS. MACMILLAN LONDON

ST. JOHN'S WOOD
[29? JUNE 1928]

Dear Sir,

Thanks for your cheque of £100—I assure you that there is plenty of room for it.

I enclose a copy of a letter from G. B. Shaw which may interest you.[1]

I intend to ask Mr. Shaw if I may make use of a part or the whole of the letter, which, I think, would look well—splendid in fact—on the jacket of the book. I will let you know when I speak or write to G.B.S.

Yrs,

Sean O'Casey

[1] See Shaw's letter to O'Casey, 19 June 1928.

To Bernard Shaw [1]

TS. O'CASEY [2]

29 JUNE 1928

Dear G B S—

May I send to Macmillans the following portions of your letter to me about the Silver Tassie?

> 'What a hell of a play! . . . a deliberately unrealistic phantasmo-poetic first act, intensifying in exactly the same mode into a climax of war imagery in the second act, and then two acts of almost unbearable realism bringing down all the voodoo war poetry with an ironic crash to earth in ruins . . . there is no falling off, or loss of grip—the hitting gets harder and harder right through to the end.'

When I got the quires of criticism from the Abbey, I galloped off to Macmillans and told them they could withdraw the book if they thought the criticisms more important, and though they held on to the book, I feel they got a shock, so when your letter came I sent it on to cheer them up, and they have asked me to seek your permission to print some passages.

Besides, as far as I can see at the moment, the coming year must be financially filled up with whatever the sale of the book may bring in and any help in this way is a gift from God.

I confirm my assurance that I have no vindictive feeling to the Abbey —I refused four offers to have the play produced in Dublin—and that I should be glad to have The Silver Tassie performed there subject to conditions mentioned which, I think, are fair and just under all the circumstances.

Warm Regards to you and to Mrs Shaw.

Sean O'Casey

[1] George Bernard Shaw (1856–1950), Irish dramatist and man of letters.

[2] Shaw replied on the back of this letter on 3 July 1928, giving permission to quote from his letter, telling O'Casey that Lady Gregory was really on his side in the controversy, and warning him that "Playwriting is a desperate trade"—"Your wife must support you (what is she for?), and when she is out of work you must go into debt, and borrow, and pawn and so on—the usual routine. Such is life."

From Lady Gregory

PS. MODERN DRAMA [1]

COOLE PARK, GORT, CO. GALWAY
SUNDAY, 1 JULY 1928

Dear Sean—

The Silver Tassie arrived yesterday afternoon—I thank you very gratefully for it—the Plough and Juno looked lonely in their shelf without it—I felt a little sad as I touched them—how the three together witness to an unbroken friendship that I value—And you are right to put 'Pride' where I put 'Humility—' for I am a life in the ebb—you a full life on the flow—that with wife and son and home (tho' I hope one day this may be an Irish one) should be and I trust will be a happy one to the end—

I enclose a cutting—you may have seen it—giving Jim Larkins views—one can't but sympathize with his anger about the banning of the poem—I am sorry I was not at that later enquiry, I should have liked to speak to him—tho' what can one do?

In church this morning, during the sermon an idea came to me very strongly that Christ Church Cathedral ought to be sold for a large sum—half a million say—it might be a whole million with U.S.A. help—to the R. C. and that money given straight to the building of houses for the labourers and the poor—I suppose I should be excommunicated if I suggested this—but Ireland will never be a Protestant country (in the religious sense tho' I hope we'll protest against wrong and injustice when we can—) I went to an afternoon Sunday service at Christ Church a few months ago—Beautiful music—beautiful singing—a long procession of choir boys and men, and clergy 30 odd—So far as I could count the congregation was one or two *under* this number. The verger had pounced on me as a prize, and wanted to show me (as if I didn't know it) Strongbows tomb—Even without the streets of houses—miles long—with little gardens, for the workers—as in American cities—Philadelphia for instance—the gathering for prayer or the Mass in so beautiful a building would surely lift the spirit heavenwards—

But this has nothing to do with our poor 100,000 or so for the Gallery—And that also will be a place of rest and beauty for the poor.

I didn't mean to go into this when I began writing—Some day I hope you will be here again. I don't believe you are as yet as wise in woodcraft as Finn—who timed his rising at the moment when he could tell the leaves of the ash from the leaves of the oak.

My grandchildren are not yet home, I am quite alone—but find

[1] From a copy made by A. C. Edwards and printed in *Modern Drama,* May 1965.

plenty of work to do. And though July has opened with floods of rain I can watch the grass growing from the windows—and think of my seedlings in the garden—

Many thanks again, and all good wishes to you and yours from yr affectionate

A Gregory

To Irish News, *Belfast*[1]

TC. O'CASEY

4 JULY 1928

'Desmond' and the Silver Tassie.

In the course of a long, long criticism of "The Silver Tassie," written by 'Desmond' in "The Irish News" of the 23rd of June, there are a number of statements that may be left to darkness and to Desmond.

But there is one that calls for a song, and it is this: "Bernard Shaw would never have put his name to 'The Silver Tassie'."

Now I would say that he might. There's a hell of a lot of the giddy kid in G B Shaw yet, and one never knows what a giddy kid may suddenly do. . . . Ah, there's the postman knocking. A letter for me, Eileen? Yes, that's right—it does look very like Shaw's writing. Be God, it is from Shaw—and about the "Silver Tassie," too! Go on, read away:

> "What a hell of play! A deliberately unrealistic, phantasmo-poetic first act intensifying in exactly the same mode into a climax of war imagery in the second act, and then two acts of almost unbearable realism bringing down all the voodoo war poetry with an ironic crash to earth in ruins . . . there is no falling off or loss of grip—the hitting gets harder and harder right through to the end."
>
> G. Bernard Shaw.

And there I'll leave you Desmond, peeping at the world beneath the legs of Shaw.

[1] This letter was refused publication by the editor. On 7 July, the *Irish News*, a Roman Catholic and Nationalist newspaper in Northern Ireland, gave the following explanation for its refusal to print O'Casey's letter: "We have received an epistle from Mr. Sean O'Casey. He begs that we will 'be good enough to publish the same unannulled and unamended in the *Irish News.*' With regret we find ourselves unable to do so. Mr. O'Casey as a correspondent is hardly less particular in his choice of words than he is as a dramatist in some of the passages in 'The Silver Tassie,' which was recently reviewed by 'Desmond' in our columns."

THE EDITOR, "THE IRISH NEWS."
Dear Sir:

The above will explain itself, and I beg that you will be good enough to publish the same unannulled and unamended in "The Irish News."

Sean O'Casey

London,
4 July 1928

To Daniel Macmillan

MS. MACMILLAN LONDON

ST. JOHN'S WOOD
4 JULY 1928

Dear Sir,

Mr. G. B. Shaw has written to me saying that you can have permission to quote "passage enclosed." [1]

I would like you if possible to print the quotation on the jacket of the book.

I understand that the Abbey Theatre think now a mistake has been made, & possibly negociations may be shortly commenced for the production of the play there (This is private for the present).[2]

Yours sincerely,
Sean O'Casey

[1] See O'Casey's letter to Shaw, 29 June 1928, for the passage he had in mind.

[2] Unfortunately nothing came of this private rumor. Apparently O'Casey was willing to give the Abbey directors a second chance, but they refused to take it.

To Bernard Shaw [1]

MS. O'CASEY

[5? JULY 1928]

Dear G.B.S.

I don't see how I can save myself from imposing conditions. The whole affair has been carried out in a cloud of conceits: I am human &

[1] Rough draft of a reply to Shaw's letter of 3 July.

can't release suspicion from my mind. I know so much about the ways of the Abbey Theatre.

I'm sure the play was rejected before it was sent in. The mode & manner was no surprise to Yeats, for when he came to London he came to me to make sure the play would be offered to the Abbey, he was told of the new manner & method of the play—that it concerned itself with the G.W. [Great War] & he made no remark of remonstrance.

The first evasion was in Robinson's acknowledgment of the receipt of the play when he said "I will read it as soon as possible. Very busy now with a new Murray (play) & a Borkman production". Though I knew he had read it, & could hardly read it quick enough.

The second was Yeats' statement in his letter to me saying [that he dictated his letter before "I opened the letters of the other directors"], which is countered by a statement in a letter from L.G. saying "that she couldn't remember writing this letter" (though she recorded in her diary that she agreed with L.R.'s opinion).

The third was (date?) an answer from R. to a letter from me suggesting a Caste saying that he would pay attention to it; he was sending in the play to Yeats & was off in a hurry on a holiday.

The fourth was the effort made to get Lady Gregory's friendship for me to make (not for me) the rejection as easy as possible for them!

The fifth: was the determination to prevent the publication of the letters shown by AE writing & wiring to me to show his fright over the possibility of an action for breach of [copyright] against him by Yeats, & the only way I could reply to the stirring of his fourth dimensional conscience was to write saying, No AE, "don't be trying to act the bloody Gaum!"

The sixth was the concealment from me of the one criticism (Dr. Starkie's) that was in any way favourable to me, & which possibly never would have been known if he hadnt rounded on his fellow-Directors in an interview with the Press.

How do I know these things! Ah! how did I know that Yeats was coming to London, & coming to see you before he stepped on the ship in Dublin Bay.

They have turned a Playhouse into a silly little temple, darkened with figures past vitality, giving vision only to see coloured-windows of Yeats, L.G., Synge, L. Robinson, and out [of] this temple what are called Abbey Dramatists step cautiously to play their little tunes of adoration on the little organ.

From Charlotte Shaw to Eileen O'Casey

MS. O'Casey

Ayot St. Lawrence
8 July 1928

Dear Mrs. O'Casey

I am so *very* sorry, but I fear we cant go & see you now because we are just starting off abroad for a holiday & have got so terribly tied up with all the silly odds & ends we have to get done before we go. We have taken our sleepers for Sunday, & are going to be down here until Thursday afternoon. Then there will be an orgie of business & packing!

I am the more sorry for this as I do feel "Sean" wants a lot of looking after just now. He is going to be very naughty & fierce & resentful—& he is a terribly hard hitter!

That idea of letting G.B.S. see his letters to his 'friends' is a grand one. Do keep him up to it. Any letters addressed to 4 Whitehall Court will be forwarded *at once,* & I will send you our address the moment we are settled, & he must write about all he is doing, & G.B.S. will answer *quickly,* & try to act as a lightning conductor!

Directly we come back we will go & lunch with you, & see Brian, if you will ask us again.

Our very kindest & most friendly thoughts to you both.

Yours sincerely
C. F. Shaw

Mr. Yeats didn't come & see us about the play, but about the Irish Literary Academy they are trying to get up. He never mentioned The Silver Tassie. It was *I* who insisted upon talking about it—& he was rather self conscious & reluctant!

From the Lord Chamberlain to C. B. Cochran

TS. O'Casey

Lord Chamberlain's Office
St. James's Palace, S.W.1.
[? July 1928]

Dear Mr. Cochran,

The following are the passages in the "Silver Tassie" which the Lord Chamberlain would like omitted or modified:—

Act I,	page 16	"God Almighty"
"	" 17	"My God Almighty"
"	" 27	"arse"
"	" 28	"We'll rape her"
"	" 29	"Christ"
"	" 31	"Jesus"
Act II	" 3	"Pissing" and "God damn"
"	" 10	"rustle a Judy"
"	" 15	"Does he whore well?" and the following line.
"	" 16	"Holy Christ"
"	" 18	"How do you do to God"
"	" 21	"every bitch's son"
Act III	" 17	"Christ Almighty"
Act IV	" 7	"Goddam"
"	" 9	"Holy God"
"	" 22	"Hurt her breast pulling your hand quick out of her bodice did you?"
"	" 23	"Peering pimp".

Yours sincerely,
(Signed) *C. L. Gordon*

To Gabriel Fallon

MS. TEXAS

ST. JOHN'S WOOD
14 JULY 1928

Dear Gaby—

Here are a couple additional reviews of the play. Read that out of 'The Munster Advocate'. Let me have back the one from the Dundee Evening Telegraph.

Haven't heard a whisper from the Abbey yet. Did you go to see 'The Rale McCoy?' [1]

How's Will?

Here is as it is at present about the possible London production of "The Tassie" (For your own private ear only).

Billy [McElroy] wants to back the play: promised me he'd ask no

[1] J. J. MacKeown's *The Real McCoy* opened at the Olympia Theatre, Dublin, on 25 June 1928, performed by Arthur Sinclair and Maire O'Neill's Irish Players.

one in his business for part of the Funds: got all, or almost all the money from business connections: I refused to let him go on. Cochrane came back from America & sent for Billy about the play: Billy told him how things were: I had a suspicion that Cochrane wanted to back out of the affair because of the Abbey criticisms—which I showed him when they were received—I was badly mistaken: he's more enthusiastic than ever: says the play must be produced: So he & I & Billy are to meet in a week's time & have a final talk. Cochrane spoke again about you, & should things come off, we shall probably call for your services. We're thinking of getting Ernest Thesigur to play the parts of Sylvester & of 'The Visitor'. If these enquiries & examinations end in a decision for production here, the play will probably go to Dublin, & so the Abbey may be cut out of a first production.

G.B.S. & Mrs Shaw are very anxious that the tiff with the Abbey should cease; & want me not to be fierce, angry & resentful, which will be as God may decide.

Barry Jackson read the play; says it's 'one of the greatest of Post-War Plays' & hesitates to produce it. 'Keeping it in his mind' he says, & is—like Will—anxious about deciding to accept, & anxious about deciding to refuse.

And I'm leaving him that way: leaving him to think it out for himself & going on in my own way.

Another offer from another producer is to be made to me in a week's time. Well, let the offer come & we'll think it over.

Be God, that's good news about T.C.D.M.[2] At the present time the Abbey couldn't select a greater or a more happy choice as a Director than T.C.M. Yours

(Love to all) *Sean*

[2] O'Casey's joke about the Irish playwright, T. C. Murray, and T.C.D., Trinity College, Dublin. Murray did not become a director of the Abbey.

To Gabriel Fallon

MS. Texas

St. John's Wood

17 July 1928

Dear Gaby—

On Friday I go to the Lord Chamberlain's Office, St James's Palace, (The Censor) to get the licence for the play.

He has passed all but a few words & phrases, & I will press for the retention of only two—the rest are unimportant.

Could you let me know—How long you could stop here during rehearsals, & When.

(I don't exactly know when the play will be performed—if scheme with Cochrane goes through, which I'm almost certain will—perhaps in late September, more probably in October) Would the latter time suit you equally?

Of course, if you come over you'll stop with us.

And, apart from your expenses, what fee would you be asking?

I imagine the main parts of the Caste will be filled by English Players for I am convinced The Irish Players couldn't do this play.

I should like you to join us, if you can with safety to yourself; the experience might possibly open out a new—and a better in my opinion—life to you.

Love to Rose & to Francis & to you.

Sean

Postum Scripta Abbeyarius: no word yet.
Verba Verum Seaniensis: Dont care a damn.

To Gabriel Fallon

MS. Texas

St. John's Wood
28 July 1928

Dear Gaby—

Have sent out inquiries about 'The Vice' & 'The Tragic Women,' & as soon as I get news of them, I ['ll] transmit it on to you. The Lord Chamberlain has passed the play, with a few omissions, & one or two modifications. The two words you liked have had to pack up & go.

I think I shall know next week definitely if Cochrane decides to go on. The fee I should say you should ask for would be for the 3 weeks £50 inclusive, or if you think this wouldn't be enough, ask for more: you can always come down, never go up. I don't like to talk in this final way till everything's settled, but I'm almost certain the arrangement will be finally sealed soon. I, of course, will think of your suggestion about Miss [May] Craig & H[ugh] Nagle—I have jotted down their names on the Caste draft. By the way could you suggest anyone that might be able to play the part of 'Fluther' for a tour in the provinces Billy is thinking of during the coming Autumn? We have to do without Sinclair (thanks be to God) & could get along if we could find a man to fit the part of Fluther. For "The Tassie" I want to get as far away from the Irish Players as possible & to break the tradition that no "Irish" play can be played without the 'Irish' players. [George] Tyler of America is trying to arrange a "Subscription Tour" next year of Juno & The Plough of a 25 weeks run, on condition that [Arthur] Sinclair stays near Trafalgar Square.

I'm sending you a review from 'The Guardian', an Anglican High Church Weekly, which blows a bugle note back which you have blown before. The Boston Sun has it that LNX R[obinson] is going this Winter to tour America lecturing about how to pattern properly Yeats's worlds of Wallpaper.

There's no use of Will talking to you Gaby, & telling you this, & telling you that, & asking you to say this & to say that—let him write to me or write to Billy & say what he has to say. Personally, I'm not so keen as I was to lift him out of his job. I'm afraid he wouldn't fight, & would go about baa, baa, baahing out of him looking for a quiet place in which to lie down & die.

See Yo's criticism? Sent a reply on Thursday.

Love to Rose Francis & yourself.

Sean

To Gabriel Fallon

MS. TEXAS

ST. JOHN'S WOOD
4 AUGUST 1928

Dear Gaby—

Pirandello's "The Vice" is in a volume published in America, & a copy is on its way to me which, when it comes, I will send on to you.

"Tragic Women" was written as a joke by "G.K" for the Beaconsfield Club. It hasn't been published & is still in M.S. G.K's Secretary asked Bumpus (& Sons) (who enquired for me) to give her an idea why the M.S. was needed.

I'll write G.K's Secretary if you like, or if you'd rather do this yourself (better get your name known to these people—it can do no harm) here's the address:

Dorothy E. Collins.
Secretary
G. K. Chesterton.
Top Meadow
Beaconsfield
Buckinghamshire.
Reference
8.143 JGW.

Yours,
Sean

To Irish Statesman

4 AUGUST 1928

Y.O. AND THE SILVER TASSIE.

Dear Sir,—A word or two to tail on to the criticism in the STATESMAN of the 21st July, 1928, about the intensity and the incapacity of *The Silver Tassie.*

As Y.O. was moved by the intensity and the incapacity of the play, so I have been moved by the intensity and the incapacity of the criticism. It reminds me somewhat of the art of the cubist painter introduced into the art of criticism: a rapid circle around Starkie, a delicate curve touching the feet of Robinson, an oblique move towards O'Casey, then a sudden swirl and off at a tangent on a bee line for W. B. Yeats. Or it may be more like the interlacing, intertwining, ever-twisting, coming back, bending sideways, going forward, never ending of what is called the Celtic Art of Illumination.

Take the statement: "That very intensity of feeling has carried O'Casey into regions of the soul to which his art is unable to give adequate expression." This is meant to mean something; it may mean everything; it seems to mean nothing. It may mean that the Art of the Drama is unable to give adequate expression in the regions of the soul; or that O'Casey's art in the Art of the Drama is inadequate in the regions of the soul; or that when he had gone in, if he had kept a cool head, he would have given an adequate expression of the regions of the soul; or that there are certain regions of the soul in which the Art of the Drama, or O'Casey's art in the Art of the Drama, is inadequate towards expression; or that there is a certain intensity of feeling that can adequately express, and another capacity or incapacity of intensity of feeling that can only inadequately express the regions of the soul; or that Y.O. has a special, peculiar and privileged knowledge of the regions of the soul, and a peculiar and privileged sensibility to comprehend the exact intensity of feeling necessary to feel comfortable and be perceptive there, and that the regions of the soul are mapped out perfectly, like the City of London, with their West Central 1, North East 2, and South West 3, and that Y.O. stands there and watches there like a Postmaster General in the Soul's Sorting Office. It seems to me that O'Casey's expression of the regions of the soul in his play is more adequate and less confusing than Y.O.'s expression in his criticism.

But let us take it that Y.O. knows all that there is to be known about the regions of the soul, and so examine his statement, or apparent statement, that O'Casey's incapacity in the play is mainly due to his excursion or incursion into these psychically sacred places. Now the big penetration into what Y.O. calls the regions of the soul takes place in the second act, yet he says that this second act is on a higher level than that of the two following acts where the penetration dwindles down to an occasional peep. So that while Y.O. says because he means it, or because he doesn't mean it, that the incapacity in the play is due to O'Casey plunging into regions of the soul, he adds that the second act, where there is more of the soul and less of the body, is on a higher level than the third and fourth acts, where there is less of the soul and more of the body. So the very cause of the incapacity in the play makes an act better where the cause is greater, than in two acts where the cause is less. Again in a paragraph (which has very little to do with the play) about Academicians and Cubists, he first seems to tell us that the Academicians are greater than the Cubists; then pulls us back to tell us that the tip-top Cubists are greater than most of the Academicians; and, finally, that apparently, possibly or probably, that the Cubists had something to say, but said it badly, while the Academicians had nothing to say, but said it well. In my opinion, this is not profound, but cross-eyed criticism.

Later on in the criticism, Y.O. says that had the Abbey produced the play, O'Casey at the rehearsals would almost certainly have felt what Y.O. calls "the unreality of some speech-making in the play." He seems unable to imagine that this may have been deliberately done; that the unrealistic speech of Harry may be truer than the realistic speech of Mrs. Foran; that while it may not be exactly what Harry would say, it may be exactly what Harry would think; and that things that hop out over the tongue (even Y.O.'s) may be less important and less real than the things that abide behind in the mind. What is wrong with Y.O. is that he wants the old and much caressed familiarities. He wants *The Silver Tassie* to be a copy of *Juno,* and he liked *Juno* because it was a copy (it wasn't) of actual life. New things are beginning to startle him. He misses in *The Silver Tassie*

All the old familiar faces,
In their old familiar places,
Talking of to-morrow's races,
Round the fire.

He says that had it been a first play sent in by a hitherto unknown writer it would have been accepted. Citizens of mine old familiar City of Dublin, I bow, though I am not certain that this is a tribute to the Abbey or to me—perhaps, in his own subtle way, Y.O. means it to be a tribute to both of us.

Y.O. says that O'Casey brought (he isn't sure) a greater intensity to the writing of this play than to *Juno* or to *The Plough*. The first act is almost as good as anything he has done. In the second act he thinks (he isn't sure) O'Casey shows a greater subtlety of imagination than in anything else he has written. He thinks (he isn't sure) that there are many moving moments in the last two acts; and that he thinks (he isn't sure) that there is enough genius in the play, for all its awkwardness and defects, to justify its production. Y.O. is probably one of those human beings who thinks (he can't be sure even of that) he can't be sure of anything in this world.

Y.O. says that he isn't familiar enough with the technique of acting to know how it would affect him if he saw it performed. He thinks (he isn't quite sure of this either) it would move him. Does Y.O. know anything at all about the technique of the Drama? I am positive he knows nothing, for if he knew ever so little, he'd realise that a play like *The Silver Tassie* would depend for its impression in performance on the technique of the production, rather than on the technique of the acting.

He believes that the play was rejected through a desire that O'Casey's reputation should not suffer. That is a cold and wretched statement to make. It was rejected because W. B. Yeats and Lennox Robinson couldn't see, or wouldn't see, that the play was worthy of production by the Abbey Theatre; that was the ethical reason for the rejection. The concern for O'Casey's reputation vanishes with its tail down when we remember that the replies to the Abbey's criticisms showed that O'Casey was prepared to risk his reputation, which was all his own business and none of theirs, to which they refused to respond by producing the play to show whether their opinions were right or wrong; by the fact that the one favourable criticism from the Abbey was hidden till the last moment; that strenuous efforts were made to prevent the publication of the criticisms, and then, when those efforts failed, by the tremendous threat of a legal action through the Society of Authors.

It is exhilarating to read that Y.O. cannot find any evidence of lessening of talent in *The Silver Tassie*. I'm sure there was a constant and a brooding search for that. I thank him for this heart-lifting concession, and in return venture to suggest to him he should look to his own.

Sean O'Casey

London with the sun out.

(DEAR SEAN,—You are creating a new character, and when you have finished annihilating your critics the portrait of the annihilator will be as vivid in the consciousness of your readers as Joxer or the Paycock. Our vision of each other's meanings is necessarily a little blurred. I do not expect from you the insight of God into my meanings, and I think you might be a little less ferocious with your critics for not having the full insight of God into your meanings. We are all as God made us, or as evolution has left us. Try to be a little good natured about our imperfections. There was something else out besides the sun when you wrote those letters.—Y.O.)

To Nineteenth Century

SEPTEMBER 1928

'THE PLAYS OF SEAN O'CASEY' A REPLY [1]

Dr. Starkie in Dublin is in literature what one would call a toff. He is a professor in Dublin University, a director of the Abbey Theatre, and a big thing in the Dublin Drama League. These powers have laid their hands on his head, and he wears a stole of authority from the literary apostolate and epistolate of Dublin, so that everything he writes is stamped with a scholarly image and superscription.

Tired but proud of the tidy literary fold of Dublin, he has gone out to instruct into order and quietness some who decline to bleat with his baa-lambs. He starts his little exercises with a criticism of the plays of the celebrated workman dramatist Sean O'Casey.

We all must admire Dr. Starkie for struggling towards new values and cheer him as he starts on a wonderful involution as a critic. But he must learn to classify his ideas, and work his criticisms up into a synthesis. Though his movements are often jerky and sometimes vertiginous, he shows many fine attitudes as he skips la, la, la, la over the pages of *The Nineteenth Century*.

[1] Walter Starkie, "The Plays of Sean O'Casey," *Nineteenth Century,* August 1928.

Dr. Starkie is a director of the Abbey Theatre that was concerned with the rejection of *The Silver Tassie,* and since he wrote about the play in this Review, it is natural that I should be interested to show that upon examination every one of his criticisms is empty-headed.

In his official criticism Dr. Starkie said that 'in order to prepare his mind for *The Silver Tassie* he read over again the three published plays of Sean O'Casey.' He read over again three old plays in order to prepare his mind for a new one! He thought that he must read *The Silver Tassie* cautiously, carefully and thoroughly, so he sat down to read, not the new play, but the three old ones. What is one to think of a critic who thinks that the best way to prepare his mind for a new play is to sit down and read three old ones? This action of his thunders out the suggestion that, if at all possible, a flaw would be found in the new play. But the silliness of the preparation got a shock, for, having read the three other old plays, he finds in the new one 'a new departure, a new art, a new technique.' But then he does a worse thing. After priming his criticism with incapacity by reading three old plays to understand a new one, he paints his criticism with incapacity by criticising the new departure, the new art, the new technique, of the new play, by the old manner, the old art, and the old technique of the old plays! Dr. Starkie says that 'the fault of *The Silver Tassie* is that it is too vague and indefinite.' He does not say where it is vague and where it is indefinite. He hints at the last two acts. There is not a docker, who is not a duffer (the percentage of duffers among dockers is low, and far less than the percentage of duffers among dons), who would fail to understand a single sentence or fail to feel a single emotion that is spoken or manifested in any one act of the play.

He says, writing about the second act of the play, 'It is difficult to imagine such scenes when we read the play.' Well, if he cannot, he has lost all that was left of his imagination. He says, 'Poor Harry has not half the personality of poor, pale little Mollser sitting outside the tenement in *The Plough and the Stars*.' Best to tell the Doctor that Harry has not any of the personality of poor, pale little Mollser sitting outside the tenement simply because he was not meant to have it. He says: 'The prayer-meeting, Bible-quoting Susie of the first act evolves into a frivolous V.A.D., but we are not shown any gradual transformation.' If Dr. Starkie had read the new play as often as he says he read the old ones, he would see that no gradual change is shown because no change takes place. Susie can show a leg in the first act as well as she can in the last. And if he had read the new play as often as he says he read the old ones, he would see that her sturdiness and decision in the first act function as strongly again in the third act of the play. And if he imagines that in the music of a jazz band a V.A.D. would hear only the moans of many patients, then one day Dr. Starkie may become a plausible critic, but he will never be a playwright. Writing of the second act, he says, 'The crude realism of the words does not suit the chant.' What does he mean? Is not one word as real as another? Is there a different kind of realism in different words? Or the same kind of realism in different words? Or a different kind of realism in the same words, or what? He says, 'The second act is a queer, fantastic scene.' The act is built up of words, and if the words be crudely realistic, how can the act be queer and fantastic? He says again in one place that 'it is hard to imagine such scenes when we read the play,' and in another place that 'the author has introduced a grotesque chanting in doggerel verse that haunts the imagination.' And this is the critic that says O'Casey in this play is vague and indefinite, and must learn to classify his ideas! In criticism it seems that Dr. Starkie does not know his right hand from his left. Again, 'The excellent first act, which suggests *Juno and the Paycock.*' Excellent, mind you, because it reminds him of 'Juno'; the rest of the play not so good because it does not, mind you, remind him of 'Juno'. He does not like the new play because it is not like the old ones. The change was nothing to O'Casey, but it has huddled Starkie into corner-cowering criticism.

Starkie says again, 'He makes his opinions and theories fit into the framework of the bourgeois play, and thus he is not an innovator in drama . . . He is still dominated by the well-made play.' Go on again, Dr. Starkie. 'In *The Silver Tassie* he has left behind him the plays of a former manner and is groping towards new dramatic values.' In the *Irish Times* he called this new manner 'a technique touched with genius and standing out above all.' He cancelled his criticism before, and he can cancel it again. How can O'Casey be still dominated by the well-made play if he has left behind him the plays of a former manner? How can he be groping towards new dramatic values if these new dramatic values are touched with genius and stand out above all? And the fact that Starkie read over again the three old 'well-made plays' in order to prepare his mind for *The Silver Tassie,* and the fright that the new dramatic values of this play gave him, show that it is the critic rather than the dramatist that is dominated by the well-made play.

Dr. Starkie says again, 'O'Casey has not lost any of his power in writing or his vivid imagination.' Will Dr. Starkie tell me for my own good what I have lost? Perhaps the will or the stamina to transform a play into a synthesis. Or is it that O'Casey has 'left the scenes of his impressionable years and has ceased to see intensely'? This opinion of Dr. Starkie, as well as being a Yeatsian echo, is a puny prod at the play when we remember that the critic spent his novitiate in the comprehension of new values by the hot-blooded study of old ones. But it is more than this—it is a mean and underhand method of trying to shoulder a prop under his opinions. In the first place, it would be impossible to lose in two years the impressions of forty; in the second place, a good deal of those two years has been infused into the production of my old plays, and the rest of the time has been spent in the writing of *The Silver Tassie,* so that about a lunar month remains in which I must have lost the 'power to see intensely.' At its worst there seems to be something spiteful in this contention; at its best it stands adjutant to the opinion of Mr. Yeats. There would be something in it if all other opinions stood in the porch with Starkie's; but, if he wishes, I will send him opinions given by those as clever as he, as Irish as he, far more experienced in the drama than he, which will tell him, saucy to his face, that the intensity and reality of the two last acts of the play endure to the end. Let Starkie try to hit it off fairly, without imagining that others must be as he himself is—able to see only the things in his own and his neighbour's garden. And if Starkie bets, and he is game, I will take a bet with him that he himself during his life has spent more of his time out of Ireland than I have. The fact is that Starkie's *leit-motif* of separation from Ireland is a veil over the conceited opinion that there must be a loss in the wider separation from that little Irish league of letters who have joined hands and dance continually around the totem pole of their own opinions.

It would be a weary thing to climb over the whole pile of his opinions, but there is one that Starkie has thrown in which deserves to be lifted out and laughed at. He says: 'O'Casey is not the dramatist of a new nation full of hope in its future progress. In this respect he is a contradiction to the optimistic spirit which has prevailed owing to the wise government of Mr. Cosgrave and his colleagues . . . Let us not see too many of such plays, for in an epoch [great word, Starkie!] of reconstruction all our energies should be set upon creating a new country.'

This smells of courage, resolution, and determination. Starkie wants things done. He wants plays of hope, plays of purity, plays of progress for his dear old country; plays that will play their part in the present epoch of reconstruction; plays to buck them up and give them peace. The Irish dramatist of the future will have to take his tips from the Irish Government. He can see everything, but the Government will show him what to look at. And Starkie thinks that this is dramatic criticism. You are a politician, my dear Starkie. Stand for the Dail, and, if elected, you will learn more quickly of the things that belong unto politics than you will ever learn of the things that belong unto the drama.

Sean O'Casey

To Gabriel Fallon

MS. TEXAS

ST. JOHN'S WOOD
3 SEPTEMBER 1928

Dear Gaby—

Got a letter from Oliver Craig—H. Sec. D.D.L.[1] saying—The Committee of D.D.L. think it possible (sic) that they might like (sic. twice) to produce "The Tassie" during season 28–29 (Sic, third & last time)

Could you let me know (if you know) if Yeats, LNXR[obinson] & Georgina [Mrs Yeats] are on Committee still; or have they resigned; or were they rejected at the last election?

Best Wishes
Sean

[1] The Dublin Drama League was founded in 1918 by W. B. Yeats, Lennox Robinson, James Stephens, and Ernest Boyd, to perform plays of international reputation. The League productions were presented in the Abbey Theatre on Sunday and Monday nights, when the theatre was not used by the regular company, and the casts were mostly made up of Abbey actors. The League ceased to exist in 1928, when its function was taken over by the newly formed Dublin Gate Theatre. See Lady Gregory's letter to O'Casey, 30 October 1928, note 2.

To Gabriel Fallon

MS. TEXAS

ST. JOHN'S WOOD
11 SEPTEMBER 1928

My dear Gaby—

Fear not. The Dublin Drama League's not going to get the play. I wanted to know the personel of the Committee for future reference. Sheila [Richards] came here on Sunday. Told me she didn't know the D.D.L. had asked for the play. She said it would be a great joke to have the Tassie played in the Abbey, by the Abbey (players) for the D.D.L. By the people, with the people for the people. Told Sheila I had a better joke even than that, to be played by O'Casey, with O'Casey for O'Casey somewhere in Dublin. I've sent the following answer to the Hon Sec. D.D.L.LLLL.

Dear Madam. I thank you for your letter to me written on the 5th of Sept 1928, saying 'the Committee of the D.D.L. think it possible that they might like to produce "The Silver Tassie" in the season of 1928–1929' & asking for terms.

It cannot be did.

Sean O'Casey

I have been asked for the play by "The Festival Theatre" Cambridge, & have had to refuse regretfully, for this little Theatre's doing far better work than the Abbey—which wouldn't be a task that would make it sweat.

Will write a longer letter soon.

Yours in Love
Sean

To Gabriel Fallon

MS. TEXAS

ST. JOHN'S WOOD
13 SEPTEMBER 1928

My dear Gaby—

I concluded things definitely with C. B. Cochrane yesterday, & the play is to be produced sometime during the next 12 months—probably in January. Billy & I talked to Cochrane about you, & pressed the venture of getting you to help in the production. He is still very interested in you, but, candidly—although he didn't say so—I'm afraid he was not sure of how you would do. I can't really blame Cochrane, for, as he's putting up all the money, about £5000, he wont take what he could conceive to be a risk.

And again he has practically decided to perform the play first in America; saying that in the American Theatre there is more courage, & more of the spirit of go on chance it, than there is here, which is easily true, for there's none here at all. It is almost impossible to make an impression unless you are here, living & working here, & constantly getting into notice. They may prate as they damn well like, but Dublin's a far way from London, particularly the theatre.

When we spoke of you he said 'that's the kind of man I'm looking for', but he seems to be content to go on looking & searching & seeking in places where everything is as it ought to be—exactly as it was before.

The trouble is to get the demand here linked up with the supply. Producers here do a few monkey-tricks: smoke cigars; draw £500 for a play; lean back in their chairs in the Garrick Club, & hear the trumpets of God blowing a salute. Supposing you drew a design for the second act of 'The Tassie' or "Porgy" or some plays other than these & send them on to C. B. Cochrane with a letter? This would at least be a beginning, & would focus his attention on you. Then, if he was in any way impressed, we might arrange a meeting. Cochrane does a hell of a lot of work—mostly revues of course—but he is to do 'Porgy', & if he makes a hit with 'The Tassie' he will go in for anything. I think there is a lot of the artist in C. B.—more than there is in some or most of those who prate Art, & dress up once or twice a year in Burkian Costumes for a Fancy Ball.

I will write again later on. How is Lyle Donaghy & where is he now?

Best Wishes
Sean

To Lady Londonderry

MS. Lady Bury

St. John's Wood
24 September 1928

Dear Lady Londonderry,

A picture in a paper showing you in a yacht at the helm has told me that you have changed the sickness that was a trouble to you when last we spoke on the phone into health again, & I am very glad.

I have just signed a contract with C. B. Cochrane for the production of "The Silver Tassie." He thinks that it may be best to have the play first performed in New York. Play production in America is nearer to courage & original effort than production here, & I think he is right. England is fifty years or more behind the present power in Drama & limping badly too. And Ireland has had to abandon Dramatic effort to allow her to concentrate all her energies toward the creation of her Peg o' my Heart Pound notes.

I have heard nothing since speaking to G.B.S. about the Abbey, finally deciding to produce the play. I expected, because of what G.B.S. said, a letter from them asking for the play again, but they have remained silent & shy. A strange thing has happened however—I got a letter from the Secretary of the Dublin Drama League saying—"The Committee think it possible that they might like to produce "The Silver Tassie" during the '28–'29 Season." And I understand W. B. Yeats, W. Starkie & L. Robinson are members of the Committee; if I had agreed the play would have been performed by the Abbey Players in the Abbey Theatre,

& the result, I suppose, would have been that the Abbey Directors had produced the play, & the Abbey Directors hadn't produced the play! Or, according to the wording of the request, that they had agreed to produce or hadn't agreed to produce the play! And they call this sort of thing honest & they think it dignified. Oh, well, let them think so if they like.

I read that Lord Londonderry has kept an unprofitable mine open to save the miners from hardship of unemployment, & this, even to my fierce, jagged Communistic outlook, was a very good deed, indeed.

I Sincerely hope you, he & all your children are well. My little boy is going along like a house on fire—double his birth-weight, though he was forced into the world two months before his time, more than a month before the double-weight was due.

Yours Sincerely,
Sean

To Mrs. Charlotte F. Shaw [1]

MS. British Museum

St. John's Wood
25 September 1928

Dear Mrs. Shaw—

Many thanks for sending me Blake's Vision of Job.[2] It was very good of you to do this. I have so far read, trying diligently to comprehend, the Notes, List, Preface & Introduction, & I have read & read the first two chapters, & looked at Illustration No 1 & Illustration No 2, but I am, at the end of it all, as mystified as Blake's admirers.

Come into my hand
By your mild power; descending down the
Nerves of my right arm
From out the Portals of my Brain—[3]

Oh, Blake, Blake, Blake.

[1] Mrs. Charlotte Frances Payne-Townshend Shaw (1857–1943), married Bernard Shaw in 1898.

[2] Joseph H. Wicksteed, *Blake's Vision of the Book of Job: A Study with Reproductions of the Illustrations,* (London, Dent, 1910).

[3] In his introduction, Wicksteed quotes these lines from Blake's poem "Milton" (Book I, 11. 5–7), to illustrate Blake's belief that "The right hand, as the one that held the brush, pen, pencil or graver, was in direct relation with the brain—the seat of Paradise in Blake's 'Human–Divine' system."

The right hand, therefore, is connected with, Poetry, Paradise, Vision. Oh, Wicksteed, Wicksteed, Wicksteed!

But I will read the book leisurely & carefully & thoughtfully, some of the coming nights, when I sit by the fire & there isn't a mouse stirring. And it was Kind of you to send it to me. Best wishes to You & G.B.S.

Sean O'Casey

To Daniel Macmillan

MS. MACMILLAN LONDON

ST. JOHN'S WOOD
15 OCTOBER 1928

Dear Mr. Macmillan,

Lyle Donaghy,[1] a friend of mine, is anxious that a volume of his poetry should be published by you. I should like you to meet him & have a talk with him about his work, which I think is well worthy of consideration.

He has the passion of the poet in his nature—which is bad—but he also has the passion of the poet in his work, which is good, & will, I believe, cause men to speak about him in time to come.

If you could grant him an interview, I'm sure you would be interested in the man, & probably interested in his work.

Very sincerely yours,
Sean O'Casey

[1] John Lyle Donaghy (1902–49), Irish poet and teacher. Yeats's Cuala Press in Dublin had published one of Donaghy's books of verse, *At Dawn Above Aherlow* (1926).

To Gabriel Fallon

MS. TEXAS

28 OCTOBER [1928]

Dear Gaby.

Well, we're all well, well, so so, well sir, thank you. Does Will swear—what does he swear by himself, he swears by himself, says she.

Perhaps, he's right; may be I didn't tell him to write to C.B—I think I did.

But, anyhow, I'm afraid, C B. wouldn't see eye to eye with me for an American Production about Will. I daresay, he'd like to have a perfectly balanced Company. London's different. Anyhow, Will ought to write to C.B.C. & ask him about the London Production. I can't carry him out of Troy the way AEneas carried Anchies out of Dublin—on me back!

I'd love to see King Lear a la Abbeyensis at The Abbey.[1] And Will doing Kent in buskins—thinkest thou that duty shall have dread to speak, when pow'r to flatt'ry bows? Oh, why don't they play it in modern dress & make Will wear his plus twos. Oh, Gaby, Gaby. I swear it will be a mighty feast for the gods! Can Will pull a bow? Is he an Archer. He'll clap his hand on a sword & say—There is a tempest raging in my boosom, & courage gives it vent. And M.J. [Dolan] I suppose will play the fool, as he does in The Minute Glass.[2] Where an Angel catches a Soul as a kid would catch a fly. Poor old Will: a great skin when all's said & all's done. By the way, who produces K. Lear?

So W. B. has gone to Rapallo—I sat me down by the waters of Babylon & wept. An English paper here says he's given up the cares of state. This is a dangerous thing for him to do, for he leaves all his material behind him. (Air. The Raparees)

King Willie he has gone away,
And left his pals behind.
And hopeless, pale & far from gay
To be whistled down the wind.
Starkie is dumb, A E is glum.
With all his plans askew
And Lennox wails to his dolls in the dales
What am I going to dooooo?
    What am I goin to do,
    What am I goin to do,
I'm left on me arse, oh, life is a farce.
Now what am I goin to do!

But whatever he does, be sure he'll do it well.

Well, Lyle has some of it over him—the worst has to come yet.

[1] The Abbey Theatre had announced a performance of *King Lear* for November, to be produced (directed) by Denis Johnston, with F. J. McCormick as Lear, Michael J. Dolan as The Fool, and Barry Fitzgerald ("Will") as Kent. It opened on 26 November 1928.

[2] W. B. Yeats's *The Hour Glass* was first performed on 14 March 1903 by the Irish National Theatre Society at Molesworth Hall, Dublin. Dolan played the role of The Fool in revivals of the play.

Just finished a short story—it isn't a story—The Star Dance [3]—who says Yeats?

Love to Frank & Rose
Sean

[3] "The Star-Jazzer," printed in *Windfalls* (London, Macmillan, 1934).

From Ernest Blythe [1]

MS. O'CASEY

BELMONT,
11 SANDFORD ROAD,
DUBLIN
29 OCTOBER 1928

Dear Sean,

Thank you for sending me a copy of "The Silver Tassie". I have read it again and I think more than ever that it is a very moving and powerful play. I only hope I may be able to see it on the stage.

If the Directors of the Abbey had said they must reject it because they were afraid of a stupid riot in which their seats would get damaged and their curtain torn I could have understood their attitude. But when they decided to have none of it because it was not good enough for the Abbey and because it was unworthy of you, their minds worked in a way that is beyond my powers of comprehension.

I shall certainly ring you up the first time I am in London. I should like very much to see yourself again and to meet your family.

With all good wishes
Ernest Blythe

[1] Ernest Blythe (1889–), Irish politician, Gaelic language enthusiast, and a director of the Abbey Theatre. In 1935 he was appointed a director of the Abbey by W. B. Yeats; and when F. R. Higgins died in 1941, Blythe succeeded him as managing director of the theatre, a post he has held for the past thirty years. He retired in 1972. See O'Casey's letter to Lady Gregory, 1 November 1925, note 1; and O'Casey's letters to Blythe, 18 November 1959, 1 September 1964, Vol. III.

From Lady Gregory

MS. O'Casey

Standard Hotel,
Dublin
Tuesday—30 October 1928

Dear Sean—

This is just to say how splendidly the Plough went last night[1]—its deep tragedy and rich comedy have never seemed finer—tho' I didnt like the new Rosie Redmond as well as the other—she was younger & had charm & pathos—not easy to find. Tonight is wet & cold & I'm staying in—rather tired—The best thing today was a copy of the report of the City Commission—in favour of building a Gallery—such a relief! (although they throw out a suggestion that subscriptions should be asked for to gauge public feeling—but this we can disregard).

There is a new idea, of abandoning Stephens Green & Lutyens, & taking Ld. Charlemt's old house in Rutland Square—(it has a fine frontage) & building on a plain gallery at the back. I went to see [Thomas] Bodkin about this—not much liking it—however he is all for it—& I said & we agreed this time I *must* not have a quarrel about a site again—I will agree to whatever is decided on. That house belongs to the Govt. They are using it for offices—but may not need it when the Custom House is rebuilt. Bodkin & I determined on the "no quarrel" to give no excuse for further delay—When the site is arranged & the estimate agreed to (probably much under the Lutyens one) we can start the fight anew in the English papers. [T. C.] Murray has just been here about a troublesome business of amateur fees—paid to [J. J.] Hayes—"Playwrights Association" & not reaching the authors. I think the Association must be broken up, especially as it gives the Abbey as its headquarters so we may be considered responsible.

I am staying here for about 3 weeks I think, to look after the Abbey—W.B.Y being off to Italy & L.R. in U.S.A. I dont know how King Lear will go. The "Gate Theatre" is very enterprising.[2] I went to see Peer Gynt—the staging & lighting wonderfully good. My grandchildren are dispersed, Richard at Woolwich—Anne in Paris—Catherine at her

[1] *The Plough and the Stars* was revived at the Abbey Theatre on 29 October 1928, with the original cast, except for Blanaid O'Carroll, who played the role of Rosie Redmond in place of Ria Mooney.

[2] The Dublin Gate Theatre Studio, later the Dublin Gate Theatre, was founded and performed Ibsen's *Peer Gynt* as its first production in the Abbey's Peacock Theatre on 14 October 1928, with Hilton Edwards in the title role. The directors of the new theatre were Edwards, Micheál MacLiammoir, Georoid O'Lochlainn, and Mme. D. Bannard Cogley.

mothers—who is now Mrs. Gough & lives at a beautiful place, Lough Cutra—5 miles from Coole, a happy marriage I think.

I hope all goes well with you & yours—you would have been pleased to see the Plough last night—& the "Far Off Hills" [3] is very amusing & went very well.

Yours affectionately
A. Gregory

[3] Lennox Robinson's *The Far-off Hills* opened at the Abbey Theatre on 22 October 1928.

To Oliver St. John Gogarty

MS. GOGARTY

ST. JOHN'S WOOD
5 NOVEMBER 1928

Dear Oliver—

Haven't you a buttie called AE? Isn't he a judge of potatoes, judge of poetry, judge of pictures, judge of plays, judge of politics, judge of all the earth?

Well read his Art article in this week's Statesman on "Illustrators of the Sixties," [1] & if you have tears prepare to shed them then.

Yours As Ever,
Sean

[1] A.E.'s review of a book on painting by Forest Reid, *Illustrators of the 'Sixties* (London, Faber & Gwyer, 1928, in the *Irish Statesman,* 3 November 1928.

To Lady Gregory

MS. GREGORY

ST. JOHN'S WOOD
[7 NOVEMBER 1928]

Be God, that's good news, Lady Gregory—that the Commissioners have decided in favour of building a gallery—though it would hardly be conceivable that they could refuse. And I imagine it was wise of you to say unto yourself—'We shall fold our hands in peace for a little while, & shall not quarrel, & store our treasures in a humble shelter till a time that's further on shall give us the opportunity of building them a fairer home'.

United to those already in the Municipal Gallery they will make a fine collection of painting, drawing & Sculpture. But there are a few Lane gave to the National Gallery that should be placed in the New Building—Rembrandt's Young Woman, El Greco's St. Francis & Goya's Spanish Woman—and some in the Municipal Gallery that should be hurried at once to some dark corner in the National Gallery among others Leighton's drawings; B. Jones Sleeping Princess & Millais's "Return of the Pigeon to the Ark."

I am getting to love the Art of painting more & more; & as I grow in days I grow in wisdom, in feeling and in choice. I have been to the Tate Gallery often & am going again this week. May I say that I think you are mistaken in thinking Daumier's 'Don Chichote' is the best of the group in the Lane Collection. There is too much of the Illustrators touch in it to be a great picture. I thought this from the first & I think the same still. Next time I shall again look at it & compare it with the others & make a final decision for myself.

I suppose when the Gallery is built in Rutland Sqr, & The Lane Pictures are back again, addition will be, from time to time, made to the collection. Some day, then, I hope to see there pictures by Van Gogh, Cezanne, Segonzac & Utrillo. But I suppose some damned old Academic Committee will rule & rule what is genius out, & rule & rule what is mediocrity in.

[Augustus] John & I are great friends & I have often been in his Studio looking at his pictures. He has given me a princely present by sending me the first portrait he painted of me, which, I think, is a very great work indeed. I am very proud of it hanging over the mantelpiece of our little sitting-room. We have six originals now, & some beautiful prints by modern artists. We have declared war on the clumsy, gaudy, garish, picture-degrading cult of gilt framing, & enclose them all in simple oak, walnut or ebony frames.

By the way did you read AE's article in this week's Statesman on "The Illustrators of the Sixties?"

Sorry to hear about J. J. Hayes. I wrote to him a long time ago asking him to write to Rugby College, that had given a play of mine without permission, but I heard nothing about it. Anyhow, I suppose, we shouldn't expect anyone to do a lot of work without payment. I cant altogether blame him.

You will have to forgive me for ceasing to care where W.B.Y[eats] is, or what L.S.R[obinson] is doing. I can't forget their sneakiness in the rejection of "The Silver Tassie". What Robinson does, or does not, doesn't matter much—he'll never add one jot or tittle to life or to literature—but Yeats's action must be counted unto him for unrighteousness. He has overthrown his own original constitution of the Abbey Theatre, in which he wrote about "the freedom to experiment which is not found in Theatres in England." We must change that now to "the freedom to experiment which is found in the English Theatre but is no longer to be found in the Abbey Theatre of Dublin."

You know, of course, that I have given the rights to C. B. Cochrane, who may produce the play first in New York. He is thinking of getting the producer of "Porgy", a Russian to produce 'The Tassie' with my help, so if this happens, I shall have to pop off to America. Some time ago, he & I went to the Censor here, & I found him a sympathetic, alert & comprehending friend. He has passed the play with the alteration of six words. Indeed our interview consisted of a very friendly & intensely interesting discussion of the Drama. I have been agreeably astonished in Cochran's knowledge of art & Drama. He has produced himself a scene called 'Dance, little Lady, Dance' in his latest Revue, which is a marvel of Expressionism. And he has some lovely pictures by Cezanne, Renoir, V. Gogh, Degas & John.

Please remember me to all the children when you see them, Anne, Catherine & Richard. Good Wishes to all at Coole.

And Warm Regards to You.
Sean

To Gabriel Fallon

MS. TEXAS

ST. JOHN'S WOOD
7 NOVEMBER 1928

Dear Gaby
Here's a lyric, a lyric for [F. R.] Higgins, and Gogarty, & A[ustin] Clarke, & [Frank] O'Connor & G[eoffrey] Phibbs, & AE—

The Abbey's old age is in one of its rages,
For Johnston is sounding the gong;
Lady G's in a flutter to pull down th' shutter,
For Johnston's just going too strong!
Will's brain's in a fuddle—things are in a muddle,—
King Lear's getting turn'd into a song;

Each day the thing worse is, but in spite of the curses,
Brave Johnston keeps rolling along! Ha, Ha.

Has Robinson done another rash thing? Has he promised Johnston success—& why? Are they calling up again to the rescue the Cohorts of Coole? "Allowing him to produce the play or give him money"! ha, ha, what does this mean? Another dark spot on the Sun? I would give something to be present when Dennis [Johnston] is rehearsing & Lady G. is watching.

But seriously what does it mean, what can have happened, why should they be afraid of Dennis. And, as usual, Robinson runs away. I had a letter from Lady G. the other day saying that the Commissioners had decided in favour of a Gallery; that she was in Dublin on Theatre business; that LNXR was in America, & W.B.Y. in Italy. I wrote a long letter to her today telling her of my happy interview with the Censor; that she must forgive me for ceasing to care where W.B.Y. was, or what LNXR was doing. 'That what LNXR does or does not, does not matter, for he'll never add one jot or tittle to either life or literature'. That I couldn't forget their sneakiness in the rejection of "The Silver Tassie" (I've since thought of the phrase, "cultured sneakiness"—good term for an article, eh?) And I told her that the original Charter of the Abbey "Freedom of experiment which could not be found in England", had been changed to 'Freedom of experiment which could be found in England but no longer in the Abbey Theatre of Dublin', & a lot more. For fear I'd forget

Evan Walters.
Grove Studio
Well Road, Hampstead. N.W.
London.

I'm afraid we have sinned in thought, word & deed against Beckenham.[1]

Dublin Opinion's opinion of "Far Off Hills" seems to say the play's not the thing.[2] Anyhow, you can't build flesh & blood structures on tea & toast. He never rose above his "The Clancy Name."[3] Did you read AE's art from the heart article on "Illustrators of the Sixties" in Last Week's Statesman? (I have asked the same question of Lady G) AE must be getting inspiration from deities that are pulling his leg about Art. Poltergeists—isn't that what they are called? Well, some damned spirit must be masquerading to him in the guise of Daksha, which is an-

[1] He had pinned to the letter a news story from a London paper headlined, "Ibsen Without Cuts," which told about the Beckenham Theatre's production of the complete *Peer Gynt,* a project supported by Bernard Shaw and J. T. Grien.

[2] "Stage and Screen," *Dublin Opinion,* November 1928, a review of Robinson's *The Far-off Hills.*

[3] Lennox Robinson's *The Clancy Name* opened at the Abbey Theatre on 8 October 1908.

other name for the moony-tired Maheshwara, god of all creatures animate & inanimate.

Got a letter from Ernie Blythe saying he couldn't understand the rejection of "The Tassie" by the Abbey, & adding that he thought it a powerful & moving play, which shows that Ernie Blythe knows more about Drama than Yeats, or Robinson, or Starkie or Lady Gregory.

How you bloody well spied out the reference to the Catholic Poetry Circle! They wrote to me asking for a signed photograph to be sold in aid of the "Crusade of Rescue for Catholic Destitute Children", & sending them a copy of a play, I told them straight I didn't like any test to be applied to hungry children. Said it sounded like Jesus Christ holding bread in His hands & questioning kids before He fed them, which I as an Atheist, refuse to accept as a characteristic of Christ. If the Catholic Faith is worth anything it is worth profession by well-fed, world-thoughtless, spirited happy children. But the duty of the Catholic Faith is to all children. Christ never, as far as I know, asked a child if he believed in Him. There was no necessity: Christ brought the kid love which is greater than Faith.

Here I'm giving a Sermon.

[O'Casey made a drawing here.]

Curtain coming down. What is wrong with Links [Lennox Robinson]? Why does he want his Give a god a — produced? [4] Think of him having fifty pounds to spare on such a play! I was talking to an Agent yesterday to whom a woman in the Theatre asked to read "The Big House" [5] saying "if he thought it good, she'd produce it here". The Agent didn't think much of it, & it was turned down. I'm afraid that I am beginning to believe that Links is writing with his two eyes on the Commercial Stage. Cochrane's Revue opened in New York yesterday evening. A month or so will bring him back here, I think, & then we'll see.

Coming near the end of the page so I'll have to say halt for a day or two. Never mind the troubles with Candida: go on, & what does it matter anyhow? Keep your tail up & wait. Love to Rose, Frankie & to you. Send me Will's address. If you meet W. Bye Bye, remember me to him.

Sean

[4] Lennox Robinson's *Give a Dog a ——*, rejected by the Abbey Theatre, was first produced in London by Nigel Playfair at the Strand Theatre on 20 January 1929. The title is based on the proverb, "Give a dog a bad name and hang him."

[5] Lennox Robinson's *The Big House* opened at the Abbey Theatre on 6 September 1926.

To Gabriel Fallon

MS. TEXAS

ST. JOHN'S WOOD
29 NOVEMBER 1928

Dear Gaby—

Just a line or two or three to tell to you that CBC is back in London again but that I haven't heard anything from him yet about you, or about The Tassie. I didn't expect to hear from him in any way so soon anyhow, & it may be a week or so before he sends word about something to say or something to do. His 'Year of Grace' is an astonishing success in New York, & is playing to packed houses booked out for the next 16 weeks, & taking £8000 a week which means the very little profit of at least £7000 a week for C.B.C & his backers. The Writer of the Revue, Noel Coward is in wages & royalties, making a £1000 a week minus income TAX, so you see my boy GENIUS & ART sometimes have a reward greater than a cup of cold water. Delighted that 'Candida' went on & off so well. These activities will bring you a little closer to the £1000 a week ideal. Though maybe when we go to God, there may be no coins rattling in our pockets. Did you see see pee see's [1] praise of King Lear? He says, says he that K.L.'s a Katabolic Kharacter—& so he is. However they seem to have done fairly well considering their inexperience, & the mightiness of the play. I've been writing a good deal these few days—well into a short story to be called—I think—

"The Flesh is Willing".[2]

and my eyes feel a little tired. Bringing a Holy Picture into a story of a man's desire for a woman. And when you write Irish write it properly. I was listening last night to a Scot, a friend of Billie's, singing some songs in Gaelic in Our House. It was Champeen!

You can't say Naċ Leirge ata art—as far as I remember. Is abarr i gceart nó ná abarr i naon cor é. Aċt ċaitfid mé ċuir deire leis an leitir seo, le cois te is 'tá an teine 'tá codlad i teact orm,[3] & cheerio.

Love to all
Sean

[1] "see pee see"—Constantine P. Curran, *Irish Statesman,* 1 December 1928, a review of the Abbey Theatre's production of *King Lear,* which opened on 26 November. Curran described Lear as "furiously katabolic."

[2] He changed the title to "I Wanna Woman," *Windfalls* (1934). See Lady Rhondda, "Notes on the Way," *Time and Tide,* 13 May 1933, and O'Casey's letter of 17 June to A. E. Harrison, about the refusal of the printer of *Time and Tide* to print this "immoral" short story. The story was also the cause of the banning of *Windfalls* in Ireland.

[3] O'Casey is correcting Fallon's Irish: "You can't say *that it isn't laziness is on you*—as far as I remember. *Say it right or don't say it at all. But I must put an end to this letter. With the heat of the fire, sleep is coming on me.*"

Commend me with all diligence to Yeats, & all the brethren that are one in the love of the things that belong to the world of art & Literature. Postum Verum rerum derum serum scriptum—

Really glad Peter[4] came out of the wreck—was it really a wreck—so well. Three hundred pounds in soft cash! T'Abbey's becoming "furiously Katabolic." Seepeesey ses Sheila [Richards] looked like a Tanagra, but in his whole criticism from East to West & North to South & NNW by S.S.E. he never blows a bloody breeze around the name of Dennis [Johnston]. Why? 'Oh, I want to go where you go, & do what you do!' 'I cannot wish the fault undone the issue of it being so improper' Seepeesee catching wild rays from the Yonian[5] Constellation says "Cordelia shines as a star of loyalty & truth through this moral chaos" Oh, I want to go where you go, & do what you do—then I shall be happy!

This romantic moral moonshine makes me sick. Lear lashing out because his hundred knights are reduced to fifty. All the world—as well as his daughters—expected to sweat for his upkeep in body & soul & spirit. 'I want to cry when you cry, & smile when you smile, & rave when you rave, then I'll be happy!'

And Dolan was a sweet fool too! One hundred & twenty pounds for light. So, So. And Dennis said Let there be light, & there was light. And Dennis said Let there be more light & it was so. And it cost One hundred & twenty pounds! Oh my poor little Teatre!

And all next week, & the week after they'll pack Shakespeare into the Abbey, till the Abbey will be vomiting Shakespeare. What kind of a Shakespeare is Mr. Martin's Shakespeare? And now I must put the poor hand into the sling again.

Sean

[4] F. J. McCormick (Peter Judge) was unanimously praised for his performance as Lear, in an otherwise undistinguished production.

[5] Yonian—an allusion to the mysticism of Y.O./A.E. (George Russell).

From Lady Gregory

PS. *Modern Drama*[1]

DUBLIN
1 DECEMBER 1928

Dear Sean—I have been here for some weeks, looking after the Abbey, but go home on Monday—McCormick is wonderfully fine in King Lear—but the audience wasn't very good, but is improving—

[1] From a copy made by A. C. Edwards and printed in *Modern Drama,* May 1965.

I am sending you *Days of Fear* [2]—because I think it a very beautiful and moving book, and I would like you to have it—

I would like to send a copy to A[ugustus] John also—please tell me where he now is—I'm not sure if he has come back from U.S.A.—Is there any photograph of his portrait of you—I should much like to have one—That was, as you say "a princely gift—"

Your affectionate
A Gregory

[2] Frank Gallagher's *Days of Fear* (London, John Murray, 1928), a diary kept during a hunger strike in Mountjoy Jail, Dublin, in 1920.

To Gabriel and Rose Fallon

MS. TEXAS

ST. JOHN'S WOOD
12 DECEMBER 1928

My dear Gaby & dear Rose—

Yes, it's bad news, very bad news indeed. But not quite so bad as you are inclined to think, imagine, & dwell upon. And you mustn't think it tragedy: it isn't tragedy. Tragedy is irremediable & this is not. It is an agonising, bloated nuisance, but it isn't a tragedy. What about me? At three or four years of age, agonising ulcerated cornea of both eyes of a tubercular origin. Sixteen or fifteen years or fourteen years of pain & many periods of blindness. Still a thorn in the flesh but yet God or Nature gave compensations. Compensations brought agony too, but still they remained compensations.

Slight erosion on top of hip-joint, tubercular erosion too—bad, but not really terrible. It can be cured. It very often is cured now. Especially in the years of infancy. They can do almost anything now if the sufferer be young & has a heart. And what in the Name of God is two or three years to a kid? And don't get panicky. He won't feel it anyway like you and Rose. And you & she must mind yourselves. You & she are more important than he is; even because of him you & she are of more importance. So don't get panicky. Of course you must stand up to it, but don't let Rose do all the standing. And where's your faith in God, man? If you believe not, take it like a man; if you believe then you must know that the very hairs in Frankie's head are numbered. And where's the tragedy of 'looking the healthiest child in the world'? He is probably healthy but for this one defect, & all the better for that. Don't you see that this will make his rearing easier? You're not going to grumble because he has qualities that will stand to him, are you? The Stronger his lungs & heart are the better for the healing of the hip joint.

And think of Billy's little girl Tessie [McElroy] (the pretty youngster we saw colouring the pictures in Billy's flat) legs cut open to tighten tendons; legs in plaster for six months; massage for months; still having special treatment. Getting better & better, & stronger & stronger. Going down on Friday to her singing carols in her school.

The doctors are right this time: the defect is young, & can the more easily be overcome. That is commonsense. The few years will be hard on you & Rose; it will really mean nothing to the child. If he be cured, & that is very likely, he won't even remember the mechanism of his cure.

I am very, very sorry, & Eileen is very, very sorry. But take it as calmly as you can. And write to me again.

With love to Rose & you
Sean

V

RESTLESS AND UNREPENTANT IN LONDON 1929-30

THIS reply was published in the Press, but for fear of future confusion among either 'English' or 'Irish' Catholics, please publish the fact that in Social and Economic opinions, I am a Communist, and in opinions that we term religious, I am an Atheist."

"How am I, & what am I doing? Well, not so well, vigorous & free in spirit as I should wish to be, which is the physical and spiritual chain that binds me to humanity. Most of us, most of the time, like the figures in Blake's pictures, have the left foot forward. But error is not far from truth, & only restlessness can bring us peace."

When *The Silver Tassie* was finally produced in London in October 1929, Lady Gregory saw it and wrote to O'Casey to tell him how much she liked it, adding that she had also written to Yeats to say "we ought to have accepted it." Unfortunately, however, this belated and generous act of contrition could not change a tragic situation and inadvertently it rubbed more salt on the righteous O'Casey's wounds. He needed more than moral victories now, for even C. B. Cochran's impressive production of the play—with a brilliantly conceived second act specially designed by Augustus John, and outstanding performances by Charles Laughton and Barry Fitzgerald—turned out to be a tainted victory. It received mixed but many favorable reviews and played to packed houses; nevertheless it had to close after two months because of excessively high operating costs. So O'Casey was winning some of his artistic battles but he was still losing the war of survival—the struggle to go on writing his new plays on his own uncompromising terms. As an innovative playwright determined to experiment with symbolic and nonrealistic techniques, he was a generation ahead of his time and ironically had to suffer for his creative insight since the theatre of London was not ready for him and the theatre of Dublin had disowned him.

Throughout these two years Lady Gregory humbled herself by writing to him as a peacemaker, asking if she could see him, begging him to forgive the Abbey and submit another play. But now it was his turn to say no. Although he later regretted his stubborn refusal to see her—he told her he wanted to avoid making vindictive remarks that might hurt her, but he hurt her more by turning his back on her—he was still under constant attack from Ireland and found it "impossible to forget, & bloody difficult to forgive." For while Lady Gregory was trying to make peace, Yeats and the Abbey and Ireland generally were extending the conflict with a series of irritants, accusations, and insults. As it had done on a number of previous occasions, the Abbey withheld O'Casey's royalty checks, and then followed this petty maneuver with a surprise lawsuit. O'Casey had given the former Abbey actor Arthur Sinclair and his Irish Players permission to perform *Juno* and *Plough* in Cork and Belfast, but the Abbey took legal action to insist that it had the sole production rights on these plays in Ireland. Whereupon O'Casey, with the aid of a solicitor and his own devastating rhetoric, convinced the Abbey directors that their rights were limited to Dublin, and the suit was dropped. Meanwhile Yeats had been quoted in the English press as having made a number of false and mocking statements on *The Silver Tassie* and O'Casey—statements which Yeats denied having made—and again the hypersensitive O'Casey swung into action to demand and receive an apology. He received no apologies, however, from the irate citizens of Limerick who in 1929 barely tolerated Sinclair's production of *Juno* but prevented him from performing *Plough,* and who a year later on second thought burned the film of *Juno* during a street demonstration against O'Casey.

Small wonder then that on some occasions the suspicious O'Casey created enemies where none existed, as for example in his controversy with A.E. over modern art, where he may have had the best of the argument but in his ruthless attack was more sinning than sinned against. Toward the end of 1930, however, his suspicions were once more justified when an Irish priest launched such a vituperative attack on *The Silver Tassie* that a Dublin production of the play had to be canceled. And there was no sign of peace on his horizon, for the unrepentant O'Casey was now writing a new symbolic play about Hyde Park which was destined to provoke artistic and religious controversy once more.

To Harry Bergholz [1]

TC. O'CASEY

ST. JOHN'S WOOD
3 JANUARY 1929

Dear Sir:

I am not sure of the year of birth; I think it was 1884.[2] I wrote a little book called "The Story of The Citizen Army," the body founded by Jim Larkin, and commanded by James Connolly, which dealt with the activities of the army before and after the Rebellion of 1916.

It would be difficult to explain why the Abbey Theatre Directorate refused "The Silver Tassie". W. B. Yeats came to me when he was in London, and asked earnestly that his Theatre should be given the first production of the play; so did Lennox Robinson. But at that time, and long before (in fact nine months before the play was written) I felt that what they really looked for was the chance to reject the play, because I refused to be fittingly reverential to their Dublin Literary clique. They thought the rejection would frighten me, and that I would withdraw it because they thought it was a very bad play. They made a hell of a mistake, for I published their criticisms, and I answered them fervently and fiercely, and since then they haven't opened their mouths, except to threaten me with "breach of copyright" because I ventured to publish adverse criticisms of my own play! I thought then, and I still think that "The Silver Tassie" is the best play that I have written. The Abbey Theatre's talk about idealism is pure hypocrisy, for many of their plays

[1] Harry Bergholz, a young German who was preparing an article, "Sean O'Casey," *Englische Studien,* LXV (Berlin, 1930).

[2] He was mistaken. The date of his birth, as he later found out, was 30 March 1880.

would do honour to the worst commercial Theatre in London. And who in the name of God would say that "The Silver Tassie" was a commercial mode in drama.

The play has been taken by C. B. Cochrane for production in New York, and here in London it is to follow the production of "Porgy" by the same producer.

Sincerely yours,
Sean O'Casey

To Gabriel Fallon

MS. TEXAS

ST. JOHN'S WOOD
8 JANUARY 1929

Dear Gaby—

AE has refused the publication of my third (and last) reply to his wonderful discoveries made in the art of painting. I want you to see if it would be published in the paper published by the Republican Party, or by the paper published by Cumann na Gaedheal.[1] I would post it myself but I know not the name nor address of either paper. It doesn't matter which publishes it, for Artists may be born in any Camp, and the rubbish written by, & the adoration of imitation Corot technique by that sceptered old myth, AE are a snare & a pit to any young spirit finding a way towards expression in colour, line & form. It makes me wild to read the statements made on Art & Literature by this old Sham who has made himself judge of politics, of poetry, of painting, of plays & judge of prayer. Fire from heaven, fire from heaven, oh God, to burn up all the silly teaching of the self styled Logos Hibernica.

Love to Rose, the kids & to you.

Sean

Sursum Corda

[1] See O'Casey's letter to *An Poblacht,* 18 January 1930.

To Gabriel Fallon

MS. TEXAS

ST. JOHN'S WOOD
9 JANUARY 1929

Dear Gaby—

A short letter just to give you a squint at things here.

Have been sick for the last two weeks—catharrh of the belly—& am under the doctor & am beginning to like hearing the birdies singing again in the garden. They did get on my nerves while I was in pain. Billy [McElroy]'s been in bed for the last week & is under the care of the same doctor. He's better now, & so am I, so tra, la, la, cum Starkie, cum Gregoriusiana, hallelujah Yeats, and Bonny bonnie, blue-bonnetted, bonnie Robbie Rob Roy McGregor O!

I don't think you need worry very much about Frankie. Look to his food, & give him air & leave the rest to God.

Have heard nothing yet from C. B. Cochrane about anything. He probably won't chance the Tassie now till the Autumn.

I think you're right about [Cecil] Salkeld. That's his place—The Theatre. Not the Gate, nor the Abbey, but the Theatre. His design in The Studio is a fine one. Nigel Playfair's producing Lynnx's Give a Dog — here soon for a Play performing Society.[1] He has sent his Far Off Hills to Sinclair, & it is now with Harwood of The Ambassadors' Theatre here who's thinking of putting it on.

Adviser of Drama to the University of Michigan—that's the place for Robbie.[2] What about holding a class in the open on the shores of the Lake? Such a fin de siecle idea! Everybody bring a cushion. Lecturer in extraordinary to Thespis. And draw me salary from The Abbey all the while.

Glad to hear that Lyle [Donahy] has got something to do in the way of a job, for he has plenty to do in many other ways.

Love to Rose, Frankie & to yourself.

Sean

Tell Will to gird up his loins & fear not

[1] Lennox Robinson's *Give a Dog a* —— was performed by the Repertory Players at the Strand Theatre, London, on 20 January 1929.

[2] Early in 1929 Robinson spent a month at the University of Michigan as a visiting guest director and professor of drama.

To Gabriel Fallon

MS. TEXAS

ST. JOHN'S WOOD
26 JANUARY 1929

Dear Gaby—

Another and another and another! Hope the new pilgrim is going on well, & that Rose is right again. You'll find Frankie will be alright in a short while.

Am just beginning to feel a little friendly towards the world again. Billy's still bad & confined to his bed. Haven't seen Cochrane since, but the papers have said he is going to get Reuben Mamoulian to produce The Tassie. It will probably go on in September. Michael Scott was here last night, & looked pale after rising from an attack of Influenza. Augustus John is going to paint me again in the coming Spring. Evan [Walters] has done a fine pastel of Eileen. Full of colour & form. Sorry that Macmillan's have refused Lyle's poems. I guessed they would. It takes a sale of a thousand copies now to cover the cost of publication, & I'm afraid Lyle wouldn't sell that number for years. There is a much better sale now for plays than for poetry, & the publishers are very shy at accepting a play. I met James Stephens the other night & he was looking drawn & pale & worried. Hadn't much chance of a talk with him for we met, twas in a crowd at Lady Londonderry's, & persons kept butting in to talk to him & to talk to me, so we hadn't much time for, as Billy would say, a 'chin wag'. I understand Boss has an infant that is weak & delicate. Hard lines on Boss & Mac.[1] Writing this just to keep in touch, feeling a little tired because of illness & of working a good deal lately.

Remember me to Rose. Best wishes to Bernard, to Frankie, to Rose & yourself.

Sean

[1] Mr. and Mrs. Arthur Shields.

From Lady Gregory

PS. *Modern Drama* [1]

[DUBLIN, ? FEBRUARY 1929]

[2] . . . the old house—to be a "Civic Museum" and a new plain gallery built at the back—It is a beautiful house—and tho' I sigh for the Lutyens

[1] From a copy made by A. C. Edwards and printed in *Modern Drama,* May 1965.

[2] The first page is missing.

building and Stephens Green, this will be made ready far more quickly, and the cost will be far less—And we can begin to fight anew "con spirito"—

What a fine collection of pictures you are getting around you—Has there been any photograph of the John picture of you? I have never seen a reproduction—

I shall get away after a couple of weeks, as L. R. is coming back after all I am glad to say. He goes first to Rapallo to stay with Yeats—My youngest grandchild, Catherine, is now at the Alexander College, and I am glad to be here while she gets fitted in—

Gogarty has been very kind coming in to see me. I like very much his little poem in the last *Statesman*.[3]

I am asking Barry Fitzgerald to come and see me tomorrow—or rather to see Mrs. Flanagin's book about the Russian theatre [4]—there are a couple of very good chapters on that and the workers in it—

I hope great things from your visit to the dentist—teeth are responsible for much ill health—You may renew your youth as the Eagle: —Good bye now and every good wish for you and yours from yr affectionate

A Gregory

[3] Oliver St. John Gogarty, "Verse," *Irish Statesman*, 9 February 1929.

[4] Hallie Flanagan, *Shifting Scenes of the Modern European Theatre* (London, Harrap, 1928). Six chapters are devoted to impressions of Soviet theatres and plays.

To Oliver St. John Gogarty

MS. BUCKNELL [1]

ST. JOHN'S WOOD
5 FEBRUARY 1929

Dear Oliver,

Billy [McElroy] has told me that you aren't well, & I send you balm & consolation with the knowledge that he has been sick & I have been sick as he & hell. Just recovering a little now after having had my teeth out, but still feeling like a 'perne in a gyre.' [2] This simile, & hyperdoxi-

[1] An imperfect copy of this letter appears in James F. Carens, "Four Letters: Sean O'Casey to Oliver St. John Gogarty," *James Joyce Quarterly*, Fall 1970, O'Casey Issue.

[2] A reference to a line in Yeats's poem, "Sailing to Byzantium," Part III, in *The Tower* (1928). The whole letter is an attack on Yeats's book, which was universally praised and won the 1928 Tailteann Games first prize for poetry.

logical symbol may be found I think if you root long enough through the millions & millions (The Milky Way) of pages of the Encyclopedia Pox Box Brittanica, "and when found, make a note on." I see WBY says when his body peels off his soul he'll take again no natural shape, but be a cup or something of hammered gold or gold enamelling, or a kind of a cock or hen sitting on a golden bough singing to passing gents & ladies on their way to Byzantium.[3] May I be one of the passing gents that listen. That's the shape I'll take to hear the little cocky cocky bird a singing. I've read Yeats's 'The Tower' in fact—as [Lennox] Robinson would say—three times in all, and it doesn't satisfy me. He builds better in wattles than he builds in stone. And all the silver-throated bugles that blew about this bloody book! There isn't a good line about life from one end of the book to the other, though there are several bad ones about death. Where is its bountiful beauty to be found—will somebody tell me that? Age like a tin can tied to a dog's tail? [4] Talk of silver candlesticks or sconce or the clipped off ears on a little covered dish? [5] Sturge Moore's swan in a fading gleam floating on a long lost reach of glittering stream, singing his long, last, little share of song.[6] I'm sitting on top of the world, just rolling along, I'm quitting the blues of the world, and singing a song, singing a song. "The death of friends, or death of every brilliant eye," [7]—& so to end is his best so far to me. But there's no fear of YO giving anyone a catch in his breath, except all the elect people of God. "An affable Irregular, an heavily Falstaffian man, comes cracking jokes of civil war." [8] Was he any worse than Yeats thinking of a pear tree broken by a storm? [9] Is he trying to be serious here or trying to be funny? Or trying to wed what is sublime to what is ridiculous? And that loud-lauded passage "Hollow of cheek as though it drank the wind and took a mess of shadows for its meat." [10] Thought of by a quattrocento mind & written by quinquagesima fingers. Take them all from Sailing to the Highlands High to All Souls' Night and we get some prate, a lot of pose, & very little poetry. You don't make verses great when you push in the names of Dionysus, Semele, Poseidon, & others names of gods that godded Greece. We are sated and sick of this heresy in Literature & in Art. O, stars, come build in the empty hive of the honey bees! [11] There is nothing natural here; it is all forced. He has polished bone till he thinks it ivory. Perhaps at your

[3] *Ibid.,* Part IV.

[4] "The Tower," Part I.

[5] *Ibid.,* Part II.

[6] In his "Note" to "The Tower," Part III, Yeats quotes and praises Sturge Moore's "The Dying Swan."

[7] "The Tower," Part III.

[8] "Meditations," Part V, "The Road at My Door."

[9] *Ibid.*

[10] "Among School Children."

[11] A parody of "Meditations," Part VI, "The Stare's Nest by My Window": "O honey-bees,/Come build in the empty house of the stare."

leisure you would send me parts that are abrim, or even brimmed with beauty. To me the stuff is court-sworded & epauletted verse. And now I hope you're well again, & maybe, when you're here the next time we'll talk of & walk through the Tower, & have a look at Sato's sword,[12] & decide whether or no S. Moore's Dying Swan is, as Yeats says, one of the loveliest lyrics of our time. God be merciful to us all.

Sean

[12] "Meditations," Part II, "My Table."

To T. P. O'Connor[1]

TC. O'Casey
[St. John's Wood]
8 February 1929

Dear Mr O'Connor—

I thank you for the honour of asking me to come with you to the Banquet which is yearly held in Liverpool, Chun Gloire De agus onora Naoimh Phadruig,[2] but regret to say that I cannot go.

I felt sure that my hesitation in speaking to your Secretary would indicate my reluctance to participate, for nothing will induce me to attend any of these organised meals.

I am sorry to hear of your physical weakness, but the Summer, which I too wait to welcome, will, I feel sure, make you much better.

Sincerely Yours,
[Sean O'Casey]

[1] Thomas Power O'Connor (1848–1929), journalist, member of Parliament, editor of *T.P.'s Weekly*.
[2] For the glory of God and the honor of St. Patrick.

From Oliver St. John Gogarty

MS. O'Casey
[Renvyle, Co. Galway]
8 February 1929

Dear Sean,

Your health is not impaired anyway! Still you keep philosophysing with an hammer. You know as well as I do (and can express or suppress it better) that the charm of Yeats is the very artificiality that you hammer—hasn't he sacrificed his personality to affectation—"greater Art hath no man . . ." The affectation, the convention. There is no greater artificiality than being natural in literature. If it were possible that naturalness were literature, you and the rest would be well superseded by a dictagraph. Where would the fashioning faculty be? All we can do with our life in Art is to form, to shape something. That is why my family is a better achievement than my verses. But since my dentist quoted me to myself the other day, I have no poetic ambitions any longer. And he would never have known that I wrote, were it not for the fact that a remainder of 500 or so of the 3000 edition is selling at a bob a copy in Hanna's! [1] If it falls to a tanner, the Censors may become aware of Art!

I was on the point of writing to you to ask what was wrong with "that assiduous valetudinarian Billy", as Augustus calls him. What is the flat in Brussels for? He would be better in a German spa. Bad Nauheim for instance. Those b——y lemons! An ulcer in the guts will be his next effort. And we could never do without his outlook on life.

It's not so much the flue but the loss of energy that follows, that has landed me. I go to France at Easter by air for a week or so (if the bank lets me out of their sight). I am supposed to print another book with the Sisters; [2] but between Lennox's awful Anthology of weeds [3] and the coming "Package of W.B. for Ezra Pound" [4] there will be little kudos left in being published by Cuala. Anyhow an edition limited to twenty for those whom I may count on to cut the pages without cutting me subsequently will do no harm. We shall see. Here's specimen one enclosed.

Lady Gregory is at the Standard Hotel. Robinson has left America for Rapallo ("Not here, O Apollo!") and the nest of echoers will keep together till May. That fellow Pound! "Taking himself so seriously that he bleeds internally" as Wyndham Lewis says. His wife is worse for keeping and encouraging him.

It was very decent of you to send me a word oversea to break into

[1] The British edition of Gogarty's *An Offering of Swans* (Eyre & Spottiswoode, 1924). The limited Cuala Press edition of 1923 was dedicated to William McElroy, best man at O'Casey's wedding on 23 September 1927. Both editions have a preface by W. B. Yeats.

[2] The Dun Emer Press, which became the Cuala Press in 1908, was founded in 1903 at Dundrum, County Dublin, by "the Sisters," Elizabeth Corbet Yeats (1868–1940) and Susan Mary Yeats (1866–1949), with the aid of their brother, W. B. Yeats, who served as editor. James Joyce's Buck Mulligan (a fictional character modeled after Gogarty) made the following pertinent remark: "Five lines of text and ten pages of notes about the folk and the fishgods of Dundrum. Printed by the weird sisters in the year of the big wind." *Ulysses* (1922; Random House ed. 1934), p. 14.

[3] *A Little Anthology of Modern Irish Verse* (Dublin, Cuala, 1928), ed. Lennox Robinson.

[4] W. B. Yeats, *A Packet For Ezra Pound* (Dublin, Cuala, 1929).

this Pompeii. What about a double bedded room in the Papal territory and plenary indulgences 10% on the bill? Service!

Tout a toi
Ever
Oliver

For Sean O'Casey.

Phildey Rua's Song.

O Boys, the Times I've seen!
The things I've done and known!
If you knew where I have been,
Or half the joys I've had,
You never would leave me alone;
But pester me to tell,
Swearing to keep it dark,
What . . . but I know quite well:
Every solicitor's clerk
Would break out, and go mad;
And all the dogs would bark!

There was a young fellow of old Marco Polo
Who spoke of a wonderful town
Built on a lake of gold,
With many a barge and raft
Afloat in the cooling sun;
And lutes upon the lake
Played by such courtesans,
The sight was enough to take
The reason out of a man's
Brain, and to leave him daft
Babbling of lutes and fans.

The tale was right enough:
Willows and orioles,
And ladies skilled in love—
But they listened only to smirk,
For he spoke to incredulous fools;
And, maybe, was sorry he spoke;
For no one believes in joys,
And Peace on Earth is a joke,
Which, anyhow, telling destroys,
So better go on with your work:
But Boys, O Boys, O Boys!

Oliver St. J. Gogarty

To Augustus John [1]

MS. JOHN [2]

ST. JOHN'S WOOD
11 FEBRUARY 1929

My dear John—

Ever so glad to get your letter, & to read that you have been able to quit the hotel to settle more comfortably in the Villa. Billy [McElroy] is much better & is beginning to open his topcoat to the icy winds, as Cassius opened his toga to the lightning. Not surprised to hear that snow has fallen in Villefrance sur mer: that invariably happens when Billy has decided to go to the Continent to see the Sun. Last year one of Billy's boys was bad, & Billy wasn't too well, either, so the boy proposed to the feyther that, as the South of France mightn't be hot enough they should go to Morocco. And Billy wanted me to go & make it a trilogy of the party. I cooed reluctance at first, & finally roared refusal. Then Billy backed out, and off went the boy to the blaze & amaze of Morocco's magnificent sun. By accident the next morning I glanced at a paper and what did I see? Shocking cold gales, tidal waves and storm in Morocco; five thousand lives lost! And when I rang up Billy to tell him the news, he said there must be some mistake.

It's a pity Yeats & other symbolical & mystical poets couldn't see the Sailors dancing & otherwise enjoying themselves with the filles de joie—it might result in something better and the picture of the fluttering frenzy of the Swan on Leda. I am having an argument with Oliver Gogarty just now about Yeats's latest book of poems, "The Tower," & Oliver's latest declaration is that "Yeats proves his Artistry by having sacrificed his personality to his Art." Wheel, o Wheel. Wheel in de middle of a wheel. Wheel o wheel, wheel widin a wheel, way in the middle of the air! That must be the radium of vicarious activity. And so mystical verse is followed by mystical approbation.

I was in Tooths the other day but saw none of your pictures hanging. There was an exhibition of oils, drawings & pastels by Benois, who uses a cook for a model. I had read that she, with Derain, had designed for the Ballet of Petrouchka, & was interested to see her work. But there was nothing there that would have prompted me to break the eighth Com-

[1] Augustus John (1878–1961), British portrait and mural painter, etcher and lithographer, born in Wales. He painted a portrait of O'Casey in 1926.

[2] From a Xerox copy made by Michael Holroyd.

mandment—protestant catechism. There are two interesting nudes, but the rest—came out by the same door as in I went.

How could there be any difficulty with you over a conception of a design for the Second act of The Tassie? [3] Just that which springs from the humility of a great man, and there the difficulty ends. I send you a cutting that appeared in The Observer, & which angered me so much, & with the cutting, I send copy of a letter I have sent to C. B. Cochran. Warm wishes to Mrs. John to Vivien & Bobbette, and my deep affection to you.

Sean

[3] John had agreed to design the setting for the symbolic second act of *The Silver Tassie*. See Lady Gregory's letter to O'Casey, 11 October 1929, note 2.

To Oliver St. John Gogarty

MS. GOGARTY

ST. JOHN'S WOOD
16 FEBRUARY 1929

Dear Oliver—

Thanks for your kind letter having in it the chrysalis of a job for Evan W[alters]. I have read it to him, & have left him to bring forth in the heat of his imagination a beetle or a butterfly. I couldn't conscientiously suggest to him that he should paint Lady L[ondonderry] or Lord L as either or both wanted to be painted.

Very well, we'll talk of 'The Tower' [1] & other things when we have time and a lot of space. Who's Ezra Pound? I think I remember that some poems of his were reviewed recently by Y.O.[2] Is he an Irish Poet, an English poet or a Continental poet? And tell me who is Sturge Moore. I have just read in Life & Letters a thing by him called 'The Closing Door', written in memory of Henry Poole R.A, that is the most pretentious pile of dullness I have ever read. A discussion between Keiron, Apollodorus & Amymone. All letters & no life; give me in preference all life and no letters.

Billy [McElroy] is himself again.

What happened to L. Robinson that he left his job as Advisor in

[1] See O'Casey's letter to Gogarty, 5 February 1929, notes 2–12.

[2] Y.O., *Irish Statesman,* 8 December 1928, a review of Ezra Pound's *Selected Poems,* edited with an introduction by T. S. Eliot (London, Faber & Gwyer, 1928).

Drama to the Michigan University? Have they increased his salary as first, second & third class Producer of the Abbey?

If you sold 2500 copies out of 3000 it wasn't bad. 3000 is altogether too big of an edition for poetry or plays. Lady Gregory sent me a copy recently of your "Offering of Swans."

Terrible frost here: hearts breaking & pipes bursting. Just off now to the Pond on Hampstead Heath to see the skating.

Best Wishes.
Sean

To Augustus John

MS. JOHN [1]

ST. JOHN'S WOOD
20 FEBRUARY 1929

My dear John—

I hope you are well as this does not leave me at present. I am passing through the transitional stage of having new teeth planted in my mouth by the gentle hands of man, and am understanding more clearly than ever the foolishness in the phrase of loving one's neighbour as oneself. The only book that might give me comfort at the moment is "The Decline and Fall of the Roman Empire." We have had terrible weather here for some days, and on every house you can see plumbers crawling over the roofs and along the walls massaging the pipes. Cascades of cursing everywhere.

I enclose cutting from "The Era" and a letter from C. B. Cochran, in reply to one from me ticking him off, pointing out that though we let live those who err because they know nothing, we can't be so kind to those who err because they know something. His letter shows he sees his sin. I think it will soon be felt what a tremendous thing it is for ~~John to~~ (that was wrongly put) the Theatre that John should stoop to lift it a hell of a lot higher.[2] And, of course, it is a tremendous thing to me that through me this should happen.

I am going tomorrow or Friday to see an exhibition of Duncan Grant's pictures. I have seen several of his before at a representative Show of the London Group, but none of them sang of greatness.

[1] From a Xerox copy made by Michael Holroyd.

[2] A reference to John's decision to design the setting of the symbolic second act of *The Silver Tassie*, in C. B. Cochran's premiere production of the play. See Lady Gregory's letter to O'Casey, 11 October 1929, note 2.

I have been inquiring a little about Daintry[3] lately, & have so far found out that "he's not bad; he's very poor, & lives somewhere in Bloomsbury."

Best wishes to Mrs. John to Vivien & to Bobbette.

Yours Affectionately,
Sean

[3] Adrian Daintrey (1902–), British painter.

To Gabriel Fallon

MS. Texas

St. John's Wood
28 February 1929

Dear Gaby—

I dont know how I am, where I am or what I am, or who I am; or whether to condemn progress that takes away teeth, or progress that gives one a new set. I have been to the dentist, & am now struggling valiantly, despairably, with a top row and a bottom row of teeth. There is wailing & gnashing of teeth. However they're feeling more hopeful now, & in years to come, I will be able to hang on to an iron bar. Yes, A. John has undertaken to do a design for the 2nd act, & possibly for all four scenes. He is very interested in the play, thinks it great, & says 'The Abbey People were stupid to refuse it'.

Thanks for the copy of 'Spread Eagle',[1] my dear Gaby, it isn't a great play. Is it even a good one? No, no, (extract, excerpt, (Larkey)[2]

from 'I met my sister t'other day')

Lady G tells me L.R. is coming back to the Abbey (the cat came back) so Michigan University didn't keep the neo professor long. Oh, he

[1] George S. Brooks and Walter S. Lister, *Spread Eagle,* a play by two New York journalists, opened in London on 27 June 1929. Fallon was probably attracted to the play by an enthusiastic comment by the London Correspondent of the *Irish Times,* 29 June 1928, who called it "one of the most scathing plays I have ever seen . . . it destroys cherished illusions and makes a mock of patriotism." Coincidentally, Raymond Massey, who directed it and played a leading role, was soon to direct *The Silver Tassie;* see Lady Gregory's letter to O'Casey, 11 October 1929, note 2.

[2] Dr. John F. Larchet, musical director and conductor of the orchestra at the Abbey Theatre.

didn't stop long, no he didn't stop long, for he loved his native land the best. I've made a note on Will's resignation, & will write C.B. [Cochran] suggesting his inclusion for the part of Sylvester in The Tassie.[3]

Just engaged now (a secret) in negotiations for the sale of the Film rights of Juno,[4] & if it comes off, it will fit into the nick of time to pay £500 debt (Secret II) & give me time to live till Christmas.

How did 'Mountain Dew'[5] taste. Did it go up to the brain? An Abbey Divina Commedia, maybe. Last letter to Lady G I said poor Shiels would never write a line worth remembering. She sang dumb. Her letters are always kind and gracious, but never an answer to a criticism about LR, or AE, or Yeats or Shiels. This may be a divine dignity, or it may be a fluttering fear. Robinson said nothing terrible, or daring, or revolutionary, or bloodily merry in his lectures in the U S A. or Canada. Got a few clippings which showed he spoke about 'Anglo-Irish Poetry', & praised Tommy Moore. His day will come, gentlemen. Let us drink to it —Der Tag!

What's the idea of the house? Is it to be more secluded so that you can think? Of course you are right, it is possible to do anything only in loneliness. I hope Frankie's going on all right and the latest that has shoved itself into the world. And Rose. And you.

Yours as ever
Sean

[3] Will Shields (Barry Fitzgerald) had temporarily resigned from the. Abbey, and he did play the role of Sylvester Heegan in *The Silver Tassie*. See Lady Gregory's letter to O'Casey, 11 October 1929, note 2.

[4] The film version of *Juno and the Paycock* was released in 1930, directed by Alfred Hitchcock, produced by British International Pictures, with the following cast: Edward Chapman as Captain Jack Boyle, Sara Allgood as Juno Boyle, John Laurie as Johnny Boyle, Kathleen O'Regan as Mary Boyle, Sidney Morgan as Joxer Daly, Maire O'Neill as Maisie Madigan, David Morris as Jerry Devine, John Longdon as Charles Bentham, Dennis Wyndham as The Mobiliser, Fred Schwarz as Mr. Kelly. For O'Casey's reaction to the film, and particularly to the change of the original role of "Needle" Nugent, the tailor, to Mr. Kelly, played in the film by an actor with a stage-Jewish accent, see his letter to Charles Rosenberg and Martin Kesselman, 23 March 1955, Vol. III.

[5] George Shiels's *Mountain Dew* opened at the Abbey Theatre on 5 March 1929.

To Gabriel Fallon

MS. TEXAS

ST. JOHN'S WOOD
MONDAY, 15 APRIL 1929

My dear Gaby—

One can write no better on an orange box than on an ebony table, but one can write as well, & the box will serve for the time being. I think you have done well in getting a place of your own—no harm to say so when you've got it—and, if you can manage to keep things going with a little over to keep things coming, then, in a year or so, you'll gradually be able to garnish the place comfortably. As little ornament as possible, straight lines ———| up & down, everything having its use, and you fill the new laws of modern interior architecture—not decoration, which is horrible. As you are trying to get some new things together, we are trying to separate old things from our Association, things that we still have to use, & which are an abomination unto us. Billy [McElroy]'s a good deal better, & one of his horses, Moscow, has won twice. I think the bould Will [Barry Fitzgerald] exaggerated a little. He said himself I was looking younger than on the day before I was born. It was just inevitable that when Will was here, a good deal of the talk was of the Abbey, & a good deal of the Abbey was about their sudden & recent manner of rejecting new lamps for old ones. But, not being a Christian, I can't pretend to cherish affection towards those who had—as I firmly believe—decided to reject a play of mine if it happened to be a good one, & to accept the play if it happened to be a very bad one. I couldn't have harboured one thought against what the Abbey would probably call Commercial Cochrane, if he had said, no, no; no use. Too much risk of a loss. But Commercial Cochrane—more of an artist than the Abbey Arties—took the play, & from what I know, the Silver Tassie will get a production that not one of my plays has ever received here or in Dublin. But the play is rarely in my thoughts, & will not be often there till the work of production starts seriously. No, I'm neither puzzled nor surprised to hear that you are to sit in the seat of Dramatic Judgment at The Father Mathew Feis. Not good enough yet, but it would be foolish to despise the day of small things.

What Sheelah lujah[1] heard, & where she heard it, I don't know. This is how it is:—my contracts with Abbey end in July & August next. So I have given leave to Sinclair to play them in Cork & Limerick. He is to play 'The Plough' too in Belfast. The moment I fixed up a production of the Plough in Belfast, the Abbey wrote to me saying they had heard this—was it true, & they wanted to do the play there. I don't see why I shouldn't get as much as I can from the plays. When the Talkie comes,

[1] Shelah Richards.

then the chance will be over. The Abbey can go on playing them in Dublin, if they wish, though one week in the Gaiety or Olympia would bring me in as much as a year's fees from The Abbey. And that's how things stand now. Oh Gaby, Gaby what can that little propaganda be? Glad to hear that you made a success of "The Wagon & the Star".[2] But did you do well to re-write "almost the whole of the first act" of the play? Duffy's a good fellow, but your brains are your own & should be used only for the family welfare.

I got a letter from Lady G this morning saying how glad she was that Juno was to be filmed, & that I—and Ireland—and the Abbey are to be congratulated that it is the first—or one of the first filmed for the talkies. Which shows that she & Ireland—and The Abbey are far more interested in it than I am. By the way, International Pictures wrote asking me to do the dialogue that is to go with "The Informer",[3] but I turned the offer down.[4]

[2] Bernard Duffy's *The Wagon and the Star* (Dublin, Talbot Press, 1929).

[3] The film version of Liam O'Flaherty's novel, *The Informer* (London, Jonathan Cape, 1925), directed by John Ford.

[4] Page missing.

To Gabriel Fallon

MS. Texas

St. John's Wood
24 April 1929

Dear Gaby—

Good. Don't take LESS than 50/50. Having asked for the play[1] they should give 60/40. In the Division you pay the Back of the house—stage workmen, manager etc.,—they pay the front of the house—programme sellers, Booking Office etc—that's how they do here anyhow—and be sure to make THEM pay for half of the Advertising & Light.

Try to knock something out of this yourself. Make an Agreement with Duffy. You will do the mule's work—see you get paid for it. In the Agreement say in case of a tour you get so much a week £2. £3 £4, or say one or two per cent of the Gross Receipts. Fagan got £25 a week for Juno & The Plough as well as 50% of the profits, with *no risk* of a loss, except his profit. Don't forget to get Duffy to sign—you

[1] *The Shadow of a Gunman.* See O'Casey's letter to Fallon, 4 June 1929, note 1.

can't begin early enough. Will be seeing Cochrane shortly now about "The Tassie". Hope Will, will well, do well. Best wishes to Will; good wishes to Peter [Judge (F. J. McCormick)] & to Frank Hugh [O'Donnell].

& Good & Best to you & Rose & Frank, & the other.

Hope Frankie's doing well. Will answer your letter later on.

Yours
Sean

To Gabriel Fallon

MS. Texas

St. John's Wood
14 May 1929

Dear Gaby—

Will has written to me telling me that your father has died. I send you my sympathy, for it is bound to prove a shock to you in some ways. One of the curses of death is that when he comes he always interferes with something. This ever-aching, never-curable bruise on the heel of man is a damned nuisance. And the present way of the present world make it a bigger burden still. The world has made Death a bigger robber now than he was in the time of the tribes. It is a bitter thing to think that death very often makes the life left behind a little or a lot more difficult to live. And huge money-stout institutions flourish on our fear that we may not be able to perform an office of charity in burying our brother or our sister in an orderly & a seemly way. Oh, well, you've many things to think about & try you besides the things dreamed in my philosophy, & I'm sorry indeed that I can only leave you to bear them as best you can. I hope though your father's death will not disconcert your economical position too much, & that after all the troubles concurrent with death, you may be shortly able to go on in the way from which this knock-about has taken you for the time being.

Love to you & Rose & Frankie & the littlest of the Fallons.

Yours
Sean

To Arthur Sinclair [1]

MS. Mair

St. John's Wood
2 June 1929

Dear Arthur Sinclair—

Gaby Fallon has written asking permission to give two weeks' performance of "The Gunman" in a Hall in Dublin. He has had a lot of bad luck lately—father dying & the only brother that earns anything in hospital waiting for a bad operation. He himself is married & has two kids, a wife & a few quid a week, so I would like to help him.

The letter of our agreement allows me to do this, but the spirit of our understanding is that you have full control of acting rights, outside the claim of the Abbey, so that it is only fair that I should get your permission, which I now ask for.

These cursed elections are a nuisance. The Theatres here are as empty as Gospel Halls, but that doesn't quit us of the desire to strain the capacity of our places of Entertainment: So better fortune for you next week—and for me too.

The list of dates you have sent to me looks fine and promising, & perhaps they will result in you & me having a chance to open a little Deposit Account in our respective Banking Houses.

Best to Mollie
& You.

Gaby doesn't act for the Abbey now, having had a difference with them more than a year ago.

[*Sean*]

[1] Arthur Sinclair (1883–1951), Abbey Theatre actor, husband of Abbey actress Maire O'Neill, co-director and actor with his wife of the Irish Players in London.

To Gabriel Fallon

MS. Texas

St. John's Wood
4 June 1929

Dear Gaby—

Well, here we are again. Yes, you can have permission to give 2 weeks' performance of "The Gunman" [1] provided you have the announcement on your bills & your programmes. 'By Kind Permission of Arthur Sinclair'.

Now I hope you are going to take no risk—or rather that any risk you take will be a very reasonable one. And don't forget that a fifty-fifty deal means division of expenses. Fifty-fifty in costs as well as in takings. There is just a danger that in the hot time of August your houses may not be quite so good as you imagine.

I'm very sorry to hear of Dan having to lie down just when a multitude of reasons are roaring at him to run about.

No news to send. Dr. [Joseph] Cummins has been over here for a few days & looks well & is as lonely minded as ever. Peter Judge [F. J. McCormick] is over here now, & rang me up yesterday to ask me to see him & Eileen. Thinking of asking him to tea on Sunday, though his association with the Abbey, & their refusal of The Tassie makes me a bit embarrassed.

Love to all.

Your Buttie
Sean

[1] *The Shadow of a Gunman* was produced at the Civic Theatre, Dunlaoghaire, County Dublin, from 26 August to 4 September 1929, by the First National Players, a company that Fallon had helped to organize.

To Gabriel Fallon

MS. Texas

St. John's Wood
6 June 1929

Dear Gaby—

Just joking when I wrote you must put Arthur Sinclair's name on bill in Big Letters. You mustn't spoil your Ad by display of mine or his name. Just the ordinary way, & if you like it better, substitute By Arrangement with A. Sinclair & Sean O'Casey.

Not only voted for Labour, but replying to a H.M. Inspector of Taxes, demanding the immediate return of a filled up Form, added a Postscript saying:

On Thursday, sir, don't forget to vote often & vote early for the Labour Man.

Yours
Sean

To R. S. Williams

TC. O'Casey

London
14 June 1929

Dear Sir—

Now, sir, what would it serve to grant you the interview you ask, or the half hour's chat you desire? Would it serve God? No, sir. Or one of His Religions? No, sir. Or King or Country? No, sir. Or even Mammon? Not even Mammon, sir.

Besides I might feel far from comfortable pilloried between your selection of Distinguished Irishmen; certainly restless if you stuck me between Y O and A E. and vindictive if I found myself back to back with Professor Magennis,[1] who, lecturing on Drama, once said that a play must have a beginning, a middle and an end, as profound a statement as any ever made by Mr York of York, York.

Remembering, sir, that I now reside in England, and that my latest play has been banished with drum beat and trumpet blast by the Abbey Theatre, I am now in the unhappy group of Extinguished Irishmen, and so, sir, would, I think, be a most unsuitable addition to your selection of Distinguished Irish Talkies.

Yours Sincerely,
Sean O'Casey

[1] Prof. William Magennis, department of metaphysics, University College, Dublin; chairman of the Irish Censorship Board, 1934–46.

To Lady Londonderry

MS. Lady Bury
St. John's Wood
16 June 1929

Dear Lady Londonderry—

I enclose you a newspaper cutting which seems to indicate that Sally Allgood has buckled herself on to another play,[1] and so the agitating prospect of having to hang on to the Dole is not quite so near as she imagined it to be.

Affectionate regards to your son & daughter, to Lord Londonderry & to you.

Sean O'Casey

[1] Frank Vosper's *Murder on the Second Floor* opened in London on 21 June 1929, with Sara Allgood in the role of Mrs. Armitage.

To John H. Perrin[1]

TC. O'Casey
London, 9 July 1929

Dear Sir—

Royalties due for the last performance of "The Plough and the Stars", for week ending May 27th, 1929, have not yet been received.

Yours Faithfully,
Sean O'Casey

[1] John H. Perrin, secretary of the Abbey Theatre.

From Lady Gregory

MS. O'Casey
Coole Park, Gort, Co. Galway
15 July 1929

Dear Sean—

It is long since I have heard news of you—though you are often in my mind. I hope all goes well with you and the boy & his mother—I have been a good deal alone and though the grandchildren return this week, this is no longer their *only* home as it was their father's. Their mother married last year our neighbour, Captain Gough—& she lives at Lough Cutra—a beautiful lake there tho' not our woods—so the children divide their time—& we all go back & forwards, over the 5 mile road. My garden is lovely just now with blue delphiniums, & phloxes, rose, white & purple coming into flower—I work in it a good deal in the evenings. The forestry is a great joy—over a million little seedlings in one field will be planted out eventually—& a good deal of planting of imported little trees has already been done.

I had never heard of Malone until his book on Irish Drama came out.[1] He speaks so highly of me that I don't like praising it! but it is the greatest help having the Abbey History put down so clearly, with its dates & facts—so many writers in U.S.A and Germany have been writing asking for information to put in their books—& can be referred to it. One German, whose innumerable questions I have already answered a percentage of, writes today asking among other things for the original M.S. of all my plays!

I hope your boy continues to grow in health & strength. And I do hope you are well & strong—and I do honestly hope for the success of the Tassie—please believe this—& believe me affectionately your friend

A. Gregory

[1] Andrew E. Malone, *The Irish Drama: 1896–1928* (London, Constable, 1929).

To Lady Gregory

MS. GREGORY

ST. JOHN'S WOOD
18 JULY 1929

Dear Lady Gregory—

Thanks for your letter, and its core of kind remembrance.

I am fairly well, though my health hasn't been always easy, & my eyes trouble me a good deal. But these are things that entrenched themselves in me in Childhood, & the only thing to do is to fight a defensive war & keep them under cover. Anyhow, I have often been worse, and as I have married a splendid girl in every way, & as we are very happy together; a girl who has never tired me for a moment, whose good taste in pictures is remarkable, & who is quickly acquiring one for good books, & who is a great mother,—then I have many reasons indeed for believing that the goodness of God hasn't altogether left me alone. We live a very simple life, and the difficulties of meeting our needs—for we have ever been faced with the fact of having none to spare—and sometimes even not enough—have brought us closer together. She has a part in "Bitter-Sweet" [1] to be produced tonight here, which will, perhaps, help her to gather a few pounds together for herself & her particular needs.

Our little plantation is beautiful too, full of Delphiniums, lupins, petunias, pansies, dahlias, & peonies, & the apples on two trees we have are getting very fat & important looking. I'm trying to make friends with a blackbird that lives near us, and though he is still a little shy, I hope to put him at his ease shortly. A. E. Malone wrote for the Labour papers some years ago, & occasionally for The Statesman & The Dublin Magazine. He is a friend of F. Hugh O'Donnell. Of course I believe you hope for the success of "The Tassie". I'm sure from the viewpoint of Drama its success is certain; its financial success of course, will mean much to me.

I see one of the American papers says Yeats refused the work because it was "an English drawing-room piece".

Best wishes to all at Coole, & to all at the other home five miles away.

Yours Affectionately
Sean

[1] Noel Coward's *Bitter-Sweet* opened in London on 18 July 1929 and ran until May 1931. Eileen Carey O'Casey played the role of Jane, one of the girl friends, for the entire run of the play.

To Whitney, Moore and Keller [1]

TC. O'CASEY

ST. JOHN'S WOOD
23 JULY 1929

Dear Sirs—

I have received from Mr P. Selby [2] a copy of a letter sent to him by you, evidently on behalf of The Abbey Theatre, saying among other things that—"Permission was given to The National Theatre to perform certain plays in Ireland, and Mr O Casey bound himself not to permit his plays to be produced except by the Abbey Co in any theatre or Music

[1] Whitney, Moore and Keller, Dublin, solicitors for the National Theatre Society (the Abbey Theatre).

[2] P. Selby, manager for Arthur Sinclair and the Irish Players.

Hall in Ireland." And that they intend to try to prevent performances of my plays in Ireland by The Irish Players.

So not being satisfied with the fine pleasure of an insult given some time ago, they now seek the coarser satisfaction of a pleasure through an attempted injury. After what was done in the refusal of "The Silver Tassie" which was sent to them as a first offering, contrary to business advice here,—which no other dramatist would do, except, perhaps, one conscious of a good reason for faithfulness, it's a bit thick for the Abbey to believe that Sean O'Casey would singing a song, chain himself to the Abbey for the sole production of his plays over in Ireland. They got, of course, permission to perform his plays in Ireland, and they are now trying to show their appreciation for a sentimental act of loyalty done even under the stress of justifiable rage and resentment. The Abbey Directorate—or some of them—are evidently determined to make the minor relations that still connect me with them, as harrassing and as painful as possible. I will give you some instances: No mention was made of a performance of "The Plough" till they heard of that to be given by The Irish Players. When they heard of the American tour, they immediately wrote to me for my plays in an American tour they were arranging. On 4th Mar, their Secretary wrote asking me to tell him by return if [Arthur] Sinclair was to play the play in Belfast. I wrote by return, and received no comment whatever, which dandy indifference is not concomitant with their reputation for unqualified courtesy, or their anxiety to produce the play themselves. On the last occasion of a production of a play of mine in Belfast, I had to write and point out an omission on their part. Numerous letters from me on important matters have been ignored by the Abbey Theatre. On one occasion, having written to the Secretary four times, I wrote to Mr Robinson, four or five months afterwards, complaining, and he thought the matter settled by the despatch of a formal postcard, and it was not till a letter had been sent to Lady Gregory that the complaint was answered five months later. When in Ireland last I had to go personally to the Theatre to find out why letters had remained unanswered, and why arrangements agreed upon had not been carried out. And it is still happening, for no reply has been received by me yet to a letter sent to the Theatre on the 9th of July. May I point out that nearly three years ago (on receiving a request from the Rosario Players) I urged the Abbey Theatre to include Belfast in their activities, but no notice was then taken of my suggestion. Then I wrote to them, after talking with Sir Barry Jackson, about a possible London season, but, as far as I am aware, no notice was taken of the suggestion. The suggested season in London, might, of course be impossible, or, if possible, unwise, but the matter was, at least, worth a passing reference.

The Abbey Theatre has had "The Plough and the Stars" for three years, and, as far as I know, never proposed playing it in Belfast till they heard it was to be played there by The Irish Players. They have had "Juno and the Paycock" for four years, and are thinking of playing it in Cork, because a production there has been planned by The Irish Players. This sudden interest in the two plays seems to be to be more significant than generous.

However, as The Abbey Theatre Directorate—or some of them—are evidently determined to make things as uncomfortable as possible for me, in little ways and big ways, for reasons guessed by me, but best known to themselves, and as you are, probably, interested only in the legal aspect of the difference, let me point out to you that the agreement made by me with the Abbey Theatre for "The Plough and the Stars", ended on the 2nd DAY OF JULY, 1929, so that their objection to the performance in Belfast by The Irish Players, is null and void; and that the Agreement made by me with The Abbey Theatre for "Juno and the Paycock", ends on the 6th DAY OF AUGUST, 1929, and as no notice of renewal was sent to me, then their objection to performances in Cork by the Irish Players is null and void also.

So I must ask you without any delay, to inform Mr Percival Selby of these facts, and to let me know immediately that you have done so, and that you will send to me an undertaking from the Abbey Theatre Co that will cease from prejudicing my rights by issuing notices of this kind.

Faithfully Yours

[*Sean O'Casey*]

To Whitney, Moore and Keller

TC. O'CASEY

[24 JULY 1929]

addendum; addenda; addendi.

Dear Sirs—

The enclosed letter had already been written when your letter to me came this morning Wednesday, July 24th, 1929., and I think nothing more remains to be put before you by me, except,

a. It will be, as far as I am concerned, necessary for The Abbey Theatre to try to enforce what you term their rights, which, I hold, do not morally or legally exist.

b. No month's notice in writing that The Abbey Theatre intended to continue the Agreement for another year, was received by me, either for

"The Plough and the Stars", on the one hand or "Juno and The Paycock" on the other.

Yours Sincerely,
[*Sean O'Casey*]

To Whitney, Moore and Keller

MS. O'Casey [1]

1 August 1929

Dear Sirs,

I have received your letter of today.

Yes, cheques have a habit of going astray when it is most necessary they should not do so. They are beginning to behave like Sheep & Christians—all cheques like Sheep have gone astray—you know the quotation from the Koran.

I appreciate your Clients' statement that they absolve me from all blame. I say ditto, absolvo omnia Latitudino aquarium.

Reply to a letter from your Clients' Sec on Mar 4th, 1929, they not only got an indication but a definite statement that my plays would be produced by A. Sinclair in Belfast, & no comment was made in this notification.

I will have to first consider your request that I should give The Abbey T. Soc the rights of my plays for Dublin. The present tendency is for my peace of mind to cast away from them altogether.

Yrs,
S. O'Casey

[1] This is a rough draft.

To W. B. Yeats

TC. O'Casey

St. John's Wood

14 August 1929

Dear Sir—

The enclosed cutting, with the statements in its lap, is appearing in the English Provincial Press—for instance in the Nottingham Journal;

the Sheffield Independent, as well as the journal from which the cutting I send you is taken—and for obvious reasons I will be forced to topple these statements over by a categorical denial.

Before doing this I shall be glad if you would kindly let me know that nothing you said during the House Party mentioned in the latter part of the cutting, could have been threaded into the statements that "Mr. Yeats, who is one of the Directors of the Abbey Theatre, suggested some slight alterations in one or two of the scenes. These Mr. O'Casey refused to consider, etc;" or that "The Silver Tassie went to America after a brief run in Dublin;" or that "the play was being produced when Mr. Yeats and I were both members of a House Party in the Wicklow district."

I am sorry to have to trouble you about this, but the writer evidently claims some intimacy with you, and his statement that you were sitting in his company "around the fire on a wet Irish night," while you "recited first your poems, and then some lines from 'The Silver Tassie' ", would lead almost any reader to associate you with the statements appearing previously about my play in the same cutting.

I shall be very glad of an early reply.

Yours Sincerely,
[*Sean O'Casey*]

I am sending this by registered post by way of The Abbey Theatre.

From Oliver St. John Gogarty

MS. O'Casey

Renvyle,
Co. Galway
17 August 1929

Dear Sean

That cheered me! It was a kindly thought of yours to send me a line. And the portrait of the Rex Sanctae Johanne lucis or Silvestri bears out what I have often been thinking: that our best deeds are our boys.

Yes, I wrote "The Charioteer"[1] to "get away" with that about the chinless or rather "neckless" natives who won't hold their heads up under any circumstances or Governments; and then "you cannot examine your conscience with a super-charger". As if, in the middle of

[1] Oliver St. John Gogarty, "The Charioteer," *Irish Statesman,* 27 July 1929, an allegorical tale.

life and the tip of existence this damned conscience should be considered at all! But no one will read me until I am dead & then only a little bit about me: Nabocliv! [2] As long as you do.

Little chance of getting over; but when I meet Mac [Billy McElroy] (Give him my love) again—God send it soon—I'll ring you. I hope Cochrane will treat you well.

Always yours
O.G.

[2] Na bac libh!, Never mind!

W. McA. McCracken [1]

TC. O'CASEY
[ST. JOHN'S WOOD]
[18 AUGUST 1929]

O'Casey V National Theatre Society.

I am unaware of any practice obtaining in past years of signing fresh Agreements each year with The Abbey Theatre. For instance the one signed with them previous to that signed in 1928, on which they stake their present claim, (The Plough and the Stars) was signed in 1926, and as in 1927 the Abbey sent me neither Agreements nor notice of renewal (they would hardly claim to have done so in this instance) then it was open to me in 1928 to refuse to have anything more to do with them. It was in this period that the dispute about the rejection of "The Silver Tassie" happened, and in the midst of this they sent me the Agreements to sign, saying that their Auditors requested them to have them signed before the accounts were passed. The spirit in which these were signed by me was that of an indignant decision not to withdraw altogether from the Abbey Theatre, backed by appeals from St John Irvine and G. B. Shaw, and in no way did I mean to confer upon them the exclusive rights of producing my plays in Ireland. The clause of giving a month's notice for renewal wasnt even noticed by me then, or when I made arrangements with Mr [Arthur] Sinclair. And this decision not to withdraw my plays from The Abbey Theatre has been carried on right through by me, as I can, I believe easily prove. While the dispute over "The Silver Tassie" was proceeding, G. B. Shaw asked me to lunch with him and Mrs Shaw, during which I was told The Abbey would produce the play if I would be forgiving enough to let them

[1] W. McA. McCracken, 24 Upper Ormond Quay, Dublin, O'Casey's solicitor.

do so. I agreed, but felt so bitterly about the whole affair that Mrs Shaw thought in correspondence that might take place about the production, I would say hard things that would again cause a break. So I arranged to forward any letter I might write to the Abbey first to G.B.S. for his approval or suggested alteration, if such was thought to be necessary by him. I imagine that I could not do much more than that, but The Abbey Theatre never indicated in any way whatsoever that they were willing to produce the play, and in this, to my mind subjected me to another humiliation. When arranging with Mr Sinclair about the production of my plays in Ireland, my thought was not how I could take them from the Abbey Theatre to give them to Mr Sinclair; but how I could give them to him without taking them from The Abbey. And so it was understood between Mr Sinclair and me that The Abbey could, if they wished, produce the plays in Belfast, while he had no permission to perform any one of the three plays before the month of August, 1929; as a matter of fact The Abbey had date pencilled in for production of The Plough and the Stars in the Opera House, Belfast for five or six months, but the Manager of the Theatre could not get them to fix it, and actually asked Mr Sinclair to take the date up that was left vacant by the Abbey. But immediately they heard of Mr Sinclair's production in Belfast in November, they at once take legal action, and say they too want to perform the play in the same City in the same Month. And so, although I held that the rights of my plays would revert to me from the Abbey Theatre after the month of August, Dublin was held back from Mr Sinclair, and reserved by me for The Abbey Theatre. All this can be proved from letters held by me, Mr Sinclair and Mr Sinclair's Agent. (The rights for the Free State were not given to Mr Sinclair, but permission only to play the plays in Cork, Limerick and Waterford.) There was no practice of signing fresh Agreements each year known to me, and I can hardly believe it was or is known to any other Dramatist. To sign an agreement containing an option of renewal for another year every year is a preposterous idea, and is unknown here even in the womb of the Commercial Theatre. Besides if they get this done, what do they want with an option? How can they turn an option into an agreement; an agreement may contain an option, but can an option contain an agreement?

The view expressed in your letter did not come to me as a surprise, because it was quite clear to me that The Abbey Directorate—or some of them—were determined to press home a legal point that existed between them and me, but not between me and them, for, as I hope I have made clear, up to the time of their clumsy-minded legal action, I had kept certain the continuance of my connection with them.

Now let me say a word or two about the contents of the Letter from Whitney, Moore and Keller:

"The outstanding desire of The Society is to be on altogether friendly terms with O'Casey." Damned funny thing to say after the rejection of "The Silver Tassie", to be followed on by the neglect of the good offices of G.B.S. towards a reconciliation. ". . . regarded them as two of their best plays, and to give up the right to produce them would have been foolish to a degree." But I had myself to increase the number of performances specified (six) in agreement to twelve as a fair number, and to fulfil this they had to put the play on during the last week of their last season. And since last January, poor stuff by one Dramatist has been put on six times, while the two of their "greatest plays" have been put on twice.

The next is an implicit statement that I received the Agreements. Anyone friend of mine—Seamus O Connor for instance—would hardly believe I would deny receiving them if they came, even under the conditions The Abbey Theatre claim their reception would impose upon me. I submit they should have been sent by registered post. They were very important to the Abbey. To "give up the right to produce these plays would have been foolish to a degree," says their letter. I submit it was foolish to a degree not to have sent these agreements by registered post. Recently I had to give notice terminating lease of a flat. The Solicitor sent one, but not seeing it actually sent I despatched another. Last year I wanted to terminate an American Play Agreement; my Agent sent a registered note; my Solicitor sent a second, and I sent a third. They say they sent the agreements on the 1st of June; they began to take legal action on July 17th, knowing that they had received no notice from me of the arrival of the agreements, the non-receipts of which would make their claim difficult, if not impossible; but they troubled to make the slenderest inquiry about them. It was only on July 22nd when they sent me a cheque due more than seven weeks before, and asked for by me on the 9th July, that they mentioned the matter in a very casual way indeed. The whole thing seems very extraordinary.

". . . the aims and objects (of the Theatre) must commend themselves to every Irishman." This from Mr Lennox Robinson is very poor rameis [2] indeed, and we take it as read. "They greatly regret that he should have found it necessary to take exception to the treatment he has received." The first record I have of delay in sending Royalties due is May, 1927, which was discovered "when checking the Bank balance." There was one before this, but I have not the written record. The next recorded are a number of Royalties a long time due, frequently written for, but enticing no reply from the Secretary. A letter was finally sent to L. Robinson, which won a postcard on which was written:—"Johnny Perrin (The Secretary) got married yesterday and skeeted off to Wales for a few days, will attend to yours when he gets back. I'm certain the cheques were sent long ago." Twenty-three days afterwards I was in Dublin and went down to The Abbey Theatre to see Mr Perrin, but he

[2] rameis, rubbish.

wasnt in. I left a message that I must see him that evening, and when I came the cheques were waiting for me at the Box Office with a trite letter of apology. Early in October, as I left Dublin, they put on one of my plays, and again the royalties were hiding somewhere in The Abbey. I wrote and received no answer. Another play was put on, but neither the royalties due on this nor on the previous one were sent to me. A third play was produced and the same thing happened. I wrote several times and never received an answer. Finally I had to write direct to Lady Gregory, who wrote to Mr Robinson, and finally I received the royalties at the end of January, 1928. Then followed the rejection and the method of rejection of "The Silver Tassie." And recently I have had to write about royalties held back for a long time (eight weeks) receiving no answer, but finally the coming of the cheque with a casual reference to the discovery that they were due when checking bank balance. I think I am justified in "taking exception" to the humiliation of having to write after royalties due, and to feel angry that my letters had been always ignored. No commercial Manager here would dare to do that. In "The New York World" recently appeared the following: " 'The Silver Tassie' was rejected by Mr Yeats because it was an English drawing-room piece." In "The Chicago Tribune" the note, "We hope The Abbey Theatre will stage 'The Silver Tassie' now that Mr O'Casey has failed to find a Producer." This in spite of the fact that it has been announced in English and Irish papers that the play was to be produced by C. B. Cochran. (The last note was sent to American paper by a Dublin Correspondent) And on August 9th, in three English papers on the one day appeared the following: "I happened to be in Dublin when the fierce correspondence on 'The Silver Tassie' was raging between Mr Yeats and the author. Mr Yeats, who is one of the Directors of the Abbey, suggested some slight alterations in one or two of the scenes. These Mr O'Casey refused to consider, so The Silver Tassie went to America after a short run in Dublin. Mr Yeats and I were both members of a house party in Wicklow when the play was produced; sitting by the fire he declaimed some of his poems, and then recited lines from 'The Silver Tassie.' We saw the difference." (I hope he saw a bloody big difference. S.O'C) I know that this is all irrelevant, and that it would be wrong to say that any Abbey Theatre Director is responsible, but it seems to me, that the writer must have had some association with those who are in immediate attendance upon Dublin's Literary Corolla, and are written, if not to injure, at least to irritate. The Abbey, too, has a habit, when they are in difficulty about the production of an advertised play, of substituting my Shadow of a Gunman, with bad results for the play and for me. The last time this was done in Feb when for some reason they were unable to produce "Mountain Dew" on the date announced, and they jumped The Gunman into its place. I protested about this, but no notice was taken.

"You will have gathered from our interview that so far from welcoming any litigation, etc." Now honestly isnt this a rather mean attempt to slide the responsibility for any legal proceedings that may take place on to me? They started it without the slightest warning to me, and their action is proving to be as clumsy and as foolish as their rejection of The Tassie.

"We have had an opportunity of discussing the matter with our Clients." It would be very interesting to know who exactly are their Clients. I have had a letter from one of the Abbey Directors, dated 15 Aug, saying that word came of the trouble with me only an hour ago. This is the sort of thing I hate and abominate, and why there is in me a strong desire to get away from The Abbey Theatre and its Hangers-on as effectively as possible and as soon as possible.

However, I will grant the concessions they ask, namely, permission to play in Dublin, 'Juno and the Paycock' and 'The Plough and the Stars' provided:

1. Before production they are advertised in the same manner as other plays, and are never substituted for any play previously chosen.
2. That all royalties due to me be forwarded within three weeks of last day's performance of a week, or less than a week's production, and that neglect to do this will give me power to cancel permission to perform the play for which the royalties are due.
3. That this concession be sent to Lady Gregory, and that acceptance by her only will be recognized by me.
4. That the implied statement that I received the Agreements and cheque be withdrawn unreservedly.

The above are offered subject, of course, to your approval.

Very sincerely,
[*Sean O'Casey*]

From F. M. Inwood

TS. O'CASEY
22 AUGUST 1929

THE STARMER GROUP
NEWSPAPER HOUSE, 170 FLEET ST.

SEAN O'CASEY ESQ.

Dear Sir,

The paragraph headed "Unwanted Advice" on which you have addressed letters to several of the Editors of the papers in this group, form part of the "London Letter" supplied by this office. The Editors concerned, therefore, have asked me to reply to you.

I was away at the time but the writer of the paragraph assures me that she was herself present last year at the house party in Wicklow and has given me the name of her hostess. Mr. W. B. Yeats was also a member of the party at the time when I believe you and he were in controversy concerning "The Silver Tassie". My correspondent obtained the statement in the paragraph regarding Mr. Yeats from that gentleman himself, and it therefore seems that some further correspondence, possibly with Mr. Yeats who I understand is at Rapallo just now, is necessary before the inaccuracy of my correspondent's statement is definitely established.

I do, however, admit the inaccuracy of the statement that the play was produced in Dublin and subsequently went to America. I understand from Major Leadlay (Mr. C. B. Cochran's press representative) that the play was not presented in Dublin on account of the very controversy to which my correspondent has made reference.

I regret that you should think that either or both of these statements is calculated to cause injury to the coming production of "The Silver Tassie". On the contrary, I should have thought the statements would increase public interest in the play. If, however, you think it would be helpful to correct that part of the paragraph which we do admit at once was inaccurate, I will gladly do so.

Yours sincerely,
F. M. Inwood
LONDON MANAGING EDITOR.

To F. M. Inwood

TC. O'CASEY

23 AUGUST 1929

Dear Mr. Inwood—

Reply to your letter of the 22nd. Aug:

Forgive me for not bothering about what Major Leadlay may, or may not have said (as it happens he is completely wrong too) for I am concerned only with what appeared about my play and about me in your Journals.

I have never denied, nor attempted to deny, that your contributor (Who is Sylvia, what is she?) was herself with Mr W. B. Yeats at a House Party in Mrs Phillimore's in Kilmaccurragh, Kilbride, Co Wicklow last year, or that there, sitting by the fire, Mr Yeats declaimed his poems, and then recited some lines from "The Silver Tassie", and that your contributor saw the difference—a bloody big difference I hope.

You have already admitted that two of the statements were untrue, and I thank you. Now will you be good enough to get your contributor to find out whether or not Mr W. B. Yeats, sitting by a Wicklow fire on a wet night, said to her that "He suggested some slight alterations in one or two of the scenes. These Mr O'Casey refused to consider. 'You will have it whole, or not at all,' was his reply."

I may add that Mr. Yeats is at present, not in Rapallo, but in 42, Fitzwilliam Square, Dublin. I myself sent him on Aug. 14th, a letter by registered post, to which, so far no reply has come.

When this is done, I will tell you why I should like you to be good enough to contradict them in some future issue of your Journals.

Best personal wishes.
Sincerely Yours,
[*Sean O'Casey*]

To W. B. Yeats

TC. O'CASEY

ST. JOHN'S WOOD
24 AUGUST 1929

W. B. YEATS, ESQ.
42, FITZWILLIAM SQUARE, DUBLIN.

Dear Sir—

On August 14th, I sent by registered post, through the Abbey Theatre, a newspaper-cutting taken from the English Press, containing untrue statements about 'The Silver Tassie' which paragraphs were associated with your name. I also sent a letter with the cutting asking you if you would kindly send me a note contradicting them. No reply has been received by me, and as I understand you have been and are in Dublin, this seems to be very curious.

I have since written to the Editors of these papers, and have received a letter from the London Managing Editor admitting three of the statements to be untrue, but adding that the statement, "Mr Yeats, who is a Director of the Abbey Theatre, suggested some slight alterations in one or two of the scenes (The Silver Tassie). These Mr O'Casey refused to consider. 'You shall have it whole or not at all', was his reply." was, according to a letter from the Contributor, obtained from Mr Yeats, himself, during the house party in Wicklow on a wet night.

As I am about to request these papers to publish a letter denying all these statements, perhaps you would be kind enough—since it can hardly be true—to let me have a personal note from you confirming the denial.

[*Sean O'Casey*]

From Whitney, Moore and Keller

TS. O'CASEY [1]

WHITNEY, MOORE AND KELLER
DUBLIN
26 AUGUST 1929

SEAN O'CASEY
19 WORONZOW ROAD, ST. JOHNS WOOD, LONDON

Referring to your letter 18th ult. National Theatre Society withdraw all claim to the right of production of the two plays referred to save in Dublin. Writing. Whitneys Dublin.

[1] Telegram. O'Casey's victory was confirmed by a letter from Whitney to McCracken written on the same day, 26 August, a copy of which was forwarded to O'Casey, and which stated in part: "We consider the matter settled. Mr. O'Casey has agreed that the National Theatre Society shall have liberty during the next twelve months to produce in Dublin the two plays mentioned above [*Juno* and *Plough*]. The Society has withdrawn all claim to the right of Production of the two plays elsewhere. Any arrangement therefore which may be made between Mr. Sinclair and Mr. O'Casey for production of the plays anywhere save in Dublin will, so far as our clients are concerned, be quite in order." (TS. O'Casey)

From W. B. Yeats

TS. O'CASEY

42, FITZWILLIAM SQUARE,
DUBLIN
26 AUGUST 1929

Dear Mr O'Casey

I never told anybody that I "suggested some slight alterations" or alterations of any kind in "The Silver Tassie", and of course your play, not having been played in Dublin, had no "brief run" there. Nor can I imagine myself declaiming verses at any house-party whatever. There is only one Wicklow house I stay in and I cannot recall meeting your critic there "on the wet Irish night" "when the play was first produced", nor anywhere else.

Yours sincerely
W B Yeats

The delay is not the fault of the Abbey. I send at intervals for my letters. I sent yesterday & got your letter.

To the Editors, Birmingham Gazette, Sheffield Independent, Nottingham Journal

TC. O'CASEY

ST. JOHN'S WOOD
27 AUGUST 1929

Dear Sirs—

On August 9th, 1929, there appeared in the above Journals the paragraph given below.

> Unwanted Advice.
>
> I wonder whether Sean O'Casey's play, "The Silver Tassie," to be produced by C. B. Cochran in September, will have a better reception here than it had at the Abbey Theatre? I happened to be in Dublin at the time when the fierce correspondence on the subject was raging between the author and Mr. W. B. Yeats.
>
> Mr. Yeats, who is one of the directors of the Abbey, suggested some slight alterations in one or two of the scenes. These Mr. O'Casey refused to consider. "You shall have it whole or not at all," was his reply. So "The Silver Tassie" went to America after a very brief run in Dublin.
>
> Mr. Yeats and I were both members of a house party in the Wicklow district when the play was produced. I shall always remember him sitting by the fire on a wet night, declaiming verses from his own works in that sonorous and most impressive voice. Then he turned to "The Silver Tassie" and recited the opening lines, which are not happy. We saw the difference.

The Silver Tassie never had a reception in the Abbey Theatre, because the play was never produced there. Though five offers were made to me for production in Dublin, the play was never produced there, so that it has had no "brief run" there, and the play has not yet gone to America. In a letter I have received from Mr W. B. Yeats, I am told that he "never told anybody that he 'suggested some slight alterations' or alterations of any kind in 'The Silver Tassie' ". And that he cannot "imagine himself declaiming verses at any house-party whatever." And that he "cannot recall meeting the critic in Wicklow 'on a wet, Irish night', nor anywhere else."

So it is plain that from side to side, and from top to bottom, the paragraph is untrue in implication and in statement, and I shall be glad if you would publish this denial, requesting your Contributor that in making future statements about my plays and me, a little more trouble be taken to verify them.

Sincerely Yours,
[*Sean O'Casey*]

From F. M. Inwood

TS. O'CASEY

THE STARMER GROUP
NEWSPAPER HOUSE
169/170 FLEET ST. E.C.4

29 AUGUST 1929

SEAN O'CASEY ESQ.
Dear Sir,

I shall be leaving London on Saturday for a fortnight, but before going I am having copies made of your letter for distribution among the Editors of the papers which published the offending paragraph. I have no doubt that the Editors will give your denial in full, but it may be necessary for reasons of space to limit the quotations of the paragraph itself to those portions the accuracy of which you dispute.

It is a great pity that Mr. Yeats has been unable to recall the incident because Miss Scott-James has satisfied me that what she wrote so far as it concerns Mr. Yeats was correct, and she assures me that another member of the House Party confirms her account of the incident.

I am very annoyed that Miss Scott-James should have been inaccurate upon facts which it was quite possible for her to verify, and in the circumstances I have no alternative but to accept unreservedly the corrections supplied by yourself and Mr. Yeats.

Yours faithfully,
F. M. Inwood
LONDON MANAGING EDITOR.

From Lady Gregory

PS. *Modern Drama* [1]

COOLE PARK, GORT, CO. GALWAY
13 SEPTEMBER 1929

Dear Sean—

The agreement came yesterday, and the Superintendent of Civil Guard happening to call served as a witness to my signature—I have sometimes to call in John or Mike: from their work—I was very glad to sign—But what about *Shadow of a Gunman*? You have not deprived us of this, have you?—the first of your plays we produced—I was glad to see it did so well at Kingstown [2]—and hope all we have done at the Abbey may go about the country—that is, if good performances are given—such as Sinclairs—

I am all alone here—but have just had a fortnights visit from Jack Yeats and his wife—he is always a pleasant visitor—His last London exhibition seems to have been a success—and he is to have one in Dublin next month—

The giving over of Charlemont House for a Gallery will be a gt help in the fight for the pictures—which I hope will begin "con spirito" when Parliament meets—AE did a portrait of my youngest granddaughter, Catherine—not very good but he promised another after the holidays—Has John's portrait of you been photographed or reproduced? I shd. much like to see it—I hope your youngster is doing well—And that you yourself are keeping well? I am all alone here now—but trying to write a bit—a sort of "aftermath"——

Every good wish—for you and those dear to you and your wife—

As always affectionately A Gregory

[1] From a copy made by A. C. Edwards and printed in *Modern Drama,* May 1965.

[2] The name of Kingstown was changed to Dunlaoghaire after the establishment of the Irish Free State.

To Gabriel Fallon

MS. TEXAS

ST. JOHN'S WOOD
18 SEPTEMBER [1929]

Dear Gaby—

Up to the neck in the whirl & sweep of the Tassie's Rehearsals. Going gloriously. Charlie Laughton's a Genius. Playing Harry with amazing strength & pathos. Will's here & doing grandly.

Copy of Elyan's letter.

Dear Mr. O'Casey,

I beg to enclose statement of receipts in connection with the production of "The Shadow of a Gunman" at the Civic Theatre Dunlaoghaire, & accompanying cheque for £7. 6. 0. calculated on a basis of 10%.

Yours L. Elyan.

Dun Laoghaire Development Committee.

This is to certify that the Account shown hereunder is a true & proper account of all the takings of the Civic Theatre during its occupation by the First National Players from Aug 26th. to Sept 4th. 1929. Inclusive

Gross recepits	£93. 2. 5.
Less Entertainment Tax	20. 0. 0.
	73. 2. 5.

W. Doody
Hon. Sec.

So there you are. As soon as [1]

[1] Pages missing.

To Lady Gregory

MS. GREGORY

ST. JOHN'S WOOD
19 SEPTEMBER 1929

Dear Lady Gregory—

Working continually now on The Silver Tassie Rehearsals. Charles Laughton's a genius, & will give an amazing performance of Harry Heegan. Expect Barry Fitzgerald to make a great hit, & then, off he goes from me forever. Baby going on splendidly. Not surprised to hear that AE's picture of your grandchild was bad—he couldn't do a good one. He knows very little indeed about painting. Just read his article in last week's Statesman about photography [1]—"The camera can give us sometimes almost all the delight of great landscape art"—and the rest of it. And this man is an authority on painting. I wouldn't let him paint a lily!

Warm Wishes, hurrying out to a rehearsal.

Yours Sincerely,
Sean

[1] Y.O., "Irish Salon of Photography," *Irish Statesman,* 14 September 1929.

To Oliver St. John Gogarty

MS. GOGARTY

ST. JOHN'S WOOD
8 OCTOBER 1929

Dear Oliver—

Don't forget your promise to be here on Monday to say whether or not a great cavity is to be made in my throat.[1] I wouldn't care to say "go," till you said so,—& we can seize the opportunity of going to "The Silver Tassie."

Feeling fairly unfit.

Yours As Ever,
Sean

[1] O'Casey was suffering from tonsilitis.

From Lady Gregory

PS. *Modern Drama* [1]

STANDARD HOTEL [DUBLIN]
FRIDAY—11 OCTOBER 1929

Dear Sean—

I have only just now realised that your play comes on tonight[2]—and though I never send telegrams on such occasions I want you to be sure that you have all my good wishes for it—and its success. I hope to see it myself very soon for I cross to England on Monday—I shall be for

[1] From a copy made by A. C. Edwards and printed in *Modern Drama,* May 1965.

[2] *The Silver Tassie* opened on 11 October at the Apollo Theatre, London, production by Charles B. Cochran, directed by Raymond Massey, and with the following cast: Charles Laughton as Harry Heegan, Barry Fitzgerald as Sylvester Heegan, Sidney Morgan as Simon Norton, Eithne Magee as Mrs. Heegan, Beatrix Lehmann as Susie Monican, Una O'Connor as Mrs. Foran, Ian Hunter as Teddy Foran, Binnie Barnes as Jessie Taite, S. J. Warmington as Barney Bagnall. In the symbolic Act II, the set of which was designed by Augustus John, Charles Laughton as the First Soldier, Ian Hunter as the Second Soldier, Barry Fitzgerald as the Third Soldier, S. J. Warmington as the Sixth Soldier, Emlyn Williams as The Trumpeter.

some days with Mrs. Phillimore—1, Upper Phillimore Gardens—And I look forward very much to a visit one afternoon if you invite me—to see and make acquaintance with your wife and your son—and your garden—

Now good bye—with affection—*A Gregory*

To Lady Gregory

MS. GREGORY

ST. JOHN'S WOOD
15 OCTOBER 1929

Dear Lady Gregory—

Thank you ever so much for your kind wishes towards the London Production of "The Silver Tassie".

The production has made my mind a-flood again with thoughts about the play's rejection by the Abbey Directorate, & bitterness would certainly enter into things I would say about W. B. Yeats, & L. Robinson if we were to meet; bitterness that would hurt you, and I am determined to avoid hurting you as much as possible.

Recently I have had to make four English papers contradict statements attributed to W. B. Yeats, that were made—it was said—at a House Party on a wet, Irish night, in a place called Kilbride, Kilcurragh, Co. Wicklow. And before me is another contradiction of a statement made in an American Literary Journal about the "public dissociation" by W. B. Yeats from the "naturalism" of The Silver Tassie. So, knowing how I feel, & guessing what I would say about the many Artistic & Literary Shams squatting in their high places in Dublin, I feel it would be much better to set aside, for the present, the honour & pleasure of seeing you & talking with you.[1]

Affectionately Yours.
Sean

[1] When I read this letter to O'Casey thirty-four years later, he groaned and remarked: "That was one letter I should never have written, especially that cruel last sentence, to my poor dear Lady Gregory! But I suppose my wounds were still raw and I wasn't strong or wise enough to forgive and forget." See his comment on the incident in "Black Oxen Passing By," *Rose and Crown* (1952), *Autobiographies II,* p. 336.

From Lady Gregory

PS. *Modern Drama* [1]

1 Upper Phillimore Gardens
Kensington
Tuesday 15 October [1929]

Dear Sean,

Your letter has grieved me—perhaps I deserve that—but I do ask you to change your mind and allow me to come and see your wife—and the boy—and the garden and the pictures and *yourself*—I do not feel that any word need be spoken on that grievous matter that has given me so much pain—I am here but for a few days (till Saturday)—Could go to-morrow afternoon—if you give me leave—as always affectionately

A Gregory

[1] From a copy made by A. C. Edwards and printed in *Modern Drama,* May 1965.

To Gabriel Fallon

MS. Texas

St. John's Wood
19 October 1929

My dear Gaby—

Sorry for not writing sooner; & sorrier that this letter must be brief. I am very busy; I have had a hell of a time with throat & ear, & am still in pain; I have a heavy, blasted cold—but cheerio. Did ja read that majestic criticism of "The Silver Tassie" hin the Irish Statesman? [1] The gilded conceit of the desperate bastard! And wily woolly-brained old AE-YO kept clear of the danger. Won't let a man . . . plunge. Busy painting his bad pictures, I suppose. I wonder what does this . . . . . psyche think of it all? The play is playing to crowded houses. The week's receipts break the record of the Apollo for the last three years.[2] "Not good theatre as *we* understand the term (therm) in tehse islands". How could it be good

[1] Sean O'Faolain, "*The Silver Tassie* Staged," *Irish Statesman,* 19 October 1929. This is a typical example of the way Irish reviewers have read sermons to O'Casey on the error of his new dramatic techniques, urging him to go back to his familiar old themes and old forms, and to return to Ireland.

[2] The play ran for eight weeks, in spite of the fact that it opened three weeks before the catastrophic Wall Street crash.

like 'Mountain Dew' [3]; "The Blind Wolf" [4] "Look at Heifernans" [5] or "Punching the Waves" [6] or L.R.'s "I'll Sing a Song of Americay".[7]

Well, God be with you, & Rose & the two kids.

Sean

Will has made a great hit.

[3] George Shiels's *Mountain Dew* opened at the Abbey Theatre on 5 March 1929.

[4] T. C. Murray's *The Blind Wolf* opened at the Abbey Theatre on 30 April 1928.

[5] Brinsley Macnamara's *Look at the Heffernans!* opened at the Abbey Theatre on 12 April 1926.

[6] W. B. Yeats's *Fighting the Waves* opened at the Abbey Theatre on 13 August 1929.

[7] An allusion to Lennox Robinson's visit to America early in 1929 as guest director and professor of drama at the University of Michigan.

From Augustus John

MS. O'CASEY

FRYERN COURT
NR. FORDINGBRIDGE, SALISBURY
21 OCTOBER 1929

My dear Sean,

Thanks for your letter. I am proud to have been of help with the splendid 2nd act. Your play has moved people profoundly. Lawrence (of Arabia) who has been sitting to me finds it the greatest thing of our time.[1]

I am truly sorry to hear you have been suffering. I'm returning to town today & hope to see you better.

Yours ever
Augustus

I don't see why you need attach yourself to any *class*. A poet, an artist is really no class at all.

[1] See T. E. Lawrence's letter to Lady Astor, 15 February 1934, printed below.

From Lady Gregory

PS. *Modern Drama* [1]

(ENGLAND)
THURSDAY, 23 OCTOBER 1929

Dear Sean,

Although I have missed the pleasure of seeing you, I should like to tell you what I have just written to Yeats about the Tassie—"I am troubled because having seen the play I believe we ought to have accepted it—We could not have done the chanted scene as it is done here, it is very fine indeed and impressive"—But I say, and think, we could have done the other acts better—Barry Fitzgerald was of course very fine—

I leave for Dublin tomorrow, just passing through London. I have had some pleasant days with old friends but am sorry not to have made the acquaintance of that "kid" [2] whose father shows such splendid vitality and of his mother. I have done a little work about the Lane pictures and have great hopes of them now—

As always affectionately
A Gregory

[1] From a copy made by A. C. Edwards and printed in *Modern Drama,* May 1965.
[2] Breon O'Casey.

To Gabriel Fallon

MS. TEXAS

ST. JOHN'S WOOD
24 OCTOBER 1929

My dear Gaby—

Six o'clock, P.M. Precisely Euston Station—Ever the time & the place. So W.B.Y. wants a Bally [1]; well, we must make a Bally for W.B.Y. Let W.B.Y.'s Wifie bring her birdies. Is AE going to dance the Faun, or Puck, or Psyche? And Robinson the gentle fool and ikey.
And what's the part will fit poor Dolan Mikey?
Will Will put on his armour strong & spikey?
And roar & sweat & threat, & then cry hikey?

[1] Yeats's *Fighting the Waves* was "A Ballet Play," with choreography by Ninette de Valois, music by George Anthiel, conducted by Dr. John F. Larchet.

While Starkie criticises from a Bikey.
While all the world will clap & say, we likey!

And Yeats is tired of realism & wants beauty! Apart from some beautiful things he has written, does this man know very much, or does he know anything about Beauty? Does he think that there is no beauty outside of his own plays & outside of a Ballet? And does he not know that a Ballet may be a ballet & not beautiful? That a ballet may be bad, as bad as a bad play. That the designs may be bad, the choreography may be bad & that the music may be bad. That a Ballet may be satirical as well as beautiful. That what he calls the realism of the Abbey Playwrights mayn't be realism at all, but colossal codology. That it is very probable that the Abbey Ballets will be worse than the Abbey plays. Or as bad as the bad pictures hanging up in the Abbey Vestibule. Or contribute as much to Art as the Irish Free State's Peg o me heart pound notes. That there's no-one in Ireland could decorate a Ballet with Derain, Benois, or Bakst. That there is no Composer (even Jack Larchet) who could give to a Ballet what Rimsky-Korsakoff gave to Scheherazade, what Scarlatti gave to the Good Humoured Ladies, or what Stravinsky gave to Petrouchka. Oh, the bloody cant & roguery of it all! What these Literary & Art controlling posers want is to be chained together & made to look at Punch & Judy Shows, visit Circuses, stare at Revues, & do years of hard labour dancing Jazz. Then there might possibly be a glimpse of God for them.

Lyle is here & is coming tomorrow. I don't think I'll write again till I see you (& then I'll talk) on Saturday at Euston, at 6 o.c.P.M. precisely.

Love to Rose & Frank.

Ever Yours
Sean

To Charles Edward Brumwell

MS. British Museum

St. John's Wood
[? October 1929]

Dear Mr. Brumwell—

No, I never spent an official moment in the British Army. Your question about the cock & the cannon wheel[1] is a bit vague. Do your officer friends mean to say that tying men to guns was never practised; or, that such a punishment was never given for stealing fowl; or, that it

[1] An incident in the symbolic second act of *The Silver Tassie*.

was measured out if the fowl stolen was a hen, but not if the fowl stolen was a cock?

I had a friend in Dublin named Barney Fay; he was a gunner in the Royal Field Artillery, & on the Reserve when I knew him. Whenever he was out of work, he gave himself an occasional meal by capturing neighbours' "poulthry." I have eaten of roast duck with Barney. He was called to the colours when war was declared, & went out with the first B.E.F. to France. And he stayed there till the war was over; came back, untouched in mind or body, the same careless, irresponsible, charming fellow. Exemplary in every other way out fighting in France, he couldn't keep (as he told me when he returned on leave) his hands off the peasants' "poulthry," & after being warned, & admonished, he was finally tied to the wheel of a gun for "choking an Estaminet cock." But why do your friends sing silently about the cruelties of the war, and secretly but loudly abjure the harmless joke of Staff pundits tying a man to the wheel of a gun for a minute or two? Can't you see how ironic & silly this attitude is? Yes, ready to admit, right enough, the blood-rotting sting from a scorpion, but refusing the humiliation of being bitten by a flea. If the war had consisted of every man (including conchies) being tied to a wheel of a gun, the countries concerned would now be just as stupid, no more happy, but they wouldn't be quite so miserable. Don't you see how ironic & foolish the repudiation of this little tomfoolery becomes in the dread darkness of all that happened!

Yours,
Sean O'Casey

To Gabriel Fallon

MS. TEXAS

ST. JOHN'S WOOD
4 NOVEMBER 1929

My dear Gaby—

The Tassie still goes very well. G.B.S. says "it is the greatest play he has ever seen"—vide Sunday Chronicle, & in 'The Observer' that "it is a magnificent play", so where's your W. B. Yeats noo? At home dancing in one of his own balleys, or droning out lines from the Hawk's Well; well, well, well; hell, hell, hell. By the way, Kernoff sent no address with his designs [1]—at least I think he didn't—and as I want to return them, I shall be glad if you would let me know where to send them. I showed

[1] Harry Kernoff, a Dublin artist, did a series of set designs for *The Silver Tassie*.

them to C.B. [Cochran] but he didn't say much, so I suppose they didn't impress him potently. I'm sorry to say this, & to say that they didn't harass me with emotion either, but don't say so to Kernoff. There seems to be too much of Gate Theatre in them, but, fairly, & frankly, I'm no judge of this kind of work. I learned a lot about painting since I came here, but nothing about Theatre design—there's nothing to be learned here. "As it was in the beginning, is now & ever shall be" is the pregnant imprimatur of the English Theatre. I have given "The Gunman" to the Abbey on the same terms as the other plays. I don't know why they decided to put it on, & then decided to take it off. Three weeks of Robbie —not bad, eh? Heard he was in last Saturday Matinee looking at 'The Tassie'. The page missing from "Nannie" [2] has been missing for years.

Can't act on the suggestion in Baumann's letter. He has been pestering me for my plays since I came here, & will keep on apparently for ever. Giving my plays to Baumann wouldn't really help Duffy—which I should like to do—he simply wants to get mine because there is a call for them. It is only recently I chose a translator, young, unknown, & poor; clever & imaginative, & I have given him mine, & since he has become an important man on the Continent. Max Rheinhart's Representative's on his way here to see "The Tassie".

I am much better now but still have to go meekly to Harley St. (Wimpole St) to be prodded & prodded by a Surgeon who says & says & says "The Tassie's a great play." Glad to hear The First National Players are bigger & better—& brighter?—than ever.

Will's doing well, & has a little room of his own & a gas fire.

Love to Frank & Barney, & Rose & You.

Sean

Return B. Duffy's letter

[2] *Nannie's Night Out.*

To Charles B. Cochran [1]

TC. O'CASEY

ST. JOHN'S WOOD

8 NOVEMBER 1929

My dear C.B.

Let's take the last part of yours of the 7th inst, first (the last shall be first, etc.) I wont bother about Sweden just now. A fortnight ago, I refused an offer from Lady Low, who already translated Juno and The

[1] Sir Charles Blake Cochran (1873–1951), theatrical producer and promoter, knighted in 1948 for his services to the theatre.

Plough. Some days before the first night of The Tassie, Sir Sydney Low left a letter with the Stage-door man, saying that Lady Low wanted to be at the first night, but when he applied at the Box Office (the terrible box office) for two tickets, he was asked for £2.8.0., which was ridiculous (oh, B C, C B, you have a lot to answer for.) Ridiculous and mad, and outside of all proportionate reasoning, so would I get him tickets, or seats, and a book of the play, that his wife might be there to make the play known at the earliest possible moment to The Best People in Sweden. A day or two after the first night, I got a letter from Lady Low, saying she'd been too ill to go on the first night. Anyhow, I wrote to say I wouldnt bother about a Swedish translation just yet, and that there was no reason for a breath-losing race towards translation.

Some day I'll write a song about The Pest People, and compose a melody to it, which I'll demand shall be played forever and only from the strings of the ukelele. I enclose a cutting taken from The Irish Statesman,[2] the journal of the Best People in Ireland, whose Editor is Georgie Russell, known as AE, or YO,—one in three and three in one—who came over here, saw the play, got a batman to write the criticism because he hadnt the guts to do it himself. It is so stupid that one can crown the stupidity in a few sentences. "O'Casey turned to a technique beyond his powers." "Found the experiment in the new technique beyond the capacities of the modern stage." If the technique is beyond the power of the modern stage, how does the critic know that the technique is beyond the power of the dramatist? Is the technique too much for O'Casey, or too much for the stage? "The second act suggests that O'Casey finds the conventions (as if I thought of the conventions) of the modern stage (the modern stage mind you—what is the modern stage?) insufficient for his purpose." Is this clown condemning the insufficiency of the stage, or the extra-efficiency of the dramatist? Does the insufficiency of the stage make the efficiency of the dramatist inefficient? "Yet," he goes on to say, "the producer must have found the second act easy game"—good term for a literary gent to use—"This sort of stuff has been done more than once before." If the thing be easy game, how can it be beyond the capacities of the modern stage? What a dim-brained clown we have here, to be sure! And this fellow is marked down by The Best People in Ireland as a sensitive judge in the things that belong to mind and imagination.

G.B.S. was with us on Thursday, and would like to write about the play, but prefers to write to you, instead of writing directly to the Press. So, if you still think well of this, you could ask him to write to you—or I can do so—and he will send the letter on to you, to do what you think useful with it.

[2] Sean O'Faolain's review, "*The Silver Tassie* Staged," *Irish Statesman,* 19 October 1929.

Lastly, I'm very sorry that you have made enemies with a cold, and hope youll be alright soon again. I have not yet got rid of the one I got at rehearsals.

Best of wishes.
[*Sean*]

From W. P. Harty to S. H. Parsons[1]

MS. Mair

St. Michael
[Limerick]
12 November 1929

Dear Mr. Parsons,

I fear there will be considerable risk in putting on "The Plough and the Stars" next week. Feeling is still running high, as far as we can gather. The idea that is rooted in thc public mind is that this is a perfectly rotten play picturing the most degrading aspects of Irish life, & insulting the national feeling. That feeling I think will remain even though many cuts have been made. Please consider this.

Yrs. sin.
W. P. Harty

[1] Forwarded to O'Casey by Maire O'Neill. See his letter to Maire O'Neill, 20 November 1929. A year later on 10 November 1930 a nationalist mob seized and burned the film of *Juno and the Paycock* in a Limerick street. For another aspect of the anti-O'Casey feeling in Ireland at this time, see O'Casey's letter to Gabriel Fallon, 11 September 1930, note 1.

From S. H. Parsons to Arthur Sinclair [1]

TS. MAIR

LYRIC THEATRE
LIMERICK
18 NOVEMBER 1929

ARTHUR SINCLAIR, ESQ.
ST. JOHNS HOSPITAL,
LIMERICK.

Dear Mr. Sinclair,

I have your note regarding your appearance tonight, and must again warn you of the foolish step you propose taking. I am confident from information received that there will be riotous scenes in the theatre if you attempt to do "PLOUGH AND THE STARS".

I am surprised at you changing your mind after giving your stage manager Mr. Quinn, and myself full authority to put on a substitute programme, and on the strength of this 300 D. C., 3,000 Hand Bills, & 500 Special programmes have been printed for "COINER" "RISING OF THE MOON" "DUTY".

Personally I would rather close the doors, as I know full well there will be trouble. You know that you have been warned several times. However, if you insist, I have no alternative then but to abide by the contract, and must give you notice that Clause 3, Clause 8, Clause 13, Clause 17 & 18 of the contract must be observed, and also in view of warnings I shall have no alternative than to hold you responsible for any damage to the property, its furnishings, and everything belonging to the Landlords, & Lessees, inside and outside the building, and also should there be any accidents or injury to any person you must be prepared to compensate them for any claim they make. I heard that practically every church in the town spoke about this play last night, and this is sufficient warning of the seriousness of the whole affair. I know you do not want to take it off, and the question must therefore be boiled down to one of mutual arrangement.

If you are agreeable, so am I, but if you insist, then the results must rest upon your own shoulders.

I take it from your note that you are leaving the hospital and are in a position to play if the need arises. But should you not be able to play and as it is rather late to commence advertising a new bill, I think it would be best to close altogether.

[1] Forwarded to O'Casey by Maire O'Neill. See his 20 November letter to Maire O'Neill.

Awaiting your reply, with kindest regards and best wishes for your speedy recovery,

I am,
Yours faithfully.
S. H. Parsons

P.S. The three one act farces suggested, will not of course be the same attraction as a once nightly show, and knowing that you have no heavy royalties, I think the terms should be reduced in the event of playing this suggested programme. Please do not take this letter in the wrong way—I must state all these things to clear myself.

Dear Sean, Please send this letter back. Mac. wants it. Molly.[2]

[2] Comment by Maire O'Neill.

To Maire O'Neill [1]

MS. MAIR
ST. JOHN'S WOOD
20 NOVEMBER 1929

Dear Mollie—

Sorry to hear Arthur hasn't been well, & hope he's alright again now. I remember saying to him that he shouldn't choose "The Plough" for Limerick—or Cork—but he would have his way. I hope he got out of the difficulties safely. I am sending back here Parson's letter—& another [by W. P. Harty].

Also receipt for Royalties for week ending Nov. 11th., 1929.

Sincerely yours,
Sean

P.T.O

I'm not surprised the people don't like 'The Plough"—they have been dosed with so much romantic stuff for so long that they like it soft & like it sweet.

I wish they would read the old Catholic Mediaeval play "Noah"

[1] Maire O'Neill (1887–1952), Abbey Theatre actress, sister of Sara Allgood; fiancée of J. M. Synge, and the original "Pegeen Mike" in his *The Playboy of the Western World* (1907); now married to Arthur Sinclair, and his co-director of the Irish Players in London.

which has something like this in it when the bold Noah is trying to get his wife away from gossips into the Ark.

Noah. Be Christ you will go in.
Wife: Be Christ I wont!

Times has changed, Joxer; times has changed.

Yr Sean

[Stamped Receipt enclosed]

20 NOVEMBER 1929

Received from Arthur Sinclair, Esq, the sum of, £14.9.0. Royalties on performances of Juno and the Paycock, in The Lyric Theatre, Limerick, for week ending, Nov. 11th, 1929.

Signed: Sean O'Casey

To Irish Statesman

30 NOVEMBER 1929

CONTRADICTIONS

DEAR SIR,—Every week THE IRISH STATESMAN welts a way into the sleepy minds of the Free State people. Every mentally active man and every mentally active woman there sits up on the day of publication and nod their nuts in salutation; they brood in its brooding, cogitate in its cogitation, for they know, or know they ought to know it thrusts for truth, and feel, or feel they ought to feel the foment of its wisdom. Like a little cuckoo clock in a soda-fountain parlour it hops out at stated times, sings its little song and bells its little chimes, then hops back for rest and further meditation, that it may be ready to hop out again to say its little say before the drinking, chattering and flirting that go on in the soda-fountain parlour. When the Editor, or one of his batmen, opens his mouth to speak, all who are straining after intelligence in art, literature or drama keep a three minutes' dead silence to hear what the psyches are saying to the people. Some of the psyches sometimes say strange things, and here are a few that follow:

In a recent issue of THE IRISH STATESMAN "Y.O.," writing of the "Reading of Poetry," [1] says: "In Japan the picture lover deals delicately with art. He does not crowd his wall with pictures, making his

[1] Y.O., "Reading of Poetry," *Irish Statesman,* 9 November 1929.

house a gallery, but displays them slowly, one after another. He will hang one picture in a room for a week, and it is then withdrawn and another picture takes its place. I have been told this at least three times by the same person, so it has got fixed in my consciousness. The surest way of becoming blind to art is to walk about national galleries, and the houses of great collectors, stopping for a moment before each picture."

In less recent issues "AE" writing about the Art of the great illustrators of the 'sixties,[2] says:

"What a delight to sit in a room where the walls are covered with little masterpieces. I advise the small collectors to start cutting these things from books, mount them on white cardboard with a thin white frame, and make his room a gallery of little masterpieces." Cut them out, cut them out quick, paste them on, frame them well and crowd the walls with the little masterpieces. "AE" hanging them on the walls and "Y.O." taking them off again.

In even a less recent issue, "Y.O." writing about photography,[3] says: —"The products (great word that—product) of the photographer's art sometimes give us a pleasure almost equal to that conveyed by great artists." Vox Aeius non vox Dei—non by a long chalk.

Less recent still, but not so very long ago:—"Folk obviously inspired by Cezanne or Picasso should be sternly suppressed. If God has not given anything for a man to say out of himself, why should that man be permitted to acquire merit by saying over again what other artists have said?" [4] In an issue before the one that made the foregoing statements, we were told that in a dream "Y.O." saw a picture coming out of an open heaven; that it was a lovely landscape by Corot; that in his dream he wondered how Corot painted the wonderful sky.[5] Suddenly the picture spread and spread itself out, so that every touch the artist had put on the picture was plainly visible, a white ground of canvas separating each spot of colour from another. Waking up, "Y.O." shouted out: "I know now how he did it," and hurried on to put touches of pale greenish blue interspersed with touches of a pale rose violet over a new sheet of canvas, so that he might be able to show everybody a sky as all-lovely as the lovely sky of Corot. It is only fair to Corot to say that, when "Y.O.'s" critical faculties got going, "Y.O." repudiated immediately any quality in the picture from the infection of Corot.

Now why should a young artist, who is impressed and influenced by Cezanne or Picasso be suppressed, while another who is impressed by Corot (though he colours the imitation by a dream conjured out of his psyche) be applauded? In painting is not the inspiration of Cezanne

2 A.E.'s review of a book on painting by Forest Reid, *Illustrators of the 'Sixties* (London, Faber & Gwyer, 1928), in the *Irish Statesman,* 3 November 1928.

3 Y.O., "Irish Salon of Photography," *Irish Statesman,* 14 September 1929.

4 Y.O., "London Artists," *Irish Statesman,* 15 September 1928.

5 Y.O., "True Dreams," *Irish Statesman,* 8 June 1929.

equal at least to the inspiration of Corot? Are we to understand (it looks like it) that "Y.O." or "AE", or both of them, would fight like the devil to get the work of Courbet, or Corot, Morizot or Mancini represented in the gallery in course of collection and erection in Dublin, but would strive like the devil to keep the work of Cezanne and Picasso out of the place?

But, artists and students and men and women, what does it matter what a man fights for, or fights against, when he says one minute that the test of an all-in love of art is to cover a wall with pictures, and the next that the test of an all-in love for art is to show on the wall only one picture at a time, and shoves up beside these two the statement that "the products of the photographer's art sometimes gives us a pleasure almost equal to that conveyed by great artists."—Yours faithfully,

Sean O'Casey

P.S.—The pedigree of "Y.O.'s" thought about the way a picture lover in Japan looks at his pictures is possibly—by W. B. Yeats, by Lady Gregory, by S. O'Casey, out of J. H. Cousin's book of "New Japan." —S.O'C.

(DEAR SEAN,—It is delightful to know that in your exile you read THE IRISH STATESMAN so intently and remember what you read for months and months. About these contradictions which trouble you so much, please consider this, that man is not a simple being, but very complex. Whitman, whom I recommend you to study, said in answer to some Sean O'Casey of his time, who probably wrote to the poet pointing out contradictions, "Do I contradict myself? Very well, I contradict myself. I contain multitudes." You yourself, dear Sean, have created in masterly fashion, characters who are full of contradictions, who now barge like angry fishwives and the next minute are kind and generous. You recognise so much complexity in human nature. Well, if you meditate more you will find that many contraries are balanced in the soul, as they are in nature. One part of our complex being may thirst after the spirit sincerely and another may delight in bodily things. The spirit in us may believe, while another part of our nature—intellectual, may be sceptic. At one time we may desire solitude, at another moment multitude. At one moment we may like to surrender ourselves to the magic of a particular picture or poem and dream into it. At another time we may like to range over twenty or thirty drawings or poems, criticising and contrasting them, and there is no evil in this; and the person who yields to these contrary impulses is not a person of feeble mind, as you suppose, but quite wise. Your own nature, dear Sean, will get enriched if you give up the search for perfectly simple rules of conduct in life or thought, and allow your many-sided and complicated nature intellectual nourishment for the various elements from which it is compounded. You might also repeat every morning this sentence from Emerson: "A foolish consistency is the hobgoblin of little minds." This will help to release you from your obsession of simplicity and unity, as for example that a man must be thinking one thing all the time, or he breaks up your idea of what is in keeping with the character you have surmised from some previous utterance. You might read also Eddington's *Science and the Physical World,* which may complete your education about the complexity of human nature. You will discover that a great scientist can also be a mystic, that he can make the nicest and most minute investigations, mathematical or by delicate instruments, into the nature of matter and energy, and yet give credit to the mystic and his intuitional method of discovering truth. You will discover also that nature is made up of opposites, each of which have their own reason for being, there are protons and electrons charged with positive and negative electricity, each of which have their own rationale. Since you have appealed to us publicly for guidance in your perplexity, and ask for assistance, our advice is, with the help of intellectual engineers like A. S. Eddington, to lay down another track in your mind. A single track mind is liable to be congested and even to bring about intellectual catastrophe when you try to get traffic of ideas going two ways on the same line. Note the obstruction in your mind, which led to your letter, and lay down another track, so that the traffic in ideas may flow freely between the opposites. Another track, dear Sean, is what the situation demands.—Editor I.S.)

To Gabriel Fallon

MS. TEXAS

ST. JOHN'S WOOD
3 DECEMBER 1929

My dear Gaby—

Damned hard to say what I think of your sketch, & just as hard to think of what to say. I really don't think there's enough in it; & amn't surprised that you got it back from The Nation & Atheneum. I don't believe any paper or magazine would publish it. You will have to put more into what you write. And even were it everything you think, where's the paper would publish your expressionistic rhythm? But remember—even in short stories—the body is more than the raiment. The rain is much more than the man in the middle of it.

Heard anything from "The Sunday Express?" You'll hardly get in there, for before the 'Tassie' went on Hannan Swaffer asked me for an interview, and I refused to give it, since when he hasn't opened his mouth about me, which shows he felt the snub. He hasn't said any thing derogatory, so that shall be counted unto him for righteousness. An Irish Reporter, refused a favour, would never end depreciating one. But I fear 'Jimmy' Douglas—the Editor, a fully-winged sentimental ranter—will be loth to let you in to his paper. However, we'll see; & if it comes off, it'll send you a few guineas anyhow.

Yes, Paul Farrell—I know a Pol Ua Fearghail—is it the same man?—wrote to me to say he had written C.B.C[ochran] for a job on the Tassie, sending him a load of photos, cuttings etc. He says, "As a genius, who has like yourself (Is this a compliment, or is it a joke?) languished in the cob-web chains of Caitlin Ni hUallachan [Cathleen Ni Houlihan] for too long, may I hope that, knowing something of my abilities, you will see what a valuable asset, etc."

I'm afraid C.B.C. won't knock his chains off, & that he'll have to stay where he is, &, if he be still in the Civil Service, that's the best thing for him to doodle, doodle doo! Don't give any addresses to these inquirers—poor G.B.S. is plagued with people bursting with genius & he can't get jobs for them all. I've no time to be answering Paul Farrell. He must plough his own furrow, & paddle his own Canoe.

The Editor of Irish Statesman replied last week to my letter, & I have today sent a reply to the sundered psyches—G. Russell, AE & YO. The Tassie comes off on Saturday.[1] Playing to fine houses—£1400 a week, but expenses are too heavy for it to go on.

Well, all the best to Rose, & Frank & Bernard & to you.

Sean

[1] *The Silver Tassie* closed on 7 December, after a run of two months.

To Irish Statesman

14 DECEMBER 1929

CONTRADICTIONS.

DEAR SIR,—Woa, there, Georgie; woa, man, and quieten your hop-about, runaway, intellectual agitation. Calm yourself, calm yourself, and try to force a definite thought or two out of the congested mass of nonsense in your nut. Questions have been put, not to Whitman, nor to Emerson, nor to Eddington, but to you, so don't put before me what Whitman wrote or what Whitman thought, but try to speak for yourself. "If God hasn't given a man something to say out of himself, why should he get an award of merit for saying something some other artist has already said?" Since you are so fond of quoting others, maybe you'd be able to tell us why.

Your statement that "one part of our complex being may thirst after the spirit seriously, and another may delight in bodily things" is stale, has been heard before—long, long years ago in the Sunday School. Well, you have determined to be like Whitman—a multitude of contradictions (you are hardly like him any other way). Then why not print on the front page of your paper, "A.E., Editor—a multitude of contradictions, guaranteed never to say the same thing twice." This would be a bit of a joke, for you say the same things over and over again, like eyes looking at red beginning to see green; eyes looking at green beginning to see red; pendulums that swing forward always swing-swong back again; nature is made up of opposites, and a lot more of little, jingling phrases, like the ringing of the toy bells on the coloured reins when the kiddies start to play horses. But what have the contradictions in Walt Whitman got to do with your contention that "artists who are inspired by Cezanne ought to be suppressed?" You yourself have gloated over your own imitation of a Corot Sky. (Eh, ask Whitman or Emerson, or even Eddington, if there isn't a difference between imitation and inspiration.) Do you think Cezanne less than Corot? Is imitation to be a meanness in others and a glory for you, glory for you, glory for you?

After having brought me to Whitman—led to him as a Salvation Army lass might lead a man to Jesus—you fetch me on to Emerson, and bid him speak for you. But why don't you speak for yourself, for if God hasn't given a seer something to say out of himself, why should he be kow-towed to when he says what some other artist has already said? You poke up Emerson to tell me to say every morning (why not every night as well?) "a foolish consistency is the hobgoblin of little minds." This is to form part of my education. At present we aren't concerned with what you think about education, but what you think and what you have said about the Art of Painting. It wasn't dear, old Waldo that said: "Photography sometimes gives us a pleasure equal to that conveyed by the work of the Great Masters," and so his "hobgoblin of foolish consistency" doesn't even suggest absolution for making a silly and a stupid statement. There is something more than the suggestion of a little mind that thinks or hopes to frighten off an attack upon a silly opinion by a boo from Emerson. For one, who—or his Y.O. contradiction—in Art Circles in Dublin is the Primate of all Ireland (God moves in a mysterious way His wonders to perform), to say that "the camera can sometimes give us almost all the delight of great landscape art," makes manifest the certainty that he plays with a shoddy gilding that he takes to be gold. If what he thinks and says be so, why bother about the Lane pictures; why not stock (stock is the right word here) Dublin's new Gallery with examples of photography that are as great and would give us as much pleasure as the works of the Great Masters of French Impressionism? I wonder has it ever struck your intuitional mind that while Emerson discovered there was such a thing as a foolish consistency, O'Casey has discovered, near at home, without the use of any delicate instruments either, that there is also such a thing as a foolish inconsistency knocking about somewhere?

Having finished with Emerson (I've finished with him, too), you lead me jubilantly to Eddington, who will tell me—one of the Editor's psyches interpreting—that "a great scientist may also be a mystic (I wonder can a great mystic also be a scientist; for this would go to prove what you say, "that nature is made up of opposites"); that he can make the nicest and most minute investigations, mathematical, or by delicate instruments into the nature of matter and energy; that there are protons and electrons charged with positive and negative electricity (my God!), each of which have their own rationale." Is there something wrong with the grammar here?

Do you know, Mr. Russell, that all this is too foolish even to be laughed at? What have mathematical investigations, protons, electrons—negatives and positives certainly might—matter and energy got to do with the A.E. sub-psyche statement that the way to Art is to cover your wall with pictures, or with the Y.O. sub-psyche statement that the surest way away from Art is to cover your wall with pictures? If you can, rationally or intuitionally, get a connection between the discoveries of Eddington in protons and electrons, with your discoveries in Art, then, I'm afraid, you know as much about Science as you do about Painting.

All these foolish remarks, urged on to fight for themselves by statements much more foolish still, have been made by a man who is one of the Vice-Presidents of The Friends of the National Collections of Ireland. A Vice-President who says that "photography sometimes equals the work of the Great Masters!"

But damn it all, a friend's a friend, and a man's a man for a' that, so to help you out of your education, which seems to fit so badly, I advise you to say three times every morning before you get up, and three times every night before you go to bed (murmur it, and it'll do just the same), "If God hasn't given a man something to say out of himself, why should he be permitted to acquire merit by saying again what some other artist has already said?" Keep at this hard enough, now, and it may save you from the bad habit of one day filling yourself, like a fattened goose, with Spengler, to spout Spengler; or, on another day, filling yourself up, like a fattened goose, with Eddington, to spout Eddington. It may deliver you, too, from having to say what has already been said by Laotze or Li Hung Chang; Waldo Emerson or Billy Sunday; Signor Eddington or Monsieur Buffon, and in the end you may be even as The Answerer,

What cannot be answered he answers, and what can be answered he shows how it cannot be answered.

Remember me to all the boys and girls.—Yours faithfully,

Sean O'Casey

(DEAR SEAN,—We are afraid, however complimentary your studies of articles in this journal may be, that a series of special lessons elucidating their meaning to you might become tiresome to others, as special instruction for a backward boy in a class rather tends to be annoying to those who understand very well. We are sorry that you do not seem to grasp the complexity of human nature, and that you still seem to believe in simple rules for the thinker. Blake says—you must permit quotation—"One law for the lion and the ox is oppression," and the emotional, intellectual, aesthetic faculties must be nourished by very different methods. And you should try to understand what is written before you base an argument against it. One of the points you bring up with an air of victory is that in a dream "Y.O." saw a picture which *in dream* he understood to be a Corot, and on waking "Y.O." remembered the picture and tried to paint it. But it was stated distinctly in the article that to the *waking consciousness the picture had none of the attributes of a Corot landscape.* It is regrettable that in order to prevent yourself drowning when out of your intellectual depth, you should have grasped so passionately at the support of so frail a straw. You contrast indignantly an opinion in dream with a straw. You contrast indignantly an opinion in dream with a waking opinion, and denounced this as an outrageous inconsistency of attitude. "Y.O." had elsewhere been critical of paintings showing too obviously that the artists had little to say for themselves, and were obvious imitators of Cezanne or Picasso. "Y.O." had exactly the same objection to obvious imitations as a literary critic would have in poetry to obvious imitations of Tennyson or Swinburne. We are sorry we cannot assist your education further about the right which every person has at times to isolate a work of art by itself for special study, and at other times to compare and discuss a number of pictures without being considered a person of inferior mind. You will doubtless understand this in the future. But as it is too difficult for you at present, you had better put the problem aside and take it up later. There is nothing to shout about in the statement that the camera can sometimes give us almost all the delight of great landscape art. We derive pleasure from looking at pictures or photographs for many reasons besides that they are great art. We may do so because a particular effect of sunlight may arouse memories of nature which have a special appeal to us. But to admit such pleasurable feelings does not necessarily imply that the person fails to distinguish between great art and a photograph. Finally, Sean, when you quote you should quote accurately. The sentence you attribute to "Y.O."—*i.e.*, "That photography sometimes equals the work of the Great Masters," does not appear in the article. It is not good literary manners to put in inverted commas sentences which are your own and attribute them to another and base an argument on them. We think that as the articles are too difficult for you, you should read in preference some of the many journals where there are no complexities or references to philosophy or psychology or science. We appreciate the intensity of study you have given to articles, even of only a few paragraphs, appearing in this journal, but we think you could employ the genius which created *Juno and the Paycock* in more profitable ways, that is, by writing about the life you understand well and not worrying about articles which cause a red haze to form before your mind so that you cannot even see what is written.—Ed. I.S.)

To Irish Statesman [1]

TC. O'CASEY

[20 DECEMBER 1929]

Dear Georgie—

It is evident, I'm afraid, that you are beginning to get a little bit ratty, and this is a condition of mind neither dignified nor prudent.

If you read again what I have already written, you will see that I allowed you the difference between what you thought when you were asleep and what you thought when you were awake. You seem to have some obsession to divide yourself into as many parts as possible. You have already divided into three, now you are beginning to divide the parts into portions, and what Y.O. thinks in a dream is repudiated by what Y.O. thinks when he's awake. But if every Y.O. in six thousand Y.O.'s were in six parts, and every part a Y.O., we shall still try to keep the main body and the main mind to the point.

The first point is, that you blame young artists for copying Matisse and Cezanne, while you hail yourself as a fine fellow for copying Corot. If, after you have talked of Corot, dreamed of Corot, and tried to paint a Corot, you delude yourself into the belief that what you have painted isnt an attempt at an imitation of a Corot at all, then the sooner Eddington or Freud renders you first aid the better. There is an excuse for imitation in the works of a young artist, for no young artist can escape an influence, but you are old enough to know better. Touching on this point, I asked a question in my first letter, and now I ask it again: would you object to, or would you rejoice at the inclusion of a work by Cezanne, by Picasso, or by Matisse in the New Gallery of Modern Art that is to be opened in Dublin?

I have no time to again follow your tedious evasions from your statements (or statutes) that the way towards a fuller appreciation of the

[1] This letter was refused publication.

Art of Painting was to crowd a wall with pictures—comparatively poor and trivial things, too—countermanded the next minute by the statement that the way to a fuller appreciation of the Art of Painting, was to put only [one] picture at a time on a wall. You even mention the number of these "little masterpieces"—a hundred. A hundred little masterpieces on the wall of some poor man's or woman's room, to be gazed at with "pride and affection".

A hundred pictures an' a' an' a',
Be Masters, me boy, that can draw, can draw,
Without one blemish or flaw, or flaw
A hundred pictures an' a'.

It seems to be clear that these conflicting statements were made, not because of any complex love or appreciation of the Art of Painting, but that the first statement was made, when A.E. was reviewing a book, because it suited him to make it at the moment; and that second statement was made when reviewing another book at another time, for the same reason, coupled with the fact that there was very little genuine feeling for Painting in the soul or heart or psyche of the man that made them. Let anyone of moderate intelligence read your articles on "Reading of Poetry", and the "Salon of Photography", and he or she will see that the esthetic principle there isnt "to isolate a work of Art for special study," and at other times to "compare and discuss a number of pictures," articles on "Reading of Poetry," or "Illustrators of the Sixties," and he or she will see that the mumbling of "every person has the right to isolate a work of art for special study, and, at another time, to compare and discuss a number of pictures," is a stealthy backing away from the contradictory dictums, the one telling your readers to crowd a wall with a hundred little masterpieces, and the other telling them that this is the surest way to blind themselves to Art.

If you think that because I wrote "photography sometimes equals the work of the Great Masters," instead of "the photographer's art sometimes gives us a pleasure almost equal to that conveyed by great artists," (I quoted you word for word in my first letter) you can dodge such statements as "There are a thousand aspects of nature which the camera can capture better than any but the greatest craftsmen in oils or watercolours," or, "the camera can sometimes give us almost all the delight of great landscape art," then you can welcome the thought, and keep it, kiss and hug it, and take it to bed with you. Of course there is nothing to shout about over your deferential enthusiasm for the glories of the camera. There is no reason that I know of, why you shouldnt go on for the rest of your life enjoying, analysing, comparing and discussing the "endless delicacies of light and tone" found swarming in the art of photography.

Since my backwardness—for which may God pardon me—and my failure to elucidate (good word, good word) the meanings contained in the articles of the "Irish Statesman" irritate you, perhaps you may be good enough to elucidate to me, and to the wide, wide world, the meaning or meanings hidden in two sentences appearing in your last reply to me. They are:

"We derive pleasure from looking at pictures or photographs for many reasons besides that they are great art," and, "But to admit such pleasurable feelings does not necessarily imply that the person fails to distinguish between great art and a photograph." In the first sentence you associate photography with great art; in the second sentence you separate great art from photography. See how clumsy your writing can be, even when you are on your guard.

Finally, George, you're wrong when you think that my criticisms of your criticisms are "intense studies" of "only a few paragraphs," that have been "isolated by themselves for special study." Quite a number have been left to sleep quietly for a time. For the present we are content to say these few things about your views on the Art of Painting, (and photography) so, fairly satisfied with the tumbling about we have given them, we'll leave you crouching in the little dug-out you have made for yourself behind Whitman, Eddington, Emerson and Blake.

and warble, cheerio.
[*Sean O'Casey*]

To Irish Statesman

TC. O'Casey

[St. John's Wood]
3 January 1930

Dear Sir—

A reply to what you said under the heading of "Contradictions", in "The Statesman" for the issue of Dec. 14th, 1929, was sent by me to you for publication in your Paper. As the letter was sent by Registered Post, you must have received it, yet, so far, it hasnt appeared.

I am inclined to assume that you do not intend to permit it to appear in your Paper. If this be so, perhaps you will manifest the good literary manners to tell me so; to say so in the next issue of your Journal, and to return the MS to me.

Yours Faithfully,
Sean O'Casey

From George Russell

MS. O'CASEY

THE IRISH STATESMAN
84 MERRION SQUARE, DUBLIN
6 JANUARY 1930

Dear O'Casey,

I see no reason why I should continue printing any rigmarole you send. As you desire it I return you the third letter. I have printed two letters from you. You said all you had to say in the first. You repeated this in the second, and again in the third. I have no doubt you have leisure to go on repeating yourself for months to come. I am not going to weary my readers and myself by these repetitions.

Yours sincerely,
George Russell

To Irish Statesman [1]

TC. O'CASEY

7 JANUARY 1930

Since you have dropped the 'Dear Seanny' business, we'll turn aside from the 'Dear Georgie' method of address, and say:

The Editor, Irish Statesman,
Dear Sir—

I have received your letter refusing to publish my last reply to your statements. You give as a reason for refusing, that what I have written would 'weary your readers'.

"But it is really much more exciting to talk to people who differ from us, than to talk to people who agree with us. Our opposites vitalise us, and we feel that complete identity of opinion rather boring. We all ought to read what we disagree with, if only for the purpose of confirming us in our truth. The article that starts a vigorous controversy between portions of our dramatically sundered psyche is mentally vitalising".

[1] This letter was refused publication.

So the synthesis of your own words seem to say that you are something of a fourflusher in the game of battling thought.

My intuitional mind told me that you would refuse to publish what I had written (though I had distinctly stated it would be my last letter on that subject) not because it would have wearied your readers (you know little of psychology, if you really think this) but because any more strokes from the Titan would have pulverised you. The fact is, of course, that you are slipping swiftly down (like an old fossil sitting on a mat tearing down, trying to look dignified, on a mountain glide in a Fancy Fair) on the descending arc of your cultural circle.

Perhaps you will be good enough to show a little of your 'fourth dimensional justice' by stating in the next issue of your Journal that my last reply to you has been refused publication.

Yours Sincerely
Sean O'Casey

P.S. A merry Christmas.

To Irish Statesman [1]

TC. O'CASEY
[ST. JOHN'S WOOD]
10 JANUARY 1930

Dear Sir—

As no intimation appears in the current number of your Journal, I must again ask you (the third time) to spare a minor space in "The Irish Statesman" so that your readers may know that by refusing to publish a letter from me, you have delivered them from weariness and pain. You can say the letter was stupid, rot, punk, foolish repetition —anything you like—but at least let your readers know I attempted to answer you, which is something of an achievement, since you are, as the stars sing, the Logos Hibernica.

Surely, one who has made of Rathgar a patch of "holy earth, a leaping place from star to star", isnt afraid to say that a letter from O'Casey has been refused publication in "The Irish Statesman".

Yours Sincerely,
[*Sean O'Casey*]

[1] This letter was refused publication.

To An Poblacht

18 January 1930

COMPLICATED CONTROVERSY
Sean O'Casey and AE in Argument
Apostle of Art

(For the benefit of such of our readers as do not read the *Irish Statesman* we note that this letter comes at the end of a prolonged controversy in the columns of that paper, in the course of which: (1) Sean O'Casey questions AE's ability to paint pictures or criticise them; (2) AE doubts the universality of Sean O'Casey's knowledge and his clarity of mind. (No prize is awarded for the solution of the problem.)

The Editor, *An Poblacht.*

Dear Sir,—Perhaps you would be good enough to permit the appearance in your paper of the enclosed letter, ... which has been refused publication in "The Irish Statesman" by the Editor, AE or YO. The letter sent by registered post was kept by him, and no acknowledgement of receipt was given till a further letter was sent asking him if he intended to publish it, to say why, if he refused, and to return the MS. He then returned the letter, and feeling that he must say something, he said that he refused to put it in because it was "a rigmarole of repetitions that would weary his readers."

And yet this Polonius of Literary Circles and Art Circles in Dublin has said himself in his very own paper, "It is really much more exciting to talk to people who differ from us, than to talk with people who agree with us. Our opposites vitalise us, and we feel that complete identity of opinion rather boring. We all ought to read what we disagree with, if only for the purpose of confirming us in our truth. The article that starts a vigorous controversy between portions of our dramatically sundered psyche is mentally vitalising." The synthesis of his own words tells that he is something of a fourflusher in the game of battling thought.

The refusal to publish becomes more significant when one remembers that once before he tried to suppress letters because, as he said in telegram and letter, if they were printed, W. B. Yeats might start legal proceedings. Imagine W. B. Yeats taking legal action against his buttie, AE! And this is the hardy, eh there, get outa th' way, big fellow who tore out into the streets to protest against a censorship of mind in Ireland.

This Apostle of Art and of freedom of thought has refused the publication of himself; has said that photography is great art; that photography isnt art; that the way to see the beauty of art is to cover your wall with pictures; that the way to blind yourself to the beauty of art is to cover your wall with pictures; that a man may speak of Corot, think of Corot, dream of a picture like a Corot; try to paint like Corot, and then stand up to all the world and say, "this picture isnt a Corot derivative at all"; that artists that find inspiration in Picasso, Cezanne or Matisse ought to be vigorously suppressed; that all this is explained in Whitman's poetry, Emerson's prose, Blake's vision and in electrical protons and electrons when they they are picked up and weighed by delicate instruments.

AE revels in "particular effects of sunlight that arouse memories of nature"; he likes Corot because Corot copied the vision of the camera; he reacts to mistiness and all the tone values of direct painting, and so declares that his emotional and intellectual experience in Painting is very limited indeed. Somewhere Lady Gregory has said that AE hides his mystical light in a turnip; but the fact is that AE hides the turnip in a mystical light.

Yours Sincerely,
Sean O'Casey

To Catholic Herald [1]
London

TC. O'CASEY

LONDON
15 MARCH 1930

Dear Sir:

I have received a cutting of a letter written by someone calling himself "Celt", which has been published in your paper.

Among other things said that do not matter to me, "Celt" says:—"At the time of his first success English Catholic papers hailed him (Sean O'Casey) vociferously as a brilliant Catholic dramatist, and, though this isnt so, I am not aware he ever troubled to correct it himself."

The writer implies here that I was anxious to creep into favour with those whom he calls "English Catholics." This is a mean thing to say. I have never tried to hide the fact that I am an Atheist (were the Catholic Church as powerful now as She was many years ago, there's no knowing what I would have to do), and I feel there is nothing to be proud of, or ashamed of in that fact. I am not quite so eager to trumpet out my Atheism, as "Celt" evidently is to trumpet forth his Catholicity, though defending his Faith and his Fatherland, he prefers to remain incognito. Recently the Catholic Poetry Society asked me to come to a reading of poetry by Padraic Colum (it was very kind of them to

[1] This letter was refused publication by the editor.

invite me, and I appreciate their kindness), and I refused, saying that I was not a poet, nor a Catholic, nor even a Christian. This reply was published in the Press, but for fear of future confusion among either "English" or "Irish" Catholics, please publish the fact that in Social and Economic opinions, I am a Communist, and in opinions that we term religious, I am an Atheist.

Sincerely yours,
[*Sean O'Casey*]

To New York Times

20 MARCH 1930

SEAN O'CASEY AND GEORGE RUSSELL

Dear Sir,

Perhaps you would be good enough to allow me to make a few remarks upon the Editorial comment that appeared in the *New York Times* in the issue of Feb. 6th, 1930, about the controversy that recently took place between George Russell, Editor of the *Irish Statesman,* and Sean O'Casey.

Russell was directly asked why in one issue of his paper he said that a way to the knowledge and love of Art was to "cover a wall with pictures," and in an issue following, "the best way to come to a love of Art was to hang on the wall one picture at a time." He was asked, too, why he condemned young artists for being influenced by Matisse or Cezanne, while he himself laboured to imitate Corot. He was asked did he really believe that "the Art of photography can sometimes give us a pleasure almost equal to that conveyed by great Artists." He was asked to explain the following sentences appearing in the same article: "We derive pleasure from looking at photographs or pictures for other reasons beside that they are great art," and "to admit such pleasurable feelings does not necessarily imply that the person fails to distinguish between great art and a photograph," for in the first sentence he associates great art with photography, and in the second, separates great art from photography. He wriggled away from the questions by glorifying inconsistency, quoting Emerson's "Consistency is the hobgoblin of little minds", too stupid to see that when he counselled me to "stick to the work I knew so well," he was advocating the manner he had just before condenmed.

I can assure you that I know as much about Emerson as Mr. Russell, and more about Whitman, both from the point of view of the poet's work, and even from the point of view recently expressed about the poet in the *American Mercury*.

I assure you, too, painting nothing, I paint as well as Russell. Criticise his poems, and those who are bent in the back worshipping him, will say, "oh, dont judge him as a poet, but judge him as a painter." Criticise his painting, and the same crowd will say, "not as a painter, no; you must judge him as a poet." The fact is that looking at his pictures, you do him justice and praise him soundly when you say, "his pictures are equal to his poems", and, reading his poems, we do him justice and praise him soundly, when we say, "his poems are equal to his pictures."

Mr. Russell as well as being in Ireland first judge of poetry, prose, plays, politics, purity, painting and auto-puffery, evidently thinks too, that New York wants something like him badly. In a poem called "New York," after talking about the "heaven assailing spires" that have outdone the work of "the children of Babylon"; after telling us that "earth has spilt her fire," in the building of these great works, he goes on to ask pathetically—

> Has she (New York) that precious fire to give,
> The starry-pointing Magian mind
> That soared from the Chaldean plains,
> Through zones of mystic air, and found
> The Master of the Zodiac,
> The will that makes the Wheel go round!

So you see Mr. Russell is longing to heave New York up a little nearer to the stars, but—sotto voce—there's more of cotton than there is of silk in the poetry.

Your comment says that O'Casey's attack left "Mr Russell serenely smiling on his throne." I'm afraid the smile was a wan one. The testy humor displayed in the letter he sent me when asked if he intended to publish my last reply to what he had written, coupled with his refusal to publish after keeping the reply secret in his bosom for some weeks, seem to indicate that the shaking up had ruffled him a little. And distrust and suspicion are spreading. In "The Star", the organ of the largest political party in The Free State, portion of a leading article, appearing in the issue of Feb. 22, 1930, says:—" . . . We hope the Abbey Theatre Directorate (though not a Director, Mr Russell is one of the bunch) will wake up. Like the majority of Free State Citizens, we have, during the last year or two, experienced a distinct loss of confidence in the judgement of the Abbey Theatre Directorate. Since the Directors have, within the last twelve months, rejected three plays worth producing, we are driven to think that the Board must, in the course of the last twenty-five years, have rejected many good plays and checked the development of a number of promising playwrights."

This is the opinion of the Party that voted the subsidy to the Theatre, and since Russell is one with the Abbey Directors in power, piety and preaching, it seems to be evident that others are assembling thoughts to show it is time to end the arrogant assumption of power and infallibility in things Artistic and things Literary by this Yeatsian and Russellian hand-picked group in Dublin.

Yours Sincerely,
Sean O'Casey
6 March 1930

To Gabriel Fallon

MS. TEXAS

ST. JOHN'S WOOD
20 MARCH 1930

Dear Gaby—

Just a line—or two—or three—to testify I remember you, & that as it was so it is now—from me to you. I have really been looking long & long at pictures, & feel how much was lost to me when some Power decided I was not to paint.

Will, as you know, is in Cochrane's 1930 Revue [1]—bad parts, but gilded and gillded & guilded with 25 Pounds per week of seven days, & a likelihood of the Revue running for 6 months. Will wants a part that he can "get his teeth into", but, if he was asked to play Falstaff for a tenner a week of seven days, I wonder would he do a buck jump forward or backward? F.H.O'D[onnell] was over here, & spent an evening with me. He says there are rumblings to be heard in the Board Room of the Abbey Theatre. I sent a letter about Yo's Art criticism to the 'Star' last week. An Editorial in that paper urged the Abbey Di's "to wake up", & I urged in addition, that Y.O. should go sleep for a little while.

Nothing startling to tell you, except that Billy fell off, or was thrown off, a grey horse he was riding, & broke a bone in his wrist.

Yeats's "Fighting the Waves" is to be produced here next week at Hammersmith by L. Robinson.

Love to Rose, Francis, Bernard & to you.

Sean

[1] Will (Barry Fitzgerald) had a number of comic roles in C. B. Cochran's *1930 Revue*, which opened at the London Pavilion on 27 March 1930.

To The Star, *Dublin*

29 MARCH 1930

Dear Sir:

From a cutting sent to me I read that, in a leading article,[1] *The Star* expresses a hope that the Abbey Theatre Directorate would wake up, and, agreeing, add another that The Abbey's best man, Y.O., would lie down, fold his hands and go to sleep for a little while, so that those who feel an urge towards depression in the Art of Painting can go on their own way unhampered by silly and fogey-minded criticism. He is obsessed with the meanest and most trivial phase of Corot's landscape art. At every exhibition of landscapes, with a maddening consistency that is enough to make Emerson squirm in his grave, he trots out his "quivering of variable and delicate grey on the water . . . some dramatic streak of light on hill or moor . . . a veil of pale violet air over the valleys, dissolving everything in harmony with itself . . . emotion of mystery in shadowy hills . . . the air is always drinking up light and shade . . . Irish air is so full of moisture that the receding of light and shade from the foreground is very perceptible." His familiar experience must be very narrow, for he seems to be for ever seeking this trickiness and sentimentality in the examples of landscape art painted by Irish Artists. When it is absent his blood runs cold; when it is present, like Stalky and Co., he gloats, gloats, gloats. Even when he looked at the products of the camera in The Photographers' Salon, he burst out into: "the happy photographer will find a group of trees as well composed as a landscape by Corot, and we miss only the figures, which with Corot seemed part of the rhythm of nature," evidently that the likeness between a photo and a Corot landscape, so far from adding to the art value of a photo, takes away the value from the Corot landscape. Let anyone with a feeling for art look at these mistiful, wistful Corot Landscapes and his soul will call for a song; if he listens reverently, he will hear the spirits hidden in the shadowy hills singing the song:

Just a song at twilight when the lights are low,
And the flickering shadows softly come and go.

Corot turned these out be the dozen, and fellows and girls following, turned them out be the hundred, so that there are now thirteen thousand of them in America, and it would seem that Y.O. will never, never rest, nor let the sword fall from his hand till there are at least one imitation

[1] "Enriching Dublin Life," *The Star,* 22 February 1930.

Corot Landscape for every head of the population in The Free State. I wonder what gave Y.O. this comic Corot complex. Perhaps because they are the kind of paintings that are easiest to imitate; perhaps because they helped him to pack his poetry with phrases about "mystic dew dropping from twilight trees" (what are twilight trees?), "blue woods of twilight" and other mistiful and wistiful thoughts; but more probably because Y.O. has no genuine feeling for colour line and form, for the youngest kid in an art school knows that the artistic value in the vague and imponderable landscapes of Corot, is very small indeed. There are a lot more things in Nature than Y.O. dreams of, or Corot saw, and some of these things were seen even by Corot's buttie, Rousseau.

Y.O. gives other indications that his feeling for Pictorial Art is faint even for examples that come intimately into his presence. In last week's *Irish Statesman* [2] (where he again gave his old, reliable, Corotesque criticism of some paintings by Mr. Iten) he says: "I liked also *The Shawls* . . . In looking at these mill-workers with their shawls, and remembering the Kerry girls I saw years ago with their shawls draped about them like the shawls in Tanagra terra-cottas, one sometimes feels a whole world full of artistic possibilities has been overlooked by artists. They had better set about painting and modelling them now. Bobbed hair and short skirts are becoming the sign of woman from Peking to San Francisco, and in the West of Ireland the old costumes are fast vanishing. Why do not the artists set down that old world beauty, as the folklorists are collecting the tales, before the Ministry of Education wipes imagination out of the mind?"

When mentioning the rhythm of *The Shawls,* which reminded him of Kerry Girls that he saw years ago, one would think that the first thing to flash into his mind would be the rhythm of the shawl-covered women in the central panel of John's magnificent *Galway*. Peradventure he has forgotten all about this work, which ought to be in Dublin instead of where it is. Why is he always telling artists what to do? Supposing they do what he tells them to do, does he think that mansions and cottages all over Ireland sporting Tanagra terra-cotta dolls will add anyhing of design and imagination to art in Ireland? He thinks they ought to be done because they are old costumes that are vanishing away. Does he think that an artist paints pictures to record vanishing fashions? Or does he think shawls should be painted because they shelter rhythm and design absent from other things? But an artist may find rhythm and design in anything. Has he seen Van Gogh's *Chair?* Or *Les Parapluies* (in the Lane Collection), by Renoir? Peradventure he has forgotten this work, which ought to be in Dublin instead of where it is. But I

[2] Y.O., "Sculpture and Painting," *Irish Statesman,* 8 March 1930, a review of the paintings of Hans Iten.

imagine he wants these things done so that picturesque memories may be revived, like old associations brought back by a faded photograph or a lock of hair. But this has nothing to do with art. *Galway* is as interesting to a Mexican as it is to an Irishman, and artists must find subjects for the play of their imagination in themselves, and not in Y.O.

This very week revueing (this spelling is correct) Grace Henry's pictures,[3] out of half that had been brought to the exhibition, he mentions four only, saying that he could "only look on half hung walls." Here's a Doctor of Literature telling us that when he came to an exhibition of pictures, he could only look on half hung walls. What are half hung walls? As well as keeping back half of the pictures, the Imp of the Perverse played another trick on Y.O.: he neglected to put names under the pictures, and so Y.O. was flummoxed. When he arrived in front of the pictures he was panic-stricken to find that none of them had a label. How can anyone with a profound feeling for painting tell us anything about a picture that is destitute of a label? So poor Y.O. could only stagger away, murmuring, "I am an ineffective guide to them." But before he got well away, he caught a glimpse of something that steadied him a little: it was a picture of some boats sailing gallantly into the old, reliable, luminous blue mist.

This kind of evasive, misty-mystical, rhetorical, sentimental criticism is of very little value to the practice and progress of art in Ireland, but will frighten young artists away from the realization that there is nothing beautiful in a landscape because it resembles a Corot.

Ireland has criticised her own ideas of political opinions in a fierce and terrible way, and it is natural that a velvet-mannered arrogance in things artistic and things Literary should be bitten into bravely when that velvet-mannered arrogance demands that the young artists in Ireland should keep alive and nourish by imitation formulas in Literature and Art that died everywhere else fifty years or so ago, and more. Y.O. came to a dead halt at the end of Corot's bad period of Landscape Art: he doesn't go so far even as the artistic statements of the Lane Collection, for here are Renoir, Manet and Degas. But are the coming artists of Ireland determined to take no step farther than the farthest step taken by the French Impressionists? Are they to be bull-dozed into a horror and a hatred of Cezanne, Matisse, Picasso, Segonzac,—not daring to mention Braque? Some days ago Y.O. was asked if he would or would not be in favour of including a work by Cezanne, Picasso or Matisse in Dublin's Municipal Collection of Modern pictures. He refused the question. Either he was afraid to say yes, or afraid to say no, or scorned to answer a question put by me. But it is a shameful thing to Art Circles that Dublin has no example of work by Cezanne, Van Gogh, Matisse, Picasso or Gaughin. A Russian letter in a French Art Journal tells us that in the Moscow Modern Art

[3] Y.O., "Grace Henry's Pictures," *Irish Statesman*, 15 March 1930.

Gallery, there are 25 Cezannes, 29 Gaughins, 55 Matisses, 54 Picassos, as well as works by those that preceded, and works by others that follow the artists mentioned. And not one in Dublin, not a whisper even of one to come, only a wistful silence of derision from him who is a clique, uplifted authority on Art, Literature, Science, Drama and Politics in Ireland. Is it right to think that Y.O.'s fawning on the pictures in the Lane Collection is stimulated only because of the circumstances surrounding their gain and their loss, and not that he feels for them a genuine emotion evoked by the pictures? Is one not right in thinking that if this collection contained a Cezanne, he would be unwilling to surrender an inch of canvas?

The Star has expressed the fear that the attitude of the Abbey Directorate during the past twenty-five years may have checked the development of promising young playwrights, and let me add that if the outlook of Y.O. and others like him, continues to run current in Ireland as an unimpeachable authority, then the three last things of Judgement, Death and Hell will be the lot forever of the Art of Painting in Ireland.

Yours Sincerely,
Sean O'Casey

From Lady Gregory

PS. *Modern Drama* [1]

STANDARD HOTEL, DUBLIN
2 APRIL [1930]

Dear Sean—

I must write—because my mind is so full of the Plough and the Stars, that I saw last evening[2]—a wonderful play.—Always next morning—even without B. Fitzgerald—though of course no one can fill his place—I cannot help hoping that you will *give and forgive*—give another great play—and give us a new opportunity. Anyhow whether you do or not, I feel I must thank you for this—and for Juno—but I put the Plough first in my mind. And the audience last night was full of enthusiasm. I hope all goes well with wife and child. Affectionately. A. Gregory.

[1] From a copy made by A. C. Edwards and printed in *Modern Drama*, May 1965.

[2] *The Plough and the Stars* was revived at the Abbey Theatre on 1 April 1930. For the first time since he created the role in 1926, Barry Fitzgerald did not play Fluther Good, which on this occasion was played by P. J. Carolan. In another cast change, Eileen Crowe, who had refused to play the role of Mrs. Gogan in the original production because some of her lines were indecent, now played the role of the prostitute, Rosie Redmond.

From Oliver St. John Gogarty

MS. O'Casey
15 Ely Place
Dublin
11 April 1930

My dear Sean

Thanks for wire. The thing I sent you was telephoned and I omitted to have the reply prepaid. I didn't think it could be done by 'phone but it seems it can. Hence the P.O.

There are a few more than amateurs here who want to do 4 plays limited to a small caste in the Pavilion in Kingstown and I was asked as I knew you (or dreamed that I did) to ascertain the author's address which couldn't be found by inquiring here. I don't think we have a Tallulah but one never knows! Did you see that perfectly marvellous portrait of that lesbian lady which the Master has painted? [1] He has made her so spiritual that it is either a caricature of Tallulah or a reminder to the nation that "some shall be saved yet so as by fire"!

Billy was lately in Bel*fast* the fastest thing he has, for I hear that his horses have been sticky of late. I do hope they wont trust him again. Could he not be taught also to save himself by fire? By sticking to the sales of coal?

I hope you and your family continue to thrive. If you know anyone who wants a hotel with salmon fishing in a beautiful place, send them to ours at Renvyle, Connemara, & come yourself "on me".

All the best to you!
Oliver

[1] Augustus John had painted a portrait of the actress Tallulah Bankhead, which is reproduced as the frontispiece of her autobiography, *Tallulah* (London, Gollancz, 1952).

To Oliver St. John Gogarty

MS. BUCKNELL [1]

ST. JOHN'S WOOD
14 APRIL 1930

My dear Oliver,

I return herewith & herein, & herewhat, & forthwith and henceforth the 2/P.O. you sent to me as payment for or liquidation on the expense of the wire I sent to you.

"Make no great sacrifice for your friends, but be ready at most times to put yourself to a little trouble & inconvenience for their sakes"—Laotze, or Blake, or Emerson, or Whitman. vide A.E. vide Y.O. vidilicet G. Rex Russell.

The play you're looking for is on tour, & amateur rights haven't yet been released, Messrs French, I understand, are negociating with the author. Where's Kingstown? Plenty of Hallelujahs with you, but a Tallulah!

No, haven't seen John's picture of the lady you mention, but from what you say it's like, it's possible Tallulah's springing towards her opposite—aha—look at red for a long time, & the eye [2] sees green! Billy [McElroy] has a lovely horse now, a grey mare, that he mounted, then the animal threw him & broke a bone in his wrist.

[1] An imperfect copy of this letter appears in James F. Carens, "Four Letters: Sean O'Casey to Oliver St. John Gogarty," *James Joyce Quarterly,* Fall 1970, O'Casey Issue.

[2] Here he drew a sketch of an eye.

So AE has been unhorsed too, arsed & unhorsed.[3] My God, my God why hast—

Yours As Ever
Sean

[3] Due to financial difficulties, A.E.'s *Irish Statesman* ceased publication with the issue of 12 April 1930. The magazine had been in existence since 15 September 1923.

To Gabriel Fallon

MS. TEXAS
ST. JOHN'S WOOD
[17 APRIL 1930]
HOLY THURSDAY

My dear Gaby—

And how are you, and Rose and the two claimants to life? It's a long time since I have heard from you, the trees bud, the birds are active, the sun strengthens a little—& you are silent—standing dumb in the heart & the mind of The Free State. Do I owe you a letter, or do you owe me one?

Well, for fear of debt, here's a repayal, small, but an instalment of more to come, & may it please you.

Will is working away in Cochrane's Revue, which promises a good run, & Will will be financially stronger at the end of it. I see him rarely, but he has settled down nicely, likes his company companions, moves easily in his new surroundings, & longs for a bigger chance to show the stuff he's made of.

I am doing a little work, & expect to start a play shortly—Half-Gods Go; Ediste Fideles, or The Whale's Belly.

I had a letter recently from Lady Gregory, saying how moved she was by the last production of 'The Plough', & how she hoped "I would forget & forgive, & give them another opportunity". Whether she meant another offer of 'The Silver Tassie' or the offer of a new play, I know not, but it would be impossible to forget, & bloody difficult to forgive. I hear that the Abbey is showing signs of going West—according to details given of my plays the audiences are subsiding—and, possibly, this is a pity, but God does not go on suffering things forever. Robinson was over here recently, & asked if I were writing a new play; that things in the Theatre were bad, & that the players were anxious. Well, they had their prophets, and, instead of listening in & listening out, they stoned & stoned & stoned them. I hear, too, The Gate is hanging off a hinge, & that the Directors are meeting to discuss the position of affairs. What a damned mess of the possibilities for Drama all these high cods & low cods are making in Ireland!

And Russell has been unhorsed too. In his last farewell, he tells us it is only fair to go, to make way for young genius, for the minds of elderly men have lost their flexibility. Before that infirmity weighs more heavily (he says) he feels it best to cease criticism & comment. Always the gilded lie, instead of the simple truth. He cannot say that he must ring off because no longer can he find the friends to find the money to pay for his wisdom in Art & Literature & Politics. We all know that, had there been more money, there would have been more comment & more criticism. Well, it's a good wind that blows no-body ill, for this release will give him more time to paint bad pictures, & to write his bad poetry. How is T. C. Murray, & do you ever see B[rinsley] Macnamara now? Lennox Robinson, I understand, has gone to U.S.A. to teach play production, or to lecture on Drama, there in one of the Universities—another reason for believing that Universities are dead trees packed with blooms & foliage made & woven by the celebrated "Mac".

Well, Affectionate Wishes,
from the old Buttie,
Sean

To Gabriel Fallon

MS. TEXAS

ST. JOHN'S WOOD
[27? APRIL 1930]

Your prayer has been answered, my dear Gaby: the house is in a state of chassis. Maid burned her foot; I got a cold; water supply broke, burst & the plumbers are in possession, so that I have had to do all the things & more recommended in your last kind letter to me.

I have been thinking of Dublin production of "The Silver Tassie", & the following thoughts & ideas are now put before you:

1. Why not produce in a bigger theatre—say Queen's or Olympia?
Good reasons for this:
    A. Chance of bigger audience & more money for (almost) the same amount of work.
    B. Consequently, you as well as I would get something out of it.
    C. C.B.C[ochran], who has the rights would, I think, prefer a bigger

theatre, because his Company gets half of whatever would be coming to me.

D. Surely it would stand as good a chance as the production of The Constant Nymph & Co?

E. Scenes for 1st 3rd & 4th Act might be got from C.B.C. on loan, but we would have to find out what the cost of transport, etc, would be, so as to make sure that this would mean a much cheaper way than the creation of a new production—I am certain it would.

Perhaps you have as good reasons to set against the above, & you—if you think still of a Tassie production—might let me know them, so that I could fully think upon your idea of production in 'The Gate.'

Above all, don't let yourself in for too much work.

Yours As Ever
Sean

From Lady Gregory

PS. *Modern Drama* [1]

DUBLIN, ABBEY THEATRE
3 MAY 1930

Dear Sean—

I have just had the pleasure of buying what I think a good drawing of you, by Kernoff [2]—I am so glad to have it—and to keep it in the country, for none of the photographs were good—and anyhow something more substantial and lasting was needed, for your fame will last, and increase, that is, at least, my belief—

I am getting up *White Cockade* [3] after its rest of 13 years—I think the performance will be fine—tho' I wish Barry Fitzgerald was at hand—I went up to see a performance in the Peacock last week "A Noise in the Street" [4]—an interesting play that the censors have cut too much out of for the author to give in to, in England—

[1] From a copy made by A. C. Edwards and printed in *Modern Drama*, May 1965.

[2] A pastel portrait of O'Casey drawn in 1930 by Harry Kernoff (1900–), Dublin artist. It is now in the National Gallery of Ireland.

[3] Lady Gregory's *The White Cockade*, a three-act history play about Patrick Sarsfield and James II after the Battle of the Boyne, first performed at the Abbey Theatre on 9 December 1905.

[4] Stephen Schofield's *A Noise in the Street* opened at the Abbey's Peacock Theatre on 22 April 1930, presented by the New Players.

My family are still at Leixlip Castle, the granddaughters come in to see the plays—

Autumn Fire [5] this week hasn't had big audiences—but it goes well—An American man wept openly at the last scene—Dolan is *very* fine in it—I get back to Coole after this week—I don't give up hope of seeing you there some day, with wife and son—

It is strange poor Good [6] having died so soon after the passing away of the *Statesman*—AE is away in the country, is going to U.S.A. soon for some lectures on agriculture—Dublin looks gay, but I don't meet people except in the Abbey—

I hope all goes well with you and yours—

As ever, affectionately
A Gregory

[5] T. C. Murray's *Autumn Fire* was revived at the Abbey Theatre on 28 April 1930, with Michael J. Dolan in his original role of Owen Keegan.

[6] James Widner Good (1877–1930), Irish writer and friend of A.E.

To Gabriel Fallon

MS. TEXAS

ST. JOHN'S WOOD
6 MAY 1930

Wha ja mean by saying, "this scrap is mine". What scrap? And if the letters were much needed letters, how could the letters have been tactically wrong letters? And what had or has Kernoff got to do with them? His name was never mentioned, neither did it enter into my thoughts during the course of their writing. I never saw a picture by Kernoff; I never met him till he came over here; he never once, even indirectly came into the row that flamed up between me and the Most Eminent & Right Honorable G.R.A.E.Y.O.D.L.I.T.T. And how could the dispute have contributed in any way to the rejection by the I.H.R.I.A. of Kernoff's pictures[?] And if Kernoff has exhibited there year after year, what of that: was it a gain to him or to The Academy? And is it the core of his ambition to have pictures every, every, every year in the R.H.A.? And is Kernoff frightened because his pictures have been rejected? O, God! And he runs to you, & asks you to ask me for Christ's sake to write no more letters that have nothing to do with the refusal or acceptance of his pictures by the R.H.A. And even if the letters made poor old AE ratty, what then? Did poor old Dublin shake, the graves stand tenantless, & the sheeted living squeak & gibber through the City Streets? Comfort in Zion, there's comfort in Zion—Lady Gregory writes to say that soon he'll be bidding you a long farewell, for some morning he'll soon be off to Philadelphia on a long, long trail, dropping on his way courses & discourses on the pains and problems & profits of Agriculture. And Lady G. says, too, she has bought a drawing of your most humble & most disobedient servant, Sean, from Mr. Kernoff, so that's one up for me, see?

And the Gate—the glittering Gate has had a bit of a blow-out with 2500 pounds sterling which was a Present from Dublin. Hold you the watch tonight? We do, my Lord.

Lady G says last week's run of 'Autumn Fire' was cheered by great audiences, & An American Man wept openly at the end of the last Act, for M. Dolan was fine! And the star-spangled banner in triumph shall wave—

Walt Whitman
Waldo Emerson

And now about that threat of yours to [do] my little play, "The Silver Tassie."

Lady G. asked me to forget & forgive & to give them another opportunity—she made no mention & she made no moan about The Tassie.

The Tassie wouldn't fit in the Gate—the production would be too much for *you* (not artistically, dramatically,—but it would mean too much bloody work—have you me)—and the result in the gate would be no good to you nor to me. We cannot afford to make the sacrifices for love of the Drama that the Abbey so readily and so hotheadedly make—oh, Jasus!—and before we could decide on anything this way, we would have to have a long & unsteady talk. Did you hear—there's a rumour here that the Irish Statesman's Dead.

Love
Sean

To Gabriel Fallon

MS. Texas

St. John's Wood
19 June 1930

My dear Gaby—

I am writing today to C.B.C. about the Dublin production of The Tassie.

Now, before anything & everything, you must send me signed a solemn declaration that *you* will take *no* risk whatsoever of losing anything on the venture. When we gather together all the details we can, then you will consider all the cost, toil & trouble, & say no, or saying, yes, give me an undertaking that you personally will lose, fail or win, no money in the work. This must be certain.

I am, of course, very interested in the proposed production, but I would like to feel sure about the certainty of your losing nothing, but making something, out of the venture.

We had Boss & Charlie Saurin[1] to dinner here on Sunday, and Will & [Evan] Walters.

Paul Farrell sent me some days ago a letter asking for "The Tassie," but I haven't answered it—I'm finding it impossible to answer letters now—so if you drop on him anywhere, tell him that you have the thing in hand—with Mr. Gallicker, it's in good hands.

May Sun & Sea do you all good.

Sean

[1] Charles Saurin, brother-in-law of Arthur Shields (Boss) and Barry Fitzgerald (Will Shields).

To Mrs. Charlotte F. Shaw

MS. British Museum

St. John's Wood
23 June 1930

My dear Mrs. Shaw—

I was delighted to hear that you had again rallied yourself back into our ranks. I felt your fight would be a good one, & that you would get better again.

And now you must be careful of yourself—more careful than before—for a hard fight leaves us a little weaker for a long time.

I suppose you did well, but did you do wisely, to go to the Plough and the Stars,[1] and lose your sleep over it. Wait till you are quite well before you plunge into anything that will keep you from resting, besides it isn't the sick poor sinners that should be called to repentance, but the righteous that are filling the world with institutions for our physical & spiritual redemption.

Of course, my dear Mrs. Shaw, I am really gratified that you & G.B.S. thought so well of the play, & of the acting by little Kitty Curling, who has talent, & who has had a pretty rough time of it in Dublin.

Don'[t] forget to take care of yourself till you are quite strong again.

Give my affectionate regards to G.B.S.

Yours Affectionately,
Sean

[1] *The Plough and the Stars* opened at the Duchess Theatre, London, on 4 June 1930, for a limited run of six weeks, presented by Arthur Sinclair and Maire O'Neill's Irish Players, with the following cast: Arthur Sinclair as Fluther Good, Maire O'Neill as Mrs. Gogan, J. A. O'Rourke as Peter Flynn, Tony Quinn as The Young Covey, Kitty Curling as Nora Clitheroe, Sara Allgood as Bessie Burgess, Fred O'Donovan as Jack Clitheroe, Bernard Kavanagh as Captain Brennan, Joyce Chancellor as Mollser, Kathleen Drago as Rosie Redmond.

To Gabriel Fallon

MS. TEXAS

ST. JOHN'S WOOD
27 JUNE 1930

Dear Gaby—

I enclose here a letter got from C.B.C[ochran]'s Secretary, which you might return when you've read it & made a note on. This morning I rang up A. Sinclair, & he is to find out from Bromley traffic manager of the L.M.S. what the approximate cost would be for transportation to Dublin & back of the scenery. It would be much cheaper if a company were traveling with it. However, we'll see. I suppose it would hardly be less than £50 exclusive of the £20 fee asked for by C.B.C.

Best Wishes to All.
Sean

To Gabriel Fallon

MS. Texas

St. John's Wood
30 June 1930

Dear Gaby—

According to what has been told to me the cost of using the scenery for 1st, 3rd & 4th acts will be:

A. Cochrane's fee	£20. 0. 0.
B. Cartage to train (about)	6. 0. 0.
C. Freightage back & forward	30. 0. 0.
D. Insurance (about)	5. 0. 0.
	61. 0. 0.

It may even be something more.

So you see the expense of a production will be pretty heavy, unless you could do these things yourself for less.

I earnestly hope you will quietly & sensibly review, examine & ponder upon all the difficulties before you definitely do anything.

Hope the Sea & the Sun have done you all good.

Best Wishes
Sean

To Gabriel Fallon

MS. Texas

St. John's Wood
8 July 1930

My Dear Gaby—

Enclosed is what may satisfy you in the shape of an official letter giving consent to the Dublin Production of "The Silver Tassie." I have written to C.B.C. asking him to do the same, & I daresay you may have already got his official consent.

Would it be wise to raise the price of the seats? I don't think so; but the affair is in good hands, & you know best.

Aha, so J.A.P[errin] is being watched! Not a minute off the day, not a penny off the pay. The Abbey instead of looking ahead is looking behind. Well, it's none of our business.

J. B. Fagan is shortly to put on in the Duchess Theatre here, G. Shiels' new play "The New Gossoon" which will link us up with Euripides.

Best of Wishes
Sean

Right, I'm Glad you've got Mrs. Cogley[1] to help you. Good luck to you both.

[1] Madame D. Bannard Cogley (1883–1965), actress, theatre promoter, a founder-director with Micheál MacLiammoir, Hilton Edwards, and Georoid O'Lochlainn of the Dublin Gate Theatre in 1928. See O'Casey's letter to Fallon, 3 September 1928, note 1.

To Gabriel Fallon

MS. TEXAS
ST. JOHN'S WOOD
10 JULY 1930

My dear Gaby—

I have got from C.B.C. a copy of a letter which he has sent to you, giving his sanction to the proposed production of 'The Tassie' in Dublin, so that you have now, I imagine, all the materials for a definite proclamation.

I think you are wise to get together your own scenery if possible, for it will probably save a lot of trouble in the end. The one fault, maybe, with the Gaiety, would be the lighting system.

I don't quite get your meaning out of the "attack of Juliannalaneity",[1] from which Dublin is suffering. Can't guess who she may be.

Eileen & I have talked about possible meanings, but can find none. The only visitors (feminine) that we have had here are Mrs. G. B. Shaw, Mrs. Julian Huxley, some friends of Eileen's, who know not Dublin, & a girl (with her boy) on a visit to London from Australia. These are all that I can remember. It's very mysterious. No-one has ever been here that could be associated with us to the extent of talking about it in Dublin. Perhaps, you will let me know who this young lady may be.

Yours As Ever
Sean

[1] See his reference to "Dora Lane" in letter of 28 July 1930 to Fallon.

To Lady Londonderry

MS. Lady Bury

St. John's Wood
14 July 1930

Dear Lady Londonderry—

How am I, & what am I doing? Well, not so well, vigorous & free in spirit as I should wish to be, which is the physical and spiritual chain that binds me to humanity. Most of us, most of the time, like the figures in Blake's pictures, have the left foot forward. But error is not far from truth, & only restlessness can bring us peace.

I am not doing much with an earnest heart and definite mind at the moment: lounging through some of the distance that still lies between my restlessness that is called life, & the quietness that is called the end. Enjoying the fullness of Summer as it is circumscribed & trinity fashioned in the Parks & gardens of the North Western end of London. Sauntering through Hyde Park, "taking upon me the mystery of things, & acting as if I were one o' God's spies." What a place is Hyde Park.[1] From the little cock'ey'd sparrow watching a crumb in the hand of a fellow full of pity for the bird, & destitute of pity for himself, to the red-coated, gorgeously braided Salvation Army officer thunder-voicing God's love, & whining out about the terrible day of wrath that is to come. Secular Societies saying that even "where there is nothing" there is no God; Public Morality Councils fainting with dignified terror at the prospect of man's desire for woman, & woman's desire for the desire of man; circles of people tossing troubles away into the singing of "Danny Boy", or, "Oh God, our help in ages past," led by conductors tense as steel moving their slender white wands as if from their tips flowed the energy that gave majestic & immortable motion to the planets and the stars. The gaudy-coated household troopers gibbering with their lassies, whose minds have a vision little farther than the vision of the ducks & drakes swimming on the pond. And here and there a lonely, static-faced preacher appealing piteously for someone to come along & shake the hand of Jesus. Riders in the Row, walking their horses, trotting their horses or galloping their horses from end to end and back again, having eyes that see not, ears that hear not the things that moan and mutter all around them. But "matter has cohered together from its diffuse float, and the sail is on the surface, water runs and vegetation sprouts" for all, for everyone of them.

I suppose you are very busy with & in the change that has been creeping, & now is rushing wildly into present-day politics here. Beaverbrook is busy waking up the dead with bugle calls, and the Bankers have become the prophets of the people. Didn't some editor say that if Beaver-

[1] The following passage suggests a series of motifs for his next play, *Within the Gates* (1933).

brook didn't think as he thought, & say what he says, & did not what he doeth, it would be "contrary to the lesson of the Parable of the Talents, the value of which we have proved by long experience." So there you see that England's intellect in its way of expression is waxing fat and prosperous. And a clergyman has hung a notice outside St. John's Wood Church, saying: "It ought to be a part of every man's religion to see that his country is properly governed." Well, the Bankers have made a confession of their faith, anyhow—we believe—. But I'm afraid the vision has come a little too late, but still we will do well to burn the night with torches.

But I hope you are well & fully enjoy your moiety of life with Lord Londonderry, your fine boy and fine girls, & hope to have the pleasure of seeing you one of these days. Eileen is well, but a little fagged from working so constantly, & our boy's digging the sand at Margate, plunging into the sea & going from strength to strength.

With Affection & Warm Regards,
Sean

To Gabriel Fallon

MS. TEXAS

ST. JOHN'S WOOD
28 JULY 1930

Dear Gaby—

I have sent the sketch asked for on to you, & hope you may get it safely.

Yes, C.B.C. is really a very decent fellow in every way, and is, I think, fond of me—why? there I'll leave you.

There you are! Dublin talking about the dirty trick Fallon's played on Farrell, & Sean's heart-friend, bosom friend, soul-friend (anam-chara) M. Scott. The play was never intended to be given to Paul Farrell or anyone else, bar G. Fallon of Ballybrack, North Strand & Glasnevin. I wished the same G. Fallon to have produced in London, as you know, & C.B.C. knows. There is no-one in the world, I think, with whom I disagree so much & agree so often as the same identical aforesaid Gaby Fallon of Ballybrack, etc. And everybody in Dublin whom I knew who had eyes to see & ears to hear ought to know that same & more, if it went to that.

But never mind, let them talk & talk & be damned to them. But I don't think J.B.F[agan] would have financed the "Tassie"—I don't think he'd finance anything—even if he had the dough to do it.

Oh, I met "Juliana" (I knew her as Dora Lane) twice in my life. First more than three years ago, when she rang me up, & said Will had asked when she was in London to come & see me. Well, she came to Clareville St. talked & wept (but it wasn't weeping) about her helplessness (she wasn't helpless) told me she was stopping at a hotel & hadn't the money to pay her bill. Gave her the money, went with her to the hotel, not as a cavalier, but to verify my suspicion that she was lying (as she had a perfect right to do about herself) found she could find no admittance; brought her back to Clareville St, let her sleep the night there, when she left next morning as pure as she came in, & let him who hears believe this or no. She rung me up several times after, sent me a book which I didn't want, & once after going out, met her on her way to my place bringing me a bunch of Flowers! But I had nothing to do with her or her flowers, & never once has she set her foot inside 19. Woronzow Rd. I had completely forgotten her, & didn't bring her to mind even when you first mentioned Juliana. All she knows about me & you has been undoubtedly got from Will. If she rang me up, she'd hear a mouthful, not because I am more virtuous than she (surely I am a bloody sight worse, all things considered) but because from the first I disliked her strongly & would have nothing to do with her. It is usually those who try to injure you. But I don't mind—she really couldn't make me out worse than I am. Paul even calls himself the 'chief of sinners', & who then is poor Juliana Lane or poor Sean O'Casey?

So let us close on the low note of contrition, & hope you, Rose & the two kiddies are O.K.

Yours
Sean

To Gabriel Fallon

MS. TEXAS

1 AUGUST 1930

Dear Gaby—

Glad to hear that you have good hopes of a great success: I, myself, am positive of a big attendance for at least a fortnight. The circumstances around the play make this certain.

Considering everything,—I ask that my royalties shall be ten per cent of the gross weekly receipts, with 50% of the net profits.

Yours Sincerely
Sean O'Casey

To Gabriel Fallon

MS. TEXAS

"WINSTANLEY" 26 WARWICK ROAD
CLIFTONVILLE
MARGATE
19 AUGUST 1930

Dear Gaby—

Here trying to get a little life back into a war-worn body & mind. Only got your letter this morning.

Cranfield [1] is evidently trying to make as much as possible—keep your eye on him. I am sending you a formal letter saying 50% of net profits wouldn't be acceptable, & adding more on as you will see, but, I am, of course, in this instance, ready to adjust things as they may happen to commend themselves to you. You understand that, between you & me, things are to be arranged after the event as they will be commended by you, providing, of course, that you don't want to make a bloody fool of yourself by giving me too much & yourself too little.

If enclosed letter isn't suitable, write one yourself, send it to me, & I'll copy & send it back.

Sean

[1] Lionel Cranfield, Fallon's business associate in the venture.

To Gabriel Fallon

MS. TEXAS

"WINSTANLEY". 26 WARWICK ROAD
CLIFTONVILLE, MARGATE
[19 AUGUST 1930]

Dear Gaby,

I am forced to ask 50% of profits, as well as 10% of gross weekly receipts, for C.B.C.—who holds rights of play—must, according to contract —which I can let you see, if necessary—receive half of whatever may be coming to me.

So you see it would be impossible for me to take less.

The billing of the play *must* take the form of "By Arrangement with C. B. Cochran", for, as well as holding the rights of the play, C.B.C. wouldn't be pleased if his name was omitted, so it *must* be Produced by G. Fallon, by Arrangement with C. B. Cochran.

Yours
Sean

To Gabriel Fallon

MS. TEXAS

ST. JOHN'S WOOD
4 SEPTEMBER 1930

Dear Gaby,

1. No, not a spot of truth in it. There never was any effort or any talk about a tour; circumstances made that impossible. And, even had there been, the Gaiety would have been a far-away contingency. But a tour was never contemplated, so the statement is a lie.
2. I don't know, you don't know, & who the hell knows anything about the auditing of the Abbey Accounts? There is one thing hidden that shall never be revealed, & that is what the Abbey do, or do not do with the dough.
3. Yes; it was [P.] Selby whom the Abbey threatened with an action when Sinclair had arranged to produce my plays in Belfast. Later on, if you think well of it, I might write to Selby. I don't think he wants to be unfriendly with the Abbey, & that there is little more than this (apart from commercial thoughts) in his opposition.
4. To a reasonable extent. All the Obscene expressions, & a few redundancies.
5. I have answered immediately

And now, my dear Gaby, think it all over once again. I'm certain you will have the cold-blooded (more dangerous than hot) antagonism of the Abbey. Under the best of conditions the production would be a whole-time job of difficulties, but under opposition, it will be a burden to the spirit—not to mention the flesh—& it would be well & wise to ponder on whether it is worth while to go on with it. Count the cost, Gaby, & if you decide to draw away from it, Sean won't mind in the least. Get away for that week or two & think & think it over & over again. Don't go down any lower than 50/50—it should be 60/40.

Selby's statement to Telford [1] is incomprehensible. Once without my knowledge, Sinclair wrote to Selby suggesting a week of "Juno" in Dublin —he thought I had separated finally with the Abbey—& Selby said this would be useless because of the many times the play had been produced there: perhaps, for some reason, he colours the name of "Juno" over with the name of "The Silver Tassie". You may take it for certain that he was never asked about the Tassie, for a tour was never thought of.

Yours
Sean

[1] David Telford, manager of the Gaiety Theatre, Dublin.

To Gabriel Fallon

MS. TEXAS

ST. JOHN'S WOOD
11 SEPTEMBER 1930

My dear Gaby—

Gaffney [1] stands on a molehill & takes it for the Mount of Olives. He mocks the sovereignty of his Saviour by offering Him a paper crown. He washes his hands in front of his flock & says behold, now, we are clean

[1] Rev. Michael Henry Gaffney, O.P., Dominican priest and playwright. Fallon had sent O'Casey a cutting of Father Gaffney's article, "Dublin's Draught From *The Silver Tassie,*" *Catholic Mind,* September 1930, Dublin, reproduced in its entirety below. Alarmed over the announcement that the play was to be produced in Dublin (he mistakenly assumed that the Abbey Theatre had changed its mind and was now planning a production), Father Gaffney wrote:

"There have been several tentative announcements in the press recently of the forthcoming production of Mr. O'Casey's play *The Silver Tassie,* at the Abbey Theatre. The Abbey once rejected this play to which it now offers the hospitality of its boards.

"Dublin is to have the opportunity in the Autumn of drinking deep from *The Silver Tassie.* But I fancy that Dublin is a little too wise in 1930 to put its lips to a cup that may possibly have been filled from a sewer.

"The play has been published in London, and is in our hands for cold inspection. It defies analysis. It is a vigorous medley of lust and hatred and vulgarity. And a Dominican Nun, who acts and speaks like a Salvation Army Lass, is dragged into the whirl of the movement in order to give point to the chanting *off* of the *Salve Regina.*

"In attempting to analyse this play, I have fallen into despair. One can do nothing with it without being coarse—at least in quotation—and alienating many readers of this periodical. I have no hope of conveying any adequate idea of its deliberate indecency and its mean mocking challenge to the Christian Faith.

"This play was produced in a London theatre last year. I choose, from many criticisms, one from the pen of the sanest and wisest dramatic critic attached to the every Whit, & our hearts are full of reticent perfection. If he had said that the Silver Tassie was a challenge to the application & practice of Christian ethics by a Christian people he might have been nearer the mark, but, as far as I can see, it fails to be a challenge, mean, noble, serious or mocking, to the Christian Faith. But even if it were he ought to be able & willing to stand up to the challenge. Has he none of the battle spirit of either Peter or Paul? He is threatening the poor Pagan, not with the sword of the Spirit, but with the Sword of the Secular arm—the Free State Government. God isn't enough, so he calls for President Cosgrave. It is comic how few of these men of miracles have so little confidence in the strength of the mighty arm of their God. No amount of Celtic romantic reticence can hack man's humanity away from him. We are still being created a little lower than the angels. It will take something more than poor Gaffney's glibness to make Ireland a little greater than she is. The poor man hasn't even an elementary understanding of his own thoughts. He says, "in attempting to analyse this play I have fallen into despair. It defies analysis". Stepping from this heart-broken statement, he plunges into—"it is a vigorous medley of lust, hatred and vulgarity", so, after all, he analyses the play very easily indeed. But there is no value to me or to you in wasting time & sacred thought with Father Gaffney. Let him go on damning himself with good plays, like mine, & bad plays, like his own. So don't bother anymore about him. In the course of the last twelve months I have destroyed most of the Press-Cuttings that came to me, and cannot remember all that was said and written about the play. I have one pasted in a book, which appeared in "The Universe" saying:—

"The sharp criticism that appeared in these columns about "The Silver Tassie" last week has been followed by *one* or *two* (sic) dissenting letters from our readers. One reader says that our critic saw more bitterness in the play than it actually contains, while another says our critics under-

---

London Press [*The Universe*]. '*The Silver Tassie* is,' he says, 'a terrible mixture of horror, indecency and violent blasphemy.'

"If this dramatic dose turns out to be too bitter and a revulsion takes place, the Abbey Theatre will not be in the same position as it was when Mr. Yeats called the policemen to quell the *Playboy* troubles before we, young men, were born. For, firstly, the Abbey Theatre is now in tutelage to the Government elected by the Irish Nation. And, secondly, the Abbey Theatre has now to reckon with a vigorous opposing force which is not alien to the genuine and authentic spirit of the Irish people.

"The row over the *Playboy* was but a flash in the pan, a child's cracker, in comparison with the hostility with which the Abbey is confronted if it persists in defying Catholic principle and flouting that delicate reticence which is a characteristic of our people.

"Dublin people are not prudes or puritans if they exact from a Government theatre a recognition and observance of the norms of plain etiquette. And plain etiquette *will not tolerate horror, indecency or blasphemy, on or off the stage*."

See Father Gaffney's almost verbatim letter to the *Irish Press*, 14 August 1935, printed below, on the occasion of the Abbey Theatre's first production of *The Silver Tassie*.

valued its dramatic importance. All we can say about these objections is that whatever its theme, the play certainly expresses, if only in particular passages, sentiments from which a Catholic must recoil, & that our contributor himself, while critical of form, made it quite clear that The Silver Tassie was an unquestionably powerful work . . . . . it however contains blasphemies, perhaps without intention[,] to which the most serious exception must be taken. One at least of these is vital to the interpretation of the play. The words of our Lord taken from the canon of the Mass are parodied in a scene that expresses the terrible bitterness of a maimed soldier. In the circumstances, we doubt if a Catholic writing in a Catholic paper could have done otherwise than regret a performance that so offends against his creed."

This from "The Irish Rosary"—Sept. 1928 ". . . . Considered as a piece of Dramatic literature 'The Silver Tassie' is a remarkably fine piece of work, but the pagan spirit of it all is almost intolerable at times, & the author is—shall we say—brutal in his unremitting search for realistic details". No mention of blasphemy here.

But leave him to his Corotian vision of how sweet & fair is the fight against the world the flesh and the devil. The truth is that Catholic Journalism, here & in Ireland, is resonant with ignorance & soppy with fear, controlled & contributed to by cock-shy & merry-go-round minds.

Aidee Blockem [2] is a virulent case in point.

Catholics writing for a Catholic Press—
"Oft they have not that which they possess".
So says Shakespeare, & we cry, amen.

"Oh, silver trumpets be ye lifted up,
And cry to the great race that is to come." [3]

So cries Yeats, and AE gets a testimonial of £800,[4] and Aidee Blockem edits the Catholic Standard.

My dear friend, get back to your writing; leave "The Silver Tassie" alone,[5] & turn again to your writing. A blast long & loud must be blown on trumpets of ram's horn before they will listen to the trumpets of silver.

Verily yours in affection to all.

Sean

[2] Aodh de Blacam (1890–1951), Irish journalist and author, editor of *The Standard,* and writer of a regular column for the *Irish Press* under the pseudonym of "Roddy the Rover."

[3] The Young Pupil in W. B. Yeats's *The King's Threshold* (1904).

[4] On 3 September 1930 the Governor-General of the Irish Free State, James McNeill (1869–1938), presented a check for £800 to George Russell (A.E.), a sum raised by Lyon Phillimore, Oliver St. John Gogarty, Joseph M. Hone, and other friends, "as a token of public esteem for George Russell's character and work in Ireland."

[5] As a result of adverse criticism by people like Father Gaffney, Fallon had to abandon the plans for a production of *The Silver Tassie* in Dublin at this time.

From Lady Gregory

PS. *Modern Drama* [1]

COOLE PARK, GORT, CO. GALWAY
4 OCTOBER 1930

Dear Sean—

In reply to enclosed I have sent Mrs. Vaughan the Daily News article I wrote [2] after the giving of the Hawthornden Prize—as you had seen it and "passed" it—I have asked her to let me have it back. Prague played one of Synges plays long ago—and the then Director of the theatre came and spent some days here getting 'local color'—I remember his being taken into a room in one cottage—and rushing out with a trophy he thought was something peculiar to Ireland that could be reproduced on the stage—But it was a gourd: sent by a daughter in U.S.A. as it was oddly shaped—

I have not heard from you for a long time—but I hear rumors that you might come back to Ireland—and I hope these have foundation—It would be a pleasure to me to see you again—and make acquaintance with your wife and son—so be sure to let me know if you do come—

Yours sincerely and affectionately
A Gregory

[1] From a copy made by A. C. Edwards and printed in *Modern Drama,* May 1965.

[2] Lady Gregory, "How Great Plays Are Born: The Coming of Mr. O'Casey," *Daily News,* London, 27 March 1926.

To Gabriel Fallon

MS. TEXAS

ST. JOHN'S WOOD
22 OCTOBER 1930

My dear Gaby—

What's wrong? Haven't heard a whisper from you for years . . . and years. I earnestly hope you aren't, or haven't been ill. You never can tell: Eileen's been away sick in hospital for the past few weeks, but she's better now, & hopes to be back this week end.

Not much news here. Will's Revue ends on Saturday, & no one knows what'll happen then. Robinson's "Far Off Hills" ran for a few weeks here, but didn't do well. The Everyman Theatre Guild among its plays for next Season, lists "Mountain Dew". Why doesn't Father Gaffney have a try with his "Sweet Miracle (4M.2.F)" [1] here, too. I have just read "Look at the Heffernans", [2] & it should prove an inspiration to many not to write plays.

Yours Affectionately
Sean

[1] Rev. Michael Henry Gaffney, O.P., *Sweet Miracle* (Dublin, Talbot Press, 1928), a play adapted from the Portuguese of Eça de Queiroz.

[2] Brinsley Macnamara's *Look at the Heffernans!* opened at the Abbey Theatre on 12 April 1926. By coincidence, Macnamara and Gaffney led the bitter fight against O'Casey and *The Silver Tassie* when it was first produced at the Abbey Theatre in 1935. See O'Casey's reply to them, *Irish Times*, 11 September 1935, and also the series of letters and statements in the *Irish Times* between 14 August and 7 October 1935, printed below.

To Gabriel Fallon

MS. Texas

St. John's Wood
4 November 1930

My dear Gaby—

Well, it can't be helped, & we must be satisfied. Or we must pen up our dissatisfaction in patience, and suffer poor young Gaffney to go on setting up his candle against the Sun & calling out all true Irishmen & Catholics to view the illumination.

I'm not surprised that the clergy who differ from the member of the Friars Preachers prefer to remain unanimously anonymous. They are only a little worse than he, for he has said what he had to say, though he said it badly.

I'm glad they're offering you the job (I hope it's not only the work) of acting as Director of the Catholic Theatre. I hope they won't expect you to work miracles with five barley loaves & two small fishes.

Yes, of course, I've heard of Murray's Flutter of Wings in & Flutter of wing out! [1] But Murray has preserved a rare dignity throughout it all. Praise God, as the Salvationists say in Hyde Park. Yes, I heard about

[1] T. C. Murray's new play, *A Flutter of Wings*, was rejected by the Abbey, then accepted by Hilton Edwards and Micheál MacLiammoir of the new Gate Theatre. It was produced at the Gate on 10 November 1930.

Father Brady.[2] Sooner or later an Archdeaconship comes along to St. Laurence O'Tooles. How strange it would feel to me to walk slowly & pensively through that district now.[3]

[2] Rev. James Canon Brady, P.P., St. Laurence O'Toole's Church, O'Casey's old friend and patron of the St. Laurence O'Toole's Pipers and Athletic Club, was appointed archdeacon of Dublin in October 1930.

[3] Pages missing.

From Lady Gregory

PS. *Modern Drama* [1]

COOLE PARK, GORT, CO. GALWAY
28 DECEMBER 1930

Dear Sean—

It is long since I have had news of you—I hope all goes well with you and your wife and the son. There was a rumor a while ago that you were coming back on a visit to Ireland—but it died away—

I am alone here—but my grandchildren, Robert [Richard] and Anne are with their mother, Mrs. Gough—only 5 miles away—so they are often at the door—But the youngest, Catherine is at school in Switzerland—I have been but little in Dublin of late—The Forestry dept. are busy in the woods here—cutting poor parts and replanting—this is very comforting. I like to think the woods will continue to flourish and even increase—our govt. is very good about forestry—and all my own little plantations are very healthy and tall—My garden is in my own hands and was very beautiful this year—and even now in this mild weather I have roses in bloom:—Now I must wish all happiness for Christmas and for the New Year to you and yours.

Affectionately
A Gregory

[1] From a copy made by A. C. Edwards and printed in *Modern Drama,* May 1965.

To Gabriel Fallon

MS. TEXAS

ST. JOHN'S WOOD
31 DECEMBER 1930

My dear Gaby—

Very glad indeed to get a letter from you & to find that you are still standing well away from the land o the Leal.

No, you mustn't give away any of your time and energy to the German Production of the "Plough". You have enough to do for yourself, and too much to think of already, so don't let this idea worry you any longer. As a matter of fact—as enclosed letter will show—music, photos etc were asked for from me, & these were sent on some days before I got your letter. I have never come into direct contact with Ernst Pabst, as all things have been done through Erich Glass, the writer of letter enclosed. It seems unkind to cross your kindness out, but it is necessary that all effort on your part should be made entirely for your own interests. When you are more safely & comfortably fixed in the world it will be time enough to get you to take thought for the things of O'Casey. There's no news to send you at present. Will went home, & you say he intends to stay there. Well, there's no place like home, is there? At the immediate present I am trying to fix a film scenario,[1] & have written as part of the talkie, an Artist-Atheist's hymn to God!

The Sun is but a wee brooch in his breast
The moon a fair stone in the ring he is wearing
The stars are the beads that gleam in his robe
When the evening is fallen etc amen

And take all the rest you can, Gaby, for you will need your energy in the days to come. God, if I had now the energy I gave to the Gaelic League & other Institutions!

Glad to hear the boys & the wife are well; remember me to them all.

Yours As Ever
Sean

[1] This was the first version of *Within the Gates,* which he initially conceived as a film about Hyde Park, at this time tentatively titled *The Green Gates.* See his comments on this early version of the play and the cinematic art, the day Mr. and Mrs. Alfred Hitchcock came to dinner in "A Long Ashwednesday," *Rose and Crown* (1952). Hitchcock had directed the film version of *Juno and the Paycock,* released on 22 September 1930.

VI

WITHIN THE GATES OF BUCKS AND NEW YORK, 1931-34

GOD be my judge that I hate fighting. If I be damned for anything, I shall be damned for keeping the two-edged sword of thought tight in its scabbard when it should be searching the bowels of knaves and fools."

"The people here have no time to wait for help from heaven, and are a strange contrast to the Gaels of Skye or Connait. The Irish here—and there are thousands of them—hurry along life with the rest of them, and shove away the day that is with them for the day that is to dawn. It is a mill-race of life; fascinating, but terrifying when one stops to think of it. In Ireland, America seems to be very close; but in America, Ireland is a long way off."

"You can't go on writing fine things, Sean, unless they bring some material reward," C. B. Cochran wrote in 1933, explaining why he admired O'Casey's new play, *Within the Gates,* but couldn't risk producing it. In view of the fact that he had lost money on his courageous production of *The Silver Tassie* four years earlier, Cochran had sound reasons for insisting upon a compromise between "fine things" and "material reward," and he reluctantly but realistically urged O'Casey to return to the safer dramatic form of his early successes. Since O'Casey was to be confronted by this practical advice throughout his life from friends and enemies, especially the latter in Ireland, his forthright reply to Cochran provides the best and only justification for his motives as man and artist: "Your advice to go back to the genius of 'Juno' might be good for me, but bad for my conception of drama."

So there were to be few material rewards for the dedicated O'Casey. In 1932 he was so deeply in debt that he was forced to sell part of the amateur rights of *Gunman, Juno,* and *Plough* to the Samuel French Company for £300, although Bernard Shaw warned him not to do it: "My advice is to let wife and child perish, and lay bricks for your last crust, sooner than part with an iota of your rights." But again it was apparent that O'Casey was not one to take advice about money for his own good. And it was equally apparent that in spite of his protest to Mrs. Shaw that he hated fighting, he wielded his "two-edged sword of thought" with such exuberant indignation that he could not avoid becoming involved in many fights that were not good for him. In October 1932 he made a public announcement of his angry refusal to accept the offer of membership in Yeats's newly formed Irish Academy of Letters. In May 1933 he wrote a short story, "I Wanna Woman," which was accepted for publication in Lady Rhondda's *Time and Tide* but her printer refused to set the type for this "immoral" work, and when it finally appeared a year later in his *Windfalls* the Irish censorship board, not about to be outdone by an English printer, and ignoring the magnanimous defense of O'Casey by Yeats, banned the book. In February 1934 when *Within the Gates* was produced in London, after he had fought with the temperamental director during rehearsals, O'Casey assailed the London critics who wrote unfavorable reviews, especially the formidable and wasp-tongued James Agate. O'Casey had a devastating sting of his own, but once more he was winning battles and losing wars.

Nevertheless, he was also winning some new and enduring friends, like the influential American theatre critic George Jean Nathan. It was Nathan who in 1932 printed some of O'Casey's early articles in his *American Spectator,* Nathan who worked unceasingly to arrange the New York production of *Within the Gates,* Nathan who became a loyal confidant and champion of O'Casey for a quarter of a century. They met in New York when O'Casey went to America for the opening of his play in October 1934. There he also met and developed close friendships with one of his heroes, Eugene O'Neill, with the important theatre critic

Brooks Atkinson, and with the teacher and writer Horace Reynolds, who arranged O'Casey's lecture at Harvard University.

O'Casey was now an international figure, but he was penniless when he arrived in New York, wearing a new suit made from cloth given to him by Lady Astor, and with a £200 guarantee from Lady Londonderry in his pocket. The Irish proletarian had humbled himself to accept help from aristocratic ladies. And several years earlier in 1931 he had humbled himself before Lady Gregory, his dear and unhappy friend in Ireland, by writing her a letter of reconciliation a year before she died.

To Lady Gregory

MS. GREGORY

ST. JOHN'S WOOD
6 JANUARY 1931

Dear Lady Gregory—

Many thanks given in good measure for your kind thoughts and kind wishes to my wife, the kid and me. All are well, and facing front in this mysterious Universe of ours.

I had decided never to look Westward in thought again, but your kind letters have (like a still small voice) whispered in my ears that it would be something lower than bad manners if I continued to ignore them.

I have had lately another cause for bitterness, for I find that one of the patrons of the clique that ruined my play in America is Dr. Lennox Robinson; [1] and another, who lately acted especially in the Abbey, & who, according to a Press report, warned Irish Dramatists against cliques of this kind, is one of the patrons, too—Mr. Dudley Digges. However, we can smile at a mind that, in Belfast says, 'plays will tend to become less national & more international', &, when in Cork, says the local play's the thing to ask for & to encourage—he tempers the shorn lamb to the wind.

I have been occupied lately in sending coloured sketches, photos etc. of the "Plough" to [Ernst] Pabst who is arranging for a production in Germany this month. The work has been a bit of a nuisance, for to me,

[1] On 24 October 1929 the Irish Theatre, Inc., produced the American premiere of *The Silver Tassie* at the Greenwich Village Theatre, New York, directed by Michael Breathnach. They were an inexperienced company and the production received bad notices, closing after 40 performances. The names of Lennox Robinson and Dudley Digges were listed among the patrons of the Irish Theatre, Inc. See the exchange of letters between O'Casey and Digges on 24 November and 27 December 1931.

all work done is dead, and interest lies only in work that the future will bring to life.

I am glad to hear that your grandchildren are well, & so near you, & that they often bring their voices & energies over to Coole.

Again many thanks for your Kind Thought.

Sean

To Erich Glass [1]

TC. O'CASEY

ST. JOHN'S WOOD
10 JANUARY 1931

Dear Erich—

You must take [Basil] Dean's offer and Ashley Dukes as well—as we say in Irish, 'there's no getting away from it.' Dont waste time thinking about me—under the circumstances, I'd rather step aside and let Dukes creep into the adaptation of the play.[2] He is a clever fellow, used to this work, and might, probably would, do it better than I. You see, I might thrust my personality into the work and overthrow the balance of the play: there is no fear of Dukes doing this. And we have the heirs as you say, to consider. Besides, my dear Erich, I cannot gather myself into a wrangle as to who shall or shall not do this adaptation of poor Chlumberg's work. I would much prefer to let the work be done by another, especially when I believe the work will be well done. I have never done adaptation before, and it isnt my work. Besides I'm in the midst of a job myself, and to turn away, even for awhile, would be foolish and might be fatal. Your affection for me tends to blunt your judgment, and I might not be quite so good as you think. Anyhow, first of all, we must think of those whom poor Chlumberg left behind, and since the play has got such publicity in Germany and America, it would be well to hurry up the production over here as quickly as possible. So then, the only and the best thing to do is to take Dean's offer, labouring only to make it as good as possible. For your sake, Erich, I'd like to be able to look at the thing as you do, but, honestly, I cant; I was reluctant from the beginning, and now that I have heard about this move on the part of Dean and Dukes (the dean and the duke) I must withdraw, and advise you to make the best terms you

[1] Erich Glass, O'Casey's continental agent based in Vienna, later in London.

[2] Hans Chlumberg's *Wunder um Verdun*. The play was translated from the German by Edward Crankshaw under the title *Miracle at Verdun,* and was produced in London on 21 September 1932.

can for Mrs Chlumberg, and yourself with Basil Dean. Your suggestion that I should try to see Dean's impossible: I wouldnt ask Basil Dean for a breath of air if I was dying. Try to get the translation for yourself with Dukes as adaptor, or get a share as final advisor of Dukes—you translated Drinkwater, Ervine and O'Casey—and if you cant get this, then get the best terms you can for the heirs. Of the two, Dukes is much the better for I'm afraid Dean's a bit of a money-shark, and his paw on Melpomene is always near her pocket, much nearer to her pocket than to her belly or her breasts. So you see by what I have written, that I have decided to withdraw, so go ahead, banishing me from your mind, and do the best for Mrs Chlumberg and yourself.

I was delighted to get your cable saying that 'The Plough' was a 'colossal triumph', and hope it will be so everywhere. Here's the telegram I sent to Herr Pabst; [3]

> I find it impossible to be present at the production of 'The Plough and the Stars'; wife not well; deep and earnest wishes for success; affectionate regards to you, the company and to the great German People. O'Casey.

Offices of Basil Dean, according to telephone book, are: 5, John Street, London, W.C.2. Tel: Temple Bar: 3891. Never offered any play to Film Co. The Internat Pictures Co asked for 'Juno'. Will write fully in a day or so, and send you back American clippings about Wunder Um Verdun.

Affectionate Regards,
[*Sean O'Casey*]

[3] Ernst Pabst, who produced a German translation of *The Plough and the Stars* at the Stadtheater, Osnabrueck.

To Erich Glass

TC. O'CASEY

SUPPLEMENTARY. 12 JANUARY 1931

Got your letter and copy of letter to The Play Co. For me, now, Erich, the thing's impossible. There are now a thousand reasons for refusing to adapt—even if Mr Dean were willing. Principally because I am in the throes of a work myself. And supposing we did it and the play over here was a failure—which, of course is possible—it would mean torture to me for many long months. Basil is used to this sort of thing;

it is his business, and he would bear up remarkably well, but I would be in a woeful state thinking of Mrs Chlumberg, and of the chance she might have had, had the play been done by someone else.

No, Erich, I have finally decided that I can have nothing to do with it, and I am going to write to Dean saying that, as far as I am concerned, he will have no more trouble. There is no doubt that Dukes will do the work well—as I said before, possibly better than I could.

Give Mrs Chlumberg my deep sympathy and warm regards. I hope the play will be a great success here.

Yours,
[*Sean*]

To Gabriel Fallon

MS. TEXAS

ST. JOHN'S WOOD
6 FEBRUARY 1931

My dear Gaby—

I can hardly congratulate you on having to fill another mouth, for, nowadays, manna no longer falls from heaven, & we have to seek a bit of bread now and again in places difficult to find: we often seek now, but do not find; knock, and the bolts are shot tight to keep us out. However, it may do good by compelling you to cling more closely to yourself.

The address of the Authors' Society Secretary is:

D. Kilham Roberts,
Society of Artists, Authors and Composers
11 Gower Street, London W.C.1.

whether poets would be willing to give their work is a question—2/6 for a hundred lines is a very small payment. However, no harm to try.

About Broadcasting plays, I suggest you should write to,

Val Gielgud
B.B.C.
2, Savoy Hill, London W.C.2.

Gielgud's the manager of the Dramatic Dept, & might give you the information you are looking for. I attach above a stamp so that you can send him an addressed envelope for reply. English stamps are probably difficult to get in Dublin.

No news to send you except that just now I'm learning the words & the tune of "Fead an iolair", which, being interpeted, means, "The Eagle's Whistle". Why? Oh, there I'll lave you!

I see the Abbey, the other week, put on "The Plough". Curious, the curious comings in & goings out that have taken place in the Abbey. Robinson seems to be top dog & bottom dog there now.

Well, well.
Yours as Ever
Sean

Love to all

To Horace Liveright [1]

TC. O'CASEY

ST. JOHN'S WOOD
10 FEBRUARY 1931

Dear Sirs—

The condition of my eyes at the moment forces me to do as little work as possible, so I must content myself with adding a fervent amen to whatever admiration may be shown and praise given to Eugene O'Neill by the writers you have chosen to put down what they think of the fine work and the great work this man has done for the Drama in the English tongue.

Besides it might be a little impertinent for me to say why and how O'Neill is a great dramatist when, always in his published books, and often on the stage, his work is always bearing witness to the things great and the things beautiful which have saved the Theatre from the shame of a house of illfame and a den of thieves, and have kept the ground in and around the Theatre as holy as the ground around the burning bush.

Look into this man's work closely, but look deeply as well, and you will find he is like unto the surge of a great orchestra, cancelling with its deep and thundering rhythms the tiny tinkle of the castanets ashake in the hands of the minor dancing dramatists.

Eugene O'Neill, like all men born with original sin in their souls, has, I suppose, what we, in a pensively critical mood, would call, his weak moments. I remember several little playwrights, whose eyes are ever closed, whose ears are ever stopped, pointing out to me what they called

[1] Horace Liveright, American publisher of Eugene O'Neill. In preparation for a plagiarism case against O'Neill, Liveright, and the Theatre Guild, over *Strange Interlude* (1928), Liveright wrote to O'Casey asking for a testimonial for O'Neill. From the nature of O'Casey's reply, Liveright probably didn't mention the trial due in March 1931, which was eventually decided in O'Neill's favor by Judge John M. Woolsey, who two years later gave the historic decision lifting the ban on Joyce's *Ulysses.*

weak moments in O'Neill's plays. Well, a weak moment in an hour of strength and power isnt quite so dangerous as a strong moment in a hour of weakness, so we'll leave O'Neill to himself, and the little playwrights to God.

A playwright reviewing in a Dublin Literary Journal a book written about the work of O'Neill, said, "O'Neill at any time may write a great play." There you are, a vaudeville playwright, dancing his little dance of drama, shaking his castanets of dialogue, says "at any time O'Neill may write a great play," failing to understand that to him, since he sees nothing great in what O'Neill has already done, there will never be greatness in anything O'Neill has still to do.

Another, not a playwright, in the same Journal, criticising a performance of "The Fountain," and complaining about the literary quality of the play, said, "We prefer O'Neill in his rougher manner, when he uses, shall we say, 'sailor talk'." But the same man, if he heard seven syllables of sailor talk bellowed into his ear would be knocked unconscious for a week, and, even then, it would take a very, very holy saint to be able to say effectively, "sir, I say unto thee, get up out of thy faint and walk."

But never mind; Eugene O'Neill's alright, and, please God, will be given a long life to go on giving a fuller nobility and a greater power to the Drama and to the Theatre and all that is in them.

Sincerely yours,
[*Sean O'Casey*]

From Charlotte F. Shaw

MS. O'CASEY

MALVERN HOTEL
MALVERN.
27 AUGUST 1931

Dear Sean

It is delightful to hear of you even with such troublesome tidings as you send. I am glad you are in the country as I know you both wanted to get away from London & it will be so good for you—and, another thing is I think you will be just within a drive of us—a long one—but unless I am very much mistaken, quite a possible one. I have no Bucks maps here: we are away for a holiday, which always means rather a more busy time than usual. Of course they are all at G.B.S. to write about Russia, & he finds it rather difficult to do. He can talk by the hour, but when he starts to write he doesn't seem to know where to begin! However one article is finished now, & another is nearly done. He had a wonderful experience there, & he has got a wonderful uplift from it. They seem to be the only hope of the world just now—the Russians.

I *am* so sorry about the Broadcast. You should never tell anyone your ideas for plays, for sometimes even the best people forget they are yours and fancy they thought of it themselves: I am so sorry, I can't remember you ever telling me anything about Hyde Park. I remember perfectly your saying you were working on a *film*, & not a play, when I last saw you: because I was sorry & wanted the play. That is all I remember. Earlier than that you told me you wanted to write about English workmen—dockers I *think*.

Dear Sean—is your play very far advanced? & will this Broadcast matter? I can't help feeling anything you write will be so original, & so different from other people's work, that nothing they do will harm you that way.

And oh! dear Sean, don't be too belligerent!

Love to you both from your friend

C. F. Shaw

What a dear little book Lady Gregory has written about Coole.[1]

[1] Lady Gregory, *Coole* (Dublin, Cuala Press, 1931). This was a shortened version of the original manuscript, and for the complete text see Liam Miller's new edition, *Coole* (Dublin, Dolmen Editions X, 1971), completed from the manuscript, and edited by Colin Smythe, with a foreword by Edward Malins.

To Charlotte F. Shaw

PS. *Rose and Crown* [1]

[? September 1931]

I do not know how much I must read into your advice "not to be too belligerent." God be my judge that I hate fighting. If I be damned for anything, I shall be damned for keeping the two-edged sword of thought tight in its scabbard when it should be searching the bowels of knaves and fools. I assure you, I shrink from battle, and never advance into a fight unless I am driven into it. I give you a recent instance: The Abbey Theatre are going on a tour through America; notices appeared in the Press, mentioning the plays, which included *Juno*. I wrote to Mr. Robinson about this, and he replied that he had asked the Chicago Lecture

[1] A copy of this letter, a reply to her letter of 27 August, appears in "Black Oxen Passing By," *Rose and Crown* (1952).

and Concert Association months ago to get into touch with my American agents. I left the matter there, and said no more. Then I got a letter from my agents, Samuel French, Ltd., saying that the Lecture and Concert association were asking for *Juno*, and that they had asked for an advance of five hundred dollars; this was refused, and the demand was reduced to two hundred and fifty dollars; this, also, was refused, with the statement that all the other dramatists were satisfied to do without an advance. I rang up the Authors' Society, explained the situation, and was strongly advised to press for the advance. The intimation (that the Abbey had selected *Juno*) came so recently that I had no time to write about the matter, and so to avoid any suspicion that I wished to hurt the success of the tour, I wrote to the agents telling them not to bother about any claim to an advance of royalties. So, in face of a possible misapprehension, I shrink even from insisting on a very modest demand.

On behalf of James Joyce, before me now, is a letter I received this morning, which tells me that someone has translated a story into German, and has had it published in a German paper over the name of this writer. Joyce declares that he never wrote the story, and that his signature is a forgery. And, worse than all, the thing is altogether beneath the genius of Joyce. Now should I sing silently in my heart of the meanness of this deception against an artist; or should I give this man the comfort of indignant sympathy from a comrade in the evil that has been brought upon him? I shall not keep silence, and the song in my heart and on my lips shall be in harmony with the indignant song of Joyce.

To Jack Carney [1]

TC. O'CASEY

2 MISBOURNE COTTAGES,
CHALFONT ST GILES, BUCKS.
18 SEPTEMBER 1931

Dear Jack,

We're living just now in a little cottage in South Bucks. I got your letter asking for a photo of the wife, the kid and myself, but as everything

[1] Jack Carney (1888–1956), Irish labor journalist and union organizer; assistant to Jim Larkin in the Irish Transport and General Workers' Union, and helped Larkin edit the *Irish Worker;* met O'Casey in Dublin during the 1913 general strike; a free-lance journalist in London at the time of his death. In 1966 Carney's widow sold one hundred and twenty-six O'Casey-to-Carney letters to the New York University Library, but the man who arranged the sale of the letters, Prof. David H. Greene of NYU, refused to give me permission to see them or make copies. Among O'Casey's private papers I found three typed carbons, the above letter, and two others, 15 January 1947 and 16 March 1949, Vol. II.

we have is in store it is impossible to get them for you. Besides, I wouldnt care to have the family portraiture, even if these things should interest your readers, which is hardly likely, splashed all over the pages of "The Irish Worker". I have always disliked this kind of display which seems to me to be grafted on to pride and vain-glory of imagination. Later on, if you wish it, I'll send you on pictures of us all for your own personal possession.

I have read G. B. Shaw's article on Russia in "The Worker",[2] which you so kindly sent to me, and, of course, what he says about what he saw and what he heard there is so simple and so charged with commonsense, so necessary to the vital welfare of man, that no-one in power or in place will hear, or hearing, will refuse to understand, and the holy church will go on appealing to God to give unto the lords of the council and all the nobility, grace, wisdom and understanding. The church fails to realise that, even if God gave to the lords of the council and the lords of nobility all the grace he had to give, all the wisdom he had to give and all the understanding he had to give, the lords of the council and the nobility of the present system, could do no more than what theyre doing now: slipping ten per cent off the dole, and slipping a penny on to the pint of beer. The change in Russia is a great change but it is a simple one. They have put away from them the problems of party and creed, and have settled down to solve the problems of life. Were everything done by the leaders under the present system the correct things to do, they would have in them the fundamentals of falsehood; were everything done by the leaders in Russia at the present time the incorrect things to do, they would have in them the fundamentals of truth. If the present things that we know which are called the system of civilization, continue to be sanctified by custom, God's will and the guns, for a long enough period of what is called time, then the soul of man will turn into a huge arse. But in fairness it must be said that the lords of the council and all the nobility have as much grace, wisdom and understanding, as those Labour leaders who bring into the House and out of the House their squadrons of ayes and regiments of noes.

You arent right about the film of "Juno" in Germany; it has never been, and possibly never will be, done there. The play, as an artistic venture may be done in Berlin, with [Albert] Bassermann as "The Paycock" and that alone will be a great honour. Affectionate regards to yourself and to the one and only Jim [Larkin], less wise in his generation than what are known as the children of light.

Yours, the same yesterday and today.
[*Sean O'Casey*]

[2] Bernard Shaw, "Shaw Visits Russia," *Irish Worker,* 19 September 1931. O'Casey's letter to Carney, minus the first paragraph, appeared in the following issue, 26 September, which also contained a leading article by Carney, "The Success of Sean O'Casey."

From Barry Fitzgerald [1]

MS. O'Casey

On Board the Cunard R.M.S. Aquitania
8 October 1931

Dear Sean,

I rang your old 'phone no. on Tuesday, when I was in London on my way to Southampton, & as I couldn't get any reply I went out to Woronzow Rd. I came away feeling very desolate & lonely, for the stranger who answered the door told me you had left. She didn't know your address but referred me to the House Agents, who told me they would forward you any letters sent in their care. The nice quiet thoroughfares around Woronzow Rd. seem so closely associated with you that I felt very dismal to find you were there no longer. The agent told me you had gone to live in the country, & I remembered you told me last year that you thought of doing this.

I am with the Abbey people on this boat, on the way to New York for our American tour. The party consists of Boss [Arthur Shields] & his wife (she's engaged for small parts & wardrobe work—hairy enough!), [F. J.] McCormick, [Eileen] Crowe, [P. J.] Carolan, [Michael J.] Dolan, Fred Johnson, Denis O'Dea (a new man, who you've never probably seen —a juvenile lead kind of young man), Sheila Richards, [Maureen] Delaney, Kate Curling & May Craig & myself. Thirteen in all—an unlucky number! Lennox Robinson & his wife have gone on in advance. He is to lecture (hairy enough!) at each place we play in a week or so before our visit, keeping always a week ahead of us. The plays on our list are "Juno," "W. H. Boy" [2] (hairy enough!), "Autumn Fire," [3] "John Ferguson," [4] "Professor Tim," [5] "Hyacinth Halvey," [6] "Kathleen Ni Houlihan," [7] "Rising of the Moon," [8] but we have besides prepared many others, in case they are wanted, including "OEdipus Rex" & "OEdipus at Co-

[1] Barry Fitzgerald (1888–1961), stage name of William "Will" Shields, Abbey Theatre and cinema actor who first established his fame as a comedian as "Captain" Jack Boyle and Fluther Good in the original Abbey productions of *Juno* and *Plough*.

[2] Lennox Robinson's *The Whiteheaded Boy* (1916).

[3] T. C. Murray's *Autumn Fire* (1924).

[4] St. John Ervine's *John Ferguson* opened at the Abbey Theatre on 30 November 1915.

[5] George Shiels's *Professor Tim* (1925).

[6] Lady Gregory's *Hyacinth Halvey* opened at the Abbey Theatre on 19 February 1906.

[7] W. B. Yeats's *Cathleen Ni Houlihan* was first performed by Frank and William Fay's Irish National Players at St. Teresa's Hall, Dublin, on 2 April 1902.

[8] Lady Gregory's *The Rising of the Moon* opened at the Abbey Theatre 9 March 1907.

lonus." [9] It is thought however that the affair will resolve itself into a one play tour & that the play might be the "W. H. Boy."

We go out under the care of "The Alber Agency" of Cleveland, a concern that no one I've met seems to know anything about. I think it's a pretty obscure organization & I fancy the Abbey people haven't got very good terms. We travel out Tourist Third Class, play mainly in small towns & universities—mostly "one night stands" & get very small salaries (double our ordinary Abbey salaries—which will leave us pretty close hauled in America). It looks as if we were really going to support Robinson's lectures. Our return passages are booked for April next year.

It's just as well we are leaving Dublin for awhile because business there has been pretty bad. The theatre has been running at a pretty heavy loss, particularly during last winter. I will say without being too cocky that things improved a wee bit when I went back. I fancy, however, I'm not as popular as I used to be; perhaps I haven't as much vigour as I had or perhaps people who go away as I did are disapproved of by Dublin people. I found it frightfully hard to get used to Dublin again & I was generally pretty unhappy when I got back there, but I'm hoping that I may, by some good fortune, be able to stay away for good & all this time.

How are things with you Sean? & how are Eileen & the Juvenile? Are you working at all on the play you spoke of? I'm wondering if I'm likely to be too late for a part, if there is one for me, when I get back to London in the Spring.

I don't know that I've any news of interest for you. Only one new play was produced while I was in Dublin, a one act play, "The Disciple", [10] by a woman called Deevy who had a one act play produced once before. "The Disciple" was really very bad. It had a childish ingenuous air about it, however, that made it fairly amusing.

I saw nothing of Gaby [Fallon] while I was in Dublin. Lady Gregory came up from Gort to see us off. She's got bad rheumatism & is obviously failing.

My address for the next 6 months will be:

Barry Fitzgerald
Abbey Theatre Co.
C/O Alber Agency
3608 Euclid Ave.
Cleveland, Ohio, USA.

Maybe you'd drop me a line sometime, Sean, & let me know how things are with you.

God bless you,
Will

[9] W. B. Yeats's version of Sophocles' *Oedipus the King* opened at the Abbey Theatre on 7 December 1926, and his version of *Oedipus at Colonus* on 12 September 1927.

[10] Teresa Deevy's *A Disciple* opened at the Abbey Theatre on 24 August 1931.

To Gabriel Fallon

MS. Texas
Hillcrest
Chalfont St. Giles
24 October 1931

My dear Gaby—

We have just settled down in above address after a long sojourn in the Wilderness. We came to Mid Bucks for a holiday with the kid & liked it so much that we decided to remain there. After some months of search, Eileen found the place we were looking for, & here we are & 'ere we stay. The intervening time spent between 19 Woronzow & the getting of the house in which we now are was a big bit of a nuisance, for I found it impossible to do anything where we were; but I hope & intend to get going again immediately.

Well, how are you, & how's all the care—& heaven knows you have enough to think of now! I thought I might have been able to go over to Dublin for a few days last Summer, but I found it impossible to do so. I had a letter from Will yesterday—he wrote it on the boat—& in it he says he saw nothing of you while he was in Dublin. Poor Will. It's really a sad thing that he didn't succeed over here. He has the talent, but something was missing. Perhaps, the American Tour may help him to find a higher level of thought & determination.

I have, at last, got a chance of again using the hack & shovel, & have worked hard here with these glorious tools every day in the garden. Some of the old muscles are beginning to appear again & all Hail to them! I worked today hacking out a path facing the setting sun, with a heavy frost falling, till, sore & tired when darkness came, I returned to a simple meal & a warm fire. Once a labourer always a labourer!

Curious that we should have been scattered so—you in Dublin, Will on the Atlantic & I out here in the belly of Bucks!

Well, good fortune, Gaby, & Good health first of all to all.

Yours As Ever
Sean

I enclose photo of myself in my new Court Uniform.

To Mrs. Charlotte F. Shaw

MS. British Museum

Chalfont St. Giles
28 October 1931

Dear Mrs. Shaw,

We have settled in & are now breaking bread in our new little home. Its aspects & atmosphere are very pretty, & we feel that we shall like it sincerely. After having been tossed about since July, I hope to be able to begin work again soon. I have arranged order from confusion, & everything is sorted out in readiness to begin again. I have, in a way, returned to type, & have done a lot of labouring with shovel & pick in the garden.

Any time you & G.B.S.—whom God preserve—chance to be in or near Mid. Bucks, we should be delighted if you would come to see us.

I sincerely hope you & he are well.

Affectionate Regards,
Sean

From Lady Gregory

PS. *Modern Drama* [1]

Coole Park, Gort, Co. Galway
30 October 1931

Dear Sean,

It gave me very great pleasure to see your writing again—And also to read that pleasant account of your new home—It seems an ideal place to bring up your little fellow in—tho' of course I would rather know you were in Ireland where I might have a chance of seeing you all some day—I don't think I am likely to cross the Channel again, for I am at present crippled by a rheumatic attack, and at my age it is not likely to pass away—However I can get to the garden—And in the house the books and other pleasant surroundings keep me content—W. B. Yeats has been here most of the summer—goes up to Dublin now and then. But Dublin seems very empty now with the Abbey closed—The players had a rough passage, but I hope the plays will go well enough to cheer them up—I have hardly been at all in Dublin these last months—Mrs. Gough (Mrs.

[1] From a copy made by A. C. Edwards and printed in *Modern Drama,* May 1965.

Gregory that was) is only 5 miles away, at Lough Cutra Castle and grand-daughter Anne is there now. Richard, now in the Royal Engineers is at Trinity College, Cambridge for another year—(part of his training) And little Catherine is learning domestic and other work at a Dorset school. Mr. Gough has bought Celbridge Abbey (Co Kildare) for a winter residence—there is more society there than here—Yeats is working well—has just finished a big book *The Vision* he has been working at for some time.[2] Perhaps one day you will bring your wife here. I am sorry not to have met her—Affectionately

A Gregory

[2] Yeats was working on the revised edition of *A Vision*, which was published in 1937. The first edition had been published privately in 1925, and the last edition with Yeats's final revisions came out in 1956.

To Mrs. Charlotte F. Shaw

MS. British Museum

Chalfont St. Giles
[? November 1931]

Dear Mrs. Shaw—

Thanks many times & more for your kind letter. Go away to the Sun if you can for the sun is more than raiment or than meat.

Of course we wouldn't expect you or G.B.S. to come over to us on a dark &, probably, cold & gloomy afternoon. And why should he bother to take trouble to see me anyhow? And, besides, G.B.S. is never absent. He is one of my great friends, anam-chara—soul-friend—as we say in Ireland, & has been so for many years, long before I met him in the flesh.

I daresay, according to the register of Time, that G.B.S. is ageing, but in reality he is a babe and a suckling out of whose mouth cometh wisdom & understanding. And this present-day cant of youth makes me sick! A young fogey is a worse nuisance anyday than an old fogey, & there are thousands of young ones strolling about today.

I'm looking forward to the publication of "Too True to be Good" [1]—it's a rare title, & contains in itself a terrible philosophy.

Should I go to London on a Thursday or a Friday—& you be there—I shall ring you up, but, if you have friends with you, or are tired, or G.B.S. wants to be with his own thoughts, or if you should have any reason

[1] Bernard Shaw, *Too True To Be Good* (1931), first performed by the Theatre Guild in Boston on 29 February 1932.

whatsoever which would prompt you to be by yourselves, you must tell me, & I shall be content to wait for a more favourable day.

Brian's in splendid condition, & is growing in strength & wisdom day by day.

I'm afraid the moving did interfere a lot with my work but it can't be helped. We were to come into where we now are in June, but the tenant stayed on till October, so we had to live in a little furnished cottage till the place became vacant. We had to use oil lamps there, & as I couldn't give up my reading, I used to place a lamp on the floor, lie down beside it, &, leaning on my elbow, do the best I could. The interest I had in the books I read prevented me from noticing a growing pain in my elbow, & one day I found there a painful & ugly swelling. I had got "housemaid's knee" on the elbow! Surgeon said it would probably mean an operation to have the swollen sacs removed, but, when we got into our new place, I dug, hoed, rolled, fixed bookcases, cupboards, shelves, & various other things, exercising the arm tremendously & foolishly, so that now the swelling is gone & the arm is practically well again!

I began last week to get back to the play or film [2]—or whatever it may turn out to be—& to the semi-biography to be called, A Child is Born.[3]

Love to you & to G.B.S.

Sean

[2] This was the script of *Within the Gates* (1933), which had been interrupted by the move from London to Chalfont St. Giles.

[3] This was the earliest indication that he was writing his "semi-biography" or impressionistic autobiography. "A Child is Born" became the first chapter of *I Knock at the Door* (1939).

To Dudley Digges [1]

TS. N.Y. Pub Lib

Chalfont St. Giles

24 November 1931

Dear Mr. Dudley Digges—

When you spoke to me over the phone I was not in the best of humour for a few days before I had received a Press cutting reporting

[1] Dudley Digges (1879–1947), Irish actor who first appeared in Dublin in Yeats's *Cathleen Ni Houlihan* and *The Hour Glass* in 1902–03 with Frank and William Fay's Irish National Players; went to New York in 1904 and became an outstanding actor, appearing with the Theatre Guild from 1919 to 1930, in many films, and gave his last performance as Harry Hope in Eugene O'Neill's *The Iceman Cometh* (1946).

a warning given by you to Irish dramatists against giving plays to any Society other than those certain to give a good production, and mentioning plays—mine among the number—that had been ruined by bad production. Yet a few days before I had received a prospectus from the Irish Theatre Society of New York—who had ruined my 'The Silver Tassie,'—and among the list of patrons of this Society was the name of Dudley Digges.[2]

I thank you for the kind interest you take in my work. I am working on a play at present, but cant say when it may be finished. When it is completed it will, I hope, be published in the usual way. I may say that several important American Producers have asked me to send them any play MS I may have now or in the future. I had hoped that when you were connected with the Theatre Guild that you might have been interested in the production of my work by that important Organization. It would have been an honour to have rubbed shoulders with the great Eugene O'Neill.

Best Wishes,
Sean O'Casey

[2] See O'Casey's letter to Lady Gregory, 6 January 1931, note 1.

To Lady Astor [1]

MS. ASTOR

CHALFONT ST. GILES
4 DECEMBER 1931

Dear Lady Astor—

Forgive me for failing to reply more courteously than in telegraphic form before this to your kind invitation to luncheon.

I have been very busy trying to evolve order out of chaos. We expected to enter where we now are in June last, but the tenant remained on till October, & we had to spend the intervening time—having abandoned our house in London—in a furnished cottage sans everything but shelter from the wind & the rain. When the shadows fell we got what light we could from an oil lamp, &, when I wanted to read—which was often—I had to put the lamp on to the floor, stretch myself beside it, & leaning on my elbow, do the best I could. The weight on the elbow with the

[1] Viscountess Nancy Astor (1880–1964), born of an old Virginia family, married Viscount William Waldorf Astor in 1906; became an M.P. in 1919, the first woman to sit in the House of Commons; famous as a political and literary hostess in London and at the Astors' country house, Cliveden; was an ardent Christian Scientist.

friction of the hard floor gave me a damned swelling that the surgeon said was housemaid's knee; complete rest & possibly an operation. But when I came into the Bungalow, I dug, & hoed & barrowed, & in two weeks' time the elbow was well.

All my papers notes, books were trey nah hyayle [2]—as we say in Irish—and many days were spent sorting them out, finding a place for everything, & putting everything in its place.

It was kind of you to ask me to luncheon, & I thank you for the invitation. But I never like going to these meals, for I know that where they are there can be no intimate & serious interchange of thought. The time is invariably giddied into talk about trivial things. And I refuse to waste the time of an intelligent woman.

Now, if ever you chance to be in Mid-Bucks, we, my wife & I, should be very pleased if you would honour us with a visit. You were recently in High Wycombe, & that town isn't a thousand miles away from us. And I have read that you were one of the Judges at an oratorical display given by very young men & very young women. Eight hours of it, too! Oh, Lady Astor, Lady Astor! An' all about passages from the King's speech in Parliament. Oh, Lady Astor, Lady Astor! All the time that God in the Whirlwind, & God in the still small voice is calling out to us to scrap the present political system!

Chalfont St Giles is midway between Amersham & Chalfont St Peter. Our house is a little way up past the village of Chalfont St Giles on the way to "The Three Households".

Warm Regards, and we shall always be pleased to see you with us here.

Sean O'Casey

[2] trí n-a chéile, upside down.

From Dudley Digges

MS. O'Casey

2273 Holly Drive
Hollywood, California
27 December 1931

Dear Sean O'Casey,

I wish I had seen you in London to explain how my name came to be on that prospectus because I too was feeling sore about "The Silver Tassie" having been done by inexperienced people, however laudable their aims might be, and it was to prevent a repetition of that sort of thing that I sounded a warning in Dublin. I am afraid it has made me unpopular with the young people who are trying to do something in the way of an Irish Theatre in New York but I can't help that. I did not see the performance and cannot speak from first hand knowledge but I read and heard on all sides that it was pretty bad. I was glad to observe however, that you received the circular after and not before the production here, and were not influenced in giving the play by the fact that my name appeared on it as a patron. Beyond wishing them well in their effort to start an Irish Theatre I knew very little about them. They were an amateur group at that time, beginning in a very modest way but when in a few months I heard that they had raised money enough to undertake the rent of a small theatre and announced "The Silver Tassie" I felt doubtful of the result although I had to admire their enterprise. After all one can never tell what is going to happen in the theatre next and it doesn't become any of us to be too critical over the efforts of young people.

It was a pity that they chose such a difficult play and that you were not better informed as to their abilities before you let them have it. I believe they had some professional actors in the cast, not that that means anything, but the first production of The Silver Tassie called for a much finer performance than I'm afraid they were able to give it.[1]

[*Dudley Digges*]

[1] Pages missing.

From J. Ramsay MacDonald [1]

PS. O'CASEY [2]

CHEQUERS
PRINCES RISBOROUGH, BUCKS
19 FEBRUARY 1932

My dear O'Casey,

I was so glad to have your letter. You understand so many things which the ordinary person does not. I would like very much if you would come and see me here one week-end when I am down, and I shall write to you when I get back from my holiday. Thanks to an upbringing something like your own, I am getting better by leaps and bounds.

With kindest regards to your wife and yourself, I am

Ramsay MacDonald

[1] James Ramsay MacDonald (1866–1937), British statesman; prime minister: 1924; 1929–31; 1931–35.

[2] Printed in "Rose and Crown," *Rose and Crown* (1952), *Autobiographies II* (1963), p. 332.

To J. R. Storey [1]

PS. EILEEN O'CASEY [2]

[? JULY 1932]
CHALFONT ST. GILES

Dear Sir,

I have now only Twenty pounds in the whole world, but I send you, as ordered Five pounds to keep the wolf from the door, leaving myself with Fifteen to keep myself, wife and kid, and help to promulgate the Gospel in foreign parts.

I appreciate your point that my debt to the Inland Revenue is now £236 odd, but it won't be higher on account of last year's income, for there was none, for which I cannot thank God. With your permission, I should like to make a point myself, and it is this: when we poor devils of Artists get anything, we get it all at once, and not regularly, as others do, so that we have to pay more taxation than most persons. There seems to be a core of injustice in that. I'm not referring, of course, to the official personnel of the Inland Revenue, for, from Commissioners to Collectors, I have been treated with courtesy, and, in many instances, kindness.

I have just finished a little one-act play,[3] which I hope to see on the Halls; this may make things a little easier, and allow me to get down that £236 a little lower.

I hope, too, within the next three or four months, to finish my big play [4] which I am sure will be anything but popular, but may, I hope, add to the honour of drama written in the English tongue. So in this way, I will bless them that curse me, and be praying for them that despitefully use me.

I hope the Conversion Scheme [5] will be a success, for everybody seems to think that this is much more important than the conversion of the heathen.

Sincerely yours,
Sean O'Casey

[1] J. R. Storey, H. M. Inspector of Taxes, 7 Amersham Hill, High Wycombe, Bucks. O'Casey owed personal taxes for the years 1930–32.

[2] Eileen O'Casey printed this letter in her *Sean* (London, Macmillan, 1971).

[3] *A Pound on Demand,* printed in *Windfalls* (1934).

[4] *Within the Gates.*

[5] On 30 June 1932 the Chancellor of the Exchecquer Neville Chamberlain announced the British government's scheme for the conversion of the five percent war loan of 1927–47 into a three and a half percent loan in order to save thirty million pounds in interest yearly.

To Dudley Digges

TS. N.Y. Pub Lib

Chalfont St. Giles
22 July 1932

Dear Dudley Digges—

Mr Anderson,[1] Critic of one of the N Y Dailies, has visited me here, and spoke about you. I have written a One Act Comedy [2] which might interest you. From what was said by Mr Anderson, I gather that I had wrong opinions about things, for which I'm sorry.

The play I mentioned has Four characters—two men and two women—has many funny incidents, a very good song, and lasts for about half an hour. I think I remember you saying years ago that a one act play would be useful in the U S A.

If you feel in any way interested, I shall send on a copy of the work to you.

Yours Sincerely,
Sean O'Casey

[1] John Anderson (1896–1943), dramatic critic of the *New York Evening Journal.*
[2] *A Pound on Demand.*

To Sean O'Faolain [1]

TC. O'Casey

10 August 1932

Dear Sean O'Faolain—

Thanks for your letter. I couldnt do the suggested article about Madame Markiewicz. I dont like taking a hand in these contributory articles; and, even if I did, in a hand of court cards, the joker would be out of place. By the way, I've no reverence for the de mortuis nonsense. To launch an attack on the living is much more dangerous than to launch an attack on the dead, and I did this on M. de Markiewicz, when she was

[1] Sean O'Faolain (1900–), one of Ireland's outstanding writers of fiction, biography, history, and criticism.

living, when she was popular, and when those who were greater and higher than I was then, were afraid to say boo to the goose.[2]

It was kind of you to remember me in connection with a series of articles for publication. Several Journals have asked me to do this; I have often thought of doing so, but, up to now, never had the time. As soon as I get my next play—the one I am at work on now—into definite shape, I shall think of it seriously. I hope you may have a pleasant holiday.

Sincerely Yours,
[*Sean O'Casey*]

[2] In 1914 when he was secretary of the Irish Citizen Army, O'Casey challenged the right of the Countess Constance Gore-Booth Markiewicz (1868–1927) to serve as an official of the Citizen Army at the same time that she was one of the leaders of the rival Irish Volunteers. By a one-vote majority O'Casey's position was defeated, and when asked to apologize to the countess, he refused and resigned in October 1914. For an account of this incident, see O'Casey's *The Story of the Irish Citizen Army* (1919), reprinted in *Feathers From the Green Crow* (1962). See also his letters on the Citizen Army and the Volunteers in the *Irish Worker,* 14 January to 13 June 1914.

From Barry Fitzgerald

TS. O'CASEY

7 NORTH FREDERICK ST.
DUBLIN
11 SEPTEMBER 1932

Dear Sean,

Excuse the typewriter; I can't lay my hands on a decent pen.

The tablets you sent have been a great boon. I took them according to your directions and after the second day's treatment I felt much improved. I've been almost completely well ever since though today I have a slight return of the complaint. I'm infinitely obliged to you. I'm sure there's no organic trouble; it's just excess of acid aggravated sometimes by the beastly stuff we take on the stage which represents whiskey. It's the ordinary bottled ginger beer that I used to delight in when I was a kid and I always feel bad during the weeks when I have to drink it on the stage. I've insisted on another substitute for the future.

I can't get over to London after all. I'm wanted here for "Spreading the News"[1] which at the eleventh hour they decided to put on with the new play [*A Disciple*] of Miss [Teresa] Deevy's. I'm very disappointed.

[1] Lady Gregory's *Spreading the News,* which was first performed at the opening of the Abbey Theatre, as part of a double bill with Yeats's *On Baile's Strand,* on 27 December 1904.

I hoped to see you to tell you of all my troubles and confess my sins and now I suppose I must keep them under hatches until I get back from America. I'd love to hear from you meanwhile.

There is no particular news here. Carroll's play [2] was on again last week: good houses early on in the week but they thinned down considerably by Saturday. The play does not seem to wear well. I found it tedious after the first few nights. Carroll by the way has written to me and hints (I think) that you might like to read the play in its original form. He is sending it to me anyway to read myself. Would you be interested enough to read it if I send it on?

Lennox Robinson has been commissioned to put into Irish form the dialogue of an Irish Film called "Blarney Castle" written for Tom Walls. It is said that he is to get £400 for the job.

The Metro-Goldwyn people have brought Kitty Curling over to London for a picture and sound test. Two of their representatives saw her in the Carroll play and apparently think highly of her. It seems likely they will offer her a contract and if they do I shouldn't be surprised if she tears up her Abbey American contract and refuses to travel with us to the States.

She would be a damned fool to let the chance slip and I don't know that the Abbey people would succeed in getting much damages if they took legal action. It appears that the picture representatives asked Robinson if he could suggest any other artists who might be suitable for the Screen. He told them we were all under fast contract and didn't encourage them to interview us. It's hard luck on us but I suppose we can't blame Robbie.

We are getting our few things together for the tour already. We leave Galway on the 1st Oct. and open in Hartford Connecticut on 10th Oct. Then to New York for four weeks.

Give my compliments to Eileen and Breon.

God bless you Sean.
Will

[2] Paul Vincent Carroll's *Things That Are Caesar's* opened at the Abbey Theatre on 15 August 1932.

To George Jean Nathan [1]

MS. CORNELL

CHALFONT ST. GILES
28 SEPTEMBER 1932

Dear Mr. Nathan—

I have been busy for the last few weeks typing out Prompt Copies of three plays of mine from memory, which job [2] has prevented me from replying to your letter before this.

The horrible work is over now, and I hasten to say that, first, it is a great honour, & then, a rich pleasure to be asked to contribute an article to the magazine you and your friends propose to publish.[3]

I shall try to write something called, "Laurel Leaves and Silver trumpets," [4] written around the newly formed Irish Academy of Literature, which—according to reports in the Press—I have been asked to join, a step I do not intend to take, for I am utterly opposed to the idea & scope of the venture.

I am sorry that you hadn't time to visit London so that I could see you & talk to you for a little while; but, then you have often talked to me,

[1] George Jean Nathan (1882–1958), drama critic, author, editor; wrote over thirty books on drama and theatre; began writing reviews for the *New York Herald* in 1905; co-editor with H. L. Mencken of *Smart Set,* 1914–24; regular drama critic of the *New York Journal American,* 1943–56; early champion in America of the works of Ibsen, Strindberg, Shaw, O'Neill, O'Casey, and Saroyan. From 1907 until the day of his death, 8 April 1958, he lived in the same book-lined studio apartment in the Hotel Royalton on 44th Street in New York. In 1955 at the age of seventy-three he ended his bachelorhood and married the actress Julie Haydon, and he was converted to Roman Catholicism shortly before he died. For O'Casey's reaction to his conversion and death, see his letter to Brooks Atkinson, 16 April 1958, Vol. III.

[2] In August 1932 O'Casey was forced to sell half of the amateur rights of *Gunman, Juno,* and *Plough* to the Samuel French Company, for his lifetime plus fifty years, for £300, in order to pay his debts. He was now preparing the prompt copies of the plays for French. In a letter of 23 July 1932, Bernard Shaw had warned O'Casey against this "absurdly bad bargain," adding: "My advice is to let wife and child perish, and lay bricks for your last crust, sooner than part with an iota of your rights." Shaw enclosed a loan of £100, but it was not enough to pay the debts, and O'Casey was a long time in repaying it. As it turned out, ironically, the sale of his rights was unnecessary for he discovered some time later that the New York office of French was holding £350 due to him in royalties but claimed they could not locate his address. For his explanation of these unfortunate events, see his letter to to Beatrix Lehmann, 28 February 1945, Vol. II.

[3] *The American Spectator,* a literary newspaper, began monthly publication in November 1932, under the editorship of George Jean Nathan, Ernest Boyd, Theodore Dreiser, James Branch Cabell, and Eugene O'Neill. From 1935–36, Charles Angoff served as editor, then M. Lehman took over until the final issue in May 1937.

[4] Sean O'Casey, "Laurel Leaves and Silver Trumpets," *American Spectator,* December 1932. See also his letter, "The Academy of Letters," *Irish Times,* 11 October 1932.

long and earnestly, in the articles and books which you have written, as have Dreiser, O'Neill, Cabell, & Boyd.

I shall start the article at once, & hope to let you have it soon.

I pray that your magazine may be a great success.

With Best Wishes &
Warm Regards
Sean O'Casey

To George Jean Nathan

MS. CORNELL

CHALFONT ST. GILES
5 OCTOBER 1932

Dear Mr. Nathan—

Enclosed is the article called "Laurel Leaves and Silver Trumpets," which I hope you may find suitable for inclusion in "The American Spectator."

If it be possible, I should like you to let me have it published in some English Journal after it has appeared in your Magazine. It doesn't matter if this should not be agreeable to you.

I am working on my new play; but the work is hard, and the going is damned slow. My wife has just read O'Neill's "Mourning Becomes Electra," [1] and the play has made a powerful impression on her. I will not read it till I have finished my own, for if I did, I know my mind should be full of it for months, and this influence would be a handicap to my own thoughts. But the temptation to read it is growing stronger every day, and in the end, I suppose I shall yield, and curse O'Neill for being such a powerful writer.

Should you be writing to him, give him my deep admiration and sincere affection for his great contribution to the Art of the Night,

and to all those who are with you on the Spectator,

and a big share of the same feeling for yourself.

Sean O'Casey

[1] Eugene O'Neill, *Mourning Becomes Electra* (1931), first performed by the Theatre Guild in New York on 26 October 1931.

To Irish Times

11 OCTOBER 1932

THE ACADEMY OF LETTERS [1]

Dear Sir—

Would you be kind enough to find space in your Journal for me to say that I cannot permit or persuade myself to accept the offer of membership in the new Irish Academy of Letters.

Unlike Mr. [Daniel] Corkery, I haven't a hundred reasons for refusing, but I have a few.

There's no use of saying anything about the official censorship; for, though the Circular issued by the Founders of the Academy implies antagonism, Mr. Yeats has said that he "did not see they could do much in the matter". Mr. Robinson has said that "it might be perfectly right and proper to condemn a book or author"; and again, that "the attitude of the Academy to the censorship had not been defined". [Mr. O'Sullivan refused to say anything, and Mr. T. C. Murray, hairy enough, prefers to keep an open mind.] [2] What the attitude towards the official censorship may be does not, in my opinion, matter much; for the censorship of dull authority embattled in this Irish Academy of Letters will be much more dangerous to the Irish authors of the future than the *Domine dirige nos* censorship exercised by the State and the Church. Once upon a time a Cardinal condemned a play written by Mr. Yeats.[3] The Cardinal is gone and forgotten, but the play is as great today as it was on the day the old Cardinal cursed it. But the members of this Academy will weave round themselves a power far beyond that which they venture to assume now. They will become—maybe even to themselves—to the young writers of the future as "sages standing in God's holy fire, as in the gold mosaic of a wall," [4] and the young writers will fall down and worship them, and call upon them for their names' sake, but there will probably be a casting forth and a denial of all who will not submit to the ritual of Academic conformity. It isn't likely that the young writers gathered into the Academy will do much to hurry up the younger writers who follow on, for they will naturally aim at keeping all who come later on a lower plane of honour

[1] The Irish Academy of Letters was publicly inaugurated at a meeting in the Abbey's Peacock Theatre on 18 September 1932, on the occasion of a lecture by W. B. Yeats on the subject of the New Ireland. Lennox Robinson presided and read out the letter, signed by Bernard Shaw, president, and Yeats, vice-president, addressed to the thirty-five writers who had been invited to become members. Seven who refused membership were: Daniel Corkery, Lord Dunsany, Douglas Hyde, James Joyce, Stephen MacKenna, George Moore, Sean O'Casey.

[2] Passages in square brackets omitted by the editor.

[3] In 1899 Cardinal Logue condemned Yeats's *The Countess Cathleen* as heretical, though he had not seen or read it.

[4] From Yeats's poem "Sailing to Byzantium" (1928).

and distinction. [I have a vivid recollection of how at least three of the chosen tried to belittle the work of an author shortly after he had refused to take the lead in an effort to down the very men whom they have asked to form this Irish Academy of Letters.]

The statement that there is still in Ireland "a deep respect for intellectual and poetical quality" is a little above the truth. This is simply tickling Kathleen Ni Houlihan under the chin. But I imagine this statement is rather an attempt on the part of the Academicians to fortify themselves with a literary cocktail, than an attempt to flatter Ireland. I should say that Brian Boru O'Higgins [5] is considered by the Irish People, at home and abroad, to be a greater poet than W. B. Yeats.

When we remember what has been done and left undone by Academicians who have been on the Board of The Abbey Theatre; when we remember what has been done by an Academician in awarding a prize at an assembly of the Tailteann Games; [6] [when we remember that the Provisional refused to answer the simple question of whether he would or would not welcome a picture by Cezanne, Gauguin, or Matisse into the Municipal Collection of Art in Dublin:] when we remember the action of four of the younger Academicians against an author who ventured to differ from them—then we can have but little confidence in this Coalition Government of Irish Literature.

"We can at least," says Mr. Yeats, "tell our own people what writers are valued most by their fellow-craftsmen." Yes, that's just it; they'll tell us what they value most; but will what they value most be the most valuable of the contributions to Irish Literature; or will what they chose be valued most because it has in it an echo of their own ideas and their own craftsmanship?

And if Ireland gives birth to an original and creative artist, how much will he care for the craft of his fellow craftsmen, who wont be fellow craftsmen at all? He wont care a damn, but they will. They will, and, especially, in my opinion, the younger members, try in various ways to dull the gleam of his work so as to keep the polish on their own.

No; an Academy can only be an Academy, and nothing else.

Yours, etc.
Sean O'Casey

Buckinghamshire, 8 October 1932

[5] Brian O'Higgins (1882–1963), Irish Republican journalist, editor, publisher, writer of nationalist and religious greeting card verses.

[6] An allusion to the fact that Lennox Robinson was one of the judges who awarded the Tailteann Games first prize for drama in 1924 to Kenneth Sarr's *The Passing,* ignoring what was undoubtedly the best play of the year, O'Casey's *Juno and the Paycock*. See O'Casey's letter to Gabriel Fallon, 21 June 1928, note 1. For the background of the Tailteann Games, see his letter to James Stephens, 12 August 1924, note 2. As O'Casey explained it to me in 1963, the Tailteann prizes for drama were exclusively reserved for nonentities: Sarr's *The Passing* won in 1924; David Sears' *Juggernaut* won in 1928; Ulick Burke's (Lillian Davidson) *Bride* won in 1932. The Tailteann Games were abandoned after 1932.

To Sara Allgood

MS. NAT LIB, DUBLIN

CHALFONT ST. GILES
4 NOVEMBER 1932

Dear Sally Allgood—

I find that we shall be going out next Sunday week, so I'm now asking you to come down on Friday, the 11th instead. Come for lunch, if you can. You'll have to take the Bus from Oxford Circus at 5 minutes before 11:o'c. This will bring you to Chalfont St. Giles by 12:30, & so in time to have a meal with us. If you let me know that you are coming, someone will meet you at "The Pheasant."

Take a *return* ticket—much cheaper.

Yrs,
S. O'Casey

To George Jean Nathan

MS. CORNELL

CHALFONT ST. GILES
26 NOVEMBER 1932

Dear Mr. Nathan—

Thank you for the Check, for which I enclose receipt.

Even if payments shouldnt rise proportionately, I hope you may make a profit out of the Magazine, and that this profit may increase immediately.

It would be a grand thing if sincerity and intelligence, now and again, could buy a little cake, as well as making enough to buy its daily bread.

By the way, the Abbey Players, as you probably know, are going about the Eastern States of U.S.A. If you had time, I should like you to go to a play in which Barry Fitzgerald was playing a good part. I think him the finest European comedian in the English language. He was the original "Boyle" in "Juno," and the "Fluther" in "The Plough."

I have belled his cleverness everywhere, but no-one seems to take notice. I imagine him to be far more subtle than [Arthur] Sinclair. I should like to know what you think of him.

Yours Sincerely,
Sean O'Casey

Received from THE AMERICAN SPECTATOR, the sum of Nineteen Dollars, in payment for article entitled, "Laurel Leaves and Silver Trumpets."

With Thanks,
Sean O'Casey

By Lady Rhondda

Time and Tide
13 MAY 1933

Notes on the Way
By Lady Rhondda

As we announced in our last issue we had intended publishing this week in TIME AND TIDE a story by Sean O'Casey whose subject is indicated by its title.[1] It is a story which would, I know, have shocked and distressed some amongst our readers. It shocked me when I first read it, shocked me into realizing how fine a piece of literature it was. We hear a great deal today about the beauty of the flesh and of the desires of the flesh, and that they have beauty I make no doubt, but that taken alone uninspired by anything beyond themselves and mingled as desire must then almost inevitably be, with a cold malignant selfishness and very often a subconscious antagonistic cruelty (a hating of the person who has made one hate oneself) they have a revolting horror that is almost beyond endurance, I make also no doubt. One feels oneself to be then at the very core of selfishness. That is a thing which the world has known for many thousands of years. But just at the moment it seems to be in danger of forgetting it. That is why just now this story of Sean O'Casey's seemed to me to be especially worth publishing.

Here we have one of the masters of literature of this generation showing us the thing in its bare loathsomeness. Here is one of the ugliest things

[1] "I Wanna Woman," eventually published the following year in *Windfalls,* led to the banning of the book in Ireland.

in the world portrayed with a faithfulness of which only a very great artist is capable. There is no description of outward physical ugliness whatsoever in Sean O'Casey's story, none save that in the man's and the woman's mind, yet its horror is, to me at least, unforgettable. Here is the lust of the flesh and the shrewd bargaining in the flesh market shown in two people of whom the woman certainly and the man probably is not devoid of physical beauty nor probably in other ways and in other relations devoid of decent human attributes, shown unaccompanied by kindliness, by love, by decency, by humanity, shown for the horrible thing it then becomes.

I had hesitated long before I decided to publish the story. I was well aware that its appearance must call forth a great deal of criticism and of censure. But it seems to me a cowardly policy to decide against the publication of a thing which one believes to have real value merely because it lays one open to criticism. When I had finally made up my mind to print it I was quite clear that I was right. It was not the kind of story TIME AND TIDE had ever published before, probably it was not the kind of story that we should use again—but that it was profoundly moral and that we were right to publish it in this instance, of that I was absolutely assured.

I had reckoned, however, without sufficiently taking into account the established English habits of the day. When our printers received it from us they refused to print it. We immediately got into touch with Mr. Sean O'Casey and received his permission to excise certain passages which might we supposed be the cause of their decision. We took it back to the printers. They still refused to print it. At first I was surprised, for I am quite clear that I have read many things in print that seem to me very much more likely to cause offence than can this story. But when I reconsidered the matter I was not so much surprised. The things I have read that seem to me much worse are for the most part directed to pointing out the charms of and often to sentimentalizing a thing of which this story is directed to pointing out the horrors. When Sean O'Casey means us to see and feel a thing we do see it—see it, feel it, touch it. He has that gift more markedly than almost any other of his contemporaries. The case against this story and the reason that the printers have refused to print it seems to me to be that it faces unflinchingly up to its facts.

I am not in any way blaming the printers. It is not their business to judge literature. It is their business, as printers with a big reputation to lose, to keep most carefully within the confines of the public opinion of the day. I do, however, regret that that public opinion is what it is. And I regret still more the interpretation which is often given to it in official quarters, which makes it apparently impossible to publish a very fine, moving and socially valuable piece of literature. For the moment the printers' action has left me with no alternative save to allow this week's

TIME AND TIDE to appear without the promised supplement. It may be, however, that I may yet discover some way round the difficulty with which we are faced.[2]

[2] In the June 10 issue Lady Rhondda announced that she had appealed to several other printers without success and finally had to abandon the attempt to publish the story in *Time and Tide*.

From W. B. Yeats to Time and Tide

27 MAY 1933

"Sean O'Casey's Story"

Sir,—That public opinion should permit, or encourage, the censorship of printers is intolerable. What is there in their trade to guarantee their judgment? Where is such judgment to stop? Is some new "Origin of Species" or "Madame Bovary" to be forbidden by some combination of printers? The issue is between Lady Rhondda and her public. If she cares to risk her popularity and the circulation of her paper, no mechanic, or employer of mechanics, should be allowed to interfere. I am glad that Mr. Sean O'Casey has broken his long silence; he has moral earnestness and great dramatic genius. Perhaps if I am permitted to read his story I may dislike it, but that is not the issue.

I am, etc.
W. B. Yeats

To George Jean Nathan

MS. CORNELL
CHALFONT ST. GILES
30 MAY 1933

Dear George Jean Nathan—

I am very glad you and your comrades liked the little article about Ibsen on the one hand and Hannan [Swaffer] on the other.[1]

I look forward to the coming of The American Spectator every month, and pray to the great God that it may have a long life.

[1] Sean O'Casey, "Dramatis Personae Ibsenisensis," *American Spectator,* July 1933.

Should you be able to come to London, I indeed hope that I may be able to meet you.

I am working hard towards the completion of my new play, "Within The Gates." It is the hardest job that I have ever attempted, making me exclaim with Yeats, "my curse on plays that have to be set up in fifty ways!" [2] All the action takes place in a Park; it is in four scenes, Spring (morning), Summer (noon), Autumn (evening), and Winter (night), so, to keep the action in the Park, and keep it going, is a job. There will be music, songs sung singly and in chorus, and though the work may not be a great one, or even fine, I'm sure it will be interesting.

By the way, I wish you wouldn't refer to me as "Mister." I heard of you first in the Abbey Theatre many years ago; I have read some of your books, and a great many of your articles in "The American Mercury," so I look upon you now as an old and valued friend. I dont put the title before your name, for I think you are too big to need it.

With Best Wishes.
Very Sincerely Yours,
Sean O'Casey

[2] W. B. Yeats, "The Fascination of What's Difficult" (1910):

"... My curse on plays
That have to be set up in fifty ways,
On the day's war with every knave and dolt,
Theatre business, management of men."

From Wyndham Lewis to Time and Tide

3 June 1933

"Sean O'Casey's Story"

Sir,—Having been given the opportunity of reading Mr. Sean O'Casey's story, "I Wanna Woman," I can only say that I consider the scruples of the printer absurd, and I regard it, of course, as most important that such hold-ups should be discouraged. The tone of the story—on the theme of The Expense of Spirit in a Waste of Shame (with full accent on the *shame*)—is moral. What more does a printer want? He knows that there *are* lots of prostitutes in Maida Vale; and, for his further comfort, this piece of "realism" is at least not calculated to increase their number. "Realism" is highly moral in its effect. The foolish bachelor, with the twenty-guinea ladies' wrist-watch, can only be an object-lesson, too. Snitzler was somewhat less explicit in his expressions, but only somewhat.

What does that matter, a little more or less? So the question presents itself to my incorrigibly coarse mind.

I am, etc.
Wyndham Lewis

To A. E. Harrison [1]

CHALFONT ST. GILES
17 JUNE 1933

Dear Mr. Harrison—

It was good and kind of you to send the cheque for £15.15.0. in recognition of all the trouble "I Wanna Woman" gave your Editor and her Staff; but as the story hasn't been published, I dont see how I can accept the money. I'm afraid the statement that the story indirectly benefited your Journal springs from a kindness rather than a fact.[2]

I enclose the cheque with this note and remain,

Sincerely Yours,
[*Sean O'Casey*]

[1] A. E. Harrison, general manager of *Time and Tide*.

[2] The printer of Lady Rhondda's magazine, *Time and Tide,* refused to print O'Casey's short story, "I Wanna Woman," on moral grounds. Lady Rhondda had originally written to O'Casey on 24 February 1933 asking him for some short stories; on 31 March she wrote thanking him for three stories, "I Wanna Woman," "The Star-Jazzer," and "The Job"; on 5 May the printer said no; on 24 May, after several judicious cuts had been suggested, the printer still said no, although Lady Rhondda began to receive many letters in strong support of O'Casey from Shaw and Desmond MacCarthy and even W. B. Yeats; on 13 June, speaking for Lady Rhondda, the general manager wrote to O'Casey: "We enclose a cheque for £15.15.od. in payment for your literary contribution. Although it has not appeared in the columns of *Time and Tide* we are satisfied with the indirect benefit which has resulted from the interest it created." But now the proud O'Casey said no.

To Secretary, Society of Authors

TS. SOCIETY OF AUTHORS

CHALFONT ST. GILES
23 JULY 1933

Dear Sir—

I have a question to put before you, and shall be grateful for an answer. Here it is:

I sold a half share of the Amateur rights of three of my plays for a lump sum of £300. I hold the opinion that this sum doesnt constitute a taxable portion of my income. The Inspector holds, however, that it is what he calls "an ordinary item of income," and is, therefore, subject to assessment. How a thing that can never happen again can be called "an ordinary" thing I don't know; but I suppose the Tax Authorities can transform a miracle into a purely natural phenomenon.

I should be glad if you would give me your opinion on the matter.

Sincerely Yours,
Sean O'Casey

To George Jean Nathan

MS. CORNELL

CHALFONT ST. GILES
27 JULY 1933

Dear George Jean Nathan—

I amnt at all surprised that you have been and still are associated with Eugene O'Neill. If you werent, who would be?

I shall not forget your kind letter about my play, and I have sent a copy of it to C. B. Cochran. I have still to get the airs of the songs and choruses in the play taken down. They are modifications, done by myself from Irish folk tunes. I shall send you a copy of the play to read as soon as I can.

I hope The American Spectator is doing well, and I welcome the enlargement. Only one reads it too damn quick, and wants to remember almost all the articles contain. It's the brightest Journal I have ever read, and it is, as we say in Ireland, a "caution" of a paper.

Give my love to Eugene O'Neill. I have read his "Mourning Becomes Electra" six or seven times, and wish to Christ I was the author of it.

Best and Warmest Wishes,
Sean O'Casey

From Charles B. Cochran

TS. O'Casey

49, Old Bond St., London W1.
1 August 1933

My dear Sean,

I am worried about "Within the Gates." I don't believe I could produce it without financial loss. It is true that I might incur this with less worthy material.

You have written some grand stuff and I am intrigued by your manner of introducing the singing, although you have created another difficulty for the producing manager, who must find an actress who can sing. The non-singing actress is difficult enough to find—the combination is very rare. I wish I could see my way to risk the production, but frankly I can't.

I am glad you are changing the Bishop's wife to the Bishop's sister. I read your play before your letter and I felt that you were limiting what the Bishop stood for by giving him a wife.

Please send me your sketch, "End of the Beginning," and I might be able to place it for you, although I sha'n't have use for it as I am not contemplating any more revue productions.

I hope ever so much that I am all wrong about your play and that somebody will do it and earn royalties for you. You can't go on writing fine things, Sean, unless they bring some material reward. I suppose you are tired of people advising you to get back to the method of "Juno." I wish you would.

Yours as ever,
C. B. Cochran

To Charles B. Cochran

TC. O'Casey

Chalfont St. Giles
2 August 1933

Dear C.B.—

Here I am searching you out with a letter to ask you a couple of additional questions. Macmillan's are listing my play in their Autumn catalogue, and I am anxious to get it into shape for publication as soon as possible. I cant do this finally till I have all the airs for the songs noted down. Now what I want to ask you is this: do you think it would be a good thing to have a simple arrangement made to the airs—say on three or four instruments? I, personally, would like this, for it would simplify the singing of them, and I have no fear of characters breaking into song, accompanied with music, during the performance of the play;—in fact, I think there should be more of it in the newer drama.

Herbert Hughes is willing to do this for me. I have since added airs myself to the two choruses and the songs, which I at first thought of getting Martin Shaw to do. All I have to do now is to get chants, or, preferably, intonations, for the dialogue in the latter part of the final act and the air for the dance done by the Dreamer and the Young Whore in the last scene.

You neednt tell me what you think of the play, if you havent yet made up your mind about it. Take your time, but I should like your advice about the above question so as to be able to go and talk over the printing with Macmillan's.

By the way, what's all this about the National Theatre at His Majesty's? One of the papers has rung me up to ask me what I think about the scheme. They think because I write an odd good play, or a good, odd play, now and again, that I know all that there is to know about the Theatre. J'ever hear such nonsense!

Sincerely Yours,
[*Sean*]

To Charles B. Cochran

TC. O'CASEY

CHALFONT ST. GILES
7 AUGUST 1933

My dear C.B.

Thanks for your kind letter telling me what you thought about "Within The Gates", and, alas, telling me that you couldnt take the risk of its production. Although I hadnt asked you, I, of course, had a hope that the play would appear under your name. But I clearly understand your fear, and, though I have a feeling that this play stands a far better chance than stood "The Silver Tassie", I realise that a "feeling" is a poor thing to put before any sensible Manager. But I cant see why the play, being at least above the average, should be cluttered with costly accessories, and that, since a risk must be taken, why that risk shouldnt be as simple a risk as possible, with a simple scene, and a group of actors ready to act in a good play—a play that gives each a good part—for a reasonable salary.

As regards the sketch ["End of the Beginning"] I have an air of a song to get, and when I have this, I shall send it on. It wouldnt be suitable for any revue that you might put on, for it was written for Sinclair—who pestered me into doing it when he was out of work—and then didnt do anything with it.

I have been able to afford only two elaborate typed copies of the play, and I should be glad if you could let me have back the copy I sent to you.

Your advice to go back to the genius of "Juno" might be good for me, but bad for my conception of the drama. And the fault of finding it almost impossible to get a good play produced is not in us, neither in you nor in me, but in an ignorant public that have nothing, and who, eventually, shall lose even that which they have.

Please give my best wishes to Mrs Cochran.

And good luck to you till you are in a position to do any damn think you like.

Yours As Ever,
Sean

To Herbert Hughes [1]

TC. O'CASEY

CHALFONT ST. GILES
21 SEPTEMBER 1933

Dear Herbert—

Got your letters this morning. Your remarks about royalties were, to me, rather vague, so we'd better get this straight. I understood you were to ask Macmillans about a small royalty for the inclusion of the airs in the book of the play; but as you didnt mention anything about this in either of your letters, I got into touch with Mr Harold Macmillan, and they are now considering the question, and will get into touch with you.

Now about performing rights, with which, of course, Macmillans have nothing to do: this, I imagine must be, or can not be, definitely decided till we get a Manager willing to take on the play. Anything that we agreed upon could only be tentative, and would depend on the contract offered by the Manager, taking all the circumstances of production into

[1] Herbert Hughes (1882–1937), Irish composer and music critic.

consideration. For instance, you suggest inclusion of Brass into the Orchestra, which would send up the costs, and reduce my (and yours) chance of making the play possible. As a matter of fact I, after thinking it over again, don't want any blare in the play. The whole tenour of the play is, I think, if not solemn, at least dignified.

However, I think we could come to a preliminary understanding between ourselves about your fee during the run of the play.

1 £4 weekly during run of piece.
2 £25 advance royalties.
3 Fifty-fifty on gramophone record receipts.
4 I'm afraid the question of Film fees must remain over. We may have to give most of the film money to the Managers. They usually ask a big percentage. 50% was allowed in the American for Juno, and the same for The Silver Tassie.
5 5% on Amateur performances. (fees)
6 On programmes and Posters to be written: Music adapted and arranged by Herbert Hughes.

I think above covers all points. Mr Gibbons hasnt said anything yet. I'd like you to let me have the old copy of the play, and the additional 3rd act you took in mistake, as I like to keep these old copies. Dont bother about the old music M S, for I have copies wrapped up with the stuff that went to make the play. Hope you and Susie are well. I've had another attack of the ear, but I'm better now.

Addendum to enclosed letter.

Re Band parts, or instrumental music.

You say you think that Macmillans wont want to have anything to do with this. Why? I always thought that these were to form part of the Appendix. That all the music was to be in the book. Do Macmillans think this would be too costly? If they do, that's another matter. Cant you make sure about this? The music to Yeats's play was all there. I think four strings would be enough, with flutist, and drummer. But no Brass, Herbert, it would spoil the pathos of the play.

But for goodness sake make sure that Macmillans dont want to include the parts mentioned. A scene of hiring would be a hell of a bother to everyone concerned, and might put off many a production in the future.

I hope this is clear, Herbert.

Yours as ever.

[*Sean*]

To Harold Macmillan [1]

TC. O'CASEY

CHALFONT ST. GILES
23 SEPTEMBER 1933

Dear Mr Harold—

This to confirm our talk over the telephone. Mr Hughes to receive a percentage on his music included in the book of the play, "Within The Gates", of 2% from royalties allowed by you to me; or, a sum of money down not exceeding £25.

If this figure doesnt seem fair, I am quite willing to leave the final decision to you, though, in fairness to myself, it is necessary to say that all the airs, except the "Dance of Jannice", the "Gardeners Song", and "Summer Chorus" are adapted from airs chosen by me, and even the last two of these spring, I imagine, from the tunes hummed into, and hummed out of my own head.

However, we dont want any bother, and I repeat that I am perfectly willing to leave the matter in your hands, if you should think the above proposal inadequate.

You are right in taking for granted that I should like the play to come out as soon as possible, for I am anxious to send an advance (or proof) copy to George Jean Nathan of America as soon as I can.[2]

[1] Harold Macmillan (1894–), Macmillan & Co. Ltd., London; British publisher and statesman; prime minister: 1957–63.

[2] Page missing.

To Gabriel Fallon

TS. TEXAS

CHALFONT ST. GILES
24 SEPTEMBER 1933

Dear Gaby—

'member the tale of the "Pound On Demand?"

You told it to me four, five, six or seven golden years ago. Well, I've written a short story to it, and will send it to a Magazine for consideration. You often told me to use it, and at last I've done so.

Now the point is this:
would you be willing to take 10% on whatever I may get on the yarn?

If so, write and say so.

I have also written a one acter round it, and again ask you if you would take ten per cent of each fee received, should the thing ever be produced?

I don't mean, of course, would you be too proud, but if you think this offer fair.

I intend to get, if I can, a hetergenuous volume, called "Windfalls" published containing verses, stories,—not including Pound On Demand— and two sketches, including Pound On Demand.

The sketch may never be done, but I think it was worth doing.

My new play is in the printers' hands, and Macmillans think it the best work I've ever done.

Had a bad time with nerve, heart attack inflammation of the ears and other minor afflictions. When I lay on my back, and wanted to turn, had to do it by numbers.

A doctor with a telescope found out that the heart wasn't really bad; the nerves are well once more and I'm beginning to skip about again.

Best of wishes to Rose, the children,
and to You, old boy.
Yours as ever.
Sean

To Herbert Hughes

TC. O'Casey

Chalfont St. Giles
24 September 1933

Dear Herbert—

The possible terms quoted by me in last letter were for the usual commercial production. They couldnt hold in a Rep or a Stage Society production. Let's hope the commercial Production will be with us and not against us.

Let me deal with your points as they occur.

1. A sum of £50 as advanced royalties seems to me to be altogether too much for the work done, as well as adding to the first cost of the play. It would amount to half of the maximum I could possibly get, though I have done nine tenths of the work. For instance I've been working for nearly two years, while you've done four weeks. And dont forget my share, even in the music.
2. Very well: £5 per week for the run of the piece. (let me know precisely what you mean by the run of the piece)
3. Re Macmillan: Quite so: I said that you should have a small pro-

portionate royalty on the published book. But since you were friendly with one of the Directors, and that you brought your script personally to him, I assumed that you would settle this yourself, especially after I had written saying that I would be willing to leave the arrangement with them. However when I got a letter from them about the book, and nothing was said about you, I got into touch with them, and you have probably heard from Macmillans by now.

4. 3 pounds weekly from the tour in the big towns, Edinburgh, Liverpool, Manchester, Glasgow, and £2 weekly in each of the others.

Notes.

Conversations are of no use: I want to get all possible points down on paper, which action is as fair to you as to me.

Of course I shall have to pay these royalties, for the simple reason that they will be taken from mine.

My royalties will have to be modified to meet the expenses of a collaborator, as in the case of the published version of the play, and, of course this is quite fair. The thing to decide is what is a fair division. I think my proposals are very fair, indeed.

If we cant agree on these points, I propose we leave the question to the Composers' Committee of the Authors' Society.

I dont think I can remember anything more at present, except that even an advance royalty of £25 would represent a proportion of a third of what I would get, for that sum would have to come off the £100 (if I get this) advance royalties due to me.

I have heard nothing yet from Mr Gibbons. Nathan has written to me again. I think I shall send on the script of the play—the music can follow later on.

Yours as Ever.
[*Sean*]

To Harold Macmillan

TC. O'CASEY
CHALFONT ST. GILES
30 SEPTEMBER 1933

Dear Mr Harold—

This is a formal confirmation of our conversation over the telephone today regarding the percentage to be given to Mr Hughes.

I agree with Mr Daniel [Macmillan]'s suggestion that "a fixed royalty of 2½% on all copies sold would be appropriate."

I should like to remind you of the two proof copies needed by me—one for G. J. Nathan of America, and the other for my Continental Agent, Mr Glass.

And I thank you for telling me how much you thought of my play [*Within the Gates*]. I must honestly say that I was delighted to hear that you thought it the finest thing I had yet written.

My Very Best Wishes,
Sincerely Yours,
[*Sean O'Casey*]

To Macmillan & Co. Ltd.

TS. MACMILLAN LONDON

CHALFONT ST. GILES
1 OCTOBER 1933

Dear Sirs,

I shall be in London on Monday next, and, if I may, shall call in between 11 and 12 to leave with you for consideration the material to form the volume called "Windfalls."

I should like to say a few words to you about the work.

I telephoned your Publications' Department yesterday asking for a proof copy of the music which is to form an appendix to the play, so that I could send it on to G. J. Nathan of America, who is, as he says, "setting about at once to get the best production possible for the play." More than a week ago, Mr Hughes told me these would be available in a few days, and, when on a visit here, yesterday, he said that he could in no way account for the delay, as the proofs had left his hands long ago. I thought that these would be included in the proof copies you so kindly sent to me. Of course I dont want the rough proofs, for these would be altogether too bulky, but the proofs as they will appear when they are made to fit the book, thirty-one *small* pages.

Yours sincerely,
Sean O'Casey

To Herbert Hughes

TC. O'CASEY

CHALFONT ST. GILES
5 OCTOBER 1933

Dear Herbert—

I am glad that you have finally arranged with Macmillans about royalty on book sales.

There seems to be now only one item on which we dont agree namely, the question of preproduction advance.

I cant agree that whatever may be received by you before production should be considered as a fee, and not as advance on royalties. If there was one thing clear to me, and which was insisted upon by me, it was that the venture was a gamble, and that we should both share it. I insisted upon this, so that it might be prominent in your mind before you consented to work. What you ask for now (a fee) removes all the uncertainty from you, which, to my mind, is an unfair breach of our understanding, and, frankly, I wont agree to it.

If you cant see your way to look upon any advance as advance in royalty, I shall be glad if you would say so finally.

I don't mind what you got from Fagan: I am not J. B. Fagan, and "Within The Gates" is not "And So To Bed".[1]

It is hardly necessary to remind you that my work, too, is only half done, and that work on rehearsals will be, I think, much heavier than yours.

I think your point about getting these things down "in writing fairly soon," is answered by the fact that they have already been put down clearly and, I hope, precisely by me.

There is just the one point of advanced royalties: it is for you to say finally whether you will agree that the fee you ask for and get from any producer is to be considered as advanced royalty or not.

If not, then I must go my own way.

Yours Sincerely,
[*Sean*]

[1] A reference to J. B. Fagan's light comedy, *And So To Bed* (1926), a Pepysian comedy.

To Harold Macmillan

TS. MACMILLAN LONDON

CHALFONT ST. GILES
7 OCTOBER 1933

Dear Mr Harold

I enclose here the revised Agreement you sent me, and have, as you suggested, destroyed the one first sent to me.

I shall be glad if you would kindly reserve 25 copies of the play for presentation to particular friends, and send them on to me as soon as it may be convenient to you.

Could you let me have, too, a copy of "The Winding Stair" by Yeats,[1] and a copy of "The Avatars," by George Russell,[2] followed by a copy of "Is Life Worth Living?," by Robinson.[3]

I have almost completed arranging the volume to be called "Windfalls," consisting of two Humourous One Act Plays, Four Stories (short) and a number of poems, ancient and modern. I think these will make an interesting book; you can consider them apart from my plays, and use your own judgement as to whether you'd like to publish them or not.

Dont forget to let me have the two advanced proof copies as soon as possible.

Give me a couple of days notice, and I shall be delighted to see you.

Yours sincerely,
Sean O'Casey

[1] W. B. Yeats, *The Winding Stair* (London, Macmillan, 1933).

[2] A.E. (George Russell), *The Avatars: A Futurist Fantasy* (London, Macmillan, 1933).

[3] Lennox Robinson, *Is Life Worth Living?* (London, Macmillan, 1933). This play was originally produced as *Drama at Inish* at the Abbey Theatre on 6 February 1933.

To George Jean Nathan

MS. CORNELL

CHALFONT ST. GILES
7 OCTOBER 1933

Dear George J. Nathan—

Here's the script of "Within The Gates." The writing of the arrangement for the songs has been delayed, and I decided to forward the script without delay so as to let you see what the play was like. I will forward the music in a few days, but, of course, this is of far less importance than the play itself.

I sincerely hope that you may think it good.

It is very kind of you to take such interest in the work, and I hope it may be possible to have a production in America.

I have almost recovered again from my illness, and am flitting about again like a new born butterfly.

Best Wishes.
Very Sincerely Yours,
Sean O'Casey

P.S. MS. sent in separate registered cover.

To Herbert Hughes

TC. O'CASEY

[CHALFONT ST. GILES]
14 OCTOBER 1933

Dear Herbert Hughes—

I have now got from the Printers two advanced proof copies of the play, but the arrangements arent included. I have already sent the script of the play to G. J. Nathan, and told him the music would follow in a few days. Has anything happened to delay the printing?

Could you let me have a copy of the music that it may be forwarded on to him?

A proof would do well, and afterwards, I could send him on a full copy of the play.

It's important that there should be as little delay as possible.

I'm discussing the London Production with another Manager, and I hope something definite may come out of the conversations.

I hope you have had good news about your book on Chopin.

Best Wishes.
[*Sean O'Casey*]

To George Jean Nathan

MS. CORNELL

CHALFONT ST. GILES
17 OCTOBER 1933

Dear George Jean Nathan—

I daresay you've read my play by now, and I sincerely hope that you may be able to say a few good things about it.

I wish to write a few words about the business side of the venture, so as to let you know how things stand, and possibly save you from trouble later on.

I have almost settled terms with a Manager for an English production, but he is a little troubled about America. The custom here is that the English Manager gets an option on the American licence to produce it there. He is quite willing to come to an arrangement with any American Manager you may select to produce the play. And he is willing to go fifty-fifty with the American Producer on what ever may be finally settled as to the Fil [full?] share given by me. At present he wants 50%, but I am fighting for 40%, so that will mean 25% or 20% to whichever American Manager takes the play.

I think it good and wise that you should know all this.

Delighted, really delighted to hear of O'Neill's success,[1] and glad that he is happy about it. He deserves it for singing his great songs as he passes through the wilderness.

Affectionate Regards,
Sean O'Casey

[1] Eugene O'Neill's *Ah, Wilderness!* opened in New York on 3 October 1933.

From Oliver St. John Gogarty

TS. O'CASEY

15 ELY PLACE
DUBLIN
23 OCTOBER 1933

My dear Sean, I have just got back from the fretted edge of Europe which is the West of Ireland, Connemara, the Land of the "Sons of Conn who dwell by the Sea," as Donal O'Sullivan translates it:—and no nonsense about "inlets of Ocean". Your letter was a great joy to me and an invigorating transfusion where I am bled white. Anyway, I will get you, or, rather, put you in the way of getting, the articles on George Moore's Urn Burial which I wrote for the Manchester edition of the Daily Express.[1] They owe me £20; and, if a man in your position asks for the back numbers containing the stuff by the only member not of the family who had the audacity to attend the boycotted obsequies, you will be giving a "literary brother" a big lift. And you know what that means: to be helped. I would not ask you to write direct and in your own name to Manchester if I had a copy. But the copy I had went in with the bill; and I have not heard since. But I get requests to write every week and with 2 weeks long back in arrear, I don't reply. If they think that you think my work worth rescuing, not only shall I be paid, but I shall be appreciated. It needs only a well-known man to give them the lead and a kick behind at the same time: an Oirish Bull, by Gad!

I had a letter from Robinson Jeffers, the grimmest poet of them all in the U.S.A. Ulster descended . . . Ossian's Grave: [2]

"This is the proper Fame to have, not cornered in a poem . . .

Fabulous, a name in the North".

inveighing against AE, for not turning up at George Moore's Urn Burial. "Plato was sick" I said (but safe)!

Moore had intended to have his ashes spread "where the donkeys are on Hampstead Heath" but his Mother's side produced another oddity in his sister, Mrs. Kilkenny, whom I had to row in lieu of local aid, to the Castle Island for the internment, and she staged the funeral as if "The great green rath's ten-acre tomb", lay heavy on his urn. Great! Up Mayo! and "The Gap of the Two Bushes and the wide Plains of Mayo".

Daily Express, Manchester. O. Gogarty's account of the Urn burial. I forgot the date. But you'll get the articles and I the cash!

Also, you asked me to call on you for aid when publishers did me down. I send Putnam's last agreement. Nothing signed or written about yet. I want to keep the American rts. separate, for the U.S.A. (Macmillan) pay me well.

Poplar are looking for our Billy [McElroy] and I hope that they won't get him! He got into the wrong geological epoch about the coal. It seems that there were no seams where he sent it from! Have you heard? I love

[1] Oliver St. John Gogarty, "Who Will Be a Legend in His Own Land," 22 May 1933; "Silent Vigil By a Lake That is Always Green," 29 May 1933; *Daily Express*, Manchester Edition. This was Gogarty's tribute to George Moore (1852–1933), on the occasion of the urn burial of Moore's ashes under a pagan cairn of stones on an island in Lough Carra, County Mayo, opposite the ruins of Moore Hall, where he was born. See also Gogarty's account of the incident in *I Follow St. Patrick* (London, Rich & Cowan, 1938), p. 235.

[2] Robinson Jeffers (1887–1962) spent the summer of 1929 in a cottage at Cloghbrack, Knocknacarry, County Antrim, two and a half miles from Ossian's Grave, a circle of prehistoric standing stones. Later he wrote the poem, "Ossian's Grave," *Give Your Heart to the Hawks* (New York, Random House, 1933).

Sean O'Casey in his Sunday best, 1910.

The St. Laurence O'Toole Pipers' Band at Bodenstown in 1913. The hatless figure marching alone on the left is O'Casey.

James Larkin in action on Dublin street during 1913 strike.

HARRY BOLAND

Merchant Tailor,

ALL IRISH GOODS

64 Middle Abbey Street, Dublin.

Insist on getting Rubber Stamps MADE IN IRELAND

J. W. BROADBERRY, Rubber Stamp & Fountain Pen Specialists,

32 Capel Street, Dublin.

The only firm making Rubber Stamps in IRELAND who can use the Irish Trade Mark.

cumann uí tuatail

Concert and Play

IN THE

EMPIRE THEATRE

(By kind permission of the Management)

Sunday, Nov. 25th, 1917

Total Proceeds of Concert will go to provide Meals for Necessitous Children and the Poor.

PROGRAMME **ONE PENNY**

P. CONWAY & CO.,

TOBACCONISTS

31 EXCHEQUER ST. Established 1894

The Story of Thomas Ashe

BY SEAN O'CATHASAIGH

On Sale Everywhere Price Twopence

Issued by FERGUS O'CONNOR & CO., 44 Eccles St., Dublin

Pictorial and Republican Publishers. Trade only Supplied

WEST, T.U. PRINTER, CAPEL ST., DUBLIN.

—YOUR FRIENDS WANT—

Sinn Fein Xmas Cards

Largest Selection in City from

P. J. DOOLEY, Tobacconist, Newsagent, &c.

40 AMIENS ST.

"THE NABOCKLISH,"

A Comedy in Two Acts - - By Thomas K. Moylan.

CHARACTERS:

Jeremiah Cullinan (a well-to-do Farmer)	...	P. MacDonnell
Molly (his Servant)	... ...	Bridie Sheils
Pat Carmody (a Cardriver)	... ...	Michael Smith
George Herbert Chantilly Smith (an English Tourist)		S. O'Cathasaigh
Matty Moroney (a Shoemaker)	... ...	M. Colgan
Mick Considine (a Blacksmith)	... ...	William Byrne
Jamesy Linnane (a Publican)	... ...	P. Mitchell

The Scene is laid in Cullinan's Kitchen in Bandharan, Co Clare. A few hours are supposed to elapse between Acts I and II.

Time—The Present.

An Xmas Dinner for 2d.

CAN BE HAD AT THE

Sean Connolly Sinn Fein Club,

77 AMIENS STREET,

By the lucky winners of their GOOSE CLUB. The only Sinn Fein Goose Club. Several Prizes of various kinds.

XMAS CARDS

Before purchasing, be sure you inspect our magnificent selection—10.000 Cards.

BUTLER'S, 41 AMIENS STREET.

"ORDERS BOOKED FOR PRIVATE CARDS."

PROGRAMME—PART I.

1. Band Selection,	O'Toole Pipers		—
2. —	"The Nabocklish"		—
3. Dance ...	Jig BRIDIE McKENNA.		—

INTERVAL

Mrs. Sheridan will play a Selection of Irish Airs.

Accompanist - Mr. Joseph Crofts.

PATRICK DELANEY,

Furniture Dealer,

SPENCER ROW.

GUINAN BROS.,

GROCERS AND . . .

WINE MERCHANTS

55 & 56 TALBOT ST.

PROGRAMME—PART II.

1. Song ...	"Fir an Iarthair," ... MOLLIE O'BYRNE		*Dr. Maguire*
2. Dance ...	Hornpipe ... THOMAS BOLGER		—
3. Recitation	..."Pearse's Oration at Bodenstown"... ILIAM PAUL		—
4. Song	..."Wrap the Green Flag Round Me," SEAN MAGH FHLOINN		*P. Reilly*
5. Song	"My Dark Rosaleen," ... JOAN BURKE		*Mangan*
6. Dance ...	St. Patrick's Day ... JOSEPH BREWER		—
7. Song ...	"Shipmates o' Mine," ... J. NEILAN		—
8. Song ...	"The Brave Volunteers," ... CONNIE O'HANLON		—
9. Song	"The Constitutional Movement must go on," SMYTH AND O'CATHASAIGH		—

Accompanist Mr. JOSEPH CROFTS

MICHAEL SARGENT,

Victualler,

17 LR. SHERIFF ST.

Lady Augusta Gregory. Portrait by John Butler Yeats, the Elder. Courtesy of the National Gallery of Ireland.

(LEFT) On these four pages of the Concert and Play Program for the Empire Theatre, 25 November 1917, O'Casey appears as author, actor, piper, and singer.

O'Casey's room in Dublin tenement at 422 North Circular Road, where he wrote his first three plays. He lived here from 1921 to 1925.

O'Casey in Dublin, 1924.

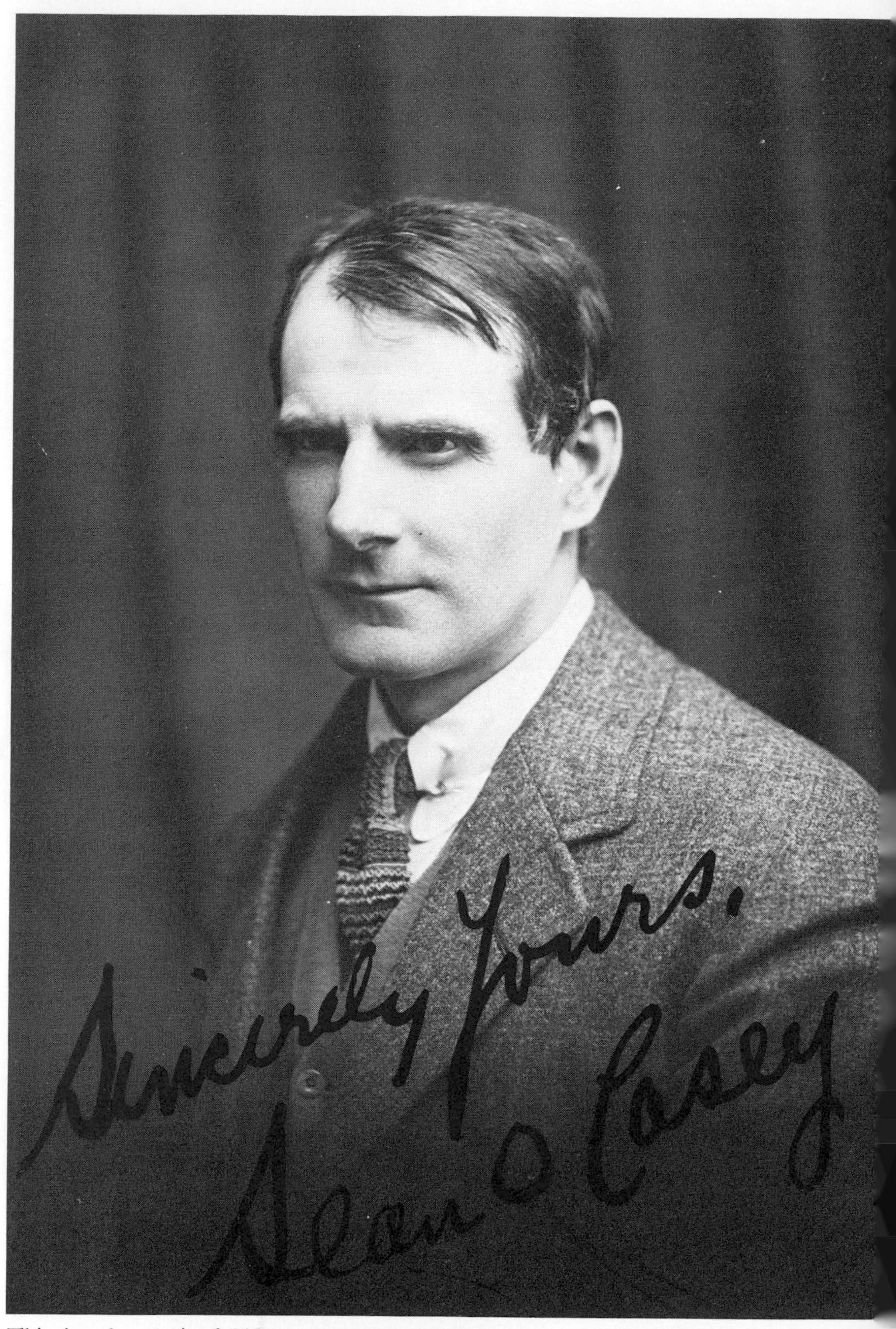

This signed portrait of O'Casey was taken in 1925.

(RIGHT) O'Casey with a London bobby, 1926.

Augustus John and O'Casey in Chenil Gallery, Chelsea, 1926.

George Bernard Shaw and O'Casey, 1930.

Drawing of James Joyce (1921) by Wyndham Lewis. Courtesy of the National Gallery of Ireland.

Eileen and Sean O'Casey on the day of their marriage, 23 September 1927, outside Roman Catholic Church of All Souls and the Redeemer, Chelsea, London.

William Butler Yeats. Portrait by John Butler Yeats, the Elder. Courtesy of the National Gallery of Ireland.

Sketch by Charles E. Kelly of Yeats kicking O'Casey out of the Abbey Theatre. Courtesy of the *Irish Statesman*, 9 June 1928.

MR. W. B. YEATS "Of course, Mr. O'Casey, you must on no account take this as being in the nature of a rejection. I would suggest that you simply tell the Press that my foot slipped."

O'Casey, New York, 1934.

the "billie". Is there a play in a rich merchant Bohemian going to prison to escape from the incongruous results of his Chelseisms? Health exercises put for "misconduct" and food enthusiasms for "crim.con".?

But have either of us time?

Your new play's proofs means that you have a new one finished. Great! Get it off on the screen before trusting to the evening papers for a London audience. And then put McElroy, Prince of Men, but not merchants,—on the stage to give the Londoners a play with "Pep" in it. All their purges and patent medicines would advertise you. And what country takes more? He cannot sleep with a woman without sterilised air!

The "Gate" here is producing about 40 plays a year. The Abbey . . . . . . Lennox is again in the States! I have characteristically, *half* a play on the Hospitals (Sweep) written. It gets to disease being the norm and health, "Concupiscence of the Flesh, and the Pride of Life"! Now stay in your stall as Willie of Stratford did; and pass not personal opinion! Sean! But is Health to become a desideratum and not the birthright of men? What has happened? Were we pre-Lenined by the Christians? I must get it staged by the Innocents of the Abbey.

Why did you mention AE? You have . . . see what you have done to me! I am mesmerised. I find the Halls of Indra, "Twalf Pillars an a Roof" forming round me. It's a bit draughty, but not so open as the Gaelic equivalent . . :

"Bryan O'Lynn had a House, to be sure:
With the Stars for a roof and the Bog for a Flure:
A Way to go out; and a Way to go in.
'Shure, it's mighty convenient', said Bryan O'Lynn!

Scoffers and Heresiarchs! Yes; both of us. You for reading me; and I for cocking myself up to you to be read. Joyce would denounce us; but we got in first, and laughed last.

Now I have got over the intoxication of having a letter in your cuneiform and I am cooling down like my, not Red Hanrahan, but Fresh Nellie who might stand for the Race, fresh, frolicsome and faithful, and am beginning to be alarmed at the spate of talk you induce in me. Is it that I too, like you, need a plain MS. with no "delirium of the Braves"? And an inferior Race to frame me with non-historical prejudices and passions? Or is it that I am so sunk in this bog that I testify at too great a length to the first full-length friend who gives me a friendly word? No matter! God be glad because of you, Sean! And put a punch into your son, the next generation. To your wife, that unperturbable and patient hostess, who always gave me a welcome no matter when or with *whom* or how I came, give a picture of me bowed in salute to her as Billy would like to bow in slendering. "Sweet-spoken".

Yours always, Oliver

And to think that the Daily Express could not understand "lambent hyaline" when I raved about Lough Carra on the telephone! Blind Raftery could see it (before he was *retrospectively* converted to Wordsworth by Lady Gregory and Douglas Hyde).

Tell your Missus not to bother to acknowledge the enclosed.

To Norman MacDermott [1]

TC. O'CASEY
CHALFONT ST. GILES
23 OCTOBER 1933

Dear Norman MacDermott—

In reply to your letter of the 21 inst:

1. Very well, then; Six months from the 1st of January, 1934.
2. No arrangement can be made about America till I hear from G. J. Nathan. He has, as I told you, been interested in the play for the last nine months, and I gladly promised to let him be my sponsor in the U.S.A. If he secures a Manager, my royalties and advance will have to come from him. I have written to G. J. Nathan, saying that an English Manager was in touch with me, and that I would probably arrange with him for the London Production; I added that an arrangement might be arranged between the two managers, and pointed out that 20% of what might be received for the film, would go to the American Manager.
3. This will really make it less of a gamble for you. Nathan may think nothing of the play; or, he may think it unsuitable for America; so you'll have plenty of time, and good guidance before you ask for an option. And if he does decide to take it I will try to get a percentage for you, though this may be difficult to get.
4. I thought of the clause about my name appearing on bill, Etc, but dont care a damn about this, for when the book is published, all the world'll know who wrote the play. Anyhow, my style is, for good or evil, unconcealable.
5. I will look into your suggestion about provincial royalties.

I and Eileen will do our best to get to London to see Jessica. I havent heard from Hughes yet. What about the Censor? Oughtnt we to send a copy

[1] Norman MacDermott (1889–), founder-director of the Everyman Theatre in Hampstead in 1920; directed the premiere of *Within the Gates* in London on 7 February 1934.

to him? I could let you have a proof copy for this purpose. I am sending this copy here.

Yours Sincerely,
[*Sean O'Casey*]

To Gabriel Fallon

MS. TEXAS

CHALFONT ST. GILES
27 OCTOBER 1933

My dear Gaby—Thanks for your letter. And thanks for the little medal.[1] I cannot consent to wear the symbol, but I shall keep it as a dear and kind wish from a dear and kind friend. I've sent the story to The Strand Magazine; but they returned it as unsuitable. I'm afraid it was really unsuitable for those who form the crowd that read that Magazine. Or, maybe, the story's style is too much akin to the Drama. I shall send on the Sketch to you, if you'd like to read it. I saw it announced that "Gabriel Fallon & His Company" were Broadcasting recently; I tried to connect, but I don't seem to be able to get Dublin or Athlone on our set, though it is a 5 valve Pye. I've often longed to hear oul Dublin's (or Cork's) voice again.

I am "conducting conversations"—as the politicians say—for the production of "Within The Gates" in London, & hope they may be satisfactorily concluded.

George Jean Nathan is interesting himself in the American Production—without my ever asking him or speaking to him or even seeing him. He asked me to let him do this 7 months before the play was finished. I sent him the MS a fortnight ago, & I enclose here his opinion of the play.

How's The Abbey? I hear it is dying—which is a pity—without having even a swan song to sing.

Yours as Ever,
with Love to Rose, Frankie, Bernard & the little Rose, & to
Yourself
Ever Yours
Sean

[1] The Miraculous Medal of St. Catherine Labouré.

To Oliver St. John Gogarty

MS. GOGARTY

CHALFONT ST. GILES
[27 OCTOBER 1933]

Dear Oliver.

I've sent away for 3 copies of the Express Dairy Daily, saying, I'd sent my copy to a friend, who sent it on to another, & I never got it back. Two more friends had asked for the article; I wanted to send a copy to each & retain one for myself, so I wanted 3 copies myself.

I cant help you over the Putnam question till I know more about it. Putnam's have an American Publishing Branch, just like Macmillans, so why not let them publish in both places. Macmillans invariably want the American licence for a work as well as the English Licence. Do you prefer Macmillans? If so why not withdraw from Putnams, provided you are certain Macmillans will do the job? Do you think the book is of fair commercial value? Would it be certain to sell 1500 or 2000 copies? If Macmillans take [George] Shiels to their bosom—as they have—I don't see why they shouldn't take Gogarty!

Why hasn't Beaverbrook paid you for your article? Did you contract for £20? A pretty big fee, you know, for an Article in the Manchester Edition. However, not too big, if you contracted for it. But did you, or did you just do one of Billy [McElroy]'s gambles?

You have to be damned careful of these people. They're always on the lookout for something for nothing. I wrote a fine article about a National Theatre for England, just because I felt hot about it; it was splashed over a Front Page; but I didn't get a red rex for it. "Thank you kindly; and it was so charming of you to write it". Charming—!

I know some of R. Jeffers work. I have read his "Cawdor",[1] & by God, it's a fine poem. I'd love to read what *He* has to say about A.E., the prime blower of the Age! But have you read "The Avatars"? [2] George Russell's dhry dhream. Bad style, bad composition, bad grammar, bad poetry, & no imagination. He has passed away in his own Nirvana. Well, no-one'll try to hook him out of it again.

All the Best.
Sean

[1] Robinson Jeffers, *Cawdor* (New York, Liveright, 1928).
[2] A.E., *The Avatars: A Futurist Fantasy* (1933).

To Harold Macmillan

MS. MACMILLAN LONDON

CHALFONT ST. GILES
27 OCTOBER 1933

Dear Mr Harold,

I send you here a quotation from a letter received from G. J. Nathan, the celebrated American Dramatic Critic. He is trying to get a suitable production for the work in the U.S.A.

I am very pleased to get ths tribute from such a man & such a critic. He is, of course, the foremost critic in America.

I am sure you, too, will be pleased to read what he thinks of the work.

Sincerely yours,
Sean O'Casey

Quotation from a letter received from George Jean Nathan, the celebrated American critic.

> I read the manuscript of "Within The Gates" last evening, and want to tell you, in all and heart-felt critical sincerity, that it is one of the most beautiful plays I have read in a very long, long time. I am thoroughly delighted with it. It has an *overwhelming* beauty.
>
> George Jean Nathan

To George Jean Nathan

MS. CORNELL

CHALFONT ST. GILES
1 NOVEMBER 1933

My dear George Jean Nathan—

It's difficult to reply to such a letter as the last one I got from you. It is something splendid to read what you think of my play. It is as the dew unto Israel, grapes in the wilderness, and the firstripe in the fig tree. It is a proud thing to me to fondle in my mind the high opinion you have of my play. For a long time now, I have desired the good opinion of

George Jean Nathan. This opinion will always be an important opinion to me. I thank you.

I am, of course, quite content to allow Eugene O'Neill's Agent [Richard J. Madden] to handle the financial end of the play. I have almost fixed up here with a London Manager, but I have eliminated from our agreement all things connected with the American Production.

Thank you again for your great kindness.

Sincerely Yours,
Sean O'Casey

To Oliver St. John Gogarty

MS. GOGARTY

CHALFONT ST. GILES
9 NOVEMBER 1933

Dear Oliver—

You didn't say anything about Putnams. Why not ask the Authors' Society's advice? And let them apply to The Express for your fee? I think I remember seeing your name on the list of membership recently. You should insist on that fee. It isn't fair to yourself, or to *other authors* that you should write for nix. They'll think all the more of you if you stick out for your due. And when you send an article, give them only "the first serial rights"; for these articles are often sold again to other papers—provincial & American—when they have a value. Insist on your fee: tell them I kicked up a row, & am threatening to report the matter to the Authors' Society.

Is it true that AE is in London painting sickey after sickey [1] in a back room? What do you make of a soul "buoyed up by air and exults"?

No, no; not AEolus; but Aloysius AEolianus—that's the fit & proper name of this wandering psyche. Billy's doing well, & in great fettle, for all the air in his neighborhood has been carefully and suitably sterilized.[2]

Best of Wishes.
Sean

If you ever get a copy of your article send it to me; I'll let you have it back allright.

S.O'C.

[1] Pun on "psyche."
[2] McElroy had installed an air-purifying machine in his coal company office.

To George Jean Nathan

MS. CORNELL

CHALFONT ST. GILES
23 NOVEMBER 1933

My dear George Jean Nathan—

I am sending you here a copy of my play in print which may be useful to you.

I should very much like to send you a signed copy of the play when I get them from Macmillans.

I am very pleased to think that there is a chance of the The [Theatre] Guild doing the play.

I have always wished for this, but have been invariably unfortunate in this matter. What a difference it would have made to me had "The Silver Tassie" been produced by The Guild!

I hope that O'Neill's play, "Ah, Wilderness," is doing well. Some over here who have grumbled because he wrote tragedy, now grumble because he has written a comedy. Peepers-in at the hole in the wall in the Temple of Drama.

My best wishes to him and to you.

Sean O'Casey

To George Jean Nathan

MS. CORNELL

CHALFONT ST. GILES
30 NOVEMBER 1933

My dear George Jean Nathan—

I got your kind letter this morning, and I thank you for it. Alas, you will know by now that the play has been published. I had no chance to postpone the publication, for I was in desperate need of the advance royalties given by Macmillans. I have had a bad two years of it, and they came just in time. It cant be helped now, and I can only hope the publication of the play wont harm the production there or here.

Madden may have no fear about the sale of the film rights—I will consult him first of all, and refuse all English offers till I am convinced none will come from California.

I hope I am not giving you too much trouble over this play.

I venture to send you a copy of the English edition of the work.

Gratefully Yours, and with
Warm Regards.
Sean O'Casey

To Evening Standard [1]

TC. O'CASEY

CHALFONT ST. GILES
9 DECEMBER 1933

THE EDITOR, *Evening Standard*, LONDON.

Dear Sir,

Some days ago a review or a criticism of "Within The Gates" written, I believe, by Howard Spring, appeared in the columns of *The Evening Standard*.[2] Your critic shows that he carries a banner in the group of mentally Down and Outs when he complains that the play is not a study of the whole seething brew of life. Who is the man and where is the play that could make a study of the whole seething brew of life? I have no time to waste commenting on his views of "order, truth, and goodness," nor on his plaintive statement about this land "trying to live according to its ancient lights." They are, indeed, ancient lights in more ways than one.

The play is obviously above his powers of intelligence to understand, so I will content myself by adding a comment on a reference to the character of The Dreamer that appears in the play. He says, "The character who arises out of the ruck is called 'the Dreamer' and that's a pity, for, if one thing is more certain than another in these troubled times it is that the day for dreaming is behind us—far, far behind."

Now what the world wants more than anything else at the present moment is a Dreamer, for it is always the Dreamer who first rises out of the ruck of things. Hail to Faraday and Florence Nightingale! Last year the Bible Society says it sent out nearly eleven million copies of the Bible, but not a single copy apparently, came the way of Howard Spring. This is

[1] This letter was refused publication by the editor.

[2] Howard Spring, "On New Books," *Evening Standard,* London, 30 November 1933, a review of *Within the Gates,* published by Macmillan in November 1933.

a pity, for in that book is a lovely description of the first Dreamer rising above 'the ruck of things'. One of his own greater poets says of this Dreamer:

> Thou from the first
> Wast present, and with mighty wings outspread
> Dove-like satst brooding on the vast Abyss
> And mad'st it pregnant.[3]

The First Dreamer is the Holy Ghost.

Spring pushes the Dreamer behind. He wants progress so that the land may live according to its ancient lights: in him ignorance and bliss have kissed each other.

Sincerely Yours,
Sean O'Casey

[3] Milton's *Paradise Lost,* I, 19–22.

To Lady Astor

MS. Astor
Chalfont St. Giles
12 December 1933

Dear Lady Astor—

We haven't yet chosen the Caste—we find it hard [to] find a girl for one of the principal characters—but we expect to have this done soon. Then there will be a reading which may, I hope, take place before Christmas. I should like to spend the night before this reading in London, but shouldn't care to venture into your home, unless you were there yourself. Afterwards, the Rehearsals will start—following Christmas—and then I should be glad if you could accommodate a stranger within the gates. But not if it gives you much inconvenience. Frankly, it would save me a lot of hotel expenses, which at the moment, I can ill spare. One doesn't get a lot of money for what one wants to write, though a great deal is offered for what suits certain journals. But I don't want to be heralded into hell for that sort of thing.

I'm afraid you'll find me an unshakable materialist: baptised into it, confirmed in it, and in daily communion with that faith. Scientifically and spiritually, I am a materialist. Our God the gold sovereign has hidden his face from us, and we are in a nice plight! However, we can, I hope, talk of these things anon.

With Warm Wishes
Sean O'Casey

From Eugene O'Neill [1]

TS. O'CASEY
THE MADISON HOTEL
FIFTEEN EAST FIFTY EIGHTH STREET
NEW YORK
[15 DECEMBER 1933]

My dear Sean O'Casey,

I have been meaning to drop you a grateful line ever since I finished reading your "Within The Gates". It is a splendid piece of work. My enthusiastic congratulations to you! I was especially moved—and greenly envious, I confess!—by its rare and sensitive poetical beauty. I wish to God I could write like that!

All who admire your work here—and there are a lot of us!—are hoping the play may be placed with the right management to give it the New York production it deserves. And when it is produced I hope you may come to this country and that while you are here you and Mrs O'Casey will find time to visit Mrs O'Neill and me in our home in Georgia.

I have just seen the English edition of "Within The Gates" and I deeply appreciate your generous reference to "Mourning Becomes Electra".[2] If anything about that play has suggested anything which was of the slightest service to "Within The Gates" I am only too flattered and I like my trilogy all the better for it!

Good luck to you! My admiration for your work—and all personal good wishes!

Eugene O'Neill

[1] Eugene O'Neill (1888–1953), the American playwright. Mrs. Carlotta O'Neill informed me that all of O'Casey's letters to O'Neill were destroyed. Only two letters from O'Neill to O'Casey have been found in O'Casey's papers, this one, and the letter of 5 August 1943, Vol. II.

[2] See "Notes for Production," *Within the Gates* (1933): "If possible, the Curtain intervening between the opening of the play and the scenes following, should be one showing the Park Gates, stiff and formal, dignified and insolent. . . . The above idea of a front curtain was derived from Eugene O'Neill's suggestion of a front curtain for his great play, *Mourning Becomes Electra*." O'Neill's play was first performed in New York on 26 October 1931.

P.S.

For years, every time I've read a new play of yours, I've meant to write to you to this same effect—and my only excuse for not having done so is that where letters are concerned I'm the laziest man on earth!

To Time and Tide

16 DECEMBER 1933

MR. ST. JOHN ERVINE

Sir,—Though St. John Ervine is well fitted to give an answer for the hope and faith that are in him, I should like to say how close I am to him in his denunciation of the vulgarity and sensationalism that stems out of certain sections of the press.[1]

A short time ago a fellow, Gordon Beccles, attached to the very paper St. John Ervine mentions, rang me up and asked if he could jump into a car and come down to talk to me about my play. My wife told him that I was busy and did not wish to be disturbed. He then asked her about the condition of my eyes, and was requested by my wife in my own presence to say nothing about this. This request was made to him several times, and he promised to say nothing. The next morning the subject was used as a splash-line in the paper. It is abominable that a person's private feelings should be abused in this way simply because Peer Beaverbrook wishes to lift the circulation of his paper by a few copies. If I were as hefty now as I was twenty years ago, this fellow would not do it a second time, even with Beaverbrook behind him.[2]

In my opinion, St. John Ervine is one of the cleverest and most forcible writers we have, and his articles are invariably stimulating and sensible. The *Daily Express* lost something when they lost him. I do not agree with all his views—for instance—I differ wholly from the views he has given of Eugene O'Neill as a dramatist—but there is no doubt of St. John Ervine's character and force in everything that he writes. I cordially yield him my earnest admiration and good wishes.

I am, etc.,
Sean O'Casey

Chalfont St. Giles,
Buckinghamshire.

[1] A reference to the views St. John Ervine had expressed in the "Notes on the Way" column in *Time and Tide,* which he had written for the month of November 1933.

[2] Gordon Beckles did "do it a second time." See his review of the London production of *Within the Gates* in the *Daily Express,* 8 February 1934, and the letters by O'Casey and Beckles in the *Daily Express,* 12 February 1934.

To The Theatre Guild

TC. O'CASEY

26 DECEMBER 1933

MESSRS THE DIRECTORS,
THE THEATRE GUILD,
NEW YORK.

Dear Sirs—

Mr George Jean Nathan has written to [me] saying that The Theatre Guild has decided not to interest themselves in my play, "Within The Gates." It was with the deepest regret that I heard of the refusal.

Now that no ulterior motive can be tacked on to what I say, may I express my sincere admiration for all that The Theatre Guild has done for the Drama, and add to my admiration my sincere wish that many new and many great things may be done by the Guild in the future.

I Am,
Sincerely Yours,
[*Sean O'Casey*]

To George Jean Nathan

MS. CORNELL

CHALFONT ST. GILES
27 DECEMBER 1933

Dear George Jean Nathan—

I am indeed sorry to hear that the Theatre Guild decided against taking up the production of "Within The Gates." I suffered the same set-back with expectations about "The Silver Tassie." C. B. Cochran told me that he was almost certain they would produce it, but, afterwards, told me that they had changed their mind. But their rejection of the play isnt anything like the rejection of "The Silver Tassie" by The Abbey Theatre some years ago. That forced me into a fight that lasted a long time, and many echoes of it are lingering in many places still.

All that is worrying me now is that you should be giving yourself too much trouble to get the play done. You are a busy man, and have a hell of a lot to do without spending energy and time over my work.

If you could let me have a copy of anything you have written about the play I should be grateful. I have got a few very sensible notices here. I enclose one from "The Times." [1]

I have got a fine letter from Eugene O'Neill, and will answer it in a day or so.

I have taken the offer of a young producer here who is being backed by some Jewish friends, in preference to an ordinary commercial production. This man did "splendid work some years ago under impossible conditions," according to Shaw; he is coming back to the theatre—he should never have been allowed to leave it—and I have given him my play as a first venture. I hope it may be a great success for my own sake and for his. Now dont worry too much about my play. Thanks and thanks again for all you have done for me.

Warm Wishes
Yours As Ever.
Seen O'Casey

[1] "Mr. O'Casey's New Play, *Within the Gates*: Return of Poetry to the Theatre, From our Dramatic Critic," *The Times,* London, 28 November 1933.

To Lady Astor

MS. Astor
Chalfont St. Giles
30 December 1933

My dear Lady Astor—

I thank you again for your fine kindness in giving a room in your London home to Eileen & me during the rehearsals of "Within The Gates". Margery Mars will be playing the very important part of "The Young Whore". The rehearsals of this play will be particularly hard, so a room in London will save me a tremendous lot of energy by setting aside the necessity of going down to, & coming up from Chalfont St Giles.

I should like to let you know that the weakness of my eyes, directly or indirectly, is in no way infectious whatsoever.

Again I thank you for your kindness & look forward to the chance of thanking you once more in person.

Yours Sincerely
Sean O'Casey

To Oliver St. John Gogarty

MS. GOGARTY

C/O LADY ASTOR
4, ST JAMES'S SQUARE
LONDON, S.W.1.
[5 JANUARY 1934] [1]

Dear Oliver—

You seem to be in a hell of a mess. 90,000! Do they think they'll sell 90,000? [2]

It looks as if there was a lot of doubt about Murphy. If he got the £125 as for work done, he wouldn't be willing to facilitate any re-arrangement. Leave this open till you're sure of how much of the £125 Putnam's will give him for "expenses in his journey to Dublin". He journeyed to Dublin for other reasons besides that of helping you in your book.

Who is Mr. Medley?[3] Solicitors to the Authors' Society? never 'eard of 'im!

However, I'll make inquiries today. What about sending the whole thing to the Authors' Society?

I'm just off to rehearsal now, & will write you again later—the whole thing seems damn curious.

Sean

[1] Postmarked date.

[2] A reference to the book of reminiscences Gogarty had just contracted to write, *As I Was Walking Down Sackville Street* (London, Rich & Cowan, 1937).

[3] C. D. Medley, the literary executor of George Moore.

To Lady Astor

MS. ASTOR

4 ST. JAMES'S SQUARE, LONDON
6 JANUARY 1934

Dear Lady Astor—

Here I am now in your home as comfortable as I ever hope to be or wish to be saeculo saeculorum. It is so cosy & agreeable that I have ventured to stay here during the week-end, rather than take on myself the fatigue of a visit to Chalfont. You have been very kind & very generous, and I thank you very heartily indeed.

We have now plunged into the work of reheasals, & have all the Caste (30) arranged, except one part only. "The Young Whore" is to be played by Margery Mars; "The Bishop" by [Douglas] Jeffries; and "The Dreamer" by Sir Basil Bartlett.

I think the Caste is a good one, & am pleased with it.

The Producer [Norman MacDermott] is, I think, a very clever fellow, and an Artist. He has been out of the Theatre for some time, is returning to Management, & his first venture is my play.

Again I thank you for your kind thought and action, and will quietly take advantage of both, understanding, of course, that you will at once let me know if you want the suite, or whenever my presence may prove to be inconvenient to you.

With Warm Regards,
Sean O'Casey

From J. Ramsay MacDonald

TS. O'CASEY

10, DOWNING STREET
WHITEHALL
10 JANUARY 1934

PERSONAL & PRIVATE.
SEAN O'CASEY ESQ.,
AT 4, ST. JAMES'S SQUARE,
S.W.1.

My dear Sean,

I was very glad to have your letter. Nothing would give me greater pleasure than to see your play, but I have almost had to forget that there is such a thing as a theatre in existence, as my work continues late into the evening and, at best, is so uncertain in its calls from day to day that I rarely can make engagements ahead, unless imposed by necessity.

I have read Macmillan's book [1] and find in it many echoes of what I myself have been saying and writing for years. Before I had read the book I had begun a series of conferences somewhat on its lines. Here one has to meet actual difficulties and deal with actual persons, and that is a totally different job from working out ideas. If, for instance, you remember what he wrote in his chapter about the co-ordination of certain industries, including coal, and would look at 'The Times' during the last day or two and read this morning's leading article on the subject of coal, you will understand something of the obstacles we have to surmount in

[1] Harold Macmillan, *Reconstruction: A Plea For a National Policy* (London, Macmillan, 1933).

our attempts to apply what, in Macmillan's book, is such a reasonable proposal. Again and again he very wisely says that he is not producing a detailed plan. If he did attempt that, and had gone on to present the details of the machine which he would construct, he either never would have finished his book at all, or would have shown his readers what those who are working on the lines of his plan have to surmount. At the same time, I welcome the book, because it will raise a more general interest in the problem, so that if we have to come into conflict with certain of the interests concerned, we may have an intelligent public opinion to support us. The gap between an idea and the working it out in detail is very wide and contains really all the difficult problems, as I am sure you know when you first get hold of an idea for a play and then sit down and work it out in its stage situations.

I wish I saw you oftener, but life seems to be taken up with an endless stream of "concerns".

Yours always,
J. Ramsay MacDonald

To Norman MacDermott

TC. O'CASEY [1]

[CHALFONT ST. GILES]
[? JANUARY 1934]

Alteration in Scene 1, Page 19-21

O. Attendant:— . . . gitewye to a fuller 'en a nobler life!

Bishop's Sister (a little frightened)—Gilbert, come away before this develops into a common quarrel.

Atheist (mockingly, indicating the C. Attendants—, to the Bishop's sister) —Let the right 'en reverend gennelman 'ave a look at wot is anxious ('opes) to pass through a gitewye to a nobler life, before you tike 'im to a plice of sifety!

Bishop (roused to indignation—to The Atheist)—A soldier, fighting under Christ's banner, sir, flies from nothing, flies from nothing, sir!

Bishop's Sister (catching the Bishop's arm, and vigorously pulling him off) Oh, for goodness' sake, Gilbert, come away and look at the swans!

Bishop (relieved at being carried off—as he goes off)—Swans? yes; quite.

---

[1] Rough draft of changes in the published text of *Within the Gates,* and some comments on the staging.

Alteration Same scene, page 24.

Couldnt the boy who comes in with the two nursemaids knock down the chairs, so leaving the subsequent entry of C Attendants as it is?

Dreamer:—Kill off, O God, the creeping things that crawl about and soil the glorious fancies of Thy brooding mind!

Notes About The Summer Chorus.

1 It is, I think, necessary to have the Chorus done as differently as possible from The Spring Chorus. In The Spring Chorus the whole scene, almost, is done in action—marching and counter-marching. I suggest that there should be less of this in The Summer Chorus, and that grouping and movement should take place on the front of the stage as much as possible.

2 The good singers as close to the front as possible, boy and girl, say, standing beside tree to right, and boy and girl standing beside tree to left. Couple to right at an appropriate moment could move to left, and vice versa. Girls might carry coloured sunshades.

3 Opening: Two couples could be seated, or reclining against Rostrum front. Groups or couple strolling about under the trees; or some might march in as before across Rostrum, and then march about among the trees. During this The Bishop could come on with a child walking backwards, or frontways before him, the child holding on to that part of his (Bishop's) cord girdle hanging down behind; the second child, in the same way, holding girdle, following on behind. The crowd rise from their languid positions, standing up, if they be seated, forming a lane, or a circle, in respectful attitudes as the Bishop comes down steps to front. Then The Bishop does a circular movement, standing, as it were, as a living maypole, while the children go round him, the Bishop moving round with the movements of the children; the others could do movements in contrast to the action of children and Bishop. (The children could hold girdle left and right, if this were better than back and front)

4 Picture: The Guardsmen, one at each side, looking over the bushes. On Rostrum, first the Dreamer, then the Bishop, then the Two Chair Attendants crossing over Rostrum, stopping for a moment or two to look at The Bishop playing with the children.

5 First verse of song could be sung as the Bishop is crossing Rostrum with children, and as they are coming down the steps. Second verse as the Bishop plays with the children, and, then, breaking up to end, the last verse could be sung so as to allow suitable exits.

6 The Picnic idea, I'm afraid, wont work.

Perhaps these few hints will help.

[*Sean O'Casey*]

To Norman MacDermott

TC. O'CASEY

[CHALFONT ST. GILES]
28 JANUARY 1934

Dear Norman MacDermott—

I feel it necessary to say a few words in reply to your letter of the 27 inst.

You say "I am very hurt that you left rehearsal last night without a word at the very time during production at which your help was needed most."

You will probably remember that, in the first instance you said that "when I wasnt sure of anything, or thought anything was wrong, or wanted to make a suggestion, I was to do so without hesitation." You will remember that on the night in question I went over to you to ask a question, you turned round, placed your hands on my shoulders and said "Look here, Sean, you mustnt be interrupting me in this way. You must have complete confidence in me—though there was no question of confidence or lack of it—and you must let me go on in my own way." You will see that, as this was said before the whole Company, there was nothing for me to do but to leave you to it for the time being till you got a little cooler. So I left it to you, and went away. Now you come along and in your letter say that "I left when my help was most needed." You ask for help, and, in the same breath, refuse it. Even you cant have it both ways.

You will remember that I was very anxious—as were you—about the movements. That Miss Peters was teaching things that would turn the play into a farce. For instance the hopping about of The Dreamer and The Y. Whore during the dance in the last scene. Here, I understand, when the incident of dying was mentioned, the advice to "gnaw your knuckles" was given. You will remember that when Miss Wilson took up this job of arranging movements, you gave her two days to see what she could do without interference from you, though I was never told of this. When I got to the rehearsal I found that steps were being taught that could never be performed. This, after two days trial, was admitted. So, I think, three days were wasted.

You will remember that when the Spring Chorus was in first rehearsal, I went up to your Office and told you what I thought of it. You will probably remember your answer. You came down to the rehearsal and, when I had pointed out what I thought to be wrong, you said, "well, go down on to the stage and show us precisely what you want." Not a very helpful answer.

You will probably remember when I made a suggestion to help about the figure of the Memorial, you turned on me and hotly told me that "this was your production, and that you wouldnt have this interference," though the interference was connected with trying to save expense. Yet last night you asked my advice about particular costumes.

You frequently quote your experience, but you fail to see, I think, that experience is only of comparative value when new problems are to be solved.

And I beg of you, should we be discussing any problem in your Office, not to pace about the room and shout your opinions at me. Both of us must try to keep our heads clear, and quietly meet any difficulty that may arise.

Sincerely Yours,
[*Sean O'Casey*]

By Gordon Beckles

Daily Express
8 February 1934

A CHALLENGE TO SEAN O'CASEY
WHAT IS HIS NEW PLAY REALLY ABOUT? [1]

Sean O'Casey—his chin cupped in his hands—sat in the stage box with George Bernard Shaw last night, peering down on the darling of his seven-year-long dreams.

Eight years ago, in this very theatre, his first play had been produced. O'Casey was then so nervous that he hid in his Bloomsbury temperance hotel!

"Juno and the Paycock," however, was passionately realistic and full of real people. "Within the Gates" is passionately *un*realistic and peopled with characters that not even poetic drama can justify.

[1] *Within the Gates* opened on 7 February 1934 at the Royalty Theatre, London, directed by Norman MacDermott, with the following cast: Sir Basil Bartlett as Dreamer, Douglas Jefferies as Bishop, Gertrude Sterrold as Bishop's Sister, Richard Caldicot as Atheist, Marjorie Mars as Young Whore, Alan Wheatley as Gardener, Ronald Waters as Guardsman, Walter Herbage as First Chair Attendant, Jack Twyman as Second Chair Attendant, Isobel Scaife as First Nursemaid, Daphne Scorer as Second Nursemaid, Marie Ault as The Old Woman, Molly Tyson as Policewoman, Patrick Barr as Salvation Army Officer, Edward Mervyn as Man in Bowler Hat, Richard Caldicot as Man in Burberry, Denis Alban as Foreman.

The chief characters are a Park prostitute and a Bishop.

They meet within the Park's gates, and their meetings sustain the continuity of the play.

There is music and dancing, in the manner of Greek drama: a Poet, an Atheist, a Policeman, an Evangelist, and so on. O'Casey is obviously trying to say something, desperately, but incoherently.

The piece is a cry from the heart.

It is not a play.

But O'Casey didn't seem to mind last night. He sat, with a twisted smile, listening to his own ranting denounciations of the world's hypocrisy. Miss Marjorie Mars, as the young prostitute, was giving a fine performance; but, like every other character (Cockneys included), she was handicapped by the Hibernian atmosphere and rhetoric.

Indeed, dialogue and characterisation alike, were devastatingly Dublin.

The end?

The young prostitute dies; the Bishop is overwhelmed; *she is his illegitimate daughter.*

Yet I challenge Mr. O'Casey to tell the world what this play is *really* about.

G[ordon] B[eckles]

By James Agate

Sunday Times
11 February 1934

BEYOND THE AGATES
A Difficult Play

WITHIN THE GATES
A Play. By Sean O'Casey

Royalty Wednesday, 7 February

Sainte-Beuve said—and I apologise for so many good things occurring in French—that there were three legitimate kinds of criticism. The first was the critic's own private judgment to be delivered between four walls and to intimate friends, the note of such judgment being predilection or antipathy. But since the critic is not the universal model and other opinion may follow other moulds, the second sort of critic should put himself on one side and even think against his own grain. Compromise, if you like, but compromise informed by equity and intelligence. The third kind of critic shows lenience and consideration on the score of an author's standing. So far Sainte-Beuve, in as nearly his own words as I can remember. What a case is one in, then, who on leaving the theatre would have whispered to any of the four walls the words "pretentious rubbish," knew that he had left an audience violently disagreeing with him, and now remembers having loudly spoken of Mr. Sean O'Casey as the greatest living dramatist but one! So we will cross out "rubbish" and leave the word "pretentious." Next we will try to see what Mr. O'Casey was pretending, informing our guesses with as much "equity and intelligence" as we can muster. Last, we will endeavour to decide to what extent we were taken in.

But first we must do a little ground-clearing and explain that "pretentious rubbish" is not nearly so offensive as it sounds. Grandeur of form may well go with vacuity of content, and it is the latter which makes the thing rubbish and the combination of the two which makes that rubbish pretentious. See Swinburne. Mr. O'Casey is a most distinguished craftsman as well as a poet, and as such is obviously incapable of thinking of any subject except in terms of art. "Within the Gates" is obviously a work of art, just as some pictures are works of art in which everything judged by any but the artistic rule is manifestly cock-eyed. Now carry this a step further. We know to our amazement that pictures which make no appeal to the eye may still be works of art, and we have learned to our chagrin that musical compositions which make no appeal to the ear are to be placed in the same category. Is it similarly laid down that a play which runs counter to the mind in its rational functioning may still be a work of art in virtue of its appeal to eye and ear?

Mr. O'Casey's eye-appeal is the old business of Rodinesque, Volga-Boatmannish stage-grouping—in this case a conglomeration of Down-and-Outs with heads uniformly bowed and all of them thinking everything bloody. The appeal to the ear consists in the splendour of Mr. O'Casey's beautifully muscled prose—or is it poetry?—which is sometimes overlaid and spoiled by music. I find a note scribbled in my programme to the effect that not one word of the great chant at the beginning of the second act reached me. But this was only an unhappy detail. Mr. O'Casey, as we have known, can write all kinds of great stuff, from the scrumptious majestic to the overheard bar-parlour, and he fits both into his pattern adroitly. But does or doesn't it matter what people in a play say? Or is the manner of their talk the only thing? An eminent colleague in a passage of enthusiasm for this play's essential rhythm either let slip or was careful to insist upon the parenthesis:—"Whatever one's view may be of its opinion." [1] "Not 'arf hedgin', aint 'e!" as one of Mr. O'Casey's park-keepers

[1] Along with this parenthesis, Charles Morgan, drama critic of *The Times,* 8 February, stated in his review: "Mr. O'Casey's fierce play is that very rare thing—a modern morality play that is not a pamphlet but a work of art." And he concluded: "Except in Strindberg and the early O'Neill, there are no precedents for Mr. O'Casey. He is opening up a new country of the imagination from which, by its rigid photography, the fashionable theatre has hitherto been shut out."

might easily remark. There is a famous line of French poetry—I again apologise—which runs:—"Qu'importe la coupe pourvu qu'on ait l'ivresse?" Modern fashion and my colleague would appear to put it the other way round:—"What does the wine matter so long as the cup is gold?" The alternative view is that what Mr. O'Casey's characters say does actually matter. What, then, do they say?

The answer is—a lot of things all couched in the form of groans, moans, grunts, sneers, snarls, yells of rage, and whoops of despair. Everything in the garden's unlovely, and there is no health in either flowers or weeds. There is a Bishop who prattles about establishing contact with his fellow-creatures, thrusts his nose in where it isn't wanted, and when appealed to in a case of real distress can only offer the empty formality of words. She who appeals is a street-walker, and his own daughter, for alas, the Bishop was once a naughty boy! Is Mr. O'Casey's sock in the episcopal jaw what my distinguished colleague means by the persons in this drama being "not particular instances merely, but universals also"?

The young street-walker is the idealised harlot that intellectual Bloomsbury is always running after. She prates rather than prattles, uses words like "oblate," and talks about "composing hymns to intellectual beauty." And then she is, I submit, unreasonably inconsistent. She complains that her customers want no more than the French pigeons—third apologies!—to wit, "bon souper, bon gite, et le reste." And again: "A sigh, a sob of pain, a thought higher than their own from a woman, and they're all hurrying home." But of course! Since at home and from a wife they can get sighs and sobs and thoughts higher than their own in plenty! Yet this idealist takes a man's money and then bilks him. When her drunken old mother complains that she is going to die, she screams at her: "I'd dance and sing if I thought you'd die in an hour!" The Old Woman who begins as harridan ends in the Kathleen-Ni-Houlihan vein, depositing a wreath at the foot of a War Memorial and speaking in purple prose: "O soldier in bronze, cold guard of remembrance for those who rode out on swift horses to battle and fell. . . ." Yet only a few minutes previously she had been threatening to tear every stitch off her daughter.

And so one might go on through the whole cast from the park-gardener with his unusual lyricism to the Down-and-Outs continually chorussing off-stage another wholly unintelligible chant. Do we imagine that in these victims of society we have at last fastened Mr. O'Casey down to something, if only a break in the evening hate? Never were playgoers more mistaken, for the play has a Dreamer, the ethereal offspring of Galsworthy and Mr. Drinkwater, who at the end of the play says roundly that the Down-and-Outs are scum and ought to be down-and-outed. After which he expresses the opinion that the street-walker is the best of the lot, since she has courage, if only of the despairing sort.

It is difficult to separate one's disagreement of opinion from the place of that opinion in a work of art. That we should impatiently ask what is biting Mr. O'Casey does not affect his right to be bitten, with, if he likes, unending objurgations; still, it would be a little boring if all Shakespeare's sonnets had been written on the theme of "Tired with all these, for restful death I cry." This play is obviously non-realistic, and therefore one must not put it to a naturalistic test. What a pity, then, that Mr. O'Casey should make it so difficult for us by making his characters both real and unreal, earthbound and fantastic, so that his play reads like "Alice in Wonderland" interleaved with Euclid!

But perhaps this is the new medium which the unusual rhythm of this play is said to usher in? If that is so, then there is one dramatic critic who will have to go out of business. I think I can understand park-keepers, prelates, and, at a pinch, prostitutes, and I try to grapple with symbols, sublimations, subfuscations, and substantiations whereby an author shelves his characters to substitute himself. But I find it difficult to do these two things at the same time, and in my view the characters in every play should decide at the beginning whether they are going to be a metaphysical all-my-eye or a real Betty Martin. The trouble is that Mr. O'Casey is essentially an Irishman who, while labelling his characters English and dropping the accent, still retains the Irish idiom. Take the Old Woman, for example. Any drunken old lady who is Irish has that poetry in her which befits her for Kathleen-Ni-Houlihan, whereas the capacity to soar is not in the English Mrs. Gamp. If this play were translated back into the Irish in which it was conceived one might take a very different view of it.

The acting is uneven. The two park-keepers of Messrs. Walter Herbage and Jack Twyman were admirable, and so too were the nursemaids of Mesdames Isobel Scaife and Daphne Scorer. But there was a Guardsman who had obviously left Oxford in order to enlist, and a singing gardener who perhaps could not be blamed for bringing a musical-comedy air to the twofold task of bedding-out the daffodils and crooning about his girl. And then the ecstatics were all wrong. The street-walker of Miss Marjorie Mars struck one as a plain sensible girl whose head would run not to nonsense about intellectual beauty, but merely to keeping herself spruce and her room clean and tidy for the gentlemen. The Old Woman was played by Miss Marie Ault, who was obviously flummoxed at having to be the embodiment of whatever it is the old girl embodies, and so sought and found refuge in a portrait which might have been that of a theatrical landlady mothering low comedians at Kensal Green. Mr. Douglas Jefferies had a fair shot at the Bishop, though Mr. O'Casey obviously contemplated an oilier scoundrel.

The Dreamer is a nightmare part for any young actor, and Sir Basil Bartlett played the character as if he were still at Oxford amid whose circumspection nobody, of course, could be expected to see a dream walking. The crowd or chorus was excellent, and with admirable discretion the producer gave us the minimum of that intoning of which half a loaf is so much better than a whole one. The mood of the occasional music alternated between coronachs, dirges, and the smash hit of a musical show, and one got rather tired of those Park railings in front of which the whole thing took place.

To Daily Express

12 February 1934

SEAN O'CASEY AND GORDON BECKLES AT LOGGERHEADS

A remarkable controversy has arisen following Gordon Beckles' criticism in the "Daily Express" of Mr. Sean O'Casey's new play, "Within the Gates." Yesterday the Editor of the "Daily Express" received the following letter:—

To the Editor of the
"Daily Express"

SIR,—In the "Daily Express" for February 8 your dramatic critic, Gordon Beckles, gave what he thought to be a criticism of my play, "Within the Gates."

He prefaced his criticism by stating that, when I first came to London, I was so overwhelmed by nervousness that I was afraid to go to the Royalty Theatre, where a play of mine was then running.

If I felt that Gordon Beckles had in him the germ of a gentleman, I should ask him politely to withdraw this statement; but, knowing him to be what he is, I simply say that this statement is a lie, and a shabby lie, too.

Passing into his criticism, he says that the Young Whore is the illegitimate child of the Bishop, and he puts this phrase into italics, which, I imagine, demonstrates the mind of the man. The tailoring of this phrase into italics, I repeat, demonstrates the mind of the man, and needs no comment from me.

Gordon Beckles challenges me to tell him what the play really means. My mission in life is not to give to Gordon Beckles a higher mind than he has, for I am not a worker of miracles.

I always felt inclined to believe in the survival of the souls of animals, and now I know my belief to be well founded, for here we have an instance of the reincarnation of Balaam's ass, whose mouth no angel has yet opened.

Sean O'Casey

Hillcrest, Chalfont St. Giles, Bucks.

This letter was shown to Mr. Gordon Beckles, who wrote the following reply:—

To the Editor of the
"Daily Express"

SIR,—Both Mr. O'Casey's letter and play exemplify one of the distinguishing characteristics of this muddle-headed age: *the increasing disinclination of the cobbler to stick to his last.*

Ten years ago Mr. O'Casey proved himself a master of stage realism. He wrote "Juno and the Paycock" and "The Plough and the Stars," both plays of outstanding power, in a Dublin tenement.

Eight years ago he came to London, arriving on March 4, 1926. The late James Bernard Fagan arranged that he should stay at a Bloomsbury hotel a few yards away from the Fagan flat.

On the night of March 5 I met O'Casey in this hotel; he drank ginger-ale while I drank—I am almost sure—something stronger.

O'Casey discussed with me an unwritten play, which he called "The Red Lily."

"It is the drama of a fallen woman," he said. I wrote the word "prostitute," that same night, while recording the conversation for the defunct "Daily Graphic." A sub-editor altered it back again to "fallen woman"!

O'Casey admitted that he had not visited his own play on the previous night. Indeed, it was not until a week later that Fagan persuaded the shy and highly-strung Dubliner to see his first English audience.

Shortly afterwards O'Casey settled down to a life of artistic self-indulgence, discarding all the tools of his trade. "Within the Gates"—which apparently grew out of his "Red Lily" idea—is a perfect specimen of an undisciplined mind ranting against the world in general.

Now, when ordinary people give way to self-indulgence it is bad enough; but when genius—great talent, call it what you will—goes astray it is almost criminal.

For genius belongs not only to the man in whom it is born, but to the world at large.

If great scientists, doctors, and others concerned with the physical welfare of humanity indulged their genius in any way that passing fancy dictated—if a surgeon, say, decided to retrogress to experiments in barbering—he would be condemned as wilfully prostituting his talents.

How much worse when a man gifted with the power to sway millions by his plays prostitutes his natural gifts by meandering experiments in dramatic forms that were born and perfected in the heyday of Greece some thousands of years ago; and ranting Socialistic nonsense expressed in dialogue as obtuse in texture as the closing reference, in his letter, to Balaam's ass.

I should be flattered by this reference; for it was Balaam's ass who first saw the vision, while Balaam himself was a silly and pig-headed fellow.

I am, Your Dramatic Critic,

Gordon Beckles

From T. E. Lawrence to Lady Astor [1]

PS. LAWRENCE

15 FEBRUARY 1934

Mi Piresse, If you see O'Casey again, before this letter grows cold, will you bless him from me? For I have seen his Park play twice, and it has cost me only half-a-crown in all. That is real kindness.

I don't want to see it again, for it is too painful, despite its beauty. How far he has gone since he was in Ireland, on paper! This play is London and human (and inhuman) nature: all of us, in fact; and about as helpless.

And talking of inhumanity, how dare he pile loads like these upon his actors and actresses? He asks the impossible, but gets, I think, more than he deserves. Poor dumb laden beasts.

The poignancy of Act ii, *The Tassie*, is not here: it could not be, for much lay in the contrast of that act's neighbours, in the wonderful lighting and setting; in the experience which came rawly upon those new from the war. This play deals with the life we all have to lead (temporarily) and we dare not detach ourselves from it and criticise or pass judgement. That's why I do not want to see it again. However I shall read it once more, in the peace of my cottage, which is ever so far away from his park—and equally solid, too, God be praised.

I was right in feeling that this play would be bigger seen and heard, then merely read.

Bless him again. He is a great man, still in movement. May it be long before he grows slow, stops, returns on his tracks! I have learned a great deal from him.

Your Airman

[1] *The Letters of T. E. Lawrence,* edited by David Garnett (London, Jonathan Cape, 1938), Letter 510. And at the end of a letter of 31 December 1933 to Lady Astor, Lawrence writes: "O'Casey? Shawn? Indeed yes, I have just finished his new play [*Within the Gates*]. The second act of *The Silver Tassie* was my greatest theatre experience, and here is a whole play in that manner. It will play better than it reads."

When a rare Irishman does go on growing, you see, he surpasses most men. Alas that they are so rare.

Making for Southampton again.

T.E.S.

To Sunday Times

18 FEBRUARY 1934

[*The Editor,*
Dear Sir—

The Shaping of an Agate] [1]

Mr Agate heads his criticism of my play "Within The Gates" with the front curtain phrases of "Beyond The Agates," and "A Difficult Play." Then up goes the curtain on the criticism and we see Mr Agate being prompted by Sainte-Beuve, an author famous, I'm told, for being afraid to attend his friend's funeral. Encouraged by Sainte-Beuve, Mr Agate tells his audience that "Within The Gates" is "pretentious rubbish." He gently takes the word "rubbish" away, and, a few sentences farther on, he quietly puts it back again. Now we have been told by Mr Agate that the play was beyond him—which we regard as a joke—and that it is a difficult play. If the play be difficult how can it be dismissed by the breezy or the whispered term of "pretentious rubbish"? He tells us that "grandeur of form may well go with vacuity of content. See Swinburne." In this instance grandeur of form can hardly go well, or well go, with vacuity of content, for in this play the content must make the form, and how can grandeur of form blossom out of pretentious rubbish? Has it ever done so? Sending me running after Swinburne wont do, not for me, anyhow, thank you kindly, for I refuse to build an opinion on my play out of Agate, into Swinburne, and back into Agate again.

"O'Casey," he says, "is obviously incapable of thinking of any subject except in terms of art, and, obviously, 'Within The Gates' is a work of

[1] On 12 February O'Casey wrote this fifteen-hundred-word reply to James Agate's review of *Within the Gates,* titled "Beyond the Agates," *Sunday Times,* 11 February. The editor cut the letter to a third of its original length, omitting all the material in square brackets, and printed it with the following lead: "MR. SEAN O'CASEY AND MR. AGATE, CRITIC'S RETORT. Mr. Sean O'Casey sends us a long reply to Mr. James Agate's criticism of his play 'Within the Gates,' which appeared in the *Sunday Times* last week. We are unable to give the whole letter, but the salient parts of it follow:—" O'Casey sent a typed carbon of the original to Nathan in his letter of 22 February. For a continuation of this controversy, see O'Casey's *The Flying Wasp* (London, Macmillan, 1937).

art." If obviously, how can the play be difficult; if it be a work of art how can it be rubbish. And, if O'Casey be incapable of thinking in a form other than a form of art, how can the play be pretentious? How can a man pretend in the doing of a thing if he be incapable of doing it in any other way? And does Mr Agate object to a play being a work of art? Is he anxious to exile art out of the Drama?

[He instances "pictures which, though making no appeal to the eye, are works of art, and of music which, though making no appeal to the ear, are to be placed in the same category." The criticism becomes more difficult than the play, and Mr Agate goes a curious road to find fault or find favour with the work.]

"The appeal to the ear in the play," he says, "consists in the splendour of O'Casey's muscled prose." A work of art, splendour of muscled prose, grandeur of form, and yet the thing is nothing more than pretentious rubbish!

["Not one word of the splendid chant in the beginning of the second act reached me." How did Mr Agate know that the chant was splendid if he didnt hear a word of it? And even if he heard every word of it how could he call it splendid, if it was nothing but pretentious rubbish? See Swinburne again, I suppose.

Mr Agate asks if it matters what people say in a play, or is the manner of the talk the only thing. The answer is obvious—to use a phrase of Mr Agate's—: the manner and the matter are important, even if they be not equally so. What does the wine matter so long as the cup is gold, questions Mr Agate. If we think of the wine then the composition of the cup matters little; if we think of the cup, then what fills the cup is immaterial; but in a play—if he insists on the simile—the cup and the wine, mingling as cup and wine never mingle, form one whole of splendour of muscled prose and grandeur of form. The gold cup which is the grandeur of form, and the wine which is the vacuity of content together form the play, and I hold that vacuity of content in a play could never rise into grandeur of form. Mr Agate is simply trying to praise and blame at the same time, and he does it clumsily.]

The play's content is, says Mr Agate, "moans, groans, sneers, snarls, yells of rage, and whoops of despair." The world is full of them today—whether Mr Agate hears them or not—and I am not responsible for them. [But the play is not all a moan; we have the Spring Chorus, the Summer Chorus, and Land of Hope and Glory—which should appeal specially to our critic—and the Dreamer's call to waken up our courage.

Mr Agate doesnt like The Young Whore; he sees no symbolism in the word "Young," and calls her an "idealised harlot that intellectual Bloomsbury is always running after." A big sneer and a little snarl here. Though knowing little of Bloomsbury, I venture to say that Bloomsbury has persons as intelligent and as important to England as persons who live in Beaconsfield or Buckingham. "Yet this idealised harlot," says

Mr Agate, "takes a man's money and bilks him." This, he thinks, is unreasonably inconsistent. Here Mr Agate obviously shows that he doesnt know what he's talking about. There was an idealist once who was asked whom he thought his master to be, and the idealist answered, "Thou art the Christ, the Son of the living God." A few minutes later, when his master was about to be apprehended, the same idealist drew his sword and cut off the ear of the high priest's servant; a few minutes later the same idealist, when he was taxed with friendship for his master, cursed and snarled and shouted that he knew not the man. This character in this drama was unreasonably inconsistent, too, wasnt he, Mr Agate? Our critic would pardon the old saint, but he would condemn the Young Whore. He sneers when he calls her an idealised character, and snarls when he finds out that she is not.

As for The Old Woman, she begins her "purple prose" long before she reaches the Memorial, and her *end* is not at the Memorial, but in the ranks of the Down And Outs. If Mr Agate opens his eyes he will see hundreds of these women on any Armistice day, busy at the worship of the dead, and he will find, if he follows them, that they may be very different at home. Unfortunately, there is a terrible germ of fact in their worship, for a large part of the golden infancy of England's life is tarnishing now in the bellies of the worms, but Mr Agate either out of complacency or fear, calls a reminder of this fact "pretentious rubbish."]

But the creed of the play is that all this must be faced and overcome. That force and power must be created out of what we have. That only the brave and wise should govern, and that all the rest must serve. [Doesnt Mr Agate agree that the mental and physical must be down and outed? Or is he one of those who delights in the hideous frieze against which the rest of the Nation plays out its life?

He asks to be told what is biting O'Casey: nothing that is not biting him as well, though he may not know it. If he read his own Journal he'd realise that many things are biting into the very heart of England.

Again the play does not call for "restful death," but active life through The Dreamer; life with less of its sham mercy and more of its rough-edged force.

Leaving politics, let us get back to the play.] Mr Agate says "The characters in any play should decide at the beginning whether they are going to be a metaphysical all-my-eye or a real Betty Martin." That is Mr Agate's view, and, in my view, a pitiful view indeed. He would keep poetry and fantasy away from realism or what he thinks is realism, and complains that I make my characters real and unreal, so that the play reads like *Alice In Wonderland* interleaved with Euclid. I do so, sir, because, first, a change is needed in the Theatre, and, second, because life is like that—a blend of fantasy and realism.

There is fantasy and mathematics in the movement of the stars. There is fantasy in the common activities of life. When Mr Agate goes again to a Critics' Circle Dinner, let him, if he can, detach himself from the function, let him gaze and listen, and he will, if he has anything of the artist in him, find a strange fantasy in it all. Fantasy can never be separated from life, except, artificially, on the stage which pretends to portray it.

[Mr Agate moans that if this unusual play—see, he wants plays that are usual—be the new medium of the Drama, he will have to go out of business. If Mr Agate is determined to groan, moan, sneer, snarl, and whoop with despair at any unusual play, at any play that may be difficult, or be beyond him, any play that differs from what he knows to be the truth, the whole truth, and nothing but the truth, so help him, God; if he is going to hiss at "poetry, splendidly muscled prose, and grandeur of form," then, in all humility, I submit that the only honest thing he can do is to give his job to someone else.

I never intended the character of the Bishop to be oily or to be that of a scoundrel.

Mr Agate says that "the capacity to soar is not in the English Mrs Gamp." That is his opinion of the English-woman, and he seems to like this incapacity to be in her; and, in booing fantasy and poetry out of the Theatre, he is doing his bit to keep her from seeing the shadows of stars shining in the mire.

Had I had my way, Mr Agate would have seen more fantasy and formalism in the play, and less of that realism which he seems to like so much, and which has nothing whatever to do with life, and less to do with the Theatre whose elemental vigor is to be found in the phrase of "let's pretend."

Sincerely Yours,
Sean O'Casey]

Mr. Agate makes this rejoinder:—My defence is that of the thief who pleads that he was not the man who asked to be shown some diamond tiaras, and alternatively that the pearl necklace found its own way into his pocket and so stole itself.

I therefore plead Walt Whitman's "Do I contradict myself? Very well, then, I contradict myself!" Alternatively, I plead that the contradictions of which Mr. O'Casey complains were resolved in my article and shown to be no contradictions.

The difficulty is that I write in English and Mr. O'Casey thinks in Irish. This being so, I suggest that if Mr. O'Casey will get some Anglo-Hibernian to explain my article to him, he will realise that his letter was unnecessary.

To George Jean Nathan

MS. CORNELL

CHALFONT ST. GILES
15 FEBRUARY 1934

Dear George Jean Nathan—

Never mind; it cant be helped. I'm sorry you gave yourself so much trouble. It was very kind of you to put yourself out so much for me and the play. I have gone through a pretty bad time of it here, too. The Producer (and Manager) was all enthusiasm at first for the "striking originality of the work," but as the rehearsals went on, he began to get frightened, and cut out almost all the symbolism, and adapted the play "to the human needs of the audience." The result was a production from which the guts and soul were gone. The irony of the thing is that what was to give it life, struck it dead. The Drama has a big battle before it.

Forgive me for not replying to your letter sooner, but I have been very busy indeed.

I return to you the letter sent to you from Sydney Phillips. Please give him my thanks for all he tried to do.

Again, never mind.

With the Warmest Regards.
Sincerely Yours,
Sean O'Casey

To Time and Tide

17 FEBRUARY 1934

STAGE AND SCREEN [1]

Sir,—Mr. Sydney Carroll in his reply to my criticism of the Cinema, calls me a "true Irishman." There is no such person as a "true Irishman." A man is an Irishman, or he isn't—the qualifying adjective is meaningless.

He follows this with the close-up statement that my ignorance of the Film is simply abysmal; but we shall leave that to the judgment of those who read what I and he have said about the matter.

[1] O'Casey wrote the guest column, "Notes on the Way," in *Time and Tide* for the month of February, on the 3rd, 10th, 17th and 24th. On the 3rd he criticized the cinema, in contrast to the stage, and Sidney W. Carroll wrote a reply in the 10 February issue.

Mr. Carroll says he could compile a list of two thousand and more films that owe nothing to the work of the stage; and a list of two thousand and more films that have relied for their method and technique upon theatrical ideas. Does Mr. Carroll go to the Cinema after each meal? What a majestic mind Mr. Carroll must have: five thousand films and he remembers them all! Those that were bad and those that were good; those that owed nothing, and those that owed all to the method and technique of the stage. Mr. Carroll knows two thousands films and more, and he challenges me to point out in any one of them the smallest indebtedness to the stage proper. He remembers every move and every point in two and more thousand films. What a marvellous mind Mr. Carroll must have! And what is the stage proper, for I should very much like to get in touch with the stage improper?

Our friend says that "the farther a film director flees from the Theatre, the nearer he will get to artistic, cinematic salvation." He contradicted this statement himself, but more of this later on. I am now going to ask Mr. Carroll a few questions, which he, as a theatrical manager, ought to be able to answer: when a dramatist offers him a play and he accepts it, does he insert a clause in the contract asking for fifty per cent. of the film rights, and, if he does not, does he know of any other manager who neglects to do so? And if he and they do this, why do they do it? And is it not a fact that, if a dramatist objects to this exaction, the manager will tell him that a production will greatly add to the film value of a play?

Mr. Carroll gives me a list of fifteen films as an example of what can be done by the camera. Of these fifteen I have seen two—"End of St. Petersburg," and "Thunder Over Mexico." Well, we all know the kingly welcome that Hollywood gave to Eisenstein, the creator of "Thunder Over Mexico," so the less Mr. Carroll says about him the better. "The End of St. Petersburg" is a fine film, but I would hesitate to call it a work of art. And, in my opinion, "Thunder Over Mexico," in spirit and in truth, transfigured by colour, line and form, could be done on the stage for a fraction of the cost that went to form the film.

Mr. Carroll says that the film director must look "for Life, Reality, and not stage artifice." Neither Life nor Reality can ever appear on a film. The life will always be a shadow, and the reality will always be a fake. A ship on a sea will always be a celluloid ship on a celluloid sea, and no power on earth or in heaven can ever make it otherwise. On the score of Reality the Film has no advantage over the Theatre. On the score of life the Theatre has a decided advantage over the Film.

It was Mr. Carroll himself who said "the film will always seek help and encouragement from the people of the theatre, and those should not be denied it." Now he tells us that "the farther a film director keeps from the theatre the better." Here we have Mr. Carroll looking in at one window and out of another at the same time. Magic of film technique, I suppose.

Mr. Carroll asks his readers if they ever read anything so nonsensical as my statement that imagination cannot be supplied (this word is his choice and not mine), and that it is within us like the kingdom of heaven. He adds "from where did O'Casey get *his* imagination? Was it planted in him before he was born, before he was educated, before he had the smallest experience of life?" Yes, Mr. Carroll, it was planted in me before I had the smallest experience of life, before I was educated, before I was born: the seed was there as I lay in my mother's womb. "Imagination," says Mr. Carroll, "is a plant that requires a seed, and the seed is supplied by reading, by association, and by the actual contact of life." My dear Mr. Carroll, these things can no more supply us with imagination than they can supply us with intelligence, if the intelligence is not already there to take advantage of them.

Mr. Carroll says that my contention that the camera is boss is nonsensical (everything I say is, apparently nonsensical), and that "the actor, if he likes, can boss the camera and the camera-man into absolute subservience." Mr. Carroll need not tell me what I already know; but if the actor bosses the camera, then the art that appears upon the screen is the art of the actor, and not the art of the camera, and, consequently not the art of the cinema.

Lastly, Mr. Carroll says that if a "picture of aesthetic pre-eminence and intellectual distinction were presented to the millions who patronise the Cinema, they would feel the same sense of exaltation as a true work of art always causes even in an untrained and uneducated mind."

It would be a sinful waste of time and space for me to make any comment on this last statement.

May I suggest to Mr. Carroll that he should hold his peace till he knows a lot more about the art of the film, and a little more about life.

I am, etc.,
Sean O'Casey

Chalfont St. Giles, Bucks.

To Lord and Lady Astor

MS. Astor

Chalfont St. Giles
22 February 1934

Dear Lord & Lady Astor—

I have to send you many thanks, jewelled thanks, for your great kindness, during our stay in London, to Eileen & to me. No ease and no comfort greater could have been found or given than the comfort and ease enjoyed by us at 4, St James's Square. And the grace and charm of Lord Astor and of yourself gave a dear delight to the comfort and the ease. More thanks, too for your kind and generous way you entertained the company playing in "Within The Gates", & the fair & fine way you and Lord Astor waited on them. "He that is greatest among you, let him be your servant". I thank you both, and thank you deeply.

With Affectionate Regards,
Sean O'Casey

To Oliver St. John Gogarty

MS. GOGARTY

CHALFONT ST. GILES
22 FEBRUARY 1934

Dear Oliver.

I am returning here the contracts you sent to me. I don't like them very much. They seem to be bad. 7500 copies is a huge "first edition", almost that of a "best seller". And there seems to be a big muddle between Murphy & you. You ought to be clear as to what "out of pocket expenses" really mean. The libel clauses, too, seem a bit dangerous.[1] The cheap edition is a bad clause, too. Twelve months isn't long enough time to give a book to sell. Why not send all to the Authors' Society & see what they will say?

I hope you will get out of it allright; or, have you abandoned the scheme?

I have been so busy lately that I hadn't a second to write to you, or to return the contracts.

I suppose you've read what I wrote in 'Time & Tide'.

Ever & Always Regards.
Sean

[1] This turned out to be a prophetic comment, for when *As I Was Walking Down Sackville Street* was published in 1937, Henry Morris Sinclair of Dublin sued Gogarty for libel and won, Gogarty having to pay damages and costs amounting to £2000. For an account of the libel case, and Samuel Beckett's appearance as a witness for his friend Sinclair, see Chapter 19 of Ulick O'Connor's *Oliver St. John Gogarty* (London, Jonathan Cape, 1964).

To George Jean Nathan

MS. CORNELL

CHALFONT ST. GILES
22 FEBRUARY 1934

Dear George Jean Nathan—

Thank you for [Richard] Madden's letter. I don't think I can blame the various Managers for being shy of the play. It is a difficult play, and would mean great work & no little risk.

I return Madden's letter here, & suggest that he shouldn't give himself too much trouble about the work.

I also enclose the criticisms of "Within The Gates"—two of the best, & one of the worst, the last written by Agate of "The [Sunday] Times." With the last criticism is a reply of mine which "The [Sunday] Times" partially published.

There's a Robert Milton here, a Russian, who, I understand, spent a good part of his life in America, & who has asked for a talk about a possible New York production. I am to see him on Saturday or Monday, but, of course, will do nothing without yours or Madden's advice. This talk will be preliminary merely, just to see what he may have to say. Afterwards, I shall let you know—you or Mr. Madden.

With Warm Regards
Sean O'Casey

P.S. I agree: it would be foolish to do anything this Spring.

To Time and Tide

3 MARCH 1934

STAGE AND SCREEN

Sir,—Mr. Sydney Carroll can have the last word and welcome.[1]

I am in agreement with almost all Mr. Grierson says.[2] My contention that Cinematic expression did not, and never could be an art form was simply a doubt, and I am not foolish enough to turn that doubt into a dogma. But Mr. Grierson can kick the back wall out of the theatre and the theatre would still remain the theatre. But kick the camera away, and where's the cinema? The idea that by simply kicking down a back wall the cinema can climb out of space and time, won't, in my opinion, hold. That can only be done through the imagination of a poet Director—say

[1] This is a reply to Carroll's letter in the 10 February issue.
[2] John Grierson's letter appeared in the 24 February issue.

Pudovkin, for instance—and then only by the imagination of the poet finding a communion with the imagination of his audience. But are these Cinema poets free to let their visions and dreams flow out into pictures on the screen? A poet's dreams take form in stone and bronze—Epstein, for instance—into colour and line—John, for instance—into lovely word imagery—Yeats and Joyce, for instance—but is the Cinema poet free to let his vision and his dream flow out into pictures on the screen?

I agree that the real curse is, not that it is destroying the common imagination, but that it is failing to use a vast opportunity for the recreation of the common imagination.

I can't see any division, even the division of a back wall, between Mr. Grierson's opinions and my own.

I am, etc.,
Sean O'Casey

Chalfont St. Giles
Bucks

To Richard J. Madden [1]

TC. O'Casey

Chalfont St. Giles
14 March 1934

Dear Mr Madden—

I thank you for your letter, for the three copies of contract, and for all that you have done in the way of getting a production of "Within The Gates" in America, thanks for each and thanks for all. I enclose the two specified copies of contracts signed as you directed.

There is still an obstacle in the way of a determined agreement connected with the Adaptor of the music to be used in the performance of the play, namely, Mr Herbert Hughes. I will briefly set down the position which he holds and the position he takes up regarding the work he has done in the arrangement of the music.

I had heard of Hughes as an arranger of Irish airs, and, as I knew him, I asked him to do the arranging for airs that I had selected for the songs in the play. The amount of work he did is as follows:

The Summer Chorus, composed and arranged.

I'm not thinking of Blossoms at All, composed and arranged.

Jannice's Dance, composed and arranged.

Arrangements to all other airs which were selected by me, so that he

[1] Richard J. Madden (1880–1951), author's agent and international play broker; O'Casey's American agent. Among his clients were Eugene O'Neill, T. S. Eliot, and W. Somerset Maugham.

is responsible for three airs and I for seven. For this work he has received 12% of my book royalties, £25 advance royalties on the English production, and has been granted 5% of future Amateur fees received by me, and 50% of Gramaphone recording fees that may be received by me.

I have got into touch with him through Mr Aubrey Blackburn, the Secretary of the British League of Dramatists (of which I am a member), and have received from him the following, to me, preposterous demands in return for the use of his music:

$500 advance. 1% on the gross weekly receipts. The $500 to be paid on the delivery of the score.

I told Mr Blackburn what I thought of this demand, and pointed out to him the amount of work I had done with the music, and suggested that the demands made on behalf of Mr Hughes should be the same as those in the English contract so that I might conveniently deduct them from my royalties, and give you no further trouble. However, Blackburn insisted on knowing first the name of the Producer, and seemed to think that American Producers simply loved to fling their money away. I also pointed out that only for the help and enthusiasm of friends, there would be no American production, and so no money for me or for Hughes.

If it were at all possible, I should prefer that someone in America should make a simple arrangement to the tunes which are my selection, and should compose and arrange the airs for the three items mentioned above which are Hughes's composition, and so do without his music altogether. If this wouldnt cost more than say £50 the amount could come out of the advance given to me. If this be impossible, then I would not agree to more than £25 advance royalties to Hughes, plus a ½% on the gross weekly receipts. This, in my opinion, would be a very fair share in return for the work he did.

In my opinion, the terms asked for "the use of my music" are really ludicrous. If you should agree that the music should be done in New York, I could get a groundwork air for the Gardener's song, "I'm not Thinking of Blossoms at all," and send it on to you. Of course Hughes's demands are only "suggested demands," but they are so high that I, for one, should be inclined to do without his music. I enclose a copy of the letter I got from Hughes to which I replied through Aubrey Blackburn, Sec, The League of British Dramatists, 11, Gower Street, London, W.C.1., telling him that I wouldnt consent to such a big demand for such a small amount of work, and saying that the play wasnt a musical comedy, but a serious attempt at drama, and securing a production in America only through the generous efforts of a few friends.

With many, many thanks,
Yours Sincerely,
[*Sean O'Casey*]

To George Jean Nathan

MS. CORNELL

CHALFONT ST. GILES
31 MARCH 1934

Dear George Jean Nathan—

Many thanks for your kind letter. I have returned the contracts signed to Mr. Madden, and hope, of course, that "all things will work together for good for them who love the Drama." I am a little nervous that the play may not be as capable of the fulfillment of its promise as I and you would like. However, it got no chance here for the Producer strained himself trying to make it appear as "human as possible." He withered up before every suggestion of symbolism that was in the play, & laboured to bring it into close touch with the audience so succeeding that he carried it out of their sight altogether. [Charles] Morgan is right when he says—from a cutting sent to me by Mr. Madden—"A great part of . . . the dialogue ought to be chanted and orchestrated with the deliberate intention not of conciliating those who are wedded to the naturalistic convention, but of divorcing them from it." To make it as different as possible from the conventional lies—in my opinion—the hope of success. Our producer failed to see this & shattered the play on the rocks of conventionality.

I am enclosing a skit of an article which you might find suitable for "The American Spectator." [1] If it isn't so, perhaps you would let me have it back. Also a cutting written by a fine young poet [Hugh Mac Diarmid] who wrote "A Drunk Man looks on the Thistle."

Warm Regards.
Sean O'Casey

[1] Sean O'Casey, "Why I Don't Wear Evening Dress," *American Spectator,* November 1934.

To Macmillan & Co. Ltd.

TS. MACMILLAN LONDON

CHALFONT ST. GILES
5 MAY 1934

Dear Sirs,

If you think it advisable or good, I have no objection to the use of the excerpt from "Juno and the Paycock" in Messrs Collins Sons & Co's manual of English Literature for use in schools, though it is funny to think of Capt Boyle fitting himself into a manual for the use of schools. Curious they cant see that "Within The Gates" is better literature than "Juno." So there one has an example of the use of manuals and the use of schools!

I think we should ask for a fee, and, as you suggest, this might be made £6/6/-, to be divided between us.

Sincerely Yours,
E. O'C.
P.P. Sean O'Casey

To Harold Macmillan

TS. MACMILLAN LONDON

CHALFONT ST. GILES
30 MAY 1934

Dear Mr Harold,

Thank you for your letter concerning the MSS of "Windfalls."

I have good and fair copies of the short stories and rough ones of the verses and sketches. These last are now being retyped, and I can let you have them all in a few days.

Mr [Desmond] MacCarthy is to mark for me a part in "I Wanna Woman" that needs a change to permit of publication.[1] I will send all to you, and, perhaps you could let him have this story so that he may mark it and return to me for alteration.

I am to have a production of "Within The Gates" in America—New York—in the fall. Looks as if it will be very different to the one given here. Here is an extract from a letter sent by my Agent, R. J. Madden:

"I must tell you I am more than delighted with the scenic and costume layout prepared by Mr Reynolds. I have seen his sketches, all in colour, from the front curtain to the very end, including every costume to be worn in the play through the four different seasons. Mr Nathan was with us and he hadnt a single criticism to make—nothing but praise."

I thought your American Firm would like to know this. The play will be done under the management of Messrs Tuerk and Bushar.

I'm sorry the loss of the MS gave you and Mr MacCarthy such anxiety; if he had let me know earlier, I could have saved him a deal of trouble.

With Best Wishes
Sean O'Casey

[1] For the controversy over O'Casey's short story, "I Wanna Woman," see his letter to A. E. Harrison, 17 June 1933, note 2.

To Macmillan & Co. Ltd.

TS. MACMILLAN LONDON

CHALFONT ST. GILES
20 JUNE 1934

Dear Sirs,

Enclosed is the short story, "I Wanna Woman," with the passages marked by Mr Desmond MacCarthy modified.

I sincerely hope the changes will be suitable—they are much more discreet than the original passages.

Sincerely Yours,
Sean O'Casey

To Jack Daly [1]

MS. DALY

CHALFONT ST. GILES
21 JUNE 1934

My dear Jack—

I'm afraid I have to disappoint you again—and myself, too, to be candid—for I'm booked to spend that week-end with a friend [2] in Sussex whom I haven't seen for years. He is one of my few friends, a doctor who gave up a splendid West-End practice to take charge of a kids' clinic in Poplar.

He has asked me down a thousand times, & I consented a few weeks' ago to make this trip, then return to see his clinic in the East End. So I can't get out of it. Do you be free on each week end? Could you come some Saturday afternoon & stop till Sunday Evening? We could give you a rough & ready doss for the night. Let me know if you are generally free in the week-ends, & I'll write when a suitable Saturday comes.

And Dont Apologise for any letter you may send to me, at any time,

[1] Jack Daly, a close friend of O'Casey's when they were in Dublin in the St. Laurence O'Toole Club, now living in Oxford.

[2] Dr. Harold Waller, who attended Mrs. O'Casey when Breon was born.

day in or day out, year come, or year gone. I can only be sorry that I neglect to reply to some you send to me, but I have much to do, & take a hell of a long time to do it. I'm always glad to try to read your abominable writing, and delighted to think that my affection for you is accepted & returned to me. We shall soon have a long talk.

With Sincere Affection.
Sean

To Harold Macmillan

TS. MACMILLAN LONDON

CHALFONT ST. GILES
28 JUNE 1934

Dear Mr Harold,

Thank you for your very kind letter accompanying the offer of publication by your Firm of "Windfalls," and thank you for telling me that I can have an advance of what is owing to me for the present financial year.

I have had to write quite a number of letters to America concerning the coming production of "Within The Gates," and had no opportunity of replying to your letter immediately.

I am waiting to hear from America about the advance to be made for the musical arrangements, before I ask for any money on account. Mr Hughes unfortunately demanded a fee—exclusive of royalties—of £100 for the use of his arrangements to the airs, and thinking this to be exceptionally heavy and severe, I decided, on advice from the American Agent, to allow them to secure the services of an American Composer, who, I understand, will not expect anything like the fee demanded by Mr Hughes.

So I will leave the money with you, on reserve as it were, for the present, till I definitely hear from America, when I shall be glad to take advantage of your kind offer.

By the way, I've just read a bit in "The Five Silver Daughters"—chapter called "Dinner in Cardiff" [1]—which, if not as bad, is worse than anything in "I Wanna Woman."

I heard you speaking on the Wireless on The Trades' Unions, and admired your address greatly. But why did the Trades' Unions choose

[1] Louis Golding, *The Five Silver Daughters* (London, Gollancz, 1934).

such a name as "Tolpuddle" [2] to juggle inspiration into the hearts of their members? The damned English, they have no sense of humour. They had no reason to go back farther than 1913,[3] when a battle was fought for the principle of collective bargaining that Tolpuddle never knew.

With The Warmest Regards,
Sean O'Casey

[2] In March 1934 the Trades Union Congress dedicated a memorial to the Tolpuddle Martyrs, six English laborers who in March 1834 had been sentenced to seven years in a penal colony for organizing trade union activities to improve working conditions in the village of Tolpuddle, Dorset. As a result of protest demonstrations all over England, the men became popular heroes, and after two years their sentences were remitted. For a reference to Miles Malleson's play about the Tolpuddle Martyrs, see O'Casey's letter to Peter Newmark, 19 February 1937, note 2.

[3] The 1913 general strike and lock-out in Dublin.

To Lady Astor

MS. Astor

Chalfont St. Giles
17 July 1934

Dear Lady Astor—

Thank you for your very kind letter. Of course I understand that every corner of your kind heart & house was crowded with claimants on your hospitality. I expected that this would be so, & wasn't disappointed.

It was very agreeable to read in your letter that you would like to see the two of us again, but, I'm afraid, we shouldn't be very agreeable company, for, at the moment, we are, &, for some time to come we shall be, in the midst of very worrying activities. For various reasons we are leaving Chalfont St Giles, & have practically settled on a flat in Battersea. Eileen's to have a baby some time in December, & that is one reason why we wish to be in London—to be close to the doctor who is attending to her. There is to be a New York production of my play in October, & the Producers are urging me to go over for rehearsals, which would mean unceasing work & interminable anxiety; but there is no escape. I am just now correcting proofs of a new volume of short stories, verses, & sketches, to be called "Windfalls", which Macmillans are to publish in the Autumn, so you can see what a "tide of woes come rushing on this woful head at once!"

But God never shut one door, but he opened another, as we say in

Ireland; and so we go forward as bravely & as correctly as we can towards an unseen exit that may afford escape & leave all the highly-coloured problems behind us.

I hope you are keeping well, & leaving things alone, now & again, to go apart into the desert for a moment or two away from crowded life.

I read in a local paper of the invasion of Cliveden by hordes of women with trumpets & banners, and of all you said about the weakness that is in man, & all the strength that is in women, but we have all sinned & come far short of the glory of God. But so far, leaving aside the glory of God, we have come far short of the glory of men, & this is that we all must work to recreate.

I hope Lord Astor is well, & your children, Philip, Will, David, Michael, & your married daughter.

With sincere thanks for your many kindnesses.

Sean O'Casey

Don't bother to reply to this.

To George Jean Nathan

MS. Cornell

Chalfont St. Giles
21 July 1934

My dear George Jean Nathan—

I pray you excuse me for not sending you a note before this, but I have had a lot to do, & more than a lot to think about. I am getting a volume of sketches, short stories, & poems published in the Fall, & am now working on the proofs. The Publisher's Reader went on a holiday carrying my MS. in a suitcase; somewhere the case was stolen, & I had to retype the stuff from rough copies, which took a lot of time.

I am getting a bit excited about the American production of "Within The Gates." I thought I should never come to life again after the production given here; but I have heard so much of what is to be done in New York that I feel like one new-risen from the grave.

I have met Messrs Tuerk & Markle, and I like them very much indeed—though I'm a little nervous about the money they are to spend on the play. Anyway, it looks as if the American production will be a memorable one, and it will be, really, the first production of the play—for the one here was a casting out of everything that was in the play.

I think Messrs Tuerk & Markle were pleased with me, & I have arranged to go to New York, sailing on the 13th Sept in The Majestic bringing with me a little prayer & a lot of hope for the success of the venture.

I am looking forward to seeing you, & talking to you, & thrilled at the idea of an introduction to the new life in The States, on, "The New Island," as we call America in Ireland. Strange, that, while England to the Irish seems a far-away land, America is looked upon as the next parish to Galway!

It is great to hear that Lillian Gish is to play the chief part in the play. This is a fine gift to the chance of a great success.

Well, it will be good to meet you & to thank you for all that you have done for me; & to meet, maybe, Eugene O'Neill; & Richard Madden; and to walk on a new earth, & sleep under a new sky.

With Affectionate Regards
Sean O'Casey

To Macmillan & Co. Ltd.

TS. MACMILLAN LONDON

CHALFONT ST. GILES
25 JULY 1934

Dear Sirs,

If you could let me have the advance suggested by you in a previous letter (£100), I shall appreciate it very much.

Could you let me have the following, to be put against my account:

1 Two Plays.[1]
1 Juno (caravan edition).
1 Plays and Controversies.
1 The Celtic Twilight—both by W. B. Yeats.[2]
1 Within The Gates.

Yours Sincerely,
Sean O'Casey

[1] Sean O'Casey, *Two Plays* (1925), *Juno and the Paycock* and *The Shadow of a Gunman.*

[2] W. B. Yeats, *Plays and Controversies* (London, Macmillan, 1923), *The Celtic Twilight* (London, Lawrence and Bullen, 1893).

To Lady Astor

MS. Astor

Chalfont St. Giles
17 August 1934

Dear Lady Astor,

I got a cable from America telling me that tickets were secured fixing up a passage in The Britannic, sailing from Cobh on the 8th of September. I have to sail a little earlier than I first thought so as to be in New York in time to help in selection of Cast for play. I expect to spend four or five days in Mount Stewart [1] before I set off to Philadelphia in the morning. You flew away last Sunday before you showed me what you called "God's Acre" in Cliveden. What with all sorts & kinds of talk, I've seen very little of "The Big House". Even the night on which you asked us to stay with Mr. David [Astor], I saw the river, but little of the house.

I am hard at work on the "page proofs" of my new book, & hope to have this done before I have to pack up my troubles in my old kit bag, & hurry off to the land of Hoover & Walt Whitman.

Thank you for the suit-piece—is this the right term?—you gave me some time ago. I have just had it made up by a local man, & it looks just swell. I shall probably reserve it for the opening night of the play.

It is, however, a nuisance to have to go & leave all the worry & work of moving to Eileen, but it can't be helped.

I hope Jake got well away with his bowling. I looked through some papers, but couldn't find a report of the play.

With Every Good Wish
Sean O'Casey

[1] Leaving his pregnant wife in England, O'Casey went to Northern Ireland to spend a week with Lord and Lady Londonderry at their home, Mount Stewart, in Newtown Ards, County Down, before he sailed to America. The Londonderrys arranged to guarantee a sum of £200 at O'Casey's bank so that he could make the trip, for he had used his last few pounds in preparing for the journey and the promise of royalties in America. For an account of his visit to Mount Stewart, see "Star of the County Down," *Rose and Crown* (1952).

To George Jean Nathan

MS. CORNELL

CHALFONT ST. GILES
18 AUGUST 1934

My dear George Jean Nathan—

Mr. Madden has written me about a [Ben] Hecht invitation, & the invitation came with Mr. Madden's letter. I have refused it in a very polite and affable way. Mr. Madden has mentioned that he understands that I am to be a guest of yours during my stay in America. If that be your personal wish, then I couldn't & wouldn't ask for a greater honour. I will, of course, make every effort to be worthy of such kindness. I should love to be close to you during the heat & burden of the rehearsals. It would be a decided help & a great comfort. Anyhow, I am determined to do nothing without your & Madden's advice, for, on the whole, I have some commonsense left. Without your generous help first, and Mr. Madden's afterwards, there would have been no production of the play in America during my or my kid's lifetime, and it stands to reason that those who did so well for me are the only ones from whom to seek advice and help in coming difficulties.

Anyhow, & under any circumstances, it will be a pleasure and a genuine honour to be first received by G. J. Nathan.

With Affectionate Regards
Sean O'Casey

To Daniel Macmillan

TS. MACMILLAN LONDON

CHALFONT ST. GILES
27 AUGUST 1934

Dear Mr Daniel,

As I told you over the telephone, the American Consul is asking a reference from a Firm of repute before he puts his visa on my passport.

I think the following wording ought to do:

We have pleasure in certifying that Sean O'Casey's visit to The United States is for the purpose of assisting in the production of his play, "Within The Gates," under the auspices of Messrs Bushar, Inc., 137 West 48th Street, N. York,
and

that his duration of stay in the United States will be for six months or less, and
that he is financially sound.

With very many thanks for your kindness. I shall call in on Tuesday or Wednesday.

Sincerely Yours,
Sean O'Casey

To Gabriel Fallon

MS. Texas
Chalfont St. Giles
29 August 1934

My dear Gaby,

Just a line to tell you that "Windfalls" will be published soon,[1] & that you aren't to buy a copy. I will have one sent on to you. I am off to America next month to help in the production of "Within the Gates"—they demanded me, & I had to go.[2] I enclose inscription for "Windfalls",[3] for I expect to be faraway when it comes out. We shall be leaving here in a week or so, &, after the 10th Sept, our address will be—

4, Overstrand Mansions,
Prince of Wales' Road
London S.W.

I hope you & Rose and all are well.

Yours As Ever
Sean

[1] Sean O'Casey, *Windfalls* (1934), a collection of early poems, four short stories, and two one-act plays. The book came out in October, and on 4 December it was banned by the Irish Censorship of Publications Board.

[2] He sailed from Southampton on the Cunard *Majestic* on 13 September and arrived in New York on 19 September.

[3] "To my old buttie, Gaby Fallon, with all the affection of old-time memories. When we forget thee, O Dublin, let our right hand forget its cunning."

To Macmillan & Co. Ltd.

TS. MACMILLAN LONDON

CHALFONT ST. GILES
31 AUGUST 1934

Dear Sirs,

Please note that after September the 11th, the address above is to be abandoned, and the following substituted:

4, Overstrand Mansions,
Prince of Wales Road
Battersea Park,
London, S.W.11

also that Mrs O'Casey has authority to take charge of financial affairs while I am in America, and that amounts due, or advance on "Windfalls" can be endorsed by her P.P. Sean O'Casey, so they can be sent on as usual.

Sincerely Yours,
Sean O'Casey

To Lady Londonderry

MS. LADY BURY

THE ROYALTON
44 WEST 44TH STREET, NEW YORK
5 OCTOBER 1934

Dear Circe,[1]

Here I am floating about in the centre of the Lion of Commerce, a little bewildered by the amazing swiftness of the come and go of life here.[2] Yet the hotel where I stay is like a London hotel growing old with a quiet dignity. I have been surrounded with interviewers who have asked me all

[1] Lady Londonderry was known as "Circe the Sorcerer" at her famous Wednesday parties at "The Ark," Londonderry House, where O'Casey met her in 1928. See his letter to Winston Churchill, 4 July 1942, note 1, Vol. II.

[2] Arthur and Barbara Gelb in *O'Neill* (New York, Harper, 1962), pp. 787–88, make the following comment on his arrival: "O'Casey, in his first (and only) trip to the United States, arrived in a brown suit and a cap, bringing with him nothing but an extra set of underwear, a single shirt, a pair of socks and a sweater. He registered at the Royalton Hotel, where Nathan lived, and spent the first hours after his arrival testing all the electrical gadgets in his room and carefully distributing his few items of wardrobe among the drawers of his bureau."

the things that happened to me since I gave my first cry coming into the world. The people are very kind and hospitable, placing all New York at my feet; but I have selected cautiously, and am living as quietly as I would were I lounging round London—except for Rehearsals, which take up a lot of my time. The play is coming to life winningly and the production will be, I think, a very interesting one. The Costumes are in key with the symbolism of the play, and many of them—for the Summer & Spring choruses—are very beautiful. I am hoping it may be a success.

The people here have no time to wait for help from heaven, and are a strange contrast to the Gaels of Skye or Connait. The Irish here—and there are thousands of them—hurry along life with the rest of them, and shove away the day that is with them for the day that is to dawn. It is a mill-race of life; fascinating, but terrifying when one stops to think about it. In Ireland, America seems to be very close; but in America, Ireland is a long way off.

Radio City is a magnificent building, that cost countless millions to build, but the artistic life that goes on inside isn't worth the spending of a five-cent piece. But, any way, New York isnt America and I have a lot to see yet as soon as the Rehearsals slow down a little.

I hope you and Lord Londonderry are well, and that lovely Mount Stewart will come close to me soon again.

Please give my affectionate regards to your husband, to Lord Castlereagh, Lady Margaret, Lady Helen, & Lady Mary.

God be with you & them forever.

With Love,
Sean

To George Jean Nathan

MS. CORNELL

THE ROYALTON
44 WEST FORTY-FOURTH ST.
NEW YORK
[17] OCTOBER 1934

My dear George—

Messrs Tuerk, Markle, Lusk, Douglas, & myself assemble in the National Theatre tomorrow, Thursday afternoon to judge between the music of Mr. Lusk on the one hand, & the music of Engel on the other. Could you be with us to hear the airs, & give your blessing to the music that you think to be the better of the two?

And God defend the right![1]

Sean

Hour of trial: Between 5 & 5:30 PM.
Place of " : National Theatre

[1] A compromise decision was reached and the incidental music was credited to Milton Lusk and A. Lehman Engel. *Within the Gates* opened on 22 October 1934 at the National Theatre, New York, directed by Melvyn Douglas, sets and costumes by James Reynolds, dance arrangements by Elsa Findlay, produced by George Bushar Markle and John Tuerk, with the following cast: Bramwell Fletcher as Dreamer, Moffat Johnston as Bishop, Kathryn Collier as Bishop's Sister, Morris Ankrum as Atheist, Lillian Gish as Young Whore, Barry Kelley as Gardener, James Jolley as Guardsman, Barry Macollum as First Chair Attendant, John Daly Murphy as Second Chair Attendant, Vera Fuller Mellish as First Nursemaid, Mary Morris as The Old Woman, Jessamine Newcombe as Policewoman, Edward Broadley as First Evangelist.

To Horace Reynolds[1]

MS. REYNOLDS

THE DEVON
70 WEST 55TH ST., NEW YORK.
2 NOVEMBER 1934

Dear Horace Reynolds,

I should like to visit Harvard, very much indeed, and I shall eagerly consider all you say about a visit; but I don't lecture and anything I should say would be in the nature of an informal talk, not as a master to apprentices, but as an apprentice to apprentices.

I should love to meet these fresh young men you write about, & shall do my best to accept your kind invitation a little later on.

To you & to the young men, my warmest wishes.

Yours Sincerely
Sean O'Casey

[1] Horace Reynolds (1896–), writer and teacher, taught at Harvard and Brown universities.

To Brooks Atkinson [1]

MS. ATKINSON

THE DEVON HOTEL, NEW YORK
4 NOVEMBER 1934

My dear Brooks Atkinson:

I thank you quietly & earnestly, from my heart out, for the two splendid articles you wrote about my play.[2] First, & the best thing to say about them, is that you can write damn fine prose yourself.

The second article stirred me greatly, for it gave to me again the spirit that moved me as I wrote the play. In that article I can say—as we say in Irish—my soul within art those!

Very sincerely yours,
Sean O'Casey

P.T.O.
I enclose a letter sent to me by a Catholic priest, which may interest you.

I have inscribed a copy of "Windfalls" to you & a photograph which I hope you may be kind enough to accept.

SOC

[1] Brooks Atkinson (1894–), American dramatic critic and author; dramatic critic of the *New York Times,* 1926–60; conducted a special column, "Critic at Large," for the *New York Times,* 1960–66.

[2] Atkinson's review of the opening of *Within the Gates, New York Times,* 23 October 1934, and his Sunday column devoted to the play, *New York Times,* 28 October 1934.

To Horace Reynolds

MS. REYNOLDS

THE DEVON HOTEL, NEW YORK
30 NOVEMBER 1934

My dear Horace—

Forgive me for not writing before this to thank you & your wife for your great kindness to me during my stay in Cambridge. I have been very busy, hurrying here & hurrying there & finding that twenty-four hours is only a faint resemblance to what a New Yorker expects a day to be. Please give my love to Mrs. Reynolds, & to your girl and boy.

As you have heard, maybe, one of our principals dropped dead, & we have been at it rehearsing a new man for the part.

I am sending you a copy of "Windfalls" under another cover; & "The

Sun Also Rises" with it. Honestly, I don't like the book. I read it quietly & found no touch of kinship with it. As I read it my thoughts followed afar off. I must read some other of Hemingway's work.

Affectionate Regards.
Sean

To Lillian Gish [1]

MS. GISH

ON BOARD CUNARD WHITE STAR
"BRITANNIC" [2]
22 DECEMBER 1934

My dear Lillian:

Many, many thanks for your kind telegram, and many more thanks for your grand presents—they're swell!

I sincerely hope that I may soon have the pleasure of seeing you all again.

It was a great experience and a real joy.

Earnestly yours,
Sean

[1] Lillian Gish (1896–   ), American actress.

[2] He left New York on the *Britannic* on 14 December and arrived in Liverpool on 23 December.

To George Jean Nathan

MS. CORNELL

ON BOARD M. V. "BRITANNIC"
[22? DECEMBER 1934]

My dear George and my dear Friend—

Thanks for all your kindness, Prince of Dramatic Critics & Prince among men. Were New York nothing but a place of ruins, it would be a great city having you there.

What a jabbering crowd the critics are. "Because thou art neither cold nor hot," said the Spirit to the Church of Laodicea, "because thou art neither cold nor hot, I will spew thee out of my mouth." Their best would be bad, but they have lost the power even to do their best, lost it in their infancy.

Mimsie [Taylor] looked lovely on Friday as she stood on the deck of the boat. The stars come close, dear George, the stars come close in the forms of beautiful women.

I will write when I reach London; meanwhile, take care of yourself—you are the one champion of the Drama, ever standing in the gap o' danger.

God be with you.
My love to you.
Sean

VII

BACK TO LONDON AND IRELAND AND YEATS, 1935

NEXT month I may be going over to the land of my birth—hear the birds singing?—for a week or two. It is nearly nine years since I saw Ireland's shore, & I am longing to see it again—birds singing louder than ever!"

"Many are determined to drive me bodily, soul, & spirit out of Ireland, and they are using me as a lever with which to down the Abbey. W. B. Yeats is an old man now, but he is as big a fighter as ever, & will surely die with harness on his back. I enclose a few press-cuttings to give you an idea of the kind of fight we are waging. Curiously enough, I was met with a hail and hearty welcome everywhere I went—from worker, priest, monk, & literary gent. except the critics. The fight, however, is a little tiresome, & I don't think I'd join in were it not necessary to stand by Yeats."

This was a year of rows and reconciliations for O'Casey. Shortly after he returned from his trip to America he was once again involved in his continuing public battle with censors and critics early in 1935; but the most important personal events of the year were set in motion several months later when he began to make up his quarrel with Yeats and Ireland. On 15 January, the day his third child, Niall, was born, the mayor of Boston, acting under heavy pressure from outraged religious groups, banned the production of *Within the Gates,* which was about to start a tour of thirteen cities after its artistically successful New York run. Teachers and students from many New England colleges quickly defended O'Casey and his play from the usual charges of "blasphemy" and "obscenity," but the ban remained, the tour collapsed, and down the drain went the anticipated royalty checks for the O'Caseys.

Meanwhile back in London O'Casey had been trying, not very successfully, to earn some money by writing reviews, and he touched off a literary controversy with his uncompromising dismissal of *Love on the Dole,* the printed text of a popular play about the British poor which was enjoying a long run on the West End, and which O'Casey felt contained too much patronizing propaganda and too little artistic merit. By a series of coincidences Yeats's friend Ethel Mannin was one of those who wrote letters of protest against O'Casey's review, and she indirectly brought the men together. A day after he read Miss Mannin's savage letter in which she defended proletarian propaganda at the expense of art and abused him, the distressed and lonely O'Casey instinctively turned to a kindred artist and wrote a friendly letter to the ailing Yeats in Ireland—Yeats his old antagonist who had rejected *The Silver Tassie* because of its propaganda, Yeats with whom O'Casey now shared a common ground of artistic inviolability. Whereupon Yeats, who was following the controversy, wrote to Miss Mannin to defend O'Casey, to warn her about the dangers of propaganda in art, and to thank her for inadvertently provoking O'Casey into a mood of reconciliation. O'Casey was softening toward Yeats and Ireland, but his mood was understandably belligerent toward England and especially Kingsley Martin, the editor of the *New Statesman and Nation* in which the review and protest letters had appeared in February, who refused to print O'Casey's letters of reply to his critics because he was too "abusive." O'Casey finally had a chance to present his case in April and May in *Time and Tide,* exposing the devious censorship of Martin and cheerfully illustrating that when it came to insults a liberal British editor could be as abusive and underhanded as the reactionary critics of O'Casey in Boston and Dublin.

Those reactionary critics in Dublin had another chance to abuse O'Casey in August when the Abbey Theatre, after a delay of eight years, finally presented *The Silver Tassie* in the new mood of reconciliation. The dispute over his play was still raging when O'Casey arrived in Dublin in

September for his first and last visit to his native land since 1926, but apparently the ordinary people of the city gave him a warm welcome. At the theatre and in the press, however, things were different. There were many virulent objections by men like Father Gaffney and the playwright Brinsley Macnamara, who was a director of the Abbey and subsequently resigned as a protest against O'Casey and Yeats. When some newspapers printed reports that the Abbey's production of the play was a repudiation of Yeats, O'Casey was quick to present the truth in open letters to Dublin and New York: "Mr. Yeats will never be anything less than a great poet and a great man."

To George Jean Nathan

MS. Cornell

49 Overstrand Mansions
Prince of Wales Road
London S.W. 11
10 January 1935

My dear George—

Just a line to let you have a letter I got from the B.B.C. in reply to one asking them if the one-act plays we spoke about have been published. You will see that, apparently, they are not to be had in bookform. I did not tell the B.B.C. anything about the purpose for which they might be needed, as I thought you mightn't like them to know. It might be possible that they would be willing to let you have a loan of the MSS., &, if you should so wish, & let me know, I shall write and ask Val Gielgud if this can be done. You will remember the plays mentioned by me were,

The Use of Man, Dunsany
The Kingdom of the Blind, Wells
Dr. Abernethy—His Book

The plays published mentioned in the addition to Gielgud's letter wouldn't, I'm afraid, be of any use to you—except, possibly "Squirrel's Cage." They were all written by young, emphatic, artistic, show-you-how-you-live-in-a-sentence young men.

The baby hasn't come yet, & the delay may mean what is called an "induction operation." So I shall write more fully when this event is given the definite shape of a boy or girl.

Remember me to Lillian [Gish] & to Mimsie [Taylor], & to Frances [Langford] & to Sylvia [Sydney].

With Affectionate Regards
Sean

To Lady Astor

MS. Astor
Forty-Nine Overstrand Mansions
16 January 1935

Dear Lady Astor—

Eileen had her baby yesterday evening—a boy [1]—fifteen minutes, or so, after we were about to go for a walk from the Nursing home; both she & the child's going on well. So far so good, for I was beginning to get a little anxious about her.

Don't bother your head about "Windfalls"—it's but a thing of shreds & patches. It was a great pleasure to me to send you a copy as an appreciation of your kindness, cleverness, & good-will towards most men, & especially to me and mine. Whether we be beasts or men, my dear Lady Astor, we are all pathetic.

I'm sorry to hear about your boy. I, too, when I was young grew fast & furious; & so did my own boy, but he has steadied in his growth now. Don't bother too much about your boy's college & schooling culture. Let him have all the air & seemly exercise he can get, & many hours of sleep & he will come out of the dangerous time safely. The first security of life is good health, & this gift is not given freely. We have to work hard to give it to our children. Keep him far from cocktail food; furnish his body only with a simple and nourishing diet, & leave the rest to God.

I shall be delighted to see you again, & to talk to you of many things.

I hope all your other boys & girl are well, & that Lord Astor is as vigorous as he was when I last saw him.

And when we meet again, I hope you may have a good story to tell about your dear & youngest boy.

With Affectionate Regards
Sean

[1] Niall O'Casey.

To Richard J. Madden

TC. O'CASEY

49, OVERSTRAND MANSIONS
17 JANUARY 1935

Dear Dick—

Letters and cheque received. So Boston has said, thus far shalt thou go, but no farther. The priests and the proletariat are evidently out to down poor S O'Casey.[1] And while I was in America a husband shot his young wife and a Catholic priest dead because he found her in the priest's bedroom. Coming home on the boat an Irish Consul told me that Cardinal O'Connell's [2] heart was palpitating trying to stop his priests from gambling the church collections away on the stock exchange; and that a great and well-known Catholic [3] had been stung for $15,000 to get out of an action for damages because a wife of another man had been found in his bedroom, or he had been found in her bedroom. And this particular specimen of the holy faith had visited and denounced my play as anti-christian! And in Chalfont St Giles, before I left, a Superior of a Community of Discalced Carmelites was removed from his post, and, for all I know, defrocked, for carrying on with some of the women of the district. But this action only amounts to the church driving another nail into her own coffin. And in Ireland [they] are offering Mass for anyone who will buy a sweepticket. Heaven must be issuing Stop Presses to keep pace with the news.

Glad indeed to hear of the continued progress of "Everything Goes." [4] How did "Mother Lode" [5] go?

You should have received by now a registered packet containing details and contract concerning my connection with French & Co, ending in April. They retain as my letter explains, the *Amateur* rights of "The Gunman," "Juno," and "The Plough." [6] The Professional Agency of these will revert to you. The "The Silver Tassie" is free—they have no rights

[1] On 15 January Frederick W. Mansfield, mayor of Boston, banned the production of *Within the Gates,* which had been scheduled to open a week's run at the Shubert Theatre on 21 January. Roman Catholic and Methodist clergymen had led the campaign to ban the play on the grounds that it was "anti-religious and obscene."

[2] William Cardinal O'Connell of Boston (1859–1944).

[3] John McCormack (1884–1945), the Irish tenor.

[4] *Anything Goes,* by Guy Bolton and P. G. Wodehouse, revised by Russel Crouse and Howard Lindsay, music and lyrics by Cole Porter, opened in New York on 21 November 1934, and ran for four hundred twenty performances.

[5] *Mother Lode,* by Dan Totheroh, revised by George O'Neil, produced by John Tuerk and George Markle, opened on 23 December 1934, and closed after one week.

[6] For details on the sale of the amateur rights, see his letter to George Jean Nathan, 28 September 1932, note 2.

over this, and you can deal with this play without delay. And also the two humorous sketches in "Windfalls." [7]

To you and Tessa every good wish and warm regards.
Yours in seculo seculorum,
Sean

[7] *The End of the Beginning* and *A Pound on Demand.*

To George Jean Nathan

MS. CORNELL

49 OVERSTRAND MANSIONS
? JANUARY 1935

My dear George—

Ever so sorry to hear that you have been down with the grippe. I pictured you buzzing about in the snow, & felt that you'd be laid up. I myself got a whoreson cough coming home, & haven't been able to shake it off yet. However, it's fine to hear that you are on your feet again, & at least, looking out of the window. My God the way these illnesses take the pep & pip out of a man!

Yes, Dick [Madden] has told me a lot about Boston, & that, now, they are to ban the book. Well, let them, & be damned to them. But the whole thing's hard lines on John Tuerk & George Markle. Two plucky divils, these, mind you. I wish I were there to help them—but possibly, I'd be in the way, & raving like a fool. John & George have put up a great fight for me, & it worries & maddens me to think of the fight made by these "Commercial men" & the indifference & secret hostility of "non-commercial" bastards out for the higher & better-class Drama. Well, the Garden of Gethsemane before the Resurrection.

I miss you, George, as you miss me.

Give my love to dear Lillian [Gish], & say I shall write as soon as things slow down a bit.

God's Right Hand over you.
Sean

From Richard C. Boys

TS. O'CASEY

LOWELL HOUSE E-42
CAMBRIDGE, MASS.
17 JANUARY 1935

Dear Mr. O'Casey,

A few of my friends and I, all students of Harvard College, are now in the midst of the furor created by the banning of your play, *Within the Gates,* in Boston by Mayor Mansfield. Realizing the injustice and stupidity of such an action we have circulated petitions to the prominent colleges of the Boston area (Harvard, Radcliffe, Wellesley, Tufts), and have received the backing of several of Boston's leading newspapers. Already the response has been great. In two hours last night nearly four-hundred signatures were obtained in Harvard alone. These were sent to Mayor Mansfield last night. This morning the Mayor re-affirmed his position.

And although our cause is lost for the moment we intend to carry on with the matter, bringing as much pressure as possible on the Mayor to avoid any such debacle in the future. For we feel that the banning of *Within the Gates* is a retrograde step in the cultural enlightenment of Boston and of the United States.

My friends and I were part of the interested audience to which you spoke in the Fogg Museum this fall;[1] and we wish to pay our respects to you as a master playwright and as a crusader in the drama.

I am enclosing a copy of the petition sent to Mayor Mansfield.

> We, the undersigned, do protest that the action of Mayor Mansfield in banning *Within the Gates* on grounds of immorality and irreligiousness is not warranted, and we urge a reconsideration of his decision.
>
> Immorality, such as is allegedly personified in this play, does exist in Boston as well as [London]; certainly it is not to be encouraged. *Within the Gates* neither encourages immorality, nor does it show it in an attractive light.
>
> The knowledge that the allegedly immoral parts and lines are only parts and lines in a play, instead of real persons and real words in real life makes it no more conducive to personal immorality than some of the statues and paintings in the Museum of Fine Arts are conducive to nudism, or than some of the movies shown in Boston are conducive to crime and immorality. Such knowledge makes attendance at this play very much less conducive to immorality than many newspaper stories about real immorality and real crime.
>
> The very nature of the play and the reputation of the playwright, to

[1] On 16 November 1934, O'Casey gave the Morris Gray Poetry Talk at Harvard, on "The Old Drama and the New," an attack on William Archer's book of that title, written in 1923.

say nothing of the price of admission, make it an attraction to thousands whose tendencies towards immorality are much more controlled than most of those persons who attend movies and feast on lurid newspaper stories.

If religion today has not developed in its many adherents a moral and religious attitude capable of withstanding the "insidious attack" allegedly made in this play, it is a criticism not of the play, but of the religion, which should be able to stand against the gates of hell. It would appear furthermore that the play does not attack the essence of religion, but only those external and ossified fripperies which in the play, as so often in real life, are presented to the communicant as true religion.

Sincerely,
Richard C. Boys

To George Bushar Markle and John Tuerk
Nlt Via Western Union

TC. O'CASEY
[21? JANUARY 1935]

BUSHAR AND TUERK,
THE NATIONAL THEATRE,
WEST FORTY-FIRST STREET, NEW YORK.
The Ban on Within The Gates shows that not the play, but the priests are holding the church up to ridicule. stop. Play published year ago but no protest in Boston. Why no protest while I was in the city? Why wait till I had gone from America to ban play and book? They neglected to give me a chance to personally defend the work from their attacks. This is the Jesuit and Wesleyan idea of fairplay and decency. stop. I dont write plays to please priests. stop. Father Sullivan [1] asks what play symbolises. stop. Him and his friends, obviously, for one thing. stop. Play evidently startled them as the sacring bell did the Cardinal when the brown wench lay kissing in his arms—see Shakespeare. stop. The two Jesuits would probably be happier seeing Zeigfeld Follies—see Passing Judgements, page 184. The play tries to face some of the world's problems and the priests ban the play. Priests in plus-fours with only one idea in their heads. Father Terry

[1] The Rev. Russell M. Sullivan, S.J., Boston College, head of the Legion of Decency, and the then newly formed Boston College Council of Catholic Organizations. Bishop Charles Wesley Burns of the Methodist Church, although he was in Maine at the time, allowed his name to be added to Father Sullivan's protest.

Connelly [2] reported saying that only unhealthy and abnormal persons do not swoon at sight of human flesh exposed. What a midget mind we have here. He forgets only hour ago ten million men were killed in war, and fifty millions more were mangled and thousands of delicate women bore up against human flesh exposed, and nursed these poor devils back to some sort of life. Better banned with O'Neill than blessed by these paupers in mind and courage. Is it true Mansfield made Mayor of City of Zion? Is the City of Franklin, Emerson, and Poe going to stand for this sort of thing?

Greeting to you both and God be with the fight against cowardice, stupidity, and the indecent attempt to veil the truth.

O'Casey

[2] The Rev. Terence L. Connolly, S.J., Boston College, and drama critic of the Jesuit magazine *America*. At a hearing of the Boston Censorship Board, Father Connolly said of the play: "In spots it is unspeakable filth, drenched with sex and written to point out the futility of religion." (*Boston Globe*, 17 January 1935). For his published attack on O'Casey and the play, see "Critics, Interviews and Sean O'Casey," *America*, 19 January 1935. For Father Connolly's attack on Yeats's *Purgatory*, see O'Casey's letter to the *Irish Times*, 29 August 1938, note 1. For O'Casey's comments on Father Connolly, see "Within the Gates," *Rose and Crown* (1952), *Autobiographies II* (1963), pp. 422–23.

To George Jean Nathan

MS. CORNELL

49 OVERSTRAND MANSIONS
30 JANUARY 1935

My dear George—

Very sorry that a thousand and one things kept me from writing to you before this. However, you should have got a note from me carrying in its hand a letter from the British Broadcasting Co telling us that the short plays we spoke about as possible material for broadcasting, have not yet been published—&, possibly, never will be. I hope you got this letter allright.

When I reached home I was very, very tired—had a cold & miserable passage home, & could do nothing but lie about & try to get back a little energy. So after a few seconds rest I set about getting books & papers in order for all had been jumbled together in one mass when the Missus moved from Chalfont St. Giles to London. After this had been done I had to go with the Missus for walks so that she might have continuous exercise to help bring about a healthy and a normal birth. The kid was expected on Christmas Day, or thereabouts, but it didn't come, & it didn't come, till we got blue in the face waiting for it. Doctor said, it'll come today, it'll come tomorrow, it'll come the day after tomorrow, & kept us waiting. So we waited till the middle of January, a little anxious, but still walking about, & going back to the Nursing Home when the sun set. One evening in the Home the missus in pain, & the Matron fussing about going for "a little walk, a little walk; just a little walk to keep things going"; the missus protesting & half afraid to stir, & I arguing with her, seeing with a layman's eye that the moment wasn't far off, & telling the Matron her business. But the Lady-Matron kept on "Just a little walk," & we were fully cloaked & on the steps to go out, when the missus rushed back, tore off her clothes, & the kid was born inside of twenty minutes! And after four weeks in which to prepare, when the time came nothing was ready, & the poor kid actually had the baby herself while the nurse was telephoning for the doctor, & the Matron was washing her hands & looking for the chloroform. However, we were lucky, for it was only by the merest accident that the kid wasn't born in the street. It suffered a bruised head & a bruised eye; & the missus had to have some stitches in her; but all's well, or almost well now, & she comes home today to depend on her own judgement—and on mine, & thank God for that, for what I have told you is but a little of the bungling that went on & on in this highly recommended & expensive Nursing Home. And this is English order & English care, English method, and the English glory of competency & skill! God be praised that there are a few intelligent Irish still in the country. Their skill is as good as my Latin, George, & according to some accounts, that isn't of a first-class order. I'm telling you for the last few weeks, I haven't been feeling like a Princeps Pace.

I got "Passing Judgments,"[1] George, and I thank you for a fine addition to my collection of books on things of the Theatre; the Theatre of the past, of men & women; the Theatre that fills the empty heads of the Critics with an angry confusion. I am simply proud of having my name as a dedication to your book. I don't agree with the second remark you give as you pull the curtain up.[2] A critic never becomes tolerant of, or indifferent to, a bad play. Are you tolerant of, or indifferent to a bad play? My dear George I can see you vividly rising from your seat, gathering your cloak & your hat in your hands, & leaving the theatre in recessional order to an unheard chant, after the fall of the curtain on the first-act of a bad play. And the look on your face as the look of a soul in hell.

I was specially delighted to read your chapter on Charlie Chaplin. For years I have listened to wild talk about this artist, & have argued that

[1] George Jean Nathan, *Passing Judgments* (New York, Knopf, 1935). The book is dedicated to Sean O'Casey.

[2] "The tolerance that often comes to a critic in his later years is simply the result of a belated consciousness of the complete and utter unimportance of nine-tenths of the persons and performances he is brought to criticize. Its synonym is indifference." *Passing Judgments,* p. 3.

he really hadn't got some of the gifts the talk gave him. I was brought fettered & silent to see "City Lights," and, save for a few scenes, the whole Film disappointed & bored me. But the talk went on, and hearing so much of it, I finally began to think that the world was right & I was wrong. Now, I see that George Jean Nathan stands against the world, & the world has become a very small place to me now. And this is very comforting. Anyhow, it's grand to have your book, & grander to have my name in it.

I've had a remarkable letter from Brooks Atkinson (haven't answered it yet), but haven't time to tell you about it now—Missus & kid just home from Nursing Home, but will tell you about it in my next letter. Poor old Brooks! He likes you, anyway, & God will regard him highly for that.

You've had pretty bad weather in New York, & all over America, I see by the papers. We had a little snow here—about enough to fill a cup, but the days are mostly damp & the skies gloomy. I miss the sparkle of the New York Sky. The city has a glorious canopy. I got a cable from Mimsie on the birth of the boy. I shall write to her in a few days. Give her my love. And give Frances my love, too. And give Sylvia my love, three. My good God, George, you know how to pick! You lay hands suddenly on no woman. It looks as if you choose after long & earnest prayer & fasting.

Well, God be with my Anam-cara—Soul-Friend—as we say in Irish —till we meet again.

Yours with love,
Sean

PS. I enclose note for Sylvia thanking her for a present for my wife, sent by her in my cabin, & found there by me when I went aboard the boat.

By Sean O'Casey

New Statesman and Nation
9 February 1935

THE THING THAT COUNTS

Love on the Dole. Ronald Gow and Walter Greenwood. Cape. 3*s.* 6*d.*
Seven Plays. Ernst Toller. Lane. 8*s.* 6*d.*

Love on the Dole is a play delivered by Ronald Gow and Walter Greenwood out of a novel of the same name. It was either dead before it was taken from the belly of the novel, or the two drama surgeons killed it as they were taking it out. There isn't a character in it worth a curse, and there isn't a thought in it worth remembering. It is a dead thing from the head down and from the feet up. Each act of the play is honoured with such bracketed titles as "The Gods Defied," "Worship in High Places," "Catastrophe," and "Resurrection." Curious gods, indeed, and highbrow worship on Hampstead Heath. The catastrophe consists of the death of the hero by a blow from a policeman's baton as he is leading a demonstration of the unemployed, and if ever a bobby did a thing worthy to be counted unto him for righteousness, he did it when, with a welt from his baton, he put an end to the life of Larry Meath.

The jacket round the book of the play carries medals of praise on its breast given by a squad of critics to the novel from which the play is taken. Laski calls it "a superb novel"; the Bishop of Durham tells us that "it is remarkable and poignant"; and the *Spectator* says that the book is written with "vivid clarity; a gesture, a turn of speech, a cough, and the whole man lives." Well, if the novel isn't a hell of a sight better than the play, then these critics and this bishop deserve to meet the fate, and be finished by a policeman with a heavier baton than that which put an end to Larry Meath. As it is in the play, a gesture, a turn of speech, a cough, and the whole man dies. Touching on the first production of *Love on the Dole* in London, the *Star* tells us that "Labour Leaders are taking considerable interest in the event, and are to turn up in force." They would. This is the sort of stuff to give them. The Proletariat looking up and the Labour Leaders looking down. This is the kind of drama pap that will make them feverish and make them fat. Ernst Toller in the Introduction he writes to his Seven Plays hisses at the practice of patronage that artists enjoyed in days gone by, and that this patronage made the artist forget "that it was not his task to serve the tastes of the day, but to serve the eternal powers of life—truth, joy, beauty, freedom, the mind and the spirit." Beauty, truth, and justice have different shapes to different minds. We see to-day how artists are condemned to finding Helen's beauty in a brow of Egypt. Crowds scan the statue of Peter Pan, and smear with tar the Rima done by Epstein. The truth as it is in Christ Jesus—is to be found in the Pope and his Cardinals; in the Archbishop of Canterbury and his Convocation; or in Evangeline Booth eked out with a word or two from Lord Rothermere? And is justice to be vindicated by Black Shirts kicking the bellies out of the Red Shirts, or by Red Shirts kicking the bellies out of the Black Shirts? Oh, what has the artist got to do with the honest and careful reconciliation of these things? He is above the kings and princes of this world, and he is above the Labour Leaders and Proletariat, too. And under the patronage that draws a hiss from Toller many of the greatest and finest works of art were born. Under the patronage of the Proletariat we have got, so far—as far as the drama is concerned—such things as "Singing Jailbirds," a terrible thing, from Upton Sinclair; [1] *Love on the Dole* from Ronald Gow and Walter Greenwood, and seven Soviet plays from Russia. No, the artist is answerable only to himself and his work is

[1] See O'Casey's letter to Lady Gregory, (?) October 1924, note 1.

for those finer minds among men who hold varying views upon all other things.

Now a word or two about Ernst Toller and his *Seven Plays*—a holy number, and in many ways a holy book. They are published by John Lane, and the book costs 8*s*. 6*d*., and it is well worth the money. Of the seven plays, *Masses And Men* and *The Machine Wreckers* are the best, I think, but each has something to say, and all have in them that fierce outcry against the world's woe that is the strongest and shrillest note in every song that Toller has to sing. Here are plays for the modern theatre whether one likes them or not; whether they glorify one's pant for politics, or whether they provoke one to a hasty and hot condemnation of their implication. Each play is a serious reflection from a worthy and intelligent dramatist on the impact with which life has shaken him and made him reel, but still has left him standing on his feet. And all the plays are coloured deeply—some of them recklessly—with the imagery of a poet's mind. Almost all the plays cry out against, and cry in screams, what Toller thinks to be an inadequate social system for the working-class, and who to-day cannot see the present system will allow few souls to go back clean to God? But this present social system inadequate to the need of the worker is just as inadequate to the need of the rich. We all walk in its slime whether we go barefoot or go with feet sheltered in satin shoes. In the scene of the Stock Exchange in *Masses And Men,* while the bankers and brokers are bidding, one of them says:

Third Banker: Did you hear?
A mine disaster it seems.
People in want.
Fourth Banker: Then I suggest
A charitable entertainment,
A dance around the desk of the Exchange.
A dance to cope with want;
The proceeds to the poor,
Gentlemen, if you please,
A dance.

These who hold out hollowed hands to gather in such flimsy help are in need no more than those who think they give out life from charity.

But Toller's a dramatist, and that's the thing that counts. England will be striding nearer to a finer drama when Toller has his London season. That dawn seems to be a long way off, for, as I write, in London, and, probably all over England, of all the plays presented there are but three or four that can be said to come within the circle of drama, and of these, one was written by an Irishman, and the other two were written hundreds of years ago.

Sean O'Casey

To Horace Reynolds

MS. Reynolds
[49 Overstrand Mansions]
[10?] February 1935

My dear Horace—

I havent had a painless minute since I returned to England, & have only managed to write what couldn't be set aside—letters to my American Agent, & two articles—one cabled [1]—on the banning of the play in Boston. The Producers asked me to write these, & so it had to be done. It is really hateful that I should be compelled to turn my thoughts to the pious shinanachin [2] of a few Jesuits & a group of Methodist Preachers. My God, are they going to allow on the stage only the things that come out of the Tabernacle? Is the circumference of the world to be measured by the bottom hem of a friar's frock? Good job for them they waited till I was well away out of sight & out of hearing! We have had another kid born to us, a boy, & a strenuous time it was, too. The birth was nearly three weeks over time, &, at the end, it was just there with us that the missus hadn't it out in the street. The Nursing Home wise ones were shoving us out to take a walk, ignoring the fact that the woman was in pain; and only for my doubt, & Eileen's fear—for she had barely time to strip herself & get to bed when the child was born—, the kid would have certainly been born in the street. And she practically delivered herself; for, though they had been preparing for weeks & weeks, when the moment came, nothing was ready. Sister couldn't find her overall, & the chloroform had disappeared. The consequence was, all was over when the doctor came; the child's head & eyes were bruised, & we were in a state of raging indignation. However, no harm was done to the kid, fortunately, & the bruises are practically gone. All this time I have been bad with a chill, but am getting better now, & looking round me a little.

It was grand of you to take my part in this damned controversy about the play, & I give you my sincere thanks.[3] I hope Mrs. Reynolds & the two

[1] For the cabled article see (21?) January 1935 telegram to George Bushar Markle and John Tuerk; for the other article see "The Church Tries to Close the Gates," *Blasts and Benedictions,* ed. Ronald Ayling (London, Macmillan, 1967).

[2] shinanachin (shenanigain), trickery; possibly derived from the Irish sionnach, fox: foxy or tricky.

[3] Then an instructor at Harvard, Reynolds was one of the leaders of the movement to defend *Within the Gates,* with, among many others, Richard C. Boys, Harvard undergraduate; Prof. Henry Wadsworth Longfellow Dana of Harvard; Dr. Clarence Skinner of Tufts Theological School; Edward F. Melvin, drama editor of the *Boston Transcript.*

children are well. I'm afraid I seemed a bit dull on the boat, Horace; I felt so, for I was too tired to think or talk.

I have looked in lots of places for that article about "Letters to the New Island",[4] but haven't laid hands on it yet.

Love to you all.

Sean

Ad Valorem Dei Gloriam to the sons of St Ignatius Loyola, who may himself have had a secret son or two: he did his best.

[4] W. B. Yeats, *Letters to the New Island,* ed. Horace Reynolds (Cambridge, Mass., Harvard Univ. Press, 1934), a collection of letters and articles Yeats wrote for the *Pilot* and the *Providence Sunday Journal.*

To Norman Collins

TC. O'CASEY

49 OVERSTRAND MANSIONS
11 FEBRUARY 1935

Dear Mr. Collins:

Thank you for sending me an advance copy of "The Clergyman's Daughter." [1]

I am not essentially a book reviewer, and rarely like to give on a book the valuation you seek. You have only to glance at your own advertisements to see that there are more than enough of literary mariners who see a tidal wave in every ripple on the sea's surface. However, I've read the "Scene in Trafalgar Square," and I cannot for a moment agree with your high opinion of it.[2]

I advise you to suggest to your Author that he keeps such things as "and so on, and so forth, etc, etc, etc," out of any future work.

I'm afraid, dear Mr. Collins, that it will hardly serve your firm to send advance copies of books your Firm may be publishing.

Very Sincerely Yours,
Sean O'Casey

[1] George Orwell's *A Clergyman's Daughter* (London, Gollancz, 1935).

[2] Collins had singled out Chapter III, "Scene: Trafalgar Square," written in dramatic form, mostly in Cockney dialogue, as "one of the most remarkable pieces of imaginative writing I have ever read." See "Rebel Orwell," *Sunset and Evening Star* (1954), where O'Casey suggests that his refusal to write a puff for Orwell's novel may have provoked Orwell's bitter review of *Drums Under the Windows* in the *Observer,* 28 October 1945, reprinted in Vol. II. See also O'Casey's reply to Orwell in a letter to the *Observer,* 29 October 1945, Vol. II, which was refused publication.

To Richard C. Boys

MS. Boys
49 Overstrand Mansions
13 February 1935

My dear Mr. Boys—

Hail to you & to your fellow students of Harvard for standing to arms and forming a square round me and my work against the arrows of ignorance, superstition, dulness, & fear that are today flying about thick & fast in Boston. I should have written before this, but for the fact that I haven't been too well, & our elder boy came back from school with the whooping cough, & we were afraid the newest arrival would be infected; so care has to be taken, and, of course, I have to share this vigilance with my missus. So you see I am well still in the centre of the things that belong to this world; but am ever ready to fix an arrow to a bow & send it out in the hope that some country humbug or other may get it in the neck, lie down with his legs kicking, give up the ghost, & leave a vacancy for a better & more courageous man. I have already fired a few words in reply to what the learned and reverend Jesuits have said about "Within the Gates"; but it is a grand feeling that on my right hand and on my left are many comrades of Harvard, Radcliffe, Wellesley, & Tufts Universities ready to bend forward and fight against the relics of Congo taboos set up & honoured in the heart of the city of Boston.

I have read that one objection to the play was that it "showed a Bishop who had erred." What a terrible thing to do—to portray a Bishop who had erred, & come short of the glory of God! Well—judging the play from the standard of common realism—he wasn't the first Bishop who erred, &, it isn't necessary for a man to be much of a prophet to say that he won't be the last either. Any way, even the Catholic Church allows that a Saint is spiritually higher than a Bishop, & even some of these have strayed from God's way, like lost sheep. The Jesuits' own particular patron, for instance, the famous Saint Ignatius Loyola, in his young days, was a great man with the women, & may possibly have had an illigitimate kid or two before he felt the wound he got at the battle of Pampeluna. And during many periods there was quite a decent lot of naughtiness & high-spots in the History of the Church. Indeed, in the district where I last lived here there was a Superior of a Discalced Carmelite Community removed from his job because of scandals concerned with women, which were related to me with gusto by Catholics themselves! And who is the American

Bishop whose heart is broken trying to keep his Parish Priest from gambling away the Church Collection on the Stock Exchange?

Anyhow, what right has the Catholic Church to turn the Civil into Canonical Law? Are all our thoughts & all our movements to be hedged round by the taboos of Canonical Law? Take the "immoral" Dreamer of the Play: he loves a young woman, worships her with his body; endows her with his worldly goods; is faithful till death parts them, & these ignorant priests have damned impertinence to call the man "immoral"!

But these fellows are fit leaders of the world's derelicts. The Blind, the lame, the halt, the deaf, the dumb, the epileptic, the mean, ignorant, & superstitious fill up this army and come on, with their tethered flags of resignation & death, to trample on the strong, the fearless, and the fit. We must meet them on the spearpoint, drown their trumpeting sobs with the sound of the silver trumpets calling on the great race that is to come.

Give my love to all the boys of Harvard, & to all that have hurried to help a lonely fighter.

My love & thanks to you.
Sean O'Casey

From G. Wren Howard to New Statesman and Nation

16 February 1935

"Love on the Dole" [1]

Sir,—What on earth is the matter with Mr. Sean O'Casey, and why, Sir, do you accept such trash from him as you printed last week?

A timid and apologetic note from "Critic" on page 166 of the same issue suggests that Mr. O'Casey might have had the courtesy, or have taken the trouble, to go and see the play which he so roundly condemns before having the effrontery to denounce it in such extravagant, ill-considered and offensive terms. I should have thought so too, but much more vehemently. But no, Mr. O'Casey's Irish temperament has run away with him, and he damns the thing outright, though he has neither seen it, nor troubled to read Mr. Walter Greenwood's most admirable novel, *Love on the Dole,* on which he and Mr. Ronald Gow have based the play of the same title.

Lower Wyldes. *G. Wren Howard*
3 Hampstead Way, N.W.11.

[Mr. Sean O'Casey is entitled to express his own views about a book

[1] See O'Casey's review, *New Statesman and Nation,* 9 February 1935, and his reply, "Notes on the Way," *Time and Tide,* 13 April 1935.

sent him for review. His opinions, based on a reading of the book differed from those of "Critic," who formed a very different impression of the play which he expressed in a notice which was not, in our view, either timid or apologetic. *Love on the Dole* was an admirable novel, favourably reviewed in this paper and elsewhere. The play, excellently acted, will, we hope, prove a great success. People should go to the play themselves to judge who was right—"Critic," after seeing the play, or Sean O'Casey, before seeing it.—ED., *N.S.&N.*]

From Ethel Mannin to New Statesman and Nation

16 FEBRUARY 1935

"Love on the Dole"

Sir,—I am moved to protest, as I have no doubt a great many people who saw the play will be, whether they write to THE NEW STATESMAN AND NATION about it or not, by the abominable unfairness of Sean O'Casey's attack on Walter Greenwood's play, *Love on the Dole*. Can it be that Sean O'Casey is jealous because several critics likened the play to *Juno and the Paycock?* Perish the thought. (Isn't there room for all at the top of the tree—or the ladder, or whatever it is?)

Sean O'Casey says that there isn't a character in the play worth a curse. Can it be after all, along with a character in one of Aldous Huxley's novels, the author of *Juno and the Paycock* believes the proletariat to be worthless—"dam" the poor, drat the poor, blast the working class! It is up to Sean O'Casey to state *why* he thinks none of the characters in the play worth a curse? If he dismisses them as worthless he dismisses the great masses. He declares that there isn't a thought in the play worth remembering. I suggest to him that at the very beginning of the play there is a thought worth remembering, and it is this: "Unemployment and pauperdom, that is the legacy of the Industrial Revolution. That is the price we pay for the system. And that is the price you'll go on paying till you waken up to the fact that the remedy's in your own hands."

The sum total of all the thought in the play forms a complete statement of the case for Revolution—the overthrow of the system responsible for such lives as those shown in the play. It is an (implicit) indictment of the existing social system, as is Galsworthy's *Silver Box*. It is as much "an outcry against the world's woes" as Ernst Toller's *Masses and Man.*

Oh, to hell with "the artist" as "above the kings and princes of this world," and "above the Labour Leaders and the Proletariat, too." Art doesn't fill the empty belly, or pay the rent, or mend the kids' boots. Let

Sean O'Casey go spouting that stuff on Clydeside or Tyneside or in South Wales—and get a kick in the pants from the proletariat he considers not worth his artistic (sic) curse. Since when was art—worthy of the name—self-conscious, anyhow?

Oak Cottage, *Ethel Mannin*
Burghley Road, S.W. 19.

From Ronald Gow to New Statesman and Nation

23 FEBRUARY 1935

"Love on the Dole"

SIR,—I feel sure there is a profound truth somewhere behind Mr. Sean O'Casey's criticism of my adaptation of Walter Greenwood's fine novel, *Love on the Dole,* but I cannot imagine what it is. As Mr. O'Casey says—truth has different shapes to different minds. But I have too much respect for Mr. O'Casey as a playwright to condemn his denunciation of our play as "trash," as Mr. Wren Howard does, or suggest a jealous motive, as Miss Ethel Mannin does.

There is an old custom at the Abbey Theatre of smashing the seats when you don't like the play, but is not dramatic criticism expected to be more explicit in this country? Why does Mr. O'Casey think the play so bad? How have we pandered to the proletariat? In what way is it politically prejudiced? I think he ought to be more precise in his criticism and not just kick us in the belly like the fine broth of a boy he is.

"There isn't a thought in it worth remembering," says Mr. O'Casey. Should there be? Shouldn't the thoughts be outside a play? Isn't it the thoughts the audience get that matter? I think he refers to *The Moon in the Yellow River* at the end of his notice. A fine play. I suppose Mr. O'Casey would say there were "thoughts" in it. If there were I can't remember them, nor can anyone else. All I can remember are my own thoughts that the Irish are a funny lot, eternally talking about nothing, having queer notions and doing stupid things—and I submit that that is the point of the play. Where are the thoughts worth remembering in *Juno and the Paycock?* I remember fine tragic exaltation, and that has nothing to do with thinking.

Is there a tear in it worth remembering? That's the point, surely? That is the ultimate object in going to the theatre—to have the emotions stirred. Mr. O'Casey is old enough to know that all this business about "thoughts" means ruin to the theatre. A play is such an inadequate vehicle for thoughts, as Mr. Shaw has so often proved. When Mr. O'Casey talks about the artist being answerable only to himself, he talks like a very young man. The playwright is under a severe discipline. Otherwise he is nothing more than a literary playboy.

Oakleigh, Portland Road, *Ronald Gow*
Bowdon, Cheshire.

From W. B. Yeats to Ethel Mannin [1]

PS. YEATS

RIVERSDALE
4 MARCH 1935

My dear, I have not written because, being somewhat better, I have used each day's brief energy on work—proof sheets and Abbey Theatre—but now I am much better. I was out in the garden to-day and played croquet with my daughter.

I have had a friendly letter from O'Casey, about my illness. He must have written it the day after he read your letter in the *New Statesman*.[2] He is very emotional, and your attack, perhaps, made him lonely. Since we quarrelled with him years ago he has refused to speak to anybody belonging to the Abbey Theatre. Only two years ago he refused an invitation to lunch because he heard I was to be there. Though your defence of propaganda has had this admirable result do not let it come too much into your life. I have lived in the midst of it, I have been always a propagandist though I have kept it out of my poems and it will embitter your soul with hatred as it has mine. You are doubly a woman, first because of yourself and secondly because of the muses, whereas I am but once a woman. Bitterness is more fatal to us than it is to lawyers and journalists who have nothing to do with the feminine muses. Our traditions only permit us to bless, for the arts are an extension of the beatitudes. Blessed be heroic death (Shakespeare's tragedies), blessed be heroic life (Cervantes), blessed be the wise (Balzac). Then there is a still more convincing reason why we should not admit propaganda into our lives. I shall write it out in the style of *The Arabian Nights* (which I am reading daily). There are three very

[1] *The Letters of W. B. Yeats,* ed. Allan Wade (London, Rupert Hart-Davis, 1954), pp. 831–32. And several days later Yeats made the following remarks in a letter to Olivia Shakespear: "O'Casey has written me a friendly letter about my illness, and this—the first sign of amity since our quarrel—has given me great pleasure. He has attacked propaganda plays in the New Statesman and that may have made him friendly to me." *Ibid.,* p. 833.

[2] This would indicate that O'Casey wrote the letter to Yeats on 17 February 1935, but unfortunately it has not been found.

important persons (1) a man playing the flute (2) a man carving a statue (3) a man in a woman's arms. Goethe said we must renounce, and I think propaganda—I wish I had thought of this when I was young—is among the things they thus renounce.

When do you get back to London if ever? Yours always

W B Yeats

From John Tuerk

TS. O'CASEY
137 WEST 48TH STREET
NEW YORK CITY
5 MARCH 1935

Dear Sean:

"Within the Gates" no longer lives. It has crept back between the covers of the book whence it came. We finally closed on Saturday Night, February 23rd.[1] Through the forced gaiety of the farewells many a sly little tear was shed. Four happy months and one day exclusive of the rehearsals with the nicest company that I ever had contact with, will not be forgotten over night. I feel quite lost though we immediately go into rehearsal with "The Dominant Sex" this week. Weaving courage with pain and the unending struggle against those stupid censors kept me from writing you in detail what was happening then. Several times I sat down only to be interrupted. This time I shall carry through.

First of all I know you will be interested in my interview with his 'eminence' the Mayor of Boston after we had been assured that there could be no possible objection to "Within the Gates". Upon my arrival to make arrangements for the play I heard rumors that there might be trouble—little bits of gossip here and there—Boston is like a village—but I disregarded them as just theatre talk. Nevertheless, I felt uneasy and as the talk continued I pressed the Boston management for an explanation. They assured me that it was nothing, but still it persisted, and I knew that when I was requested to go to City Hall and explain what the play was about that something unusual was about to happen.

As we entered the Mayor finished some business, inquired as to whom we were, and on being told 'the show people' grunted, furtively dismissed his stenographer (evidently the subject about to be discussed was unfit for

[1] The play ran for a total of 141 performances in New York; 101 for the initial run, and a return run of 40 after the Boston ban forced the cancellation of the scheduled tour of thirteen cities.

her ears) and confronted us with a snort of disapproval muttering something about there being no room for dirty plays in Boston. Guided by the censor he fingered through the book to the diseased spots which were listed on a pink paper headed 'Office of the Mayor' as follows:

"Whore"

"Oh Jesus is there etc."

"God Damn You" "bastard" For Christs sake etc"

Regarding the first he said it was just pure filth—to put an indecent word like that on a program or anywhere. *"It must not be used in Boston."* I replied that if he objected we would change it to whatever he suggested. He then outlined all the words meaning the same thing, but that terribly objectionable word he would not even pronounce, so we finally compromised on 'Young Woman' as you suggested. As regards 'bastard' there was no excuse for it. And emphatically there must be no cursing in the play like "For Christ's sake go home" and "Oh Jesus is there no rest anywhere". To this I replied that if I could read the passages in the way they were meant to be interpreted he would see they were not blasphemy. This I did with great success so he raised his objections. As for 'God Damn you' that was out of the question and there was no excuse for it. Why not change it to "God be with you" (I nearly fell under the table at that suggestion) and then glowering he added that he had had lots of complaints from church people about the play, and he wanted to know what *kind* of a Bishop it was—whether a married Bishop, or a Bishop that couldn't marry—as if that made any difference to a Bishop who had begat a bastard daughter. I don't think he was wise to this part of the play or I would have been out on my ear by this time. I replied that there was no denomination or sect involved as the Bishop was a symbol and the play a fantasy, to which he replied, "I didn't know fantasies required any words, and particularly words like these" (pointing to the unmentionables). By this time I realized I was in the hands of a very *clever* lawyer and it were best to get out before he objected to anything more, so said we would make these changes, shook hands, he wishing us 'Good Luck' and 'I hope you make money'.

Elated we sped away, though I was a bit sick at the stomach over the fact that the Mayor of a City of over a million should have to fiddle with the lines of a play and at the same time be so stupid.

But this didn't end the matter. The following week the censor suddenly appeared in New York to see for himself. After the performance he expressed himself as pleased with the play, saw no reason why it shouldn't be presented in Boston, but suggested as a diplomatic measure that the little pink paper changes . . .[2]

[2] Page missing.

To Lady Astor

MS. ASTOR

FORTY-NINE OVERSTRAND MANSIONS
7 MARCH 1935

Dear Lady Astor—

Thank you for asking us to go with you to the theatre. We were very sorry that we could not go. We were alone on that day & our boy was down with the whooping cough & had to be watched. He is much better now, out of quarantine, & will be going back to school.

As well, I had a lot of correspondence with America over the banning of my play; and got into a tiny row here because of a sharp criticism of a play called "Love On The Dole", which was thought to be a bugle call to the workers. Two organizations that cant bear criticism—the Church & the so-called Labour Movement. I see the Bishop of London is writing about "God in the Slums". I wonder is He in the Bishop's Palace? Butler to his Reverend Lordship.

I see by the papers that L[loyd] G[eorge] has knocked at 10, Downing Street, & some are looking out of the window wondering if it would be wise to open the door!

Well, God be with you & Yours.

Sean

To George Jean Nathan

TS. CORNELL

49 OVERSTRAND MANSIONS
10 MARCH 1935

My dear George—

Thanks for forwarding the letter to Sylvia [Sydney]—may she never be less charming, and may you spend many more happy evenings with her. I have a friend here who raves about her beauty on the films; but beauty on a film is not much to you or to me, George. It must be closer up than a close up on a picture.

I have just been reading over again your many kind letters leading up to the production of "Within The Gates," and, now that the run is finished, I thank you again for all you did for me, realising that, but for you, the play, probably, would never have had a chance at all. I am writing to John [Tuerk] and George [Bushar Markle] to thank—not forgetting Dick

[Madden]—them for all they did, and the great fight they made, and for the great kind way they received me, and for all the help they gave me during the rehearsals, and the lavish courage and kindness they showed so that everything might be done to make the play a success. John has just written to say that the play finished "in a blaze of glory," and that is a lot to be grateful for. My cough is practically gone, and I hope yours is gone, too.

Today I've been reading "Since Ibsen," [1] and I must say that it is a devastating and terrible indictment of the theatre. I read it long ago, but today, thinking of realism in the drama, I re-read it, and it told me in bitter laughing phrases that by that way there is no salvation.

I havent had time to write to Eugene [O'Neill] yet, but I havent forgotten that grand fine fellow, and as I admired him before so I love him now. I have been reading [James] Agate's criticism of Strange Interlude—published in "First Nights," and I shall probably write something about it later on.[2] At the moment I can only say curse o' Jasus on the bastard.

I havent written to Mimsie [Taylor] yet, either, but I havent forgotten her. I've got myself into a minor row over here by the criticism of a play called "Love On The Dole," which, in book form, was sent to me to review, and I referred to it in some phrases of a Nathanesque manner, and—it was hailed by the Trades' (the play) as a great Socialist masterpiece—immediately there were screams against what I'd said, one asking "what on earth has happened to Mr Sean O'Casey!" I sent a reply to a squeal from a Miss Ethel Mannin, who is now a labour Revolutionary, but the reply hasnt yet been published, and as the paper—The New Statesman and Nation—is a Socialist periodical, the reply may be suppressed. I am waiting to see what will happen. They previously repressed a line critical of a statement about Othello made by Ivor Brown, because, if you please, "he was a contributor to the paper."

I liked the joining of the two of us together in the mystical cryptogram of George Sean Nathan, and feel inclined since to sign myself Sean Jean O'Casey. From my point of view there couldnt be a better combination. Or, better still, Gene, Jean, and Sean—trinity of Drama. So we can laugh at poor Brock Pemberton, the middle-aged man on the flying trapeze.

I must write to Brooks Atkinson, too, for he stood by us well, and, what is more, he really likes you and is your friend, and has in him a love and respect for the drama.

I've just got your letter telling me that you are down with the old complaint. I am sorry, but you will probably be allright by the time you get this. I hope you may. And every doctor willing, but none of them able to give you a hand. Writing the sign of Zeus on their precious prescriptions

[1] George Jean Nathan, *Since Ibsen* (New York. Knopf, 1933).
[2] See "It's All Very Curious, Isn't It?", *The Flying Wasp* (1937).

when, to save time at least, they might as well write the sign of the cross or the sign of the three pigeons. I do hope that you will soon be well again, and able to raise hell and bring down heaven with the things you do and say.

It's a pity that The Spectator has to go.[3] All the same, I'm in a way glad, for it was taking too much time and energy from you. While I was with you it seemed to me that you were working too hard, and, although the paper was worth it—for I never saw or read anything quite so brave and curious and stimulating—still it called for too much concentration and attention on your part. The other Editors seemed to take it easy. How is Ernie [Boyd]? He is, I fear, out with me. He was too fond of watching the dawn break for me.

I am glad that John Tuerk seemed so pleased over his connection with "Within the Gates," though God only knows why, for it gave him more trouble and worry than any play he had ever handled or probably will again. He and George Markle must be business saints. He sent me a letter amounting to an apology for taking the play off, and I feel ashamed to think that I shall be able only to give them my thanks for all they did.

With a prayer that you will soon be well again, and another for the success of Messrs Gene, Jean, & Sean, unlimited liability Co.

With Affectionate Regards to you and love to Lillian and Mimsie.

Yours As Ever,
Sean

[3] Nathan and his friends left the *American Spectator* in the spring of 1935, and it stopped publication in May 1937. See O'Casey's letter to Nathan, 28 September 1932, note 3.

To George Jean Nathan

MS. CORNELL

49 OVERSTRAND MANSIONS
[? MARCH, 1935]

My dear George—

As chance happened, I had written a letter to you before receiving yours containing news about RKO. I hope the Film may be a great success, though I am certain that there will be many rows over its appearance. The screen displaying "Juno" was slashed many times, & once, in Limerick, it was seized & set on fire; [1] so if they do that to "Juno," what will they

[1] Two reels of the film of *Juno and the Paycock,* directed by Alfred Hitchcock, were burned in the streets of Limerick on 10 November 1930 as a public protest against O'Casey and his "anti-Irish" play. For details of the film production, see O'Casey's letter to Gabriel Fallon, 28 February 1929, note 4.

do with "The Plough"? [2] However, it was a grand thing for me that RKO took the play, & we must wait patiently to see what the reaction to the Film may be.

I am delighted to hear that you are going to write the dramatic criticism for "Saturday Review of Literature," though you mustn't overtire yourself. But you have a bewildering vitality as well as a fine mind and a cool courage. It will be grand a la grand to see you again in June, if you can manage the trip. It will be delightful to have George Jean Nathan breaking bread in our home.

I am a poor correspondent with those who are mine. A letter's a poor symbol. Like making one poor leaf do instead of a long walk through a great wood. I am sending this to 44—I suppose you are still there. Ah, New York, New York—Like Shenandoah to me! I have a pile of good wishes to answer I got from America during the New Year. God be with you.

Ever yours with affection,
Sean

[2] The film of *The Plough and the Stars,* directed by John Ford, was released on 15 May 1937. For details of the film production, see O'Casey's letter to Horace Reynolds, 15 February 1937, note 1.

To Richard C. Boys

TS. BOYS

49 OVERSTRAND MANSIONS
31 MARCH 1935

Dear Mr Boys—

Many thanks for your kind letter packed with details about the banning of "Within The Gates," and for the clipping from [*The Harvard*] *Crimson.* This clipping tells us that Father Sullivan said that "as good taste demands reticence about physical deformities in an individual, so the good taste of the majority of the community, as embodied in the laws, demands the same reticence about certain morbid and unnatural vices."

As embodied in the laws! What laws? What has the law got to do with good taste? The good taste of the majority! Good taste never has and never will spring from the majority. Man in the mass is vulgar, and Sullivan can see this if he opens his eyes in his own churches with their shocking and tawdry images, ornaments, and windows. The Catholic Church is rotten with bad taste. Just listen to her mission hymns. Look at her churches—apart from those built in the middle ages—read her popular literature, talk to and discover the refined tastes of the majority of her clergy, talk to her communicants, look at her holy pictures, her images, her devotional Easter and Christmas cards, her scapulars, her miraculous medals; stare in at the window of a Catholic Repository and enjoy the horrors of good taste therein, or at the things for sale in the booths erected outside a church when there is a mission in progress. Good taste—my God, Sullivan ought to be the last one to blather about it. Nine out of every ten of the Catholic priests would probably fling away a fine reproduction of a painting by a del Sarto, a Fra Lippi, or a Fra Angelico. I have in my room a lovely reproduction of an Angel of the Annunciation by Simone Martini and every Catholic who came to see me, priests included, have always passed it by with a casual and uninterested glance. It says nothing to them.

But what have laws got to do with good taste? If bad taste were illegal, most of the Catholic priests would be behind prison bars. It is good taste to eat with the implements custom has provided for that purpose, but it is not against the law for a man to eat with his fingers. Instead of being reticent about deformity, it should be against the law to ignore it. If it can be prevented, then all intelligent and decent men should be prepared to face it, and get rid of its vileness forever. Doesnt this priest know about such a disease as rickets, and what causes it? Is it a bad thing to see that every child gets food and treatment in its infancy so that this horrible thing may not inflict it with a revolting deformity? Or to take measures to insure [against] the results of incipient consumption in an underfed kid. We see in the many deformities around us as the result of ignorance and stupidity, and this priest counsels reticence about these things in the name of good taste. Well, God is something more than the God of good taste. But he is the God of greatness in literature and drama, in sculpture and painting, the God of greatness in life, but this fellow would have Him nothing more than a suave, respectable, decorous deity. Sullivan tells us that the Church is still effective in the salvaging of the world's derelicts. Well, if it goes on much longer the work will be done, for the world will be a world of derelicts. They love to be forever paddling and playing among the derelicts. But Christ didnt come into the world to found a Church that was to spend its time salvaging derelicts. He came that we might have life, and have it more abundantly. But His followers revel in this lust for the mean, the miserable, the crippled, and the whining—the Down and Out.

In one place this Jesuit said that my play was a symbol of death. Imagine a Jesuit—how many of their saints are shown staring at a skull? —banning a play that sings of life, and calling it a symbol of death. And the members of his own church, rightly or wrongly, are fed on the symbols of torture and death. How often have I seen the poor people of Dublin forking out their weekly penny or tuppence to keep up the membership of the Sodality of the Bona Mors, every thought outside of their day to day needs, a thought of fear; fear, fear, fear, never realising that how they lived was more important than how they died. And are they not now trying to get the glory of canonization for a Dublin workingman who was found with hoops of steel round his body that had been there for years, and that had eaten into his flesh.[1] And this Jesuit talks of "Within The Gates" as a symbol of death.

It is something slanderous to suggest that I, as a foreigner, indirectly or directly, offended the embodied law of the United States. What he means, of course, is that the play may have affronted the laws of the Roman Catholic Penny Cathechism, but the laws of this catechism arent the Laws of The Federal States of America, or, indeed, the State Laws of Massachusetts. Or the play possibly affronted the Canonical Laws of the Councils of Nice or of Trent, but the laws of these Councils arent the Federal Laws of the United States, or, indeed, the laws of the State of Massachusetts.

The truth is, my dear friend, I know these gentlemen too well, and they know I know them. Why in the very district in which I lived just before I came to your country, a Superior of a Catholic Community of monks was removed because of scandals going the round about him.

As for good taste again, someone should ask Father Sullivan if it be good taste to promise a man a share in the Holy Sacrifice of the Mass if he sold a book of Sweep tickets—as I was. As for sex, let the gentleman Jesuit read the History of Sacerdotal Celibacy in The Christian Church, and he will get far more of it than he got in my play.

It is simply a damned lie to say that there is in "Within The Gates" from beginning to end, one line or one word dealing with "unnatural vices." Sex is not an unnatural vice, and the priest that says so maligns his faith.

The reticence he is so fond of is another and a fairer name for cowardice, and those who refuse to face the things that trouble us in this life is guilty of a dastardly rejection of the courage that comes from God.

I understand your interest in The Catholic Faith, and it is a natural interest to have in a country where Catholicism is not a dominant power. It is a very different thing in a country where it overpowers everything and everybody from the President to the newest born infant.

Please give my thanks and good wishes to Mr [Edwin F.] Melvin, drama Editor of The Boston Transcript. And to Dr [Clarence] Skinner, too.

[1] A reference to Matt Talbot (1856–1925), a Dublin laborer who had been a dissolute drinker until the age of twenty-eight when he suddenly reformed and went on to live a life of holiness and mortification. When he died chains were found on his body, rusted into the flesh. Many unsuccessful attempts have been made to canonize him. See O'Casey's letter to Honor Tracy, 1 September 1946, Vol. II. O'Casey mocks him as "Mutt Talbot" in "In this Tent, the Rebubblicans," *Drums Under the Windows* (1946).

God be with you all in Harvard, and with all men and women who fight fearlessly that we may have life and have it more abundantly.

Ever Yours,
Sean O Casey

To Macmillan & Co. Ltd.

TS. MACMILLAN LONDON
49 OVERSTRAND MANSIONS
5 APRIL 1935

Dear Sirs,

Could I have the following books?
Modernismus. Sir Reginald Blomfield. 6/0
Short History of English Words. Bernard Groom. 5/0
Wheels And Butterflies. Yeats. 6/0
This Was My World. Miscellany Ed. Lady Rhondda. 6/0
More Plays: All's Over Then? and Church Street. [Lennox] Robinson. 5/0
Irish Literary Portraits. John Eglinton.

I should like to draw your attention to the non-receipt of £18.18.0. as detailed in financial account for year 1934. This sum, I believe, should have been forwarded on the 1st of January. Perhaps you will be good enough to deduct cost of above books from my account.

Yours Sincerely,
Sean O'Casey

To Lillian Gish

TS. GISH

49 OVERSTRAND MANSIONS
8 APRIL 1935

Dear Lillian:

Thanks for your kind letter and the interesting account of the last performance of "Within The Gates", though, I'm afraid, it wouldn't have had so long a run were it not for the courage and generosity of Mr. [George] Bushar Markle. The last performance must have been a strange experience and I should have given a lot to be there, though not so much as I should have given to be present when the ban was declared in Boston. I got a whole pile of correspondence about it, and a lot of press-cuttings, but these couldn't give the thrill I'd have got from standing and hitting out in the center of the fight. Though the ban caused some excitement and a lot of talk, I should have preferred the tour and it is a pity that the Jesuits of Boston were able to stop it.

I haven't heard anything about a Summer Tour through the Colleges and imagine that might prove a difficult thing to do with the company scattered everywhere. Still, considering the great difficulty that was in the play for production and acting, I think we have had a wonderful time and everything turned out a hell of a sight better than I at first thought they would. It was a terribly difficult play for all, and everyone was good and some great—you, for instance—and only one definitely poor—the poor Gardner, though he did his best. And let me thank you, Lillian, for a grand and a great performance; for your gentle patience throughout the rehearsals, and for the grand way you dived into the long and strenuous part of "The Young Whore".

I hope George is well again. I'm glad he's decided to chuck up "The Spectator", for he was wasting himself away on it. With its 5 Editors, it was too much of a one man job. Still it's a pity, too, for there wasn't its like in the whole English-speaking world. It was a unique paper and one cannot murmur about its departure that it may rest in peace! It will be a definite loss, but the loss is bearable since it releases the one and only George Jean Nathan for other work.

I hope Dorothy's well; I'll never forget that terrible quotation she gave us from "Brittle Heaven", a quotation that was neither prose nor poetry. Well, authors have something to put up from bad actors; but actors have a lot to put up with from bad authors! And remember me to your dear mother. I have written several times to George, and hope my letter don't bother him too much. I was hardly here till I rushed into a row for damning a play that everyone praised. George has infected me with his terrible propensity to dismiss with a look from his eyes the play he doesn't like.

Affectionate regards,
Sean

To Brooks Atkinson

MS. ATKINSON
49 OVERSTRAND MANSIONS
9 APRIL 1935

My dear Brooks:

Now when the last song has been sung, the last word said, & the last tear shed, let me thank you again for all that you did to help me and my friends throughout the run of "Within The Gates". I shall never forget my stay in your country where I felt no strangeness, though full of wonder at many things I saw in your great city, regretting that I hadn't time to look long enough or close enough at all I saw. It was a bright time with a streak of bitterness in it, but there is no brightness so bright as the brightness that is slashed with a gleam of bitterness, and the controversy over the play was, with a few of the critics—the ban was another thing altogether—did me good, for a general and royal salute given to a play is a bad thing for the Dramatist to get—not that I am ever likely to get it, Brooks. I have just been reading your article called "Fiddling at the old Tunes",[1] & I agree with the most of it. It isn't silly to expect the Theatre to be in advance of its time. If a man is a Dramatist then he must be in advance of his time; just as a man if he is a critic must be in advance of the Drama of his time. If the statesmen & bureaucrats can't set the world to right, then the Dramatist must set the Bureaucrats & statesmen to rights, or send them to the right about with a quick-march following them. The activity of the Left you write about, it seems to me, is more a sign of life in the American Theatre, than a sign of life in the Left. Here there is a sign of life neither in the Right nor the Left, nor in the middle. But the article is fine & terribly true. But there's always a chance in America of a fight; here everyone's sunk up to the neck in a scented bog of politeness, and all the Dramatists here are parked into padded cells.

But I mustn't weary you with my loud cries, but confine myself to an expression of joyous appreciation of all you did for me.

Give my good wishes to Messrs. Gabriel & Mason-Brown, hoping as I do, that they & I shall live to have another fight.[2]

And give my love to Mrs. Atkinson, whom I hope to meet again in West 12th Street, & enjoy her good food & excellent wine.

My love and thanks to you,
my dear Brooks.
Yours as Ever.
Sean O'Casey

[1] Brooks Atkinson, "Fiddling at the Old Tunes," *New York Times*, 17 March 1935.

[2] Gilbert W. Gabriel, drama critic of the *New York American*, and John Mason-Brown, drama critic of the *New York Post*, had written unfavorable reviews of *Within the Gates* in their papers on 23 October 1934. Mr. Mason-Brown's review, "Without Mr. O'Casey's Gates," is reprinted in *Two on the Aisle* (New York, Norton, 1938), pp. 126–130.

To Harold Macmillan

MS. MACMILLAN LONDON

49 OVERSTRAND MANSIONS
9 APRIL 1935

Dear Mr. Harold Macmillan,

Thanks for your kind letter about the proposal from your American House to incorporate—which seems a right word to use—my plays, stories, & all into one great volume. I am quite willing to agree to your fine suggestion that "Juno & the Paycock," "The Plough & the Stars," "The Shadow of a Gunman," and "The End of the Beginning," should be popped into one cover & keep together till death do them part.

I don't know why they want to get rid of "Within The Gates" so suddenly, for I know there is a good demand for this play owing to the production in New York, & afterwards, on account of the ban in Boston, Cleveland, & Toronto.[1] All this has stirred up interest in the other plays, & when I was there, there was a lot of interest shown in "The Silver Tassie." I should be glad if you would write for me to America.

Yours Sincerely,
Sean O'Casey

[1] For the ban and controversy over *Within the Gates* in Boston, see O'Casey's letter to Richard Madden, 17 January 1935, note 1; and the letter from John Tuerk, 5 March 1935, note 1.

By Sean O'Casey

Time and Tide
13 APRIL 1935

NOTES ON THE WAY [1]
By Sean O'Casey

(In order to preserve the essentially individual character of NOTES ON THE WAY, we allow those who contribute them an entirely free pen. We must not be taken as being necessarily in agreement with the opinions expressed.—EDITOR, *Time and Tide.*) [2]

[1] This article is a reply to several letters in the *New Statesman and Nation,* in which G. Wren Howard and Ethel Mannin, 16 February, and Ronald Gow, 23 February, objected to O'Casey's review of *Love on the Dole* in the 9 February 1935 issue of that magazine.

[2] The controversial column was usually assigned to a guest author, and before O'Casey, from January to April, it had been written by T. S. Eliot, Lady Rhondda (The Editor), Wyndham Lewis, and Louis Golding. O'Casey had written it on four previous occasions in 1934, on February 3, 10, 17, and 24.

English criticism has long lost its virility, and is fast losing its courage. So many have been conscripted for the battle of the books, each equally armed and each afraid of the other, that the business—for it is a business—has become a hollow game of you touch me gently and I'll do the same to you. All are now so fond of saying things softly, of letting things down gently, of the soft answer that turneth away wrath, that they have created a land bulging with geniuses who write novels, plays, and poems, giving a grandeur to England that is a mockery and a shame. Criticism now is unacceptable unless it is performed with pleasantry and barbed only with a bow. The art has dwindled down to a village pageant flushed with toy spears, wooden swords, and grand garments, where herald-authors trumpet each other in and out of the display; where everyone wins and each is given a garland. Most of the reviewers are mere polishers of brass, a job, even if well done, that wouldn't do much harm if we were made aware that the metal polished bright was brass; but the reviewers breathe on the brass, handle it fondly, and hold it up to the light as if they were polishing gold. If this should continue much longer, England may remain a land of hope, but she will cease to be a land of glory. On the big Sunday weeklies we have, of course, a few who have the courage to say out plainly what is in their minds to say on the things belonging to literature and art. We have plain speaking in the golden gentleness of Desmond MacCarthy, in the vigorous and sturdy outlook on life and drama by St. John Ervine; and Ernest Newman, the Music Critic of *The Sunday Times* who, out of his dignity, speaks plainly when he finds it necessary to do so, as he did some time ago when he told Constant Lambert and us all the difference between the symbols of *rubato* and *tenuto* on a musical score; and recently, when he thought there was reason for blame, gave it out good and large to Kreisler. But, on the whole, every week seems to be a jubilee year to the books reviewed.

A little time ago I read an advertisement of a book that was then causing a stir, and took a note of what was said. We were told that the book had been praised by hundreds—a suspicious thing in itself—and that it had been described as magnificent, brilliant, intense, majestic, a masterpiece, unequalled, noble, vigorous, terrifying, epic, thrilling, enormous, astonishing, beautiful, fascinating, profound, exciting, significant, unforgettable, passionate, symphonic, swift, monumental. Quite a hurricane of qualities; but if one went to the trouble to gather into a bunch the adjectives applied week after week to the books reviewed, the average of acclamation wouldn't be very much below the example given above, though, if bare justice and kindly justice were done, most of them would be banished broken by a critical thunderbolt.

This ceaseless downpour of praise has left us all in such a soft and damp condition that when any author, critic, or clergyman gets a sudden and sharp prod of adverse criticism, he or she is breathless and, without a word of warning, throws a swoon. Many critics have a tendency, too, if one ventures to reply to them, of falling down in a dead faint, evidently thinking that their criticisms are written, not on desks or tables, but on the tops of holy altars. And sometimes, though the critics and the author be brave, the press, daily or periodical, is cowardly, and is afraid of its life of a fight, though a fight between two who have an interest in what they do, even though it be for the very fight's sake, is more promising and exciting than to go on forever encouraging those who sit or lie listlessly murmuring well done to everything. Damn braces; bless relaxes, cried Blake, and Blake, in spite of his fantastic mysticism, had a deep knowledge of the deepest things of life.

As it is with the novel, so it is with the play. Kid-gloved criticism of the English drama is responsible for a stream of commonplace plays that have in them neither the colour of mirth nor the dim magic of mourning. Criticism of the drama has been so great-grandmotherly for so long a time in England that many are stunned when what ought to be said is said about a commonplace play. Some little time ago I received from *The New Statesman and Nation* a number of plays with the request that I should review them. One of these was a play called *Love on the Dole*. I ventured to say what I thought, or half of what I thought, for, actually, I thought then as I think now, that this play, with many more to keep it company, is part of what ought to be swept up and thrown out of the house of drama. *Love on the Dole* uses the Means Test as its hero at the beginning, the middle, and at the end of the play, as if the Social problem that faces us all, rich and poor, learned and ignorant, could be solved by the retention or abolition of The Means Test. The play was generally praised—as usual—by the critics as a fine play, and hailed by those who are prominent in their devotion to the masses as a great and golden vindication of the proletariat. My criticism of the play raised a loud yell from a Mr. G. Wren Howard, and a louder yell from Miss Ethel Mannin, both yells duly broadcast by *The New Statesman and Nation*. I replied with another yell which the periodical refused to publish. This seemed to me to be a strange way of behaving on the part of a periodical that stands as a pioneer for untrammelled thought around the things that interest and concern us all. The paper asked me for my opinion about the play, and was frightened into silence when they got it, as if a difference of opinion about a play between Miss Ethel Mannin and me would bring about the collapse of capitalism or labour, or even lead to the fall of the Government. The boys of the bull-dog breed seem to be developing into charming old ladies of Quality Street.

Mr. G. Wren Howard wanted to know why *The New Statesman and Nation* accepted such trash from Mr. O'Casey, and vehemently protested that O'Casey should have gone to see the play before he denounced it in such "ill-considered and offensive terms." You see, a plain outspoken opinion is ill-considered and offensive. This in itself is an indication of the bitter need for outspoken opinions on what is so often thought to be and is called literature and drama. Mr. Wren Howard should know that I was asked to review the book of the play, and not to say what I thought of the acting in it. Acting cannot give to a play what a play hasn't got, and, if Mr. Wren Howard thinks it can and did, that is his funeral and not mine.

Miss Ethel Mannin was stung to fury by the criticism. She suggested that I might have been jealous because some of the critics likened *Love on the Dole* to *Juno and the Paycock*, but she added, for my benefit, I suppose, that there was room for everyone at the top of the ladder or the top of a tree. She told me that by dismissing the characters in the play I dismissed the great masses. To hell with the artist as above the princes and proletariat, she cries, and then exultantly commends a visit to the Tyneside or Clydeside so that I could get "a kick in the pants for spouting that kind of stuff." This young lady, who evidently thinks herself to be a revolutionary, has a lot to learn. If the dismissal of the characters in a poor play constitutes the dismissal of the great masses, then the great masses aren't quite so great as this young ladylike revolutionary thinks them to be. And her "room at the top of the tree" thought is, I fear, the thought of a petty bourgeois. How often have we heard it said before—every soldier carries a marshal's baton in his knapsack; the road is a straight line from log cabin to White House; every industrious apprentice can become a Lord Mayor of London, *a la* Dick Whittington. There isn't room on the top of a ladder, or on the top of a tree, or on the top of a hill, for that matter, for everyone. Under the highest possible form of Communist Government, with the enlightened practice of centuries behind it, there would be room only for a few at the top of things. The great masses would still be at the bottom. By implying that if I spoke my mind on the banks of the Clyde or the banks of the Tyne, I'd have a rough time of it, she pays a high tribute to the higher instincts and intelligence of the Proletariat.

As for jealousy, well, I am frankly jealous of many fine things done by Eugene O'Neill, Shaw, Strindberg, Ibsen, Toller, and Maugham, but this is a jealousy of admiration and affection, and in its avowal I feel not the slightest sense of shame. But if Miss Mannin includes *Love on the Dole* in this jealousy, then my thought is the thought that hummed in the mind of W. B. Yeats when he wrote:

> "To a Poet, who would have me praise certain bad poets, imitators of his and mine"
>
> You say, as I have often given tongue
> In praise of what another's said or sung,
> 'Twere politic to do the like by these;
> But was there ever dog that praised his fleas?

Which, passing on, is a valiant example of self-consciousness in art worthy of the name.

In the body of my criticism of the play I ventured the opinion that there wasn't in it a thought worth remembering. This got Miss Ethel Mannin going madly. Up she stood and told us that in the very beginning of the play there is a thought worth remembering, and she quoted it. Here it is: "Unemployment and pauperdom, that is the legacy of the Industrial Revolution. That is the price we pay for the system. And that is the price you'll go on paying till you waken up to the fact that the remedy's in your hands." Well, men and women of poverty and plentitude, what do you think of it? There's an example of original and beautiful English prose for those at the top and those at the bottom of the tree. Saucy, eh? Three hackneyed phrases in one short sentence. One: price we pay for the system; two: waken up to the fact; three: the remedy's in your own hands. And, from the Socialist point of view, the statement isn't true. The Industrial Revolution has left the proletariat a legacy, not of unemployment and pauperdom, but a legacy of abundance and material security. The Industrial Revolution has gathered together a legacy of wealth and an abundance of all things for all men. That the legacy hasn't yet been claimed doesn't alter the fact that the legacy is there. And the Industrial Revolution can hardly be called a "system." Under a Socialist or Communist Government this "system" that has provided us with a legacy of "unemployment and pauperdom," instead of being checked or abolished, would be intensified. It is both meet and right for Miss Ethel Mannin to say "to hell with art," for the hero of her "Pilgrims" is made to say that "the art of Rubens, Rembrandt, and Hals is technique without inspiration," which declaration shows us that what Miss Mannin knows and doesn't know about art isn't worth knowing.

But though E. L. in the March number of the *Adelphi* says that "*The New Statesman* is to be congratulated on its treatment of *Love on the Dole*," the fact that Wren Howard and Ethel Mannin began the controversy; that I was denied the right of replying; that I wasn't even accorded the courtesy of an announcement that a reply had been received but could not be printed, are things that make the congratulation look very shabby and dull indeed. Yes, it looks to me as if the boys of the bull-dog breed are developing into timid and charming old ladies of Quality Street. . . .[3]

[3] In the remaining seven-hundred-odd words of the article, O'Casey moves on to different topics to contend with three reviewers: James Agate, Ivor Brown, and Edward Shanks.

From Kingsley Martin [1] *to* Time and Tide

20 April 1935

SEAN O'CASEY'S NOTES ON THE WAY

Sir,—I enjoyed Mr. O'Casey's Notes on the Way, and look forward with considerable interest to the effects of the precedent that you and he have set. You realize, of course, the novelty of the procedure. To publish an attack based on the private correspondence between an author and Editor (who had not, by the way, until he saw the article, any idea that he was not on good terms with the author) certainly opens the way to a quite new type of liveliness in weekly journalism. Some differences of opinion must arise in every paper. There must be some rejected and disappointed suitors even for the hand of TIME AND TIDE. Indeed, I think I know of one. But knowing the Editor for an honourable and fair-minded person who might have excellent reasons that I cannot estimate, for his rejection of letters or articles—such as space, libel, decency and a hundred others—it had not occurred to me to invite possibly aggrieved people to make an article out of their grievances against TIME AND TIDE and publish it in the *New Statesman and Nation*. I do not deny that it might be good copy, but neither the *New Statesman and Nation* nor TIME AND TIDE have hitherto made good copy the sole reason for acceptance or rejection, and I should be sorry if they did so. I am far from accepting the old newspaper adage that "Dog does not eat dog," meaning that no newspaper should ever attack another. But the attack should, I think, be based on public policy, and a charge of suppression only made where the facts are established and not on very doubtful cases in which the only evidence is to be found in private correspondence about which the public cannot judge.

Now let me come to the particular case of Mr. O'Casey. Having a great admiration for Mr. O'Casey as one of the few first-class playwrights of our time, I was glad when he agreed to review some plays for the *New Statesman and Nation*, and, knowing his reputation, was not surprised that he slanged Walter Greenwood's "Love on the Dole." Unfortunately he only slanged it and did not review it. Now it has always seemed to us on the *New Statesman and Nation* that a review should give some idea of what a book is about. The reviewer should say what is wrong with a book in relation to what the author has tried to do, not merely be content with saying that he hates it. However, we printed Mr. O'Casey's bit of mud-slinging which was very amusing, and which was not continued in the case of the other book which he covered in the same review, and which he dealt with excellently. His attack on "Love on the Dole" produced vehement replies to which "yells" he replied, in his own phrase, with another "yell."

[1] Kingsley Martin (1897–1968), a leading British socialist and editor of the *New Statesman and Nation*, 1931–60.

I had not his letter before me because he asked for it back. But I remember that it was extremely abusive. As I could see no progress in the controversy, nor any reason why the yells should ever stop of their own accord, I did not print his letter or other attacks on him that I received. He then wrote a second letter which might have been printable, but said he only wanted it printed if the first was also printed. So I sent them both back and asked my secretary to write to Mr. O'Casey saying that I could not see much point in continuing the controversy in that spirit and asking him to come and see me. This seems an odd and trivial story on which to base an attack on the *New Statesman and Nation* for suppressing "untrammelled thought."

With much of what Mr. O'Casey says about the softness of criticism and the excessive politeness of reviewers and critics I am entirely in agreement, though I have never before heard these attacks levelled at the *New Statesman and Nation*. My only difference from Mr. O'Casey is that he identifies outspokenness with abuse. To me they seem quite different things. No doubt the tone of this letter seems to him namby-pamby and fit for an "old lady of Quality Street." What fun—and what a waste of time—it would be if we all copied his example! Instead of sincerely replying to him I should, in that case, have merely written something about Irish guttersnipes and poltroonish attacks by papers that are only fit for the lavatory. But you, Sir, would not have printed my letter and, in my view, you would have been right. And then, of course, according to your precedent I should have printed in the *New Statesman and Nation* a vehement attack on TIME AND TIDE for suppressing free speech.

KINGSLEY MARTIN,
Editor.

"The New Statesman and Nation,"
10 Great Turnstile,
W.C.1

(We regret that Mr. Kingsley Martin should feel that we ought not to have published Mr. Sean O'Casey's Notes on the Way, but in our opinion, since at least half the correspondence he refers to was intended for publication, it could scarcely be described as "private." It has always been the declared policy of this paper to allow the writers of Notes on the Way an entirely free pen. We can certainly imagine circumstances in which we should feel obliged to make exception to this rule. But the storm in this particular tea-cup did not appear to us to be large enough to justify interference. It is indeed true that every paper suffers from a long list of disappointed and often indignant would-be contributors, but for our part we should not object to any of these airing their grievances elsewhere.—*Editor*, TIME AND TIDE.)

To George Jean Nathan

MS. Cornell

49 Overstrand Mansions
22 April 1935

My dear George—

It was a pleasure to get your note telling me a lot of good news, & making it plain that you are still alive and still busy. I hadn't heard from you since I learned that you were on the rack with the old neuralgic complaint, & I often wondered how you were, & murmured to Eileen (the wife) "wonder how's George?" I take it that, as far as the old enemy goes, you are allright again, & busy disposing of the things that belong to "The American Spectator." I'm afraid I'll miss it a great deal—it was the only paper in the world to which I was a yearly subscriber—for, when it came I used to dive into it, & rarely came to the surface again till it had been read through. It was, while it lived, the Sword of the Lord & of George, Jean Nathan. Undoubtedly, it was taking too much out of you, & that couldn't go on very much longer without injury to your health and work. Besides, it seemed to me, you had on your shoulders, as well as the Journal, the Four Associate Editors, & had to carry yourself on your own shoulders, too. So God be thanked it's all over, & you will be free to do more important work.

I see by the New York "The Stage," that our old comrade Ernest Boyd was running round doing things in "The Post Depression Gantics," & that five of the critics, including John A[nderson], gambolled about in a sketch called "Custard's Last Pie." I'd have given something to see this.

Gambol, gambol all you can,
For you will soon be like a man,
A year or less, an also ran—
So gambol, gambol all you can,
John Hammond & John Anderson.

I am still in the middle of the row over my review of "Love On The Dole." The Editor of the paper that wouldn't put my letter in has now, in Time & Tide, referred to me as "an Irish Guttersnipe"; & I have in a quiet way replied to him, & to another defending Communism in such a way as to show he doesn't know the first or last thing about it.

Now, I thank you for [referring] Mr. Sisk to Dick Madden. I understand R.K.O. have offered $10,000 for the Film Rights, & Dick is trying to get $15,000 or $12,000, which will be grand and more than grand, for it is badly needed. Thank you, my dear George. G. B. Shaw's latest play [1]

[1] Bernard Shaw's *The Simpleton of the Unexpected Isles* was first performed by the Theatre Guild in New York on 18 February 1935.

must have been pretty bad according to your brief note in April's "Vanity Fair."

Every fine Wish & Affectionate Regard.

As Ever,
Sean

To Time and Tide

4 MAY 1935

SEAN O'CASEY'S NOTES ON THE WAY

Sir,—No, I don't think Mr. Kingsley Martin's letter [1] fit for an old lady of Quality Street, for it is hardly straightforward and dignified enough for that.

None of my letters was meant to be private, and as Mr. Martin's correspondence came to about eleven lines, his grip on the privilege of privacy is a very slender one. I am in no way proud that he agrees with some of the things I have said, so we shall let these consents pass by and be forgotten, and deal only with those things that have evidently got him on the raw.

Mr. Kingsley Martin complains that I "only slanged *Love on the Dole,*" and did not review it, and refers to my comments on the play as "a bit of mud-slinging." I did not consider the play worth reviewing, and that ended the matter as far as I was concerned. If there was more of this kind of criticism shot hotly at commonplace plays that totter on and off the English Stage, the English drama would have in it, at least, a faint hope for the future, instead of being, as it is, without hope or God, or a courageous critic in its world of make-believe. I will leave the charge of "mud-slinging" to those who read *The New Statesman* to decide for themselves whether or not this term is a fair comment on what I wrote about the play.

Writing of my reply to Miss Ethel Mannin and to Mr. Wren Howard, which he refused to publish, Mr. Martin says, "I had not O'Casey's letter before me, because he asked for it back. But I remember that it was extremely abusive." He implies by the statement that the letter was "extremely abusive," that he did well to keep it out of his paper, and by saying that he "had not O'Casey's letter before him" gets away from a challenge by implying that he may have been mistaken. Now the letter contains nothing that did not appear in the article written for TIME AND TIDE, and the readers of this Journal can decide for themselves whether the

[1] *Time and Tide,* 20 April 1935.

letter was extremely abusive or just a sharp but a fair comment. Besides, Mr. Martin had time to remember the letter backwards, for he had it for a fortnight before I asked for its return. Then he must have had another look at it, for I got a letter from his secretary, saying that Mr. Martin had not kept the letter, though a week or so afterwards Mr. Martin found the letter and returned it to me.

We are told that the second letter (a short reply to letters from Messrs. R. Gow and Edward Sackville West) sent by me to *The New Statesman* "*might have been printable*" (italics mine), which statement seems to convey that this letter was pretty hot stuff, even for Mr. Martin. Well, here it is:

> THE EDITOR,
> *The New Statesman.*
>
> DEAR SIR,—I have no intention of prolonging the discussion around *Love on the Dole,* or of extending it to a *Causa O'Casey contra Anglidecorum mundi.*
>
> "The Playwright" says Mr. Gow "is under a very severe discipline." Quite; the plays that are poured out on the English stage show it. The artist is answerable only to himself—he alone can make or mar his work. Mr. Gow thinks that thought should be outside a play. Most of the playwrights seem to think so, too. Mr. E. S. West thinks art should be kept out of it too. Curtain.

Is there anything libellous, indecent, or of the nature of mud-slinging in this letter? If there be, I hope Mr. Martin will be good enough to point it out to me.

Mr. Martin ends by saying that if he had adopted my manner he would have written something about "Irish guttersnipes and attacks by poltroonish papers only fit for the lavatory." Now we know where we are. And this from a paragon of virtue in the printed word. Here is a sentence worth remembering. Let us repeat it as a text as that we may fix it in our minds: Irish guttersnipes and attacks by poltroonish papers only fit for the lavatory. Well, there it is, and there I will leave it—a fit tail to Mr. Martin's kite.

Mr. Basil J. Green [2] comes rushing along breathlessly saying a lot of things, one of which is the mention of the restriction of the rights of free speech by the Government. But what about the restriction of free speech by the Editor of the Radical *New Statesman*? Not a word about this, so Mr. Green's love of freedom does not seem to go down very deep. He says that I said "Under a Socialist or Communist Government matters would be made even worse than they are at present."

I never said anything of the kind, and until Mr. Basil Green learns

[2] *Ibid.*

to read me right, I see no reason why I should waste my time in trying to reply to his questions.

My thanks to Mr. J. Daly [3] for his kind appreciation, and for the generous and effective support contained in his letter.

I am, etc.,
Sean O'Casey

London.

[3] *Ibid.* This was O'Casey's friend Jack Daly.

From W. B. Yeats

MS. O'CASEY

17 LANCASTER GATE TERRACE,
[LONDON] W.2.
[7? MAY 1935]

Dear O'Casey

I am dictating this letter to my wife. I have been in London for the last six weeks & am slowly recovering from my second attack of congestion of the lungs since January. I got well of the 1st attack & came to London on March 25th & got ill again. I wish I could see you. I cannot go out, I wonder if you could dine with me at my lodging (7 pm) on Wednesday or Friday. I shall be alone as my wife is not staying here at present as there is no room.

Yours sincerely,
W. B. Yeats

To George Jean Nathan

MS. CORNELL

49 OVERSTRAND MANSIONS
11 MAY 1935

My dear George—

Indeed, I was glad to get your letter saying that you hoped to get to England in June, et al, that you must be your own self again, & free from that damned neuralgic attack. I got a letter from Lillian the other day, written in a jungle populated with Black Shirts, & this letter told me she had seen you just before she left for the Continent, & added that you were looking fine. We are very near to heaven when we look fine and feel fine—as near it as we wish to be anyhow.

I'm really glad—and sorry—to hear that "The American Spectator" will soon be quick-marching into the past. The mainstream of G. J. Nathan's energy was dividing into too many rivulets of other interests to be good for the man, or for those who revelled in his work. I'm trying to keep in touch with America by Vanity Fair & The Stage, and, as the days flit by, I feel the flap of the Stars & Stripes more than ever. Things will happen between Hollywood, Harvard, & the Hudson.

G.B.S.'s latest must have been pretty bad. I wish he'd ca' canny for a while. I'm certain there's fire in him still, if he'd only wait till it got to a glow. But he won't, for I hear that he has written another while on a Cruise round Africa! And Coward, evidently, has climbed a step lower down with his "Point Valaine."

I enclose cutting of a dispute I had over "Love On The Dole," which Broadway will probably see next Fall.

Also, a letter for Mimsie, and I shall be gratified if you could give or send it to her, first censoring anything censorious in it.

I haven't started anything in earnest yet.

And so till June which wouldn't come quick enough if it came on a hare's back.

Ever Yours,
Sean

To Time and Tide

11 MAY 1935

SEAN O'CASEY'S NOTES ON THE WAY

Sir,—Just a final word to say that I am a little tired of the dispute about *Love on the Dole*, and, I imagine, everyone else, except Mr. Ronald Gow,[1] must be tired of it too. Anyone with an elementary knowledge of dramatic technique knows everything in a play, from the rise to the fall of the curtain, is part of the play. The word "political," though Mr. Gow dazzles us with it in italics, wasn't, as far as I remember, used once by me in anything I have written about the play. I called the play poor and commonplace, and I call it commonplace and poor still. If the play be noble, fine, moving,

[1] *Time and Tide,* 4 May 1935.

and great, as he and many others think it to be, then he can afford to laugh at my ignorance of dramatic value and dramatic technique. Let me be unto him even as one of those noises off that he thinks so very little about.

I am, etc.,
Sean O'Casey

To W. B. Yeats

TS. NAT LIB, DUBLIN

OVERSTRAND MANSIONS
1 JUNE 1935

Dear Mr. Yeats—

A few days ago I received a letter from Messrs French saying that an amateur society wished to give some performances of "The Silver Tassie." I replied saying that owing to the new nature of the play all amateur applications would have to be dealt with personally. They then sent me on the application which, strangely enough, comes from the Dramatic Society of Belfast University. I enclose a copy of the letter.

As a Dublinman I don't like to refuse anything to Belfast, but seeing that the Abbey are thinking of performing this play, it seems to me that the first production in Ireland should be given by your theatre. If you think so, too, I shall write to Mr. James and tell him that the Amateur rights have not yet been released.

I have got the supplementary catalogue of plays issued by The British Drama League, but ninety-nine and three quarters of them are rubbish, and the rest, or almost all the rest, we know, so the catalogue isnt of much use.

It has just entered into my mind that, since The Free State has declared the independence of its citizenship, all English plays can now be classified as foreign works.

I hope you are getting stronger every day.

Yours Sincerely
Sean O'Casey

2 enclosures.

From W. B. Yeats

TS. O'CASEY

17 LANCASTER GATE TERRACE
LONDON, W.2.
2 JUNE 1935

Dear O'Casey

Thank you very much for your letter. I agree with you that it would be better for the Abbey if it can give the first Irish production of your play "The Silver Tassie". A little later the amateur Society might be allowed to do it. I have just written to Blythe [1] who is, now that Lennox is away, the most representative member of our Board, telling him that you have permitted us to produce both "The Silver Tassie" and "Within the Gates". I have suggested putting "Within the Gates" into immediate rehearsal and including it in the programme for Horse-show week.

Thank you for the enclosures & all else

Yours
W. B. Yeats

[1] Ernest Blythe was appointed as a director of the Abbey Theatre on 8 April 1935.

To George Jean Nathan

MS. CORNELL

49 OVERSTRAND MANSIONS
[?] JULY [1935]

My dear George—

I'm writing these scant lines on the chance of your being still inside the boundary of New York. I daresay you have come back from Gene [O'Neill], who, I hope you found well, & left well. It will be fine to see you again, should circumstances let you come to Europe. I have started nothing definite yet in the shape of a play, but may do this a little later on. W. B. Yeats was over here recently, & asked me to come to see him. I went several times; we talked over many things, & he asked me for "The Silver Tassie," which, of course, was always there for them to do. The [Abbey] Theatre is to change its policy, & is to get away from producing purely peasant plays, substituting the best of European & American Drama, &, of course, giving a chance to any good Irish play that may come along—

a policy that they should have adopted years ago. So God be with them in the new venture. Macmillans here are issuing my Five Irish plays in one volume,[1] & I am busy looking over the proofs—curse o' God on them!

Love to Mimsie, Frances, Sylvia, three in one & one in three. & love to you—three in one yourself.

Yours Ever,
Sean

[1] *Five Irish Plays* (1935): *The Shadow of a Gunman, Juno and the Paycock, The Plough and the Stars, The End of the Beginning, A Pound on Demand.* The book is dedicated "To George Jean Nathan, drama critic, without fear and without reproach."

To Time and Tide

6 JULY 1935

A LETTER OF THANKS[1]

Sir,—I first realized that things weren't well with those who had enough money to demand respect and secure attention when, with a friend, I visited a nursing-home in the heart of the West End. While waiting for a moment in the hall, I remarked to my friend how dark, dull, and slovenly the place appeared to be. I ran a hand along a ledge and showed it to myself and friend thickly covered with the dirt one might expect to find in a wine-cellar. Not so very long ago I was acquainted with a maternity case which placed itself under the care of a nursing-home in a swell part of London. The baby was sometime overdue, and the expectant mother was receiving special care and attention—at least, so it was supposed. The woman had been under special observation for two weeks—or so it was supposed. She was encouraged to take walks to hasten the birth, and the walks were helped by the injection of drugs. One afternoon she with her husband was exhorted to go "for a good brisk walk" though the woman complained of severe pains, and was reluctant to go out. The husband protested to a nurse that it was risky to leave the home, but the two were almost shoved out of the door. Realizing her state much better than the competent nurses, the woman rushed back, and, in great pain, insisted that she was sure the baby was about to be born. She hurried to her room while the husband shouted at the hesitant nurse to ring for the doctor. The woman had just time to reach her room, whip off her clothes when the real labour began, and she actually supervised the birth of the child herself, the doctor ar-

[1] In response to a controversy which arose from a short story by Winifred Williams, "A Letter of Thanks," *Time and Tide,* 8 June 1935.

riving long after all was over. Nothing was ready when the time came, and the frightened woman tore herself in her efforts, and received a shock that she remembers to this day. The room was stuffy, the furniture primitive and ugly, and the curtains were heavy, and, apparently, dustladen. There seemed to be only one medicine glass, for it was frequently borrowed for the use of a patient in a bad way with bronchitis. Next door to the maternity case was a woman-patient almost out of her mind with drink. Attached to the home was a mangy-looking dog that continually annoyed the patients with its barking and yelping. The meals, served on dirty-looking trays, were brought in by kids of maids who looked very unhealthy, and had, apparently, been got from hard-up districts for a very small wage. The little baby was washed beside a gasfire, and seemed to be half roasted during the ordeal. When the baby was weighed by a fully competent nurse it was found to have gained ten ounces in one day, and no notice was taken of a remark that this seemed to be a physical impossibility. On this report the doctor cut down the child's allowance of food, and it was not discovered for some time that, instead of having gained ten ounces, the kid had lost weight, had become peevish because it was getting insufficient food through the incompetency of the nurse that had weighed it. At night the babies were brought upstairs and put to sleep in the operating theatre, having the comfort of breathing the ether fumes that, possibly, made them sleep nicely. The bathroom was at the top of the house, and it was often ornamented with the soiled bandages taken from the wounds of the patients. The nurses were overworked, and, so some of them told me, were fed on such things as tinned salmon and rehashed spuds. One day a doctor came in half carrying a woman screaming, apparently, in the pain of childbirth. The doctor shouted to a nurse for a room. The nurse replied that the matron was out, and that she'd have to ring her up first. The doctor shouted to ring her up and be quick about it. The nurse rang up while the doctor fumed impatiently, and the woman kept on screaming. The nurse, turning aside from the telephone, said that the matron wanted to know what price room the patient wanted? The doctor roared out any room, any room, woman, and for God's sake get it quick! The average fee in this home for a room was twelve guineas a week. But why is there a mention of second-rate, third-rate, or fourth-rate nursing homes? Shouldn't every institution of the kind be first-rate? Are women who have little money to spare to give birth to babies under fourth-rate conditions? What do the Prime Minister, the Lord President of the Council, the progressive members and the unprogressive members of the Conservative Party think of women, rich, middle-class, or of women workers having their children under fourth-rate conditions? The glorious English Government has to keep its eyes on Mussolini, on Stalin, on Japan rushing round China, but it can't waste its precious time keeping an eye on a fourth-rate nursing-home. Why call a place where those who have a lot or those who have a little money are cared for in sickness, a nursing-home? Why change the graceful, dignified, and sacred name of hospital to that of nursing-home? Snobbery, damned snobbery, peers of the realm and gentlemen of the Commons.

I am, etc.,
Sean O'Casey

To George Jean Nathan

MS. Cornell

49 Overstrand Mansions
3 August 1935

My dear George—

A Mhurie is truagh! (Oh Mary what a pity) that you find it impossible to come to Europe this year. Like the Pope's Holy Year in Rome, it would have been O'Casey's holy year in London. But, after all, considering all that can be seen in America, that is only outside your own halldoor, it would be strange to come thousands of miles to see little England; though it might be worth while to go a step farther and plant your feet for a night or two on the soil of Ireland. Next month I may be going over to the land of my birth—hear the birds singing?—for a week or two. It is nearly nine years since I saw Ireland's shore, & I am longing to see it again—birds singing louder than ever!

I think you ought to take the offer made to you by the Hearst people. The more American people who read what you have to say about the Theatre, the better for all of us. The Apollo of Dramatic Criticism can't send his steel-tipped or his golden-tipped arrows far enough in the park of Vanity Fair or Life. They should be sent flying from one end of the States to the other, and the Hearst papers give you that chance with a more powerful bow. Take it, my darling George, in the Holy Name of God! You wrote a fine article—"A Dramatic Critic Goes to The Movies"—in this month's Vanity Fair. It should have been read by Hearst's ten millions of readers.

I'm afraid I sounded sad & heavy when you spoke to me over the sea a few weeks ago. It was four o'clock in the morning, & I was full of sleep. However, it was a thrill to hear that rich deep voice of yours again. George Markle sounded as if he had had some champagne taken. Well, champagne or no champagne, he's a dear man, & I never cease regretting that he lost money on "Within The Gates." And dear old John, too; and Gertrude—there's no-one quite like them over here. I wish I were with you all again.

I've just got a letter from Barry Fitzgerald, who has just arrived back in Dublin. He says:—"I'm home again and utterly miserable. I should do anything to get back to the United States—it's the only live vital country I know of." I wish to Christ he wouldn't be reminding me of these things!

I've seen a play here called "Noah," [1] an English translation of Obey's "Noe," & it seemed fine to me. John Gielgud does Noah, & does it well. I have written an appreciation of the play for "Time & Tide," [2] & will send it on when it comes out next week. I imagine the play might go in New York, & it might be worth while considering by John. I will let you know later on how it goes here.

Thanks ever so much for the article on Gene [O'Neill] that you sent to me. In a way, I don't blame him for keeping out of the Theatre; but the Theatre with you, with all its faults, is something of a Theatre: here it is a gilded house. I must write to the great Eugene soon. I hope his next will be greater than anything he has written yet, if that's not asking too much of him. He's a great man, George.

With deeper love than Ever.
Yours
Sean

[1] Andre Obey's *Noah,* translated by Arthur Wilmurt, opened in London on 2 July 1935.
[2] Sean O'Casey, "Three Cheers For Noah," *Time and Tide,* 10 August 1935; reprinted in *The Flying Wasp* (1937).

To New York Times

11 AUGUST 1935

Mr. O'Casey Dissents

To the Drama Editor:

Underneath an interesting article around the recent Tour of The Abbey Players in The United States,[1] there is an additional article about the affairs of The Abbey Theatre in Dublin.[2] After mentioning the dispute between me and The Abbey Theatre over the head of "The Silver Tassie", the article goes on to say: "One of the first fruits of the reconstituted Abbey Theatre Board will be a production of 'The Silver Tassie' in August. The former Board rejected the play mainly on the grounds that it was not his metier. The new Directors—unlike W. B. Yeats, Lennox Robinson, or Dr

[1] "Earmarked for Dublin," *New York Times,* 14 July 1935.
[2] "And Back Home," by Hugh Smith, dateline "Dublin, 1 July," *New York Times,* 14 July 1935.

Starkie—feel that 'The Silver Tassie' was a bold and courageous experiment, and they are out to encourage new and progressive tendencies in the drama."

It would seem from the above that Mr. Yeats had practically no hand in this policy of the Abbey Theatre, and that he was almost superseded by the new element on the Board. Such is far from being the case. Mr. Yeats has been for some considerable time in favour of the change of policy now about to begin, and it was mainly through his persuasion that worthy additions have been made to the Board of the theatre. He is actively engaged in promoting this new movement and is still the guiding star of the theatre. The coming production of "The Silver Tassie" is to be given with his hearty approval and co-operation.

It is unnecessary for me to say that the production of the play by The Abbey Theatre gives me very deep pleasure, for, so far from "ignoring the Abbey Theatre", I have always looked forward to its renewal and re-creation. Mr. Yeats will never be anything less than a great poet and a great man.

Sincerely Yours,
Sean O'Casey

London, 26 July 1935

From Father M. H. Gaffney, O.P., to the Irish Press [1]

14 AUGUST 1935

Readers' Views

"The Silver Tassie"

Dear Sir—There have been several tentative announcements in the Press recently of the forthcoming production of Mr. O'Casey's play, *The Silver Tassie,* at the Abbey Theatre.[2] The Abbey once rejected this play to which it now offers the hospitality of its boards. Dublin is to have the opportunity of drinking deep from *The Silver Tassie*. But I fancy that Dublin

[1] A copy of this letter also appeared in the *Standard,* 16 August 1935. See also Father Gaffney's almost verbatim letter to the *Catholic Mind,* September 1930, reprinted in O'Casey's letter to Gabriel Fallon, 11 September 1930, note 1.

[2] *The Silver Tassie* opened at the Abbey Theatre on 12 August 1935, directed by Arthur Shields, with the following cast: Barry Keegan as Sylvester Heegan, Ann Clery as Mrs. Heegan, Michael J. Dolan as Simon Norton, Eileen Crowe as Susie Monican, May Craig as Mrs. Foran, P. J. Carolan as Teddy Foran, F. J. McCormick as Harry Heegan, Aideen O'Connor as Jessie Taite, Fred Johnson as Barney Bagnal, John Stephenson as The Corporal, Edward Lexy as The Visitor, Tom Purefoy as The Staff Wallah and Surgeon Maxwell, Soldiers: Denis O'Dea, Cyril Cusack, J. Winter, J. Hand, P. J. Carolan.

is a little too wise in 1935 to put its lips to a cup that may possibly have been filled from a sewer.

The play has been published in London, and is in our hands for cold inspection. It defies analysis. It is a vigorous medley of lust and hatred and vulgarity. And a Dominican nun, who acts and speaks like a Salvation Army lass, is dragged into the whirl of the movement in order to give point to the chanting *off* of the *Salve Regina*—in a setting that is brutally offensive.

In attempting to analyse this play, I have fallen into despair. I have no hope of conveying any adequate idea of its deliberate indecency and its mean, mocking challenge to the Christian Faith. This play has already been produced in a London theatre. I choose, from many criticisms, one from the pen of the dramatic critic attached to the *Universe: "The Silver Tassie* is," he says, "a terrible mixture of horror, indecency and violent blasphemy."

If this dramatic dose turns out to be too bitter and a revulsion takes place, the Abbey Theatre will not be in the same position as it was when Mr. Yeats called the policemen to quell the *Playboy* troubles before we were born. For, firstly, the Abbey Theatre is now in tutelage to the Government elected by the Irish Nation. And, secondly, the Abbey Theatre has now to reckon with a vigorous intellectual force which is not alien to the authentic spirit of the Irish people.

The fracas over the *Playboy* was but a flash in the pan, a child's cracker, in comparison with the hostility with which the Abbey is confronted if it persists in defying Catholic principle and flouting that reticence which is a characteristic of our people. Dublin people are not prudes or puritans if they exact from a Government theatre a recognition and observance of the forms of plain etiquette. And plain etiquette will not tolerate horror, indecency or blasphemy, on or off the stage.

For the rest, the Irish Dominicans have reason to resent most bitterly the use in this play of their canonical Habit: both Catholics and Protestants have equal reason to resent the dramatist's prostitution of one of the most delicate antiphons in the Christian Liturgy, as well as his barbaric abuse of the Divine Names held sacrosanct beyond the confines of Christendom.

M. H. Gaffney, O.P.

Holy Cross Abbey, Sligo
11 August 1935

To Irish Press

20 AUGUST 1935

Readers' Views

"The Silver Tassie"

To the Editor, THE IRISH PRESS.

Sir—Perhaps you will be good enough to allow me to make a few comments on the criticism of "The Silver Tassie" that was published in your paper on August 13. It is hard lines for a poor dramatist to have to reply to a critic who is, apparently, a scientist and theologian as well. Your critic is, obviously, much more intelligent and much fairer than the "epileptically clever" J.A.P. that writes dramatic criticism for the *Irish Independent,* and so, I take it, will not be over annoyed when he finds some of his statements contradicted. He says "the word in the play was always the word the author wanted." Very agreeable, but I haven't yet reached the height of invariably getting the words I want. "Few would suggest," he goes on to say, "that the characters represented life, even life at its worst." There is no best or worst in life yet. Each can always sink a little lower, or rise a little higher. Bad and good remain relative. A sin committed by a man of the world is not so bad as a sin committed by one consecrated to God. Even Dion Boucicault knew this when he makes Con the Shaughraun say "Sure, father, he'd rather have the irons on his hand than the sin upon your soul." No-one fell so low as Lucifer.

Your critic says: "Not more than half the people one meets are hypocrites, blatant naked hypocrites. *The Silver Tassie* would have us believe that we are all hypocrites." There is such a thing as national hypocrisy when all in a nation are enfolded in its heavy cloak, and let Ireland beware of this. We see it working now in England having her paw on all she wants, standing guard over the rights of Abyssinia. But your critic, I gather, is raising the question of purely personal hypocrisy. Let me remind him that hypocrisy implies the acting of a part, and the concealment of the real nature of the man; in that sense there is only one hypocrite in the play—The Visitor. Hypocrisy that is "blatant and naked" ceases to be hypocrisy. He goes on: "the principal character is seen in the first scene drunkenly extolling his football victory." The script says, "Harry is excited with the innocent insanity of a fine achievement, and the rapid lowering of a few drinks." He is not drunk by any means. Has your critic ever seen or participated in the wildness felt by an Irish team that has won an important match? I have, and have been as drunk as no wine could make me. For God's sake do not let us become like the English who think a man must be drunk when he is vehemently in earnest. Again he says: "Another uncalled for blasphemy is to be found in the soldiers' prayer calling on God to slay the enemy." Well, this last is really a bit too thick! Didn't the fighting countries in the last great war pray in all the churches for the success of their arms? Will your critic tell us how these prayers could be answered without the slaying of an enemy? The churches in various countries asked God to vanquish their enemies, that is, in other words, to slay them. Blasphemy, if you like, but not from the mouth of Sean O'Casey.

"Susie Monican, another of the characters, crudely recalls long-exploded Freudian theories." The Freudian theory here is simply that of a young woman who has reached a marriageable age desiring a mate, or to use a Dublin phrase, "a woman mad for a man." If that be a Freudian condition, as your critic says it is, and he seems to know all about it, then I must agree, for I have never read a line of anything written by Freud or any other major or minor psycho-analyst. Again your critic says "the soldiers at the front openly gibe at God, retaining merely a superstitious reverence for the crucifix while they are in safety." Nowhere in the play, as far as I can see, do the soldiers openly or furtively jibe at God. (As a theologian your critic ought to know that there are many worse things than a verbal jibe at God.) For soldiers at the front there was no safety; some places were safer than others—that was all. The words "superstitious reverence" show the Catholic mind over-anxious to rise above any suggestion of superstition. He is so superior that he would probably strike a match on an altar as carelessly as he would strike one on his pants. Well, I wouldn't, though I am an atheist and hate crucifixes. Long years ago I read a story that appeared in a Catholic journal called "The Messenger," and I still remember it. The story told of three French atheist soldiers on active service in 1871 who, coming upon a wayside shrine of the Blessed Virgin, fired at it in mockery and mutilated the image with rifle bullets. Later on, after a battle, these three were found dead with bullet wounds exactly similar to those inflicted on the image. This was superstition if you will, but it was more than that: implying, as the story did, that vindictiveness was an attribute of the Blessed Virgin, it was blasphemy, for, according to Catholic teaching as I know it, the Heart of the Blessed Virgin is a fount of everlasting sympathy and love. In the play the touch of superstition is forgiveable, for it comes from the heart of a war-weary, simple soldier, half terrified to meet what may yet be in front of him.

So I have tried to answer some of the objections raised, not by a dramatic critic, but by a theologian, and, with all respect, I hold that he has something to learn about theology, as I am certain that he has a lot to learn about dramatic criticism.—Yours sincerely,

Sean O'Casey

London, 15 August 1935.

Our Dramatic Critic writes:—

Mr. O'Casey has made the same mistake in his criticism of my review of the "Silver Tassie" which Mr. W. B. Yeats made in conversation with me. Both say it was attacked from a theological point of view. There is no theology in the criticism. It is natural philosophy. Philosophy searches for ultimate causes. I was trying to discover the causes in the author's mind, the ideas he was "putting over" in his play.

I have succeeded more than I had dared to hope. For Mr. O'Casey feels he must answer; yet in his answer he is reduced to gymnastics in formal logic, to quibbles on words rather than a search for their meaning in the manner "popularly" attributed to decadent Scholastic philosophy.

He must allow me in turn to make one distinction—one with a foundation. No religion ever prayed to God to slay its enemies because they were its enemies. For victory, yes, though victory may entail their slaughter. We do not pray for the pain of the operating knife. We tolerate it. Let not Mr. O'Casey appeal to Biblical texts. That would transfer the issue to theology, where I think he would come off very much second best.

Mr. O'Casey says there is only one hypocrite in the play. In my opinion all are hypocrites. It is for the public to decide. I withdraw the word "drunkenly." I had not wished to emphasise it, but rather the badly chosen—for I cannot claim always to get the word I want—"extolling," by which I would recall the disgusting self-praise of a semi-intoxicated person crying "I won the match," ignoring (hypocritically) the other ten players. And if Mr. O'Casey means Susie Monican in the play to be what he asserts in his letter, then he has written his play very badly. As to the story from *The Messenger,* I hold no brief for that periodical. Merely the story has no point here.

And lest Mr. O'Casey may now object to a *philosophical* interpretation of his play, I wish to point out that that is the only possible one. For dramatic criticism, if it is anything, is a diagnosis of drama as representative of life and truth. And philosophy is the science of life. The philosopher is the lover of wisdom (which is truth).

To George Jean Nathan

MS. CORNELL

ARDWYN
CELYN AVENUE
PENMAENMAWR
NORTH WALES
[? SEPTEMBER 1935]
C/O MRS. ROBERTS

My dear George—

I am, with wife & the two children, down in Wales wedged tightly in between sea and mountain; and, God forgive me, terribly interested in the Welsh Language, first cousin to my own Irish. It's as much as I can do to keep myself from trying to learn it, but it behooves me as an honest man to put no further burdens on my back. Besides, I have a new play to write; but what it is to be about, God only knows!

I got your new book, "The Theatre at the Moment," [1] this morning, & I shall be dug into it at once. A thousand thanks for letting me have it. The curse of your books on the Theatre is that one would want to memorise every line of them. To quote from them all that one would want to say about the Theatre would mean to write them all over again. However, that curse is a curse worth suffering. I have written a short article called "Hail Columbia" [2] trying to show how the Theatre in the U.S.A. is miles ahead of the Theatre in England. Surely, the Theatre is next door to death here. And the critics here are busy embalming the ribbish so that it may be preserved forever. What a Goddamned lot of jitney jacks they are.

I was very sorry that your shadow didn't fall on the pavements of London this year; but what, in the holy name o God, would bring you over from America to a city of people dead to everything but the height of their own bellies. There is more of God in Radio Center than there is in Westminster Abbey, though the one be built for work and the other for worship.

By the way, have you read Charles Morgan's (the dramatic critic of the London Times) latest book, "Sparkenbroke"? [3] It has been acclaimed a masterpiece in art by almost all the critics, & everybody is reading it. Morgan is, in the opinion of many, one of the finest artists in English Literature of the moment. I had (till I read Sparkenbroke) read only one work of his—his little "Epitaph on George Moore," [4] and looked forward to the reading of Sparkenbroke. I have just read it. To me it is the dullest book I have ever read. I should be glad (if you have read it) to hear what you think of it.

You may find this writing hard to make out—I am far from my typewriter, & the light here is very bad.

Give my love to Lillian, & to Mimsie, & to all those who were kind to me when I was in America—B. Atkinson, for instance, when you see him, and take my special love for yourself.

Yours, dear George,
As Ever,
Sean

I shall be back again in London about the 10th or 12th of September.

[1] George Jean Nathan, *The Theatre of the Moment* (New York, Knopf, 1936).

[2] Sean O'Casey, "Hail Columbia," *Time and Tide,* 1 August 1936; reprinted in *The Flying Wasp* (1937).

[3] Charles Morgan, *Sparkenbroke* (London, Macmillan, 1935), a best-selling novel.

[4] Charles Morgan, *Epitaph on George Moore* (London, Macmillan, 1935), a 56-page essay on Moore.

Irish Times

3 SEPTEMBER 1935

STATEMENT BY ABBEY DIRECTORS

Reply to Mr. B. Macnamara

The following statement was issued for publication by the Directors of the Abbey Theatre last night:—

Mr. Brinsley Macnamara writes in a statement to the Press of August 29th: "I was not at any time in favour of the production of 'The Silver Tassie.'" At no board meeting did Mr. Macnamara state his objections to the production of this play. There is not one word in the minutes on this subject. His protest against the production of the play was only made when attacks in the Press began. Comment seems unnecessary. His whole statement is an obvious breach of confidence, according to the procedure of all public and private boards. He then goes on to attack the players for speaking the author's words as they had been given to them. All players are expected to speak the words that are given to them, and the charge receives a touch of comedy precisely because it is made by Mr. Macnamara.

Owing to representations made by him at a recent meeting of the Board instructions were issued to the company that no word of a play's text should be altered or omitted by a player. As any breach of this regulation would have caused serious consequences to the player, it is obvious that the Directors of the Theatre alone are responsible for what is spoken on their stage. Mr. Macnamara goes on to state that the players in performing Mr. O'Casey's plays "have shown a reverence for his work which has not been given to any other author who has ever written for the Theatre," and this vague sentence means, we suppose, that they act O'Casey better than they act anyone else. This is a matter of opinion, but in our opinion our players have played whatever work has been put into their heads to their utmost ability.

He complains that our audience for the last ten years "has shown a wholly uncritical . . . . almost insane admiration for the vulgar and worthless plays of Mr. O'Casey." We do not consider our audience uncritical, and we point out that it is this audience which has made the reputation of his own plays.

W. B. Yeats,
Walter Starkie,
Lennox Robinson,
Richard Hayes,
F. R. Higgins,
Ernest Blythe.

From Brinsley Macnamara to Irish Times

7 SEPTEMBER 1935

An Abbey Theatre Play
Director's Divergent Opinions

Mr. Brinsley Macnamara, in the course of a statement, says:—

"Certain directors of the Abbey Theatre, having made their individual statements concerning the recent production of 'The Silver Tassie,' by Sean O'Casey, I feel obliged to make mine. I was not at any time in favour of the production of 'The Silver Tassie,' but it seemed to be the overwhelming desire of the other members of the Board that a former decision of the Theatre rejecting the play should be reversed. The matter arose through a sudden attempt on the part of Mr. Yeats to rush the production of what was to me a more objectionable and, artistically, even worse play by Mr. O'Casey—namely, his recent and unsuccessful 'Within the Gates.'

"I succeeded in preventing this production, but, as Mr. Yeats had evidently committed himself to Mr. O'Casey's return to the Abbey, and as this was thought to be of importance, I was powerless to prevent the production of 'The Silver Tassie.' It was to be the Theatre's gesture to Mr. O'Casey, which did not seem to me at all necessary or desirable. Mr. Lennox Robinson, who previously had been associated with the rejection of the play, was absent from Ireland at the time.

"Feeling that certain portions of the play would be wantonly offensive to the largest section of our audience and to the country from which the Theatre derives its subsidy, I took immediate steps to have certain excisions from and amendments of the printed version of the play made, particularly with regard to the travesty of the Sacred Office in the second act. I warned the Secretary of the Theatre, Mr. Eric Gorman, just when the rehearsals were beginning that, as the only Catholic director available at the moment, I urgently desired this to be done, and asked him to acquaint the producer, Mr. Arthur Shields, of my wishes in the matter. Two other directors, Senator Blythe and Mr. F. R. Higgins, were aware of the action I had taken, and were in agreement with me.

"In the course of the intervening weeks, I repeatedly inquired from Mr. Gorman if this had been done, and I was repeatedly informed that Mr. Shields had been acquainted. And so the matter rested until the production came on. I had been unable to attend the rehearsals of the play or its final dress rehearsal, but I was confident, in view of the warning that had been given, that the good taste of the producer and the fact that the majority of the players taking part in the production were Catholics, would be sufficient security against Mr. O'Casey's obscenity or insult to their own religion, and that the best that could be done with a bad play in the circumstances would be done.

"I did not see the play until the second night of its production, and my immediate feelings were that an outrage had been committed. Not alone had nothing been done to reduce the offensive quality of the play, but it was even more brazenly offensive than when I had seen it in its London production in 1929! Next morning I got into communication with the secretary and requested him to call a special meeting of the directors by telephone to consider the question of the withdrawal of the play, or, at least, its amendment for subsequent performances. This meeting was held the same evening, and it was agreed that the objectionable portions already indicated by me should be amended. I made it plain at the same time that so long at least as I remained a director of the theatre this play would not again be seen on the Abbey stage.

"I have considered it my duty to the theatre and to myself to reveal the facts as above stated, but there is another aspect of the matter to which I wish to call attention. The audience of the Abbey Theatre has for more than ten years shown a wholly uncritical, I might say almost insane, admiration for the vulgar and worthless plays of Mr. O'Casey. There has been no attempt until now to voice any serious objection to any of them, although they have all some almost equally objectionable quality.

"On the contrary, at the bidding of the present half-witted 'culture' of London and New York, the cry in Dublin has been for more and more O'Casey to the artistic detriment of the Abbey and its players. The players themselves, borne wildly upon this wave of spurious Dublin popularity, have shown a reverence for his work which has not been given to any other author who has ever written for the theatre. The producer of 'The Silver Tassie' was one of the players, and, at its first performance, not a line, however irreverent, was cut, not a word, however obscene, was blurred.

"May I say that, having made this statement, it is not my intention to engage in any controversy with Mr. O'Casey concerning the alleged merits of his plays or his own fantastic opinion of his importance. He is best at his gutter level in controversy with Mr. Yeats, who has replied after silently enduring years of the foulest abuse with this 'gesture' which forced our audience to endure 'The Silver Tassie,' even though it was only for one week."

To Irish Times [1]

11 SEPTEMBER 1935

"The Silver Tassie"

Sir,—Perhaps you will be good enough to allow me a few last defensive words on the moral, theological, scientific, critical and philosophical controversy that my play, "The Silver Tassie," has evoked in the Irish Press and Irish pulpit.

Mr. Brinsley Macnamara tells his world that he "has no intention of entering into a controversy with O'Casey on the alleged merits or demerits of his work." I beg to second his resolution; for I have no desire to waste time or intelligence over Mr. Macnamara. His statement, made publicly, that "he was not at any time in favour of the production of 'The Silver Tassie,' " has been countered by a statement made by the other directors of the theatre, who say unanimously that "his protest was made against the production of the play only when the attack in the Press began." Mr. Macnamara has not challenged this contribution, so I, for one, would hardly care to have a controversial chat with him. But when he first crept out of his shell, out of which he had been trying to peck himself for the last ten years, he made several statements that are not borne out by the well-known facts, statements that cannot be allowed to go by the board without a brief rejoinder.

He says: "At the bidding of the present half-witted 'culture' of London and New York (where O'Casey's plays consistently fail), the cry in Dublin has been for more and more O'Casey." Now, according to the souvenir programme issued by the Abbey Theatre on the occasion of its twenty-first birthday, "Juno and the Paycock" was first produced in 1924. The play was performed to crowded houses, and the reception was so cordial that the directorate decided to run the play for another week. More than a year passed before the play was first performed in London, so we see it was Dublin, rightly or wrongly, sanely or insanely, that gave the bid to London, and not London that gave the bid to Dublin. Mr. Macnamara must be aware of this, and I venture to remind him that it is not a good thing for a good Catholic, which Mr. Macnamara is now busy proving himself to be, to bear false witness against his neighbour.

Besides, as my plays are "vulgar and worthless," and as they have "consistently failed" in London and New York, why does he shout out that the culture of these cities is only a half-witted one? And if they consistently failed in London, how did London give them popularity in Dublin? And if a half-witted culture in London made a deep impression on Dublin, then the only culture in Dublin must be held tight in the head

[1] A copy of this letter, with several deletions made by the editor, appeared in the *Irish Press*, 11 September 1935.

of Mr. Macnamara alone, a thought that gives Mr. Macnamara a terrifying importance. Mr. Macnamara has tried to spit out in a high wind, and the moisture has spattered his own face.

Whatever my sins may be, I have never set sail in quest of popularity ("The Silver Tassie" proves that), and I leave that condition of misery to Mr. Macnamara himself. I venture a guess that he would not be terribly reluctant to have his own plays performed before the "half-witted culture" of London or New York. If I remember rightly, I remember his exultation years ago when there was talk of his "The Glorious Uncertainty" going on the boards in that city: and when I was in New York his last play was in the hands of an agent seeking performance there with, I am sure, the knowledge and approval of Mr. Macnamara. Lastly, so far as Mr. Macnamara is concerned, his statement that "Mr. Yeats had evidently committed himself to Mr. O'Casey's return to the Abbey" is not true, as touching myself. Neither directly nor indirectly did Mr. Yeats commit himself to me for the production of any play of mine. The plays were there for the Abbey to use or neglect as the Theatre thought fit, though I reserve the right to think that my plays are intrinsically as worthy of performance by the Abbey Players as are the plays of Mr. Macnamara.

The Rev. M. H. Gaffney, O.P.,[2] makes many charges, but proves none of them. I protest against his practice, and the practice of other lay and clerical critics, of calling a man's mind a "sewer-pipe" because one does not conform to the peculiar, sentimental, and sometimes silly, idea of Christianity that many members of Catholic societies favour. I would remind the Rev. Father Gaffney that Plainsong is not a monopoly of the Irish Catholic Church; that few Catholic congregations know anything about it, and that His Holiness the Pope, if I remember rightly, has had to make special efforts for its restoration in church Services. I imagine, too, that music in itself is not sacred, and that all rites of the Church are as effective said as sung.

The Rev. Father says that my play contains an insult to the Blessed Virgin. Will he be good enough to tell us what constitutes the insult he complains of? Even in a criminal court no accusation is made without evidence to support it; but this son of St. Dominic makes an accusation, and leaves it there. His protest against the "insult to the Canonical Habit of his Order" puzzles me. The garb worn by the Sister in the play is that worn by nursing Sisters of Charity when on duty, and has nothing to do with the Dominican Habit; if he would like to know, it was actually modelled on the nursing garb worn by the Sisters of St. Vincent's Hospital in Dublin. He thinks I made the Sister speak "like a Salvation Army lass." That the words she uses are semi-Scriptural is the only likeness. Besides, though there is little, if any, Catholic ceremonial attached to Salvation Army practice, there is something Salvationist in the practice of the

[2] See Father Gaffney's letter to the *Irish Press,* 14 August 1935.

Catholic Church, such as the fervour of missions, the visitations of sisterhoods to the homes of the poor, the saying of Mass in the vernacular to members of a Church that His Holiness is trying to bring into the unity of the Catholic fold, and the uniforms worn by the Orders. (For fear of misunderstanding, let me say I use the word "uniform" with all respect.)

I recently quoted a story that was written by a Catholic and appeared in a Catholic journal published by an Order; in this story vindictiveness was attributed to the Blessed Virgin. Was this blasphemy, or was it not? And, if it was, why was there never a word of condemnation spoken? The Dramatic Critic of the *Irish Press* [3] dismissed this story as having nothing to do with the dispute, but I think it has a lot to do with it; for it seems to show that even Catholic journals sometimes do not know how to do proper reverence to Her whom they call the Mother of God. He claims that the criticism he wrote round my play was not theology, but philosophy. No Christian can think of philosophy without thinking of God; for, as philosophy is the study of truth and wisdom, and as, to a Christian, God is the beginning and end of both, then the study of philosophy is the study of the relation of God to the world of man; and the critic of the *Irish Press* can tell us where the distinction begins and ends.

Some of the C.Y.M. Societies have proclaimed their affinity to Shakespeare, but it cannot be a very close one; for Shakespeare was a very tough guy, and said many thinks that, if they were written by me or Brinsley Macnamara, would give cause to Father Gaffney for shouting. Let them read "Hamlet," "Othello," or even "Romeo and Juliet," and they will find that O'Casey is quite a respectable boy compared with Shakespeare. I will write down a few of them if the Catholic *Standard* will guarantee to publish them.

Let me say that all the naughty words complained of in the play are to be found in the authorised version of the Holy Scriptures.

Finally, I am in no way whatsoever ashamed of one single, solitary word or phrase appearing in "The Silver Tassie," and the storm of abuse that the play has received only convinces me that "The Silver Tassie" is a greater play than I thought it to be. Thank you.—Yours. etc.,

Sean O'Casey

[3] A letter from "Our Dramatic Critic," *Irish Press,* 20 August 1935.

Irish Times

17 SEPTEMBER 1935

SEAN O'CASEY IN DUBLIN

Mr. Sean O'Casey, whose play "The Silver Tassie," gave rise to such a controversy when produced at the Abbey Theatre some weeks ago, is at present in Dublin. He attended the Abbey Theatre last night—for the first time in many years—and saw the performance of the new play by Mr. F. R. Higgins, "A Deuce O' Jacks." [1] His presence seems to mark the end of the quarrel between him and the directors of the Abbey Theatre, following their original rejection of "The Silver Tassie." Since that time, Mr. O'Casey has been living in London, where he wrote his latest play, "Within the Gates."

When interviewed, Mr. O'Casey was not inclined to talk much about himself. "I am over in Dublin for a holiday," he said, "and I don't know how long I shall be here. It may be for three days, or for three weeks." As regards the reception given to his play, he would say little, except that he was not impressed by the arguments which had been brought up against it. "I can take Father Gaffney and the other people who share his views," he said, "to places within two minutes' walk of the Pro-Cathedral, and they would agree with me that they are not places to be sentimentalised over."

[1] F. R. Higgin's *A Deuce O' Jacks* opened at the Abbey Theatre on 16 September 1935. This one-act comedy was based on the life of "Zosimus" (Michael Moran, 1794–1846), a blind minstrel-poet who was a well-known figure and "character" in Dublin, and many of whose street ballads survive today. See Yeats's "The Last Gleeman," *The Celtic Twilight* (1893).

From Brinsley Macnamara to Irish Times

7 OCTOBER 1935

The Abbey Theatre
Resignation of Director

The following statement was made on Tuesday night by Mr. Brinsley Macnamara, one of the directors of the Abbey Theatre:—

"Since issuing my statement concerning the production of 'The Silver Tassie,' it has been suggested to me by the Board of the Abbey Theatre that I should withdraw it. I have refused, and still stand by the action I took with regard to the play. The statement of the six other directors, published to-day, occupies itself mainly with criticism of me, but makes no reference to the deletion from the production on the Wednesday and following nights of its week's run of certain objectionable features as a result of the special meeting of the Board which I caused to be convened.

"It was obvious to me from the first that certain portions of the play were likely to cause grave offence and be detrimental to the best interests of the theatre. When I had spoken of the matter to two directors and they had agreed with me, and I had asked the Secretary of the theatre to communicate my wishes to the producer, particularly concerning the second act, and when I knew he had done so, I felt that my duty to the theatre, as the one Catholic director present at the time, was fulfilled. My attitude was then so obvious that it did not appear to me to be necessary to discuss the matter at any meeting of the Board, because there could be no possible difference of opinion on the subject, a fact which the reception of the play has proved. The onus lay upon the other directors and upon the producer to respect the suggestions I had made and to act accordingly. Their duty was clear, and I did not wish to be unduly insistent in pointing it out to them further. At the same time I did not altogether leave out of consideration what I felt must be the reactions of the players to the offensive portions of the play; but since the publication of my statement Mr. F. J. McCormick has made an explanation on behalf of the players that these reactions were such as I might have expected, and that he himself, were he a free agent, would not, as a Catholic, have appeared in the play. On Friday last I expressed my regret to the players that my statement should have involved them, and I now take this opportunity of saying that I whole-heartedly accept Mr. McCormick's explanation.

"The statement of the six other directors evades the main issue, which is: Are they, or are they not, prepared to defend the production of the play as it was given to the public on the first and second nights of its production? I was never prepared to do so, and, therefore, when two of the directors made vague public statements about the play, I felt it was urgent, in the best interests of the theatre, that the position should be made clear. I found it necessary to explain to the public that at least some steps had been taken to mitigate the offence of the production, so that it might not be taken as a lasting disgrace to the Abbey. This is now naively described as "an obvious breach of confidence," and the description is, on the part of the replying directors, an exceedingly easy attempt at evasion, which will not deceive anyone. I cannot any longer remain a member of a Board whose directors have such an inadequate conception of their duty when faced with a serious situation, and I have sent in my resignation.

"The six directors have not replied to the facts contained in my original statement. They have, however, a perfect reply if they wish to make it. If they still think that my action at any point was not taken in the best interests of the theatre, they can surely put on 'The Silver Tassie' again exactly as it was given on the first and second nights of its production. Will they do it?"

To Betty Purdon

MS. PURDON
49 OVERSTRAND MANSIONS
11 OCTOBER 1935

My dear Betty Purdon—

I was very glad to get your letter, & to hear that you were the child of your mother, Alice Griffin, who is very well remembered by me. Indeed, I remember every member of your mother's family—Miss Jenny, Robert, Edward, Sammy, Harriet, Gracie, & Charlie. Tell your mother that her father, my dear friend, Mr. Griffin,[1] often comes into my mind, awakening many, many affectionate feelings for that fine, generous, and saintly man. And give my love, if she be alive—please God she may be—to the gentle & kindly mother of Alice, & of her sisters & brothers, all. I hope & pray that they are all well.

You write a fine letter for one of only eleven years.

With affectionate regards
to your mother & to you,
Sean O'Casey

[1] The Rev. Edward M. Griffin, rector of St. Barnabas Church, Dublin.

To Harold Macmillan

TS. MACMILLAN LONDON
49 OVERSTRAND MANSIONS
12 OCTOBER 1935

Dear Mr Harold,

I have just returned from a trip to Ireland, and have got your letter asking me to read "Time To Kill" [1] so that I may be able to tell you what I think of it. I hardly like to put myself forward as a judge of what a man may do out of what he has done for the first time. Generally we may be sure that an acorn holds an oak, but what a man may hold in him-

[1] Rearden Conner, *Time To Kill, A Plain Tale From the Bogs* (1936); rejected by Macmillan and published by Chapman. In America the book was published by Knopf under the title *I Am Death* (1936).

self will always be a mystery. However, as you wish me to read the work, I shall do it for you, and give you an opinion that, I'm sure, will be no better than your own.

I met a young fellow in Dublin who, too, may have a future. He is young, enthusiastic, clever, broadminded, and brave. He has written a book called "Stand and Give Challenge" [2] which has called for praise from the Irish critics—though, God knows, that's not saying a lot. I havent had time to read the book, but suggest that you should do so, and then tell me what you think of it. It is published by "The Talbot Press."

I have just come out of a hell of a row over the production of "The Silver Tassie" in Dublin by The Abbey Theatre.[3] Many are calling for the suppression of all my plays, and the control of the Abbey by the Government. However, enemies in Ireland always mean the birth of many friends.

I hope you and Lady Dorothy and all the little ones are well, as we are.

Ever Yours,
Sean O'Casey

[2] Francis MacManus, *Stand and Give Challenge* (Dublin, Talbot Press, 1935).

[3] For the whole controversy over the Abbey Theatre's production of *The Silver Tassie,* see the letter from Father M. H. Gaffney, O.P., to the *Irish Press,* 14 August 1935; O'Casey's letter to the *Irish Press,* 20 August 1935; the statement by the Abbey Directors, *Irish Times,* 3 September 1935; Brinsley Macnamara's statement to the *Irish Times,* 7 September 1935; O'Casey's letter to the *Irish Times,* 11 September 1935; Brinsley Macnamara's statement to the *Irish Times,* 7 October 1935; O'Casey's "A Stand on The Silver Tassie" in his letter to W. B. Yeats, 23 November 1935.

To George Jean Nathan

MS. CORNELL

49 OVERSTRAND MANSIONS
[? OCTOBER 1935]

My dear George—

I have been able only to think of you for some weeks past, for I took a holiday that I had planned for five years, and went to see my own home town, Dublin. A quiet holiday it was to be, spent meandering through many old familiar places. I went, and, be God, I found myself in the midst of a fierce and fiery battle! The Abbey had put on "The Silver Tassie," and all the critics & some of the clergy were yelling and snapping

& biting at everything they saw or pretended to see in the play. The whole Free State tottered, & it is tottering still. All the Irish critics & most of the Irish dramatists like to get a welt at me; and, indeed, I sometimes return their welts with an ungrand and a hundred thousand welcomes. At the moment the opposing forces are withdrawing to their bases to prepare for a renewal of the fight whenever the play goes on again. Many are determined to drive me body, soul, & spirit out of Ireland, and they are using me as a lever with which to down the Abbey. W. B. Yeats is an old man now, but he is as big a fighter as ever, & will surely die with harness on his back. I enclose a few press-cuttings to give you an idea of the kind of fight we are waging. Curiously enough, I was met with a hail and hearty welcome everywhere I went—from worker, priest, monk, & literary gent. except the critics. The fight, however, is a little tiresome, & I don't think I'd join in were it not necessary to stand by Yeats.

I wonder did you stretch far enough to take on the job of writing criticism for the Hearst papers? I hope you did. By the way, when I was in Dublin I met a young & ardent Catholic, a member of the Legion of Mary, busy reading your "World in Falseface." [1] I met you there, first, too; so Dublin has her good points as well as her bad ones. I hear John's in the middle of rehearsing a new play—may it rise well with him and George. Ireland has banned "Windfalls." [2]

There's quite a lot of your books out of print, me boy, & it might be a good thing to think of getting a volume containing some of each of them published here in England. Harold Macmillan was looking forward to meeting you—I told him of your possible visit—& would have discussed the possibility of a volume. You should be better known here.

I enclose a few snaps of the missus & the kids. All of us are well.

Love to Mimsie, & to Lillian.

As Affectionately as Ever Yours
Sean

God be with New York.

[1] George Jean Nathan, *The World in Falseface* (New York, Knopf, 1923).

[2] O'Casey's *Windfalls* (1934) was "prohibited" by the Censorship of Publications Board on 4 December 1934, mainly because of the short story, "I Wanna Woman."

To Gabriel Fallon

MS. TEXAS

FORTY-NINE OVERSTRAND MANSIONS
24 OCTOBER 1935

My dear Gaby—

Enclosed is a letter which will explain itself. I hope you will get the script when "Paddy Comes Marching Home!" I daresay they didn't do "The Silver Tassie" in Cathair dhil bhreagh Chorcaigh.[1] I have been very quiet & a little tired since I came back from Ireland, & haven't ventured yet to think of anything to do. In a week or so, I shall again quietly read a lot of what has been said about the play in the Irish Press, & see if I can make any sober or sane thing out of the talk, the high talk & the low talk, the talk that says little & means a lot, & the talk that says a lot & means nothing, which includes the mutterin' of Father Gaffney. Well, thanks, oul son for all your & Rosie's kindness when we were with you. I hope you & Rose & all the buds are well, & that soon all things may be a little easier for him & you. Give my love to Frank McM[anus].

As the Best as Ever Yours
Sean

[1] The beautiful little city of Cork.

From Lady Astor

MS. O'CASEY

3, ELLIOT TERRACE,
THE HOE,
PLYMOUTH.
8 NOVEMBER 1935

Dear Comrade O'Casey,

You don't know what great pleasure your letter gave me. I agree with you there is something in Communism, and there is certainly something in Capitalism, but there is nothing in Socialism. I would like to take you to Russia—I don't know anybody who would be less fitted to live under an autocracy than you, unless it is myself!

Once this election is over, and I have recovered, I do want to see you. We won't be able to live at St. James's Square until February, the flues are all wrong, and the house won't be habitable, so I am going to try and do my work from Cliveden. Perhaps you and Mrs. O'Casey will be able to come down. How are the children. How are you. I do long to see you both. I miss Lawrence [1] so much—I never saw him a great deal but he meant a lot to me—especially since here.

God help Bill at Fulham!

Yrs
Nancy Astor

[1] Thomas Edward Lawrence (1888–1935), "Lawrence of Arabia," died on 19 May 1935 as the result of a fall from his motorcycle while trying to avoid some children in the road.

To W. B. Yeats

MS. NAT LIB, DUBLIN
49 OVERSTRAND MANSIONS
23 NOVEMBER 1935

Dear W. B. Yeats—

You may remember when I had the pleasure of being with you in your home in Terenure,[1] I suggested that I should send you a few words on the controversy about "The Silver Tassie," which was to include some passages from the Bible giving expression to "indecent" words. I enclose with this note what I have written, & you will see that even The Lord God of Israel Himself has said a mouthful!

You can do as you wish with the article, print it whole, or in part, or ignore it altogether. It might be useful if you can again put on the play. This I can't commend, for the quieter you keep yourself the better, and another row might cause you to expend too much energy—needed for greater work—on controversy. I sincerely hope that you are in good health. I stole in to see your three plays here, but didn't like the production.[2]

Good wishes to Mrs. Yeats & your boy and girl.

Yours Sincerely
Sean O'Casey

[1] During his final visit to Ireland in mid-September 1935, O'Casey visited Yeats for the last time at the poet's house, Riversdale, in the Dublin suburb of Rathfarnham, which bordered on Terenure. For a description of that visit see "The Friggin Frogs," *Rose and Crown* (1952).

[2] In honor of Yeat's seventieth birthday, Nancy Price, manager of the People's National Theatre Company, produced three of his plays on 27 October 1935 at the Little Theatre, London: *The Player Queen, The Hour Glass,* and *The Pot of Broth.*

Enclosure

"A Stand on The Silver Tassie" [3]

The most serious objection alleged against *The Silver Tassie* is that a travesty of the Mass is to be found in some nook or cranny of the play. Mr. Macnamara has been particularly vocal about it, but, like Father Gaffney, he hasn't told anybody where the travesty is to be found. Is it to be found in the first, second, third, or fourth act of the play? And will Father Gaffney or Mr. Macnamara tell us what part or passage in the play forms the travesty of the Sacred Office? There is no travesty of the Mass in the second act of the play. As far as I know, and I ought to know, there is no travesty of the Mass, stated clearly or furtively implied, from one end of the play to the other. The murmuring or singing of part of the Service in the second act, which was put in by me to imply the sacred peace of the Office compared with the horrible cruelty and stupidity of war, constitutes the only irreverence in the play as touching the Sacred Office of the Mass. If the portrayal of the infinite peace and mercy implied in the Sacrifice constitutes an irreverence to the Catholic Faith as conceived by Father Gaffney and Mr. Macnamara, then it is an irreverence and it will remain an irreverence; for I refuse to take my conception of the Catholic Faith from the conception held tight in the minds of Father Gaffney and Mr. Macnamara, now, or in any hour of the time to come.

Perhaps the travesty of the Mass may, in the mind of either Mr. Macnamara or the mind of Father Gaffney, be associated with the words spoken by the crippled Harry Heegan in the last act of the play. They are these: "No, white wine, white, like the stillness of the millions that have removed their clamours from the crowd of life. No, red wine; red, like the blood that was shed for you and for many for the commission of sin". Now the last sentence is taken—with an alteration of one word—from the Anglican Rubric of the Service of Holy Communion, and so cannot be a travesty of the Mass. The Eastern Rite of the Mass is recognised by the Catholic Church, but the Anglican Rite is not so recognised, and so the sentence cannot be an insidious insult to the Mass. Let me say here that, neither directly nor indirectly, is the quotation meant to be a stab at the Anglican Rite of Holy Communion. The sentence was introduced in an effort to convey a suitable symbol of the anguished bitterness that the unhappy Harry might conceivably feel for what he thought to be the fell waste of the war.

Father Gaffney tells us that he "cannot give an adequate idea of the play's deliberate indecency and its mean mocking challenge to the Christian Faith". What is the Christian faith? Isn't it to be found summarised in the creeds, the Athanasian Creed, the Apostles' Creed, and that Creed that particularly expresses the faith of Catholics? Now is there one phrase in the play from the start to the finish that in any way, directly or indirectly,

[3] This article is reprinted in *Blasts and Benedictions* (1967).

challenges any part of the Catholic Faith as expressed by the Creed of Pope Pius? If Father Gaffney had said that the play was a challenge to the faithful rather than to the Faith, he would have been nearer to the mark. Let me suggest to Father Gaffney that the Faith is a perpetual challenge to the faithful.

Father Gaffney says that "plain etiquette will not tolerate indecency or blasphemy on or off the stage." This is nonsense. He has his job cut out for him if he thinks plain etiquette will banish indecency or horror off the stage or out of life. There are many indecent things in life outside of sex, things more seriously indecent than the common language of the streets and the workshops. There are indecent things in politics, in home life, in business, even in religion, that we never or rarely hear a word about. Plain etiquette won't do very much to soften them down. The Seven Gifts of the Holy Ghost and the Twelve Fruits of the Holy Spirit have to do with mightier things than the paltry things he calls plain etiquette. If I were a Christian priest I should put more trust in the Sword of the Spirit than I would put in Father Gaffney's Etiquettical Catholic Catechism.

There were some who raved about a few naughty words in the play that were peculiar to the characters that spoke them. Some of them are to be found in the Bible, naked and unashamed. Turning to the Second Book of Kings, the Eighteenth Chapter and the Twenty-seventh Verse, we find this: "But Rab-Shakeh saith unto them, hath my master sent me to thy master, and to thee, to speak these words? Hath he not sent me to the men which sit on the wall, that they may eat their own dung and drink their own piss with you?" We find this, almost word for word in the Gaelic of Bedell's Irish Bible. In the First of Samuel, Twenty-fifth Chapter, Twenty-second Verse: "So and more also do God to the enemies of David, if I leave off all that pertain to him by the morning light any that pisseth against a wall." And let all concerned have a squint at the Seventh and Tenth Verse of the Fourteenth Chapter of First Kings. Here is written, "Thus saith the Lord God of Israel . . . I will bring evil upon the house of Jeroboam, and will cut off from Jeroboam him that pisseth against the wall." Each, of course, appearing in the Irish Bible as translated by Bishop Bedell. Hot and biting words indeed. What do the two chancellors of the spoken word think of them? But there is something more to come: in a play called *The Satin Slipper*, written by a well-known Catholic, the words, bastard, son of a bitch, and arse are flaunted in our faces. Worse still, these are translated from the French by a Catholic priest, the Reverend Fr. John O'Connor, and the book is published by a Catholic firm, Messrs Sheed & Ward. What have Father Gaffney, Mr. Brinsley Sheridan MacNamara, Red Handed Cu Uladh, or the Doxological Professor of Galway, Mr. J. Murphy, got to say to me now, and what have I to say to them? I have only to say this:

What to such as they, anyhow, such a poet as I? Therefore leave my works,
And go lull yourself with that you can understand, and with piano tunes,
For I lull nobody, and you will never understand me.[4]

Sean O'Casey

[4] From Walt Whitman's poem, "To a Certain Civilian."

From W. B. Yeats

MS. O'CASEY

RIVERSDALE, WILLBROOK,
RATHFARNHAM, DUBLIN.
27 NOVEMBER 1935

Dear O'Casey

Your letter has given me great pleasure. I have had a long illness, six or seven weeks, but am convalescent now, out of bed for certain hours, & doing a little work. I regret the loss of all that time but at any rate it has been a rest.

Yours always
W. B. Yeats

I am following your controversy in "The New Statesman". Ethel Mannin's quotation from "Love on the Dole" seems rather to prove your case. I like her & am sorry she has taken that side so hotly.

To George Jean Nathan

MS. CORNELL

49 OVERSTRAND MANSIONS
1 DECEMBER 1935

My dear George—

The enclosed letter will explain itself. I hope you may come to an arrangement that will allow your thoughts on the Theatre to get into some of the heads here. Harold Macmillan is one of the young Conservatives—

full of resolution to bring about a better state of things. In my opinion nothing can come but Communism.

This time, last year, I was in New York—probably hurrying along Sixth Avenue to Forty-fourth Street—ah well!

I have just been reading a book called "Dictionary of American Usage," &, in my opinion, it should be called, "Dictionary of Dublin-American Usage," for it is heavy with expressions familiar with me from childhood. (see the use of "with" here—an Englishman would say "to") The second one "aboard"—"climbed aboard the train," is Dublin. "Getting new members of a Club acquainted." "Government" in England instead of "Administration." "The Englishman in the street," says the book, "wouldn't know what you meant if you asked him if he was for or against the Administration." Well, the Dublinman would know at once. Newsdealer is common in Dublin. Omission of *the* where it would be required after *all* in England. "The Senator was troubled with Lumbago all Summer." Pure Dublin. "Didn't help matters *any*." Dublin again. . . .[1]

[1] Pages missing. The enclosed letter from Harold Macmillan indicates that O'Casey was urging the Macmillan Company to publish Nathan's selected critical writings.

To Time and Tide

14 DECEMBER 1935

"STORM OVER ASIA"[1]

Sir,—Regarding the difference of opinion between Mr. Campbell Northcroft and Mr. Brophy[2] about the incidents in this film, it seems to show how ineffective human eyes often are in seeing the same things in the same way. Here are two men who watched with concentrated attention brightly lighted objects moving about in a small space for an hour or so, and yet neither saw exactly as the other. One sees a cliff, the other a bank; one a rifle, the other a revolver and a rifle, and so on. And yet we want to see on the stage the things that in life we have seen with our own eyes! Now mine eyes have seen a little differently from their eyes. It was distinctly stated that the soldiers appearing in the film represented no particular army, and Mr. Brophy has, I imagine, no reason to connect them definitely with the British Army. They symbolized Imperialism. If

[1] *Storm Over Asia* (1928), a Russian film directed by V. I. Pudovkin.

[2] In a review, John Brophy made some satiric remarks about *Storm Over Asia*, *Time and Tide*, 16 November 1935; and T. Campbell Northcroft defended the film in a letter to the editor, *Time and Tide*, 23 November.

I remember right, the officer who gave the order for the shooting of the Partisan was a Colonel, and not a General. Neither Mr. Campbell Northcroft nor Mr. Brophy seemed to remember that the Partisan had his hands tied behind his back, which handicap would possibly add to his injuries as he rolled over the cliff or down the bank. It isn't impossible that a General, even a British General, would give a second or two to the interrogation of a peasant, provided the "peasant" was of sufficient importance to attract the officer's attention. Michael Collins was a peasant and so was Dan Breen, and many a high officer in the British Army in Ireland would have been glad to have put a question or two to either of them. As for the method of execution, strange things are done by "competent military authorities" when they are putting down a rebellion. Once in Dublin two young I.R.A. soldiers were captured and taken in a motor-car to a field used for dumping rubbish, by two Auxiliary Officers. With hands tied behind them, the I.R.A. soldiers were put sitting against a wall that surrounded part of the field. The Officers put two old galvanized buckets, taken from a rubbish heap, over their heads. Then standing a little distance away, they plugged many holes in the buckets with revolver fire, leaving the bodies where they were, when they thought the two I.R.A. chaps were dead. One survived, however, long enough to give a sworn description of the whole affair. Indeed, strange things are sometimes done in the holy name of law and order.

However, surely Mr. Brophy does realize that the film was, apart from any political significance, a fine one? Hasn't he only to give a glance round at the others running now in London to see that Pudovkin is something more than a Hollywood hack. I should advise him to go to see *The New Babylon*,[3] now showing in the same theatre. It is propaganda, but it is something more than that.

I am, etc.,
Sean O'Casey

[3] *The New Babylon* (1928), a Russian film directed by G. Kozintzev and L. Trauberg.

VIII

THE HOLY GHOST AND THE FLYING WASP, 1936-37

ISN'T it nearly time that England realised that this self-righteous hypocrisy is a sin against the Holy Ghost? England has one chance left by, as Shaw says, choosing the red flag in preference to the white one."

"I shouldnt think of giving anything I said about the theatre such a title as 'Towards a Living Theatre,' for such a title would be too academic and professorial for me to use. Besides 'The Flying Wasp,' is more lyrical, and much more to the point. Why should I leave out an article in reply to criticism of my own work? My works are, at least, additions to the drama, and defending them, I defend the drama. Am I to leave it out because 'it is not done,' or because it is not 'good form'? I hope I know something about good manners, but on a question of principle, good form can go to the devil. Invariably, I have done the things that are not done, and have left undone the things that are done, and I amnt much the worse for it. The

> theatre is more than good manners. As for 'brawling in church,' well, Jesus Christ did it before me, and I occasionally follow in His steps."

In defending his provocative book of essays on the theatre, *The Flying Wasp*, the sting of which his well-meaning publisher Harold Macmillan urged him to remove, O'Casey explained with considerable candor and accuracy: "Everything I have written, up to the present, has been 'combative,' and the sword I have swung so long is now stuck to my hand, and I can't let go." He took an Irishman's pleasure as well as revenge in swinging his sword of the spirit at what he considered to be the hypocrisies of British life and the mediocrities of British theatre. In an informal talk at Cambridge University he warned the students that the liberating power of the Holy Ghost—his metaphor of truth—would abandon England unless Englishmen began to pursue revolutionary ways of thinking and living, free from the smug deceits of their conventional existence. In magazine articles and letters he continued to attack the commercial theatre of the West End for its cheap standards, and he was a generation ahead of his time in calling for the artistic independence of a national theatre. In his direct assault on reigning critics and playwrights like James Agate and Noel Coward, he chose what he felt were the most visible and vulnerable targets of British theatre because he believed that audiences constantly exposed to the safe and conventional plays of Coward and his brittle imitators would be incapable of appreciating the bold and superior plays of O'Neill and Pirandello, would not recognize the need for a national theatre; and apparently he was right.

Probably O'Casey's public dilemma was that he was too often too right; he was so vigorous in his sword-swinging literary battles that he succeeded in alienating as well as outscoring his influential opponents. He had always been more honest than prudent, and it did not increase his popularity or further his career to offend the most powerful theatre critic, Agate, and one of the leading magazine editors, Lady Rhondda. He read ironic lessons in Scripture to both of them, under the banner of the red flag as if he were a paradoxical prophet armed with biblical rhetoric and communist intuition. He was his own unique kind of eclectic communist, more emotional than political, inspired by the Holy Ghost as well as Karl Marx, and in one of his disputes with Lady Rhondda in May 1936 he wrote: "Under Communism human nature would not automatically become angelic, but human nature would automatically become orderly, and order is heaven's first law, and so human nature would be a step nearer the angelic state." He assured his friends in England, Ireland, and

America that they were all unconscious communists, and he proclaimed that he himself was, as he wrote to Shaw in 1937, "a born Communist." He urged Shaw to write a play about the rebellion of Jack Cade: "You could make a Communist St. Joan of him." He must have confounded his good friend George Jean Nathan, the sybaritic New York theatre critic, by calling him "a great proletarian critic. . . . You want the best that can be given to the art of the theatre, and that is the creed of the Communist." For the visionary O'Casey, who all his life had witnessed deprivation and exploitation, communism, not capitalism, offered the best promise of freedom and justice in this world.

Meanwhile in his worldly endeavors as a writer several important things were happening early in 1937; *The Flying Wasp* was published; he was working on the first volume of a "curious autobiography"; and he started to write a new symbolic play, *The Star Turns Red*, which was to reflect the power of the Red Star and the Star of Bethlehem. He was, as he wrote to Harold Macmillan, a communist following in the footsteps of Christ.

To Alfred A. K. Arnold [1]

MS. O'Casey

49 Overstrand Mansions
18 January 1936

["The Holy Ghost Leaves England"]

It was very kind of your secretary and your committee to think of asking me to come to see you all to get to know you, and to say a simple word or two to you. This is the first time I have formally spoken in an English University. I have spoken in several in The U S and many fond memories of men I met there still linger with me, and will remain for a long time. Ten years ago when I first came to Eng I paid a visit to Oxford to see the Conferates then performed by Oxford Players, and was guided round the many buildings that constitute the college or University. I have wandered through the National University of Ireland, and I have cooked sausages in the dead of night with a Lecturer in trinity college Dublin, so that, as we say in Ireland, if I didnt go to

[1] Mr. Arnold, in behalf of the Shirley Society at St. Catherine's College, had invited O'Casey to give a talk at Cambridge University, and the following rough notes are an early draft of the talk, "The Holy Ghost Leaves England," which he delivered in February during his visit to Cambridge. See the chapter "Cambridge," *Sunset and Evening Star* (London, Macmillan, 1954).

school itself, I had a good look at the scholars. Often in Dublin wandering about the streets, I have looked up at the beautiful and graceful facade of trin coll and have wondered what wonderful mysteries of happy life were going on inside of the building. I have seen groups of gay well-dressed young men going in and coming out; occasionally I have seen a solemnfaced young man going with books in his hand or under his arm, and have wondered on what tremendous things his mind was concentrating. Afterwards I have concluded that his mind may have been full of thoughts about a girl but a young girl to a young man is a wonderful thing to think about. But one fact has come into my [mind] since and it is this: that whether we come from Cambridge, oxford, trinity, or harvard, we all each of us has to take a degree from the college of life. (or a L.L.C. School) each of us has to enter into the problem, each in his own way, of how in the name of God to live. Life is no certain or surer to the young man stepping bravely from the gates of a university with a degree hanging round his neck like a confraternity scapular, than it is for the man of the proletariat stepping out nervously for the first time to put down his name for a job at the nearest labour exchange. So, my friend in this sense, perhaps the most important sense, we are all fellow coll and you who have never gone to a primary school and I who have never gone to a university, are equals in the great college of life where every man must be a pupil, and everyman may become a teacher, for each of us has a lot to learn, and each of us, if there be anything in us at all, ought to have something to teach to others. I want to remind you all that I am not a practised speaker. It is seven months since a word in a formal way was spoken by me, and it was well over a year before that that I ventured to allow my tongue to wag a little in the U.S.A. I find it difficult to fix even a few clumsy sentences into a tidy frame, so I beg of you all to be as patient and as discreet as you possibly can with me. I daresay that almost all who are here tonight are englishmen, who will live their lives generally wherever they may be or whatever they may be doing as englishmen generally do, which is, in my opinion, a little too decorously, a little too solemnly, a little with a little too much devotion to what is called the law, order, and peace of the realm. Now, I dont mean that I want you all to become burning and blasting revolutionaries, for the law, the order, and the peace of the realm that I want to say a few words about tonight, are about the things of the mind, and it is the things of the mind that the englishman is too fond of peace and quiet, law, and the order of custom, habit, and convention. The thoughts of our minds must change before we can change our manner of living; or our manner of living will be roughly changed some day by those who at the moment are unable to change their thoughts . . . . . .

twelve years in Bedford gaol, wrote The Pilgrim's Progress. So Luther, shut up in the Wartzburg, translated the New Testament for the Germans. (And then—One wishes they had made better use of it.) There, you see, goes the old cant again. As if other countries hadnt got the New Testament as well as Germany, and made as little use of it too. The other day I marched myself through the British Museum, and was in no way astonished to find the place a huge dump of treasures from all countries of the world—most of them plundered treasures too. Where did the teaching of the new or the old testament come in while these treasures were being gathered together, I wonder. There's no nation at the present time can benefit by the new testament. We may leave the new testament out of it. Beer is Best is a far more important slogan than do unto others as ye would others should do unto you. It is more blessed to give than to receive, and it would be better and greater for England instead of gathering riches of art and literature out of the world, should give of these treasures herself to the world. You will all remember not very long ago a little chit of a schoolgirl writing some kind of an essay wrote something like "England is the greatest country in the world." The Master criticising the essays of the children remarked to Maud that this sort of thing was out of date and silly. When Maud went home she told her ma, and her ma kicked up a row. Beaverbrook took up the cudgels for Maud and England, and wrote article after article about this terrible insult to England given by a man payed by the state. Then, you will remember, the matter was raised in parliament, a day was set aside to debate the question, and somebody paid Maud's expenses to London so that she could be present in the House while the premier, the lord president of the council, Privy councillors, chancellor of the exchequer, president of the duchy of lancaster, knight of the black rod, knight of the white rod, and divers other parliamentary potentates debated the solemn question as to whether the schoolmaster was or was not within his rights to say that maud was silly. This, to me is a typical instance of the English people's dread of the slightest and most trivial criticism of their national glory.

Things countries are not made great by things done by others but by what is done by themselves.

the other day a catholic priest home from nine years mission work in China, visited the Abbey Theatre to see Juno and the paycock, and got the shock of his life. In a letter to the press going for the play he refers to the Irish people as the grandest and finest people in the world. Now I would like to believe that there was no other people in the wide world. . . .

From Phoebe Fenwick Gaye

TS. O'CASEY

Time and Tide

20 JANUARY 1936

Dear Mr. O'Casey,

Lady Rhondda asks me to thank you for sending her your article *Let the Wheel Turn*[1] and to say she is delighted to print it this week. There is just one small point and I hope you will not feel that we are being unduly fussy about it. The point is that Lady Rhondda feels herself under rather a debt of gratitude to Dick Sheppard[2] for his good services at the time of Miss Holtby's death and does not feel she could conscientiously make a disparaging reference to him in Time and Tide. We have consequently taken the liberty of deleting the reference and the sentence seems to run on very well without it. If you do mind perhaps you will ring me up and let me know. Of course the last thing we want to do is anything you would disapprove of.

Yours very sincerely
Phoebe Fenwick Gaye
Assistant Editor

PS. As the article works out at about half the length of your usual ones will a fee of Four Guineas be adequate?

[1] Sean O'Casey, "Let the Wheel Turn," *Time and Tide*, 1 February 1936; reprinted in *The Flying Wasp* (1937). The article was written in praise of the Mercury Theatre production of T. S. Eliot's *Murder in the Cathedral*, which opened in London on 1 November 1935, with Robert Speaight as Thomas Becket.

[2] Canon Richard Sheppard of St. Paul's Cathedral. The deleted passage referred to O'Casey's view that Londoners were more concerned with the muscular Christianity of Canon Sheppard's popular radio sermons than with the martyrdom of Thomas Becket. See O'Casey's letter to Lady Rhondda, 1 December 1937, on the death of Canon Sheppard.

To Lillian Gish

TS. GISH

49 OVERSTRAND MANSIONS

28 JANUARY 1936

Dear Lillian:

It was a welcome surprise to hear that you are in London, and that you are coming to see us one Saturday evening. I should have gone to see you but I have had a slight cold—almost gone now—and I did not wish to run the risk of giving it to you. I shall be very glad to see you and so will Eileen. I wonder what you will think of the London theatre world? A little more kindly of it, I daresay, than would George—or I! I am very interested in all I have heard of "Winterset",[1] have read the play and think a lot of it. However, we'll leave all this till Saturday.

I enclose a rough plan showing where we live. If you take a 19 bus from the Ritz, going toward Hyde Park, the bus will pass the park, go down Knightsbridge, turn into Sloane Square, go down King's Road, turn into Beaufort Street, pass over the Thames by Battersea Road Bridge and let you down at the corner of Prince of Wales Road. Come down this road and running in line with the park are blocks of mansions. Our block is down a little way and 49 is the one just before a pillar-box, indicated in the plan. I hope this will be clear to you. The bus fare is four-pence and it takes about half an hour to get to us. A taxi all the way would be about a dollar and 25 cents—about 4/6 or 5/1; from Sloane Square—there is a rank there—it would be about 50 cents, or two shillings.

I hope you had an easy crossing and that you left George well.

With affectionate regards,
Sean

[1] Maxwell Anderson's *Winterset* opened in New York on 25 September 1935.

From Phoebe Fenwick Gaye

TS. O'CASEY

Time and Tide
4 FEBRUARY 1936

Dear Mr. O'Casey,

I am so *very* sorry and Lady Rhondda asks me to say that she feels very guilty about the whole affair, but she cannot help thinking that the Coward controversy has gone far enough already in Time and Tide, as the amount he merits is not, in her opinion, equal to that you rightly devoted to the National Theatre. She would have made a special effort to get it into the paper, however, had it not been for its length, but this factor put it right outside the bounds of possibility for this week (It is 2600).

You have behaved so generously to us in the past that I am sure you will realise how mean we feel about it; we would, of course, like to pay for the article if this is not adding insult to injury?

With renewed apologies,
Yours sincerely,
Phoebe Fenwick Gaye

To Phoebe Fenwick Gaye

TC. O'CASEY

[49 OVERSTRAND MANSIONS]
5 FEBRUARY 1936

Dear Miss Fenwick Gaye—

I'm sorry about the second article [1] dealing with Mr Coward's position in the English Theatre. You may remember that I took on the job of writing about the theatre very reluctantly, and warned you that things I write might precipitate peculiar battles in Time And Tide. Well, here is one now, and I, of course, being the antagonist, cannot with a free will strike my colours. I must say, very reluctantly, that I think Lady Rhondda to be wrong. Mr Coward merits every word that I have said about his work; what he does not merit is the praise he has got from Press and People and the chittering critics. Mr Coward is, at present, the focus of the English theatre, and as such he was selected by me for an attack against the forces that are besieging the English theatre with the trivial and the commonplace. "The point I want to make is that the English theatre is in process of starvation," says Mr Agate in 1925, dealing with a play by Mr Coward (Contemporary Theatre, 1925); Agate has forgotten what he said then, and I am out to remind him, and raise the siege. It may seem strange to say, but it is true, that Mr Coward and the poor spirit he gives to the English theatre stands in the way of a National Theatre. So long as Mr Coward remains the chief force in the English theatre, so long as he stands pat on his pinnacle of fame, there can be no National Theatre; there will be no will to create it, for the spirit will be as unwilling as the flesh is weak. These things arent said in disappointment, for I'm used to this by now, and I can wait for publication later on, in book form, maybe. One must fight, and then stand still when the time comes to stand still as the battle goes against one, if one is to have a share in the peace of God. Nor are these things said to provoke you to change your attitude, for I wouldn't like the article to appear now. I shall be glad, however, if you could return it to me. Perhaps I may be allowed to reply to some things said about me in the cor-

[1] Sean O'Casey, "Worms in a Winecup," rejected by *Time and Tide;* printed as "Coward Codology: II, Design For Living," *The Flying Wasp* (1937). His first article, "Coward Codology: Noel Coward's Position as Playwright," appeared in *Time and Tide,* 11 January 1936; reprinted in *The Flying Wasp* as "Coward Codology: I, Cavalcade." See the controversial letters on this article, *Time and Tide,* 18 and 25 January 1936.

respondence, that is in the form of a brief letter. And, of course, I cannot accept payment for the article.

With all Good Wishes,
Sincerely Yours,
Sean O'Casey

To Lady Rhondda [1]

TC. O'CASEY

[49 OVERSTRAND MANSIONS]
8 FEBRUARY 1936

Dear Lady Rhondda,

I have been thinking over the suggested letter, and I have decided that it would be better to make no further mention of the matter in "Time And Tide" or in my prayers.

There are many points raised by correspondents other than those touching myself personally, and if these were dealt with the controversy would bloom again. On the other hand, if these points were ignored, it would appear that I was afraid or unable to deal with them, which would be untrue. It would be far more dignified for me to say nothing than to say too little.

I'm sorry that I managed to plant only one shell in the key position, the G.H.Q. of the popular theatre, and that the general attack failed owing to a mutiny among the reserves. So as the trumpet has sounded a retreat, it is wiser to fall back in good order, and wait for a more suitable time to advance on the entrenched forces that are making the English theatre a byword the world over.

With All Good Wishes.
Sincerely Yours,
Sean O'Casey

[1] Lady Rhondda (1883–1958), Second Viscountess Margaret Haig Thomas; publisher and journalist; campaigner for women's rights; owner-editor of *Time and Tide*.

To Peter Newmark [1]

TS. NEWMARK

[49 OVERSTRAND MANSIONS]
25 FEBRUARY 1936

Dear Mr. Newmark—

Dont handicap the hand that's fighting for you. I have enough to contend against without contending against my friends. The trifles of articles in Time and Tide were an effort to blaze a trail for "young, earnest, uncorrupted critics" by getting in a blow at the fogified critics that dominate the English Press today. I have manhandled the giants and not one of them has ventured a blow in reply. The articles arent so trifling as you think. You were, strictly speaking, out of order at the meeting, for my article in Time and Tide on Coward was not the subject under discussion. This only by the way. It was quite natural for you to think that my article did not deal with Coward's work, and I had already written one called "Worms in a Winecup" about the play you mentioned —Design For Living. It will be seen somewhere, sooner or later. If you want to know what the humour and wit of Design For Living is like, read George Jean Nathan's Passing Judgements, and see for yourself. The question is not one of morality or immorality; Coward seems to think that sexual chastity is the only virtue. He makes Otto say "We're not doing any harm to anyone. We're not peppering the world with illegitimate children". They'd be a damn sight nearer to life if they were. And "not doing any harm to anyone" is nonsense. No one can do a thing without that act having an effect on someone or something. These creatures aren't men and Gilda's not a woman. None of them ever gets away from the edge of the bed. Coward, for all his spouting, is just as much a Victorian as any little old "woman in a jet bonnet". Read Maugham again: Coward doesnt come within a patch of him. Even Coward's commercial success has been exaggerated. Other plays have had a longer run than even Bitter-Sweet, and St Joan, The First Mrs Frazer, and The Barretts of Wimpole Street come very close to it. His last Two plays Conversation Piece and Point Valaine, have been bad failures in America. But let's not bother about him any more for the present. I dont know what you mean by an anti-Christian bias. Do you mean an anti-sacerdotal bias? You say Eliot's play glorifies God, not Christ. Have you forgotten the Christian Creed? The Father is God, the Son is God, and The Holy Ghost is God. And yet they are not three Gods; but one God. It is Eliot here that jibs at theology, and not I. The Church is the Church of God, and also the Church of Jesus Christ. He it was Who founded it; He is

[1] Peter Newmark, an undergraduate at Cambridge University who had attended O'Casey's talk for the Shirley Society earlier in the month.

the Bridegroom, and the Church is the Bride. You say that there are trivial bits in Within The Gates that "dont come off". You are perfectly right and you are the first English critic that has pointed this out. Its dullness in places puzzled me for a long time. I hope I am wiser now. I think I remember being introduced to you, but cant remember talking to you, which is a pity. You should have come to me after my talk (not lecture) was over. And dont despise trifles; perfection is made up of trifles says Michael Angelo. I do not despise the trifles in Within The Gates that hurt the play. An atom is a very important power.

With all good wishes.
Very Sincerely Yours,
Sean O'Casey

To Peter Newmark

TS. NEWMARK

[49 OVERSTRAND MANSIONS]
28 FEBRUARY 1936

Dear Peter Newmark—

The remark "We're not peppering the world with illegitimate children" is attributed to Coward because it is obviously one of his thoughts. There is no getting away from it. There is no characterization in Design For Living. Otto could be Leo, and Leo could be Otto, and either of them could be Gilda. All the sayings are Coward's sayings. Coward is as evident, more evident, in his plays than Shaw is in his. Another objection to this play is that he evidently means them * to be taken for artists. I dont believe the man was ever in the company of an artist for five minutes. Advanced opinions, and leader of the intellectuals! He is actually in opinion, a worn-out old Victorian. It isnt a question of Menages a trois, as you call it. Coward could have had the design of a bed for almost every play he wrote. "Coward" says a big publisher, "is an institution seperate and apart which may not be garnished or embellished . . . an interpreter of the world and humanity . . . a philosopher . . . with the serious purpose of a propagandist and protagonist . . . God alone knows how long Coward will survive and to what heights he will attain". That, I submit, is the general opinion held of Coward by critics and people, if not by Mr Newmark.

In the Christian Faith the truth in every conception is only to be found in Christ Jesus.

* the characters, of course

It is not that I am very busy, but that my eyes are not too good, so I have to spare them as much as may be possible. So I wont write anything about the present cult of naturalism on the stage, but wait till some day you happen to be in London, when you can come along and we'll talk about it from one end to the other.

With Best Wishes
Sean O'Casey

To William W. Hadley [1]

TS. O'CASEY

[49 OVERSTRAND MANSIONS]
29 FEBRUARY 1936

Dear Mr. Hadley—

Thank you for your letter of the 28th inst. I should like to point out that the reference made by Mr. Agate came to me through a press-cutting (I'm sorry to say that I do not read every word written by Mr Agate), but, even so, my comment on what he said of me was no more belated than my reply to that same comment.[2] The fact that the letter is in type is as satisfying to me as was the statement that Home Rule had been placed on the Statute book was to the Irish People. And, after all, rightly or wrongly, my name in the Theatre is just as important as the name of Mr. Agate, so I must request that my letter (a very short one) be published, if not in the current issue, then in the following issue. Hundreds of letters are published in the year by The Sunday Times, and I think that I have some claim that my letter (a very short one) should be one of them.

With great respect,
I remain,
Sincerely Yours,
[Sean O'Casey]

[1] William W. Hadley, editor of the *Sunday Times*, 1932–50.

[2] Mr. Hadley had refused to publish O'Casey's reply to James Agate, a letter he wrote on 16 February. It was eventually printed on 1 March.

To Sunday Times

1 March 1936

Agate, O'Casey, and Coward

Sir,—In a recent issue of your widely read journal Mr. James Agate writes:—

> I see, by the way, that Sean O'Casey has just declared that "Noel Coward hasn't yet put even his nose into the front rank of second-class dramatists, let alone into the front rank of first-class dramatists." Were I a dramatist of genius like Mr. O'Casey I think I should try to say something more generous about Mr. Coward.[1]

He is not sure, though, for he says "I think I should try." Now what does "more generous" mean? Does it mean that the generosity should push Mr. Coward plumb into the front rank of second-class dramatists, or should it go further, and push him plumb into the front rank of first-class dramatists? Or does it mean that the work of Mr. Coward deserves a place in one of these two ranks, and, if so, in which one? If his work does not deserve to be put in either place, why should I try to put him in a place of which he is unworthy?

Does Mr. Agate expect me to give an opinion directly contrary to what my conscience and intelligent judgement tell me to be the right one? If he expects me to do that, then what are we to think of him as a critic? Does he expect me to show more generosity to the trivial work of Mr. Coward than he showed to the great work of Eugene O'Neill? I heard a critic say once that "a critic who is kind, that is to say, who gives praise where it is not deserved, betrays his calling." Who said that? Ah, go and guess.

[Before Mr. Agate whimpers anymore for generosity][2] Let Mr. Agate read again the article he wrote not so long ago called "Swat That Wasp." Well, I am a flying wasp that Mr. Agate will never be nimble enough to kill. I am as heartless over the triviality of Mr. Coward's work as I am over Mr. Agate's pathetic tears.

Sean O'Casey

London.
[16 February 1936]

Mr. Agate writes: With bronchitis and one or two other quarrels on my hands, I am too busy to start a row with Mr. O'Casey. I therefore merely refer him to certain laws governing this question of generosity in criticism laid down by Sainte-Beuve. Mr. O'Casey's secretary will doubtless know the passage.

[1] James Agate, "The Theatre When King George's Reign Began," *Sunday Times*, 26 January 1936.

[2] Phrase in square brackets omitted by the editor.

To Irish Press

3 MARCH 1936

"Murder in the Cathedral"

Mr. Sean O'Casey, in a letter to the Editor, writes:—

Dear Sir—There is at present a play called "Murder in the Cathedral", written by T. S. Eliot, the poet, doing extraordinarily well in a little theatre called The Mercury in London; and I should like to draw the attention of your many readers to this work in the hope that, as soon as the London run ends, the play may be seen in Dublin. Catholic Ireland, if she has any interest at all in the drama, ought to see this play. The play deals with the murder of Thomas a Becket, and is a very fine and trimly done poetic play, glittering with gaily coloured and somber-hued Christian implications. I suggest that the Directorate of the Abbey Theatre should bring over the play, the actors, and the producer for a few weeks' visit to Dublin.

To Lillian Gish

TS. GISH

49 OVERSTRAND MANSIONS

4 MARCH 1936

Dear Lillian:

We hope you did well and are doing well in Glasgow.[1] You should do very well if you let yourself get warm with a little courage. It's hard, I know, to be here alone in London—harder than to be alone in New York—but, after all, one can feel very much alone even in the midst of one's friends. The feeling of loneliness has to be conquered, that's all!

So gird yourself with courage and face all, even failure, if it comes, coolly and calmly; this is the only way to bring success a little nearer.

I hope Glasgow isn't any colder than London—it's the damp here & the yellow fog that make London so unpleasant.

So be brave; there can be no such thing as failure to him or her who does the best.

[1] Miss Gish made her first appearance on the British stage at the King's Theatre, Glasgow, in March, as Charlotte Lovell in Zoe Atkins' *The Old Maid,* but the play closed before it reached London.

Is lear do dhuire as dhichill, we Irish say—"His best is enough". Let all who look on like it or lump it.

With all good wishes,
Sean

To Lady Rhondda

T.C. O'CASEY
[49 OVERSTRAND MANSIONS]
5 MARCH 1936

Dear Lady Rhondda—

I wonder did you get the note I sent to you—addressed to Frognal—some days ago? You remember that you suggested a little talk together, and were to ring me up to make an arrangement to meet.

I have since been down in Cambridge, and have talked to the members of the Shirley Society, on "The Holy Ghost Leaves England." Did you see that they have had a strike in Oxford? I saw things in Cambridge that no man ought to speak about that "knows his catechism."

I hope you are well.
Yours Very Sincerely,
Sean O'Casey

To Gabriel Fallon

MS. TEXAS
FORTY-NINE OVERSTRAND MANSIONS
23 MARCH 1936

My dear Gaby—

Enclosed is a cheque for Ten Shillings, Share in two performances of "Pound On Demand" one, by Irish Literary Society, & the other by Darlington Grammar School, Durham, at One Guinea per performance, as per arrangement long ago between us.

Love to All. You, Rose, & the little Fallons.

Give my warm Regards to Rose. I have written to you before, & will write again when I hear from you.

Remember me to Frank McM[anus].

Your Buttie
Sean

To Phoebe Fenwick Gaye

TC. O'CASEY

49 OVERSTRAND MANSIONS
26 MARCH 1936

Dear Miss Fenwick Gaye—

I am going to ask you a few questions in the friendliest possible way relating to the recent reluctance to publish an article of mine—the one about Mr Coward's place in the English Theatre. I am not going to speak about the past, but only about the future. I have not been sure since the incident happened that Time And Tide then made a clean cut forever between itself and me, and that you wish no further connection with O'Casey. Or, on the other hand, am I to retain the assurance that any future article I may submit will receive the consideration of the Editor for publication. Candidly, I dont wish to be cast out, but if you think it better for your Journal that I should cease to be a contributor, then, of course, there is no more to be said. For instance I have an article called, "St Beuve, Patron of Poor Playwriters, Pray For Us," [1] which I should like you to read, and then publish or reject, as you see fit. But before I send it on, or any other article, I should like to know first whether what I have already written has upset you so much as to convince you (or even leave you in doubt) that Time And Tide is better without me. I have already been asked (between ourselves) by Routledge & Co to allow what I've written in Time And Tide to appear in book form, so, rejected or accepted, all I write will eventually be published, which makes things more easy for me. I have a great affection for your Journal, and should like to continue to be a contributor, and, as well, the occasional cheque comes in handy, for I have a lot to do, and I am far from being safe off financially.

So, whatever way things go,
I remain, sincerely hoping that
Lady Rhondda is allright, or nearly allright;
again,

Yours As Ever,
Sean O'Casey

[1] Sean O'Casey, "St. Beuve, Patron of Poor Playwriters, Pray For Us," *Time and Tide,* 9 May 1936; reprinted in *The Flying Wasp* (1937).

To John Ford[1]

TC. O'CASEY

[49 OVERSTRAND MANSIONS]

29 MARCH 1936

Dear Mr Ford—

Many thanks for your kind letter sent on to me by Mr George Jean Nathan. I fully appreciate your points about the appropriateness of putting something in the Film of "The Plow" that would, in some little way, show some appreciation of the achievement of our Irish fighters in the war with England, which brought the worst of England's stupidity and persecution to a stop, and gave Ireland—or part of Ireland—the Irish Free State. Of course Ireland isnt yet free in any sense of the word, even politically, for Ulster is yet cut away from her, and kept away by the help of England's power. However, we wont, at present, argue about that point. How to get into the Film what you and I want to get in is the question, and it is something of an awkward question to answer. I have pondered your suggestion, and I'm afraid that to carry it out would mean a big alteration in the whole theme of the play. Besides, I think it would be unlikely that Clitheroe—if we kept him alive so long—would hardly give expression to the speech at the funeral of his own baby (his baby is in the coffin with Mollser). Too, he could hardly say these things marching through lines of swaddies—it would be very dangerous. And there is just the possibility of it feeling a little foolish, which would be bad for the Film, as well as giving a lot of trouble to alter the play to fit it in. I have two alternative suggestions to make to you. They are as follows:

a. In one of the photographic flashes of the fighting couldnt one be given of Clitheroe and his men, hemmed in, making a last stand; dialogue something like, "we are cornered, it is death or surrender.

Clitheroe: You surrender, if you like: I shall fight on to the end. Men: Imprisonment for Ireland. Another: Or wounds for Ireland. Clitheroe: Or death for Ireland! (repetition of dialogue in 2nd scene, which might be very effective) Man: The Flag is falling!" Then Clitheroe could make his little speech of faith in the future. The undercurrent here would be "The Soldiers' Song." I think I might be able to write out some suitable dialogue for this situation; but dont want to try for fear you'd reject the suggestion, and, for my eyes' sake, I must write as little as possible.

b. Lieut. Langon who is wounded in the 3rd act could be brought along on a stretcher, his companions having had to abandon him, along the line of swaddies who are watching the flag, and seeing it fall, make remarks that would call forth a dying confession of faith from Langon.

I hope these may prove helpful.

[1] John Ford (1895–1973), American film director; RKO Studios, Hollywood.

Miss Reitzer, your London Representative, came to see me last night. We discussed the cast. I shouldnt recommend you to choose Miss [Eileen] Crowe for the part of "Bessie Burgess". She wouldnt look the part, and, in my opinion, couldnt possibly put the feeling and earnestness in the part that it needs. One of the best actresses in the Abbey Co is a Miss [May] Craig whose name seems not to have been mentioned. I feel sure she would play this better than Miss Crowe, or make a fine Mrs Gogan. Or Sally Allgood who would as Bessie Burgess, be best of all. I suppose you have plenty of choice for a pert and pretty girl to play the Prostitute, Rosie Redmond. I dont see Miss Crowe as a success in this part. I am delighted to hear of your high opinion of the play, and that "all concerned with the production of the play will strive to make it as fine a picture as it is in the stage form." I am sure you will, and that is one reason why I sincerely hope my two suggestions may be of use to you.

I'm afraid I dont see much of Liam O'Flaherty. I havent seen him for four or five years. Between ourselves, I dont get into close touch with him, though few have as great an appreciation for the work he has done than I have.

If I can do anything else for you, let me know.

With all good wishes to you and all who are working with you.

I am, Sincerely Yours,
[Sean O'Casey]

To Robert F. Sisk [1]

TC. O'CASEY

[49 OVERSTRAND MANSIONS]

29 MARCH 1936

Dear Mr Sisk—

Thanks for your kind letter, and for the letter from Mr Ford which I have answered and have forwarded by the post that brings this to you. I have made some suggestions that may meet the point about appreciation of the achievement of the Irish Soldiers that brought the Free State into existence. I hope they may prove to be satisfactory.

I have received the marked copy of the play, and feel a little furious about some of the cuts. Some of them are God damn ridiculous. Your London Representative came to see me last night, and she very kindly promised to do what she could to arrange a meeting between me and

[1] Robert F. Sisk, RKO Studios, Hollywood.

the Censor, so that he and I could talk the cuts over again. I may be able to prevail on him to give a concession or two. I shouldnt like to chance any guidance to your screen writers, for frankly, I know next to nothing about Film production, and possibly, on account of my name, the screen writers might do what I might suggest, which again might be the worst possible thing to do. Perhaps you mean that I should rewrite the marked passages in a way that the Censor would pass, and, if this be so, I think I ought to wait till I know what the Censor may finally say to me. I daresay that you will yourselves have to make some cuts in the dialogue for the easier and slicker movement of the film. For instance, the dialogue in the 3rd act between Nora and Clitheroe would, I think, be too long, and would make the action heavy. However, you know more about these things than I do.

Mr Nathan has told me that the "Plow" is in good hands, and he has a fine opinion of Mr Ford and of yourself. He thought a lot of the "Informer".

I may say that some of the cuts are the actual words spoken by Patric Pearse, Commander-General of the Irish Volunteers, at a meeting which I helped to organise. I cant see why they should object to this. However, I'll wait to see what the Censor will say to me.

With Every Good Wish.
Sincerely Yours,
[*Sean O'Casey*]

To George Jean Nathan

MS. CORNELL

49 OVERSTRAND MANSIONS
30 MARCH 1936

My dear George—

Thanks for sending me on the letters from Messrs Sisk & Ford of RKO. I have answered them as well as I could, & have sent suggestions for additions to Film that, I think, will take away the necessity to keep Clitheroe alive.

I've just got a letter from Lillian [Gish] which seems to show that she is feeling much better about the whole business of the play [*Within The Gates*]. She tells me my letter to her did her a world of good, bucked her up, & gave her courage, which is all to the good, & adds to the glory of S.O'C.

I seem to be bombarding you with letters these days!

The Theatre here today is the Theatre of yesterday—only a day older & a day worse.

However, I saw a group of Schoolboys give a grand production of Midsummer Night's Dream,[1] the other night, & that will last me for a while.

Ever Yours,
Sean

[1] Performed by the pupils of Guy Boas's Sloane School, Chelsea. See "Shakespeare Lives in London Lads," *The Flying Wasp* (1937).

To Horace Reynolds

MS. Reynolds

[49 Overstrand Mansions]
17 April 1936

My dear Horace—

Thanks for the book by Paul Green.[1] I liked it greatly. There is in it something of the lyrical quality to be found in his plays. It is rather a terrible story. However, I'm no judge of a novel. I find it getting harder & harder for me to read a novel—why, I don't know. I skip and skip & skip.

And thanks for your letter. I'm afraid, I'm sure, that my ancient lays & stories are valueless in quantity & quality. The "Story of Thomas Ashe" [2] is, I believe, gone but for one copy in The National Library. The Librarian sent me a photographic copy. Strangely enough, some time ago, I inscribed a copy for a Katharine Gregory of New York. These two are the only ones I know of. They are useless except as curiosities, & poor even as that. No: "Three Shouts on a Hill" [3] never appeared in "The Nation," or anywhere else. I sent it to Maunsel's of Dublin, but they would have none of it; & so a year after I committed the MS to the flames—in plain English I burned it. My published work appearing before my plays would make only a good-sized pamphlet. Altogether in "The Nation" or "The Irish Nation" edited by W. P. O'Ryan, afterwards Editor of "The Daily Herald" appeared only 2 short articles—one "Sound the

[1] Paul Green, *This Body the Earth* (New York, Harper, 1935).

[2] And in its slightly expanded second edition, *The Sacrifice of Thomas Ashe* (1918).

[3] See Bernard Shaw's letter to O'Casey, 3 December 1919.

Loud Trumpet"[4] & the other a criticism of the methods of The Gaelic League. An Irish priest recently reminded me that I once wrote a one-act play called "The Seamless Robe of Roisin (Ireland)",[5] which, he says, was printed by Erskine Childers in "The Common People", a paper founded to combat those in favour of the Treaty before the Civil War broke out. I had, & have forgotten it. I'm sure it must have been terrible! Then there was a terrible article, critical of De Valera's policy—from the point of view of Labour—in "Dublin Saturday Post",[6] & that, I think, is all, apart from National satirical—satirical of England—songs that I sung at National Gatherings. "The Constitutional Movement Must Go On" was started by a Fergus O'Connor who wrote the first 2 verses; I added the rest.[7] Where the song is now, God knows. Then there was "The Man From the D. Mail" "If the Germans Come to Ireland in the Morning", two verses of which I still remember; "I Dont Believe it, Do You?" a satirical parody of a music-Hall song; "How do you doodle oodle oo" another parody, both of which I have entirely forgotten. Some were published in little 2d sheets called "Songs of the Wren".[8] Even the names of others have passed completely out of my memory. Then there was the "The Story of The Irish Citizen Army"[9]—bashed about by the then Censor—which can be got still. All of them wouldn't make a book fit for a chiselur to read. I don't remember writing anything for "The Workers' Republic"; whatever I wrote then—& it was little—appeared in "The Irish Worker", Jim Larkin's paper. Most of my work (of this kind, particularly National) first appeared in Manuscript Journals that National Clubs gathered together, & read to their members once a month. "Sound The Loud Trumpet" first appeared this way. Anything else, or almost all the others have perished forever, & a good job, too. There's just a chance —a bare one—that I may go to Ireland this Summer; and if I do, I hope I shall see you there.

I am indeed glad to hear that the Critics in America, headed by the one & only George Jean, have given the palm to "Winterset". It was easily the best play of the year. Here, be christ, the critics would give the palm to the second worst play of the year, & never know they'd done so.

I hope you are getting articles into the American Press. I read one that was in "The N.Y. Times".

[4] In *The Peasant and Irish Ireland,* 25 May 1907; reprinted in *Feathers From the Green Crow* (1962).

[5] Apparently only a prose version has survived, "The Seamless Coat of Kathleen," *Poblacht Na h-Eireann* (Republic of Ireland), 29 March 1922; reprinted in *Feathers From the Green Crow* (1962).

[6] See his letter, "Labour and Sinn Fein," *Dublin Saturday Post,* 22 September 1917.

[7] See his letter to Fergus O'Connor, 4 March 1918.

[8] *Songs of the Wren No. 1; No. 2; More Wren Songs* (1918); some reprinted in *Feathers from the Green Crow* (1962).

[9] P. O'Cathasaigh, *The Story of the Irish Citizen Army* (1919). The "P" was a misprint. Reprinted in *Feathers From the Green Crow* (1962).

Give my love to Mrs. Reynolds. I hope she is keeping fit and getting stronger daily; & my love to your two children.

My Affectionate Regards to all at Harvard. I spoke a few weeks ago in one of the Cambridge Colleges here on "The Holy Ghost Leaves England", & had a good time.

With Fondest Regards.
Yours As Ever.
Sean

To Peter Newmark

MS. NEWMARK

[49 OVERSTRAND MANSIONS]
28 APRIL 1936

Dear Peter Newmark—

Many thanks for your kind letter. I don't think I should like to talk to a crowd again for some time. After talking in any public way, I like to take a holiday for a long time. I'm afraid I belong to the contemplative order of talkers—silence is more eloquent.

But, whenever you & she will, I shall be glad to come one day & have tea with you both—you & your friend. I have just read the MS of what I think to be a fine play—"Daughters of Atreus".[1] It was written a year ago & has not yet been published or produced. I have written a few words about it to Time and Tide. I hope they may publish what I have said, & that it may draw some attention to the play. I understand The Theater Guild, after keeping it a year, let it go. It has come to London, & has passed out of it again. What a great Theatre the Great Empire of England has!

I'm glad to say we are all well.

With Warm Regards
Yours Sincerely
Sean O'Casey

[1] Robert Turney's *The Daughters of Atreus* opened in New York on 14 October 1936.

To Lillian Gish

MS. GISH

49 OVERSTRAND MANSIONS
29 APRIL 1936

Dear Lillian:

I'm sending MS of play ["Daughters of Atreus"] and book by District Messenger as I find I shan't be able to run over this evening. The maid's out for the day and we have to keep an eye on the kids. Perhaps we shall see you soon in London again.

God be with you, and think well of the part of Electra in "Daughters of Atreus". A thousand "Old Maids" wouldn't make a scene of it.

With love,
Sean

To George Jean Nathan

MS. CORNELL

49 OVERSTRAND MANSIONS
[? MAY 1936]

My dear George—

Greetings! If I haven't heard from you, I've heard about you—from Lillian [Gish], who has been with us since she came to London, & who seemed to be a little depressed about her part in "The Old Maid." I'm afraid she felt lonely with the other English players. The English are, of course, much colder than you Americans; & I'd rather be "on my lonesome" in New York, than here in England. However, some of the papers in Glasgow—where the play opened—say Lillian made a hit—which God strengthen—& so she must be feeling a little happier now. I wrote to her in Glasgow, & so did Eileen, but we haven't heard a word—she's probably very busy. It has been very disappointing to me to find that Vanity Fair has turned into Vogue—Fox into Lady—& I shall miss this American monthly very much indeed.

I have had a bad time for the past eight weeks—eight years cut a little short—with a cold and a touch of bronchitis, but am nearly OK again. You've had a tough winter of it in New York, &, by the papers, floods are pretty bad in Pennsylvania. I daresay George Markle is up too high to be bothered. I got quite a flood of cards for Christmas from friends in America. I haven't yet started on a new play. I have felt tired for a long time, & no impulse came for a beginning; but I suppose, I shall set down a thought or an idea soon. The Theatre is worse than ever, poor as a mangy churchmouse. The Editor of an advanced paper came to see me, & begged me to write a few articles on the Theatre. Reluctantly, I consented. I wrote gaily about an English National Theatre, & all applauded. Then came the first of a few articles called "Coward Codology," &, bang! the shutters were put up at once! Just think, over the whole land there hasn't been yet one performance of O'Neill's "Mourning Becomes Electra." I've just written an article—semi-political—saying that one way to promote friendship between England & the U.S.A. is to produce more O'Neill. We have "The Old Maid," "Men in White," & "Three Men On a Horse," but "Mourning Becomes Electra"—no! Well, God Damn them anyhow.

My deepest affection,
Sean

To Gabriel Fallon

MS. TEXAS

FORTY-NINE OVERSTRAND MANSIONS
12 MAY 1936

My dear Gaby—

I sent the two books to you, & hope you got them allright—mine in a green-and-gold cover. Why the hell do they cage Irish writings in green-and-gold, & spangle the design with shamrocks? God, how I hate shamrocks! These God damned English still think we're a nation of Irish National Foresters. No wonder Parnell loved them!

There was an arrangement made over "Pound On Demand" some years ago. I put a copy of what I sent to you in a *safe* place, & I can't find the copy, & I can't find the place. You must have the letter *somewhere*. I got on splendidly with the young in Cambridge, & spoke of politics, sport, literature, & drama, in a quiet way, mind you, in a quiet way. Montague Slator has been Editor of a monthly called "Left Review" for some time. It is—or was—a good magazine from the Communistic point of view, but, I think it is gone now. I enclose a criticism of "Easter" [1] which appeared in a weekly here. "Easter" is as much a revolutionary play as is "Abie's Irish Rose". The MS of the play was sent to me by a

[1] Montagu Slater's *Easter 1916* was produced in London by the Left Theatre on 8 December 1935.

comrade in the Communist Party of Ireland; so I read the play, & agree with my Communist comrade that it is a bloody bad one!

What is The Marian Arts Guild, & has it anything to do with The Christian Academy of Art—or is it of Christian Art? There's a great hillaballoo here over Beverly Nichols standing up for Jesus. He's busy blazing a new trail for the Christian Saviour in England—and J. H. Thomas & his son are having a little chat over the Budget prospects!

No, I shall never forgive Father Gaffney for his bad plays.[2] He would compress all dramatic art into the compass of his own plays, & coffin his own Faith in them, too. Just think of the world as it is, & then think of the part his plays will take in its salvation. Don't go too far, he says to Christ, don't go too far. But when Christ will venture into the heart of man—as Gaffney's Faith, I think teaches—He would venture anywhere.

But I mustn't go on like this, old son.

And so my love to Rose, to your little ones, & to you.

Your Buttie
Sean

13 May 1936
ADDENDUM

I just got your note this morning. I'm glad you liked "Murder in the Cathedral"; it is a very fine play, and was produced delightfully here. I wrote to The Irish Press some time ago suggesting that all the Christian Catholic Academy of art, & all the C.Y.M.S., so interested in Shakespeare, should combine & pay for the bringing over of the London Co for a spell in Dublin. The I. Press graciously turned my letter into the suggestion that The Abbey Theatre should do it! I wonder why is there this terrible fear of the criticism of simple things? If we don't get used to this kind of criticism—another name for judgment—what way shall we feel before the last terrible criticism of all! And there'll be no side-steppin' allowed either. Do they forget that St Paul criticised St Peter, & fought tooth & nail against the imposition of Jewish Law on the Christian Gentiles? I have never seen or read "Hotel Universe",[3] but the name sounds bad. And Christ's own criticism of His own Seven Churches in Asia.

But I mustn't go on like this, old son.

My Communist comrade tells me the Gate is closed; & that Willmore & Edwards [4] are never coming back. Will ye no come back again! Tho' to be fair, their acting and production here were very good, & far above

[2] See O'Casey's letters to Fallon, 11 September 1930, note 1; 22 October 1930, note 1.

[3] Philip Barry's *Hotel Universe* was produced in New York in 1930, London in 1932, and in Dublin by the Gate Theatre on 29 May 1936.

[4] Micheál MacLiammoir and Hilton Edwards of the Dublin Gate Theatre.

those of the same class of Dramatic English Groups—except that of "Murder in the Cathedral".

My Affectionate Regards again to all & Frank McM[anus] & to the Franciscan Father & Brother, & to all Irishmen & Women.

Sean

To Melvyn Douglas [1]

MS. LEHMAN ENGEL
49 OVERSTRAND MANSIONS
17 MAY 1936

My dear Melvyn—

I want to ask you, if you still happen to be in touch with Lehman Angell [sic], to see if he could let me have a copy of the music he composed for "Within The Gates." [2] The Old Vic Theatre here—that specialises in Shakespeare productions—(and often does them badly) thinks of putting it on next season, & I much prefer the American score to the Irish score (most of it my own, & terrible!). I have often thought of Lehman, & think he has a fine talent, & hope he may get something often that will be worth his while to help,—like "Within The Gates," for, my dear Mel, with all its faults, & God knows (and you know) the play had many; but it, I think & still believe, it was worth his trouble, & all the energy & thought you put into it. I hope you still think so too. If it only had been a little better! But we all did our best, & it was a great fight.

I shall never forget my stay in New York, & regret only that it was not much longer so that I could see more of what was to be seen, & get into closer touch with the American people. I hope you & Mrs. Gahagan (Helen, if I may call her so)[3] are doing well. I have another kid now, & it takes some doing to keep things going.

I haven't started another play yet, but hope to start one soon. I suppose you never meet "Jimmy" Reynolds now.[4] Poor Jimmy! He meant well.

Affectionate Regards to You Both
Yours As Ever,
Sean O'Casey

[1] Melvyn Douglas (1901–), American director and actor.

[2] Lehman Engel, with Milton Lusk, composed the incidental music, and Melvyn Douglas directed the New York production of *Within the Gates,* which opened on 22 October 1934. See O'Casey's letter to Nathan, 18 October 1934.

[3] Mrs. Helen Gahagan Douglas, wife of Melvyn Douglas, and former actress and member of congress from California.

[4] James Reynolds designed the sets and costumes for the New York production of *Within the Gates.*

To Time and Tide

23 May 1936

"WORSE THAN MUSTARD GAS"

Sir,—The urging on and on of the Negus to fight the Italians with the promise of the League of Nations in front of him and the armies and navies of great nations hurrying up behind was, of course, far worse than anything the Italians ever did or could do; for this to the Negus and his family was a spiritual as well as a material betrayal. There never was, as G.B.S. says, the faintest chance of any such intervention, and yet a host of people refused to hear it denied, wouldn't stay to listen to Shaw when he shouted it at them a long time ago. Well, they know it now. And isn't it just like England and Sir Norman Angell to dance around and cry out against the use of poison gas by the Italians, while all the time she has herself tons and tons of it in hot storage ready to pour it down without fear or favour on any civilized or uncivilized people that would venture to give her the grand go-by? Isn't it nearly time that England realised that this self-righteous hypocrisy is a sin against the Holy Ghost? England has one chance left by, as Shaw says, choosing the red flag in preference to the white one. It's a God's act that today the defeat of Communist Russia by a Capitalistic Japan would be a serious thing for England, and, perhaps, for the United States, too. Every anti-Communist in England, France and America is asking for a German hegemony in the West and a Japanese one in the East. I was delighted to read this opinion by G.B.S., for I said the same thing last month in the *Manchester Evening News*.[1] England, France, Russia and the United States can keep peace, not for a year and a day, but for ever and ever without the dropping of a thimbleful of mustard gas or the shooting of a popgun. If the human race is to have time to breathe, then there must be an understanding with the power of the Soviets. All people of decent intelligence ought to make a beeline for the union of Russia, France, the United States, and England, though a foolish fear of Communism bellows in their ears, for without the aid of Russia, no peace can come to the world. And yet we find a brave and cultured woman, Lady Rhondda, saying in her "Notes on the Way" that to Communists "only capitalists are vile," and that they hold that under Communism "human nature would automatically become angelic." Communists say nothing of the kind. TIME AND TIDE, we are told, welcomed Mr. Shaw's views on the present situation. Why? Surely because of his intellectual outlook on life, his commonsense, and his proved integrity. Did this

[1] Sean O'Casey, "Personal View," *Manchester Evening News*, 24 April 1936.

Irish Communist ever say that "only capitalists are vile"? I, too, am a Communist with none of Shaw's intellect, some of his keen intelligence, much of his ardour, and all of his convictions, and did I ever say that "only capitalists are vile"? We believe that Capitalism is a vile thing, but that is another matter. When Lady Rhondda (I write this with all respect) and her father were just about to leave the sinking *Lusitania*,[2] she tells us she heard him murmur in the rush to get the boats out and the people marshalled, if my memory serves me right, "Inefficiency, inefficiency"; yet the deck he stood on was not the deck of a Communist ship. When he eliminated the wait of the poor people for food, the mind that thought out the scheme was the mind of the Communist, and not the mind of a Capitalist. Yet the gage of world-war everywhere threatened to be thrown down is nothing else but the declaration of a world-wide inefficiency. Under Communism human nature would not automatically become angelic, but human nature would automatically become orderly, and order is heaven's first law, and so human nature would be a step nearer the angelic state. What order have we now? Capitalism is the regimentation of life towards death, but Communism is the regimentation of life towards life, and that is the only difference, but it is a big one.

I am, etc.,
Sean O'Casey

London

[What I actually said in the course of referring with some enthusiasm to a letter from Mr. Brailsford published in the *New Statesman* of May 9th was: ". . . it may be that that bee buzzing in so many Socialist bonnets (the counterpart, it is true, of even more trying opposite number bees in the bonnets of their opponents) that only capitalists are vile, and that in a Socialist world human nature would automatically become angelic, buzzes a shade too loudly in his . . . ." Mr. O'Casey will note that I did not say that *all* Socialists—or Communists—held this view. I know well that Mr. O'Casey himself is incapable of holding it, poets have imagination. Nevertheless it is to be found. As for what he has to say about Capitalism I would reply that I should be the last to suggest that the Capitalist system functions perfectly. It certainly does not. But to say so is not, as is sometimes supposed, to say that the Socialist system (which by the way we have for some thirty years or so been slowly and tentatively beginning to substitute for it in this country—a fact which—except by the diehards—is apt to be overlooked) would function perfectly.

Is Mr. O'Casey really certain that if the *Lusitania* had been owned by Soviet Russia my father would have found no cause to murmur "Inefficiency, inefficiency" as she sank? (The story that he did so is not mine,

[2] Lady Rhondda and her father were rescued from the ill-fated *Lusitania*, which was torpedoed off the coast of Ireland by a German submarine on 7 May 1915. Of the 1,959 persons aboard, 1,198 were lost.

by the way. We never found each other in that great crowd on the boat dock. We only met again at Queenstown. Still, it may very possibly be true.) If we are to believe that, then we must believe that human brain-power in emergencies is an entirely different thing under Socialist from what it is under any other rule. No one has ever questioned the courage of the officers on board the *Lusitania,* but they were faced with a situation which needed not merely courage but almost superhuman ability. They were asked to save the lives of two thousand frightened people in twelve and a half minutes. If in such circumstances the ship's organization did to a considerable extent break down, and fail to live up to the very high standard of efficiency which we have come to expect on board our boats, it was not perhaps altogether surprising. At least I cannot see what on earth that has to do with the Capitalist system.

I find it difficult to believe—human beings being as naturally disordered as they are—that under any system of government all disorder would be eliminated, though it is of course possible that it might be minimised. By all means let us select the system of government which will, we believe, function the least imperfectly. But let us not forget that all systems of government are ultimately based on that still most imperfect organ, the heart of man, and that until and unless human beings themselves become perfect, no system of government which they evolve is going to lack the faults which men themselves possess.—RHONDDA.]

To George Jean Nathan

MS. CORNELL

49 OVERSTRAND MANSIONS
30 MAY 1936

My dear George—

Just a line to give you a greeting. I daresay Lillian has told you all about the unfortunate end of "Old Maid" (by Zoë Atkins, adapted from Edith Wharton's novel of same name). It was a pity, but maybe, it was all for the best. I shall look forward to your new book in September. The cutting about your Critics' Circle's prize for the best drama of the year is a fine one, & has borne a fine first-fruit already in [Maxwell] Anderson's "Winterset." I haven't read the play next in order, but "Winterset" certainly wins over the title of [Robert E. Sherwood's] "Idiot's Delight." Your New York Drama Critics deserve praise for this fine idea. There would be no chance of anything like that here, & less chance—if there were—that such a play as "Winterset" would not get the palm.

Lillian game me the MS of "Daughters of Atreus" [by Robert Turney] to read, and, my dear George, I found this to be a play! I forget whether or no you mentioned it to me when I was in New York, but I find you do in an article on Critics praising second-rate plays. It is, in my opinion, one of the best things I've read for a long time. I wrote an article called "I Spy A Fine Play," about it, but the papers here weren't interested, so I got the article back. I hope "Daughters of Atreus" may soon be seen in New York.

Dick [Madden] tells me he is joining up with a partner & is going to live in Paramount Buildings. I hope this change may be for a great success.

I have opened out on the critics here (at the request of "Time & Tide," who, I think are sorry now they asked me) & maybe they'll go into book form later on under the ensign of "The Flying Wasp."

God be With You.
Yours as Ever
Sean

To Horace Reynolds

MS. REYNOLDS

[49 OVERSTRAND MANSIONS]
[?] JUNE [1936]

My dear Horace.

No, the early essays are of no value whatever. You see I didn't know how to spell words of more than two syl till I was of a marriageable age—I'm not quite sure of some of them even now! And, anyhow, they wouldn't make a book of fifty pages. The first important publication (to me) was called "The Story of the Irish Citizen Army", which was hacked to pieces by the then "Competent Military Authority" in Ireland, who wouldn't even allow a quotation from St Paul to appear in the book. This is now, I believe, rare, & out of print years ago; but I have one or two copies knocking around somewhere, & will send you one, if you like. I quite agree that you shouldn't embalm your essay on my work in Vol 19 of "Harvard studies & notes in Philology & Literature". After all, neither of us want to be buried in a Museum; I'd rather lie in a People's Park myself. I hope you may get the grant you hope for, & that the expense of a trip to Europe may be saved. With a wife & two children, you can hardly, as I know, travel about in a Queen Mary & enjoy life, which isn't life at all, & is simply living in a Museum with the figures strolling about the place. I liked your articles very much, particularly the one on Yeats's book. He, I think, has made a big mistake in so savagely attacking Moore, & turning a blind eye to "Hail & Farewell". But Yeats never really forgives a forcible criticism of himself. He has had too many pedlars of praise around him all his life to be able to stand fairly up to an attack on himself. It is a pitiful weakness in such a great man, for Yeats is one of the giants of our time.

No, there's no chance of me going to Hollywood unless something out of the way happens. I'd love to read about old times on the Mississippi & the Ohio, & it would be grand of you to let me have them to read. I shall send them back to you safely. I think Barry Fitzgerald will play "Fluther" in the Film.

I am, at the moment, writing some articles critical of the London Dramatic Critics, which, I hope, may this year or next, appear as a book called "The Flying Wasp".

All my love to Kay, the two children, & you.

Sean

To Time and Tide

6 June 1936

RED FLAG OR WHITE?

Sir,—Lady Rhondda cannot see that inefficiency on the *Lusitania* has anything to do with the Capitalist system. Surely everything that happens in a Capitalist state, things efficient or inefficient, has to do with Capitalism, just as everything that happens in the Soviet has to do with Communism. I did not question the courage of the officers of the ship (she does not mention the crew), but Lady Rhondda must know that courage of itself cannot create efficiency. A ship is a community, and efficiency on the part of officers and crew must be supplemented by efficiency on the part of the passengers. I was on a liner once and I found that lifebelt and assembly drill was a farce. A lot of ladies and gents simply sniggered at the officer who was trying to instruct them, and wouldn't even try to put the lifebelts over their heads. The efficiency of the accommodation in the cabin class and tourist was grand, but I ventured through a dungeon door to the steerage, and didn't find the same efficiency there. The next time Lady Rhondda is on a liner, let her go through the crew's quarters and see what they are like. There she will find a distinction and a great difference. I'm sure efficiency on a Soviet boat in these parts would be better. And Lady Rhondda must remember that Capitalism has had a long innings, unhampered save by its own competition, whilst Communism in Russia has only just started, handicapped by every obstacle that every Capitalist country can throw in its way. She asks if "human brain-power in emergencies be an entirely different thing under Socialism from what it is under any other kind of rule?" In emergencies or outside of them, human brain-power under Communism (not Socialist, like the present mealy-mouthed Labour Party) is an entirely different thing from what it is under any other kind of rule—there is only one other—Capitalism. We saw this proved during the Great War, but this communizing of brain-power and energy was, unfortunately, the Devil's Communism. We saw the force of communizing brain-power and energy in Ireland when England feared to force conscription on her. I suggest that Lady Rhondda should read *The Russian Revolution,* by Chamberlain (no sympathiser with Bolshevism), published by Macmillan. There she will find that soldiers of rotten cardboard under the Czar became soldiers of steel under Communism; there she will find that out of ruin, famine, bewildering disorder, and pitiful impotence, Communism has created one of the strongest, if not the greatest nation in the world, and all done in a few years against the hatred and opposition of the whole Capitalist world.

Her remark that for the last thirty years Socialism is being tentatively substitituted for Capitalism seems to show that Capitalism improves when we begin to get away from it. So far the grandest scheme that Capitalism has devised is the Dole which Shaw rightly calls a monster, for it is the dirtiest devil that has crawled out of the pit of Capitalism. It is essential that some infants sleep some hours under the sky each day. A deputation was sent to a Cabinet Minister asking him to make it necessary to provide thrust-outs in all flats that were to be built so that babies could be sure that air would give them a chance. Did he say Yes? No. Life can't be allowed to interfere with the holiness of property.

And no matter what Lady Rhondda may say, the mind that thought out the scheme that did away with food queues and thought out the scheme for a Ministry of Health was the mind of a Communist. I don't altogether agree that the heart of man is naturally a hive of disorder. If Lady Rhondda had a full conception of how the workers had to struggle for a bare life, she would realise that there was very little chance given them to have the conveniences necessary to live decently, or time to keep the few things they possess always reposing in their proper places.

I am, etc.,
Sean O'Casey

To Dorothy N. Cheetham [1]

TC. O'CASEY

[49 OVERSTRAND MANSIONS]
20 JUNE 1936

Dear Miss Cheetham—

I wish that Lady Rhondda would again consider the publication of "Murdher In the Theatre," [2] if the only objection to the article is that the play with which it partly deals is ending its London run. It was precisely because I knew that the play was coming off that I included a criticism of this play in the criticism of the critics' idea of what is "realism" in the theatre, which, of course, is the very core of the article. I never knew that when dealing directly or indirectly with the qualities or claims of a play that it was necessary the play dealt with should be in public performance at the moment of writing or publication (As a matter of fact one and the chief reason for not writing the article till the play ended its run was that I didnt wish to interfere with its commercial success.).

I'm sure if Lady Rhondda were so good as to read it again, [she would see what] J.G.B. used or called into the forefront by an obvious reference to "Night Must Fall" as an example or model of what a realistic play should be like; and my article tries to show that the realism in the play selected is purely made up of inventions much more obvious than the inventions found in Strindberg's most imaginative work.

The article is an attempt to show that "realism", or "matter-of-factness" so much honored by present-day critics is outworn and limp and soiled as a medium in drama, and that it is time, if we really think anything about the theatre, and wish it to live in any worthy way, some other and more original medium must be introduced into the drama of the future. So, perhaps, Lady Rhondda would like to give the matter reconsideration.

Sincerely Yours,
Sean O'Casey

[1] Dorothy N. Cheetham, assistant secretary, *Time and Tide.*

[2] Sean O'Casey, "Murdher in the Theatre," *Time and Tide,* 10 October 1936; reprinted in *The Flying Wasp* (1937). It is an article on Emlyn Williams's *Night Must Fall,* which opened in London on 31 May 1935.

To Time and Tide

TC. O'CASEY
12 JULY 1936

Dear Editor—

I enclose article called Hail Columbia [1] for consideration.

If it isnt suitable, perhaps you will be kind enough to return it, and shove in Murdher In the Theatre alongside, which I forgot to take away with me when I was at the Office of Time And Tide.

With all good wishes,
Yours Sincerely,
Sean O'Casey

[1] Sean O'Casey, "Hail Columbia," *Time and Tide,* 1 August 1936; reprinted in *The Flying Wasp* (1937).

To Gabriel Fallon

MS. TEXAS
FORTY-NINE OVERSTRAND MANSIONS
6 AUGUST 1936

My dear Gaby. The "But I mustn't go on any more like this" was simply an indication that the old mind had failed to think of anything more to say, just as some writers who have nothing to say, but want to convey the idea that they still have a lot to say, write down, etc, & so on & so forth. It had no connection with the desire to be left alone—so rest you merry gentleman. What's coming over you, at all, at all? And besides, you must remember that my eyes give out quickly now. To type for half-an-hour is as much as I can do, or read for the same length of time, and then must come a rest of a few hours, with the eyes closed; the lids heavy, like unto the lid of Balor's one eye that took—was it ten men, to lift up with hooks. Doing one's work well is the only religion, if you ask me, & a pretty stiff religion I find it, too. I do believe in psychology, but not in a lot of psychologists. I know one well here who is clever, so clever that he has a lovely little daughter of his in a state of compos dementis by always watching her. I am to go to see him & have a long talk with him soon, because I told him that whenever I was in Piccadilly I had to get out of the place quick, because I felt always an almost irresistable desire to climb to the top of the Eros statue & sing bawdy songs to the English people. You are, I think, right about "The Star-Jazzer" [1]—it is easily the best thing in the book.

[1] "The Star-Jazzer," one of O'Casey's short stories in *Windfalls* (1934).

Now about the play: It is very hard to judge a first play, unless it be an exceptionally fine one. "Alarm Among the Clerks" [2] is good for a beginner, &, I think, deserves production by the Abbey. As you say, the presence of Selsker in the office in the last act is a bad flaw, & can only be overcome, as you say, by the action taking place in the pub as a kind of fantasy. The dialogue is too much concerned with gossip, & rarely rises high enough. The routine & monotonous life of the staff is not shown clearly enough—as in [Elmer Rice's] "The Adding Machine", for instance. The love affair between Plus & Miss Noone is poorly done. I'm afraid there would be no hope of a London production. The Embassy which does plays by unknown authors, might do it, but I doubt it. It isn't good enough as a plain, commercial play, or good enough as an art form of Drama. The author's one hope is the Abbey. Even if they decline, won't he go on? The life in the Bank should be much harder. The characters are in no way lost among the symbols of pounds, shillings, & pence. I hope the Abbey will do the play—they have very often done far worse.

My Love to Rose & the Children, & to you, oul son.

Sean

Alarm Among the Clerks—there's not enough alarm among them. It should be sterner & more vicious.

[2] Mervyn Wall's *Alarm Among the Clerks* was performed at the Abbey Theatre's experimental Peacock Theatre on 5 April 1937.

To Horace Reynolds

MS. Reynolds

[Wales]
[? August 1936]

My dear Horace—I am spending a few weeks with the wife & two children in a village in Wales, beside the sea, backed by the mountains. My time is taken up with keeping an eye on all they do, or try to do. I have looked around for a copy of "Story of the Irish Citizen Army," but, so far, haven't laid hands on one. There should be one knocking about somewhere. I'll have a good look when I go back to London.

I don't know what the usual fees are that are given to Time & Tide, but, as you say, Two Guineas seem a poor fee indeed. I can tell you what I get for articles accepted from me: At the beginning (of course, they asked me to do these) I wrote articles about the Theatre (they don't seem to be so well pleased now as at first), & the fee was to be 6 guineas an article, each to be about 1500 words. For the first two articles I got the fee named by Time & Tide. Then for the third, they rang me up and said as the article wasn't quite so long, would a fee of 5 guineas be enough. I agreed. Since then 5 guineas is the highest fee received by me. For shorter articles Say 900 to 1000 words, I get a fee of 4 guineas. That's how it stands with me now. I'm afraid the paper isn't as prosperous as it used to be. I don't know why, but experience prompts me to think so. I was offered 15 guineas for the short story—"The Star-Jazzer"—but the printers refused to set it up for them, & it came back.[1] They sent me the cheque, but I returned it. At the beginning, I wrote four articles for them in the "Notes On The Way" series, & got 8 guineas an article. From 6 to 8 guineas, I believe, used to be the usual fee, but things aren't quite so rosy now, apparently. I really know nothing definitely. But the final thought is that, in my opinion, 2 guineas fee is too small. I should hold out for a minimum of 3.

About the suggested article for Scribner's: It wouldn't be possible. I know nothing of the way in which RKO is doing "The Plough". They are, I believe, making changes, but what they may be, I know not. Besides, I've been inside a Film Studio once only, & know nothing about the technique of the Film, except a deep conviction that the Film as an art or an Institution is very poor at present. I have my ideas of what a Film should be, as I have my idea of what the Drama should be, too; but there is no way yet in which to break through, & get them—the Film people—to realise that if they go on as they are going, nothing—not even the Censor—can save them. I should very much like to do something for Schribner's; but the article suggested is out of the question. Perhaps, something else may come into my mind. I expect to have enough articles consisting of home-thrusts on the state of the Theatre & the critics here—in Merry England—in a month or so, that may make a book to be called "The Flying Wasp". It will bring me a little money (I hope) and a lot of trouble.

I am thoroughly enjoying "Sycamore Shores".

Love to you & Mrs. Reynolds & your two children.

Yours As Ever
Sean

You've written a fine article on B. Fitzgerald. He deserves it. I've been shouting his praises for years, but no-one would listen. If he gets off now, I'll be glad, though no-one will be left to play the parts in my plays. I do hope Hollywood won't kill his exquisite artistry in humor.

Sean

[1] The short story was "I Wanna Woman," not "The Star-Jazzer," which was also in *Windfalls* (1934). See Lady Rhondda's article on the incident in *Time and Tide,* 13 May 1933, reprinted below, and also the May–June 1933 letters.

To Harold Macmillan

TS MACMILLAN

49 OVERSTRAND MANSIONS
25 SEPTEMBER 1936

Dear Mr Macmillan—

Thanks for your letter about the proposed publication of "The Flying Wasp." I wouldnt ask, nor do I expect indeed, I shouldn't care to allow you to publish anything of mine about which you had the slightest uncertainty. So, the question of publication by your Firm set aside, I can freely say a word in reply to what you have said about the articles.

Most of the articles will be fresh enough, too damn fresh for a lot of people, when they are offered in book-form. Everything I have written, up to the present, has been "combative," and the sword I have swung so long is now stuck to my hand, and I cant let go. These things that are said by me, need to be said, and must be said, for England has no critic like George Jean Nathan of America, whose works are rarely read, and never mentioned here. I shouldn't think of giving anything I said about the theatre such a title as "Towards a Living Theatre," for such a title would be too academic and professorial for me to use. Besides "The Flying Wasp," is more lyrical, and much more to the point. Why should I leave out an article in reply to a criticism of my own work? My works are, at least, additions to the drama, and defending them, I defend the drama. Am I to leave it out because "it is not done," or because it is not "good form"? I hope I know something about good manners, but on a question of principle, good form can go to the devil. Invariably, I have done the things that are not done, and left undone the things that are done, and I amnt much the worse for it. The theatre is more than good manners. As for "brawling in church," well, Jesus Christ did it before me, and I occasionally follow in His steps. I believe these articles will give to young men coming into the theatre courage to say what they think,

> Let us our native character maintain;
> 'Tis of our growth, to be sincerely plain.

It is so easy to be nice. I know these sayings will not make it easier for me, and I love ease; but not enough to change what I believe to be the truth into politeness and nicety of speech and manner. All this is said in the friendliest manner, and in fair and full appreciation of your effort to prevent me from making a fool of myself. But the fact is that there is here in England no criticism of things theatrical, and all truth is lost in cowardice, good feeling, and polite deportment. I hope, and believe, that my articles will have some effect in bringing about a change.

Both of us should be pleased to see you again, but we shant be free till the beginning of October—maid going away for a holiday. Perhaps you could come to see us on the 6th, 7th, or 8th of October.

I hope you, Lady Dorothy, and your little ones are all well.

With All Good Wishes.
Sincerely Yours,
Sean O'Casey

Could you let me have typescript as soon as it may be convenient to you?

To Harold Macmillan

TC. O'Casey

[49 Overstrand Mansions]
27 October 1936

Dear Mr Harold Macmillan—

I delayed returning the contract you kindly sent to me because I was thinking of an alternative title to "The Flying Wasp;" but after much thought, I have decided that the first title chosen ought to stand.

So with this letter, I return the contract signed, together (under another cover) with the articles that are to form the book. Should the number be too many, so as to exceed the 50,000 words agreed upon, or exceed that number to such an extent as to prevent the publication of the book at 5/–, let me know, and I shall take an article out. However, I estimate that the number of words in the total number of articles will be about what we said would be convenient.

With all good wishes.
Sincerely Yours,
Sean O'Casey

To George Jean Nathan

TS. CORNELL
49 OVERSTRAND MANSIONS
28 OCTOBER 1936

My dear George—

Greeting first and foremost to you, and I wish the greeting could be given under the sky of Manhattan, or even the sky of Le Coque Rouge would do splendidly. I have read your book "The Theatre of the Moment,"[1] and it is fine reading. The old head is still abuzz with thought. You deal it out to playwrights, producers, actors, and you dont forget the critics. There is certainly no-one writing about the theatre to come within many many miles of Nathan. But you are hard on "The Little Red Writing Hoods." All the same, I think you are perfectly just, though I'd like to be able conscientiously to say that you werent. However, in getting money from Hollywood, there may be something in it of spoiling the Egyptians—though one may spoil one's art at the same time. As yet, there is nothing outstanding—bar O'Neill and M[axwell]. Anderson, of course, for they are proletarians—in the way of proletarian writing on the stage, as far as I know, or off it. But it will come—we are still too busy with the gun. I have read last week Odets' "Awake and Sing,"[2] and, honestly, cant see a line of music in it from start to finish. To me the great proletarian dramatist of America is the bould O'Neill. And the great proletarian critic is—G.J.N. For, my dear George you are a red. You may say you dont give a damn about this or that, but you are a red revolutionary in the theatre, and you always have been one—at least since I began to know you, and that's twelve years ago. You want the best that can be given to the art of the theatre, and that is the creed of the communist. It's not for nothing that your profile on the cover of your last book stands out against a background of Red.

I expect my little book—an onslaught on the critics here; not in the manner of Elmer Rice, but an effort to confound them out of the words of their own mouths—called "The Flying Wasp," will appear in January next. I will send you the first copy printed. Between ourselves, Macmillans jibbed a little at it, and gave me some fatherly advice to keep it back, saying that it would make many enemies. They said something about "brawling in church," and fell silent when I told them that the first to create a brawl in church was Jesus Christ. And then the murmur that defending oneself isnt done, it isnt quite the thing. But I do the things that shouldnt be done, for to me there is no such thing as gentlemanly behaviour in the art of the theatre (you have said it yourself), and a nice gentleman in criticism

[1] George Jean Nathan, *The Theatre of the Moment* (New York, Knopf, 1936).
[2] Clifford Odets's *Awake and Sing!* opened in New York on 19 February 1935.

cant be a critic. I dont, of course, pretend to be a critic, but here it is the easiest thing in the world to be a great dramatic critic, for truth to tell, there isnt one at the moment in the English theatre. They have made themselves great by silently enacting a law declaring that no criticism must be answered. Unless it deliberately misrepresents, or the critic confutes himself, there must be no appeal, even against the most ignorant and stupid of criticisms. Nice law, isnt it? The funniest thing is that most of them frequently confute themselves, and this fact is, I believe, made manifest in my book. Anyhow, in my opinion, no real critic cares a damn about contradiction, for this only gives him the opportunity of proving himself to be a critic. Poor old Agate is weeping over some articles already published. I shouldnt have bothered only I thought something ought to be done to prepare a way for some young Nathan that may be growing up here in the theatre of today, to show him that true criticism is greater than a mere job.

And, now, give my love to Lillian; I hope she has done well as Ophelia—though I wish she had played Electra in "Daughters of Atreus" —to which may God give a fine performance and a great success. Remember me, too, to Mimsie, and give her my love. And to Brooks Atkinson. And to all who love you. Not forgetting the great O'Neill.

And first love to you.
Sean

To Gabriel Fallon

MS. Texas

Forty-Nine Overstrand Mansions
29 October 1936

My dear Gaby—

Many thanks for the Irish Press. It is grand to read that the Slums are under a heavy bombardment at last [1]—after my sniping. How well I remember fighting at meetings of the Labour Movement over a report issued by Sir C. Cameron [2] ten, twenty years ago, in the thrilling days under the flag of Jim Larkin's Union! The Slums are one of the finer legacies left by the Grand 'oul Dame Britannia to the young & supple Irish State. Well, the old Dame has a lot of her own problems now. One of my (principal one) re-creations here is to spend some morning

[1] At the beginning of October the *Irish Press* had launched a month-long "crusade" to abolish the slums in Dublin and all the main cities of Ireland.

[2] Sir Charles Cameron, *Report on the state of public health and the sanitary work performed in Dublin during the year 1909* (Dublin, Hodges, Figgis, 1909).

hours watching the teams of Elementary Schools play football in Battersea Park. Here the effects of poverty are plain. Haggard faces tense & anxious as the ball goes from one place to another. But they are great kids. No deliberate foul play; no deception; no professionalism; all eager that their own School should win. And the ragged clothes, the pinched faces, old football boots, but brightly coloured jerseys, nursed into a long life by the School authorities. And many of the kids (and Schoolmasters) are Irish. They play on what is called "the cinder field"; there is no grass field here for footballers. I have rows already over keepers stopping kids from kicking a ball on a grass patch. "They ought to keep the bloody park under a glass-case"—remark by a Schoolmaster (MacCarthy) to me. And this Labour Council (London C.C.) preserves in this working-class district the best piece of grass-land in the park (brushed & combed three times a day) for the tottering, tender-footed old fogies that play bowls! God, it makes me blood boil! They won't let a bird light on the plot. In the way of sport, youth must be served first. Well, well, there I go again. I should have written sooner, but I am re-reading & editing articles for a book, "The Flying Wasp", to be published in January. I'll send you a hot copy.

I'm glad you're writing again. I'm just as sure as ever I was that there is something in you besides the Civil Service Sanctity.

I'm sorry Father Senan [3] didn't ring me up. I've already had a Discalced Carmelite with me in Chalfont, & he & I were great friends. And a brother Gerard (Paddy Nolan, once baker in Bolands) came to lunch one wet day, (& had to sit in a shirt & old jersey of mine while his clothes were dried for him) & when leaving, the two old Dublin boys, Carmelite & Communist, embraced & kissed each other. Father Seanan would have been most welcome, & I should have been delighted to share a meal with him. A friend of St Francis, too, to be shy of a man who, if he had no share in the Saint's virtue, at least shared his poverty. And, if you ask me, St Francis was more of a Communist than he was a Bourgeois or a Conservative or a Fascist—and a gentleman, for all that. It is the timid prelates that are always in fear trying to close the Gates of the Church; it is the Saints who are always flinging Them open.

But there I go again, my dear Gaby, blathering dogmatically as usual, who should be the least dogmatic of men; but it is in the desire that all men should be one in sympathy as we go blundering on through this life.

So give my love to Father Seanan, & to all his Brethren. Thanks again for the copies of "The Irish Press", and I hope Dev is well, & God be with Ireland, & F. McM[anus].

My Love to Rose, the children, & to you.

Yours as Ever
Sean

[3] Father Senan, O.M. Cap., editor of the *Capuchin Annual*.

To Harold Macmillan

MS. Macmillan London

49 Overstrand Mansions
13 November 1936

Dear Mr Harold Macmillan,

I don't think that I shall be likely to make additions or deletions in what I have written, so let us save the expense of issuing galley proofs. I am praying to God that the Spanish Communists may win. I wish I could be with them. However, if I haven't manned a tank, or fired a rifle for the cause of Communism, I have, at least, in my day, fired stones at the police.

Yours as ever,
Sean O'Casey

To Gabriel Fallon

MS. Texas

49 Overstrand Mansions
[?] December 1936

My dear Gaby:

It is good and grand to read that Rose is now better than ever she was. It would be a serious thing for you and the children if Rose was separated by ill health from her skill and energy and goodwill and never-ending thought for her home. That, my dear Gaby, would indeed be a grievous burden to bear. It's a shame that a man like you isn't in a position to make things easier for her & for yourself. It is a stupid thing in life that money should command in things of this kind. But if Rose be well, then most things will be well with her—though take all care, oul' son, to save your own energy as much as possible. There's a lot leaning on you, too. I have a lot to thank you for—the papers, "A Candle to the Proud",[1] your letters, and "The Capuchin Annual".[2] I don't know what

[1] Francis MacManus, *A Candle For the Proud* (Dublin, Talbot Press, 1936), a novel.

[2] *Capuchin Annual–1937* (Dublin, November, 1936), ed. Father Senan, O.M. Cap.

to say about Frank's book. There's nothing I hate in the world more than to give a written opinion of a book or a play—unless both or one of them be bloody bad; then it is easy to get going. I am prepared to give an infallible—an infallible judgment, mind you, me bucko,—on a worthless play or a worthless book. But how am I to give an opinion on what is far from bad or middling—in my opinion? It isn't great, but there's something in it that I'm not fit to discover or explain. That part of the story dealing with the killing of Colthurst is as bad a bit of work as ever appeared in a Catholic Periodical, & that is bad enough, God knows. Frank will have to renounce the world, the flesh, & the devil in literature as in life. And the money taken from the Major should never have been restored—and hidden under the floor after a lot of labour. Money taken in such circumstances, from such persons, if the act doesn't glorify God, vindicates man. Then think of Seumas O'Braonain—was there ever such a prig born from the mind of man! He is too good to be true. But the priest's devotion to the old poet is good, very good, I think, & this touched me deeply. The fight for the common is well done, too. There is something in MacManus, & he will be much better when he escapes from what I'd call the cod canonicity of the Talbot Press. But there is certainly something in Seumas MacManus. If anything I have said would hurt him, say in all & though all in dear affection, & that I have read better, far better books than "A Candle to the Proud", destitute of the curious quality that is in the work of Seumas.

I am very sorry to hear that he has been ill, and glad that Joe Cummins found out what was wrong with him. I imagine that this supra-orbital neuralgia is the same thing that periodically lays George Jean Nathan low—he calls it "neuralgia of the eyeball". It is the one terror of Nathan's life, &, when it comes, it just knocks him bawways for a week or so. He tells me that it is very painful while it lasts—isn't everything very painful "while it lasts"?—&, I think it is a very rare defect in the body of man. However, it's more painful than serious, & that same's some comfort. Strangely enough, Nathan has beautiful eyes & very keen sight. Where does all this pain come from? Hunted or haunted by pain from the cradle to the grave; millions of doctors busy night & day, beating it back, while they themselves are hunted & haunted by it, too. Anyway, one thing is certain: there's no mystery about the most of it: it comes crawling or lepping out of the stupidity of man. Here I am gettin' goin' again!

I have read every bit of "The Capuchin Annual", including the advertisements. The Magazine was full of astonishment to me. I was disappointed that a Catholic (or Christian) Magazine could be so good. It can be read by all intelligent men; possibly only by intelligent men (and women, too, of course). It can be read with respect (and that's a lot), if it can't be read with belief. I sincerely congratulate (if I may, & if it be not damned presumptuous so to do) the Capuchin Fathers on their Magazine Annual for 1937.

By the way, Francis McManus (alias Frank) is wrong when he says that the reasoned counsel of Pope Leo XIII was in neglect during the big Lock-out of 1913.[3] This counsel was quoted far more frequently than the letter written by AE.[4] Larkin (Jim) often and often sent it flying over the heads & into the ears of the men to whom he spoke. It was quoted in The Irish Worker; and it was quoted by me—to be honest, rather as a weapon than in any reverent faith as a Catholic outlook on social life. He (Frank) is right in saying that it was scorned or ignored (which is worse), but not by the workers.

I was disappointed in the work of Sean O'Sullivan.[5] Yeats had spoken to me about him, & seemed to think highly, very highly of him. Although one cannot say surely from reproduction, there is, it seems to me, no sign or coming sign of greatness. Go to The National Gallery, look at St Francis in Ecstasy, & see what great painting is; or to the Dublin Gallery, & see the John's—we have been there, already—and then look at poor AE's! The R.H.A, The R.H.A, Gaby! God will choose very few of his saints in painting out of the R.H.A.

I haven't heard from Will [Barry Fitzgerald] since he went to Hollywood; but R.K.O. wrote to say he was "superb". What he is doing or has done since, I don't know. They may have signed him up. But nothing comes from Hollywood, regarding Will, save silence.

I'm afraid that some of the Abbey Players have become a little stiff and uninteresting. There should be a flow of new blood into the acting-side of the theatre; but how they are going to solve the problem is a poser. No Repertory Theatre here give[s] an esto perpetua contract to its actors. But then they can go elsewhere. Where can the Abbey Actors go when they say farewell to the Abbey? The Torch? [6]

My dear Gaby, when you say that the pen is a heavy thing to lift, who are you tellin'? Look at me: years an years ago since I wrote "Within The Gates"; and what have I done since? A few oul' scrawls of would-be criticism that aren't worth a tinker's damn. And Cummins says I'm something like a genius, & F. Mc. says I may be something more! Well, God knows better than the pair of them, an so do I. Anyway, your little gift to The Capuchin Annual wasn't a bad one. [7] You gave quite a few of us a dig now and again, me boy, with your "I will arise & go now". And that

[3] Francis MacManus, "One Man's Years," *Capuchin Annual–1937*, an article on Matt Talbot (1856–1925), "the holy workingman of Dublin." See O'Casey's comments on Talbot in the opening pages of "The Temple Entered," *Inishfallen, Fare Thee Well* (1949).

[4] George Russell (A.E.), "To the Masters of Dublin," *Irish Times*, 6 October 1913; reprinted in *Letters From AE*, ed. Alan Denson (London, Abelard-Schuman, 1961).

[5] A series of "Drawings and Paintings" by Sean O'Sullivan, R.H.A., appeared in the *Capuchin Annual–1937*.

[6] The Torch, a Dublin theatre that specialized in melodramas.

[7] Gabriel Fallon, "Abbey Interlude: Being Passages from a Pastiche in Progress," *Capuchin Annual–1937*.

"Oh-ho" of yours! It was intensely interesting & cunningly done, & I don't think it was the personal connection that made it interesting to me; it was much more than that.

I know all about the children and bread & clothes & boots & school besides. I am up against all those things, too. We can only do our best—a big painful best, to be sure,—and then leave the rest to . . . . ?

I haven't seen Oliver [St. John Gogarty] now for years, six or more years since I laid eyes on him. I don't think his book has been published yet—indeed, has it even been written. Many months ago I was told he had received £2,000 advance royalty on the book, but publishers don't do these wild things nowadays. Anyhow, I've heard nothing of the book. Won't it be a lonely Dublin for Gogarty when W.B. [Yeats] goes! Gogarty has been in London several times, but comes not to me—why I don't know.

I have been harrassed for the last six weeks by the old stomach & nerves, & have but faintly continued to get up & lie down, and work has been a dream. We can but stay as quiet & as patient as possible, sharing with all other men the greatness & littleness of life.

Well I'll end this by adding love to all in Ireland, especially to those who have incensed my life with friendship—Frank, Father Senan (if I may) his comrade Brother, Rose & her little ones, & you,

my old Dublin buttie of long ago & of today.

Eileen & all are well, & she sends her love.

Yours as of old
Sean

To Horace Reynolds

MS. Reynolds

49 Overstrand Mansions
5 January 1937

Dear Horace.

I have just come across a copy of "The Story of the Irish Citizen Army", & am sending it on to you here with this letter. The bowels were cut out of the effort by the then "Military Competent Authority in Ireland", but even with bowels an' all, the thing isn't much—only an interesting item of days long since gone by. I enclose, too, an invoice from Time & Tide, showing that what I said before was true—that my payments have been £6.6.0, £5.5.0, £4.4.0, & £3.3.0 for articles, showing, I'm afraid, that the Weekly isn't so prosperous as it used to be. I have ceased to contribute articles on the Theatre, through no fault of my own. It was clear that they didn't like them, & went a very round-a-bout way to show it. However, it's no new thing for me to find that what I may have to say is very much disliked by many people; but I'm too damn old to change now—and, anyhow, I believe that Im right. The truth is that one mustn't speak above a very respectable whisper in this country.

Soon my little book of criticism of the English critics will come out, the articles that appeared in Time & Tide, and quite a number that didn't! When it appears I shall send you on a copy.

I am glad Rooseveldt won. We shall have to wait a day or two longer for Communism to come into its own. Japan will possibly be the next country to go Red. However, I suppose, that doesn't interest you greatly —as for me, once a Communist, always a Communist. Everything here is the same as it was—England, in the affairs of Spain, trying to be all things to all men—and succeeding everywhere, apparently, save in Ireland. It looks as if Ireland would be split in two very viciously indeed, over the Spanish War. We have a "Christian Front" here (in Ireland) which worships France, & lives to exterminate Communism; & this Front is being used politically to bring about the Decline & Fall of Fianna Fail, led by DeValera.

I hope Mrs. Reynolds & her little ones (they must be pretty big be now) are well. Give them my love.

All the Best.
Sean

To George Jean Nathan

MS. CORNELL

49 OVERSTRAND MANSIONS
23 JANUARY 1937

My dear George—

This is a good time insofar as the year ended & the year began with the giving of the Nobel Prize to our Gene [O'Neill]. I sent him a letter to join in the cheers. It is good, as you say in "The Saturday Review," that the prize goes to a Dramatist. After all, the best Drama is as good as the best novels, & bad drama is no worse than any other bad form in literature. Any way, the award is a well-deserved slap in the snot to the London Dramatic Critics who have never given O'Neill a branch of palm. There hasn't been a mention of it here—not by any of the critics, anyway. Isn't it strange & isn't it terrible! Coward is the Kingly one here. I have tried to scrape off some of the gilt from the crown in "The Flying Wasp." But it's astonishing the grip he has here. After the first article I wrote in "Time & Tide" on Cavalcade, there was a coolness in the air; no other article on him would be admitted; & the coolness grew till I was quietly shut out of the warmth of its pages altogether. And, although the proofs have been finished weeks ago the book hasn't come out yet, which, with other things, makes me suspicious that the publishers aren't very keen about it either.

I'm so glad that Lillian has had a good run in Hamlet.[1] I hope she is pleased about it.

I have been laid up & laid down with influenza, & I am not rightly over it yet. I hope you escaped. All of us, except Eileen, got it, & she had a bitter time nursing us back to the consciousness of life.

As far as I know, [St. John] Ervine was the only critic (& he's one no longer—officially) that mentioned your "The Theatre of the Moment," & I send it on—it may interest you.

Mr. Howe of Cincinnati [2] has sent me another case of "Foster Pinks," & they were the most delicious Grape-fruit I ever tasted. Hail, Columbia! I have read in "The Stage" that Miss Hellman's second play [3] isn't anything like "Children's Hour." What a pity.

My love to New York, to all my friends there, to Lillian, Mimsie, & deepest of all to you.

Sean

[1] Lillian Gish played Ophelia in John Gielgud's *Hamlet,* which opened in New York on 8 October 1936 and ran for 132 performances.

[2] W. T. H. Howe, president of the American Book Company, Cincinnati, Ohio, whom O'Casey met in America in 1934 through James Stephens.

[3] Lillian Hellman's *Days to Come* opened in New York on 15 December 1936 and closed after 7 performances.

To Harold Macmillan

TS. MACMILLAN LONDON

49 OVERSTRAND MANSIONS
29 JANUARY 1937

Dear Mr Harold Macmillan,

I think your idea of a 2/6 edition of the "The Plough and the Stars" to be offered along with the showing of the Film, a very good one. I have already telephoned this view to your Secretary. I like the blue cover on Juno, and think it much prettier than the original reddish-brown one. I haven't arranged anything about the Film; all that is in the hands of Radio Pictures, Wardour Street, and they will probably be glad to tell you all particulars. I have told this, too, to your Secretary. I think I like the YELLOW cover suggested for "The Flying Wasp" better than the BLACK one. It is, I think, brighter, and suggests the idea quite as well. If the book meant the death of the critics (which God fulfil), then the Black cover would be the more suitable. But God for His own good reasons, will go on trying us in this vale of tears, and He will let the critics live on longer, perhaps to give them a further chance to make their souls.

I am sorry to hear that you have had the damned influenza. I am just recovering from it myself. We have all, except Eileen, had it, and she has had a bitter time nursing us back to normality. I hope you are not trying to do things before it is wise to do them. You are young and hardy, but the young and hardy at times dont get everything their own way; so take care of yourself.

With all good wishes,

Yours Sincerely,
Sean O'Casey

2 Covers Enclosed

To Horace Reynolds

MS. REYNOLDS
49 OVERSTRAND MANSIONS
15 FEBRUARY 1937

Dear Horace.

Thanks for your letter & cuttings & for the strange & interesting book about Lead Belly. I agree with almost every phrase of your article on the Film.[1] I've seen the Film, and I know. However, I hope it may be a big success.

I haven't sent it on to Time & Tide. I'm certain it wouldn't be taken. As far as copyright goes here, it is best, if it can be done, to have an

[1] The film version of *The Plough and the Stars,* directed by John Ford, produced by RKO, had been shown in previews and was released in March 1937, with the following cast: Preston Foster as Jack Clitheroe, Barbara Stanwyck as Nora Clitheroe, J. M. Kerrigan as Peter Flynn, Denis O'Dea as The Covey, Eileen Crowe as Bessie Burgess, Una O'Connor as Mrs. Gogan, Bonita Granville as Mollser, Barry Fitzgerald as Fluther Good, Neil Fitzgerald as Lieutenant Langon, F. J. McCormick as Captain Brennan, Cyril McLaglen as Corporal Stoddart, Brandon Hurst as Sergeant Tinley, Erin O'Brien-Moore as Rosie Redmond, Robert Homans as A Bartender, Arthur Shields as The Figure in the Window.

article published in America & England. It all depends on the agreement made with the Magazine, or, if no agreement has been made, the author's usual custom, or that of the Magazine—all very complicated. I don't suppose The Stage would mind its publication here, but where is it to get in? I don't know enough about these things to tell you. I'm sorry about the delay in publishing or payment of your story. Time & Tide is curious these days; but I imagine you'll get there allright sooner or later. I haven't been in touch with them for months. I do hope you may get the Guggenheim Grant; but do you really think it worthwhile to spend a year delving in old unhappy far off things in Ireland? I don't think I wrote much for Irish Freedom—a tottering line or two—they wouldn't have me. Yes, I was all for a Union of Labour & the Republican Movement—not "Nationalism", if I remember rightly, & a Committee of the I.R.B. was formed to hasten & encourage it, mareadh! [2] But the tin hat was soon put on that! It was I first put the I.R.B. marching to Bodenstown on the Cinema, & introduced the ceremonial of saluting the Republican Flag. Fancy that! I wrote two "poems" about Thomas Ashe (he was a friend of mine, & sympathetic with Labour), but can't remember anything about Anna Long. There is nothing denationalizing in Socialism—[Arthur] Griffith was a mug, aping Parnell & Kossuth & Grattan, & had no conception of Communism or Culture. He soon snapped in two when the tug came. I am more *national* than ever. Griffith knew ten words of Irish; I could speak in it for an hour. He was an English-speaking Irish Liberal—& not very liberal either. Auxurs., I.C.A., I.R.A., I.R.B., Staters, Republicans, Sinn Feiners, Irregulars, Black an Tans, don't forget the A.O.H. the Molly Maguires, & A.O.H. American Alliance—all republicans. Molly Maguires, of course, followers of "wee" Josie Devlin, one of the Party M.P.s. All "Catholics" eagerly looking after No. 1.

I see by an American clipping that Lady Rhondda is in the U.S.A. trying to evoke interest in Time & Tide, so, perhaps, things are not too well with the paper. I may try them again with "Dreamschool",[3] a part of my peculiar biography—"His Father's Dublin Funeral" [4] was another. But I'd like to see your story published first. However, you try to get most—all, if you can—of your stuff printed in America—they pay much better. I wish I was there—I'd show England the back o' me hand. Here there's just a nest of cliques which unite together to down anyone who dares to say boo to them.

I've sent "The Flying Wasp" on to you, some days ago.

My love to Kay & your two little ones.

All the Best.
Sean

[2] Literally: by the way, idiomatically: not likely!

[3] Sean O'Casey, "The Dream School," *Yale Review,* June 1937; reprinted in *I Knock at the Door* (1939).

[4] "His Father's Funeral," printed in *I Knock at the Door.*

To Peter Newmark

MS. NEWMARK

49 OVERSTRAND MANSIONS
FRIDAY 19 FEBRUARY 1937

My dear Peter:—

Thanks, we are all well, though we have had influenza. And a store of thanks for asking me to come to Cambridge. But I have too much to think about to come to Cambridge. Shirley Society was kind enough to ask me to spend a weekend with them, but I had to refuse. I'm not going to be the one to dare to come even before the daffodils. When the swallows have settled down, ask me again. My book "The Flying Wasp" is to be published on March the 5th. I hope you'll review it in "The Gownsman" [1]—and send me a copy. What a terrible name—"The Martyrs of Tolpuddle". [2] Have the English no sense of humour? Tolpuddle! Good God! Tolpuddle—Jesus ha mercy on us! And the fight going on in Spain, too! I am doing a little with my "Autobiography". Have just finished a chapter on "Sunday-school & Church", ending—not beginning—with the text, "and God said let there be light & there was light".[3]

Cambridge is doing well—apart from Tolpuddle, though God be with Sybil—in Drama. Tourneur's Tragedy should be a great event. I hope that it may be well done. Read the bastard Archer's book,[4] & then you'll realise how the great live & the mean die. "He who saves his life shall lose it".

Here, I'm blathering again!

With many thanks & affectionate Regards.

Sean O'Casey

[1] A student magazine at Cambridge University.

[2] Miles Malleson's *Six Men of Dorset,* a play about the Tolpuddle Martyrs, was performed at the Arts Theatre, Cambridge, starring Sybil Thorndike and Lewis Casson. It was reviewed by Peter Newmark, "To Change the World," *The Gownsman,* 6 March 1937, Cambridge. For the memorial to the Tolpuddle Marytrs, see O'Casey's letter to Harold Macmillan, 28 June 1934, note 2.

[3] See "A Child of God," *I Knock at the Door* (1939).

[4] William Archer, *The Old Drama and the New* (London, Hinemann, 1923).

To Irish Times

23 FEBRUARY 1937

"THE END OF THE BEGINNING" [1]

Sir,—Would you be kind enough to give me room to say a word about the criticism given to "The End of the Beginning" by a learned dramatic critic in Dublin? [2] The play is one of O'Casey's later, and not "one of his earlier efforts." It has not "gone the rounds for quite a long time," for O'Casey has never asked any manager of a theatre or music-hall to produce it. The "shoddy material of the play" is derived from an old and honoured folk-tale. Long years ago I bought "News From No-where," by William Morris, the classic craftsman and poet, and there in the preface to this early edition was a reference to this honourable tale, man and cow at either end of the rope, and all. Some time after I bought a well-worn book of Norse folk tales in a second-hand bookshop kept by a Michael Hickey, of Bachelor's Walk, and there in the middle of it was the old story mentioned by William Morris—man and cow at either end of the rope, and all. Faber and Faber, of London, publish the story under the name of "Gone is Gone" as a folk-tale from Bohemia.

But strangest of all, the learned dramatic critic mentioned before (and this in the ear, too, of the Dublin dramatic critic of *The Times* [3]) will find the story written in Irish—and fine and vigorous Irish, too, if I am any kind of a judge—in *An Baile Seo 'Gainne-ne*, by "*An Seabhac*," [4] cow and man at either end of the rope, and all! Each of the stories differs a little in details, but the "clowning," broad and genuine, is all there, and the Irish story is blessed by no less than Seosamh Laoide, member of the Royal Irish Academy. It seems to be quite evident that these Irish dramatic critics are ignorant of the activities of their own country.

I suggest to *An Comhar Dramuidheachta* [5] that the story by *An Seabhac* would make a fine funny one-act play for them, and if the tech-

[1] O'Casey's one-act comedy, *The End of the Beginning*, first published in *Windfalls* (1934), was first produced at the Abbey Theatre on 8 February, directed by Arthur Shields, with the following cast: P. J. Carolan as Darry Berrill, Maureen Delany as Lizzie Berrill, F. J. McCormick as Barry Derrill.

[2] Reference to an unsigned review of *The End of the Beginning* in the Dublin *Evening Herald*, 9 February 1937. The quoted passages in the next two sentences are taken from this review, which attacked O'Casey and his play.

[3] See *The Times*, London, 12 February 1937, a review of *The End of the Beginning* by the Dublin Correspondent.

[4] *An Baile Seo 'Gainne-ne* (Dublin, Talbot Press, 1913), a book of short stories ("This Town of Ours") by "An Seabhac," the pen-name of Pádraig Ó Siochfhradha (O'Sugrue).

[5] An Comhar Dramuidheachta, the Drama Co-Operative, a group which received an annual subsidy from the Irish government to aid in the production of plays in Irish, and which after 1942 operated in conjunction with the Abbey Theatre.

nique or anything else in "The End of the Beginning" be of any use to them, they are welcome to use it.

We all act the clown at times, but the saddest clowning that I have ever known is the clowning done by some of those who venture to profess and call themselves dramatic critics.

Yours etc.,
Sean O'Casey

London, 20 February 1937

To Gabriel Fallon

MS. Texas

Forty-Nine Overstrand Mansions
5 March 1937

My dear Gaby,

I am sending you a copy of "The Flying Wasp" under another cover, & hope you'll like it. I was sorry to hear that you & Father Senan had been down with Influenza. So have I, so have we all—except Eileen, who had a tough time nursing us all. The younger kid got it from the woman who comes daily to help in the house, the younger gave it to the older kid, & the older kid gave it to the oldest—me, & I had to hurl meself into bed. Well, it's all over—for the present, as I hope it is with you.

I see poor Dev [De Valera] is going to have a handful in [Paddy] Belton. He and his party (Dev) will have something to fight in the next election. I shouldn't mention anything about Irish politics—or is it Politics?—only I, Eileen, and the two boys are now, as you may have heard, fully-fledged citizens of An tSaorstát Eireann;[1] so we can speak as de jure & de facto (how's that for French?) citizens! To me it seems a funny thing to link up Dev & his followers with Communism. One might as well call Father Senan a Communist, though—don't tell him I said it—I have no doubt there's quite a lot of Communism in them all. I wonder why do so many priests say that Communism emphatically denies the existence of God, & that a Communist must necessarily be an Atheist? If they would read the Communist Manifesto—our Creed—they'd find there no denial of God's existence. Communists are no more concerned with this matter than are Conservatives, except that Conservatives (and, maybe, Belton) make use of God for peculiar & personal purposes, and that, if

[1] The Irish Free State.

God exist, is a terrible thing to do. "It shall be more tolerable for Sodom & Gomorrah in the day of judgment"—of course, I don't include in these the poor fellow or girl praying to God or lighting a candle to a harrased (is this spelled right) saint for a job—this is but asking for one's daily bread; but to do it out of vanity, or ambition—well! But no-one ought to have to pray to God or a Saint for a job. In a sensible community—much more in a Christian Community—we shouldn't be able to find hands for all the jobs to be done. Over here there's a row on in Parliament about a Communist Poster that has superimposed a hammer and sickle on the Cross. This seems funny to me, for what holier symbols—in a very high earthly sense—have we than the sickle & the hammer? And, if I may say so, from what I have often read about Christ, I'd go bail He often used a hammer, & probably knew, & knows, how to use it well; & possibly, He knew something about a sickle, too, for we're told in Revelations that "And I looked, & behold a white cloud, and upon the cloud one sat like unto the Son of man, having on His head a golden crown, and in His hand a sharp Sickle". So you see. And these damned fools complaining about a hammer & sickle, are busy getting together 1,500,000000 to be spent on bombs, guns, & gasmasks! And the Archbishop of Canterbury says there ought to be more heartiness in the saying of the prayers said before Parliament business begins.

I haven't had a line from Will since. Never a single line. Where he is, or what he's doing, I haven't an idea.

And, now, my dear Gaby, I think you ought to stop sending me "The Irish Press". Your kindness costs money, & God knows, & I know, you have little to spare; & the packing, etc, takes time, & you have little of that to spare, either; so never mind about them from now on, & my deep thanks to you for your thought & kindness.

I hope Rose and all the little ones are well. Give her & them my sincere love. And my love to Frank & Father Senan & the Brother.

Donald O'Cahill—of The Irish Film Co—rang up—saying you had told him to—when I was very horse dee combat with Influenza; I, or, rather Eileen, I was in the centre of the bed—told him to ring a few days later, but he didn't. I'm sorry, for I should like to have seen him.

Well, my love to you.

Sean

To Peter Newmark

MS. NEWMARK
49 OVERSTRAND MANSIONS
5 MARCH 1937

Dear Peter.

Thanks for your criticism & letter. I think your criticism well-written, but you'll be better able to practice off some other boyo's plays—we are too friendly. I agree about Miss [Eileen] Crowe—monotonous & lacking emotion—Not about [Maureen] Delany—she's a bouncer in every play. (bouncer) All parts are the same to her—she takes them in her stride. Well, if I ever went to Cambridge again, you can see that I would have to go on a Shirley Society Invitation—they asked first. I've sent "The Flying Wasp" to you, &, if you review it, forget all friendliness between us, & say what you really think—I feel sure you will.

Yours
Sean O'Casey

To George Jean Nathan

MS. CORNELL
49 OVERSTRAND MANSIONS
8 MARCH 1937

My dear George—

I have, under another cover, sent on a copy of "The Flying Wasp," first, & most probably last, effort in "Dramatic Criticism." It is just that I felt that something ought to be said about the way the English Critics thought about the Theatre. The shots fired were mostly made from ammunition, high explosive and shrapnel, supplied in the talks and writings of a fellow called George Jean Nathan. There is, as you know yourself, no-one here worth enough to make a patch on the seat of your trousers. I hate the whole bunch of them, and it must be something big in badness in them, for a lot of your boys are as bad (in criticism) but I can honestly say that I've no grudge against any one of them—they were all really likeable fellows—even Gilbert Gabriel, for I did savage him a little too much, & I a raw stranger in his country. However, the book will reach you allright, I hope, and then you can see for yourself—as you always do. I'm so glad you escaped all the season's ills so far. I hope you may continue to do so. I am grieved to hear of Gene's illness; I hope to God he may be quite well when you get this.

I want to ask you if you have a copy of "The American Spectator" holding the article "A Protestant Kid Thinks of the Reformation"? [1] When I was in the U.S.A. the wife moved from the country to London; she was ill with pregnancy, & couldn't look after things as she wanted to, so some of my papers were left behind, & among them, I'm afraid was the article in question. I am, now & again, writing a "curious autobiography," & the article was really part of it. I can remember only bits of it, so if you have the copy handy, would you send it to me to type out, &, of course, I'll let you have the article back; but if the article isn't to be found readily, please don't bother about it.

I haven't started a new play yet. I am a little tired of all the rows that my plays caused. I haven't written one yet that didn't create a blaze—some are saying here even about the Film (of "The Plough and the Stars"), that because it criticises the way of England in Ireland, it should be banned!—and I really hate quarreling although I like an argument as well as the next one. I am thinking about a play to be called "The Star Turns Red"—Star of Bethlehem, that is—but amn't sure that I'll go on with it, for it would sure cause another bloody big row! I miss your "The American Spectator" greatly, for in it there was always a welcome for the strange story or article. But it's gone now, for even its ghost doesn't look a bit like it.

Mike Gold has been using the Hammer & Sickle on me in "The Daily Worker," calling me all sorts of names because of the Film, & saying a lot of things that show he knows a lot less about Ireland than I do of the U.S.A. If Communism were the power in America, his hysterics would have him liquidated in the twinkling of an eye. I think I remember you liquidating him once in a critical reference.

I'm afraid I shant be leaving London for the Coronation,[2] & will be stuck fast in the middle of all this waste & foolery. The funds don't allow more than a few weeks' simple holiday at the sea in the Summer, usually in the last week of July & the first weeks of August. At the moment I'm helping in a mild way, a production of Macbeth by a School near where I live—a County Council School.[3] Last year they did A Midsummer Night's Dream, & did it splendidly, & I am acting as "Godfather" for this year's Macbeth, God help me.

Do you ever see Ernest Boyd, now, & if you do, how is he? I daresay the same hurry about and do nothing that he seemed to be when I met him in New York.

Remember me to all friends, especially Lillian & Mimsie & Gene, John & George & Dick.

With deep affection,
Sean

[1] Sean O'Casey, "A Protestant Kid Thinks of the Reformation," *American Spectator,* July 1934; reprinted in *I Knock at the Door* (1939).

[2] The coronation of George VI on 12 May 1937.

[3] The Sloane School, Chelsea.

To Horace Reynolds

MS. REYNOLDS

49 OVERSTRAND MANSIONS
19 MARCH 1937

Dear Horace.

Enclosed is "Dreamschool",[1] part of biography I am trying to write in moments of spare time, & laziness can be driven off. I take it for granted that you have sincerely promised that you will not give yourself any trouble to get the thing placed—provided always that you think it worth placing—& that should you not be able to do so readily, you'll skeet the thing back to me without worrying.

There is a little cold consternation here over "The Flying Wasp". It is "splenetic, wanton, unfair, poor Coward shouldn't have been mentioned, malicious", & most of the big critics are saying nothing—not even Ervine—so far. This week's "Time & Tide" seems to be bloody bad —or is this thought due really to the fact that it very quietly shunted me out of its columns.

Frank Ryan, who leads the Communist Irish in Spain is coming up to see me—he has been wounded—& it was he who led the attack on "The Plough" [2] long ago—& I expect to have a fine evening with him & two others who have gone thru hell.

Love to Kay & the young ones & to You

Sean

[1] See O'Casey's letter to Reynolds, 15 February 1937, note 2.

[2] See Mrs. Hanna Sheehy-Skeffington's letter to the *Irish Independent,* 15 February 1926, note 2, and O'Casey's letter to F. R. Higgins, 5 June 1939, note 1. Frank Ryan (1902–44), I.R.A. leader and Marxist, who with Mrs. Sheehy-Skeffington had led the Republican protest against *The Plough and the Stars* in 1926, had been wounded fighting for the Loyalists in the Spanish Civil War in 1936. Later in 1937 he returned to Spain and was captured by the Fascists, who kept him in prison until the outbreak of World War II, when he was transferred to the Germans. He died in Germany, after the Nazis had tried unsuccessfully to use him to stir up an Irish revolt against the British. See also O'Casey's letters in defense of Ryan, *Irish Times,* 5 April, 10 and 21 May 1952, Vol. II.

By James Agate

John O'London's Weekly
19 March 1937

"My Reply to Mr. Sean O'Casey"

Mr. Sean O'Casey has written a little book * of two hundred and one pages, in which he has mentioned me one hundred and sixty-six times. "I know, because I counted them yesterday," said the little boy in the story of the Bishop and the Caterpillar. I know how many legs go to make up Mr. O'Casey's caterpillar because I gave a little boy sixpence to count them. At a rough guess, I should say that one hundred and sixty-four of these mentions are dishonourable, not to say abusive. Why? Can it be because in 1936 I did not hold the same opinion of Mr. O'Casey's dramatic talents that I did in 1926?

One hundred and sixty-four vituperative gobbets have induced me to look up the things I have written about Mr. O'Casey during the last dozen years. In 1925 I find that I wrote:—

> *Juno and the Paycock* is as much a tragedy as *Macbeth,* but it is a tragedy taking place in the porter's family. There are some tremendous moments in this piece, and the ironic close—in which the drunken porter returns to his lodging unconscious of his son's death, daughter's flight to river or streets, and wife's desertion—is the work of a master.

In 1926 I was writing of *The Plough and the Stars*:—

> Mr. O'Casey has done what Balzac and Dickens did—he has created an entirely new gallery of living men and women. These projections of his imagination live, and live with such an urgency and veracity that you feel moral censure to be impertinent.

Then, in 1929, apropos *The Silver Tassie*, I wrote:—

> There is no "if" about this play; all London must see it, or at least all those Londoners who can think back three hundred years to a time when the English stage had breadth and size and vision and its audiences managed to keep awake when the play was something other than old Polonius's "tale of bawdry." . . . I shall take what racing parlance calls a long shot and name Mr. O'Casey as the biggest playwright in the making for the last 300 years . . . only a man of genius could have produced these sprawling, disjointed canvases, tingling with life and veracity and power and humour and character. And as for his dramatic sense, why, it sticks out like a bull's-eye on a target!

* The Flying Wasp. By Sean O'Casey. (Macmillan, 6s.)

A little over four years later Mr. O'Casey, having migrated to England, wrote an English play entitled *Within the Gates*. I thought that this was a bad play and said so. Whereupon Mr. O'Casey launched into a campaign of vulgar disparagement culminating in this book. He proceeds by the age-old and dishonest method of quoting a little of what one has said, drawing deductions not borne out by the full text, and thus misrepresenting the entire tenor of an argument. For example, in an article on the National Theatre, I said that it would have to be "the theatre of a people, and not that very different thing, a people's theatre, which means slum dramas performed by unfashionable actors and dowdy actresses before ill-dressed audiences." Obviously by "the theatre of a people" I must mean a theatre for *the whole of a people*. In my article I elaborated this, the argument being that just as a National Theatre should not deal entirely in unfashionable drama, so it should not be "merely highbrow or coterie." The main plank of my argument was that "a universal theatre should exist solely for plays of universal appeal."

Now it may be that I was wrong here, that, as Mr. O'Casey maintains, there are not enough plays of universal appeal to go round. Perhaps I ought to have argued that the deficiency should be made up by dramas labelled "highbrow and coterie," "slum and fashionable." Even so, a theatre which should be *the theatre of a whole people* must, in the absence of universal plays, devote *equal and impartial* attention to the different kinds of plays likely to appeal to different sections of the community. This is self-evident, and there was nothing in my article which can be quoted in opposition, because my article did not envisage sectional plays at all. It stopped at the statement that "The universal theatre should exist solely for plays of universal appeal."

Now mark how Mr. O'Casey deals with my sentence about the theatre of a people:—

> Here we have the apostle of elegant, well-dressed Pinerovianism speaking. He wants fashionable actors and actresses with all the loveliness of Worth and Rozane off their backs but on their bottoms, parading their trivialities before him. He wants a National Theatre to be a theatre of the people in contradistinction to a people's theatre. I smell a rat there. Now a National Theatre to be of any use must be, not in fashionable actors and actresses, but in dignity and integrity, a theatre of the people; and it must be in dealing with the whole life of those who live, a people's theatre as well. This man pines for Pinero with his expensive clothes, his yachts, villas, grand cigars, liqueurs with golden names, French *hors d'oeuvres,* added to plots that instead of painting the lily or perfuming the violet, gild the louse.

I am not surprised that a controversialist who can take so much trouble to misrepresent a single sentence should misrepresent the whole burden and point of whatever one is trying to say. Mr. O'Casey pretends that I am opposed to a National Theatre. I am not, and never have been. What I am opposed to is sitting tight till we have collected another £350,000 to build a play-house which London has shown no sign of wanting. That one should be saddled with a white elephant is no reason for erecting a rose-pink marble palace in which to stable him! The National Theatre fund has £150,000 in hand, and my idea has long been to get Parliament to pass a Bill whereby that £150,000 should be sent on tour as a nucleus of a travelling National Theatre.

We now come to Mr. Coward, whose success irks Mr. O'Casey so terribly. About *Bitter Sweet* I wrote:—

> *Bitter Sweet,* the new operetta at His Majesty's Theatre, may be correctly described as a triumph. The plot, the dialogue, the lyrics and the music are all by Mr. Coward. He also produced the play. I suppose it is possible, even probable, that the late W. S. Gilbert could have written a wittier book, and that Sullivan's music would have been possessed of greater enchantment. But Mr. Coward has achieved in not much lesser degree what it took the combined efforts of Gilbert, Sullivan, and D'Oyly Carte to achieve—that is, the sustained entertainment throughout an entire evening of a cultivated and critical London audience. It is said that the only reason why Mr. Coward did not act, sing, and dance in the play—for he is capable of appearing as actor, singer and dancer—is that he would not be able to conduct; and that the only reason why he did not conduct is that he could not bear *not* to see himself on the stage. The piece is full of good lines and amusing situations. It has a comic-opera plot which differs from the usual musical-comedy imbroglio in this, that one can pay attention to it without loss of self-respect. Perhaps one can give no better notion of the sustained brilliance of this well-thought-out entertainment than by the simple statement that it contains no low comedian, without at least one of whose kind no musical comedy that I have ever listened to could run two nights. *Bitter Sweet* presents many delightful pictures to the eye, and it is with the greatest delicacy and tact that Mr. Coward chaperons us through the daring 'seventies and the admittedly naughty 'nineties.

That was *the whole of my comment on this piece,* and it is of this that Mr. O'Casey writes:—

> Not, of course, that Mr. Agate said that *Bitter Sweet* is a great work of art, or even a great play; but it seems to me that what he says of the play in "My Theatre Talks" gives the play a value so high—he seems so eager to make the most that can be made of it—that when he praises greater work his praise loses the power that praise ought to have.

And now for the analogy with the tribe of hymenoptera. In May, 1933, I wrote an article entitled "Swat that Wasp." This was all about the highbrows who objected about *Cavalcade* that it was not a masterpiece. I said:—

> That it found work for a great number of actors and stage-hands, and that it kept the film wolf from the door of our nearest approach to a national theatre—these were pot-boiling arguments unworthy of highbrow consideration. According to these august fellows, it were better that Drury Lane should be pulled down than that pieces like *Cavalcade* should succeed. . . . In the theatre our highbrows like low stuff provided it is genuinely low, because then it is "amusing." Red-nosed comedians, pantomime dames, burlesques at the old Elephant and Castle and under the aegis of Mr. Carroll—these things they permit. But there must be nothing else in the theatre between them and the masterpieces. Say you point out that not all of the public has the stomach for these last, that just as man cannot live by bread alone, so he cannot exist on an exclusive diet of nectar and ambrosia, that there must, in short, be middling plays for middling people. With this they are unmoved. You point out that if their policy prevailed all the threatres must close. They shrug their shoulders. Ask them if they, the exquisitely sensitised, are sufficient in number and able and willing to support a theatre providing nothing except masterpieces, and they shrug again.

Mr. O'Casey's comment is:—

> This august fellow must be told that no one with the slightest reverence for English drama could be interested in the filling for a year of our nearest approach to a National Theatre; that *Cavalcade* is a tawdry piece of work, a halfpennyworth of bread to an intolerable deal of sack; and that the intellectual one per cent. among the people have always and will always, whether Mr. Agate likes it or not, decide the fate of a play.

Here I nail down Mr. O'Casey to a demonstrable misstatement. It is the whole of the public, ninety-nine per cent. of whom are non-intellectuals, who decide the fate of any and every play. There are not enough intellectuals in London to keep its smallest theatre open. And London has forty theatres.

Even better than nailing your opponent down is to let him perform the operation for himself. On page four of *The Flying Wasp* Mr. O'Casey says:—

> Let us see who have been the high lights and the limelights and the leading lights of the English Theatre during the last ten years or so. Here they are, standing to attention with their chests out: Coward, Lonsdale, Phillpotts, Sherriff, with Beverly Nichols peeping around the corner. And their plays: *Bitter Sweet* and *Cavalcade; Maid of the Mountains* and *Spring Cleaning; The Farmer's Wife* and *Yellow Sands; Evensong.* Here we have the highest mountain peak and the deepest sea of modern English drama.

If Mr. O'Casey knows his English theatre during the last ten years, then this passage is reckless beyond words; if he does not know his theatre, it is opinionativeness unsupported by knowledge. Only two of Mr. O'Casey's five names, Coward and Sherriff, could reasonably appear in any list of leading playwrights during the last ten years. Mr. Lonsdale's *Maid of the Mountains* was produced in 1916 and *Spring Cleaning* in 1923. Mr. Phillpotts's *The Farmer's Wife* was produced in 1924 and *Yellow Sands* in 1926. Mr. Beverley Nichols has had one success, and one only. The whole passage is a libel on the English theatre in the last ten years, whose high and lime and leading lights during that period are as follows: First and foremost Mr. O'Casey himself, and I have conceded Mr. Coward and Mr. Sherriff.

But how dare Mr. O'Casey omit Mr. Maugham, who in 1927 and since has produced *The Letter, The Constant Wife, The Sacred Flame, The Breadwinner, For Services Rendered* and *Sheppey?* How dare he omit Mr. Priestley, who in this period has produced *Dangerous Corner, Laburnum Grove, Eden End* and *Cornelius?* How dare he omit Mr. Bridie, with *The Anatomist, Tobias and the Angel, Jonah and the Whale, A Sleeping-Clergyman* and *The Black Eye?* How dare he leave out Ronald Mackenzie, who gave us *Musical Chairs* and *The Maitlands?* How dare he ignore Mr. Rodney Ackland? How dare he snub Mr. Van Druten, whose first success, *Young Woodley,* came within the period? Or Mr. Benn Levy or Mr. Rudolf Besier? Or has Mr. O'Casey never heard of *The Barretts of Wimpole Street,* produced in 1930? Or Mr. Clifford Bax, with his three magnificent plays, *Socrates, The Venetians,* and *The Rose Without a Thorn?* Or Mr. Shaw, whose *Apple Cart, Too True to be Good* and *On the Rocks* are well within the period?

These are the playwrights and the plays of the last ten years, and I say, without fear of contradiction by anybody except Mr. O'Casey, that Mr. Aldous Huxley's *World of Light,* Mr. Richard Oke's *Frolic Wind,* and Mr. Denis Johnston's *The Moon and the Yellow River* are more typical of the period under discussion than *The Maid of the Mountains, Spring Cleaning,* and *The Farmer's Wife.*

Were I to think any more about the matter I should become nearly as bad-tempered as Mr. O'Casey himself. I am tempted to conclude by giving him the advice tendered to Mrs. Gogan by his own Bessie Burgess: "You mind your own business, ma'am, an' stupefy your foolishness by gettin' dhrunk!"

But I will put it more gently. I will say that Mr. O'Casey is the broth of a boy, and that the broth has gone to his head.

To John O'London's Weekly

9 APRIL 1937

"My Rejoinder to Mr. Agate"

Sir,—What Mr. Agate said about me yesterday or today or what he will say about me tomorrow is not the question. The question is whether the comments in *The Flying Wasp* on Mr. Agate's criticisms and the criticisms of the other critics are justified in substance and in fact. Whether I was prompted or provoked to "launch out in a campaign of vulgar disparagement" because Mr. Agate thought *Within The Gates* "a bad play and said so," is not the question. The question is whether the comments appearing in *The Flying Wasp* on the criticism given by Mr. Agate, under his hand and seal, on that play, are in substance and inference justified.

Mr. Agate said the play was bad, but he did more: he set out to prove it in one of the silliest dramatic criticisms I have ever read. Anyone interested in the matter can read his criticism in *First Nights,* and my comments on that criticism in *The Flying Wasp*. But let me say this: If Mr. Agate had a substantive memory, he would remember that my campaign against the English Dramatic Critics began long before *Within The Gates* was thought of.

It began a few months after O'Casey had "migrated" to England, under the noses and in front of the faces of the dramatic critics themselves. It was begun at the Critics' Circle Dinner in 1926, in response to the "Toast of the Drama." Taking the first opportunity that came to me, I gave a speech in reply to the Toast, and told the critics (Mr. Agate included) what I thought of the English theatre as mothered by them, and of their adulation of the trivial things that strutted on the English stage, and the only one, as far as I know, who enjoyed that speech was the distinguished guest of the evening Lord Cromer (for he told me so afterwards). So that the statement that I waited to criticise the critics till *Within The Gates* was declared to be a bad play, is misrepresentation.

Mr. Agate is not, I fear, very clear or concise in his use of the English Language. Some time ago he was brought to book by Mr. Ernest Newman for stating that Mr. Newman had said that before a composer's music could be analysed one would have to know if the composer liked roast pork and beans.

In an article called "The National Theatre: Clearing Away Cant," Mr. Agate derides, and shows hearty opposition to the scheme for a National Theatre, which he calls "The National Theatre That Nobody Wants." He says there that "he is, at least, as keen as anyone else in England on a National Theatre," and supports this by adding that "Nobody in England wants a National Theatre!" Now what is the quality of a keenness as keen as the keenness of anybody else if nobody else has any keenness to be keen about? Let him read what the Spirit said to the Church in Laodicea.

It runs like this: So then because thou art lukewarm, and neither cold nor hot, I will spue thee out of my mouth.

He says many curious things in this same article; for instance, "The State realising that National Galleries and Museums were good for the nation, the State gave them to the nation." This statement needs a lot of qualification. Most, if not all, of these things were at first, and are even now, largely due, not to the enlightened consciousness of the State, but to the cultured taste and public spirit of Private Persons. I always thought The Tate Gallery was founded by Sir Henry Tate, a sugar merchant, and the Municipal Art Gallery of Dublin owes its presence and its life to Sir Hugh Lane, nephew of Lady Gregory. Highbrows and Coteries, Mr. Agate, have done a lot for these things.

Mr. Agate is evidently flummoxed over his "universal theatre, universal plays and his theatre for the whole of a people." He seems to be hedging. His argument was not that a National Theatre should "not deal entirely in unfashionable drama," or that it "should not be merely highbrow or coterie." He ruled out anything that was "slum, coterie or highbrow" according to him, probably. Now he puts the word "wholly" in front of "slum", and admits, grudgingly, I'll allow, the coterie and the highbrow. His "main plank" in the argument for a theatre that "Nobody in England Wants" is that "a universal theatre should exist solely for plays of universal appeal."

Well, there's no plank, main or minor, in his argument, for the simple reason that there's no such thing as a universal theatre or a universal play. And his "Nobody Wants a National Theatre" is manifestly a misrepresentation, since hundreds signed a petition for one, and Mr. Agate says he wants one himself. Look at this as an example of English: "The National Theatre has £150,000 in hand, and that £150,000 should be sent on tour as a nucleus of a travelling National Theatre." Fancy £150,000 going out on a tour!

In his review of *Bitter Sweet,* Mr. Agate says: "I suppose it is possible, even probable, that the late W. S. Gilbert could have written a wittier book, and that Sullivan's music would have been possessed of greater enchantment." Now there is no "possibility" or "probability" about it. Gilbert's librettos are there to be read and Sullivan's music is there to be heard, and Mr. Coward's librettos can't come near the one, nor can his music come near the other. If Mr. Agate doesnt know this, he ought to, and if he does, and didnt say so—well, we all know our own know, dont we!

When Mr. Agate tries to "nail O'Casey down," he hits himself with his hammer. When I wrote about the "highlights of the theatre" I said "for the last ten years *or so*." Mr. Agate makes this a period of ten years exactly. Doesn't Mr. Agate understand the idiom of his own tongue? What kind of a "lowbrow" or "non-intellectual" is he not to know that the little Saxon word *so* after the little Saxon word *or* means *more or less,* so that what I said was "for the last ten years, more or less," so that the list of playwrights given by me can reasonably appear "as prominent for the last ten years Or So."

Of the playwrights with which he tries to pin down my criticism of the English-Shaftesbury Avenue Theatre, three are Irish, two Scots, one, probably, a Jew; and the other, born in Java, has a foreign-sounding name. Mr. Agate's attempt in *The Sunday Times* at the miracle of turning Welsh, Scots, Manx, and Irish writers into English ones won't work. God has given England 35,000,000 *or so* living souls, and I can believe (if Mr. Agate can't) that this tremendous mass of mind and energy can give England (the critics kept in their place) dramatists to stand in line with the best. If Mr. Agate looks at *The Flying Wasp* with his eyes open, he will see that most of the plays he mentioned were listed by me as worthy of all honour and regard. *Young Woodley* I leave hanging round his neck.

It is not I, but Mr. Agate, who insults the English Theatre by his fear about England's intellectual poverty. Never mind these fellows, friends. I assure you they dont know much when one has courage to call their bluff. The average intelligent man, like you or me, knows as much, and more, about the Theatre than they do.

Yours, etc.
Sean O'Casey

To Country Life

10 April 1937

"BUZZ, BUZZ" [1]

Sir,—Your dramatic critic, Mr. George Warrington, evidently thinks that I should bury myself in silence because "O'Casey has earned more critical praise than that accorded to any other dramatic writer of our day." I am to sing dumb when such plays as O'Neill's "Strange Interlude" and Pirandello's "Naked" are contemptuously dismissed, while "The Combined Maze" is passionately praised. Well, Mr. Warrington realises now, I hope, that I am as likely to be bought by praise as I am to be frightened by blame. Mr. Warrington says "Mr. O'Casey boils with fury at the success of an ingenious theatre-piece like 'Night Must Fall.'" That statement is incorrect. In the article dealing with that play there is not one word of "fury at the success" of the play from beginning to end. As a matter of fact the article was held back from publication till the end of the London

[1] Mr. Warrington reviewed The Flying Wasp in an article titled "Buzz, Buzz," *Country Life*, 20 March 1937.

run had been announced.[2] The play was criticised because it was held up by the critics as an example of "realism", of a real-life play and "brilliantly matter of fact." All its little tricks were exposed by me and it was shown to be destitute of the very qualities the critics claimed it to have. Now your critic protects it with the name of a "theatre-piece". I did not say "the leading lights of the last ten years." I said "the leading lights of the last ten years, *or so*." Doesn't Mr. Warrington know that the little Saxon word "so" after the little word "or" means "more or less"? The leading lights of the English theatre for the last ten years Or So, have been the names I mentioned, and not those of Priestley or Maugham. We can't speak that well of the English theatre yet. I'm sorry Mr. Warrington doesn't understand the simile of the shell. There is a lovely poem called "The Shell" in *The Collected Poems* of James Stephens; if he reads it, he will understand. I did not know that critics write as they do because they are afraid they'll be sacked if they don't—it explains a lot, but it doesn't increase my respect for them. Finally, with all respect, I suggest that if Mr. Warrington murmured "our Shakespeare," instead of murmuring "our Noel," he would be doing more honour to himself and to the English Theatre.—Sean O'Casey

[Mr. Warrington writes: "I have conceded Coward and Sherriff to Mr. O'Casey. If he thinks in all seriousness that the leading lights in the English theatre during the last ten years or so have been Lonsdale, Phillpotts and Beverley Nichols to the exclusion of Maugham and Priestley, I can only say that we do not regard facts with the same eyes, use the same brains, or speak the same language."—ED.]

[2] See O'Casey's letter to Dorothy N. Cheetham, 20 June 1936, note 2.

To Horace Reynolds

MS. Reynolds

49 Overstrand Mansions
16 April 1937

My dear Horace.

Enclosed is the little Book on Thomas Ashe incribed as you wished. I have been "laid up" for the last few weeks with a pain in the heart that comes on me now & again, & which is caused by cramping of the stomach against the heart after days of stooping over work. My eyes make me bend too low. There is nothing to do but to wait patiently till the ache wanes, &

then start all over again. I'm nearly free from it now, & so I send you on the booklet. With it I enclose letter from Neil Fitzgerald. The letter tells a fine story. The Police are meeting in Belfast to decide if the Film [of *The Plough and the Stars*] should be banned, & there were quite a number of people here who thought it should be banned in England, too, though it was carefully modified to suit the English people.

Haste to catch mail

Love to Kay & her & your little ones.

Sean

To George Jean Nathan

MS. CORNELL

49 OVERSTRAND MANSIONS
4 MAY 1937

My ever dear George—

Thanks for your very kind reception of "The Flying Wasp." I'm glad you saw something in it. It was really a rough & tumble attack on the infallible fools we have here. The added title of "Essays on the Modern Theatre" is Macmillan's genteel touch—I saw it first when I got my copies. The critics here have said nothing—except Agate, who fired a salvo in "The Times" & "John o London's Weekly." I replied, & the rest is silence. Agate is now well on his way to your City to write about the American Theatre. I will cut out & send the articles on to you. You have another English Critic with you (G.H.)[1] who is telling us about your Theatre in "The Observer," & I enclose two of his articles. This is the Gent who with some members of the Royal Society of Literature (English), acclaimed "Night Must Fall" as Magnificent! I hear that the English Critics are about to give a Gold Medal for the Worst Play of the Year (unknowingly).

I'm sorry "Daughters of Atreus" didn't capture the critics' prize. It is, I think, a very beautiful play; but, as you say, the critics made an honorable choice. I have more respect for the American critics than ever I had—if they're not members of a royal society of literature, they're members of the royal society of life. Do you know (with the exception of a lunch in New York which I[vor] Brown attended; and a Critics' Circle Dinner given a few months after I had landed in England (1926) at which I told them off), I've never had even a drink with an English critic; while I'd never

[1] "G.H.", who wrote the regular "Dramatis Personae" column in the *Observer*.

hesitate to lower a drink or two with any one of them in New York. Fallible as they are, & as we all are, they are fellows whose hands one can shake.

I've had a sketch (autobiographical & unconventional) accepted, through Horace Reynolds, by the Yale Review, a sketch called "Dream School," which no-one would take here. My autobiography'll be a curious thing, if I can get to the end of it.

I hope to get away to Wales in June for seven weeks or so, by the sea, & stroll about & splash about with the Welsh people. Here, everyone is up to the neck in the Coronation, with a bus strike that has emptied the streets of Buses, & has shocked those who think the workers should ever be amiable. Up Communism! & up the Theatre, & up all who truly love & honor her! My love to all my friends in America, & to you, dear George.

As Ever,
Sean

To Horace Reynolds

MS. Reynolds

49 Overstrand Mansions
5 May 1937

Dear Horace:—

Many thanks for your kind letter. Of course forty dollars will be very acceptable.[1] The sketch has not been published in England (it was offered to no-one on the certainty, almost, of no-one wanting it), & I won't offer it to anyone abroad, now that Yale Review has very kindly taken it. Unfortunately, an unconventional biography doesn't appeal to me. I have often been asked to write my "reminiscences", but, alas! this I don't seem able to do. I find that anything I want to say about myself must take a colour & a form which seems to hunt all editors away from me. May the most of them go to hell! A week ago I was offered £100 (I could easily have got £150) to write, 1500 words each, six articles about six "great Irishmen of the Century", for a popular Weekly; but I turned the offer down. This is the sort of thing the editors want here. Well, may the lot of them go to hell! I'm glad you like "Dreamschool", though your liking for me may color your liking for the sketch. I have written quite a lot in this line about myself: Father's Wake; His Father's Dublin Funeral; Inheritor of the

[1] Payment for "The Dream School," *Yale Review,* June 1937.

Kingdom Heaven; Dream Review—a sketch of a military Review that used to be held in Dublin's Phoenix Park on the "24th May the Queen's Birthday", at which I am still working.

Madden was, I fear, a little premature about the play. I didn't think he'd hear about it. I started one to be called "The Star Turns Red", & have written a song for a "Leader" & his men, called "In the Morning Early" one verse going like this:

Leader: What shall we do with the Bishop prating,
Bishop prating,
Slyly stating
God's love for the workers' patient waiting,
In the morning early?

The workers: Advance on him with the Red Flag o'er us,
Tearing down all the
Things that tore us;
We've a world to win on all before us
In the morning early! & so on.

I wasn't well when I wrote you last. Bending low over work (on accounta eyes) cramps my insides, & when I get a spot of indigestion, the heart aches, & I have to quietly wait for the pain to go. It's almost gone now. We are being dazzled here by billions & billions of [2], smothered in them, be God! Representatives from all "the free peoples of the Empire" are over here doing Whoopee! I'm glad you liked "The Flying Wasp"; the critics didn't like it here. They've kept a dead silence. But young fellows in Cambridge, Oxford, & Edinburgh have sung an anthem about it. I got a review from Two American critics: Mason Brown & J. Anderson. I liked your article on Gogarty's book,[3] but were you holding yourself in a little? What is Gogarty? My opinion is that he has lost himself looking for too many things. His hatred of De Valera is extraordinary. St. John Ervine hates him, too. He once called Dev "the pinchbeck Parnell"; [4] but the real pinchbeck Parnell was poor old [Arthur] Griffith, himself. Griffith never did, & never would, had he lived to be a hundred years & a day, have got a grip of the Irish People. But I mustn't waste your time venting political opinions, so let me thank you warmly for your good offices in getting a nest for the "Dreamschool", & my love to you, Kay, & the two children. How is Kay, by the way?

All the Best.
Sean

[2] Here O'Casey drew a small picture of a Union Jack, for the occasion of the coronation of George VI on 12 May 1937.

[3] Oliver St. John Gogarty, *As I Was Walking Down Sackville Street* (1937).

[4] St. John Ervine, "The Pinchbeck Parnell," *Time and Tide,* 1 April 1933, a review of Denis Gwynn's *De Valera* (London, Jarrolds, 1933).

To Helen McAfee [1]

MS. YALE
49 OVERSTRAND MANSIONS
11 MAY 1937

Dear Miss McAfee:

Thank you for your kind letter & galley proof of "Dream School", which I return with this note. I have heard from Mr. Reynolds, & have written thanking him for getting a place in "The Yale Review" for my little sketch. I am very pleased indeed that you like it. I am quite satisfied with the alterations, but can't understand how I came to write "relinquished" for "missed". In Ireland I'd rarely think of using "relinquished"; "I wouldn't miss a second of it" would spring to my tongue. This damn country is corrupting my use of English. Even in the phrase "he relinquished all claim to it", I'd use "he gave up all claim to it". Thank you for hauling out that terrible word.

Here they call a lot of phrases "Americanisms" that are known to me since childhood in Dublin, & they are old English expressions which England has forgotten! I picked out 100 of them in the "Dictionary of American Usage".

With All Good Wishes.
Sean O'Casey

Enclosure

[1] Helen McAfee, *Yale Review*, New Haven, Connecticut.

To Peter Newmark

MS. NEWMARK
49 OVERSTRAND MANSIONS
16 MAY 1937

Dear Peter:

We were probably over the road in the Park when you rang. If you ring anytime before 12. there will always be someone to answer. I'm very sorry I missed you.

I'm afraid the "debate" is postponed sine die, or sine qua non, or whatever it may be. Your friend, the President, in choosing as subject "that the English Theatre is going to the dogs", not only gives Agate a "loop-hole" of escape, but presents him with a wide wilderness to play in. He is caught in the net of 'The Flying Wasp', & he can't get out of it. A much more appropriate subject for discussion would be "That Drury Lane is our nearest approach to a National Theatre". However, I'm afraid I'm not willing to waste my time, or yours or your President's, blathering in a friendly way with old Agate. If James Agate be representative of the English Theatre, then the English Theatre is stiffening in rigor mortuis, & thats the end o't, & all the heraldry of Agate's & his comrades' bunkum wont bring it to life again.

I see that he's gone over to have a peep at what America is doing. I am cutting out his articles, & sending them over to Nathan, so another wasp may begin to buzz buzz there.

Ivor Brown is still plodding his weary way in The Observer.

Well. All the Best.
Sean O'Casey

I guessed that our friend Michael wouldn't stay the day.

To George Jean Nathan

MS. Cornell

49 Overstrand Mansions
25 May 1937

My dear George—

I enclose the first bloom in the bouquet Mr. James Agate is presenting to us from the Theatre of America.[1] I'm afraid that in color and size, it isn't very imposing. Is he right about the waiters & lift boys? I always found them to be good-mannered & courteous, and I didn't go through New York with my eyes shut. Indeed, I found the Furnace-man at the National Theatre a gracious host, & often had tea with him & his colleagues under the stage. But, although invited, I never went to the Century Club—I don't care a damn about "period houses or august furniture," & I rarely find them lovely—bar the cathedrals of the middle-ages. But then they are just on a par with the cathedrals of New York—the cathedrals of the present day. I suppose it is beginning to get warm in New York, as it is here. In the middle of next month I hope to get away

[1] James Agate, "The New York Scene: First Impressions of the Theatre," *Sunday Times,* 23 May 1937.

to the mountains & sea of Wales. Not to climb the mountains, or to swim in the sea, but just to look at them.

The Theatre here is worse than ever it was—the only thing worth while is "Tobacco Road," & that is being played in a shack.[2] It horrified some of our "classic critics" who are always applauding "realism." We have eight thrillers on here at the moment, including "Black Limelight,"[3] which got great praise from the London critics—& all this when London is packed with foreign visitors. Not even a whisper of "Mourning Becomes Electra." And the Archbishop of Canterbury is sending out a new call to come to God again!

God be with you
With love
Sean

[2] Jack Kirkland's *Tobacco Road,* based on the novel of the same title by Erskine Caldwell, opened in London on 19 May 1937 at the 167-seat Gate Theatre.

[3] Gordon Sherry's *Black Limelight* opened in London on 12 April 1937 at the "Q" Theatre, and ten days later moved to the West End at the St. James's Theatre, where it ran for 414 performances.

To George Jean Nathan

MS. CORNELL

49 OVERSTRAND MANSIONS
2 JUNE 1937

My dear George—

Just a note to hand you another chapter of the Theatrical Gospel by Agate.[1] I'm afraid it isn't the voice of wisdom speaking at the Gates of the City: and to tell you that I have found "A Protestant Kid Thinks of the Reformation." It is in the "American Spectator" of July 1934. I had carried it in a clip-file all the way with me to New York & back; & had forgotten where it was. Of course, dear George, there's room for great improvement on the American Stage & in the minds of the American Critics, but both are immeasurably bearably better than what we have here. When you point me to articles in "Scribner's" & "Esquire," you point me to a Critic whose shadow even isn't to be seen in England.

I am deeply grieved to hear of Gene's illness;[2] & pray to God that

[1] James Agate, "The New York Scene: A Talk with Mrs. Patrick Campbell," *Sunday Times,* 30 May 1937.

[2] Eugene O'Neill was suffering from a rare disease similar to Parkinson's in which the cells of the cerebellum were subject to a slow, degenerative process. The main symptoms were speech impairment and trembling hands. First afflicted by the disease in 1937, he suffered a bad attack in 1942 and thereafter was subject to chronic attacks until he died on 27 November 1953.

he may recover quick, & be with us till he gives all that is still in him to the Theatre we all love. Give him my love & fond prayers. I'm glad you are thinking of going to see Mexico. How any American leaves his country to see the cities, lakes, rivers, or hills in Europe, baffles me! And there is a simplicity in the people that I cannot find in the people here. Fancy me singing songs with George, John, Milton Lusk, & Mrs. Markle (Gertrude), & Mrs. Lusk (Alice), & even at a dinner with [W. T. H.] Howe & his grandees; & then fancy me singing songs with the equivalent of these among Englishmen! Good God, it simply couldn't be done.

With love & dear Remembrance,
Sean

To George Jean Nathan

MS. CORNELL

49 OVERSTRAND MANSIONS
7 JUNE 1937

My dear George—

Here's another of Agate's cushioned thunderbolts.[1] Didya ever read such God-damned piffle? Is the poor brain getting soft? Ruth St. Denis "the first approach he has seen to anything he can call a manner." New York's evidently Agate's Tragedy of manners. But it is said that Agate's a pansy, so that would explain why he takes more interest in the form of a pony than in the form of a woman. Well, my dear George, you are reading the impressions of England's greatest Dramatic Critic, and is it any wonder that I think well of the poorer ones of your own? Well, New York wont fall down, any way.

With Love.
Sean

[1] James Agate, "The New York Scene: Selections From James Agate's Diary," *Sunday Times,* 6 June 1937.

To Peter Newmark

MS. NEWMARK
49 OVERSTRAND MANSIONS
7 JUNE 1937

Dear Peter—

Thanks ever so much for "Granta" and "Cambridge Review". I liked your review,[1] and take the praise offered into my open hands, for I'm sure you meant what you said. A good point where you said A [Agate] hadn't reviewed a play by Auden, Eliot, or Toller. Ashley Dukes some time ago rang me up to say that A [hadn't] even seen M. in the Cathedral. He wrote a letter to "The Sunday Times" about this, but the letter never appeared; but there is a perfectly free expression of opinion in England.

Hope you succeed as well as you wish in Trinity. And hope to see you when you come to London. If Michael be with you, bring him along.

Hail to the Coming of Communism.

Yours
Sean O'Casey

[1] Of *The Flying Wasp.*

To Brooks Atkinson

TS. ATKINSON
49 OVERSTRAND MANSIONS
16 JUNE 1937

My dear Brooks:

Et tu Brute! I've just got your larrup, welt, or blow at The Flying Wasp.[1] You call it names, and then go all out for a column and a quarter to prove me right! Why did I knock Agate so much about? Simply because he is the Chief Critic of England, Ireland, India, S. Africa, Kenya, and Tanganyika. Because he publishes most of his criticism (some in buckram), and has done so for the last twenty years or so, and his opinion is on record, arranged, modified, and selected by himself. He who publishes his criticisms in books, isn't a day-to-day boy. Who wants the

[1] Brooks Atkinson, "A Note on Reviewing," *New York Times,* 6 June 1937, in which Mr. Atkinson says *The Flying Wasp* "is a scrappy and truculent volume with some bright retorts tucked away in its pages but with no strong line of argument or reasoning. It is petty in attitude." The article is mainly a defense of the "journalist" play reviewer, as distinct from the "literary" drama critic.

dramatic critics to be St. Beuves? Who brought Sainte-Beuve into the discussion, anyway? O'Casey? No, sir; it was Agate. I've never read a line of his, or Arnold's, or Saintsbury's criticism, and scholastic criticism can be as bad and worse that what you call day-to-day comments. Agate's isn't "newspaper" criticism: it is to be found in permanent book-form. He claims infallibility; for himself and for all his friends. He holds that the criticised should never reply to a criticism. Do you? Are you infallible? Do you know anything about the theatre in Drury Lane? If you do would you call it "England's nearest approach to a National Theatre"? Do you really believe that "the function of play reviewing represents the audience's point of view"? My dear Brooks, I believe that the personal association of a critic is, not with the audience, but with his criticism. He sits in the audience, right enough, but he isn't part of it. The theatre may be, but the Drama is not an institution; it is an art as great as the art of Beethoven, of Angelo, or of Tintoretto. It is despised here. Everything new is treated with contempt—for example O'Neill's Mourning Becomes Electra. Everything said for it is smothered in a silent censorship. Half of the articles in my book were refused publication, and a number of them by the very paper that had pleaded with me for over two weeks to write for it about the theatre. Why? Because I said what I thought. In an article (a reply) Agate brought in Murder in the Cathedral to show the value of the English Theatre. He had never reviewed it, he never saw it. Ashley Dukes who was responsible for the production, in a letter to the Sunday Times, pointed this out, but the letter wasn't published. There is a censorship here, my dear Brooks, that is remarkable for its stupid cleverness. I'm out to shatter it, and I have given a good first blow, and it is having a bigger effect than I thought it would have. I send you a cutting which shows that C. B. Cochran agrees with me about the American Theatre topping the Theatre here. And another giving Agate's recent review of "The New York Scene." See what he says about "Tobacco Road," and about "High Tor." [2] He'd have to have "American Eyes" to get them into him! And yet this Playboy of the Eastern World commenting on my arguments for a National Theater said that his idea of a N Theater was "A universal theater for the production of UNIVERSAL PLAYS to which everyone would flock as a matter of course." Out for universal plays, and he can't understand one written in his own language by one named Maxwell Anderson, a descendant (though I hope not) of the same stock; universal play, how are you, and he says that he felt no nearer to an American than an Irishman does to a Japanese (If he read James Cousins [3] work—Dr Litt in Kieto University—he'd see

[2] See O'Casey's letter to George Jean Nathan, 7 June 1937, note 1. Jack Kirkland's *Tobacco Road* opened in New York on 4 December 1933; Maxwell Anderson's *High Tor* opened in New York on 10 January 1937.

[3] Dr. James H. Cousins (1873–1956), Irish poet, critic, teacher; settled in India in 1915, and was admitted to Hindu worship in 1937; traveled on lecture tours to America, Europe, and Japan, where he taught briefly at the University of Kieto.

that an Irishman could get pretty close to a Japanese. And I knew a Corkman who married out there, had a big family, taught English in the schools, and felt at home in a kimona for half his life.) I declare to God, to man, and to you, that—barring a decent place to live and enough to keep my wife and two kids going—I strive only for the integrity I know and for what I believe to be the truth. And now, dear friend, farewell for the present, with remembrance of all your and your wife's kindness to me when I was in your City with its grand crown of a sky, and to dramatic critics, decent fellows because they never forgot to be human.

With warm and affectionate regards, I write this for your private ear, and remain, as ever,

Yours in friendship,
Sean O'Casey

To George Jean Nathan

MS. Cornell

49 Overstrand Mansions
3 July 1937

My dear George—

Yes, I read Sydney Carroll's attack on you in the Daily Telegraph, & sent a brief remark on what he said; but it never appeared. We have a silent censorship here. The bastard was wrong even about the Magazine [*American Spectator*], calling it "luxurious & frivolous" though it (that very issue) contained a story, "Christ in Concrete," [by Pietro Di Donato] that no Journal here, I bet, would publish. But, my dear George, God has long ago gutted him of any brains he ever had. Two years ago I had a set-to with him over Films, & I had to leave him braying like a brazen ass. He wanted to make out that imagination comes *only* through experience, & no man can be born with it, against the fact that a man born without imagination can never get it through experience, just as the oak is in the acorn. Jasus, George, we have some ripe "gaums" over here! Your article on effeminacy on the Stage is giving rise to a lot of talk here. The more they attack you the better, for it will create a greater interest in what you say, & your views on the Theatre are badly needed here. Already, a young man has written an attack on the same theme in a Provincial Journal; probably, led by yours. "The Flying Wasp" has raised a lot of indignation, too; but, as you say, these things dont affect our Health. We havent gone to Wales yet. Waiting for our elder boy to finish school term. He is to play the King in Hamlet next week, & we're going to see him do it—then off to the sea. I hope you've had, and are having a glorious time in Mexico. The only play on here worth a damn is "Judgement Day";[1] but the success of W. Shakespeare in America has shocked them a lot. They'd almost forgotten him, just as they blather about "American idioms" that we use day by day in Dublin, idioms that come straight out of Shakespeare's mouth, or the mouths of his companions. Reading comments by J. Anderson & Brooks on "The Flying Wasp," I sent personal & friendly comments on their comments, & maybe they'll be saying something to you about them. I enclose two more articles on "The New York Scene," written by Agate. He has, apparently, gone everywhere, & has seen next to nothing. He said here (arguing against me) that "when he thought of a National Theatre, he saw a Universal Theatre producing universal plays to which all people flocked as a matter of course"; & about "High Tor," that "he failed to understand it; that it had to be seen through American eyes; & that an Englishman could understand an American about as much as an Irishman could understand a Japanese." So I have asked him (thro the Sunday Times) where does his "universal play" come in? But the letter hasn't been published yet. If one can't understand a play written in the Same language, by an Author claimed to be of the same fundamental stock, then how, in the name o' God, is one justified in thinking that there can be such a thing as "a universal play to which people will flock as a matter of course"? This is what we have to listen to here. Contradictions, not after 20, ten, five, or even after one year's thought; but contradictions heel to heel, with arms around each other's neck.

I haven't seen or read "Shadow & Substance."[2] A young Irish poet (a lot in him, I think) who is, in real life, a cobbler, visiting me in a down an out muddle, told me the play "was a terrible one." But young Irish writers don't see very much in the work of their brothers, &, when I hear an opinion like this of a new work, I invariably assume that there's something in the new author. Unfortunately there's but a bare chance of an Irish play coming this way. What would we do without the U.S.A.? I think I'll have to buy (cant get it here) the play with the Stars & Stripes, & tack it on the wall.

I'm still doing all I can to speed on the good work in Spain where the workers & thinkers & poets are alive in the flames of the barricades.

With a fond embrace,
Yours
Sean

[1] Elmer Rice's *Judgment Day* opened in London on 10 May 1937.

[2] Paul Vincent Carroll's *Shadow and Substance* opened at the Abbey Theatre on 25 January 1937. It opened in New York on 26 January 1938, and won the New York drama critics' award for the best imported play of the year.

To Horace Reynolds

MS. REYNOLDS

49 OVERSTRAND MANSIONS
19 JULY 1937

My dear Horace:

Many, many thanks for sending me copy of "Yale Review" with "Dreamschool" as a nosegay in its bosom. Curious, seeing it in print, I don't think it so good as I thought it before it settled down. But everything I write dims down when I see it printed. Oh, God, for satisfaction! Nay, God, not satisfaction, for that way is death.

Thanks, too, for suggesting that I should send you other things written, but I don't see why I should worry you with the task of placing them—you've got enough to do with your own.

By the way, looking over notes in an old book yesterday, among notes for songs to be written, I found one of "The Bonnie Bunch o' Roses", so, maybe, the one you found was written by me, after all.

I hope you have a gorgeous time on the American rivers.

Love to You All.
Sean

To Harold Macmillan

MS. MACMILLAN LONDON

C/O MRS ROBERTS
ARDWYN, CELYN AVENUE
PENMAENMAWR, N. WALES
13 AUGUST 1937

Dear Mr Harold Macmillan,

Thank you for your kind letter. You can see from above where I am at the moment—as far away from "Juno" & London [1] as I can be. Wales is the next best place to Ireland. Here I am, getting the sea breezes, & the mountain air, & trying to persuade the Welsh people I meet that Wales should, must break away from England, & establish her own independence. National Freedom must, unfortunately, come before Communism. I am speaking at a gathering here next Tuesday, & hope I may persuade some

[1] *Juno and the Paycock* was revived at the "Q" Theatre in London on 12 July 1937 by Arthur Sinclair's Irish Players, with Sinclair as Captain Jack Boyle and Sara Allgood as Juno Boyle. It was transferred on 9 August to the Haymarket Theatre, and on 6 September to the Saville Theatre, where it closed on 2 October.

who havent yet joined the National Movement, to fight for a flag, and a government of their own—and learning a little Welsh, in the meantime. So you see, the Communist, instead of trying to reduce life to a dull standard of tone & activity, is actively in favour, vehemently in favour, & will fight to make a people preserve & honour & love its own peculiar national identity. I should love to see you again. We shall return in the middle of September, but then you'll be—under Soviet Skies, saluting the Red Flag? Thanks for mentioning "Juno": the proceeds, I hope, will more than pay for our holiday.

With all Good Wishes to Lady Dorothy, your Children, & yourself.

Sean O'Casey

To Harold Macmillan

MS. MACMILLAN LONDON

C/O MRS ROBERTS
ARDWYN, CELYN AVENUE
PENMAENMAWR, N. WALES
27 AUGUST 1937

Dear Mr Harold,

Could you let me have a copy of *"Five Irish Plays"* for a friend here who wants to translate one or more of them into Welsh to be played by Dramatic Societies here. We are having a good time here. I am going next week to a Harper's home high up on Snowdon, & then to an allnight gathering in Anglesea. How I wish I knew Welsh—I know a little already. The Welsh are a lively & graceful people—like the Scots & Irish.

Affectionate Regards to you, Lady Dorothy, & the children.

Sean O'Casey

To George Jean Nathan

MS. CORNELL

49 OVERSTRAND MANSIONS
16 SEPTEMBER 1937

My dear George—

Here I am back from Wales, & there you are, I suppose, back from Mexico! I hope you liked the country & the people who have come so close to Communism, & who have done so much to help the Republicans fighting in Spain. Wales is now developing a vigorous National Party claiming independence from England, and England is carrying on the old game she tried so long in Ireland, caused so much bloodshed, & finally failed, & it will certainly fail in Wales. I hope you are in the best of health, & that New York will have a fine Theatre season, & that you may be able to pick one flower, at least, from the thousand & one weeds. The Abbey Players are to tour America again this year. They haven't signed with me, yet. I, of course, referred them to Dick [Madden], & they wrote to him. A week or so ago, they suddenly got my London agent to send me a telegram (I suppose it was "they") asking if I would send a telegram permitting a revival of "Juno" in New York (there's a revival here, at the moment). I, of course, am always in favour of a revival of "Juno" or any play of mine in N.Y., but this needed thought, for it would, apparently, clash with the Abbey production, & I couldn't arrange with my English Agent [1] (a clever young Austrian Jew, by the way), for Dick was my agent in America. So I phoned my English Agent up from the Welsh hills, told him I'd no objection to a revival in New York but that Dick would have to handle it. Mentioning the possible clash with the Abbey, I then learned that it was the Abbey who were applying through Shubert's London Agent (Shuberts are in charge of the tour), & all this while the Abbey had in their hands a Contract made out by Dick on my behalf. Doesn't it look as if an effort had been made to trick me away from Dick? Well, it looks odd to me. However, the Abbey Players are probably in America now, & they will have to deal with Dick. Previously, I had written them that I would try to meet them in every possible way, but reserved the right to decide finally, only on Dick's advice. This is the nth time the Abbey has tried to give me one in the eye.

Now, I'll try to take up my next play again from where I left off, before I went to Wales, & pray that God may help me to do well by the Drama. I hope Gene is nearly himself again. Give him & Carlotta my love.

My deep love to you.

As Ever,
Sean

I enclose cutting from an Irish Magazine which touches you. You have plunged your critical spear deep into many vitals, George, me boy!

[1] Erich Glass.

To Brooks Atkinson

TS. ATKINSON

49 OVERSTRAND MANSIONS
[17] SEPTEMBER 1937

My dear Brooks:

Thanks for your letter of two months ago. I have been journeying in Wales, like [George] Borrow, doing all I could to enjoy myself, and give a God speed to those Welshmen who were anxious for Wales to have a Government of her own. As for my book, I'm sure it's all you say, but—I wish I could take your advice, and never publish anything that isn't a work of art. You think more of me, Brooks, than I do of myself, and I am glad of that. How am I to know that what I have written or what I shall write will be or are works of art? Ah, if I could only know. All I dare venture to say is that I have never yet written anything I didn't want to write. I have never been pressed for time, I don't know what time is, but I have often been pressed for that which is called money. I once had to sell the world half-rights, amateur of my plays for three hundred pounds, and re-write them all in prompt-copy form before they would be taken.[1] And when I went to America, I brought twenty pounds in my pocket, left twenty-five with the wife—who was having a baby—and owed two hundred.[2] And since we have been living on what I got for the film of The Plough and what I got from Within The Gates. America—that is The United States—has been a godsend to me, but all the same, The Flying Wasp wasn't written just to make money, for damn little will come out of it. It came about this way: the two Editors of Time and Tide came to me, and begged me to write monthly articles on the theatre. I held out for two weeks. They came again, and, at last, I consented to write. After (though I warned them I would be controversial, and they said, so much the better) some six articles they cooled, every excuse possible was thought of to refuse the articles, and, finally, I discontinued sending them. So I determined that all that had been refused would be published, and so The Flying Wasp was born. I know YOU don't assume the role of dictator, but many of your English comrades do, and that is, or was my complaint. And, of course, you do try to be the Artist's advocate. I hope you and Mrs. Brooks Atkinson had a glorious time at Prink Hill, and that you will enjoy the kindly fruits of the earth that you have nursed around you. All the above, of course, is for your personal ear.

And now, my affectionate regards to you and your wife.

Yours as ever.
Sean

[1] See his letter to Nathan, 28 September 1932, note 2.
[2] See his letter to Lady Astor, 17 August 1934, note 1.

To Horace Reynolds

MS. Reynolds

49 Overstrand Mansions
17 September 1937

Dear Horace:

Whether I owe you a letter, or you owe me one, I know not, but here's one to give you a hallo. We have just come back from a six week's ramble in North Wales, where there is a movement growing like the movement that grew in Ireland years ago, & startled England in 1916. The Nationalist Movement is growing in Wales, rank hatred of England is spreading amongst the young, & I have spoken to many young people with a "fierce light in their eyes". I was "well in" with them all. At a Concert given by Gor Telyn Eryri—Harp Quior of Eryri (a range of hills near Snowdon), I spoke (as chairman) in favour of the three Welshmen imprisoned by England in Wormwood Scrubs, & a number of English visitors got up & walked out! They call the recent tour of the English King in Wales "The Royal Circus", & many of the old loyal Welsh people are heavily shocked. The Nationalists have a paper called Y Ddraig goch (The Red Dragon, symbol of Wales) & a vigorous paper it is. I have impressed on all young (& old) Nationalists I met, that Communism isn't against Nationality, but will always help, instancing China's Red Army going into action against Japan. Strangely enough, the President of the National Party, Saunders Lewis, is a Catholic, & all the members of the Party seem to know the recent history of Ireland from A to Z.

I was glad to see your little story appearing at long last in Time & Tide.

All the Best to Mrs. Reynolds, the boy & girl, & to you.

Sean

To Gabriel Fallon

MS. Texas

Forty-Nine Overstrand Mansions
[? September 1937]

My dear Gaby: Hail! I've been busy over many things—children & a new play started—& haven't had time to answer your gracious letters with enclosures. I've been—as you know—in Wales, & have plunged there into the National Movement, & haven't forgotten to speak a few words for Communism. There's trouble brewing in Wales, & I think it will develop a Sinn Fein Movement. Everything is like what it was in Ireland some years before " '16". There's a flame in the eyes of a crowd of young people. I had meals & long talks with permanent-way men, quarry workers, professors, Schoolmasters, Clergymen, Students, & people that live in the little sheep farms in the mountains of Eryri (Snowdonia). At a late-night (Nosaulawm)—means a pleasant evening—in Glas Morin, in Anglesea, near the sea, & many miles from a road, I joined in the gathering, & sang a song in Gaelic 'The Palatine's Daughter'. All those who are in the National Movement have an amazing knowledge of Irish affairs, & follow them step be step. I had to hold meself in, or I'd ha been roarin out again the oul cries of hatred to the Saxon—not that I love them overmuch. Ready to weep at the least little thing, ready to laugh at the least little thing —& yet they are never moved. Forever talking—yet silent sods, the whole of them—bar the Communists, & their one representative in Parliament is a Saxon called Gallogher—the name may be familiar to you.

I am very sorry that I was away in Wales when Father Senan rang up. You see, we try to give the children as long a time as we can near the sea, after a nine or ten months' stay in a London flat. We, in Wales, live in "digs", & so get into close touch with the Welsh people. I acted as Chairman at a Concert in Penmaenmawr where hardly any English was spoken, & had (for lack of energy) to refuse lots of calls to speak in various places. I hope F. Senan will take my regrets that I missed the great chance of having a chat with him. Give him my respectful & warm regards, &, also, to Father Leo.

Thanks for "The Irish Monthly", the little magazine of which I heard so much in the "Reminiscences of a Maynooth Professor".[1] Your critical article [2] was, I think, the best of yours I've read, so far. I hope you're getting something to help keep things going by this work—for work it is, me boy.

[1] Dr. Walter McDonald, *Reminiscences of a Maynooth Professor* (London, Jonathan Cape, 1925). Shortly before his death in 1920, at the age of sixty-six, Dr. McDonald appointed Denis Gwynn as his literary executor, and Gwynn edited this posthumous volume of controversial reminiscences. For a chapter devoted to the memory of Dr. McDonald, see O'Casey's "Silence," *Inishfallen, Fare Thee Well* (London, Macmillan, 1949).

[2] Gabriel Fallon, "Stage Wasps and Stinging Irishmen," *Irish Monthly*, May 1937, a review of *The Flying Wasp*. O'Casey liked the review, even though Fallon's general praise of the book was mixed with some hard judgments: "Instead of wielding that sword of drama criticism which he would like to wield, he uses, as often as not, any old weapon that comes to hand. So we find him pelting away with personal prejudice or heaving whole hodfuls of mixed opinions. This is a pity, a great pity, for Mr. O'Casey possesses a strong *feeling* for what is right in the theatre. But for many reasons he is like a child in the dark. He has sufficient courage to shout for a light but not enough to leave the darkness to go and search for one. He has possibly done the English theatre some service by this stinging business, simply because he has stung hard enough to make people think. But he has done it at his own expense."

I enclose a playbill of the Abbey's activities now going on in New York.[3] "Katie Roche" was a bad flop, & got very bad notices. Why not, Gaby, send that "young Frenchman" on to Brinsley [Macnamara]? It would be gorgeous reading his account of O'Casey. I return the letters you sent to me: you might want them.

My Love to the children, to Rose, & to you.

Yours As Ever
Sean

[3] The Abbey Players offered a repertory season in New York, from 2 October to 18 December 1937, with the following plays: Teresa Deevy's *Katie Roche*, O'Casey's *The Plough and the Stars,* Lennox Robinson's *The Far-Off Hills,* J. M. Synge's *The Playboy of the Western World,* George Shiels's *The New Gossoon,* O'Casey's *Juno and the Paycock,* Frank O'Connor's *In the Train,* Lennox Robinson's *Drama at Inish.*

To Macmillan & Co. Ltd.

MS. MACMILLAN LONDON

49 OVERSTRAND MANSIONS
29 OCTOBER 1937

Dear Sirs,

The English Association are to publish a second volume of "Poems of Today," covering the period of 1922 to the present day.

In this volume they wish to include "Spring Chorus" & "Chant of the Down And Out" from "Within the Gates."

I shall be glad if you would let me know whether you approve of this; or if you have any objection to the use of these songs by them.

Sincerely Yours,
Sean O'Casey

To B. Douglas Newton

MS. NEWTON [1]

[49 OVERSTRAND MANSIONS]
29 OCTOBER 1937

Dear Mr. Douglas Newton:—

I have no letters written by T. E. Lawrence—I wish I had. I met him once only, in G. B. Shaw's house, & I was too damned shy to try to deepen

[1] From a copy made by Mr. Newton.

the acquaintance. I'm certain that I should have got to know him better had not a terrible accident taken him clean away from us.

Yours Sincerely,
Sean O'Casey

To Macmillan & Co. Ltd.

MS. MACMILLAN LONDON

49 OVERSTRAND MANSIONS
2 NOVEMBER 1937

Dear Sirs,

Could you send me the following books:

1 Copy of "The Flying Wasp."
1 " " "AE: A Memoir." [1]
1 " " "The Living Torch." [2]
1 " " "The Dead March Past." [3]
1 " " "A Ploughman's Songs," [4] I think is the name of this book: a small collection of poems (1/–?) by a young Irish poet.

Sincerely Yours
S. O'Casey

PS. Will you put above against my account.

[1] John Eglinton, *A Memoir of AE, George William Russell* (London, Macmillan, 1937).

[2] *The Living Torch, AE,* edited by Monk Gibbon, with an introductory essay (London, Macmillan, 1937).

[3] Gerald Griffin, *The Dead March Past, a Semi-autobiographical Saga* (London, Macmillan, 1937).

[4] Patrick Kavanagh, *Ploughman and Other Poems* (London, Macmillan, 1936).

To Bernard Shaw

MS. CORNELL

49 OVERSTRAND MANSIONS
24 NOVEMBER 1937

My dear G.B.S.

I hope you are well. I've heard that Mrs. Shaw has been poorly, & I send, through you, my true sympathy. I'm just beginning to read (having read the preface) your "Immaturity," [1] lent to me, by the way, by a hard nut of an Irish Communist who was for a long time assistant to Jim Larkin in Dublin, & who is now here busy with the development of milk bars! "Immaturity" is the one novel of yours I've never read—never even heard of it, till my friend brought it along. I read all the others, bought second-hand years & years ago in Dublin. It amused me to read of your Irish shyness, & ceased to amuse me when I realised that this very shyness & pride is deeply set in my own nature. However, it's better, thank God, than the frightful hypocrisy & maddening complacency of the English. No wonder Swift went mad. I was struck with the idea that a Communist is born a Communist, and (if he be not aware of it) is tormented till he discovers himself, or God's grace shows him his inborn nature.[2] I am a born Communist (as well as being practically born into Communism), for often as I have been filled with anger at what Labour Leaders did & did not do; I have always come back to the belief that the workers alone have the words of eternal life.

I am just considering an offer from America of a house & garden, a car, and all arrangements made for the education (I & Eileen have our own views on Education) of our two boys; and though I have great faith in the youth and vitality of the people of America, I'm afraid I'm a little too far spent to make a new life for myself & family outside of this poor, timid, half-dead country—with a keen eye on the possibility of Ireland. A year or so ago I got an offer to help with the Theatre in Dartington Hall, but the offer seemed to stand in the way of free expression (I was to be very limited in my choice of work), so I reluctantly gave the back of my hand to it. Anyway, I won't decide on anything till I finish, for good or ill, the writing of "The Star Turns Red." I thought some time ago of writing something around the rebellion of Jack Cade. I was reading Froissart's Chronicles, & it interested me very much. What about you? You could make a Communist St. Joan of him.

All here (except myself, who have a cold) are well. The two Boys, Brian & Niall growing into big intelligent Irishmen—each heavier & bigger than the scheduled size for their ages.

My love to you & Mrs. Shaw.

Sean

PS. Don't bother to reply—just wanted to keep in touch with you both.

[1] *The Works of Bernard Shaw,* Vol. I, *Immaturity* (London, Constable, 1931).

[2] In the preface Shaw wrote: "The born Communist, before he knows what he is, and understands why, is always awkward and unhappy in plutocratic society. . . . As it happens, I was a born Communist and Iconoclast (or Quaker) without knowing it; and I never got on easy terms with plutocracy and snobbery until I took to the study of economics, beginning with Henry George and Karl Marx."

To Lady Rhondda

TC. O'CASEY

[49 OVERSTRAND MANSIONS]

1 DECEMBER 1937

Dear Lady Rhondda,

You may remember that you cut a criticism—a mild one—of The Reverend Richard Sheppard from an article of mine a long time ago.[1] I have just read in the Daily Telegraph that The Reverend Richard Sheppard has died [2] leaving more than £40,000 after him; that his canonry brought him £1000 a year and a house (I have heard that his vicarship of St Martin's brought him 3000 a year—the wages of sin is death, but the gift of God is 3000 a year) and that he made more than 3000 a year on his bacon-and-egg articles about the love of God. Is it any wonder that there was always a smile on the smug commonplace face that was forever looking into the face of Jesus? We materialists sometimes seem to hear poor Jesus sigh.

Yours Sincerely,
Sean O'Casey

[1] See letter from Phoebe Fenwick Gaye to O'Casey, 20 January 1936.

[2] Hugh Richard Lawrie Sheppard (1880–1937), vicar of St. Martin-in-the-Fields, 1914–27; he kept the church open day and night and made it famous through his radio sermons; dean of Canterbury, 1929–31; canon of St. Paul's Cathedral, 1934–37. He died on 31 October 1937.

To Lady Rhondda

TC. O'CASEY

[49 OVERSTRAND MANSIONS]

[?] DECEMBER 1937

Dear Lady Rhondda—

I did not call, nor did I imply, that Canon Shepherd was a "villain". He had none of the greatness in him that a villain needs. When you say "you are too big for this or that," I'm afraid I feel no catch in my breath. You have said it before; the same thing has been said by many others—[James] Agate, [St. John] Ervine, [Charles] Morgan, and a number of priests and peasants, so the term falls off me, like water off a duck's back. It is simply one way of trying to shut an honest man's mouth. I am not responsible for the facts stated in The Daily Telegraph—with, it seems to me, an implied reproach. It wasnt I who said "Where your treasure is, there shall your heart be also", and Shepherd must have thought at times of his £40,000. I dont criticise him "for the money that passed through his hands." Jesus does; especially when it passed through his hands into a bank. I'm not arguing that Jesus is right; but Shepherd did. He believed, or said he believed, told everyone he believed, preached that he believed every word that Jesus said. That was the Mission he took upon himself to carry out. It isnt my mission, neither is it yours; therefore the reference to yourself is of no value. Not many would look on you as a saint; from your writings, I shouldnt even call you a Christian. Besides, your face is neither smug nor commonplace. His was one of the most commonplace faces I have ever seen (I know something about form in the face), and, judging from his writings, his mind was as commonplace as his face. His articles didnt show one sign, even one sign, of the beauty and terror of Christ's teaching, no more than may be heard any evening from any of the commonplace preachers in Hyde Park.

Now Canon Shepherd was regarded by thousands, if not millions of people as a saint. The other day the Archbishop of Canterbury (a good authority) hinted at it; you yourself—or a deputy—in "Time and Tide" writing about Pacifism, said as much. This saint when he was vicar of St Martin's had £3000 a year; as Canon of St Paul 1000 a year and a house; and as a soul-saving journalist more than 3000 a year, and he left £40,000 behind him in storage. By saying "I have more than my fair share of money in an unfair world," you, by implication, condemn England's popular saint, for he was a priest of God by his own choice, by his own avowal, an example for all the world to follow, to follow him as he followed Jesus. He didn't even confine himself to a parish, to a diocese; he preached in letters, in the pulpit, in the street, in articles, over the wireless to the world that he could reach, and you must admit that he was well paid for it. Money for jam. You say "he spent money lavishly on the causes he believed in." Easy to spend money given by others especially when you've a lot of your own. And what do you mean, or did he mean by "causes"? To the Christian, much more to the priest, much more again to the saint, there is only one cause—the truth as it is in Christ Jesus. You say that "his friends say that he was one of the most generous men alive." That is just emotional nonsense, on a par with the preaching and spiritual poaching of their pastor. What can a limited experience tell of the generosity to be found among men the world over? Compare his with the generosity (and faith) revealed in the story of the handful of flour and the cruse of oil. But here we have to consider not generosity, but Christian charity—a very different thing. You say "they say he kept numbers of individual people." I say, we say, you say, they say. How did "they" get to know this—for kept people dont, as a rule, tell it from the housetop. Let me say that the keeping of individuals is a very dangerous thing for a priest to do—more so when it is known. A priest, much more a saint must always avoid every occasion of spiritual pride. The church—to give her her due—realising this, dispenses most of her charity communally, that is through the medium of charitable organizations. Evidently this wasnt good enough for Canon Shepherd. To him be the kingdom and the power and the glory. And what are these "kept people" going to do now? And think of the horror of "these are they who are kept by Canon Shepherd." You say that he had a wife and children, and ask if "he ought to have left them penniless?" Well, someone said "take no thought for your life, what ye shall eat, or what ye shall drink; nor yet for your body, what ye shall put on." He was evidently afraid that they would be in the position of those "kept by Canon Shepherd." But to leave them penniless or not, is not my concern, nor is it yours. That was a question for his own conscience. I dont blame him for the decision he made. I'd do the same myself. But that isn't the point. The point is that he hadnt the faith in God that he so persistently preached to others. That is the whole point. And as he hadnt the faith in God that he so persistently preached to others, then his preaching was a mockery and a sham. The preaching of faith in God by a man having over a thousand pounds a [year] income, a fine house, and forty thousand pounds in the bank, to penniless men with wives and families was and is a hypocrisy, and a hypocrisy of a very high order. The Irish priests have a reputation of screwing money out of their flocks, and some of them deserve it; but I can say that there isnt a priest from one end of Ireland to the other (nor do I know one here, and I know a good many, Redemptorists, Franciscans, Discalced Carmelites, and some secular priests) who has or ever had a salary of 3000 pounds a year for administering the sacraments or preaching the gospel. Don't read bitterness into one who says a thing that shocks. Jesus was bitter: Oh, generation of vipers. So was the gentle Blake: his poem about Hayley, part of which is so obscene that it hasnt been printed whole; so was Shelley. Beware of entering into a sham, lest you become part of the sham yourself.

Yours sincerely,
Sean O'Casey

To George Jean Nathan

MS. Cornell

49 Overstrand Mansions
28 December 1937

My dear George—

Your new book on the Theatre [1] has just been popped into my hands by the postman. It is a grand opening for the New Year, & I shall set

[1] George Jean Nathan, *Morning After the First Night* (New York, Knopf, 1938).

aside most things that the book may be read. Thank you very much indeed, for the gift. The picture on the cover is something I've never seen before. Where does it come from? It looks like a drawing, & is a very good head of G.J.N. It's the best I've seen as a symbol of you by a long chalk. (The wife talked of "the handsome head.") Have you a copy of it? Or a photo of it, if it be a drawing? If you have one to spare, send it along, send it along, so that it may hang where I can have a dekko at it, now and again.

A few days ago I and the wife saw a performance of Eugene's "Mourning Becomes Electra" here in the Westminster Theatre. To my thinking, it was a grand performance & production of a great play. I (and she) was delighted with it. I was spell-bound, & my envy of Gene's great work grew enormously. I am so glad that his play got such a fine production. It was to run for 4 weeks, but became so successful, that it was continued over Christmas, and it is running yet. Imagine "Mourning Becomes Electra" running in London during Christmas, bang in the middle of Pantomimes & Peter Pans! The old theater is not dead yet. I thought I should never see the play in this life; but here it is, & doing well, and done splendidly.

I enclose a review of the play done by Agate,[2] & a slip of his saying something about "High Tor." Christmas here with the two boys has interfered a little with my work; but I hope to take up the shovel & the hoe again in a day or so.

As soon as I have dived into & swam about your new book, I shall write again. And many more thanks for "The Morning After The First Night."

With all the Old Affection
Yours
Sean

[2] James Agate, "Wuthering Depths," *Sunday Times,* 21 November 1937, a review of Eugene O'Neill's *Mourning Becomes Electra,* which opened in London on 19 November 1937.

IX

ON THE RUN FROM LONDON TO DEVON, 1938-39

I AM a fighter as G.B.S. is a fighter; neither so great nor so amiable a fighter, to be sure. But, then Peter wasnt so great nor so lovable as his Master; but he was a forcible fellow, and I really believe that I am a forcible fellow, too."

"There is a time when a fellow has to take up his gun, and run! But I am out against the condition of life in which under such circumstances, a man has to think of his wife and children. A man should be able to do anything, go to jail, die, anything, without his children having to suffer (in the way of necessities) for it."

It is abundantly clear in his letters that O'Casey had a special gift for provoking and enjoying a verbal fight, that he rushed into his celebrated battles with a sense of impetuous pleasure that was equal to his tone of moral outrage. He could swing his sword of the spirit with comic gusto, and he could aim his metaphorical gun with a rapid-fire barrage of consequential words, to use his own weapon imagery. From March to June of 1938 in letters and articles he was involved in a bitter and lively fight with Malcolm Muggeridge over the Moscow treason trials, for O'Casey the polemicist was suspicious of all anticommunists and automatically exposed them to the devastating scorn he reserved for enemies of the Russian revolution, the proletarian struggle to which he remained idealistically and uncompromisingly loyal throughout his life.

When the right-wing *Daily Telegraph* refused to print his letter attacking Muggeridge's anti-Russian article on the trials, O'Casey sent his extended reply to the left-wing *Daily Worker,* and the fight then overflowed into the columns of several other journals with new participants. The socialist Emrys Hughes, in whose *Forward* some of the battle was fought, was probably right in describing O'Casey as "a sentimental and emotional communist"; and O'Casey was probably right in justifying his emotional defense of Russia on the grounds that many a British journal "fears Russia as the devil is said to fear holy water." Unorthodox and self-taught communist that he was, he delighted in flogging the capitalists with modified Christian homilies, and he liked to appeal to God and compare himself with Christ and Peter. In the summer of 1938 when he had a brief encounter with an overly pious Catholic in Ireland, he stated in a letter to the *Irish Times* that, "like George Bernard Shaw, I'm an Atheist, and I thank God for it." In a serious and confidential mood, however, in a March 1938 letter to one of his best friends, George Jean Nathan, he revealed that he was aware of his critical and combative shortcomings: "I am altogether too vehement to be a good critic. I can't keep calm."

The first volume of his autobiography, *I Knock at the Door,* was published in March 1939, and his friend of earlier years Oliver St. John Gogarty attacked the book in a review in the *Observer,* attributing its failure to the fact that "O'Casey has, after all, a grudge against Life." O'Casey quickly counter-attacked with one of his vehement letters which the editor of the *Observer* refused to print, but which finally appears here, in which he replied: "On the contrary, I love Life. But I have more than one 'grudge' against the futilities, shames, stupidities, and romantic nonsense that distort and maim Life." Then, as if to confirm his protest against the follies of life, Ireland, in a futile and shameful grudge against O'Casey, banned the book.

It was his hope for a better life for his children which prompted him to leave London in September 1938 and go to live in the little village of Totnes in Devon, where they could attend the progressive and creative school, Dartington Hall. In his autobiography and new plays he was now developing affirmative themes with the use of dream techniques and symbolic fantasy, and in a letter to Brooks Atkinson in April 1939 he defended his new forms: "I get a tremendous joy out of the writing of fantasy, more than out of anything else. A lot of joy, & maybe, a little money." The money was slow in coming, for he was unable to pay his dues to the Society of Authors, now acting as his agent. But his joy increased, for late in 1939 he was working on the second volume of his impressionistic autobiography, and he had begun a new comic fantasy, *Purple Dust*.

To Horace Reynolds

MS. Reynolds

49 Overstrand Mansions
1 January 1938

My dear Horace:

A good New Year to you an' all. Yes, I probably would have loved Vic Faust.[1] There's a few of them knocking about now. When a kid, I used to sit on a wall, & hang up my hat, bringing on a loud laugh from other kids at the look of mystification on my kisser when the hat fell! Yes, we do miss Nathan's "American Spectator" badly. The "tone" of the papers that's going hasn't much of a sound. One has to be deaf to hear it. Television here asked me to do a 3 minute talk on any subject I liked. Here's an easy-earned 3 quid says I. So I wrote it out & learned it by heart—a talk on the proposed National Theatre. Did they take it? Like hell. The subject was "too controversial!" So my trouble went for nothing. Nice thing for a kid to be seven years in a Sanatorium. And Jesus died that we might live! I haven't read Colum's "Road Round Ireland"; [2] but I had just undergone an operation, & while waiting for a vacancy in a "Convalescent Home", had a row with a Nun over Jim Larkin, and gathered all my property in a handkerchief, & stalked out of the hospital.[3] You are right, I think, about the Gate Theatre—I can't see the American people yelling themselves hoarse over their productions. They are a good—sometimes a very good—Repertory Co, & that is all. However, I think The Abbey should put on a certain number of International Dramas each year, so that Irish playwrights can see manner & method other than their own.

Sally [Allgood] was as good as ever here in "Juno",[4] but the others

[1] Vic Faust, a music-hall comedian who performed on Billy Bryant's Houseboat.

[2] Padraic Colum, *The Road Round Ireland* (New York, Macmillan, 1926).

[3] See "St. Vincent Provides a Bed," *Drums Under the Windows* (1945).

[4] See his letter to Nathan, 16 September 1937, note 1.

did a lot of clowning, & have sadly fallen away from grace. Ever so many thanks for saying that you would try to place another biographical sketch. I have one called "A Child of God",[5] & when it has been typed out clean & fair, I shall send it on to you.

I am working at the new play, & I think it is doing well.

My love to you, Kay, & the two children.

As I was before I listed.

Sean

[5] See "A Child of God," *I Knock at the Door* (1939).

To John Bradley [1]

MS. BRADLEY

49 OVERSTRAND MANSIONS
6 JANUARY 1938

My dear John,

Yes, of course, I remember you. I missed your company on the boat coming back. I'm glad to see you're in Yale. I hope you'll do well. But depend more on yourself than on Yale. I missed Yale when I was in America. Pity I did. I've been very busy doing damn all since I saw you. However, I must do something soon. Money getting dangerously low. The theatre here in London looks remarkably handsome in its coffin.

Give my regards to your Father & Mother. I am still sorry it won't be possible for me to have a meal with you all.

My warm regards,
Sean O'Casey

[1] John Bradley, a student at Yale University, had met O'Casey on the Cunard *Majestic* during the voyage to New York in September 1934.

To Horace Reynolds

MS. REYNOLDS

49 OVERSTRAND MANSIONS
[?] JANUARY 1938

My dear Horace

Many thanks for your kind letter, and for demanding scripts of my RADIO TALK of three minutes on the NATIONAL THEATRE, which was shut up and shut off and shut out. No, I wont send you that, for it simply isn't worth a damn. It was made as peaceable as possible so that it wouldn't come bang on the Saxon ear, & so is worthless. God, the way they all fluttered about to stop this talk: letters, interviews, & telegrams—they must have thought that the BARRICADES would be flung up in the streets if I had given the talk. They're a funny lot. A day or so ago they wanted to broadcast my one-acter. "Pound on Demand". Would I be willing? Yes. Would I take three guineas? No; five guineas. Fight. Very well, 5 guineas. Would I permit adaptation? Yes, of course. Very well; contract for one performance for 5 guineas signed, sealed, & skeduled. Next day letter proclaiming the abandonment of the broadcast! They're all asweat with fear in this country.

I saw the first production of "A Deuce o' Jacks" at the Abbey when I was last in Dublin; [1] but the production was, I fear, a very bad one. [F. R.] Higgins has, I think a lot in him; but (between ourselves, Sinn Fein) he's inclined to be, I imagine, a little too Yeatsian, if you know what I mean.

I read your article with gusto on Billy Bryant & the gay goins on in his Houseboat. There's more of the theater there than there is here. I'd give a lot to see Billy playing Hamlet.

I enclose, as ordered, the sketch called "Child of God." It brought me back to the days when life was largely pain & Church & Sunday School and a lot of laughter & some vision in dreams.

You didn't say how your little ones (bigger & bigger now) are, & Kay.

God grant them fullness of life.

Yours As Ever.
Sean

[1] See "Sean O'Casey in Dublin," *Irish Times,* 17 September 1935, note 1.

To Harold Macmillan

TS. Macmillan

49 Overstrand Mansions
[? February 1938]

Dear Mr Harold Macmillan—

I have read "Tribunal" by G. R. Malloch. May God, in His mercy, forgive Macmillan & Co for sending me such a play to read. It flashed forth on the first page what it was. However, I read it to the bitter end. Judging it by the lowest standards, it is one of the crudest things I ever read. It's an atrocity. Theatre Managers are stupid enough, God and I know, but they arent stupid enough to produce a play like this one. Nancy Price [1] ought to be ashamed of herself to have given it even the light of a reading.

I am returning it to you by registered post.

I should like to see you again. I have a few things in hand (doing something with a play, and a few fantastic pages of biography),[2] but they havent reached the stage yet that would interest a publisher.

Perhaps I may ring you some day this week?

God be wi you.
Sean O'Casey

[1] Nancy Price, manager of the People's National Theatre Company.

[2] He was working on *The Star Turns Red* and *I Knock at the Door*.

To Horace Reynolds

MS. REYNOLDS

49 OVERSTRAND MANSIONS
6 FEBRUARY 1938

Dear Horace:

First greeting to Kay, the children & to you. I fail to see how birth in Belfast would be the indictment of a crime. "Scorn not Irish-*Born* man" —Davis [1]—let them listen to Davis. And what of the unity of Ireland? But I'm sorry not to be able to oblige them. During a life of more than fifty years, I've been in Belfast but for an hour or so, & then without seeing it—in a boat that had taken me from Liverpool, waiting for a car to come to take me to Mountstewart in Co Down. It was from this place, I went back to Liverpool, & then on to the United States—the time you & I first met. I was born in Dublin 78, or 85 Dorset Street (I think 85) [2] an apartment house kept by me da which nearly ruined him—it is now a Branch of some bank. I was baptised in St. Mary's Church, Mary Street, the upper end of Henry St, Dublin. There me ma & me da had been married, & all their children were baptised there. My father came from Limerick, my mother was born in Dublin; her mother was a Wicklow woman. I really started life in 9 Innisfallen Parade, Drumcondra, to which we came when I was 2 years old or so, & it was here my father died when I was about five years old [3]—"His Dublin Father's Funeral". I went to Sunday School & to Day School (for a year) to St Mary's National

[1] From "Celts and Saxons," a poem by Thomas Davis (1814–45).

[2] 85 Upper Dorset Street.

[3] Michael Casey died on 6 September 1886 at the age of forty-nine, and O'Casey was six at the time.

School for Boys & Girls, 25 Lower Dominick St, (See "A Child of God"), & then, later on, for a year or so to No 2 School, Central Schools, Marlboro St. Not only was I born in Dublin, but I was 25 or 26 before I ever crossed the border of the city, that is when I got a job that sent me out on country jobs. Then it was when I first saw corn growing, the plough at work, & some other activities of country life. So I am a Dublin man from head to foot & from top to toe. There is a drop of Norman blood in me, however. My mother's mother married a man named Archer (That was my mother's maiden name), but this Archer family, according to Alderman Tom Kelly, an authority on old Dublin, had lived in Dublin for 700 years, so even with this drop in me, I'm pure Dublin and wholly undefiled Dublin—except the Limerick blood of me da. That's all, for the moment about Dublin.

Now the answers to your questions around Easter Week.

I had been for a good number of years a member of the Irish Republican Brotherhood, & an ardent Nationalist. Then came the preaching of Jim Larkin and the books of Bernard Shaw. (By the way, it was a young Dublin Nationalist named Kevin O'Loughlinn, member of the third order of St. Francis, who introduced me to Shaw, by persuading me to read the sixpenny edition of John Bull's Other Island). These two great men swung me over to the left, & I became critical of pure nationalism. But, still more was I critical of the workings of the I.R.B. It was making no progress, & appealed only to clerks & artizans—the great body of the workers were set aside. Hardly a man of them knew how to use a hack or shovel, & nothing about the building of defences. But particularly, I hated Bulmer Hobson,[4] who was the white-haired boy of Tom Clarke. Once Tom put me out of his shop because I criticised Hobson as a Leader, & as Editor of Irish Freedom; Tom telling me he "loved Bulmer as his own son".

The I.R.B. took every help they could get (and they got a lot) from Jim Larkin's Union, & I did most of the work, for Jim was very fond of me. (I had him with me the other evening with a friend, & we talked from the early evening to the coming of the morn) However, at a general meeting of the I.R.B. in Dublin, I criticised its working, I was howled at by a lot, and supported by some; Bulmer, on the platform drew a gun, & there was pandemonium. So, afterwards, with some others, I left the I.R.B, & flung myself into the Labour Movement, though still doing all I could for the National Movement, & for P. H. Pearse's School St Enda, & St Laurence O'Toole's Hurling & Football Club & Pipers Band, which I founded & brought to a fine band,[5] with the help of chums, out of a first

[4] Bulmer Hobson (1883–1969), Irish Republican, editor of *Irish Freedom* in 1912, secretary of the Irish Volunteers in 1914 when O'Casey was secretary of the rival Irish Citizen Army. See O'Casey's letters attacking the Irish Volunteers, to the *Irish Worker*, 24 January, 21 February, 7 March, 13 June 1914.

[5] See his letter on the founding of the St. Laurence O'Toole Pipers' Band, (?) September 1910, and his letter to Lord Castletown of Upper Ossory, 14 May 1911.

capital of 3/6. I collected hundreds for this band. At the time of Easter Week, I was living at Abercorn Rd North Wall, with my mother only. She did not die till November, 1919.[6]

I wasn't working anywhere at the time. After 1913 strike, I found it damn hard to get a job; & had to be content with scratch jobs now and again—for instance pulling down a few old houses. So this unemployment meant very little food, & in consequence I got into a bad way. Then glandular swelling appeared in the neck (I got it in the neck!) & I had a lump there as big as an apple. I went to a clinic, & the doctor there gave me a note saying I needed surgical attention. I got a note to the Adelaide Hospital, saw the head surgeon who called the House Surgeon, showed me to him, & said "Let him in, & give the poor devil a chance". But the "poor devil" got no chance, for the H. Surgeon showed him out, saying "we wont have a bed for years". Finally, under the patronage of the Irish Transport Union, I got into St Vincent's Hospital & was immediately set down for operation.[7] But they decided to feed me up for some weeks first, & I had a fine time in a fine bed & enjoyed fine food while it lasted. First I was under a Sister called Sister Gonzaga, but, alas! was shifted to a ward under Sister Paul, who didn't like Jim Larkin. However, I didn't know this then, so I talked & laughed & sang for all I was worth. The operation took place, the bad gland was removed, & the wound began to heal quickly. Then Sister Paul sent for me to her office, & told me I was to stay in the hospital till a vacancy occurred in the Convalescent Home, where I was to spend a fortnight, & go home fit & well. I thanked her for her kindness. Then she asked me if I was to go back to work when I went home. I said work was hard to get, & mentioned one reason why. Then she came out on poor Jim Larkin, & I listened till she had done. Then I said what I felt I had to say, left her, wrapped up brush & comb in a handkerchief, & walked out of the hospital. I attended, however, to get the wound rebandaged, etc, & carried on my connection with St Laurence O'Tooles boys, many of whom were in the Volunteers. I knew that a Rising was to take place, but not the exact day; but knew definitely that it would take place (it was obvious to me) on Easter Sunday, when the Parade was announced. (I was a friend of C. Monaghan, one of the boys who went over the Kerry cliff, in the car sent to fetch [Sir Roger] Casement).

But the Parade was declared off by Eoin MacNeill, & B. Hobson, & then, as you know, the Dublin I.R.B. & the Irish Citizen Army struck on the Monday. I saw the Lancers coming back from their gay attempt to frighten the men in the G.P.O, and though feeling rotten, I wandered round

[6] Susan Casey died on 9 November 1918 at the age of eighty-one.

[7] He was in St. Vincent's Hospital, Dublin, from 15 August to 1 September 1915, for an operation on his neck for tubercular glands. For an account of the incident that follows, see "St. Vincent Provides a Bed," *Drums Under the Windows* (1945).

the city. Most of the fighting I saw, was the sniping—two soldiers killed in the North Strand, & one in Amiens St. I saw the body of what may have been the first casualty, a young boy, Jim Fox, son of a friend of mine, lying in the morgue, with a bluish mark in the centre of his forehead—shot in Stephen's green. Where I lived wasn't held by the British for a few days. Coming home the second night, I think, they had put a detachment to hold the North Wall (the docks), & to get to our road, I had to cross a bridge (Spencers Dock) crossing a canal leading to the Liffey. The night was dark, & with my sight, I could see but a yard in front of me. They had put sentries on the bridge; crossing I heard the challenge, halt, who goes there, but couldn't see where the sentry was, nor did I know the challenge was meant for me. Again came the challenge, this time sharp & full of threat; luckily, I called out, a friend, & went by, but it was a narrow shave. Another bugger was a little further on. He simply lowered his rifle & bayonet, & I just halted on the top of it. Who goes there again, & again, I answered, friend. "Pass on, chum", ses the bugger, "but you came very close".

That night, I think, they closed the bridge, & would let no one pass without a pass. However, there was a roundabout way over the railway by which anyone who wanted, at a risk, to get to the centre of the city, could do so. And hundreds took the risk, for no-one was afraid. We had had no experience, & flying bullets didn't trouble us. Later we knew, & got more canny. During the week the number of civilians killed was three times, or more, the number of combatants killed. Previously, I had seen the looting—it began almost immediately, when the people saw the police flying for safety to their barracks. This was a funny sight, with many an old striker trying to trip up, or get a knockout home to the chin of the "flying cowardly bastards!" I must say my sympathy was with the looters. They were trying to snatch a few seconds of joy & trying to bring a few good things into homes that were bare from their birth, & would be bare to their death. The world was theirs for an hour or two. Then one evening alone with the mother, she went near a window, there was a burst of fire, & the room was filled with powdered particles from a cut-up wall. A volley had come in through the window. Then an officer & a file of men visited the people house by house to find the house that had been fired at. They came up to me & the mother, found the shattered wall, & sent the mother down stairs to the people below. Then the search began! The few pillows we had were ripped open, & the feathers scattered on the floor; the bed [clothes] were flung about; every little thing we had was tossed down on the floor; the upholstery of an old sofa (one of the father's relics—indeed all the furniture was from my father's time, but now down & out)—was prodded & slashed with bayonets, while the officer stood beside me with a revolver ready. They were searching for an automatic! Corporal reported "nothing knocking abaht, sir", & I was brought down to the street, put against a wall, & searched from top to toe. Then the Helga, a gunboat, opened fire from the Liffey, aiming at Liberty Hall, & half a dozen of the shells fell & exploded about 60 feet from us. All the soldiers ran, including the officer, for shelter, & I was left standing by the wall. I returned to the house, & that night I was taken to the Protestant church mentioned in the Plough. All the night, with two others, I sat in a pew. The next morning, the Church was crowded—they had decided to round up all the men on account of the sniping. That night we were all shifted to a grain store, filled with maize, the Indian corn so great a favourite of the U.S.A. I've always looked on it with suspicion since. Previously, that is before the visit from the soldiers, I had thought it wise to take off the bandage from my neck, & pull up the collar of my jersey to hide the wound—they might have thought it was a wound received in action—& I payed for it later on. I slept as best I could in the corn, & some of the dirt & dust of the place got into the wound. After all was over, the wound became septic, and for many a month I had a bad time of it. However, that's a long story, & doesn't much matter now.

Let me end This bloody long letter by saying that I, the missus, & the two boys are citizens of Eireann, & with all, & in spite of all the attitude of mind towards me by some of the Irish, I wouldn't think of surrendering my Irish citizenship. By the way, the missus, too, is Dublin-born—more Irish than I, her mother from Mayo, & her father from Westmeath.

You'll be tired out be the time you get to the end o' this.

So my Love to you all.

Sean

To Horace Reynolds

MS. REYNOLDS

49 OVERSTRAND MANSIONS
11 FEBRUARY 1938

Dear Horace:

I sent a few points to you by Registered post. One word more: It has been often said—it has again been said in an article appearing in the Post Despatch, St Louis, Mo. that "while continuing at his labouring work, O'Casey learned dramatic technique by watching plays at the Abbey Theater after work"—a nice little romantic idea, without a word of truth. Before the production of "The Gunman", I had been to the Abbey *twice,* & saw Gogarty's "Blight" [1] with a one-acter that I've forgotten; and

[1] *Blight* by "Alpha and Omega" (Oliver St. John Gogarty and Joseph O'Connor) opened at the Abbey Theatre on 11 December 1917.

"Androcles & the Lion." [2] And these two were seen as in a glass darkly, for I was in the cheap seats, & couldn't see well, so far away. There was no use of going to the Abbey unless I got near the front, & 3/6 was far beyond me then. It's still about as much as I can give now. I learned more from reading plays than from seeing them on the stage. Those I saw were mostly in the old Queens & the old "The Mechanics" that is the old Abbey, minus The Morgue. The plays, "The Shaughraun", "Arrah na Pogue" "Colleen Bawn" "The Octoroon," all Boucicaults! "Face At The Window" "The Harbour Lights", "Peep o Day Boys" "The Unknown" & such like. I read lots of paper-covered ones for, I think, 3d each, Dick's Standard Plays, they were called, & Orange paper covers. The only one I can remember of these is "Fish out of Water".

But the Abbey has had nothing whatever (bar producing my plays) in my evolution as a playwright—though, of course, production is damned important.

Yours
Sean

[2] Bernard Shaw's *Androcles and the Lion* opened at the Abbey Theatre on 4 November 1919.

To George Jean Nathan

MS. Cornell
49 Overstrand Mansions
14 February 1938

My dear George:

Thanks for the photograph of your handsome boyish face. It will make the companion of one of Augustus John. I am very glad & pleased to have it.

And I've read your book, "The Morning After The First Night," and enjoyed it immensely. I enclose a cutting written by the Great God Ivor Brown in "The Observer" on the Theatre in America—he has evidently been over there lately. You'll see that in the tail of the article, he tries to stun you with a balloon. You'll notice that he markedly draws attention to the American liking for bawdiness; and you'll remember that this was the puritan bugger who, when he was in America the same time as myself, took the first choice of the American Theatre, then on in New York, by selecting the dirty farce, called, I think, "Personal Appearance." [1] That was this gem's first choice. The damned hypocrisy of

[1] Lawrence Riley's *Personal Appearance* opened in New York on 17 October 1934, and ran for 501 performances.

these gutties! And looking at the list of London Theatres, today, Feb. 14th, 1938, I find that, in my opinion, there are but two plays worth seeing, one by a dead Russian called Tchehov,[2] & the other by a living American named Eugene O'Neill.[3] With these are two by Priestley, called "Time & the Conways," [4] & "We've Been Here Before," [5] that the English Critics call great ones, but I can't see any greatness peeping out of Priestley's Plays. What's more, I don't believe Brown has even heard of "Daughters of Atreus," [6] so one of the best has passed him by, & how then can he speak of the value of America's Theatre? I wish I had your calm spirit. I am calmer since I met & talked to you, & more patient. But these bastards make me mad. I still believe that the American Theatre has the firmest shape of finer things in the drama. This belief can't be bias because of what you and America did for "Within The Gates" [7]—you see, I've examined my conscience. If I followed the bias of my heart, I would proclaim Russia to be the Leader, for she is a Communist Country, & I am a Communist. But America holds—as we Irish say—the Branch (of palm).

I am more than sorry to read in your book that "Anderson is ferociously out to wrench O'Neill's present standing as the foremost American dramatist away from him." This is a great pity, & will do Anderson no good. It seems to be envy—not of the right sort—& it will do Anderson harm. No-one can pull O'Neill down from where he stands. He is a great Dramatist, & there is no more to be said—except to thank God for him. (By the way, between ourselves, the wife some weeks ago got a letter from Lillian [Gish] saying that, if I still wanted to come, all arrangements had been made to bring us all to the U.S.A. Maxwell Anderson had left his house for another, & the house he left was at my disposal. It was very near to the one he now lives in. A "Rich Man" was to pay our passage out. Arrangements had been made by Maxwell for the education of our children, & a hearty call was given for us to come, Maxwell saying how glad he'd be to have me near him. (He mightn't be so glad when he got to know me!) The wife wrote to Lillian, saying I was at work on a play, & wouldn't think of stirring till it had been finished. I have to write to Lillian myself about the proposal yet, and will have to try to find suitable words for refusing the very, very generous offer. It would be impossible to accept; but it seems strange that Maxwell should

[2] Michel Saint-Denis's production of *The Three Sisters*.

[3] *Mourning Becomes Electra*. See O'Casey's letter to Nathan, 28 December 1937, note 1.

[4] J. B. Priestley's *Time and the Conways* opened in London on 26 August 1937, and ran for 225 performances.

[5] J. B. Priestley's *I Have Been Here Before* opened in London on 22 September 1937, and ran for 210 performances.

[6] See O'Casey's letter to Peter Newmark, 28 April 1936, note 1.

[7] Nathan had worked behind the scenes to arrange for the American production of *Within the Gates*. See O'Casey's letters to Nathan from 7 October 1933 to the New York opening on 22 October 1934.

want one whom he doesn't know to live beside him. It's a dangerous thing to do.

About the new Irish plays that have come to us, especially Miss Deavy's "Katie Roche," [8] the idea of which is "hard to put down on paper," vide Charles Morgan, I have a word to say, & an idea to let loose. This peculiarity is due, I think (softly) to the fear of dealing openly when dealing at all with the strange ways of a man with a maid. I've noticed this appearing (or disappearing) in novels as well as plays. You see Katie Roche is never allowed to do "Anything evil." So in "Autumn Fire" [9] (& all Murray's plays) the young girl who marries the old man, & then falls in love with his son, goes no farther than a chaste kiss. In a novel written by Lynn Doyle (I think) a farmer fiddler likes his fiddle better than farm or wife, & loves a pretty maid, tho, who "understands him." He & the maid eventually leave the farm, & go wandering with the fiddle, but, the Reviewers are at pains to point out, everything is perfectly innocent between the two people. So we find the same chaste caution in the latest novel "This Was My House" by F. MacManus.[10] The men & women go to the edge, but never even look over it. It isn't necessary that the jump should be always made, but it is ridiculous to imagine that it can never happen. That is, roughly, my idea of the curious vagueness found in a lot of recent Irish writing. You meet the same kind of caution in "Call It a Day." [11]

I'm glad "Night Must Fall" was such a failure in America.[12] It strengthens my belief in the goodness of Broadway. And "Black Limelight" is still going strong here! [13]

I'm still doing a little to the new play. And also carrying on biographical sketches to make a book. One appeared in "The American Spectator"—"A Protestant Kid Thinks of the Reformation." [14] I've done nine or ten of them, & if I can get the play & this volume done by the end of the year, I'll expect George Jean (if they be well done) to say bravo!

With Sincere Affection
Sean

[8] Teresa Deevy's *Katie Roche* opened at the Abbey Theatre on 16 March 1936.

[9] T. C. Murray's *Autumn Fire* opened at the Abbey Theatre on 8 September 1924.

[10] For O'Casey's comments on Francis MacManus's *This House Was Mine* (Dublin, Talbot Press, 1937), see his letter to Gabriel Fallon, 11 September 1938.

[11] C. L. Anthony's *Call It a Day* opened in London on 30 October 1935, and ran for 509 performances. (C. L. Anthony is the pseudonym of Dodie Smith.)

[12] Emlyn Williams's *Night Must Fall* opened in New York on 28 September 1936, and ran for 64 performances. The London production opened on 31 May 1935, and ran for 435 performances. For O'Casey's attack on the London production, see his letter to Dorothy N. Cheetham, 20 June 1936, note 2.

[13] See O'Casey's letter to Nathan, 25 May 1937, note 3.

[14] See O'Casey's letter to Nathan, 8 March 1937, note 1.

To Time and Tide

5 MARCH 1938

"Sigma's 'Notes On The Way' "

Sir,—In his "Notes on the Way" in your issue of February 26th, Sigma blows Satan about with his breath, finding himself breathless when he finds Satan everywhere he looks and everywhere he turns. Then he has a spell trying to poke transcendent Truth (with a capital capital Tee) and love of country out of their coffins. Let us listen to a few things he says, and then slap in a few questions quick.

Will Sigma tell us where are the geniuses who "are doomed to wither in isolation because they refuse to prostrate themselves before the mob"? And where are those who have, and have got the mob panting after them? How does Sigma know that "new and more frightful inequalities are being established in the name of equality?" Has Sigma got information? Have greater inequalities been established in Ireland (after a bloody fight —love of country, if not transcendent Truth) by the winning of semi-independence? By the new powers conferred on India? Or, his pet horror, the dictatorship of the proletariat—or that of the "despot Stalin," if he likes —in Russia? To whom is Christianity "the religion of religions"? To the Mohammedans or the Buddhists? Or only to the Christians themselves? If Sigma only opens Sigma's eyes a little wider, Sigma will see many kids knocking about who are nearly as bad (and no war on) as were the kids in Germany during and after the war, for inadequate food, clothing and shelter may lead to anything, and does lead to every physical evil. And Sigma will find these kind of kids outside the distressed areas, too.

He makes, in brackets, a sneering reference to the workers, implying that Communism looks upon the worker as a "godlike being." Where did he hear this about Communism? He may find this in AE's poetry, but not in the teaching of Communism. Now Sigma is, apparently, a Christian, and Sigma ought to know (or else keep his mouth shut) that it is Christianity that makes this claim, and not Communism. Man is the image and glory of God—that isn't our Karl Marx or Lenin, Sigma, but your St. Paul. And doesn't the worker become, after baptism, a member of Christ, a child of God, and an Inheritor of the Kingdom of Heaven? Learn this, sweet Christian Sigma, and cease to jeer at the worker. There is something godlike in these privileges, isn't there? One thing is certain—the worker has one godlike (devilish, in my opinion) quality, the quality of patience, and woe to him for having it!

Sigma says that "the wrongdoing of an English policeman (is he a godlike being?) in Shanghai is worth a hundred executions in Spain or Russia." Well, in Russia it is the Russians who execute Russians, and (as Shaw said in another case) who has a better right to cut a Russian's throat than another Russian? And what's the English policeman doing in Shanghai? Wouldn't it be funny to see a Chinese policeman ordering the English about in Piccadilly? Love of country would start beating in Sigma's breast then. The English policeman has as much right in Shanghai as a Black and Tan has in the City of Cork. Sigma says that Communists and National Socialists hunt in packs. There's no other way to hunt. So do the Conservatives, and so do Sigma's broadminded Christian Liberals hunt in packs as big as they can gather together.

What is Transcendent Truth and what is love of country? In England Maudie Mason's love of country led to a Cockney Durbar in the House of Commons, and in Ireland love of country brought the bullet and the hangman's rope. Before Sigma says anything more, Sigma should learn a little more about Communism, and a little more even about Christianity.

I am, etc.,
Sean O'Casey

London

To Daily Telegraph [1]

TC. O'CASEY

[15 MARCH 1938]

Moscow Confessions [2]

Dear Sir:

Mr. Muggeridge says, "if Mr. Graham knew anything at all about conditions in Russia, he would be aware that it is inconceivable for anyone suspected of heresy to hold the post of editor of *Pravda* as for a Presbyterian to become Pope." [3] Well, it is conceivable that a Presbyterian, or even a Calvinist, by conversion and ordination, might, one day succeed to or rather be elected to the supreme Pontificate of the Catholic Church;

[1] This letter was refused publication.

[2] This controversy was originally provoked by Malcolm Muggeridge's article, "Significance of the Soviet Trials," *Daily Telegraph,* 9 March 1938, based on the conclusion of the Moscow trials in early March when Bukharin, Zinoviev, Radek, and others were convicted of murder and treason and sentenced to death.

[3] A. C. Graham of Corpus Christi College, Oxford, attacked Muggeridge's views in a letter to the *Daily Telegraph,* 12 March; Muggeridge replied to Graham on 15 March, and O'Casey is here responding to and quoting from Muggeridge's reply.

might even be raised to the altars of that Church. It is also conceivable that a man, suspected of doctrinal heresy on the one hand, or political heresy on the other, might continue to be a teacher of a faculty in religion, or the editor of a political journal. Heresy isnt heresy to be condemned till it be judged to be heresy. Bishop Barnes, for instance, seems to hold views that are, according to the canons and doctrines of Anglicanism, heretical, yet he continues in the church, and, as far as I know, remains a Bishop. The Reverend Walter McDonald. D.D. had many books condemned by the authority of his Church, yet he continued in the position, till his death, of theologian on the staff of Maynooth and Dunboyne. Even Communism, even the Communism that simmers in the mind of Malcolm Muggeridge, cant be always and ever condemning mortals for a mistake or two. Besides, those recently on trial in Moscow, were tried, not for heresy, but for far and away worse crimes. Let us ask by what means Mr Muggeridge claims a fuller authority to speak about "conditions in Russia" than that of Mr Graham or any other intelligent man? Are the confessions to be set aside as not authentic because Mr. Muggeridge says so? I have looked up Mr. Muggeridge in a Who's Who book, and I find it recorded (probably by himself) that he was "correspondent in Moscow for the M[anchester] G[uardian] from 1932 to 1933," so I suppose there's no gainsaying anything he has to say about Russia. He must know all. But I've seen myself the results of this kind of knowledge expressed about "conditions in Ireland" by such correspondents after a hasty cup of tea in Dublin. So the opinion of any intelligent man in favour of the new life in Russia stands up as straight as the opinion of Mr. Muggeridge who hates it. Straighter, in fact, for what is the "authentic" judgment of Mr. Muggeridge worth? Not much, I'm afraid, judging, not by what others say, but according to what he says himself. For instance: Reviewing a book some time ago in *Time And Tide* about "conditions in Russia," he said, of the book, "It is sincere, and because it is sincere, it is authentic." Whatever, then, is said or written sincerely, must be authentic! No, Mr. Muggeridge's not a Daniel come to judgment.

Yours, etc,
Sean O'Casey

London, 15 March 1938

To Daily Telegraph [1]

TC. O'Casey

[? March 1938]

Dear Sir:

I have never met, nor have I ever clapped eyes on Mr Muggeridge, so my letter couldnt possibly be an attack on Mr Muggeridge. All the comments made were comments on statements issued publicly by Mr. Muggeridge. You say my letter was too long. Well, some time ago you published columns and columns in the *Daily Telegraph* about Haig's Horse. Surely the Soviet Union, even a "villainous" Soviet Union, is of more importance than Haig's Horse. By the suppression of my letter, you show a very safe and rather common desire for the "elucidation" of the question of the Moscow confessions. Your refusal to print my letter convinces me, at least, that you are afraid of argument, and that your Mr. Muggeridge—in spite of the fact, proclaimed by you, that he "lived in Moscow for some time, and is well acquainted with the work of those political leaders who have recently faced a State trial on charges of treason"—is a cock who cant or wont fight.

Sincerely Yours,
Sean O'Casey

[1] This letter was refused publication.

To Time and Tide

19 March 1938

Sigma's "Notes on the Way"

Sir,—Sigma hasn't given us the name of the "genuises who are doomed to isolation because they have refused to prostrate themselves before the mob," or the names of those who have, and are cheered by the mob; he hasnt told us of "the more frightful inequalities" established, for instance, in Ireland since semi-independence was secured, and native government has taken the place of the viceroys and the chief secretaries and their staffs; he hasn't explained transcendent Truth to us, poor people; nor to whom Christianity is "the religion of religions." He just shouted these things to all men, and then ran away to get busy establishing his own peculiar church (something new, at last, under the sun), turning it outside in to make it "a challenge," and keeping it well away from *real* life.

It is to challenge real life, and at the same time have nothing to do with it. And it wasn't Christianity (that is but a name), but Jesus that descended from eternity into time. Sigma doesn't like facts, and this Advent is the central fact, material fact, of Christianity—and the Word was made flesh, and dwelt among us. And this miracle of the Word made flesh did away with all—not some—of the condemnation of the Fall which he is insistent about—as in Adam all die: even so in Christ shall all be made alive. And when a church becomes secular or modern, it still remains a church. It is for Christ, and not for Sigma, to remove the candlesticks. I'm afraid Sigma's transcendent Truth, even his transcendent Christian Truth, won't do.

Permit me to say a word in the ear of Pride of the Fancy, gay and free: There is a big difference between the attitude to oppression in the Soviet Republic and the oppression in the British Empire. If the "oppression" in Russia was given a vote, an almost unanimous vote in favour would be given to it. It is being given now, even before it is asked for. Had a vote been taken in Ireland during the British oppression, it would have received universal condemnation. The Sinn Fein elections rejected England's policy, the entire nation would have cursed her executions. These are facts, and have nothing to do with transcendent Truths. I never said that England should disarm (I hold it would be good for all nations to do so, but that's another question), and that statement by Pride of the Fancy is misrepresentation. I never said or hinted that the "godlike worker was as much Sigma's idol as his own"; that, too, is misrepresentation. On the contrary, I asked Sigma what Communist declaration of creed or policy claimed godlike qualities for the worker. I pointed out that the claim was made, not by the Communists, but by the Christians. Evidently, Pride of the Fancy knows as much about Christianity as does Sigma. According to Christianity, the "Marxian worker" and the "Christian man" *are* the same being. And Sigma didn't qualify the word "worker" with the word "Marxian"—that is Pride of the Fancy's addition; but even the "Marxian worker" and the "Christian man" *are* the same being.

In a recent issue (still dealing with Christianity) Margery Allingham reviewed Mr. Hilton's novel, called *That State of Life*.[1] Margery Allingham says of a character in the novel, "Mrs. Ritchie married a trifle beneath her, and in her old age her considered view was that (quotation from novel) 'the way of peace and of true liberty is sticking to that state of life to which it has pleased God to call you.' " The novel has apparently been built from this "quotation" taken from the Catechism of the English and Irish Episcopalian Churches. There is no such command in the Catechism: it is "And to do your duty in that state of life into which it *shall* please God to call you." The "quotation" usually given is very nice as an induce-

[1] Margery Allingham's review of Hilton Brown's *That State of Life* (London, Geoffrey Bles, 1938), in *Time and Tide*, 5 March 1938.

ment to the poor to remain pat in their misery unto which "it *has* pleased God to call them," but it doesn't run that way, and so it won't work, even for learned Christians like those who see or do not see godlike qualities in the workers.

I am, etc.,
Sean O'Cosey

To George Jean Nathan

MS. CORNELL

49 OVERSTRAND MANSIONS
27 MARCH 1938

My dear George:

So. I thought as much. I was afraid, before I got your letter that you knew, & had a little sympathy with Maxwell Anderson's idea. I'm very glad you haven't. Under no circumstance could I have fallen for the offer. It would be a mad mad thing to turn one's life (and family) upside down in order to live rent free with someone unknown & unmet. I'm so glad you didn't like the idea. It would have been as bad, very probably, for poor Anderson as for me. I wouldn't be, altogether, an angel in his house. I'm glad he didn't write to me personally about it. So I escaped a very awkward letter. Eileen answered Lillian's, & I was to follow on with another letter; but I think I'll let the whole thing drop now.

Lately, Agate, supporting his contention that "French Without Tears" isn't much of a play (which it isn't), quoted your opinion of it appearing in "Morning After the First Night." That is good, but it isn't enough. I wish a book of your criticisms could be published here—not for your sake, but for ours. You have plunged your probe into the centre of Priestley's conceit—his passion for profundity. I understand he's writing a play now about what happens after death. I'm afraid the pure English have very little sense of humour. Priestley's mad to be a great thinker. You settled Coward's standing once for all in your criticism of him in the same book. I wish I could have written that way in "The Flying Wasp." I am altogether too vehement to be a good critic. I can't keep calm. You gave Coward a grand little pose on his little pedestal. However, I think "The Wasp" did some good. Agate's attack on "French Without Tears" was his bravest for a long time. And he has rebuked Coward for his "operetti." I enclose an article by [St. John] Ervine from this weeks "Observer." I can't understand Ervine. He is always, it seems to me, contradicting himself. And how he could say that one "Ah, Wilderness!" was worth a dozen "Mourning Becomes Electras" I don't know. And yet he loves the Theatre.

I thought he (would) "go" for me over the "Wasp," but he hasn't mentioned it, though I thought I'd draw him out by the article about him in the book, but he didn't bite. I talked to Ivor Brown at a cocktail party—first, & last, since I came back from America—, & he was sore about the Theatre in America. Perhaps, the failure of "Time & the Conways" (his wife produced it) had something to do with it, for we're all human. He said he couldn't understand how "Nathan could be so profound, & then occasionally so ridiculous in his criticism." I asked him, bluntly, to tell me where Nathan had written ridiculously? I've been reading Nathan, now, (said I), for 15 years, & I've never found him ridiculous; & I read close, as some of you critics know. Hardly a week goes by, but I read him, new books, & books written years ago, and never yet have I found him contradicting himself—over years, mind you; while you boys are contradicting yourselves more than once a week. He went into silence, & manoeuvred (had to look up this) out of range. That's the worst of our critics—they won't stand up to an attack; they just sidle off, & go into a rest camp. I enclose Brown's criticisms of this week. You may be interested in what he says about "Idiot's Delight." But aren't they written dull! I think I'll have to give up getting "The Observer"—this sedateness is maddening.

I've just read "Winterset" again, & this fine play makes me sad to think of the author's envy of O'Neill. His envy won't do O'Neill any harm, but it is bound to injure Anderson. Let's hope he'll get over this foolishness before long.

My Love.
Yours as Ever,
Sean

To Forward [1]

16 April 1938

SEAN O'CASEY DEFENDS "THE SWORD OF THE SOVIET" [2]

Sean O'Casey, the Irish poet and playwright, sends us the following reply to Emrys Hughes:—

[1] *Forward,* a socialist weekly newspaper published in Glasgow, edited by Emrys Hughes.

[2] When the *Daily Telegraph* refused to publish his 15 March letter of reply to Malcolm Muggeridge, O'Casey expanded his remarks into an article, "The Sword of the Soviet," and had it published in the *Daily Worker,* 25 March 1938. Emrys Hughes replied to O'Casey in "'The Sword of the Soviet': An Open Letter to Sean O'Casey," *Forward,* 2 April 1938.

LONDON, 1938

If I were Emrys Hughes, I shouldn't think too much about the Archbishop of Canterbury—it's bad for him. When he sees a similarity between me and the Archbishop, it's no wonder he sees nothing in the confessions of those recently tried in Moscow.

The title "Sword of the Soviet" was chosen merely because of its vowel sounds and alliteration, a bad habit acquired by me in playwriting.

The article was written spontaneously in reply to an article written by Mr. Malcolm Muggeridge, printed by the "Daily Telegraph". The "Daily Worker" hadn't asked for it, they knew nothing about it, till they received it in the ordinary way. There was no use in sending it to the "Daily Telegraph"—that paper wouldn't publish even a letter of mine replying to points raised by Mr. Muggeridge.

Mr. Muggeridge has sung dumb about the article, and is evidently a cock that won't fight. And Emrys Hughes is a cock that fights badly.

First by bringing in the Archbishop. Then by an unworthy attack on the "Daily Worker". I chose the "Worker"; the "Worker" didn't choose me. Perhaps this confession will be attributed to Tibetan drugs or torture, or some of the abracadabra conjured up to explain the confessions given in Moscow. Emrys Hughes says, "Outside official Communist parties throughout the world there are now precious few people with as much child-like faith as you." Few or many doesn't alter one jot or tittle of the points made in my article.

This sort of argument shows the weakness of Emrys Hughes' case. Emrys Hughes says, "Judging from your article you are a sentimental and emotional Communist." He has gone now to a column and a half, and he hasn't yet touched on one point in my article—bar the title. Nothing easier for me than to retort, "you are a sentimental and emotional Trotskyist," but where does that sort of stuff bring us?

Emrys Hughes asks, "What has Ireland and Parnell got to do with the Moscow business?" There is more similarity between Parnell, Ireland, and "the Moscow business" than there is between me and the Archbishop of Canterbury. The successful betrayal and hounding to death of Parnell brought about the temporary ruin of Ireland, and still leaves the curse of partition hanging round our neck, just as the successful betrayal of Stalin would have brought about the partition of the Soviet Union and the ruin of Socialism there. Parnell hadn't the power to save himself because the most of the people were against him, and so Ireland suffered; Stalin had the power, because the most of the people were with him, and so Socialism was saved.

I hope this is plain to Emrys Hughes.

Emrys Hughes calls Mr. De Valera a revolutionary. Mr. De Valera "emerged as the Leader of the Irish State," not as a revolutionary but as a constitutionalist. He and his party accepted the constitutional formulas, entered the Dail, constitutionally abolished the oath, the Governor-generalship, and constitutionally created a new constitution which is as revolutionary as the articles of the Church of England. He is an able man, and has many fine qualities, but he is not a revolutionary.

My article was a reply to an article written by Mr. Muggeridge, and not to the various great authorities mentioned by Emrys Hughes. And, up to the present, as far as Mr. Muggeridge is concerned, my article, if not unanswerable, is unanswered. I'm sure that in "Le Populaire" denial after denial has appeared from people with whom the prisoners confessed to have plotted in places where these people have never been.

We have heard of these denials before.

Emrys Hughes has a child-like mind, if he thinks these people would acknowledge their plotting. Time and again, Chamberlain denies all knowledge of Italian intervention in Spain. Innocent Mr. Chamberlain. Emrys Hughes says, "if you hadn't swallowed all the dope, you wouldn't have figured so prominently in the 'Daily Worker'."

Now the points made by me in support of the theory of Trotsky's envy of Lenin and Stalin were taken, not from the pages of any journal or book sympathetic to the Labour cause, not even from "Forward", but from a book, "The Russian Revolution," written by W. H. Chamberlin, a man antagonistic to the aims and objects of Socialism in general and to the Soviet Union in particular. The publishers (Macmillan & Co.) tell us that Mr. Chamberlin took twelve years to write the book, most of which were spent in Russia; it was published in 1935, so that it was begun in 1923, a year before Lenin died, and six years before Trotsky's deportation from Russia. In volume one there is a full-page picture of Lenin, and in volume two, a full-page picture of Stalin, which seems to be of some significance. I had often heard that Trotsky had organised the Red Cavalry, but, strangely enough, in this book there is a photo of the review of the first Red Cavalry in 1919, and the force is being reviewed not by Trotsky, but by Stalin.

The alliance of Stalin and Lenin prior to and after 1917, declared to be a myth by Emrys Hughes, is pretty well indicated, just as Trotsky's opposition to Lenin and Stalin is indicated too, and by one who must have known what he was writing about. In "Everyman's Encyclopaedia," Emrys will find it stated that "To Lenin Trotsky seemed too moderate; their association ceased in 1903."

Emrys Hughes alleges torture to have extorted confession from the accused men. "Prisoners confess anything after being in the jails of the O.G.P.U.". (He knows all about it.)

"If they cannot be prevailed upon to confess they are shot without public trial. I wonder if you would hold out if you were in the clutches of the O.G.P.U. Or would you not confess if only to be shot and end the misery of it all?" Emrys is sadly confused here.

There was no evidence of torture. There wasn't even a black eye among the lot of them. The O.G.P.U. evidently couldn't hold a candle to the Black And Tans. Emrys Hughes assumes they confessed to get a public trial; but what was the use of a public trial, when the result was only a much more elaborate confession than that said to be given in order to secure a public trial?

You see where your confusion is leading you?

Did they confess in order to be shot and put out of their misery; or confess to get a public trial in order to confess and be shot and put out of their misery?

And Emrys Hughes says I have swallowed a lot of dope!

As to the personal question, I can't say "yes" or "no" to it. I can only say what I believe: I believe that I wouldn't stick much; but because there is weakness and cowardice in me, it doesn't follow that there isn't fortitude and courage in others.

I have given past and present examples in my article in the "Worker", and Emrys Hughes daren't deny them.

They are neither sentimental nor romantic, but simply facts.

Finally Emrys Hughes and his friends ought to get together in a conference, and decide, once for all, what induced the confessions in Moscow. Whether they were due to Tibetan drugs, hypnotism, torture—as alleged by Mr. Hughes—or ritual ecstasy as alleged by Mr. Muggeridge. Some of us can swallow a lot, but few of us can swallow all these things. I'm afraid Trotsky is as bad as he is painted, though from what has been said and written, I shouldn't be at all surprised if some people shortly began to refer to him as "a gallant Christian gentleman."

Sincerely yours,
Sean O'Casey

To Harold Macmillan

MS. MACMILLAN LONDON

49 OVERSTRAND MANSIONS
28 APRIL 1938

Dear Mr. Harold Macmillan,

Thank you for your letter asking me about "the book," but mercifully leaving out the bell and the candle. I'm hard at work on it [1] and expect to be able to let you have a look at the first batch of sketches soon.

[1] Here he drew a picture of himself writing.

I hope you and your family are well, & that Mr. Maurice [2] has started in as a publisher.

Sincerely Yours
Sean O'Casey

[2] Maurice Victor, Macmillan's seventeen-year-old son.

To Forward

30 April 1938

SWORD OF THE SOVIET [1]

London
20 April 1938

SIR,—Emrys Hughes and I cannot agree and, I'm afraid, could never agree, so a continuation of the discussion would be a waste of time for him and me.

But perhaps I may set down a few further explanatory, non-argumentative sentences, and then cry finis—as far as I am concerned.

I submit that the place for Mr. Muggeridge to reply is, not the "Worker," but the "Daily Telegraph." The "Worker's" power and space is limited, and it has its work cut out to fight for the workers. To open its columns to those who are against the workers would be, in my opinion, foolish. With all respect, I think that "Forward" is foolish in doing this.

I wonder what Emrys Hughes means by a "Donnybrook Fair"? I have lived most of my life in Ireland and have never seen one.

I do not read the Russian papers simply because I do not know the Russian language—I wish I did. If Emrys Hughes means the papers dealing with Russia, and published in the English language, well, that's a different thing. I know something about the Russian Constitution, but that did not enter into the dispute. I have not laughed at the executed Russians. It is a great tragedy that such men should have done such things. But I claim the liberty to have a laugh at the ridiculous things said by Mr. Muggeridge in the "Daily Telegraph" and, possibly, at some of the things said by Mr. Emrys Hughes.

Sincerely yours,
Sean O'Casey

[1] Emrys Hughes had replied to O'Casey in "O'Casey and His Sword," *Forward*, 16 April 1938.

[Sean O'Casey's grievance against the "Daily Telegraph" is that it wouldn't publish his reply to Muggeridge, who therefore was "a cock who wouldn't fight."

But if O'Casey were the editor of the "Daily Worker" (it would be much more readable and livelier if he were) he wouldn't let Muggeridge reply either.

We open our columns to all-comers, from Sean O'Casey to the Earl of Glasgow, because we believe it is the more honest method to let our critics have their fling and then answer them. If we adopted the "Daily Worker" attitude, O'Casey wouldn't have had his laugh.

As for the "Donnybrook Fair" (that is O'Casey's last desperate effort to divert the controversy to Ireland), I do not wish him to disappear with a grievance; I apologise to Ireland.—E.H.]

From Malcolm Muggeridge to Forward

30 April 1938

O'CASEY CHALLENGED TO DEBATE

Reply from "A Cock that Won't Fight"

We have received the following from Mr. Malcolm Muggeridge whose article on the Russian Trials in the "Daily Telegraph" has been recently criticised by Mr. Sean O'Casey in the "Daily Worker" and in "Forward."

[Editor, "Forward".]

To the Editor of "Forward"

Whatlington
23 April 1938

Sir,—My attention has been drawn to some correspondence published in your columns relating to an attack by Mr. Sean O'Casey in the "Daily Worker" on an article of mine, published in the "Daily Telegraph," dealing with the recent Moscow trial.

When I first saw this article I considered whether or not to reply to it, and decided not to. The article is so confused and incoherent that it did not seem to me worth a reply; and in any case, since I knew that the "Daily Worker" was bound in all circumstances to approve of the actions of the Soviet Government, whatever they might be, any views it might publish about the Moscow trials, or about remarks of mine on them, had as little significance, as far as I was concerned, as views published in the "Angriff" about the burning of the Reichstag.

Since, however, Mr. O'Casey has now accused me of being "a cock that won't fight," I felt bound to send the enclosed letter to the "Daily

Worker," and, as the matter has been given some prominence in your columns, I should be grateful if you would publish it, too.

I should like, also, to take this opportunity of stating publicly that I am ready at any time and in any place to debate with Mr. O'Casey, or by any other means provide an opportunity for his and my attitude towards the Soviet regime to be put before others with a view to their deciding which of us has the better case.

Yours etc.,
Malcolm Muggeridge

LETTER SENT TO "DAILY WORKER"

Sir,—In your issue of March 25 you published an article by Mr. Sean O'Casey attacking an article of mine, published in the "Daily Telegraph," which dealt with the recent Moscow trial. I did not reply at the time because it seemed to me not to be worth it, nor should I have expected you necessarily to publish my reply if I had sent one. Now, however, Mr. O'Casey has accused me in "Forward" of being, among other things, "a cock that won't fight," and has suggested that I have not hitherto replied to him because I could not. This makes a reply necessary and, in view of Mr. O'Casey's insinuations, I assume that you will give it the same prominence you gave Mr. O'Casey's article.

The following, as far as I can unravel them, are the main points (apart from personal abuse) which Mr. O'Casey makes:—

(a) If, as I wrote, no one really believes in the validity of the Moscow trials, why should I have bothered to disprove them?

If Mr. O'Casey will read my article he will see that I did not bother to disprove them.

I assumed that no one capable of forming a reasoned judgment would suppose that the Russian Revolution was brought about and the Soviet regime established by three honest men whose associates were all in the pay of foreign powers concerned to destroy the regime which they had been at such pains to establish.

What I tried to do was to explain why the trials happened. That is important because of its bearing on the whole character of the Soviet regime.

(b) My contention that it is absurd to suppose members of the Soviet Government would plot to bring about their own downfall is false because (i) Padriac Pearse "plotted against English power in Ireland," and therefore "plotted his own downfall"; and (ii) Parnell's followers, in plotting against him, were "plotting their own downfall."

There is no parallel in either case. Padriac Pearse was not in the English Cabinet; and Parnell's followers openly rejected him as their leader and did not plot against him in alliance with England.

If they had been in the pay of the Conservative Party, and had engineered Parnell's affair with Mrs. O'Shea and as part of the bargain had agreed to the extirpation of the Catholic faith in Ireland, and total destruction of all opposition to British rule there; and then had confessed to all this with slobbering repentance after months of imprisonment, without a shred of documentary evidence being produced, and with every externally verifiable detail of their confessions being proved false—then their case might be compared with that of Radek, Bukharin, Zinoviev and the others.

(c) Servetus's death took place in the Middle Ages, and therefore no one knows anything about it.

Servetus's death did not take place in the Middle Ages, and his trial is one of the best documented and also one of the most famous trials in history. My authority for the statement that Servetus was reduced, on the night before he was burnt at the stake for heresy, to begging Calvin's pardon, is Professor James Mackinnon's "Calvin and the Reformation," published last year.

(d) Because there have been cases of men subjected to imprisonment, intensive cross-examination and even torture without being thereby induced to make confessions, it follows that when confessions are made in similar circumstances they may be assumed to be true.

I do not dispute that there have been in the past brave men who have endured suffering without breaking, but the Russian revolutionaries who have been put on trial are not among them. There is no parallel between, for instance, a martyr dying rather than recant his faith and a gangster pouring out inconceivable confessions in the hope of saving his skin. Because the martyr could not be induced to confess himself a villain it does not follow that the gangster's confession is to be believed.

(e) I "hold that the Russians are a mystic people," whereas in fact they are not.

I do not hold, and have nowhere stated that the Russians are a mystic people.

(f) I should read William Henry Chamberlin's "The Russian Revolution" and from it learn of "the opposition to and envy of Lenin and Stalin by Trotsky" which was "evident before even the Revolution of 1917 began."

I have read and reviewed at some length William Henry Chamberlin's "The Russian Revolution." I have also read what Stalin wrote about Trotsky in "Pravda" in the issue of November 6, 1918:—

> "The whole task involved in the practical organisation of the rising was conducted under the immediate leadership of the chairman of the Petrograd Soviet, Comrade Trotsky. That the garrison passed over so rapidly to the side of the Soviets and that the work of the revolutionary soldiers' committee was so audacious is something the Party owes principally and above all to Comrade Trotsky."

(g) Since Gorki "planned a trilogy of plays" in 1927, and wrote two of them, one being produced in 1932 and the other in 1934, my description of him as in his later years "senile, decrepit and bewildered," is absurd.

Opinions about Gorki's later work differ. I have a low opinion of it, and the impression he made on me when I saw him in Moscow in 1932 was of decrepitude, senility and bewilderment.

The main drift of Mr. O'Casey's article, in so far as it has one, is that I basely and maliciously cast doubts on the impartiality of Soviet justice, whereas Mr. O'Casey knows that all these trials which have taken place are fairly conducted, all these confessions freely made and true in every particular, and all these executions amply deserved.

Mr. O'Casey is so fine a dramatist that I cannot help being surprised at such folly in him. He, an Irishman, with a vigorous independent mind, not to be brow-beaten by authority in any guise—he, of all people, comes forward and insists on the validity of a series of charges, so fantastic that if they were made in a British or German, still more an Irish court, he would be the first to laugh them to scorn; insists that confessions often containing obvious absurdities (as at the Ramzin Trial, when interviews were confessed to with men dead at the time the interviews were supposed to have taken place), unsupported by documentary or other evidence, are to be implicitly believed; that Yagoda, in his capacity as head of the G.P.U., was discovering traitors at the same time as, in his capacity as a German-Japanese spy, he was being one; that . . . . But why go on?

The Dean of Canterbury, Professor Laski, the Duchess of Atholl, Sir Bernard Pares, the Webbs—these I can understand; but the author of "Juno and the Paycock"—I admit I was surprised.

Yours etc.,
Malcolm Muggeridge

To Time and Tide

7 May 1938

THE RUSSIAN TRIALS

Sir,—Permit me, at the risk of becoming a nuisance, to agree with H. Walsh [1] over your curious and constant attacks (rather sly, some of them) on the Soviet Union. The acceptance (or rejection) of the Soviet Power is surely something more than a question of "taste".

[1] Letter to *Time and Tide,* 30 April 1938.

Editorially, the recent trial is declared to be "fraudulent", and a "horrible farce." That is certainly a positive statement to make. We seek the truth. Will TIME AND TIDE tell us how and where and when the Journal became privileged to know the facts proving the trial to be fraudulent and a horrible farce? For a start, the statement that "Stalin has exterminated all those who were of importance in the revolution" isn't true.

I am, etc.,

London *Sean O'Casey*

[We base our statements on material to which Mr. O'Casey has the same right of access as ourselves, on the official reports of the trials. He seems to have drawn different conclusions. It would appear that we must agree to differ.—Editor, TIME AND TIDE]

To Forward

14 May 1938

SUPPRESSED BY THE "DAILY WORKER"

London
May 1938

SIR,—Mr. Muggeridge has no reason to be alarmed at the simile of the cock. This bird is, I believe, the symbol of France, he shook up St. Peter into shame, and Shakespeare calls him, "the trumpet to the morn," so Mr. Muggeridge need not let his spirit be troubled, for even the cock that fights and runs away, will live to fight another day.

But for once I find myself in happy and enthusiastic agreement with Mr. Muggeridge when he says that when I "conduct controversies I should be well advised to choose for his purpose some other organ than the 'Daily Worker.' "

The article of mine that did in Mr. Muggeridge's article should have appeared, not in the "Daily Worker," but in the "Daily Telegraph." But the "Daily Telegraph" so far from allowing an article from me in reply to Mr. Muggeridge's, refused to publish a short letter slashing at a few points raised by Mr. Muggeridge. Mr. Muggeridge, hairy enough, keeps a dead silence about this, though he knows it well. It is easy enough to "raise the neck and clap the wing, red cock, and crow" [1] in front of the "Daily Worker," dependent on the shillings, sixpences, and pennies of the

[1] See the Musician's song in W. B. Yeats's *Dreaming of the Bones* (1919).

militant workers; but not quite so easy to do the same thing in front of the elegant and opulent "Daily Telegraph and Morning Post." Why doesn't Mr. Muggeridge condemn this big journal for suppressing, in the first instance, my letter in reply to his, when he condemns the "Daily Worker," in the second instance, for suppressing his letter in reply to mine? Like Gorki, I am a little bewildered about this.

I promise I shall be "chary" about talking of cocks again when replying to Mr. Muggeridge. Between him and me, I'm frightened, and am worn out making acts of contrition since he raised his clenched fist at me; but, all the same, sometime and somewhere, there remains something more to be written about the things said by Mr. Muggeridge in his article and letters on the recent Soviet Trials.

Yours, etc.
Sean O'Casey

From Malcolm Muggeridge to Time and Tide

14 May 1938

"Press Censorship?"

SIR,—The following episode may interest your readers. Last month I contributed an article to the *Daily Telegraph* dealing with the recent Moscow trial. Subsequently, letters criticising this article were published in the same newspaper, but not, apparently, one from Mr. Sean O'Casey.

Mr. O'Casey thereupon contributed an article to the *Daily Worker* attacking me personally, and the views I had expressed in the *Daily Telegraph*. This article did not seem to me to be worth a reply. As it upheld the now so familiar official justification of Stalin's slaughter, one after the other, of his former associates, there seemed nothing to say about it except, perhaps, to express surprise that as fine a dramatist as Mr. O'Casey should be so credulous.

Mr. O'Casey then taunted me, in a letter published in *Forward*, with being a "cock that wouldn't fight," and boasted that my not answering his arguments proved them to be unanswerable. This made a reply necessary. I therefore sent one to the *Daily Worker*, but it was refused publication.

This, it seems to me, is yet another example of the utility of the French law which makes it obligatory for a newspaper, when it publishes a personal attack, to provide an equal amount of space for, and to give the same prominence to, the victim's reply. Especially is such a provision necessary when, as in the case of Mr. O'Casey, the attacker, not content with his immunity from a counter-attack, actually indulges in public boasts that the absence of one proclaims the invincibility of his arguments and the cowardice of his victim.

There has been plenty of, often justified, fulmination from the Left about the unfairness of the "Capitalist Press"; but it is important to realize that a newspaper like the *Daily Worker*, no doubt basing its practice on as it takes its views from, the Soviet Press, outdoes all others in its intolerance of criticism.

I am, etc.

Whatlington *Malcolm Muggeridge*

To Horace Reynolds

MS. REYNOLDS

49 OVERSTRAND MANSIONS
23 MAY 1938

My dear Horace:

Never mind trying to find a foster-father for the "Child of God".[1] I have written, now, 17 sketches on the same lines, & will be bringing them to Macmillans this week to scc if they (or some more) will make a book to be called, "First The Green Blade".[2] If you could let me have the MS back, I'd be glad—for when the copy goes to Macmillans, I'll not have a note of it left. Long ago, the MS of "Windfalls" was lost by Macmillans Reader, & I had to type the blasted lot all over again. But if it's any trouble to get the MS. dont bother.

I hope you'll have a big party, & a good time in Dublin during August. It should be very interesting to see the Abbey at its worst, or at its best. The Tour, I'm afraid, hasn't been a roaring success.

I wonder are you right about the "terrible impact" of "Child of God"? I hope you are. But the impact may be strengthened because you know me—a friend's often a bad critic.

I've been busy polishing up the biographical sketches, & have had no time to write to anyone; and now I'll be busier writing more of them; & the play—my God!

I hope Kay and the two youngsters are well. Ours are growing fast

[1] "A Child of God" became the fifteenth chapter of *I Knock at the Door* (1939).

[2] "First the Green Blade," tentative title of the first volume of the autobiography, became the second chapter of *I Knock at the Door.*

& furious—Jasus, where's the money goin to come from! Different to the time of "when me hat's on, me house is thatched".

However; eyes front; quick march & keep a steady step.

My love to All.
Yours As Ever.
Sean

To Time and Tide

28 May 1938

PRESS CENSORSHIP?

Sir,—I see Mr. Muggeridge complains in TIME AND TIDE that an article replying to an article of mine was suppressed by the *Daily Worker*; and that in my article replying to his that appeared in the *Daily Telegraph*, I "attacked the views he expressed, and attacked him personally." I have never clapped eyes on Mr. Muggeridge, to my knowledge; I know nothing big or small about him; my knowledge of him is wholly based on what he writes in various journals. So how on earth could I possibly make a "personal attack" upon him? His article appeared in *Forward* (he doesn't say so), but an article of mine replying to his couldn't appear, because the controversy had already been closed. He seems to think that no one should have anything to say about the Soviet Trials of a different nature to what he says himself. He doesn't condemn the *Daily Telegraph* for suppressing a letter of mine dealing with a few points raised by him. Oh, no; the big, elegant, powerful *Daily Telegraph* is not to be blamed; but the little *Daily Worker* gets a slap in the kisser. Let him go, and hit his match, as we say in Ireland. I have never claimed, nor do I claim to be invincible in argument; but I reserve the right to think myself as infallible as Mr. Muggeridge. But I hope my arguments will be weightier than such as "There seemed nothing to say about it except to express surprise that as fine a dramatist as Mr. O'Casey should be so credulous." The fact of one being a dramatist, fine, or finicky, or fairy, had nothing to do with the matter. I suppose I have the right to contest, or laugh at, some of the things said by him, just as I (being an Irishman, and having felt it) laugh at Mr. Voigt kneeling in breathless adoration before the altar of Pax Britannica; or at Mr. Muggeridge's statement that "Hesketh Pearson manages to enjoy life without needing to merge himself in any collectivity." As if anyone at all could even live without merging himself in some sort or measure of "collectivity."

I am surprised that such a fine writer as Mr. Muggeridge should be so credulous.

I am, etc.
Sean O'Casey

London

From Idris Cox to Time and Tide

28 May 1938

"Press Censorship?"

SIR,—The letter published in the name of Mr. Malcolm Muggeridge in your issue of May 14th has been brought to my attention.

Mr. Muggeridge admits that the reply of Mr. Sean O'Casey to this letter in the *Daily Telegraph* was not published. In other words, the *Daily Telegraph* refused to give Mr. Sean O'Casey an opportunity to reply to Mr. Malcolm Muggeridge's assertions on the Moscow trial.

Mr. Sean O'Casey then asked the *Daily Worker* to publish this reply, and, in view of the press censorship exercised by the *Daily Telegraph*, it was agreed to publish his letter.

Some time afterwards Mr. Malcolm Muggeridge sent to the *Daily Worker* a reply to the article published by Mr. Sean O'Casey.

It is interesting to note that Mr. Muggeridge knew the *Daily Telegraph* had refused to publish Mr. O'Casey's letter. He does not complain of that. But knowing that Mr. O'Casey had not been given the right to reply to him in the *Daily Telegraph*, he expects the *Daily Worker* to give him the right to reply to Mr. Sean O'Casey.

This might be Mr. Muggeridge's view of the freedom of the press, but I am quite confident it is not the view of the *Daily Worker*.

I am, etc.
Idris Cox

Daily Worker
Nelson Place, E.C.1

From Malcolm Muggeridge to Time and Tide

4 JUNE 1938

"Press Censorship?"

SIR,—In their letters in your last issue Sean O'Casey and Idris Cox completely distort the circumstances of the *Daily Worker's* refusal to publish my reply to O'Casey.

This is what happened:—

(a) I contribute an article about the Moscow trials to the *Daily Telegraph.*

(b) O'Casey submits a letter to the *Daily Telegraph* criticizing this article. Two letters criticizing it with some severity are published in the *Daily Telegraph*, one on the leader-page, but O'Casey's letter is rejected.

(c) O'Casey thereupon contributes a long article to the *Daily Worker* criticizing my article, questioning my qualification to write it at all, and generally knocking me.

(d) I ignore this, and O'Casey, in *Forward*, calls me a "cock that won't fight" and boasts that his arguments are unanswerable.

(e) I then write to the *Daily Worker* pointing out that he has thus boasted publicly, and that I have no alternative but to reply. My reply is refused publication.

O'Casey and Idris Cox contend that this refusal to publish my reply was justified because the *Daily Telegraph* had rejected O'Casey's letter. The two cases are utterly dissimilar. As stated above, the *Daily Telegraph* published two letters criticizing my article. (Has the *Daily Worker* ever published a letter criticizing anything which appeared in it? I doubt it.) My article made no reference to O'Casey. If I had made in it the kind of personal references to him which he made in his article to me, I should certainly agree that he was entitled to be allowed to have his say. Still more should I agree he was entitled to have his say if I had called him a cock that wouldn't fight, and boasted that, since he had left my article unanswered, he obviously found its arguments unanswerable.

O'Casey, you know perfectly well that you have behaved badly. You know perfectly well that no newspaper can be expected to publish every letter which may be submitted criticizing articles which have appeared in its columns, and that every other newspaper in England except the *Daily Worker*, and perhaps the *Catholic Times*, would have allowed me to reply to an abusive article like yours about my *Daily Telegraph* article.

Even then, I did not try to reply. "I've had my say," I thought, "and he's had his. Leave it at that." All I got for my forbearance was an extra kick in the pants from you.

If you have decided to plump for Stalin and throw in your lot with his Comintern sycophants inside and outside the U.S.S.R., then cut out talk about fair play and the freedom of the press. That kind of cant I expect from Idris Cox, but not from you, who must know that if you went through a *Daily Worker* file, and through a file of every Soviet newspaper ever published, you would not find one single word criticizing the Soviet Government, its acts or policy or extant personnel.

I am, etc.

Whatlington, Sussex *Malcolm Muggeridge*

From Emrys Hughes to Time and Tide

4 JUNE 1938

"Press Censorship?"

SIR,—I do not wish to interfere in the controversy in your columns between Mr. Sean O'Casey and Mr. Malcolm Muggeridge. But I would like to point out that Mr. O'Casey does not explain exactly what happened as far as *Forward* is was concerned. We printed all the letters we received from Mr. O'Casey and from Mr. Muggeridge and Mr. O'Casey had the last word to the extent of three quarters of a column. The article by Mr. O'Casey was not suppressed "because the controversy had already been closed." It may be quite true that the *Daily Telegraph* suppressed Mr. O'Casey and the *Daily Worker* suppressed Mr. Muggeridge, but *Forward* published the views of both, including the letter by Mr. Muggeridge, which was suppressed by the *Daily Worker*. Mr. Sean O'Casey no doubt has a grievance against the *Telegraph* and Mr. Muggeridge a grievance against the *Worker*, but neither of them can have any grievance against *Forward*, which, like *Time and Tide*, allows the expression of many different points of view even when they disagree with its own.

I am, etc.

Forward *Emrys Hughes,*
26, Civic Street *Editor.*
Glasgow, C.4.

To Time and Tide

11 JUNE 1938

"Press Censorship?"

Sir—Last week or so Mr. Muggeridge said I claimed that my arguments were invincible; now he says that I have boasted they were unanswerable. This is what I said: "My article was a reply to an article written by Mr. Muggeridge, and not to the various authorities mentioned by Emrys Hughes. And, up to the present, as far as Mr. Muggeridge is concerned, my article, if not unanswerable, is unanswered." If Mr. Muggeridge reads a boast into that mere statement of fact, then either he or I know not the meaning of English. He says, "O'Casey knows perfectly well that no newspaper can be expected to publish letters critical of articles appearing in its columns." What I know or do not know is not the question: what I do know is that they refused to publish mine. That refusal of the *Daily Telegraph* was neither fair nor unfair: it was their policy. What is more, I knew they would refuse it. It is Mr Muggeridge, and not I, who has been bellowing out of him about "fair play". I simply oppose that policy of the great and powerful, without wasting time weeping over a knock or two. Of course I "knocked" him in my articles—that was what I set out to do. Did he want me to fall on his neck and kiss him? Now he wants to act the censor on my behaviour.

From the beginning of my life (judging myself from Mr. Muggeridge's standard) I have behaved badly, and I will do so till the end of it. But I dont boast, even about arguments. What have any of us got to boast about, in the name of God? He says, "In my article I did not mention Mr. O'Casey." I know he didn't. But how could he expect me to reply to an article without mentioning the writer of the article? Can't he understand that all replies of this nature must, of necessity, become personal? *Time And Tide*, last week, teemed with it in reply to statements made by Mr. Voigt. I have no comment whatever other than comments on statements made by Mr. Muggeridge written down for all to read.

These camouflage cries of "personal attacks", and "Abusive articles" are wearing a bit thin by now. He says, "Search every Soviet newspaper ever published, you will not find one single word criticising the Soviet Government, its acts, or policy, or extant personnel." This is the sort of statement common with Mr. Muggeridge. How does he know? Has he searched them all? I thought all along that he was complaining about the grim effectiveness of Soviet criticism. Mr. Muggeridge has an irritating habit of forgetting what he has written before. In his first article he says, "No-one beyond a few incorrigible friends of the Soviet Union, like the Dean of Canterbury, really believes in the validity of these trials." Then

I who do am one against millions (*Athanasius contra mundi*), so where does the sycophancy come in? If he has millions on his side, why grudge Stalin one or two foolish friends? I have always stood for the U.S.S.R. and I stand for her now, and for Stalin, too: and it will be a wise day for England when she lines up beside this great country.

All that Mr. Emrys Hughes says is true, and more. All I sent to *Forward* was published. My last article was not sent, so was not suppressed. All was published, followed by a cheque (unasked and unexpected) and a kind invitation to contribute an occasional article to *Forward*. I sent a letter to Emrys Hughes thanking him for his courtesy (long before the cheque came), and, with your permission, I thank him again, now. And you, too, Mr. Editor, for allowing this last letter on this dispute with Mr. Muggeridge to appear in *Time and Tide*.

I am, etc.,
Sean O'Casey

To Harold Macmillan

TS. MACMILLAN LONDON

49 OVERSTRAND MANSIONS
21 JUNE 1938

Dear Mr Harold Macmillan,

Many thanks for your letter. I'll do my best to add the 15,000 words wanted. I've already done two sketches—"The Tired Cow" and "The Street Sings," with another—"Vandhering Vindy Vendhor"—well on the way. A few more should make a volume.

I'm not satisfied with the title "The Green Blade"; and I am trying to think of another—"Father of the Man," or "Of Such is the Kingdom of Heaven"—too long?

'Studies' in Autobiography seems to have too much of a scholastic touch about it for me. I'll have to try to make the sub-title simpler.

I am doing a bit of broadcasting next Saturday—"The Playwright and the Box-Office";[1] but I'd rather be going ahead with the sketches.

I hope Lady Dorothy and all the Family are well.

Like everything else, punctuation is changing. I havent been indifferent to it. "Modern English Punctuation" [2] is never far from me. But

[1] "Playwright and Box Office," BBC broadcast of a discussion between Maurice Brown and Sean O'Casey, published in the *Listener*, 7 July 1938; reprinted in *Blasts and Benedictions* (1967).

[2] Reginald Skelton, *Modern English Punctuation* (London, Pitman, 1933).

in certain sketches, or part of sketches, I must allow the rhythm or lilt to flow free. Besides, I think the practice of handcuffing all dialogue between inverted commas an abominable one. I will, however, have another look through the chapters. I really have pondered over this a lot.

With All Good Wishes.

Sincerely Yours,
Sean O'Casey

To George Jean Nathan

MS. CORNELL

49 OVERSTRAND MANSIONS
28 JUNE 1938

My dear George:

I got your letter a moment ago. It gave me a bit of a shock. I could imagine you laid up with a cold; but I couldn't imagine & shouldn't care to imagine you as seriously ill. And to think you have been so isn't a pleasant thought. God be praised you're coming to yourself again. What was it that came on you? I wish I had known you were ill—at least I could have sent you a message of love. Are you trying to do too much? You know you do hammer away at that long desk of yours, with the three lights going overhead, for a long, long spell at a time. Try to take things a little easier. G.B.S. has been down for some weeks, too; but is now nearly himself again. Trying to do too much. And you must have more rest, & not wear yourself away too quick. My eyes compel me to rest often, & though I hate it, it's good for me, & keeps me, or helps to keep me from over doing it. Anyway, the least little things would prevent me from doing too much. Once again, God be thanked you are getting allright again.

The play is as it was when I last wrote to you. At present I'm writing four more chapters to make a volume to be published by Macmillans—they're waiting for it, and when this is done, then, with the help o' God—the play. Though things are so curious in the Theatre, I'm not over anxious to come into contact with it again. I dread the dumb look of reproach in so many eyes when a play's a financial failure; and I don't expect any play of mine to be a financial success. However, the new play, success or no, has got to be written; & maybe, more when that's done.

Lately I & the missus have been busy taking stock of things—kids' education, etc.; & we have decided to leave where we are for the country. Of this, more anon.

I enclose article by Agate admitting that the American Theatre is more alive than the English Theatre. He's getting on, though it took him some time to see it—a helluva time. Better late than too late, as we Irish say.

My love, dear George, & prayers that you will soon be your own self again.

Yours with all affection renewed.
Sean

To Horace Reynolds

MS. Reynolds

49 Overstrand Mansions
28 June 1938

My dear Horace:

Just a line to say that a volume of sketches (containing "Child of God") is to be published by Macmillan's as soon as I have written 3 more; so I cant let "The Yale Review", even if they want to, publish the sketch. So, if you can, tell Miss [Helen] McAfee that the story is now in the hands of Macmillans, & can't be published by any magazine.

I'm very sorry to give you all this trouble; but it is largely your own fault for being so kind as to try to place it for me. The things I write are a damn nuisance to most people, & invariably give a helluva lot of trouble before they appear in print or on the stage. I am now in the middle of writing the other "reveries", & so haven't time to bless meself.

I sympathise with the job of paying for music lessons, etc—we have had to cut out this fee for Brian—our money didn't cover it. Give my congratulations to John.

My love to Kay & Peggy, & many thanks to you for your kindness.

Yours As Ever.
Sean

To Harold Macmillan

MS. MACMILLAN LONDON

49 OVERSTRAND MANSIONS
20 JULY 1938

Dear Mr Harold Macmillan,

I've been thinking and thinking over your anxiety about punctuation. I'll have to see you about it. I'm no innovator—I wish I was—; this has been done years & years & years ago.

In some parts of the book, the usual method is impossible—it would murder the lilt of the sentences. In "Modern English Punctuation," the continued use of inverted commas for dialogue is questionable. And in the same book is an example of speech without any punctuation taken from—Punch! Perhaps, we could come to some compromise—there is, of course—a lot in what you say—; but in many parts of the book conventional punctuation's impossible.

I think I ought to wait till the whole thing's written before signing contract. Then you can see what you think of it, as a whole.

I hope you & yours are well.

Yours As Ever
Sean O'Casey

To Harold Macmillan

MS. MACMILLAN LONDON

49 OVERSTRAND MANSIONS
23 JULY 1938

Dear Mr. Harold Macmillan,

I've no plan; others are planning for me. At present we wait to see if the Devon Landlord will accept some modification in the agreement sent to us. If all goes well, we go to Devon about the middle of August, or beginning of September, or middle of September—not much of a plan here; but we have to wait on the will of others.

I want to get as much of the new book done as I can, before the turmoil starts—even some proofs read, if possible. I've done three more chapters, & a fourth well on the way. Two more should do it. But, if we agree about , ; : — . these little things, I'll be glad to put the MS in your safer hands, before things begin to move.

So could you come to us? Wednesday, Thursday, or Friday, next week, at 4-o'c for tea; or 7-o'c for a meal with us? Or any day the following week? Any of them may be less convenient for you than for me. So I could go to your office, if you can't come to us; though, of course, I'd rather you came here. I'd like to stick at this work till it's finished.

Yours As Ever,
Sean O'Casey

To Irish Times

29 AUGUST 1938

O'CASEY QUESTIONS MAURICE LEAHY

Sir,—It is reported in your important journal, that during Dr. Starkie's talk about O'Casey,[1] Maurice Leahy asked the lecturer two questions, namely:

(a) What is O'Casey's attitude to Christianity? and

(b) Why is O'Casey one of the "Wild Geese,"

In the first place, "attitude" is a sickly word to use in reference to what I think or don't think about Christianity. Maurice Leahy is more of an Attitudinarian than I am. As a Catholic, much more as a "Catholic writer," he should know that the only possible person to answer such a question was not Dr. Starkie but O'Casey himself. Maurice Leahy is, evidently, one of those Catholics gadding around who think that Catholic Action is the Catholic Church. Let an ignorant unbeliever tell him that it isn't, and never can be. It is recorded that Maurice Leahy is a co-founder of "The Catholic Poetry Society." This society isn't the Catholic Church either, and never can be. Some years ago I was asked to attend a meeting of this society. Quite frankly, I replied that, as an unbeliever,

[1] The Abbey Theatre presented a dramatic festival of plays and lectures, 6 to 20 August 1938. A report of Dr. Walter Starkie's lecture on O'Casey, and the questions raised by Maurice Leahy, appeared in the *Irish Times,* 17 August. The lectures have been printed in *The Irish Theatre,* ed. Lennox Robinson (London, Macmillan, 1939), lectures delivered during the Abbey Theatre festival held in Dublin in August 1938. For the contents of the book, see O'Casey's letter to Macmillan & Co. Ltd., 5 April 1940, note 2. Several other incidents provide the background for the O'Casey-Leahy letters. As part of the festival, the Abbey presented Yeats's new play, *Purgatory,* on 10 August; and in the *Irish Times,* 18 August, it was reported that a controversy had arisen over the play, with the Rev. Terence Connolly, S.J., as one of its opponents. This was the same priest whose attack on O'Casey had contributed to the banning of *Within the Gates* in Boston in 1935. Maurice Leahy, in a letter to the *Irish Times,* 19 August 1938, defended his friend, Father Connolly, adding another provocation for O'Casey. For Father Connolly's attack on *Within the Gates,* see O'Casey's cable to George Bushar Markle and John Tuerk, 21? January 1935, note 2. See also O'Casey's letter on Leahy to the *Irish Press,* 17 October 1938.

I should be very much out of place there, and refused to attend. Does he resent this honesty? To ease his mind, I tell him, once for all, that, like George Bernard Shaw, I am an Atheist, and I thank God for it.

The really important question is: What is Christianity's "attitude" to O'Casey? Not as an individual, but in the mass; for there are millions and millions asking these same questions now.

The second question is an innuendo, implying that he knows the reason why O'Casey became a "Wild Goose;" or that he met someone who heard the reason from someone else. If he has any reason to believe that I left Ireland for any reason, direct or indirect, other than my own personal choice, let him have the honesty to say so. Let him tell us what it is, and if he be right, I'll admit it; and if he be wrong, let him keep his tongue still.

One more point: In *The Boston Evening Transcript* for April 6th, 1938, it is reported that Maurice Leahy, in the course of a lecture before the Jeanne d'Arc Academy Alumnae Association, "will give a few personal memories of Sean O'Casey, the romantic realist." What personal memories could Maurice Leahy give of me? I never knew the man. As far as I know I never even saw him at a distance. There you are. Yours, etc.,

Sean O'Casey

London, 26 August 1938

From Maurice Leahy to Irish Times

2 SEPTEMBER 1938

"Atheism a la Mode"

SIR,—I have seen Mr. O'Casey's letter in your columns. He seems extraordinarily angry because I asked a few questions about his work and himself. Here are the facts. My remarks at the "festival" were not reported *verbatim* or *in toto*. If Mr. O'Casey were at this Dublin lecture he would have known this. In response to the invitation for comments I told the lecturer that Irishmen in America were protesting against the importation from Ireland of vulgar plays in which Christian Ireland was derided while being commercially exploited. I proceeded to say that among the many questions asked in America the following frequently occurred: Does Sean O'Casey nationally represent Ireland, which prides itself in being a Christian country, with Christian rulers and a Christian Constitution? And what, if any, were his views on Christianity? And why is he considered to be one of the "Wild Geese"?

Is he indignant with me for having imported these questions—asked by sincere Irishmen in America, where I was told a play of his was suppressed as being unfit for Christian consumption?

Some years ago Mr. O'Casey stated in a letter to me some of his views on Christianity. Is he now angry with me for having casually referred at the lecture to what he now openly proclaims in his letter to your paper—that he is an atheist?

I am sorry to have to disappoint Mr. O'Casey, but I did not do him the honour of lecturing on him in America on that occasion in April last to which he refers.

It is significant that Mr. O'Casey's Press quotation says that Maurice Leahy "will" talk about him. It is much more significant that Maurice Leahy did not talk about him at all. Nor am I responsible for what the Press in America thinks I am thinking of talking about, nor for the imaginativeness of American journalists who seek me when I am visiting America. Nor have I seen the Press statement to which he refers. I do not indulge in the vanity of paying a subscription to a Press-cutting agency to find out how often my name appears in print. My lecture actually was on the Poetry of Ireland—real and romantic: in this lecture I specially dealt with a Christian representative of Ireland—Padraic Pearse. I showed that Pearse saw in the tear-stained, dirt-stained faces of the dumb suffering poor people the Holy Face of God. I fear I could not put Mr. O'Casey in such company.

Qua cursum ventus!

Yours, etc.
Maurice Leahy

Greystones, County Wicklow
31 August 1938

To Time and Tide

3 September 1938

Walt Whitman

SIR,—In the book telling all about Whitman,[1] and the review that buttered it up, mention was made of the poet's small white hands as hardly connected with hard graft. This shows all they know about it. I myself worked with a man who handled all things, from a pick and shovel to a newly creosoted sleeper—no nice or easy thing to handle; I know, because I've handled them myself. Yet this man's hand could

[1] Esther Shepard, *Walt Whitman's Pose* (London, Harrap, 1938), reviewed by Malcolm Muggeridge in *Time and Tide*, 6 August 1938.

wear a girl's glove, and his foot could wear a girl's shoe. I've worked with him wearing his mother's (who'd a small foot) while his own were in pawn; and given a rest and a little care, his hand could have become as fine and as fair as the hand of a gentle ladie. So there you are.

I am, etc.,
Sean O'Casey

To Irish Times

6 SEPTEMBER 1938

ATHEISM A LA MODE

Sir,—Maurice Leahy is indeed unfortunate. Two reviews have not represented him fully, one has not represented him at all. *The Boston Transcript* did not say he was lecturing on me (I do not think I said so either), but that in a lecture on A.E. he would also give personal memories of Sean O'Casey. The statement smacks of accuracy. Maybe the Maurice Leahy of one place differs from the Maurice Leahy of another. Just as the Maurice Leahy who wrote asking me to come to a meeting of the Catholic Poetry Society was a different Maurice Leahy to the one who asked the questions at Dr. Starkie's lecture. He evidently disliked my refusal to become better acquainted.

He admits having a letter from me stating "some of my views on Christianity," yet he takes the trouble to ask Dr. Starkie what they are, with this letter in his breast pocket. I presume he knows that a letter is the property of the writer, and not the property of him who receives it; and that publication would be a breach of copyright. Well, should he think that the letter would do me the slightest or the greatest harm, I hereby give him full, plenary and public permission to publish it.

After "attitude" we have: "I was told a play of his was suppressed as being unfit for Christian consumption." A glorious sentence from the co-founder of the Catholic Poetry Society. "Christian consumption"—my God!

The collection of Press-cuttings is based on a far lower level than that of the childish vanity of seeing one's name in print. Maurice Leahy has nothing to be envious about. Like most human pleasures, that of seeing one's name in print soon loses its thrill. If Maurice Leahy was an author of any popularity or importance, he would know they were collected for the very mercenary reason of assuring himself that payment was made for a work produced.

"Padraic Pearse saw in the tear-stained, dirt-stained faces of the dumb suffering poor people the Holy Face of God." Here's a double edition of smug slobbering for you. Greystones rhapsodising over Gloucester street. Did Padriac Pearse see this wonder because of, or in spite of, the tear-stained, dirt-stained disfigurement on the faces of the "dumb suffering poor people"? And what are these things doing in a Christian country, with Christian rulers, and a Christian Constitution?

Other than in the fact of representing Ireland as an Irishman, I represent Ireland in no way whatsoever. No one does, no one can (except, perhaps, Dr. Douglas Hyde, and he as a symbol only). I do not pretend to represent even my own family. I represent myself, and that gives me enough to do. I am doing it now.

Maurice Leahy has not told us why he launched the innuendo in the question of "Why is O'Casey considered one of the Wild Geese"? He has, as I thought he would, remained tear-stained, suffering, poor, and dumb. He has not, evidently, the courage of his own little convictions.

In reply to J. M. J. Martin: Speaking at a meeting G. B. Shaw was frequently interrupted by someone (a Cockney Leahy, probably) bawling: "You're an atheist; you shouldn't be listened to; you're an atheist." Whereupon Shaw suddenly retorted: "You are right, sir; I am an atheist, and I thank God for it."

And so do I, especially when I listen to the silly remarks of Cockney Leahys here, and Gaelic Leahys over in Eireann.—Yours, etc.,

Sean O'Casey

London, 4 September 1938

To Harold Macmillan

MS. Macmillan London

49 Overstrand Mansions
9 September 1938

Dear Mr Harold,

I hope you had a good holiday—short & sweet, like an ass's gallop.

I want you to hold book proofs of "I Knock At The Door" till I am settled (or unsettled) in Devon. I go there 9 days from now, & don't want the proofs tumbling into an empty flat; & I'm not sure of the actual day on which we shall enter our new home. I'm glad you think you will be able to include photo of Mrs. Casside.[1]

[1] The photograph of O'Casey's mother, Susan Casey, who is characterized as "Mrs. Casside" in the autobiography, is the frontispiece of the first volume, *I Knock at the Door* (1939). The baby she is holding is not Sean but her grandchild, Susan Beaver, the daughter of O'Casey's sister, Isabella.

I thought to give out news through the "Sunday Referee" by letting a reporter come to see me—she said the editor had insisted she must see me, or—so my kind heart gave way. Never again, by God! These creatures never say what you say. I see she says I called children "bloodthirsty little devils"; whereas what I said was that, "children, when they played at soldiers or cowboys, killing imaginary foes, should never be repressed." It is the pacifists who prevent this, who are the "bloodthirsty big devils." And again: I said "Chamberlain should be a railway porter", whereas what I said was that "comparing him, as P.M. with men I knew, he sank into the insignificance of a porter." Never again, so help me God.

What's wrong with Harold Nicholson? Isn't he one of your party? In reviewing a book, "The Communist International," he says "The Commintern failed in Bulgaria, Germany, England, Hungary, China, & in Spain." Does he know what a Revolution is? He thinks it's the blazing of guns. That may be a part, & a very important part (given certain circumstances) of a revolution; but it is not The Revolution. I am part of The Communist International. How do I act? By doing all I can to make myself a better human being. By using the intelligence I have for the good of all men. When I talk to you, I am in the Revolution; & when you talk to others, you are in the Revolution. How? Because we are intelligent men; & intelligent men must ever be thinking of bringing about a change. Like the Catholic Church (or the Christian), Communism has a soul, & many unattached from the body, are well within the Soul of Communism. They have been baptised, not by water; but by the Spirit.[2]

Well, this was meant to be a business letter.

So could you let one of your Staff send me one copy of "The Flying Wasp," & one copy of "Two Plays."

With All Good Wishes

Sean O'Casey

[2] Harold Macmillan, in the first volume of his autobiography, *Winds of Change, 1914–1939* (London, Macmillan, 1966), p. 187, made the following comment on O'Casey and his communist faith: "Among my greatest friends in this group was Sean O'Casey. He and his talented wife used to come to stay with us in Sussex, and I watched with growing delight his rise to face. Although he claimed to be a Communist and, I think, an atheist, his was a truly Christian nature; one of the kindest and most genuine men that I have known. He and Ronald Knox—in their very different ways—were saintly men."

To George Jean Nathan

MS. CORNELL

49 OVERSTRAND MANSIONS
[?] SEPTEMBER 1938

My Dear George:

I hope you are back to your old form again, working away at the old desk, under the old lights, keeping your brother critics in sight of the right road. And I hope, too, you won't work too hard.

I've just sent the MS of my life—in the form of chapter stories—up to twelve, under the name of "I Knock at the Door," to Macmillan, & expect to be working at the proofs in a week or so—the damned proofs! The book is to be published in the early Spring. I'll let you have the first copy I get. I think, on the whole, the work is good. It contains "A Protestant Kid Thinks of the Reformation" & there are many more that would have, I'm sure, gone into your "American Spectator" had people not lost interest in it. I often sigh for it. I think it was the liveliest & finest monthly I ever handled. How quick it shut down when you departed. "Cover her face; mine eyes dazzle; she died young."

Soon, too, I shall be in the middle of a move—the 19th of this month—down to Devon, near Plymouth, close to Dartington Hall, of which you may have heard. The shift is mainly taken for the children's sake. School is a big & difficult question here, unless you've a good deal of money. I must say, I go regretfully. But it will not be complete isolation. Dartington Hall School carries on a big activity in other ways: Pottery, Textiles, Farming, Sawmills, Furniture Making, Cider brewing, Ballet (Joos), Indian Dancing (Shan Kar)—Theater, & a training school for Opera. I've spent some pleasant days there before; & am very interested in what is being done there. A couple of years ago, I was offered a job in the Theatre; but, as it seemed to indicate a curtailment of freedom in my work, I declined to take the job; while still remaining very affectionately interested in the success of the venture. When we go down, I'll send you some literature about the activities. The venture is financed by a very wealthy American woman, her husband & her daughter—the Straights—& now Mrs. [Dorothy] Elmhirst, in Dartington Hall, Devon. They have lectures, concerts, & all sorts of things; & I'm sure, it won't be so lonely as it was for me when in Buckinghamshire, which I left to come straight to New York & G. J. Nathan. Actually, I never met before a more charming couple than Mr. & Mrs. Elmhirst. I don't intend to enter actively into any of the interests there; but hope I shall be able to enjoy them when I'm a little tired of my own work. But if I had the power to live my own way, I'd live in Ireland; or, if I was younger, take a boat to the next County from Cork—the U.S.A.

So, if you don't hear from me for a few weeks after you get this, you'll know I'm trying to fix up things in our new home.

I've been reading some of the dialogue already written for my new play, "The Star Turns Red"; I haven't looked at it for the last two months or more; & so may possibly be more critical, than if I had written it yesterday. Well, the most of it, to me, sounds good, which has pleased me a little. I begin to think of it again today, & hope to make progress tomorrow, & continue till the upheaval of moving really starts.

I have your photograph safely packed away in my desk already. It has been looking at me from the mantelpiece since it came.

I hope you will have a good theatrical season this year. Morgan's "The Flashing Stream" has had its first night; [1] & the only critic I've read, so far, praises it highly. But I can't see Charles Morgan writing a fine drama, can you? "I believe in the quick & the dead" says the Christian Catechism; well, I believe, all right, in the dead here; but I haven't much faith in the quick.

Give my love to Lillian, & to all old friends.

With my love to You.
Sean

Yes, they're admitting, at last, that the American Theater is alive. About time they did. I wasn't long in the U.S.A. till I saw that. And I said so when I came back. They didn't like it. So I said it again.

I enclose a view by Agate of "The Golden Boy" [2] which may interest you.

[1] Charles Morgan's *The Flashing Stream* opened on 1 September 1938 at the Lyric Theatre, London.

[2] James Agate's two-part review, *Sunday Times,* 26 June and 3 July 1938, of Clifford Odets's *Golden Boy,* which opened on 21 June 1938 at the St. James's Theatre, London.

To Gabriel Fallon

MS. TEXAS

49 OVERSTRAND MANSIONS
11 SEPTEMBER 1938

My very dear Gaby:

It was a very great pleasure to look on the old, neat graceful writing again. There is never a silence between you & me. If we don't write, we think of each other, & what could be betther than that?

I'm a little annoyed (with meself) that you anticipated me by a day or two; for this week I had to write to you. We leave London on Monday for a little place near Totnes in Devon; so I, at least, was about to tell you of this change, & to send you our new address.

This sailing from one place to another is a nuisance, but it can't be helped. We think it may be cheaper (between you & me and Father Senan & Francis & Dr Cummins & Brother . . . . . ? &, of course, dear Rose). The rents here are going up; & we have to tighten our belts. We have been on the job of getting a place for months, & only a few weeks ago managed it. Now I hope in God (in Whom I don't believe) that the change may be a comfortable one.

I kept putting off writing to you, from day to day. You see my eyes get very tired after working, & I have to keep them shut for a long time, or they would get very painful entirely. Only a week ago I got a letter from Nathan asking the reason of a long silence; &, now, I am free in conscience having written to you & him & to Joe Cummins. Another reason: I've been working on a volume for Macmillans; a work I started two years ago, & just completed (in MS) a few days ago. It is biographical, & deals, in stories, with what I saw & heard & felt during the first 11 or twelve years of my life. It is called "I Knock at the Door". I thought I'd have it in, to have it out this Autumn; but I failed; & it won't appear till the early Spring. Needless to say, you'll have one of the first copies. I think it good, & it may even be unique—but I'm not sure.

However, when you read it, you'll say your say, like a man. About Frank's book: that's a teaser, Gaby! I don't like giving an opinion about another's book. Because I've got something of a name, there is an importance given to an opinion given by me (not by you, of course; for you're a real buttie) which makes me feel uncomfortable. "Sean O'Casey says—" you know the thing. Of course my opinion's an intelligent one, but it's not infallible. I'm right about as often as anyone else. And I'm afraid that even Frank would attach too much important to it. To you I say that Frank's last book is more free from Catholic "bias" than his previous one; but it is not so good. I seem to imagine that he is struggling between the influence of [Daniel] Corkery on the one hand, & of [Liam] O'Flaherty on the other; (Corkery in "A Candle For The Proud"; [1] & O'Flaherty in "This House Was Mine" [2]) & to be dominated by either of them is bad for him. He must fly himself, though he may have, here & there, a Corkery or an O'Flaherty feather in his wings. "This Was My House" seems strained. Though there's a lot of conventional rot in "Candle for the Proud", the story flows; the story in "This House was mine" doesn't. There are fine bits in it, of course, but, no; it isn't so good as "Candle For The Proud".

There; & I may be wholly & entirely wrong. After all, Frank himself knows best.

[1] Francis MacManus, *A Candle For the Proud* (Dublin, Talbot Press, 1936).
[2] Francis MacManus, *This House Was Mine* (1937).

Anyway, let him not bother about keeping within the centre of gravity of the (so-called by so many) Catholic Faith. It makes me laugh to hear some persons blathering about "The Catholic Faith". If the Catholic Faith be what he thinks it to be, then, so long as he remains a Catholic, he can never step or wander outside of it. What is the Catholic Faith (in the sense of The Catholic Church) anyway? No-one really knows. Not even St Thomas Aquinas. If it be what the Faith is claimed to be, then there is no end to it. The man who limits the Catholic Faith (as I understand it) limits God.

Oh, Lord, Gaby, here I am flowing out into an Atheistical pastoral! But I honestly do think that many who are defending "The Faith" are doing the Faith a good deal of harm. And, I fear, that sometimes, it isn't love of the Faith that gets them going; but a kink of personal conceit in themselves.

About Father T. Connolly, S.J: He, I think, was one of the Boston Band that barred the way of "Within The Gates",[3] but I do not count him an enemy for that reason. He could have had no personal reason for his resistance. I lost by it; but he gained nothing, so his motive must have been good (though I think he was mistaken). And one gets a little bewildered by these things; by curious differences of opinion. For instance: Father Connolly of Boston condemning me; & Father McGinley S.J. of Pennsylvania praising me! Only complaining of my bad Latin, & sending me his Breviary to prove it. I have it here still. So there you are.

But should Father Connolly ring me up, I shall be delighted to ask him to come up & have a cup of tea—if he does so before Sunday, my last day in London.

Isn't it a pity that Peter [Judge: F. J. McCormick] should be so unfriendly? It's a puzzle to me. I like Peter, & wish him all the best; and Brinsley [Macnamara], too.

But I do not like Maurice Leahy. I never met him; but I do not like his ways. Some time ago a friend in Harvard (near Boston) wrote to me saying that things were being said in Boston that I should contradict. So I had to write a lot about myself, defending myself from attacks I knew very little about. Particularly about my connection with Ireland—a pretty long & intimate connection, you'll admit. That stung me on the raw. I am as loyal to Ireland as any man living or dead. When this friend mentioned the name of Maurice Leahy, it brought nothing to my mind. I thought I had never heard of him. It was only when I read that he was connected with the Catholic Poetry Society, I remembered. He had written to me begging me to come to a meeting of the Society. I wrote a courteous reply, refusing; pointing out that, as a Non Catholic, & more, an unbeliever, I would be out of place there. Nothing else, & all perfectly true. He, seemingly, has had it in for me, ever since. But I have nothing

[3] See O'Casey's letter to the *Irish Times,* 29 August 1938, note 1.

against the Catholic Poetry Society, save to believe that great "Catholic Poetry" is poetry for us all. At least—for I haven't the letter beside me—that is, I think, the tenor of what I wrote.

Is this damned letter getting too long?

A few more words, Gaby.

Oddly enough, sometime ago, I had to cut out my subscription to the Press-cutting Agency, in an effort at economy, & the news of what Leahy said was told to me here, & I asked Joe Cummins to send me any references. The cutting about his lecture in Boston came to me accidentally (was it an accident?) while I was burning rubbish, preparatory to our flight to Devon. I have let a lot of things go that have been said about me; but I can't let everything go. After all, Gaby, if I don't care much about what a lot of people think of me, I do care about what some think of me in Ireland. And so, I imagine, I was justified in hitting out this time at Maurice Leahy.

If Father Senan knew as much about me as I know myself, he'd say things to make me blush—in a very different way. My life has been full of villainy; but God (if there be a God), as far as my observation goes, makes a lot of allowances; & I will, I hope, when the time comes, have the courage to reverently claim my share.

Anyway, villain or no, give him my love, & my love, too, to Brother . . . . . . who I know is now Father . . . . to Frank; & my affectionate regards to Peter Judge.

And my love to you, Gaby, & to the children, & to dear Rose.

The other day I read a letter in which you told me Francis had been taught by Rose to point to a picture of me when she said "Show me Sean".

I hope you & they are all well. Remember, though, not to question yourself about me. That is a *little* unjust. You should know how I feel for you & yours. We differ from each other in a lot of ways; but there should be no such thing as silence between us. We have thought of you, of Rose, & of the children, often & often; & will continue to send thought to you, even though no Postman carries it in his bag.

And so, dear buttie, Goodbye for the present.

Yours As Ever
Sean

To Mrs. Charlotte F. Shaw

TC. O'CASEY

[49 OVERSTRAND MANSIONS]
[? SEPTEMBER 1938]

Dear Mrs Shaw:

Thank you for the kindness you showed to us yesterday. The trek from here to Devon will, I'm sure, be a good thing for the two youngsters—and that matters most.

I have been searching my conscience, since you spoke to me, about my tendency towards quarrelling; But I dont think this tendency goes down deep in me. In all productions of my plays, I have had but one quarrel (with Norman Macdermott),[1] and that's saying a lot. The "quarrel" with the dentist landlord [2] was just a flash rejecting the idea of "references". I can, and did, ask for a financial guarantee; but I'm not going to ask anyone to guarantee my morals. I cant say myself what sort I'll be a week from now. To be asked to get a moral guarantee from others, or one from myself, is, to me, stupid, and makes me mad. A long time ago I was asked to declare that a worker looking for the job of caretaker, was sober, honest, truthful, reliable, and industrious. I replied saying that what was wanted was a saint, and not a worker. And the man got the job!

I think my "Flying Wasp" did a little good. Recently, [James] Agate spoke at Toynbee Hall in favour of Government support of Music and Drama. Anyway, the book was just a continuation of what I said at a dinner given by the Critics' Circle in 1926, when I, foolishly, I suppose, told them my mind. They havent asked me since.

I have always had to fight like the devil for life; but you must blame your husband, G.B.S. for whatever sharpness and wit that have come into my fighting qualities; and my young Dublin comrade, member of the Fourth Order of St Francis, who first put the green-covered copy of "John Bull's Other Island" into my then reluctant hand. I am a fighter as G.B.S. is a fighter; neither so great nor so amiable a fighter, to be sure. But, then Peter wasnt so great nor so lovable as his Master; but he was a forcible fellow, and I really believe that I am a forcible fellow, too.

With many thanks and affectionate regards.
Yours Sincerely,
Sean O'Casey

[1] For the details of O'Casey's quarrel with Norman MacDermott, director of the London production of *Within the Gates,* see O'Casey's letter to MacDermott, 28 January 1934.

[2] For the details about O'Casey's dentist landlord and the broken lease at Overstrand Mansions, see Bernard Shaw's letter to O'Casey, 17 October 1938, and O'Casey's letter to Gabriel Fallon, 25 August 1939.

To Harold Macmillan

MS. MACMILLAN LONDON

DEVON [1]
30 SEPTEMBER 1938

Dear Mr Harold Macmillan,

All's uneven, & everything's left at six & seven. We are all in the midst of chaos. I am praying for a miracle.

I'm not sure of the exact address. Some say this; some say that. However, the following will find me:

O'Casey
Tingrith
Ashburton Road
Totnes
Devon

What do specimen pages mean, anyway? I daresay, you know I havent had the Proofs yet. So I suppose the pages are not of the printed pages of the future book. And, as I am dealing with the pages, let me say a word about the cover: if possible, don't have it green; & let no shamrocks blossom on the cover; or harp either. The format of the first volumes—"Two Plays," etc., was fine; but, if I remember right, the green cover of "Five Irish Plays" has shamrocks on its edges. The green immortal shamrock! I dread the look of them in book or picture. They represent a dead & sentimental Ireland to me. And I am neither dead nor sentimental.

I see Russia has been kept out of the Four Power Conference; and yet I'm told Russia has gone back, or is fast going back to "as you were before you listed."

They are busy giving out gasmasks down here. All the workers here are against Hitler. That's something, anyhow.

I hope Lady Dorothy and all your children are well. Remember me to Mr Maurice.

With all Good Wishes

Sean O'Casey

PS. Send on Specimen pages, or any other news (except Proofs) as soon as you like. S.O'C.

[1] The Totnes, Devon address, hereafter Devon, in Volume I should not be confused with the St. Marychurch, Devon address in Volumes II and III.

To Horace Reynolds

MS. REYNOLDS

NEW ADDRESS: TINGRITH
ASHBURTON ROAD,
TOTNES, DEVON. ENGLAND
3 OCTOBER 1938

My dear Horace:

I haven't heard from you for years & years. We have moved to Devon, & this is a line to give you new address as above. There is a good school here (I hope) for our two boys; modern, & cheaper than the same kind (not so good in London) in London. I'll tell you more later on. I don't like the country, but the children do; & I am praying to God; so I am very busy.

I've sent in the MS to Macmillan's; & the book—"I Knock At The Door", is to be published in the early Spring. It brings me up to twelve or thirteen years of age. I hope to write two more—1. "Come On In"; & "The Lighted Room"; but when—. I think you'll like the book; it's written, I think, in an unusual way.

Love to Kay & the two children.

Yours as Ever
Sean

To Gabriel Fallon

MS. TEXAS

NEW ADDRESS: TINGRITH
STATION ROAD
TOTNES, DEVONSHIRE
5 OCTOBER 1938

My dear Gaby:

Just a line to say we are here. What a time of chassis! Putting everything back in another place, & finding the place the wrong one. And the whole place gutted with dugouts, caverns, pits, trenches, with gas men & electric men yelling havoc all the time. When the most of the devastation was over, it was found out that the gas-men had put their pipes too near the electric cable, & so all had to be done over again—British Brain.

Well, Father Connolly S.J. never came, never rang up, never wrote, never made a sign that he would come to see me. And I often stopped in waiting for him to ring; & always left someone at home, with explicit instructions to insist, if he rang up, to come & have a cup of tea and a talk. But he made no sign. So everything turned out as I expected. Men like these don't give an answer for the hope that is in them. It is a pity, but it is true. Wasn't it Father Connolly who said that "the greatest critic in America said there were but two playwrights of real worth in the world—Claudel and T. C. Murray". Claudel & Murray! Poor Claudel!

Later on, we'll talk more about these things—meanwhile I'll have to go on settling things straight.

The country feels very curious after London. The change is a gamble, & we must abide by the hazard of the die.

I hope all are well with you. My love to Rose & the children.

With All the Old Affection
Sean

To Harold Macmillan

MS. MACMILLAN LONDON

DEVON
7 OCTOBER 1938

Dear Mr. Harold Macmillan,

You are right, and I am wrong. I was positive that the cheque was due "on the signing of the contract"; so positive that when I got your letter, I was certain a mistake had been made by Macmillan & Co. So when things had been placed somewhere in my room, I looked up the contract, feeling, I'm afraid, a little happy in the assurance of confirming your mistake: but you were right, and I was wrong. What made me so sure about my own idea of what had been written, I don't know. Perhaps, it really was because I wanted it, & the wish was father to the thought. I hope you wont call out *your* army over the mistake.

The Specimen Pages.

I return them marked according to Eileen's choice, namely,

1st Choice: Specimen E.
2nd " " C.
3rd " " D.
4th " " A.

Frankly, neither she nor I know anything about these things. This is the first time I have seen a "specimen page." So, I think, the final choice must be with you.

The Proofs:

I can receive the proofs now. So Clark's [1] may send them on anytime they like. Some time ago, I wrote to them asking, because of possible alteration in the songs, to hold back the proof of "The Street Sings." I have seen the published version of these songs, & find my own is better; so please tell them to carry on with "The Street Sings."

I dont want a separate half-title for any of the chapters. I prefer it to be done as I have written it; or, as it appears in Specimen A—that is the words

THE PROTESTANT REFORMATION

standing out in large print, just as they have printed it. To put a secondary title such as "Biographical Sketch" under any chapter would spoil it. The Book—the 23 chapters or sections is an organic whole—at least, I hope it is—; and the whole book is autobiographical, from Alpha to Omega, of the first twelve years of my life. I have thought of two more volumes: "Come On In"; and the third "The Lighted Room." The second to consist of what happened till I joined the Irish Movement, & the last to deal with all or most of what happened afterwards.

The proofs are to be sent to

TINGRITH,
STATION ROAD,
TOTNES, DEVON.

POLITICS.

I dont know what to add to what I have already said. One thing is certain: you'll have to get rid of the old gang before you can find room to plan. I wish I could have a talk with you & [Lord] Hartington and [Ramsay] MacDonald & the rest of your comrades—if Mac be one. I know more about politics than I do about Specimen pages—may the Lord God forgive me! I have spoken at many surging meetings surrounded by police; have sat on Election Committees; and have sent many "dead men" in to vote. Your chance is now, or as the Irish say "anish no riamh, anish ar go brath" "Now or never; now & forever." England sits in the shadow of death. Who is to say "Let there be light"?

You & your comrades who have imagination & who have conquered the worst of selfishness that sprouts green in the human heart.

With Affectionate Regards,
Sean O'Casey

[1] R. & R. Clark, Ltd., Edinburgh, printer.

To Guy Boas [1]

TS. Boas

Devon
9 October 1938

My dear Guy,

Here we are. Just breath enough for a word or two out of the turmoil. Sorry we couldn't see you before we folded our tents to leave London, but we simply hadn't a second. We'll miss the yearly joy the Sloane School gave us, miss it truly, and very much indeed.

I'll never forget the production of "Twelfth Night" in Modern Dress—if it really was played in modern dress. It was done so brilliantly that, to me, it might have been done in the old Globe, with the finest caste Shakespeare could gather together. I've never seen a better performance of the play; never even one so good, and I've seen many. Although I've delayed to tell you this, I can't let the world pass away before I tell you how proud I was and am of you, the woman who does the costumes, and the grand group of boys who showed us Shakespeare in all his jollity and great glow. I've never seen the comic parts done so well before; the ones I saw before were dead; this was of the quick; and in the theatre I believe in the quick, but not in the dead. Aguecheek, Toby, Maria were grand; and so was he who played Fabian; the singing of the song at the end of the play was, I think, simple and beautiful. Malvolio was the best Malvolio from a long list. He was given a manliness others never had. He was, apart from his love-madness, a worthy steward, though a little too concerned over trifles. But the originality of the creature was great and very pleasing to me. They all made the play live—except for the first few minutes; then it appeared to be dull, and I cursed that I had come; but it soon became real and stately and merry; and a glorious night was passed—; live vigorously and well. Give my best thanks to all who took part in it; and may each of them, wherever they may be in the future, or whatever they may do, be well rewarded for the great things they have done for Shakespeare.

I'm very sorry that I may not possibly be in the midst of you all next year. I will, in spirit anyway.

Love to Mrs. Boas and your boy and to you.

Sean O'Casey

[1] Guy Boas, headmaster of the Sloane School, Chelsea.

To George Jean Nathan

MS. CORNELL

NEW ADDRESS
TINGRITH, STATION ROAD
TOTNES, DEVON
ENGLAND
10 OCTOBER 1938

My dear George:

Here I am fastened down in the above little Town—a lot different from New York, or even the Virgin Islands. However, the two youngsters are enjoying themselves, & that is something. Whether I shall bloom or wither here, I don't know—it's too early to say yet. I've lived four years in another part of the English Countryside, & it was terrible; but the Devon people—those I've met so far—are much better, more likeable, & greater characters than the people in Buckinghamshire. I've had a tiring time moving furniture, sorting books, & hanging pictures; but the house looks a little shapely now, & in a few more days, I hope to be able to start work.

Agate in last "Sunday Times" says that of all the English plays now on in London, only one, "The Flashing Stream"—Morgan's—is worth mentioning. And they're all afraid (it seems to me) to say a word 'gainst Morgan. They walk in fear & trembling before him. Where he stands is holy ground, & where he sits is very holy ground. Well, if the play be as good as the Masterpiece called "Sparkenbroke", give me a long long drink in a Soda-fountain Parlour. I can manage Shakespeare, Milton, Herrick, Whitman, Joyce, & a score or so of others; but "Sparkenbroke" gets me down. I couldn't even bear to look at the cover. I can't see it, either as an honest to God novel, or as a lovely work of art. AE [George Russell] of Ireland was another who desired worship, & got it. When I criticised his painting, his poetry, & his wisdom, Ireland's heart stood still for a long time. But even poor old AE is plainer & more to be pitied than Charles Morgan. Well, more of this anon. There are still some books to be sorted & some pictures to be hanged, so I'll end this till I hear from you.

I hope your health is fine.

With deep affectionate Regards and Remembrance.
Sean

To Gabriel Fallon

MS. TEXAS

DEVON
13 OCTOBER 1938

Dear Gaby:

Just a copy of a letter received some years ago from Maurice Leahy.[1] Isn't it good?

"Angelic of me!"

"As an ardent admirer of your work, I thank you over & over."

God forgive us, we're all a curious gang.

Sean

Enclosure

[1] See O'Casey's letter to the *Irish Press,* 17 October 1938. He gave Fallon a copy of Leahy's letter of 31 October 1928.

To Lady Astor

TS. ASTOR

DEVON
14 OCTOBER 1938

Dear Lady Astor:

Talking over the telephone to Eileen, I understand you fired a shot at me, saying that "Russia was killing all her intelligent people". Poor Russia. Hitler will have an easy road to Moscow. If he does, I'll be there to give the Nazi salute. But if Russia kills "all" then one instance will be enough to declare this happy wish to be an idle dream. What about the great Russian scientist who died a few weeks ago? He hated the Bolsheviks, and never lost a chance to say so privately and publicly. Was he killed? No; they turned a deaf ear to his cries of hatred, and, for the sake of the science in the man, gave him everything that he asked for; fitted him up with a laboratory that the Czar and all his tribe could never have seen, even in the dimness of their minds' eye.

In "The Russian Revolution", by Chamberlin (not the Prime Minister —the book would be beyond him), mention is made of a Professor who hated the Communists. He shrank back into his conservative shell. Lenin called on the Soviets to offer special salaries to Scientists; the professor wrote an angry letter to Pravda, saying that scientists were not to be bought; and then waited for the Police. Did they come to destroy him? I dont think so. And Chamberlin belongs to the right; the book is published by Macmillans. Besides, an intelligent being can be a dastard. Highly intelligent men betrayed the great Parnell. Had Parnell lived long enough to free Ireland, these intelligent (some of them intellectual) would have had an unhappy time. An intelligent traitor's more dangerous than a stupid one. The Red Army's none the worse for the loss of a few of Hitler's friends. In the Great War it might have benefited England if she had lost some of her generals before it started. I remember, in your own house, Lloyd George saying of a prominent general that "he hadn't an idea in his head". And it took the great English experts twenty years to decide whether justice or injustice had been done to General Gough. Intelligence is often used in the cause of rascality. Judas Iscariot was, probably, as intelligent as Peter, James, or John. These yarns of "killing all intelligent people" are as bright as the one saying that "Papanin tried to walk across the ice-floes to escape to America". And isn't England doing all she can to destroy intelligence? Don't you remember the instance of Maudie Mason? Wasn't that enough to show the softening of England's brain? And your own experience in the Women's Movement showed you the dear broad-mindedness of the English mind. Shaw said many years ago that the English lived in mortal dread of a new idea, and they live in mortal dread of it still. But Lady Astor isn't English, therefore—

And Communism hasn't come to Russia yet. But it is on the way. Everything isn't perfect there; but nothing is perfect here. Their one bright spot is—Chamberlain. The head of the house. In the sense of science, art or Literature, a Brumagem doughboy. Beggared of imagination, England accepts him as her prophet. He pleases her by prophesying good things. So did another prophet mentioned in the bible.

And Education: we send our boys to the school we think best for them as long as our means will allow. It is, of course, exercising a privilege of money no less than those who send their boys to Eton. I don't blind myself to that fact. I think it unfair, and I think it bad, viewing education as a National benefit. It doesn't alter the fact because they happen to be intelligent, and so are worthy, or, I hope, will be worthy of the trouble taken by the teachers and by us. I think that all intelligent boys and girls should have the same chance; and so do you in your heart of hearts.

I take an interest in the Council schools. But the teachers, many of them, are not of the best. They aren't the pick of the nation. They cant be, seeing the conditions under which they fit themselves for the job. I saw them at work in Cambridge, and I was shocked. I'll write about these things when I have the time. The enclosed letter will show I took an interest in these boys. I've spoken with them, taken tea with them, and helped in their productions. Guy Boas is Headmaster of Sloane School, situated in the slum part of Chelsea. He is a grand man, and a Conservative. What the Council School here is like, I don't know—I haven't seen it yet. I wouldn't try to fatten a pig in the one in Chalfont St Giles.

But Education is a big question. We who are Communists cannot standardise the problem no more than can the Conservatives. Many fine minds have long been convinced that there is a hell of a lot wrong with the present methods. Your own Nursery Schools are a cry that something is wanted. You yourself are the mother of a group of fine boys. Now do you mean to tell me that these intelligent boys got perfect encouragement (looking at it from the best point of view) at Eton or Harrow, or wherever they went to school, from first to last? I don't think so. Their children must have better times.

I believe that it can come only through Communism. With all your faults, you have a good heart, as I, with all my faults, and they are many, have a good heart; but there are many who have not, though they be high in the plane of intelligence; and these are enemies.

With all good wishes,
Sean O'Casey

To Irish Press

17 October 1938

"Invitation to Mr. Sean O'Casey" [1]

Dear Sir—In shifting to another place, I came across the following letter from Mr. Maurice Leahy:

35B Queen's Gate,
London, S.W.7.
31 October 1928

Dear Mr. O'Casey:—

It was perfectly angelic of you to respond so generously to our appeal (what it was, I haven't the slightest idea—S.O'C.). We cannot quite express our gratitude to you for your kind thought.

I am sorry if I expressed myself unhappily about "Crusade of Rescue for Catholic Children"—I meant first of all that it is under Catholic direction and that it is composed mainly of Catholic children; but of course the only qualification for entrance is destitution. I can appreciate your horror at the thought of making theological tests or tags the criterion of

[1] See O'Casey's letters to the *Irish Times,* 29 August and 6 September 1938, and Maurice Leahy's letter to the *Irish Times,* 2 September 1938.

bestowing a bed to the little ones. I should myself recoil with horror from such a prospect. But the Crusade of Rescue is not so.

And now as I hail from the same land as yourself, dare I ask a further request—if my cheek is not insufferable. We are having other charity readings and fixtures. Mr. Chesterton is doing one and Shane Leslie is doing another. Would you preside at Shane Leslie's fixture? I could give you dates if you are willing to honour us thus. As an ardent admirer of your work I thank you over and over.—Yours very sincerely,

(Signed) Maurice Leahy

In fairness to me, would you be good enough to publish this, or part of this letter, in your valuable journal? Yours sincerely,

Sean O'Casey

Devon, 12 October 1938

From Bernard Shaw

MS. O'CASEY [1]

4, WHITEHALL COURT,
LONDON, S.W.1.
17 OCTOBER 1938

My dear Sean,

Your landlord, being a dentist, has developed an extraction complex. He proposed a lease in which I was not only to guarantee all your covenants, but indemnify him for all the consequences. I said I did not know his character, but knew enough of yours to know that the consequences might include anything from murder to a European war; so I redrafted the agreement. The lawyers, knowing that their man was only too lucky to get a gilt-edged (as they thought) security, and that his demands were absurd, made no resistance. I mention it as you had better watch your step, not to say his, with the gentleman. Anyhow I had a bit of fun with him.

I seem to have picked up completely. The anaemia was not really pernicious.

[1] O'Casey printed a copy of this letter in "Shaw's Corner," *Sunset and Evening Star* (1954). The occasion was the O'Casey family's move from London to Devon, in order to be near the school, Dartington Hall in Totnes, which, on the recommendation of Shaw, the O'Caseys had chosen for their children. For the background see *Sunset and Evening Star, Autobiographies* II, pp. 614–16.

I am glad to learn that the two miniature O'Caseys are happy among the young criminals at Dartington, and that their mother is now one of the Beauties of Devon.

Charlotte sends all sorts of affectionate messages.

G.B.S.

To Timofei Rokotov [1]

TS. INTER LIT, MOSCOW

DEVON

20 OCTOBER 1938

The world has lost a golden opportunity of assuring peace to a frightened world; peace, not for an hour or two, but peace long enough to allow us all to move certainly, to plan sensibly, and to learn that war solved no problem. How was the golden opportunity lost? By (as G. B. Shaw showed years ago) a combination of the power of England, France and the USSR in a declared policy of political and military union against the use of force. But England failed through fear. No; not England, really, but a little group in England whose personal interests curtain them off from the mighty interests of their own people. It is, to me, as plain as a pikestaff that the interests of England and those of Nazi Germany and Fascist Italy cannot grow harmoniously together. Sooner or later, Germany and Italy will strike at England; and when she strikes (even though England had France before or behind her), if the USSR isnt there to help, Germany will bite her heart out. With the USSR and France by her side, The U.S.A. would almost signal her assistance. But to England today, the power of the USSR is even more important than the power of the U.S.A. Then the thing for England to do (even for her own selfish sake) is to bring to power in England a Party that, so far from being afraid of the USSR, will seek in every possible way to gain her support. Of all the Powers in the world, the USSR is, to me, the only Power that is impregnable. What the USSR did in 1917 with her half-starved, untrained, and tattered army shows what she can do with her mighty power today.

A union with her brings the certainty of peace; and in peace alone, can the Arts and Sciences blossom. In the USSR alone can mighty experiments be made, and these mighty experiments are a vital necessity, if life is to march forward. Any Policy that excludes the USSR is a Policy, not

[1] Timofei Rokotov, editor, *International Literature,* Moscow.

of a fine mind gone weak, but of a mind that never had any strength at all.

Sean O'Casey

T. Rokotov, Esq.

Jack Lindsay suggested I should write something for you on above subject.

To Harold Macmillan

TS. MACMILLAN LONDON

DEVON
27 OCTOBER 1938

Dear Mr Harold Macmillan,

A month ago the Literary Editor of The Sunday Times asked [me] to review a book called "Robert Loraine." I did so.[1] The Editor wrote saying that the review pleased him very much, and suggested that should I hear of any book that took my fancy, he'd be pleased to send it to me. I have just done a review of two more books for him.[2]

This is what I really want to say:

If you ever have a book coming out that you think "might take my fancy," would you be good enough to let me know—if this be not infra dig with the publishing clan.

Or, in sending a catalogue, you might put a mark on a book likely to attract my attention.

I am unsettling down in Totnes fairly well. I'm tired after hanging pictures, arranging books, and doing other odd jobs, but that's nearly over now.

I hope you and yours are all well.

Yours as ever,
Sean O'Casey

[1] Sean O'Casey, "A Prophet in the Theatre," *Sunday Times,* 18 September 1938, a review of Winifred Loraine's *Robert Loraine: Soldier, Actor, Airman* (1938); reprinted in *Blasts and Benedictions* (1967).

[2] Sean O'Casey, "Portrait of Jack London: A Light That Failed," *Sunday Times,* 30 October 1938, a review of Irving Stone's *Sailor on Horseback* (London, Collins, 1938); "From Prison Cell: A Smuggler's Journal," *Sunday Times,* 20 November 1938, a review of Sergiusz Piasetski's *Lover of the Great Bear* (London, Routledge, 1938), a novel, translated by John Mann.

To Gabriel Fallon

MS. TEXAS

DEVON
28 OCTOBER 1938

My dear Gaby:

Howja like our new notepaper? Swell, isn't it? Thanks, dear thanks for your kind letter, & kindest offer. It won't be forgotten. We are unsettled in here, at last; & things feel a little better—not so much danger of breaking one's neck over a pipe or a cocked up carpet. Now, I'm trying to arrange the light to suit my eyes, & it's a devil of a job. And in the middle of the proofs for "I Knock At The Door", too. But it'll sort itself out—it's only a matther of measurement.

Is it that you haven't a photo of my old Kisser, at all, at all? Haven't I ever given you one? Well, I'll search for one for you. The one that appeared in the Abbey Souvenir should be here, somewhere; will that do? I'll have a look round for some other, too. I've a letter here from J. J. Hayes asking for a photo. Writing a series of articles (4) on Irish Dramatists & "O'Casey's to be one, to be sure". And he wants a photo, to finish it off. Says, if he buys one, it'll cost him a guinea; but he seems to think I've nothing to do but pick them up wherever I go. He's another who'll be saying "I want me name in the Press as often as possible"—& he after putting it in himself—and gettin' paid for it. Well, he can wait for the photo.

Father Connolly *didn't* say "Murray & Claudel are one." A mistake of mine. You'll see by enclosed cutting that F. Connolly isn't such a fool as I thought he was. I'd give something to know who did say it.

The letter sent wasn't the letter from Leahy that came first into my mind. He sent me several. I don't like the man. Father Connolly's different: I don't know his motive; but I believe it to be an honest one; so there's a cup of tay for him, anytime he comes along. And the Same for Father Gaffney. (By the way, Liam Pilkington, ex Chief Commandant of the Western I.R.A; now Redemptorist Priest, stationed at Streatham, says Father Gaffney's a "fine fellow," & he's probably right)

I don't know Leahy's motive, either; but I believe it to be a dishonest one; &, so, I don't like him; & there's no cup of tay for him. I haven't yet risen to the Christian virtue of loving one's enemies.

I don't know what to think about the Abbey. Things seem to be changing there—and I'm not to blame, this time. I'm anxious about it all. I've been asked to join in the discussion (all Faolain's articles & O'Connor's letters in The Irish Times [1] have been sent to me), but I've

[1] Sean O'Faolain and Frank O'Connor debated the subject "Ideals For an Irish Theatre" in a series of contentious letters to the *Irish Times,* 3, 6, 12, 15 October 1938.

determined to keep well out of it all. As a matter of fact, from the cuttings, I can't get the hang of it. I don't quite know what either of them's seeking —if I know at all.

I agree about poor Hunt [2]—he couldn't produce a play, without the earnest help of God; & God, in this respect, chooses whom He will. Hunt hasn't even been called. The Abbey should never have let you go away, banging the door after you. Had I been in a high place there, I'd have hung on to you, like grim death—&, possibly, have persuaded you to throw your job to hell! Well, maybe it's better the way it is—not, in my opinion, for the Abbey, though.

(it's gettin' long, this)

How we can write, other than out of our poor opinions, I don't know; & W.B.Y. doesn't know either (Is there an echo somewhere here?) Well, that was a long time ago; & I've forgiven Yeats: I hope he's forgiven me—though there wasn't anything to forgive, really. It was a principle, & I'd do it agen, Ma; I'd do it again (another echo?).

No, I didn't hear [Paul Vincent] Carroll's new play has been rejected. I read (Faolain's letter) in the I. Times, that "it was fighting for it's life", & that's all I knew. I wondher now? Ah, Gaby, when I think, had I had the chance, of the fine band of actors, Scenic Designers, & Producers I'd have gathered round me in the Abbey, I am sorrowful; but these tears are idle tears; & the day (and the chance) is over forever.

I've read "Church Street"; [3] and I'm afraid it's a bad play; & what could be worse than that?

And I'll look for a photo when I get books & papers sorted out.

And, now, my love to Rose (how *is* she; you didn't mention her name; & I'm very fond of Rose & so is Eileen),

to the little ones,
& to you.
Sean

P.T.O.

I thought of writing to St John [Ervine] about "Guff" & "welcome". They aren't exclusively Ulster words. Failte [4] is one of the commonest (& most beautiful) words in the Gaedhilge. "Guff" is the Gaedhilge for the "speaking voice", (guth) spelled guf (guf) & so pronounced in the Gaedhilge of Connacht.

But—

[2] Hugh Hunt, an Englishman who had served as a producer (director of plays) at the Abbey Theatre since 1935, resigned in October 1938. A letter from Hunt on his resignation appeared in the *Irish Times,* 7 October 1938. In January 1970 Hunt returned to the Abbey to become its artistic director.

[3] Lennox Robinson's *Church Street* opened at the Abbey Theatre on 21 May 1934.

[4] failte (pronounced *fall*-cha), joy, greeting, or welcome.

To Time and Tide

5 NOVEMBER 1938

"The Light of the World"

Sir:—*Time And Tide* has, undoubtedly, many fine and fair qualities. But, it seems to me, that your Journal fears Russia as the devil is said to fear holy water. It seems to stiffen when Russia's name is mentioned, ay, just as the most Conservative of papers stiffen when Russia's name is whispered. There seems to be a terrible commotion in the minds of many English people because Russia (according to accounts) has got rid of some of her generals. Strangely enough, too, because their loss has been "the ruin of her army." Well, generals may lose battles, but, as in the Great War, damn few of them seem to win them. Wouldn't it have been a good thing for England (her men, anyhow) if she had got quit of some of them before the war started? Didn't it take the Military experts twenty years to find out that General Gough was an intelligent soldier? I heard, myself, a famous statesman say that a certain famous general (up and doing during the war) "hadn't a single idea in his head." And what about the might of Russia's army when she had hardly a single superior whom she could trust? What did her starving, tattered armies do to the many attempts of her enemies to overthrow the Revolution, even when they were backed with the help of most of the countries of Europe?

Read Chamberlin's "The Russian Revolution". Even Stalky & Co had to scuttle out of Baku as fast as he could. What can her armies do now, well fed and powerfully armed? Stalky & Co have a lesser chance than ever.

And wasn't there a suicide the other day of a young man who left a note behind saying, "There seems to be no place in the world for me." Where was that, now? In Moscow? Some damned rogue told me it happened in either Oxford or Cambridge.

And, mentioning the recent flight of Soviet women from Moscow to the Amur, the *Daily Telegraph* said, "Russia is the only country in Europe who would trust such a fine machine to women." A writer in your own Journal said recently that "the creation of civil aviation was a stroke (or thought) of genius." Such a scheme is old-fashioned in Soviet Russia. And in England everyone has to fork out half-a-crown for an hour's jaunt. What worker can do this?

I notice in all the terrible things mentioned as happening in Russia, one appalling thing isn't in existence there, namely, A National Society for the Prevention of Cruelty to Children.

Didn't they tell us that one of the Soviet Arctic Explorers tried "to escape across the ice-floes to America." Doesn't that show you what a Soviet man could do, if he's put to the push?

Besides, they (and all us Communists) are ignorant, lacking all the grace of Christianity and the fineness of long established culture. Wasn't there a group of graceful, Christian members of parliament profoundly shocked recently because we "superimposed the Hammer and Sickle on the Cross of Christ"? Though, if the thick heads had any power of thought at all, what lovelier symbols could be placed upon Christ's Cross than these two symbols?

Ye have the light: two thousand years of grace from God and, through the Bible or the Sacrements, the wonderful Gifts of the Holy Ghost; but yet there is the National Society for the Prevention of Cruelty to Children; and the *Telegraph* tells us that the finer airplanes are not to be trusted to women.

Up the Soviets!

I am, etc.,
Sean O'Casey

To George Jean Nathan

MS. CORNELL
DEVON
[? NOVEMBER 1938]

My very dear George:

Peaceful & contented! Hardly that. I am more likely to be content in a town than I am in the country. But we thought it might be cheaper to live here; and there is a fine school (at least we hope it's fine) for the two boys. So I just smothered my doubts & anxiety; & came here, bag & baggage. At the moment, I'm awaiting the Page Proofs of "I Knock At The Door"; the galleys are done, thank God. And I can never be peaceful or content about the work I do. I never seem to be satisfied. Maybe, it is just as well.

And only the other week I had a row with a boyo (well known in Boston), called Maurice Leahy.[1] It was that Walter Starkie gave a LECTURE about me at the Abbey Theatre Festival; & when it was nearly over, this boyo got up & asked questions about O'Casey's attitude to Christianity, etc. So I replied in the Irish Press; there was a lot of

[1] See O'Casey's letters to the *Irish Times,* 29 August 1938, note 1, and to the *Irish Press,* 17 October 1938, note 1.

talk in Dublin about it, especially when I sent a letter got from this boyo some years ago, praising my work and me up to the nines. (I discovered the letter, quite by accident, when I was burning waste, just before packing things to leave London). The letter has silenced him in Dublin. With Leahy, too, was a Rev. Father O'Connolly S.J. who led the fight in Boston (with a Father Sullivan) against "Within the Gates".[2] A Franciscan Father, friend of his & mine (I have friends in heaven & hell) told Father Connolly he'd have to come to see me in London, & talk things over. Just what I'd love to do; so I sent word to Dublin that I'd love to see Father Connolly, & we could talk of many things over a cup of tea or a ball o'malt—whichever he preferred: he never came.

As well, a kind of split or conflict has developed among those who have to do with the Abbey Theater; and, I'm afraid, it will do the Abbey no good. There has been a big correspondence in the Press, giving this opinion, & giving that opinion. Privately, I hear that it is a fight between Yeats & [F. R.] Higgins on the one hand, and Lennox Robinson & Sean O'Faolain on the other. Yeats, it appears, is out to drive all "Realism" from the Abbey Stage; &, I think, incidently, to drive my plays out as well. (To be fair, this is but a suspicion, & I have no proof of it whatsoever, except that, I'm sure, he's never forgiven me for daring to argue with him over the rejection of the "Silver Tassie". Even when I saw him in Dublin two years ago,[3] & was his guest in his house, he forgot his duty as a host by rebuking me once more for publishing the correspondence—a deed I would do a dozen times, if I once thought it necessary). What this "Realism" is I can't guess. I do feel terribly ignorant when these titles to things theatrical are brought up for discussion. The Editor of "The Irish Times" sent me the Press Cuttings, & pleaded that I should join in; but I refused, & am determined that this or these problems must be solved by themselves—I have neither the time nor the brains to help. I've read the correspondence three times, & can't get the hang of it. I don't know what they want. I am enclosing it with this letter to you. It may interest you, or even provoke an article. When you've finished with them, you can post them back; but, if this be irritating in any way (for you've a lot of work to do), just burn the bloody things.

Candidly, my dear George, I should be delighted to get "Newsweek"—with your articles in it—from you. I've begun to get "Esquire", & enjoyed your layout on acting. And, be God, it came at a curious moment. Listen! I think I told you that there was a great enterprise going on here, called "Dartington Hall Activities"—Textiles, Pottery, Woodwork, Cider making, etc.—organised by a very wealthy American woman, Mrs. Elmhirst (nee

[2] See O'Casey's cable to George Bushar Markle and John Tuerk, 21? January 1935, note 2.

[3] It was in September 1935, on his final trip to Ireland, that O'Casey visited Yeats at his home in Riversdale, Rathfarnham. For his account of the visit, see "The Friggin Frogs," *Rose and Crown* (1952).

Straight) & her husband, helped by a Board of Trustees. A very fine enterprise, & doing grand work. The School is part of the activity. Well, this woman's daughter (as well-off as her mother), Miss Beatrice Straight, established a theater, called The Dartington Hall Chekhov Theater Studio. They set out to train themselves for three years in acting, & then go on tour, here & in the U.S.A. Two years ago they asked me to take on the job of helping the work by writing bits for them to act, under the supervision & direction of Chekhov.[4] I sent a short note refusing. Mrs. Elmhirst sent me a letter pleading with me to reconsider the matter, & accept. Then I launched a letter criticising the whole thing, & again refusing. I imagined I saw then, that the methods were wrong, & that the venture would fail. I'm afraid I was right. (After my refusal, I never mentioned the matter, one way or the other). Last issue of "News of the Day", programme of activities about Dartington, it was published that the Theater Studio was leaving Dartington, to make its headquarters in the U.S.A. And when it had been established there, it was to go on tour—with what, I don't know. A lot of money has been spent, & the results are, I'm afraid, small. Anyway, Mrs. Elmhirst, just before her daughter left for America, asked me to advise her as to whom Miss Straight would go to in America for council & help. I suggested Dick Madden, pointing out that he, of course, would have to be paid for his time. (I have written to Dick about it). Then Mrs. E. mentioned Brooks Atkinson, & I said she couldn't go to a better man—bar you, though you would be certain to be less kind to anything in the nature of codology. Beatrice Straight is a pretty, charming, & intelligent girl; & I do wish & I do hope that all her work & enthusiasm will show results. To go back to your article in "Esquire": it seemed, nay it did, counter every, or almost every, canon of acting held sacred by the Chekhov Studio. It was funny that it came into my hands at such a time. It confirmed all I had been thinking about the acting practised by the Students here: all & every way of doing things beautifully, gracefully, & delightfully—except that unimportant thing of acting in a play! As some seem to think Dress clothes make a gentleman; so others think that fantastic conduct & strange dress make an artist. An artist or a gentleman can wear what he chooses; but his clothes have little to do with the making of him. Anyhow, what I wanted to say is that I gave "Esquire" to one of the Secretaries to read; & I pray God that the article has been read, too, by some of those connected with the Theater Studio.

I'm so glad to hear Gene is getting on so well with his new work. I pray God it may be great. Gene is indeed a lovable & great man. When next you write to him, give him my undiminished love and admiration—& Carlotta, too.

I envy you your chances of being so close to the beautiful American

[4] Michael Chekhov (1891–1955), director and actor, nephew of Anton Chekhov.

girls—in this respect, the wealthiest nation in the world. "An honest man's the noblest work of God" me neck! A lovely girl's the noblest work of God, say I.

Isn't Charles Morgan a curious gift from God? Funny enough, he's an idol here—every one that counts breathless with adoration. Well, he leaves me cold, & I have to say so, or lose my temper. The figures he loves have little to do with love—at least, not in my experience.

I hope to be able to get on to the play soon. I've ideas for several in my head.

This letter (so long) has probably tired you out; but it's my only chance of having a chat with you.

So farewell for a week or so.
With deep affection.
Sean

To George Jean Nathan

MS. CORNELL

DEVON
9 DECEMBER 1938

My dear George:

Wc are fairly unsettled in here at last. This is just a note to thank you for "Newsweek." With that, Esquire, & the Theatrical magazine, parts of "The New York Times" & "The Herald-Tribune", I am able to see America, as if in a glass, darkly; but not clear enough to write a book about it—as so many do, after a visit to New York to look at the dock. I'm glad you are beginning to go to the Country for a week-end—about enough—if you ask me; but a little is fine. I hope your health is OK again.

The chief news is—notwithstanding a few reviews for the Sunday Times; & an odd dash into print for Communist, Irish Front, & Democratic Activities—that I am in the middle—more than the middle—of the new play: First Act & Second done; 3rd Act nearly so; & 4th partly. Out of a hugh mountain of chaos, order is, I think, beginning to appear.

With Love,
Sean

To Forward

10 DECEMBER 1938

WOULD YOU VOTE FOR THE DUCHESS?

We have received the following replies from well-known public men and women [1] in reply to our question, "If you had a vote in West Perthshire, would you vote for the Duchess of Atholl?"

Sean O'Casey

Irish Playwright:

"Lady Atholl is a woman in whose head a mind is looking forward; she has courage to join in the thoughts of the people on great and deep questions vitally concerning Democracy. A mean effort is being made to close her mouth, and so close her mind against revealing the things that belong to our peace. There are too many closed minds in England; and a thousand times too many in the Conservative Party.

They are trying to down her because she has refused to remain dumb and pat, sitting still among the coot and hern Conservative crowd.

If I lived in West Perthshire, and had a vote, my vote would be early in the ballot box, and the X on the paper would be directly opposite the name of Lady Atholl."

[1] Replies in support of Lady Atholl also appeared from Bernard Shaw, Ethel Mannin, Victor Gollancz, Kingsley Martin, and others.

To Michael Casey [1]

MS. MURPHY

DEVON

18 DECEMBER 1938

Dear Mick,

Enclosed will get you some tobacco for Christmas.

I'd have sent more, but with two kids it's hard to make both ends meet.

We've come to Devon, finding London too expensive to live in; & here there's a school we like for the two boys.

Hope you are well,

"Jack"

[1] Michael Casey (1866–1947), O'Casey's brother, who was living in Dublin with their niece, Mrs. Isabella Murphy, the daughter of their sister, Mrs. Isabella Casey Beaver. See O'Casey's letters to Mrs. Murphy, 20 January 1947, Vol. II, on the occasion of his brother's death.

To Gabriel Fallon

MS. TEXAS

DEVON
27 DECEMBER 1938

My dear Gaby:

Well that is a surprise and a shock—the Abbey taking to the law over a criticism.[1] Surely the report from the Stationer's Office was sufficient foundation for any reasonable man on which to fix a statement. Why have they taken exception to this particular criticism? Is it because it deals with money? But surely, if we know anything, to criticise the acting or the production of a theatre is far more serious than to criticise how they spend the money; for it is from acting & production money comes. Surely they discovered this during the last American Tour when the New York critics almost as one man chorussed out at them about the serious deterioration in Abbey acting & production. National or Non-National, the support depends (after the plays) on acting, & production. I can't see that they have a case. You, I'm sure, mentioned no name, & did not, even in your secret mind, assume any thing like personal speculation. Money can easily be squandered (& is in cartloads) on bad plays, bad acting & bad production. Here there is waste everywhere. The Abbey isn't a bud or a bloom of perfection. I can't see that they have a case against you. I feel sure you've been sending a critical arrow in, now & again, through loopholes; but why not? They need a critic above & beyond the things calling themselves critics in the Daily Newspapers. If you haven't already gone to a Solicitor Go to McCracken & McCracken of Ormond Quay: they were the men who stood by me when the Abbey threatened law proceedings. And don't worry—it's not much, when you are used to it. At the moment, I'm threatened with a law action over 49. Overstrand Mansions; writing to solicitors, etc, but it's all in the day's work.

And, in my experience, something was wrong with the business of the Abbey some years ago; for I had a hell of a job to get royalties due.

[1] In a lecture given at the Dublin Literary Society on 9 December 1938 and reported in the Irish newspapers, Fallon stated in reference to the Abbey Theatre that "a theatre which in four years work lost £8,280 despite the fact that it had been receiving £1,000 a year was a theatre which was in need of something more than financial assistance." In reply to this accusation, F. R. Higgins, managing director of the Abbey Theatre, stated in the *Irish Times,* 14 December 1938, that the theatre had in fact lost the trivial sum of £42 during the four-year period, 1934–37. See Fallon's public apology in his letter to the *Irish Times,* 20 January 1939, where he retracts his accusation and indicates that he has "indemnified the theatre against the legal costs incurred by them in the matter."

Enclosed copy of letter will show you of it, in 1934. (Let me have it back) Ervine once wrote asking why letters of his weren't answered, asking for Royalties due. I myself wrote to Mr. Robinson, Lady Gregory, The Secretary—numbers of times; & even to W.B. The letter enclosed was to Starkie. So you see, everything then wasn't going the way it should have gone.

Don't bother about "heavy damages". How the hell could you pay them? Sixpence a week, & a bob at Christmas. And, if you agree to their conditions, strike some of them out. Agree to no more than, at least, you can pay without hurting your family. If the Abbey is determined to be vindictive, then it's the beginning of the end.

A letter acknowledging your mistake (if it be one) should be enough for them. There was no personal attack; no malice behind the criticism; it was in the public interest you spoke; so where can the libel be?

Yours as Ever
Sean

I send back your
cuttings
2 Enclosures

To Eric Gorman [1]

TC. O'CASEY
[DEVON]
30 DECEMBER 1938

Dear Mr. Gorman:

I have heard that the Abbey Theatre is contemplating legal action against Gaby Fallon for something he said in a lecture recently given in Dublin. Without knowing much about it (beyond a few cuttings sent to me), I would venture an appeal to the Directors not to go on with this intent. Fallon, as you know, is an old Abbeyite, and, whatever may be said by others or even by himself, loves the Old Theatre still. I haven't the slightest doubt about this. I think the Abbey, fighting as she has and is against all kinds of censorship, should hesitate before she establishes a legal one herself. Certainly, there was something wrong some years ago. I remember Con O'Leary telling me he got no royalties for the production of a one act play of his; and St John Ervine wrote asking me "what was wrong with the Abbey," for he couldn't get any reply to letters sent in-

[1] Eric Gorman (1886–1971), secretary of the Abbey Theatre and an actor in the company.

quiring about royalties due to him; and I, myself, had quite a lot of trouble about this matter, too. The recent correspondence between O'Faolain and O'Connor showed there was a difference of opinion about other matters. Incidentally, I was asked to join in this discussion, but, not knowing enough, and being too far away to even get my ear to the ground, I refused. But the Abbey has made mistakes; I think one was to get an English Producer [Hugh Hunt]—not because he was English, but because Ireland has nothing to learn from the English theatre of the moment; it couldn't be much deader than it is. I thought at the time, too, that it was a mistake to get Shubert to patronise the recent American tour—I think I said so in a letter to you. But these things are over, and we all wish the Abbey to live and thrive. To prove oneself virtuous before the law isn't a great thing to do. I have no business, of course, in interfering in this matter, but I have still some connection with the Theatre (even were it only the mercenary one of getting royalties which come in very useful) still, and so wish the venture well. Therefore, I am bold to appeal to the Directors to come to some understanding that will fend this action off, satisfactory to themselves, and that will not exact too big a penance from a well-intentioned criticism.

I enclose Agreement signed. And thanks for your good wishes. I wish the same to you, to the Theatre, and to all who have it in their care.

Very Sincerely,
Sean O'Casey

To Gabriel Fallon

TS. Texas

Devon
9 January 1939

Dear Gaby: The enclosed is a letter I sent to the Abbey Theatre. That is, it is a copy of one I sent. They seem to be convinced that your lecture overstepped the mark, and that your remarks about their financial circumstances stepped well into defamatory libel. I am told that a letter was sent to you, that afterwards F. R. Higgins sent a letter to the Press asking three questions arising out of your statement and F.R.'s reply, and that no reply was given. It seems that had a reply been given [it] would have relieved the situation. Now, be this as it may, they are clearly concerned about the financial implications, and no-one can blame them. If one was making a lot out of a thing, it wouldn't matter much; but when one makes nothing out of it, then it is really maddening to rest under the implication of having got away with something. I wish the whole matter could be solved quietly, without recourse to blows—for these will do neither you nor the Abbey Good. If you have been mistaken, and it would seem you have been, then there is nothing else to do but to go and say so as loudly as you can. There is nothing to be ashamed of in making a mistake; It is the cowardly non-acknowledgement of them that shows the vanity and brings the danger (says Stalin), and Stalin is right.

If you have been mistaken, and say so, I think the Abbey Directors will meet you. As you have said, you've really no grudge against the theatre—in fact, I've always held that you should never have left it—, and so there is no reason why you and they should not shake hands—even if you call each other a gang of bastards when you get home again.

Law business is a painful thing, and the less you have to do with it, the better; and, anyhow, win or lose, it's bound to cost money that can ill be spared, really by either side.

I am assured that there is no vindictiveness behind all this, and that the Directors are honestly angered and grieved over this imputation (which you never meant), and that they would be willing (with you willing, too) to pass over it by a generous recognition by you of the way in which the Public look upon the implication of a particular part of your lecture.

So up with the flag of Conciliation, my dear Gaby, and let the matter end forever and a day.

Yours As Ever,
Sean

Enclosure

To Gabriel Fallon

TS. TEXAS

DEVON

13 JANUARY 1939

My dear Gaby:

You are quite right; the letters of dec 27 and jan 9 though written by the same man, were written under a very different feeling; and the Abbey had nothing to do with it. The first was in a gay, damn it all, fight it out way; the second was written—after a talk with Eileen—with your Missus and kids staring me in the face. I was afraid my fist * letter would cock you up to fight, and so I sent the other to (first having written to the Abbey to blunt their spear, if possible) you, to make sure that the

* fist should be "first," but fist is better, so let it stand.

first letter wouldn't prompt you to do anything unwise. There is a time when a fellow has to take up his gun, and run! But I am out against the condition of life in which, under such circumstances, a man has to think of his wife and children. A man should be able to do anything, go to jail, die, anything, without his children having to suffer (in the way of necessities) for it. The children are never to blame. To tell me that, if you had gone on with the case, it might have meant the loss of your job, and, even under things as they are, it will mean a postponement of what you call promotion, is to tell me of the tyranny of the present system of social life. And they blather about Russia! Don't worry your head about my "righteous anger"; it was a suitable term for the moment. My anger against a man's danger of seeing his children suffer because of something he has done (right or wrong) is righteous anger. But it is hard to say whether our anger be righteous when it is the result of some personal impact. Then we have to be on our guard, for many things enter into it.

Without going into details, I still think the Abbey made a mistake by resorting to the law. On one occasion, they sent their solicitor's letter to me, demanding cancellation [of] a performance in Belfast by Sinclair, built on the technicality of Perrin sending me notice of renewal of contract.[1] But they had to agree to the very point that I had inserted in Sinclair's agreement, giving them free use of Dublin performances. That gave me (and them) a lot of trouble, over nothing at all. I'm afraid I was very rude to Kildare St—if that be still the place where their solicitor hangs out. What they should have done was to challenge you to public debate, and to thresh out the financial question, and any other criticism you had given against their various activities. The Abbey, in my opinion, must be wary of any kind of censorship by them. But the Abbey must find it hard to make both ends meet. I remember when I was in Dublin, that it cost something like eight or ten thousand to do it (or, so I was told). Now, it must cost a hell of a lot more, and the Government grant doesn't go far. So far they have my sympathy. And the Abbey has done well, in the past, and, I hope, may do well in the future (not if they are prone to run to the law), and I would do a lot, and, maybe, pray a little, rather than let the Abbey die. But their first mistake was to let you go. The theatre is in your blood; and you were bound to be of use to them. I would have had you—if you were determined to give up the acting—on an advisory staff; if necessary, I'd have punched you into the position. They weren't able to pick their men, Look at that kid (she played Mollser) whom they let go, too—I've forgotten her name.[2] I met her

[1] For the right of Arthur Sinclair's Irish Players to perform *Juno* and *Plough*, see O'Casey's letter to Whitney, Moore and Keller, 23 July 1929, and subsequent letters up to the settlement in the 26 August 1929 telegram from Whitney, Moore and Keller.

[2] Kitty Curling.

afterwards at a theatrical exhibition in Philadelphia, looking wistfully at the examples of theatrical art there. Oh, well, we all make mistakes.

As I said before, there, to me, seems to have been no cause for an action against you. If anyone should have been held to account, it was the Minister who gave the details of what the Abbey had lost during the past couple of years. It was the implication of "mis-management", I suppose, that got them riled. But there are many other ways of "mis-managing" a theatre, or anything else. Maybe, more dangerous ways too. But the Abbey has, in my opinion, always been too sensitive to criticism. You know yourself the row I got into for criticising the performance of Man And Superman.[3] That was what began the dislike of me in the Greenroom. Yet I know that every word was justified. Suppose I had then been under the actors' thumbs? The Inquisition would have been nothing to it! And look at what happened over the The Silver Tassie. They were to criticise me, but I wasn't to criticise them. But this sort of thing has followed me all my life, and I'm getting used to it. Read the enclosed letters got the other day, and let me have them back when you're writing to me again. And you'd hardly believe how every effort has been made to smother the "The Flying Wasp".

Well, in the middle of a play, and with my eyes aching, I've sat down to write to an old and well-loved buttie, this letter of explanation. I eventually thought it was a time for you to run, and I did what I could to get you started—and that is all. I think that many, very many of your criticisms about the Abbey are correct, and I think this last one should never have been the cause of a threat to bring the law on to you.

But, by the way, there seems to be a mistake in the adding of your figures. If you take the profit of £983 away from the loss, you have less than the figure you give—namely £4,341. It seems to be £3,341.

Meanwhile, my love to Rose and to the five children. And next Christmas this turmoil, will be forgotten, I hope (not to leave the thing till after Christmas was mean). Yours til the day when no man will risk his job by saying what he thinks he should say.

Yours as Ever
Buttie Sean

Enclosure

[3] See O'Casey's letter to Michael J. Dolan, 13 August 1925.

To George Jean Nathan

MS. CORNELL

DEVON

13 JANUARY 1939

My dear George:

Good wishes for the New Year. I read your articles with delight, those in Newsweek & those in Esquire. You gave a fine mallavoging [1] to Priestley. Poor Priestley! Time and Mr. Priestley—what will Time do to him? I enclose some notes written by J. B. [Priestley] in Time and Tide. It appears that he "feels something hostile & even menacing to him in New York." There's egoism for you! Imagine the 5 or 6 million of New York feeling hostile to him! Why, probably, not more than two in every hundred heard of him. One can feel hostile to a city; but a city can't feel hostile to us. That is simply impossible. He felt hostile to New York because his play failed to go. So, to save his feelings, he must believe that the City was hostile to him. He "went to great trouble to find a guest room." Fancy that! Well, I've had experience of four hotels in New York: The Royalton with you; The Dorset, with [John] Tuerk & [George] Bushar [Markle]; the Devon, with myself; & the big Biltmore with James Stephens, & in each I found the rooms quiet—nothing but the sound of our own voices. Here, where I am now, in the County of Devon, is as noisy, even noisier than the places I stayed in during my visit to New York. You are right in saying Priestley writes a play while Gene is sharpening his pencil. Priestley has another one ready now! The English have determined among themselves that Priestley's a great Dramatist, & he can't understand the New York critics giving him the frozen mitt. Has he really written one yet as good as O'Neill's or Shaw's worst? I enclose an Agate criticism of Gene's "Marco Millions." [2] How Agate seems to hate him! While, writing about "Paradise Lost" (Odets) [3] he does everything he can to make it good; yet he tries in every way to make any work (as far as I know) by O'Neill bad. And the silly things he says to prove it. "But the difference between being & not being matters a lot, dear Mr. O'Neill." How can it matter? How can being matter to one who has ceased to be? This fellow, evidently, thinks that one who has ceased to be, yet is.

It was good of you to let me have "Newsweek." It does give a fair idea of the American scene & fair synopsis of foreign news. So with that, Esquire, the theatrical parts of "Herald-Tribune" & "The New York

[1] mallavoging, from the Irish mealbhóg, a bag, i.e., a bagging or beating.

[2] James Agate, "The Higher Fudge," *Sunday Times,* 1 January 1939, a review of Eugene O'Neill's *Marco Millions,* which opened in London on 26 December 1938.

[3] James Agate, "A Good Bad Play," *Sunday Times,* 18 December 1938, a review of Clifford Odets's *Paradise Lost,* which opened in London on 11 December 1938.

Times," & the Commentary of Raymond Gram Swing, I do hear a word or two from America.

I have just finished "The Star Turns Red" & have to add a line or two, & go through it once more to see & feel (or try to, rather) how it moves.

"I Knock at the Door" is to be published in March. Macmillan of New York are publishing it on the same day. I'll mail you—so don't get one) the first that comes to me. I'm still getting censored here: I wrote an article called "Ulster For Ireland" for a Labour paper called "Forward." [4] They thought it so good, that they sent it to their usual agency to get it printed in the U.S.A., but the agency sent it back, saying that it "wasn't in the best interests of Socialism to have it published." And an article on a book about John Mitchell (whose sons fought for the South) for the Sunday Times (at their own request) hasn't appeared yet, though it has been in their hands for two weeks before Christmas.[5] However, we'll wait & see.

How is your health? Are you keeping fit?

My love to you.
Sean

[4] Sean O'Casey, "Ulster For Ireland: Some Plain Truths For Protestants and Catholics," *Forward,* Glasgow, 7 January 1939; reprinted in *Irish Freedom,* London, May 1939.

[5] His review of Seamus MacCall's *Irish Mitchel* (London, Nelson, 1938) had already appeared, "From Prison Cell," *Sunday Times,* 20 November 1938; however, he wrote another review of the same book, "Ireland's Tongue of Fire," which was soon to appear in *Irish Freedom,* March 1939.

To David Astor [1]

TC. O'CASEY
17 JANUARY 1939

Dear Mr David Astor:

Thank you for your card and very kind wishes. As for choosing between dogs and haloes, it depends very much on how theyre done in paint or stone. Many haloes are very beautiful—Raphael, Giotto, Fra Angelico, and many others. But these dogs depicted in the card you sent to me are as bad as the worst of haloes. It is such a medley of forms that no form is shown in it at all. And because it is bad art (which means it isnt art at all), it doesnt much matter whether it be coarse or refined.

[1] David Astor (1912–), Hon. David Langhorne, son of Lady Astor and Second Viscount Astor; editor of *The Observer* since 1948.

Rembrandt, you remember, could make a lump of beef beautiful. But, then, that was Rembrandt, that was! Who is the young man standing looking at the dogs? Is that meant to be the Honorable David Astor? If the Honorable, well enough; but if it is meant to be the intelligent, nervous, imaginative young man I once knew—David Astor—then, what a falling off is there! Jasus, man, youre not going to see the universe in a pack of snarling curs? You are young; you are intelligent; you have, I think, imagination that which, according to Blake, links us close to heaven.

Dont waste these tremendous gifts on dogs. After throwing away the dollars, dont go to the dogs. But, if you are beginning to take an interest in art, then a bad beginning's no great harm. We all make bad beginnings. I began with the Victorian story-telling pictures, and ended with the Old Masters (as new as ever) and Cezanne, Van Gogh, John, Utrillo, Matisse, and others.

But it was very kind of you to remember me. We are down here in Devon, now. I am to have a new book out in March. Life story up to twelve years of age. Hope you'll buy it. Hope you'll read it. Hope you'll like it. Called "I Knock at the Door."

I return your kind wishes most sincerely,

Yours,
Sean O'Casey

To Brooks Atkinson

TS. ATKINSON

[DEVON]
19 JANUARY 1939

My dear Brooks:

Remember saying some time ago that I should write nothing but works of art?

Well, since then I've written a lot of stuff that had nothing to do with Art; but a new book by me (dealing with my life up to twelve years of age—one of three, I hope), called "I Knock At The Door", is coming out in March, & I think it has something in common with a work of art. But has it? How do I know? I don't know; I simply feel it has; but I may be a helluva long way out in my reckoning. I feel you'll like it (again I don't know), & will say, "O'Casey has done something at last!"

By the way, I read your article every week on the Theatre in "The New Y. Times"; agreeing with you & disagreeing with you as often as you would agree & disagree with me. In your article about the Abe Lincoln play,[1] you mentioned the word "Wrastler", putting it in brackets as I Love Alone. That was the way in which I, as a kid, pronounced & always heard the word wrestler spoken. "He's a great wrastler"; & I often watched men wrestling in the Phoenix Park for a colored garter—for that was the reward of the Championship. I think it was called "heel & toe" wrastling; & it was always very thrilling. I've got some ugly falls myself in the game. It is amazing how often Ireland peeps out in American manners. I've a book here called "Modern American Usage" giving about 270 examples of "American" modern idioms, unacquainted with the King's English. Over a hundred of them were common (& still are) in Ireland when I was a kid; most of them, I think, survivals of the Elizabethan way of speaking. The English don't know their own tongue.

I hate the London Critics as deeply as ever. Did you see the row they kicked up over "Death Takes a Holiday"?[2] Brown condemned & ridiculed it bitterly because of dialogue & situation that, it was revealed afterwards by Richard Watt, Junr., an English dramatic improver had put into the play. But not a word from Brown. Oh, they're a mangy lot—as we say in Dublin—I wouldn't be found dead with them.

I hope you're well, & that Mrs. Brooks Atkinson is as well as you are.

And so farewell for the present.
Yours Very Sincerely.
Sean O'Casey

[1] Brooks Atkinson, "Lincoln's Prairie Years," *New York Times,* 23 October 1938, his Sunday column review of Robert E. Sherwood's *Abe Lincoln in Illinois,* which opened in New York on 15 October 1938, and ran for 287 performances.

[2] Walter Ferris's *Death Takes a Holiday,* based on Alberto Casella's *La morte in vacanze* (1924), opened in New York on 26 December 1929.

To L. E. Carroll [1]

TC. O'CASEY

21 JANUARY 1939

Dear Mr Carroll:

You are quite right—the artist is altogether on the wrong track. Neither of the pictures has anything to do with the spirit, the manner, or the temperament of the book.[2] The place is Dublin; and the two places in Dublin most prominent are Nelson's Pillar and The Bank of Ireland

[1] L. E. Carroll, editorial staff, Macmillan & Co. Ltd., London.

[2] *I Knock at the Door,* to be released in March 1939.

(Old House of Parliament). The regemine or regime or regiment then was that of Victoria and the Lion and the Unicorn; and its chief enemy Parnell. The Church, too, had a hand in it; so these, or symbols of them, should, I think be the picture on the jacket.

I enclose two horrible sketches of a faint idea of what I mean. No 1, has the pattern of the Celtic Cross peculiar to Ireland, as the principal panelling of the door. In the corners are 1, the Arms of Dublin; 2, Lion and Unicorn; 3, Nelson's Pillar; 4, a church; and at each side of the cross's circle, a head of Parnell and a head of Queen Victoria.

If these ideas or connections could be stylised somewhat, so much the better, or they could be made so as to appear like carvings on the door, like the carvings on the panels of the Celtic crosses. I have inserted a little door into the main design, but maybe it would be better to make the whole design into one big door. The figure of the boy should be as small as possible—it is the door of life that he is supposed to be knocking at it. If this design is to be followed, Nelson's Pillar and the Lion and Unicorn ought to be on a slant, not the Dublin Arms, as shown in draft; or, if the artist thinks it better harmony, then all upright, or all on the slant.

The 2nd Sketch shows the Arms of Dublin forming the door, with the other panels imposed. I prefer the first one. Perhaps the mother might be shown at the corner, watching the boy knocking at the door. Anyway, realism wont do. I prefer a plain jacket to that. Maybe these thoughts will give you a little help. I hope so.

Yours sincerely,
[*Sean O'Casey*]

Instead of green
Crimson, or Blue or
purple, or Red & black.

To Horace Reynolds

MS. Reynolds

Devon
22 January 1939

My dear Horace,

Just a line to keep in touch with Harvard & you. I'm very busy at the moment with "I Knock at the Door". (Macmillans have asked me for ideas to make a picture jacket—the artist doing the job hasn't the slightest idea of what it should be like, so Shaun has to help him out), & my play;

& trying to make the Commissioners of Inland Revenue wait a minute or two for some tax owed to them. They're done singing "God rest you merry, gentlemen", & Jesus is quietly hid in the lumber room for another year or so. However, in my next letter to them (with, I hope, a cheque on account) I'll put in a big request to them to buy my book out in March, & so help me to please them. "I hope you'll buy it; I hope you'll read it; I hope you'll like it, gentlemen". I think I've finished Maurice Leahy in Ireland. In the move here, while burning papers, I came across a treasure, copy of which I enclose here. I sent a copy to Dublin & it was published in the press & put the caidp bháss [1] (Kybosh) on Leahy.[2] Isn't it a nice example of what a crawling bousey can do?

We are all well here, but I'm a bit lonely. Love to Kay & the children & to you.

Sean

[1] caidhp bais, cap of death.
[2] See his letter to the *Irish Press,* 17 October 1938.

To Michael A. McInerney [1]

TC. O'CASEY

[DEVON]
24 JANUARY 1939

Dear Mr McInerney:

Thank you for your letter. I'm afraid I could be of no active use to your Club. Many Labour activities write asking me to give my name, and, if I consented, that name would appear in many places, giving it an importance I shouldn't like it to have, and which it in no way deserves. Rightly or wrongly, I dont like my name to be too prominent, for I am shy about appearing to pose in any way as a sir oracle. I suggest that a far more suitable name for a Vice-Presidency of your Club, is the name of Jim Larkin. Jim, as you know, was and is a great Irish Labour Leader.

As for a message, how can I, to follow Stalin, say anything that I have not already said? Your policy is the only possible policy for Irishmen earning a living in England, or earning a living anywhere else, for that matter. It is labour alone that keeps the world going, and it is labour alone, labour with hand and brain that alone can make life, not only worth living—that wouldnt be a very great thing to do—, but a vigorous and joyous experience. Workers unite, not only to secure what the clergy call "a living wage"—that is a mere existence—, but workers are uniting and

[1] Michael A. McInerney, secretary of the James Connolly Club, London.

fighting to bring about a condition of things giving the workers all that life can give—that is to all human beings, for in that world all will be workers.

"An honest day's wage for an honest day's work" is a phrase that is a cod and an outcast. To hell with it. There never was such a thing and there never will be.

I wish your efforts every success.
Sincerely Yours,
[*Sean O'Casey*]

To George Jean Nathan

MS. CORNELL

DEVON
8 FEBRUARY 1939

My very dear George:

I am sending on the play, "The Star Turns Red" to you, under another cover; and a copy to Dick Madden, too, who, every fortnight, asked me if the play was coming on next week. First, the copies are a bit shaggy. The old typewriter is a bit worn—it's gone to be mended, now—, & I didn't want to go to the expense of having fair & elegant copies typed. So try to forgive the tax on your eyes and nerves, for my sake. Next, I hope you'll see something in it. As well as being something of a confession of faith, it is, I think, a play; &, possibly, the best of its kind which has been written—which isn't saying a lot. There are, anyhow, some good lines in it. It is, I think, much more compact than "Within The Gates," though I don't yet know just how much of the verse form ought to go to a play dealing with present-day life. There was too much singing in "Within The Gates," or, maybe, as is most probable, the singing was in the wrong place; or the chanting, or whatever we can call it. The action takes place during the last few hours of a Christmas Eve; & by this means, I've managed, I think, to give an ironical twist here & there. And I've tried to give a symbolism in the coloring of the 4 scenes, as you will see. However, you will judge for yourself. For the past two weeks, the house here has been upset with influenza (the Grippe) but, though surrounded on every side, I came clear so far. I hope you escaped it. I see by the N.Y. Times, that Brooks was laid low. I wrote him a week or so ago telling him of my new book. He once wrote to me (after reading the "Flying Wasp") advising me never to write anything save a "work of art." (as if I could ever tell whether what I was writing was a work of art or no), and I told him I hoped he'd take "I Knock at the Door" as a work of art. This morning, I got a New Year's card from Carlotta [O'Neill]. I'll be writing to thank her soon (and him), & hope you may be able to forward the letter on for me. It's great news that Gene has four of his plays in hand. Go neartiaghidh Dia é! May God strengthen him—in Irish. What a mind that boy (for he's only a boy—as you are—me, too) has for keeping his thoughts together to carry a series of plays from beginning to end! As in "Strange Interlude" & "Mourning Becomes Electra" I wish to God I had such a mind. And you seem to be able to remember the Theatre from Alpha to Omega, too! It takes me time to think of a thing that happened an hour ago. I'm glad that your "The White Steed" [1] is a success, & that Fitzgerald is so good in it—though the bastard hasn't sent me a line since he acted in the Film of The Plough & the Stars. I enclose Agate's criticism of Coward's "Design for Living," & what he said about Odets' "Paradise Lost." "This play," says he, "is American"—in italics. Good Christ! I can't understand this sort of talk. Every play written by an American is an American play; & this plea of unfamiliarity in an American play maddens me. I've seen some; read many, & never found one of them unfamiliar.

Well, this will leave it.

My love, & the expectation of seeing you in late May.
Yours
Sean

[1] Paul Vincent Carroll's *The White Steed,* with Barry Fitzgerald in the leading role of Canon Matt Lavelle, opened in New York on 10 January 1939, and ran for 136 performances.

To Evan Walters [1]

MS. MEINEL [2]
DEVON
8 FEBRUARY 1939

My dear Evan,

How are you at all? We have been down here in Devon for some time. Last I heard of you was that you had been ill, & had gone back

[1] Evan Walters (1893–1951), British painter, born in Wales. See also O'Casey's comments on Walters' life and work, in an interview and letter to David Bell, 5 June 1952, Vol. II. Walters drew a portrait of O'Casey in 1936.

[2] From a copy made by Erna Meinel, executor of the Walters estate.

to Llangyfelach to live; but, apparently, you are back in London again. How are things with you, & are you able to keep body and soul together? We came here thinking to live cheaper, but, I'm afraid, we'll find it something of an illusion.

God be with the times you and I used to say what art was & was not, sitting cushy by the fire! I do hope you manage to sell a picture or two. Most of us have just got over influenza. I'm sending this note to the National Society in the hope you'll get it.

Affectionate regards.
Yours as Ever,
Sean

To Gabriel Fallon

MS. Texas

Devon
9 February 1939

My dear Gaby:

I agree with you: You've done enough; job or no job, I'd do no more. They're trying to rub it in a bit too roughly. I'm sorry you've been blasted with the influenza. Our house, too has been topsy turvy with it—all except myself. I came free háunig mé slán.[1] I enclose a few cuttings from American papers that may interest you—pictures of Boss, Shelah, & the bould Will.[2] By all accounts, Will is giving a great show in "The White Steed". The boyo hasn't written a line to me since he went to America. His interview will possibly amuse you. Not a word about you & me, or the way we had to coax, shout, drill, & threaten him into the part of Boyle & Fluther—principally you. Well, he has the goods, anyway, & that covers a lot of sin.

I've just had a busy time knocking out a design for the jacket of "I Knock at the Door". The "artist" who was given the job hadn't the slightest idea of what was expected of him; but he'll get the fee for all I did myself. I'm very sorry that W.B. went so soon.[3] He'll be missed. The B.B.C. wanted me to do a wireless talk about him, &, down here, they wanted me to lecture on him; but I declined both, for, somehow, I can't abide the idea of rushing to talk about those who have just passed out. Am I right, or am I just a bloody fool? Well, the Abbey has lost a fighter

[1] tháinig mé slán, I escaped.
[2] Arthur Shields, Shelah Richards, and Barry Fitzgerald.
[3] W. B. Yeats died on 28 January 1939 at Roquebrune, France, at the age of seventy-four.

& a friend. Strange to think of them all gone, now—Lady Gregory, AE, & W.B. And, I hear (from the local P.P.), that Gogarty's started practice in London.

Well, a new age and new men must carry the burden now. May they be greater than those who bore it earlier.

Give my love to Rose & all the Youngsters. I hope they're back at school again. Mine went back today after a fortnight's absence. Oh, that damned influenza.

Thanks for Frank's book, "After The Flight".[4] It was very interesting; but a little tantalising—I wanted much more of each story. Is he at anything now. And, lastly, I hope the recent bother won't make you give up your writing.

Ever Yours
Sean

[4] Francis MacManus, *After the Flight* (Dublin, Talbot Press, 1938), "Being eyewitness sketches of Irish History from AD 1607 to 1916."

To Harold Macmillan

TC. O'CASEY
[DEVON]
9 FEBRUARY 1939

Dear Mr Harold:

You propose a problem. I cant quite understand Allied Newspapers wanting "I Knock at the Door." I believe the book to be something in the way of a work of art, and I dont associate the love of art with the Sunday Graphic or the Sunday Chronicle. However, if a work of art should appear in either paper, so much the better. Shaw has made a success of his Pygmalion in the film world, and, maybe, the newspapers are about to turn over a new life. Of course there are many among the people who would read the story in a newspaper, yet wouldnt be able to give 10/6 for the book. I imagine I might have a big circle were the book to be got for say 3/- or 2/6. Then there's the money—very important. Now this is where you come in: Will this suggestion or offer suit Macmillans? Will it hit the 10/6 book? Will it hit a future cheap edition? (if you should publish one) I have nothing against the scheme—provided we get a good return for it, and you dont think it will damage the sale of the book. I'd just as soon get money from Macmillans as from the Allied Neswpapers. If, on the other hand, it may mean a net gain for you and me, then go ahead full steam. And, anyway, they may jib when they see what the book is like, though there is much of it might suit (and improve) either paper. It may, too, be a good advertisement. You should know. I have had no experience of serial matters of this kind. They could, I think, get twelve weeks or so out of the whole story. So, if you think well of it, go ahead, but dont forget to let me know what they may offer, before you accept.

With all good wishes.
[*Sean O'Casey*]

PS. I've just finished the play "The Star Turns Red," and will write to you about it when this thing is out of the way.

To F. R. Higgins[1]

TC. O'CASEY
[DEVON]
19 FEBRUARY 1939

Dear F.R.

Many thanks for your kind letter asking if I had any work in progress suitable for The Abbey Theatre. I would not venture to say whether present or future work would be suitable for the Abbey—you'll have to use your own judgement on that question. I have, as a matter of fact, just completed a play—"The Star Turns Red"—and have sent the only two copies typed to America: I dont think it would go down in Dublin, and, perhaps, not in many other places either. This time, if possible, I shall have the play produced before publication, because very often a little alteration becomes necessary, and, once the play has been published, I'm too lazy to make any alteration in a future edition. If you care to read it, then, whenever a copy comes to hand again, I'll let you have it, on condition you'll let me have it back, if it be of no use to you. Or, if it be published first, then, of course, you are always at liberty, under the usual contract, to have it in the Abbey; but not in England till such time as that province of ours shall be free.

Isnt it a pity that W.B. [Yeats] didnt last another ten years? I'm sure you'll all miss him very much. The B.B.C. here, wanted me to give a talk about him, but I dont like the idea of rushing to speak about great men the moment they have died. Probably a lot of rot, this idea. Wonder what would Freud say about it?

With all good wishes to you and your charge—the Abbey.

Yours sincerely,
Sean O'Casey

[1] Frederick Robert Higgins (1896–1941), poet, playwright, managing director of the Abbey Theatre.

To Cyril Clemens [1]

TS. CLEMENS

DEVON

4 MARCH 1939

Dear Mr. Cyril Clemens:

I have received your kind letter after it had travelled about a good deal, and hasten to acknowledge it now.

I am more than pleased to hear that your Society has elected me to an honorary membership.[2] It is an honor and a great honor for my name to be attached to that of Mark Twain. He, of course, has been my friend for a long time (through his works) and it is now an added pleasure and joy to be allowed to come closer to this great man by being a Member of the Society that holds his great and delightful name in honor.

Please give my warm thanks to all those of your Society who helped, by their sanction and approval, to make me one with you all.

Very sincerely yours,
Sean O'Casey

[1] Cyril Clemens, president, International Mark Twain Society.

[2] In 1955 O'Casey was made a Knight of Mark Twain, an honor he shared with Yeats and Shaw, among many others.

To Timofei Rokotov

TS. INTER LIT, MOSCOW

TOTNES, DEVON, ENGLAND

4 MARCH 1939

COMRADE T. ROKOTOV.
EDITOR,
INTERNATIONAL LITERATURE

Dear Comrade Rokotov:

Thank you for your letter, and for asking me about the work I am doing at the moment.

First, let me say that I [am] very glad you liked what I wrote, and that you honored my thoughts by publishing them in your Magazine. Two or three years ago, I wrote in the Manchester Evening News [1] for a union of the USSR, France, The United States, and England, as the only possible shield between us and war. I hold the same view still. Without any ag[g]ression, this Union would keep the peace for centuries, and give us time and a chance to make life well worth living.

I am, indeed, an old lover of the USSR, for I raised my voice at the Dublin meetings, held to protest against the interference waged by the powers in order to down the struggling Revolution.

I have just published a book dealing with the first twelve years of my life. It is written objectively—that is to say, I am a member of and a mover in the life around me. As well, I have written a play which is called, "The Star Turns Red", dealing with the impact of Communism with "The Saffron Shirts," the clergy, and the self-seeking officials in the Labour movement. I have by me a copy of the play, and I will send it on to you in a day or two. As my eyes are not too sound, the typing isnt as well done as I should like it to be; but, truth to tell, at the moment, I cant spare the amount it would cost to have it professionally done. I will send it by registered post. Twice I have tried to get into touch with your Radio Center by letter; but, probably, the letters never got as far as Moscow. This one will be registered.

I hope you may get the play safely, and that you will think something of it.

With deep regards to All who are working to add to the power and greatness of the great Soviet Nation, for in building up your own power and greatness, you are building up ours.

With all good wishes,
Yours,
Sean O'Casey

[1] Sean O'Casey, "Personal View," *Manchester Evening News*, 24 April 1936.

To Harold Macmillan

MS. Macmillan London
Devon
7 March 1939

Dear Mr Harold,

Thank you for your kind words about the good notices. As a matter of fact, I have read only one—that in The Listener.[1] Having an Agent here, & one in America, I get no Press-cuttings as a matter of economy

[1] *I Knock at the Door* was reviewed in the *Listener*, 13 February 1939.

at the moment. And strange as it may seem—I am a curious character—I have abandoned the pleasure of praise years ago. Everything of every grade & kind is praised so much now, that praise has lost its value. But on the point of the good notices possibly sending the sales up—ah, there I'm with you; link your arm and do the goosestep! I have finished a new play—"The Star Turns Red," & have sent two copies to America, hoping for a production there. I don't think I'll try for publication till a production comes my way—if it does come—, as there are usually a few things to change in Rehearsal; & these changes are the devil to do in the book when the play has once been printed. I hope the good notices of "I Knock At The Door" will go on, & that the sales will go up and up and up.

I daresay all this war business has contributed to the apathy of the book-buying public; and, too, there's less money knocking about.

Thanks again for your kind letter. My best wishes to Lady Dorothy, & yours & her children.

Yours sincerely
Sean O'Casey

By Oliver St. John Gogarty

The Observer

12 March 1939

BOOKS OF THE DAY
"The Unlocked Heart"
Sean O'Casey's Autobiography
"I Knock At The Door." By Sean O'Casey. (Macmillan, 10s. 6d. net.)
By Oliver St. J. Gogarty

Should a dramatist unlock his heart? The answer is, No. Nor anyone else for that matter. There is a decorum of Life which has to be observed, because within its bounds most of the world moves. To that one-third of the world's population which is in China decorum is religion. And though I like to imagine and to seek for my friends supercharged people, men and women so rammed with Life that they outsoar its mediocrities, I know only too well that there are others which compose the greater part of the earth's population who hardly live at all. Thus, below the surface, life becomes blurred, while above it it tends to disappear in ecstasy. In medio stat virtus. I only accept that when I cannot help it.

Had Shakespeare unlocked his heart we would have had an autobiography in which he would have told us his grudge against the Queen, why he never praised her with one melodious tear, why he ran off to

Scotland and came back full of honours from the throne of James. He might even have confessed to a little disagreement with the dagger-men who were the shadows of our gunmen from those days, for he lived on the edge of the law, he had to consort with "harlotry players" and to take the risk which arose from his status of vagabond of having his corpse handed over to the medicos. Hence his grave fifteen feet deep and his title, "armiger."

There are some parts of this capable and terrible book which should have been buried full fathoms five or deeper. I am not thinking (for they affect me little) of what must be passages of insufferable poignancy to others, but I have in mind the parts where the dramatist merges into the lyricist at the cost of the dramatic mask. These are passages where the tremendous odds against which O'Casey, blind almost from birth and for the twelve years or so covered in this book, had to contend. It makes me remember Dr. Johnson's great translation; for everywhere as in this autobiography

> This mournful truth is everywhere expressed:
> Slow rises worth by poverty oppressed.

And yet where could that knowledge of life to the bone which the O'Casey plays show have come from unless from experiences such as these so powerfully and painfully set down in this volume? When you cast your mind back over the dramatists of the ages the law that seems to rule them is that they all learned in sorrow, and as often as not in poverty, what they taught in song. The serenest among them accepted Life; they did not gird at it. It would seem that O'Casey has, after all the unsurpassable hilarity of his plays, a grudge against Life. It is all very well for people such as I, who prefer to sit on an avalanche than under it, to pose as being in love with it all. But if I had been submerged as O'Casey has been submerged I would have tried essay writing in gall and wormwood. That is, if I ever emerged. He got out because of his worth and genius. There are some passages of "I Knock At The Door" which recall scenes from "The Silver Tassie"—not that they are repetitions by any means, but examples of the experiment of mixing prose and poetry together. These, being contradictory, will never mix. They turn Parnassus into a purlieu, and, by mixing ancestral and traditional forms with modern usages, make a kind of slum. The author may have done this deliberately to show the effect of environment on the mind. There is much strange and original writing in this book. It strikes me as the author tells us the first reading of Scripture in the vernacular struck Luther:—

> He was greatly astonished at what he read therein, for it wasn't a bit like anything he had read himself, or had heard read by anyone else, it was all so good, so bad, so reading on and reading ever, he prayed when he was puzzled and reviewed in his mind all that had been written, and all that had been preached afore time about the heavens and hell, the earth, and all that was under the earth, the sea and all that is in it, till he got to know just where he was standing and found out that there were differences here and differences there which wouldn't bear investigation, and had a dangerous tendency to deceive and corrupt innocent, simple and stupid people who were anxious to serve God in spirit and in truth to the best of their ability, so long as they could get bread from heaven in a less laborious way and at a reasonable price.

Those who read this book can interpret the famous plays of O'Casey with a new understanding and sympathy. They will know where he learnt how to hold the mirror up. It is a powerful and unsparing book, but to use a form of speech which deserves a place in the grammars, the Irish bull, Everyman, should have his autobiography written by someone else.

To The Observer [1]

TC. O'Casey
[Devon]
[? March 1939]

The Unlocked Heart.

Dear Sir:

In his review of "I Knock at the Door", Dr. St. J. Gogarty says, "O'Casey has, after all, a grudge against Life". (Dr. Gogarty, himself, gives Life a capital letter). Well, the doctor's wrong. His diagnosis is mistaken. On the contrary, I love Life. But I have more than one "grudge" against the futilities, shames, stupidities, and romantic nonsense that distort and maim Life, and end it before its natural time. As a surgeon scientist, he knows as well (he ought to know better) as I do that the loss of any sense or faculty, or the maiming of any limb, reduces the correspondence of life with Life to the extent of the loss or the gravity of the maiming. If his out of date indifference were logically accepted, then we should have nothing to do but sweep away all thought and every effort to improve Life's standard and make it, [at] least, a little more worth the living. I am interested in a far bigger and wider Life than the Life that ravishes Dr. Gogarty. I am not so much interested in this (O'Casey) or that (Gogarty) life, as I am in the life of all. His idea and ideal of Life is, apparently, himself, like a little bird singing from the centre of a tree bending with blossom. That is, of course, very interesting, indeed, very charming, but it is relatively unimportant.

He says, "Some parts of the book should have been buried full fathoms five or more". Oliver St. J. Gogarty is frightened. A scientist, and he is frightened. Oh, Oliver Gogarty, Oliver Gogarty! A tip for the Doctor: The skin may cover cancer, but it cannot hide it.

"There is", he says, "a decorum of life which has to be observed, because within its bounds most of the world moves. To that one third of the world which is China decorum is religion." Is Dr. Gogarty alive at all? Can't he see, can't he hear, doesn't he know that the most of the world is smashing his corcon of decorum into smithereens? And he dumps China in front of our faces, mind you! Hasn't he heard from China lately? That lovely decorum that is, as Dr. Gogarty says, a religion has landed China into a pretty mess. The Eighth Army will do more for China than its religiodium decorum.

Then he brings in Shakespeare. Has he read him? Doesn't he know that Shakespeare sometimes unlocked his heart, and showed he had grudges against what Dr. Gogarty calls Life? Doesn't he remember "as flies to wanton boys", the most blasphemous expression, as G.B.S. says,

[1] This letter was refused publication by the editor.

that was ever uttered by the mouth of man? Shouldn't that have been buried full fathoms five or deeper?

"Being contradictory", says he again, "poetry and prose won't mix". Does he mean a mixture, or a chemical affinity, or what? Does he mean that because he or I can't mix them, no one can? Is this one of Dr. Gogarty's immutable laws? But they have been mixed. Shakespeare does it; so does Marlowe; so does Strindberg, and many others, so that my little venture follows a long way behind. What Dr. Gogarty seems to mean is that no one can break through precious rules that have long since sunk into interesting dust. If he and I live long enough, we'll see strange things mix that never mixed before.

Finally, Dr. Gogarty can no more escape from the "mediocrities" of life than anyone else—though, of course, he may think he does. They will as often trip up the golden feet of the poet as they trip up the clay feet of him who follows afar off, or goes the other way.

Yours sincerely,
Sean O'Casey

To George Jean Nathan

MS. CORNELL

DEVON
14 MARCH 1939

My very dear George:

Just a few lines. I'll write a long letter when I think you're steadier, & your eyes are stronger. Mine have been tormenting me, too; but that's usual with me. It is a pity yours trouble you, for they are lovely eyes. I do hope they will soon be well again.

About the play—just this: I think you are right; so I'm trying to make the difference between the B[rown] Priest & the R[ed] Priest clearer; to make the girl more consistent; & to do something about Kian.

I enclose a notice of Priestley's new play. It has been a failure. It was, I understand, his first attempt at a big, big play. Now, he'll find a hostility in London—he will, in me neck!

Please don't put yourself out for "The Star Turns Red." I'll write to Dick soon.

Now, get well.

With my love.
Sean

To Ivor Brown [1]

MS. BROWN
[DEVON]
24 MARCH 1939

Dear Ivor Brown:

Thank you very much for your kind letter on appreciative review of "I Knock at the Door".[2] I'm glad you found the book a fine tribute to Mrs. Casside. She was, really, a great woman. With her help, I knocked a way out of a hard time. But no-one ought to have to knock a way out of a hard time. It is a sinful waste of energy. Now, it appears, the whole of England will have to knock a way out of a hard time. I have been arguing for years for a Union with the U.S.A & Russia; but managed only to get an article more than two years ago into "The Manchester Evening News" & some Australian papers; and, of course, the Daily Worker. I wish that England would decide on a Representative Government, united on a policy we can all support.

But all this, though it's here, is not there; and all I should do is to thank you for your letter & your Review.

This I do again, & join good wishes with the thanks.

Yours sincerely,
Sean O'Casey

[1] Ivor Brown (1891–), English dramatic critic and author.
[2] Ivor Brown, *The Observer,* 12 March 1939.

To Timofei Rokotov

TS. INTER LIT, MOSCOW

DEVON
26 MARCH 1939

My dear Mr Rokotov:

I should be glad to hear if you have safely received the play, "The Star Turns Red", which I sent to you some time ago under registered post. Since then I have made a few alterations in the text—trying to make clearer the meaning between the "Brown Priest of the poor", and "The

Red Priest of the Politicians." I have altered the character of "Julia", making her more consistent in her attachement to the Red Star; and I have again brought in the character of "Kian", feeling that he was dropped too suddenly in the first act. If you dont like the play, I should, if it be not too much trouble to you, [like it] to be sent back to me; for I have but one ragged copy, and at the moment, I cant afford to have another typed, and that job is too troublesome to do myself. My eyes arent too good, and the extra work would mean a great strain. However, if the sending of it back would be any trouble, please dont bother.

A new book of mine—dealing with the first twelve years of my life—has just been published. It is called "I Knock at the Door;" and, if you like, I shall ask Macmillan & Co to send you a copy. It is, I think, good and interesting.

We are trying to get a move on in arousing some sort of preparedness here against the positive and long apparent determination of Fascism to make all men and all things walk their way.

With brotherly greetings,
sincerely yours,
Sean O'Casey

To Lady Astor

MS. Astor
Devon
30 [March] 1939

The Viscountess Astor.

Dear Lady Astor.

I will be defendant in a law case shortly, & I have to go to London some day next week—that is some day between the 7th: & 14th of April, —to talk over the affair with "Counsel"; the case is, I believe, to follow a few weeks later.[1]

This is the point of my note to you: can I stay for the night (or two) at your place? If a visit like this (isn't the "season" on?) should cause you much, or even any, inconvenience, don't bother. I can sleep in a police Kiosk.

Yours sincerely
Sean O'Casey

[1] See O'Casey's letter to Fallon, 25 August 1939, where he explains the case of the broken lease at 49 Overstrand Mansions.

To Gabriel Fallon

MS. Texas

Devon
3 April 1939

My dear Gaby:

I am glad to hear that you think so well of "I Knock at the Door". George Jean thinks it "a grandly beautiful job"; so I'm well away! I think you're right about Rabelais—I've never read him—the indecency is all my own. Like W.B. & L.R. once saying I was the present-day Swift (maybe I am), but no thanks to Jonathan—I never read him, either —not even "Gulliver's Travels". All I know of him is "The Writing on the Window Pane", & "Yahoo".[1] I've been very busy (and still am) making out hundreds of questions for the threatened law-case, which I imagine is a swindle (a claim for £170) & a K.C. whom I've asked says the same. But preparations have to be made—in case; & it's all a damned nuisance. I've got in my mind just this about "Green Gravel!"—

Green gravel, green gravel,
The grass is so green;
She's as pretty a fair maid as ever

was seen—& there I stop. Am I right so far? I seem to remember it. But can't recollect ever hearing "The Lady on the Mountain-top", didn't come into our street. The local P.P. tells me Barry's coming home in the Summer with £15,000 in the bank! I wonder how much will go to the "aged parent"? Hasn't he done fairly well? Better than he thought he would. I hear, too, that Brinsley has been co-opted to the Abbey Directorate.

We're all well here, except the "Daily", who is ill; so things have to be done that are usually left alone. O'Faolain has given a slating to "I Knock at the Door" in the London Mercury.[2] He says "I'm a genius at plays, but". And the only time he criticised a play of mine was when AE got him to criticise "The Silver Tassie"; & some day, if I live, I'm going to criticise the criticism of the play.

But back I have to go now to the proper & fair lay-out of the case for the K.C.

I hope you, Rose, & all the bairns
are well & thriving.
Longer letter, next time.

Yours As Ever
Sean

[1] W. B. Yeats's *Words upon the Window-pane* (1934) and Lord Longford's *Yahoo* (1933), two plays about Jonathan Swift.

[2] Sean O'Faolain, "Sean O'Casey Wallops at the Door," *London Mercury,* March 1939.

To George Jean Nathan

MS. Cornell

Devon
4 April 1939

My dear George:

I hope your eyes are better by now. It is a trial to have to work with troublesome eyes. And the one thing one likes to do & has to do, is the one thing that does them no good.

Yes, of course, I've read your "Vas you dere, Sharlie?" [1] Charles Morgan has been a puzzle to me for a long time. He is a powerful literary influence here; and although the other dramatic critics occasionally make an anonymous joke about him, they are all, I think, really afraid of him—the dramatic critic of "The Times"! [2] He has said very nice things about me; but what's the good of that? I, myself, don't share the awe of others; don't really believe he's of the theatre—don't even think he's alive to the world—so what good is his approbation? I've neither seen nor read "The Flashing Stream"; but from what I've heard & the few comments I've read, I know it wouldn't appeal to me. I've read a lot of his criticisms; his "The Fountain"; [3] his "Epitaph on George Moore"; [4] & "Sparkenbroke",[5] and, to me, they're all uninteresting, & a lot of all of them damn dull. He's married & has two children, so he ought to have some savvy. I simply can't make him out—or the English that made "Sparkenbroke" a best-seller. I, honestly, had to skip leagues of it, & Eileen skipped it altogether. But, anyway, the man who says Shakespeare had no sense of humour, is hardly worth a lively thought. I've always lived in the idea that Shakespeare had a glorious sense of humour. Well, this is a case, I think, or Charliensis contra mundi. God must have been in a curious mood when He made Morgan. I'll look forward to reading your article in "Esquire."

I've made a few alterations in the play, trying to make it appear that one Priest is the Red Priest of the Politicians, & the other the Brown

[1] George Jean Nathan, "Vas you dere, Sharlie?", *Newsweek,* 27 March 1939, a satiric article on Charles Morgan, whose *The Flashing Stream* opened in New York on 10 April, and closed after 8 performances.

[2] On the death of A. B. Walkley in 1926, Morgan became dramatic critic of the *Times* and held that position until September 1939.

[3] Charles Morgan, *The Fountain* (London, Macmillan, 1932), a novel for which he won the Hawthornden Prize.

[4] See O'Casey's letter to Nathan, ? September 1935, note 3.

[5] See O'Casey's letter to Nathan, ? September 1935, note 2.

Priest of the Poor; have brought in Kian again twice; & have made the girl a consistent (with a moment's lapse) upholder of the Red Star. But I don't want Dick to put himself out about its production. I think I'll try to get it published, & just let it take its chance.

You may not hear from me for some time for this reason: I'm defendant in a lawsuit against a claim for recovery of rent, a claim that I think is a swindle (A K.C. agrees with me) & so ought to be fought. So I shall be busy for some time preparing points for the case, & won't be able to think of much else till it's over, one way or the other. It's a nuisance, but it can't be helped.

Tell Carlotta [O'Neill] how glad I was to hear that her lovely eyes are allright again: & I hope yours will soon be the same.

I am so glad you liked "I Knock at the Door." I sent a copy to Brooks. Wonder what Charlie would think of it? C. B. Cochran has written saying Elizabeth Bergner would like me to write a play for her. All seem to think writing's an easy trick to do.

I never met Morgan, did you?

With deep affection
Sean

To George Jean Nathan

MS. Cornell

Devon
4 April 1939

My very dear George:

Just a line to keep a hold of your hand. That last article of yours in "Newsweek" about does it to Bonnie Prince Charlie! If the article gets to be known in the literary circles of England, you'll be excommunicated. In my woebegone & invincible ignorance, I agree with you. Charlie wants to be content with a room, a light, & a pen. No girls. Monks will be monks. Yet he was married, & has, I believe, a son. Curious, isn't it? He's a F.R.S.L. educated in Osborne, Dartmouth, & Brasenose College, Oxford (B.A. Honors, History) so, mind your step, me boy. Did you ever meet him? I never have; & don't want to. Still it was a hard knock to have the play off after only four nights. As a Dramatist, I feel for him here. Venal or non-venal, a fellow feels bad after such a knock-out blow.

I am busy with this law case; getting ready a dossier of cross-examination, etc. I tried to do some more of the biography; but had to give it a miss till this damned thing is over. I suppose you'll be going to the Fair. It's a little lonely here; but the kids like it; & are growing big & strong.

My Love to you,
as ever.
Sean

To Brooks Atkinson

MS. ATKINSON
[DEVON]
[?] APRIL 1939

My dear Brooks:

I'm glad you liked the book. And many thanks for your fine tribute to the things that are in me.[1] I differ from you—and don't mind the difference, for differences between you & me doesn't amount to much, seeing how we like each other & respect each other—if we didn't, I don't think I should argue—in your contention that my "dream fantasies & streams of consciousness" are "foreign to my best style." They may indeed be so to my best style, but not to my style; & I'll tell you why I think they aren't: The first thing written by me, that ever appeared in print, some 28 years ago, was a satiric fantasy throwing a mockery of glory over Augustus Birrell's policy of Education in Ireland. It appeared in "The Irish Nation", after having been read in many Irish National Clubs, & it was called "Sound the Loud Trumpet." [2] Strangely enough, it was that article that convinced me (because it had convinced others) that I could write. So I went on writing a lot badly (as I do now), & a little well (as I do now). So you see, I led off with a fantasy—having then heard nothing of the bould & (to me) great James Joyce. It was in my blood. And another one act play of mine (it just appeared in a paper before the Civil war began here) was a fantasy called "The Seamless Robe of Roisin" [3]—Roisin is Ireland—; &, I think, it tried, through ridicule to halt the Civil war. But hungry, tattered O'Casey then was of no account; & the war began. It was in my blood. And there is another thing that puzzles me: How am I to choose between differing opinions?

Yours, which you have put before me; and those of Austin Clarke,

[1] Brooks Atkinson, "Insurgent Penmen," *New York Times*, 9 April 1939, a review of *I Knock at the Door*.

[2] "Sound the Loud Trumpet," *The Peasant and Irish Ireland*, 25 May 1907, written under one of O'Casey's early pseudonyms, "An Gall Fada," the Tall Foreigner or Protestant; reprinted in *Feathers From the Green Crow* (1962).

[3] See O'Casey's letter to Lennox Robinson, 10 April 1922, note 1.

the Irish Poet, & a fine one, too. Now, I've never laid eyes on Clarke, so personal contact has had nothing to do with what he says. Here it is:

"The book is largely an exploration of the dream-world in which youngsters live so vividly, & here the glories of Empire and of Sunday School march, prance, & gallop past in mad-cap comic procession, bringing a ferocious & idiotic splendor into the dirty purlieus of Dublin. All this in its savage satire is set down in a rhythmical deludhering extravagance of vernacular that recalls the masterful blarney & gab of Joyce, but has a lyrical spontaneity of its own." Here is another from an Irish Novelist, Sean O'Faolain:

"The remainders are wearisome bellyaching, a corrosion of self-pity, or the most embarassing *litherachure*—o the most darlint litherachure, half prose, half verse, a kind of rhapsodical continuum of rhetoric, ingenuous beyond discription. The few objective chapters save the book from being completely boring." [4]

There you are, Brooks: Where does the truth lie? I must say, I don't know. I can do naught, but feel my own way forward—or backward, as the case may be.

But this I know: I do get tremendous joy out of the writing of fantasy, more than out of anything else. A lot of joy, & maybe, a little money. Take the chapter of "A Protestant Kid Thinks of the Reformation." That appeared in "The American Spectator" years ago; [5] & it, I understand, delighted the then four or five Editors of the paper. I loved writing it. I really think there is some Elizabethan gusto in it. And of another thing, dear Brooks, I am as positive as a human can be: there is no posing in the book from one end to the other—that is "art" posing. For I can honestly say I don't care a tinker's damn about art, simply because I know nothing about it. But I love the way I imagine the Greeks wrote (from English translations) & I love the way I know the Elizabethans wrote; & I am anxious & eager to try to make use of both in the things I try to write. Ambitious? Damnably so; but, even so, what is success (if I succeed) or what is failure? (if I fail). Who can tell?

Here I am writing reams to you, when I know you are busier than I doing your own important job. But, old son, tread lightly when you tread on my dreams. And thanks again for your dear kind words about me—I shall try to deserve them, for I value all you say, & don't exclude in value those things you say that go against the grain.

To Mrs. Brooks Atkinson, my love:
& my love to you.
Yours as Ever.
Sean

[4] Sean O'Faolain, "Sean O'Casey Wallops at the Door," *London Mercury*, March 1939.

[5] Sean O'Casey, "A Protestant Kid Thinks of the Reformation," *American Spectator*, July 1934.

To Timofei Rokotov

TS. INTER LIT, MOSCOW

DEVON
17 APRIL 1939

Dear Mr Rokotov:

Thank you very much for your telegram and very kind letter. First about printing the play in your Magazine: 1. In the Russian Edition, go ahead, complete or abridged, just as you think fit—I shall be honored in having it there. 2: The English Edition: As you may be aware, Macmillans, up to now, have published all I have written, and so I will write to them first about your proposal, for they will, probably, publish "The Star Turns Red." I daresay, they will have no objection to the publication of the play in the English Edition of your Magazine.

I, of course, take no objection to anything you may say. I am, more or less, aware that religious beliefs (or what are called religious beliefs), and the very language connected with religion, have disappeared, or have almost disappeared from the minds of your people. That doesnt shock me in any way for I have long given up any attachement to any form of institutional religion. But—and you will, I feel sure, understand this—"religious beliefs" still hold a fast sway here and in many other countries, and that many forms of organised religion still bolsters up a nefarious form of economic life in numerous countries outside the Soviet Union. I have to take into my regard many things that would be something of a puzzle in your country. We cant ignore them; they encircle us even as Capitalism still encircles the Soviet Republics. We have to criticise and fight them. The path to Socialism "doesnt go straight, but takes a zig zag course." Now there are many in these religious organizations who are beginning to examine their attitude towards those questions dealing with the economic factors that control and determine the life of man; and, it seems to me, that it is a good thing to try to confound them with the words that come out of their own mouths. I have come into collision with many clerics—some who like me very much, and some who would down and damn me with the greatest glee. I know their ways well, and I am fit to fight them. They—or many of them—rose up wrathfully against my "The Silver Tassie," and an American Tour of "Within The Gates" was stopped by a union of Methodist and Catholic clergy. They were afraid of what was in them. Militant Labour here is up against what is called the "Church", but many followers, both Protestant and Catholic, are becoming bewildered at the church's support of Franco, and its insistent backing of those who represent the power of the privilege of birth and wealth. So, in my opinion, it is good to make them more bewildered, and so I use their own language to criticise and denounce them. That has been done in "The Star Turns Red," under a symbol that all will recognise, namely the Star, showing, or trying to show, that the new faith is that one fixed on the Star that will lead to Communism. So well, I fear, and so well understood, that there will be some, if not great, difficulty in getting the usual production. I dont think anyone here or in say America, intimately or remotely connected with Christianity, would think that Red Jim uses "religious language!"

Were Red Jim to speak as a Marxist, the audience here or in America —that is, if there ever be an audience—would take no notice; only the converted, those already Marxists would listen. Now I dont want to talk to those who are already [in] our way of thinking—they are already on the march; but I do want to get into touch with those who are lagging behind, especially those who [are] among the crowd of workers attached to the Catholic religion. One instance: A dear friend of mine in Ireland who was what is called "A Member of the Third [Order] of St. Francis" was a fierce supporter of the "Hands off Russia" movement during the time the Interventionists were trying to crush out the Revolution in your country; and, I imagine, we can do with many more of these friends, and try to make them more definite and numerous.

But do write in detail on those points which, you think, could be improved in the play; I will be ready to try to fall in with them, if I think they would make the play better. The changes already made were due to the suggestions of a critic and a friend.

I thank you deeply for sending me the original play and a copy so that the changes may be inserted into one of them, and the amended copy sent back to you.

I am asking Macmillans to send you a copy of "I Knock at the Door" by registered post.

I will let you know about the publication of the play in International Literature as soon as I hear from my publisher; you will understand, I'm sure, that their opinion is important, seeing that I get a good deal of my royalties from the sales of my plays published by them.

With warm wishes and best regards,

Sean O'Casey

To Gabriel Fallon

MS. TEXAS
DEVON
8 MAY 1939

My dear Gaby:

Got your letter & all the news. Where's it all going to end? This censorship! [1] Though I don't see why dirty & smutty things shouldn't be given the go-by. But that's what censorship is either unable or unwilling to do. The Rabelaisian O'Casey has often felt uncomfortable listening to things on the Halls & even over the wireless. And Nathan has often squirmed in his seat when a dirty phrase, without meaning or wit, hit him & me in the eye.

Of course (The "of course" again), were I never so willing, I couldn't enter into O'Connor's controversy,[2] for I know next to nothing about it, or, indeed, of the ways & intentions of the Abbey either. The publication of "The Arrow" [3] was Yeats's idea: he spoke of it to me some two years ago when he was in London, & when I was in Ireland, & went to see him. But I do hope the Abbey won't come to grief. I didn't see Robinson's estimate of Yeats—at least, I can't remember seeing it, so I suppose it passed me by. Yeats was certainly something more than Tennyson or Moore—the two of them, mingled into one corporeal, intellectual, & poetical (and, maybe, spiritual) unity, couldn't make a Yeats. Whatever he was, he was a man & a poet. One can see his right stature, now that he has become a handful of dust. You're right about the Old Lady [4]—she was a dramatist. And both of them, man & woman, had, each of them, the child in them, & of such is the Kingdom of Heaven. Where are the children now? I'm afraid, too, you're right about them "dying to be Directors!" Isn't it a pity that any should strive for the mere place of honour, instead of the proper place for work? These honours! place & praises! I am to get £90. for the serial [of *I Knock*

[1] The news of the banning of *I Knock at the Door* in Ireland broke early in the month, and the book was officially "prohibited" by the Irish Censorship of Publications Board on 16 May 1939, according to a report in the *Irish Times,* 18 May, because it was "in its general tendency indecent." The ban was "revoked" on 16 December 1947.

[2] One of the new directors of the Abbey Theatre appointed by Yeats in 1935, Frank O'Connor was opposed by several of the other directors after the death of Yeats early in 1939, and by 23 August of that year he was forced to resign. For a pro-O'Connor account of the controversy, see Peter Kavanagh's *The Story of the Abbey Theatre* (New York, Devon-Adair, 1950), "New Directors," pp. 167–78; "Betrayal," pp. 179–84.

[3] *The Arrow,* an occasional magazine of the Abbey Theatre, edited by W. B. Yeats. Five issues were published between 1906–09. The sixth and last issue was the "W. B. Yeats Commemoration Number," Summer 1939, edited by Lennox Robinson.

[4] Lady Gregory.

at the Door] in Sunday Chronicle. Macmillans first asked me would I take £50 for twenty thousand words—instead of rejecting it, in scorn. So I had to bargain on that basis; & I demanded £200. The enclosed telegram will show the net result. Ten per cent, the £100 goes to Macmillans, so I get £90. Keep this telegram to show those who, I suppose, think I got a £1000. Had I not been hard-up, I wouldn't have had it serialised at all. How the book has gone, I don't know yet. I'll know in October. I guess, if I'm fortunate, that it'll sell about 2500 or 3000 copies. I get 15% on the first 1500, & 20% afterwards, & I make that out to be about £232, of which £100's paid in advance, & was handed over to the Inland Revenue for tax owed; so, with the £90, there's a net reward expected (if it goes as well as I hope) of £322—not a fortune for three or four years' work. It hasn't come out yet in America; so I can't say what may happen there. I'm off to London now to "see Counsel". The Case isn't one of libel—it's one of £140 rent claimed by our late Landlord, for remainder of lease, which was, for certain reasons (I allege) taken over by them; & which reasons had to be abandoned by them on the head of the "crisis." I'm fighting what I believe to be a swindle on the part of a great Property Trust.[5] I'm glad your youngsters have got rid of the mumps. What a job are children—& we're expecting another in September!

Pardon hasty ending. Love to F. J. McManus.[6] I like him too well to mind what he thinks of my work. Love to Rose, the little ones, (getting bigger now) & you.

Sean

[5] He lost the case. See his letter to Fallon, 25 August 1939.
[6] He meant Francis "Frank" MacManus.

To Lady Astor

TS. Astor
Devon
17 May 1939

Dear Lady Astor:

I've received a letter from the Solicitors, saying, "Short Cause Actions are liable to be taken at a moment's notice; in fact they often do not appear on the lists until 4 o'clock on the day before that on which they are heard. I gather that your case is almost certain to be heard between now and the end of the term which is on Friday week. I may, therefore, have to telegraph you urgently to come up immediately towards the end of the week, or, more likely, at the beginning of next."

So from this you will see that not only can I give you no decent notice, but I can give you no notice at all. I, of course, could send you a telegram which might help your servants, instead of just popping in at an unexpected hour. Eileen is coming with me, for, I understand, she may be required as a witness in the case. Can you possibly manage both of us? If this should not be possible, Eileen will try to stay with a friend.

Looking over what has been written, I find this letter troubling my mind, for it seems to be imposing a good deal upon your and Lord Astor's kindness, but what in the name of God am I to do!

However, I am a little comforted by feeling sure that if you cant put us or me up, you'll say so, knowing that I can well understand the many calls upon your generous goodwill.

Very sincerely yours,
Sean O'Casey

To Timofei Rokotov

TS. INTER LIT, MOSCOW

DEVON
20 MAY 1939

Dear Mr Rokotov:

Thanks for your letter and the play safely received. I am sending (under another cover, registered) the amended play. I, of course, understand that, if it be published in Russian (as I sincerely hope it may be), it will have to be adapted to suit the idiom and different understanding of your great people. So I have no objection to the Translator doing what he thinks necessary to the play in order to bring it more vividly to the receptiveness of USSR audiences or readers.

I send you back your own copy of the play amended, feeling sure that this copy, on the whole, would be clearer to you for all purposes, than the additional one I have typed for myself and the publisher.

I got into touch with Macmillans, my publishers, and they think that the publication of the whole play in International Literature would hit the sales badly; but they would have no objection to the publication of one act of the play. Should this suit you, I suggest that the First Act would be the best to print. Macmillans is a conservative Firm, but they are a straight one, and have never refused to publish anything I have written—I wish I could say the same of many others, papers and magazines—and the Director, Harold Macmillan has travelled through your country, and is one of the leading Left Wingers in the Conservative Party in the English House of Commons.

So, if one act of the play would meet your wishes, I shall be delighted to see it in your International Magazine.

I'll think over your request to write an article for the Autumn number. I imagine I'd prefer to write about the English Theatre (though, really, there isnt an English Theatre—it died long ago), rather than about Irish Literature. There's a fight starting in Ireland about the censorship (though a lot of them say you cant open your mouth in Russia!), which has existed some time now over Literature, and is, I fear, about to be applied to the Drama. My last book was banned in Ireland,[1] and, now, as you will see from enclosed cutting, "I Knock at the Door" has been banned, too. A good many are up in arms against this, and so the banning will serve a good purpose by seeing more plainly the fear in ecclesiastical eyes. I should have written sooner, but have been defendant in a case with a Landlord, and was too occupied.

With all good wishes for the work in your hands.

V. sincerely yours,
Sean O'Casey

[1] See O'Casey's letter to Gabriel Fallon, 29 August 1934, note 1.

From James Joyce

MS. O'Casey

[26 May 1939] [1]

34 rue du Vignes
Paris XVI[e]

Dear Mr. O'Casey: I wonder whether you have seen already the Dublin paper [2] I sent you with its curious misprint—if it is a misprint. I hope it may be prophetical and that we may some day meet. When my wife recovers from an attack of influenza we are going to see your play [3] at the Theatre de l'Oeuvre and if I find that it is attributed to me I shall certainly send you on the programme. Anyhow I hope you will take the printer's error, as I do, for a happy and amusing omen.

With all good wishes
Sincerely yours
James Joyce

[1] Postmark.

[2] The *Irish Times,* 6 May 1939, in its "Publications Received" column announced *"Finnegans Wake,* by Sean O'Casey."

[3] *Juno and the Paycock* was produced in Paris by Edward Sterling and his English Players Company.

To James Joyce [1]

MS. Buffalo

Devon

30 May 1939

My dear James Joyce:

I was very glad to get a letter from you, and to find that you weren't annoyed at 'Finnegans Wake' being put against my name. My mind is still far away from the power of writing such a book. I wish I could say that such a power is mine. I am reading it now, and though I meet many allusions, the book is very high over my head. A friend here (a painter) and I often read it (or try to) together; and I, it is fair to say, am better than he, and lead him into many a laugh and into the midst of wonder and wonderland. It is an amazing book; and hardly to be understood in a year, much less than a day. I've had constant contact with you in 'Dubliners' and 'Portrait of the Artist'; and in 'Ulysses'—that great and amazing work. As you see, we are now living in Devon,—meself and herself, two kids and another coming, so I don't suppose you'll ever be near here. But God is good, and we may meet some day, I sincerely hope so.

I don't think the reference was a misprint. I know many of Dublin's Literary Clique dislike me, and they hate you (why, God only knows), so that 'misprint' was a bit of a joke. Well, Oxford's (or Cambridge) going to hang the coloured gown of a D.Litt. over the shoulders of Wodehouse, whom, Belloc says, is the greatest living writer of English. So 'Finnegans Wake' will, I fear, be a wake in earnest.

Them and their Academy of Letters [2]—all in all, and in spite of all,

A deep bow to James Joyce,

Yours very sincerely
Sean O'Casey

I do hope your wife is all right or much better by now.

[1] James Joyce (1882–1941), the celebrated Irish author.

[2] Joyce and O'Casey had rejected the invitation to become members of the newly formed Irish Academy of Letters in 1932. See O'Casey's letter to the *Irish Times,* 11 October 1932.

To M. Apletin [1]

TC. O'CASEY

[DEVON]
31 MAY 1939

Dear Mr Apletin:

Thank you for *The Moscow News* and your kind letter. The articles in No. 17, setting out some of the ways in which Shakespeare has been honoured and enjoyed in the USSR is something to be proud of, and I fervently wish that I could say the same, or half as much, ay or quarter as much about the honour they gave the great poet in his own country. The English had a Shakespeare Festival of a week or so in the Memorial Theatre in Stratford on Avon (where the poet was born); a place where only those who have a lot of money and time on and in their hands can go. One theater in London—called the Old Vic gives performances of Shakespeare's plays constantly. Some of these are done well, and many of them are done badly. The people who keep the commercial theater going give it the miss—dont care a damn about it; and the theater is always in a bad way financially. The bare truth is that Shakespeare is nor wept nor sung nor honoured in his own country. As for the workers, it may be said that they never come into touch with Shakespeare from the cradle to the grave. Millions and millions have never seen a play of his, and he has been so neglected that very few actors are able to play a principle character in any of his plays. This is not my opinion alone. Here's a quotation from Ernest Newman, the Music critic of The Sunday Times: "Most of the actors and actresses gabble verse as if it were a paragraph from a newspaper. If blank verse is spoken as it is by the majority of these people, I shall continue to prefer my Shakespeare in my study." Again, from [James] Agate, Dramatic Critic of the same paper: "Despite the efforts of the Old Vic, the art of acting Shakespeare is nearly lost to this country. We have not the players today who can really stand up to Lear and Othello and Richard the Third. Our actresses have lost the power to play Lady Macbeth, Volumnia, and Cleopatra. We have lost the knack of playing Shakespeare by not playing him, and through no other reason."

I have written, time and again, about this; have fought with the critics over it; have published a book attacking the state of the theatre here; have been held back and censored; so you see with what joy and encouragement I read that in the USSR Shakespeare is seen and heard so often, and that the theatre there is a great and an honoured art.

By the way, dear friend, I'm an Irishman, and it's rather amusing

[1] Mikhail Apletin, secretary, Foreign Commission of Writers' Union of U.S.S.R., London.

that an Irishman should have to rebuke England for the stupid neglect of one of her greatest sons.

With affectionate regards and good wishes.
Yours very sincerely,
Sean O'Casey

To George Jean Nathan

MS. CORNELL

DEVON

[? JUNE 1939]

My very dear George:

It's some time since I wrote to you, due, in a large way, to the damned law case. It was simply a case in which the gaum [1] Sean was made a sucker of by a big Property Trust agent.[2] He undertook to do certain things in return for our immediate vacation of the flat; the "Crisis" upset his rosy plans, & we were had. It's over now, & we shant die; & I have had an experience with the higher law, & now I know its rascality & futility.

By the time you get this, I daresay you'll be far away from New York. I think you did well not to come to Europe this season; the voyage over, or the voyage back wouldn't be pleasant, if the war broke out. Anyway, what does an American want with lingering looks at a dying Europe? (except the Soviets, old man). You show the decay of the European theatre in your last article in Newsweek. How anyone who has the American Continent under his feet, wants to come here, beats me. Pack up your troubles in your oul kitbag, & blaze the trail to California. There's No Eugene O'Neill here (bar myself), & I'm a long way from London now. Ever since we came down to "glorious Devon", the weather has been terrible. As I write, a cold rain is pelting against the windows. It's a bit lonely here; but the kid[s] love it—so that's something.

I daresay you heard "I Knock at the Door" has been banned in Ireland. I don't ever seem to be able to get rid of some kind of banning. Of course, you know Carroll's "White Steed" hasn't been performed there, either. They'll make the country a Finnigan's Wake yet.

I'm enjoying Joyce's book; & am quietly getting a grip on some of it. That was a raking article on Morgan's "Flashing Stream" in "Esquire."

[1] gam, fool.

[2] See his letter to Fallon, 25 August 1939.

From the quotations you give, I'm a lot nearer to James than I am to Charlie. "The Fountain" made me weak; and the story of "Sparkenbroke" finished me. I'm afraid, George, there's something coarse in me—and, maybe, in you, too. There's some peculiar affinity that brings us close together. It's strange when I think of it—the esthetic, aristocratical critic & the plebian red-minded Communist. But what a lonely bird I'd have been in New York, N.Y. if I hadn't had you to lean on! I'll never doubt the existence of God again.

I do hope you'll take a good long holiday somewhere in the open sun, & that you won't be tempted to stay too near the Fair & the Show Girls in Aquacade.

I am, with an odd article or two, writing a little of the second part of "I Knock at the Door", & am trying to think of a theme for a new play.

God be with you.
My sincere love.
Sean

To F. R. Higgins

TC. O'Casey
[Devon]
5 June 1939

Dear F.R.:

I am sending "The Star Turns Red" to you, under another cover. The copy contains almost all the alterations made, and so is as I should wish it to be—that is the final draft, bar one or two very minor amendments.

I have heard nothing about the banning of "The Plough," and think the reference a mistake. There will be no row of the kind manifested over "The Plough" over this present play. The "Abbey" row was, as you know, due to the indignation of the Republican element, and that antagonism has died out, as far as I am concerned. The Leader of the attack then [Frank Ryan] has now become one of my friends—I was never an enemy of his; and we often played hurly together, more than twenty golden years ago. He fought in Spain, and came to see me in London when he was over recovering from a wound, to talk over the fight there was around the performance of "The Plough." He is now in prison in Spain, sentenced to thirty years in jail, and only the day before yesterday, I was speaking to the "Referee" about him, and the efforts being made to get him out. He is really a splendid fellow.[1] When I last saw W. B. [Yeats] he mentioned how there was no row in the Theatre over "The Silver Tassie", saying that the play in no way hit the Republicans, so that the opposition to it was, not political, but "religious". So—if there be a row—it will be with the present play; the fight will be non-political, but strictly sectarian.

It is the clergy—or some of the clergy—and the Confraternities that will raise the right hands to smite.

You are right when you say that the banning has no quality, not even an advertising one.[2]

I think you are wise to have the tour sponsored, instead of you taking all the risk. The difficulty to get a sponsor. If anyone should know of one, it should be Walter [3]. Anmer Hall of the Winminster Theatre might do it—he is said to be pretty well off, and is, I know, intensely interested in the theatre. He had the Gate in his theatre for three weeks.

I hope you may get one, for something is needed to refresh the terrible theatre here.

With all good wishes,
Yours sincerely,
[*Sean*]

[1] All attempts to release or rescue Frank Ryan failed, and he died a broken man in Germany in 1944 at the age of forty-two. For earlier references to Ryan see Mrs. Hanna Sheehy-Skeffington's letter to the *Irish Independent,* 15 February 1926, note 2, and O'Casey's letter to Horace Reynolds, 19 March 1937, note 2. See also O'Casey's letters in defense of Ryan, *Irish Times,* 5 April, 10 and 21 May 1952, Vol. II. For an account of Ryan's imprisonment and death, see Francis Stuart's two-part article, "Frank Ryan in Germany," *The Bell,* November, December 1950.

[2] In his 2 June letter to O'Casey, Higgins made the following comment on the Irish government's banning of *I Knock at the Door:* "Well, my dear Sean, you have I think the honour of being the first Irish protestant, pagan, author to be included in the four or five hundred banned books. The banning is of no quality, not even an advertising one. I read the book, and as an Irish country protestant pagan, thoroughly enjoyed it." (MS. O'Casey)

[3] Walter Peacock, who was casting director of the London production of *The Silver Tassie* in 1929.

To D. Kilham Roberts

MS. Society of Authors

Devon

6 June 1939

Personal

D. Kilham Roberts, Esq.
[Society of Authors]

Dear Sir:

I have been having a lean time for the last two years, & have had, or will have to pay a large sum in a recent case which is good law & poor equity, so I am, at present unable to pay what I owe to your Society.

I enclose £1.10.0 in an effort to hang on; &, if this doesn't do, then there's nothing left for you to do but to knock my name & title off your list of members.

Yours.
Sean O'Casey

To Harold Macmillan

TS. Macmillan London

Devon

23 June 1939

Dear Mr Harold Macmillan,

Thanks for your letter and draft agreement. I enclose the agreement, signed with a fair signature. I am, at the moment, bargaining with a proposed production of the play [*The Star Turns Red*] to be given in the Autumn, when I would like the play to be published, alongside the first night (if it comes off—or on), or thereabouts.

I havent a duplicate copy of the play, so, if you please, let your New York House have a galley proof, if you think they should desire one.

There will be a few airs set to music for inclusion at back of book, but they will not be more than half a page—three short tunes.

Arent these Anglo-Russian talks taking a long time? Theyre getting me down! When will English Governments become realistic? I have just written a short article for Picture Post called "Value of Violence." [1] A lot of pacifists down here are turning me into a wild man. And Judge Humphreys in a hurry to settle the Irish question by sending young Irish-

[1] Sean O'Casey, "The Value of Violence," *Picture Post,* 5 July 1939.

men to prison for 20 years.[2] And nothing done about the 100 lost in the Thetis [3]—worse than these Irishmen have done since they started throwing bombs about. And Balfours Mandate [4] flying, like an angel, over Jew and Arab blowing each other to smithereens. Finnegans Wake.

Well, I hope you are standing up well to it all. I wish I could see you again, for I and Eileen are very fond of you.

My warm regards to Lady Dorothy and all your children.

Yours Sincerely,
Sean O'Casey

Enclosure

[2] On 3 April 1939 in London Justice T. Humphreys sentenced seven Irishmen to long prison terms for possession of arms and explosives.

[3] On 5 June 1939 the British submarine Thetis was reported missing with ninety-nine men lost during diving trials in Liverpool Bay.

[4] Arthur J. Balfour, British foreign minister, had issued the controversial Balfour Declaration in November 1917, calling for the creation of a Jewish national state in Palestine.

To Tom Hopkinson [1]

TC. O'CASEY

[DEVON]
28 JUNE 1939.

Dear Mr Hopkinson:

Many thanks for your letter. I am glad that you liked the article.

You say in your letter "I think a good many readers will take up your criticism of the imprisonment of Irishmen on bombing charges. 'If the government is not to shut them up' they will want to know 'what is it to do with them?' Violence must work both ways, and cannot always be right when used by the weak against the strong, and used by the strong in reply."

You are right, of course. It is inevitable that the government will shut up all they can capture. My point is that this has been, and will be ineffective. That is the big flaw in the business that will render it useless. More and more will join the I.R.A., and the bombings will go on. Now there's a bigger question behind the whole thing. England cant afford to make enemies at the moment—or rather, it is well for her to have as many friends as she can gather together. Particularly America. I am anxious for a complete union between England and The United States. The Irish

[1] Tom Hopkinson, assistant editor, *Picture Post.*

number, at least, 20 millions there. A large proportion of them are against partition, and these will sympathise with the "bombers". Their vote will be in favour of isolation, and so a block in the way of Union. So you see, to me, these 20 millions are of more importance than old Craigavon's outworn nonsense about Protestant Ulster. Maybe, later on, you would let me write an article on this question. It does nearly concern the understanding that should exist between the U.S.A. and England. Anything that checks that should be, if at all possible, removed.

Very sincerely yours,
[*Sean O'Casey*]

To Timofei Rokotov

TS. INTER LIT, MOSCOW

DEVON
2 JULY 1939

My dear Mr Rokotov:

I enclose an article called Literature in Ireland,[1] seeing that you think such an article preferable to one on the English Theatre—you are probably right; and I sincerely hope the article may suit you. It is informative rather than analytical, for, you will understand, to write an analytical work would require an article, and more, on each writer mentioned in it.

In case it doesnt suit you, I send the following names to whom you might write on the possibility of getting one to write it for you.

Frank O'Connor. c/o The Abbey Theatre, Abbey Street, Dublin. C.8. Ireland.
(I personally believe that this young writer isnt in love with the USSR; but might write for International Literature)

Sean O'Faolain. Killough House, Kilmacanogue, Co. Wicklow. Ireland. (This is, I'm afraid, another of those liberals who hate Communism and Fascism equally, and so steer a safe course—as they think—by thinking of themselves.)

Peadar O'Donnell's address is unknown to me, but I will try to get it for you, if you like. Peadar is one of the best, a fighter, and a member of the Left fighting a dour fight in Ireland.

[1] Sean O'Casey, "Literature in Ireland," originally published in *International Literature*, December 1939, Moscow; reprinted in *Blasts and Benedictions* (1967).

The publication of the book of my play will depend on the date of production here. I am at the moment negotiating for a production, which, in this case, is more difficult than an ordinary commercial play. As soon as I have definite news, I'll let you know.

I know Jim Phelan, but havent read his book,[2] so cant say anything about it. He's a fine fellow, and I do hope it will go well. Some time ago, he rang me up, and said he was going to America, and I havent heard about him since.

Very sincerely yours,
Sean O'Casey

Enclosure

[2] Jim Phelan, *Green Volcano* (London, Peter Davies, 1938), half fiction, half reminiscence about the Irish revolutionary period, 1916–22.

To Harold Macmillan

TS. MACMILLAN LONDON

DEVON
7 JULY 1939

Dear Mr Harold,

I dont think I like keeping anything absolutely uniform, the same yesterday, today, and forever. I like change, not for the sake of change, but because a change might be better—and very often is. I think the change in the format suggested by you would be a distinct change for the better. I like the new idea greatly. I hope it wont cost much more.

I will sent you on the music MS tomorrow—just three short tunes. I should like, if possible, to get a few proofs of these when they are pulled to be sent to those who may decide to produce the play.

I have written an article called "The Value of Violence" for "Picture Post,'" that touches on the question of partition, and the bombings that are startling things in various parts of England. This Ulster question is a serious thing, and should be settled, even if Craigavon has to be put in a concentration camp all on his own. England wants all the friends she can get now; and Halifax is talking through his hat when he says (the other day) that Ireland is friendly. She isnt, and cant be while Ulster's outside. And he thinks, as others do, too, that Ireland's just the three provinces: she isnt just that; she had more than 20 millions in The U.S.A., a million and a half in Australia, and as many more in Canada. All these, or most of them, will not cheer to read of Irishmen going to jail for twenty years.

Long ago, in a speech Padruig Pearse, referring to the English Governments, said "The fools, the fools, the fools;" [1] I say ditto, now. I believe Ireland will be friendly, if England says to Ulster, oh, go in for God's sake, and dont be making a fool of yourself.

All the best to you and yours,

Sincerely,
Sean O'Casey

PS. I enclose Music herewith.

[1] Pearse's funeral oration over the remains of O'Donovan Rossa delivered in Glasnevin Cemetery, Dublin, on 1 August 1915: "They think that they have provided against everything; but the fools, the fools, the fools! they have left us our Fenian dead, and while Ireland holds these graves, Ireland unfree shall never be at peace."

To Cedric Belfrage [1]

TC. O'CASEY

[DEVON]
22 JULY 1939

Dear Mr Belfrage:

Thanks for your very interesting letter about the proposed Organization [Associated Film Audiences] to create film-minded audiences. Anyone with a mind at all would wish for something better than the terrible stuff that is usually put upon the screen. I am heartily in sympathy with your scheme. I have read your recent articles on Hollywood that appeared in Reynold's. Things are pretty bad there. I dont altogether agree that the Film is the most potent media by which to reach the people. To me, the drama is that. But I wont argue over that question, for the Film is popular, and it should be potent instead of being impotent as it is at present. But let me get to the core of your letter: you wish my name to be added to the Advisory Council. Well, honestly, I have nor time nor energy, nor, what is all-important, the knowledge of the Film to readily agree to your proposal. It's the young men who dream dreams who must do all that. I am too old and weary now for this kind of work (and, concerning the

[1] Cedric Belfrage, British-born journalist who lived in the United States after 1937; founded the *National Guardian,* a left-wing weekly newspaper, in 1948 in New York, with James Aronson and John T. McManus. For Belfrage's difficulties with the House Un-American Activities Committee, 1953–55, see O'Casey's letter to Belfrage, 16 January 1956, note 1, Vol. III; see also Belfrage's book, *The Frightened Giant: My Unfinished Affair With America* (London, Secker & Warburg, 1957).

Film, too ignorant). But as I agree with all you have said in the circular, and if my name alone would be of any use to you (or you think it might), well, then, you are welcome to it for the purpose mentioned in your letter and circular.

Very sincerely yours,
Sean O'Casey

To R. T. House [1]

TC. O'CASEY

[DEVON]

15 AUGUST 1939

Dear Mr. House,

James Joyce.

Thank you for giving me the honour of nominating an Author I think would be most deserving of the recognition you propose to give who has presented the world with the most distinguished book or group of books from 1918 to now.

James Joyce is my choice for his Ulysses and his recent Finnegans Wake.

They are unique and, I think, tremendous. There can be no question of the artistry of this man, of his strange originality, and of the rich tragic and comic poetry that blossoms in all that he has written.

For the third time—James Joyce.

With all good wishes.

Yours very sincerely,
[*Sean O'Casey*]

[1] R. T. House, editor, *Books Abroad,* Norman, Oklahoma.

To F. R. Higgins

TC. O'CASEY

[DEVON]

21 AUGUST 1939

Dear F.R.:

I daresay you've read "The Star Turns Red" by now, and, as I told you, found it most unsuitable.

If you can I shall be much obliged for its return so that I may send it along to another who wants to read it, too.

I hope the Abbey is doing well. One hears little about it here. The Dublin Correspondent of The Sunday Times is so busy telling everyone in Ireland what they should do that he hasnt any time to mention the Abbey or the Municipal Gallery, or anything, apparently, that has to do with outside of the money coming into or going out of the National till.

Best of luck.
Yours sincerely,
Sean O'Casey

To Peter Newmark

MS. NEWMARK

DEVON
24 AUGUST 1939

My dear Peter

I've read "There's no Escape"; no better & no worse than a thousand others. Shall I post it back, or wait till you come down some day when the missus's allright again?

Now for the main point: You said, if I remember rightly, about giving my play to the Unity people. The D. Worker has just asked me to write an article on Unity—a People's Theatre—going into the Kingsway Theatre. I've scribbled one for them; but this has sent me thinking; & I've told them if they can assure me of a good production & reasonable royalty, I may enter into talk with them about "The S. Turns Red". What do you think?

Perhaps, you have your own difficulties in trying to enter the Civil Service, & can't think at all. If that be so, Don't bother to answer; but I somehow think I heard you say you were interested in Unity. So am I; but more so in my play.

All the Best.
Sean

To Gabriel Fallon

MS. TEXAS
DEVON
25 AUGUST 1939

My dear Gaby: No, not in Dublin (wish I was), but here, in Devon still. Since writing last, I've had a lot to do & much to think about, including an experience in the King's Bench. It was, briefly, like this: The big property trust owning our flats were improving them, tiled kitchens, parquet floors, etc, & adding a huge sum on the rents as the leases fell out. Ours had to run more'n a year & a half. When the Trust heard we were thinking of going, they sent their Manager to encourage us to go off so that they might do the alterations, & promised us release from the rest of the lease. Like fools, we fell for it. All would have been well, but for the crisis: then, instead of people falling over themselves to get into the flats, they fell over themselves thrying to get out; & the blighters repudiated their promise—horns of a cow, hoof of a horse, smile of an Englishman. The judge found against us, & it will cost us about £300. That's that, as you say yourself. Eileen's having another kid—it seems you've heard of it—& she's having a fidgety time of it, & some sleepless nights. (In any letter to me, don't mention this, oul son, or say anything about it).

Vera Kennedy's yarn is a very interesting one; but, so far, I've heard nothing about any Hollywood interest in "I Knock at the Door". I can't see how they could be. Two years ago, they were interested in "Juno", but nothing came from it; & I don't think anything will now. However, I hear, through George Jean, that the book had a fine "press" in America; but how it went there or here, I don't know yet. I just sent a biographical Sketch, "Royal Risidence", account of a visit with a Crimean veteran Uncle Tom, who was also a "Purple Ordher Orangeman" to Kilmainham Jail when I was a kid, "Virginia Quarterly Review",[1] for $5.00 a page. (five, not 500) & I've written three more, about a dog's drowning, "Dung-dodgers over the Border" & "The Cat 'n Cage",[2] which you may have heard of. Didja ever hear of such a place?

Haven't had a half a line from Will. However, I've "heard" that he's sitting on a cushion of gold: has about £25,000 in the sack; so he's allright, so far. An "no chick or child to lave it to". But he's an artist, anyway, & deserves it; but he might have written to you or me, for, after all, we had a hand in dhriving him out to do his bit, hadn't we?

[1] Sean O'Casey, "Royal Risidence," *Virginia Quarterly Review,* Winter 1940; reprinted as the third chapter of *Pictures in the Hallway* (1942).

[2] Sean O'Casey, "Cat 'n Cage," *Virginia Quarterly Review,* Summer 1940; reprinted as the fifth chapter of *Pictures in the Hallway.* The title of "Dungdodgers over the Border" was changed to "The Hawthorn Tree," which is the fourth chapter of *Pictures in the Hallway.*

Didn't see "The Arrow".[3] Robbie asked me to write on Yeats, but I don't care to do that just yet, there. Wrote an article on "Irish Literature" [4] —God help me—for International Literature (on request) published in Moscow, & said a few words about him.

I've finished the "play" long ago—"The Star Turns Red". (entre nous, between ourselves, sub rosa) I (on request) sent it to the Abbey, but assured them it wasn't, in my opinion, suitable. It's a Communist play, for, as you know bloody well, I write only for money.

There's an awful panic over here since Moscow gave the kiss of peace to Germany. We have a bunch of gasmasks waiting for us in one of the rooms.

If England goes to war with Germany, for Poland, it's—wallops.

All love to Rose, you, &
the kidgers.
Sean

If Vera wants an autograph, let me know what way to write it for you.

[3] See O'Casey's letter to Fallon, 8 May 1939, note 3.

[4] Sean O'Casey, "Literature in Ireland," *International Literature*, Moscow, December 1939; reprinted in *Blasts and Benedictions* (1967). His "few words" in memory of Yeats appear in two relevant passages: "The greatest of these big figures was, undoubtedly, Yeats, the strange, dreamy, faraway poet, who could, all in a moment, be so practical in the affairs of the theatre. He is the great poet of the period, and so far, possibly (to me, certainly), the greatest poet writing in the English language. At the first go-off, and, indeed, for some time, Yeats built all, or almost all, his poetry on the legends and romances that sparkle in the literature of the Gaelic past, though, to no little extent, he fled too far away from the common people, turning the poet into a cold aristocrat who turned his head up to the heavens, looking at no-one below the altitude of a star; failing to see that many, especially among the workers, were themselves, in their own way, seeking a vision, more roughly, perhaps, but no less deep than his own." (p. 176)

"Yeats, too, was a fine and fearless fighter, raising himself against the intimidation, the stupid intolerance, the ignorant opposition of the religious societies, anxious to make sure that nothing outside of their own seedy, senseless, and lackalight lumber should be said or sung in the land.

"In the last years of his life, Yeats became much more human, drew nearer to the world's needs, and, as he told me himself, became intensely interested in the new voice of the resurgent working-class speaking in its own way, and demanding the earth and the fullness thereof. He is gone now, and Ireland will miss him sorely, for he was Ireland's greatest poet, and a great warrior to boot." (p. 178)

To Peter Newmark

MS. NEWMARK
DEVON
31 AUGUST 1939

My dear Peter:

Thanks for this, that, & t'other details, which will be very useful, if Unity Proposals prove interesting. It was very good of you to take so much trouble. Anyway, there's no room for anything, but war, at the moment.

I've gone back in memory over my whole, whole existence, & can't remember that you have ever offended me in thought, word, or deed, so help me God! Will that do? As soon as things permit, we hope to see you here again. I do hope you'll come out of your exam with honour; or, at least, that you may get a job, & so have some little useful routine in your life. By the way, were you ever asked to write an article on "The English Theatre", by "International Literature"? I was asked to do this, or one on "Irish Literature". I eventually did the second, & mentioned your name for the one on the Theatre, in preference to the bloody oul' fossils who are always at it. We are all well, though Eileen is feeling the job of bearing a baby a bit. I am (between putting up curtains & blinds to darken rooms, & make ready for kids coming here from London) trying to do a little more of the biography. I think you're wrong about Russia. What was done was, in my opinion, the best that could be done under the circumstances. It's puzzling them all. Stalin isn't only an "as I roved out kind of a man". An Irishman knows what that means.[1]

Yours As Ever
Sean

[1] An allusion to the happy wanderer who figures in many of the "As I roved out" Irish ballads. See "The Bonny Labouring Boy" or "The Sporting Races of Galway" in *Irish Street Ballads* (Dublin, At the Sign of the Three Candles, 1960), collected and annotated by Colm O Lochlainn.

To George Jean Nathan

MS. CORNELL
DEVON
[?] SEPTEMBER 1939

My dear George:

Better send you a greeting, before the going gets too bad. Here we are in the midst of darkness: every window blinded & the right hand on a gas mask. We have three poor kids from London stopping with us;[1]

[1] The children of the London slums were sent to stay with families in the country to escape the German bombing raids.

these with our own two, & one more coming, makes things lively. I have to give a hand with the making of the beds, etc. A good job I've been used to kids from my youth up. All theatres and cinemas are closed, so fare you well for awhile. Concerning the theatre, O'Casey's occupation's gone. I'll have to try to look around for some other things to write about to keep the kettle on the hob.

I wish New Theatre would think a little more sensibly before they write down things. Most Communists are better with politics than with the things of the theatre. They've told Chamberlain what would happen, told him years ago. I was one of them. It has happened. But they must think a little more deeply about the theatre. You're right (in your "England goes Yankee Doodle" [2]) about them here plunging into the American theatre; & giving it greater recognition. With all immodesty, I think I had a hand in it. My "Flying Wasp" helped them to see how poor they were, & how, comparatively, healthy the American Theatre is. You should take all the chances you can get to loaf by the sea in the sun's centre. It is a job to go so often to a play house; to sit; to listen expectantly before the curtain rise; & then, after the curtain has risen, to be unable to listen any longer.

You did well not to come to Europe this year. I imagine it would have been an unpleasant experience. Your own townland is much more comfortable. I hope you had a chance to see Gene. I wish I had been with you in Bermuda—where the sun has a chance to shine. I got a number of American reviews of "I Knock," & they were good. I haven't heard from Macmillan how the book went. I hope it went well—the American Dollar's very precious just now—God forgive me for thinking of it! I amnt surprised to hear what you said about Carroll's new play. I had a cinch that he was writing too much; but one has to be very careful about professional jealousy—the human heart is deceitful above all things. I agree with you that English dramatists are silly when they try to be philosophical about sex & love. And just as silly about "Time-Space" or "Space-Time." I hope they wont be so silly over war—but they have Irish & Scots & Welsh to help them there.

For the present, I have to hark to my

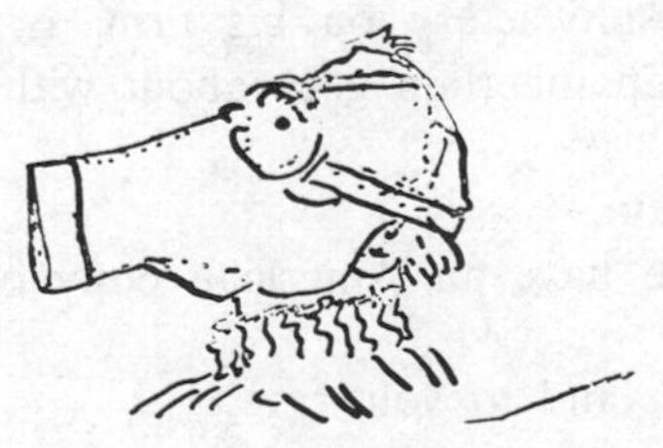

To you, too, all my ald love.
Ever Yours.
Sean

[2] George Jean Nathan, "England Goes Yankee Doodle," *Newsweek*, 17 July 1939.

To George P. Brett[1]

TS. MACMILLAN, N.Y.
[DEVON]
20 SEPTEMBER 1939

My dear Mr. Brett:

I am sending you back, with this letter, the Agreement, signed and all, for the publication of my new play, "The Star Turns Red".

However, I should like you to read the play before you decide to publish it. If, on reading it, you don't feel fervent about it, I won't mind you backing out of your promise to scatter it among the American people. I invariably send anything to Messrs Macmillans here on this understanding—that they are, of course, at liberty to refuse what they don't like—they haven't refused anything so far, but that isn't the point. An understanding, to me, is always to be preferred to a formal contract. You can sometimes depend on a man's word; rarely on a contract. And, anyway, I like you very much; and I like Harold and Daniel Macmillan very much, too; and I venture to look upon you as friends—no matter how the hell we may differ—rather than as the fellows who publish my books. I wish to Christ most of the Conservatives here were like Harold Macmillan.

England has landed herself in a right mess. It is the price they have paid for the planned stupidity of Chamberlain. All for war when peace is best; all for peace when war was best. In politics today there are only four remarkable men: Stalin in Russia; Hitler in Germany—however we may hate him—; and your own Man in the White House; and Jim Larkin the Dublin Labour Leader—Dublin's always in it.

We are up to the neck here in gasmasks; everyone's carrying—except meself—it like a Jew carries a phylactery on his arm, or a Catholic carries a scapular on his chest. Chamberlain goes about with it, too—to show a good example.

I hope your leg is allright again.

A favour: could you let me have an American copy of "I Knock at the Door?"

Warm regards to Mrs. Brett and to you.

Sean O'Casey

enclosure

[1] George P. Brett, president, Macmillan Company, New York.

To Richard J. Madden

TC. O'Casey

Devon
19 October 1939

My dear Dick:

Youve said it, Dick: my mind is not only hectic, but hazy as well, over my own affairs, in particular, and over the affairs of a good deal of the world in general. We are caught up and whirled in a tornado of stupidity. England has as much chance of winning this war as I have of winning the Grand National, or the fight against the world, the flesh, and the devil. It is simply appalling to go on witnessing the chaos, the waste, the rushing here and there, the building up, and then knocking down of the multitude of incompetents doing their bit for King and country. England's one chance is to make for peace, and make for it quick. She ought to get into close touch with Russia without delay, no matter what she may think of Russia's policy. Even though it be, to her, unrighteous—though what she has had to do with righteousness from Bunker's Hill down to today, I dont know—she, to take Christ's advice, should make friends with the mammon of unrighteousness, if she wants to live a few days longer.

Of course I realise that the chance of a production of "The Star Turns Red" has gone down below zero. Things here are even colder.

The fact of an understanding between Nazi Germany and Communist Russia is a long story; but it was inevitable, and anyone who watched things for the past couple of years could see it coming. I myself shocked some Liberals here nearly a year ago by saying that an understanding between Germany and Russia was not only possible but certain, if England and France refused to take their chance of forming a peace front. Had Russia undertaken to fight Germany, she would have been left in the lurch as Poland was left; but Stalin is no fool, whatever else he may be. People make the mistake of thinking that Communists are idealists. On the contrary, we are realists. It is simply this, Dick: England's Statesmen have no longer the power or faculty of seeing an inch in front of their noses. When the U.S.A., years ago, prompted England to take action with her over the invasion of Manchuria, England turned the deaf ear and the blind eye to America's suggestion. She ignored your country in every way as she ignored Russia. Why, when I was over with you, I spoke of these things to the English Speaking Union, stressing the ignorance of England about America's life, her literature, and her art.

I have argued for years for the proper recognition of O'Neill, have rowed with the critics over him, have suffered for it, but not half as much as England will suffer for her assumption that there is only one country in the world—herself. Bloody cheek of them! And Russia, anyway, has taken only what is or was her own—part of Ukraine and Byelo-Russia. They are as close to Russia as the people of Fermanagh and Tyrone are to Erinn.

But these are big questions, and would take reams to write about. So let us return to our own personal or, rather, my personal problems. I hope "The Plough" will go on after the "Journey's End," though I have grave doubts about the success of Sheriff's play now; for, like Armistice Day, it is well outworn. But we'll hope for the best. I hope, too, in the name o God, that the deal of the film will go through. I am working spasmodically at the 2nd vol of "I Knock at the Door", but that wont be finished for a year and a lot of days, and I must think of something to keep the pot boiling for the next few months.

Which brings a question: Do you act as Agent for short stories, sketches, or articles? Or only for plays? I might be able to get some of the sketches of the 2nd vol taken by some magazine or other, and should like to ask your advice on this point. For instance, a year or so ago, I had a sketch from the 1st vol in "The Yale Review" for which I got fifty dollars (I think), and in the Fall, I have one out of the 2nd vol appearing in "The Virginia Review" attached to Virginia University which comes out quarterly. Again, I was thinking of writing an article on the similarity of American usage of words with their use in Dublin. A book has been published here on Modern American Usage, and I find the 75% of the words are common in Dublin, and are probably old Elizabethan words that Dublin has retained, and probably, carried to the U.S.A. That article might do for the Sunday Edition of "The New York Times". Or, again, my views about the political situation here. But if you dont [handle] this kind of thing, you must promise me that you wont bother to do it for me. For, I know, you damned communist, you'd put yourself out a lot for my sake, and I cant let you do too much, for you have your own big business to see to, and a job it is to keep things going. So I take it, my dear Dick, that you will be quite frank about this, and answer as a realist, and not as a dear friend.

The "Star Turns Red" is to be published by Macmillans here, and will probably be published by their American house in the New Year. Meanwhile, let us hope the war will end soon—I believe it will be over before Christmas—and so let us all get on with work far more important than that of killing each other.

With my love to Tessa and you.
As ever,
[*Sean*]

To Harold Macmillan

TS. MACMILLAN LONDON

DEVON
22 OCTOBER 1939

Dear Mr Harold,

Mother o' God. I daresay youre right, more than right, and that it would be better to publish in the New Year than at the present moment, when everyone's trying their worst to keep their hearts up. Listen to the B.B.C., listen to the band. I must say, frankly, that I was thinking solely of the money, but even with that, I think I'll have to go out and look for a job somewhere here, somewhere there, anywhere at all. I've no news of the play being put on here or in America, but plenty of news about it not going on anywhere, at home or yonder. Everyone's a little afraid of it. I had an offer here—before the war of course—, but they wanted the American rights as well, and these I wouldnt give. Even had I done so, it wouldnt have gone on. So do whatever you think to be best; you know better than I about these things.

I should have written sooner, but I'm just getting away from an attack of bronchitis.

Yes, we have another member of the family, a girl,[1] this time,—another blessing, yes; but another burden, too.

I am buried down here, and I'm afraid I must remain buried, for it takes a lot of money to be able to go from place to place. Willy nilly, we must stay here till our lease is up, and then, well one place seems as good as another. Anyway, with six kids [2] in the house, now, one has a lot to do for oneself.

But the war wont last as long as the lease. It darent. Neither side can win. They can only hope to destroy each other. The thing is futile. The young will be destroyed again. But they are asking questions at last. Three of them from Exeter college were with me yesterday—one, just joined the army, from Clonakilty, in Cork. I tried to tell them what I thought of everything. If the damned fools that rule only planned in peace as they try to plan in war, things would be better, for sooner or later the fools would be thrown out—liquidated, if you like—, and the able would take their place. And it is far far more important to plan in peace than it is to plan in war.

[1] Shivaun O'Casey was born on 28 September 1939.

[2] Three O'Casey children plus three refugee children from London. See O'Casey's letter to George Jean Nathan, ? September 1939, note 1.

I'm sure you and Lady Dorothy will be happy in a cottage. You and she, I think, are Communists in heart. She and you must be anxious about your son. Sons, sons, sons of guns, literally. The young, the young, if England can spare them, life cant.

With sincere affectionate regards to you and all.

Sean O'Casey

To Macmillan & Co. Ltd.

MS. MACMILLAN LONDON

DEVON
9 NOVEMBER 1939

Dear Sirs,

In connection with Unity Theatre, a "cultural & political group in N. London," are publishing a Magazine, "Youth Review," & want to make an article of excerpts from "The Flying Wasp." They can't pay fee. I've no objection—I rather like the idea. Do you agree? I'll get them to mention book & Publisher.

Yours sincerely,
S. O'Casey

To Picture Post

11 NOVEMBER 1939

What Are Our War Aims

Sean O'Casey, the Irish Playwright, in a statement to *Picture Post*:—

Our first aim ought to be at an immediate peace, bringing a sudden and unprovided end to the pitiful struggle now going on for what is called the destruction of Hitlerism. For ever, the Versailles Treaty has vanished, and Smigly-Ridz and his henchmen who laboured in the wealthy lord's vineyards are bygones by this time.

Why do they want to destroy Hitler, when, according to the words of their own mouths, Hitler has been destroyed already? By Stalin—Churchill has said as much in a broadcast; *Punch* has shown Hitler, the man, and Stalin, the master, in a cartoon; and J. L. Garvin has bellowed it out in the wide spaces of the *Observer*. Mr. Eden has said that Russia blocks Hitler in the East, and Turkey in the south-east; and the Maginot Line surely blocks him in the west. Then what prevents us from making peace with him and with all the world? Even if he would, he can't bear the world on his back, so the yell of world dominance is simply sunshine. The world must get together to end this curse of world dominance everywhere. With England no less than with Germany; in India no less than in Czecho-Slovakia, and in all places where there is a Rajah, white, brown, or black. With forces as they are, there can be no victory in this war—only senseless destruction. France will destroy Saarbrucken, Germany will destroy Mulhouse; France will destroy Carlsruhe, Germany will level Strasburg—so said Hitler, but we refuse to believe the devil even when he speaks the truth. Like the last war, all the mouths are open again, spraying boast and bombast all over the world. Hore-Belisha boasted that 150,000 men had been carried to France without a single casualty. But will this 150,000 be brought back to England without a casualty? That is the point that concerns these men, their relatives, their friends.

The only war aims that can ever be are the aims of the guns, and we know what they are.

Peace at once, and then war. War to throw down the barriers to keep us from the practical things being done in the U.S.S.R. and to force us into the madness of the impracticable things they want us to do here; peace communism, instead of war communism; war on the sham hypocrisies, and stupidities in high places; war to drive the rottenness out of our children's blood and bones; war for citizenship for our young men who are good enough to die, but not good enough to vote; war on the cant of physical fitness for a half-starved nation; war on Mr. Duff Cooper's schoolboy essay that "the German people should be given every assistance in finding for themselves a form of government which will create confidence in their future determination to pursue peaceful methods." See the sign of it? Blather. Receive every assistance from whom? Mr. Duff Cooper and the rest of them. The God-sent wisdom of the English governing classes is over and done with; away with them, and him; peace abroad, and war at home against these things, here and now.

To George Jean Nathan

MS. CORNELL

DEVON

28 NOVEMBER 1939

My very dear George:

I hope this may float into the Royalton; but things being as they are here & on the ocean, it is hard to be certain. I've been ill since—a London kid carried home a bad cold, & got it—, &, having welcomed (dubiously) another kid with the family—a girl this time; & Eileen's mother coming to live with us, on account of the war, I haven't had time to bless myself. However, here I am again, sending you my deep affectionate greeting. Things are getting worse every day here, & we are continually halloed & woohed with the most stupid & inept Government time & space ever saw. For instance, a lot of jacks in brief authority are running round shouting for things to be done. A local bank manager lives next door to us. He is a "special constable," & any time he sees the slightest slinking clink of a light thru' our curtains (black-out ones, too) he crushes his bobby's hat on his thick head, & rushes out, torch in hand, to batter at the door (& he half drunk), commanding that "the damned light be put out at once!" England's brain is going soft.

I had a great personal delight in your article on the revival of "Journey's End." [1] That backboneless & ribless play got a drubbing. I was especially glad, for when it came out first, I ventured to say it was no good, & England's heart stopped beating. I got into an infernal row, for all said I said it because of "The Silver Tassie" being a war-play, too; &, of course, I was jealous of "Journey's End." Well, time has shown I made more than a guess. I wasn't quite so glad to read your laughable criticism of "The Possessed," [2] & the "new" style of acting by the [Michael] Chekhov Studio. It was, in a lot of ways, sad reading. So much might have been done, in another way, & by another man. It is heartbreaking to see so much time, energy, & money resulting in mass monkey antics. I guessed (really knew) that your onslaught was a sure thing. I warned them more than a year ago that they were going back, instead of going forward. I think I wrote to you about it. They wanted me to be Chekhov's assistant; he wrote a lot to me about his views of what a theatre—produc-

[1] George Jean Nathan, "Appeasement Drama," *Newsweek,* 2 October 1939, a review of a revival of R. C. Sherriff's *Journey's End,* which opened in New York on 18 September 1939, and closed after 16 performances.

[2] George Jean Nathan, "In Two Directions," *Newsweek,* 6 November 1939, a review of George Shdanoff's *The Possessed,* based on ideas from the writings of Fyodor Dostoievsky, translated by Elizabeth Reynolds Hapgood, produced by Michael Chekhov, which opened in New York on 24 October 1939, and closed after 14 performances.

tion, acting, & playwrighting—should be; & I told him what I thought of his ideas; & then there was a dead silence. I often meet his disciples wandering round here—like a group of discalced Carmelites—, & many of them used to halt me, & insist in pouring into my dull ear millions of abstract phrases, Stark & Youngian, about the soul of acting & of writing plays. They frightened me, by God, for I saw what was coming. And, now, you have given it the theatrical anathema. So be it.

I shall look forward to, & wait expectantly for your big work on the Theatre. It will be a great gift. Don't forget me. I enjoy most thoroughly, & with great elation all you have to say. So don't forget me. I am glad about Saroyan. If you ever write to him, give him my greeting for bringing gold and myrrh & frankencense into the theatre.

I have had to pass off, for the time being, my vague scheme for a new play. The times are too bad. But I am attempting a sort of a comedy to be called—, I think, "Purple Dust," and which I hope may be done, or nearly done, early on in the new year. As well, I do an odd chapter of 2 vol. of "I Knock at the Door"; to be called, I think, "Rough House." One of the Chapters, "Royal Risidence"—a visit paid as a youngster, with an Uncle—to Kilmainham Jail—is to appear in Dec. or Jan. number of "The Virginia Quarterly". Curious how I can't get any of these sketches published here, isn't it? The Land of Hope & Glory. Well, she's got herself into a cleft stick now.

Don't forget me when your book comes out.

My love.
Sean

To Peter Newmark

MS. NEWMARK

DEVON
10 DECEMBER 1939

My dear Peter.

Thanks for your letter. A question: Would you really have the time, & if the time, the willingness to take an authoritative hand in Unity's production of "The Star Turns Red"; in other words, would you act as my deputy. I have practically refused the play; but they have appealed, & I am hesitating as to what to finally decide.

All the Best.
Yours as Ever.
Sean

To Harold Macmillan

TS. MACMILLAN LONDON

DEVON
11 DECEMBER 1939

Dear Harold Macmillan,

A line or two about your letter stating the terms offered by your American Firm: The royalties are allright, but I cant pledge myself to give them, or anyone else, any other thing that I may write. However, as you know, I'm hardly likely to wish to change my publisher for the love of change, and cant see much sense in gadding about with MS to this fellow and that fellow, so that, for what they may be worth, your American brother may be easy about where my next book will probably go.

One grumble: I have noticed that "Windfalls" and "The Silver Tassie" were "sold off" in large quantities. Not much can be said for "Windfalls" (though I think it deserved more support than it got—that is, from the reading public)—vanity again!—, but the selling off of "The Silver Tassie" was a pity. And doesnt this selling off hit your English sales, too?

I hope they wont have to do this with "I Knock At The Door."

We're all well here, but a little upset about a roving leopard that escaped from a PRIVATE zoo, and that hasnt been caught yet. This fellow who owned the leopard has put a whole community to a lot of trouble. Parents are all anxious about their children. I know what I'd do with people who kept leopards in their back yard! We had, of course, the usual trouble during the cold spell.

If you ever come down anywhere near here (we have bed to spare), I hope you'll call on us. They say it's beautiful here in the Spring (I hope theyre right), and early Summer, so maybe you'd like to see the pastures of violets and primroses flooding the whole land with (so they say) colour.

My best wishes to you, Lady Dorothy, and your family. Remember me to Lord Hartington and his Lady.

Yours Sincerely,
Sean O'Casey

To Peter Newmark

MS. NEWMARK

[DEVON]
14 DECEMBER 1939

My dear Peter:

Many thanks for your kind letter. Allright, I'll choose Beatrix [Lehmann], if she'll be foolish enough to take the part. I don't think Unity will take it on, however. They seem to be funking it. Jack Selford came down here & stopped a night. He argued a lot about the play; wanted Red Jim modified; & the girl's escapade with Joybell cut—seemed that because of her teasing Joybell, audience might think she deserved a lashing. So with the cuts made by G. or by T.G. & the silencing of Gladonzov's music, & God knows what else, it would hardly look like an O'Casey play. Well, neither G. nor T.G. are going to have their way with my play. The flowers are not for them to pick. I took a year & a half to write it; they took a few hours to read it; so I ought to know more about it than the whole of them put together. The truth is they're all a little afraid of it. They're afraid of the melodramatic in it; but it is curious melodrama, & they cant see it. I like your Goyavian idea: that's the sort of thinking production wants. They, I think could make that part of the last scene very effective with the living discussion between Red Priest & Red Jim going on in the midst of stiff lay figures in various attitude of death. That's the sort of stuff we need in Production. These would-be intellectuals give me the sick!

I daresay you have heard about the Chehkov Theatre Studio? They gave a performance of a play "The Possessed" taken from Dostoevksy's works in Broadway, New York.

The result was terrible! It came off the second or third night. Nathan was hilarious & cruel about it. But the boyo deserved all he got, & more. While the stars shine, he'll never build a theatre. And all the money that's gone west.

I enclose a few clauses I gave to Selford, & which are to be fixed into any contract offered to me. Keep it safe.

Eileen, I, Brian, Niall, & our new arrival (a girl), Shivaun, are all splendid.

Affectionate Regards.
Sean

enclosure

The Unity Theatre and S. O'Casey.
Clauses to be included in Agreement.[1]

a

The licence to perform "The Star Turns Red" is given only to the Unity Theatre. Transference to any other theatre or Club is not allowed except only by written permission.

b

No alterations or cuts whatsoever to be made in the play without written permission. Or additions.

c

The Author to have the final decision regarding selection of Cast, Producer, or any other point dealing with the play's production.

d

This authority may be given to one who the Author thinks is the most fully conversant with the Author's idea in the play. A friend may be chosen to act as the Author's representative.

e

The Royalties to be a flat rate of 5% on the gross weekly receipts.

f

This Royalty applies only to the Unity Theatre; in any other theatre, the terms to be by a new written arrangement.

g

If English actors perform in the play, no attempt whatever to be made to speak the "Irish brogue;" or "Irish accent;" there are 32 counties in Ireland, and each has a different accent, so there is no such thing as "an Irish accent." The dialogue is to be spoken in a straightforward way.

h

The licence to last only for the run of the play.

i

No other licence or right given, but that of performing the play.

[1] This is a typed carbon copy which I found among O'Casey's papers. Newmark had returned the original to O'Casey.

j

The Theatre to allow the book of the play to be sold in the Theatre during the performances, should the book be then published.

To Gabriel Fallon

MS. TEXAS

DEVON
22 DECEMBER 1939

My dear Gaby:

A hasty, but a hearty greeting to you and all. I have been terribly busy since: a London kid came back with a foul cold, & gave it to me; & for some time I was a prisoner in a medicine bottle; then we had another arrival—a girl—Shivaun, & that left me breathless; then came the Blackout, & I had to make all kinds of gadgets to fit paper & old clothes to the host of windows looking straight out into Germany; with A.R.P. men & policemen knocking at the door every day & twice on Sundays, to point out a jink of light escaping through the closed curtains.

And so I couldn't find time to sit down & write a letter. Besides I do all the chopping of logs that make up our fires. So you see, though I'm not a drawer of water, I'm a hewer of wood.

The country's in a terrible state, & getting beautifully worse; & it's meself is thinking, when all's over, the British Empire'll be a Nursery Rhyme.

I've just been looking over "The Capuchin Annual—40", a fine work; but am heavily disappointed that the names of Fallon & Macmanus are missing. There's a silly article by a Dennis on the Theatre [1] —the old guff about Abbey realism, when the Abbey—nor me either—could venture to put things real we saw, & heard, & handled in our time.

The oul' wan cursin' Healy, & the boyo surrounded with his ai de camps, sailin' into the Abbey, for instance—who could put that on the Abbey stage.

But how is it, now, neither you nor Frank wrote for the Annual? And what is Frank doing? And what are you doing?

I know he's married. I told him years ago—he blathered about giving a girl up—to go the whole hog. I hope I didn't say wrong.

"The Star Turns Red" is going to be produced here by a Left Group,

[1] Alfred Dennis, "A Citadel of the Theatre," *Capuchin Annual-1940,* Dublin, an ironic attack on the Abbey Theatre and Yeats based on nationalistic and religious views.

called Unity Theatre. How it will be done, God knows; but I've a young friend, whom I picked up in Cambridge, watching the show for me. At the moment he's a Stretcher-bearer, but, like you, he should be chained to the Theatre. When are you Catholics going to have a Theatre worth a visit?

The book of the play, which was to be published in the Autumn, is now to come out, I hope, in February; when it comes, I'll let you have a hot copy.

And, now, for the moment, Goodbye, with
love to the children, to Rose, & to you.

Ever Your Buttie.
Sean

To George Jean Nathan

MS. Cornell

Devon

27 December 1939

My very dear George:

Just a word to say your fine book [1] —fine outside, & finer inside—came yesterday, & there is a loud hurrah to be given. I hope it may have the sale it deserves. At the moment, I'm going over "The Star Turns Red" with Unity Theatre producer, a charming fellow, with, I think, the theatre alive in him, & a young Jew, a dear friend of ours, who is representing me at the Rehearsals. He is a keen critic, & a lover of George Jean. The Unity Theatre's a Labour Group who do "Left" plays, & they first did "Waiting for Lefty" here. How they'll make the Red Star Shine, I don't know. I read them your page on "Left Propaganda," [2] & the three of us had to admit that you were right, or as right as a man can be.

I, to speak honestly, hesitated to read them what you said of "The Star Turns Red," but I did read it to them; & there was silence; & then

[1] George Jean Nathan, *Encyclopaedia of the Theatre* (New York, Knopf, 1940).

[2] "Left Propagandists," in *Encyclopaedia of the Theatre*. Here is the passage O'Casey probably had in mind: "The fault of the proletarian boys is that they believe the only way you can make an argument impressive is to put it into a sandbag and hit the other fellow over the head with it. As a result, the plays they write and the plays they endorse are largely indistinguishable from so many holdups. To persuade an audience fully, the weapons must be equally distributed between the play and the audience. A play can't hold a pistol against an audience's head and command it to give up." (p. 225)

demur. I'll write about this later on. I took the chance of showing how, by this example, that nothing on earth would make you say you like a play you didn't like. I pointed out how deep was your affection for me (one of the few things I am proud of, & justly proud of, too), & that this deep affection wouldn't weigh the fraction of pennyweight with you, when a play was in question.

I've had a busy Christmas with the youngsters, & with these Unity men, ay & four workers from different parts of England, who were visiting Totnes, & came to see the "Bolshevist Playwright"; and grand skins they were: an engineer, 2 Electrical workers, & a sheet-metal worker. We arranged the way of the world between us.

You're not to answer this; for it is but an intimation that your book has arrived, & that my nose is close to its pages. I haven't had anything like it since "Finnegans Wake."

Thank you, old son, dear friend, for not forgetting me.

Will write again when I've read more of it. So far, an Amen goes with every sentence.

Yours with love.
Sean

X

RED STAR AND PURPLE DUST, 1940-41

"I DONT agree that the publication of the play [*The Star Turns Red*] would do me immeasurable harm—and, even if it did that would not prompt me to hold back. The flesh might be unwilling to bear opposition, but the spirit would ever be strong to fight it. So, I think, it has been all my life, and I shant change now. . . . However, writing to you, personally, I dont think that the poor play is so terrible as you think. There is little more in it than there is in the American Constitution (which I read when I first began to educate myself. It was in an American book called 'The Comprehensive Summary,' owned by my father, and published in your country) or in Lincoln's declaration of 'Government of the people, by the people for the people'; or in the prophecy by the prophet Amos, accepted as canonical by all the Anglican Communions —which they have conveniently forgotten; as they have forgotten many other things."

> "I have been thinking that since I started, I've never written anything that didnt cause a dispute, a row, a difference, or something. Never mind. Though I wrote PURPLE DUST with the idea that here was a play that would cause no commotion, I have evidently builded better than I knew."

O'Casey was hardly a good Protestant, but he was certainly a splendid Shavian "protest-ant." In his savage and sly letters to the press he reminded the British that their brutal treatment of the Irish was no less real than the Nazi brutality, and his urgent call for the unification of Ireland in 1940 was still painfully relevant thirty years later. In October 1940 he became involved in a public dispute over Russia with a British M.P., and when one of his letters was refused publication by an editor because the language was "too foul to print," the earthy O'Casey promptly replied in another rejected letter: "Sorry that the word 'balls' gave you such a sudden stroke. But you won't be able to do much to win a war, if you run away from a word." For an uninhibited word-fighter like O'Casey, there were appropriate words for every occasion, and in January 1941 he rebuked one of his Irish critics, the playwright T. C. Murray, who in a review of *Purple Dust* had objected to O'Casey's extravagant language. O'Casey's reply was one he often had to make in defense of his plays: "Take away from the drama of the world those plays that are crowded, ay, crammed with rhythm and music in dancing words, and you have left but a handful of grey and pathetic dust."

His words could dance or damn, and when the London *Daily Worker* was banned by the minister of home security, O'Casey wrote a letter to the *New Statesman and Nation* in August 1941 defending the communist paper in an eloquent plea for freedom of the press. One passage in this letter celebrates what might be called O'Casey's communist manifesto: "There is a Persian proverb which says: 'If you have two pennies, with one buy bread, and with the other a lily.' But if we have but one penny, we can buy only bread. It has been my fight for a long span of years now to try to bring about a condition in which the worker spending his penny on bread will have one left to buy a lily."

Although *The Star Turns Red* was published in February 1940 by Macmillan in England, it was rejected by the firm's American office because, as its president George P. Brett protectively explained to O'Casey, due to the war, and the Russian alliance with Germany, "America is rabid against Communism, and I should hate to see the book brought out over your name now because I feel that it would be a sure way of alienating your friends among the readers in this country." O'Casey replied in March 1940 in a firm but friendly letter which characteristically indicated why, without any concern for what it might cost him in friends or readers, he could never isolate his life or his work from the fate of all mankind: "I agree that war is a stupid and bloody business. I have seen a lot of it in my day. But intelligent and fair men must begin to bring about a condition of things in which the bounty of the earth will be possessed by all. If this war spreads, it will end in revolution, bloody revolution. A peaceful, if possible, revolution would, in my opinion, be wiser. 'Come, let us reason together, saith the Lord of Hosts.' The 'The Star Turns Red' is a warning."

James Agate ignored the warning and praised O'Casey's artistry. Perhaps Agate, who had been sharply stung by O'Casey's counter-attacks on several previous occasions, took the precaution of overstating his response this time, for in his review of Unity Theatre's London production of the play in March 1940 he hailed it as "a masterpiece," not for its prophetic communist warning but for what he called O'Casey's rich comic poetry and compassion. Bernard Shaw, in an April 1940 letter to O'Casey, praised the politics and above all the poetry of the play: "It shewed up the illiteracy of the critics, who didn't know that like a good Protestant you had brought the language of the Authorized Version back to life. Splendid!"

To Irish Freedom

JANUARY 1940

SEAN O'CASEY'S MESSAGE
Ireland Should Be Against the War

I hope your Commemoration [1] will be a great success. Mellows was a great loss to us all. I send my affectionate greetings to all who will gather together there to think for Ireland, to speak for Ireland, and to act for Ireland. To think, speak, and act so as to bring Ireland into full step with all men and women who are discontented with the present mean mass life of the peoples, and to insure that the earth and the fullness thereof shall be, not for the few, but for all. To think, speak, and act for this, and for no less.

I am against Ireland's neutrality in the war. I think it would be wise

[1] As part of its campaign for Irish neutrality, the James Connolly Club in London planned to hold a commemoration in honor of Liam Mellows, one of the Republican martyrs of the Irish Civil War, executed in 1922 by the Irish Free State Government.

for Ireland to go out definitely against it. For the many, it is a stupid war; for the few it is a profitable war. I think that all those whose profit out of it will be a rich endowment of penury and want should go all out to bring it to an end. Those who shout for it are no more out for liberty and justice than God is out to make a bit on the Stock Exchange. To think of their freedom and their justice, we have only to think of Ireland and India. Apart from India and Ireland, if countries far less than they in origin and achievement, can't produce a better government than the scuts of minds that form one here, the world is in a bad way indeed. In the higher qualities of art and literature and science, England has often been great and noble; in the quality of her government of subject peoples, from my own experience in Ireland, England is the lowest of the low. But it is sickening to hear that English government has the hallmark of heaven; it hasn't, and never had.

Anthony Eden, speaking at Birmingham the other day, said: "The rule of the rubber truncheon, torture, and the lash will never hold sway here as long as an Englishman lives and breathes."

Well, these things held sway in Ireland for a hell of a long time, and Eden is old enough to know it. This is the talk of a sentimental, ignorant kid. I, myself, helped to organise the funerals of Dublin workingmen whose skulls were battered and scattered to bits by truncheons. It is true they weren't rubber ones; they were made of sterner stuff, mercifully made by an English Government to bring death sharp and sudden to whomsoever happened to come under them. And that was only the kind, kid glove; the iron fist came later.

So, with Mitchel, to hell with all this hypocrisy and sham; and on with the fight for Ireland's freedom, for India's freedom, for freedom of all men till the earth and the fullness thereof is wholly ours.

Sean O'Casey

To Peter Newmark

MS. NEWMARK

DEVON

4 JANUARY 1940

My dear Peter:

Enclosed—one copy [1] —is all I could get; so here it is for you, or for them—whichever you like. Please let John [2] know it was all I could get.

[1] An advance copy of the printed version of *The Star Turns Red,* which was released for publication by Macmillan in London in February 1940.

[2] John Allen, who was directing the play for Unity Theatre.

Has the new ukase caught you in the web, with the other million young men, to go fight for freedom in Finland—Finnegan's Wake. God, what a crowd they are!

Chamberlion; Fee Simple Simon; Whore Belisha; Whinstone Churchyell; Morrowsin; Lord Hailafix; & the rest of them. Young hands & strong tight on their Throats—my New Year's wish to them.

Ever yours.
Sean

To Peter Newmark

MS. NEWMARK
DEVON
13 JANUARY 1940

My very dear Peter:

Any of the ladies you mention would do fine; but—they're not to be got; & if they were, they'd cost Unity too much. Jessica Tandy would be fine; but would she act for Unity, or in such a play? I doubt it.

If the Cambridge has talent, perhaps she could do fairly well. If she doesn't get a chance, how can she advance? Though we must think of poor Jack, as well.

I am hard at work on "Purple Dust", a joke in three acts. You should have kept Nathan's book, till you'd finished with it.

We are all OK, here.

Yours as ever
Sean

To Alfred Knopf[1]

TC. O'CASEY
DEVON
[? JANUARY 1940]

Dear Sirs:

I am very happily obliged to you for sending me G. J. Nathan's ENCYCLOPAEDIA OF THE THEATRE. It is a grand book. It is what one expects from G. J. Nathan, and that's saying a hell of a lot

[1] Alfred Knopf (1892–), American publisher.

in a quiet way. The sentences come floating before one's mind, like lovely iridescent bubbles, to burst with the shattering force of high explosives, breaking in pieces all the shams sheltering in the arms of playwright, actor, actress, and even those sheltering in the arms of his comrades, the critics. Here is a true knight of the theatre: thinking with Hamlet, dying with Othello, and roaring out a bawdy song with Falstaff. There is none like Nathan; no, not one; and long may he be spared to further use his marvelous memory and remarkable gifts in the service of the theatre.

Very sincerely yours,
Sean O'Casey

To Gabriel Fallon

MS. TEXAS

DEVON
18 JANUARY 1940

My dear Gaby: You know more about the "The Arrow" [1] than I do. Robbie [Lennox Robinson] asked me to write an article on Yeats for the 1st number (as the B.B.C. asked me to Broadcast about him), but, somehow or other, I didn't like the idea of making money on a man so soon dead. "Don't be superstitious, mon!" Well, there it was (and is), & I didn't do either. I haven't seen the Magazine, & so it lies. But I'm really glad to hear that they have asked you to write a critical article for them; & very glad that you have consented. You ought to be connected with the Abbey, because of your close & very intelligent connection with the Theatre. And, when all's said & done, the Abbey has done great work, & we dare not do otherwise than wish it well—so long as it continues to do good work. We all know its faults (knowing damn all about our own.), but it has done well, & so it's not quite time for bed. At their own request, I sent them my last play, fully assured that the theme, the tout assembly, & the whole thing would be too much for them, & so it is.

I suppose you heard "Kindred" [2] lasted only a few days in New York? They've put on "Juno" [3] for a few weeks' run, instead, so, God

[1] See his letter to Fallon, 8 May 1939, note 3.

[2] Paul Vincent Carroll's *Kindred,* produced by Edward Choate and Arthur Shields, directed by Robert Edmond Jones, starring Barry Fitzgerald, opened in New York on 26 December 1939, and closed after 16 performances.

[3] *Juno and the Paycock,* revived by Edward Choate and Arthur Shields, in association with Robert Edmond Jones, directed by Arthur Shields, opened in New York on 16 January 1940, and ran for 105 performances, with Sara Allgood as Juno Boyle, Barry Fitzgerald as Captain Jack Boyle, and Arthur Shields as Joxer Daly.

help us, it's an ill-wind that blows no-one good. We're iced down & snowed up here; & life is TERRIBLE! Glorious Devon, they say! Last Summer was so bad, I went round asking the natives "was the winter always like this?" but they didn't catch on.

Sorry to hear about Francis [MacManus]; but no matter how big the head may swell, so long as there's something in it. And I think Frank has something in that nut of his. And why does Ireland ban "Picture Post"? It's all so God damn silly! You should hear them talk here about the censorship in Ireland! I gave a few home truths to Captain Liddell-Hart about the English Censorship: silent, cute, cunning, & sinister—the hypocritical bastards! We do that sort of thing as if we were blowing down the walls of Jericho with all Ireland's Brass Bands blowing together, & a few Pipe Bands to keep them company. Here—not a word. It's done in the silence of death.

Well, a word more: I've ⅔rds of a new play done; & the last of it roughly written—a comedy to be called "Purple Dust".

So the black-out didn't make me sing dumb.

All Well here.
Love to Rose, You, & all the
bairns from Eileen & from me.

Yours as Ever
Sean

To Peter Newmark

MS. NEWMARK
DEVON
24 JANUARY 1940

My dear Peter:

Just as well you cant lay sudden hands on Jessica Tandy: she, or Wendy [Hiller], would overwhelm the balance of the other acting—& it wouldn't be Unity acting either. They'll have to depend on themselves, if they're to do anything. I'm glad you're going to Rehearsals, it will do you good; give you experience, & show you what a terrible place the Theatre is! What drab & hopeless things—apparently—rehearsals are. An actor, coming to the footlights, bending over, & asking, "how did I do that, Sean?" And I saying, out loud, "not bad; not bad, at all" & to myself, "Jasus, you couldn't be worse!"

Don't be too anxious. John [Allen] can only do his best; & that he'll do, I know. We must be satisfied with what Unity can give.

Let the Red Priest say his part as he thinks best, & in a way that will make him feel comfortable. The direction to "drone" it doesn't come from heaven; & may be, probably is, altogether wrong. Let him get out the porterey of the lines in his own way, with yours & John's help. Don't mind what I say; mine was a guess.

I'm sure the talk about the play is only beginning. Wait till it comes to the Stage!

I've just ended, roughly, the last act of "Purple Dust". I'm writing an alternative end; then I'll think for a while; & so eventually choose which will be the better one.

Not a word to be heard since about Dartington Hall Theatre: dead silence. Nothing left, I'm afraid but purple dust.

We're all well here, but damned cold.

My love.
Sean

By George Jean Nathan

Newsweek
29 JANUARY 1940

The Best of the Irish
by George Jean Nathan

In a letter taking me to task for expressing in a recent book certain unfavorable opinions on the present English theater, my friend St. John Ervine continues: "And stop talking about Sean O'Casey as if he were heaven's only light. He is superb music-hall with a hint, now and then, but rarely, of a poet—that's all." If, indeed, that's all, your commissionaire knows so little of dramatic criticism that he should be booted out instanter. Also, unless he is mistaken, St. John should be booted down the stairs right after him for knowing not very much more.

These distressing thoughts bemuse me particularly now that O'Casey's JUNO AND THE PAYCOCK has again seen revival here. For, to my mulish way of looking at it, not only is this O'Casey, Shaw alone expected, at his best the best of all living Irish playwrights but even at his worst so much better than three-quarters of them at their best—and some of them are pretty blamed good—that only an Ulster Irishman who dislikes the Irish as much as St. John does could possibly persuade himself otherwise. If "The Plough and the Stars" isn't one of the finest dramas in the modern world theater, if this "Juno" isn't one of the richest tragicomedies, if "The Silver Tassie" with all its readily admitted weaknesses isn't one of the most honorable experiments, if "Within the Gates," for all its lapses, isn't beautiful, brave song, and if even the incontrovertibly poor "The Star Turns Red," the feeblest play O'Casey has written, isn't peculiarly invested with a poet's prophetic vision—if these plays aren't these things than I bow my head in shame for my ignorance and stand prepared to ship over to St. John my resignation from my critical job, along with my first-night dress clothes (including the two pearl studs and the red carnation), my opera glasses, my gold lead-pencil, and letters of introduction to all the bartenders in the theatrical zone.

To derogate O'Casey's rare comedy scenes as mere superb music-hall is not only obvious critical snobbery, for superb music-hall remains nonetheless still superb, but equally obvious critical superficiality, inasmuch as it overlooks their deep roots in dramatic character, their deep penetration into human eccentricity, and withal their beautiful, drunken dramatic literature. They are Molière full of Irish whiskey, now and again Shaw off dietetic spinach and full of red meat, Nervo and Knox (if Mr. Ervine insists) in the classical costumes of Falstaff and Dogberry. Furthermore, to derogate O'Casey as a mere hint of a poet is even more sadly to relegate oneself to the critically dubious. Where in the drama of living Irishmen is there greater and more genuine dramatic poetry than you will find in the mighty sweep of "The Plough and the Stars," or in the boozy low melody of parts of "Juno," or in the people of "Within the Gates" and their periodic utterance, or in even passages of the otherwise largely meritless "The Star Turns Red"?

Inasmuch as I am hired to answer questions rather than to ask them, I'll answer. Nowhere. Dunsany has his dramatic poetic moments, and so, surely, has Carroll, and so has Denis Johnston (I am thinking of "The Moon In the Yellow River"), but even at their most deserving and eloquent, I feel, there is missing in them something of the profundity of feeling, the real pity and sorrow and pain and joy, the true shooting beauty of life tragically experienced and life desperately lived that lies innermost in and is awakened by the O'Casey pen.

The present revival of "Juno," though it gets everything it needs from the admirable Barry Fitzgerald and Sara Allgood, isn't otherwise all it should be. The Joxer of Arthur Shields is the especially weak point. But even so it is a pleasure to have it again with us.

To Peter Newmark

MS. NEWMARK

DEVON
31 JANUARY 1940

My very dear Peter:

Allright, oul' son; absolvo tuo—I hope this is good Latin. Thanks, very much for your letter. I have written to John [Allen] giving him my opinions of Alan's "incidental music"; of "black as an undramatic colour" (telling him I conceived the scene as a cubic black coffin in which the people lived; touched by the Church spire & the Factory chimney; & the sky with a star in it.); and the drop-curtain with the clenched fist threatening with death the unfortunate audience. If a curtain is to symbolise the play, I suggested it should have on it, a huge church; a huge factory chimney; a long vista of tiny houses; a star in the sky; & behind the star, a "cloud no bigger than a man's hand"—see bible—showing the form, in a cloudy way, of a clenched fist.

I'm sorry you had words with John. He is a grand fellow; & is doing his best against tremendous handicaps. We can only let the play take the best shape possible under the circumstances. He has a terrible job; & why he should do it for nix or next to nix, I don't know. A little out of his mind, I suppose; as you are, & I am. I have never really had an ideal cast for any one of my plays—"Juno" included. Anyhow, I am not going to allow myself, or my play, to be a cause of trouble between you & Jack. I'd rather take the play away, & burn the blasted thing, than separate two comrades by it. So, Peter, oul' boy, just give him all the hints you can, & don't you kill yourself over the oul' play either. I will do my best here to give any hints I can. At all events, the production mainly depends upon the Cast; & Jack, here, is dependent on material at his hands. He cant send off a note to some bugger big in the acting way, & say eh, here's a £100 a week for a good show as Red Jim, or the Red Priest. It will have to be as it can be; but I do manage to believe that Jack will put up a good show; &, if with your help, he does, then O'Casey won't say a single curse about the thing.

I've also mentioned the "red drapery over the door" put as "an indication of the crime committed". Oldfashioned, oldfashioned. They did this donkey's years ago; &, on the whole, it didn't work; & it wont work, now. Everyone'll think its a red flag hung up in a home, as banners are hung up in a church.

An idea: Wouldn't even a Red Star on a curtain, be better than a clenched fist?

Love to You, Peter.

Ever Yours
Sean

To George Jean Nathan

MS. CORNELL

DEVON
4 FEBRUARY 1940

My very dear George:

I've been very busy: the kids in the house (my own); putting up the makeshift blinds to keep every blink of light in for the blackout—why God only knows; if as much as a pin point of light goes out, a policeman knocks at the door—; & finishing the play. "Purple Dust". I just getting a fair copy typed for Dick; & will send it on to him in a week, or so. I won't bother you, for it isn't quite fair to impose upon your affection for me; & to expect you to go about forcing a production for me, as you did with "Within The Gates"—though it was damned lucky for me you did from the low down financial point of view—not to mention anything else.

I have read your "Encyclopaedia" twice over, & a grand book on the theatre it is; outside & in, for Knopf have given it a fine cover. I have written to Knopf's thanking them for sending me your book. I have spent a very happy & stimulating time with it. How you can manage to be ever the same & always different, beats me. Excluding this one, I've read seventeen of your books; & this one is as fine & as fair & as merciless & as true & as witty as the best of the others. As far as the theatre goes, you are an amazing man; & amazing in a lot of other ways, too. I don't think there is anyone in the world who has the same love for the theatre as you have. Certainly, no one with the same knowledge; & where's the other boys who have the same courage? My volume of 5 Irish Plays (Juno, Plough, Gunman, End of Beginning & Pound on Demand) published by Macmillan's here [1935], I dedicated the volume "To George Jean Nathan, Drama Critic, without fear & without reproach" & anything you write adds a bar to the needed. I hope the Abbey authorities may read your "Erin go blah." [1] It should do them good.

[1] George Jean Nathan, *Encyclopaedia of the Theatre* (1940), "Erin go blah," pp. 120–21. In the relevant passage he wrote: "But the infelicitous fact remains that, lovely and musical speech aside, the present Abbey Theatre company has put the dub in Dublin. Not so long ago one of the finest acting organizations in the world, it is now a caricature of its former self and, save when it offers itself in the more trivial comedies of its repertoire, as generally lack-lustre a theatrical outfit, whether in the way of group acting, stage direction, scenic and lighting skill, or compositional manuscript interpretation, as one may encounter this side of the fashionable London stage or the average summer cow-barn theatre."

As I've read your "O'Casey," [2] & have pondered over it; & am still pondering over it. One thing I'm certain of: Communism need not injure a playwright. Almost everything I've written (except juvenile stuff) was written as a Communist. I've been a Communist for more years than I care to remember. But I fully agree with you that writing a play on Communism is a pretty hard thing to do. To write a play on Das Kapital is, I suppose, impossible; or as hard to do as to write a play about "Time & the Conways." [3] I, myself, had largely to throw my play into the antagonism of the political church to the claims of the workers. It is being done by a Labour Group, & we shall see how it may work; though I'm too busy & too far away to go to rehearsals. By the way, it was a great Irish Labour Leader [4] (a Communist) who first brought me into touch with O'Neill. He had been to the U.S.A. & had seen "The Hairy Ape"; [5] & came back to Dublin full of it—long before I thought a play of mine would appear on the stage. And, God and you forgive me, I regard you as a Communist, too! Look at the simple life you lead; indifferent to most things really, [except] for a good play & a lovely lass.

Your criticism of Carroll's "Kindred" in "Newsweek" shocked me.[6] You are a merciless fellow. I've had a story in The Virginia University Quarterly; [7] a fancy man from Jacksboro, Texas, has sent me a Thesis, bound in red leather, & gilded, with a large picture of myself on it, on me and my plays; & got his M.A. for it; and a letter from a Sister of Charity of St. Paul, Minnesota, asking me a few questions, because she wants to write another Thesis! What would I or my family do, if it were not (seriously) for the U.S.A.?

I got a card from Gene & Carlotta [O'Neill], for the New Year; & I will write to them in a day or two.

Thanks again, George, for your grand book.

My love as ever.
Sean

[2] Ibid., "O'Casey," pp. 186–88. In the relevant passage he wrote: "The two worst influences on present-day playwrights are, very often, Strindberg and Communism. Strindberg, for example, did all kinds of things to Paul Vincent Carroll before he reformed, as his *Things That Are Caesar's* sufficiently attested. And Communism, one fears, has now adversely affected Sean O'Casey as a dramatic artist, as a perusal of his latest play, *The Star Turns Red,* disturbingly hints."

[3] See O'Casey's letter to Nathan, 14 February 1938, note 4.

[4] Jim Larkin, upon whom he based the character of Red Jim in *The Star Turns Red.* See O'Casey's letter to the *Irish Worker,* 8 March 1913, note 4.

[5] Eugene O'Neill's *The Hairy Ape* opened in New York on 9 March 1922.

[6] George Jean Nathan, "Post-Holiday Spirit," *Newsweek,* 8 January 1940, a review of Paul Vincent Carroll's *Kindred.* See also O'Casey's letter to Gabriel Fallon, 18 January 1940, note 2.

[7] See O'Casey's letter to Gabriel Fallon, 25 August 1939, notes 1 and 2.

To Peter Newmark

MS. NEWMARK
DEVON
7 FEBRUARY 1940

My very dear Peter:

I have had the Set Designs under my eyes; & I find that Gowing[1] was right, & I was wrong. With the whole conception of the play, the closed in coffin-room won't do. The influence the Spire, the Chimney, & the Star were to have would then be lost. I forgot these, till Lawrence Gowing reminded me of them; & also of the mingling of "realism" & symbolism in the play, suggesting the same thing in the designs. I agree with him. And I think, and so does Eileen, that he has cleverly done this in his designs. I like them very much; & I don't see how they can be bettered for the purposes of the play; unless we had a big theatre & a bigger pursc: two things that might ruin the play and the production. I have disagreed with the idea of a Clenched-Fist curtain; & hope they wont do it. Anyway, a poor theatre, to avoid expense, should have a neutral curtain, suitable for any play. But I understand the desire of the Artist to paint anywhere & everywhere. I hope you won't be going into the army. Perhaps, you'll manage to escape it. I've just sent my roughly typed copy of "Purple Dust" to be professionally done; & hope for the best in the U.S.A. No hope here. What happened to the play you sent to the Westminster? Did you get it back; if you did, let's have a look at it.

With Affectionate Regards
Yours as ever.
Sean

[1] Professor Lawrence Burnett Gowing, painter and teacher, who designed the sets for the Unity Theatre production of *The Star Turns Red.*

To George Jean Nathan

MS. CORNELL
DEVON
14 FEBRUARY 1940

My very dear George:

Just a line to say I've sent the typescript of "Purple Dust" to you & Dick. I think it is, in some ways, an odd play. A young lady comes in in riding-dress; but I don't think you'll go for me over that. At first it was to be just a skit on the country; but it changed a little into, maybe, a kind of an allegorical form. The idea crept into my head after a visit to a family living in a Tudor House here; suffering all kinds of inconveniences because of its age & history; going about with lantern, & eating in semi-gloom. Terrible torture for the sake of a tumbledown house with a name! I've never gone there since. I was perished with the cold, & damaged with the gloom. However, you'll read the play; & of course, I hope you'll find something in it. A lot of the humour is, I think, pretty broad, & a little exaggerated, but we Irish are fond of adding to things.

You know, I suppose, "Juno" is on in Broadway. Dick [Madden] sent me a bag of United States dollars out of it; & welcome they were. They came in mighty handy. That was a terrible article on "Kindred." I will say something about it when I write again. Now I want to catch the post, & get the play away as soon as possible. Dick's impatient for it.

With fond love.
Sean

From George P. Brett

TS. O'CASEY

THE MACMILLAN COMPANY,
PRESIDENT'S OFFICE
60–62 FIFTH AVE. NEW YORK.
16 FEBRUARY 1940

Dear Mr. O'Casey,

Our editorial department has just got around to presenting the publishing order for THE STAR TURNS RED, and in doing so they have called my attention to the reader's report depicting the content of the play. Having read this I am mindful of your kind letter of September 20 in which you say in part—"However, I should like you to read the play before you decide to publish it. If, on reading it, you don't feel fervent about it, I won't mind you backing out of your promise to scatter it among the American people."

It is not for us to judge the works of Sean O'Casey. His work stands apart. It represents his own character and style, which is of such nature, I am happy to say, that any publisher would be glad to have it on his list. But I am prompted to take advantage of your kindness and refrain from publishing this particular play because of the nature of the world in which we live, especially because of the public temper in this country today.

Not only do I feel that the publication of this play in America at this time would do you immeasurable damage, but by the same token it would damage us too. America is rabid against Communism, and I should hate to see the book brought out over your name now because I feel that it would be a sure way of alienating your friends among the readers in this country. This would hurt us too, because if, as I hope, we are to have the pleasure of publishing for you for years to come, I fear that publication of THE STAR TURNS RED would make our road a difficult one in so far as your books are concerned for the future, at least for the immediate future.

To sum up then, from the point of view of American publication, the thought of bringing this play out now is ill timed, and I think we had better not do so.

Plays, you know, can be copyrighted in America without actually being set up here, so I am arranging to obtain copyright on THE STAR TURNS RED so as to protect your interests.

Now I do not want to stand in the way of your having this play published here if you wish to do so, so if you like we will draw up a formal release cancelling the contract between us for the publication so you will be free to offer it elsewhere if you choose to do so. Of course, if you have no intention of publishing it at this time, as a result of my advice, this letter will suffice to indicate that we understand each other, namely that The Macmillian Company is not going to publish it.

So that I may know that you got this letter—we never know these days what happens to our mail—so that the record may be complete, I am sending this letter to you in duplicate with the request that you kindly acknowledge its receipt by signing one copy and returning it to me for my files.

I wonder when this dizzy world will settle down to realism and give up the thought that war can settle anything to the advantage of anyone. Of course, we are all up against it now, but would that there were a way out, a way to prevent this war from swinging into "high", for otherwise surely civilization as we would hope to have it will disappear from this earth.

With the kindest personal regards,

Faithfully yours,
George P. Brett Jr.

To Picture Post

24 FEBRUARY 1940

"Ireland—A Dramatist's View" [1]

The partition of Ireland is a double partition. It divides Ireland from Ireland, and separates Ulster from herself; for Cavan, Donegal, and Monaghan are separated from her. So the Ulster that Englishmen speak about isn't Ulster at all, but only part of Ulster. Ulster is as much a part of Ireland as a limb is a part of a human body. The Irish people, work-a-day and militant will never allow her to become, at the vain desire of England, the little state of Cragavonia. A clique isnt going to keep Dal Riada, Oriel, Tirowen, and Iveagh from the rest of Ireland. Ulster is as Irish as they make them. [In Ulster is Cave Hill, beside Belfast, where the Founders of the United Irishmen took the oath to drive the English out of Ireland. These men were Protestants, by the way. Here is Emain Macha, the home of the Red Branch Knights; here's the mountain on which St. Patrick, as a slave boy, minded his master's herds; here is the first church he had where he dispensed the Lord's Supper (Protestant view), or celebrated Mass (Catholic view); and here he lies in his last sleep. Here is the See of Columbkille, Protestant Saint as well as a Catholic one (see Stoke's Keltic Church); here are the homes of Hugh O'Neill, Owen Roe O'Neill, and Shane the Proud; Here lie sleeping hundreds of Irish Protestants who in 1798 fought against the English: Orr, McCracken, Russell, Jimmy Hope, Betsy Gray. And the name of Ulster's chief town (city) is Beilfeirste,[2] as Gaelic a name as Cathair dhil bhreagh Chorchaigh[3]. The ballads in the Ulster Orange Song Book are as Irish in form and spirit as any sung in the streets of Dublin.] [4] And its name is "Northern Ireland." If Northern Ireland hasnt an unbreakable connection with East, West, and South Ireland, then geography doesnt exist.

A word or two on Hulton's recent article: [5] "The British are the supreme example of orderliness and unity." We have never had such an exhibition of orderliness as that shown when Mafeking was relieved. It gave a new word to the language.

The unity for Irish self-government is a thousand years old, and is still there. We understand the English far better than they understand us. There is no use mentioning "Nazi tyranny" to an Irishman. English Government in Ireland, setting aside the Black and Tans, has often been soft-brained, but never soft-handed. The Irish Censorship is largely a

[1] O'Casey's original title was "Ulster for Ireland, or Trouble."

[2] Belfast.

[3] The dear and beautiful city of Cork.

[4] This passage in square brackets was omitted by the editor.

[5] Edward Hulton, "What is Happening in Ireland?", *Picture Post,* 20 January 1940. Hulton was editor of the magazine, which was subtitled *Hulton's National Weekly of London.*

farce: it is comic; but here, as I can prove, the censorship is silent, sinister, and severe. And the Irish will never permit Holland Guards to come into the country. We must settle this question ourselves. Let England clear out of it. That is the only hope. It will be settled one day; but not by England; only by ourselves. It can never even be hidden by dumping it down into a quicklime grave.

Sean O'Casey
Devon

To George Jean Nathan

MS. CORNELL
DEVON
27 FEBRUARY 1940

My very dear George:

We have been overwhelmed here with influenza, & have had a busy time nursing ourselves. Myself, the missus, & our two boys are nearly on the Qui vive again, but the little girl of six months is still laid up with it. They say it is carried about from the soldiers' camps that are every where here, now. I sent Jim & Dick the MS of "Purple Dust." But more than a week afterwards, the P. Master General sent me a note refusing registration; & asking me what he would do with the parcels. And there is no notice of the refusal in any P. office. So, stupidity promotes delay, expense, & anger. To this day—more than a fortnight after—I don't know if the parcels have been sent on. I am getting two more copies typed to send on in unregistered parcels, so when you get either or both depends on the King's Navee. I also sent you a copy of "The Star Turns Red", & hope you'll get it allright.

And evermore thanks for your answer to St. John Ervine's onslaught on O'Casey.[1] Though he won't be pleased at your revealing what he'd consider a confidential communication. That was Yeats's contention with me over the Silver Tassie row: that I should never have published what was private correspondence. He even tried to move the Author's Society to promote an action for breach of copyright! Poor Yeats. A very great poet & a very great man; & I loved him more than many who fawned on him. He began to like me very much towards the last; & I have even played Croquet with him.

[1] George Jean Nathan, "The Best of the Irish," *Newsweek,* 29 January 1940, which is reprinted above in its chronological order.

But I wonder why Ervine wrote to you about me? He knows of the bond of friendship between us; & it was curious of him to select you for the blow that he aimed at me. Some time ago, he sent me, in pamphlet form, a lecture, called "The State & the Soul", &, also, "The Essex Hall Lecture," delivered by a different person every year, under the auspices of The General Assembly of Unitarian & Christian Free Churches. This he sent to me, inscribed "to Sean O'Casey, from St. John Ervine." I read it; pondered on what was said in it; & ventured to send a few criticisms in my letter of thanks to him for remembering me. He never replied. In all his writings, he has never referred to the "Flying Wasp", though it was concerned, wisely or foolishly, with the Theatre. He has never referred to "I Knock at the Door", though he has given columns to biographies such as you laugh at in your last book. I daresay, he resented my criticism of his State & his Soul. Well, I did it all in good sport, for I have an affection for St. John. But, strangely enough, quite a lot of Ulstermen consider themselves to be something of an oracle; 5 of them for instance: Robert Lynd, Literary Editor of "The News Chronicle"; our own St. John; England's Garvin Angel, Editor of the Observer; James Douglas, Spouter in the Sunday Express; & the late A. E., of the Irish Statesman & Irish Homestead.

Isn't it a pity that your book isn't published here as well as in America? It's rather a commentary on the state of the English theatre that it isn't. The English theatre is now a little theatre in every sense of the word.

And by the way, I don't altogether agree about business men and art, so bitingly set down in your criticism of "Kindred." Certainly, over here, business men have small conception of anything in the way of art. Or the aristocrats either; or, indeed, the Proletariat, though there is small blame to them. I must say your business men—the few I've met—seem to be different. I've never met any here like G. Bushar Markle, for instance. He even tried to paint pictures in the basement of his house; could play the piano; & sing a song. Well, when we meet again, we'll talk of these things. But Carroll forgot one big business man who was interested in more things than one—Engels, the friend and partner of Karl Marx, & co-author of the Communist Manifesto. But Carroll, I suppose, doesn't stand for Communism. I've just read in "World in Falseface" [2] that a certain man's content with "plenty of sharpened pencils, lighted cigars, & paper." When he has these, the world is his. Well, I'll throw in a lovely girl; &, as far as desires of this world go, that means a Communist.

And God be wi' him.

My love.
Sean

[2] George Jean Nathan, *The World in Falseface* (New York, Knopf, 1923).

By James Agate

17 March 1940
Sunday Times, London

A MASTERPIECE
By James Agate

Unity

Thursday, 14 March[1]

"THE STAR TURNS RED"
A Play. By Sean O'Casey.

> "Germinal" is a work of compassion, not a revolutionary work. In writing it my desire was to cry aloud to the happy ones of this world, to those who are the masters: "Take heed! Look underground, observe all those unhappy beings toiling and suffering there. Perhaps there is still time to avoid a great catastrophe. But hasten to act justly, for, otherwise, the peril is there: the earth will open, and the nations will be swallowed up in one of the most frightful convulsions known to the world's history."—Emile Zola.

The blurb to the printed version of Mr. O'Casey's new play has this: "The voices of the workers proclaim that life must give an equal chance to all, that wasteful beggary must be replaced by fruitful labour, that leisure must be the lot of all, and that charity, great or small, must be strained away from the energies of man. The play says that if these things are not given they will be taken, for the Star will turn red and shine the wide world over." Thus 1940 finds Mr. O'Casey saying exactly what Zola said in 1885. In the meantime Bolshevism has come, but alas, not gone! And for fairness' sake, and since what follows is written by a dramatic critic who cares for nothing in politics except their drama, let it be noted that in the same period Fascism also has come, and alas, not gone!

Mr. O'Casey's play is a masterpiece. "Aljaybra," says a character, "has nothing to do with hanging festoons at a right angle!" The passion, pathos, humour, and, above all, poetry with which this great play is hung, are there for all the world to see and hear, and I shall leave it to the Y.C.L. to decide whether the festoons are at the correct left angle or not.

[1] Sean O'Casey's *The Star Turns Red* opened on 12 March 1940 at Unity Theatre, London, directed by John Allen, with sets by Lawrence Burnett Gowing, and a cast of amateur actors divided into two separate companies which played on alternating nights.

The angle, as another Irish playwright would have said, is immaterial. Further to be advanced on this play's behalf are its drive, its variety—the four acts constitute a globe of four continents—its perfect setting in the Ireland of "to-day or to-morrow." I find the piece to be a *magnum opus* of compassion *and* a revolutionary work. I see in it a flame of propaganda tempered to the condition of dramatic art, as an Elizabethan understood that art. To one such a proud prelate was a prelate whose pride was whole and absolute, and free of those erosions and nibblings insisted on by an age which realises that nothing is whole and absolute. That is why the Red Priest in this play is more than a whole-hogger for things as they are; he is a medieval whole-hogger. It is a pity and must confuse many that this Priest should be called Red when his politics are what is known as anti-Red; the fact remains that he is as much of an out-and-outer as the Red Queen in "Alice."

Opposite, as the films have it, to the Red Priest is the people's leader, Red Jim, who is as much a model of Communist virtue as, let us say, Shakespeare's Henry V was a model of manly excellence. And, of course, Priest and Leader go to it hammer-and-tongs, like those English and French armies. Remember how single-mindedly Shakespeare drew the two camps the night before the battle, one busy at prayer, the other given over to idle chatter. Did Shakespeare worry whether there were serious-minded exceptions in the French lot, or wanton fellows in the English? No! Mr. O'Casey's play is Elizabethan. One side says "Ding," and the other "Dong." And that is all there is to it, excepting, possibly, the Brown Priest who, as the spirit of compromise, tries to bring ding and dong together by saying, "Dell"! Let me insist again upon this play's Elizabethan quality. No Shavian nonsense here, whereby the protagonists, in this case meaning antagonists, put their knees under the mahogany and obligingly put each other's cases!

Now perhaps one should give some idea of the action-plot. In the first act a Saffron-Shirted Fascist shoots a Worker whose Communist daughter the Red Priest has ordered to be whipped. In the second act a Worker beats up half-a-dozen corrupt Trades Union leaders. Let those who blame the Unity Theatre audience for vocalising their delight at this ask themselves how an Elizabethan audience took Fluellen's beating up of Pistol, and Pistol's beating up of the French soldier. The third act, which begins with the halt and the blind, the phthisic, and the deformed processing round the dead man's bier, is, pictorially speaking, sheer Webster, though exactly what the mourners stand for is a little baffling. For while these are the victims of poverty, they are not proposing to do anything about it. Perhaps they are the equivalent of those cross-bench or mugwump angels who, as the ancient legend has it, were neither on the side of Jehovah nor on that of Satan in the day of battle. After the procession the two sides square up to each other over the coffin, the Priest deploying all his powers of rhetoric and casuistry against the lava-like flow of the leader's impassioned oratory, whose speciousness is at once innocent and over-riding.

Then follows the fourth and weakest act, weakest perhaps because its forerunner simply does not permit of any sequel, or perhaps more simply because Mr. O'Casey just couldn't keep it up! There is an alleged comic scene between two workmen which reminds one of Mr. Shaw's letter to the late James Welch: "You will never be as funny as the Brothers Griffith." In the matter of paper-hanging Mr. O'Casey is not so good as the Brothers Anybody. The play concludes with the siege of the Workers by the military and the police, done in dumb-show, and a sudden change of heart on the part of these two bodies. During this the Star, coldly glittering from the beginning, now turns red, in which change of colour the playgoer can choose between the blush of a new dawn and the conjuring trick of a dramatist at a loss for an ending.

I came away impressed above all by a verbal splendour which can throw away: "Where's his 'Workers of the world, unite!' now? Hid in the dust of his mouth and lost in the still pool of his darken'd eyes!" upon a minor character. Shakespeare's prodigality again, which could give the "lated traveller" jewel to a First Murderer. Now, at last, Mr. O'Casey has achieved that towards which in "The Silver Tassie" and "Within the Gates" he was feeling his way. Now in this great play are eye, ear, and mind all satisfied, provided they are the eye, ear, and mind of a playgoer sitting in a theatre, and not of a politico-economic actuary totting up this and tatting about whether it comes to that!

The piece is being acted by two alternating companies of amateurs. The company I saw was the second one, and I thought it did well enough. The spirit of the play shone through each and every one of the players, some of whom had a distinct measure of competence.

To George P. Brett

TC. O'Casey

[Devon]

21 March 1940

My dear Mr Brett:

Thanks for your kind letter dealing with the question of publishing "The Star Turns Red."

I enclose the letter sent to me, signed, so that the contract for the publication of the play is thereby cancelled. I guessed, at the start, that you might, from a business point of view, hesitate about the play. That was why I suggested that you should read it before you sent a contract. Pity you didnt. I dont agree that the publication of the play would do me immeasurable harm—and, even if it did that would not prompt me to hold back. The flesh might be unwilling to bear opposition, but the spirit would ever be strong to fight it. So, I think, it has been all my life, and I shant change now. That it might do you damage, I'll have to allow; and that you cant have that, I'll allow, too; for business as a body, must do as business does.

Therefore, I don't blame your hesitation in the least; and my first warning will, I think, support this statement.

However, writing to you, personally, I don't think that the poor play is so terrible as you think. There is little more in it than there is in the American Constitution (which I read when I first began to educate myself. It was in an American book called "The Comprehensive Summary," owned by my father, and published in your country) or in Lincoln's declaration of "Government of the people, by the people for the people"; or in the prophecy by the prophet Amos, accepted as canonical by all the Anglican Communions—which they have conveniently forgotten; as they have forgotten many other things.

The play has been produced here by a Labour Group; and I enclose some of the reviews, which may make interesting reading.

If any opportunity presents itself, I will, of course, be delighted to have the play published. I must refuse to fear results.

I agree that war is a stupid and bloody business. I have seen a lot of it in my day. But intelligent and fair men must begin to bring about a condition of things in which the bounty of the earth will be possessed by all. If this war spreads, it will end in revolution, bloody revolution. A peaceful, if possible, revolution would, in my opinion, be wiser. "Come, let us reason together, saith the Lord of Hosts." The "The Star Turns Red" is a warning. With good and warm wishes to you and Mrs. Brett, and to my friends and brothers in America.

Very sincerely yours,
Sean O'Casey

To Peter Newmark

MS. NEWMARK

[DEVON]

30 MARCH 1940

My dear Peter:

Sorry you have to go, but, in the Summer, anyway, Margate wont be bad. I know it well. Dont try to change to the Infantry, no matter how dull the Pay Corps may be. Dont fall out with good luck. I don't know what to say about your play. It is hard to analyse. Anyway, first, I think there's no hope of production. It strikes me that the great fault of it is that it is (lots of its & ises) all on the level. It doesn't change in tempo. It seems, too, to be a blend of Coward & Shaw, and has in it an odd hint of Harwood's "The Immortals".[1] And the tumbling scene comes out of [Shaw's] "The Apple Cart"; doesn't it?

If I be right, then two phases of advice to you: Shaw's mind is too bright & intellectual to be imitated; & Coward's so dull & brittle that it isn't worth imitating. However, Eileen's going to read it; & I'll see what she will say, before I give my final malediction. She is getting good at judging a play. She reads (on the Q.T.) all my M.S. as I'm writing it; she reads them when I amn't looking; & so she's got an idea of how it shouldn't be done; & her opinion's good. So I'll see what she says. Yours reminds me of my first efforts: better on the whole, but inferior to the spurts I managed occasionally to get into mine.

I have had a sore chest for a week, now. Niall crashed into it with his head, in play, & bruised a rib; & it's damned sore still.

It's a pity you will be losing sight of John [Allen]. What a job he had. Eileen says, if you get any leave, you should come down here for a few days—though it's a long way from Margate; but, if you do, we'll all be very glad to see your young face again.

"Purple Dust" has found an American manager, so my Agent has cabled; but what they really think of it, I don't know.

I am busy on my autobiography, (now isn't lifestory a better word than that?) & hope to have most of another volume done by the end of the year.

Take care of yourself, & come to see us as soon as you can. Write to us, now & again, too. Shall I send your play—when Eileen's read it—back to 66?

With love from Eileen, Brian, & me.
Yours
Sean

[1] Probably H. M. Harwood's *These Mortals* (London, Hinemann, 1937).

P.S. The double-named authorship of the play makes it more difficult—which is Newmark & which is Urban? [2]

[2] Fritz Urban, a teacher of mathematics, who had also translated some of the works of Lord J. M. Keynes into German.

To Picture Post

DEVON
30 MARCH 1940

"Dramatist O'Casey Replies"

That was a jovial little outburst from Dora Treloar, that was, in the issue of your journal of March 9.[1] While she shouted for all Irishmen to be booted out of the House of Commons and the House of our Lords (a helluva tragedy that would be to both England and Ireland) she, with commendable sense, didn't even suggest that they should be booted out of the Army and Navy. That shout of hers was a dear little poppy wreath laid on the graves of the thousands of Irishmen lying asleep in Flanders or in the stony plains of Gallipoli. I suppose she'd boot out the American Ambassador, too, because his name happens to be Kennedy. Wasn't that the name of the Captain who went down on the *Rawalpindi*? Dora Treloar should have had sense enough to know that my reference was, not to the English people, but to their rulers. They are spending heaps of money keeping a tiny clique in North East Ireland, money that could be more wisely spent on English Social Services. They keep troops there, too, that would be more usefully employed elsewhere fighting for Democracy. She, like us all, has to pay her whack of the expense. If she likes that, she hasn't what I would call a hard nut. But she has shown that it isn't only an Irish Paddy that can sometimes go wild.

Sean O'Casey

[1] Dora O. Treloar, in a letter to the editor, wrote: "Irishman Sean O'Casey is quite right, the English are soft-brained, otherwise he and his kind would be 'booted' out of England back to their wonderful East, West, and South Ireland, and never allowed to return to this country on *any* pretext. If an Englishman in *Ireland* had had such a letter printed abusing Ireland he would be riddled with bullets. English people in *England* writing letters abusing Ireland cannot even get their letters printed. Yes, we are soft-brained. Let's boot them all out, from the House of Commons, the House of Lords, and pack Bernard Shaw off with them."

To George Jean Nathan

MS. CORNELL

DEVON
31 MARCH 1940

My very dear George:

Yes, I got your article "Best of the Irish," one from you, one from Dick [Madden], & one from the Newsweek itself; & have read the three of them—more than once. My modesty cracks up before an article like that, & the flesh & spirit rejoice together. Thanks, ever more; it was a grand article; hard to live up to; but well worth the effort. I sent you a long letter in reply, which I hope you have received by now. I have still a warm corner in my Southern Irish heart for St. John. He is, at least, a virile writer. "The Flying Wasp" stung him, I'm afraid. But what the hell about a sting! We all get one, at times.

I am, of course, very glad & very proud of your good opinion of "Purple Dust." I was somewhat uncertain about the play, myself. I knew there were good passages in it, & that it was odd—that's the word I thought of—; but was afraid to fancy it had more than those things in it. Eileen—the wife—read it, & thought a good deal of it beautiful; but I was afraid her near connection to me interrupted her clear view of it. Well, you have supported her view, handsomely; &, though your connection is very near to me, too, I know it doesn't interrupt your view of what I do; & so I am very proud & exhilerated; but a little anxious of what my next work may be like. Enough for the present, anyway.

Dick has cabled to say that Eddie Dowling has taken the play. I am still working on the second book of my life. I have ten chapters done; & I think some of them are very good. And through all & in all, I share a good deal of my life with the three children. I've just finished reading "David Copperfield" to the eldest. So far Mark Twain is his favourite. I must say that I did enjoy reading Tom Sawyer & Huckleberry Finn, myself, while I was reading them to him. Mark was the rale McCoy. So you see, I haven't much spare time. I haven't had a chance to write to Eugene [O'Neill] yet; but I must do it this week. A day or two ago, I read his "Moon of the Caribbees" again; & had a lovely half an hour, & a lovely time thinking of it afterwards. I wish I could write as good a one act play. A great boy!

Dick mentioned a few over-done in "Purple Dust"; & I'm going to look them over to see what parts would be best to knock out of them.

I'm afraid this damned war will make it impossible for me to go over. No one can tell what may suddenly happen here; and I shouldn't care to leave the missus & three kids to their own resources. However, please God, the strife will be over by then.

Thanks again, dear friend, for your article & your letter.

With much love.
Sean

To Horace Reynolds

MS. Reynolds
Devon
31 March 1940

My dear Horace:

I've been wondering how you are? & Kay & the two children—big children now! I've been very busy since—with the law case again; with another baby born to us—a girl; with influenza & German measles; & with the damned war. And with a new play. So there were a few reasons for not writing to you. Anyway, let me hear how you & all are. And the boy at Harvard. I wish my boy was with him. I understand Gogarty is over there with you, now. I am working on the 2nd volume of my life story; & hope to have it ready for the publishers by the end of the year. One of the chapters, "Royal Residence", appeared in the Virginia Quarterly Review; & another, "Cat'n Cage" may appear in their Autumn or Winter number. You are still reviewing. I read your "Gogartian Explorer in England". I must get Gogarty's "Going Native".[1] "Tumbling in the Hay"[2] was disappointing to me. Gogarty must miss W.B.Y[eats] a lot. I wonder what is Dublin like, now, with W.B.[,] L. Gregory, & AE (pious oul' fraud) gone? It will be a long time, I'm afraid, before Ireland gets another Lady G; & longer before she gets another W.B; though there is a young poet rising in P[atrick] Cavanagh, I think. And [F. R.] Higgins can be damn good, too. Have you ever read [Sean] O'Faolain or [Frank] O'Connor; &, if so, what do you think of them? Although I occasionally review a book here (when I'm asked; & to scrape a couple of guineas into (the oul' sack), between you & me (keep it dark) I'm not a good reviewer! Have you read —or tried to read—Finnegan's Wake? I never tire of it; but, of course, only able to hit it out here & there; but aware of the grand comic-tragic scheme of the work.

I daresay, you've heard of the short survival of "Juno" in New York.[3]

[1] Oliver St. John Gogarty, *Going Native* (London, Constable, 1941).

[2] Oliver St. John Gogarty, *Tumbling in the Hay* (London, Constable, 1939).

[3] The revival of *Juno and the Paycock* in New York was soon to close, on 13 April, after a run of three months, having opened on 16 January. See O'Casey's letter to Gabriel Fallon, 18 January 1940, note 3.

It couldn't have come at a more critical time. It has enabled me to face without flinching too much the £200 owed in the recent law case. Up the U.S.A!

Well, Horace, old boy, all the best, till the next time. Love to Kay & the two children.

Yours as ever.
Sean

To Michael McInerney[1]

PC. *Irish Freedom*

April 1940

SEAN O'CASEY TO IRISH EXILES

Dear Mac,—I wish your Assembly of Irish men and women every success. It is becoming more and more important that we Irish should take a fuller interest in and a sturdier part in the changes that are taking place around us. There is, I think, a hardening of heart here against the recognition of the people's needs. The ruling classes, like the fool Pharoah, won't let the people go. They are busy building Mannerheim Lines all around them. Well, we will have to break through them. It won't be easy; but do it, we must. The Irish here ought to be with the militant working-class. Perhaps, many with you now heard the roar in "Picture Post" from Dora Treloar, shouting at her loudest that the Irish, including myself and Bernard Shaw, should be booted out of England. Well, that wouldn't affect us very much, would it. But I notice that the loud-voiced lady said nothing about booting the Irish out of the Army or the Navy. Not bloody likely! Come along and die for us, and we'll give you an indecent burial. A fine reward, surely. A fine tribute from Dora Treloar to the fifty thousand Irishmen lying dead in Flanders and the plains of Gallipoli.

I hope Irishmen and Irishwomen will merge with all those who see that it is worthless to fight for anything less than the right to own the things they fight for; when the talent, not of this class or that class, but the talent of all men will be free to flourish to its full; when all those who profit out of a worker's energy, and even out of a worker's burial, will be buried themselves, and our children will never have heard their name.

Sean O'Casey

[1] Michael McInerney, editor of *Irish Freedom,* and secretary of the James Connolly Club in London, had invited O'Casey to attend the club's commemoration of the Easter rising of 1916, and this letter was O'Casey's reply, printed in *Irish Freedom,* April 1940.

To Macmillan & Co. Ltd.

TS. MACMILLAN LONDON

TINGRITH, STATION ROAD
TOTNES, DEVON
5 APRIL 1940

Dear Sirs,

Would you kindly send a copy of "The Star Turns Red," for review in Irish Freedom,[1] to
M. McInerney,
31, Norfolk Road,
New Barnet, Herts.

And to me
One copy of "Abbey Theatre Lectures." [2]
" " "The White Steed," by P.V. Carroll.[3]
" " G Treasury of Scottish Poetry. MacDiarmuid.[4]
" " Dickens' "Tale of Two Cities"; good print (for reading to my boy), with original illustrations.
" " "Our Mutual Friend," by Dickens, with the same print and pictures (kind of, you know)
and, if you publish it, one copy of The Count of Monte Cristo.

Yours sincerely,
Sean O'Casey

Please add "Pickwick Papers"—same kind of quality as the others—to order sent, & oblige, S. O'Casey.

[1] The review appeared in *Irish Freedom,* April 1940.

[2] *The Irish Theatre* (1939), lectures delivered during the Abbey Theatre festival held in Dublin in August 1938, edited by Lennox Robinson: "Foreword," Lennox Robinson; "The Early History of the Abbey Theatre," A. E. Malone; "Synge," Frank O'Connor; "Lady Gregory," Lennox Robinson; "Yeats and Poetic Drama in Ireland," F. R. Higgins; "The Rise of the Realistic Movement," A. E. Malone; "George Shiels, Brinsley Macnamara, etc.," T. C. Murray; "Sean O'Casey," Walter Starkie; "Gaelic Drama," Ernest Blythe; "Problem Plays," Micheál MacLiammoir.

[3] Paul Vincent Carroll, *The White Steed* (London, Macmillan, 1939).

[4] *The Golden Treasury of Scottish Poetry,* selected and edited by Hugh MacDiarmid (London, Macmillan, 1940).

To George P. Brett

TS. MACMILLAN, N.Y.

DEVON
12 APRIL 1940

Dear Mr. Brett:

I got your letter, sent via the American Atlantic Clipper, today.

The "Squib" was correct in its statement, though I don't know whether the play [1] is of modern or ancient Ireland. Ireland is always modern and always ancient. I still have one or two unimportant emendations to make —though Angelo has said that perfection is made out of trifles, so they aren't important, after all.

So far, I have but mentioned the play to your Colleagues here. The MS is with Mr. Richard Madden, who, I understand, is making arrangements to have it produced next season. I don't think it is very like anything else I have already done. It is, I think, gay, original, and imaginative. So others, who ought to know, say.

Of course, I am going to offer it to Messrs Macmillan & Co; I'm afraid I'd feel very strange offering it to anyone else. I have a great respect and a great affection for the Firm.

My agent in America has told me that Random House (this is private news) are eager to publish it; but I have told him that though I am not bound to you in a commercial sense—that is by laygal contract, I am more or less bound to you in honour; and so, if you like, I think it ought to be published in conjunction with your Colleagues here. I don't want it published before production; and I shall write to Mr. Harold about this soon—he has promised to come down here next month—; and, if he takes the play, he can get into touch with you about it.

I sent you a letter some time ago, and some cuttings of reviews about the Red Star that may interest you—if you get them. I am working at the second volume of my biography, and hope to have it finished by the end of the year, if things don't get too bad here. It looks as if we were to have another world war again, a Mhuire is truagh! [2]

Warm regards to Mrs. Brett and to you.
Sean O'Casey

[1] *Purple Dust.*
[2] O Mary it is a pity; idiomatically, more's the pity.

To Bernard Shaw

MS. British Museum [1]

Devon

29 April 1940

My dear G.B.S.

Fine to hear that all's well in Ayot St. Lawrence.

I've no play for Malvern.[2] "Purple Dust" has been taken by Eddie Dowling of New York; & he'll be getting an option on the English License. He is very much struck with the play; & has, I believe, a part in it for himself. Dowling's father & mother were Irish, & he is Irish, too! We're all Irish. Mr. Elmhirst [3] was telling me he had lunch with you lately. They're doing part of your Film [4] here. Good luck. Don't worry about Malvern & their mania for new plays. Haven't they hundreds to choose from. And a lot of yours, too.

God be wi' you,
Sean

[1] Postcard.

[2] In a postcard of 22 April 1940, Shaw had asked O'Casey if he had a new play for the Malvern festival. He also made the following comment on *The Star Turns Red*: "It shewed up the illiteracy of the critics, who didn't know that like a good Protestant you had brought the language of the Authorized Version back to life. Spendid!" (MS. O'Casey)

[3] Leonard Elmhirst of Dartington Hall.

[4] Shaw's *Major Barbara,* directed by Gabriel Pascal, released in 1941.

To Timofei Rokotov

TS. Inter Lit, Moscow

Devon

3 May 1940

My dear friend:

It is very pleasant to get a letter from you again. There ought to be a broad and easy way to Moscow; but, at the moment, it seems to be narrow, but, I feel sure, the way will widen year by year, and, maybe, even day by day.

I am glad to say that I got the two Magazines safely the other day. I am glad you liked my article on Irish Literature.[1] No, I didnt know that the article on Irish Literature had been reprinted in "The Sunday Worker" of New York. I am pleased to hear that it has been.

[1] See O'Casey's letter to Gabriel Fallon, 25 August 1939, note 4.

I havent yet read GREEN VOLCANO;[2] but will do so as soon as I can. It isnt always possible to lay hands on every book one would like to read. I have just read his JAIL JOURNEY,[3] and a remarkable book of prison life it is.

When I last heard of Jim Phelan,[4] he was about to leave the house he lived in through lack of money because of the fact that the publication of his book had been postponed on account of the war. It is now in print, and perhaps, he is in a better position. He asked me for help, and, though I couldnt give him all he wanted, I gave him a little that, I hope, helped him. I am writing to him through his publishers, about his last book; and when I get a reply, I'll send you on his address. I have told him of his book being printed in your Magazine.

Yes, "The Star Turns Red" is doing well in Unity Theatre. It is a small theatre, built by the workers themselves, and the war is handicapping them; but they are a brave lot, and I think the success of my play will bring them a little money which they needed badly.

Of course I am delighted to hear that "I Knock at the Door" is to be printed in the Russian Edition of your Magazine. May I say how glad I was at the smashing of the Mannerheim Line by your Red Army. The gigantic force and mighty bravery is what one would expect from the Army of the people of The U.S.S.R., and the Army of the Working Classes of the world.

Victory and Blessing to the U.S.S.R.

Yours very sincerely,
Sean O'Casey

[2] Jim Phelan, *Green Volcano* (Davies, 1938).
[3] Jim Phelan, *Jail Journey* (London, Secker & Warburg, 1940).
[4] Jim Phelan (1895–1960), Irish writer who lived most of his life as a proletarian tramp, and at various times was an actor, blacksmith, and prisoner.

To Horace Reynolds

MS. Reynolds
Devon
19 May 1940

My dear Horace.

Thanks for your very welcome letter. Here's one for you, if it can get to you. I enclose with it the copy of "The Star Turns Red". The run of "Juno" in N. York was a godsend, & saved me from setting out to slay the Directors of "The Clarendon Property Co".[1] I don't know what to say

[1] See the comments on the broken lease in his letter to Fallon, 25 August 1939.

about Gogarty. I'm disappointed, but in no way surprised. I told him, myself, ten years ago what would happen, if he didn't organise his pose of gaiety & irresponsible betrayal of the more serious things of life & art. Gogarty is joined to idols—there's nothing to do but to leave him alone. I am sorry to hear about Kay; but glands aren't very dangerous things, if care is taken. I've had a lot myself. A bad time with one, I had, after an operation. Let her take the Sun as much as she can. The flaming sun's much more of a friend than an electric lamp—violet ray'd, or red, white, & blue-ray'd. The blessed Sun! And, anyway, ten hours a day's enough for any woman, & far too much for any man.

"Finnegan's Wake" is me darlin'! The dream of Finnegan's the world's nightmare, & the clap of thunder is in our ears (Earwicker's ears) once more. We are waiting here for it to break in flames over our heads. "Sheshell ebb music wayriver she flows", is Joyce's own parody, & a lovely parody it is, too. In Literature, my dear Horace, I'm sure Joyce is the great man. Very glad, indeed, to hear good accounts of John & Peggy. How they must have changed & grown since they came on to the boat at Boston, & clamoured for us to "Show them something exciting!" Well, they'll find life exciting enough, now. God be wi' them! I haven't read Mark Twain's "Life on the Mississippi". But Breon, at the moment, curious enough, has a craze on the bould Mark. We have both read together "Huckleberry Finn" & "Tom Sawyer", & laughed violently together, too. Now he has eight volumes, & is reading "Yankee at the Court of King Arthur". I'm afraid W.B. [Yeats] was disappointed in his children. Anyway, I don't think he mixed with them as much as he should. And "I begin to feel my children living my death" is nonsense. Rather do they make one live one's life over again. That's the way I find it; & you find it that way, too. At the moment I'm reading "a Tale of Two Cities" with Brian; kicking football with Niall; & peek a boo with Shivaun—seven months old—Doing it all over again, & doing it better. Capitalistic Industry likes men to be as alike as pins or dots. But that's dying; & the "Spectre over Europe" is becoming a living thing; & industry will assume its proper proportion. Only Communism can find places for the Johns & Peggies & Brians & Nialls & Shivauns. I've thought so all my thinking life; I think so now; & I fight, in my own way, ever & always, without ceasing for the life that will give life to the young. "Oh, silver trumpets, be ye lifted up, & call to the great race that is to come!" [2]

Their blast is heard in many places.

With love to Kay, John, Peggy, &, my dear friend, to you.

Ever Yours
Sean

[2] "Oh, silver trumpets be ye lifted up,
And cry to the great race that is to come."
The young pupil in Yeats's *The King's Threshold* (1904).

To George Jean Nathan

MS. CORNELL
DEVON
26 MAY 1940

My very dear George:

Things are terribly tense here; & all things & all thoughts are concentrated on & confined to the things that have to do with our war. We expect, in a day or two, crowds of children to come down here out of the "danger zones", though, it seems to me, every square inch of the country is now, if not an actual, then a potential danger zone. We are having to pay a bitter price for the years of Chamberlain's regime. However, we can only go on, & do our best. I am trying to keep going at the "Biography;" but with a nation in arms around one, it's slow going.

I have sent on a few alterations in "Purple Dust" to Dick [Madden] which he suggested himself; & which he said you approved of. "Newsweek" has been reaching me fairly well; but I haven't had a copy for some weeks now. Anyway "The Best of the Irish" came to cheer me up, & send me whistling along with the oul' head up higher than ever.

I will forward to Dick the up to now finished MS of the projected new volume of Biography, for safety. No-one knows when the place may be bombed, & all go up in smoke; & I'd like to have what I've written in safe hands. Besides, there's a chance of publication ceasing here altogether. God be praised for the "Juno" run; that brought a great relief to me.

"Virginia Quarterly Review's" Summer number is to have a chapter of the story, called "Cat 'n Cage," [1] a once well-known country tavern, then astride the City of Dublin boundary. I think some of the chapters are good.

I have started to smoke a pipe, me son; the cigarettes here have become too damn expensive, except for one who can dig up gold in his back garden. It looks as if Finnigans Wake was going to be enacted to the final curtain of most men. One thing seems certain—we don't seem to possess any descendent of the warriors Grant or Lee here. The battles are being lost on the playing fields of Eton. Any way, Eton, & all the stupid things that are hallowed there, are, I think, ended forever; & thank God for that! Most of our Drama Critics crept out of those places. There isn't one of the Universities here has a magazine that's a patch on the magazine of the University of Virginia. And, if you read Dublin's magazine "T.C.D." mother o' God!

[1] See O'Casey's letter to Gabriel Fallon, 25 August 1939, note 2.

The theater here is, of course, dead. Not that that's any fine loss. It is a relief rather than a loss. Some day, something better may awake out of the ashes: when we dead awaken.

I'm sorry to hear that Eddie Dowling wouldn't take "The Foolishness." [2] I've read "Shadow & Substance," & it promised a lot of fine things. What can have happened to o' Carroll? Perhaps the two rejections may have a good effect on this. A jolt, now & again, is a good thing. Complacency, complacency (Priestley) is a dangerous thing in a playwright. Anyway, a good job—in anything—is always a hard job; & one cannot afford to be complacent when doing a hard job—even in breaking stones, for one has to constantly look for the vein.

My warm Regards to all friends,

& my love to you.
Ever.
Sean

[2] Paul Vincent Carroll's *The Old Foolishness* was later produced in New York on 20 December 1940, and closed after three performances.

To Daily Worker

LONDON
10 JUNE 1940

O'CASEY ON DAILY WORKER

When Sean O'Casey, the author and playwright, was asked to become a member of the new Editorial Board [1] of the *Daily Worker* he wrote in his letter of acceptance:—

"For the *Daily Worker* to go would mean the piercing of the drum of the worker's ear and the splitting of the worker's tongue.

[1] On 8 June 1940 the *Daily Worker* announced the formation of a new advisory editorial board composed of the following members: J. B. S. Haldane (chairman); William Rust (editor); Dean of Canterbury; J. R. Campbell; Jack Owen; Arthur Horner; J. R. Scott; A. F. Papworth; R. Page Arnott; Beatrix Lehmann; L. C. White; Sean O'Casey.

According to the current editor, George Matthews, in a letter which he wrote to me on 29 March 1963, the board was in existence for about a dozen years: "It was discovered in the early 1950s that the members of the Editorial Board could be held legally responsible if any actions were taken against the Daily Worker. Since they were not in fact responsible for the day-to-day running of the paper (the Board acted in an advisory capacity and met approximately monthly) it was obviously not desirable or fair that they should be placed in that position. The Board was consequently wound up in order that there could be no question of any legal liability on the part of its members, but they continued to associate with the paper as supporters and contributors to its columns."

"The *Daily Worker,* becoming a broader forum, is more necessary than ever today," he continued.

"Above all, it is well to remember, though a maddening thing to remember, that had the *Daily Worker's* policy of some years ago been followed, or even listened to, we should have had to face far less loss of sweat, less toil, and far less sacrifice than we are called upon to face today."

To George P. Brett

TS. Macmillan, N.Y.

Devon

2 July 1940

Dear Mr. Brett:

A good few hours before you get this, you should receive from Messrs Macmillan's of London, a copy of my new play, PURPLE DUST. I sent two copies of the play to Mr. Daniel, and he answered, saying that he would forward a copy on to you at once.

If you should accept publication of the play, perhaps you'd set down the terms expressed in the Agreement you sent to me for THE STAR TURNS RED.

The one thought here in the minds of all is "the best way of sheltering from the bursting of bombs." Eileen (the missus) has passed her exam for First Aid; she is helping to serve dinners to children sent here from London; and she even thinks of learning how to use a rifle—I wonder if she's thinking of using it on me?

For myself, I'm just thinking of how a bunch of simpletons, picked at random from the first asylum met, would have been as effective at the head of affairs as those who have been there for the last ten or fifteen years of this, our Lord's era. They have given kingdoms, arsenals, and armies away to the enemy.

Since 1914, this is the fourth war I've gone through—the Great War; the Easter Rising; The Black and Tan war; The Irish Civil War; and now this one! I'm a bit sick of the sound o' shooting. A lot here are very jittery, roaring and running about to get to the U.S.A. or Canada; but we have decided to stay put—if they'll let me.

With the warmest of wishes.

Yours sincerely,

Sean O'Casey

To George Jean Nathan

MS. CORNELL

DEVON

20 AUGUST 1940

My dear George:

I haven't heard from you for a long time, & so am sending this note to touch your hand again. I daresay, you have been on a holiday, & I hope you have. Up to now, I've kept in touch with you through "News-week", but that line has broken, for you no longer speak from its pages.[1] That is a sore disappointment. John O'Hara isn't even the ghost of a substitute. God forgive him for having an Irish name. An O'Hara, & to write such stuff. Some men earn their living easy.

As you can guess, things are very near the sound of the guns here. German aeroplanes drone over our heads almost every night, & the sound of them isn't "like a melody that's sweetly played in tune." We have a kind of a cellar that we are to go to when the siren sounds. I went once; but haven't gone since; & wont, unless I hear the bombs exploding near by. I shouldn't mind, if it weren't for the three children, the eldest 11 & the youngest a year. But, we'll just have to do our best. Your country's feeling it, too; & Dick tells me taxes are rising. I hope it won't hurt the theatre. Commercially, the theatre here's doing a lot better; from any other angle—mother o' Jasus! The only plays on, worth a curse, are "Margin for Error," [2] "Thunder Rock," [3] & "The Devil's Disciple" [4] two American plays, & one from an Irishman. I'm afraid, I'm afraid, I'm afraid, George, the cultural civilization the English Leaders are always blowing about is all Baloney. "England treats her artists generously," says the Daily Telegraph, in a Leader (referring to Gracie Fields, who hooked it to America with a heap of dollars), but that's baloney, too. If I be an artist, & I think there's something of an artist in me, I have little to thank England for; something to thank Ireland for; & a helluva lot to thank the U.S.A. for. So far, I've kept myself & the missus, & brought up the kids on American dollars, which seems to me to say something.

I wonder did you go to see Eugene [O'Neill] lately? If you did, let me know how he is, & Carlotta, too.

I've made inquiries about James Joyce (he was in Paris during the

[1] Nathan had served as dramatic critic of *Newsweek* for three years and wrote his last column on 1 July 1940. He was succeeded by John O'Hara.

[2] Clare Boothe's *Margin For Error* opened in London on 2 August 1940.

[3] Robert Ardrey's *Thunder Rock* opened in London on 18 June 1940.

[4] Bernard Shaw's *The Devil's Disciple* was revived in London on 24 July 1940.

recent fighting), & can't learn a thing about him. I do hope he managed to keep safe.

Well, my love to you, George.
Yours as ever.
Sean

To Peter Newmark

MS. NEWMARK
DEVON
18 SEPTEMBER 1940

My dear Peter:

Glad to hear from you. I agree with you that most of the people think, can only think of their own worries. The first law of nature yesterday is the first law today. And that a part of them, destitute of mind, are doing the comic for the sake of a little glory. Well, it was the first law of nature that made the Russian soldier in 1917 turn his back upon the trenches, to plunge into a war, worse than what he'd left; but which gave us our first Socialist State. Will the English people awake, at last? Umm.

Anyhow, we'll chat about these things when you come to stay with us. I'm looking forward to seeing the smiling, hasty, nervous, good-natured dial of you again—& don't leave anything behind in the train.

Love.
Sean

To Herbert Marshall [1]

TS. MARSHALL
DEVON
19 OCTOBER 1940

Dear Mr. Herbert Marshall:

Thanks for your two letters. Several sculptors (one, even down here) have tried to get me to sit for them; but that's a thing I dont like doing, so I have always refused so far, and, I'm afraid, must continue to do so.[2]

I am very busy with work, and with a family, and dont get much time to answer many letters—a job I hate.

[1] Herbert Marshall (1912–), theatre producer, director, writer, translator of Mayakovsky's poetry, founder-director of Unity Theatre in 1935. He directed Robert Ardrey's *Thunder Rock*.

[2] Marshall's wife, Fredda Brilliant, F.I.A.L., a sculptor, wanted O'Casey to sit for her.

The play "Purple Dust" isnt available for English production. Ninety-five (possibly more) of whatever I get from my work comes from the U.S.A, and so I always make every effort to secure attention there. At present, the play is to go on in New York, I believe, this Fall; and he who is to do it there, has an option on the English rights. Anyway, I'm not terribly interested in the English theatre as it has been for a long time now.

Of course, I've heard all about the play, "Thunder Rock" ever since it was first done in New York. I have read it, and, I've heard, they are to give a reading of it soon up in Dartington Hall. I daresay you'd like me to give an opinion on it. Well, I'm not a judge of a play that has merit; all I venture to do, as a rule, is to condemn a damned bad one.

I sincerely hope that your tour may be a financial success, and that your partnership with the OLD VIC may be a very fruitful one.[3]

Your letters are a bit of a thunderclap, arent they? How do you get time to do all the things you have in hand? I wish I had a spot of your energy.

With all good wishes to you and
Mrs Marshall,
Yours sincerely,
Sean O'Casey

[3] Marshall was appointed a director of the Old Vic in 1940.

To Tribune [1]

TC. O'CASEY
19 OCTOBER 1940

MESSRS. THE EDITORIAL BOARD
(INCLUDING MR. ANTHONY HERN) OF "THE TRIBUNE."

Dear Sirs:

I have received your letter refusing to publish my last reply to Mr. Strauss.[2] I am not surprised—I expected the refusal. I am becoming accustomed to this kind of thing in the Commonwealth of Free Nations; and from those who are the trumpeters of free expression of thought for

[1] This letter was refused publication by the editorial board of the *Tribune.*

[2] Originally the *Tribune* had printed an article by O'Casey, "O'Casey Writes," on 4 October 1940, which was a reply to an earlier article by George Strauss, M.P., "Some Questions For Communists," *Tribune,* 13 September 1940. Strauss's reply to O'Casey also appeared in the 4 October issue, and O'Casey's second reply to Strauss was rejected by Anthony Hern, assistant editor, and the editorial board, for reasons explained by the editor, Raymond Postgate, in "From the Editor's Chair," *Tribune,* 1 November 1940, which is reprinted below in chronological order.

all men. In Mr. Strauss's reply to me he says, "O'Casey has absorbed into his writing the worst characteristics of the 'Daily Worker'." You say in your reply to me, "In view of the fact (cliche) that Mr. Strauss's reply to your first article was not printed in the 'Daily Worker', we cannot see our way (cliche cliche) to printing your final piece." You are, evidently, absorbing some of the bad characteristics of the paper yourselves. Because "The Worker" didnt print his, you refuse to print mine. A high-souled outlook on freedom of thought, isnt it? Though the "Worker" may have refused (I am unaware that they did so) to print Mr. Strauss's reply, surely you proud and superior intellectuals should be an example to others. The discussion that took place concerned the "Tribune" primarily; it was in your paper that Mr. Strauss's article appeared. The "Tribune", therefore, must be indicted for refusing to print an answer to an attack, an attack calculated to poison the goodwill of those who read it against the defender. If you think that the correspondence is closed, you err greatly: freedom of thought isnt stamped out quite so easily. If not now, then again; if not so soon, then years ahead of us, the question may be before us, and certainly, sooner or later, I will deal with it, in my own way and in my own good time. To me, it simply shows that Mr. Strauss (or the Editorial Board) couldnt sit down to the challenge. The yarn about the "Daily Worker" refusing to print Mr. Strauss's reply is merely all balls.

Yours sincerely,
Sean O'Casey

To George Jean Nathan

MS. CORNELL
DEVON
29 OCTOBER 1940

My very dear George:

I got your reviews of "Purple Dust," one from "Esquire" [1] & one from the breast of "Liberty" [2] (I presume, tho' no name of periodical appeared on the pages), & grand they were, full of good tidings, bearing branches of praise from one whose praise is worth having.

Before I got "Esquire," I quoted from your letter to Macmillan's, without mentioning your name (I quoted as from a famous critic), but asked them to hold quotation till they heard from me again; for I don't like quoting from private letters. But (of course) when the opinions were made public, I sent pronto the views to the publishers, &, I daresay (and

[1] George Jean Nathan, *Esquire,* September 1940.
[2] George Jean Nathan, *Liberty,* 12 October 1940.

hope) some of them will appear on the jacket & in advertisements. Dick sent me the one from "Esquire," & said it would be a great boost for the play.

I'm glad you had a good time in New Jersey—you need all of that you can scrounge out of your full-time critical life.

I'm sorry about "Newsweek"; as far as the Theatre is concerned, it's a dry well now. And what a clever fellow O'Hara thinks he is! Is it any wonder that humility is the first step to heaven? I can understand now the rage in "The Man Who Struck O'Hara."

I'd have written sooner, but for the fact that evacuees (it is said, tho' the country can do a bit of its own in this way) brought Influenza to our Townland. Anyhow, I got it badly, & had to stay in bed for more'n a week; & then had to crawl about helping the missus, who was stricken down when I got up.

A great pleasure & pride it is to me to hear of your good accounts of Gene's new play, "The Iceman Cometh".[3] A great fellow. The only time I think another life possible after this, is that it might give a chance to me to spend a long time with a fellow called Nathan & another called O'Neill. Curious how we fell for each other so quickly. Grand it was for me, & grand it will be forever.

I have been a little disturbed by the war. It upsets the regular way of living. As well, I'm a member now of the Editorial Board of 'The Daily Worker',[4] & these, & three kids, fill up a lot of time. But I am working at "The Biography", & in a chapter just written, I've included a song, that I like, called "She Carries a Rich Bunch of Red Roses for Me". I have a few thoughts swimming around in my head for another play, too; & hope things will let them grow into a decision.

The "I Knock at the Door" sold, so far, in U.S.A. 1800 copies; & I'm hoping it will do as well again, for, I think, the accounts closed for the year in June. Anyway they're eager to get the next volume, which is good, for English customers are nearly nil, now. As you know, the theater here has been dead for ages; the morgue door is ever closed now. I understand the Abbey is struggling along bravely. It had to go without its usual Horse Show Bumper week. Resurgam: no Angli—bad Latin, but the meaning's there.[5]

Ever yours with love.
Sean

[3] Eugene O'Neill's *The Iceman Cometh* was completed in 1939, but it was not produced until 9 October 1946 in New York.

[4] See O'Casey's letter to the *Daily Worker,* 10 June 1940, note 1.

[5] He meant that the Abbey Theatre would rise again without the aid of the English tourists.

By Raymond Postgate

Tribune
1 NOVEMBER 1940

"From the Editor's Chair"

I expect my readers have had enough of the O'Casey-Strauss controversy, but as the *Daily Worker* has dealt with the matter again in its usual inaccurate way, I must give the facts. They are these; George Strauss wrote an article for the TRIBUNE, of permanent value and paramount importance, in my opinion. It dealt with the present Communist policy and showed it was, in its results, treachery to the working-class and aid to Hitler.

O'Casey, as a member of the *Daily Worker* editorial board, sent in a reply, which we, in accordance with our principles, printed in full, with a rejoinder by Strauss. But I perceived that before the TRIBUNE had printed O'Casey's article, the *Daily Worker* had begun to publish it. (The *Daily Worker* says publication was "simultaneous": it is queer how these people cannot tell the truth even in matters of minor importance). Therefore, I immediately sent round to it Strauss's rejoinder, to give it the opportunity of publishing it and acting decently by its readers. I was not greatly surprised when it suppressed it, as TRIBUNE readers know. I was, however, a little surprised to receive after this yet another article from the unblushing O'Casey. As I was going for a week's holiday, I left it for the Editorial Board to do as they pleased with: they, with considerable restraint, merely told O'Casey that as his paper had failed to publish Strauss's reply, they were not going to print his. (I might have been tempted to add that as it was incoherent and only comprehensible in places, it wasn't publishable anyway).

Thereafter came a letter from O'Casey which ranks as a curiosity. It cannot be printed in full, for the language of one sentence is too foul to print. (Only an extract appears even in the *Daily Worker*). But it contains three interesting things. The first is the information that this alleged director was "not aware" of the suppression of Strauss's article by the *Daily Worker*. The second is the statement that "the discussion concerned the TRIBUNE primarily": it did not. Primarily, secondarily, tertiarally, and every other -ally it concerned the stabs which O'Casey and his lot are delivering into the backs of anti-Fascist armies the world over. Finally, it has this superb piece of insolence: "Freedom of thought is not stamped out quite so easily."

Indeed and indeed, you poor ranter, that is truer than you know.

[*Raymond Postgate*]

To Macmillan & Co. Ltd.

TS. MACMILLAN LONDON

DEVON

5 NOVEMBER 1940

Dear Sirs,

Would you let me have

1 Five Irish Plays.
3 The Star Turns Red.
1 Boswell's Johnson. 6/6. I think.
1 Plough & Stars—Caravan Edition.
1 Napoleon's Marshals.[1]
1 Making of Ireland and Its Undoing—Green.[2]
1 Walt Whitman—Men of Letters, New series,[3] 3/6.
1 Robespierre. A Study in Deterioration.[4]

And greatly oblige,
Yours sincerely,
Sean O'Casey

[1] Archibald Gordon Macdonnell, *Napoleon and His Marshals* (London, Macmillan, 1934).

[2] Alice Stopford Green, *The Making of Ireland and Its Undoing, 1200–1600* (London, Macmillan, 1934).

[3] John Cann Bailey, *Walt Whitman* (London, Macmillan, 1926).

[4] Reginald Somerset Ward, *Maximilien Robespierre: A Study in Deterioration* (London, Macmillan, 1934).

To Raymond Postgate [1]

TC. O'CASEY

[DEVON]

6 NOVEMBER 1940

Dear Sir:

I do hope youre feeling a little better now. Sorry that the word "balls" gave you such a sudden stroke. But you wont be able to do much to win a war, if you run away from a word. Is there any other "Tribune" taboo?

You do, you know, leave yourself open to a laugh. "Give Eire back the Catholic counties, and keep the Protestant ones," because the Catholic counties are Republican, and the rest are mmm—what? Monarchical? Is Protestantism, then monarchical? Wolfe Tone, Parnell, Napper Tandy, Henry Joy McCracken, Betsy Gray, Jimmy Hope, William Orr—and

[1] Raymond Postgate, editor, *Tribune,* who refused to publish O'Casey's letter of 19 October 1940.

quite a lot of others, all monarchical; not forgetting "The Man from God Knows Where," of whom, possibly, you have never heard.

Again, "isnt Priestley essential to our hearts and minds?" The peace of God which passeth all understanding, keep your hearts and minds in the knowledge and love of J. B. Priestley—the new benediction. Seems a little raw on Jesus Christ.

Why not have a little gawk, now and again, at FINNEGANS WAKE? It might do you good.

Well, so long, and all the best.

Sean O'Casey

To Peter Newmark

MS. NEWMARK

DEVON

6 DECEMBER 1940

My dear Peter.

This must be a short note. My one good eye has troubled me lately. An Eye Specialist has advised me to rest it as much as possible; & all my beloved log splitting has to be given up, for fear of a detached retina.

I hope you are still safe & well. I sent the copy of "The S. Turns Red" to Mrs. Paull of Bristol. I hope she got it safe; & that she's safe herself.

Things here are just as they were—save that I have said farewell to the axe. Latest news from the U.S.A. is that "Purple Dust" is to go on in January. Got a letter from Hugh Willitt saying he had joined up.

Eileen sends her love. Am trying to do a little with the biography. Beware of the Coshies.[1]

Ever yours.
Sean

[1] Fascists

To Irish Freedom

JANUARY 1941

SEAN O'CASEY WRITES TO "IRISH FREEDOM"

You have asked me to give an opinion on the dispute over the holding or the surrender of the Irish Ports.[1] It is, indeed, a terribly difficult

[1] In the early period of World War II the Irish government, which had declared its neutrality, was subjected to pressure from London to allow the British navy to use the Irish ports of Berehaven, County Cork and Lough Swilly, County Donegal.

question to answer. The true facts to British opinion (as a whole) are not the true facts that circumstances present to the Irish people. And, just because I happen to have written a few plays, my opinion is in no way more important than that of any other sensible and intelligent man. For me to claim an importance I haven't got on a question that may involve the loss of thousands of lives would be doing a thing full of murderous impudence. The lives of the Irish people are very valuable possessions, not only to Ireland, but to the whole world over; for the Irish race, in energy, in imaginativeness, and in colour of personality, is second to no other race in the world. The Irish have scattered these grand qualities with a lavish fervour wherever the English language is spoken, and in many places where it is not.

Under the present circumstances, then, what is the better thing to do in order to prevent the killing off of many more of this fine people, surrender the ports to England, as Shaw suggests, or hold tight to them against all comers?

Shaw is right when he says these ports belong not to Ireland alone, but to Europe and to civilisation, as indeed do all ports, London as well as Hamburg. Under Socialism they would belong, not to this or that group, but to all men.

The civilisation of England, as Ireland has known it, has been a bitter, blasting, and vulgar one, from the day they first landed up to recently, when it was manifested in the lousy robbery of the Lane pictures. You can see what W. B. Yeats thought of it on page forty-nine of his "Dramatis Personae"; and what an English poet, Mr. Masefield, thinks of it in what he has written about what should be done when peace comes to us all again. And it has been shown to many people who never bothered about it before, by the half-fed, tattery-clothed, lice-lorn children scattered now over England by the falling bombs, worthy symbols of life gone mad with the desire of the things thieves steal and moth and rust corrupt. No, England gains no points on the score of civilisation.

I can see no reason, on God's earth, or man's earth, why Irish bodies should mingle with the mangled squirming mass wriggling in pain, here and in Germany. One would imagine that this war had gone far enough. Anyway, it seems certain that the Irish people don't want to mix themselves up in this struggle for justice, righteousness, truth and honour—not, of course, forgetting freedom, the loss of which would prevent the workers from streaming to the Riviera the time the winds begin to get any way cool here.

I think the English Government (for the English people have really very little to say in the matter) will make a big tactical mistake if they seize with force the Ports held by the Irish Government. Three-and-a-half millions is a low estimate of the power of the Irish people. There is America, where, probably, seven times that number of Irish will ask the reason why. But what is really needed is a revolutionary change of Government in both countries. Guarding England is the trinity of rent, interest, and profit; and I'm afraid the same powers stand watch over Ireland, too. Till Socialism strangles these three evils, there will be war, and men, women and children will be mangled senselessly, with malice and with calculated brutality. Ay, and even in peace, without Socialism they will be mangled just as effectively by poverty and disease.

The vigil for security, peace, and the sensible rush of life has lasted long enough. It is time to end it.

> I sweep my eyes o'er the scene fain to observe it all,
> Faces, varieties, postures beyond description, most in obscurity, some of them dead,
> Surgeons operating, attendants holding lights, the smell of ether, the odour of blood,
> The crowd, O the crowd of the bloody forms, the yard outside also filled,
> Some on the bare ground, some on planks or stretchers, some in the death-spasm sweating.
> It is time to end it all.

Sean O'Casey

To Daniel Macmillan

TS. MACMILLAN LONDON

DEVON
12 JANUARY 1941

Dear Mr Daniel,

I am sending, under another cover, three more chapters for the second part of "I Knock at the Door,"

Cat 'n' Cage.
Alice, Where Art Thou?
To Him That Hath Shall Be Given.

and I hope your Premises are still standing after the terrible attacks of explosion and flame on London. Two of my friends [1] had an extraordinary escape. They live (or lived) in St Paul's Churchyard, and had to pass through miles of flame before they reached safe standing.

Last night we were shaken to a degree by a great explosion caused (it is said) by a land mine dropped in the Town. I was at work on another chapter at the time. I hope all yours are safe and well.

Yours sincerely,
Sean O'Casey

[1] Jack and Mina Carney.

To Irish Press

17 JANUARY 1941

O'CASEY'S ADVICE TO DRAMATISTS

Dear Sir,—Would you let me say a few words about the comments on "Purple Dust," made by T.C.M.[1] in a recent issue of your daily and important Journal?

Assuming (quite rightly) that I pay attention to the sound and sparkle of words in a play, and make it an "artistic creed," he says, "this is a dangerous one for the dramatist whose purpose it is to show life in action on a stage." One might as well say that colour was a dangerous creed to a painter. Rather is this a dangerous and a cowardly warning to the young dramatists in Erinn. I say to them, don't believe a word of it; and put your finest thoughts into the finest words you can think of into any play you write; the finer, the more musical they are, the better. Take away from the drama of the world those plays that are crowded, ay, crammed with rhythm and music in dancing words, and you have left but a handful of grey and pathetic dust. "Life in action on the stage," and "bearing little relationship to the life we know," are just jargonistic phrases. Maybe it has no relationship to the life he knows; but, even if a play has no apparent, realistic relationship to the life "everyone knows," the play may be a very fine one. What relationship to this "life" has *The Ghost Sonata*? Or *The Dream Play*? or *Hassan*? Or *Heartbreak House*? or even *St. Joan*? or *The Tempest*? to mention only a few. [I would remind the critic that the cow has a sacred signification in some countries; and that even in Erinn it was a symbol of grand things, which the critic would have known, had he ever sung Drimin Donn Dilis.[2] He needn't have travelled as far as Hollywood to find a parallelic lion to the appearance of the cow in *Purple Dust*; he could have found one on his own doorstep. I remember seeing on the Abbey stage a lion padding after an Emperor, Gladiators, and Christians, and sending them "scuttling in all directions".[3] Evidently, his mind is looking over the wall of Hollywood.] [4]

Finally, dear young playwrights, put the best you have into any play you write. Don't be afraid to make low life on the stage lower than the

[1] T. C. Murray, "Sean O'Casey's New Play," *Irish Press*, 20 December 1940.
[2] "Sweet Brown Cow."
[3] A reference to Bernard Shaw's *Androcles and the Lion*, which O'Casey had seen at the Abbey Theatre during the week of 4 November 1919.
[4] Passage in square brackets omitted by the editor.

"life we know"; and high life on the stage higher than the life we know; for unimaginative realism dies as it is being written. And as for his statement that the clergy have never denounced the wearing of low-cut bodices, shorts, and picnic panties, then the poor man must be a little deaf.—*Yours etc.*

Sean O'Casey

Devon
12 January 1941

To Peter Newmark

MS. Newmark

[Devon]
9 February 1941

My dear Peter:

Thanks for Hansard.[1] Whether the bastard story be true or not doesn't matter much. Bastards sometimes are fine fellows—Dunois, Falconbridge, &, I think, Don John of Austria. Change the B. to D. & there you have a fit label for those who sell their class for handfuls of silver & ribbons to stick in their coats. Acland is close to Gollanz & Gollanz is close to Bevin, & Bevin is close to Churchill, & Churchill is close to God.

I hope you're writing no more books for Michael Young.[2] Write your own books, if you write any. I haven't seen Young since. I daresay, I'll never see him again. That'll be sorrowful. Curious he told you I'd probably be at the People's Convention. He was certainly pretending an intimacy he hasn't got with me. Let him go on measuring the earth's surface, & putting it all down in books. A new map of the world, by Michael Young.

Regarding Joyce, McCarthy doesn't know what he's talking about. His essays were a shabby-genteel tribute to a genius. Green boys are round the head of the dead Joyce; [3] artificial flowers round the dead head of McCarthy. Take his plaint that Joyce could think only of Dublin, Dublin, Dublin. Well? McCarthy doesn't know that Dublin isn't one, but fifty cities. Eblana, Dyflin, Dublin, B'la Cluath; English Kings came there; Cromwell, Shelley; Dickens; Thackeray; Grant; Parnell & a host of others, including W. Wilkie. Every stone in every street has the name of a Man

[1] The official record of daily proceedings in parliament.
[2] A lecturer at Cambridge University.
[3] James Joyce died in Zurich on 13 January 1941, at the age of fifty-eight.

carved on it. And, anyway, if McCarthy can't understand the greatest Everyman that so far has ever been written; if he can't understand the written symbolism that makes him a mourner at Joyce's Finegans Wake; he'll soon (if he doesn't already) understand that he's a mourner at the Finegans Wake of the world he knows. It is finished—last words of Christ; last words of Desmond Florence McCarthy.

So you expect leave on the 17th March. St Patrick's Day, be God! Fine. Come down, if you can. We shall all be delighted to see you again.

Ever Yours.
Sean

Eileen sends her love.

To Gabriel Fallon

TS. TEXAS

DEVON
10 FEBRUARY 1941

My very dear Gaby.

It's years and years since I wrote to you (I've decided to write the rest in type so's to give the Censor a better chance of reading it.) but we've often thought about you; and, once or twice, have heard your voice on Radio Eireann. Thank you ever so much for the Calendar, having on it a bit of the oul country—I seem to recognise a strip of the Royal Canal in the picture. Am I right or am I wrong, Mr. Gallicker? I sent you a long time ago, a copy of "The Star Turns Red", and assumed that you liked it so little, that you didn't bother to say you got it. I also sent, recently, a copy of "Purple Dust", through Macmillan's and hope that came safely. One to Joe Cummins got there allright. I couldn't send it direct, with the usual inscription; but the authorities wouldn't let it pass. If you like, I'll tear out the Inscription, and send it on to you.

I am hard at work at a second volume of "I Knock at the Door", and hope to have it in print by the end of the year—if the invasion doesn't hunt us all from our peaceful homes. I've had some trouble with my eyes; and have to take things easier; and, worst of all, have to give up anything in the nature of heavy physical work, for fear of a detached retina. The left eye went west years ago; and I now have to depend on the right one; so must go canny. I have been using an axe—a woodman's one—chopping blocks—a bit of old times, that swinging of the axe—; but have to give it up, just as I was quietly growing into a Samson.

"Purple Dust" was to be done in New York in November last; but the Manager, Eddie Dowling, was on tour in Saroyan's "Time of Your Life", and it had to be put off; I understand it is to go on this month. They're trying to get Spencer Tracy (at least G. J. Nathan is trying) for the part of O'Killigan. It's hardly likely he will consent to play it.

I've got word from America that Carroll's play, "The Old Foolishness" got a bad press, and had to be taken off after a short run. That's hard lines; but we all meet with that sort of thing. I've heard a rumour that F. R. Higgins is dead; [1] but it hardly seems credible to me. Terrible, if it's true.

I hope you, Rose, and the children are all well. We are here, bar occasional bouts of the flu, colds, measles, and other simple disorders. Our doctor, you'll be glad to hear, is a Dubblinn Man, one of the Varian's who used to have a Brush Factory in Talbot Street. A fine fellow, too. He and I recently, bellowed out together Who Fears to Speak? [2]

My love to Rose the children, and to you. Eileen joins her wishes with mine,

Ever Yours,
Sean

[1] Frederick Robert Higgins, poet, playwright, and managing director of the Abbey Theatre, died on 8 January 1941 at the age of forty-five.

[2] A well-known patriotic poem by John Kells Ingram (1823–1907), "The Memory of the Dead," about the rising of 1798. The first stanza reads:

Who fears to speak of Ninety-Eight?
Who blushes at the name?
When cowards mock the patriot's fate,
Who hangs his head in shame?
He's all a knave, or half a slave,
Who slights his country thus;
But a true man, like you, man,
Will fill your glass with us.

To Lovat Dickson [1]

MS. Macmillan London

Devon
10 March 1941

Dear Mr. Lovat Dickson,

Well, here you are—what you asked me for—or the nearest I can get to it. It is always hard for me to write anything—even a letter—in which my mind, like the wind (or the Holy Ghost), can go where it

[1] Lovat Dickson (1902–), writer and publisher; editor at Macmillan, London.

listeth. The request of the Macmillan Co still puzzles me. They never asked for anything like this before. Is it really that they're getting nervous of my work? If that be so, I should be the last to expect them to go on publishing it. We Irish are all a critical crowd of realists. Goldsmith (softhearted tho' he was), Sheridan, Swift, Sterne, Shaw & Joyce; particularly the first-class writers. And I believe, if I'm not up to them, I'm holding on to their tails.

Give my warm regards to Mr. Daniel & to Mr. Harold—if you ever see him now.

All good wishes.

Yours sincerely,
Sean O'Casey

To Richard J. Madden

TC. O'Casey

[Devon]
20 March 1941

My dear Dick,

Got your letter dated Feb. 20th, 1941, with enclosed Statement of Accounts (all precise, clear, and nicely done), and your news that PURPLE DUST is not to go on this season. That is, of course, very disappointing to me and all; but no worse, and not so bad as some disappointments that have come my way since I first saw the darkness. However, even were things allright, the season's so far gone now, that it wouldnt be much good to put it on till next Fall. Eddie Dowling's reluctance to give up his tour means, I suppose, that he is doing well with Saroyan's play [*The Time of Your Life*]. Well, that's something to the good. It is a pleasure to think that a man who helps on good work does well by it. I am very glad of his success (if I have assumed right). As far as my play goes, I'm primarily concerned from the economic point of view; but that cant be helped, and certainly nor you nor Dowling nor any of my friends in the U.S.A. started the war. I am working on the "Biography", and hope to have the 2nd volume in the publisher's hands before the next snow comes.

As you say, it is idle to comment on the political or military situation. Still, I venture to say that I think there's not so much danger of a Pacific conflict as there is of one in the Atlantic. It, I imagine, would be dangerous for Japan to move forward (or backward) to have a skelp at the

U.S.A. The Soviet Red Army, I'm sure, would get going into north China then, and join up with China's 8th route army—youve heard of it, I daresay. As for us here, we're safe so far; but ready with pads, bandages, splints, et al (as George would say), for what may happen any minute.

I enclose a copy of a letter I got from Lichtig & Englander, Motion Picture Representatives. I am writing to say that you are my Representative for play and film in America, and have been so for years, and that in you I have not only an oul' reliable, but a most pleasant man, and a valued friend.

I have had two tentative inquiries about PURPLE DUST here, but I am not doing anything about them, and wont till I hear for certain about Eddie Dowling's decision; and then only on what you may think of the principal details.

I should say that I wasnt altogether unprepared for your news about the play; I had read Richard Watts' reference in a theatrical note in "The Herald Tribune". Please forgive me for feeling it curious that the defence of democracy would be evident in the hiding up of artistic expression (I believe there's some art in the play). I've been thinking that since I started, I've never written anything that didnt cause a dispute, a row, a difference, or something. Never mind. Though I wrote PURPLE DUST with the idea that here was a play that would cause no commotion, I have evidently builded better than I knew. The thing to do is to go on with the work. And now my love to Tessa and to you. If you see George, say I'll write soon. I have to spare my eyes these days.

Love again. Ever Yours,
Sean

To Gabriel Fallon

TS. TEXAS

DEVON
29 MARCH 1941

My dear Gaby:

It was good to get your letter; but, Et tu, Brute! I never got the criticism of "The Star Turns Red", which was a pity, for I should like to have read it. You are, I believe, partly right about that play, though there are, I think, some good things in it. For instance I like the third act of the play, as an act per see—as Agate would say—better than any other act of any other play of mine, bar the second act of the "Silver Tassie". Nathan agrees with you, and holds it's the feeblest play I've written, though

"peculiarly invested with a poet's prophetic vision". [1] Anyway, as a whole, it isn't too well done. At least, not as good as it might have been. But I don't think you're quite right about "Purple Dust". And who are you to talk about the abolition of symbolism? Oh, Gaby! "The Star of the Sea", the Litany of the Blessed Virgin, the Cross, In hoc signum vincit—if this Latin be right, but you'll guess what it is, or ought to be. Oh, Gaby! As a matter of fact, the play was begun, and well on its way without a thought of symbolism, being named simply, a "Stay in the Country." I, being tired of controversy about my plays, determined to write at least one that wouldn't cause any comment (adverse), and that would go on, and be seen through bursts of laughter; and, incidentally, bring me in a few quid badly needed. Even the poor cow—that troubled T.C.D.M.[2] so much—was a perfectly innocent animal. The play simply grew out of what I first thought, and, only when it was finished in its rough form (which means three quarters done), did I see its implications. I'm afraid, I've builded better than I knew. Anyway, the production of the play in New York has been postponed till the Fall, because it makes some of the English look ridiculous. It was to be done last December, then, at latest, in Feb; but, in spite of my first determination, it seems I am still writing things to make people uncomfortable. "I always feel uncomfortable with O'Casey", said Sir Hugh Walpole—and thereby hangs a tail. Another few chapters, and I will have written another volume of "I Knock at the Door." That, I daresay, will make more persons uncomfortable. Well, (with all reverence) Jesus, Himself, made and brought a hell of a lot of discomfort to a lot of poor people. And I will go on doing it; not to make them uncomfortable out of malice or spite or pride; but because I feel uncomfortable myself in the midst of things as they are. No sensible man can be satisfied. To take one thing alone: the civilization that could let Joyce die in poverty, and crown with an Litt.D a thing like Wodehouse,[3] deserves fire and brimstone from heaven; and it is getting it. We are all at the bier of Finnegans Wake. Well, let's get away from all this for a second. What happened to F. R. Higgins? I'm afraid things will go bad for the Abbey. Have you read "The Bell",[4] the new O'Faolain monthly? It seems good, though, I imagine, the last number isn't so good as those that went before. No, Gaby, oul' son, we're not gettin' younger; but we're not gettin' ouldher; we're stayin' put—as they say here. Yes, you told me of the challenge, and I was looking forward to seeing it in "The Arrow", but no sign came. Bad sign that they didn't take up the arrow (yours), and send it back

[1] See his letter to Nathan, 22 September 1941, note 1.

[2] T. C. Murray, with an allusion to T.C.D., Trinity College, Dublin. See O'Casey's letter to the *Irish Press,* 17 January 1941.

[3] P. G. Wodehouse received a D. Litt. degree from Oxford in June 1939. See O'Casey's letter to the *Daily Telegraph,* 8 July 1941.

[4] *The Bell,* a literary magazine founded in Dublin by Peadar O'Donnell in October 1940, and edited by Sean O'Faolain. O'Donnell took over the editorship in 1946, until it ceased in November 1954.

again. Well, so Frank [McManus] has gone into the [Irish] Academy of Letters. Member or Associate, or both? Who are its officers now? They have lost a lot recently—Yeats, AE, Higgins, Lawrence. Are O'Faolain and [Frank] O'Connor in it too? A double-harness team they. These two seem (to me) to be amusingly cocky, bestriding Ireland like a twin collossus. Castor and Pollocks. (Literary Collossussuss I mean.) They go along in literature like two little neatly dressed colleens, arm in arm, out for a walk. But I don't see how an A membership is going to raise Frank's prices. If he thinks of the market here, then the only way to do that is to have a big sale; and even then, he'd have to be careful over a contract; except with Macmillan's, and one or two other Firms. I don't believe it will bring him in another fiver a year. I may be wrong, not knowing what influence the A may have. Colaiste Mhuire? [5] Usen't that be the Leinster College of Irish? I think you did well in your selection. However, education is tumbling to pieces; and the old method has a rattle in its throat. Thank God for that. I've fought it for years. Not that all the old things are bad. At present I'm reading Ivanhoe to our eldest and to an Evacuee. I've already read, Moby Dick, David Copperfield, Barnaby Rudge, Nickolos Nickelby, C. of Monte Cristo, Huckleberry Finn, Tom Sawyer, Life on the Mississippi, Tale of Two Cities, Pickwick Papers, and the Devil's Disciple. We had a good time with them all. All of us are safe so far, though the house rocked all the time the guns barked and the bombs burst over Plymouth—one of the dances at Finnegans Wake.

How's Brinsley Macnamara? Give him, if you ever see him, my good wishes. And Father Senan and Father Gerald? I see Shelah Richards is doing Gertrude Lawrence in "Private Lives." [6] What on earth does she want to waste her time on this sort of thing? Did you see D'Alton's "Money Doesn't Matter" [7] ? Is this he who once wrote "Sable and Gold" [8] as well as "The Man in the Black Cloak" [9] ? He has a play—"Tanyard" [10]—on in New York now, and Barry Fitz is in it. Never yet got a line from Barry. Curious, isn't it!

Well, Love to Rose, and to all the big and little ones.

Ever Yours,
Sean

[5] St. Mary's College, a secondary school in Dublin where all subjects are taught "through the medium," through the Irish language.

[6] Noel Coward's *Private Lives* opened at the Abbey's Peacock Theatre on 17 March 1941, with Shelah Richards, Leo McCabe, and Stanley Illsley.

[7] Louis D'Alton's *The Money Doesn't Matter* opened at the Abbey Theatre on 10 March 1941.

[8] Maurice Dalton's *Sable and Gold* opened at the Abbey Theatre on 16 September 1918.

[9] Louis D'Alton's *The Man in the Black Cloak* opened at the Abbey Theatre on 27 September 1937.

[10] Louis D'Alton's *Tanyard Street,* directed by Arthur Shields and starring Barry Fitzgerald, opened in New York on 4 February 1941, and closed after 21 performances. See O'Casey's letter to Nathan, Vol. II, 10 March 1942, note 1.

To Workers' Action, Dublin Trades Council

TC. O'CASEY

[DEVON]
[? APRIL 1941]

Greeting to Workers' Action.

I wish the Workers of Eireann all success in the struggle to strangle the new Trades' Union Bill, aimed obviously at weakening the rising resolution of the working-class to have a finer and a firmer share in the world's good things. If the workers are alive, half alive, even, they can strangle the thing, that, if they dont, will soon have the power to strangle them. It is a significant thing that the one class Governments think themselves free to bandy and bully about are the workers; but it is time, surely, for the workers to say now that they have had about enough of it. They are out, or ought to be out, to live, not the Franconian life, not the Salazarian life, not even the De Valerian life; but a life evolved in themselves outwards towards all men of good will, creating and building their own life, a great life, out of their own energy and skill. It is they who make all things, and it is they who rightly own them; as they surely will, and as they surely do in the Soviet Union. Looking over the list of those attending the recent R.H.A. Exhibition, among the many worthy names recorded, I saw no mention of Mr Tom Healy, Docker; Mr Jim Cogan, Railway Worker; Mr Pat Fitzsimons, Tramway Employee; or Mr Pat Mooney, Stableman. Why? They were damn well all hard at it in the docks, in the stable, on the tram, or on the permanent way. The time has gone by now for us to be content with a shilling a week rise, and the cost of living going up another shilling by the same tick of the clock. We want all life can give us; and, believe me, life has a lot of grand things to give to all men who earn them. This new bill is, to me, a wily attempt to create a system of labour conduct and control that will be half governmental and half ecclesiastical—red tape and rosary beads—conceived to give the worker the least possible share of the things life has to give. Then battle with it, and beat it down; give it the frozen mit; and determine yourselves what ye shall eat, what ye shall drink, and the wherewithal that shall clothe ye. Dont crawl with gratitude when hard up a lean hand called charity gives you a crust and a glass of water. You've earned more than those things. Dont listen to the blandishments of your spiritual pastors and masters on this question, my comrades. They've brought the world between them to a nice pass, havent they—looking after their interest, their rent, and their profit. Dont think I said that; or that I learned it first from Lenin: I didnt; no fear, but from one of your own Saints. Listen to what St Thomas More says: "Therefore when I consider and weigh in my mind all those commenwealths, which now a days any where do florish, so God help me, I can perceive nothing but a certain conspiracy of riche men procuring theire own commodities under the name and title of the commenwealth." And of the charity, mentioned above, here's a remark from an Irish rebel, J. Boyle O'Reilly—whose book, by the way, got a blessing from Cardinal Gibbons—:

> "The organised charity, scrimped and iced,
> In the name of a cautious, statistical Christ."

Yours.
[*Sean O'Casey*]

To Peter Newmark

MS. Newmark

[Devon]
28 April 1941

My dear Peter:

Thanks for the longest letter youve written—bar the one criticising WITHIN THE GATES. It was good hearing from you after the fire that came from the skies, and to know that you crept safe out of it all. Yes, they've done it in the Balkans again. Just what was bound to have happened. They cant escape it. The most incompetent bunch that England ever had, and she's had a few, me boy. It's all very well to talk of oppressed countries: It's my belief that each of these countries have a helluva lot who regard England as a worse enemy than Germany. If it were not so, Hitler's line of communications is so long that there would be a great feast going for a partizan movement everywhere. But the quislings are numbered in millions. It must be so. Anyway, as far as oppressed countries go, England has a damned bad record; so she cant honestly shout at another, die villain. I'm afraid Iraq is as good as gone: and maybe the Suez, too. The latest news should send down Churchill's stock with a bang. Poor man, swimming on blathers made out of Garvin's [1] balls. I think you'd do well to take the idea of a commission seriously, get rid of your depression, and go in for an officer's job. You should have

[1] J. L. Garvin, editor of *The Observer*.

done it long ago. Straighten yourself out, and run for it. Delighted to hear John [Allen]'s allright on a sweeper. Sorry to hear of the dulness of P[alme] Dutte and [Roy] P[age] Arnot. Perhaps they speak too often. Anyway, they keep too much to the one thing; not enough imagination with them. They, like Lenin, should take a greater interest in literature and the theatre. No, I havent seen Michael [Young] since, and never think of him. He may, as you say, be too much under Mrs [Dorothy] Elmhirst's influence, but I have no desire to bring him under mine. Havent heard of Nathan's book; but have just written to him, asking him to send me a copy. I've just seen a contract, signed by my agent, saying that Purple Dust will be produced on November next, the 1st: so I live on in hope. Yes, my dear Peter, I got the pipe safe, and Hemingway's story [2] and the sweets allright. I think I ought to pay for the pipe, so let me know what you flung away on it. Curious, I cant get Hemingway. He seems to be writing in a faraway land from me. I'd have written sooner, but we all got colds, and I was some time getting back my breath. Well, goodbye for now. We must wait for the worst, for not heads, but skulls govern us now. Ever Yours,

Sean

[2] Ernest Hemingway, *For Whom the Bell Tolls* (New York, Scribner, 1940).

To Dorothy Elmhirst [1]

MS. ELMHIRST

DEVON

2 MAY 1941

My dear Mrs. Elmhirst:

I have just heard that you are ill in bed; some time ago, I heard the same thing about you. What on earth are you doing to yourself? Are you flinging yourself about on the bare chance of keeping well? The last time I saw you (when I went up to copy a picture of a Tudor room), you had a cold, a bad one, too; the day was sharp & bitter; yet there you were in a cold room, without a fire! That sort of thing is not good enough. You know, or you ought to know, that your personality is important to Dartington; & so you should do all you can to keep fit & vigorous. I have long thought (when I heard you were taking your meals in the White Hart [2]) that this was unwise (foolish is a better word). You ought

[1] Dorothy Whitney Straight Elmhirst (1887–1968), with her husband Leonard Elmhirst, founder-director of Dartington Hall, Totnes. At this time O'Casey's two sons, Breon, thirteen, and Niall, six, were students at Dartington.

[2] The student restaurant at Dartington Hall.

to give yourself all the comfort necessary to the keeping of yourself in good form, that you can stride about & see to things. You are too good to be laid up. I am sorry to hear of your illness; & this is written because I am sorry. But do (if not for God's sake), then for Dartington's sake, look after yourself in a good way.

Ever affectionately yours
Sean O'Casey

To News of the Day [1]

TC. O'CASEY

[DEVON]
26 JUNE 1941

Dear Sir:

Fifteen years or so ago, the Drama Critic of the Dublin "Irish Independent", in an attack on the Abbey Theatre activities, made the stunning remark, "The Critic goes to the theatre to see the performance, to report upon it, and to assure that the public get a fair deal—fair value for the money they pay at the door."

In the last issue of "News of the Day", A. N. Onymous makes the equally stunning remark of "What a Critic is supposed to be doing is telling his readers what they will get for their money."

It is amusing, after so many years, to hear the bray of a Dublin jackass echoed down here in Dartington.

Yours sincerely,
Sean O'Casey

[1] The newspaper at Dartington Hall. The letter was refused publication.

To Daniel Macmillan

TS. MACMILLAN LONDON

DEVON
1 JULY 1941

Dear Mr Daniel,

I have been surprised that the stuff I sent in was so full of words. I have since looked over and looked over the list of chapters, and find it undesirable to evict any of them from their holding. They, one by one, follow the years, and any of them would be out of place in any succeeding volume. I had thought of four altogether, with the last one to be called, "The Clock Strikes Twelve." What the intervening one may be called, God only knows; if indeed any other thing can be written. If there be, it will be per ardua ad astra with a vengeance. However, I can drop out the last chapter—"He Paints His First Picture," and end the volume with the part that gives the title to the book: "Pictures in the Hallway."

Do you think these others will form too big a book? I should like, if at all possible, to include them all—bar the last one mentioned.

With this letter, I am sending a photo of myself when I had grown from a gasun [1] into a bouċhal.[2] Could this be given as a frontispiece? I wanted, if possible, a picture of The Rev E. M. Griffin,[3] a Rector of a parish I lived in for a long time, a very dear friend of mine, and a beautiful character, inset, too; but although I've written his daughter whom I taught in Sunday School [4] (God forgive me!) for a photo, she tells me she has but a snapshot of her father (he has been dead quite a while; but his memory is very vivid with me still). She has written to her brother, the Rector of a parish in Offaly; but I haven't heard from him yet. I think I shall dedicate the volume to this dear friend of mine.[5]

When the last vol was in print, your Mr Carroll wrote asking me for ideas about a design for a jacket. Should circumstances allow a jacket, I shall be glad to send a design that might be a good guide for a suitable one.

[1] garsún, boy.

[2] buachaill, young man.

[3] Rev. Edward Morgan Griffin (1852–1923), rector of St. Barnabas Church, North Strand, Dublin, 1899–1918. His picture is the frontispiece of the third volume of O'Casey's autobiography *Drums Under the Windows* (1946).

[4] O'Casey taught Sunday school at St. Barnabas from 1900–03.

[5] He dedicated *Pictures in the Hallway* (1942) "To the memory of The Rev. E. M. Griffin, B.D., M.A., one-time Rector of St. Barnabas, Dublin. A fine scholar; a man of a many-branched kindness, whose sensitive hand was the first to give the clasp of friendship to the author."

With all good wishes, and prayers for the success of the Red Army, and the sincere hope that you and yours are well.

Yours,
Sean O'Casey

To News of the Day [1]

TC. O'CASEY
[DEVON]
6 JULY 1941

Dear Sir:

Mr C. Martin [2] has certainly made some curious published remarks recently, such as (I quote from memory) "We are, of course, glad, if the community and the people at large have enjoyed the activities of our Arts Department"; showing in a bright light the pompous courtier of the Pouncet-box whom the bloodstained and sweaty Harry Hotspur rated so roundly. The above remark seems to be a close and rather laughable confinement of the Holy Ghost. Perhaps the most singular statement made by a Director of an Arts Department is that of "Perhaps the peak moment in the life of the Arts Department occurred in June, 1938, the end of the Paris season of the Ballet Jooss and there was an anti-war demonstration when the curtain fell upon THE GREEN TABLE."

Certainly, the ballet was successful in one respect for we know now that the curtain fell only to rise again to show us the Vichy Government almost hand-in-glove with Hitler. Joking apart, however, the statement quoted above seems to imply that this "anti-war demonstration" gave the ballet its whole glory, or added an artistic value to it. We read somewhere that St Paul "withstood the Prince of apostles to his face, because he was to be blamed," so I venture to withstand the statement of the Director, and dub it untrue and misleading. No demonstration, hostile or favorable, can take away from, or add to, the intrinsic value of a work of art. It stands alone, or it doesnt stand at all. And bringing in the statement of the demonstration, not in praise of the play, but simply against war, touches the claim with a sparkle of ridicule. And this from a Director of a Department that obviously thinks so much of itself and so little of others!

Oh! vanity, vanity.

Yours, etc,
Sean O'Casey

[1] This letter was refused publication.
[2] Christopher Martin, secretary of the arts department at Dartington Hall.

To Daniel Macmillan

MS. MACMILLAN LONDON

DEVON

8 JULY 1941

Dear Mr Daniel,

I have now received a photo of The Rev E. M. Griffin from his son the Rev R. S. Griffin. This I should, I think, like to have in "Pictures in the Hallway." If it should prove too costly to include the two, I think I'd prefer the photo of Mr Griffin to form the Frontispiece.

Please don't do anything with the photo you have, till we decide.

Yours sincerely,
S. O'Casey

To Daily Telegraph

8 JULY 1941

"Wodehouse in Berlin"

Sir—It is amusing to read the various wails about the villainy of Wodehouse.[1] The harm done to England's cause and to England's dignity is not the poor man's babble in Berlin, but the acceptance of him by a childish part of the people and the academic government of Oxford,[2] dead from the chin up, as a person of any importance whatsoever in English humorous literature, or any literature at all. It is an ironic twist of retribution on those who banished Joyce and honoured Wodehouse.

If England has any dignity left in the way of literature, she will forget for ever the pitiful antics of English Literature's performing flea.[3] If Berlin thinks the poor fish great, so much the better for us.

Yours, etc.
Sean O'Casey

Devon

[1] It had just been announced in the press that the novelist P. G. Wodehouse was released from internment in Germany and would make a series of radio broadcasts from Berlin.

[2] Wodehouse had received a D. Litt. degree from Oxford University in June 1939.

[3] Wodehouse used this phrase as the title of his "Self-portrait in Letters," *Performing Flea* (London, Herbert Jenkins, 1953; Penguin, 1961). This book contains the texts of the five Berlin broadcasts, and the following comment by Wodehouse: "With Sean O'Casey's statement that I am 'English literature's performing flea,' I scarcely know how to deal. Thinking it over, I believe he meant to be complimentary, for all the performing fleas I have met have impressed me with their sterling artistry and that indefinable something which makes the good trouper." (p. 254, Penguin)

To Peter Newmark

MS. NEWMARK

[DEVON]

9 JULY 1941

My dear Peter:

We were glad to get your letter, "a damned piece of crabbed penmanship as ever I saw". Hitler's attack on the U.S.S.R. has somewhat bewildered me too. I thought Hitler would go Left. Well, there they are now, locked in a fight that, however it goes, will destroy a lot of fine work done by the Soviets. I, too, find almost all Communists certain of a[n] overwhelming victory. I have even been accused of spreading despondency for setting forth some doubts about the utter defect of the German War Machine. I have, in my day, studied, as well as I could, a few things about military tactics & strategy; & looking at things from this view (out of the tiny window of the news), there is no doubt that the Red Army is hard set. If, as a young fighting force, they don't rashly fling away their planes & tanks, & are able to pull their armies back when the pressure becomes too fierce, then the Germans are done. That they may lose too many of those three is the only thing I'm afraid of. Somehow, I don't believe they will. As for the gains in geographical miles, they don't matter a damn. Some extraordinary good men are bound to come out of this terrible experience. The men & women of the Soviet have had a chance to think for themselves—what we have never had in our possession—those means were always locked up safe in the strong rooms of the Banks. "Look here" said the Polish poet, Mickieviez, shaking the Pope's arm, when the Poet was irritated by the Vatican's suave diplomacy, "Look here, the Holy Spirit is in the Jackets of the people of Paris". I believe that the Spirit has now outspread, & is in the jackets of the peoples of the world.

I have just finished the second biograph vol. to be called "Pictures in the Hallway". I've overshot the mark in amount of material, writing over 100,000 words; & have now, I fear, to think of what can come out to make it sell for less than a quid. I daresay, if all goes well, I'll soon be working at the proofs. We are all well here; but very busy. To cut down expenses, Eileen has had to send away our girl, & now does the cooking & general house keeping; so I've to help now & again: a bit of a nuisance, but it cant be helped. George Jean N. often refers to "Purple Dust". According to an article in "Liberty", he likes it as much as he did seven months ago, but doesn't think it'll be a box-office draw. A travelling

Rep Co came here, & caught on; but Dartington's Art Dept has ordered it off; & there's a bit of a rustle going on—perfectly polite & daintily-spoken. I have sent in a few sharp comments on remarks made in the News of the Day. I should, indeed, love to have a gawk at your chairmanship. I agree with you. Chairmen, as a rule, are too much like dummies for me. We grow speechless from the fear of hurting somebody's feelings.

Of course, the loss of the maid doesn't mean that you can't come down to us when you get leave—if you are content to muck in with us, & take things as they are. Eileen's growing into a grand cook.

I hope the Germans dont get Leningrad, for that would make it damned awkward for the Red Fleet.

Affectionate Regards from Eileen & me.

Sean

To Daniel Macmillan

TS. Macmillan London

Devon
10 July 1941

Dear Mr Daniel,

With this note, I enclose the photo of my friend, Mr E. M. Griffin. His son who sent it to me, asked that great care should be taken of it, as it was the only one of his father the family had. I have promised to return it safely to him—making a mental reservation about a possible bombing, of course. I also enclose the rough sketch for a possible jacket, and explanation of the sections are pinned to the design.

In thinking over the size of the book, and wishful that it wouldnt be too big, I imagine I could, at least, take out the chapter called "Thy Servant a Dog," and possibly the last one too, called, "He Paints His First Picture," though, if Mr Griffin's photo goes in, that chapter, I think, should be left, for it mentions him a great deal; much more than does the one preceding. I have looked the others over and over, and think each of them too good to abandon—what I'll think of them a year or two from now, God knows.

I see by the papers that Mr Harold is busier than ever. I hope you are keeping well, for you must be hard set, too.

Economic dislocation has forced us to get rid of our maid, so the wife does the cooking and housework for eight of us; and I have to give an occasional hand; so you see we're in the running for being hard pushed too. However, if the job doesnt take too long, we'll all be the better for it in the long run.

Yours sincerely,
Sean O'Casey

To Jack Daly

MS. DALY

JULY THE TWALFTH [1] 1941
TOTNES, DEVON

My dear Jack:

It was good to hear from you again. I often wondered what had happened to you—if you had been engulfed by the war, or become an Oxford don—and the last state shall be worse than the first. We are all OK here, so far; four children—one evacuee—in the house, & plenty to do. The missus does the housework (I help) now; for we had to say hail & farewell to our maid of all work. I have just finished the 2nd vol of "I Knock at the Door", 100,000 words & more, & am waiting for the first rush of proofs. It will be called "Pictures in the Hallway"; & I think some of it is very good. Well, the U.S.S.R. is with us now; & "The Internationale" will ring out on every piano. I have just sent a cable to T. Rokotov, Editor of "International Literature", Moscow, linking myself up in spirit with the Soviet people. He sent me a cable asking me to do it; so I daresay he thinks a message from me will be of some use—what, God knows.

So poor Margarita [2] has gone the way of all flesh! I am still convinced, Jack, that she, unintentionally, committed slow suicide. I didn't believe then, & I dont believe now, that she really had an organic defect. She persuaded herself she had; & then there was no hope. As well, I'm afraid, she married unwisely. Margarita had some rare delicacy in her, & should have made a more careful choice. But it was as it was to be; & there's the end of it. How is the child she left behind her? I hope she'll never hear tell of her mother's illness—the nature of it. We are trying to get the Daily Worker out again; but I don't think [Herbert] Morrison will

[1] July the 12th, celebrated in Northern Ireland as the yearly commemoration of the Protestant victory of William of Orange over the Catholic James II at the Battle of the Boyne in 1690.

[2] Daly's sister.

change his great mind.[3] I see he's arrested Cahir Healy, M.P.[4] Jasus, is there to be no limit to their stupidity. Healy is as much a Revolutionary as the parish priest of Ballinamuck.

Well all the best to you & Floss, who, I hope, is well. Are you still in the old job?

Yours as ever.
Sean

[3] See O'Casey's letter of 2 August 1941 to the *New Statesman and Nation* on the banning of the *Daily Worker.*

[4] Cahir Healy (1877–1970), a Northern Ireland member of parliament for forty years, was arrested in the summer of 1941 and interned in Brixton Prison for nearly two years "because the Home Secretary had cause to believe that Mr. Healy had recently been concerned in acts prejudicial to the public safety or the defence of the realm." Healy had made a visit to neutral Southern Ireland in 1941.

To Totnes Times

12 JULY 1941

"Worthless Leadership in Art"

Dear Sir:

In an address given recently on the retention of the T.R.T.[1] the Rev. R. A. Edwards [2] made the remark that "the theatre was an art that the man in the street could understand," implying either that all other arts were beyond his comprehension and outside his power of enjoyment; or that the art of the theatre was so commonplace that anyone with an absentee mind could grasp and enjoy all that it had to give. But the fact is that no other art is any farther from man than the theatre, and the levels of enjoyment are about the same in all instances. The M. in the S. has as much (in some cases much more) experience of them as he has of the theatre. Is there a house anywhere that hasnt a picture on the wall? Is there a town that hasnt some kind of a statue? And is there one of us who hasnt whistled a tune, not counting the hosts who have played on the fiddle, the concertina, the mouthorgan, or the dulcimer? Even the Salvation Army has the big drum and the tambourine. The child using his pencil and crayons, or moulding his coloured clays, gets as much experience of painting and sculpture as he gets of the theatre when he elects to play the part of a soldier, a cowboy, or a redskin. But these young and delightful imaginations are corrupted when they grow bigger because almost all

[1] The Traveling Repertory Theatre.

[2] The Rev. R. A. Edwards, vicar of Dartington parish, gave a talk, "Art and the Man in the Street," reported in the *Totnes Times,* 5 July 1941.

the art around them is venal and vulgar—in other words, isnt art at all. It isnt that the M. in the S. accepts them; but rather that they are forced upon him by the higher-up persons whom he is taught to respect and frightened into revering. Not everyone who paints a picture, digs a design out of a stone, composes a tune, or writes a play, is an artist. Many are called, but few are chosen. The commonplace in other arts reach the M. in the S. as readily as do the commonplace in the theatre. The proof is before our eyes, in Totnes itself: it lies in the War Memorial; that to Queen Victoria; the one to those who first crossed the bush in Australia; the numerous advertising pictures on the hoardings; and the coloured war poster that hangs, or recently hung, on the railings of the parish church of the Borough—all pathetic examples of atrocious art, destitute of imagination, design, or dignity; desperately dull and commonplace. It isnt the M. in the S. that is to be blamed; it is those who pose as the leaders of the people, and impose their own ignorant and unimaginative dicta on the common people. It is this leadership that banned James Joyce and crowned Wodehouse. It is this ignorant and worthless leadership in art that has got to go, with many other things that have lost their value, and are fast losing their power. To end, perhaps Mr. Edwards will be good enough to tell us how the M. in the S., or, indeed, any other man can *understand* a work of art as, say, one may understand a problem in Euclid?

Yours sincerely,
Sean O'Casey

6 July 1941

To Gabriel Fallon

TS. TEXAS
DEVON
17 JULY 1941

My dear Gaby:

Well, I shall be glad to see Father Declan, should he ever be good enough to look me up. What does C.P. mean? Congregation of the Passion? Is he what we used to call "a Passionist Father"? The Five Lamps [1] have

[1] On 31 May 1941 three German bombs dropped on Dublin, killing over thirty people and injuring over one hundred. One bomb exploded in the North Circular Road area, causing heavy damage and death on the North Strand Road from Seville Place to Newcomen Bridge. The Five Lamps, a familiar landmark still standing today in the heart of this "O'Casey country," is a pile of wrought-iron Victorian street furniture, a combination horse-trough and street light with five hanging lamps, at the bottom of the North Circular Road where four streets intersect—Amiens Street, Portland Row, North Strand Road, and Seville Place, which leads into the parishes of St. Laurence O'Toole (R.C.) and St. Barnabas (C. of I.).

had a hot time of it since I last wrote to you. And was 422 N.C.R.[2] left standing? And Newcomen Bridge! How often have I warmed me backside sitting on the parapet on a fine fair sunny evening! Ay, an' will again, please God, as a Dublin man would say, were he by my shoulder. I can't remember the Convent of the Cross and Passion. Maybe the oul' memory's goin'.

You are just as likely to be right about my last plays as I am to be wrong about them, though I don't know where my moral judgement comes in; In "The Star Turns Red"—you say "Shines Red", a better title than mine—I just tried to put, in my own way, to show the feeling of millions of workers to things as they are. There is really nothing noble in Communism as Communism; but there is something necessary in it. We'll have to leave it at that till I see you face to face, and end it all or end each other.

I am up to the neck here with all sorts of things. The woman who did the housework has gone, so Eileen does it, cooking, etc, and I try to give her a hand. I am back at the old work of doing anything that I'd like to do, feeling that any risk is better than corpulent idleness.

I've just finished the 2nd vol of biography—if it can be called a biography. When it was measured, it was found to extend to well over 100,000 words; so I've had to lift some of it out to make it a semi-reasonable length. I am calling it "Pictures in the Hallway". When it may be in print, God knows, with things as they are; but there is a little hope that it may appear this year. I'll let you have a quick copy of course, though I shan't be able to write in the usual greeting.

What do you think of this, taken from "The Kerryman"; "A splendid night's entertainment was provided in the Carnegie Hall, Kenmare, on Easter Sunday night, when the Bernadette Players from Dublin, staged the famous play, NIGHT MUST FALL. The hall was packed to capacity, and the prolonged enthusiastic applause . . . . ." Bernadette, Kenmare, Easter Sunday night, and Night Must Fall—a curious harmony, to say the least of it. The Reds in Charlemont Lane,[3] or wherever it is, couldn't do as bad as that; and "Draw The Fires",[4] even at its worst, is not quite as bad as N M F, performed on an Easter Sunday night. It certainly shocked a hardened oul' bugger like me. I'm not blaming you, now, or the Church; only showing what we are all up against, meself as well as yourself. (The above was read in The Kerryman of April 19th of this year.) The scarcity of tea must have you all in a lamentable state. So far, all well here. Louis D'Alton is thinking of doing an Irish tour of JUNO. Have written this after listening to the 12 o'clock news, and am anxious about the Soviet Army fighting in front of Moscow. If they can pull back their armies before the

[2] O'Casey's last Dublin address in 1926 on the North Circular Road.

[3] The New Theatre Group (1937–45), a socialist theatre in Charlemont Road, Dublin, which performed plays by dramatists like Gorki, Toller, and O'Neill.

[4] Ernst Toller, *Draw the Fires!* (London, John Lane, 1935), translated by Edward Crankshaw.

pressure, Hitler's done; if not, the war will last for years. Remember me to Father Senan, and his comrade; to P. White, and Francis—if you meet now. My love to Rose and the children, and to you. Eileen sends her love, too.

Ever yours,
Sean

You will be interested to hear that the Totnes P.P. is a Doublin man —Father E. Russell. His brother founded the Free State Air Force. He is a grand chap, & often spends an evening chatting with me & Eileen. A Dublin Priest an' a Dublin Doctor—be god, they're everywhere! He's a fine Bohemian, fitting in with us well & hearty. There's an awful commotion here over Wodehouse blathering over the Berlin Wireless—as if it mattered a tinker's damn where he wirelessed or how he wirelessed. God, Gaby, it's amusin'!

Yours as ever again,
Sean

To Daniel Macmillan

MS. Macmillan London
Devon
17 July 1941

Dear Mr Daniel,

Very well; we'll leave out "Thy Servant, a Dog" and "He Paints His First Picture." I can start the next vol with the 2nd sketch; &, by a change, include the other one, too. I think I shall dedicate the book to Mr Griffin; & perhaps, his picture can be in the next volume (planning ahead, isn't it?). I'm afraid, now, I won't be able to get the photo back to Mr R. S. Griffin. Doesn't the censorship prohibit all pictures to Ireland?

I give the wife an odd hand: make my own bed, help wash up, & amuse the youngest on occasions. I've just written an article for A. Fadeyev of the Commission of Foreign Writers, & hope it may get to Moscow; with a greeting to the Russian People. They think it may have an encouraging effect—I can't see how. However, if they think it, they must have it. Anyway, I've been sending them greetings for the last five years, so they know me well. I do hope things may go well with them.

Yours sincerely,
S. O'Casey

To Totnes Times

26 JULY 1941

"Worthless Leadership in Art"

Dear Sir:—

I am sorry that part of my letter appeared to be obscure to Jane Copeland.[1] My main point was that the people are as familiar with all other arts as they are with the art of the theatre. Every street, every house is an example of the lay-out of the art of architecture; every illustration in a book, every picture on a wall, and every poster on a hoarding is an example of the art of colour and line and form; and every hymn or song we sing, every tune we whistle is an expression of the art of music; and every statue or memorial in every Church garden or corner of a street, or centre of a square, is an expression of the art of sculpture. They are mostly very bad examples, but no worse than most of the things seen in the theatre. The generally held opinion that the people are more familiar with the art of the theatre than they are with the other arts is, in my opinion, a very mistaken one.

The people who sit in high places are many, and more than few of them, while possibly good at the job for which they may be chosen have a bad habit of acting as judges of everything. The meaning of "higher-up persons" should be plain. Let us say "higher placed persons" instead. Here are three examples of what I mean: W. E. Gladstone, who went down on his knees to kiss the hand of Marie Corelli, the (as she and he thought) second swan of Avon; The Earl of Baldwin parading around with Mary Webb; and the "higher-up persons" of Oxford University giving the degree of Litt.D. to Wodehouse, English Literature's performing flea. Jane Copeland will get a grand account of a little lesser Fry gathering pompously together to help Pecksniff lay the foundation of a Grammar School, in Dickens' *Martin Chuzzlewit*. The "cranks" dont matter. Nobody lets a "crank" design a bank or a warehouse. It's the fellows with titles on their brows and ribbons in their coats that do most of the damage. We are forced to buy things that are worthless, and this extends from pictures to patent medicines. The people, in every possible and plausible way, are forced to deceive themselves into the honouring of the fraudulent and valueless. The man in the street doesnt know what is second-rate, for his leaders and guides are too busy forcing the third-rate things into his life. The old town might look strange without its Australian memorial,

[1] Jane Copeland's letter to the *Totnes Times,* 19 July 1941, which is a reply to O'Casey's letter of 12 July.

but that sentimental feeling cant make it look less ugly. The Plains, with its Island and its river, with a little planning and a little taste, could be made to look both dignified and beautiful. It is anything but that now. The natural beauty of England is for all and there must be restrictions (as the Government is beginning to realise) to prevent interested persons from building where and how they like.

The War Posters were simply crude, commonplace and childish, without a child's charming quaintness usually apparent in their efforts. They were no more "modern" than the Memorial beside them.

I had no intention of being hard on Mr. Edwards. He is a man, by all accounts, who is taking a vigorous and intelligent interest in the community around him (his interest in T.R.T. showed so), and I would be the last to sneer at such an activity. I merely set out to point out a misconception generally held about the people's familiarity with the theatre.

Yours sincerely,
Sean O'Casey

To H. Cowdell

TS. MACMILLAN LONDON

DEVON
2 AUGUST 1941

MESSRS MACMILLAN & CO.
Dear Mr Cowdell,

Thank you for sending me the copy of proposed Jacket for PICTURES IN THE HALLWAY. I think it quite good, but would suggest some changes.

I think that GREY would be better in the Circle, in the top and bottom border, and in the spine panels than the DUSTY PINK tint as shown in the design.

I want the figure of the Spectator, in the right bottom corner, taken out, and the figure of the man marching with a flag substituted—this is attached to the jacket design.

And the tops of the drumsticks removed: Orange drums are usually beaten with long canelike sticks, without the felt balls on the top of them. And King Billy is in Ireland always shown with a Baton in his hand, not a pistol.

Sorry for troubling you; but perhaps these changes wont give too much trouble.

Yours sincerely,
S. O'Casey

To New Statesman and Nation

2 AUGUST 1941

THE DAILY WORKER

Sir,—If fair is fair, there are quite a lot of things and persons that deserve banning much better than the *Daily Worker*.[1] It wasn't those of the *Daily Worker* who went to Hitler with gifts of gold and frankincense (leaving the myrrh out). And there can hardly be any doubt that at one time, not very long ago, the democracies of France and Britain were bent over the decision to go for the Soviet Union with horse, foot and artillery, in order to "bring help to Finland." It was only the good earth herself who stood between us and almost certain war with the Soviet Union. These are things in the oul' history books by now.

As you say in your Journal, friendship, at least, alliance if possible, with the Soviets has always been among the main notes played on the Communist trumpet; a call, for some reason or another, many people here hated to hear. I, personally, have no doubt that this enthusiastic approval of the U.S.S.R. was one of the hidden reasons for the suppression of the paper. I, for twenty years and more, have been arguing with and tormenting people into my own admiration for almost all the things done by active Socialism in the Soviet State. Six or seven years ago a Christmas message of mine to the Australian papers urged a closer union between the U.S.A., Britain and the Soviet Union. An article of mine, just as long ago, voicing the same thing appeared in the *Manchester Evening News.* I always argued, not only for a closer political union, but for a closer cultural union as well. I have appealed for a fuller recognition and a higher honour on the English stage for the finer examples of American drama than it has ever received. And as I have tried to keep up this connection with New York, so I have tried to keep up the same connection with Moscow. This morning, July 23rd, I got a letter, dated April 24th, from Timofei Rokotov, Editor of *The International Magazine,* with a grand special number of a magazine, almost entirely devoted to Shakespeare. Here is part of the letter:

> I was extremely delighted by your letter of January 28th, which I received only yesterday. We always remember you, and experience joy

[1] On 21 January 1941, Herbert Morrison, home secretary and minister for home security, announced that he had issued the necessary orders under Defense Regulation 2 D for the suppression of the *Daily Worker*. The paper was banned for nineteen months and resumed publication on 7 September 1942. See O'Casey's letter to Winston Churchill, Vol. II, 4 July 1942.

whenever we see your name on the pages of the English press. . . . Several days ago I read the splendid letter you wrote to Comrade Apletin with regard to the Shakespeare Jubilee in 1939. Now we are again honouring the memory of the world's greatest dramatist, on the occasion of of the 325th anniversary of his death. In connection with this event, I have taken the liberty of publishing excerpts from your letter in both *International Literature* and *Moscow News*. Might I ask you to do me a favour that would be of exceptional importance for the magazine? Our connections with British literature have been interrupted. We have hardly any new English books, and we are in great need of them. Perhaps it would not be too much trouble for you to select, at your own discretion, several of the recent literary publications you might consider worthy of the attention of our readers, and send them to us. You would be doing us an invaluable service. Any book we might receive from England at the present time would be highly appreciated here. We are particularly interested in contemporary English plays. Naturally, we will cover all expenses incurred. T. ROKOTOV.

As a member of the Editorial board of the paper, I should like to ask Mr. Morrison if this kind of thing was likely to hamper the war effort? Of course, Communists have to deal with other things beside literature—with bread, for instance; but Christ dealt with that: the bread is given, right enough, but we don't get it—we have to fight for it. There is a Persian proverb which says: "If you have two pennies, with one buy bread, and with the other a lily." But if we have but one penny, we can buy only bread. It has been my fight for a long span of years now to try to bring about a condition in which the worker spending his penny on bread will have one left to buy a lily.

I think it will be allowed that those connected with the *Daily Worker* have done what they could to bring the Soviet Union and Britain together; they can do much now to keep them together; and much more, if they have the *Daily Worker* to help them. With all deference, the combined energy and single-mindedness of the Communists is as important as the energy and single-mindedness of Mr. Morrison.

Sean O'Casey

Devon

To H. Cowdell

TS. MACMILLAN LONDON

DEVON

14 AUGUST 1941

Dear Mr Cowdell,

Thank you for sending me the completed design for the jacket of PICTURES IN THE HALLWAY.

I think the design looks rather graceful, as well as giving some idea of the general scope of the book's contents.

There is but one other point: The words TIRIS TEANGA are three in number, like TIR IS TEANGA: they mean simply "Country and Language." If this could be rectified without trouble, it would be good. If not, then it's not important, and dont trouble. It is my fault, for I saw the defect in the rough design, and stupidly forgot to point it out.

I like the Jacket very much indeed.

Yours sincerely,
Sean O'Casey

PS. If the alteration be any trouble at all, don't bother.

To Peter Newmark

MS. NEWMARK

DEVON

13 SEPTEMBER 1941

My dear Peter:

Eileen asks me to send you a note to say that you are to come along in Sept, & take Pot-Luck with us. We shall all be delighted to see you again. I have been busy with proofs of my new vol "Pictures in the Hallway" to come out in the Autumn. Let's know the day & the hour when you leave London for our townland. I hope you don't land in the Artillery. I've been busy, too, cabling & writing to Moscow. I, too, am anxious, not only about the Ukraine, but about the whole line. Murmansk is nearly as important; & if the British let this port go—well. Leningrad, too, is of first-class importance. Don't worry about Budenny. He's old fashioned, ri' enough; but he has a name; & a staff: & all depends on the Staff. I believe the Red Army will eventually produce good leaders—Galitzy for instance. If the young officers can keep alive through their experiences, then all will be well: that is just what all of them need. Just what Lady Astor would say to a Corporal; but, apparently, the corporal hasn't a sense of humour. Just what I would say, too: "Ye's must all bloody well run to my house, if there happens to be a Blitz, & put the fires out there first". Nathan sent me years ago the clipping you were kind enough to send.

I'll look forward to seeing you soon.

Ever yours.
Sean

To Jack Daly

MS. DALY

DEVON
21 SEPTEMBER 1941

My dear Jack:

I got the "Life of C. Cohen" [1] allright. Forgive me for not thanking you sooner. I have been busy with proofs of 'Pictures in the Hallway', a second vol to 'I Knock at the Door'; the missus now has to do the cooking & housework, & I give her a hand, as well as keeping the weeds from our little plot in the back; I have had to do a few things for Moscow; & I have had a flare-up again of the old swelled neck gland. I'm better now; & so, at 1 in the morning, when all's quiet on the Sou'Western Front, sit down to thank you for sending me Chapman Cohen's fine book. Though not a Biography in the ordinary sense of the word, it was much more interesting than those ones like Buchan's "Memory Hold the Door", retailing & wholesaling all the eminent men met in a life's day-walk. I'm glad of the contempt he poured out on the Bishop of London, Winnington Ingram. This was the fellaheen who carried about with him the yarn mentioned in "The Star Turns Red", of how he heard a little girl, in rags & tatters, saying as she knelt before the altar: "Bless God for everything!" [2] The ill-got, ignorant, blatherin' bastard! The flower o' the flock, wha'? Oh, wouldn't I like to clothe him in rags & tatters, & send him out to sing

[1] Chapman Cohen, *Almost an Autobiography, The Confessions of a Freethinker* (London, Pioneer Press, 1940).

[2] The First Workman in Act IV of *The Star Turns Red*: "(*mimicking the Lord Mayor*). Remember what the Purple Priest said! I remember him damn well telling us one day of hearing a rustle in church, and of creeping down to see what it was. (*He attempts to mimic an ecclesiastical voice.*) And there, brethren, kneeling before the altar, was a wee girl, clad only in rags and tatters, busy mumbling, "Thank God for everything'!"

[in] the streets for a living. A bollocks, if ever there was one! And now a lot of them think they'll beat the Nazis with peals of prayer. By God, if the Red Army has to fall back to the Urals, they'll feel the weight of the Nazi prayers—tons of them to set the cities & the towns aflame.

All the best to you & Floss.
Yours as Ever.
Sean

To George Jean Nathan

TS. CORNELL
DEVON
22 SEPTEMBER 1941

My very dear George:

Your letter, dated the 25th of August has just rambled in to me, and I was damned glad to hear from you. I was thinking of you as you, evidently, were thinking of me. I was wondering and wondering why you didn't write. I certainly sent at least two letters to you to which no answer came. I often said to the missus that it was a wonder George didn't write, and hoped you weren't ill. I sent a letter to Dick [Madden] mentioning that you owed me an answer to two letters. Indeed, I haven't heard from him now for some time—since I wrote telling him not to bother about my suggestion concerning the putting on of the STAR TURNS RED; and telling him I received nothing in the shape of a book from him—the Book of Irish Plays, with your preface.[1] In one of my

[1] *Five Great Modern Irish Plays,* edited with a foreword by George Jean Nathan (New York, Modern Library, 1941). The book contains *The Playboy of the Western World* and *Riders to the Sea* by J. M. Synge; *Juno and the Paycock* by Sean O'Casey; *Spreading the News* by Lady Gregory; and *Shadow and Substance* by Paul Vincent Carroll. In his foreword, Nathan defended O'Casey's *Juno* from attacks by St. John Ervine, who called it "superb music-hall . . . that's all," and Nathan also wrote: "Of all the still living, this O'Casey, Shaw aside, is in every respect the foremost. Not only is he at his best the best of the Celts but even at his worst so much better than three-fourths of them at their best—and some of them are surely not to be sniffed at—that to fail to perceive it must remain the privilege of amateur criticism. If *The Plough and the Stars* is not one of the finest dramas in the modern theatre, if *Juno and the Paycock* is not one of the richest human comedies, if *The Silver Tassie* with all its admitted deficiencies is not one of the most honorable experiments, if *Within the Gates,* for all its lapses, is not beautiful, brave and thrilling song, if *Purple Dust* is not a ringing, moving melody orchestrated with a resounding slapstick, and if even the incontrovertibly poor *The Star Turns Red,* the feeblest play O'Casey has written, is not oddly invested with what may conceivably turn out to be a poet's prophetic vision—if these plays are not these things, then I am not the man to have been engaged to write this foreword." See also Nathan's "The Best of the Irish," *Newsweek,* 29 January 1940, reprinted above.

letters to you, I asked if you could let me have an article on Walt Disney, that had appeared in ESQUIRE, about which a friend of mine spoke glowingly. Well, George, it'll be a long time before I forget you. I am so glad to hear that Eddie Dowling is getting on with plans for the production of PURPLE DUST, and that his pictorial idea of the play is good. That is a thing, I think, we lack in the theatre. Pictures on the Stage, of the play and in the play. I wish you and I could have a theatre of our own. What a chance [Michael] Chekhov of the Dartington Hall Studio has missed. I hear he's going about now playing "The Cricket on the Hearth," a revival, I suppose, of what was played in Moscow fifteen years ago. We can but go on fighting, you there, and I here; and, after all, the theatre is nothing to be ashamed of. Great names are there as well as in any other art.

I got neither the book you sent to me, nor the one sent by Dick—and I longing to read your preface. But we have suffered so many things lately, that we bear disappointments now more calmly than before. Perhaps they may come yet; but I fear Hitler has sent them fathoms down. I have just finished the galley-proofs of the biographical second volume—PICTURES IN THE HALLWAY. I'll send you the first copy out. I have an article in it showing how I first came to the theatre, or how, perhaps, the theatre came to me. I think you'll find it interesting, especially the curious blend of Shakespeare and Boucicault. I think there is some good writing in it. At the moment, I am trying to think out another play, in the midst of writing a few things for Moscow, and a song for a revue the Left Wing are thinking of putting on some time later on; and doing things about the house giving a hand to the wife who does the cooking and housework now; and a bit of digging in the back garden to furnish us with an odd spud—God be wi' the days when I trampled on thousands of crimson tomatoes growing wild in [George] Buschar [Markle]'s garden on the mountains of Pennsylvania! [2] It is extraordinarily good of you to take so much interest in Purple Dust for my sake. I am sending on a carbon copy of this letter later on, in the hope that one may reach you. Anyway, the warships of the U.S.A. will make it a safer journey. My love to Eugene and Carlotta, and all friends.

My love, as deep as ever
to you.
Sean

[2] See "Pennsylvanian Visit," *Rose and Crown* (1952).

To Jack Daly

MS. Daly

Devon

4 October 1941

My dear Jack:

I don't know the publication date of the book, 'Pictures in the Hallway', nor does Macmillans. It will depend on the printers & the binders. I am now editing the Page proofs. The book is expensive—15/–, & I'm not flush enough, at the moment, to send you one. But I could get you it at cost price—10/–, sign it, & send it on to you, if you like. Anyway, 5/– is 10/– these days. I know, only too well, how low down in thoughts many of the workers are; but all the things you mentioned are conditioned purposely to keep the workers where they are. They have God's blessing, the opportunity to punt & ride, which the system puts before the glory, hardship, & responsibility of citizenship. But there is a core of intelligent & awakened workers. Most of them, when they are near, come to see me; and we chat together. Some of them have very fine minds. They are mostly craftsmen, but one or two have been labourers, like myself. And 90% of the Russians, not long ago, could neither read nor write. Anyway, they know little less about literature & art than their "betters". The 'oul neck is well; but I have been down & up with Influenza since; & so has the missus. The woman who tidied the house went on war work; & I had to do my bit here; but I'm well used to these things, & take them silently in my stride. There can be no going back: forward till the breath is gone, & the heart stops beating.

Ever Yours.
Sean

To Horace Reynolds

TS. Reynolds

Devon

4 October 1941

My dear Horace:

Ay, it seems a long time since I heard from you, and it was good to get your letter telling me that Kay's glands are cured. I have had a flare-up of a youthful trouble—a swelled neck-gland, but it has subsided again, and a crown of rejoicing is on the old head once more. I dont hear much from

Eirinn meself; but I've just got the music and words from the Deputy Chief of Broadcasting of "A Bhean ud thios ar bhruach an tsruthan," [1] a song I knew long ago, but had forgotten, and which has a lovely air. It is a lullaby, and I want—or think I shall want it—for a new play. I heard it on the Radio Eireann, and all the old memories came back again. But the Director says nothing about Ireland, only wishing for better days, a wish we all can share. I envy you your trip down the Ole Man River. What grand names live along its steep banks! When the last Packet goes, what way will they sail the river? Man isnt the same under all systems. Health, for instance, would banish many irritations; a healthy child is rarely irritable; it is troublesome, of course, for it is always moving, but that is all. Try a child that has to be coaxed to eat with one that swallows food down in the glory of a vigorous appetite. And financial security would banish many more. Men and women are naturally kind, not naturally criminal. History has always been determined by the way the people live; and not by the romantic escapades of kings and princes. I am more convinced than ever that Communism alone will bring about a safer and a much more active world; ay, and a much more colorful life, too. Of course, it doesnt undertake to banish jealousy, or envy—though there wont be much of a chance for that, except a holy envy of desiring to share the greater gifts of another. When I last talked with Yeats,[2] he was full of childlike eagerness to hear why I was a communist; but he was too old then to tempt me to display meself before him, so we had a long and animated talk about the Elizabethans instead. But he had got as far as "The Weavers", The "Machine Wreckers", and poor Toller's "Draw The Fires". He has left at long last; but his letter in defence of us when we were in the throes of the great Dublin Lock-out in 1913 showed that he was never very far away from the masses.[3] I dont agree with O'Leary. If he meant the people when he said the Nation, then he was wrong. One lie to free a people is nothing to the millions blathered to keep them cool. Poor Gogarty! He'll get on well with Brockhurst.[4] You are quite right about the Bucks.[5] But Gogarty will never write anything of a first order—even about the Bucks. He is quite the irredeemable, and, in a wide way, ignorant, hapless individualist. Your query about cigarettes brought me a warning from the censor that it was agin the law to ask for anything; and that anything from overseas must be an unsolicited gift received on an

[1] "Oh Woman down there on the banks of the stream."

[2] In September 1935 when O'Casey made his last visit to Ireland. See his account of that meeting with Yeats in the opening pages of "The Friggin Frogs," *Rose and Crown* (1952).

[3] Yeats's open letter in defense of the workers of Dublin during the 1913 general strike and lock-out, "Dublin Fanaticism," *Irish Worker,* 1 November 1913.

[4] Gerald Brockhurst, the painter.

[5] The eighteenth-century Irish "bucks" or dashing young blades, such as the notorious Buck Whelan; hence, Joyce's name for the character based on Gogarty in *Ulysses,* "Buck Mulligan."

isolated occasion. So there's an example of isolation for you. Happily, I'm not interested in cigarettes, for I gave them up two years ago. Now I smoke a pipe, and wouldnt give you a thank you for a hundred cigarettes. The pipe is the only thing that gives me satisfaction in the way of a smoke; but a thousand thanks all the same. I'm glad to hear about John; and what a young lady Peggy must be now.

By the way, your quotation of "You dont know about me without you have read a book", and your liking for the "without" is interesting. It seems to be a Gaelic idiom. The word "Gan", meaning without, is an idiomatic word in Gaelic. "Is Truagh *Gan* Mise in Sasana", "I wish I were in England", is really, It's a pity without me in England, or without me to be in England. He stood there without as much as a word out of him, and it comes into hundreds of phrases. The "only", of course, is a common saying in Dublin. Another lovely one is "I up with me fist, an' let him have it in the snot!" But the common talk of Ireland sparkles with Gaelic phrases and twists.

I don't expect I'll ever hear again from Barry Fitzgerald. It's five years since I got a word from him.

My Love to Kay, and congratulations. My Love to John and Peggy. My Love to you

Ever Yours,
Sean

To Peter Newmark

MS. Newmark

Devon
18 October 1941

My dear Peter:

Just a line to say I've got a copy (at last) of D. McArdle's "Irish Republic" [1] & to thank you for trying to get me one; & to thank you a second time for Freud's grand book on Moses.[2] I'm reading it, & finding it enthralling; & am convinced he's right. Niall's down with whooping cough, & we're afraid Shivaun's getting it, too. Between them, they've given me a cold, & I'm hoarse & heated. So excuse this terse letter till things cool down a bit.

Bad news from the U.S.S.R.

Yrs
Sean

[1] Dorothy MacArdle, *The Irish Republic* (London, Gollancz, 1937).
[2] Sigmund Freud, *Moses and Monotheism* (London, Hogarth, 1939).

To Irish Times

25 NOVEMBER 1941

An Irish Institution [1]

Sir,—In a recent issue of your Journal, a letter written by the Rev. Dudley Fletcher tells us that "Since its disestablishment seventy years ago, the Church of Ireland is a thoroughly Irish Institution, and, for that reason, should be an object of interest to every patriotic Irishman." [2] That was not my experience when I was a member of her communion. I invariably found Her, not only passively unirish, but actively hostile to all, or almost all, things distinctively Irish.

Take the Irish Language for one thing: What support did the Church give, what sympathy did the Church show to the Irish language revival movement? None. She hampered it in every way she could. Dr. Douglas Hyde could tell him a lot about the attitude of Trinity College then to all things Irish. I remember (for I was one) a Committee being formed to combat this hostility and ignorance. It was called "The Gaelic League Mission to Protestants." A Mission, mind you; and hard work it had to do. If I remember rightly, a deputation went to see the then Dean of St. Patrick's (Dr. Bernard, I think) to get him to agree to an Irish Service in the Cathedral on St. Patrick's Day. He refused, coldly and emphatically. I wasnt respectable looking enough then to go with the deputation, but I heard all about it. [A deputation went to see the Rev. Phineas Hunt, then Rector of St. Kevin's, I think, on the S.C.R. (South Circular Road.) While two of the deputation talked to Mr. Hunt, I talked to his wife, for I saw plainly that the decision would lie with her. I did my work well, and the Service was agreed to, because, as she said, what matter the language so long as the pure gospel was preached to the people. That was her knowledge of, and sympathy for, the tongue of St. Patrick, St. Bridgid, and St. Laserian.] [3]

I have an Irish New Testament presented to me by the then Rector of St. Barnabas, Dublin, the Rev. E. M. Griffin (a scholar, a saint, and a democrat, if ever there was one) who apologised for the book's mean appearance and archaic form. Few could read the primitive print, even with hard striving. A smaller one, bought by myself, years after, has the same

[1] O'Casey's original title was "Protestantism in Ireland."

[2] *Irish Times,* 5 November 1941, a letter from the Rev. Canon William Dudley Fletcher (1863–1948), St. Laserian's, Old Leighlin, County Carlow. A brother of Canon Arthur Henry ("Harry") Fletcher, Canon William Dudley Fletcher was the rector at Kilbanagher, Laois, 1907–27, and canon at St. Laserian's, 1927–46.

[3] Passage in square brackets omitted by the editor.

primitive print, ornamented with crudely coloured pictures illustrating texts out of the Old Testament. So much for the Language.

What did the Irish Church ever do to secure the right of the Irish soldier in the English Army to wear a sprig of Shamrock in his helmet, busby, or glenageary? It appeared in Royal ensigns, but it couldn't show in the Irish soldier's bosom.

What did the Church do to prevent the robbery of the Lane Pictures from Dublin? Nothing.

The Church may be steadier now than in the days of Swift; but is it livelier, or as lively? Swift was there, then, and that's saying a whole lot. As for Roe's and Iveagh's restoration of the two cathedrals,[4] that, in my young days, was a mockery among the Irish Protestant poor, who said "One was built be whiskey, and the other was built be porther."

I reluctantly go against Mr. Dudley Fletcher in any way, for I know him to be Irish and a democrat, and I have had a curious connection with members of his family. When we first came to the Parish of St. Barnabas,[5] his father (I think), the Rev. John Fletcher, D.D. was the Rector, and I sat in the same Sunday School class, if my memory serves, with the Doctor's daughter. Seemingly democratic, but I remember how the Teacher, a Miss Ballantine,[6] welcomed the young lady, and kissed her, gave her all the easy questions, and, if she hesitated, helped her out with a hard one—sympathy that didnt flow to any other member of the class. Of course, neither the father nor the child was to blame, but there it was. His brother, Mr. Harry Fletcher, afterwards came to the parish, and a fine fellow he was, lifting my brother, dying from pneumonia, into the Adelaide Hospital, and saving his life for the time being. A chapter in my next biographical book deals with this memorable incident.[7] I met Mr. Dudley Fletcher in Liberty Hall, in the middle of the Big Lock-out, in 1913, when he came to offer his sympathy with the workers.[8] So I should be the last to say a word against him; but he will forgive me, I'm sure, for saying that, in my experience, the Church of Ireland was never Irish, and never democratic, and didn't know how to be one or the other either.

Yours sincerely,
Sean O'Casey

[4] In the 1870s, Henry Roe, the Dublin whiskey distiller, paid £250,000 for the restoration of Christ Church Cathedral; and Sir Benjamin Lee Guinness (Lord Iveagh), the Dublin brewer, paid £160,000 for the restoration of St. Patrick's Cathedral.

[5] The Casey family moved from 9 Innisfallen Parade, off Dorset Street, to 22 Hawthorne Terrace, in the parish of St. Barnabas, in 1889, when O'Casey was nine years old.

[6] See O'Casey's letter to the Rev. Canon William Dudley Fletcher, 30 January 1942, note 3, Vol. II.

[7] See "Poor Tom's Acold," *Drums Under the Windows* (1945).

[8] See "Dark Kaleidoscope," *Drums Under the Windows,* where O'Casey describes meeting the Rev. Dudley Fletcher with Jim Larkin in 1913.

To Rev. Canon Arthur Henry Fletcher[1]

TC. O'Casey
Devon
1 December 1941

My dear Mr. Harry,

Right glad I was to get a letter from you, forming a coda to a chapter that I thought had ended forever; though it's a queer thing to hear from one after such a big fistful of years had been flung away into the past. You could hardly remember me, for I was a lot shyer then, and kept safely in the background. Still I had tea with you twice, among a number of others after you had given us the final lessons in preparation for Confirmation.[2] I remember once arguing with you about the "militaristic influences of the Boy's Brigade." Well, we know better now what militarism is. I remember you presented each candidate with a coloured certificate, having on it a golden cross which shocked a lot of people; and a copy of Bishop Walsham How's "Holy Communion", a small blue-covered book, with red edges. It told us first of all that the best preparation for Communion was a holy life. "Easier said than done," as one of the Confirmed, Nicholas Stitt, said to me when we were looking over the book together.

It's strange youve forgotten the help you gave when my brother Tom was sick of pneumonia. By the way, he wasnt "a little brother"; but a big full-grown man of twenty-three or so. You discovered that he was sick quite accidentally; and helped to hold him down in bed (he was delirious) once when he had overpowered me and my mother. You lived then in Gt. Charles St.—25, I think—and your father lived in Miltown. I have told of it all in a chapter called "Death on the Doorstep"[3] in a book of mine to be published in the beginning of the year that is before us. I left your right name in the story, feeling that, if you ever read of it, or heard of it, you wouldnt be ashamed of a good deed done for others. Do you not remember coming to bid me goodbye when you were leaving the Parish, owing, it was said, to the displeasure given to Orange-minded and low-church members of the Parish by your "Puseyite" views, and your wearing

[1] Rev. Canon Arthur Henry Fletcher (1867–1949), Killaloe, County Clare; curate of St. Barnabas Church, Dublin, 1896–98.

[2] O'Casey was confirmed on 29 March 1898, at Clontarf Parish Church, Dublin, and the certificate of confirmation was signed by Henry A. Fletcher, curate, St. Barnabas.

[3] See "Death on the Doorstep," *Pictures in the Hallway* (1942).

of the Romish garment, called a cassock, during divine service? [4] I remember you (it was a bitter night) warming your hands round the little chimney of a little lamp that gave light to let me read and study in the room. I had an Irish friend with me that night, and all the time he was hidden behind an old sofa, for he was in deadly fear of having to meet a Protestant Minister. Do you not remember the little Debating Society you started in the Parish? I remember a young man, named Blake, reading an essay on "The Ishmaelites of Modern Society," crying for sympathy to be shown to the bad men and bad women in the world; and Now I can see the Schoolmaster, Hogan,[5] climbing on to a desk to be close to the gasjet so that he could belch out the speeches of Burke and Fox and Pitt. I never thought, nor do I think now that you were one of the Sandford and Merton type. You presented yourself as a fine man to me, and I had a great affection for you, as had my mother, too. You wouldnt know "The Wharf" now. I, too, often snibbed eels under the bridge, and climbed about looking for mussels under "The middle arch." Of course the Church of Eireann may be more democratic than the C. of Rome, but that's not saying a lot. In contact with the people, it isnt. Ninety per cent of the priesthood of the C. of Rome in Eirinn spring from the people, the plain people, the artizans and the peasants. Willy nilly, that makes them bone of their bone and flesh of their flesh. And they are much more at their ease (with notable exceptions, of course) with all sorts of people than are the average Protestant clergymen, Eireannach or Sasanach.[6] I know that by a wide and deep experience. However, I dont think it matters much now, for when this great world convulsion ends, life will be more active and more promising than the life that you and I knew.

I, too, should very much like to have a chat with you, about things past, things present, and things to come; but we must wait. When this terrible strife ends, and if a play of mine happens to have a fortunate passage over the stage, I should like to visit Eire again with my wife and three children.

Yours very sincerely,
Sean O'Casey

[4] See "Sword of Light," *Pictures in the Hallway*, for O'Casey's account of these incidents and the Rev. Harry Fletcher's farewell. See also his use of some of this material in Act IV of *Red Roses For Me* (1942), in the scenes between the rector of St. Burnupus and Dowzard and Foster.

[5] See "Crime and Punishment," *I Knock at the Door* (1939), for O'Casey's characterization of John Hogan, the teacher at St. Barnabas School, as schoolmaster Slogan.

[6] Irishman or Englishman.

To Peter Newmark

MS. NEWMARK
[DEVON]
9 DECEMBER 1941

Dear Peter:

Well, how are you? Seems a long time since us heard from you. The whooping-cough is all gone where the bad niggers go, & we're waiting now for the Nipponese to come over & take the old Guildhall. I've been in a bit of a mess lately, having stamped on my spectacles, & the Home Guard reserve ones I have aren't too good; so I went about in the twilight. Had a twilight sleep, so to say. The Red Army seems to be doing a little better now; & experience is giving them younger & newer generals with a sharper vision than the older one of Budenny, who, of course, did his work well long, long ago.

"Pictures in the Hallway" has been put off till the beginning of the year; & now that men up to 50 have to go to the front, it may be postponed forever. I've heard nothing further about the New York production of "Purple Dust". The new call on America's man-power may mean the putting-off of the play; & then there'll be nothing for it, but a job in the M.O.I.[1] We are all fairly well, but a little tired. But we look forward to the sound of the Church bells at Christmas. I'm afraid the Japs are going ahead in Maylaya. Took them by surprise! The leaves falling from the trees are taking them by surprise, too.

Eileen sends her love.

Labour Monthly got me to write a criticism or review of "Distant Point".[2] I did so, and told them, next time, they should ask you, for you had a better gift than I for this work.

Affectionately Yrs.
Sean

P.S. Unity Theatre lately staged a "Living Newspaper" showing the struggle for a Free Press.[3] I understand copies are available for anyone wanting them. Could you get me one? I'd like to have a squint at it. It is to be got from

Daily Worker League
150. Southampton Row
London. W.C.1.

[1] Ministry of Information.

[2] Sean O'Casey, "Connolly Speaks Again," *Labour Monthly*, May 1941, a review of the Soviet dramatist Alexander M. Afinogenov's *Distant Point* (1934), translated and adapted by Hubert Griffith, first produced on 25 November 1937 at the Gate Theatre, London; revived by Unity Theatre on 10 August 1941, and at the Westminster Theatre on 28 October 1941.

[3] Unity Theatre's production of *This Our World* opened in London on 19 October 1941.

To Peter Newmark

MS. NEWMARK

DEVON
MONDAY.
[? DECEMBER 1941]

My dear Peter.

Just a line to say I got Freud's book on Dreams [1] all right, & to thank you for it.

Just now, it's too hard to read—I'm climbing cautiously out of an attack of damned Influenza. Burns came to see me, sodden with it, & of course, two days later I was soaked with it, & had to hide myself in bed for a week.

Hope you are keeping fit, & that the bombs are falling far from you.

Yours as ever.
Sean

[1] Sigmund Freud, *The Interpretation of Dreams* (London, Allen & Unwin, 1933, rev. ed.).

To John Burns [1]

TC. O'CASEY

[DEVON]
10 DECEMBER 1941

Dear Mr Burns:

I have read the letter you wrote to Eileen. Respecting myself, you say, "I hope Sean is not too detached from the bloody conflagration. We still seem so very remote from it all round here but the flames are sure to lick and engulf us—perhaps sooner than we expect." Apart from the futility of fighting flames that are "sure to engulf us," there are implications in your comment on me that should, I feel, be opposed and contradicted. In the first place, you cant be aware of what I do, or dont do. Concerning

[1] John Burns, Greygarth, Budleigh Salterton.

this remoteness, I wish you would speak more for yourself and less for others. Maybe you are, unconsciously, speaking for yourself. This struggle has never been remote from me, or I from it. It has been beside me and in me years before it happened. Your rather gratuitous remark of being "too remote" from what is happening cannot be let go unresented. Months ago, when the comrades were going about saying the Red Army would be in Berlin in a week, I told them what would happen, and added that what they should show was what the Red Army was up against, and what would happen to us, if the Red Army couldnt hold the Germans. But most of them went on with their fairy thinking. I would remind you, my friend, that when the Execution of the Trotsky group of traitors had taken place, and almost all England—including many who are cheek by jowl with you now—were howling destruction to the U.S.S.R., I stood by what had been done, and publicly, too, as you can see by looking up the files of the Daily Worker and the Glasgow Forward. Again, when the Soviets set out to make their Finnish border more secure, again, when the howl went up, I defended the U.S.S.R. as you can see by looking up the files of the Tribune. Again, when the Daily Worker was threatened, I allowed my name to go on the Board, though I wasnt stupid enough to hold the view that my name would be any protection. Again, when you decided to hold Marxist classes in Totnes, you will, perhaps, remember that the first decision arranged to hold them alternately at our place and at the County Girls' School, at the instance of your friend, Miss Barton. One class, only, was held in the school, for reasons better known to yourself. Miss Barton, too, soon kept away from the classes, presumably, because she feared for her position and quite rightly so. May I remind you that you, too, were, or seemed to be a little reluctant to appear publicly, on account of your position, and quite rightly so, too. But now, when it is easy to be brave and brisk, you come along with an implication of indifference about one who stood by the U.S.S.R. when, to say the least of it, most others were somewhat afraid to take her part. If you want to [do] good work, do it; but dont go round with an implied boast in your allusion to others, who, to say the least of it again, have done as much as you have. I would remind you that you go on teaching your mathematics, so please allow me to go on with my job of trying to write; and dont assume that because I do as you do (in another way), I must necessarily be "too remote" from everything that is happening around us.

Yours, etc,
Sean O'Casey

To Irish Times

15 DECEMBER 1941

An Irish Institution

Sir,—Cordial greeting to Mr. Dudley Fletcher, and to his tribute to Jim Larkin,[1] the Irish Labour Leader. Jim is a great orator, but he is much more—a great man. God made something when He made Jim Larkin.

I came to the Parish of St. Barnabas some fifteen or sixteen years after Mr. Dudley had gone into Trinity, so I wasn't there in his time. He asks me a good many questions, one of which is: "If I do not recognise a great change from my point of view during the last fifty years or so." Not from my point of view, but that doesn't hinge on the present discussion. I prefer to look, for the moment, at it from the general point of view. The other day I got a letter from the daughter of a Protestant Rector who sometimes preached in St. Barnabas's, and whom I heard preach in his own church. This lady says she "knew the Griffins and the Fletchers (as she calls them) well." This is part of her letter: "We surely have evoluted a bit from the Gaels (quite a lot, if you ask me), so why bother to revive their ways, dress, and language, when we have now, what suits our purpose and our need. Gaelic is ugly to hear and hard to learn (perhaps that's why she doesn't like it), and we can be just as Irish without it, can't we?" Not much change here.

The changes brought to Ireland were mainly brought by The Gaelic League, the Irish Republican Brotherhood, and by the Abbey Theatre. The Church of Ireland had little or nothing to do with it. (The Catholic Church, *per se,* hadn't a lot to with it, either.) Political freedom has been brought to twenty-six of the thirty-two counties: so far, so good. But the British Federation of Free Nations (or the Fountain Head) declares that the Primate of All-Ireland lives in one country, while the Primate of Ireland lives in another. The mount where Patrick toiled as a herd, the barn that formed his first church, and the little bed of ground where he now sleeps, lie, so this Federation says, in a foreign country. So does St. Colmkille's old home. A change, right enough, but hardly for the better. He asks me "was I not perfectly free to study any side of a question, and to form his opinions according to the dictates of his own reason and conscience?" I was, certainly, because I came but little under its educational influence.

Mr. Fletcher knows as well as I do that a boy or girl passing through the mill of a National School, and having the Bible bored into his or her brain, they were left with little courage to ask a question, and little desire to form an opinion other than those taught to them. He answers, I imagine, the last question himself when he says "I am always proud to see the

[1] *Irish Times,* 1 December 1941, a letter from the Rev. Dudley Canon Fletcher, in reply to O'Casey's letter to the *Irish Times,* 25 November 1941.

National and Gaelic element in our Church coming to the front, so long as it is not inconsistent with the wider loyalty to the British Confederation of Free Nations." If the Church comes from Saints Patrick, Brighid, Colmkille, Aidan, and the rest, she should be National, not only in an odd element, here and there, but National through and through. But to go deeper, what right has any bishop, priest, or deacon to refuse a welcome to the Communion of the Church a Gael who is tinctured with disloyalty to the British Federation of Free Nations? Imagine St. Patrick, or Colmkille, or Brighid saying to a Gael at the gate of heaven, "You cant come in here, me boy (or me girl), for you havent been loyal to the B.C. of F.N."

I am no teacher, and have never tried to teach, though I am still hard at it trying to learn. I have just set down things that were simple facts, at least, to me.

Deep feelings of good will to him whom I regarded as a friend when he was Rector of Coolbanagher, ay, ever since the day he stood with us in Liberty Hall, deepened when he shocked the bit of a cod, D. P. Moran, editor of *The Leader* (who had criticised him), by sending him a reply in Irish that Moran couldn't read.

Yours sincerely,
Sean O'Casey

Devon, 4 December 1941

To Lovat Dickson

TS. MACMILLAN LONDON

DEVON
20 DECEMBER 1941

Dear Mr Lovat Dickson,

This is a reply to the letter you sent to [me] on the 15th.

Some time ago, I wrote to your Firm saying that I had received a contract, dealing with PICTURES IN THE HALLWAY from your American House, and mentioning that for the reason of the difficulty of getting into touch with them on any question, I was asking my American Agent,

Richard Madden,
The Richard Madden Play Co,
515, Madison Avenue,
New York City,

to act on my behalf. I got a reply from your Firm acknowledging this letter (ref: DM/AS, Date Oct 29th) and adding that you thought I was quite right to ask Mr Madden to act for me.

I have sent the draft contract, with a letter explaining what I wanted done, to Mr Madden, long ago; and followed this later on with a copy of the letter; but I have received no reply. I have since cabled him. I also sent a letter to your American House telling of what I had done; following it with a copy some weeks later; but again, I got no reply; so that it seems they have all gone where the good niggers go.

So that it comes to this: I have forwarded the draft contract to Mr Madden, with a request that he should deal for me about the matter with your American House. Today I got a letter from your American Firm, enclosing a few dollars royalty on sale of PURPLE DUST, and as this has, previously, been done through you, it seems to be a little puzzling.

I wish you, and all who work with you, a fair share of whatever merriment may be knocking about this Christmas time. We are getting up here a little show of Soviet Pictures of life and achievement in the Soviet Union, and the Mayor has promised to open it for us. Stalin is becoming a household name in Totnes. As well, I am trying to write another play to be called, I think, Asea in a Gold Canoe [1]—if one can say ashore, surely one can say asea.

Well, all the best.
Sean O'Casey

[1] This was the beginning of *Red Roses For Me* (1942).

(Continued in Volume II, 1942–54; and Volume III, 1955–64.)

APPENDIX

The following two letters to *Sinn Fein,* the earliest extant letters, were discovered too late to be included in their proper order at the beginning of this volume.

To Sinn Féin [1]

19 MARCH 1910

OUR READERS' OPINIONS

The Emmet Commemoration Concert

A Chara—May I ask, through the medium of "Sinn Fein," the Wolfe Tone Memorial Committee, who organised the recent Emmet Commemoration Concert, a question or two? When do they intend to declare that they have eyes that see, and ears that hear, the sights and sounds of the Irish Language Revival? When—we are patient people—will they deign to bow their crested heads before its power, its vigour, and its dignity? At the recent concert many, many songs were sung in English; few, few indeed, in the tongue of our land. In one particular case a song, marked on the programme—that was the name given to the list of items, and which was lustily chorused by those selling them through the hall—"Maire of Ballyhaunis," was exchanged, actually exchanged, for one in English!

An Gall Fada [2]

Bothar Abercorn, a 4, Marta.[3]

[1] *Sinn Féin* ("Ourselves Alone"), an Irish nationalist weekly newspaper owned and edited by Arthur Griffith. Tone and Emmet were symbolic heroes of the national movement for Irish independence: Wolfe Tone (1763–98), a United Irishman, one of the leaders of the Rising of 1798; captured by the British during the French invasion of Ireland; committed suicide in prison. Robert Emmet (1778–1803), leader of the abortive Rising of 1803 in Dublin; executed by the British.

[2] *An Gall Fada,* the tall foreigner or Protestant, one of O'Casey's early pseudonyms. He was born a Protestant in a predominantly Catholic country.

[3] Abercorn Road, 4 March.

To Sinn Féin

2 APRIL 1910

OUR READERS' OPINIONS

The Emmet Commemoration Concert

A chara dhil [1]—The knightly champion of above [2] gallops into the field with a pointless lance. The arguments he uses and the excuses he pleads are weak and unsustained. An effort to see our language honoured by those who lead us in the ways of national life is not an effort "to create a grievance" or perpetuate "squabbling about personalities." If it be a national disgrace that Dublin should show no visible sign of its approval of the great sacrifices of Wolfe Tone, it is also a grave national disgrace and constitutes a graver national danger that her advanced political leaders should, by ignoring it, despise the language of our Motherland. It is a fact that the introduction of the lecturer, the address that young Irishman gave, the vote of thanks, the seconding of same—save a few words by our friend Sean, and the concluding remarks of the Chairman, were all at this function carried out in the language of Sean Buidhe.[3] This after fifteen years' work on the part of the Gaelic League in the capital of Ireland.

Oh! the pity of it all—the shame and the dishonour! Sean says they made their Clár, in the present state of the language revival in Dublin as Irish in speech as possible. I am glad to say that I believe that the knowledge of the language in our city is more extensive than Sean seems to imagine. If what Sean contends to be true, then it is urgent that the importance of our language should be evidenced in speech before those by whom it is lightly esteemed. One speech in Irish is not much to demand, and next year, and on all occasions such as these, the Wolfe Tone Committee will do well and wisely to honour above all, and before all

[1] A chara dhil, Dear friend.

[2] S. Ua huadaiG (Sean O'Huadhaigh), secretary of the Wolfe Tone Memorial Committee, had replied to O'Casey in *Sinn Fein,* 26 March 1910, stating that a critic should use his own name rather than hide behind a "nom-de-plume"; that the Committee's minutes were kept in the Irish language; that the concert programme (clár), though written in English, was Irish in sentiment; and that "it is puerile to discuss such points as that of the children who sold the programme calling it a programme instead of a clár. There is too much of this quibbling about trifles in Ireland." See also below the "Wolfe Tone Committee" report in the *Irish Worker,* 19 July 1913, which indicates that three years later O'Casey became secretary of the Wolfe Tone Memorial Committee.

[3] Sean Buidhe, John Bull or the English.

things, the sweet language of Banban.[4] It is good that the minutes of this Committee are kept in Irish—whom may we thank? Not the Committee, but that body's secretary, Sean himself, whom we know, and whose work for Ireland we know as well. Does it, a Shean, betray foolishness to be careful about trifles? I do not think so. Michael Angelo pointing out some little imperfection in the work of a young student received the reply, "Oh! that's only a trifle." "Oh! yes," said the great master, "but the care of trifles ensures success, and success is no trifle." "Yea," says Father O'Leary, "to get one word of Irish spoken in a place where none was spoken before, is a good work for Ireland." Oh! Sean, neither you nor I, nor even yet the Wolfe Tone Committee, can afford to despise the day of small things. This Committee wears in its helmet the Plume of National Independence—it is no shame to lower in salute that sacred symbol before the majesty of our National Language. This must be done. If our leaders do not lead us towards an Irish Ireland, then we must choose those who will. We do not want to hinder their great work—God forbid! We want to help them on, and we love them none the less because we love Ireland more. For we believe that Ireland shall be free, not when the figure of Tone stands in a Dublin street, or when German shells are bursting round the dome of St. Paul's—as some of the Commemoration speeches suggested—but:

Nuair a chifar Gaedhil
Go Gaedhealach Groidhe
I dteangaidh, i mbeas, i ngiomh.[5]

Before closing I would like to praise the National Council for the truly superb concert on St. Patrick's night. It was a good night's work for them and Ireland.

I suppose I had better wear my beaver up in this last joult[6] with Sean, whom I am proud to look upon as a dear friend in our strife for an Irish and a free nation.

Mise le meas mor,[7]
S. Ua Cathasaigh, nó "An Gall Fada"

[4] Banban, a poetic name for Ireland, from a queen of the Tuatha Dé Danann.
[5] When Irish people will be seen
To be Irish and spirited
In tongue, in manner, in deed.
[6] This could be a typographical error; he might have written "joust."
[7] With great respect.

INDEX OF LETTERS AND DOCUMENTS BY O'CASEY

INDEX OF LETTERS AND CRITIQUES ABOUT OR TO O'CASEY

INDEX OF REPORTS AND REVIEWS ABOUT OR BY O'CASEY

GENERAL INDEX

Note: Footnote page entries in boldface indicate references with biographical or background information.